COLUMBUS
WORLD TRAVEL ATLAS
10th Edition

ISBN: 1-902221-93-1

Columbus Travel Guides, Media House, Azalea Drive, Swanley, Kent BR8 8HU, United Kingdom
Tel: +44 (0)1322 660 070 • E-mail: booksales@nexusmedia.com

• **Cartographic Editor:** *David Burles.*

• **Production Editor:** *Brian Quinn.*

• **Additional Cartography:** *Anderson Geographics Ltd, Berkshire.*

• **Contributors:** *Patrick Fitzgerald, Tony Peisley, Patrick Thorne, Penny Locke, Graeme Payne, Jon Gillaspie, Bill la Violette, Ned Middleton, Sachiko Burles.*

• **Continental Introductions:** *Brian Quinn.*

• **Cover Design:** *Antonio Manuel of Nexus Media Communications.*

• **Printed by:** *UP Group, Lithuania.*

• **Founding Editor:** *Mike Taylor of the University of Brighton.*

• **Publisher:** *Pete Korniczky.*

This publication has been created from a wide range of sources and where appropriate these have been credited on the relevant maps, charts or articles.The publishers would like to thank all the many organisations and individuals who have helped in the preparation of this edition, with particular thanks to Ian Alexander of Battlefiels Tours; Bill Adams of Safari Consultants; Isobel Falk of JLA; Keith Wright of Amusement Business; Brad Smith of Foremost West; John Knighton of African Pride; Maria Hinayon of ACI; Kate Pirie and Natalie de la Porte of Southern Skies Marketing; John Douglas of Malawi Tourism; John Haycock of Africa Explorer; David Ezra of the Saltmarsh Partnership; Maria Polk of Tours.com; Cathy Keefe of Travel Industry Association of America; Graham Johnson; Dirk Triep of the German National Tourist Office; Theresa Mancini of IACO; Olaf Schoonhoven of the World Travel School; Ivo Siebens of KHM; Ann Tack of Spermalie Hotel & Tourism School; Jeff Bertus of Bertus Leisure; Elliot Frisby of Visit Britain; Simon Hampton and Anne-Marie Hansen of Kuoni; Jane Voss; Dan Josty; Steve Jackson; Leila Carlyle; and Michael Knop. Apologies to organisations or individuals omitted from this list in error.

The publishers welcome comments as to how future editions could be improved still further. Please contact booksales@nexusmedia.com

For more information on • ordering additional copies • bulk purchase rates • overseas rates and distributors • overbranded editions • content licensing • cartographic commissions – please contact the publishers at the above address.

See also... Country Contents (4-5); Thematic Contents (6-7); Index (211-256)

The listings above refer to a selection of related themes.

General Contents

This General Contents provides a summary of the main subjects and areas covered in this Atlas. For clarity, many of the individual countries and topics covered are not listed separately here. Many countries have focus maps which give detailed coverage of areas of particular importance. For further help with locating countries or topics, see the Country Contents (4-5), the Thematic Contents (6-7) and the navigation panels which appear at the top of every page and which refer to a selection of related themes.

See also... Country Contents (4-5); Thematic Contents (6-7); Index (211-256)

The listings above refer to a selection of related themes.

General Contents

KEY TO TOPOGRAPHIC MAPS

Communications

- Airport *main international gateways and domestic hubs*
- Motorway/expressway or equivalent *focus maps only*
- Main road • Road in tunnel
- Main passenger railway, with station • Railway in tunnel
- Dedicated high-speed rail line *focus maps only*
- Ferry route *selected passenger routes: focus maps only*

Boundaries & boxes

- International boundary • Disputed international boundary
- Internal administrative boundary *sometimes shown as solid line for clarity*
- National park, wildlife reserve
- Area featured in a focus map

Settlement

- Towns and cities *size of dot is determined by population; darkest red indicates a city with over one million inhabitants*
- National capital/capital of overseas territory *named in CAPITAL LETTERS*
- Built-up area *larger scale focus maps only*
- Archaeological site, ruins • Important building/s (e.g castle, temple)
- Other place of interest (e.g. park, reserve, natural feature) *focus maps only*

Physical features (see individual map pages for elevation tints)

- Mountain peak • Land depression *with altitude in metres*
- Pass, canyon *with altitude in metres*
- River, with waterfall, with dam • Seasonal river
- Lake • Seasonal lake • Salt lake
- Canal
- Coral reef

See also... General Contents (2-3); Thematic Contents (6-7); World Pointers (10); Countries A-Z (202-210); Index (211-256)
The listings above refer to a selection of related themes.

Country Contents

This section lists the countries of the world as they have been defined for the purposes of this book. For more information on what is and what is not a country – a less clear-cut matter than might be supposed – please see the World Pointers section on page 10, the introduction to the Countries A-Z section on page 202 or the Columbus *World Travel Dictionary.* Countries are here prefixed with a dot, the colour of which indicates the section of the book in which they are covered (see map on page 14). Only one page number has been given per entry, even where (as is often the case) the country is covered more extensively, and this generally refers to where a map of the entire country can be found. A selection of other destinations are also shown, in *italics*. If preceding ≈, this is not, or no longer, the official name of the country: the official or current name follows the symbol. If preceding >, this is politically part of another country: the 'mother' country follows the symbol. (For ease of reference, the page number has been given where this is different from that of the 'mother' country). If preceding Δ, this is a geographical area: the countries it comprises follow the symbol. The list of such ambiguities could be many times longer and only those regarded as being the most important for the purposes of this Atlas have been included here. For further help with locating places, see the General Contents (2-3), the Thematic Contents (6-7), Appendix 1: Geographical Definitions (192), Countries A-Z (202-210), the Index (211-256) and the navigation panels which appear at the top of every page and which refer to a selection of related themes.

● Asia ● Africa ● Australasia & Oceania ● Europe ● Latin America & The Caribbean ● Poles ● USA & Canada *See map on page 14.*

See also... General Contents (2-3); Thematic Contents (6-7); Countries A-Z (202-210); Index (211-256)

The listings above refer to a selection of related themes.

Names preceded by > are politically part of another country; by ≈ are old/unofficial titles; by ∆ are geographical areas. *See introduction on page 4.*

See also... General Contents (2-3); Country Contents (4-5); Index (211-256)

The listings above refer to a selection of related themes.

Thematic Contents

This Thematic Contents gives page references for around 280 of the topics covered in the Atlas. It can be seen that many of these (diving, travel statistics, railways, airports, cruising and religion, for instance) are touched upon in different ways in different parts of the book. The abbreviations SIs and CSs mean that the theme is covered in one or more of the section introductions or the country sections. For further help with locating topics, please see the General Contents (2-3), the Country Contents (4-5), the Index (211-256) and the navigation panels which appear at the top of every page and which refer to a selection of related themes.

CSs = See Country Sections SIs = See Section Introductions

See also... World Political (14-15); Travel Indicators (24-25); Other Introductions (see Contents)

The listings above refer to a selection of related themes. For more information, see the Contents (2-7).

World

Key facts

Number of Countries	226
Area ('000 sq km)	135,477
Population ('000)	6,450,988
Population Density (per sq km)	48
Gross National Income (US$m)	39,659,845
Visitor Arrivals ('000)	766,000
Visitor Receipts (US$m)	601,726

GNI figures are for 2004. Population figures are taken from the most recent reliable source. Travel figures (UNWTO) are based on overnight stays, not same-day visitors, and are for 2004. For more information see the Countries A-Z section from page 202.

There are many opinions as to how big the worldwide travel business really is. Like all service-based sectors it has no physical product that can be weighed or counted. Many problems of definition follow from this – an airline pilot or a travel agent is clearly part of the industry; but what about a small-town taxi driver, or the owner of a convenience store that also sells local souvenirs? Different countries and organisations will take different views on such points. Despite such challenges, widely accepted estimates are produced by several respected bodies. One such, the World Travel and Tourism Council, suggests that 10.6% of the world's GDP and 8.3% of the world's jobs depend directly or indirectly on travel and tourism, making it the world's largest industry: in the 1960s it was not even in the top ten. The World Tourism Organisation further suggests that travel is the world's fastest growing one, with an annual average increase in receipts of 9% between 1984 and 2000. Various projections put the real growth per year at around 4 to 5% between 2006 and 2015. By any estimate, travel is clearly big business – a multi-trillion dollar industry, driven by people's frequent desire to be elsewhere.

The *World Travel Atlas*, now in its tenth edition, provides a unique overview of the travel industry in the early 21st century. The focus maps which complement the conventional regional and country plates offer detailed, travel-specific coverage of the most-visited areas. A large number of themes, ranging from economic indicators to UNESCO World Heritage Sites and from ski resorts to time zones, are covered throughout the book, supplemented with detailed appendices. There are also six continental introductions, which provide an overview of each region, a discussion of some of the key travel-related issues, a summary of the main travel destinations and a selection of statistics. Themes covered here include low-cost airlines, the cruise industry, intra-regional travel patterns, the changing role of the travel agent, responsible tourism, regional economic change, the internet, the problems of the major airlines, globalisation and niche markets. Many of the maps and charts are new to this edition and all pre-existing ones have been updated. Another first-time feature is the navigation aid panel at the top of each page which refers to maps or charts of related interest. There is also are also two additional contents providing thematic and country-by-country, overviews of the numerous topics that the *World Travel Atlas* addresses. Overall, the book's aim is to provide a clear, balanced and accurate picture of the world for a wide range of readers in the travel industry and elsewhere.

Past, present and future

Apart from 1982 (due mainly to the Gulf War) and 2001 (due mainly to the 11 September terrorist attacks), visitor numbers and travel receipts have risen in every year since accurate records began in 1950. Aviation figures go back even further than that: in 1926 the US domestic air travel market involved some 8,000 passengers, about the number that took to the skies for domestic flights in America every seven minutes in 2005. As for international flights from the USA in 1926, there were none recorded. It was not until 1946 that US international departures broke through the one million mark. They have increased by an average of about one million per year ever since.

By whatever means of transport, Europe remained comfortably the most-visited continent in 2005. What is encouraging for the global health of the industry is that, while Europe's market is still growing, arrivals to other regions – notably Asia – are growing at a faster pace. The WTO's Tourism 2020 Vision forecasts that worldwide international arrivals are likely to exceed 1.56 billion by 2020. Under this model, Europe will remain the most-visited region, but with a market share reduced from 60% in 1995 to 46% in 2020. As regards outbound travel, Europe will continue to dominate, but Asia will, by 2020, have doubled its number of visitors compared to 1995 whereas those of the Americas will only have increased by 50%. The report goes on to predict that long-haul travel will grow at a faster rate than regional travel during this period.

The leading countries in the travel-numbers league seem to have their positions assured, for the next few years at least. The six top countries in terms of visitor arrivals were the same in 2004 as in 1997, with France comfortably in the lead and the chasing pack bunched some way behind them, occasionally changing their positions from year to year. On the other three basic indicators, the Germans travel more and (having recently overtaken the USA) spend the most, while the Americans receive the most money. The most significant medium-term change is likely to be the emergence of China, not only as a destination but also as a source of travellers. The increase in number of countries being granted Approved Destination Status, the relaxation of travel restrictions and China's rapidly growing prosperity have already led to international departures more than doubling between 2000 and 2004. By many estimates, China will be supplying more tourists than any other country by 2010.

Travel remains something of an exclusive market: the 11 most visited countries accounted for over 50% of all tourist arrivals in 2004. It is also something of a crowded one: in 41 of the world's countries the annual visiting population in 2004 exceeded the native one, on four occasions (Andorra, Macau, the British Virgin Islands and Aruba) by a factor of more than 10.

Prospects for 2006 and beyond appear good on the basis of recent performance and medium-term trends, although there are several potential problems ahead. The WTO has identified terrorism, rising oil prices and the spread of the H5N1 avian flu virus as three of the most important factors which could disrupt the industry during the coming years.

Travel trends

2005 was another record year for the travel industry with visitor arrivals reaching 808 million according to the WTO, an increase of 5.5% and over 40 million travellers compared to 2004's 766 million. All this was despite a catalogue of problems including natural disasters, health scares, terrorism and oil price rises, all seemingly striking at the very heart of the industry. The strongest continental growth was recorded in the less mature markets, with Africa (10% up) leading the way: further good news for an industry which, like any other, is seeking to diversify its appeal. Even the airlines prospered better than many would have predicted a couple of years ago, with RPKs (revenue passenger kilometres) of IATA members up by nearly 8%. Still more surprisingly, many observers predict that the aviation industry as a whole will return to profit by the end of 2007. It was another excellent year for many niche markets: cruising, for example, attracted double the number of travellers in 2005 than ten years earlier. New holiday options are constantly being offered and new ways of doing business developed. In addition, a new ethical dimension is being added, with an increased emphasis on responsible and sustainable tourism. All things considered, the travel business is clearly both very adaptable and very robust.

An important area of the industry, but one that is often overlooked, is domestic tourism. The extent of this is for obvious reasons very hard to quantify. Although this generates no new revenue from foreign countries, it at least keeps money flushing through a national economy and keeps travel-related businesses healthy even at times when people are, for whatever reason, disinclined to venture abroad. Around 95% of all trips taken by Americans are domestic, according to TIA – 'See America First' was first used as a slogan by the National Parks Service in 1906 and has been popular ever since – while the UK Tourism Survey estimates that over 126 million such journeys were made in Britain in 2004. Many national tourist offices now devote a good part of their budget to encouraging their own citizens not to travel abroad.

Special-interest holidays have been growing steadily in recent years and the trend shows no sign of slowing. Adventure holidays, cruising, winter sports and city

Visitor arrivals

The world's 25 most visited countries in 2004 (millions)
Source: WTO

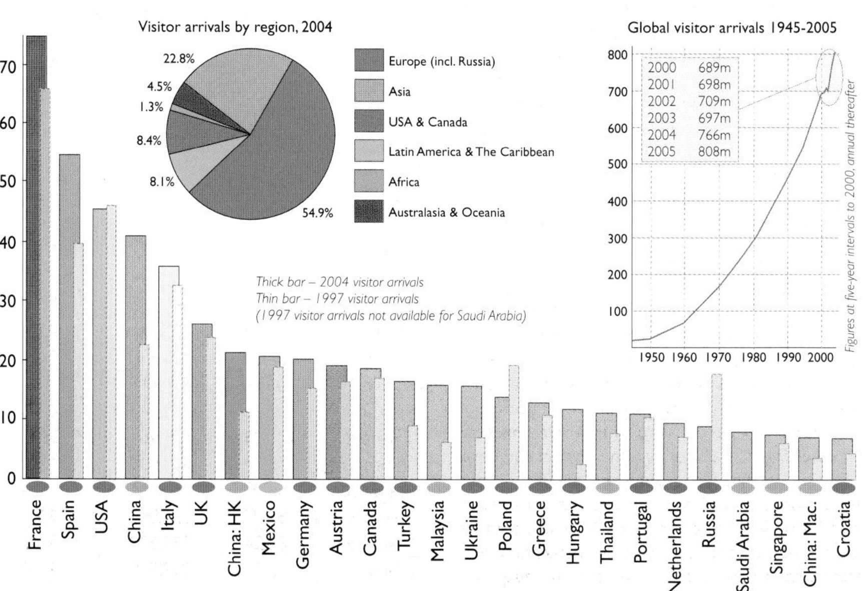
Visitor arrivals by region, 2004
22.8%
4.5%
1.3%
8.4%
8.1%
54.9%
Europe (incl. Russia)
Asia
USA & Canada
Latin America & The Caribbean
Africa
Australasia & Oceania
Thick bar – 2004 visitor arrivals
Thin bar – 1997 visitor arrivals
(1997 visitor arrivals not available for Saudi Arabia)
Global visitor arrivals 1945-2005
2000 689m
2001 698m
2002 709m
2003 697m
2004 766m
2005 808m
Figures at five-year intervals to 2000, annual thereafter
1950 1960 1970 1980 1990 2000
0 10 20 30 40 50 60 70
France
Spain
USA
China
Italy
UK
China: HK
Mexico
Germany
Austria
Canada
Turkey
Malaysia
Ukraine
Poland
Greece
Hungary
Thailand
Portugal
Netherlands
Russia
Saudi Arabia
Singapore
China: Mac.
Croatia

- In economic terms, international travel and tourism receipts are classified as exports, and international tourism expenditure as imports. According to the WTO, travel and tourism is one of the top five export categories for over 80% of countries.
- In 2004, Air France-KLM carried 47,190,000 international passengers, more than any other airline. Delta carried the most domestic passengers (79,289,000).
- 19 countries received over 10 million international visitors in 2004. 60 others received over 1 million.
- 17 countries supplied more than 10 million international travellers in 2004. 40 others supplied more than 1 million.
- 17 countries received in excess of US$10billion from international travel in 2004. 46 others received in excess of US$1billion.
- 14 countries spent in excess of US$10billion on international travel in 2004. 28 others spent in excess of US$1billion.
- The biggest travellers, the Germans, have, on average, 35 vacation days a year: Americans have only 13.
- The world's population grew from 1.6 billion to 6.1 billion during the 20th century and is expected to exceed 7 billion by 2015.
- In an average year, Carnival Cruise lines puts 10 million chocolate mints on their guests' pillows.
- Saudi Arabia is the most generous aid donor measured by contributions as a proportion of national income.
- 41 countries (including France, Hong Kong, Portugal, UAE, Ireland, Singapore and many Caribbean states) receive annually more visitors than their population.
- According to ACI, the world's airlines carried 6.7% more passengers in June 2005 than in June 2004.
- Over 55% of cruises in 2005 were in the Caribbean or the Mediterranean.
- The first commercial flight took place in 1914.
- More people are killed on the roads of the USA in an average six-month period than have been in all commercial aviation accidents since 1960.
- The WTO predicts that international travel arrivals will exceed 1.5 billion by 2020.
- And finally, a few thoughts from some other travellers:

'Like all travellers, I have seen more than I remember and remembered more than I have seen.'
(Benjamin Disraeli)

'Maps encourage boldness. They're like cryptic love letters. They make everything seem possible.'
(Mark Jenkins)

'The traveller sees what he sees – the tourist sees what he has come to see.'
(GK Chesterton)

'The destination is never a place, but a new way of seeing things.'
(Henry Miller)

'Everywhere I go, I find a poet who has been there before me.'
(Sigmund Freud)

Visitor receipts

The 25 countries that received the most from international travel in 2004 (US$ millions)
Source: WTO

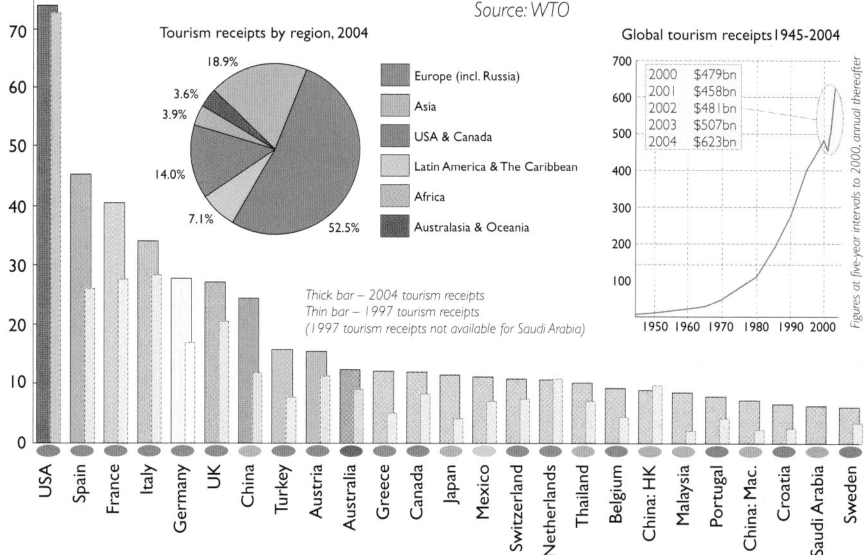
Tourism receipts by region, 2004
18.9%
3.6%
3.9%
14.0%
7.1%
52.5%
Europe (incl. Russia)
Asia
USA & Canada
Latin America & The Caribbean
Africa
Australasia & Oceania
Global tourism receipts 1945-2004
2000 $479bn
2001 $458bn
2002 $481bn
2003 $507bn
2004 $623bn
1950 1960 1970 1980 1990 2000
Figures at five-year intervals to 2000, annual thereafter
Thick bar – 2004 tourism receipts
Thin bar – 1997 tourism receipts
(1997 tourism receipts not available for Saudi Arabia)
USA
Spain
France
Italy
Germany
UK
China
Turkey
Austria
Australia
Greece
Canada
Japan
Mexico
Switzerland
Netherlands
Thailand
Belgium
China: HK
Malaysia
Portugal
China: Mac.
Croatia
Saudi Arabia
Sweden

breaks are four of the most important and travel agencies able to offer specialist advice and services in these areas have benefited. Travellers are also becoming more discriminating, demanding and adventurous, a trend fuelled by the internet. In Europe, for example, the low-cost airlines are offering a complete one-stop range of short-break options – flights, hotels, car-hire and insurance – through their web-sites. Many of these involve destinations that ten years ago would have been almost unknown, and the list is growing. The number of European city breaks doubled between 2000 and 2004, and many cities have seen year-on-year growth of over 30% in this period.

The low-cost airlines are one sign of change, and of a kind that few would have predicted 15 years ago. In fact, the distinction between low-cost and other kinds of airlines is already starting to blur. With varying degrees of success, many traditional carriers now compete on cost, and some have started up their own low-cost operations. The business model of successful entrants into any market is usually based on a mixture of addressing the failings of the incumbents and utilising new technology, and the new breed of airlines have exploited both. Furthermore, it is easier to start with a blank slate, free of long-established and possibly outdated labour contracts, marketing perceptions and partnership arrangements, than it is to adapt an existing business. Low-cost airlines have been highly successful in re-defining the travel business.

So to has the internet, the other major force for change of recent years. Numerous statistics, some of which are reported elsewhere in this book, testify to the internet's dramatic growth as a medium for travel information and bookings, and appear to suggest an irreversible trend towards direct sales. The reality is rather more complex. The more successful agencies are now making use of the internet as a 24-hour marketing and sales tool, while at the same time ensuring that their levels of knowledge (often in specialist areas) and customer service keep pace with consumers' increasing expectations. In the same way, many on-line companies are looking to provide a human face to their services by using retail outlets. In time, these developments are likely to blur the distinction between 'on-line' and 'traditional' travel suppliers. Throughout the travel industry, as in others, the companies that thrive will do so because they manage to provide the best and most cost-effective service to their customers.

Big spenders

The 20 countries whose residents spent the most on international travel in 2004.
Source: WTO/IMF/World Bank

	Expenditure (US$ millions)	GNI (US$ millions)	Expenditure as % of GNI
Germany	72,271	2,488,974	2.9%
USA	65,635	12,150,931	0.5%
UK	55,930	2,016,393	2.8%
Japan	38,129	4,749,910	0.8%
France	28,636	1,858,731	1.5%
Italy	20,544	1,503,562	1.4%
China	19,100	1,676,846	1.1%
Netherlands	16,539	515,148	3.2%
Canada	16,017	905,629	1.8%
Russia	15,730	487,335	3.2%
Belgium	13,954	322,837	4.3%
China: HK	13,258	183,516	7.2%
Spain	12,156	875,817	1.4%
Austria	11,416	262,147	4.4%
Sweden	10,123	321,401	3.1%
Korea, Rep.	9,499	673,036	1.4%
Australia	9,407	541,173	1.7%
Switzerland	8,797	356,052	2.5%
Norway	8,428	238,398	3.5%
Taiwan	8,170	317,070	2.6%

The reasons for travelling, the means by which the arrangements are made, the choice of possible destinations and the activities to engage in one arrived are all more numerous than ever before. Business trips or beach holidays, cruises or kayaking, safaris or skiing – they are all available somewhere, as long as one has the necessary leisure time and disposable income.

Travel and wealth

Sadly, many people in the world are currently no more than spectators of this glamorous industry. According to the World Bank, the percentage of the population in developing countries who live on a purchasing power parity of less than US$2 a day (defined as describing what US$2 will actually buy in that country, rather than what it will buy in the USA) was 62.1% in 1990 and had only fallen to 55.6% by 2000 and 52.9% in 2004. This is over 3.4 billion people. In subsistence economies, leisure time as it is understood in the developed world is non-existent. For such people, international leisure travel is an impossibility.

As beneficiaries, directly or otherwise, of the leisure time and spending of others, however, travel and tourism becomes rather more relevant. For many countries, incoming travel represents a large, if not the largest, source of foreign exchange and jobs. The infrastructure required is generally less damaging or divisive than that needed for an industrial operation, there is less danger of its being sold out to a foreign government or corporation and at least as good a chance of the wealth it creates reaching the local economy. Moreover, the 'product' itself is generally already in place, in the shape of beaches, jungles, temples or local culture. The demands of tourism have in many cases reversed trends of destruction and development; without tourists, many national parks and game reserves would not be financially viable. The world's number-one industry may have its share of faults and cause its share of problems, but it also has much to be proud of.

Ethical tourism

All forms of travel have an impact on the planet, as do the creation and maintenance of what visitors expect on arrival: while mass tourism can cause change and disruption to the destination societies, and not always for the better. All sectors have been forced to become more aware of the effects of their transient presence. A number of organisations such as the The International Ecotourism Society, The Pro-Poor Partnership, Tourism Concern, The Travel Foundation and Just a Drop, sometimes in conjunction with major airlines and bodies as the WWF, ABTA, PATA, AITO

▶ World – to page 53

Europe from 54
Africa from 112
Asia from 124
Australasia & Oceania from 144
USA & Canada from 152

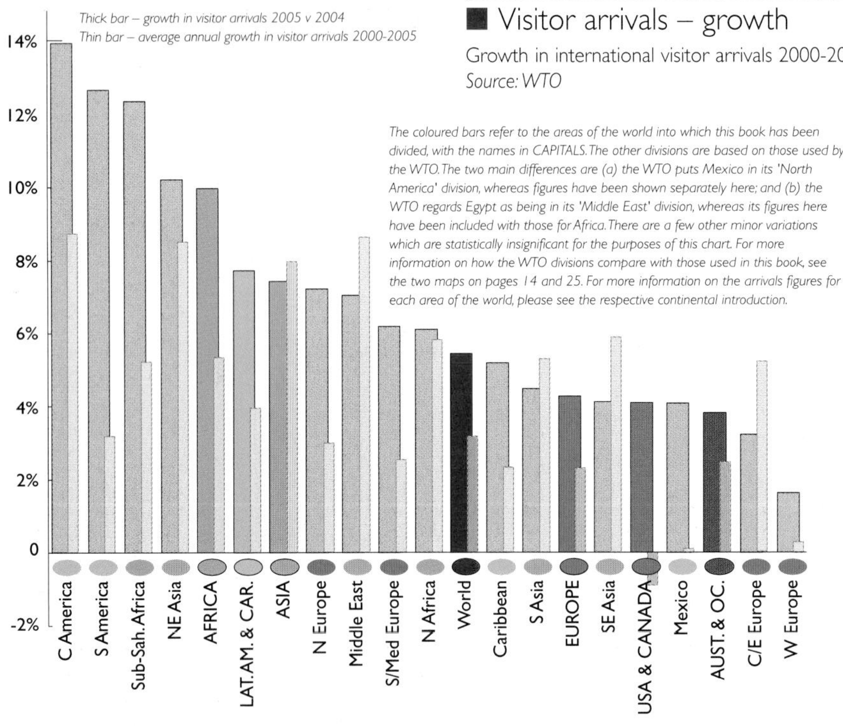
Thick bar – growth in visitor arrivals 2005 v 2004
Thin bar – average annual growth in visitor arrivals 2000-2005
14%
12%
10%
8%
6%
4%
2%
0
-2%
C America
S America
Sub-Sah. Africa
NE Asia
AFRICA
LAT.AM. & CAR.
ASIA
N Europe
Middle East
S/Med Europe
N Africa
World
Caribbean
S Asia
EUROPE
SE Asia
USA & CANADA
Mexico
AUST. & OC.
C/E Europe
W Europe

■ Visitor arrivals – growth

Growth in international visitor arrivals 2000-2005
Source: WTO

The coloured bars refer to the areas of the world into which this book has been divided, with the names in CAPITALS. The other divisions are based on those used by the WTO. The two main differences are (a) the WTO puts Mexico in its 'North America' division, whereas figures have been shown separately here; and (b) the WTO regards Egypt as being in its 'Middle East' division, whereas its figures here have been included with those for Africa. There are a few other minor variations which are statistically insignificant for the purposes of this chart. For more information on how the WTO divisions compare with those used in this book, see the two maps on pages 14 and 25. For more information on the arrivals figures for each area of the world, please see the respective continental introduction.

and the EU, have emerged in recent years, all in their different ways dedicated to the idea of improving, or at least mitigating, the impact of travel. An increasing number of awards, such as Tourism for Tomorrow, are designed to motivate good practice, and newspaper travel supplements frequently devote their entire edition to the subject of ethical tourism. In a world dominated by globalisation, it is increasingly hard to be know how much expenditure will benefit the community, or even the country, being visited. To pick but one example, in 2005 nearly 75% of Kenyan hotels were foreign-owned, as were all of the charter airlines serving the country. Such statistics suggest that the benefit of tourism is not being equally shared.

Fortunately, steps are being taken to address these problems. Many operators have become involved in projects ranging from water conservation to sponsorship of schools. Local bodies, like ASSET in the Gambia, have emerged in recent years to offer representation, business training and marketing advice to small local businesses such as local guides and restaurants which depend on visitors. Bodies ranging from national tourist offices to small hotels are increasingly keen to stress their ethical credentials. There is certainly no shortage of innovative ideas in this area. The challenge for the industry as a whole is to reconcile growth with sustainability and responsibility, in all the ways these terms are now used, while at the same time offering value for money. So far, the signs are encouraging, but much still remains to be done.

World pointers

This section provides information or definitions for a selection of the global events, industry trends and technical terms which are directly or indirectly relevant to today's travel business, many of which are referred to throughout this Atlas. This list is not intended to be exhaustive, but merely an Editor's selection. More information on these and many other points may be explored in more detail elsewhere in this book, or in the *World Travel Guide* and the *World Travel Dictionary*, also published by Columbus Travel Guides. Pages where the topic is explored in more detail are indicated by >.

11 Sept 2001 • The date on which Islamic terrorists hijacked four planes in the USA and destroyed the twin towers of the World Trade Centre in New York and damaged the US Defense Pentagon building in Virginia with the loss of around 3,000 lives. Often referred to as 9/11. For the travel business not least, the scars have been psychological as much as physical and plunged airlines in particular into a sharp decline. On a wider level, the event has served to redefine the nature and focus of US foreign policy.

Adventure travel • Originally, this was a general terms for a type of holiday, such as trekking, white-water rafting or jungle expeditions, which involved a fairly high level of physical exertion and often an element of danger. Increasingly, the term covers a wider field: skiing, diving, cycling and walking holidays are now often referred to in this way.

AIDS • Acquired Immune Deficiency Syndrome, a loss of cellular immunity as a result of viral infection generally through sexual fluids and blood, which leaves the body vulnerable to a wide range of often fatal infections. The first reported case was in December 1980. Estimates as to how many people are, or will be, infected vary greatly, but many experts predict over 40 million worldwide by 2007. The majority of cases are in sub-Saharan Africa. *>39.*

Bird flu • The common name for avian influenza, a viral disease believed until 1997 not to be transmittable to people. The H5N1 strain of the disease has been identified as causing human deaths initially in south-east Asia and increasingly elsewhere. The first confirmed avain case in the UK was in April 2006. The World Health Organization has warned of the risk of a global pandemic.

Climate change • The effects of industrial pollution and in particular the burning of fossil fuels has, according to most estimates, caused measurable increases in average global temperatures and sea levels. Travel and tourism, along with many other industries, is now taking some steps to redress these potentially very serious problems. Most remedies are, however, seemingly incompatible with economic growth. *>17*

Concorde • The world's first and, to date, only supersonic passenger aircraft. An Anglo-French co-operative venture, it made its maiden flight in March 1969: regular trans-Atlantic services started in May 1976. Only 20 were ever built, though the original plan was for over 300. On 25 July 2000, an Air France Concorde crashed on take-off from Paris with the loss of 113 lives. Services were resumed the following November. British Airways and Air France announced in April 2003 that all Concordes would be withdrawn from service and the last scheduled flight landed at London Heathrow on 24 October 2003.

Continents • There are anything between five and eight of these depending on which source one consults. The six divisions used in this atlas have been created to make the title easy to use and have no political or other significance. *>14-15*

Countries • As with continents (qv), there is no clear definition as to how many countries there are in the world. Many 'countries' have varying degrees of connection with an independent state which might in some cases amount to practical independence. In other cases, a conflict has created differing views as to the 'country's' status. French Guiana, Gibraltar, Jersey, Guam, Palestine, the Cook Islands, Taiwan, Western Sahara and Bonaire all provide different examples of this ambiguity. For travel purposes the distinction is often unimportant but can lead to confusions with paperwork such as visas. The most important examples are Hong Kong and Macau which, though now part of China, are still regarded as separate destinations by, for example, the World Tourism Organization for statistical purposes. *>14-15*

Cruising • One of the fastest-growing sectors within the travel business, and one of the areas which has shown continued growth throughout the problematic years of the early 21st century. In 1985 there were 2.75 million worldwide cruise passengers: this had risen to 4.5 million in 1990, to 11 million in 2000 and to 14 million in 2005. The industry is developing additional itineraries and introducing new ports of call, particularly in the Indian sub-continent and the Far East. *> 46-47, 191*

Ethical tourism • The increasingly popular type of, and attitude to, travel which seeks to ensure that tourism development and activity respects the geographical and social environment. This includes involving local communities in the creation and management of tourism projects, sharing the socio-economic benefits fairly with them, and ensuring that any development makes as much use as possible of sustainable local resources. (The term is often used in conjunction with the overlapping concepts of 'responsible tourism' and 'fairtrade tourism' (qv) and also other terms such as 'ethical tourism' (qv). Such terms are often used interchangeably, but all convey a similar attitude.)

Eco-tourism • Tourism which respects the environment being visited. (The term is often used in conjunction with the overlapping concepts of 'fairtrade tourism' and 'responsible tourism' (qv) and also other more general terms such as 'ethical tourism' (qv).)

Euro • The common currency of 12 of the members of the European Union, introduced in January 2002 and replacing the previously used local currencies. Other countries, notably the UK, may join in the future. *> 60-61*

European Capital of Culture • An initiative, formerly known as the European City of Culture, run by the EU since 1985 to reflect, promote and celebrate Europe's cultural diversity. Until 1999, one city a year was selected, but in the millennium year of 2000 there were nine (Avignon, Bergen, Bologna, Brussels, Cracow, Helsinki, Prague, Reykjavik & Santiago de Compostela). Since then, the cities have been/will be: 2001 – Oporto & Rotterdam; 2002 – Bruges & Salamanca; 2003 – Graz; 2004 – Genoa & Lille; 2005 – Cork; 2006 – Patras; 2007 – Luxembourg & Sibiu; 2008 – Liverpool & Stavanger. The UK's only previous representative was Glasgow in 1990. *>68*

European Union expansion • In 1957, there were six founding members of the then-European Economic Community: from mid-2004 the European Union had 25 members and now, for the first time, has a frontier with Russia. Several other countries including Bulgaria, Romania and Turkey are waiting to join. *>60-61*

Fair-trade tourism • Tourism which is developed and operated in partnership with local communities, and which is designed to be at least partly for their social and economic benefit. This will include ensuring a fair remuneration for

Conclusion

Change, renewal and growth appear to be the three words that best sum up the prospects for the travel business. The world is changing fast, and the best companies are adapting to it. Few industries have such a solid record of performance stretching back several decades to help underpin their future. The desire for new destinations and new experiences seems to be insatiable. Public demand for new ethical standards is growing and will shape future supply. The industry has long since shifted away from its traditional commission-driven pattern of package holidays and monopolistic airlines. It is also shifting away from its well-established Europe-North America axis. To a certain extent, every traveller has become their own travel planner. Do any certainties remain?

Quite possibly not. It seems more than likely that entrepreneurial companies and new technology will continue to challenge all our current preconceptions about travel. So – what's next? Space tourism? In fact, it already exists. Denis Tito was the first (in 2001). Others have followed since, and many more plan to boldly go in the future. Low-cost space tourism, booked through the internet? Now there's a thought…

International departures

The 25 countries that provided the most international travellers in 2003 (millions)
Source: WTO

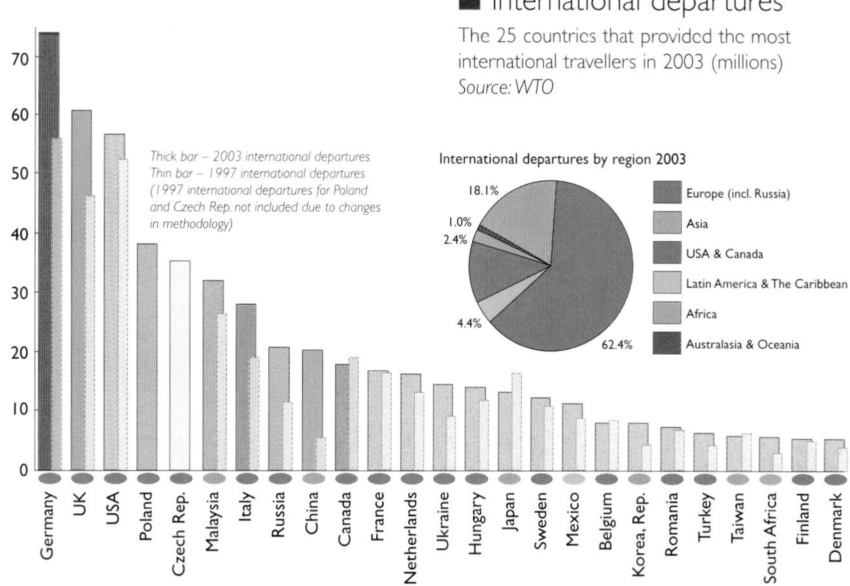
Thick bar – 2003 international departures
Thin bar – 1997 international departures
(1997 international departures for Poland and Czech Rep. not included due to changes in methodology)
0
10
20
30
40
50
60
70
Germany
UK
USA
Poland
Czech Rep.
Malaysia
Italy
Russia
China
Canada
France
Netherlands
Ukraine
Hungary
Japan
Sweden
Mexico
Belgium
Korea, Rep.
Romania
Turkey
Taiwan
South Africa
Finland
Denmark
International departures by region 2003
18.1%
1.0%
2.4%
4.4%
62.4%
Europe (incl. Russia)
Asia
USA & Canada
Latin America & The Caribbean
Africa
Australasia & Oceania

workers, maximising the level of local (rather than foreign) ownership of the tourism facility, encouraging the use of local suppliers of products and services (such as food and tour guides) and establishing sustainable relations between all parties involved. (The term is often used in conjunction with the overlapping concepts of 'responsible tourism' and 'ecotourism' (qv) and also other terms such as 'ethical tourism' (qv).)

GDP and GNI • In crude terms, GDP (Gross Domestic Product) is the value of the wealth produced by a nation – 'the gross value of all resident producers in the economy' as the part of the World Bank's definition puts it. GNI (Gross National Income) is increasingly used in many publications, including this one. The two measures are broadly comparable: in essence, GNI also includes income derived by residents of the country in question from abroad, such as from external investments. >22

High-speed rail • Many countries, particularly in Western Europe and Japan, have invested massive sums in dedicated high-speed lines and trains offering city-to-city services at speeds in excess of 200 kph. The network is constantly expanding and major projects are being planned in many countries, including China and the USA. New Maglev (magnetic levitation) trains represent the new generation, and should run at over 550kph. In Europe, the low-cost airlines have provided considerable competition. *>62-63, 139*

Indian Ocean tsunami • The devastating tidal wave resulting from an undersea earthquake near Northern Indonesia on 26 December 2004. Over 200,000 people were killed and 500,000 left homeless, mainly in Thailand, Indonesia, Sri Lanka, India, the Maldives and the coastal regions of East Africa.

Internet • On-line sales and information services have revolutionised the travel business in recent years, and the trend is increasing. There are countless statistics to illustrate this, and the growth in web usage generally. It took radio 38 years and TV 13 years to build an audience of 50 million in the US: the internet achieved this in three and a half years. The internet had over one billion worldwide users in April 2006. *>37*

Iraq war • After years of diplomatic stand-off and unsuccessful UN attempts to locate Iraq's alleged weapons of mass destruction, US-led coalition forces began attacking the country on 20 March 2003. The war itself, and in particular its protracted count-down, caused a slump in the travel industry worldwide, although the relatively quick resolution of the initial phase of the conflict saw a fairly quick recovery in airline bookings. Despite elections in 2005, the long-term future of Iraq and the nature of its government remains uncertain, as does the question as to whether the intervention will have calmed or inflamed the volatile situation in the Middle East.

Long-haul charters • The introduction of medium-sized wide-body aircraft such as the Boeing 767 and Airbus A300 in the 1990s facilitated the growth of package holidays to destinations further afield such as Goa, Sri Lanka and the Maldives. These areas suddenly became very affordable and, as a consequence, have rapidly developed as a result of the arrival of charter flights from Europe. Many local authorities are currently reviewing the desirability of receiving such flights.

Low-cost airlines • The terms 'budget' and 'no-frills' are also often used. The concept began in the USA in 1971 when Southwest Airlines started services between Dallas and San Antonio. Numerous other airlines have since followed suit, including Jet Blue, Ryanair and easyJet. Their low prices and commercial flexibility result from following very precise and efficient business models.

Mega cruise ships • Any ship with a gross registered tonnage of 100,000 is regarded as mega. The first of these arrived in the late 1990s as *Voyager of the Seas* owned by Royal Caribbean Line at GRT 142.000 GRT: it took 21 million man-hours to build and is (so far) the only cruise vessel with its own zip-code (33132-2028). These massive ships of up to 22 decks high have become resorts at sea opening the cruise market to a much wider audience. On 12 January 2004, Cunard Lines' 150,000 GRT *Queen Mary 2* entered service on the traditional transatlantic scheduled route. RCI's 156,000 GRT *Freedom of the Seas* made its maiden voyage in June 2006.

MICE • 'Meetings, incentives, conferences and exhibitions', which have in recent years become a distinct and increasingly important part of the the global travel business. *>34-35*

Olympic Games • Last held in Athens in August 2004. The next Olympics (the 29th) will be in 2008 in Beijing. *>40*

Pets Travel Scheme • Introduced in 2000, this allows cats and dogs to travel between the UK and a number of European and long-haul destinations (though currently not North America) without the need for quarantine on arrival back in the UK. Pets must be micro-chipped, be issued with an appropriate pet passport, and have a valid vet's certificate certifying vaccination against rabies.

Responsible Tourism • The increasingly important principle that guides touristic development and behaviour, particularly in respect of developing countries, with the aim of ensuring that its impact is as positive as possible. Exact definitions vary, but the Cape Town Declaration of 2002 provides possibly the most comprehensive summary. Its key points are that responsible tourism should: minimise negative economic, environmental, and social impacts; involve local people positively and generate economic benefits for them; contribute to the conservation of natural and cultural heritage; offer more rewarding experiences for tourists through more connections with local people and a greater understanding of local cultural, social and environmental issues; and provide access for physically challenged people. (The term is often used in conjunction with the overlapping concepts of 'fairtrade tourism' and 'eco-tourism' (qv) and also other more general terms such as 'ethical tourism'(qv).)

SARS • Severe Acute Respiratory Syndrome, an air-borne virus which causes flu-like symptoms and sometimes death. The first reported case was in Hanoi in February 2003 and it rapidly spread to other parts of Asia, and to Canada, causing havoc in the travel industry for several months.

Set Jetter • A person who makes holiday destination decisions based wholly or partly on being able to visit the sets or locations of films or novels. By some estimates, up to one in four outbound travellers from the UK could be so described. *>26-27*

Travel statistics • There are a multitude of these available. organisations, cities, states, countries and regions all produce their own, for a variety of purposes; while the most authoritative global figures are compiled by the World Tourism Organization (WTO or, more formally, UNWTO to distinguish it from the Would Trade Organization), which is based in Madrid. Statistics concerning movement of people and money as a result of travel can most conveniently be divided into inbound and outbound, of which the former are generally more complete and reliable. Because of the time spent collating and analysing them, many statistics are not published for months or even years after the period to which they refer and historical data is often revised retrospectively. Comparisons between figures produced by different organisations may be misleading due to possible different methodologies used or time periods covered. *>24-25*

USSR • The Union of Soviet Socialist Republics (also known as the Soviet Union). Dominated by Russia, it came into being in 1922 in the aftermath of the Russian Revolution and Civil War. During the early 1990s it fragmented into 15 independent states in Eastern Europe and Central Asia. All of the former states apart from the three Baltic republics formed the Commonwealth of Independent States in 1991 which still retains some co-ordinating powers.

World Cups • Many sports, notably rugby, cricket and football, organise regular international tournaments, usually every four years. Flights and accommodation for such events may need to be booked months or even years in advance. *>40*

See also... Continental Physical maps (see Contents); World Political (14-15); Geographical Definitions, Longest Rivers, Highest & Lowest (192)

The listings above refer to a selection of related themes. For more information, see the Contents (2-7).

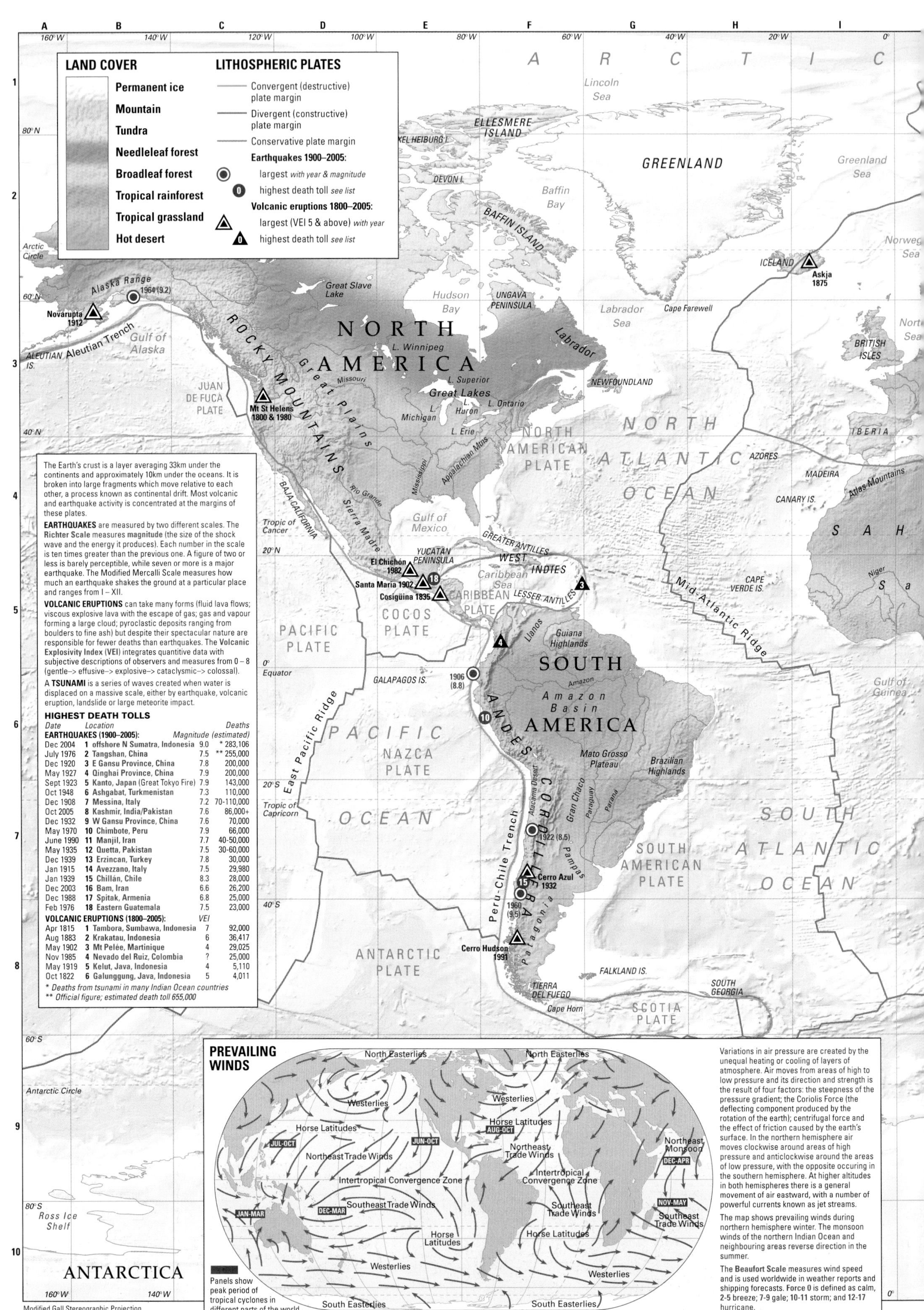
LAND COVER
Permanent ice
Mountain
Tundra
Needleleaf forest
Broadleaf forest
Tropical rainforest
Tropical grassland
Hot desert
LITHOSPHERIC PLATES
Convergent (destructive) plate margin
Divergent (constructive) plate margin
Conservative plate margin
Earthquakes 1900–2005:
largest with year & magnitude
highest death toll see list
Volcanic eruptions 1800–2005:
largest (VEI 5 & above) with year
highest death toll see list
ARCTIC
Lincoln Sea
ELLESMERE ISLAND
DEVON I.
GREENLAND
Greenland Sea
Baffin Bay
BAFFIN ISLAND
Norwegian Sea
ICELAND
Askja 1875
Alaska Range
1964 (9.2)
Novarupta 1912
Great Slave Lake
Hudson Bay
UNGAVA PENINSULA
Labrador Sea
Cape Farewell
ALEUTIAN IS.
Aleutian Trench
Gulf of Alaska
NORTH AMERICA
ROCKY MOUNTAINS
Great Plains
L. Winnipeg
Labrador
BRITISH ISLES
North Sea
Missouri
L. Superior
Great Lakes
L. Huron
L. Michigan
L. Ontario
L. Erie
NEWFOUNDLAND
JUAN DE FUCA PLATE
Mt St Helens 1800 & 1980
NORTH AMERICAN PLATE
NORTH ATLANTIC OCEAN
IBERIA
AZORES
MADEIRA
CANARY IS.
Atlas Mountains
Mississippi
Appalachian Mts
Rio Grande
Sierra Madre
BAJA CALIFORNIA
Tropic of Cancer
Gulf of Mexico
GREATER ANTILLES
YUCATAN PENINSULA
El Chichón 1982
Santa Maria 1902
Cosigüina 1835
WEST INDIES
Caribbean Sea
LESSER ANTILLES
CARIBBEAN PLATE
COCOS PLATE
PACIFIC PLATE
CAPE VERDE IS.
Mid-Atlantic Ridge
Niger
Llanos
Guiana Highlands
SOUTH AMERICA
Amazon
Amazon Basin
GALAPAGOS IS.
1906 (8.8)
Equator
Gulf of Guinea
East Pacific Ridge
PACIFIC OCEAN
NAZCA PLATE
ANDES
Mato Grosso Plateau
Brazilian Highlands
Atacama Desert
Gran Chaco
Paraguay
Parana
CORDILLERA
Tropic of Capricorn
Peru-Chile Trench
1922 (8.5)
Pampas
SOUTH AMERICAN PLATE
SOUTH ATLANTIC OCEAN
Cerro Azul 1932
1960 (9.5)
Patagonia
Cerro Hudson 1991
ANTARCTIC PLATE
FALKLAND IS.
SOUTH GEORGIA
TIERRA DEL FUEGO
Cape Horn
SCOTIA PLATE
Antarctic Circle
Ross Ice Shelf
ANTARCTICA
Modified Gall Stereographic Projection
PREVAILING WINDS
North Easterlies
Westerlies
Horse Latitudes
JUL-OCT
JUN-OCT
AUG-OCT
Northeast Trade Winds
Northeast Monsoon
DEC-APR
Intertropical Convergence Zone
Southeast Trade Winds
JAN-MAR
DEC-MAR
NOV-MAY
South Easterlies
Panels show peak period of tropical cyclones in different parts of the world

The Earth's crust is a layer averaging 33km under the continents and approximately 10km under the oceans. It is broken into large fragments which move relative to each other, a process known as continental drift. Most volcanic and earthquake activity is concentrated at the margins of these plates.

EARTHQUAKES are measured by two different scales. The **Richter Scale** measures **magnitude** (the size of the shock wave and the energy it produces). Each number in the scale is ten times greater than the previous one. A figure of two or less is barely perceptible, while seven or more is a major earthquake. The Modified Mercalli Scale measures how much an earthquake shakes the ground at a particular place and ranges from I – XII.

VOLCANIC ERUPTIONS can take many forms (fluid lava flows; viscous explosive lava with the escape of gas; gas and vapour forming a large cloud; pyroclastic deposits ranging from boulders to fine ash) but despite their spectacular nature are responsible for fewer deaths than earthquakes. The **Volcanic Explosivity Index (VEI)** integrates quantitive data with subjective descriptions of observers and measures from 0 – 8 (gentle–> effusive–> explosive–> cataclysmic–> colossal).

A **TSUNAMI** is a series of waves created when water is displaced on a massive scale, either by earthquake, volcanic eruption, landslide or large meteorite impact.

HIGHEST DEATH TOLLS

Date		*Location*		*Deaths*
EARTHQUAKES (1900–2005):			*Magnitude*	*(estimated)*
Dec 2004	**1**	**offshore N Sumatra, Indonesia**	9.0	* 283,106
July 1976	**2**	**Tangshan, China**	7.5	** 255,000
Dec 1920	**3**	**E Gansu Province, China**	7.8	200,000
May 1927	**4**	**Qinghai Province, China**	7.9	200,000
Sept 1923	**5**	**Kanto, Japan** (Great Tokyo Fire)	7.9	143,000
Oct 1948	**6**	**Ashgabat, Turkmenistan**	7.3	110,000
Dec 1908	**7**	**Messina, Italy**	7.2	70-110,000
Oct 2005	**8**	**Kashmir, India/Pakistan**	7.6	86,000+
Dec 1932	**9**	**W Gansu Province, China**	7.6	70,000
May 1970	**10**	**Chimbote, Peru**	7.9	66,000
June 1990	**11**	**Manjil, Iran**	7.7	40-50,000
May 1935	**12**	**Quetta, Pakistan**	7.5	30-60,000
Dec 1939	**13**	**Erzincan, Turkey**	7.8	30,000
Jan 1915	**14**	**Avezzano, Italy**	7.5	29,980
Jan 1939	**15**	**Chillán, Chile**	8.3	28,000
Dec 2003	**16**	**Bam, Iran**	6.6	26,200
Dec 1988	**17**	**Spitak, Armenia**	6.8	25,000
Feb 1976	**18**	**Eastern Guatemala**	7.5	23,000
VOLCANIC ERUPTIONS (1800–2005):			*VEI*	
Apr 1815	**1**	**Tambora, Sumbawa, Indonesia**	7	92,000
Aug 1883	**2**	**Krakatau, Indonesia**	6	36,417
May 1902	**3**	**Mt Pelée, Martinique**	4	29,025
Nov 1985	**4**	**Nevado del Ruiz, Colombia**	?	25,000
May 1919	**5**	**Kelut, Java, Indonesia**	4	5,110
Oct 1822	**6**	**Galunggung, Java, Indonesia**	5	4,011

** Deaths from tsunami in many Indian Ocean countries*
*** Official figure; estimated death toll 655,000*

Variations in air pressure are created by the unequal heating or cooling of layers of atmosphere. Air moves from areas of high to low pressure and its direction and strength is the result of four factors: the steepness of the pressure gradient; the Coriolis Force (the deflecting component produced by the rotation of the earth); centrifugal force and the effect of friction caused by the earth's surface. In the northern hemisphere air moves clockwise around areas of high pressure and anticlockwise around the areas of low pressure, with the opposite occuring in the southern hemisphere. At higher altitudes in both hemispheres there is a general movement of air eastward, with a number of powerful currents known as jet streams.

The map shows prevailing winds during northern hemisphere winter. The monsoon winds of the northern Indian Ocean and neighbouring areas reverse direction in the summer.

The **Beaufort Scale** measures wind speed and is used worldwide in weather reports and shipping forecasts. **Force 0** is defined as calm, **2-5** breeze; **7-9** gale; **10-11** storm; and **12-17** hurricane.

▶ See also... Continental Physical maps (see Contents); World Political (14-15); Geographical Definitions, Longest Rivers, Highest & Lowest (192)

The listings above refer to a selection of related themes. For more information, see the Contents (2-7).

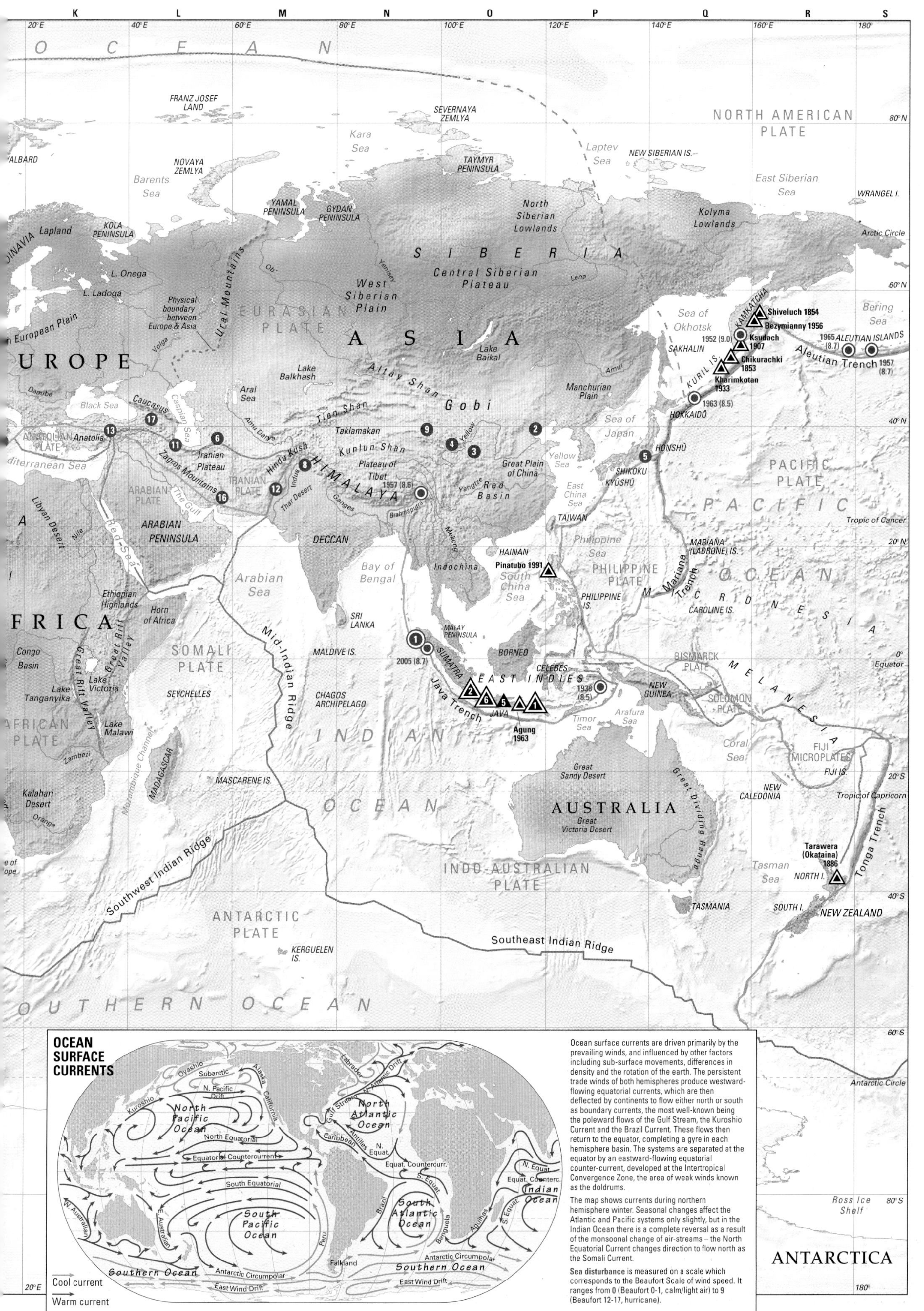
K
L
M
N
O
P
Q
R
S
20°E
40°E
60°E
80°E
100°E
120°E
140°E
160°E
180°
80°N
60°N
40°N
20°N
0°
20°S
40°S
60°S
80°S
O C E A N
FRANZ JOSEF LAND
SEVERNAYA ZEMLYA
NORTH AMERICAN PLATE
Kara Sea
Laptev Sea
NEW SIBERIAN IS.
NOVAYA ZEMLYA
TAYMYR PENINSULA
Barents Sea
East Siberian Sea
WRANGEL I.
YAMAL PENINSULA
GYDAN PENINSULA
North Siberian Lowlands
Kolyma Lowlands
KOLA PENINSULA
Lapland
Arctic Circle
S I B E R I A
Central Siberian Plateau
L. Onega
West Siberian Plain
Lena
L. Ladoga
Ural Mountains
Ob'
Yenisey
Physical boundary between Europe & Asia
EURASIAN PLATE
European Plain
Volga
A S I A
Sea of Okhotsk
KAMCHATKA
Shiveluch 1854
Bezymianny 1956
Bering Sea
1952 (9.0)
Ksudach 1907
1965 (8.7)
ALEUTIAN ISLANDS
SAKHALIN
Chikurachki 1853
Aleutian Trench
1957 (8.7)
Lake Baikal
KURIL IS.
Kharimkotan 1933
UROPE
Lake Balkhash
Altay Shan
Amur
Manchurian Plain
Danube
Aral Sea
1963 (8.5)
Black Sea
Caucasus
Tien Shan
Gobi
HOKKAIDŌ
Sea of Japan
Caspian Sea
Amu Darya
Taklamakan
Yellow
ANATOLIAN PLATE
Anatolia
Iranian Plateau
Kunlun Shan
HONSHŪ
Mediterranean Sea
Zagros Mountains
Hindu Kush
Plateau of Tibet
Great Plain of China
Yellow Sea
SHIKOKU
KYŪSHŪ
PACIFIC PLATE
IRANIAN PLATE
HIMALAYA
Indus
Red Basin
Yangtze
ARABIAN PLATE
The Gulf
Thar Desert
1957 (8.6)
East China Sea
Ganges
Brahmaputra
P A C I F I C
Libyan Desert
ARABIAN PENINSULA
TAIWAN
Tropic of Cancer
Red Sea
Nile
DECCAN
Mekong
Philippine Sea
MARIANA (LADRONE) IS.
HAINAN
Pinatubo 1991
Bay of Bengal
Indochina
South China Sea
Arabian Sea
PHILIPPINE PLATE
Mariana Trench
O C E A N
Ethiopian Highlands
PHILIPPINE IS.
M I C R O N E S I A
CAROLINE IS.
FRICA
Horn of Africa
SRI LANKA
Great Rift Valley
Mid-Indian Ridge
MALAY PENINSULA
Congo Basin
SOMALI PLATE
MALDIVE IS.
BORNEO
BISMARCK PLATE
Equator
2005 (8.7)
SUMATRA
CELEBES
M E L A N E S I A
Lake Victoria
EAST INDIES
Lake Tanganyika
SEYCHELLES
CHAGOS ARCHIPELAGO
1938 (8.5)
NEW GUINEA
Java Trench
JAVA
SOLOMON PLATE
AFRICAN PLATE
Lake Malawi
Arafura Sea
Timor Sea
Agung 1963
I N D I A N
Zambezi
Coral Sea
FIJI MICROPLATE
MADAGASCAR
Mozambique Channel
Great Sandy Desert
Great Dividing Range
FIJI IS.
MASCARENE IS.
Kalahari Desert
NEW CALEDONIA
Tropic of Capricorn
O C E A N
AUSTRALIA
Orange
Great Victoria Desert
Tonga Trench
Tarawera (Okataina) 1886
Southwest Indian Ridge
INDO-AUSTRALIAN PLATE
Tasman Sea
NORTH I.
TASMANIA
SOUTH I.
NEW ZEALAND
ANTARCTIC PLATE
KERGUELEN IS.
Southeast Indian Ridge
S O U T H E R N O C E A N
Antarctic Circle
Ross Ice Shelf
ANTARCTICA
OCEAN SURFACE CURRENTS
Oyashio
Subarctic
Alaska
Labrador
N. Atlantic Drift
N. Pacific Drift
California
Kuroshio
North Pacific Ocean
Gulf Stream
North Atlantic Ocean
North Equatorial
Canaries
Caribbean
Antilles
N. Equat.
Equatorial Countercurrent
Equat. Countercurr.
N. Equat.
Equat. Counterc.
South Equatorial
S. Equat.
Indian Ocean
W. Australian
E. Australian
South Pacific Ocean
Peru
Brazil
South Atlantic Ocean
Benguela
Agulhas
S. Equat.
Falkland
Antarctic Circumpolar
Southern Ocean
East Wind Drift
Cool current
Warm current

Ocean surface currents are driven primarily by the prevailing winds, and influenced by other factors including sub-surface movements, differences in density and the rotation of the earth. The persistent trade winds of both hemispheres produce westward-flowing equatorial currents, which are then deflected by continents to flow either north or south as boundary currents, the most well-known being the poleward flows of the Gulf Stream, the Kuroshio Current and the Brazil Current. These flows then return to the equator, completing a gyre in each hemisphere basin. The systems are separated at the equator by an eastward-flowing equatorial counter-current, developed at the Intertropical Convergence Zone, the area of weak winds known as the doldrums.

The map shows currents during northern hemisphere winter. Seasonal changes affect the Atlantic and Pacific systems only slightly, but in the Indian Ocean there is a complete reversal as a result of the monsoonal change of air-streams – the North Equatorial Current changes direction to flow north as the Somali Current.

Sea disturbance is measured on a scale which corresponds to the Beaufort Scale of wind speed. It ranges from 0 (Beaufort 0-1, calm/light air) to 9 (Beaufort 12-17, hurricane).

See also... Continental maps (see Contents); World Physical (12-13); Population & Urbanization (20); Major Urban Areas (196); Countries A-Z (202-210)

The listings above refer to a selection of related themes. For more information, see the Contents (2-7).

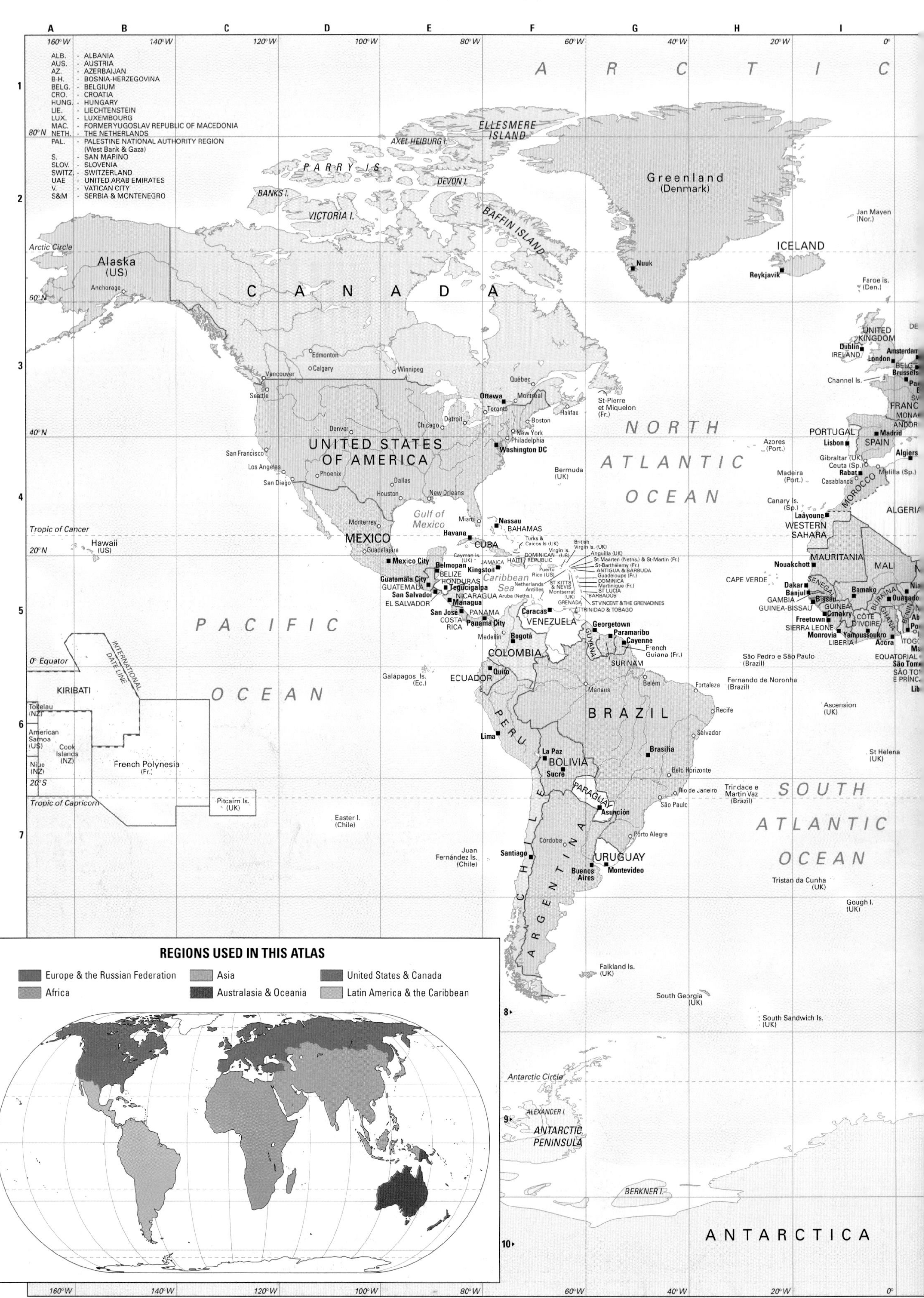
A
B
C
D
E
F
G
H
I
160°W
140°W
120°W
100°W
80°W
60°W
40°W
20°W
0°
1
2
3
4
5
6
7
ALB. - ALBANIA
AUS. - AUSTRIA
AZ. - AZERBAIJAN
B-H. - BOSNIA-HERZEGOVINA
BELG. - BELGIUM
CRO. - CROATIA
HUNG. - HUNGARY
LIE. - LIECHTENSTEIN
LUX. - LUXEMBOURG
MAC. - FORMER YUGOSLAV REPUBLIC OF MACEDONIA
NETH. - THE NETHERLANDS
PAL. - PALESTINE NATIONAL AUTHORITY REGION (West Bank & Gaza)
S. - SAN MARINO
SLOV. - SLOVENIA
SWITZ. - SWITZERLAND
UAE - UNITED ARAB EMIRATES
V. - VATICAN CITY
S&M - SERBIA & MONTENEGRO
80°N
A R C T I C
ELLESMERE ISLAND
AXEL HEIBURG I.
PARRY IS.
DEVON I.
BANKS I.
VICTORIA I.
BAFFIN ISLAND
Greenland
(Denmark)
Jan Mayen
(Nor.)
Arctic Circle
Alaska
(US)
Anchorage
60°N
C A N A D A
Nuuk
ICELAND
Reykjavik
Faroe Is.
(Den.)
UNITED KINGDOM
Dublin
IRELAND
London
Amsterdam
Brussels
Channel Is.
FRANCE
Edmonton
Calgary
Vancouver
Seattle
Winnipeg
Québec
Ottawa
Montreal
Toronto
Halifax
St-Pierre et Miquelon
(Fr.)
Detroit
Chicago
Boston
New York
Philadelphia
Washington DC
Denver
UNITED STATES OF AMERICA
40°N
N O R T H
A T L A N T I C
O C E A N
PORTUGAL
Lisbon
Madrid
SPAIN
Azores
(Port.)
Gibraltar (UK)
Ceuta (Sp.)
Rabat
Algiers
Melilla (Sp.)
Casablanca
MOROCCO
Madeira
(Port.)
San Francisco
Los Angeles
San Diego
Phoenix
Dallas
Houston
New Orleans
Bermuda
(UK)
Canary Is.
(Sp.)
Laâyoune
WESTERN SAHARA
ALGERIA
Gulf of Mexico
Miami
Nassau
BAHAMAS
Monterrey
Tropic of Cancer
Hawaii
(US)
20°N
MEXICO
Guadalajara
Havana
CUBA
Mexico City
Belmopan
BELIZE
Kingston
JAMAICA
HAITI
DOMINICAN REPUBLIC
Puerto Rico (US)
Guatemala City
GUATEMALA
HONDURAS
Tegucigalpa
San Salvador
EL SALVADOR
NICARAGUA
Managua
Caribbean Sea
San José
COSTA RICA
PANAMA
Panama City
Caracas
VENEZUELA
Georgetown
Paramaribo
Cayenne
French Guiana (Fr.)
GUYANA
SURINAM
Bogotá
Medellín
COLOMBIA
Quito
ECUADOR
Galápagos Is.
(Ec.)
MAURITANIA
Nouakchott
MALI
CAPE VERDE
Dakar
SENEGAL
Banjul
GAMBIA
Bissau
GUINEA-BISSAU
GUINEA
Conakry
Bamako
Freetown
SIERRA LEONE
Monrovia
LIBERIA
CÔTE D'IVOIRE
Yamoussoukro
Accra
GHANA
P A C I F I C
O C E A N
0° Equator
INTERNATIONAL DATE LINE
KIRIBATI
Tokelau
(NZ)
American Samoa
(US)
Cook Islands
(NZ)
Niue
(NZ)
French Polynesia
(Fr.)
20°S
Tropic of Capricorn
Pitcairn Is.
(UK)
Easter I.
(Chile)
Juan Fernández Is.
(Chile)
São Pedro e São Paulo
(Brazil)
Fernando de Noronha
(Brazil)
Belém
Fortaleza
Manaus
B R A Z I L
Recife
Salvador
Ascension
(UK)
PERU
Lima
La Paz
BOLIVIA
Sucre
Brasília
Belo Horizonte
St Helena
(UK)
PARAGUAY
Asunción
Rio de Janeiro
São Paulo
Trindade e Martin Vaz
(Brazil)
S O U T H
A T L A N T I C
O C E A N
Porto Alegre
Córdoba
Santiago
CHILE
URUGUAY
Buenos Aires
Montevideo
ARGENTINA
Tristan da Cunha
(UK)
Gough I.
(UK)
Falkland Is.
(UK)
South Georgia
(UK)
South Sandwich Is.
(UK)
8
Antarctic Circle
9
ALEXANDER I.
ANTARCTIC PENINSULA
BERKNER I.
10
A N T A R C T I C A
REGIONS USED IN THIS ATLAS
Europe & the Russian Federation
Asia
United States & Canada
Africa
Australasia & Oceania
Latin America & the Caribbean

Modified Gall Stereographic Projection

See also... Continental maps (see Contents); World Physical (12-13); Population & Urbanization (20); Major Urban Areas (196); Countries A-Z (202-210)

The listings above refer to a selection of related themes. For more information, see the Contents (2-7).

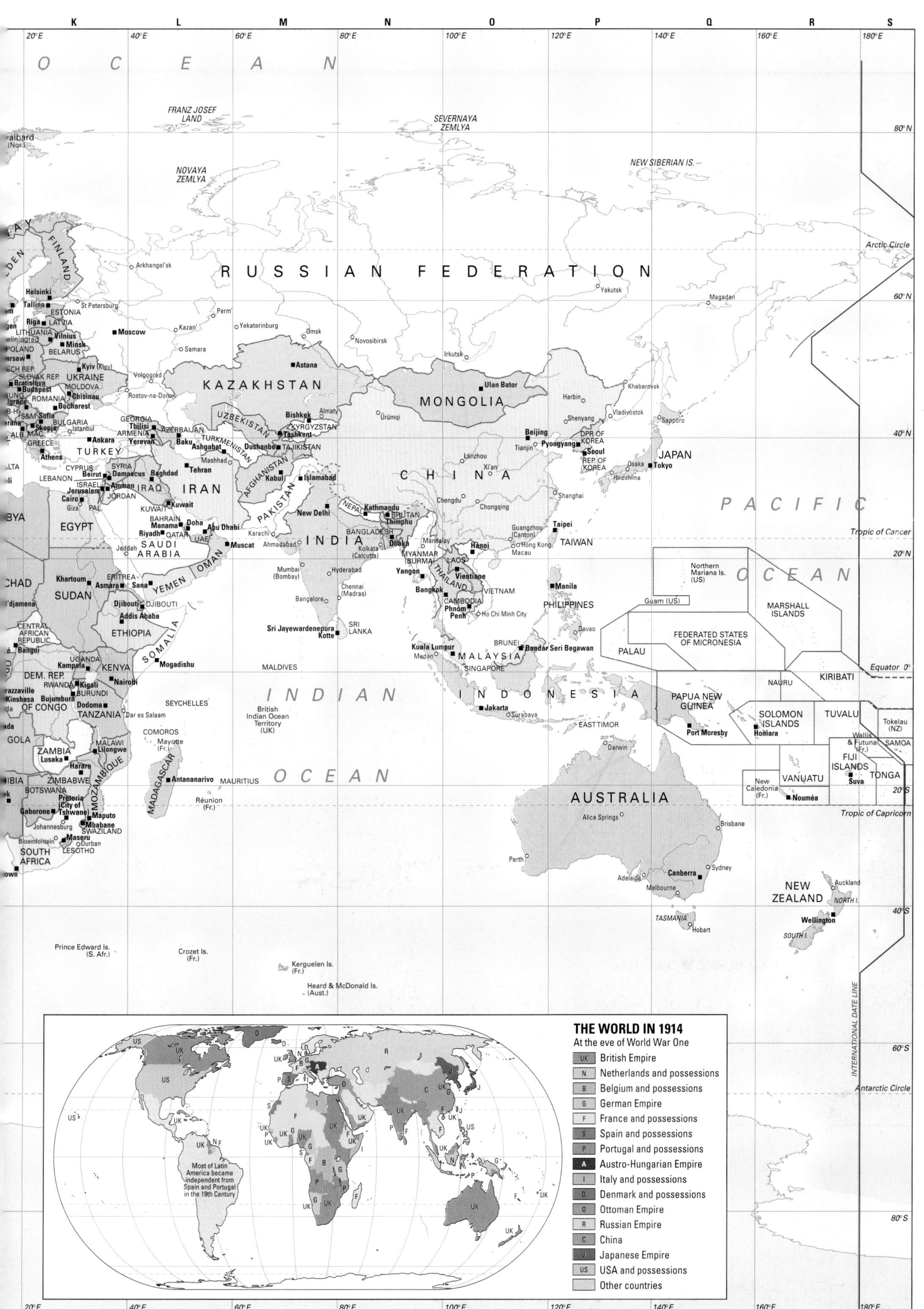
THE WORLD IN 1914
At the eve of World War One
UK British Empire
N Netherlands and possessions
B Belgium and possessions
G German Empire
F France and possessions
S Spain and possessions
P Portugal and possessions
A Austro-Hungarian Empire
I Italy and possessions
D Denmark and possessions
O Ottoman Empire
R Russian Empire
C China
J Japanese Empire
US USA and possessions
Other countries
Most of Latin America became independent from Spain and Portugal in the 19th Century
RUSSIAN FEDERATION
KAZAKHSTAN
MONGOLIA
CHINA
INDIA
IRAN
JAPAN
AUSTRALIA
INDONESIA
PACIFIC OCEAN
INDIAN OCEAN
NEW ZEALAND
INTERNATIONAL DATE LINE

See also... World Environment (17); Regional Climate Terms (196); Continental Climate maps & charts (see General Contents)

The listings above refer to a selection of related themes. For more information, see the Contents (2-7).

WEATHER EXTREMES

Highest temperature in the shade: Al 'Aziziyah, Libya
57.8°C (136.0°F) on 13th Sept 1922

Hottest place: Dalol, Ethiopia
average annual temperature of 34.4°C (94.0°F)

Lowest temperature: Vostok Base, Antarctica
-89.2°C (-128.6°F) on 21st July 1983

Coldest place: Pole of Cold, Antarctica
average annual temperature of -58°C (-72°F)

Coldest inhabited place: Noril'sk, Russian Federation
average annual temperature of -10.9°C (12.4°F)

Greatest snowfall: Mt Rainier, Washington, USA
31,102 mm (1,224.5 inches) over a 12-month period, 1972-73

Most sunshine: Yuma, Arizona, USA
averages 4,127 hours of sunshine per year

Least sunshine: South Pole
no sunshine for 182 days a year

Driest place: Atacama Desert, Chile
virtually no rain throughout the year

Wettest place: Mawsynram, Meghalaya, India
11,873 mm (467.4 inches) during a 12-month period

Most rainy days: Mt Waialeale, Hawaii
up to 350 rainy days per year

Most thunder days: Tororo, Uganda
up to 251 days per year

Highest surface wind speed
• ***Tornado:*** Oklahoma City, Oklahoma, USA
512 km per hour (318 miles per hour) on 3rd May 1999
• ***High altitude:*** Mt Washington, New Hampshire, USA
372 km per hour (231 miles per hour) on 12th Apr 1934
• ***Low altitude:*** Qaanaaq (Thule), Greenland
333 km per hour (207 miles per hour) on 8th Mar 1972

Windiest place: Commonwealth Bay, Antarctica
322 km per hour (200 miles per hour) in gales

Heaviest hailstones: Gopalganj, Bangladesh
weighing up to one kilogram (2.2 lb) on 14th Apr 1986

Polar: no warm season (warmest month below 10°C)
Ice cap (perpetual frost: all months below 0°C) and Tundra (warmest month between 0°C and 10°C)

Cooler humid: rainy climates with severe winters (coldest month below 0°C, warmest month above 10°C)
Subarctic (less than four months over 10°C), Continental cool summer (warmest month below 22°C) and
Continental warm summer (warmest month above 22°C)

Warmer humid: rainy climates with mild winters (coolest month between 0°C and 18°C, warmest month above 10°C)
Temperate (warmest month below 22°C), Humid Subtropical (warmest month above 22°C) and
Mediterranean (dry season in summer)

Dry Steppe/semi-arid and Desert/arid

Tropical humid: rainy climates with no winter (coolest month above 18°C)
Savannah (with a dry season, either in summer or winter) and
Rainforest (constantly moist or monsoon rain with only a short dry season)

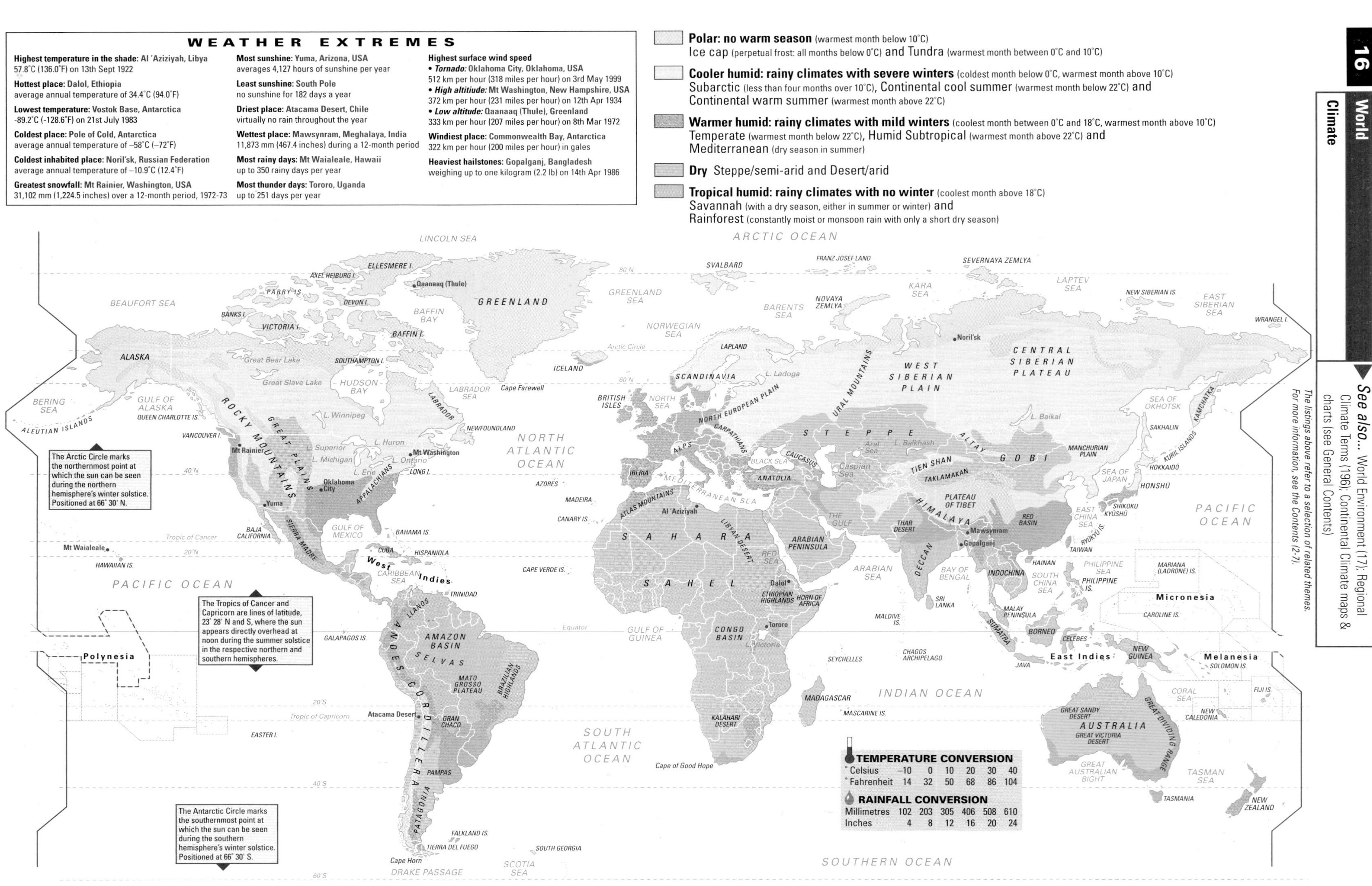
ARCTIC OCEAN
LINCOLN SEA
ELLESMERE I.
AXEL HEIBURG I.
Qaanaaq (Thule)
GREENLAND
PARRY IS.
DEVON I.
BEAUFORT SEA
BANKS I.
BAFFIN BAY
VICTORIA I.
BAFFIN I.
ALASKA
Great Bear Lake
SOUTHAMPTON I.
Great Slave Lake
HUDSON BAY
LABRADOR
LABRADOR SEA
Cape Farewell
ICELAND
GREENLAND SEA
NORWEGIAN SEA
Arctic Circle
SVALBARD
BARENTS SEA
NOVAYA ZEMLYA
FRANZ JOSEF LAND
KARA SEA
SEVERNAYA ZEMLYA
LAPTEV SEA
NEW SIBERIAN IS.
EAST SIBERIAN SEA
WRANGEL I.
BERING SEA
ALEUTIAN ISLANDS
GULF OF ALASKA
QUEEN CHARLOTTE IS.
VANCOUVER I.
Mt Rainier
ROCKY MOUNTAINS
GREAT PLAINS
L. Winnipeg
L. Superior
L. Michigan
L. Huron
L. Ontario
L. Erie
Mt Washington
LONG I.
NEWFOUNDLAND
APPALACHIANS
Oklahoma City
Yuma
BAJA CALIFORNIA
SIERRA MADRE
GULF OF MEXICO
BAHAMA IS.
CUBA
HISPANIOLA
West Indies
CARIBBEAN SEA
TRINIDAD
Tropic of Cancer
Mt Waialeale
HAWAIIAN IS.
PACIFIC OCEAN
NORTH ATLANTIC OCEAN
AZORES
MADEIRA
CANARY IS.
CAPE VERDE IS.
Equator
GALAPAGOS IS.
LLANOS
AMAZON BASIN
SELVAS
ANDES
CORDILLERA
MATO GROSSO PLATEAU
BRAZILIAN HIGHLANDS
GRAN CHACO
Atacama Desert
Tropic of Capricorn
EASTER I.
PAMPAS
PATAGONIA
FALKLAND IS.
TIERRA DEL FUEGO
Cape Horn
DRAKE PASSAGE
SCOTIA SEA
SOUTH GEORGIA
Polynesia
SOUTH ATLANTIC OCEAN
GULF OF GUINEA
LAPLAND
SCANDINAVIA
L. Ladoga
BRITISH ISLES
NORTH SEA
NORTH EUROPEAN PLAIN
CARPATHIANS
ALPS
IBERIA
MEDITERRANEAN SEA
BLACK SEA
CAUCASUS
ANATOLIA
ATLAS MOUNTAINS
Al 'Aziziyah
SAHARA
LIBYAN DESERT
SAHEL
RED SEA
Dalol
ETHIOPIAN HIGHLANDS
HORN OF AFRICA
Tororo
L. Victoria
CONGO BASIN
KALAHARI DESERT
Cape of Good Hope
MADAGASCAR
MASCARINE IS.
SEYCHELLES
URAL MOUNTAINS
WEST SIBERIAN PLAIN
Noril'sk
CENTRAL SIBERIAN PLATEAU
STEPPE
Aral Sea
L. Balkhash
Caspian Sea
THE GULF
ARABIAN PENINSULA
ARABIAN SEA
TIEN SHAN
TAKLAMAKAN
ALTAY
GOBI
L. Baikal
PLATEAU OF TIBET
HIMALAYA
THAR DESERT
DECCAN
Mawsynram
Gopalganj
BAY OF BENGAL
SRI LANKA
MALDIVE IS.
CHAGOS ARCHIPELAGO
INDIAN OCEAN
RED BASIN
MANCHURIAN PLAIN
SEA OF OKHOTSK
KAMCHATKA
SAKHALIN
KURIL ISLANDS
HOKKAIDŌ
HONSHŪ
SEA OF JAPAN
SHIKOKU
KYŪSHŪ
RYUKYU IS.
EAST CHINA SEA
TAIWAN
HAINAN
INDOCHINA
SOUTH CHINA SEA
PHILIPPINE SEA
PHILIPPINE IS.
MALAY PENINSULA
SUMATRA
BORNEO
CELEBES
JAVA
East Indies
NEW GUINEA
MARIANA (LADRONE) IS.
Micronesia
CAROLINE IS.
Melanesia
SOLOMON IS.
PACIFIC OCEAN
CORAL SEA
NEW CALEDONIA
FIJI IS.
GREAT SANDY DESERT
AUSTRALIA
GREAT VICTORIA DESERT
GREAT DIVIDING RANGE
GREAT AUSTRALIAN BIGHT
TASMAN SEA
TASMANIA
NEW ZEALAND
SOUTHERN OCEAN
80°N
60°N
40°N
20°N
20°S
40°S
60°S

The Arctic Circle marks the northernmost point at which the sun can be seen during the northern hemisphere's winter solstice. Positioned at 66° 30' N.

The Tropics of Cancer and Capricorn are lines of latitude, 23° 28' N and S, where the sun appears directly overhead at noon during the summer solstice in the respective northern and southern hemispheres.

The Antarctic Circle marks the southernmost point at which the sun can be seen during the southern hemisphere's winter solstice. Positioned at 66° 30' S.

TEMPERATURE CONVERSION

° Celsius	–10	0	10	20	30	40
° Fahrenheit	14	32	50	68	86	104

RAINFALL CONVERSION

Millimetres	102	203	305	406	508	610
Inches	4	8	12	16	20	24

See also... World Physical (12-13); World Climate (16); Energy (28-29)
The listings above refer to a selection of related themes. For more information, see the Contents (2-7).

AGRICULTURAL LAND & FORESTS

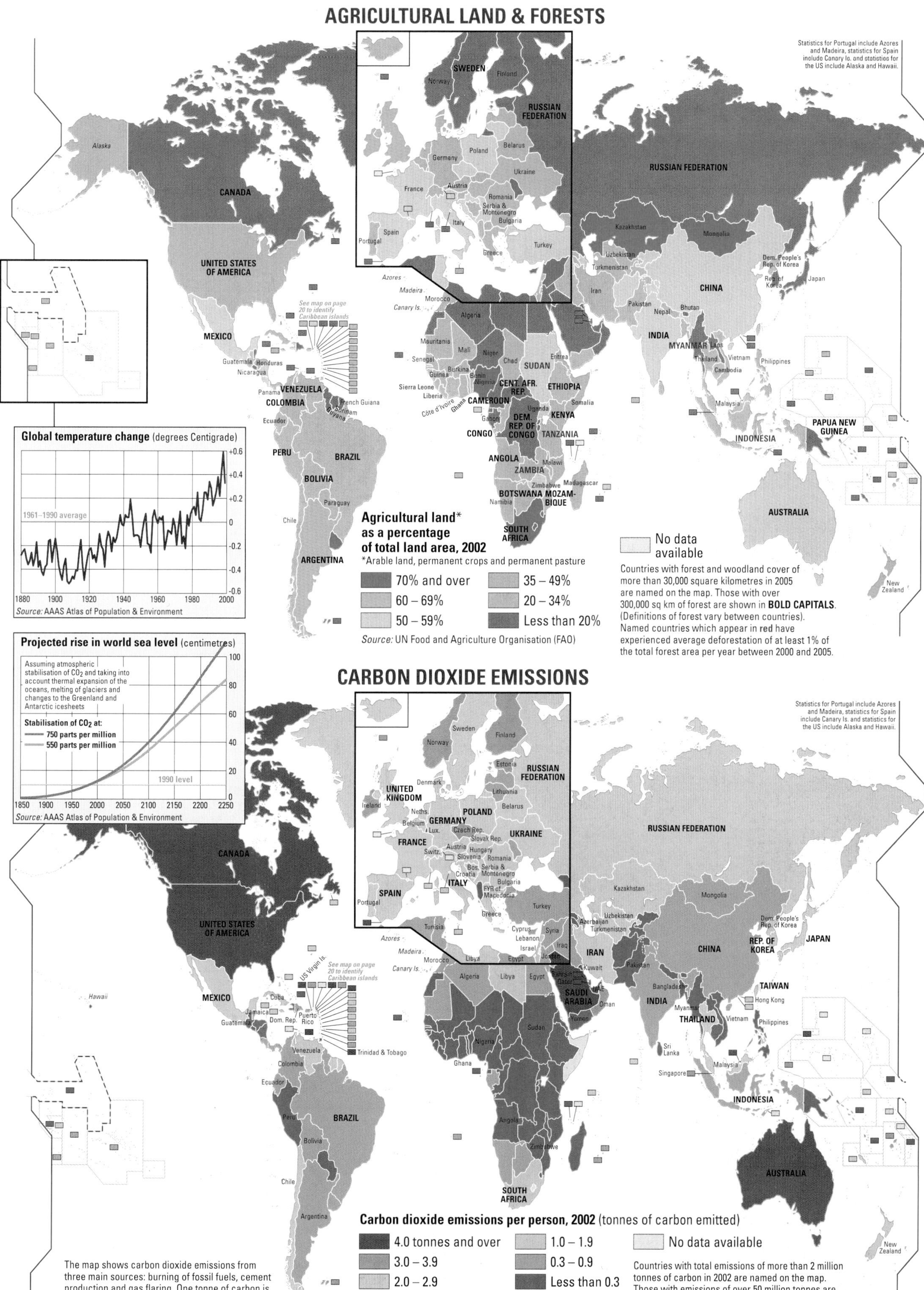
Statistics for Portugal include Azores and Madeira, statistics for Spain include Canary Is. and statistics for the US include Alaska and Hawaii.
Global temperature change (degrees Centigrade)
1961–1990 average
Source: AAAS Atlas of Population & Environment
Projected rise in world sea level (centimetres)
Assuming atmospheric stabilisation of CO_2 and taking into account thermal expansion of the oceans, melting of glaciers and changes to the Greenland and Antarctic icesheets
Stabilisation of CO_2 at:
750 parts per million
550 parts per million
1990 level
Source: AAAS Atlas of Population & Environment
See map on page 20 to identify Caribbean islands
CANADA
UNITED STATES OF AMERICA
MEXICO
RUSSIAN FEDERATION
CHINA
INDIA
BRAZIL
AUSTRALIA
INDONESIA
SOUTH AFRICA
CARBON DIOXIDE EMISSIONS

Agricultural land* as a percentage of total land area, 2002

*Arable land, permanent crops and permanent pasture

- 70% and over
- 60 – 69%
- 50 – 59%
- 35 – 49%
- 20 – 34%
- Less than 20%

Source: UN Food and Agriculture Organisation (FAO)

No data available

Countries with forest and woodland cover of more than 30,000 square kilometres in 2005 are named on the map. Those with over 300,000 sq km of forest are shown in **BOLD CAPITALS**. (Definitions of forest vary between countries). Named countries which appear in **red** have experienced average deforestation of at least 1% of the total forest area per year between 2000 and 2005.

CARBON DIOXIDE EMISSIONS

Carbon dioxide emissions per person, 2002 (tonnes of carbon emitted)

- 4.0 tonnes and over
- 3.0 – 3.9
- 2.0 – 2.9
- 1.0 – 1.9
- 0.3 – 0.9
- Less than 0.3
- No data available

Source: Oak Ridge National Laboratory, USA

The map shows carbon dioxide emissions from three main sources: burning of fossil fuels, cement production and gas flaring. One tonne of carbon is equivalent to 3.67 tonnes of carbon dioxide.

Countries with total emissions of more than 2 million tonnes of carbon in 2002 are named on the map. Those with emissions of over 50 million tonnes are shown in **BOLD CAPITALS**.

▶ See also... Flight Times (45); Russian Republics (111); US Time Zones (165)

The listings above refer to a selection of related themes. For more information, see the Contents (2-7).

This table provides time differences compared to the Universal Time Co-ordinate (UTC), now the generally accepted term for Greenwich Mean Time (GMT). Time differences , in hours and (sometimes) minutes, are coloured by whether the 'normal' (non Daylight Saving) time in the main part of the country is ahead (red) or behind (blue) UTC. Countries that use UTC are in green.

Several countries span more than one time zone. In some cases (such as the USA) these zones have names which are widely understood. In others (such as Russia) a list of the main cities within each zone has been considered more useful. The names used to describe these zones here do not necessarily follow any official term, even where one exists. Countries may change their time arrangements without reference to any international body, although alterations usually only affect Daylight Saving Time (see below) rather than the 'normal' time. One exception to this was in 2000 when part of Kiribati moved its time forward to UTC+14 in order to be the first place on earth to see in the new millennium.

Daylight Saving Time (DST) was first introduced in some European countries during the First World War, but the idea did not become firmly or widely accepted until 1960s. Today it is used in some or all of about 70 states, generally outside the tropics. Clocks are advanced by one hour in spring and put back one hour in autumn. While many countries change their clocks on predictable days from year to year, others do not. There is no universal agreement on the subject and countries, or regions within them, may make any arrangements they see fit, often at short notice. Some countries, most notably the USA, have extendied the period of DST as an energy-saving measure, and others may follow suit . All information may thus be subject to change.

The dates between which DST is effective are shown in the 'DST change' column. For the reasons described above, these may alter from year to year. The letters M, A, S, O and N refer to March, April, September, October and November. The abbreviations Su, Th, etc refer to the day of the week. The initial number (or L, for last) refers to the incidence of that day in the month. Thus LSuM-LSuO (by far the most common period, and one which applies throughout Europe) means the Last Sunday in March to the Last Sunday in October. In some cases, particularly countries in the Middle East which use different calendars, dates cannot accurately be predicted and so more general ranges have been given. Sometimes DST is not observed throughout all of the area in question. The more important of these are referred to in this column.

For reasons of space, information has not been included on several minor dependencies and overseas territories .

Country	Time	(DST time)	DST change
Afghanistan	+4.30		
Albania	+1	(+2)	LSuM-LSuO
Algeria	+1		
American Samoa	-11		
Andorra	+1	(+2)	LSuM-LSuO
Angola	+1		
Anguilla	-4		
Antigua & Barbuda	-4		
Argentina	-3		
Armenia	+4	(+5)	LSuM-LSuO
Aruba	-4		
Australia – *Western*	+8		
– *Central*	+9.30	(+10.30)	LSuO-LSuM (SA)
– *Eastern*	+10	(+11)	1SuO-LSaM *(not QL)*
Austria	+1	(+2)	LSuM-LSuO
Azerbaijan	+4	(+5)	LSuM-LSuO
Bahamas	-5	(-4)	LSuM-LSuO
Bahrain	+3		
Bangladesh	+6		
Barbados	-4		
Belarus	+2	(+3)	LSuM-LSuO
Belgium	+1	(+2)	LSuM-LSuO
Belize	-6		
Benin	+1		
Bermuda	-4	(-3)	1SuA-LSuO
Bhutan	+6		
Bolivia	-4		
Bonaire	-4		
Bosnia-Herzegovina	+1	(+2)	LSuM-LSuO
Botswana	+2		
Brazil – *Western*	-5		
– *Central*	-4	(-3)	3SuO-3SaF
– *Eastern*	-3	(-2)	3SuO-3SaF
– *Fernando de Noronha*	-2		
British Virgin Islands	-4		
Bulgaria	+2	(+3)	LSuM-LSuO
Burkina	UTC		
Burundi	+2		
Cambodia	+7		
Cameroon	+1		
Canada – *Newfoundland*	-3.30	(-2.30)	1SuA-LSuO
– *Atlantic*	-4	(-3)	1SuA-LSuO
– *Eastern*	-5	(-4)	1SuA-LSuO
– *Central*	-6	(-5)	1SuA-LSuO *(not SK)*
– *Mountain*	-7	(-6)	1SuA-LSuO
– *Pacific*	-8	(-7)	1SuA-LSuO
Cape Verde	-1		
Cayman Islands	-5		
Central African Republic	+1		
Chad	+1		
Channel Islands	UTC	(+1)	LSuM-LSuO
Chile – *incl. Juan Fernandez*	-4	(-3)	2SuO-2SaM
– *Easter Island*	-6	(-5)	2SuO-2SaM
China – *incl. HK & Macau*	+8		
Colombia	-5		
Comoros	+3		
Congo (DR) – *Western*	+1		
– *Eastern*	+2		
Congo, Republic	+1		
Cook Islands	-10		
Costa Rica	-6		
Côte d'Ivoire	UTC		
Cuba	-5	(-4)	LSuM-LSuO
Curaçao	-4		
Cyprus	+2	(+3)	LSuM-LSuO
Czech Republic	+1	(+2)	LSuM-LSuO
Denmark – *Mainland*	+1	(+2)	LSuM-LSuO
– *Faroes*	UTC	(+1)	LSuM-LSuO
Djibouti	+3		
Dominica	-4		
Dominican Republic	-4		
East Timor	+9		
Ecuador – *Mainland*	-5		
– *Galapagos*	-6		
Egypt	+2	(+3)	LFrA-LThS
El Salvador	-6		
Equatorial Guinea	+1		
Eritrea	+3		
Estonia	+2	(+3)	LSuM-LSuO
Ethiopia	+3		
Falkland Islands	-3	(-4)	3SuA-1SaS
Fiji Islands	+12		
Finland	+2	(+3)	LSuM-LSuO
France	+1	(+2)	LSuM-LSuO
French Guiana	-3		
Fr. Polynesia – *Gambier*	-9		
– *Marquesas*	-9.30		
– *Papeete*	-10		
Gabon	+1		
Gambia, The	UTC		
Georgia	+4		
Germany	+1	(+2)	LSuM-LSuO
Ghana	UTC		
Gibraltar	+1	(+2)	LSuM-LSuO
Greece	+2	(+3)	LSuM-LSuO
Greenland – *Eastern*	-1	(UTC)	LSuM-LSuO
– *Central*	-3	(-2)	LSuM-LSuO
– *Western*	-4	(-3)	LSuM-LSuO
Grenada	-4		
Guadeloupe	-4		
Guam	+10		
Guatemala	-6		
Guinea	UTC		
Guinea-Bissau	UTC		
Guyana	-4		
Haiti	-5		
Honduras	-6		
Hungary	+1	(+2)	LSuM-LSuO
Iceland	UTC		
India	+5.30		
Indonesia – *Western*	+7		
– *Central*	+8		
– *Eastern*	+9		
Iran	+3.30		
Iraq	+3	(+4)	A-O; dates vary
Ireland	UTC	(+1)	LSuM-LSuO
Israel	+2	(+3)	M-O; dates vary
Italy – *incl. San Marino, Vat.*	+1	(+2)	LSuM-LSuO
Jamaica	-5		
Japan	+9		
Jordan	+2	(+3)	M-O; dates vary
Kazakhstan – *Western*	+4		
– *Central*	+5		
– *Eastern*	+6		
Kenya	+3		
Kiribati – *Christmas Is.*	+14		
– *Phoenix Is.*	+13		
– *Gilbert Is. (incl. Tarawa)*	+12		
Korea, DPR (North)	+9		
Korea, Republic (South)	+9		
Kuwait	+3		
Kyrgyzstan	+6		
Laos	+7		
Latvia	+2	(+3)	LSuM-LSuO
Lebanon	+2	(+3)	LSuM-LSuO
Lesotho	+2		
Liberia	UTC		
Libya	+2		
Liechtenstein	+1	(+2)	LSuM-LSuO
Lithuania	+2	(+3)	LSuM-LSuO
Luxembourg	+1	(+2)	LSuM-LSuO
Macedonia, FYR	+1	(+2)	LSuM-LSuO
Madagascar	+3		
Malawi	+2		
Malaysia	+8		
Maldives	+5		
Mali	UTC		
Malta	+1	(+2)	LSuM-LSuO
Marshall Islands	+12		
Martinique	-4		
Mauritania	UTC		
Mauritius	+4		
Mexico – *Central*	-6	(-5)	1SuA-LSuO
– *Mountain*	-7	(-6)	1SuA-LSuO
– *Pacific*	-8	(-7)	1SuA-LSuO
Micronesia – *Yap, Chuuk*	+10		
– *Kosrae, Pohnpei*	+11		
Moldova	+2	(+3)	LSuM-LSuO
Monaco	+1	(+2)	LSuM-LSuO
Mongolia – *Central/Eastern*	+8	(+9)	
– *Western*	+7	(+8)	
Montserrat	-4		
Morocco	UTC		
Mozambique	+2		
Myanmar (Burma)	+6.30		
Namibia	+1	(+2)	1SuS-1SuA
Nauru	+12		
Nepal	+5.45		
Netherlands	+1	(+2)	LSuM-LSuO
New Caledonia	+11		
New Zealand – *N & S Is.*	+12	(+13)	1SuO-3SuM
– *Chatham Island*	+12.45	(+13.45)	1SuO-3SuM
Nicaragua	-6		
Niger	+1		
Nigeria	+1		
Niue	-11		
Northern Mariana Is.	+10		
Norway	+1	(+2)	LSuM-LSuO
Oman	+4		
Pakistan	+5		
Palau	+9		
Palestine NAR	+2	(+3)	M-O; dates vary
Panama	-5		
Papua New Guinea	+10		
Paraguay	-4	(-3)	3SuO-2SuM
Peru	-5		
Philippines	+8		
Poland	+1	(+2)	LSuM-LSuO
Portugal – *incl. Madeira*	UTC	(+1)	LSuM-LSuO
– *Azores*	-1	(UTC)	LSuM-LSuO
Puerto Rico	-4		
Qatar	+3		
Réunion	+4		
Romania	+2	(+3)	LSuM-LSuO
Rwanda	+2		
Russian Fed. – *Kaliningrad*	+2	(+3)	LSuM-LSuO
– *Moscow, St Pet, Astrakh.*	+3	(+4)	LSuM-LSuO
– *Samara, Izhevsk*	+4	(+5)	LSuM-LSuO
– *Perm, Yekater'g, Surgut*	+5	(+6)	LSuM-LSuO
– *Omsk, Novosibirsk*	+6	(+7)	LSuM-LSuO
– *Tuva, Norilsk, Abakan*	+7	(+8)	LSuM-LSuO
– *Bratsk, Irkutsk, Ulan-Ude*	+8	(+9)	LSuM-LSuO
– *Yakutsk, Tynda, Mirnyy*	+9	(+10)	LSuM-LSuO
– *Vladiv'k, Khab'k, Sak'n*	+10	(+11)	LSuM-LSuO
– *Magadan, Chirskiy*	+11	(+12)	LSuM-LSuO
– *Kamchatka, Anadyr*	+12	(+13)	LSuM-LSuO
St Eustatius	-4		
St Kitts & Nevis	-4		
St Lucia	-4		
St Maarten	-4		
St Pierre et Miquelon	-3	(-2)	1SuA-LSuO
St Vincent & the Gren.	-4		
Saba	-4		
Samoa	-11		
São Tomé e Príncipe	UTC		
Saudi Arabia	+3		
Senegal	UTC		
Serbia & Montenegro	+1	(+2)	LSuM-LSuO
Seychelles	+4		
Sierra Leone	UTC		
Singapore	+8		
Slovak Republic	+1	(+2)	LSuM-LSuO
Slovenia	+1	(+2)	LSuM-LSuO
Solomon Islands	+11		
Somalia	+3		
South Africa	+2		
Spain – *incl. Balearic Is.*	+1	(+2)	LSuM-LSuO
– *Canary Islands*	UTC	(+1)	LSuM-LSuO
Sri Lanka	+5.5		
Sudan	+3		
Surinam	-3		
Swaziland	+2		
Sweden	+1	(+2)	LSuM-LSuO
Switzerland	+1	(+2)	LSuM-LSuO
Syria	+2	(+3)	A-O; dates vary
Taiwan	+8		
Tajikistan	+5		
Tanzania	+3		
Thailand	+7		
Togo	UTC		
Tonga	+13		
Trinidad & Tobago	-4		
Tunisia	+1		
Turkey	+2	(+3)	LSuM-LSuO
Turkmenistan	+5		
Turks & Caicos Islands	-5	(-4)	1SuA-LSuO
Tuvalu	+12		
Uganda	+3		
Ukraine	+2	(+3)	LSuM-LSuO
United Arab Emirates	+4		
United Kingdom	UTC	(+1)	LSuM-LSuO
United States – *Eastern*	-5	(-4)	*see note**
– *Central*	-6	(-5)	*see note**
– *Mountain*	-7	(-6)	*see note* (not AZ)*
– *Pacific*	-8	(-7)	*see note**
– *Alaska*	-9	(-8)	*see note**
– *Aleutian/Hawaii*	-10		
US Virgin Islands	-4		
Uruguay	-3	(-2)	2SuO-2SuM
Uzbekistan	+5		
Vanuatu	+11		
Venezuela	-4		
Vietnam	+7		
Yemen	+3		
Zambia	+2		
Zimbabwe	+2		

** 1SuA-LSuO (2006 only): 2SuM-1SuN from 2007.*

See also... Flight Times (45); USA Time Zones (165)

The listings above refer to a selection of related themes. For more information, see the Contents (2-7).

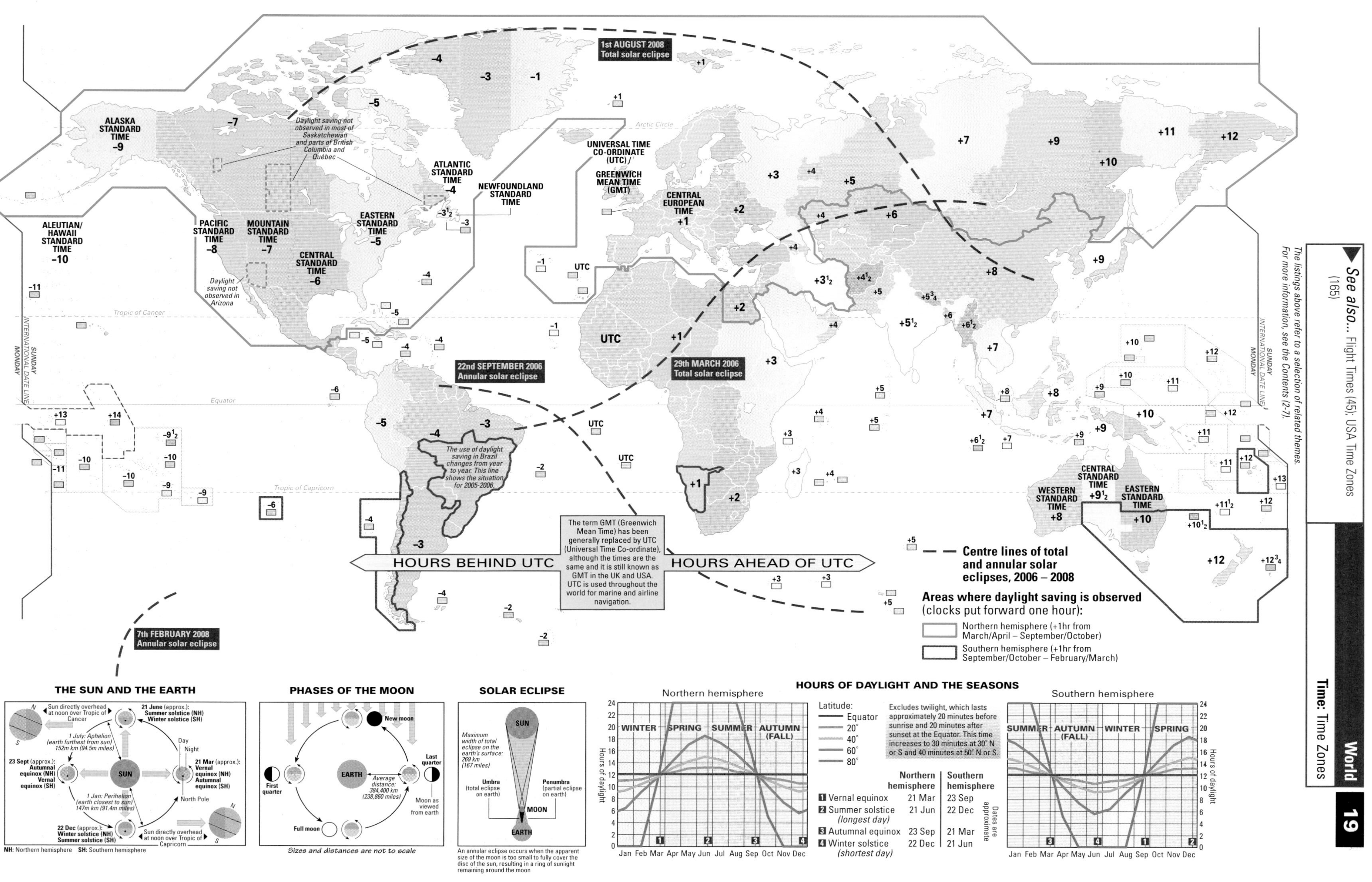
INTERNATIONAL DATE LINE
SUNDAY
MONDAY
ALASKA STANDARD TIME -9
ALEUTIAN/HAWAII STANDARD TIME -10
PACIFIC STANDARD TIME -8
MOUNTAIN STANDARD TIME -7
CENTRAL STANDARD TIME -6
EASTERN STANDARD TIME -5
ATLANTIC STANDARD TIME -4
NEWFOUNDLAND STANDARD TIME
Daylight saving not observed in most of Saskatchewan and parts of British Columbia and Québec
Daylight saving not observed in Arizona
UNIVERSAL TIME CO-ORDINATE (UTC)/ GREENWICH MEAN TIME (GMT)
CENTRAL EUROPEAN TIME +1
WESTERN STANDARD TIME +8
CENTRAL STANDARD TIME +9½
EASTERN STANDARD TIME +10
1st AUGUST 2008 Total solar eclipse
29th MARCH 2006 Total solar eclipse
22nd SEPTEMBER 2006 Annular solar eclipse
7th FEBRUARY 2008 Annular solar eclipse
The use of daylight saving in Brazil changes from year to year. This line shows the situation for 2005-2006.
The term GMT (Greenwich Mean Time) has been generally replaced by UTC (Universal Time Co-ordinate), although the times are the same and it is still known as GMT in the UK and USA. UTC is used throughout the world for marine and airline navigation.
HOURS BEHIND UTC
HOURS AHEAD OF UTC
Arctic Circle
Tropic of Cancer
Equator
Tropic of Capricorn
Centre lines of total and annular solar eclipses, 2006 – 2008
Areas where daylight saving is observed (clocks put forward one hour):
Northern hemisphere (+1hr from March/April – September/October)
Southern hemisphere (+1hr from September/October – February/March)
THE SUN AND THE EARTH
Sun directly overhead at noon over Tropic of Cancer
21 June (approx.): Summer solstice (NH) Winter solstice (SH)
21 Mar (approx.): Vernal equinox (NH) Autumnal equinox (SH)
23 Sept (approx.): Autumnal equinox (NH) Vernal equinox (SH)
22 Dec (approx.): Winter solstice (NH) Summer solstice (SH)
1 July: Aphelion (earth furthest from sun) 152m km (94.5m miles)
1 Jan: Perihelion (earth closest to sun) 147m km (91.4m miles)
Sun directly overhead at noon over Tropic of Capricorn
SUN
North Pole
Day
Night
NH: Northern hemisphere SH: Southern hemisphere
PHASES OF THE MOON
New moon
First quarter
Full moon
Last quarter
EARTH
Average distance: 384,400 km (238,860 miles)
Moon as viewed from earth
Sizes and distances are not to scale
SOLAR ECLIPSE
SUN
MOON
EARTH
Penumbra (partial eclipse on earth)
Umbra (total eclipse on earth)
Maximum width of total eclipse on the earth's surface: 269 km (167 miles)
An annular eclipse occurs when the apparent size of the moon is too small to fully cover the disc of the sun, resulting in a ring of sunlight remaining around the moon
HOURS OF DAYLIGHT AND THE SEASONS
Northern hemisphere
Southern hemisphere
WINTER SPRING SUMMER AUTUMN (FALL)
SUMMER AUTUMN (FALL) WINTER SPRING
Hours of daylight
Jan Feb Mar Apr May Jun Jul Aug Sep Oct Nov Dec
Latitude: Equator 20° 40° 60° 80°
Excludes twilight, which lasts approximately 20 minutes before sunrise and 20 minutes after sunset at the Equator. This time increases to 30 minutes at 30° N or S and 40 minutes at 50° N or S.
1 Vernal equinox — Northern hemisphere 21 Mar — Southern hemisphere 23 Sep
2 Summer solstice (longest day) — 21 Jun — 22 Dec
3 Autumnal equinox — 23 Sep — 21 Mar
4 Winter solstice (shortest day) — 22 Dec — 21 Jun
Dates are approximate

See also... The World's Major Urban Areas (196); Countries A-Z (202-210)

The listings above refer to a selection of related themes. For more information, see the Contents (2-7).

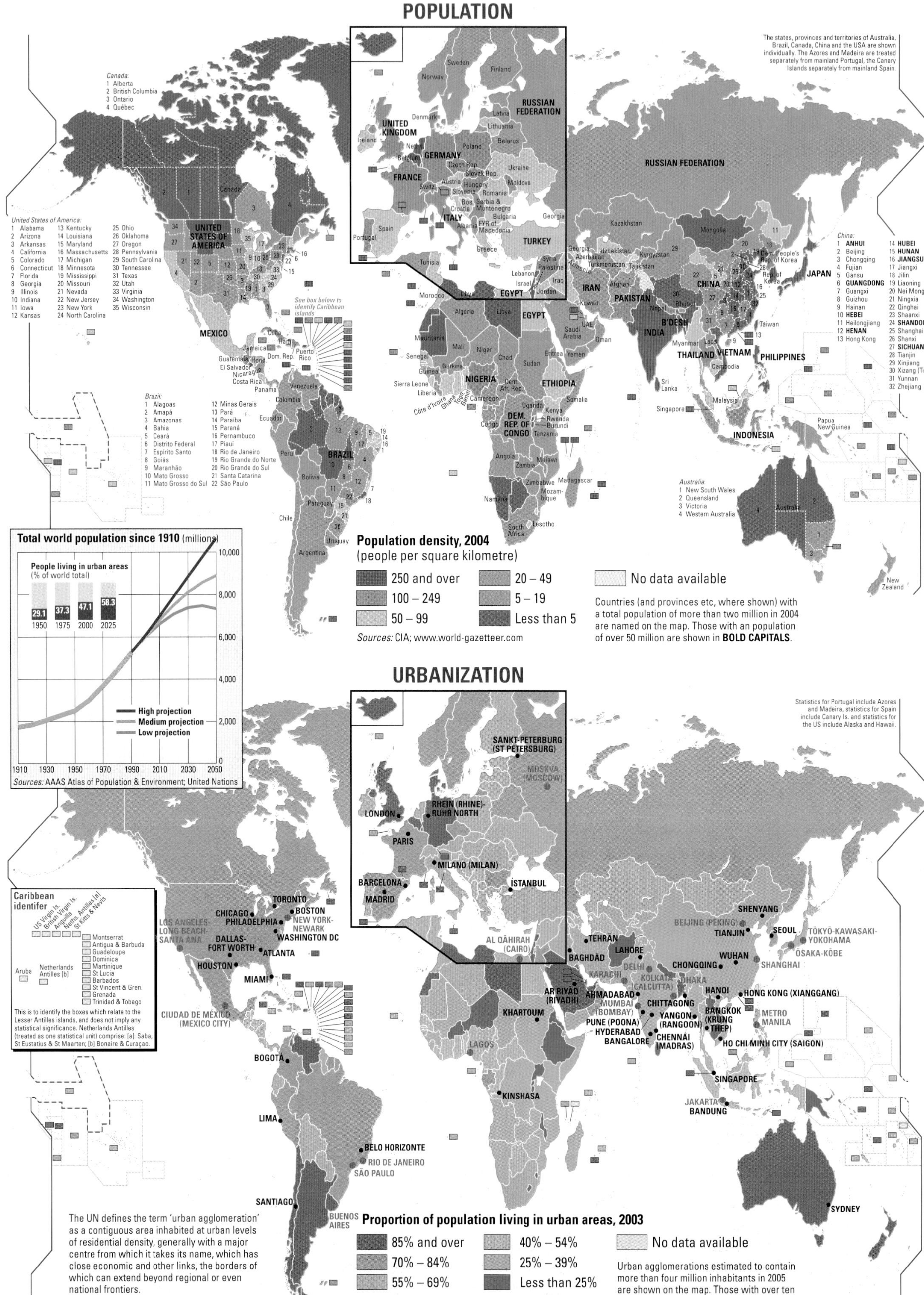
POPULATION
The states, provinces and territories of Australia, Brazil, Canada, China and the USA are shown individually. The Azores and Madeira are treated separately from mainland Portugal, the Canary Islands separately from mainland Spain.
Canada:
1 Alberta
2 British Columbia
3 Ontario
4 Québec
United States of America:
1 Alabama
2 Arizona
3 Arkansas
4 California
5 Colorado
6 Connecticut
7 Florida
8 Georgia
9 Illinois
10 Indiana
11 Iowa
12 Kansas
13 Kentucky
14 Louisiana
15 Maryland
16 Massachusetts
17 Michigan
18 Minnesota
19 Mississippi
20 Missouri
21 Nevada
22 New Jersey
23 New York
24 North Carolina
25 Ohio
26 Oklahoma
27 Oregon
28 Pennsylvania
29 South Carolina
30 Tennessee
31 Texas
32 Utah
33 Virginia
34 Washington
35 Wisconsin
Brazil:
1 Alagoas
2 Amapá
3 Amazonas
4 Bahia
5 Ceará
6 Distrito Federal
7 Espírito Santo
8 Goiás
9 Maranhão
10 Mato Grosso
11 Mato Grosso do Sul
12 Minas Gerais
13 Pará
14 Paraíba
15 Paraná
16 Pernambuco
17 Piauí
18 Rio de Janeiro
19 Rio Grande do Norte
20 Rio Grande do Sul
21 Santa Catarina
22 São Paulo
China:
1 ANHUI
2 Beijing
3 Chongqing
4 Fujian
5 Gansu
6 GUANGDONG
7 Guangxi
8 Guizhou
9 Hainan
10 HEBEI
11 Heilongjiang
12 HENAN
13 Hong Kong
14 HUBEI
15 HUNAN
16 JIANGSU
17 Jiangxi
18 Jilin
19 Liaoning
20 Nei Monggol
21 Ningxia
22 Qinghai
23 Shaanxi
24 SHANDONG
25 Shanghai
26 Shanxi
27 SICHUAN
28 Tianjin
29 Xinjiang
30 Xizang (Tibet)
31 Yunnan
32 Zhejiang
Australia:
1 New South Wales
2 Queensland
3 Victoria
4 Western Australia
See box below to identify Caribbean islands
RUSSIAN FEDERATION
UNITED STATES OF AMERICA
MEXICO
BRAZIL
NIGERIA
ETHIOPIA
DEM. REP. OF CONGO
EGYPT
IRAN
PAKISTAN
INDIA
B'DESH
CHINA
JAPAN
THAILAND
VIETNAM
PHILIPPINES
INDONESIA
UNITED KINGDOM
FRANCE
GERMANY
ITALY
TURKEY
Total world population since 1910 (millions)
People living in urban areas (% of world total)
29.1 1950
37.3 1975
47.1 2000
58.3 2025
High projection
Medium projection
Low projection
Sources: AAAS Atlas of Population & Environment; United Nations
Population density, 2004 (people per square kilometre)
250 and over
100 – 249
50 – 99
20 – 49
5 – 19
Less than 5
No data available
Sources: CIA; www.world-gazetteer.com
Countries (and provinces etc, where shown) with a total population of more than two million in 2004 are named on the map. Those with an population of over 50 million are shown in BOLD CAPITALS.
URBANIZATION
Statistics for Portugal include Azores and Madeira, statistics for Spain include Canary Is. and statistics for the US include Alaska and Hawaii.
Caribbean identifer
US Virgin Is.
British Virgin Is.
Anguilla
Neths. Antilles [a]
St Kitts & Nevis
Montserrat
Antigua & Barbuda
Guadeloupe
Dominica
Martinique
St Lucia
Barbados
St Vincent & Gren.
Grenada
Trinidad & Tobago
Aruba
Netherlands Antilles [b]
This is to identify the boxes which relate to the Lesser Antilles islands, and does not imply any statistical significance. Netherlands Antilles (treated as one statistical unit) comprise: [a]: Saba, St Eustatius & St Maarten; [b] Bonaire & Curaçao.
LOS ANGELES-LONG BEACH-SANTA ANA
CHICAGO
TORONTO
BOSTON
PHILADELPHIA
NEW YORK-NEWARK
WASHINGTON DC
DALLAS-FORT WORTH
ATLANTA
HOUSTON
MIAMI
CIUDAD DE MÉXICO (MEXICO CITY)
BOGOTÁ
LIMA
BELO HORIZONTE
RIO DE JANEIRO
SÃO PAULO
SANTIAGO
BUENOS AIRES
LONDON
RHEIN (RHINE)-RUHR NORTH
PARIS
MILANO (MILAN)
BARCELONA
MADRID
İSTANBUL
SANKT-PETERBURG (ST PETERSBURG)
MOSKVA (MOSCOW)
AL QĀHIRAH (CAIRO)
LAGOS
KHARTOUM
KINSHASA
BAGHDĀD
AR RIYAD (RIYADH)
TEHRĀN
KARACHI
LAHORE
DELHI
AHMADABAD
MUMBAI (BOMBAY)
PUNE (POONA)
HYDERABAD
BANGALORE
CHENNAI (MADRAS)
KOLKATA (CALCUTTA)
DHAKA
CHITTAGONG
YANGON (RANGOON)
BANGKOK (KRUNG THEP)
HANOI
HO CHI MINH CITY (SAIGON)
SINGAPORE
JAKARTA
BANDUNG
METRO MANILA
HONG KONG (XIANGGANG)
CHONGQING
WUHAN
SHANGHAI
BEIJING (PEKING)
TIANJIN
SHENYANG
SEOUL
TŌKYŌ-KAWASAKI-YOKOHAMA
OSAKA-KŌBE
SYDNEY
The UN defines the term 'urban agglomeration' as a contiguous area inhabited at urban levels of residential density, generally with a major centre from which it takes its name, which has close economic and other links, the borders of which can extend beyond regional or even national frontiers.
Proportion of population living in urban areas, 2003
85% and over
70% – 84%
55% – 69%
40% – 54%
25% – 39%
Less than 25%
No data available
Source: United Nations
Urban agglomerations estimated to contain more than four million inhabitants in 2005 are shown on the map. Those with over ten million inhabitants are indicated in RED.

See also... Wealth (22-23); Health (38-39); Europe Historical (59); Asia Historical (128); Holy Land (131); Latin America Historical (187); Countries A-Z (202-210)

The listings above refer to a selection of related themes. For more information, see the Contents (2-7).

HUMAN DEVELOPMENT INDEX

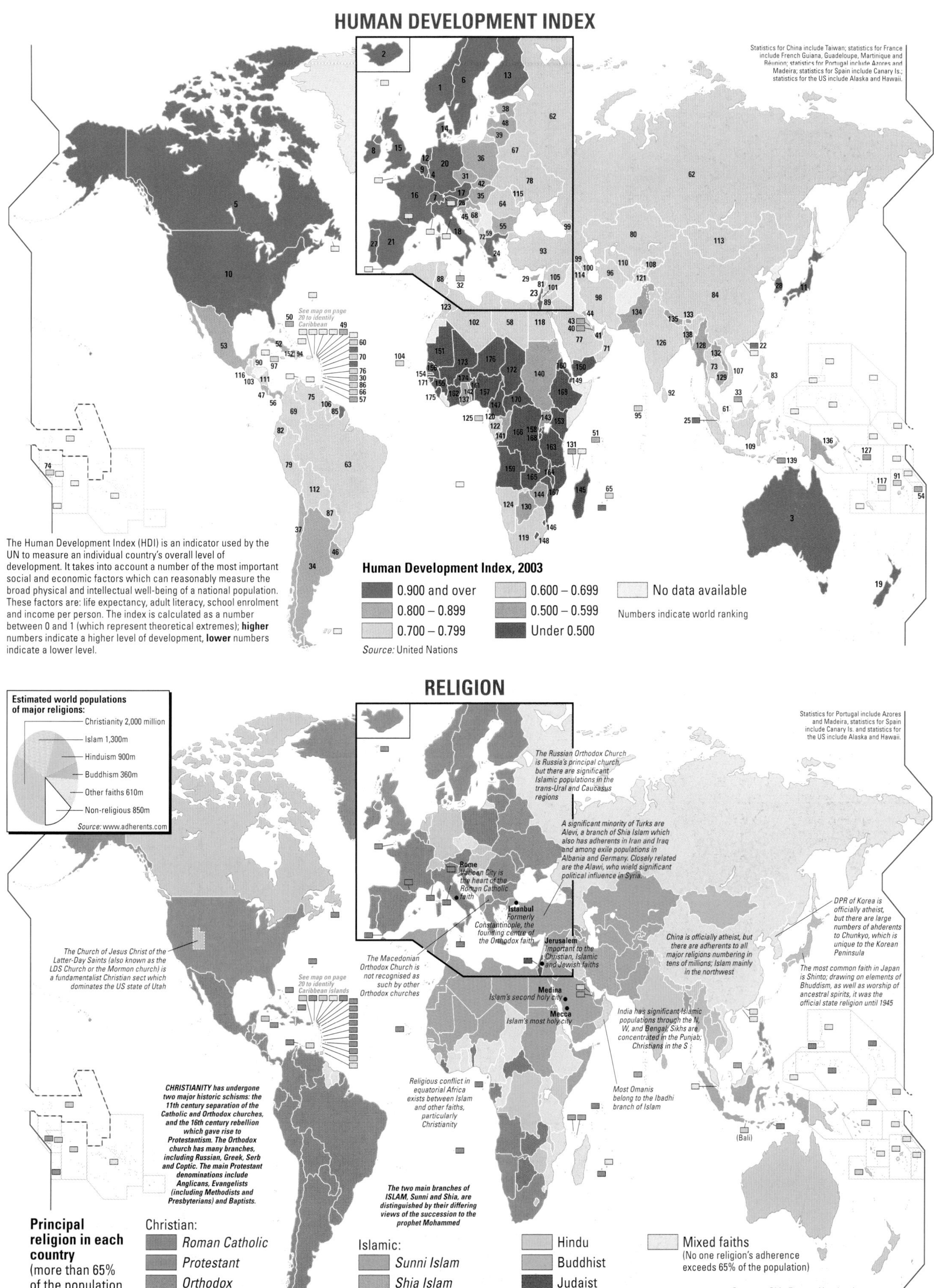
Statistics for China include Taiwan; statistics for France include French Guiana, Guadeloupe, Martinique and Réunion; statistics for Portugal include Azores and Madeira; statistics for Spain include Canary Is.; statistics for the US include Alaska and Hawaii.
See map on page 20 to identify Caribbean
The Human Development Index (HDI) is an indicator used by the UN to measure an individual country's overall level of development. It takes into account a number of the most important social and economic factors which can reasonably measure the broad physical and intellectual well-being of a national population. These factors are: life expectancy, adult literacy, school enrolment and income per person. The index is calculated as a number between 0 and 1 (which represent theoretical extremes); **higher** numbers indicate a higher level of development, **lower** numbers indicate a lower level.
Human Development Index, 2003
0.900 and over
0.800 – 0.899
0.700 – 0.799
0.600 – 0.699
0.500 – 0.599
Under 0.500
No data available
Numbers indicate world ranking
Source: United Nations
RELIGION
Estimated world populations of major religions:
Christianity 2,000 million
Islam 1,300m
Hinduism 900m
Buddhism 360m
Other faiths 610m
Non-religious 850m
Source: www.adherents.com
Statistics for Portugal include Azores and Madeira, statistics for Spain include Canary Is. and statistics for the US include Alaska and Hawaii.
The Russian Orthodox Church is Russia's principal church, but there are significant Islamic populations in the trans-Ural and Caucasus regions
A significant minority of Turks are Alevi, a branch of Shia Islam which also has adherents in Iran and Iraq and among exile populations in Albania and Germany. Closely related are the Alawi, who wield significant political influence in Syria.
Rome
Vatican City is the heart of the Roman Catholic faith
Istanbul
Formerly Constantinople, the founding centre of the Orthodox faith
Jerusalem
Important to the Christian, Islamic and Jewish faiths
Medina
Islam's second holy city
Mecca
Islam's most holy city
DPR of Korea is officially atheist, but there are large numbers of ahderents to Chunkyo, which is unique to the Korean Peninsula
China is officially atheist, but there are adherents to all major religions numbering in tens of millions; Islam mainly in the northwest
The most common faith in Japan is Shinto; drawing on elements of Bhuddism, as well as worship of ancestral spirits, it was the official state religion until 1945
The Church of Jesus Christ of the Latter-Day Saints (also known as the LDS Church or the Mormon church) is a fundamentalist Christian sect which dominates the US state of Utah
See map on page 20 to identify Caribbean islands
The Macedonian Orthodox Church is not recognised as such by other Orthodox churches
India has significant Islamic populations through the N, W, and Bengal; Sikhs are concentrated in the Punjab; Christians in the S
Most Omanis belong to the Ibadhi branch of Islam
Religious conflict in equatorial Africa exists between Islam and other faiths, particularly Christianity
(Bali)
CHRISTIANITY has undergone two major historic schisms: the 11th century separation of the Catholic and Orthodox churches, and the 16th century rebellion which gave rise to Protestantism. The Orthodox church has many branches, including Russian, Greek, Serb and Coptic. The main Protestant denominations include Anglicans, Evangelists (including Methodists and Presbyterians) and Baptists.
The two main branches of ISLAM, Sunni and Shia, are distinguished by their differing views of the succession to the prophet Mohammed
Principal religion in each country (more than 65% of the population professing adherence)
Christian:
Roman Catholic
Protestant
Orthodox
Christian overall (with no dominant branch)
Islamic:
Sunni Islam
Shia Islam
Islam overall (with no dominant branch)
Hindu
Buddhist
Judaist
Animist or 'traditional' belief
Mixed faiths (No one religion's adherence exceeds 65% of the population)
Sources: CIA; Europa Yearbook; www.adherents.com

▶ *See also...* Human Development Index (21); Energy (28-29); Business (32-33); Countries A-Z (202-210)

The listings above refer to a selection of related themes. For more information, see the Contents (2-7).

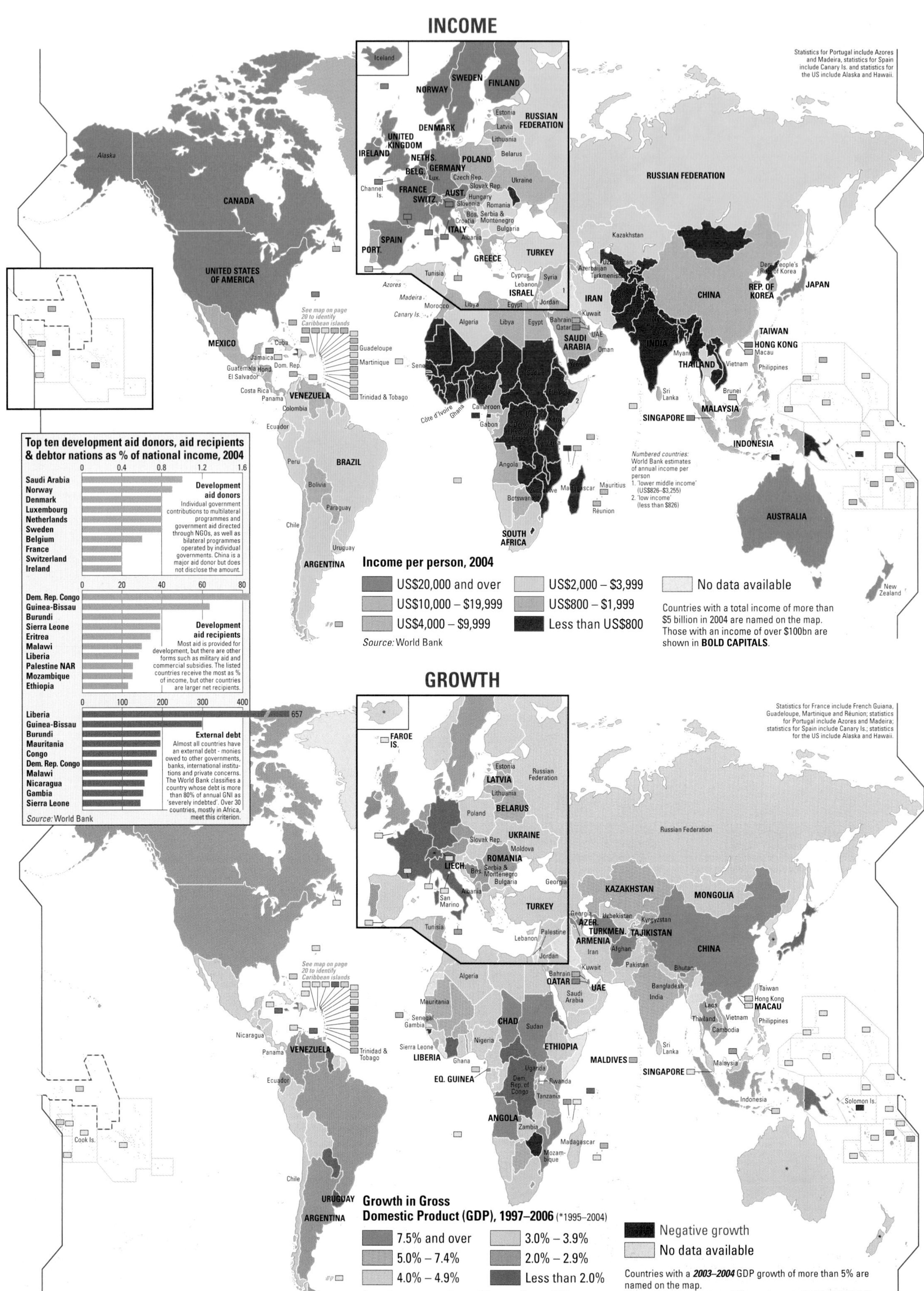
INCOME
Statistics for Portugal include Azores and Madeira, statistics for Spain include Canary Is. and statistics for the US include Alaska and Hawaii.
CANADA
UNITED STATES OF AMERICA
MEXICO
BRAZIL
ARGENTINA
VENEZUELA
RUSSIAN FEDERATION
CHINA
JAPAN
INDIA
REP. OF KOREA
TAIWAN
HONG KONG
SINGAPORE
MALAYSIA
THAILAND
INDONESIA
AUSTRALIA
SOUTH AFRICA
SAUDI ARABIA
IRAN
ISRAEL
TURKEY
GREECE
UNITED KINGDOM
IRELAND
NORWAY
SWEDEN
FINLAND
DENMARK
NETHS.
BELG.
GERMANY
POLAND
FRANCE
SWITZ.
AUST.
ITALY
SPAIN
PORT.
See map on page 20 to identify Caribbean islands
Numbered countries: World Bank estimates of annual income per person
1. 'lower middle income' (US$826–$3,255)
2. 'low income' (less than $826)
Income per person, 2004
US$20,000 and over
US$10,000 – $19,999
US$4,000 – $9,999
US$2,000 – $3,999
US$800 – $1,999
Less than US$800
No data available
Source: World Bank
Countries with a total income of more than $5 billion in 2004 are named on the map. Those with an income of over $100bn are shown in BOLD CAPITALS.
Top ten development aid donors, aid recipients & debtor nations as % of national income, 2004
0 0.4 0.8 1.2 1.6
Saudi Arabia
Norway
Denmark
Luxembourg
Netherlands
Sweden
Belgium
France
Switzerland
Ireland
Development aid donors
Individual government contributions to multilateral programmes and government aid directed through NGOs, as well as bilateral programmes operated by individual governments. China is a major aid donor but does not disclose the amount.
0 20 40 60 80
Dem. Rep. Congo
Guinea-Bissau
Burundi
Sierra Leone
Eritrea
Malawi
Liberia
Palestine NAR
Mozambique
Ethiopia
Development aid recipients
Most aid is provided for development, but there are other forms such as military aid and commercial subsidies. The listed countries receive the most as % of income, but other countries are larger net recipients.
0 100 200 300 400
Liberia 657
Guinea-Bissau
Burundi
Mauritania
Congo
Dem. Rep. Congo
Malawi
Nicaragua
Gambia
Sierra Leone
External debt
Almost all countries have an external debt - monies owed to other governments, banks, international institutions and private concerns. The World Bank classifies a country whose debt is more than 80% of annual GNI as 'severely indebted'. Over 30 countries, mostly in Africa, meet this criterion.
Source: World Bank
GROWTH
Statistics for France include French Guiana, Guadeloupe, Martinique and Réunion; statistics for Portugal include Azores and Madeira; statistics for Spain include Canary Is.; statistics for the US include Alaska and Hawaii.
FAROE IS.
LATVIA
BELARUS
UKRAINE
ROMANIA
LIECH.
TURKEY
KAZAKHSTAN
MONGOLIA
CHINA
AZER.
TURKMEN.
TAJIKISTAN
ARMENIA
QATAR
UAE
MACAU
MALDIVES
SINGAPORE
CHAD
ETHIOPIA
LIBERIA
EQ. GUINEA
ANGOLA
VENEZUELA
URUGUAY
ARGENTINA
Growth in Gross Domestic Product (GDP), 1997–2006 (*1995–2004)
7.5% and over
5.0% – 7.4%
4.0% – 4.9%
3.0% – 3.9%
2.0% – 2.9%
Less than 2.0%
Negative growth
No data available
Annual average growth over 10 years Source: IMF
Countries with a 2003–2004 GDP growth of more than 5% are named on the map. Those with growth of over 8% are shown in BOLD CAPITALS.

The listings above refer to a selection of related themes. For more information, see the Contents (2-7).

Income from each sector as a percentage of Gross National Income (GNI), 2004

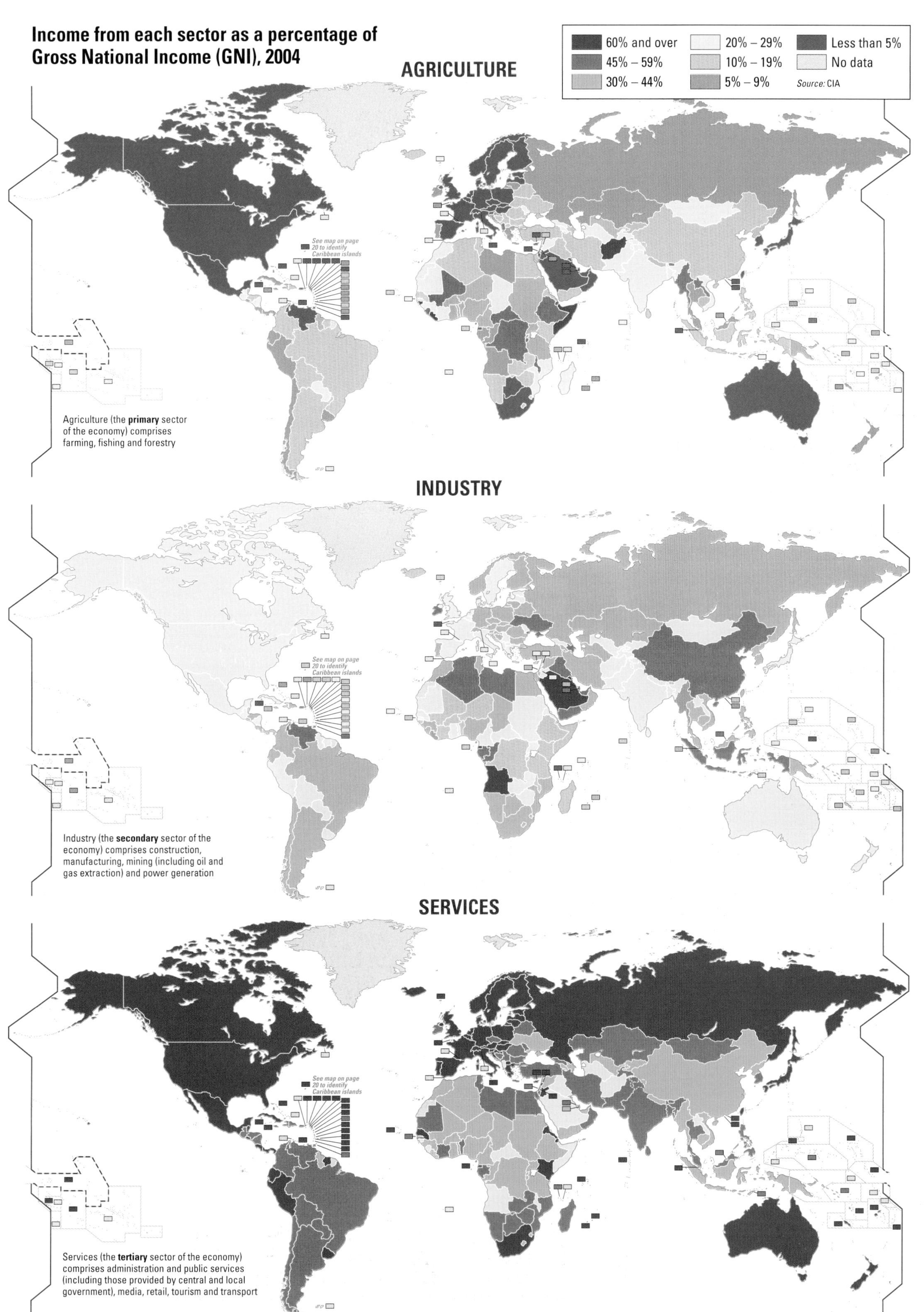
AGRICULTURE
60% and over
45% – 59%
30% – 44%
20% – 29%
10% – 19%
5% – 9%
Less than 5%
No data
Source: CIA
See map on page 20 to identify Caribbean islands
Agriculture (the **primary** sector of the economy) comprises farming, fishing and forestry
INDUSTRY
See map on page 20 to identify Caribbean islands
Industry (the **secondary** sector of the economy comprises construction, manufacturing, mining (including oil and gas extraction) and power generation
SERVICES
See map on page 20 to identify Caribbean islands
Services (the **tertiary** sector of the economy) comprises administration and public services (including those provided by central and local government), media, retail, tourism and transport

See also... World & Continental Introductions (see General Contents, 2-3); MICE (34-35); Countries A-Z (202-210)

The listings above refer to a selection of related themes. For more information, see the Contents (2-7).

VISITOR RECEIPTS

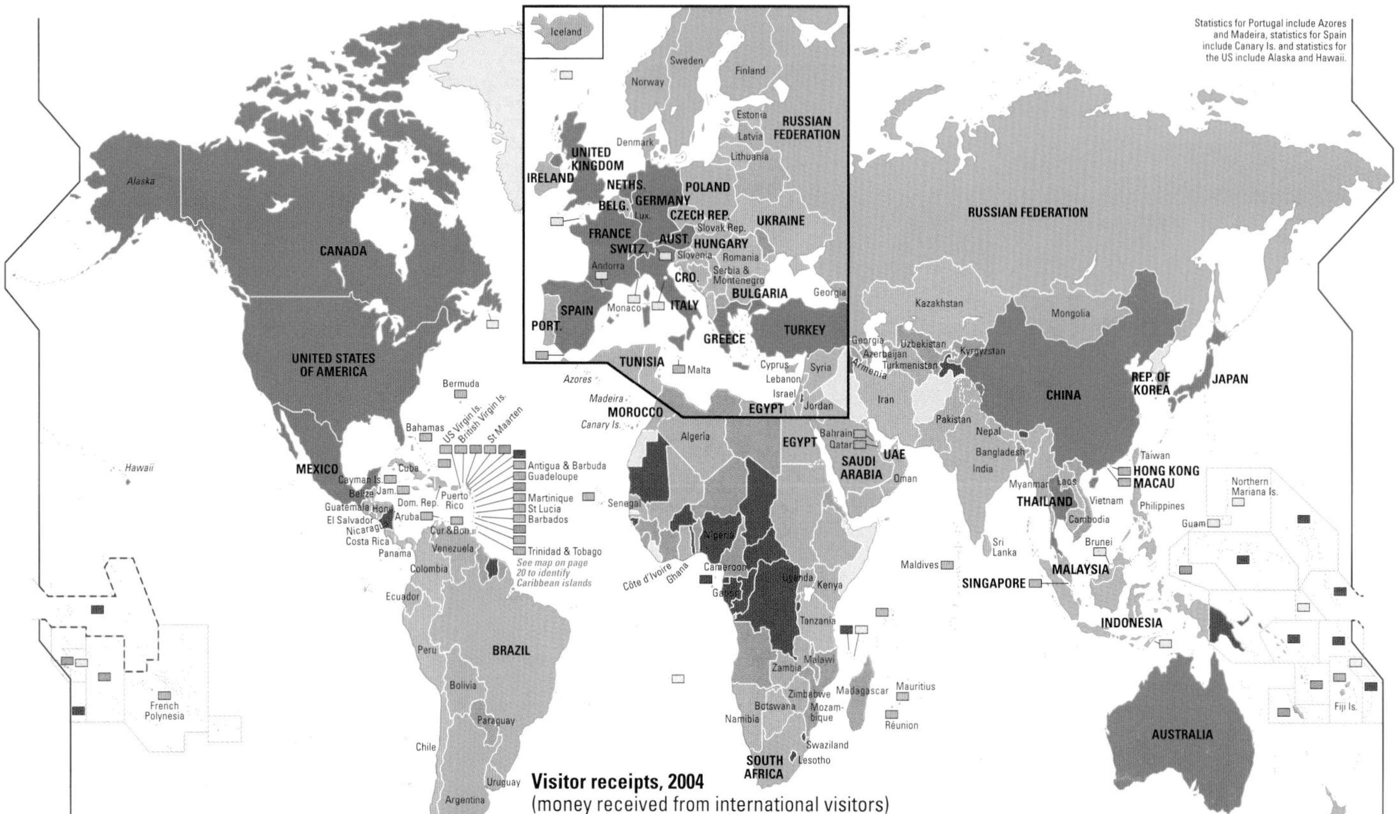

Statistics for Portugal include Azores and Madeira, statistics for Spain include Canary Is. and statistics for the US include Alaska and Hawaii.

Visitor receipts, 2004
(money received from international visitors)

- US$10,000 million and over
- US$2,000m – $9,999m
- US$500m – $1,999m
- US$100m – $499m
- US$30m – $99m
- Less than US$30m
- No data available

Excludes international transport *Source:* World Tourism Organisation

'International arrivals' are defined as people staying at least one night and exclude people arriving and departing on the same day; however in a few countries separate figures are not available and so total arrivals are shown. **This applies to all international arrivals charts in this atlas.**

Countries with more than 200,000 international arrivals in 2004 are named on the map. Those with over four million arrivals are shown in **BOLD CAPITALS**. *See note on left.*

See map on page 20 to identify Caribbean islands

VISITOR EXPENDITURE

Statistics for Portugal include Azores and Madeira, statistics for Spain include Canary Is. and statistics for the US include Alaska and Hawaii.

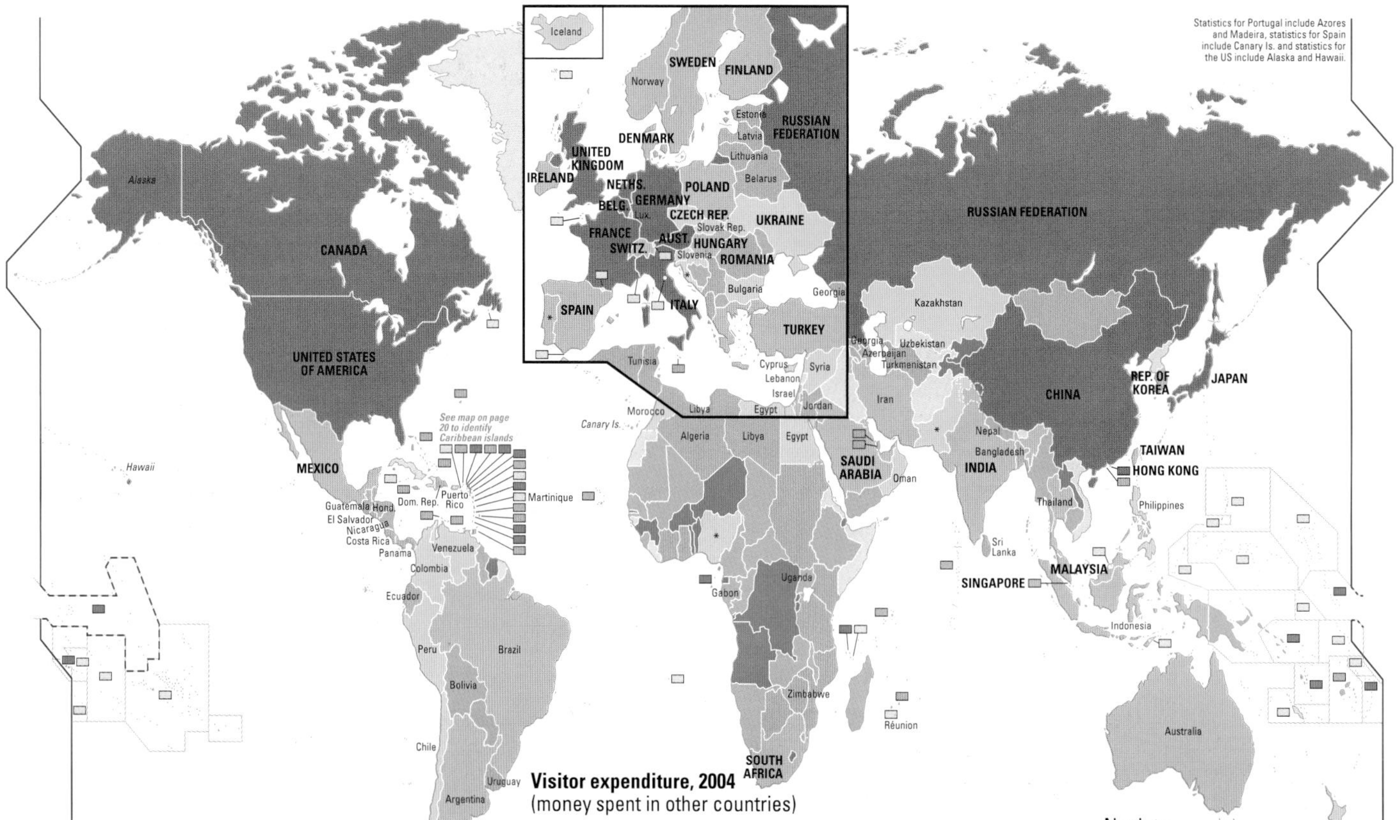

Visitor expenditure, 2004
(money spent in other countries)

- US$10,000 million and over
- US$2,000m – $9,999m
- US$500m – $1,999m
- US$100m – $499m
- US$30m – $99m
- Less than US$30m
- No data available

Excludes international transport *Source:* World Tourism Organisation

Consistent statistics for outbound travel are unavailable for a number of countries. Countries which indicate significant levels of expenditure but for which departures figures are unavailable, an * is shown. In some instances, departures figures are available but not expenditure.

Countries with more than 200,000 international departures in 2004 are named on the map. Those with over four million departures are shown in **BOLD CAPITALS**. *See note on left.*

See map on page 20 to identify Caribbean islands

▶ See also... World & Continental Introductions (see General Contents, 2-3); MICE (34-35); UK (70-76); USA (154-171); Countries A-Z (202-210)

The listings above refer to a selection of related themes. For more information, see the Contents (2-7).

UNITED STATES TOURISM

UNITED KINGDOM TOURISM

INTERNATIONAL ARRIVALS, 2004

(top ten countries of origin, thousands)

Width of bar is proportional to number of travellers

United States

Total arrivals in USA (millions)

% change on previous year

2000	2001	2002	2003	2004
+5.7	−8.4	−7.1	−5.4	+11.8

- Canada 13,849 (30.1%)
- Mexico 11,906 (25.8%)
- UK 4,303 (9.3%)**
- Japan 3,748 (8.1%)
- Germany 1,320 (2.9%)
- France 775 (1.7%)
- Rep. of Korea 627 (1.4%)
- Australia 520 (1.1%)
- Italy 471 (1.0%)
- Netherlands 425 (0.9%)
- Rest of world 8,134 (17.7%)

AK HI

United Kingdom

Total arrivals in UK (millions)

% change on previous year

2000	2001	2002	2003	2004
+0.5	−10.5	+5.9	+2.2	+12.1

- USA 3,616 (13.0%)*
- France 3,254 (11.7%)
- Germany 2,968 (10.7%)
- Ireland 2,578 (9.3%)
- Netherlands 1,620 (5.8%)
- Spain 1,465 (5.3%)
- Italy 1,348 (4.9%)
- Belgium 1,104 (4.0%)
- Australia 787 (2.8%)
- Canada 740 (2.7%)
- Rest of world 8,275 (29.8%)

Sources for all US and UK data: Office of Travel and Tourism Statistics; Office for National Statistics; World Tourism Organisation; Visit Britain

TRAVEL BETWEEN THE USA AND THE UK

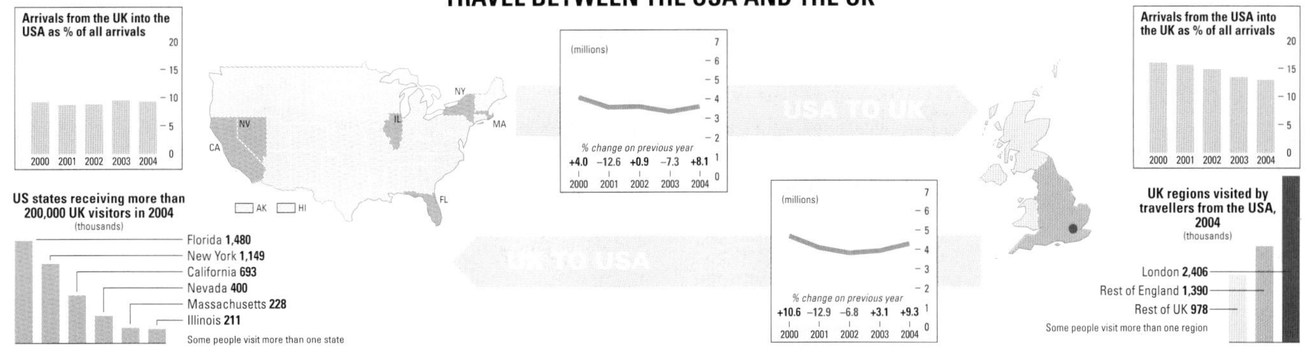

Arrivals from the UK into the USA as % of all arrivals (2000–2004)

US states receiving more than 200,000 UK visitors in 2004 (thousands)

- Florida 1,480
- New York 1,149
- California 693
- Nevada 400
- Massachusetts 228
- Illinois 211

Some people visit more than one state

NY, MA, IL, NV, CA, FL; AK HI

USA TO UK (millions)

% change on previous year

2000	2001	2002	2003	2004
+4.0	−12.6	+0.9	−7.3	+8.1

UK TO USA (millions)

% change on previous year

2000	2001	2002	2003	2004
+10.6	−12.9	−6.8	+3.1	+9.3

Arrivals from the USA into the UK as % of all arrivals (2000–2004)

UK regions visited by travellers from the USA, 2004 (thousands)

- London 2,406
- Rest of England 1,390
- Rest of UK 978

Some people visit more than one region

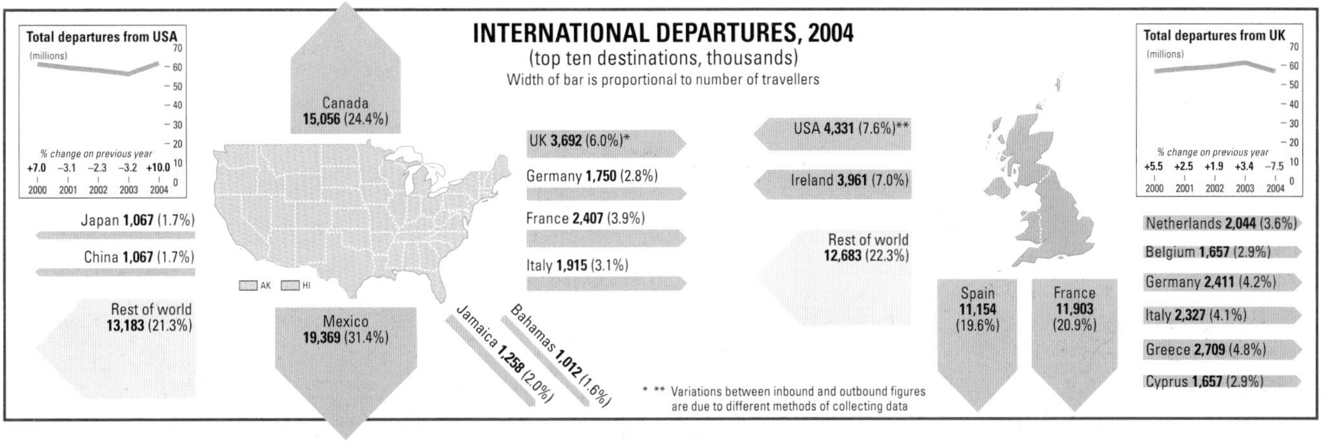

INTERNATIONAL DEPARTURES, 2004

(top ten destinations, thousands)

Width of bar is proportional to number of travellers

United States

Total departures from USA (millions)

% change on previous year

2000	2001	2002	2003	2004
+7.0	−3.1	−2.3	−3.2	+10.0

- Mexico 19,369 (31.4%)
- Canada 15,056 (24.4%)
- UK 3,692 (6.0%)*
- France 2,407 (3.9%)
- Italy 1,915 (3.1%)
- Germany 1,750 (2.8%)
- Jamaica 1,258 (2.0%)
- Japan 1,067 (1.7%)
- China 1,067 (1.7%)
- Bahamas 1,012 (1.6%)
- Rest of world 13,183 (21.3%)

AK HI

United Kingdom

Total departures from UK (millions)

% change on previous year

2000	2001	2002	2003	2004
+5.5	+2.5	+1.9	+3.4	−7.5

- France 11,903 (20.9%)
- Spain 11,154 (19.6%)
- USA 4,331 (7.6%)**
- Ireland 3,961 (7.0%)
- Greece 2,709 (4.8%)
- Germany 2,411 (4.2%)
- Italy 2,327 (4.1%)
- Netherlands 2,044 (3.6%)
- Belgium 1,657 (2.9%)
- Cyprus 1,657 (2.9%)
- Rest of world 12,683 (22.3%)

* ** Variations between inbound and outbound figures are due to different methods of collecting data

WORLDWIDE TOURISM

INTERNATIONAL ARRIVALS TO UNWTO REGIONS

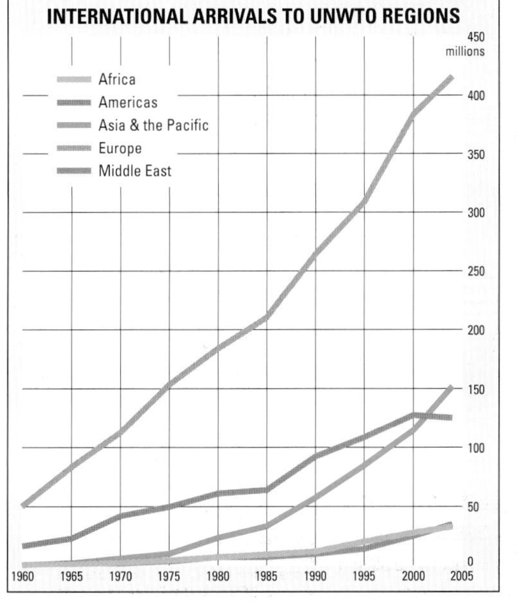
Africa
Americas
Asia & the Pacific
Europe
Middle East
450 millions
400
350
300
250
200
150
100
50
0
1960
1965
1970
1975
1980
1985
1990
1995
2000
2005

WORLD TOURISM ORGANISATION REGIONS

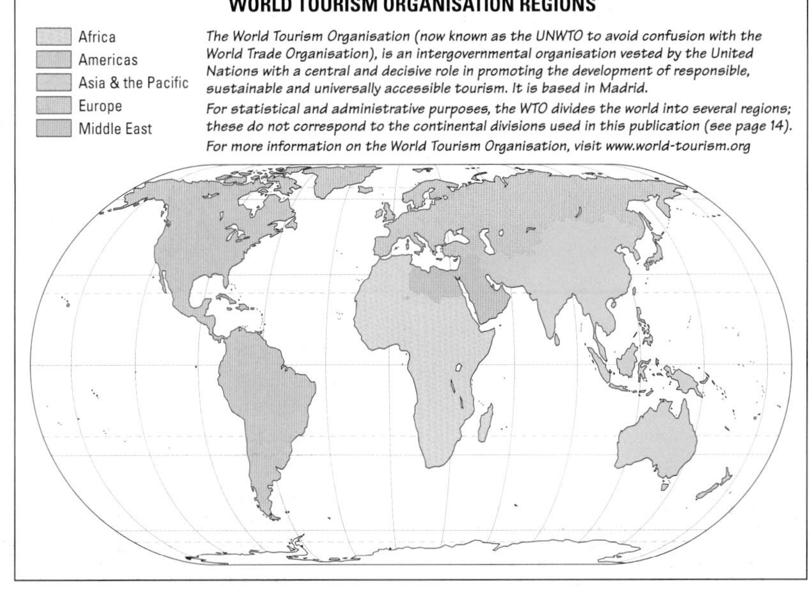
Africa
Americas
Asia & the Pacific
Europe
Middle East

The World Tourism Organisation (now known as the UNWTO to avoid confusion with the World Trade Organisation), is an intergovernmental organisation vested by the United Nations with a central and decisive role in promoting the development of responsible, sustainable and universally accessible tourism. It is based in Madrid.

For statistical and administrative purposes, the WTO divides the world into several regions; these do not correspond to the continental divisions used in this publication (see page 14).

For more information on the World Tourism Organisation, visit www.world-tourism.org

Set Jetters

▶ *See also...* Europe Leisure Parks (67); US Theme Parks (171)

The listings above refer to a selection of related themes. For more information, see the Contents (2-7).

This map shows a selection of movie locations that are likely to be of interest to 'set-jetters' – people whose choice of holiday destination is influenced by the desire to visit the location of a film. Many places from New York City's Central Park to New Zealand's Fiordland have achieved iconic status due to their celluloid stardom. An increasing number of tourist boards use such films to strengthen their country's appeal and many tour operators offer movie location-based packages.

The choice of titles is selective and subjective to provide a good geographical and chronological spread. Some locations are famous for standing in for other places, for example Helsinki has been used many times in place of Moscow or St Petersburg (Gorky Park, Reds, etc.), especially during the Cold War when the USSR was inaccessible to film makers.

Many famous films will not appear at all as they were studio-based or used temporary sets which no longer exist. Others, such as The English Patient, used multiple locations of which only the most significant are included in this map.

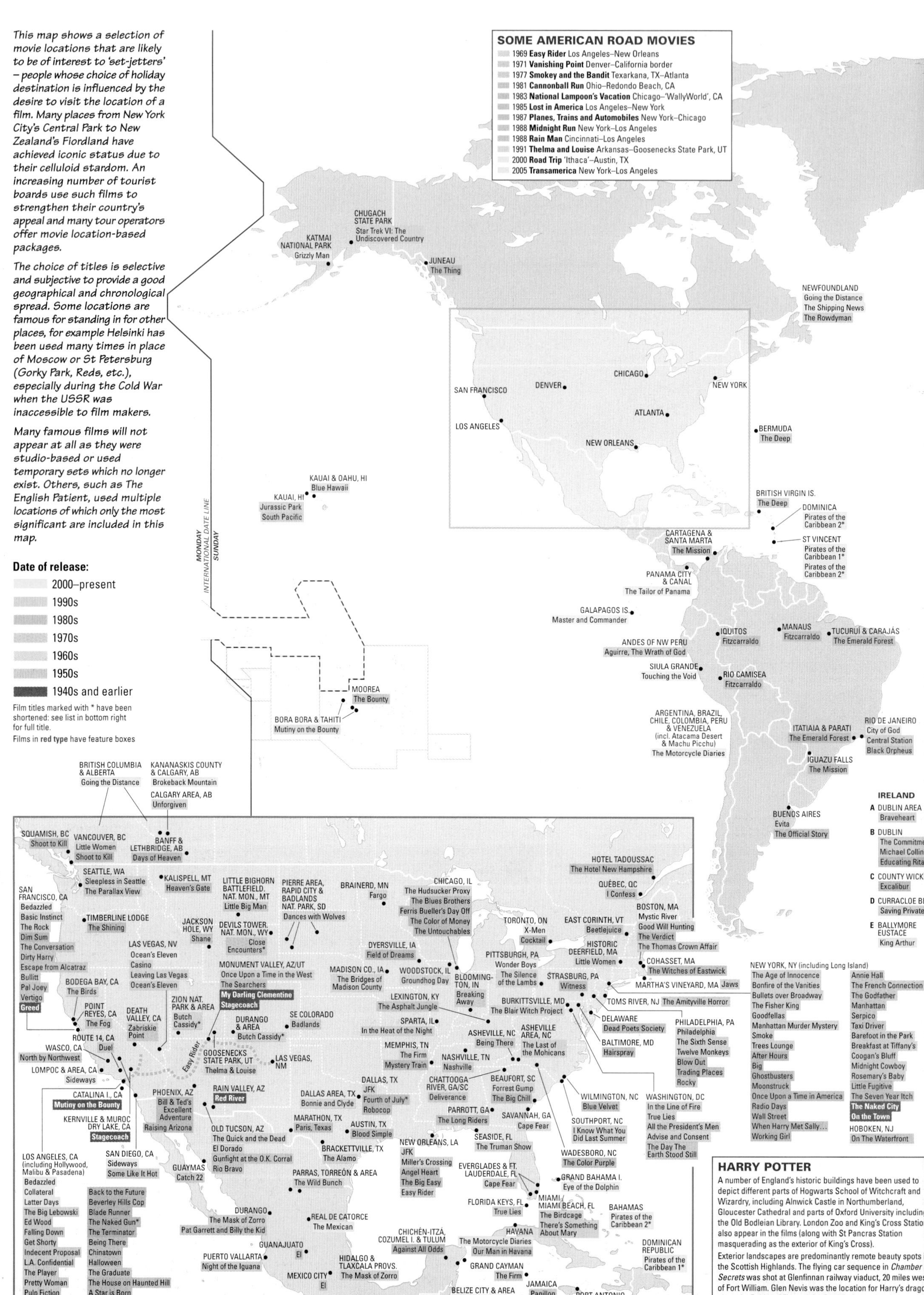
SOME AMERICAN ROAD MOVIES
1969 Easy Rider Los Angeles–New Orleans
1971 Vanishing Point Denver–California border
1977 Smokey and the Bandit Texarkana, TX–Atlanta
1981 Cannonball Run Ohio–Redondo Beach, CA
1983 National Lampoon's Vacation Chicago–'WallyWorld', CA
1985 Lost in America Los Angeles–New York
1987 Planes, Trains and Automobiles New York–Chicago
1988 Midnight Run New York–Los Angeles
1988 Rain Man Cincinnati–Los Angeles
1991 Thelma and Louise Arkansas–Goosenecks State Park, UT
2000 Road Trip 'Ithaca'–Austin, TX
2005 Transamerica New York–Los Angeles
Date of release:
2000–present
1990s
1980s
1970s
1960s
1950s
1940s and earlier
Film titles marked with * have been shortened: see list in bottom right for full title.
Films in red type have feature boxes
INTERNATIONAL DATE LINE
MONDAY
SUNDAY
CHUGACH STATE PARK
Star Trek VI: The Undiscovered Country
KATMAI NATIONAL PARK
Grizzly Man
JUNEAU
The Thing
NEWFOUNDLAND
Going the Distance
The Shipping News
The Rowdyman
SAN FRANCISCO
DENVER
CHICAGO
NEW YORK
ATLANTA
LOS ANGELES
NEW ORLEANS
BERMUDA
The Deep
KAUAI & OAHU, HI
Blue Hawaii
KAUAI, HI
Jurassic Park
South Pacific
BRITISH VIRGIN IS.
The Deep
DOMINICA
Pirates of the Caribbean 2*
ST VINCENT
Pirates of the Caribbean 1*
Pirates of the Caribbean 2*
CARTAGENA & SANTA MARTA
The Mission
PANAMA CITY & CANAL
The Tailor of Panama
GALAPAGOS IS.
Master and Commander
IQUITOS
Fitzcarraldo
MANAUS
Fitzcarraldo
TUCURUÍ & CARAJÁS
The Emerald Forest
ANDES OF NW PERU
Aguirre, The Wrath of God
SIULA GRANDE
Touching the Void
RIO CAMISEA
Fitzcarraldo
MOOREA
The Bounty
BORA BORA & TAHITI
Mutiny on the Bounty
ARGENTINA, BRAZIL, CHILE, COLOMBIA, PERU & VENEZUELA (incl. Atacama Desert & Machu Picchu)
The Motorcycle Diaries
ITATIAIA & PARATI
The Emerald Forest
RIO DE JANEIRO
City of God
Central Station
Black Orpheus
IGUAZU FALLS
The Mission
BUENOS AIRES
Evita
The Official Story
IRELAND
A DUBLIN AREA
Braveheart
B DUBLIN
The Commitme
Michael Collins
Educating Rita
C COUNTY WICKL
Excalibur
D CURRACLOE BE
Saving Private
E BALLYMORE EUSTACE
King Arthur
BRITISH COLUMBIA & ALBERTA
Going the Distance
KANANASKIS COUNTY & CALGARY, AB
Brokeback Mountain
CALGARY AREA, AB
Unforgiven
SQUAMISH, BC
Shoot to Kill
VANCOUVER, BC
Little Women
Shoot to Kill
BANFF & LETHBRIDGE, AB
Days of Heaven
SEATTLE, WA
Sleepless in Seattle
The Parallax View
KALISPELL, MT
Heaven's Gate
LITTLE BIGHORN BATTLEFIELD. NAT. MON., MT
Little Big Man
PIERRE AREA, RAPID CITY & BADLANDS NAT. PARK, SD
Dances with Wolves
BRAINERD, MN
Fargo
CHICAGO, IL
The Hudsucker Proxy
The Blues Brothers
Ferris Bueller's Day Off
The Color of Money
The Untouchables
HOTEL TADOUSSAC
The Hotel New Hampshire
QUÉBEC, QC
I Confess
SAN FRANCISCO, CA
Bedazzled
Basic Instinct
The Rock
Dim Sum
The Conversation
Dirty Harry
Escape from Alcatraz
Bullitt
Pal Joey
Vertigo
Greed
TIMBERLINE LODGE
The Shining
JACKSON HOLE, WY
Shane
DEVILS TOWER. NAT. MON., WY
Close Encounters*
TORONTO, ON
X-Men
Cocktail
EAST CORINTH, VT
Beetlejuice
BOSTON, MA
Mystic River
Good Will Hunting
The Verdict
The Thomas Crown Affair
LAS VEGAS, NV
Ocean's Eleven
Casino
Leaving Las Vegas
Ocean's Eleven
DYERSVILLE, IA
Field of Dreams
HISTORIC DEERFIELD, MA
Little Women
PITTSBURGH, PA
Wonder Boys
The Silence of the Lambs
COHASSET, MA
The Witches of Eastwick
MONUMENT VALLEY, AZ/UT
Once Upon a Time in the West
The Searchers
My Darling Clementine
Stagecoach
MADISON CO., IA
The Bridges of Madison County
WOODSTOCK, IL
Groundhog Day
BLOOMING-TON, IN
Breaking Away
STRASBURG, PA
Witness
MARTHA'S VINEYARD, MA Jaws
BODEGA BAY, CA
The Birds
POINT REYES, CA
The Fog
DEATH VALLEY, CA
Zabriskie Point
ZION NAT. PARK & AREA
Butch Cassidy*
LEXINGTON, KY
The Asphalt Jungle
BURKITTSVILLE, MD
The Blair Witch Project
TOMS RIVER, NJ The Amityville Horror
SE COLORADO
Badlands
DURANGO & AREA
Butch Cassidy*
SPARTA, IL
In the Heat of the Night
DELAWARE
Dead Poets Society
PHILADELPHIA, PA
Philadelphia
The Sixth Sense
Twelve Monkeys
Blow Out
Trading Places
Rocky
ROUTE 14, CA
Duel
ASHEVILLE, NC
Being There
ASHEVILLE AREA, NC
The Last of the Mohicans
BALTIMORE, MD
Hairspray
WASCO, CA
North by Northwest
Easy Rider
GOOSENECKS STATE PARK, UT
Thelma & Louise
LAS VEGAS, NM
MEMPHIS, TN
The Firm
Mystery Train
NASHVILLE, TN
Nashville
LOMPOC & AREA, CA
Sideways
DALLAS, TX
JFK
Fourth of July*
Robocop
CHATTOOGA RIVER, GA/SC
Deliverance
BEAUFORT, SC
Forrest Gump
The Big Chill
CATALINA I., CA
Mutiny on the Bounty
PHOENIX, AZ
Bill & Ted's Excellent Adventure
Raising Arizona
RAIN VALLEY, AZ
Red River
DALLAS AREA, TX
Bonnie and Clyde
WILMINGTON, NC
Blue Velvet
WASHINGTON, DC
In the Line of Fire
True Lies
All the President's Men
Advise and Consent
The Day The Earth Stood Still
PARROTT, GA
The Long Riders
SAVANNAH, GA
Cape Fear
SOUTHPORT, NC
I Know What You Did Last Summer
KERNVILLE & MUROC DRY LAKE, CA
Stagecoach
MARATHON, TX
Paris, Texas
AUSTIN, TX
Blood Simple
OLD TUCSON, AZ
The Quick and the Dead
El Dorado
Gunfight at the O.K. Corral
Rio Bravo
SEASIDE, FL
The Truman Show
NEW ORLEANS, LA
JFK
Miller's Crossing
Angel Heart
The Big Easy
Easy Rider
BRACKETTVILLE, TX
The Alamo
WADESBORO, NC
The Color Purple
LOS ANGELES, CA (including Hollywood, Malibu & Pasadena)
Bedazzled
Collateral
Latter Days
The Big Lebowski
Ed Wood
Falling Down
Get Shorty
Indecent Proposal
L.A. Confidential
The Player
Pretty Woman
Pulp Fiction
Speed
Back to the Future
Beverley Hills Cop
Blade Runner
The Naked Gun*
The Terminator
Being There
Chinatown
Halloween
The Graduate
The House on Haunted Hill
A Star is Born
Sunset Blvd.
SAN DIEGO, CA
Sideways
Some Like It Hot
GUAYMAS
Catch 22
PARRAS, TORREÓN & AREA
The Wild Bunch
EVERGLADES & FT. LAUDERDALE, FL
Cape Fear
GRAND BAHAMA I.
Eye of the Dolphin
DURANGO
The Mask of Zorro
Pat Garrett and Billy the Kid
REAL DE CATORCE
The Mexican
FLORIDA KEYS, FL
True Lies
MIAMI / MIAMI BEACH, FL
The Birdcage
There's Something About Mary
BAHAMAS
Pirates of the Caribbean 2*
HAVANA
The Motorcycle Diaries
Our Man in Havana
CHICHÉN-ITZÁ, COZUMEL I. & TULUM
Against All Odds
GUANAJUATO
El
PUERTO VALLARTA
Night of the Iguana
HIDALGO & TLAXCALA PROVS.
The Mask of Zorro
MEXICO CITY
El
DOMINICAN REPUBLIC
Pirates of the Caribbean 1*
GRAND CAYMAN
The Firm
JAMAICA
Papillon
PORT ANTONIO
Cocktail
BELIZE CITY & AREA
The Dogs of War
The Mosquito Coast
TIKAL
Star Wars
NEW YORK, NY (including Long Island)
The Age of Innocence
Bonfire of the Vanities
Bullets over Broadway
The Fisher King
Goodfellas
Manhattan Murder Mystery
Smoke
Trees Lounge
After Hours
Big
Ghostbusters
Moonstruck
Once Upon a Time in America
Radio Days
Wall Street
When Harry Met Sally...
Working Girl
Annie Hall
The French Connection
The Godfather
Manhattan
Serpico
Taxi Driver
Barefoot in the Park
Breakfast at Tiffany's
Coogan's Bluff
Midnight Cowboy
Rosemary's Baby
Little Fugitive
The Seven Year Itch
The Naked City
On the Town
HOBOKEN, NJ
On The Waterfront

HARRY POTTER

A number of England's historic buildings have been used to depict different parts of Hogwarts School of Witchcraft and Wizardry, including Alnwick Castle in Northumberland, Gloucester Cathedral and parts of Oxford University including the Old Bodleian Library. London Zoo and King's Cross Station also appear in the films (along with St Pancras Station masquerading as the exterior of King's Cross).

Exterior landscapes are predominantly remote beauty spots in the Scottish Highlands. The flying car sequence in *Chamber of Secrets* was shot at Glenfinnan railway viaduct, 20 miles west of Fort William. Glen Nevis was the location for Harry's dragon chase in *Goblet of Fire* and the Quidditch matches in *Philosopher's Stone* and *Chamber of Secrets*.

See also... Europe Leisure Parks (67); US Theme Parks (171)

The listings above refer to a selection of related themes. For more information, see the Contents (2-7).

THE DA VINCI CODE

In this religious conspiracy theory thriller Lincoln Cathedral substitutes for Westminster Abbey but London's Temple Church and The Louvre in Paris play themselves, as does Scotland's Rosslyn Chapel, famous for its suspected links to the Holy Grail and the Knight's Templar. Other locations include the Caledonian Hilton Hotel in Edinburgh and Château de Villette in Val-d'Oise, France.

JAMES BOND

Date	Film title	007	Principal / most memorable locations
1962	Doctor No	Connery	Jamaica
1963	From Russia with Love	Connery	Istanbul • Lochgilphead, Scotland (helicopter chase) • Venice
1964	Goldfinger	Connery	Locations in NW London • Andermatt & Lucerne, Switzerland
1965	Thunderball	Connery	Château d'Anet, near Paris • Silverstone racetrack • New Providence I., Bahamas
1967	You Only Live Twice	Connery	Gibraltar • Japan: Himeji Castle (Ninja school) & Kirishima National Park (Blofeld HQ)
1969	On Her Majesty's Secret Service	Lazenby	Lisbon area • Murren area, Switzerland (stock car rally, skating, mountaintop clinic)
1971	Diamonds are Forever	Connery	Amsterdam • Las Vegas • Vandenburg Air Base, CA (Blofeld's satellite launch)
1973	Live and Let Die	Moore	Manhattan • Jamaica (voodoo & crocodile farm) • Southern Louisiana (boat chase)
1974	The Man with the Golden Gun	Moore	Macau • Hong Kong • Bangkok (boat chase) • Phang Nga Bay, Thailand (Scaramanga HQ)
1977	The Spy Who Loved Me	Moore	Asgard Peak, Baffin I., Canada (ski jump) • Giza Pyramids (lightshow) • N Sardinia (hotel)
1979	Moonraker	Moore	Vaux-le-Vicomte, France (Drax's mansion) • Venice (boat chase) • Rio (cable car fight)
1981	For Your Eyes Only	Moore	Becton gasworks, London • Cortina, Italy (chases) • Corfu • Meteora, Greece (monastery)
1983	Octopussy	Moore	Northolt Aerodrome, nr. London • Moab, UT • Udaipur, India • Berlin (Checkpoint Charlie)
1983	Never Say Never Again	Connery	Luton Hoo, near London • Villefranche-sur-Mer, France (motorbike chase) • New Providence I., Bahamas • Antibes, France (Largo's fortress)
1985	A View to a Kill	Moore	SE Iceland • Château Chantilly, nr. Paris • Paris (Eiffel Tower parachute jump) • San Francisco
1987	The Living Daylights	Dalton	Vienna: Prater & Schonbrunn Palace • Morocco: Ouarzazate, & Forbes Museum, Tangier
1989	Licence to Kill	Dalton	Key West, FL • Acapulco • Mexico City • Toluca & I. de Mujeres, Mexico • Rumorosa Pass, near Mexicali (road chase)
1995	GoldenEye	Brosnan	Lake Verzasca, Switzerland • Monte Carlo • St Petersburg (tank chase) • SE England
1997	Tomorrow Never Dies	Brosnan	Peyresourde Airfield, Pyrenees • W London • Phuket, Thailand • Bangkok (hotel descent)
1999	The World is Not Enough	Brosnan	Guggenheim Museum, Bilbao • River Thames (boat chase) • Baku • Chamonix, France (paraglider attack) • Luton Hoo, near London • Maiden's Tower, Istanbul
2002	Die Another Day	Brosnan	Cornwall, Hampshire, Norfolk & Hawaii (Korean scenes) • Cádiz (Cuban scenes) • Jökulsárlón, Iceland (ice palace exterior) • Eden Project, Cornwall (ice palace interior)
2006	Casino Royale	Craig	*(unreleased at time of going to press: locations include Bahamas, Czech Rep., Italy, UK)*

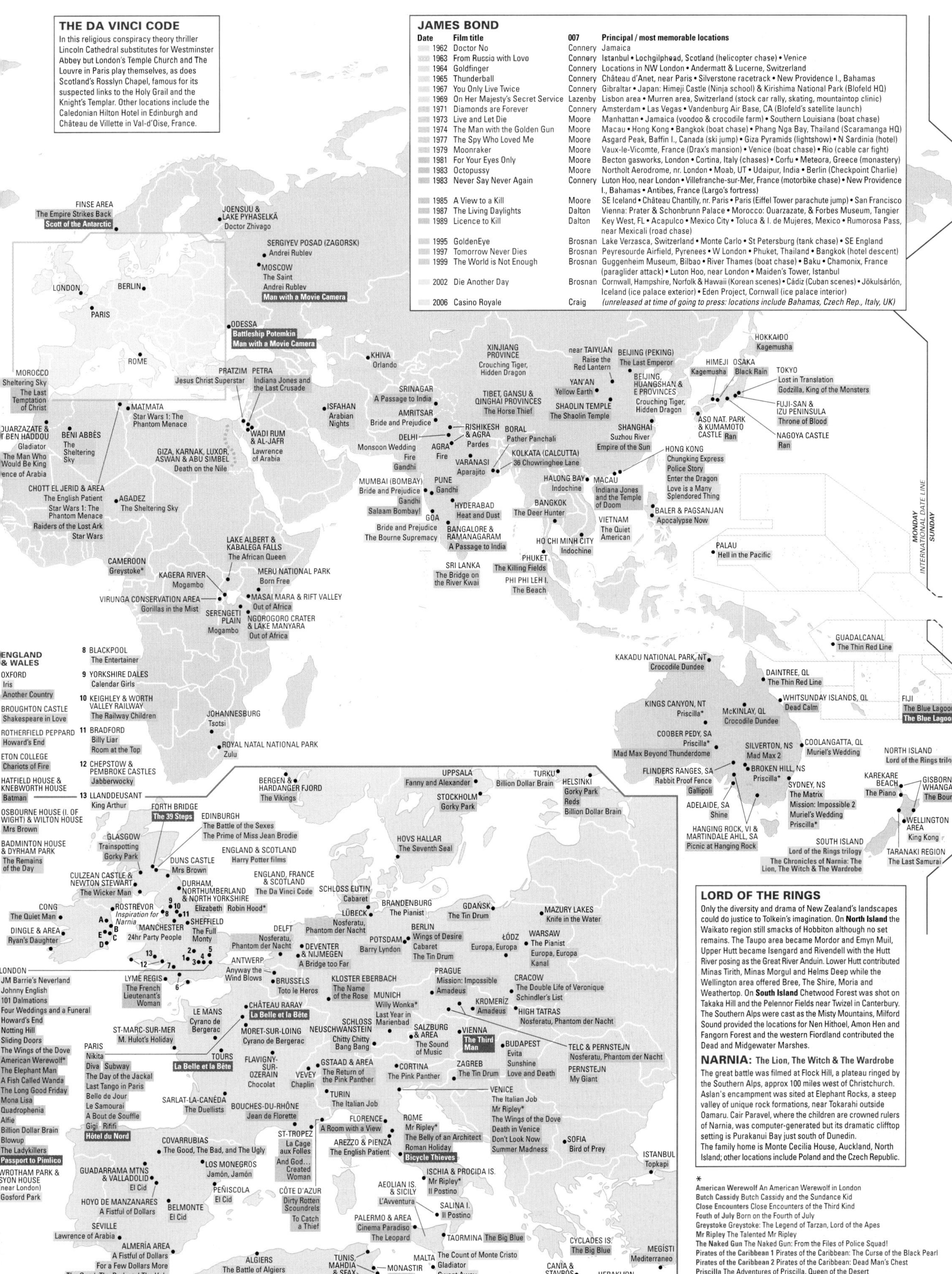

FINSE AREA
The Empire Strikes Back
Scott of the Antarctic
JOENSUU & LAKE PYHASELKÄ
Doctor Zhivago
SERGIYEV POSAD (ZAGORSK)
Andrei Rublev
MOSCOW
The Saint
Andrei Rublev
Man with a Movie Camera
LONDON
BERLIN
PARIS
ODESSA
Battleship Potemkin
Man with a Movie Camera
ROME
MOROCCO
Sheltering Sky
The Last Temptation of Christ
MATMATA
Star Wars 1: The Phantom Menace
PRATZIM
Jesus Christ Superstar
PETRA
Indiana Jones and the Last Crusade
KHIVA
Orlando
ISFAHAN
Arabian Nights
WADI RUM & AL-JAFR
Lawrence of Arabia
GIZA, KARNAK, LUXOR, ASWAN & ABU SIMBEL
Death on the Nile
BENI ABBÈS
The Sheltering Sky
CHOTT EL JERID & AREA
The English Patient
Star Wars 1: The Phantom Menace
Raiders of the Lost Ark
Star Wars
AGADEZ
The Sheltering Sky
CAMEROON
Greystoke*
LAKE ALBERT & KABALEGA FALLS
The African Queen
KAGERA RIVER
Mogambo
MERU NATIONAL PARK
Born Free
VIRUNGA CONSERVATION AREA
Gorillas in the Mist
MASAI MARA & RIFT VALLEY
Out of Africa
SERENGETI PLAIN
Mogambo
NGOROGORO CRATER & LAKE MANYARA
Out of Africa
JOHANNESBURG
Tsotsi
ROYAL NATAL NATIONAL PARK
Zulu
SRINAGAR
A Passage to India
AMRITSAR
Bride and Prejudice
DELHI
Monsoon Wedding
Fire
Gandhi
AGRA
Fire
RISHIKESH & AGRA
Pardes
VARANASI
Aparajito
MUMBAI (BOMBAY)
Bride and Prejudice
Gandhi
Salaam Bombay!
PUNE
Gandhi
HYDERABAD
Heat and Dust
GOA
Bride and Prejudice
The Bourne Supremacy
BANGALORE & RAMANAGARAM
A Passage to India
SRI LANKA
The Bridge on the River Kwai
BORAL
Pather Panchali
KOLKATA (CALCUTTA)
36 Chowringhee Lane
XINJIANG PROVINCE
Crouching Tiger, Hidden Dragon
TIBET, GANSU & QINGHAI PROVINCES
The Horse Thief
near TAIYUAN
Raise the Red Lantern
YAN'AN
Yellow Earth
BEIJING (PEKING)
The Last Emperor
BEIJING, HUANGSHAN & E PROVINCES
Crouching Tiger, Hidden Dragon
SHAOLIN TEMPLE
The Shaolin Temple
SHANGHAI
Suzhou River
Empire of the Sun
HONG KONG
Chungking Express
Police Story
Enter the Dragon
Love is a Many Splendored Thing
MACAU
Indiana Jones and the Temple of Doom
HALONG BAY
Indochine
BANGKOK
The Deer Hunter
VIETNAM
The Quiet American
HO CHI MINH CITY
Indochine
PHUKET
The Killing Fields
PHI PHI LEH I.
The Beach
BALER & PAGSANJAN
Apocalypse Now
PALAU
Hell in the Pacific
HOKKAIDO
Kagemusha
HIMEJI
Kagemusha
OSAKA
Black Rain
TOKYO
Lost in Translation
Godzilla, King of the Monsters
FUJI-SAN & IZU PENINSULA
Throne of Blood
ASO NAT. PARK & KUMAMOTO CASTLE
Ran
NAGOYA CASTLE
Ran
MONDAY
INTERNATIONAL DATE LINE
SUNDAY
GUADALCANAL
The Thin Red Line
KAKADU NATIONAL PARK, NT
Crocodile Dundee
DAINTREE, QL
The Thin Red Line
WHITSUNDAY ISLANDS, QL
Dead Calm
KINGS CANYON, NT
Priscilla*
McKINLAY, QL
Crocodile Dundee
FIJI
The Blue Lagoon
The Blue Lagoon
COOBER PEDY, SA
Priscilla*
Mad Max Beyond Thunderdome
SILVERTON, NS
Mad Max 2
COOLANGATTA, QL
Muriel's Wedding
NORTH ISLAND
Lord of the Rings trilogy
FLINDERS RANGES, SA
Rabbit Proof Fence
Gallipoli
BROKEN HILL, NS
Priscilla*
SYDNEY, NS
The Matrix
Mission: Impossible 2
Muriel's Wedding
Priscilla*
ADELAIDE, SA
Shine
HANGING ROCK, VI & MARTINDALE AHLL, SA
Picnic at Hanging Rock
KAREKARE BEACH
The Piano
GISBORNE & WHANGAREI
The Bounty
WELLINGTON AREA
King Kong
SOUTH ISLAND
Lord of the Rings trilogy
The Chronicles of Narnia: The Lion, The Witch & The Wardrobe
TARANAKI REGION
The Last Samurai
ENGLAND & WALES
OXFORD
Iris
Another Country
BROUGHTON CASTLE
Shakespeare in Love
ROTHERFIELD PEPPARD
Howard's End
ETON COLLEGE
Chariots of Fire
HATFIELD HOUSE & KNEBWORTH HOUSE
Batman
OSBOURNE HOUSE (I. OF WIGHT) & WILTON HOUSE
Mrs Brown
BADMINTON HOUSE & DYRHAM PARK
The Remains of the Day
8 BLACKPOOL
The Entertainer
9 YORKSHIRE DALES
Calendar Girls
10 KEIGHLEY & WORTH VALLEY RAILWAY
The Railway Children
11 BRADFORD
Billy Liar
Room at the Top
12 CHEPSTOW & PEMBROKE CASTLES
Jabberwocky
13 LLANDDEUSANT
King Arthur
FORTH BRIDGE
The 39 Steps
EDINBURGH
The Battle of the Sexes
The Prime of Miss Jean Brodie
GLASGOW
Trainspotting
Gorky Park
ENGLAND & SCOTLAND
Harry Potter films
DUNS CASTLE
Mrs Brown
CULZEAN CASTLE & NEWTON STEWART
The Wicker Man
DURHAM, NORTHUMBERLAND & NORTH YORKSHIRE
Elizabeth
Robin Hood*
ENGLAND, FRANCE & SCOTLAND
The Da Vinci Code
CONG
The Quiet Man
ROSTREVOR
Inspiration for Narnia
DINGLE & AREA
Ryan's Daughter
MANCHESTER
24hr Party People
SHEFFIELD
The Full Monty
LONDON
JM Barrie's Neverland
Johnny English
101 Dalmations
Four Weddings and a Funeral
Howard's End
Notting Hill
Sliding Doors
The Wings of the Dove
American Werewolf*
The Elephant Man
A Fish Called Wanda
The Long Good Friday
Mona Lisa
Quadrophenia
Alfie
Billion Dollar Brain
Blowup
The Ladykillers
Passport to Pimlico
WROTHAM PARK & SYON HOUSE (near London)
Gosford Park
LYME REGIS
The French Lieutenant's Woman
BERGEN & HARDANGER FJORD
The Vikings
UPPSALA
Fanny and Alexander
STOCKHOLM
Gorky Park
TURKU
Billion Dollar Brain
HELSINKI
Gorky Park
Reds
Billion Dollar Brain
HOVS HALLAR
The Seventh Seal
SCHLOSS EUTIN
Cabaret
LÜBECK
Nosferatu, Phantom der Nacht
BRANDENBURG
The Pianist
GDAŃSK
The Tin Drum
MAZURY LAKES
Knife in the Water
DELFT
Nosferatu, Phantom der Nacht
DEVENTER & NIJMEGEN
A Bridge too Far
POTSDAM
Barry Lyndon
BERLIN
Wings of Desire
Cabaret
The Tin Drum
ŁÓDZ
Europa, Europa
WARSAW
The Pianist
Europa, Europa
Kanal
ANTWERP
Anyway the Wind Blows
BRUSSELS
Toto le Heros
KLOSTER EBERBACH
The Name of the Rose
MUNICH
Willy Wonka*
Last Year in Marienbad
PRAGUE
Mission: Impossible
Amadeus
CRACOW
The Double Life of Veronique
Schindler's List
KROMERÍZ
Amadeus
HIGH TATRAS
Nosferatu, Phantom der Nacht
LE MANS
Cyrano de Bergerac
CHÂTEAU RARAY
La Belle et la Bête
ST-MARC-SUR-MER
M. Hulot's Holiday
MORET-SUR-LOING
Cyrano de Bergerac
SCHLOSS NEUSCHWANSTEIN
Chitty Chitty Bang Bang
SALZBURG & AREA
The Sound of Music
VIENNA
The Third Man
BUDAPEST
Evita
Sunshine
Love and Death
TELC & PERNSTEJN
Nosferatu, Phantom der Nacht
PERNSTEJN
My Giant
PARIS
Nikita
Diva
Subway
The Day of the Jackal
Last Tango in Paris
Belle de Jour
Le Samourai
A Bout de Souffle
Gigi
Rififi
Hôtel du Nord
TOURS
La Belle et la Bête
FLAVIGNY-SUR-OZERAIN
Chocolat
VEVEY
Chaplin
GSTAAD & AREA
The Return of the Pink Panther
CORTINA
The Pink Panther
ZAGREB
The Tin Drum
SARLAT-LA-CANÉDA
The Duellists
BOUCHES-DU-RHÔNE
Jean de Florette
TURIN
The Italian Job
VENICE
The Italian Job
Mr Ripley*
The Wings of the Dove
Death in Venice
Don't Look Now
Summer Madness
FLORENCE
A Room with a View
ROME
Mr Ripley*
The Belly of an Architect
Roman Holiday
Bicycle Thieves
AREZZO & PIENZA
The English Patient
SOFIA
Bird of Prey
ISTANBUL
Topkapi
COVARRUBIAS
The Good, The Bad, and The Ugly
ST-TROPEZ
La Cage aux Folles
And God... Created Woman
GUADARRAMA MTNS & VALLADOLID
El Cid
LOS MONEGROS
Jamón, Jamón
PEÑISCOLA
El Cid
CÔTE D'AZUR
Dirty Rotten Scoundrels
To Catch a Thief
HOYO DE MANZANARES
A Fistful of Dollars
BELMONTE
El Cid
ISCHIA & PROCIDA IS.
Mr Ripley*
Il Postino
AEOLIAN IS. & SICILY
L'Avventura
SALINA I.
Il Postino
PALERMO & AREA
Cinema Paradiso
The Leopard
TAORMINA
The Big Blue
CYCLADES IS.
The Big Blue
MEGISTI
Mediterraneo
SEVILLE
Lawrence of Arabia
ALMERÍA AREA
A Fistful of Dollars
For a Few Dollars More
The Good, The Bad, and The Ugly
Lawrence of Arabia
ALGIERS
The Battle of Algiers
TUNIS, MAHDIA & SFAX
The English Patient
MONASTIR
The Life of Brian
MALTA
The Count of Monte Cristo
Gladiator
Swept Away
Troy
Popeye
Midnight Express
CANIA & STAVROS
Zorba the Greek
HERAKLION
Otello

LORD OF THE RINGS

Only the diversity and drama of New Zealand's landscapes could do justice to Tolkein's imagination. On **North Island** the Waikato region still smacks of Hobbiton although no set remains. The Taupo area became Mordor and Emyn Muil, Upper Hutt became Isengard and Rivendell with the Hutt River posing as the Great River Anduin. Lower Hutt contributed Minas Tirith, Minas Morgul and Helms Deep while the Wellington area offered Bree, The Shire, Moria and Weathertop. On **South Island** Chetwood Forest was shot on Takaka Hill and the Pelennor Fields near Twizel in Canterbury. The Southern Alps were cast as the Misty Mountains, Milford Sound provided the locations for Nen Hithoel, Amon Hen and Fangorn Forest and the western Fiordland contributed the Dead and Midgewater Marshes.

NARNIA: The Lion, The Witch & The Wardrobe

The great battle was filmed at Flock Hill, a plateau ringed by the Southern Alps, approx 100 miles west of Christchurch. Aslan's encampment was sited at Elephant Rocks, a steep valley of unique rock formations, near Tokarahi outside Oamaru. Cair Paravel, where the children are crowned rulers of Narnia, was computer-generated but its dramatic clifftop setting is Purakanui Bay just south of Dunedin. The family home is Monte Cecilia House, Auckland, North Island; other locations include Poland and the Czech Republic.

*
American Werewolf An American Werewolf in London
Butch Cassidy Butch Cassidy and the Sundance Kid
Close Encounters Close Encounters of the Third Kind
Fouth of July Born on the Fourth of July
Greystoke Greystoke: The Legend of Tarzan, Lord of the Apes
Mr Ripley The Talented Mr Ripley
The Naked Gun The Naked Gun: From the Files of Police Squad!
Pirates of the Caribbean 1 Pirates of the Caribbean: The Curse of the Black Pearl
Pirates of the Caribbean 2 Pirates of the Caribbean: Dead Man's Chest
Priscilla The Adventures of Priscilla, Queen of the Desert
Robin Hood Robin Hood, Prince of Thieves
Willy Wonka Willy Wonka and the Chocolate Factory

See also... Environment (17); Wealth (22-23); International Organisations (30); Business (32-33); Countries A-Z (202-210)

The listings above refer to a selection of related themes. For more information, see the Contents (2-7).

MAJOR FOSSIL FUEL DEPOSITS & HYDROELECTRIC SCHEMES

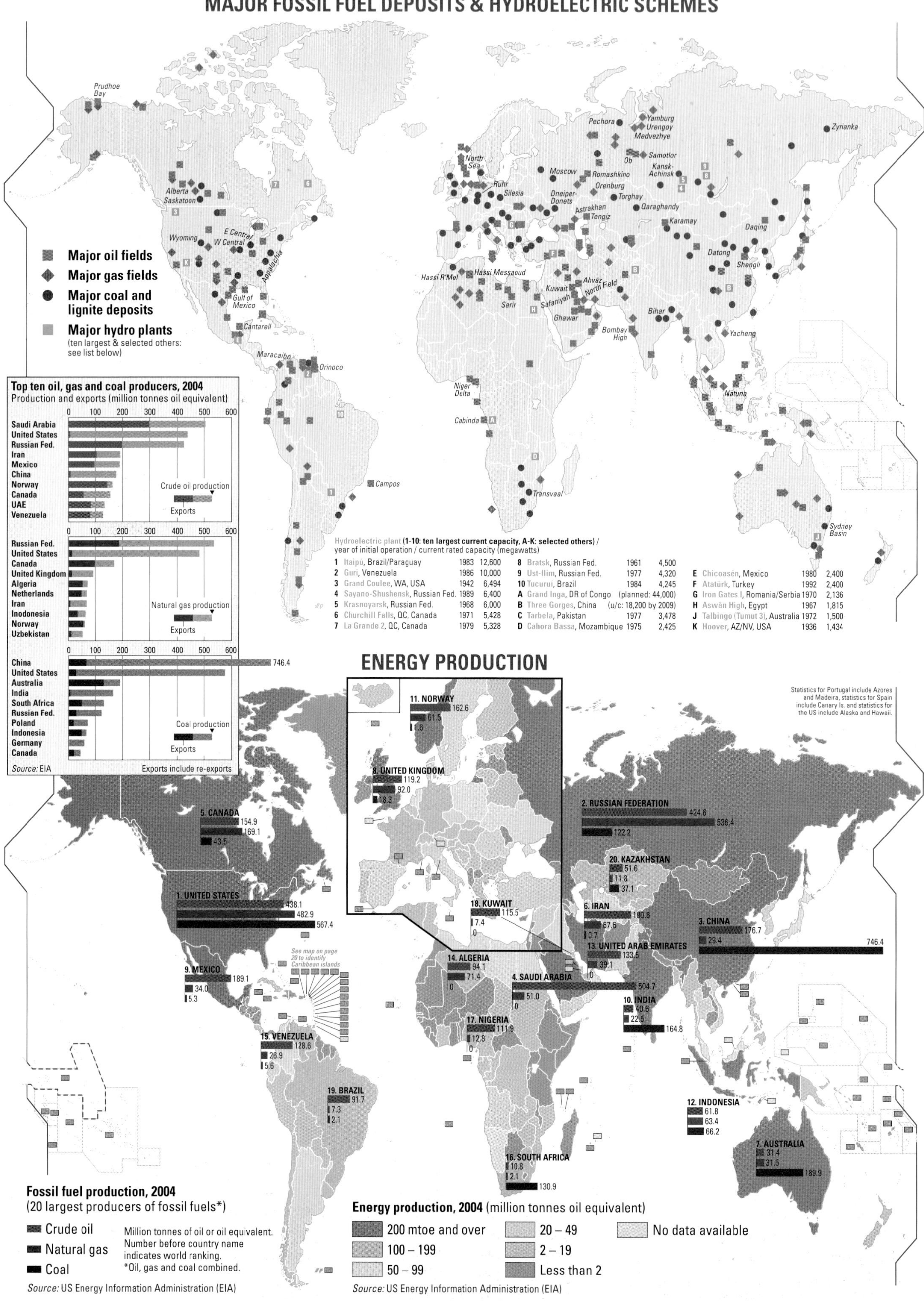
Major oil fields
Major gas fields
Major coal and lignite deposits
Major hydro plants
(ten largest & selected others: see list below)
Prudhoe Bay
Alberta
Saskatoon
Wyoming
E Central
W Central
Appalachia
Gulf of Mexico
Cantarell
Maracaibo
Orinoco
Campos
North Sea
Ruhr
Silesia
Moscow
Romashkino
Orenburg
Dneiper-Donets
Astrakhan
Tengiz
Torghay
Qaraghandy
Pechora
Yamburg
Urengoy
Medvezhye
Samotlor
Ob
Kansk-Achinsk
Zyrianka
Karamay
Daqing
Datong
Shengli
Hassi R'Mel
Hassi Messaoud
Sarir
Kuwait
Safaniyah
Ahvāz
North Field
Ghawar
Bombay High
Bihar
Yacheng
Natuna
Niger Delta
Cabinda
Transvaal
Sydney Basin
Top ten oil, gas and coal producers, 2004
Production and exports (million tonnes oil equivalent)
0 100 200 300 400 500 600
Saudi Arabia
United States
Russian Fed.
Iran
Mexico
China
Norway
Canada
UAE
Venezuela
Crude oil production
Exports
Russian Fed.
United States
Canada
United Kingdom
Algeria
Netherlands
Iran
Inodonesia
Norway
Uzbekistan
Natural gas production
Exports
China
United States
Australia
India
South Africa
Russian Fed.
Poland
Indonesia
Germany
Canada
746.4
Coal production
Exports
Source: EIA
Exports include re-exports

Hydroelectric plant (1-10: ten largest current capacity, A-K: selected others) / year of initial operation / current rated capacity (megawatts)

1	Itaipú, Brazil/Paraguay	1983	12,600
2	Guri, Venezuela	1986	10,000
3	Grand Coulee, WA, USA	1942	6,494
4	Sayano-Shushensk, Russian Fed.	1989	6,400
5	Krasnoyarsk, Russian Fed.	1968	6,000
6	Churchill Falls, QC, Canada	1971	5,428
7	La Grande 2, QC, Canada	1979	5,328
8	Bratsk, Russian Fed.	1961	4,500
9	Ust-Ilim, Russian Fed.	1977	4,320
10	Tucuruí, Brazil	1984	4,245
A	Grand Inga, DR of Congo	(planned: 44,000)	
B	Three Gorges, China	(u/c: 18,200 by 2009)	
C	Tarbela, Pakistan	1977	3,478
D	Cahora Bassa, Mozambique	1975	2,425
E	Chicoasén, Mexico	1980	2,400
F	Atatürk, Turkey	1992	2,400
G	Iron Gates I, Romania/Serbia	1970	2,136
H	Aswân High, Egypt	1967	1,815
J	Talbingo (Tumut 3), Australia	1972	1,500
K	Hoover, AZ/NV, USA	1936	1,434

ENERGY PRODUCTION

Statistics for Portugal include Azores and Madeira, statistics for Spain include Canary Is. and statistics for the US include Alaska and Hawaii.
11. NORWAY 162.6 61.5 1.6
8. UNITED KINGDOM 119.2 92.0 18.3
2. RUSSIAN FEDERATION 424.6 536.4 122.2
5. CANADA 154.9 169.1 43.5
20. KAZAKHSTAN 51.6 11.8 37.1
1. UNITED STATES 438.1 482.9 567.4
18. KUWAIT 115.5 7.4 0
6. IRAN 190.8 67.6 0.7
3. CHINA 176.7 29.4 746.4
13. UNITED ARAB EMIRATES 133.5 39.1 0
See map on page 20 to identify Caribbean islands
14. ALGERIA 94.1 71.4 0
9. MEXICO 189.1 34.0 5.3
4. SAUDI ARABIA 504.7 51.0 0
10. INDIA 40.6 22.5 164.8
17. NIGERIA 111.9 12.8 0
15. VENEZUELA 128.6 26.9 5.6
19. BRAZIL 91.7 7.3 2.1
12. INDONESIA 61.8 63.4 66.2
7. AUSTRALIA 31.4 31.5 189.9
16. SOUTH AFRICA 10.8 2.1 130.9

Fossil fuel production, 2004
(20 largest producers of fossil fuels*)

Crude oil
Natural gas
Coal

Million tonnes of oil or oil equivalent. Number before country name indicates world ranking.
*Oil, gas and coal combined.

Source: US Energy Information Administration (EIA)

Energy production, 2004 (million tonnes oil equivalent)

200 mtoe and over
100 – 199
50 – 99
20 – 49
2 – 19
Less than 2
No data available

Source: US Energy Information Administration (EIA)

See also... Environment (17); Wealth (22-23); International Organisations (30); Business (32-33); Countries A-Z (202-210)

The listings above refer to a selection of related themes. For more information, see the Contents (2-7).

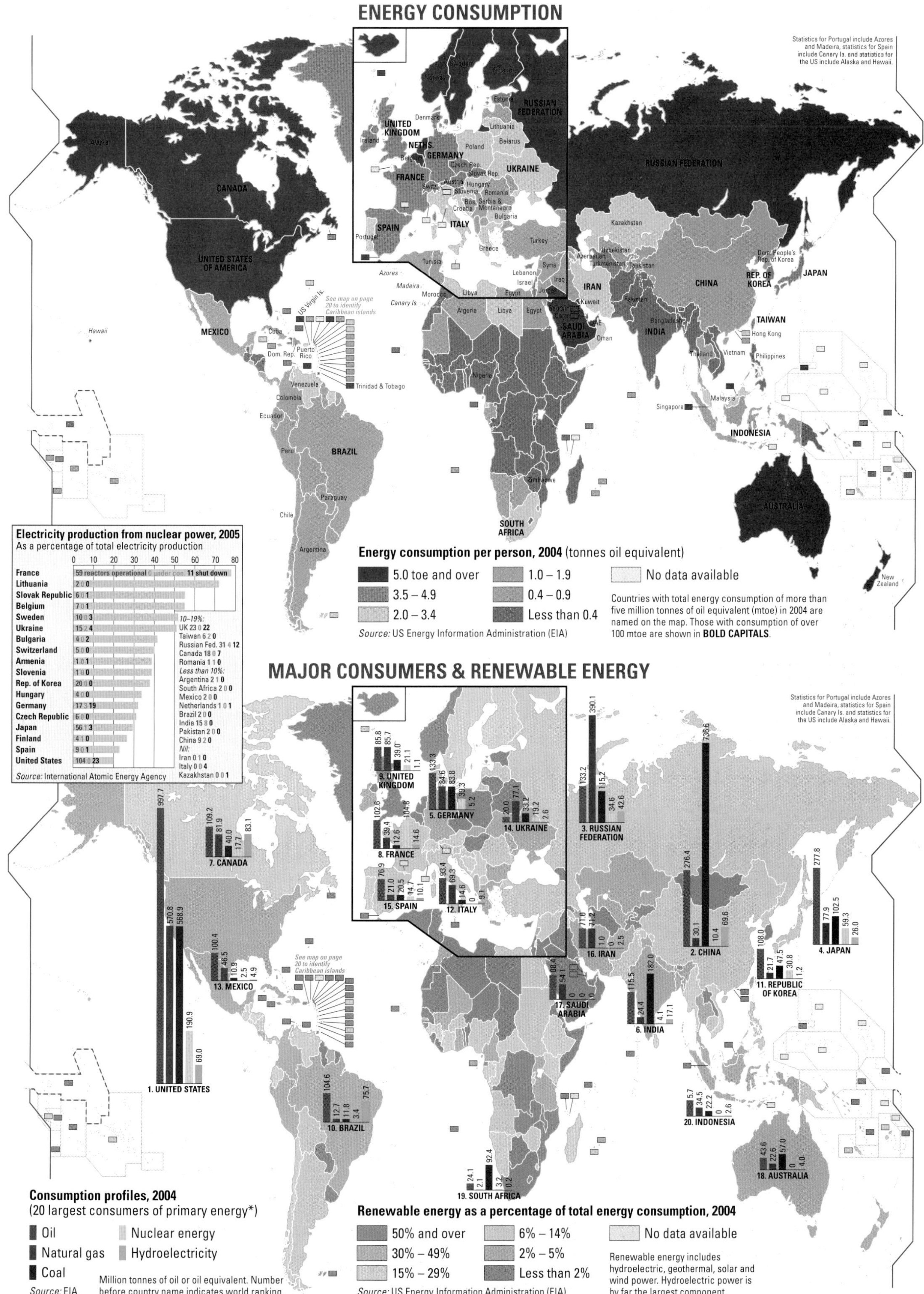
ENERGY CONSUMPTION
Statistics for Portugal include Azores and Madeira, statistics for Spain include Canary Is. and statistics for the US include Alaska and Hawaii.
CANADA
UNITED STATES OF AMERICA
MEXICO
RUSSIAN FEDERATION
UNITED KINGDOM
NETHS.
GERMANY
FRANCE
SPAIN
ITALY
UKRAINE
IRAN
SAUDI ARABIA
INDIA
CHINA
REP. OF KOREA
JAPAN
TAIWAN
INDONESIA
BRAZIL
SOUTH AFRICA
AUSTRALIA
See map on page 20 to identify Caribbean islands
Energy consumption per person, 2004 (tonnes oil equivalent)
5.0 toe and over
3.5 – 4.9
2.0 – 3.4
1.0 – 1.9
0.4 – 0.9
Less than 0.4
No data available
Source: US Energy Information Administration (EIA)
Countries with total energy consumption of more than five million tonnes of oil equivalent (mtoe) in 2004 are named on the map. Those with consumption of over 100 mtoe are shown in BOLD CAPITALS.
Electricity production from nuclear power, 2005
As a percentage of total electricity production
0 10 20 30 40 50 60 70 80
France 59 reactors operational 0 under con. 11 shut down
Lithuania 2 0 0
Slovak Republic 6 0 1
Belgium 7 0 1
Sweden 10 0 3
Ukraine 15 2 4
Bulgaria 4 0 2
Switzerland 5 0 0
Armenia 1 0 1
Slovenia 1 0 0
Rep. of Korea 20 0 0
Hungary 4 0 0
Germany 17 3 19
Czech Republic 6 0 0
Japan 56 1 3
Finland 4 1 0
Spain 9 0 1
United States 104 0 23
10–19%:
UK 23 0 22
Taiwan 6 2 0
Russian Fed. 31 4 12
Canada 18 0 7
Romania 1 1 0
Less than 10%:
Argentina 2 1 0
South Africa 2 0 0
Mexico 2 0 0
Netherlands 1 0 1
Brazil 2 0 0
India 15 8 0
Pakistan 2 0 0
China 9 2 0
Nil:
Iran 0 1 0
Italy 0 0 4
Kazakhstan 0 0 1
Source: International Atomic Energy Agency
MAJOR CONSUMERS & RENEWABLE ENERGY
1. UNITED STATES 997.7 570.8 568.9 190.9 69.0
2. CHINA 276.4 30.1 738.6 10.4 69.6
3. RUSSIAN FEDERATION 133.2 390.1 115.2 34.6 42.6
4. JAPAN 277.8 77.9 102.5 59.3 26.0
5. GERMANY 133.3 84.6 83.8 39.3 5.2
6. INDIA 115.5 24.4 182.0 4.1 17.1
7. CANADA 109.2 81.9 40.0 17.7 83.1
8. FRANCE 102.6 39.4 12.6 104.8 14.6
9. UNITED KINGDOM 85.8 85.7 39.0 21.1 1.1
10. BRAZIL 104.6 12.7 11.8 3.4 75.7
11. REPUBLIC OF KOREA 108.0 21.7 47.5 30.8 1.2
12. ITALY 93.4 69.3 14.6 0 9.1
13. MEXICO 100.4 46.5 10.9 2.5 4.9
14. UKRAINE 20.0 77.1 33.2 19.2 2.6
15. SPAIN 76.9 21.0 20.5 14.7 10.1
16. IRAN 71.0 71.2 1.0 0 2.5
17. SAUDI ARABIA 68.4 54.1 0 0 0
18. AUSTRALIA 43.6 22.6 57.0 0 4.0
19. SOUTH AFRICA 24.1 2.1 92.4 3.2 0.2
20. INDONESIA 5.7 34.5 22.2 0 2.6
Consumption profiles, 2004
(20 largest consumers of primary energy*)
Oil
Natural gas
Coal
Nuclear energy
Hydroelectricity
Source: EIA
Million tonnes of oil or oil equivalent. Number before country name indicates world ranking.
*Commercially traded fuels only.
Renewable energy as a percentage of total energy consumption, 2004
50% and over
30% – 49%
15% – 29%
6% – 14%
2% – 5%
Less than 2%
No data available
Source: US Energy Information Administration (EIA)
Renewable energy includes hydroelectric, geothermal, solar and wind power. Hydroelectric power is by far the largest component.

International Organisations

See also... Wealth (22-23); Energy (28-29); Business (32-33); MICE (34-35); Military (41); Europe Historical (58-59); EU (60-61)

The listings above refer to a selection of related themes. For more information, see the Contents (2-7).

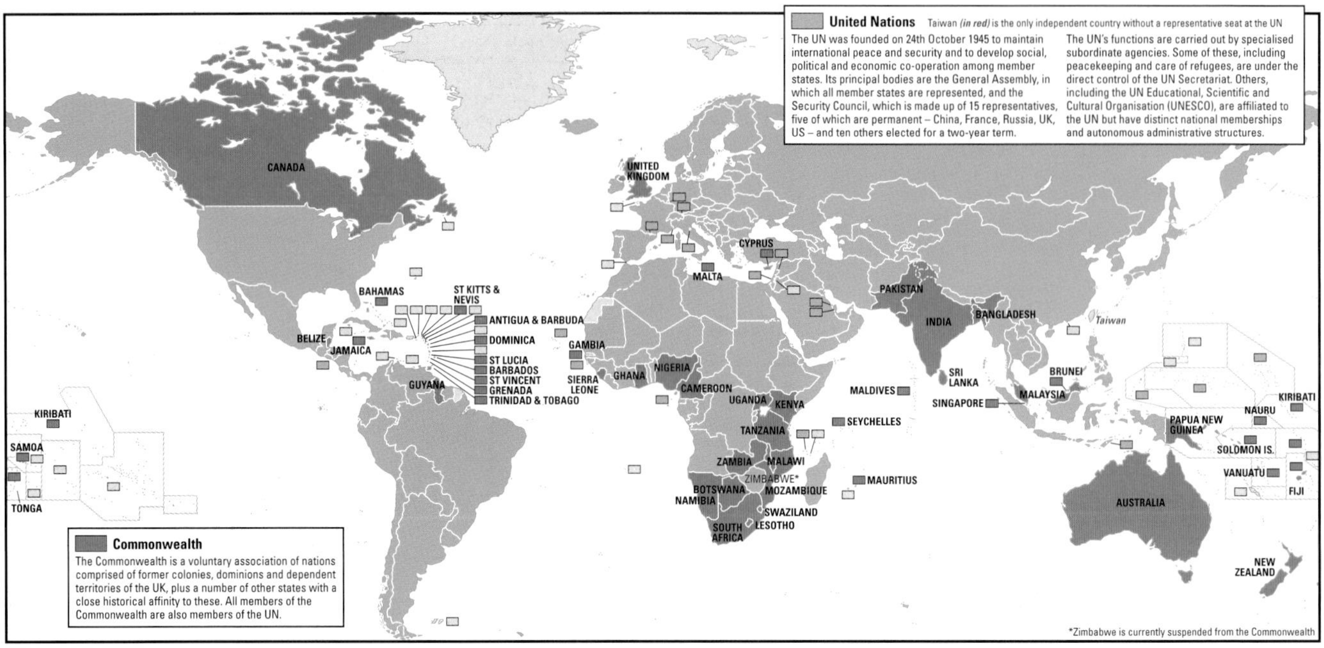

United Nations Taiwan *(in red)* is the only independent country without a representative seat at the UN

The UN was founded on 24th October 1945 to maintain international peace and security and to develop social, political and economic co-operation among member states. Its principal bodies are the General Assembly, in which all member states are represented, and the Security Council, which is made up of 15 representatives, five of which are permanent – China, France, Russia, UK, US – and ten others elected for a two-year term.

The UN's functions are carried out by specialised subordinate agencies. Some of these, including peacekeeping and care of refugees, are under the direct control of the UN Secretariat. Others, including the UN Educational, Scientific and Cultural Organisation (UNESCO), are affiliated to the UN but have distinct national memberships and autonomous administrative structures.

Commonwealth

The Commonwealth is a voluntary association of nations comprised of former colonies, dominions and dependent territories of the UK, plus a number of other states with a close historical affinity to these. All members of the Commonwealth are also members of the UN.

*Zimbabwe is currently suspended from the Commonwealth

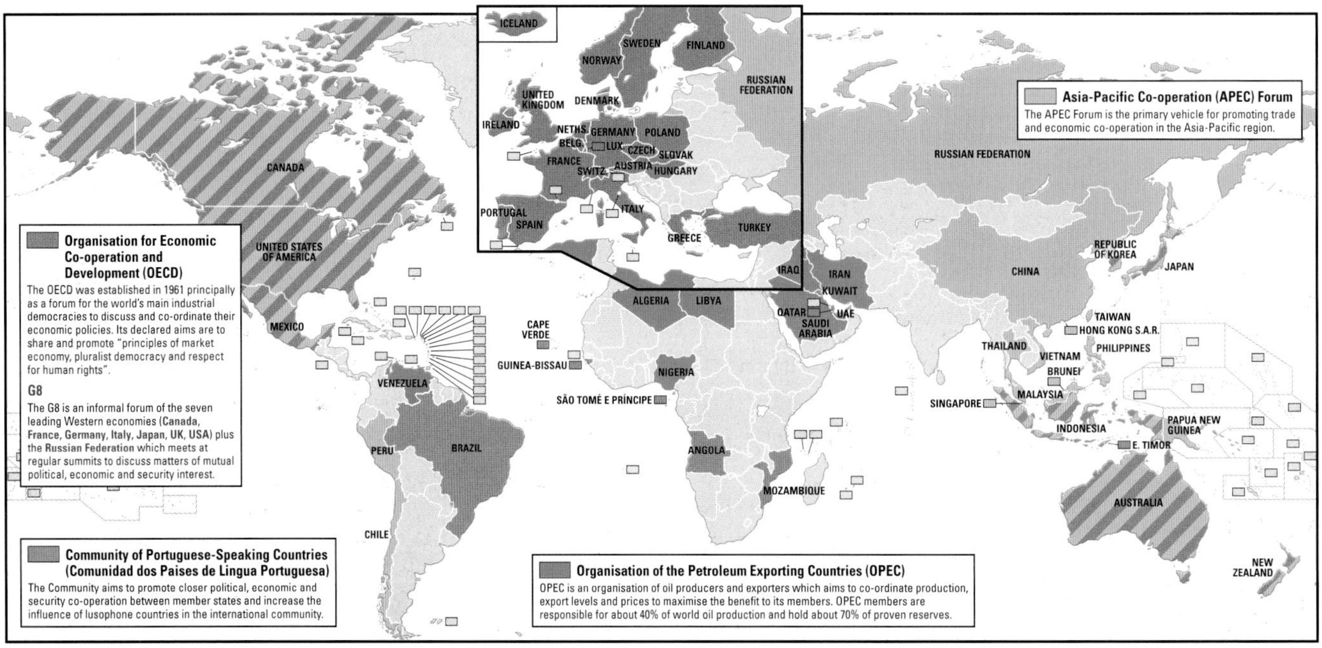

Asia-Pacific Co-operation (APEC) Forum

The APEC Forum is the primary vehicle for promoting trade and economic co-operation in the Asia-Pacific region.

Organisation for Economic Co-operation and Development (OECD)

The OECD was established in 1961 principally as a forum for the world's main industrial democracies to discuss and co-ordinate their economic policies. Its declared aims are to share and promote "principles of market economy, pluralist democracy and respect for human rights".

G8

The G8 is an informal forum of the seven leading Western economies (**Canada, France, Germany, Italy, Japan, UK, USA**) plus the **Russian Federation** which meets at regular summits to discuss matters of mutual political, economic and security interest.

Community of Portuguese-Speaking Countries (Comunidad dos Paises de Lingua Portuguesa)

The Community aims to promote closer political, economic and security co-operation between member states and increase the influence of lusophone countries in the international community.

Organisation of the Petroleum Exporting Countries (OPEC)

OPEC is an organisation of oil producers and exporters which aims to co-ordinate production, export levels and prices to maximise the benefit to its members. OPEC members are responsible for about 40% of world oil production and hold about 70% of proven reserves.

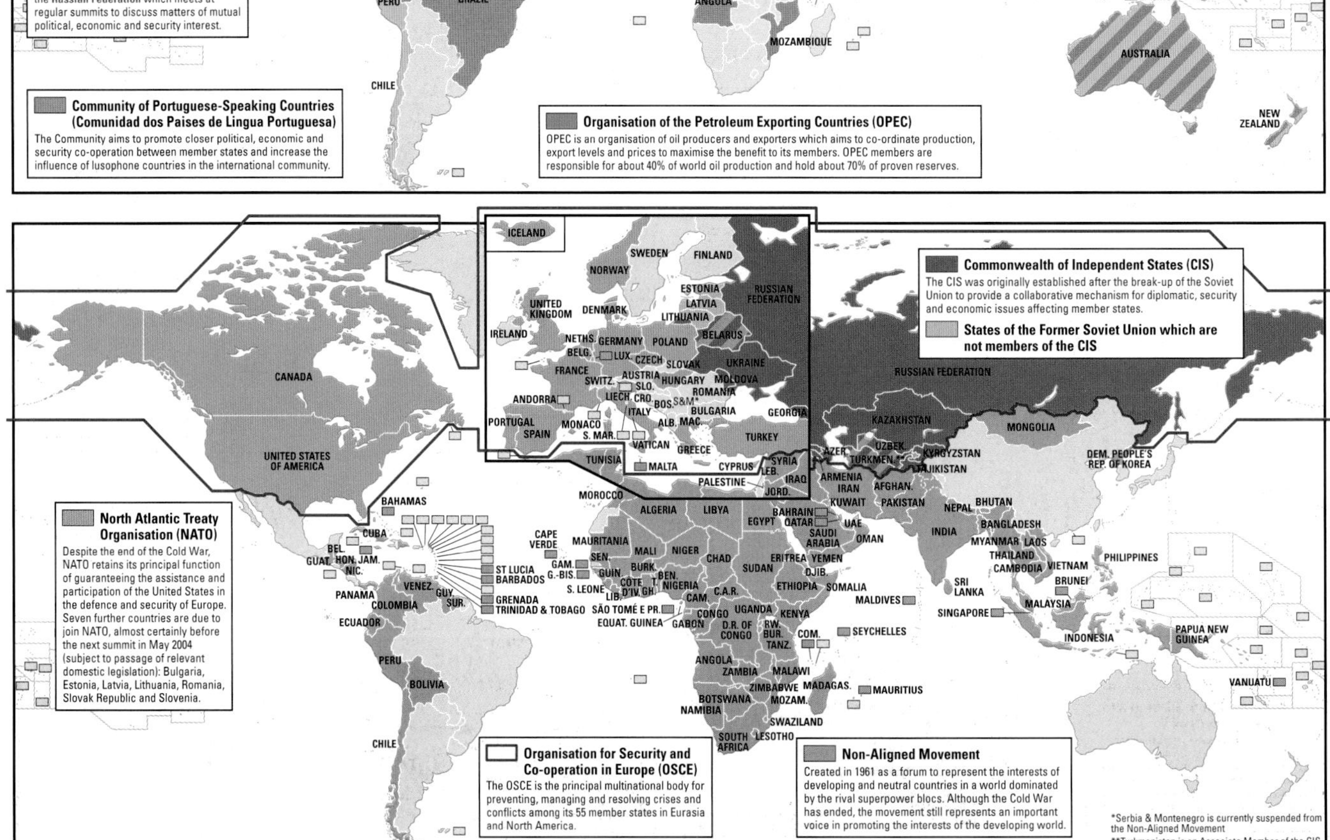
Commonwealth of Independent States (CIS)
The CIS was originally established after the break-up of the Soviet Union to provide a collaborative mechanism for diplomatic, security and economic issues affecting member states.
States of the Former Soviet Union which are not members of the CIS
North Atlantic Treaty Organisation (NATO)
Despite the end of the Cold War, NATO retains its principal function of guaranteeing the assistance and participation of the United States in the defence and security of Europe. Seven further countries are due to join NATO, almost certainly before the next summit in May 2004 (subject to passage of relevant domestic legislation): Bulgaria, Estonia, Latvia, Lithuania, Romania, Slovak Republic and Slovenia.
Organisation for Security and Co-operation in Europe (OSCE)
The OSCE is the principal multinational body for preventing, managing and resolving crises and conflicts among its 55 member states in Eurasia and North America.
Non-Aligned Movement
Created in 1961 as a forum to represent the interests of developing and neutral countries in a world dominated by the rival superpower blocs. Although the Cold War has ended, the movement still represents an important voice in promoting the interests of the developing world.
*Serbia & Montenegro is currently suspended from the Non-Aligned Movement
**Turkmenistan is an Associate Member of the CIS

See also... Wealth (22-23); Business (32-33); MICE (34-35); Military (41); Europe Historical (58-59); EU (60-61)

The listings above refer to a selection of related themes. For more information, see the Contents (2-7).

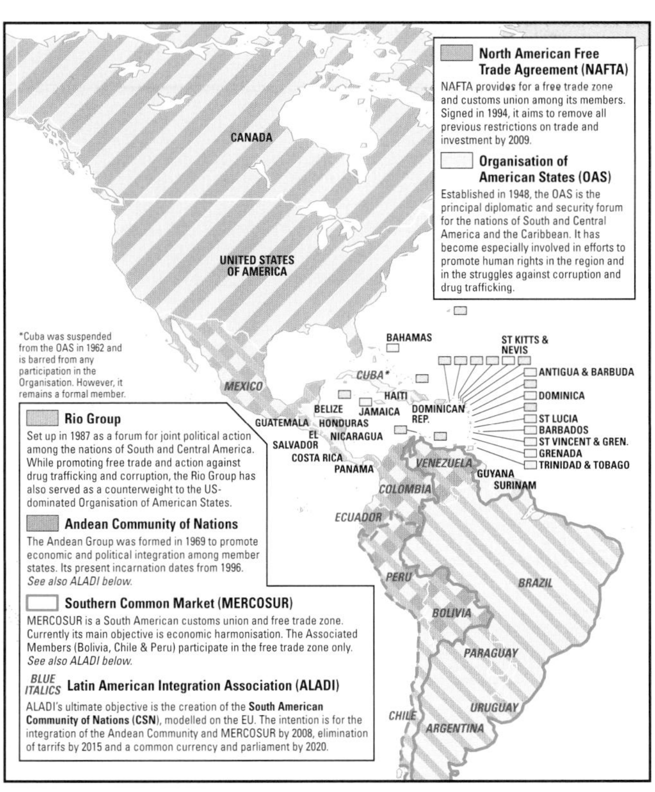
CANADA
UNITED STATES OF AMERICA
MEXICO
CUBA*
BAHAMAS
HAITI
DOMINICAN REP.
JAMAICA
BELIZE
GUATEMALA
HONDURAS
EL SALVADOR
NICARAGUA
COSTA RICA
PANAMA
ST KITTS & NEVIS
ANTIGUA & BARBUDA
DOMINICA
ST LUCIA
BARBADOS
ST VINCENT & GREN.
GRENADA
TRINIDAD & TOBAGO
VENEZUELA
GUYANA
SURINAM
COLOMBIA
ECUADOR
PERU
BRAZIL
BOLIVIA
PARAGUAY
CHILE
URUGUAY
ARGENTINA

North American Free Trade Agreement (NAFTA)
NAFTA provides for a free trade zone and customs union among its members. Signed in 1994, it aims to remove all previous restrictions on trade and investment by 2009.

Organisation of American States (OAS)
Established in 1948, the OAS is the principal diplomatic and security forum for the nations of South and Central America and the Caribbean. It has become especially involved in efforts to promote human rights in the region and in the struggles against corruption and drug trafficking.

*Cuba was suspended from the OAS in 1962 and is barred from any participation in the Organisation. However, it remains a formal member.

Rio Group
Set up in 1987 as a forum for joint political action among the nations of South and Central America. While promoting free trade and action against drug trafficking and corruption, the Rio Group has also served as a counterweight to the US-dominated Organisation of American States.

Andean Community of Nations
The Andean Group was formed in 1969 to promote economic and political integration among member states. Its present incarnation dates from 1996. *See also ALADI below.*

Southern Common Market (MERCOSUR)
MERCOSUR is a South American customs union and free trade zone. Currently its main objective is economic harmonisation. The Associated Members (Bolivia, Chile & Peru) participate in the free trade zone only. *See also ALADI below.*

BLUE ITALICS **Latin American Integration Association (ALADI)**
ALADI's ultimate objective is the creation of the **South American Community of Nations (CSN)**, modelled on the EU. The intention is for the integration of the Andean Community and MERCOSUR by 2008, elimination of tarrifs by 2015 and a common currency and parliament by 2020.

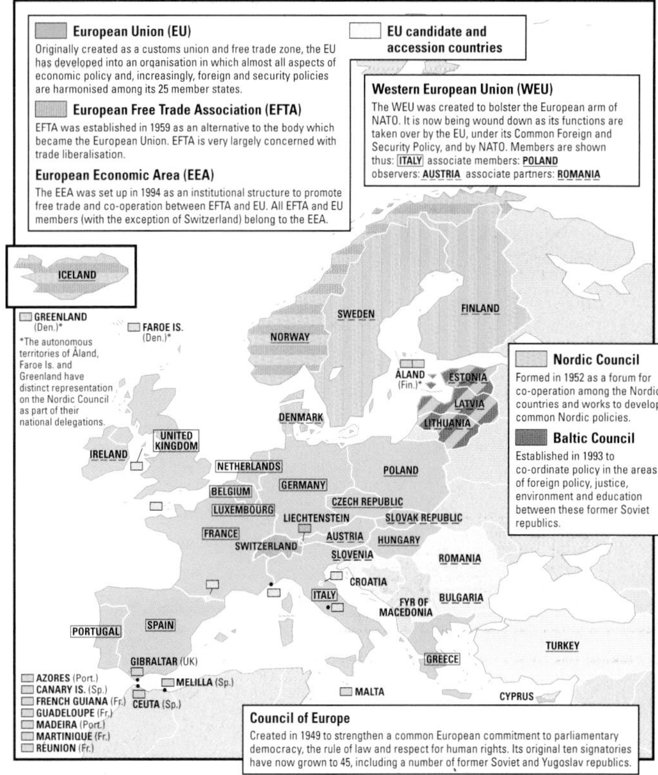
ICELAND
GREENLAND (Den.)*
FAROE IS. (Den.)*
NORWAY
SWEDEN
FINLAND
ÅLAND (Fin.)*
ESTONIA
LATVIA
LITHUANIA
DENMARK
UNITED KINGDOM
IRELAND
NETHERLANDS
BELGIUM
LUXEMBOURG
GERMANY
POLAND
CZECH REPUBLIC
LIECHTENSTEIN
SLOVAK REPUBLIC
FRANCE
SWITZERLAND
AUSTRIA
HUNGARY
SLOVENIA
ROMANIA
CROATIA
ITALY
FYR OF MACEDONIA
BULGARIA
PORTUGAL
SPAIN
GREECE
TURKEY
GIBRALTAR (UK)
MELILLA (Sp.)
CEUTA (Sp.)
MALTA
CYPRUS
AZORES (Port.)
CANARY IS. (Sp.)
FRENCH GUIANA (Fr.)
GUADELOUPE (Fr.)
MADEIRA (Port.)
MARTINIQUE (Fr.)
RÉUNION (Fr.)

European Union (EU)
Originally created as a customs union and free trade zone, the EU has developed into an organisation in which almost all aspects of economic policy and, increasingly, foreign and security policies are harmonised among its 25 member states.

European Free Trade Association (EFTA)
EFTA was established in 1959 as an alternative to the body which became the European Union. EFTA is very largely concerned with trade liberalisation.

European Economic Area (EEA)
The EEA was set up in 1994 as an institutional structure to promote free trade and co-operation between EFTA and EU. All EFTA and EU members (with the exception of Switzerland) belong to the EEA.

EU candidate and accession countries

Western European Union (WEU)
The WEU was created to bolster the European arm of NATO. It is now being wound down as its functions are taken over by the EU, under its Common Foreign and Security Policy, and by NATO. Members are shown thus: ITALY associate members: POLAND observers: AUSTRIA associate partners: ROMANIA

*The autonomous territories of Åland, Faroe Is. and Greenland have distinct representation on the Nordic Council as part of their national delegations.

Nordic Council
Formed in 1952 as a forum for co-operation among the Nordic countries and works to develop common Nordic policies.

Baltic Council
Established in 1993 to co-ordinate policy in the areas of foreign policy, justice, environment and education between these former Soviet republics.

Council of Europe
Created in 1949 to strengthen a common European commitment to parliamentary democracy, the rule of law and respect for human rights. Its original ten signatories have now grown to 45, including a number of former Soviet and Yugoslav republics.

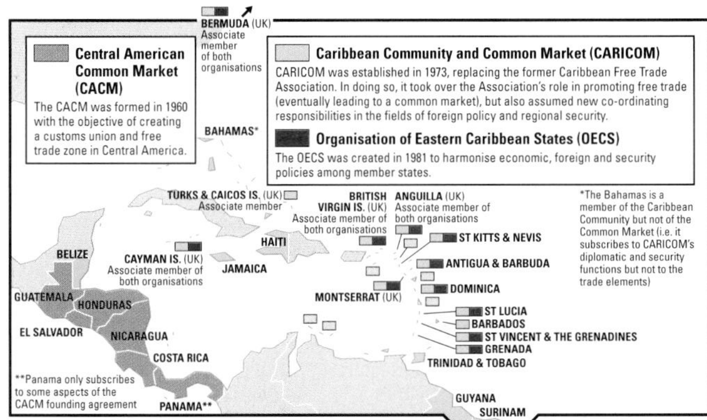
BERMUDA (UK) Associate member of both organisations
BAHAMAS*
TURKS & CAICOS IS. (UK) Associate member
BRITISH VIRGIN IS. (UK) Associate member of both organisations
ANGUILLA (UK) Associate member of both organisations
HAITI
BELIZE
CAYMAN IS. (UK) Associate member of both organisations
JAMAICA
ST KITTS & NEVIS
ANTIGUA & BARBUDA
DOMINICA
MONTSERRAT (UK)
GUATEMALA
HONDURAS
EL SALVADOR
NICARAGUA
COSTA RICA
PANAMA**
ST LUCIA
BARBADOS
ST VINCENT & THE GRENADINES
GRENADA
TRINIDAD & TOBAGO
GUYANA
SURINAM

Central American Common Market (CACM)
The CACM was formed in 1960 with the objective of creating a customs union and free trade zone in Central America.

Caribbean Community and Common Market (CARICOM)
CARICOM was established in 1973, replacing the former Caribbean Free Trade Association. In doing so, it took over the Association's role in promoting free trade (eventually leading to a common market), but also assumed new co-ordinating responsibilities in the fields of foreign policy and regional security.

Organisation of Eastern Caribbean States (OECS)
The OECS was created in 1981 to harmonise economic, foreign and security policies among member states.

*The Bahamas is a member of the Caribbean Community but not of the Common Market (i.e. it subscribes to CARICOM's diplomatic and security functions but not to the trade elements)

**Panama only subscribes to some aspects of the CACM founding agreement

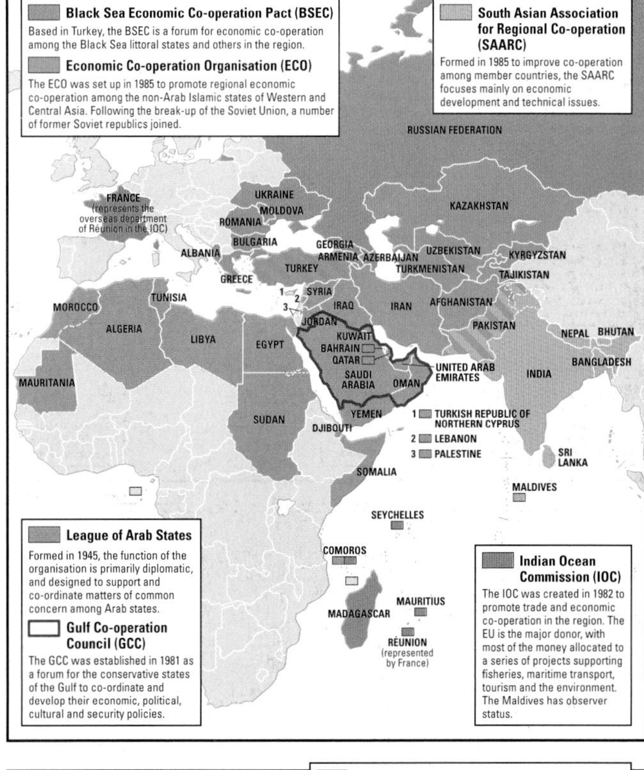
RUSSIAN FEDERATION
FRANCE (represents the overseas department of Réunion in the IOC)
UKRAINE
MOLDOVA
ROMANIA
BULGARIA
KAZAKHSTAN
GEORGIA
ARMENIA
AZERBAIJAN
UZBEKISTAN
KYRGYZSTAN
TURKMENISTAN
TAJIKISTAN
ALBANIA
GREECE
TURKEY
SYRIA
IRAQ
IRAN
AFGHANISTAN
PAKISTAN
TUNISIA
MOROCCO
ALGERIA
LIBYA
EGYPT
JORDAN
KUWAIT
BAHRAIN
QATAR
SAUDI ARABIA
UNITED ARAB EMIRATES
OMAN
YEMEN
NEPAL
BHUTAN
BANGLADESH
INDIA
MAURITANIA
SUDAN
DJIBOUTI
SOMALIA
1 TURKISH REPUBLIC OF NORTHERN CYPRUS
2 LEBANON
3 PALESTINE
SRI LANKA
MALDIVES
SEYCHELLES
COMOROS
MADAGASCAR
MAURITIUS
RÉUNION (represented by France)

Black Sea Economic Co-operation Pact (BSEC)
Based in Turkey, the BSEC is a forum for economic co-operation among the Black Sea littoral states and others in the region.

Economic Co-operation Organisation (ECO)
The ECO was set up in 1985 to promote regional economic co-operation among the non-Arab Islamic states of Western and Central Asia. Following the break-up of the Soviet Union, a number of former Soviet republics joined.

South Asian Association for Regional Co-operation (SAARC)
Formed in 1985 to improve co-operation among member countries, the SAARC focuses mainly on economic development and technical issues.

League of Arab States
Formed in 1945, the function of the organisation is primarily diplomatic, and designed to support and co-ordinate matters of common concern among Arab states.

Gulf Co-operation Council (GCC)
The GCC was established in 1981 as a forum for the conservative states of the Gulf to co-ordinate and develop their economic, political, cultural and security policies.

Indian Ocean Commission (IOC)
The IOC was created in 1982 to promote trade and economic co-operation in the region. The EU is the major donor, with most of the money allocated to a series of projects supporting fisheries, maritime transport, tourism and the environment. The Maldives has observer status.

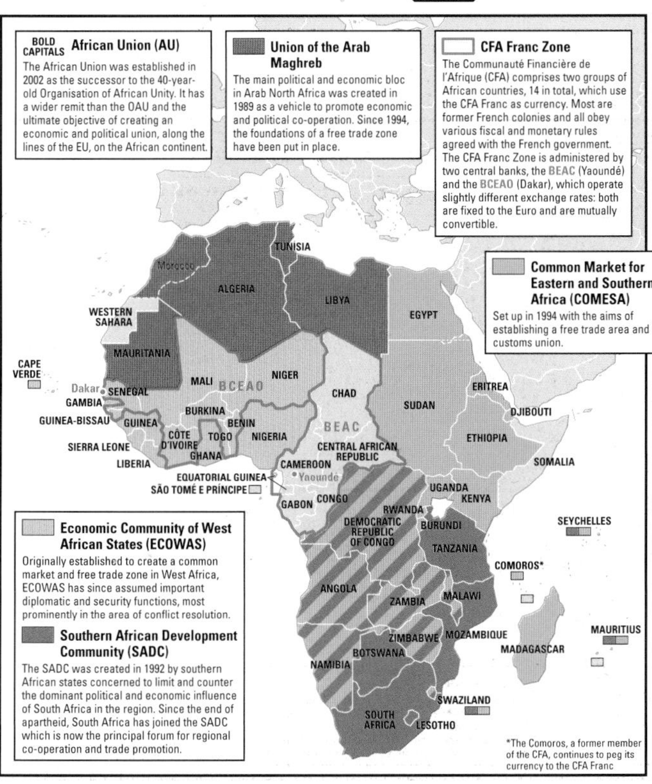
TUNISIA
Morocco
ALGERIA
LIBYA
EGYPT
WESTERN SAHARA
MAURITANIA
CAPE VERDE
Dakar
SENEGAL
GAMBIA
GUINEA-BISSAU
GUINEA
SIERRA LEONE
LIBERIA
MALI
BCEAO
NIGER
CHAD
SUDAN
ERITREA
DJIBOUTI
ETHIOPIA
SOMALIA
BURKINA
BENIN
CÔTE D'IVOIRE
TOGO
GHANA
NIGERIA
BEAC
CENTRAL AFRICAN REPUBLIC
CAMEROON
Yaoundé
EQUATORIAL GUINEA
SÃO TOMÉ E PRÍNCIPE
GABON
CONGO
UGANDA
KENYA
RWANDA
BURUNDI
DEMOCRATIC REPUBLIC OF CONGO
TANZANIA
SEYCHELLES
COMOROS*
ANGOLA
ZAMBIA
MALAWI
ZIMBABWE
MOZAMBIQUE
MAURITIUS
MADAGASCAR
NAMIBIA
BOTSWANA
SWAZILAND
SOUTH AFRICA
LESOTHO

BOLD CAPITALS **African Union (AU)**
The African Union was established in 2002 as the successor to the 40-year-old Organisation of African Unity. It has a wider remit than the OAU and the ultimate objective of creating an economic and political union, along the lines of the EU, on the African continent.

Union of the Arab Maghreb
The main political and economic bloc in Arab North Africa was created in 1989 as a vehicle to promote economic and political co-operation. Since 1994, the foundations of a free trade zone have been put in place.

CFA Franc Zone
The Communauté Financière de l'Afrique (CFA) comprises two groups of African countries, 14 in total, which use the CFA Franc as currency. Most are former French colonies and all obey various fiscal and monetary rules agreed with the French government. The CFA Franc Zone is administered by two central banks, the BEAC (Yaoundé) and the BCEAO (Dakar), which operate slightly different exchange rates: both are fixed to the Euro and are mutually convertible.

Common Market for Eastern and Southern Africa (COMESA)
Set up in 1994 with the aims of establishing a free trade area and customs union.

Economic Community of West African States (ECOWAS)
Originally established to create a common market and free trade zone in West Africa, ECOWAS has since assumed important diplomatic and security functions, most prominently in the area of conflict resolution.

Southern African Development Community (SADC)
The SADC was created in 1992 by southern African states concerned to limit and counter the dominant political and economic influence of South Africa in the region. Since the end of apartheid, South Africa has joined the SADC which is now the principal forum for regional co-operation and trade promotion.

*The Comoros, a former member of the CFA, continues to peg its currency to the CFA Franc

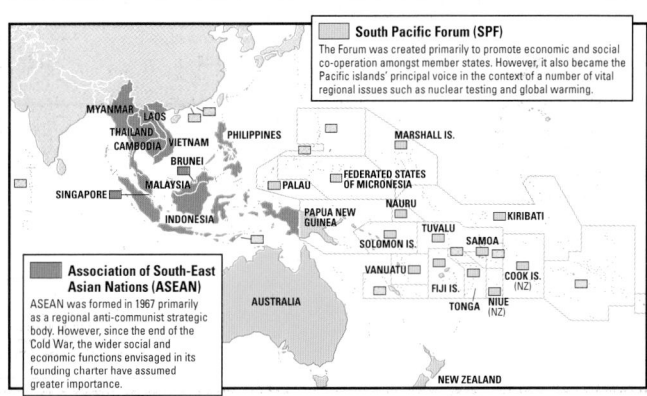

South Pacific Forum (SPF)
The Forum was created primarily to promote economic and social co-operation amongst member states. However, it also became the Pacific islands' principal voice in the context of a number of vital regional issues such as nuclear testing and global warming.

MYANMAR
LAOS
THAILAND
CAMBODIA
VIETNAM
PHILIPPINES
MARSHALL IS.
BRUNEI
MALAYSIA
SINGAPORE
PALAU
FEDERATED STATES OF MICRONESIA
NAURU
INDONESIA
PAPUA NEW GUINEA
KIRIBATI
TUVALU
SOLOMON IS.
SAMOA
VANUATU
FIJI IS.
COOK IS. (NZ)
TONGA
NIUE (NZ)
AUSTRALIA
NEW ZEALAND

Association of South-East Asian Nations (ASEAN)
ASEAN was formed in 1967 primarily as a regional anti-communist strategic body. However, since the end of the Cold War, the wider social and economic functions envisaged in its founding charter have assumed greater importance.

▶ See also... Wealth (22-23); Energy (28-29); International Organisations (30-31); MICE (34-35); Telecoms (36-37); EU (60-61)

The listings above refer to a selection of related themes. For more information, see the Contents (2-7).

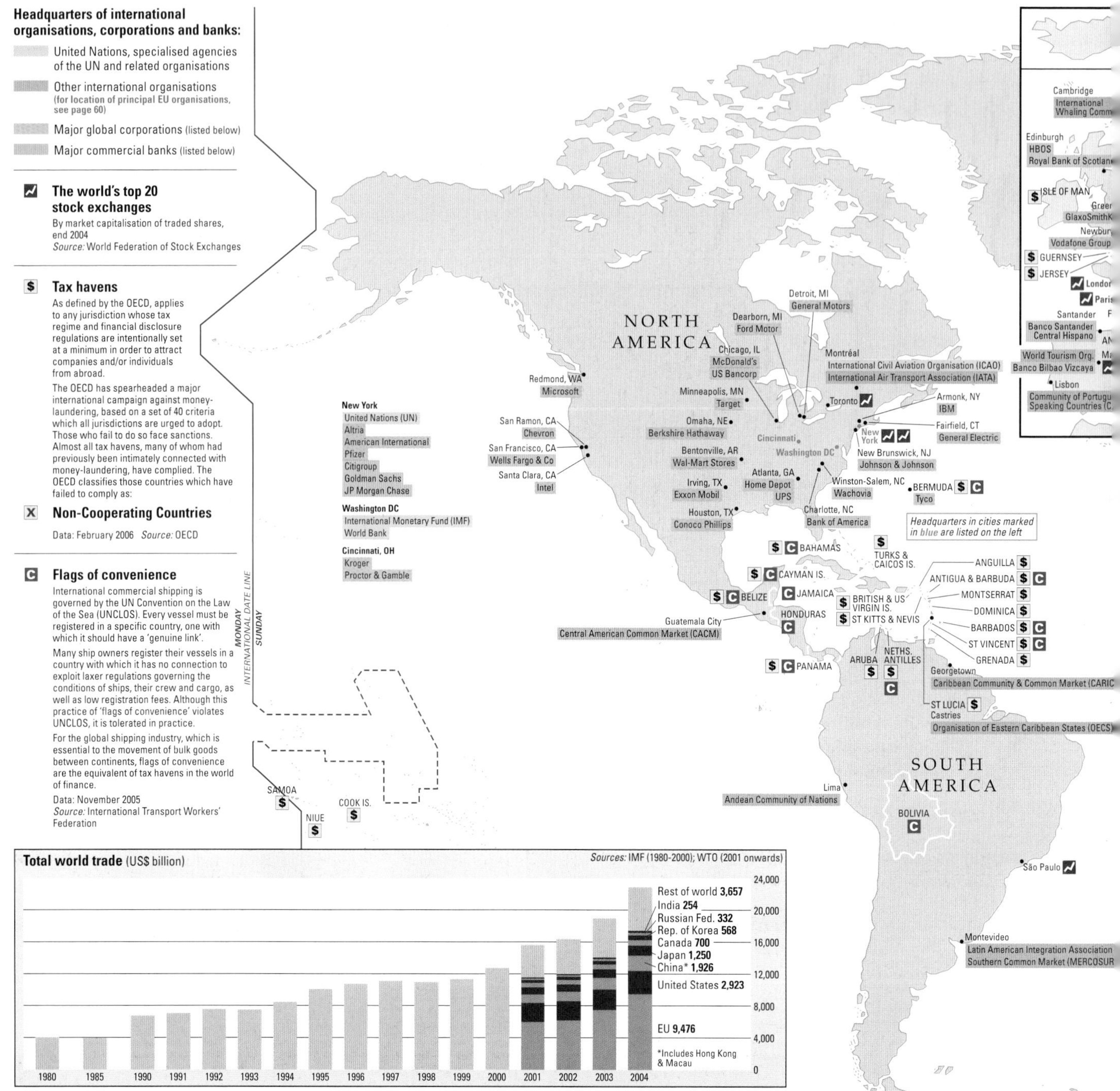

Headquarters of international organisations, corporations and banks:
United Nations, specialised agencies of the UN and related organisations
Other international organisations (for location of principal EU organisations, see page 60)
Major global corporations (listed below)
Major commercial banks (listed below)
The world's top 20 stock exchanges
By market capitalisation of traded shares, end 2004
Source: World Federation of Stock Exchanges
Tax havens
As defined by the OECD, applies to any jurisdiction whose tax regime and financial disclosure regulations are intentionally set at a minimum in order to attract companies and/or individuals from abroad.
The OECD has spearheaded a major international campaign against money-laundering, based on a set of 40 criteria which all jurisdictions are urged to adopt. Those who fail to do so face sanctions. Almost all tax havens, many of whom had previously been intimately connected with money-laundering, have complied. The OECD classifies those countries which have failed to comply as:
Non-Cooperating Countries
Data: February 2006 Source: OECD
Flags of convenience
International commercial shipping is governed by the UN Convention on the Law of the Sea (UNCLOS). Every vessel must be registered in a specific country, one with which it should have a 'genuine link'.
Many ship owners register their vessels in a country with which it has no connection to exploit laxer regulations governing the conditions of ships, their crew and cargo, as well as low registration fees. Although this practice of 'flags of convenience' violates UNCLOS, it is tolerated in practice.
For the global shipping industry, which is essential to the movement of bulk goods between continents, flags of convenience are the equivalent of tax havens in the world of finance.
Data: November 2005
Source: International Transport Workers' Federation
INTERNATIONAL DATE LINE
MONDAY
SUNDAY
NORTH AMERICA
SOUTH AMERICA
New York
United Nations (UN)
Altria
American International
Pfizer
Citigroup
Goldman Sachs
JP Morgan Chase
Washington DC
International Monetary Fund (IMF)
World Bank
Cincinnati, OH
Kroger
Proctor & Gamble
Redmond, WA
Microsoft
San Ramon, CA
Chevron
San Francisco, CA
Wells Fargo & Co
Santa Clara, CA
Intel
Detroit, MI
General Motors
Dearborn, MI
Ford Motor
Chicago, IL
McDonald's
US Bancorp
Minneapolis, MN
Target
Omaha, NE
Berkshire Hathaway
Bentonville, AR
Wal-Mart Stores
Irving, TX
Exxon Mobil
Houston, TX
Conoco Phillips
Atlanta, GA
Home Depot
UPS
Cincinnati
Washington DC
Montréal
International Civil Aviation Organisation (ICAO)
International Air Transport Association (IATA)
Toronto
Armonk, NY
IBM
Fairfield, CT
General Electric
New York
New Brunswick, NJ
Johnson & Johnson
Winston-Salem, NC
Wachovia
Charlotte, NC
Bank of America
BERMUDA
Tyco
Headquarters in cities marked in blue are listed on the left
BAHAMAS
TURKS & CAICOS IS.
CAYMAN IS.
BELIZE
JAMAICA
HONDURAS
BRITISH & US VIRGIN IS.
ST KITTS & NEVIS
ANGUILLA
ANTIGUA & BARBUDA
MONTSERRAT
DOMINICA
BARBADOS
ST VINCENT
GRENADA
Guatemala City
Central American Common Market (CACM)
PANAMA
ARUBA
NETHS. ANTILLES
Georgetown
Caribbean Community & Common Market (CARIC
ST LUCIA
Castries
Organisation of Eastern Caribbean States (OECS)
Lima
Andean Community of Nations
BOLIVIA
São Paulo
Montevideo
Latin American Integration Association
Southern Common Market (MERCOSUR
SAMOA
NIUE
COOK IS.
Cambridge
International Whaling Comm
Edinburgh
HBOS
Royal Bank of Scotland
ISLE OF MAN
GlaxoSmithK
Vodafone Group
GUERNSEY
JERSEY
London
Paris
Santander
Banco Santander Central Hispano
World Tourism Org.
Banco Bilbao Vizcaya
Lisbon
Community of Portuguese Speaking Countries
Total world trade (US$ billion)
Sources: IMF (1980-2000); WTO (2001 onwards)
Rest of world 3,657
India 254
Russian Fed. 332
Rep. of Korea 568
Canada 700
Japan 1,250
China* 1,926
United States 2,923
EU 9,476
*Includes Hong Kong & Macau
24,000
20,000
16,000
12,000
8,000
4,000
0
1980
1985
1990
1991
1992
1993
1994
1995
1996
1997
1998
1999
2000
2001
2002
2003
2004

THE WORLD'S TOP 20 GLOBAL CORPORATIONS (excluding banks)

By annual turnover (US$ billion):	
Wal-Mart Stores	285.22
BP	285.06
Royal Dutch Shell	265.19
Exxon Mobil	263.99
General Motors	193.45
Daimler Chrysler	192.75
Ford Motor	170.84
Toyota Motor	165.68
General Electric	152.36
Chevron	142.90
Total	131.64
Volkswagen	120.71
Conoco Philips	118.72
Allianz Worldwide	112.35
Nippon T&T	106.30
AXA	97.92
IBM	96.29
American International	95.04
Siemens	93.49
Carrefour	88.66

Data: 2005 *Source:* Forbes

By number of employees (thousands):	
Wal-Mart Stores	1,500
McDonald's	438
Siemens	430
Carrefour	419
PetroChina	417
Daimler Chrysler	385
UPS	355
Deutsche Post	349
IBM	329
Target	328
Ford Motor	327
Hitachi	326
General Motors	324
Gazprom	300
General Electric	300
Home Depot	299
Matsushita	290
Kroger	290
Toyota Motor	264
Tyco	258

Data: 2005 *Source:* Forbes

By market capitalisation (US$ billion):	
ExxonMobil	405.25
General Electric	372.14
Microsoft	273.75
BP	231.88
Royal Dutch Shell	221.49
Wal-Mart Stores	218.56
Pfizer	197.99
Johnson & Johnson	194.68
American International	173.99
Vodafone	170.29
IBM	152.76
Total	151.13
Intel	149.39
Toyota Motor	140.89
GlaxoSmithKline	140.39
Berkshire Hathaway	138.74
Altria	134.75
Procter & Gamble	133.92
Chevron	131.52
Novartis	122.07

Data: 2005 *Source:* Forbes

THE WORLD'S TOP 20 BANKS

By Tier One capital (US$ billion):	
Citigroup	74.42
JP Morgan Chase	68.62
HSBC	67.26
Bank of America	64.28
Crédit Agricole	63.42
Royal Bank of Scotland	43.83
Mitsubishi Tokyo	39.93
Mizuho	38.86
HBOS	36.59
BNP Paribas	35.69
Bank of China	34.85
Banco Santander CH	33.26
Barclays Bank	32.18
Rabobank	30.81
Sumitomo Mitsui	30.39
Wells Fargo & Co	29.06
ING Bank	28.79
Wachovia	28.58
UBS	27.44
ABN AMRO Bank	26.99

Data: 2005 *Source:* The Banker

By assets (US$ billion):	
UBS	1,533.04
Citigroup	1,484.10
Mizuho	1,295.94
HSBC	1,276.78
Crédit Agricole	1,243.05
BNP Paribas	1,223.91
JP Morgan Chase	1,157.25
Deutsche Bank	1,144.20
Royal Bk. of Scotland	1,119.48
Bank of America	1,110.46
Barclays Bank	992.10
Mitsubishi Tokyo	980.29
Crédit Suisse	962.78
Sumitomo Mitsui	896.91
ING Bank	839.65
ABN AMRO Bank	828.96
Société Générale	818.70
Banco Santander CH	783.71
HBOS	759.59
Caisse d'Epargne	740.82

Data: 2005 *Source:* The Banker

By market capitalisation (US$ billion):	
Citigroup	247.66
Bank of America	188.77
HSBC	186.74
JP Morgan Chase	129.98
Royal Bank of Scotland	108.95
Wells Fargo & Co.	100.46
UBS	89.16
Wachovia	84.18
Banco Santander CH	77.70
Barclays Bank	70.22
BNP Paribas	64.39
HBOS	62.13
Mitsubishi Tokyo	59.88
Banco Bilbao Vizcaya	58.83
Mizuho	58.41
US Bancorp	55.26
Lloyds TSB	52.78
Goldman Sachs	52.47
Crédit Suisse	48.52
Deutsche Bank	47.86

Data: 2005 *Source:* Forbes

See also... Wealth (22-23); Energy (28-29); International Organisations (30-31); MICE (34-35); Telecoms (36-37); EU (60-61)

The listings above refer to a selection of related themes. For more information, see the Contents (2-7).

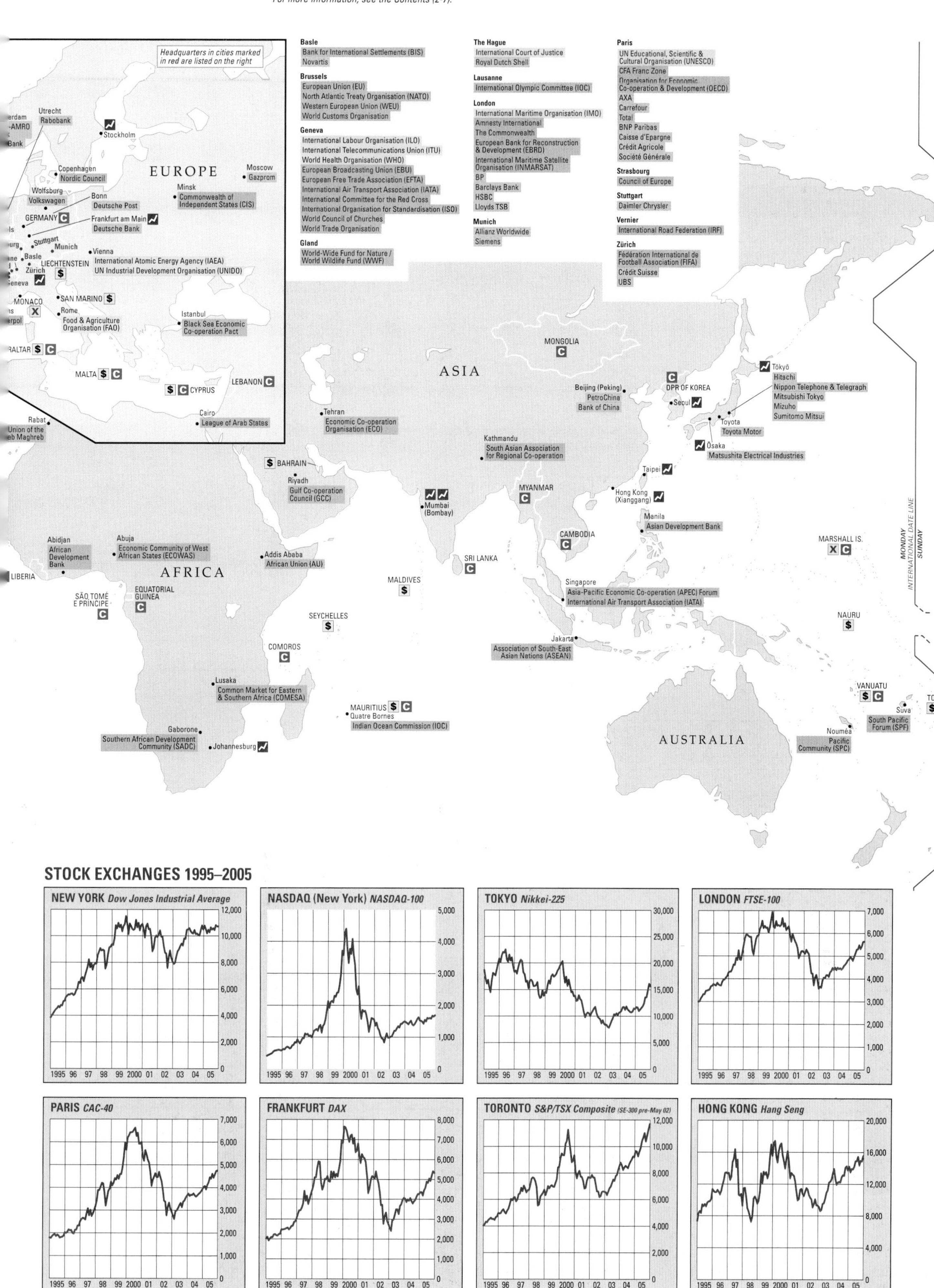
Headquarters in cities marked in red are listed on the right
Basle
Bank for International Settlements (BIS)
Novartis
Brussels
European Union (EU)
North Atlantic Treaty Organisation (NATO)
Western European Union (WEU)
World Customs Organisation
Geneva
International Labour Organisation (ILO)
International Telecommunications Union (ITU)
World Health Organisation (WHO)
European Broadcasting Union (EBU)
European Free Trade Association (EFTA)
International Air Transport Association (IATA)
International Committee for the Red Cross
International Organisation for Standardisation (ISO)
World Council of Churches
World Trade Organisation
Gland
World-Wide Fund for Nature / World Wildlife Fund (WWF)
The Hague
International Court of Justice
Royal Dutch Shell
Lausanne
International Olympic Committee (IOC)
London
International Maritime Organisation (IMO)
Amnesty International
The Commonwealth
European Bank for Reconstruction & Development (EBRD)
International Maritime Satellite Organisation (INMARSAT)
BP
Barclays Bank
HSBC
Lloyds TSB
Munich
Allianz Worldwide
Siemens
Paris
UN Educational, Scientific & Cultural Organisation (UNESCO)
CFA Franc Zone
Organisation for Economic Co-operation & Development (OECD)
AXA
Carrefour
Total
BNP Paribas
Caisse d'Epargne
Crédit Agricole
Société Générale
Strasbourg
Council of Europe
Stuttgart
Daimler Chrysler
Vernier
International Road Federation (IRF)
Zürich
Fédération Internationale de Football Association (FIFA)
Crédit Suisse
UBS
EUROPE
Utrecht
Rabobank
Stockholm
Copenhagen
Nordic Council
Moscow
Gazprom
Minsk
Commonwealth of Independent States (CIS)
Wolfsburg
Volkswagen
Bonn
Deutsche Post
GERMANY
Frankfurt am Main
Deutsche Bank
Stuttgart
Munich
Vienna
International Atomic Energy Agency (IAEA)
UN Industrial Development Organisation (UNIDO)
Basle
LIECHTENSTEIN
Zürich
MONACO
SAN MARINO
Rome
Food & Agriculture Organisation (FAO)
Istanbul
Black Sea Economic Co-operation Pact
MALTA
LEBANON
CYPRUS
Cairo
League of Arab States
Rabat
ASIA
MONGOLIA
Beijing (Peking)
PetroChina
Bank of China
DPR OF KOREA
Seoul
Tōkyō
Hitachi
Nippon Telephone & Telegraph
Mitsubishi Tokyo
Mizuho
Sumitomo Mitsui
Toyota
Toyota Motor
Ōsaka
Matsushita Electrical Industries
Tehran
Economic Co-operation Organisation (ECO)
Kathmandu
South Asian Association for Regional Co-operation
BAHRAIN
Riyadh
Gulf Co-operation Council (GCC)
Mumbai (Bombay)
MYANMAR
Taipei
Hong Kong (Xianggang)
Manila
Asian Development Bank
CAMBODIA
MARSHALL IS.
MONDAY
INTERNATIONAL DATE LINE
SUNDAY
Abidjan
African Development Bank
Abuja
Economic Community of West African States (ECOWAS)
Addis Ababa
African Union (AU)
AFRICA
LIBERIA
SRI LANKA
MALDIVES
Singapore
Asia-Pacific Economic Co-operation (APEC) Forum
International Air Transport Association (IATA)
SÃO TOMÉ E PRÍNCIPE
EQUATORIAL GUINEA
SEYCHELLES
NAURU
Jakarta
Association of South-East Asian Nations (ASEAN)
COMOROS
Lusaka
Common Market for Eastern & Southern Africa (COMESA)
MAURITIUS
Quatre Bornes
Indian Ocean Commission (IOC)
VANUATU
TONGA
Suva
South Pacific Forum (SPF)
Nouméa
Pacific Community (SPC)
AUSTRALIA
Gaborone
Southern African Development Community (SADC)
Johannesburg
STOCK EXCHANGES 1995–2005
NEW YORK Dow Jones Industrial Average
NASDAQ (New York) NASDAQ-100
TOKYO Nikkei-225
LONDON FTSE-100
PARIS CAC-40
FRANKFURT DAX
TORONTO S&P/TSX Composite (SE-300 pre-May 02)
HONG KONG Hang Seng
1995 96 97 98 99 2000 01 02 03 04 05

MICE (Meetings, Incentives, Conferences & Exhibitions)

▶ *See also...* Tourism (24-25); International Organisations (30-31); Business (32-33); Airports (42-44); Cruising (46-47)

The listings above refer to a selection of related themes. For more information, see the Contents (2-7).

Meetings, incentives, conferences and exhibitions (MICE) form an increasingly important reason for travel. Despite the advances in digital communication, there is often no substitute for meeting clients and peers face-to-face, and in recent years a large number of specialist event organisation companies and meeting venues have developed to cater for this market. This map provides information on a selection of the world's most important conference and exhibition venues and includes details of exhibition area and number of meeting rooms. This venue information was compiled with the help of Incentives & Meetings International, whose website and publications are designed for buyers and planners of international meetings, incentive travel programs, congresses and corporate events. For more information, contact www.i-mi.com or pub@i-mi.com

The following definitions of the four 'MICE' terms are based on those provided by the ICCA (International Congress and Convention Association).

MEETING: a general term indicating the coming together of a number of people in one place to confer or carry out a particular business-related activity. This can be either on an ad hoc basis or according to a set pattern, such as annual general meetings or committee meetings.

INCENTIVE: a business-related event as part of a motivational programme, which often also involves recreational and social activities, offered to its participants to reward professional performance.

CONFERENCE: a participatory event designed for discussion, fact-finding, problem-solving and consultation. A conference is normally smaller in scale and more select in character than a congress. The term 'conference' carries no special connotation as to frequency.

EXHIBITION: an event at which products and services are displayed, generally specific to a particular service or industry.

A selection of major travel-trade related events is shown in the top right.

Total exhibition space

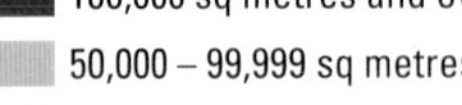

- 100,000 sq metres and over
- 50,000 – 99,999 sq metres
- 20,000 – 49,999 sq metres
- 10,000 – 19,999 sq metres
- Less than 10,000 sq metres

The number of **meeting rooms** in each Congress Centre is shown in the list: (0)

Congress Centres with **annual events** featured in the box (top right) are indicated: ▲

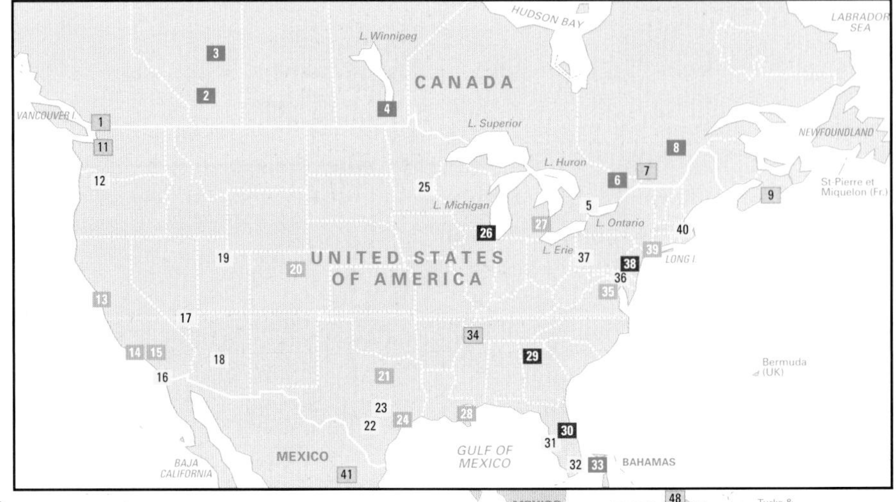
CANADA
UNITED STATES OF AMERICA
MEXICO
HUDSON BAY
LABRADOR SEA
L. Winnipeg
L. Superior
L. Huron
L. Michigan
L. Ontario
L. Erie
VANCOUVER
NEWFOUNDLAND
St Pierre et Miquelon (Fr.)
LONG I.
Bermuda (UK)
GULF OF MEXICO
BAJA CALIFORNIA
BAHAMAS

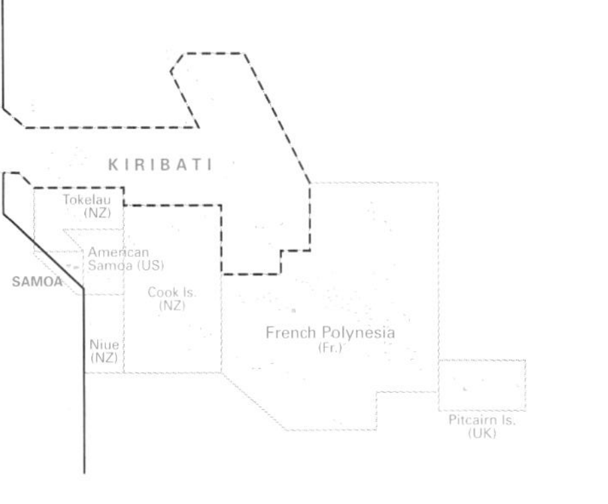
Hawaiian Is. (US)
PACIFIC OCEAN
KIRIBATI
Tokelau (NZ)
American Samoa (US)
SAMOA
Cook Is. (NZ)
Niue (NZ)
French Polynesia (Fr.)
Pitcairn Is. (UK)
Easter I. (Chile)

ICELAND
Faroe Is. (Den.)
UNITED KINGDOM
IRELAND
PORTUGAL
SPAIN
Gibraltar (UK)
Azores (Port.)

MEXICO
CUBA
Turks & Caicos Is. (UK)
Cayman Is. (UK)
JAMAICA
HAITI
DOM. REP.
BELIZE
GUATEMALA
HONDURAS
EL SALVADOR
NICARAGUA
CARIBBEAN SEA
Panama Canal
COSTA RICA
PANAMA
BARBADOS
GRENADA
TRINIDAD & TOBAGO
VENEZUELA
GUYANA
SURINAM
French Guiana (Fr.)
COLOMBIA
Galápagos Is. (Ec.)
ECUADOR
PERU
BRAZIL
BOLIVIA
PARAGUAY
CHILE
Juan Fernández Is. (Chile)
URUGUAY
ARGENTINA
Falkland Is. (UK)
South Georgia (UK)
TIERRA DEL FUEGO
Cape Horn
DRAKE PASSAGE
SCOTIA SEA

1 Puerto Rico (US)
2 Virgin Is. (US, UK)
3 Anguilla (UK)
4 St Maarten (Neths.) & St Martin
5 ST KITTS & NEVIS
6 Montserrat (UK)
7 ANTIGUA & BARBUDA
8 Guadeloupe (Fr.)
9 DOMINICA
10 Martinique (Fr.)
11 ST LUCIA
12 ST VINCENT & THE GRENADINES
13 Bonaire (Neths.)
14 Curaçao (Neths.)
15 Aruba (Neths.)

UNITED STATES & CANADA

1 Vancouver Convention & Exhibition Center (20)
2 Calgary TELUS Convention Center (34)
3 Shaw Conference Center, Edmonton (23)
4 Winnipeg Convention Center (30)
5 Metro Toronto Convention Center (64)
6 Ottawa Congress Center (17)
7 Montréal Convention Center (59)
8 Québec City Convention Center ▲ (36)
9 World Trade & Convention Center, Halifax (24)
10 Hawaii Convention Center, Honolulu (47)
11 Washington State Convention & Trade Center, Seattle (61)
12 Oregon Convention Center, Portland (50)
13 The Moscone Center, San Francisco (96)
14 Los Angeles Convention Center (64)
15 Anaheim Convention Center ▲ (10)
16 San Diego Convention Center (72)
17 Las Vegas Convention Center ▲ (144)
18 Phoenix Convention Center (43)
19 Salt Palace Convention Center, Salt Lake City (53)
20 Colorado Convention Center, Denver (60)
21 Dallas Convention Center (105)
22 Henry B. Gonzales Convention Center, San Antonio (37)
23 Austin Convention Center (54)
24 George R. Browne Convention Center, Houston (105)
25 Minneapolis Convention Center (87)
26 McCormick Place, Chicago ▲ (114)
27 Cobo Conference/Exhibition Centre, Detroit (81)
28 Morial Convention Center, New Orleans (140)
29 Georgia World Congress Center, Atlanta (105)
30 Orange County Convention Center, Orlando (74)
31 Tampa Convention Center (22)
32 Miami Beach Convention Center ▲ (70)
33 James L. Knight International Center / Miami Convention Center (0)
34 Memphis Cook Convention Center (31)
35 Washington Convention Center (66)
36 Baltimore Convention Center (50)
37 David L. Lawrence Convention Center, Pittsburgh (51)
38 Pennsylvania Convention Center, Philadelphia (52)
39 Jacob K. Javits Convention Center of New York ▲ (102)
40 Boston Convention & Exhibition Center (80)

LATIN AMERICA & THE CARIBBEAN

41 Cintermex Convention & Exhibition Center, Monterrey (19)
42 Expo Guadalajara (9)
43 Centro Banamex Congress & Exhibition Centre, Mexico City (25)
44 Centro de Exposiciones y Convenciones Las Americas, Mexico City (25)
45 Acapulco Cultural & Convention Center (45)
46 Cancún Center Conventions & Exhibitions (13)
47 Cancún Convention Center (24)
48 Havana International Conference Center (11)
49 The Jamaica Conference Centre, Kingston (8)
50 Barceló Bávaro Convention Center, Punta Cana (24)
51 Puerto Rico Convention Center, San Juan (25)
52 World Trade Center Curaçao (9)
53 Palacio de Exposiciones y Covenciones de Medellín S.A. (2)
54 Riocentro, Rio Convention & Exhibition Center, Rio de Janeiro (64)
55 The São Paulo Trade Fair Pavilion & Convention Center (9)
56 Transamerica Expo Center, São Paulo ▲ (9)
57 Centro de Convenciones Santiago - Espacio Riesco (12)

EUROPE
(including Atlantic islands, Turkey and Cyprus)

58 Trondheim Spektrum AS (13)
59 Stavanger Forum Conference & Exhibition Centre (30)
60 Norway Congress Centre - Norway Trade Fair, Oslo (34)
61 Göteborg Convention Centre (46)
62 Malmö Exhibition & Convention Center (15)
63 Elmia Congress Centre, Jönköping (12)
64 Stockholm International Fairs & Congress Centre (50)
65 Helsinki Fair Center (53)
66 Bella Center, Copenhagen (33)
67 Irish International Convention & Exhibition Centre, Dublin (20)
68 Belfast Waterfront Hall & Concert Centre (16)
69 Scottish Exhibition & Conference Centre, Glasgow (18)
70 Edinburgh International Conference Centre (EICC) (17)
71 Aberdeen Exhibition & Conference Centre (29)
72 Harrogate International Centre (12)
73 Manchester International Convention Centre (G-Mex) (14)
74 The NEC (National Exhibition Centre), Birmingham ▲▲ (44)
75 Cardiff International Arena & Convention Centre (40)
76 Earls Court ▲ and Olympia Conference Centres ▲▲, London (41)
77 ExCel Exhibition & Conference Centre, London ▲ (65)
78 Wembley Conference & Exhibition Centre, London (20)
79 Barbican Centre, London (11)
80 The Queen Elizabeth II Conference Centre, London (21)
81 The Brighton Centre (17)
82 Bournemouth International Centre & Pavilion (21)
83 Amsterdam RAI (22)
84 Royal Dutch Jaarboers, Utrecht (55)
85 Netherlands Congress Centre, The Hague (40)
86 Maastricht Exhibition & Congress Centre (MECC) (27)
87 Brussels Expo (12)
88 International Congress Center (ICC) Berlin (80)
89 Messe Berlin ▲ (90)
90 Congress Center Leipzig (Leipzig Trade Fair) (19)
91 CCH - Congress Centrum Hamburg ▲ (38)
92 Düsseldorf Congress CCD Ost / PhilipsHalle / RheinHalle / Robert-Schumann-Saal ▲ (42)
93 Congress-Centrum Kölnmesse (36)
94 Rhein-Main-Hallen Wiesbaden (16)
95 Congress Centrum Mainz GmbH (8)
96 Congress Center Messe Frankfurt ▲ (69)
97 Karlsruhe Trade Fair (151)
98 Stuttgart Trade Fair & Conference Centre (MCS) (14)
99 Kongresszentrum Messezentrum Nürnberg (19)
100 ICM - International Congress Center Munich (20)
101 Strasbourg Convention Center (26)
102 Lille Grand Palais (20)
103 Paris Expo Porte de Versailles (32)
104 PARIS-NORD Villepinte Convention & Exhibition Centre (44)
105 Paris Expo CNIT La Défense (36)
106 Palais des Congrès de Paris (70)
107 Cité de Congrès de Nantes Atlantique (30)
108 Palais des Congrès de Lyon - Lyon Convention Center (26)
109 Le Corum Conference Center, Montpellier (25)
110 Parc Chanot, Marseilles (23)
111 Palais des Festivals et des Congrès, Cannes ▲ (27)
112 Acropolis Convention & Exhibition Centre, Nice (54)
113 Grimaldi Forum Monaco (22)
114 Palacio de Congresos de Barcelona (10)
115 Fira Gran Via, Barcelona ▲ (22)
116 CCIB - International Convention Centre of Barcelona (45)
117 Catalonia Palace of Congress, Barcelona (32)
118 Feria Internacional de Bilbao (8)
119 Euskalduna Conference Centre & Concert Hall, Bilbao (25)
120 Feria de Madrid Centro de Convenciones (75)
121 Madrid Palacio Municipal de Congresos (Campo de las Naciones) (28)
122 Valencia Conference Centre (15)
123 Puebla Español y Palacio de Congresos, Majorca (6)
124 Palacio de Exposiciones y Congresos de Granada (24)
125 Palacio de Ferias y Congresos de Málaga (12)
126 Costa del Sol Convention Centre, Torremolinos (17)
127 Congress & Exhibition Center, Marbella (10)
128 Centro de Congresos de Jerez (8)
129 Palacio de Exposiciones y Congresos (Fibes), Seville (11)
130 Europarque Congress Centre, Porto (32)
131 Estoril Congress Centre (22)
132 AIP Congressos - Lisboa Congress Centre (34)
133 Atlantico Pavilon, Lisbon (14)
134 I.C.E.C. Madeira Tecnopolo (27)
135 Palacio de Congresos de Canaria, Las Palmas (11)
136 Geneva Palexpo (21)
137 Beaulieu Congress & Exhibition Center, Lausanne (31)

▶ *See also...* Tourism (24-25); International Organisations (30-31); Business (32-33); Airports (42-44); Cruising (46-47)

The listings above refer to a selection of related themes. For more information, see the Contents (2-7).

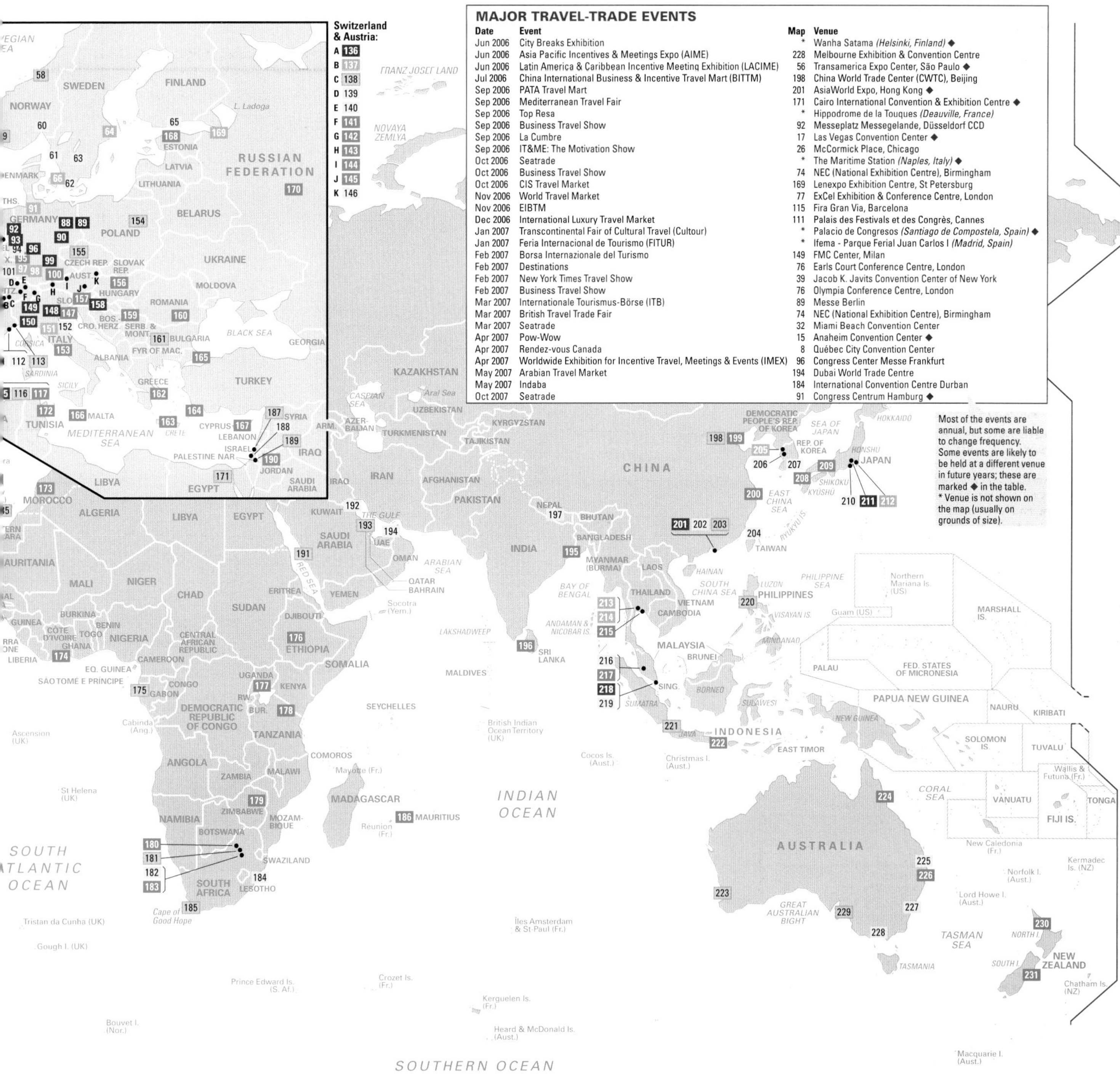
Switzerland & Austria:
A 136
B 137
C 138
D 139
E 140
F 141
G 142
H 143
I 144
J 145
K 146
Most of the events are annual, but some are liable to change frequency. Some events are likely to be held at a different venue in future years; these are marked ◆ in the table.
* Venue is not shown on the map (usually on grounds of size).
SWEDEN
FINLAND
NORWAY
RUSSIAN FEDERATION
ESTONIA
LATVIA
LITHUANIA
BELARUS
POLAND
UKRAINE
MOLDOVA
ROMANIA
HUNGARY
BULGARIA
ITALY
GREECE
TURKEY
BLACK SEA
MEDITERRANEAN SEA
TUNISIA
LIBYA
EGYPT
MOROCCO
ALGERIA
KAZAKHSTAN
UZBEKISTAN
TURKMENISTAN
KYRGYZSTAN
TAJIKISTAN
IRAN
IRAQ
AFGHANISTAN
PAKISTAN
SAUDI ARABIA
NEPAL
BHUTAN
INDIA
BANGLADESH
CHINA
MYANMAR (BURMA)
LAOS
THAILAND
VIETNAM
CAMBODIA
PHILIPPINES
MALAYSIA
SRI LANKA
MALDIVES
INDONESIA
EAST TIMOR
PAPUA NEW GUINEA
JAPAN
REP. OF KOREA
DEMOCRATIC PEOPLE'S REP. OF KOREA
TAIWAN
AUSTRALIA
NEW ZEALAND
MALI
NIGER
CHAD
SUDAN
ERITREA
YEMEN
OMAN
ETHIOPIA
SOMALIA
NIGERIA
KENYA
TANZANIA
DEMOCRATIC REPUBLIC OF CONGO
ANGOLA
ZAMBIA
MALAWI
ZIMBABWE
NAMIBIA
BOTSWANA
MOZAMBIQUE
SOUTH AFRICA
MADAGASCAR
MAURITIUS
SEYCHELLES
INDIAN OCEAN
SOUTH ATLANTIC OCEAN
SOUTHERN OCEAN
TASMAN SEA
CORAL SEA
FIJI IS.
VANUATU
SOLOMON IS.
KIRIBATI
TUVALU
NAURU
PALAU
FED. STATES OF MICRONESIA
MARSHALL IS.

MAJOR TRAVEL-TRADE EVENTS

Date	Event	Map	Venue
Jun 2006	City Breaks Exhibition	*	Wanha Satama *(Helsinki, Finland)* ◆
Jun 2006	Asia Pacific Incentives & Meetings Expo (AIME)	228	Melbourne Exhibition & Convention Centre
Jun 2006	Latin America & Caribbean Incentive Meeting Exhibition (LACIME)	56	Transamerica Expo Center, São Paulo ◆
Jul 2006	China International Business & Incentive Travel Mart (BITTM)	198	China World Trade Center (CWTC), Beijing
Sep 2006	PATA Travel Mart	201	AsiaWorld Expo, Hong Kong ◆
Sep 2006	Mediterranean Travel Fair	171	Cairo International Convention & Exhibition Centre ◆
Sep 2006	Top Resa	*	Hippodrome de la Touques *(Deauville, France)*
Sep 2006	Business Travel Show	92	Messeplatz Messegelande, Düsseldorf CCD
Sep 2006	La Cumbre	17	Las Vegas Convention Center ◆
Sep 2006	IT&ME: The Motivation Show	26	McCormick Place, Chicago
Oct 2006	Seatrade	*	The Maritime Station *(Naples, Italy)* ◆
Oct 2006	Business Travel Show	74	NEC (National Exhibition Centre), Birmingham
Oct 2006	CIS Travel Market	169	Lenexpo Exhibition Centre, St Petersburg
Nov 2006	World Travel Market	77	ExCel Exhibition & Conference Centre, London
Nov 2006	EIBTM	115	Fira Gran Via, Barcelona
Dec 2006	International Luxury Travel Market	111	Palais des Festivals et des Congrès, Cannes
Jan 2007	Transcontinental Fair of Cultural Travel (Cultour)	*	Palacio de Congresos *(Santiago de Compostela, Spain)* ◆
Jan 2007	Feria Internacional de Tourismo (FITUR)	*	Ifema - Parque Ferial Juan Carlos I *(Madrid, Spain)*
Feb 2007	Borsa Internazionale del Turismo	149	FMC Center, Milan
Feb 2007	Destinations	76	Earls Court Conference Centre, London
Feb 2007	New York Times Travel Show	39	Jacob K. Javits Convention Center of New York
Feb 2007	Business Travel Show	76	Olympia Conference Centre, London
Mar 2007	Internationale Tourismus-Börse (ITB)	89	Messe Berlin
Mar 2007	British Travel Trade Fair	74	NEC (National Exhibition Centre), Birmingham
Mar 2007	Seatrade	32	Miami Beach Convention Center
Apr 2007	Pow-Wow	15	Anaheim Convention Center ◆
Apr 2007	Rendez-vous Canada	8	Québec City Convention Center
Apr 2007	Worldwide Exhibition for Incentive Travel, Meetings & Events (IMEX)	96	Congress Center Messe Frankfurt
May 2007	Arabian Travel Market	194	Dubai World Trade Centre
May 2007	Indaba	184	International Convention Centre Durban
Oct 2007	Seatrade	91	Congress Centrum Hamburg ◆

138 Montreux Conventon Center Ltd. (3)
139 Kongresszentrum Basel / Convention Centre Basel (16)
140 MCH Zürich Exhibition (7)
141 Lucerne Culture & Convention Center (15)
142 Davos Congress Centre (20)
143 Congress Innsbruck (15)
144 Salzburg Congress Center (16)
145 Grazer Congress, Convention Center Graz (19)
146 Austria Center Vienna (14)
147 Venice Convention by Lido di Venézia - Eventi & Congressi Spa (28)
148 Centro de Congressi Veronafiere, Verona (7)
149 FMC Center, Milan ▲ (31)
150 Genoa International Fair (7)
151 Firenze Expo & Congress Spa (45)
152 Palacongressi della Riviera di Rimini (17)
153 Palazzo Dei Congressi, Rome (30)
154 Warsaw Congress Center (40)
155 Prague Congress Center (40)
156 Budapest Congress Center (19)
157 Cankarjev Dom Cultural & Congress Centre, Ljubljana (22)
158 Zagreb Fair Convention Center (10)
159 Sava Centar, Belgrade (15)
160 Chamber of Deputies - International Conference Centre, Bucharest (8)
161 National Palace of Culture, Congress Center, Sofia (15)
162 International Conference Center, Megaron The Athens Concert Hall (7)
163 Capsis Beach Hotel & Sofitel Capsis Palace & Convention Center, Heraklion, Crete (110)
164 Sofitel Capsis Hotel Rhodos & Convention Center "MarikaCapsis 2000", Rhodes (100)
165 Istanbul Convention & Exhibition Centre (26)
166 The Mediterranean Conference Centre, Valletta (17)
167 Cyprus International Conference Center, Nicosia (4)
168 Sakala Centre, Tallinn (13)

RUSSIAN FEDERATION

169 Lenexpo Exhibition Centre, St Petersburg ▲
170 World Trade Center Moscow (26)

AFRICA

171 Cairo International Convention & Exhibition Centre (CICC) ▲ (12)
172 Grand Palais des Congrès d'Hammamet (20)
173 Kempinski Mansour Eddahbi & Palais des Congrès, Marrakech (15)
174 Palais de Congrès, Abidjan (15)
175 Gabon Conference Centre, Libreville (6)
176 United Nations Conference Centre, Addis Ababa (16)
177 Uganda International Conference Centre, Kampala (5)
178 Arusha International Conference Center (10)
179 Harare International Conference Centre (16)
180 Sun City Convention Centre (19)
181 Sandton Convention Centre (19)
182 Gallagher Estate & Exhibition Centre, Johannesburg (21)
183 Expo Centre, Johannesburg (21)
184 International Convention Centre Durban ▲ (34)
185 Cape Town International Convention Centre (33)
186 Les Pailles International Conference & Exhibition Centre (6)

ASIA

187 Haifa Exhibition & Convention Centre (0)
188 Israel Trade Fairs & Convention Center (TAEC), Tel Aviv (0)
189 ICC Jerusalem International Convention Center (27)
190 Zara Expo Amman (25)
191 Jeddah International Exhibition & Convention Centre (7)
192 Kuwait International Fair (1)
193 Bahrain International Exhibition Center (12)
194 Dubai International Convention Centre / Dubai World Trade Centre ▲ (42)
195 Science City, Kolkata (11)
196 Bandaranaike International Conference Centre, Colombo (20)
197 Birenda International Convention Centre, Kathmandu (8)
198 China World Trade Center (CWTC), Beijing ▲ (19)
199 Beijing International Convention Center (40)
200 Shanghai International Convention Center (29)
201 AsiaWorld Expo, Hong Kong ▲ (0)
202 Hong Kong Convention & Exhibition Center (52)
203 Hong Kong International Trade & Exhibition Center (HITEC) (21)
204 Taipei International Exhibition Center (26)
205 Korea International Exhibition Center, Goyang City (27)
206 Convention & Exhibition Center (COEX), Seoul (51)
207 Busan Exhibition & Convention Center (BEXCO) (23)
208 Fukuoka International Congress Center (24)
209 Kyoto International Conference Hall (70)
210 Pacifico Yokohama (Pacific Convention Plaza Yokohama) (60)
211 Tokyo International Exhibition Center (Big Sight) (18)
212 Nippon Convention Center – Makuhari Messe, Chiba (16)
213 IMPACT Exhibition & Convention Centre, Bangkok (18)
214 Bangkok International Trade & Exhibition Centre (BITEC) (19)
215 Pattaya Exhibition & Conference Hall (PEACH) (21)
216 Putra World Trade Centre, Kuala Lumpur (20)
217 Kuala Lumpur Convention Centre (28)
218 Singapore Expo (19)
219 Suntec Singapore International Convention & Exhibition Centre (31)
220 Philippine International Convention Center (PICC), Manila (14)
221 Balai Sidang Jakarta Convention Center, Jakarta (17)
222 Bali International Convention Center, Denpasar (13)

AUSTRALASIA & OCEANIA

223 Perth Convention Exhibition Centre (22)
224 Cairns Convention Centre (12)
225 Brisbane Convention & Exhibition Centre (21)
226 Gold Coast Convention & Exhibition Centre (15)
227 Sydney Convention & Exhibition Centre (30)
228 Melbourne Exhibition & Convention Centre ▲ (50)
229 Adelaide Convention Centre (25)
230 Auckland Convention Centre at THE EDGE (21)
231 Christchurch Convention Centre (16)

See also... People (20-21); Business (32-33); Countries A-Z (202-210)

The listings above refer to a selection of related themes. For more information, see the Contents (2-7).

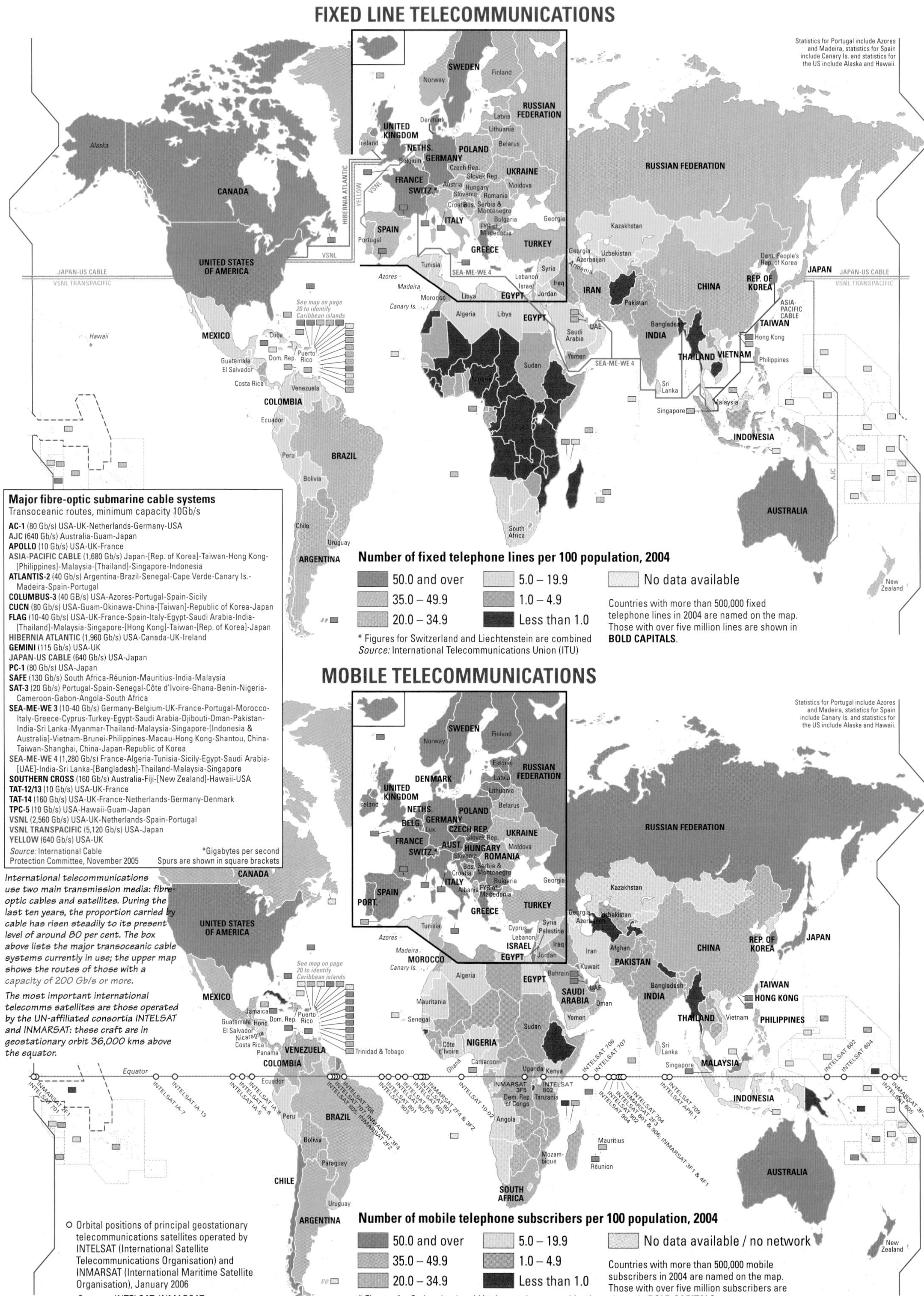
FIXED LINE TELECOMMUNICATIONS
Statistics for Portugal include Azores and Madeira, statistics for Spain include Canary Is. and statistics for the US include Alaska and Hawaii.
See map on page 20 to identify Caribbean islands
Major fibre-optic submarine cable systems
Transoceanic routes, minimum capacity 10Gb/s
AC-1 (80 Gb/s) USA-UK-Netherlands-Germany-USA
AJC (640 Gb/s) Australia-Guam-Japan
APOLLO (10 Gb/s) USA-UK-France
ASIA-PACIFIC CABLE (1,680 Gb/s) Japan-[Rep. of Korea]-Taiwan-Hong Kong-[Philippines]-Malaysia-[Thailand]-Singapore-Indonesia
ATLANTIS-2 (40 Gb/s) Argentina-Brazil-Senegal-Cape Verde-Canary Is.-Madeira-Spain-Portugal
COLUMBUS-3 (40 GB/s) USA-Azores-Portugal-Spain-Sicily
CUCN (80 Gb/s) USA-Guam-Okinawa-China-[Taiwan]-Republic of Korea-Japan
FLAG (10-40 Gb/s) USA-UK-France-Spain-Italy-Egypt-Saudi Arabia-India-[Thailand]-Malaysia-Singapore-[Hong Kong]-Taiwan-[Rep. of Korea]-Japan
HIBERNIA ATLANTIC (1,960 Gb/s) USA-Canada-UK-Ireland
GEMINI (115 Gb/s) USA-UK
JAPAN-US CABLE (640 Gb/s) USA-Japan
PC-1 (80 Gb/s) USA-Japan
SAFE (130 Gb/s) South Africa-Réunion-Mauritius-India-Malaysia
SAT-3 (20 Gb/s) Portugal-Spain-Senegal-Côte d'Ivoire-Ghana-Benin-Nigeria-Cameroon-Gabon-Angola-South Africa
SEA-ME-WE 3 (10-40 Gb/s) Germany-Belgium-UK-France-Portugal-Morocco-Italy-Greece-Cyprus-Turkey-Egypt-Saudi Arabia-Djibouti-Oman-Pakistan-India-Sri Lanka-Myanmar-Thailand-Malaysia-Singapore-[Indonesia & Australia]-Vietnam-Brunei-Philippines-Macau-Hong Kong-Shantou, China-Taiwan-Shanghai, China-Japan-Republic of Korea
SEA-ME-WE 4 (1,280 Gb/s) France-Algeria-Tunisia-Sicily-Egypt-Saudi Arabia-[UAE]-India-Sri Lanka-[Bangladesh]-Thailand-Malaysia-Singapore
SOUTHERN CROSS (160 Gb/s) Australia-Fiji-[New Zealand]-Hawaii-USA
TAT-12/13 (10 Gb/s) USA-UK-France
TAT-14 (160 Gb/s) USA-UK-France-Netherlands-Germany-Denmark
TPC-5 (10 Gb/s) USA-Hawaii-Guam-Japan
VSNL (2,560 Gb/s) USA-UK-Netherlands-Spain-Portugal
VSNL TRANSPACIFIC (5,120 Gb/s) USA-Japan
YELLOW (640 Gb/s) USA-UK
Source: International Cable Protection Committee, November 2005
*Gigabytes per second
Spurs are shown in square brackets
Number of fixed telephone lines per 100 population, 2004
50.0 and over
35.0 – 49.9
20.0 – 34.9
5.0 – 19.9
1.0 – 4.9
Less than 1.0
No data available
Countries with more than 500,000 fixed telephone lines in 2004 are named on the map. Those with over five million lines are shown in BOLD CAPITALS.
* Figures for Switzerland and Liechtenstein are combined
Source: International Telecommunications Union (ITU)
MOBILE TELECOMMUNICATIONS
Statistics for Portugal include Azores and Madeira, statistics for Spain include Canary Is. and statistics for the US include Alaska and Hawaii.
International telecommunications use two main transmission media: fibre-optic cables and satellites. During the last ten years, the proportion carried by cable has risen steadily to its present level of around 80 per cent. The box above lists the major transoceanic cable systems currently in use; the upper map shows the routes of those with a capacity of 200 Gb/s or more.
The most important international telecomms satellites are those operated by the UN-affiliated consortia INTELSAT and INMARSAT: these craft are in geostationary orbit 36,000 kms above the equator.
Equator
Orbital positions of principal geostationary telecommunications satellites operated by INTELSAT (International Satellite Telecommunications Organisation) and INMARSAT (International Maritime Satellite Organisation), January 2006
Sources: INTELSAT; INMARSAT
Number of mobile telephone subscribers per 100 population, 2004
50.0 and over
35.0 – 49.9
20.0 – 34.9
5.0 – 19.9
1.0 – 4.9
Less than 1.0
No data available / no network
Countries with more than 500,000 mobile subscribers in 2004 are named on the map. Those with over five million subscribers are shown in BOLD CAPITALS.
* Figures for Switzerland and Liechtenstein are combined
Source: International Telecommunications Union (ITU)

See also... People (20-21); Business (32-33); Countries A-Z (202-210)

The listings above refer to a selection of related themes. For more information, see the Contents (2-7).

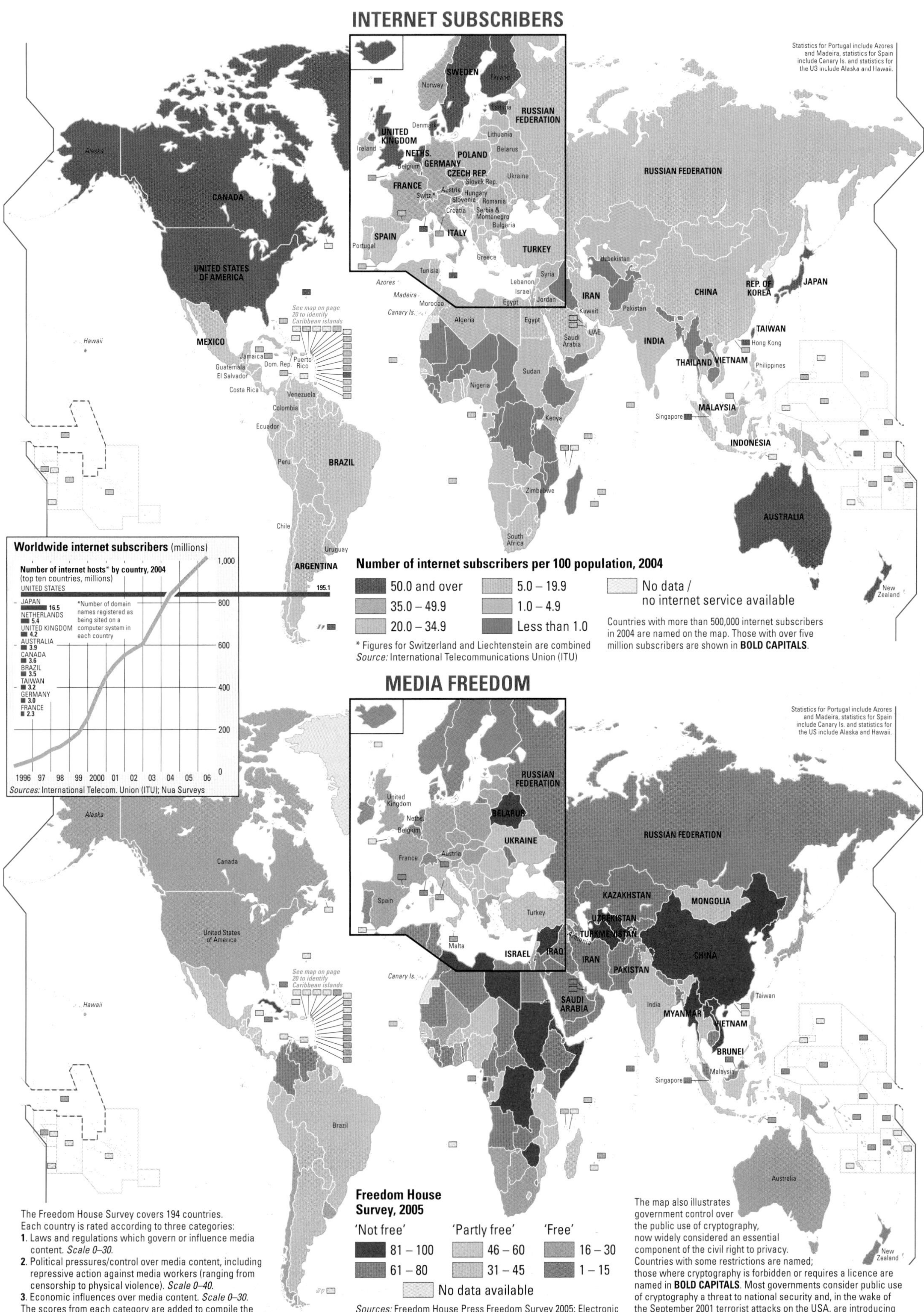
INTERNET SUBSCRIBERS
Statistics for Portugal include Azores and Madeira, statistics for Spain include Canary Is. and statistics for the US include Alaska and Hawaii.
CANADA
UNITED STATES OF AMERICA
MEXICO
BRAZIL
ARGENTINA
SWEDEN
UNITED KINGDOM
NETHS.
GERMANY
POLAND
CZECH REP.
FRANCE
SPAIN
ITALY
TURKEY
RUSSIAN FEDERATION
IRAN
CHINA
REP. OF KOREA
JAPAN
TAIWAN
INDIA
THAILAND
VIETNAM
MALAYSIA
INDONESIA
AUSTRALIA
Worldwide internet subscribers (millions)
Number of internet hosts* by country, 2004 (top ten countries, millions)
UNITED STATES 195.1
JAPAN 16.5
NETHERLANDS 5.4
UNITED KINGDOM 4.2
AUSTRALIA 3.9
CANADA 3.6
BRAZIL 3.5
TAIWAN 3.2
GERMANY 3.0
FRANCE 2.3
*Number of domain names registered as being sited on a computer system in each country
1996 97 98 99 2000 01 02 03 04 05 06
Sources: International Telecom. Union (ITU); Nua Surveys
Number of internet subscribers per 100 population, 2004
50.0 and over
35.0 – 49.9
20.0 – 34.9
5.0 – 19.9
1.0 – 4.9
Less than 1.0
No data / no internet service available
* Figures for Switzerland and Liechtenstein are combined
Source: International Telecommunications Union (ITU)
Countries with more than 500,000 internet subscribers in 2004 are named on the map. Those with over five million subscribers are shown in BOLD CAPITALS.
MEDIA FREEDOM
Statistics for Portugal include Azores and Madeira, statistics for Spain include Canary Is. and statistics for the US include Alaska and Hawaii.
BELARUS
UKRAINE
RUSSIAN FEDERATION
KAZAKHSTAN
MONGOLIA
UZBEKISTAN
TURKMENISTAN
CHINA
ISRAEL
IRAQ
IRAN
PAKISTAN
SAUDI ARABIA
MYANMAR
VIETNAM
BRUNEI
The Freedom House Survey covers 194 countries. Each country is rated according to three categories:
1. Laws and regulations which govern or influence media content. Scale 0–30.
2. Political pressures/control over media content, including repressive action against media workers (ranging from censorship to physical violence). Scale 0–40.
3. Economic influences over media content. Scale 0–30.
The scores from each category are added to compile the total score. Higher scores imply less freedom.
Freedom House Survey, 2005
'Not free' 81 – 100 61 – 80
'Partly free' 46 – 60 31 – 45
'Free' 16 – 30 1 – 15
No data available
Sources: Freedom House Press Freedom Survey 2005; Electronic Privacy Information Center (EPIC) Cryptography Survey 2001
The map also illustrates government control over the public use of cryptography, now widely considered an essential component of the civil right to privacy. Countries with some restrictions are named; those where cryptography is forbidden or requires a licence are named in BOLD CAPITALS. Most governments consider public use of cryptography a threat to national security and, in the wake of the September 2001 terrorist attacks on the USA, are introducing restrictions or tightening their regimes.

See also... Human Development Index (21); Wealth (22-23); Countries A-Z (202-210)

The listings above refer to a selection of related themes. For more information, see the Contents (2-7).

SPENDING ON HEALTH

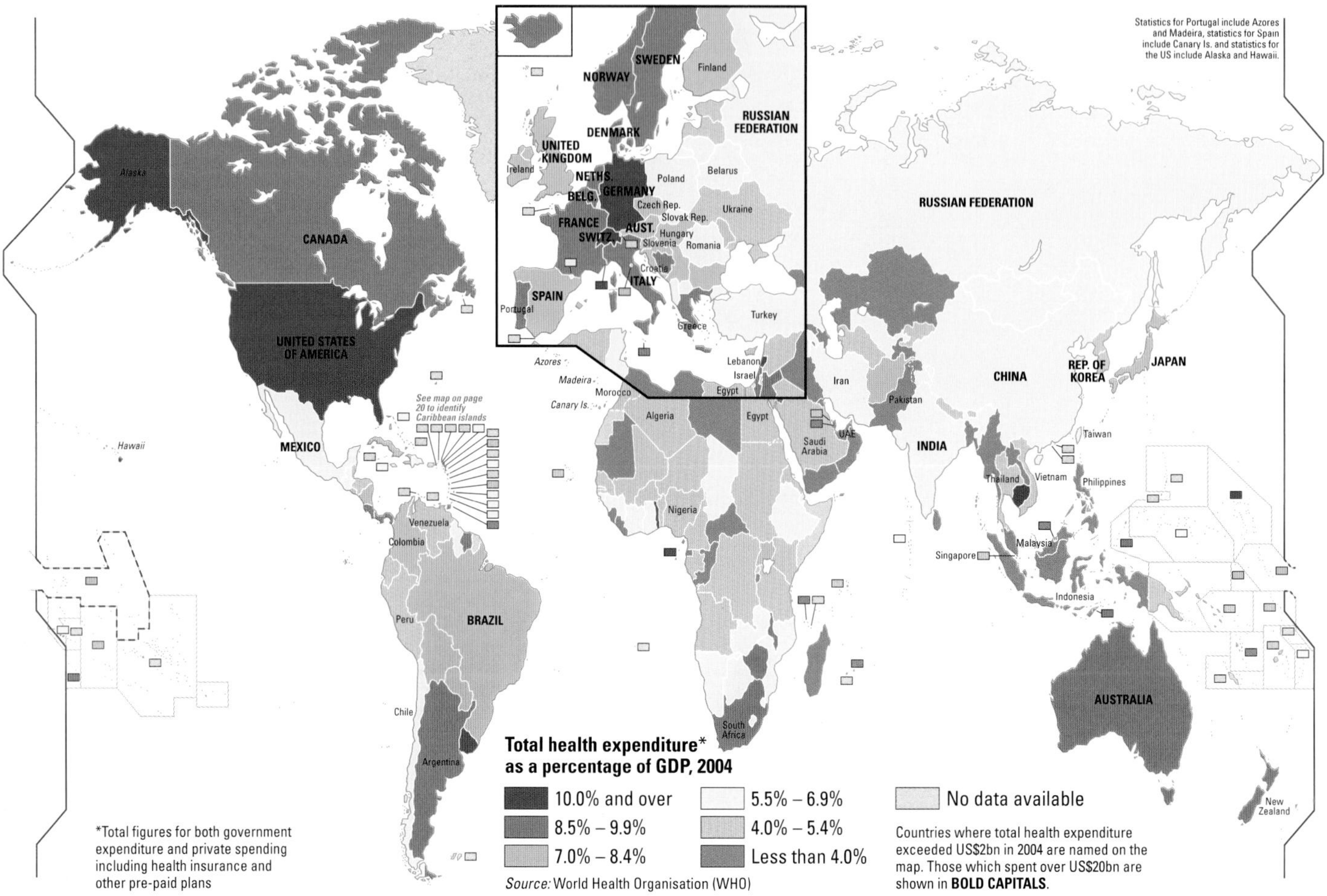

Statistics for Portugal include Azores and Madeira, statistics for Spain include Canary Is. and statistics for the US include Alaska and Hawaii.

Total health expenditure* as a percentage of GDP, 2004

- 10.0% and over
- 8.5% – 9.9%
- 7.0% – 8.4%
- 5.5% – 6.9%
- 4.0% – 5.4%
- Less than 4.0%
- No data available

Source: World Health Organisation (WHO)

Countries where total health expenditure exceeded US$2bn in 2004 are named on the map. Those which spent over US$20bn are shown in **BOLD CAPITALS**.

*Total figures for both government expenditure and private spending including insurance and other pre-paid plans

HEALTH INDICATORS

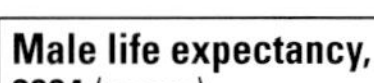

	Male life expectancy, 2004 (years)	Female life expectancy, 2004 (years)	Mortality* in childbirth, 2002 (per 10,000 births)	Infant* mortality, 2002 (per 1,000 live births)	Number of people per doctor, 2004
EUROPE & THE RUSSIAN FEDERATION	70.3	78.7	2.5	9.6	290
AFRICA	50.2	52.7	74.9	141.5	2,663
ASIA	65.4	69.3	43.5	57.4	952
AUSTRALASIA & OCEANIA	73.7	78.3	6.3	22.3	535
UNITED STATES & CANADA	75.3	80.2	1.3	7.7	194
LATIN AMERICA & THE CARIBBEAN	68.4	74.6	18.7	30.5	536
OECD COUNTRIES *(see p. 30)*	74.9	80.7	2.9	10.0	296
NON-OECD COUNTRIES	62.5	66.3	46.6	69.2	695
WORLD	64.7	68.9	38.7	58.5	663

Mortality in childbirth: Averages weighted by population. *Sources:* WHO; UNICEF. *Death of mother during childbirth

Infant mortality: Averages weighted by population. *Sources:* WHO; UNICEF. *Child under five years old

Number of people per doctor: Averages weighted by population. *Source:* WHO

Male life expectancy – LONGEST LIFE EXPECTANCY

Hong Kong, Macau, Martinique	79
Andorra, Australia, Canada, Iceland, Israel, Italy, Japan, Monaco, San Marino, Sweden, Switzerland	78
Cayman Is., Channel Is., Gibraltar, Montserrat, New Zealand, Norway	77
Aruba, Austria, Cyprus, Faroe Is., France, Germany, Greece, Ireland, Kuwait, Liechtenstein, Luxembourg, Malta, Netherlands, Spain, United Kingdom	76

Male life expectancy – SHORTEST LIFE EXPECTANCY

Angola	38
Botswana, Sierra Leone, Zimbabwe	37
Lesotho, Malawi	35
Swaziland	33

Female life expectancy – LONGEST LIFE EXPECTANCY

Japan, Macau, Monaco	85
Andorra, France, Italy, San Marino	84
Aruba, Australia, Cayman Is., Channel Is., Faroe Is., Gibraltar, Liechtenstein, Spain, Sweden, Switzerland, US Virgin Is.	83
Austria, Belgium, Canada, Finland, Germany, Guam, Iceland, Israel, Luxembourg, New Zealand, Norway	82

Female life expectancy – SHORTEST LIFE EXPECTANCY

Lesotho	40
Sierra Leone, Zambia	39
Botswana, Swaziland, Zimbabwe	36
Malawi	35

Averages weighted by population *Source:* WHO

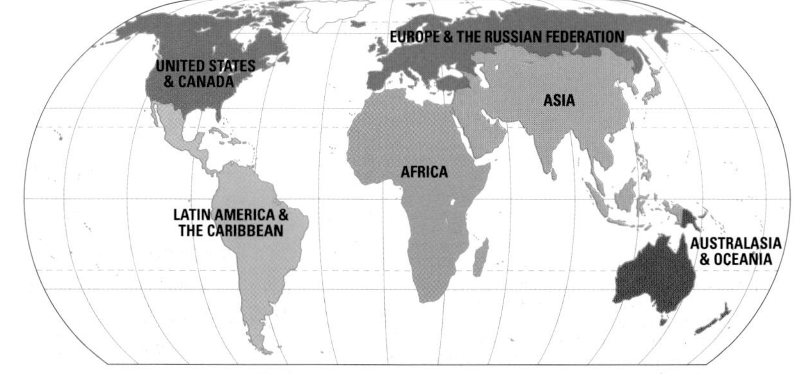
UNITED STATES & CANADA
EUROPE & THE RUSSIAN FEDERATION
ASIA
AFRICA
LATIN AMERICA & THE CARIBBEAN
AUSTRALASIA & OCEANIA

See also... Countries A-Z (202-210)

The listings above refer to a selection of related themes. For more information, see the Contents (2-7).

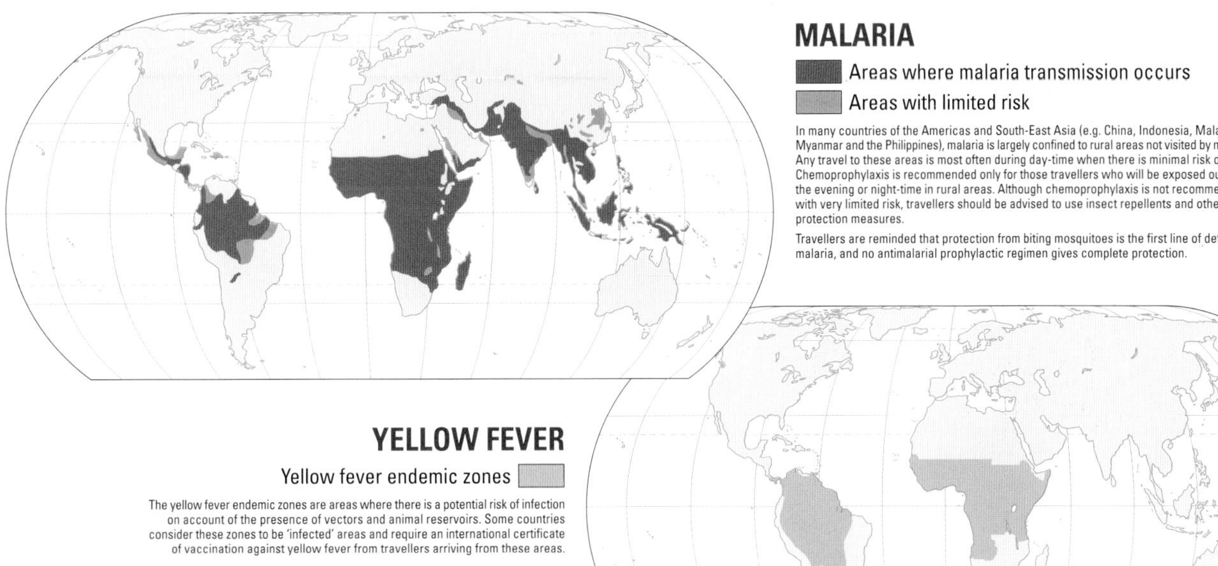

MALARIA

Areas where malaria transmission occurs

Areas with limited risk

In many countries of the Americas and South-East Asia (e.g. China, Indonesia, Malaysia, Mexico, Myanmar and the Philippines), malaria is largely confined to rural areas not visited by most travellers. Any travel to these areas is most often during day-time when there is minimal risk of exposure. Chemoprophylaxis is recommended only for those travellers who will be exposed outdoors during the evening or night-time in rural areas. Although chemoprophylaxis is not recommended in areas with very limited risk, travellers should be advised to use insect repellents and other personal protection measures.

Travellers are reminded that protection from biting mosquitoes is the first line of defence against malaria, and no antimalarial prophylactic regimen gives complete protection.

YELLOW FEVER

Yellow fever endemic zones

The yellow fever endemic zones are areas where there is a potential risk of infection on account of the presence of vectors and animal reservoirs. Some countries consider these zones to be 'infected' areas and require an international certificate of vaccination against yellow fever from travellers arriving from these areas.

TYPHOID FEVER

Areas with significant risk

Areas with limited risk

OTHER HEALTH RISKS FOR TRAVELLERS INCLUDE:

MENINGITIS
Significant risk: Sahel region and East Africa.
Limited risk: Brazil & Uruguay; Morocco; Saudi Arabia; India.

HEPATITIS A
Central & South America; Caribbean; Africa; Asia below approx. 50°N.

HEPATITIS B
Significant risk: Africa except far north & south; Arabian Peninsula; China & Mongolia; South-East Asia; Southern half of Russian Federation east of approx. 80°E.
Limited risk: Central America; Northern South America; Caribbean; Southern Greenland; Rest of Africa & Asia; North Central Australia.

HIV/AIDS, RABIES, POLIO, DIPTHERIA and **TETANUS** are risks in most areas of the world.

HIV / AIDS

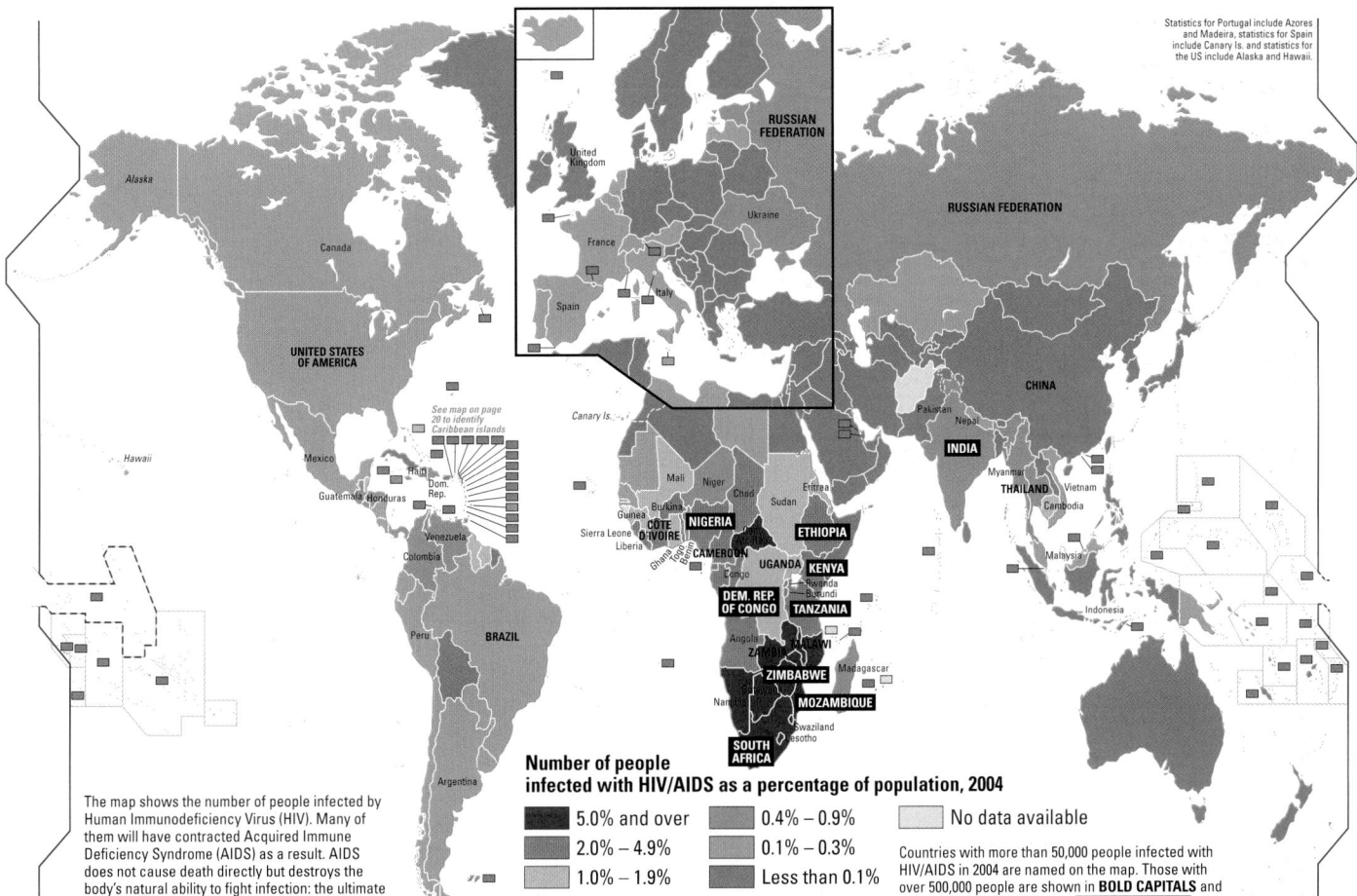

Statistics for Portugal include Azores and Madeira, statistics for Spain include Canary Is. and statistics for the US include Alaska and Hawaii.

See map on page 20 to identify Caribbean islands

Number of people infected with HIV/AIDS as a percentage of population, 2004

5.0% and over
2.0% – 4.9%
1.0% – 1.9%
0.4% – 0.9%
0.1% – 0.3%
Less than 0.1%
No data available

Estimates *Source:* WHO/UNAIDS

Countries with more than 50,000 people infected with HIV/AIDS in 2004 are named on the map. Those with over 500,000 people are shown in **BOLD CAPITALS** and those with over one million in **WHITE ON BLACK**

The map shows the number of people infected by Human Immunodeficiency Virus (HIV). Many of them will have contracted Acquired Immune Deficiency Syndrome (AIDS) as a result. AIDS does not cause death directly but destroys the body's natural ability to fight infection: the ultimate cause of death varies between individuals.

See also... Europe Winter Sports (69); USA & Canada Winter Sports (160)

The listings above refer to a selection of related themes. For more information, see the Contents (2-7).

MAJOR INTERNATIONAL SPORTING EVENTS

SUMMER OLYMPICS

The first modern Olympic Games, founded by Frenchman Baron de Coubertin, were held at Athens in 1896. They are held every four years, and a Paralympic Games is held in conjunction with the main Games. An extra Olympics held in 1906 celebrated the tenth anniversary of the 1896 Games. The next Games, the 29th Olympiad, will be held in Beijing in 2008 and the 2012 Games will be in London.

WINTER OLYMPICS

The first separate Winter Games took place in 1924 at Chamonix, France. The Games originally took place in the same year as the Summer Olympics, but are now held in between. The next Winter Olympics are due to be held in Vancouver in 2010.

COMMONWEALTH GAMES

Originally the British Empire Games, first held in 1930 at Hamilton, Ontario. Renamed the British Empire and Commonwealth Games in 1954, the British Commonwealth Games in 1970 and the Commonwealth Games in 1978. Held every four years, the next Games are due to be held in in New Delhi in 2010.

WORLD ATHLETICS CHAMPIONSHIPS

The World Athletics Championships were first held in Helsinki in 1983, and at four-year intervals until 1991. They are now held every two years. The next Championships are due to be held in Osaka in 2007 and Berlin in 2009.

FOOTBALL WORLD CUP

Association Football's premier event. Brazil kept the Jules Rimet Trophy after winning it for the third time in 1970. The teams now compete for the FIFA World Cup. Held every four years, the next competition is due to be hosted by Germany in 2006 and South Africa in 2010.

CRICKET WORLD CUP

The venue of the first Cricket World Cup in 1975 was England. Played every three to five years, it was not until 1987 that the competition was held outside England. The next World Cup is due to be held in the West Indies in 2007.

RUGBY UNION WORLD CUP

The first Rugby Union World Cup was held in 1987 and is now held every four years, with the next competition in France in 2007.

FOOTBALL WORLD CUP FINAL RESULTS

Year	Winner	Runner-up
1930	Uruguay 4	Argentina 2
1934	Italy 2	Czechoslovakia 1
1938	Italy 4	Hungary 2
1950	Uruguay 2	Brazil 1
1954	FR Germany 3	Hungary 2
1958	Brazil 5	Sweden 2
1962	Brazil 3	Czechoslovakia 1
1966	England 4	FR Germany 2
1970	Brazil 4	Italy 1
1974	FR Germany 2	Netherlands 1
1978	Argentina 3	Netherlands 1
1982	Italy 3	FR Germany 1
1986	Argentina 3	FR Germany 2
1990	FR Germany 1	Argentina 0
1994	Brazil 0	Italy 0
	(Brazil won 3-2 on penalties)	
1998	France 3	Brazil 0
2002	Brazil 2	Germany 0

FIFA WORLD RANKINGS

	May, 2002	May, 2003	May, 2004	May, 2005
1	France	Brazil	Brazil	Brazil
2	Brazil	France (2=)	France	Czech Rep.
3	Argentina	Spain (2=)	Spain	Argentina
4	Colombia	Germany	Netherlands	France
5	Portugal	Argentina	Argentina	Netherlands
6	Italy	Netherlands	Mexico	England
7	Mexico	England	Turkey	Mexico
8	Spain	Turkey	USA	Spain
9	Netherlands	Mexico	Germany	Portugal
10	Yugoslavia	USA (10=)	Czech Rep.	Italy
11	Germany	Denmk. (10=)	Italy	USA
12	England	Italy	Cameroon (12=)	Greece
13	USA	Czech Rep.	England (12=)	Sweden
14	Romania	Portugal	Denmark	Turkey
15	Ireland (16=)	Ireland	Ireland	Ireland
16	Czech (16=)	Belgium	Nigeria	Uruguay
17	Cameroon	Costa Rica	Belgium	Japan
18	Paraguay	Cameroon	Iran	Iran
19	Sweden	Paraguay	Rep. of Korea	Denmark (19=)
20	Denmark	Sweden	Portugal	Germany (19=)

RUGBY UNION WORLD CUP FINAL RESULTS

Year	Winner	Runner-up
1987	New Zealand 29	France 9
1991	Australia 12	England 6
1995	South Africa 15	New Zealand 12
1999	Australia 35	France 12
2003	England 20	Australia 17

CRICKET WORLD CUP FINAL RESULTS

1975	West Indies (291-8) beat Australia (274) by 17 runs
1979	West Indies (286-9) beat England (194) by 92 runs
1983	India (183) beat West Indies (140) by 43 runs
1987	Australia (253-5) beat England (246-8) by 7 runs
1992	Pakistan (249-6) beat England (227) by 22 runs
1996	Sri Lanka (245-3) beat Australia (241) by 7 wickets
1999	Australia (133-2) beat Pakistan (132) by 8 wickets
2003	Australia (359-2) beat India (234) by 125 runs

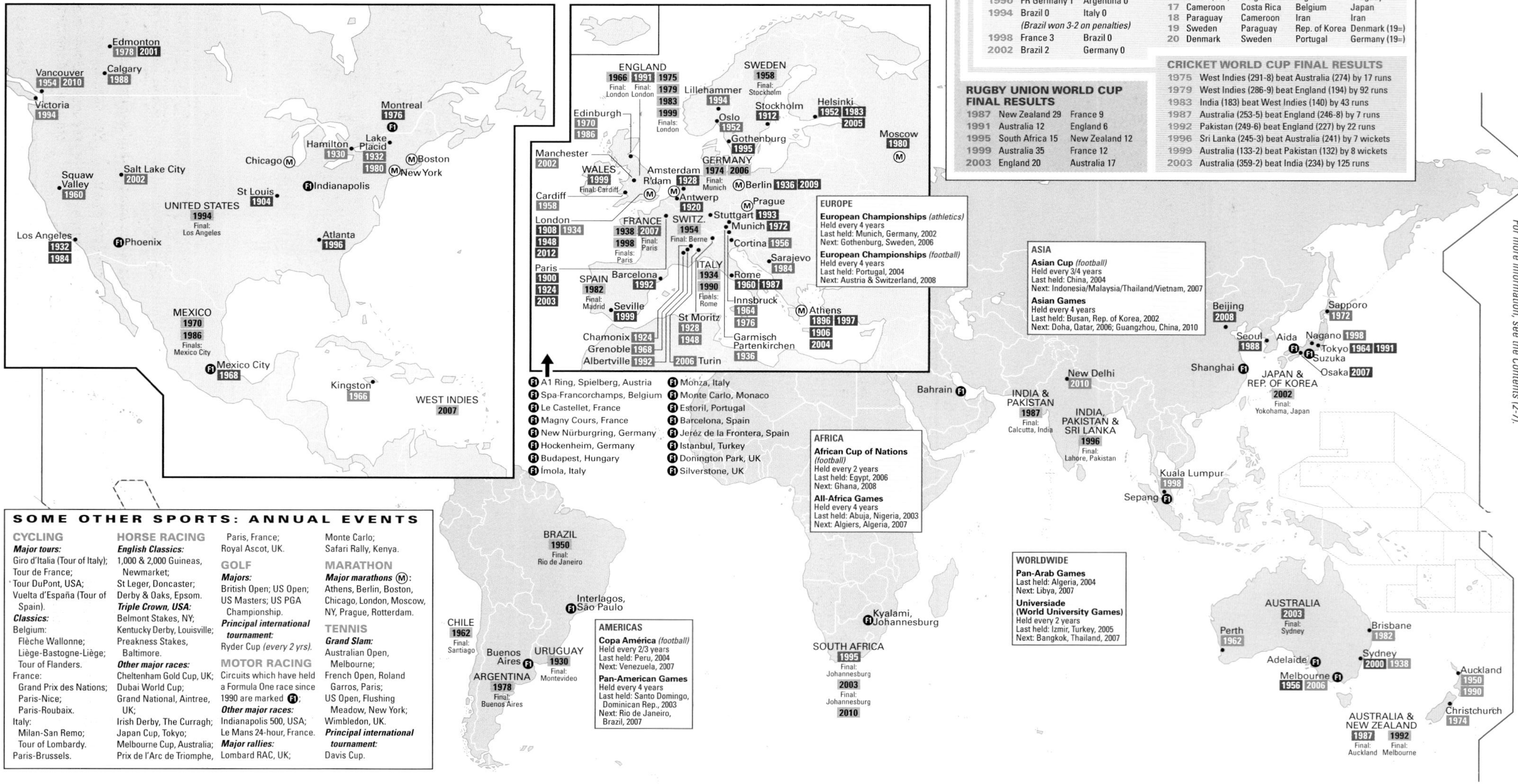

EUROPE

European Championships *(athletics)*
Held every 4 years
Last held: Munich, Germany, 2002
Next: Gothenburg, Sweden, 2006

European Championships *(football)*
Held every 4 years
Last held: Portugal, 2004
Next: Austria & Switzerland, 2008

ASIA

Asian Cup *(football)*
Held every 3/4 years
Last held: China, 2004
Next: Indonesia/Malaysia/Thailand/Vietnam, 2007

Asian Games
Held every 4 years
Last held: Busan, Rep. of Korea, 2002
Next: Doha, Qatar, 2006; Guangzhou, China, 2010

AFRICA

African Cup of Nations *(football)*
Held every 2 years
Last held: Egypt, 2006
Next: Ghana, 2008

All-Africa Games
Held every 4 years
Last held: Abuja, Nigeria, 2003
Next: Algiers, Algeria, 2007

AMERICAS

Copa América *(football)*
Held every 2/3 years
Last held: Peru, 2004
Next: Venezuela, 2007

Pan-American Games
Held every 4 years
Last held: Santo Domingo, Dominican Rep., 2003
Next: Rio de Janeiro, Brazil, 2007

WORLDWIDE

Pan-Arab Games
Last held: Algeria, 2004
Next: Libya, 2007

Universiade (World University Games)
Held every 2 years
Last held: Izmir, Turkey, 2005
Next: Bangkok, Thailand, 2007

F1 A1 Ring, Spielberg, Austria
F1 Spa-Francorchamps, Belgium
F1 Le Castellet, France
F1 Magny Cours, France
F1 New Nürburgring, Germany
F1 Hockenheim, Germany
F1 Budapest, Hungary
F1 Imola, Italy
F1 Monza, Italy
F1 Monte Carlo, Monaco
F1 Estoril, Portugal
F1 Barcelona, Spain
F1 Jeréz de la Frontera, Spain
F1 Istanbul, Turkey
F1 Donington Park, UK
F1 Silverstone, UK

SOME OTHER SPORTS: ANNUAL EVENTS

CYCLING
Major tours:
Giro d'Italia (Tour of Italy); Tour de France; Tour DuPont, USA; Vuelta d'España (Tour of Spain).
Classics:
Belgium: Flèche Wallonne; Liège-Bastogne-Liège; Tour of Flanders.
France: Grand Prix des Nations; Paris-Nice; Paris-Roubaix.
Italy: Milan-San Remo; Tour of Lombardy.
Paris-Brussels.

HORSE RACING
English Classics:
1,000 & 2,000 Guineas, Newmarket; St Leger, Doncaster; Derby & Oaks, Epsom.
Triple Crown, USA:
Belmont Stakes, NY; Kentucky Derby, Louisville; Preakness Stakes, Baltimore.
Other major races:
Cheltenham Gold Cup, UK; Dubai World Cup; Grand National, Aintree, UK; Irish Derby, The Curragh; Japan Cup, Tokyo; Melbourne Cup, Australia; Prix de l'Arc de Triomphe, Paris, France; Royal Ascot, UK.

GOLF
Majors:
British Open; US Open; US Masters; US PGA Championship.
Principal international tournament:
Ryder Cup *(every 2 yrs)*.

MOTOR RACING
Circuits which have held a Formula One race since 1990 are marked F1;
Other major races:
Indianapolis 500, USA; Le Mans 24-hour, France.
Major rallies:
Lombard RAC, UK; Monte Carlo; Safari Rally, Kenya.

MARATHON
Major marathons Ⓜ:
Athens, Berlin, Boston, Chicago, London, Moscow, NY, Prague, Rotterdam.

TENNIS
Grand Slam:
Australian Open, Melbourne; French Open, Roland Garros, Paris; US Open, Flushing Meadow, New York; Wimbledon, UK.
Principal international tournament:
Davis Cup.

See also... Religion (21); Wealth (22-23); International Organisations (30-31); Europe Historical (58-59); Asia Historical (128)

The listings above refer to a selection of related themes. For more information, see the Contents (2-7).

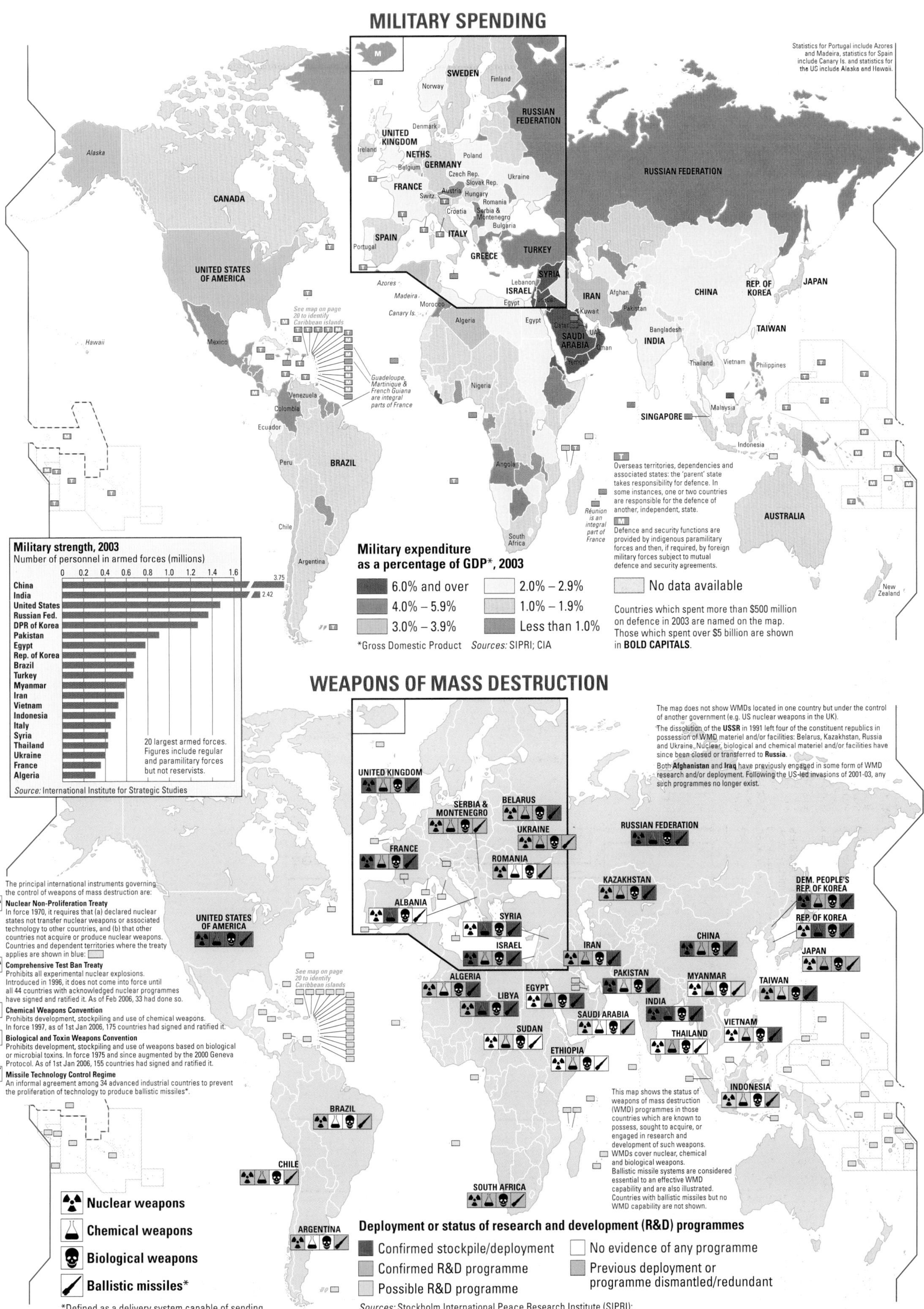
MILITARY SPENDING
Statistics for Portugal include Azores and Madeira, statistics for Spain include Canary Is. and statistics for the US include Alaska and Hawaii.
CANADA
UNITED STATES OF AMERICA
RUSSIAN FEDERATION
SWEDEN
UNITED KINGDOM
NETHS.
GERMANY
FRANCE
SPAIN
ITALY
GREECE
TURKEY
SYRIA
ISRAEL
IRAN
SAUDI ARABIA
CHINA
REP. OF KOREA
JAPAN
TAIWAN
INDIA
SINGAPORE
BRAZIL
AUSTRALIA
See map on page 20 to identify Caribbean islands
Guadeloupe, Martinique & French Guiana are integral parts of France
Réunion is an integral part of France
T
Overseas territories, dependencies and associated states: the 'parent' state takes responsibility for defence. In some instances, one or two countries are responsible for the defence of another, independent, state.
M
Defence and security functions are provided by indigenous paramilitary forces and then, if required, by foreign military forces subject to mutual defence and security agreements.
Military strength, 2003
Number of personnel in armed forces (millions)
0 0.2 0.4 0.6 0.8 1.0 1.2 1.4 1.6
China 3.75
India 2.42
United States
Russian Fed.
DPR of Korea
Pakistan
Egypt
Rep. of Korea
Brazil
Turkey
Myanmar
Iran
Vietnam
Indonesia
Italy
Syria
Thailand
Ukraine
France
Algeria
20 largest armed forces. Figures include regular and paramilitary forces but not reservists.
Source: International Institute for Strategic Studies
Military expenditure as a percentage of GDP*, 2003
6.0% and over
4.0% – 5.9%
3.0% – 3.9%
2.0% – 2.9%
1.0% – 1.9%
Less than 1.0%
No data available
*Gross Domestic Product Sources: SIPRI; CIA
Countries which spent more than $500 million on defence in 2003 are named on the map. Those which spent over $5 billion are shown in BOLD CAPITALS.
WEAPONS OF MASS DESTRUCTION
The map does not show WMDs located in one country but under the control of another government (e.g. US nuclear weapons in the UK).
The dissolution of the USSR in 1991 left four of the constituent republics in possession of WMD materiel and/or facilities: Belarus, Kazakhstan, Russia and Ukraine. Nuclear, biological and chemical materiel and/or facilities have since been closed or transferred to Russia.
Both Afghanistan and Iraq have previously engaged in some form of WMD research and/or deployment. Following the US-led invasions of 2001-03, any such programmes no longer exist.
UNITED KINGDOM
SERBIA & MONTENEGRO
BELARUS
UKRAINE
RUSSIAN FEDERATION
FRANCE
ROMANIA
ALBANIA
SYRIA
ISRAEL
KAZAKHSTAN
DEM. PEOPLE'S REP. OF KOREA
REP. OF KOREA
CHINA
JAPAN
UNITED STATES OF AMERICA
IRAN
PAKISTAN
MYANMAR
TAIWAN
ALGERIA
LIBYA
EGYPT
INDIA
SAUDI ARABIA
VIETNAM
THAILAND
SUDAN
ETHIOPIA
INDONESIA
BRAZIL
CHILE
SOUTH AFRICA
ARGENTINA
The principal international instruments governing the control of weapons of mass destruction are:
Nuclear Non-Proliferation Treaty
In force 1970, it requires that (a) declared nuclear states not transfer nuclear weapons or associated technology to other countries, and (b) that other countries not acquire or produce nuclear weapons. Countries and dependent territories where the treaty applies are shown in blue:
Comprehensive Test Ban Treaty
Prohibits all experimental nuclear explosions. Introduced in 1996, it does not come into force until all 44 countries with acknowledged nuclear programmes have signed and ratified it. As of Feb 2006, 33 had done so.
Chemical Weapons Convention
Prohibits development, stockpiling and use of chemical weapons. In force 1997, as of 1st Jan 2006, 175 countries had signed and ratified it.
Biological and Toxin Weapons Convention
Prohibits development, stockpiling and use of weapons based on biological or microbial toxins. In force 1975 and since augmented by the 2000 Geneva Protocol. As of 1st Jan 2006, 155 countries had signed and ratified it.
Missile Technology Control Regime
An informal agreement among 34 advanced industrial countries to prevent the proliferation of technology to produce ballistic missiles*.
See map on page 20 to identify Caribbean islands
This map shows the status of weapons of mass destruction (WMD) programmes in those countries which are known to possess, sought to acquire, or engaged in research and development of such weapons. WMDs cover nuclear, chemical and biological weapons. Ballistic missile systems are considered essential to an effective WMD capability and are also illustrated. Countries with ballistic missiles but no WMD capability are not shown.
Nuclear weapons
Chemical weapons
Biological weapons
Ballistic missiles*
*Defined as a delivery system capable of sending a 500kg+ payload a distance of 300km or further
Deployment or status of research and development (R&D) programmes
Confirmed stockpile/deployment
Confirmed R&D programme
Possible R&D programme
No evidence of any programme
Previous deployment or programme dismantled/redundant
Sources: Stockholm International Peace Research Institute (SIPRI); Federation of American Scientists; Carnegie Endowment for International Peace; UN

▶ See also... Time (18-19); Flight Times (45); Cruising (46-47); Europe Transport (62-65); London Airport Connections (75); • cont >

The listings above refer to a selection of related themes. For more information, see the Contents (2-7).

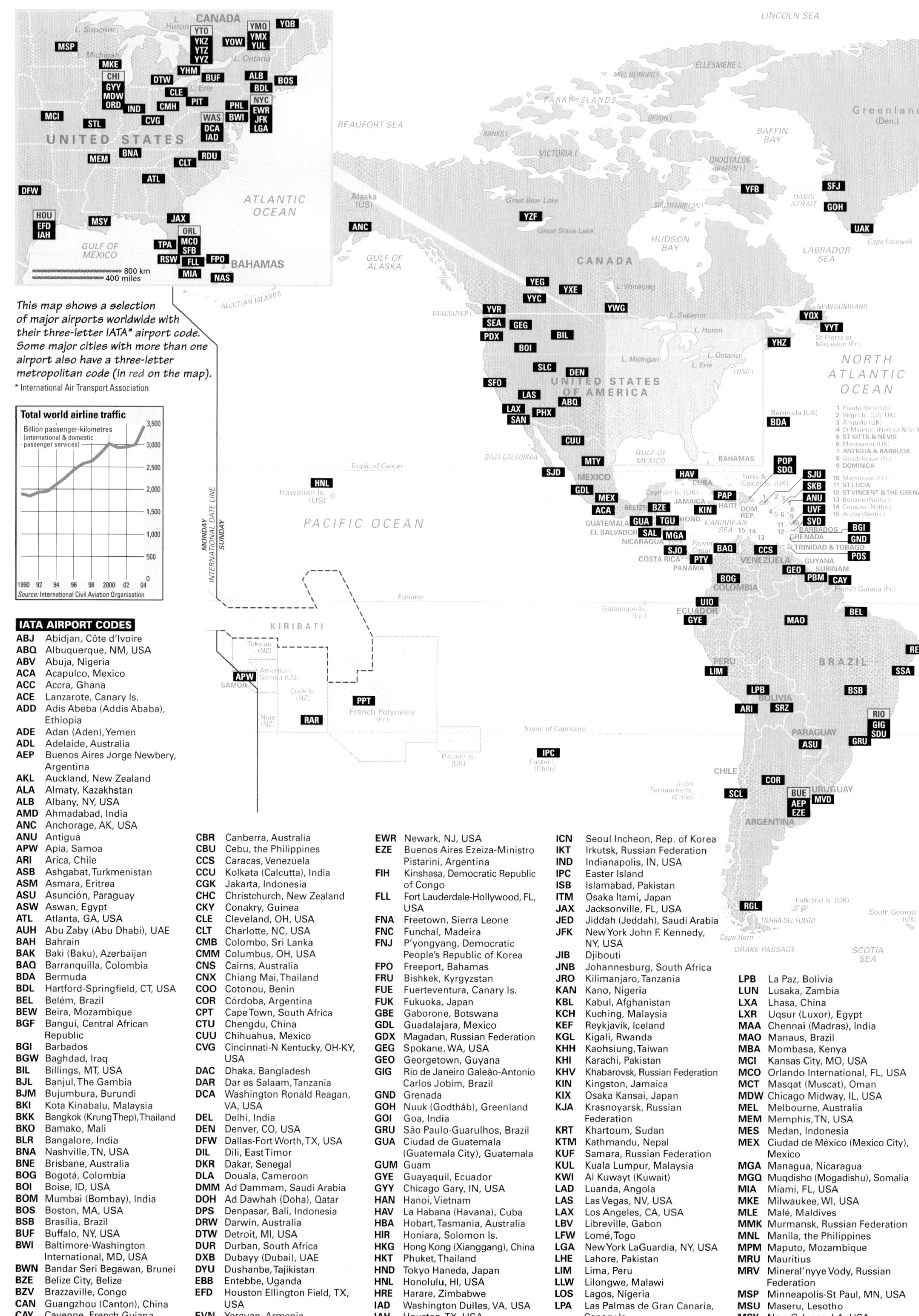
CANADA
UNITED STATES
ATLANTIC OCEAN
GULF OF MEXICO
BAHAMAS
L. Superior
L. Huron
L. Michigan
L. Ontario
L. Erie
800 km
400 miles
MSP MKE CHI GYY MDW ORD DTW YTO YKZ YTZ YYZ YOW YMQ YMX YUL YQB YHM BUF ALB BDL BOS CLE PIT NYC EWR JFK LGA PHL BWI WAS DCA IAD MCI STL IND CMH CVG BNA MEM RDU CLT ATL DFW HOU EFD IAH MSY JAX ORL MCO SFB TPA RSW FLL FPO MIA NAS
LINCOLN SEA
ELLESMERE I.
AXEL HEIBERG I.
PARRY ISLANDS
DEVON I.
BANKS I.
VICTORIA I.
BEAUFORT SEA
Greenland (Den.)
BAFFIN BAY
QIKIQTALUK (BAFFIN I.)
DAVIS STRAIT
Alaska (US)
Great Bear Lake
Great Slave Lake
SOUTHAMPTON I.
HUDSON BAY
LABRADOR SEA
Cape Farewell
GULF OF ALASKA
CANADA
L. Winnipeg
ALEUTIAN ISLANDS
VANCOUVER I.
NEWFOUNDLAND
St Pierre et Miquelon (Fr.)
UNITED STATES OF AMERICA
LONG I.
NORTH ATLANTIC OCEAN
Bermuda (UK)
BAJA CALIFORNIA
GULF OF MEXICO
MEXICO
Tropic of Cancer
Hawaiian Is. (US)
PACIFIC OCEAN
INTERNATIONAL DATE LINE
MONDAY
SUNDAY
CUBA
BAHAMAS
Turks & Caicos Is. (UK)
Cayman Is. (UK)
JAMAICA
HAITI
DOM. REP.
BELIZE
GUATEMALA
HOND.
EL SALVADOR
NICARAGUA
COSTA RICA
PANAMA
Panama Canal
CARIBBEAN SEA
1 Puerto Rico (US)
2 Virgin Is. (US, UK)
3 Anguilla (UK)
4 St Maarten (Neths.) & St Martin (Fr.)
5 ST KITTS & NEVIS
6 Montserrat (UK)
7 ANTIGUA & BARBUDA
8 Guadeloupe (Fr.)
9 DOMINICA
10 Martinique (Fr.)
11 ST LUCIA
12 ST VINCENT & THE GRENADINES
13 Bonaire (Neths.)
14 Curaçao (Neths.)
15 Aruba (Neths.)
BARBADOS
GRENADA
TRINIDAD & TOBAGO
VENEZUELA
GUYANA
SURINAM
French Guiana (Fr.)
COLOMBIA
ECUADOR
Galapagos Is. (Ec.)
Equator
KIRIBATI
Tokelau (NZ)
American Samoa (US)
SAMOA
Cook Is. (NZ)
Niue (NZ)
French Polynesia (Fr.)
Pitcairn Is. (UK)
Easter I. (Chile)
Tropic of Capricorn
PERU
BRAZIL
BOLIVIA
PARAGUAY
CHILE
Juan Fernández Is. (Chile)
URUGUAY
ARGENTINA
Falkland Is. (UK)
TIERRA DEL FUEGO
Cape Horn
DRAKE PASSAGE
SCOTIA SEA
South Georgia (UK)
ANC YZF YFB SFJ GOH UAK YEG YXE YYC YVR YWG SEA GEG PDX BIL BOI YQX YYT YHZ SLC DEN SFO LAS ABQ LAX PHX SAN CUU MTY SJD HNL GDL HAV POP SDQ MEX PAP SJU SKB ANU UVF SVD BGI GND POS ACA BZE KIN GUA TGU SAL MGA SJO PTY BAQ CCS GEO PBM CAY BOG UIO GYE MAO BEL REC SSA LIM LPB SRZ ARI BSB RIO GIG SDU GRU ASU APW PPT RAR IPC COR SCL BUE AEP EZE MVD RGL

This map shows a selection of major airports worldwide with their three-letter IATA* airport code. Some major cities with more than one airport also have a three-letter metropolitan code (in red on the map).

* International Air Transport Association

Total world airline traffic

Billion passenger-kilometres (international & domestic passenger services)

3,500
3,000
2,500
2,000
1,500
1,000
500
0

1990 92 94 96 98 2000 02 04

Source: International Civil Aviation Organisation

IATA AIRPORT CODES

ABJ Abidjan, Côte d'Ivoire
ABQ Albuquerque, NM, USA
ABV Abuja, Nigeria
ACA Acapulco, Mexico
ACC Accra, Ghana
ACE Lanzarote, Canary Is.
ADD Adis Abeba (Addis Ababa), Ethiopia
ADE Adan (Aden), Yemen
ADL Adelaide, Australia
AEP Buenos Aires Jorge Newbery, Argentina
AKL Auckland, New Zealand
ALA Almaty, Kazakhstan
ALB Albany, NY, USA
AMD Ahmadabad, India
ANC Anchorage, AK, USA
ANU Antigua
APW Apia, Samoa
ARI Arica, Chile
ASB Ashgabat, Turkmenistan
ASM Asmara, Eritrea
ASU Asunción, Paraguay
ASW Aswan, Egypt
ATL Atlanta, GA, USA
AUH Abu Zaby (Abu Dhabi), UAE
BAH Bahrain
BAK Baki (Baku), Azerbaijan
BAQ Barranquilla, Colombia
BDA Bermuda
BDL Hartford-Springfield, CT, USA
BEL Belém, Brazil
BEW Beira, Mozambique
BGF Bangui, Central African Republic
BGI Barbados
BGW Baghdad, Iraq
BIL Billings, MT, USA
BJL Banjul, The Gambia
BJM Bujumbura, Burundi
BKI Kota Kinabalu, Malaysia
BKK Bangkok (Krung Thep), Thailand
BKO Bamako, Mali
BLR Bangalore, India
BNA Nashville, TN, USA
BNE Brisbane, Australia
BOG Bogotá, Colombia
BOI Boise, ID, USA
BOM Mumbai (Bombay), India
BOS Boston, MA, USA
BSB Brasília, Brazil
BUF Buffalo, NY, USA
BWI Baltimore-Washington International, MD, USA
BWN Bandar Seri Begawan, Brunei
BZE Belize City, Belize
BZV Brazzaville, Congo
CAN Guangzhou (Canton), China
CAY Cayenne, French Guiana
CBR Canberra, Australia
CBU Cebu, the Philippines
CCS Caracas, Venezuela
CCU Kolkata (Calcutta), India
CGK Jakarta, Indonesia
CHC Christchurch, New Zealand
CKY Conakry, Guinea
CLE Cleveland, OH, USA
CLT Charlotte, NC, USA
CMB Colombo, Sri Lanka
CMH Columbus, OH, USA
CNS Cairns, Australia
CNX Chiang Mai, Thailand
COO Cotonou, Benin
COR Córdoba, Argentina
CPT Cape Town, South Africa
CTU Chengdu, China
CUU Chihuahua, Mexico
CVG Cincinnati-N Kentucky, OH-KY, USA
DAC Dhaka, Bangladesh
DAR Dar es Salaam, Tanzania
DCA Washington Ronald Reagan, VA, USA
DEL Delhi, India
DEN Denver, CO, USA
DFW Dallas-Fort Worth, TX, USA
DIL Dili, East Timor
DKR Dakar, Senegal
DLA Douala, Cameroon
DMM Ad Dammam, Saudi Arabia
DOH Ad Dawhah (Doha), Qatar
DPS Denpasar, Bali, Indonesia
DRW Darwin, Australia
DTW Detroit, MI, USA
DUR Durban, South Africa
DXB Dubayy (Dubai), UAE
DYU Dushanbe, Tajikistan
EBB Entebbe, Uganda
EFD Houston Ellington Field, TX, USA
EVN Yerevan, Armenia
EWR Newark, NJ, USA
EZE Buenos Aires Ezeiza-Ministro Pistarini, Argentina
FIH Kinshasa, Democratic Republic of Congo
FLL Fort Lauderdale-Hollywood, FL, USA
FNA Freetown, Sierra Leone
FNC Funchal, Madeira
FNJ P'yongyang, Democratic People's Republic of Korea
FPO Freeport, Bahamas
FRU Bishkek, Kyrgyzstan
FUE Fuerteventura, Canary Is.
FUK Fukuoka, Japan
GBE Gaborone, Botswana
GDL Guadalajara, Mexico
GDX Magadan, Russian Federation
GEG Spokane, WA, USA
GEO Georgetown, Guyana
GIG Rio de Janeiro Galeão-Antonio Carlos Jobim, Brazil
GND Grenada
GOH Nuuk (Godthåb), Greenland
GOI Goa, India
GRU São Paulo-Guarulhos, Brazil
GUA Ciudad de Guatemala (Guatemala City), Guatemala
GUM Guam
GYE Guayaquil, Ecuador
GYY Chicago Gary, IN, USA
HAN Hanoi, Vietnam
HAV La Habana (Havana), Cuba
HBA Hobart, Tasmania, Australia
HIR Honiara, Solomon Is.
HKG Hong Kong (Xianggang), China
HKT Phuket, Thailand
HND Tokyo Haneda, Japan
HNL Honolulu, HI, USA
HRE Harare, Zimbabwe
IAD Washington Dulles, VA, USA
IAH Houston, TX, USA
ICN Seoul Incheon, Rep. of Korea
IKT Irkutsk, Russian Federation
IND Indianapolis, IN, USA
IPC Easter Island
ISB Islamabad, Pakistan
ITM Osaka Itami, Japan
JAX Jacksonville, FL, USA
JED Jiddah (Jeddah), Saudi Arabia
JFK New York John F. Kennedy, NY, USA
JIB Djibouti
JNB Johannesburg, South Africa
JRO Kilimanjaro, Tanzania
KAN Kano, Nigeria
KBL Kabul, Afghanistan
KCH Kuching, Malaysia
KEF Reykjavík, Iceland
KGL Kigali, Rwanda
KHH Kaohsiung, Taiwan
KHI Karachi, Pakistan
KHV Khabarovsk, Russian Federation
KIN Kingston, Jamaica
KIX Osaka Kansai, Japan
KJA Krasnoyarsk, Russian Federation
KRT Khartoum, Sudan
KTM Kathmandu, Nepal
KUF Samara, Russian Federation
KUL Kuala Lumpur, Malaysia
KWI Al Kuwayt (Kuwait)
LAD Luanda, Angola
LAS Las Vegas, NV, USA
LAX Los Angeles, CA, USA
LBV Libreville, Gabon
LFW Lomé, Togo
LGA New York LaGuardia, NY, USA
LHE Lahore, Pakistan
LIM Lima, Peru
LLW Lilongwe, Malawi
LOS Lagos, Nigeria
LPA Las Palmas de Gran Canaria, Canary Is.
LPB La Paz, Bolivia
LUN Lusaka, Zambia
LXA Lhasa, China
LXR Uqsur (Luxor), Egypt
MAA Chennai (Madras), India
MAO Manaus, Brazil
MBA Mombasa, Kenya
MCI Kansas City, MO, USA
MCO Orlando International, FL, USA
MCT Masqat (Muscat), Oman
MDW Chicago Midway, IL, USA
MEL Melbourne, Australia
MEM Memphis, TN, USA
MES Medan, Indonesia
MEX Ciudad de México (Mexico City), Mexico
MGA Managua, Nicaragua
MGQ Muqdisho (Mogadishu), Somalia
MIA Miami, FL, USA
MKE Milwaukee, WI, USA
MLE Malé, Maldives
MMK Murmansk, Russian Federation
MNL Manila, the Philippines
MPM Maputo, Mozambique
MRU Mauritius
MRV Mineral'nyye Vody, Russian Federation
MSP Minneapolis-St Paul, MN, USA
MSU Maseru, Lesotho
MSY New Orleans, LA, USA

▶ *See also... cont* < • Berlin Airports (83); Paris Airports (87); New York Airports (170); North America – Railways & Airports (158)

The listings above refer to a selection of related themes. For more information, see the Contents (2-7).

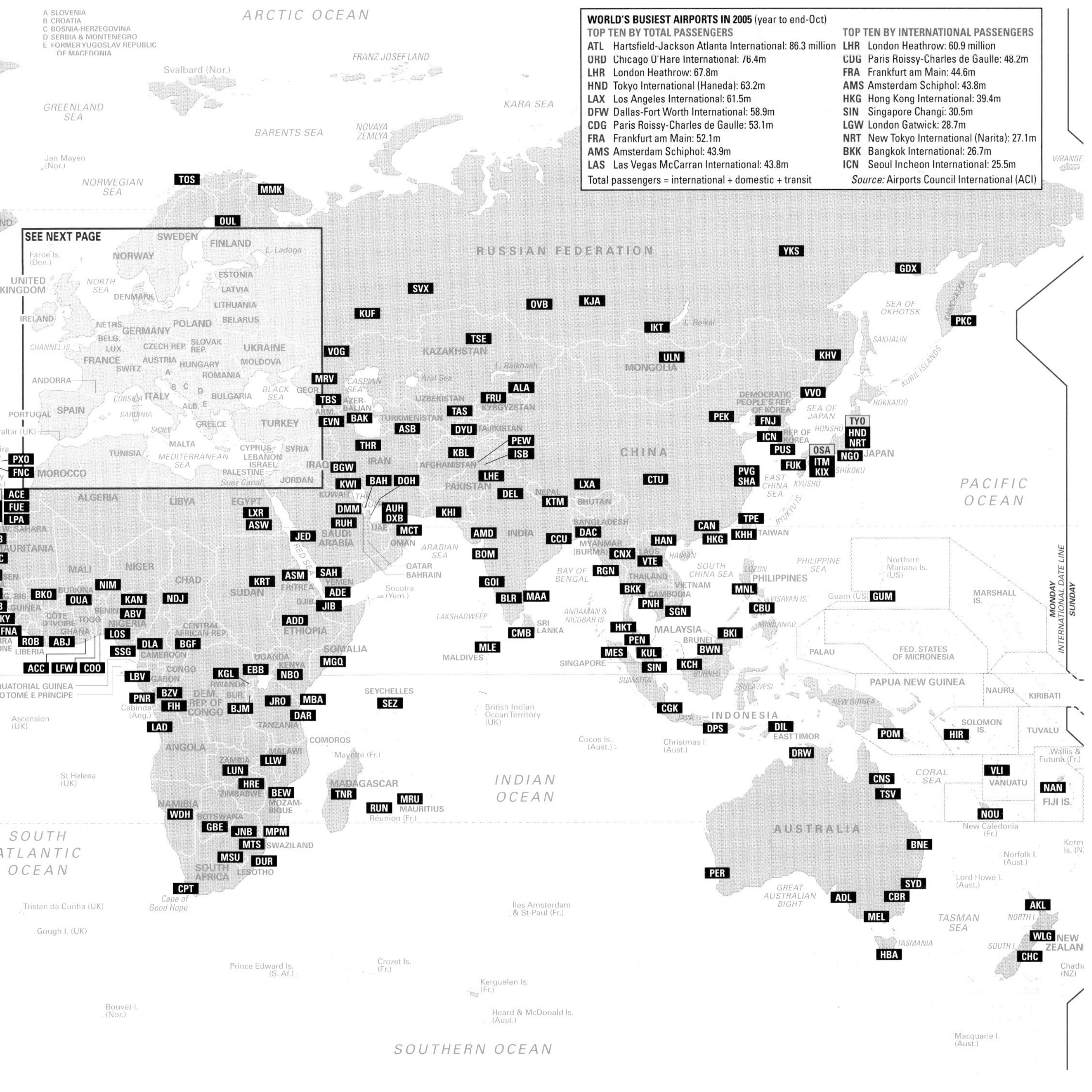
A SLOVENIA
B CROATIA
C BOSNIA-HERZEGOVINA
D SERBIA & MONTENEGRO
E FORMER YUGOSLAV REPUBLIC OF MACEDONIA
ARCTIC OCEAN
FRANZ JOSEF LAND
Svalbard (Nor.)
GREENLAND SEA
BARENTS SEA
NOVAYA ZEMLYA
KARA SEA
Jan Mayen (Nor.)
NORWEGIAN SEA
WRANGE
TOS
MMK
OUL
SEE NEXT PAGE
SWEDEN
FINLAND
NORWAY
Faroe Is. (Den.)
L. Ladoga
UNITED KINGDOM
NORTH SEA
ESTONIA
LATVIA
DENMARK
LITHUANIA
IRELAND
NETHS.
GERMANY
POLAND
BELARUS
BELG.
LUX.
CZECH REP.
SLOVAK REP.
UKRAINE
CHANNEL IS.
FRANCE
AUSTRIA
HUNGARY
MOLDOVA
SWITZ.
ROMANIA
ANDORRA
ITALY
BULGARIA
BLACK SEA
CORSICA
SARDINIA
ALB.
GREECE
TURKEY
PORTUGAL
SPAIN
SICILY
MALTA
CYPRUS
SYRIA
TUNISIA
MEDITERRANEAN SEA
LEBANON
ISRAEL
PALESTINE
IRAQ
MOROCCO
JORDAN
Suez Canal
RUSSIAN FEDERATION
YKS
GDX
SVX
OVB
KJA
KUF
IKT
L. Baikal
SEA OF OKHOTSK
PKC
KAMCHATKA
TSE
VOG
KAZAKHSTAN
ULN
KHV
SAKHALIN
MONGOLIA
L. Balkhash
MRV
CASPIAN SEA
Aral Sea
ALA
KURIL ISLANDS
TBS
AZERBAIJAN
ARM.
UZBEKISTAN
FRU
KYRGYZSTAN
VVO
HOKKAIDO
GEOR.
EVN
BAK
TURKMENISTAN
TAS
DEMOCRATIC PEOPLE'S REP. OF KOREA
SEA OF JAPAN
ASB
DYU
TAJIKISTAN
PEK
FNJ
TYO
HND
NRT
HONSHU
THR
PEW
ICN
REP. OF KOREA
IRAN
KBL
ISB
CHINA
PUS
OSA
ITM
KIX
NGO
JAPAN
AFGHANISTAN
FUK
BGW
LHE
SHIKOKU
KYUSHU
KWI
BAH
DOH
PAKISTAN
LXA
CTU
PVG
SHA
EAST CHINA SEA
KUWAIT
NEPAL
KTM
BHUTAN
RYUKYU IS.
PACIFIC OCEAN
DMM
AUH
DXB
DEL
RUH
KHI
BANGLADESH
TPE
SAUDI ARABIA
UAE
MCT
OMAN
DAC
CAN
HKG
KHH
TAIWAN
JED
AMD
INDIA
CCU
MYANMAR (BURMA)
HAN
ARABIAN SEA
BOM
CNX
LAOS
VTE
HAINAN
QATAR
BAHRAIN
PHILIPPINE SEA
Northern Mariana Is. (US)
RED SEA
ASM
SAH
YEMEN
BAY OF BENGAL
RGN
THAILAND
SOUTH CHINA SEA
LUZON
PHILIPPINES
ERITREA
ADE
Socotra (Yem.)
GOI
BKK
VIETNAM
MNL
MONDAY
INTERNATIONAL DATE LINE
SUNDAY
DJIB.
JIB
BLR
MAA
CAMBODIA
PNH
SGN
VISAYAN IS.
CBU
Guam (US)
GUM
MARSHALL IS.
ADD
ETHIOPIA
LAKSHADWEEP
ANDAMAN & NICOBAR IS.
SRI LANKA
CMB
HKT
MALAYSIA
MINDANAO
BKI
PEN
BRUNEI
BWN
PALAU
FED. STATES OF MICRONESIA
SOMALIA
MLE
MALDIVES
MES
KUL
SINGAPORE
SIN
KCH
BORNEO
MGQ
SUMATRA
SULAWESI
PAPUA NEW GUINEA
NAURU
KIRIBATI
SEYCHELLES
SEZ
British Indian Ocean Territory (UK)
NEW GUINEA
CGK
JAVA
INDONESIA
DPS
DIL
EAST TIMOR
SOLOMON IS.
POM
HIR
TUVALU
Cocos Is. (Aust.)
Christmas I. (Aust.)
COMOROS
Mayotte (Fr.)
DRW
Wallis & Futuna (Fr.)
INDIAN OCEAN
CORAL SEA
CNS
VLI
VANUATU
MADAGASCAR
TNR
TSV
NAN
FIJI IS.
MRU
RUN
MAURITIUS
Reunion (Fr.)
NOU
New Caledonia (Fr.)
AUSTRALIA
BNE
Norfolk I. (Aust.)
Kerm Is. (N.
PER
Lord Howe I. (Aust.)
SYD
GREAT AUSTRALIAN BIGHT
ADL
CBR
Îles Amsterdam & St-Paul (Fr.)
AKL
MEL
TASMAN SEA
NORTH I.
TASMANIA
WLG
NEW ZEALAN
SOUTH I.
HBA
CHC
Chath (NZ)
Prince Edward Is. (S. Af.)
Crozet Is. (Fr.)
Kerguelen Is. (Fr.)
Bouvet I. (Nor.)
Heard & McDonald Is. (Aust.)
Macquarie I. (Aust.)
SOUTHERN OCEAN
PXO
FNC
ACE
FUE
LPA
ALGERIA
LIBYA
EGYPT
LXR
ASW
W. SAHARA
MAURITANIA
MALI
NIGER
CHAD
SUDAN
KRT
NIM
BKO
OUA
KAN
NDJ
BURKINA
G.-BIS.
GUINEA
CÔTE D'IVOIRE
TOGO
BENIN
NIGERIA
GHANA
ABV
FNA
ROB
ABJ
LOS
LIBERIA
SSG
CENTRAL AFRICAN REP.
DLA
BGF
CAMEROON
ACC
LFW
COO
CONGO
KGL
EBB
UGANDA
KENYA
NBO
EQUATORIAL GUINEA
SÃO TOMÉ E PRÍNCIPE
LBV
GABON
RWANDA
PNR
BZV
DEM. REP. OF CONGO
BUR.
JRO
MBA
Cabinda (Ang.)
FIH
BJM
DAR
TANZANIA
Ascension (UK)
LAD
ANGOLA
MALAWI
ZAMBIA
LLW
St Helena (UK)
LUN
HRE
ZIMBABWE
BEW
MOZAMBIQUE
NAMIBIA
WDH
BOTSWANA
GBE
JNB
MPM
SOUTH ATLANTIC OCEAN
MTS
SWAZILAND
MSU
DUR
SOUTH AFRICA
LESOTHO
CPT
Cape of Good Hope
Tristan da Cunha (UK)
Gough I. (UK)

WORLD'S BUSIEST AIRPORTS IN 2005 (year to end-Oct)

TOP TEN BY TOTAL PASSENGERS

ATL	Hartsfield-Jackson Atlanta International: 86.3 million
ORD	Chicago O'Hare International: 76.4m
LHR	London Heathrow: 67.8m
HND	Tokyo International (Haneda): 63.2m
LAX	Los Angeles International: 61.5m
DFW	Dallas-Fort Worth International: 58.9m
CDG	Paris Roissy-Charles de Gaulle: 53.1m
FRA	Frankfurt am Main: 52.1m
AMS	Amsterdam Schiphol: 43.9m
LAS	Las Vegas McCarran International: 43.8m

Total passengers = international + domestic + transit

TOP TEN BY INTERNATIONAL PASSENGERS

LHR	London Heathrow: 60.9 million
CDG	Paris Roissy-Charles de Gaulle: 48.2m
FRA	Frankfurt am Main: 44.6m
AMS	Amsterdam Schiphol: 43.8m
HKG	Hong Kong International: 39.4m
SIN	Singapore Changi: 30.5m
LGW	London Gatwick: 28.7m
NRT	New Tokyo International (Narita): 27.1m
BKK	Bangkok International: 26.7m
ICN	Seoul Incheon International: 25.5m

Source: Airports Council International (ACI)

MTS Manzini, Swaziland
MTY Monterrey, Mexico
MVD Montevideo, Uruguay
NAN Nadi, Fiji Is.
NAS Nassau, Bahamas
NBO Nairobi, Kenya
NDB Nouadhibou, Mauritania
NDJ N'djamena, Chad
NGO Nagoya Centrair, Japan
NIM Niamey, Niger
NKC Nouakchott, Mauritania
NOU Nouméa, New Caledonia
NRT Tokyo Narita, Japan
ORD Chicago O'Hare, IL, USA
OUA Ouagadougou, Burkina
OUL Oulu, Finland
OVB Novosibirsk, Russian Federation
OXB Bissau, Guinea-Bissau
PAP Port-au-Prince, Haiti
PBM Paramaribo, Surinam
PDL Ponta Delgada, São Miguel, Azores
PDX Portland, OR, USA
PEK Beijing (Peking), China
PEN Pinang (Penang), Malaysia
PER Perth, Australia
PEW Peshawar, Pakistan
PHL Philadelphia, PA, USA
PHX Phoenix, AZ, USA
PIT Pittsburgh, PA, USA
PKC Petropavlovsk-Kamchatskiy, Russian Federation
PNH Phnom Penh, Cambodia
PNR Pointe-Noire, Congo
POM Port Moresby, Papua New Guinea
POP Puerto Plata, Dominican Rep.
POS Port of Spain, Trinidad
PPT Papeete, Tahiti, French Polynesia
PTY Ciudad de Panamá (Panama City), Panama
PUS Busan, Republic of Korea
PVG Shanghai Pudong, China
PXO Porto Santo, Madeira
RAI Praia, Cape Verde
RAR Rarotonga, Cook Is.
RDU Raleigh-Durham, NC, USA
REC Recife, Brazil
RGL Rio Gallegos, Argentina
RGN Yangon (Rangoon), Myanmar
ROB Monrovia, Liberia
RSW Southwest Florida, FL, USA
RUH Ar Riyad (Riyadh), Saudi Arabia
RUN Réunion
SAH Sana'a (Sana), Yemen
SAL San Salvador, El Salvador
SAN San Diego, CA, USA
SCL Santiago, Chile
SDQ Santo Domingo, Dominican Republic
SDU Rio de Janeiro Santos Dumont, Brazil
SEA Seattle-Tacoma, WA, USA
SEZ Mahé, Seychelles
SFB Orlando Sanford, FL, USA
SFJ Kangerlussuaq, Greenland
SFO San Francisco, CA, USA
SGN Ho Chi Minh City (Saigon), Vietnam
SHA Shanghai Hongqiao, China
SIN Singapore
SJD San José del Cabo, Mexico
SJO San José, Costa Rica
SJU San Juan, Puerto Rico
SKB St Kitts
SLC Salt Lake City, UT, USA
SMA Santa Maria, Azores
SRZ Santa Cruz, Bolivia
SSA Salvador, Brazil
SSG Malabo, Equatorial Guinea
STL St Louis, MO, USA
SVD St Vincent
SVX Yekaterinburg, Russian Federation
SYD Sydney, Australia
TAS Toshkent (Tashkent), Uzbekistan
TBS T'bilisi, Georgia
TBU Tongatapu, Tonga
TER Terceira, Azores
TFN Tenerife Norte, Canary Is.
TFS Tenerife Sur, Canary Is.
TGU Tegucigalpa, Honduras
THR Tehran, Iran
TNR Antananarivo, Madagascar
TOS Tromsø, Norway
TPA Tampa, FL, USA
TPE Taipei, Taiwan
TSE Astana, Kazakhstan
TSV Townsville, Australia
UAK Narsarsuaq, Greenland
UIO Quito, Ecuador
ULN Ulaanbaatar (Ulan Bator), Mongolia
UVF Hewanorra, St Lucia
VLI Port-Vila, Vanuatu
VOG Volgograd, Russian Federation
VTE Viangchan (Vientiane), Laos
VVO Vladivostok, Russian Federation
WDH Windhoek, Namibia
WLG Wellington, New Zealand
YEG Edmonton, AB, Canada
YFB Iqaluit, NU, Canada
YHM Hamilton, ON, Canada
YHZ Halifax, NS, Canada
YKX Yakutsk, Russian Federation
YKZ Toronto Buttonville, ON, Canada
YMX Montréal Mirabel, QC, Canada
YOW Ottawa, ON, Canada
YQB Québec, QC, Canada
YQX Gander, NL, Canada
YTZ Toronto City Centre, ON, Canada
YUL Montréal Dorval, QC, Canada
YVR Vancouver, BC, Canada
YWG Winnipeg, MB, Canada
YXE Saskatoon, SK, Canada
YYC Calgary, AB, Canada
YYT St John's, NL, Canada
YYZ Toronto Lester B. Pearson, ON, Canada
YZF Yellowknife, NT, Canada

METROPOLITAN CODES

BUE Buenos Aires, Argentina
CHI Chicago, IL, USA
HOU Houston, TX, USA
NYC New York City, NY, USA
ORL Orlando, FL, USA
OSA Osaka, Japan
RIO Rio de Janeiro, Brazil
TCI Tenerife, Canary Is.
TYO Tokyo, Japan
WAS Washington, DC, USA
YMQ Montréal, QC, Canada
YTO Toronto, ON, Canada

Airports

▶ See also... Flight Times (45); Europe Transport (62-65); London Airport Connections (75); Netherlands Airports (80); Berlin Airports (83); Paris Airports (87)

The listings above refer to a selection of related themes. For more information, see the Contents (2-7).

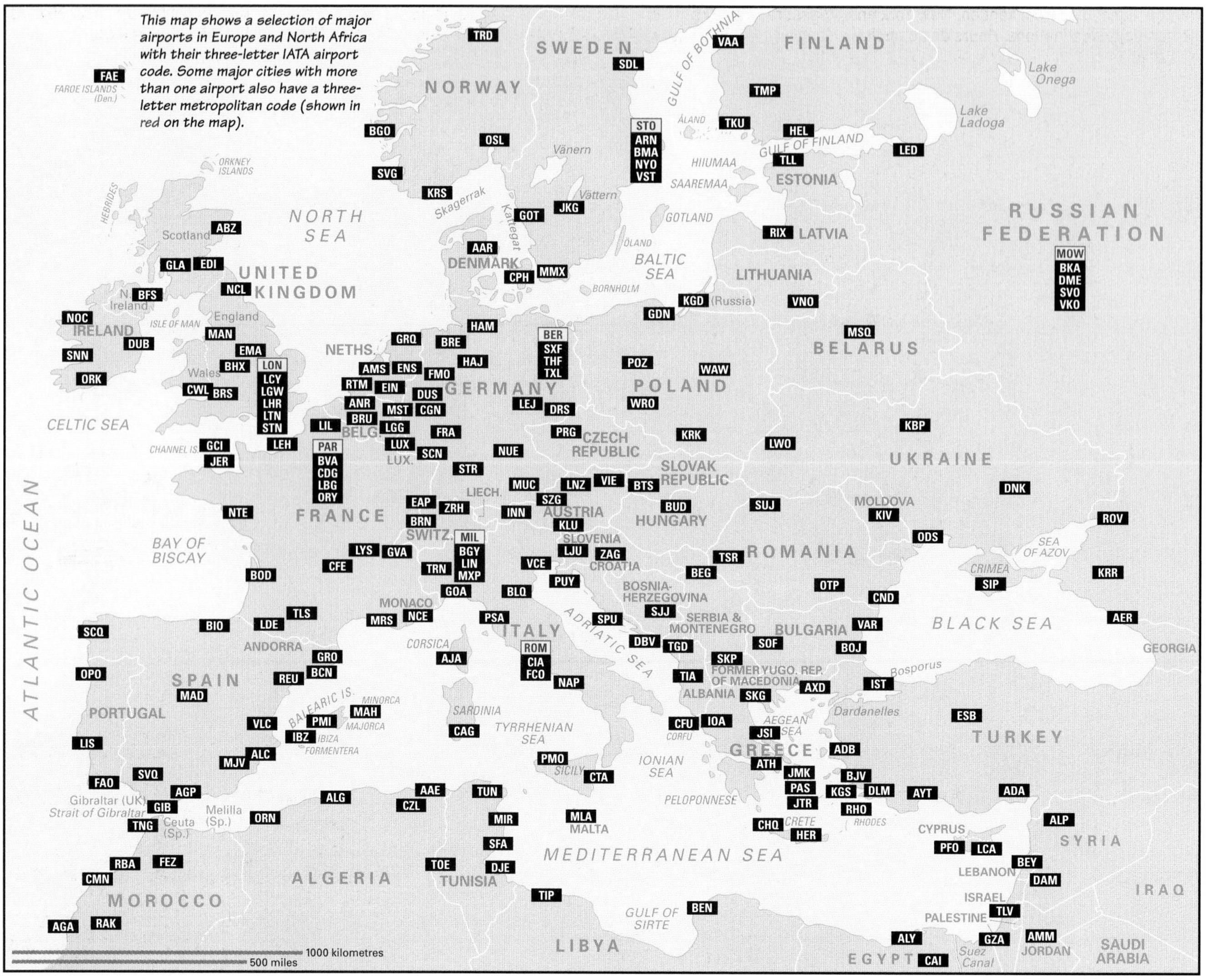

This map shows a selection of major airports in Europe and North Africa with their three-letter IATA airport code. Some major cities with more than one airport also have a three-letter metropolitan code (shown in red on the map).

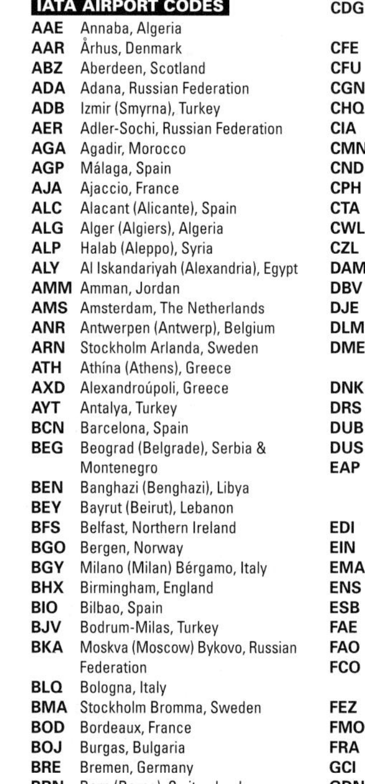
NORWAY
SWEDEN
FINLAND
NORTH SEA
UNITED KINGDOM
IRELAND
DENMARK
ESTONIA
LATVIA
LITHUANIA
RUSSIAN FEDERATION
BELARUS
POLAND
GERMANY
NETHS.
BELG.
LUX.
FRANCE
SWITZ.
AUSTRIA
CZECH REPUBLIC
SLOVAK REPUBLIC
HUNGARY
UKRAINE
MOLDOVA
ROMANIA
SLOVENIA
CROATIA
BOSNIA-HERZEGOVINA
SERBIA & MONTENEGRO
BULGARIA
FORMER YUGO. REP. OF MACEDONIA
ALBANIA
GREECE
TURKEY
ITALY
SPAIN
PORTUGAL
ANDORRA
MONACO
BAY OF BISCAY
ATLANTIC OCEAN
CELTIC SEA
BALTIC SEA
BLACK SEA
SEA OF AZOV
MEDITERRANEAN SEA
TYRRHENIAN SEA
IONIAN SEA
AEGEAN SEA
MOROCCO
ALGERIA
TUNISIA
LIBYA
EGYPT
CYPRUS
SYRIA
LEBANON
ISRAEL
PALESTINE
JORDAN
IRAQ
SAUDI ARABIA
GEORGIA
1000 kilometres
500 miles

IATA AIRPORT CODES

AAE Annaba, Algeria
AAR Århus, Denmark
ABZ Aberdeen, Scotland
ADA Adana, Russian Federation
ADB Izmir (Smyrna), Turkey
AER Adler-Sochi, Russian Federation
AGA Agadir, Morocco
AGP Málaga, Spain
AJA Ajaccio, France
ALC Alacant (Alicante), Spain
ALG Alger (Algiers), Algeria
ALP Halab (Aleppo), Syria
ALY Al Iskandariyah (Alexandria), Egypt
AMM Amman, Jordan
AMS Amsterdam, The Netherlands
ANR Antwerpen (Antwerp), Belgium
ARN Stockholm Arlanda, Sweden
ATH Athina (Athens), Greece
AXD Alexandroúpoli, Greece
AYT Antalya, Turkey
BCN Barcelona, Spain
BEG Beograd (Belgrade), Serbia & Montenegro
BEN Banghazi (Benghazi), Libya
BEY Bayrut (Beirut), Lebanon
BFS Belfast, Northern Ireland
BGO Bergen, Norway
BGY Milano (Milan) Bérgamo, Italy
BHX Birmingham, England
BIO Bilbao, Spain
BJV Bodrum-Milas, Turkey
BKA Moskva (Moscow) Bykovo, Russian Federation
BLQ Bologna, Italy
BMA Stockholm Bromma, Sweden
BOD Bordeaux, France
BOJ Burgas, Bulgaria
BRE Bremen, Germany
BRN Bern (Berne), Switzerland
BRS Bristol, England
BRU Bruxelles/Brussel (Brussels), Belgium
BTS Bratislava, Slovak Republic
BUD Budapest, Hungary
BVA Paris Beauvais-Tille, France
CAG Cágliari, Italy
CAI Al Qahirah (Cairo), Egypt
CDG Paris Roissy-Charles de Gaulle, France
CFE Clermont-Ferrand, France
CFU Kérkira (Corfu), Greece
CGN Köln (Cologne)-Bonn, Germany
CHQ Haniá (Canea), Greece
CIA Roma (Rome) Ciampino, Italy
CMN Casablanca, Morocco
CND Constanta, Romania
CPH København (Copenhagen), Denmark
CTA Catánia, Italy
CWL Cardiff, Wales
CZL Constantine, Algeria
DAM Dimashq (Damascus), Syria
DBV Dubrovnik, Croatia
DJE Jerba, Tunisia
DLM Dalaman, Turkey
DME Moskva (Moscow) Domodedovo, Russian Federation
DNK Dnipropetrovs'k, Ukraine
DRS Dresden, Germany
DUB Dublin, Ireland
DUS Düsseldorf, Germany
EAP EuroAirport [Basel (**BSL**)-Mulhouse (**MLH**)-Freiburg], France/Germany/Switzerland
EDI Edinburgh, Scotland
EIN Eindhoven, The Netherlands
EMA Nottingham East Midlands, England
ENS Enschede, The Netherlands
ESB Ankara, Turkey
FAE Vágar, Faroe Islands
FAO Faro, Portugal
FCO Roma (Rome) Fiumicino/Leonardo da Vinci, Italy
FEZ Fès, Morocco
FMO Münster-Osnabrück, Germany
FRA Frankfurt am Main, Germany
GCI Guernsey
GDN Gdansk, Poland
GIB Gibraltar
GLA Glasgow, Scotland
GOA Génova (Genoa), Italy
GOT Göteborg (Gothenburg), Sweden
GRO Girona, Spain
GRQ Groningen, The Netherlands
GVA Genève (Geneva), Switzerland
GZA Gaza, Palestine Nat. Auth. Region
HAJ Hannover (Hanover), Germany
HAM Hamburg, Germany
HEL Helsinki-Vantaa, Finland
HER Iráklio (Herakleion), Greece
IBZ Eivissa (Ibiza), Spain
INN Innsbruck, Austria
IOA Ioánina, Greece
IST Istanbul, Turkey
JER Jersey
JKG Jönköping, Sweden
JMK Mikonos, Greece
JSI Skíathos, Greece
JTR Thíra, Greece
KBP Kyiv (Kiev), Ukraine
KGD Kaliningrad, Russian Federation
KGS Kós (Cos), Greece
KIV Chisinau (Kishinev), Moldova
KLU Klagenfurt, Austria
KRK Kraków (Cracow), Poland
KRR Krasnodar, Russian Federation
KRS Kristiansand, Norway
LBG Paris Le Bourget, France
LCA Larnaca, Cyprus
LCY London City, England
LDE Lourdes-Tarbes, France
LED Sankt-Peterburg (St Petersburg), Russian Federation
LEH Le Havre, France
LEJ Leipzig-Halle, Germany
LGG Liège, Belgium
LGW London Gatwick, England
LHR London Heathrow, England
LIL Lille, France
LIN Milano (Milan) Linate, Italy
LIS Lisboa (Lisbon), Portugal
LJU Ljubljana, Slovenia
LNZ Linz, Austria
LTN London Luton, England
LUX Luxembourg
LWO L'viv (L'vov), Ukraine
LYS Lyon (Lyons), France
MAD Madrid, Spain
MAH Maó (Mahón), Spain
MAN Manchester, England
MIR Monastir, Tunisia
MJV Murcia, Spain
MLA Malta
MMX Malmö, Sweden
MRS Marseille (Marseilles), France
MSQ Minsk, Belarus
MST Maastricht, The Netherlands
MUC München (Munich), Germany
MXP Milano (Milan) Malpensa, Italy
NAP Nápoli (Naples), Italy
NCE Nice, France
NCL Newcastle, England
NOC Horan (Knock), Ireland
NTE Nantes, France
NUE Nürnberg (Nuremberg), Germany
NYO Stockholm Skavsta, Sweden
ODS Odesa (Odessa), Ukraine
OPO Porto (Oporto), Portugal
ORK Cork, Ireland
ORN Oran, Algeria
ORY Paris Orly, France
OSL Oslo, Norway
OTP Bucuresti (Bucharest), Romania
PAS Páros, Greece
PFO Pafos (Paphos), Cyprus
PMI Palma de Mallorca, Spain
PMO Palermo, Italy
POZ Poznan, Poland
PRG Praha (Prague), Czech Republic
PSA Pisa, Italy
PUY Pula, Croatia
RAK Marrakech, Morocco
RBA Rabat, Morocco
REU Reus, Spain
RHO Ródos (Rhodes), Greece
RIX Riga, Latvia
ROV Rostov-na-Donu, Russian Federation
RTM Rotterdam, The Netherlands
SCN Saarbrücken, Germany
SCQ Santiago de Compostela, Spain
SDL Sundsvall, Sweden
SFA Sfax, Tunisia
SIP Simferopol, Ukraine
SJJ Sarajevo, Bosnia-Herzegovina
SKG Thessaloníki (Salonika), Greece
SKP Skopje, Former Yugoslav Republic of Macedonia
SNN Shannon, Ireland
SOF Sofiya (Sofia), Bulgaria
SPU Split, Croatia
STN London Stansted, England
STR Stuttgart, Germany
SUJ Satu Mare, Romania
SVG Stavanger, Norway
SVO Moskva (Moscow) Sheremetyevo, Russian Federation
SVQ Sevilla (Seville), Spain
SXF Berlin Schönefeld, Germany
SZG Salzburg, Austria
TGD Podgorica, Serbia & Montenegro
THF Berlin Tempelhof, Germany
TIA Tiranë (Tirana), Albania
TIP Tarabulus (Tripoli), Libya
TKU Turku, Finland
TLL Tallinn, Estonia
TLS Toulouse, France
TLV Tel Aviv-Yafo, Israel
TMP Tampere, Finland
TNG Tanger (Tangier), Morocco
TOE Tozeur, Tunisia
TRD Trondheim, Norway
TRN Torino (Turin), Italy
TSR Timisoara, Romania
TUN Tunis, Tunisia
TXL Berlin Tegel, Germany
VAA Vaasa, Finland
VAR Varna, Bulgaria
VCE Venézia (Venice), Italy
VIE Wien (Vienna), Austria
VKO Moskva (Moscow) Vnukovo, Russian Federation
VLC València, Spain
VNO Vilnius, Lithuania
VST Stockholm Västerås, Sweden
WAW Warszawa (Warsaw), Poland
WRO Wroclaw, Poland
ZAG Zagreb, Croatia
ZRH Zürich, Switzerland

METROPOLITAN CODES

BER Berlin, Germany
LON London, England
MIL Milano (Milan), Italy
MOW Moskva (Moscow), Russian Federation
PAR Paris, France
ROM Roma (Rome), Italy
STO Stockholm, Sweden

See also... Time (18-19); Airports (42-44); Europe Transport (62-65); USA & Canada – Railways & Airports (158)

The listings above refer to a selection of related themes. For more information, see the Contents (2-7).

Average flight times from London, New York and Singapore to other major destinations. Hours do not include stopover time, when necessary, from one destination to another.

Less than 2 hours
2 hours – 4 hours 59 mins
5 hours – 8 hours 59 mins
9 hours – 14 hours 59 mins
15 hours – 24 hours 59 mins
25 hours and over

LONDON

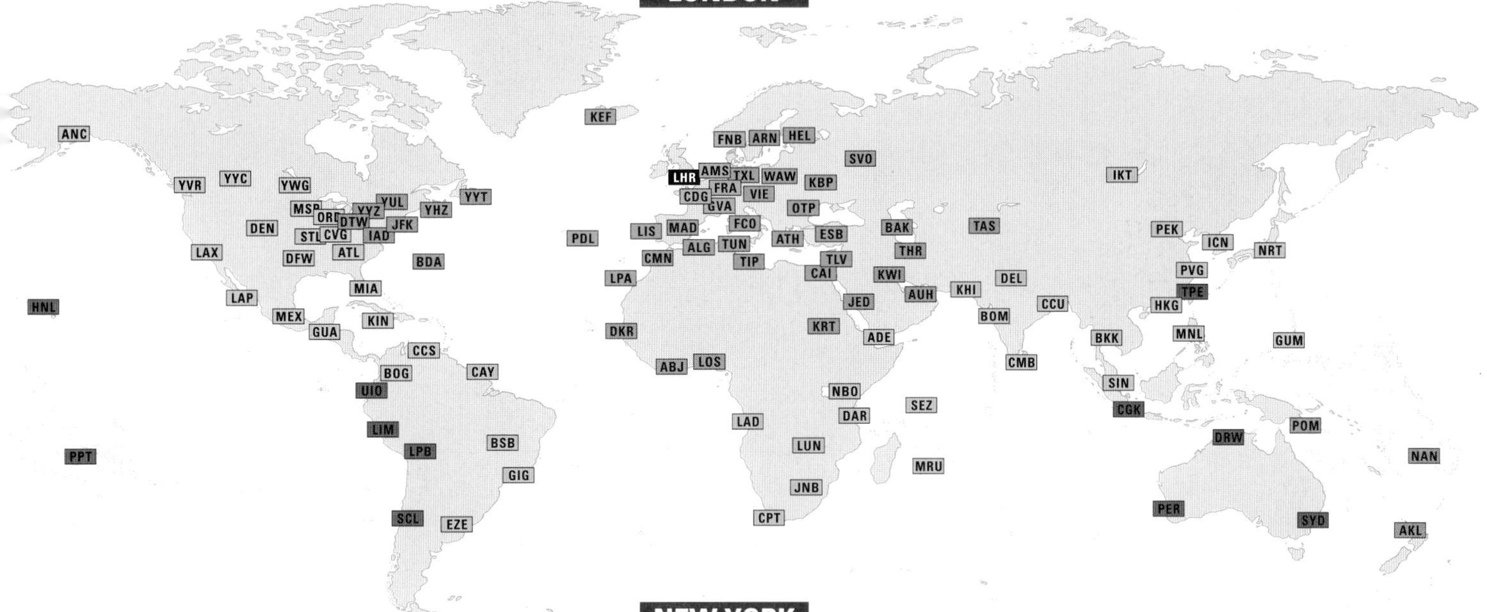

KEF ANC FNB ARN HEL SVO YVR YYC YWG LHR AMS TXL WAW KBP YYT IKT CDG FRA VIE MSP ORD YYZ YUL YHZ GVA OTP DTW JFK DEN STL CVG IAD PDL LIS MAD FCO ESB BAK TAS PEK ICN NRT LAX DFW ATL BDA ALG TUN ATH THR CMN TIP TLV CAI KWI PVG MIA LPA AUH KHI DEL HNL LAP JED TPE HKG MEX KIN DKR KRT BOM CCU GUA ADE MNL GUM CCS ABJ LOS CMB BKK BOG CAY NBO SIN UIO DAR SEZ CGK LIM LAD DRW POM BSB PPT LPB LUN MRU NAN GIG JNB PER SCL EZE CPT SYD AKL

NEW YORK

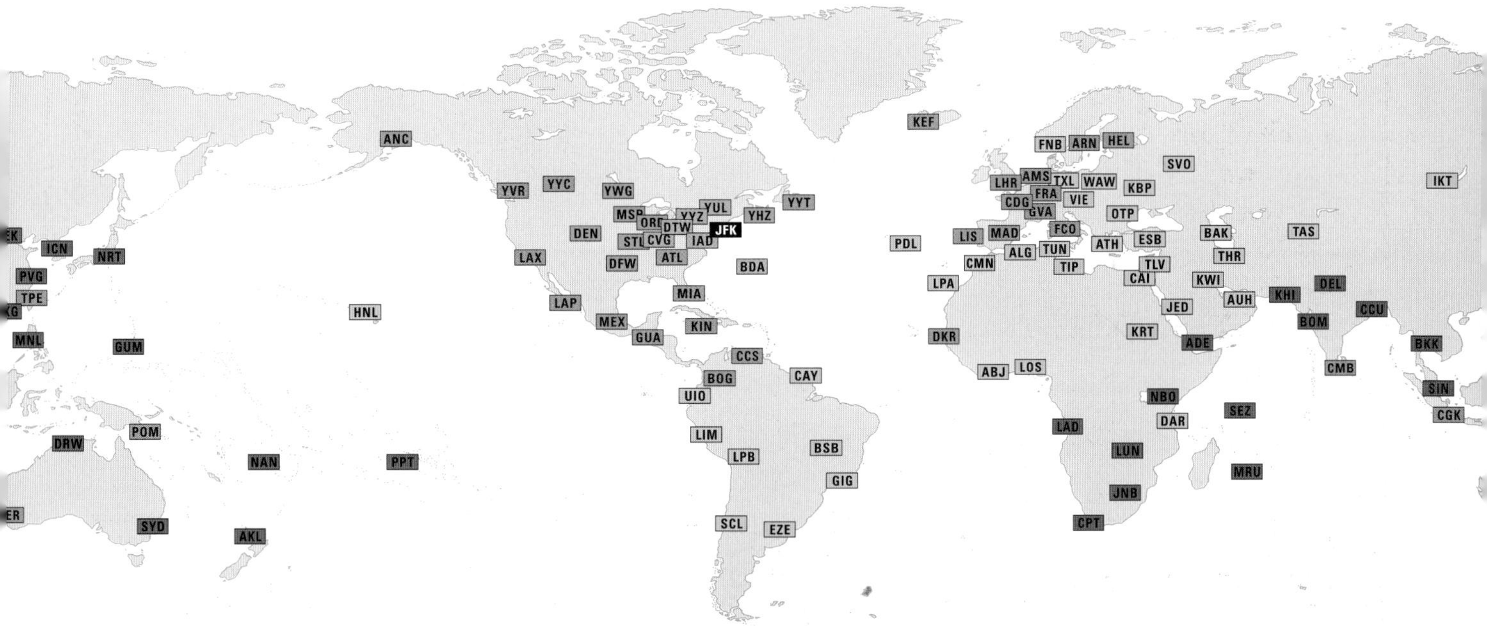

KEF ANC FNB ARN HEL SVO IKT YVR YYC YWG LHR AMS TXL WAW KBP YYT YUL MSP ORD YYZ YHZ CDG FRA VIE DTW JFK GVA OTP DEN STL CVG IAD PDL LIS MAD FCO ESB BAK TAS ICN NRT LAX ALG TUN ATH THR DFW ATL BDA CMN TIP TLV PVG CAI KWI TPE HNL LPA AUH KHI DEL MIA JED LAP CCU MNL GUM MEX KIN DKR KRT BOM GUA ADE BKK CCS ABJ LOS CMB CAY BOG SIN UIO NBO SEZ CGK DAR POM LAD DRW LIM NAN PPT BSB LUN LPB MRU GIG JNB ER SYD SCL EZE CPT AKL

SINGAPORE

KEF FNB ARN HEL ANC SVO LHR AMS TXL WAW KBP IKT YVR YYC YWG YYT CDG VIE GVA OTP MSP ORD YUL YHZ YYZ DTW JFK PDL LIS MAD FCO ATH ESB BAK TAS PEK DEN STL CVG IAD ICN ALG TUN NRT LAX CMN TIP THR DFW ATL BDA TLV CAI KWI DEL PVG LPA AUH KHI TPE MIA JED HKG HNL LAP CCU BOM KRT ADE MEX KIN DKR BKK MNL GUM GUA CCS LOS ABJ CMB CAY BOG SIN UIO NBO SEZ DAR CGK LAD POM DRW LIM LUN BSB LPB MRU NAN PPT GIG JNB PER SYD SCL EZE CPT AKL

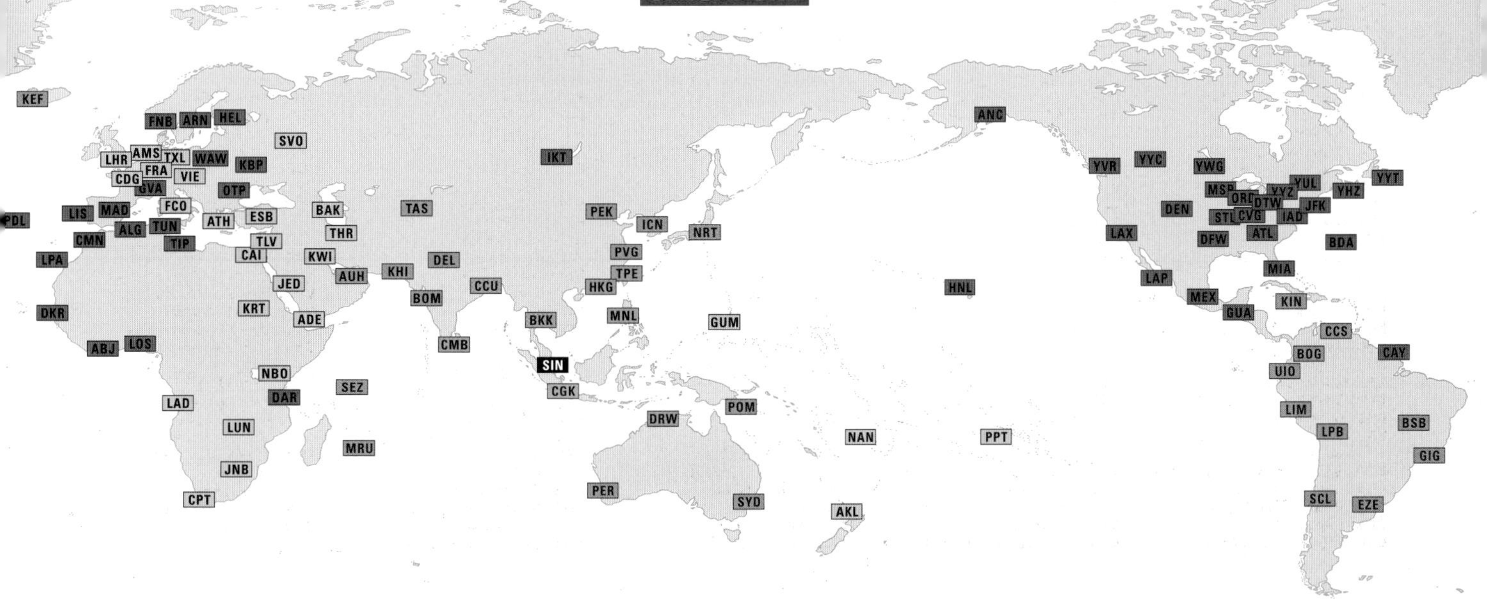

See also... Europe Railways & Ferries (64-65); UK (70-76); The Mediterranean (106); Scandinavia (107-109); The Gulf (131)• cont >

The main ocean and river cruise areas are highlighted along with the most visited ports (red dots). Follow the green line for a typical three-month world cruise route. The Mediterranean and the Caribbean, the two most popular cruising regions, are shown in extra detail below.

Not all ships can dock alongside all ports. On these occasions, ship's launches are used to tender passengers ashore. In some remote regions such as Antarctica, passengers can only travel ashore by Zodiac boats.

Cruises are year-round except in the following regions, where climate or sea conditions limit the season:
Alaska: cruises scheduled between May and September;
US East Coast May – Sep;
Baltic May – Sep;
South Africa Nov – Mar;
Antarctica & South America (Cape Horn) Nov – Feb

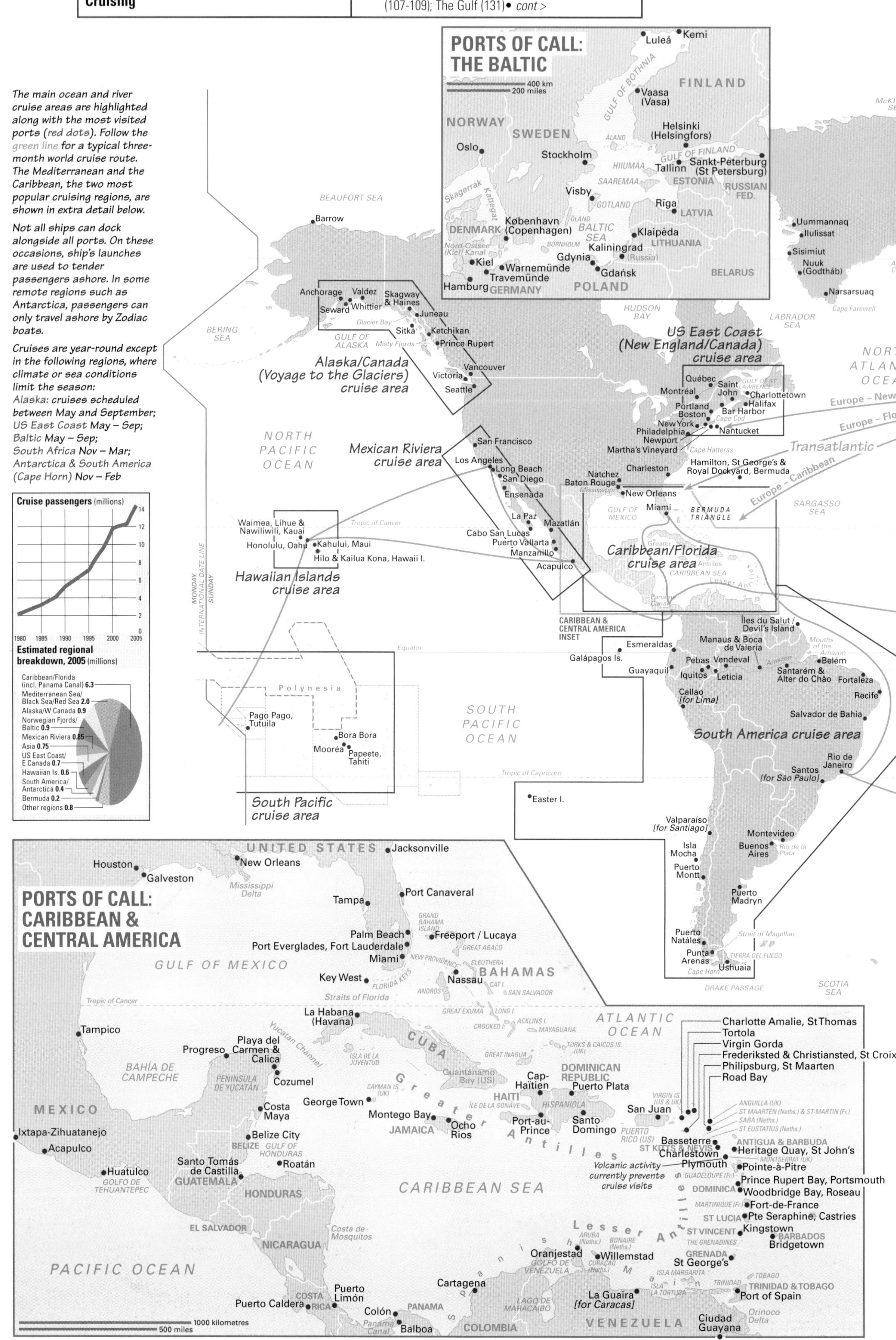
Cruise passengers (millions)
14
12
10
8
6
4
2
0
1980
1985
1990
1995
2000
2005
Estimated regional breakdown, 2005 (millions)
Caribbean/Florida (incl. Panama Canal) 6.3
Mediterranean Sea/ Black Sea/Red Sea 2.0
Alaska/W Canada 0.9
Norwegian Fjords/ Baltic 0.9
Mexican Riviera 0.85
Asia 0.75
US East Coast/ E Canada 0.7
Hawaiian Is. 0.6
South America/ Antarctica 0.4
Bermuda 0.2
Other regions 0.8
PORTS OF CALL: THE BALTIC
400 km
200 miles
Luleå
Kemi
GULF OF BOTHNIA
FINLAND
Vaasa (Vasa)
NORWAY
SWEDEN
Helsinki (Helsingfors)
Oslo
Stockholm
ÅLAND
GULF OF FINLAND
Sankt-Peterburg (St Petersburg)
HIIUMAA
Tallinn
ESTONIA
RUSSIAN FED.
SAAREMAA
Skagerrak
Kattegat
Visby
GOTLAND
Riga
LATVIA
København (Copenhagen)
ÖLAND
DENMARK
BALTIC SEA
Klaipėda
BORNHOLM
LITHUANIA
Nord-Ostsee (Kiel) Kanal
Kaliningrad (Russia)
Kiel
Gdynia
Warnemünde
Gdańsk
Travemünde
BELARUS
Hamburg
GERMANY
POLAND
BEAUFORT SEA
Barrow
BERING SEA
Anchorage
Valdez
Skagway & Haines
Seward
Whittier
Juneau
Glacier Bay
Sitka
Ketchikan
GULF OF ALASKA
Misty Fjords
Prince Rupert
Alaska/Canada (Voyage to the Glaciers) cruise area
Vancouver
Victoria
Seattle
HUDSON BAY
LABRADOR SEA
US East Coast (New England/Canada) cruise area
Québec
Saint John
Montréal
Charlottetown
Halifax
Portland
Boston
Bar Harbor
Cape Cod
New York
Newport
Nantucket
Philadelphia
Martha's Vineyard
Cape Hatteras
Uummannaq
Ilulissat
Sisimiut
Nuuk (Godthåb)
Narsarsuaq
Cape Farewell
NORTH ATLANTIC OCEAN
Europe – New York
Europe – Florida
Transatlantic
Europe – Caribbean
NORTH PACIFIC OCEAN
Mexican Riviera cruise area
San Francisco
Los Angeles
Long Beach
San Diego
Ensenada
Hamilton, St George's & Royal Dockyard, Bermuda
Charleston
Natchez
Baton Rouge
Mississippi
New Orleans
BERMUDA TRIANGLE
SARGASSO SEA
GULF OF MEXICO
Miami
La Paz
Mazatlán
Cabo San Lucas
Puerto Vallarta
Manzanillo
Acapulco
Tropic of Cancer
Waimea, Lihue & Nawiliwili, Kauai
Honolulu, Oahu
Kahului, Maui
Hilo & Kailua Kona, Hawaii I.
Hawaiian Islands cruise area
Caribbean/Florida cruise area
CARIBBEAN SEA
INTERNATIONAL DATE LINE
MONDAY
SUNDAY
CARIBBEAN & CENTRAL AMERICA INSET
Îles du Salut / Devil's Island
Equator
Esmeraldas
Manaus & Boca de Valeria
Galápagos Is.
Pebas
Vendeval
Belém
Guayaquil
Iquitos
Leticia
Amazon
Santarém & Alter do Chão
Fortaleza
Polynesia
Callao [for Lima]
Recife
Pago Pago, Tutuila
SOUTH PACIFIC OCEAN
Salvador de Bahia
Bora Bora
Mooréa
Papeete, Tahiti
South America cruise area
Rio de Janeiro
Santos [for São Paulo]
Tropic of Capricorn
Easter I.
South Pacific cruise area
Valparaíso [for Santiago]
Montevideo
Isla Mocha
Buenos Aires
Rio de la Plata
Puerto Montt
Puerto Madryn
Strait of Magellan
Puerto Natáles
Punta Arenas
TIERRA DEL FUEGO
Ushuaia
Cape Horn
DRAKE PASSAGE
SCOTIA SEA
PORTS OF CALL: CARIBBEAN & CENTRAL AMERICA
UNITED STATES
Jacksonville
Houston
New Orleans
Galveston
Mississippi Delta
Port Canaveral
Tampa
Palm Beach
Freeport / Lucaya
Port Everglades, Fort Lauderdale
GRAND BAHAMA ISLAND
GREAT ABACO
Miami
NEW PROVIDENCE
ELEUTHERA
GULF OF MEXICO
Key West
FLORIDA KEYS
Nassau
BAHAMAS
CAT I.
SAN SALVADOR
ANDROS
Straits of Florida
Tropic of Cancer
La Habana (Havana)
GREAT EXUMA
LONG I.
CROOKED I.
ACKLINS I.
MAYAGUANA
ATLANTIC OCEAN
Tampico
Playa del Carmen & Calica
Progreso
Yucatan Channel
CUBA
ISLA DE LA JUVENTUD
GREAT INAGUA
TURKS & CAICOS IS. (UK)
BAHÍA DE CAMPECHE
PENINSULA DE YUCATÁN
Cozumel
Guantánamo Bay (US)
Cap-Haïtien
DOMINICAN REPUBLIC
Puerto Plata
HAITI
CAYMAN IS. (UK)
George Town
Costa Maya
ÎLE DE LA GONÂVE
HISPANIOLA
MEXICO
Montego Bay
Ocho Rios
JAMAICA
Port-au-Prince
Santo Domingo
San Juan
PUERTO RICO (US)
VIRGIN IS. (US & UK)
Charlotte Amalie, St Thomas
Tortola
Virgin Gorda
Frederiksted & Christiansted, St Croix
Philipsburg, St Maarten
Road Bay
ANGUILLA (UK)
ST MAARTEN (Neths.) & ST-MARTIN (Fr.)
SABA (Neths.)
ST EUSTATIUS (Neths.)
Ixtapa-Zihuatanejo
Belize City
BELIZE
GULF OF HONDURAS
Greater Antilles
Acapulco
Basseterre
ST KITTS & NEVIS
Charlestown
ANTIGUA & BARBUDA
Heritage Quay, St John's
Plymouth
MONTSERRAT (UK)
Volcanic activity currently prevents cruise visits
Pointe-à-Pitre
GUADELOUPE (Fr.)
Santo Tomás de Castilla
Roatán
Huatulco
GOLFO DE TEHUANTEPEC
GUATEMALA
HONDURAS
CARIBBEAN SEA
DOMINICA
Prince Rupert Bay, Portsmouth
Woodbridge Bay, Roseau
MARTINIQUE (Fr.)
Fort-de-France
ST LUCIA
Pte Seraphine, Castries
EL SALVADOR
Costa de Mosquitos
Lesser Antilles
ST VINCENT
THE GRENADINES
Kingstown
BARBADOS
Bridgetown
NICARAGUA
ARUBA (Neths.)
BONAIRE (Neths.)
GRENADA
St George's
Oranjestad
Willemstad
CURAÇAO (Neths.)
GOLFO DE VENEZUELA
ISLA MARGARITA
PACIFIC OCEAN
Spanish Main
Cartagena
ISLA LA TORTUGA
TRINIDAD
TOBAGO
TRINIDAD & TOBAGO
Port of Spain
La Guaira [for Caracas]
LAGO DE MARACAIBO
COSTA RICA
Puerto Limón
Puerto Caldera
PANAMA
Colón
Panama Canal
Balboa
COLOMBIA
VENEZUELA
Ciudad Guayana
Orinoco Delta
1000 kilometres
500 miles

PORTS OF CALL: BRITISH ISLES

300 km
150 miles

Shetland Is.
Lerwick
Fair Isle
Orkney Is.
Kirkwall
Invergordon
Hebrides
North Atlantic Ocean
North Sea
Scotland
Greenock
Leith [for Edinburgh]
Newcastle upon Tyne
N. Ireland
Isle of Man
United Kingdom
Anglesey
Dublin
Liverpool
Ireland
England
Waterford
Wales
Harwich
Cork
Milford Haven
London
Tilbury
Bristol
Dover
Celtic Sea
Plymouth
Portland
Southampton
Falmouth
Fowey
English Channel
Isles of Scilly
Guernsey
Channel Is.
France

PORTS OF CALL: THE GULF

Iraq
Iran
Afghanistan
Kuwait
The Gulf
Bandar-e 'Abbās
Qeshm
Strait of Hormuz
Al Manāmah
Bahrain
Al Khaşab
Oman
Sharjah
Dubai
Khawr Fakkan
Qatar
Ad Dawḥah (Doha)
Trucial Coast
Fujairah
Gulf of Oman
United Arab Emirates
Saudi Arabia
Masqaţ (Muscat)
Oman
Jazīrat Maşīrah
Arabian Sea
400 km
200 miles

Arctic Ocean
Greenland Sea
Norwegian Sea
Barents Sea

Norwegian Fjords (North Cape/Land of the Midnight Sun) cruise area

Longyearbyen, Spitsbergen
Hammerfest
North Cape
Honningsvåg
Tromsø
Narvik
Ålesund & Geiranger
Baltic Inset
White Sea
Måløy & Olden
Molde
Flåm & Gudvangen
Trondheim
Tórshavn
Åndalsnes
Bergen
Helsinki (Helsingfors)
Eidfjord & Hardangerfjord
Stavanger
Oslo
Stockholm
Sankt-Peterburg (St Petersburg)
København (Copenhagen)
Uglich
Moskva (Moscow)
Volga
North Sea
Hamburg
Amsterdam
Dover
Southampton

Baltic (Northern Capitals) cruise area

Black Sea cruise area
Caspian Sea

(Western) Mediterranean cruise area (Eastern)

Funchal, Madeira
Tanger (Tangier)
Valletta
Mediterranean Sea
Al Iskandarīyah (Alexandria)
Casablanca
Southern Europe Inset
Arrecife
Elat (Eilat)
Puerto del Rosario
Las Palmas de Gran Canaria
Santa Cruz de Tenerife
As Suways (Suez)
Al Aqabah
Sharm ash Shaykh
Uqşur (Luxor)
Būr Safājah
Isnā (Esna) & Idfū (Edfu)
Aswān & Kawm Umbū

Atlantic Islands/West Africa cruise area

Red Sea cruise area
Red Sea

The Gulf Inset

The Gulf cruise area

The Gulf
Strait of Hormuz
Dubai
Gulf of Oman

Dakar
Banjul
Freetown
Monrovia
Grain Coast
Ivory Coast
Gold Coast
Slave Coast
Gulf of Guinea
Djibouti
Gulf of Aden
Bab al Mandab
Al Mukallā
Şalālah
Arabian Sea
Mumbai (Bombay)
Goa
Chennai (Madras)
Kochi (Cochin)
Colombo
Malé

Africa-India (Passage to India) cruise area

Mombasa
Zanzibar
Victoria, Mahé
Nosy Bé
Mozambique Channel
Port Louis, Mauritius
Indian Ocean

South Atlantic Ocean
Durban
Cape Town
Cape of Good Hope
Cape Agulhas

Round-the-World

Southern Ocean

Vladivostok
Hakodate
Tianjin [for Beijing]
Dalian
Sea of Japan
Incheon [for Seoul]
Yantai
Tokyo
Busan
Kobe
Yokohama
Nanjing
Wusong
Nagasaki
Chongqing
Yangtze
Shanghai
Wuhan
Ningbo
E. China Sea
Guangzhou (Canton)
Xiamen
Haiphong
Macau
Hong Kong (Xianggang)

Far East cruise area

Yangon (Rangoon)
Da Nang
Bay of Bengal
Bangkok (Krung Thep)
Philippine Sea
Port Blair, S. Andaman
Pattaya
Nha Trang
Manila
Ho Chi Minh City
South China Sea
Cebu
Phuket
Kuantan
Pinang (Penang)
Kota Kinabalu
Belawan
Melaka (Malacca)
Bandar Seri Begawan
Port Kelang [for Kuala Lumpur]
Kuching
Nias
Singapore
Ternate
Padang
Palopo
Parepare
Ambon
Strait of Malacca
Straits of Singapore
Jakarta
Java Sea
Ujung Pandang
Pulau Panjang
Semarang
Surabaya
Krakatau
Bali
Larantuka, Flores
Christmas I.

North Pacific Ocean
Micronesia
Monday
International Date Line
Sunday

Rabaul
Melanesia
Port Moresby
Honiara
Darwin
Cairns
Coral Sea
Great Barrier Reef
Port Vila, Efaté
Yasawa
Townsville, Whitsunday Is.
Suva, Viti Levu
Nouméa
Nuku'alofa, Tongatapu

Australasia/South Pacific cruise area

Perth
Great Australian Bight
Sydney
Bay of Islands
Tauranga [for Rotorua]
Auckland
Melbourne
Tasman Sea
Napier
Picton
Wellington
Hobart
Milford Sound
Christchurch
Dusky Sound
Dunedin

Antarctic cruise area
Auckland I.
Campbell I.
Macquarie I.

Grytviken, Bay of Isles & Elsehul, South Georgia
Port Stanley & West Point, Falkland Is.
Southern Ocean
Signy & Coronation Is., S. Orkney Is.
King George I.
Drake Passage
Weddell Sea
Ushuaia
Hope Bay & Paulet I.
Cape Horn
Yankee Harbour & Half Moon I.
Paradise Harbour & Port Lockroy
Antarctic Peninsula
Ronne Ice Shelf
Adelaide & Stonington Is.
South Pole
Southern Ocean
Marie Byrd Land
Ross Ice Shelf
Wilkes Land
Antarctic Circle
Ross Sea
McMurdo Station & Scott Base
Cape Hallet
Cape Evans
Cape Adare

Antarctic cruise area

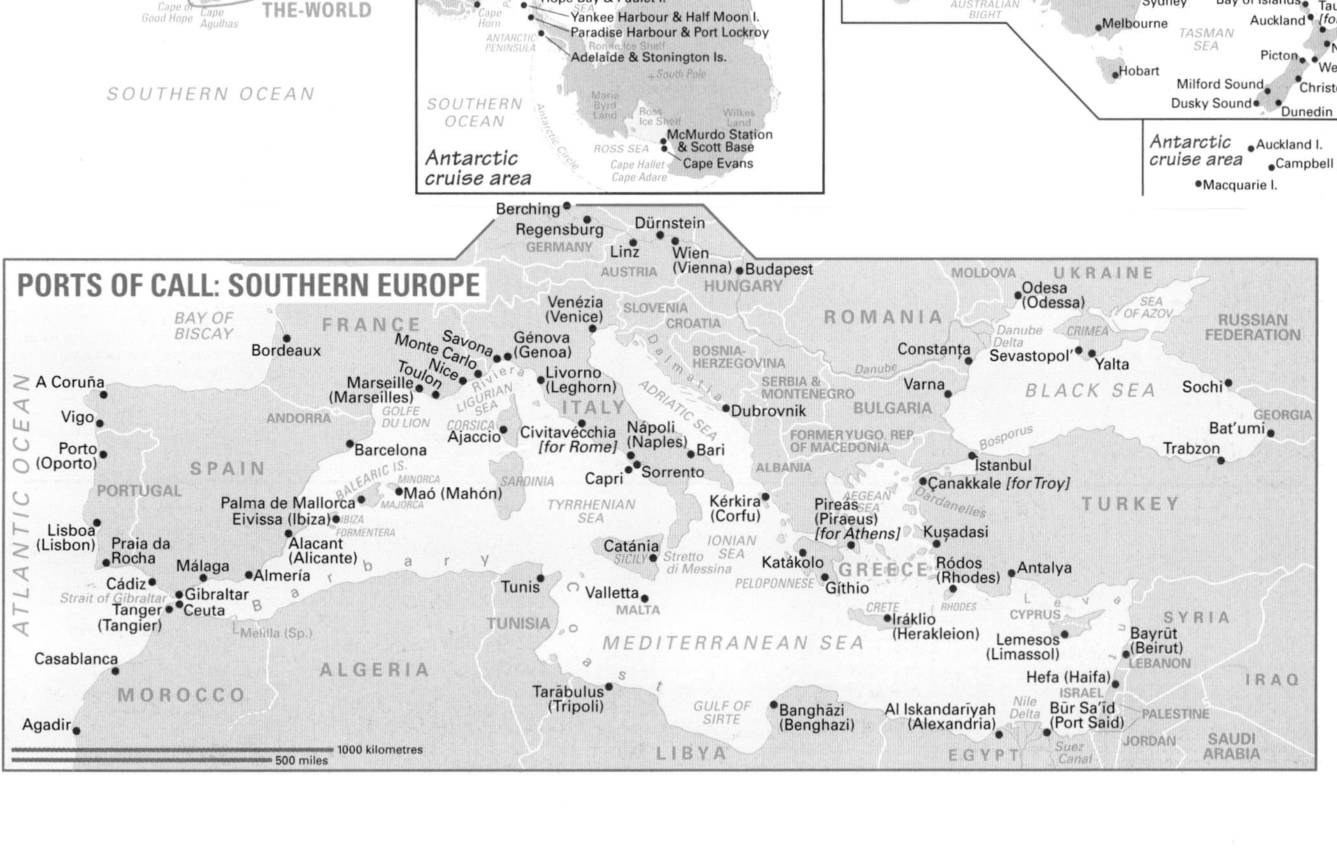

PORTS OF CALL: SOUTHERN EUROPE
Berching
Regensburg
Dürnstein
Germany
Linz
Wien (Vienna)
Budapest
Austria
Hungary
Moldova
Ukraine
Odesa (Odessa)
Bay of Biscay
France
Venézia (Venice)
Slovenia
Croatia
Romania
Sea of Azov
Russian Federation
Bordeaux
Monte Carlo
Savona
Génova (Genoa)
Danube Delta
Crimea
Constanţa
Sevastopol'
Yalta
A Coruña
Marseille (Marseilles)
Toulon
Nice
Riviera
Livorno (Leghorn)
Bosnia-Herzegovina
Dalmatia
Serbia & Montenegro
Danube
Varna
Black Sea
Sochi
Atlantic Ocean
Golfe du Lion
Ligurian Sea
Italy
Adriatic Sea
Dubrovnik
Bulgaria
Georgia
Vigo
Andorra
Corsica
Ajaccio
Civitavecchia [for Rome]
Nápoli (Naples)
Former Yugo. Rep. of Macedonia
Bosporus
Bat'umi
Porto (Oporto)
Spain
Barcelona
Sorrento
Bari
Albania
Istanbul
Trabzon
Balearic Is.
Minorca
Sardinia
Capri
Çanakkale [for Troy]
Portugal
Maó (Mahón)
Majorca
Tyrrhenian Sea
Aegean Sea
Dardanelles
Palma de Mallorca
Kérkira (Corfu)
Turkey
Eivissa (Ibiza)
Ibiza
Formentera
Pireás (Piraeus) [for Athens]
Kuşadasi
Lisboa (Lisbon)
Praia da Rocha
Alacant (Alicante)
Catánia
Ionian Sea
Sicily
Stretto di Messina
Katákolo
Greece
Ródos (Rhodes)
Antalya
Málaga
Almería
Barbary
Peloponnese
Githio
Cádiz
Gibraltar
Tunis
Valletta
Malta
Crete
Rhodes
Strait of Gibraltar
Ceuta
Tanger (Tangier)
Melilla (Sp.)
Tunisia
Iráklio (Herakleion)
Cyprus
Syria
Levant
Lemesos (Limassol)
Bayrūt (Beirut)
Lebanon
Mediterranean Sea
Casablanca
Hefa (Haifa)
Israel
Iraq
Algeria
Morocco
Tarābulus (Tripoli)
Gulf of Sirte
Banghāzi (Benghazi)
Al Iskandarīyah (Alexandria)
Nile Delta
Būr Sa'īd (Port Said)
Palestine
Agadir
Suez Canal
Jordan
Saudi Arabia
1000 kilometres
500 miles
Libya
Egypt

See also... Europe National Parks (66); African Wildlife Parks (122-123); US National Parks Service (166-167); Canadian National Parks (175)

The listings above refer to a selection of related themes. For more information, see the Contents (2-7).

The UNESCO World Heritage List consists of sites considered to be of global importance either because of their natural heritage or their significant man-made contribution to world culture. Countries which are signatories to the World Heritage Convention can submit potential sites to UNESCO, which considers each proposal under strict criteria and lists each site where one or more natural or cultural criteria have been met. Some sites satisfy both natural and cultural criteria; these appear on both maps.

The natural sites shown here are either: significant natural features, areas which constitute the habitat of threatened species of outstanding value, or areas of outstanding scientific or conservation value or natural beauty.

Properties named in red are included on the list of World Heritage in Danger.
Those **shown in italics** are joint natural and cultural sites.
Sites **marked with an asterisk** are featured in Columbus Travel Guides' 'Tourist Attractions and Events of the World'

For further information see whc.unesco.org

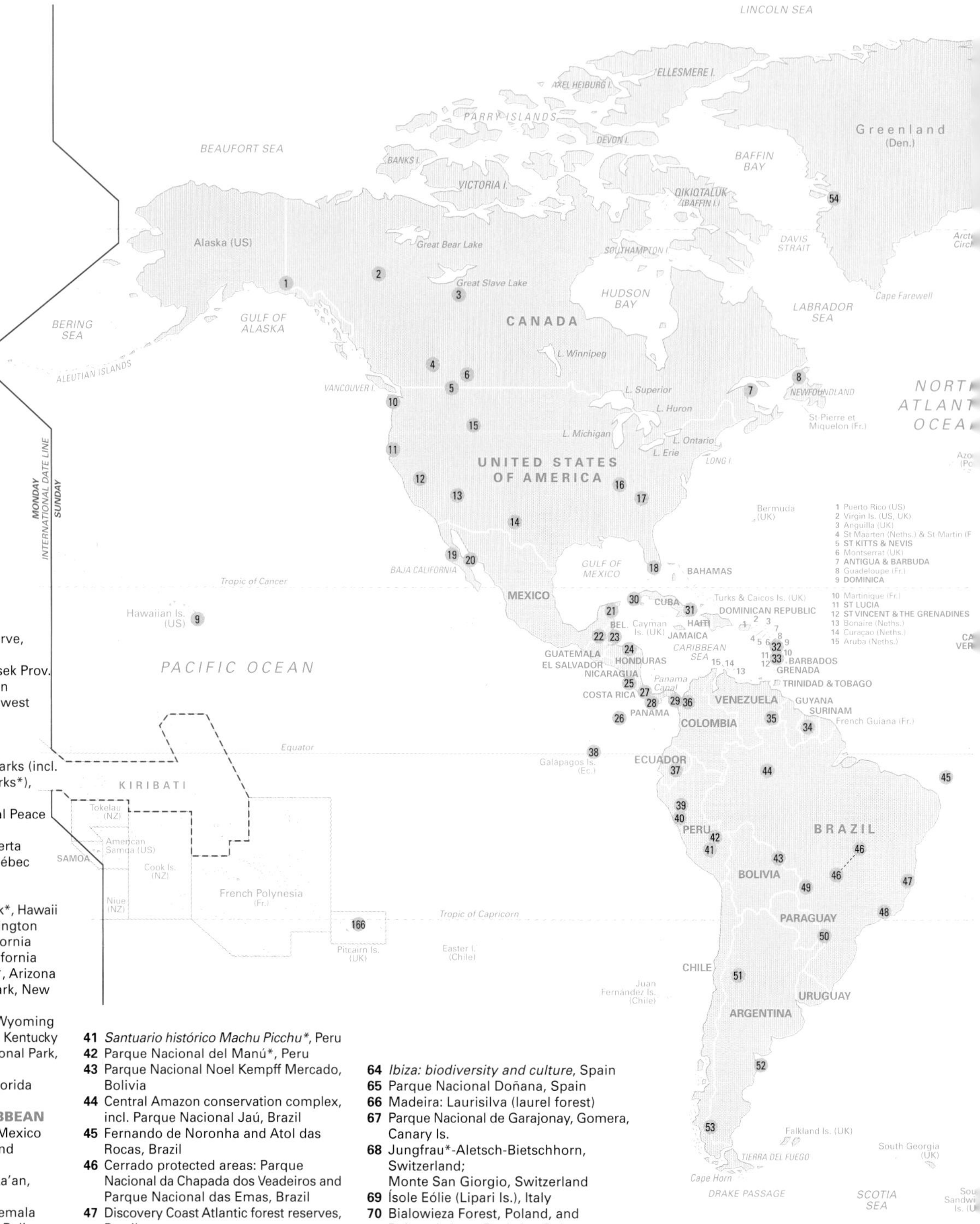

UNITED STATES & CANADA

1 Kluane Nat. Park & Reserve*, Glacier Bay Nat. Park & Preserve, Wrangell-St Elias Nat. Park & Preserve and Tatshenshini-Alsek Prov. Wilderness Park, Alaska/Yukon
2 Nahanni National Park, Northwest Territories
3 Wood Buffalo National Park, Northwest Territories/Alberta
4 Canadian Rocky Mountains Parks (incl. Banff and Jasper National Parks*), British Columbia/Alberta
5 Waterton-Glacier International Peace Park, Alberta/Montana
6 Dinosaur Provincial Park, Alberta
7 Miguasha Provincial Park, Québec
8 Gros Morne National Park, Newfoundland
9 Hawaii Volcanoes National Park*, Hawaii
10 Olympic National Park, Washington
11 Redwood National Park, California
12 Yosemite National Park*, California
13 Grand Canyon National Park*, Arizona
14 Carlsbad Caverns National Park, New Mexico
15 Yellowstone National Park*, Wyoming
16 Mammoth Cave National Park, Kentucky
17 Great Smoky Mountains National Park, Tennessee/North Carolina
18 **Everglades National Park***, Florida

LATIN AMERICA & THE CARIBBEAN

19 El Vizcaíno whale sanctuary, Mexico
20 Golfo de California: islands and protected areas, Mexico
21 Reserva de la Biósfera Sian Ka'an, Mexico
22 *Parque Nacional Tikal**, Guatemala
23 Barrier Reef Reserve System, Belize
24 **Reserva de la Biósfera Río Plátano**, Honduras
25 Area de Conservación Guanacaste, Costa Rica
26 Parque Nacional Isla del Coco, Costa Rica
27 Cordillera de Talamanca and Parque Internacional La Amistad, Costa Rica/Panama
28 Parque Nacional Coiba, Panama
29 Parque Nacional del Darién, Panama
30 Parque Nacional Desembarco del Granma, Cuba
31 Parque Nacional Alejandro de Humboldt, Cuba
32 Morne Trois Pitons National Park*, Dominica
33 Pitons Management Area, St Lucia
34 Central Surinam Nature Reserve, Surinam
35 Parque Nacional Canaima (including Salto Ángel (Angel Falls)*), Venezuela
36 Parque Nacional Los Katios, Colombia
37 Parque Nacional Sangay, Ecuador
38 Parque Nacional Galápagos*
39 *Parque Nacional Río Abiseo*, Peru
40 Parque Nacional Huascarán, Peru
41 *Santuario histórico Machu Picchu**, Peru
42 Parque Nacional del Manú*, Peru
43 Parque Nacional Noel Kempff Mercado, Bolivia
44 Central Amazon conservation complex, incl. Parque Nacional Jaú, Brazil
45 Fernando de Noronha and Atol das Rocas, Brazil
46 Cerrado protected areas: Parque Nacional da Chapada dos Veadeiros and Parque Nacional das Emas, Brazil
47 Discovery Coast Atlantic forest reserves, Brazil
48 Atlantic Forest Southeast reserves, Brazil
49 Pantanal conservation area, Brazil
50 Parque Nacional do Iguaçu*, Brazil; Parque Nacional de Iguazú*, Argentina
51 Ischigualasto & Talampaya Natural Parks, Argentina
52 Península Valdés, Argentina
53 Parque Nacional Los Glaciares*, Argentina

EUROPE (including Greenland, Atlantic islands, Turkey & Cyprus)

54 Ilulissat Icefjord, Greenland
55 Geirangerfjorden and Nærøyfjorden, Norway
56 High Coast, Sweden
57 *Lapponian area*, Sweden
58 *St Kilda*, Scotland
59 Giant's Causeway* and its coast, Northern Ireland
60 Dorset and East Devon coast, England
61 Messel Pit fossil site, Germany
62 Golfe de Girolata, Golfe de Porto, Piana Calanches and Réserve naturelle Scandola, Corsica, France
63 *Mont Perdu/Monte Perdido*, France/Spain
64 *Ibiza: biodiversity and culture*, Spain
65 Parque Nacional Doñana, Spain
66 Madeira: Laurisilva (laurel forest)
67 Parque Nacional de Garajonay, Gomera, Canary Is.
68 Jungfrau*-Aletsch-Bietschhorn, Switzerland;
Monte San Giorgio, Switzerland
69 Ísole Eólie (Lipari Is.), Italy
70 Bialowieza Forest, Poland, and Belovezhskaya Pushcha, Belarus
71 Aggtelek karst caves, Hungary, and Slovak karst caves*, Slovak Republic
72 Skocjan Caves, Slovenia
73 Plitvice Lakes National Park*, Croatia
74 Durmitor National Park, Serbia & Montenegro
75 *Ohrid and its region*, FYR of Macedonia
76 Danube Delta, Romania
77 Srebarna Nature Reserve, Bulgaria
78 Pirin National Park, Bulgaria
79 *Metéora: monasteries*, Greece
80 *Athos ('Holy Mountain')*, Greece
81 *Hierapolis-Pamukkale*, Turkey
82 *Göreme National Park* and Cappadocia rock sites*, Turkey

RUSSIAN FEDERATION

83 Western Caucasus mountain area
84 Komi virgin forests
85 Golden Mountains of Altay
86 Lake Baikal
87 Central Sikhote-Alin mountain range
88 Kamchatka volcanoes
89 Wrangel Island reserve

AFRICA

90 Wadi Al-Hitan (Whale Valley), Egypt
91 **Ichkeul National Park**, Tunisia
92 *Tassili n'Ajjer*, Algeria
93 *Bandiagara Cliffs: Land of the Dogons*, Mali
94 Banc d'Arguin National Park, Mauritania
95 **Parc national des Oiseaux du Djoudj (Djoudj Nat. Bird Sanctuary)**, Senegal
96 Parc national du Niokolo Koba, Senegal
97 **Mount Nimba Strict Nature Reserve**, Guinea/Côte d'Ivoire
98 Parc national de Taï, Côte d'Ivoire
99 **Parc national de la Comoé**, Côte d'Ivoire
100 Parc national du "W", Niger
101 **Aïr and Ténéré Natural Reserves**, Niger
102 **Simien Mountains National Park**, Ethiopia
103 **Parc national du Manovo-Gounda-St-Floris**, Central African Republic
104 Réserve du Dja, Cameroon
105 **Parc national de la Salonga**, Dem. Rep. of Congo
106 **Parc national de la Garamba**, Dem. Rep. of Congo
107 **Réserve du Okapi**, Dem. Rep. of Congo; **Parc national des Virunga**, Dem. Rep. of Congo

▶ See also... Europe National Parks (66); African Wildlife Parks (122-123); US National Parks Service (166-167); Canadian National Parks (175)

The listings above refer to a selection of related themes.
For more information, see the Contents (2-7).

A SLOVENIA
B CROATIA
C BOSNIA-HERZEGOVINA
D SERBIA & MONTENEGRO
E FORMER YUGOSLAV REPUBLIC OF MACEDONIA
ARCTIC OCEAN
Svalbard (Nor.)
FRANZ JOSEF LAND
SEVERNAYA ZEMLYA
GREENLAND SEA
BARENTS SEA
NOVAYA ZEMLYA
KARA SEA
LAPTEV SEA
NEW SIBERIAN IS.
EAST SIBERIAN SEA
WRANGEL I.
Jan Mayen (Nor.)
NORWEGIAN SEA
Faroe Is. (Den.)
SWEDEN
NORWAY
FINLAND
L. Ladoga
RUSSIAN FEDERATION
UNITED KINGDOM
ESTONIA
LATVIA
NORTH SEA
DENMARK
LITHUANIA
IRELAND
NETHS.
GERMANY
POLAND
BELARUS
BELG.
LUX.
CZECH REP.
SLOVAK REP.
UKRAINE
CHANNEL IS.
FRANCE
AUSTRIA
HUNGARY
MOLDOVA
SWITZ.
ROMANIA
ANDORRA
CORSICA
ITALY
BULG.
BLACK SEA
CASPIAN SEA
GEORGIA
AZER-BAIJAN
ARMENIA
PORTUGAL
SPAIN
SARDINIA
ALB.
GREECE
TURKEY
SICILY
MALTA
CYPRUS
SYRIA
TUNISIA
MEDITERRANEAN SEA
LEBANON
ISRAEL
PALESTINE
JORDAN
Suez Canal
IRAQ
IRAN
MOROCCO
ALGERIA
LIBYA
EGYPT
KUWAIT
THE GULF
SAUDI ARABIA
UAE
QATAR
BAHRAIN
OMAN
RED SEA
ARABIAN SEA
YEMEN
Socotra (Yem.)
KAZAKHSTAN
L. Balkhash
Aral Sea
UZBEKISTAN
TURKMENISTAN
KYRGYZSTAN
TAJIKISTAN
AFGHANISTAN
PAKISTAN
NEPAL
BHUTAN
BANGLADESH
INDIA
MONGOLIA
L. Baikal
CHINA
DEMOCRATIC PEOPLE'S REP. OF KOREA
REP. OF KOREA
SEA OF JAPAN
JAPAN
HOKKAIDO
HONSHU
SHIKOKU
KYUSHU
SAKHALIN
KURIL ISLANDS
KAMCHATKA
SEA OF OKHOTSK
EAST CHINA SEA
RYUKYU IS.
TAIWAN
PACIFIC OCEAN
MYANMAR (BURMA)
LAOS
HAINAN
THAILAND
VIETNAM
CAMBODIA
BAY OF BENGAL
SOUTH CHINA SEA
LUZON
PHILIPPINES
PHILIPPINE SEA
VISAYAN IS.
MINDANAO
Northern Mariana Is. (US)
Guam (US)
MARSHALL IS.
MONDAY
SUNDAY
INTERNATIONAL DATE LINE
ANDAMAN & NICOBAR IS.
LAKSHADWEEP
SRI LANKA
MALDIVES
MALAYSIA
BRUNEI
BORNEO
SINGAPORE
SUMATRA
SULAWESI
PALAU
FED. STATES OF MICRONESIA
PAPUA NEW GUINEA
NEW GUINEA
NAURU
KIRIBATI
JAVA
INDONESIA
EAST TIMOR
SOLOMON IS.
TUVALU
Wallis & Futuna (Fr.)
Cocos Is. (Aust.)
Christmas I. (Aust.)
British Indian Ocean Territory (UK)
SEYCHELLES
COMOROS
Mayotte (Fr.)
MADAGASCAR
MAURITIUS
Reunion (Fr.)
INDIAN OCEAN
CORAL SEA
VANUATU
TONGA
FIJI IS.
New Caledonia (Fr.)
AUSTRALIA
Kermadec Is. (NZ)
Norfolk I. (Aust.)
Lord Howe I. (Aust.)
GREAT AUSTRALIAN BIGHT
TASMAN SEA
NORTH I.
SOUTH I.
NEW ZEALAND
Chatham Is. (NZ)
TASMANIA
MAURITANIA
MALI
NIGER
CHAD
SUDAN
ERITREA
DJIBOUTI
ETHIOPIA
SOMALIA
BURKINA
BENIN
NIGERIA
GUINEA
CÔTE D'IVOIRE
GHANA
TOGO
CENT. AFRICAN REPUBLIC
CAMEROON
CONGO
GABON
UGANDA
KENYA
RW.
BUR.
L. Victoria
DEMOCRATIC REPUBLIC OF CONGO
TANZANIA
EQUATORIAL GUINEA
SÃO TOMÉ & PRINCIPE
Cabinda (Ang.)
ANGOLA
ZAMBIA
MALAWI
MOZAMBIQUE
ZIMBABWE
NAMIBIA
BOTSWANA
SWAZILAND
LESOTHO
SOUTH AFRICA
Cape of Good Hope
St Helena (UK)
SOUTH ATLANTIC OCEAN
Tristan da Cunha (UK)
Gough I. (UK)
Prince Edward Is. (S. Af.)
Crozet Is. (Fr.)
Îles Amsterdam & St Paul (Fr.)
Kerguelen Is. (Fr.)
Heard & McDonald Is. (Aust.)
Bouvet I. (Nor.)
Macquarie I. (Aust.)
SOUTHERN OCEAN

108 Parc national du Kahuzi-Biega, Dem. Rep. of Congo
109 Ruwenzori Mountains National Park, Uganda; Bwindi Impenetrable National Park*, Uganda
110 Lake Turkana national parks, Kenya
111 Mount Kenya National Park* and Natural Forest, Kenya
112 Serengeti National Park*, Tanzania
113 Ngorongoro Conservation Area, Tanzania; Kilimanjaro National Park*, Tanzania
114 Selous Game Reserve, Tanzania
115 Lake Malawi National Park*, Malawi
116 Mana Pools National Park and Sapi & Chewore safari areas, Zimbabwe
117 Mosi-oa-Tunya (Victoria Falls)*, Zambia/Zimbabwe
118 Greater St Lucia Wetland Park, South Africa
119 *uKhahlamba-Drakensberg Park*, South Africa
120 Vredefort Dome, South Africa
121 Cape floral region protected areas (incl. Cape Point* and Table Mountain*), South Africa
122 Réserve naturelle de Tsingy de Bemaraha, Madagascar
123 Groupe d'Aldabra, Seychelles
124 Vallée de Mai Nature Reserve, Seychelles
125 Gough and Inaccessible Islands

ASIA

126 Arabian Oryx Sanctuary, Oman
127 Nanda Devi and Valley of Flowers National Parks, India
128 Keoladeo National Park, India
129 **Manas Wildlife Sanctuary**, India
130 Kaziranga National Park*, India
131 Sundarbans National Park, India; Sundarbans, Bangladesh
132 Sinharaja Forest Reserve, Sri Lanka
133 Royal Chitwan National Park, Nepal
134 Sagarmatha National Park, Nepal
135 Uvs Nuur basin, Mongolia/Russian Fed.
136 Three parallel rivers of Yunnan protected area (upper reaches of the Yangtze, Mekong and Salween), China
137 *Emei Shan and Leshan Giant Buddha*, Sichuan, China
138 Jiuzhaigou Valley Scenic and Historic Interest Area, Sichuan, China; Huanglong Scenic and Historic Interest Area, Sichuan, China
139 Wulingyuan Scenic and Historic Interest Area, Hunan, China
140 *Wuyi Shan*, Fujian, China
141 *Huang Shan*, Anhui, China
142 *Tai Shan*, Shandong, China
143 Yaku-shima, Japan
144 Shirakami-sanchi, Japan
145 Shiretoko, Japan
146 Halong Bay, Vietnam
147 Phong Nha - Ke Bang National Park, Vietnam
148 Dong Phayayen - Khao Yai Forest Complex, Thailand
149 Thung Yai - Huai Kha Khaeng Wildlife Sanctuaries, Thailand
150 Gunung Mulu National Park, Malaysia
151 Kinabalu Park, Malaysia
152 Puerto-Princesa Subterranean River National Park, the Philippines
153 Tubbataha Reef Marine Park, the Philippines
154 Tropical rainforest heritage of Sumatra, Indonesia
155 Ujung Kulon National Park and Krakatau Natural Reserve, Indonesia
156 Komodo National Park, Indonesia
157 Lorentz National Park, Indonesia

AUSTRALASIA & OCEANIA

158 Shark Bay, Australia
159 Purnululu National Park, Australia
160 *Kakadu National Park**, Australia
161 Queensland wet tropics, Australia
162 Central eastern rainforest reserves, Australia
163 Great Barrier Reef*, Australia
164 *Uluru - Kata Tjuta National Park**, Australia
165 Naracoorte & Riversleigh: fossil mammal sites, Australia
166 *Willandra Lakes region*, Australia
167 Greater Blue Mountains area, Australia
168 Fraser Island*, Australia
169 *Tasmanian wilderness*, Australia
170 Lord Howe island group, Australia
171 Heard and McDonald Islands
172 Macquarie Island
173 New Zealand sub-antarctic islands
174 Southwest New Zealand parks (Fiordland*, Aoraki/Mount Cook*, Tai Poutini/Westland and Mount Aspiring National Parks)
175 *Tongariro National Park**, New Zealand
176 East Rennell coral atoll, Solomon Islands
177 Henderson Island, Pitcairn Islands

▶ *See also...* Asia Historical (128); Asia Museums & Galleries (129); North America History (156-157); USA & Canada Museums & Galleries (159); • *cont >*

The listings above refer to a selection of related themes. For more information, see the Contents (2-7).

The UNESCO World Heritage List consists of sites considered to be of global importance either because of their natural heritage or their significant man-made contribution to world culture. Countries which are signatories to the World Heritage Convention can submit potential sites to UNESCO, which considers each proposal under strict criteria and lists each site where one or more natural or cultural criteria have been met. Some sites satisfy both natural and cultural criteria; these appear on both maps.

The cultural sites are either:
(a) monuments (architectural works, works of monumental sculpture and painting or archaeological sites; or
(b) groups of buildings which are of outstanding universal value from the point of view of history, art or science; or
(c) works of man or the combined works of nature and man which are of outstanding universal value.

Properties named in red are included on the list of World Heritage in Danger. Those shown in italics are joint natural and cultural sites. Sites marked with an asterisk are featured in Columbus Travel Guides' 'Tourist Attractions and Events of the World'

The Organisation of World Heritage Cities (OWHC) was established in 1993 with the aim of assisting member cities adapt and improve their management methods in relation to the specific requirements of having a site inscribed on the UNESCO World Heritage List.

World Heritage Cities are named on the map.

For further information on Heritage Sites and Heritage Cities, see whc.unesco.org and www.ovpm.org

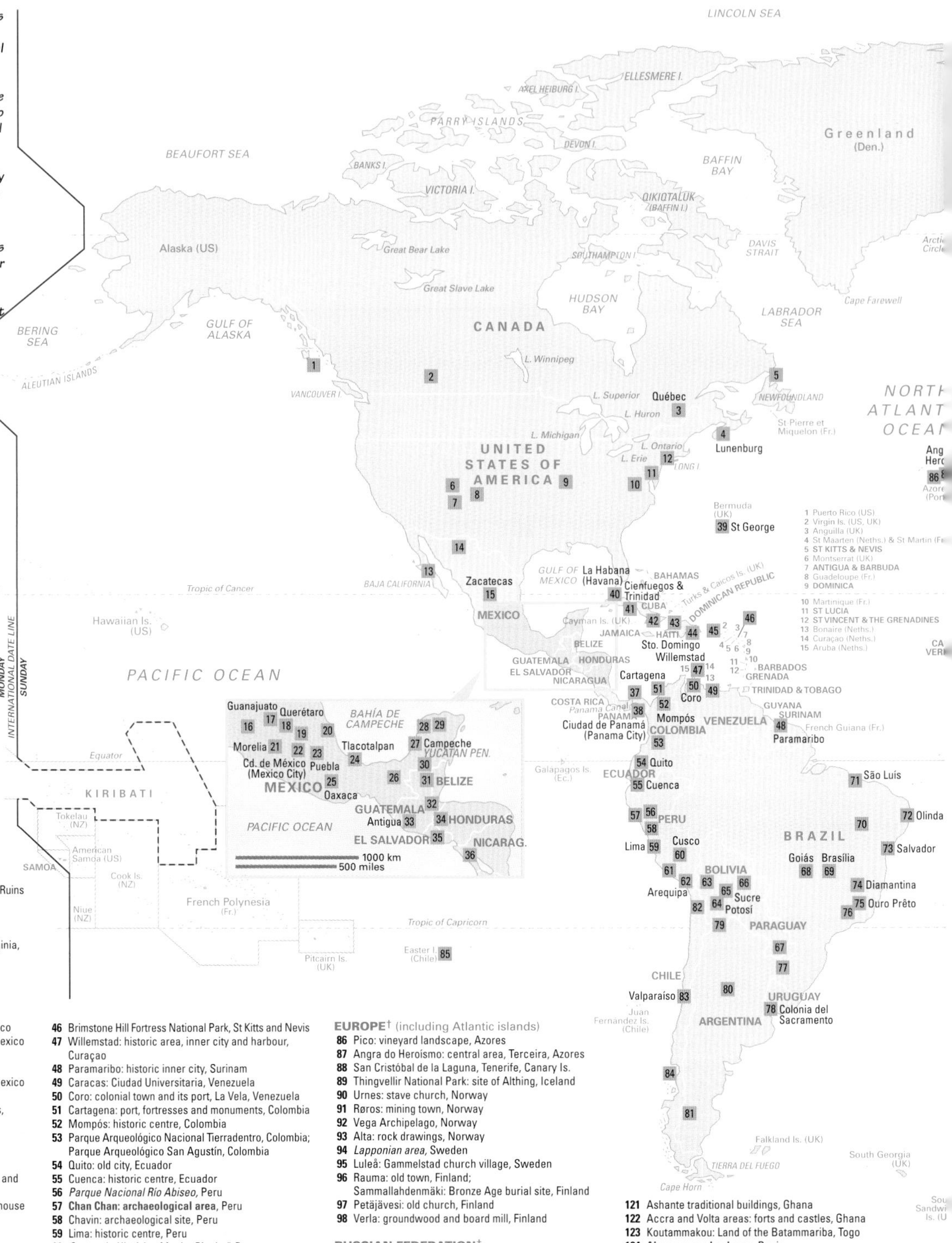

UNITED STATES & CANADA

1 Anthony Island, British Columbia
2 Head-Smashed-In Buffalo Jump, Alberta
3 Québec: historic district*
4 Lunenburg: old town, Nova Scotia
5 L'Anse aux Meadows National Historic Site, Newfoundland
6 Mesa Verde: Pueblo Indian dwellings, Colorado
7 Chaco Culture National Historical Park and Aztec Ruins National Monument, New Mexico
8 Pueblo de Taos: adobe settlement, New Mexico
9 Cahokia Mounds State Historic Site, Illinois
10 Charlottesville: Monticello and University of Virginia, Virginia
11 Philadelphia: Independence Hall, Pennsylvania
12 Statue of Liberty*, New York

LATIN AMERICA & THE CARIBBEAN

13 Sierra de la San Francisco: rock paintings, Mexico
14 Paquimé, Casas Grandes: archaeological site, Mexico
15 Zacatecas: historic centre, Mexico
16 Guadalajara: Hospicio Cabañas, Mexico
17 Guanajuato: historic town and adjacent mines, Mexico
18 Querétaro: historic monuments, Mexico; Sierra Gorda de Querétaro: Franciscan missions, Mexico
19 Teotihuacán: pre-Hispanic city*, Mexico
20 El Tajín: pre-Hispanic city, Mexico
21 Morelia: historic centre, Mexico
22 Ciudad de México (Mexico City): historic centre and Xochimilco, Mexico; Ciudad de México (Mexico City): Luis Barragán house and studio, Mexico; Xochicalco: archaeological site, Mexico
23 Popocatépetl: missionary monasteries, Mexico; Puebla: historic centre, Mexico
24 Tlacotalpán: historic monuments, Mexico
25 Monte Albán: archaeological site*, and Oaxaca: historic centre, Mexico
26 Palenque: ancient Maya city and national park*, Mexico
27 Campeche: historic fortified town, Mexico
28 Uxmal: ancient Maya city, Mexico
29 Chichén-Itzá: ancient Maya city*, Mexico
30 Calakmul: ancient Maya city, Mexico
31 *Parque Nacional Tikal**, Guatemala
32 Quiriguá: archaeological park, Guatemala
33 Antigua, Guatemala
34 Copán: Maya site, Honduras
35 Joya de Cerén: archaeological site, El Salvador
36 León Viejo: Spanish colonial ruins, Nicaragua
37 Portobelo and San Lorenzo: fortifications, Panama
38 Ciudad de Panamá (Panama City): historic district and Panamá Viejo, Panama
39 St George: historic town and related fortifications, Bermuda
40 Viñales valley, Cuba; La Habana (Havana): old town and fortifications*, Cuba
41 Trinidad and Valley de los Ingenios, Cuba; Cienfuegos: historic centre, Cuba
42 Santiago de Cuba: San Pedro de la Roca castle, Cuba; First coffee plantations in southeast Cuba: archaeological landscape
43 La Citadelle, Sans Souci and Ramiers, Haiti
44 Santo Domingo: colonial city, Dominican Rep.
45 La Fortaleza and San Juan: defensive structures, Puerto Rico
46 Brimstone Hill Fortress National Park, St Kitts and Nevis
47 Willemstad: historic area, inner city and harbour, Curaçao
48 Paramaribo: historic inner city, Surinam
49 Caracas: Ciudad Universitaria, Venezuela
50 Coro: colonial town and its port, La Vela, Venezuela
51 Cartagena: port, fortresses and monuments, Colombia
52 Mompós: historic centre, Colombia
53 Parque Arqueológico Nacional Tierradentro, Colombia; Parque Arqueológico San Agustín, Colombia
54 Quito: old city, Ecuador
55 Cuenca: historic centre, Ecuador
56 *Parque Nacional Río Abiseo*, Peru
57 **Chan Chan: archaeological area**, Peru
58 Chavin: archaeological site, Peru
59 Lima: historic centre, Peru
60 *Santuario Histórico Machu Picchu**, Peru; Cusco: old city, Peru
61 Nasca: geoglyphs and Pampas de Jumana, Peru
62 Arequipa: historic centre, Peru
63 Tiwanaku: pre-Hispanic city, Bolivia
64 Potosí, Bolivia
65 Sucre: historic city, Bolivia
66 El Fuerte de Samaipata: archaeological site, Bolivia; Chiquitos Jesuit missions, Bolivia
67 Jesús de Tavarangue and La Santisima Trinidad de Paraná: Jesuit missions, Paraguay
68 Goiás: historic centre, Brazil
69 Brasília, Brazil
70 Parque Nacional da Serra da Capivara, Brazil
71 São Luís: historic centre, Brazil
72 Olinda: historic centre, Brazil
73 Salvador de Bahia: historic centre, Brazil
74 Diamantina: historic centre, Brazil
75 Ouro Prêto: historic town, Brazil
76 Congonhas: Sanctuary of Bom Jesus, Brazil
77 São Miguel: Jesuit mission ruins, Brazil; Loreto, San Ignacio Miní, Santa Ana & Santa Maria Mayor: Guaraní Jesuit missions, Argentina
78 Colonia del Sacramento: historic quarter, Uruguay
79 Córdoba: Jesuit Block and estancias, Argentina
80 Quebrada de Humahuaca: Camino Inca cultural route, Argentina
81 Cueva de las Manos, Rio Pinturas, Argentina
82 **Humberstone and Santa Laura: saltpeter works**, Chile
83 Valparaíso: historic quarter, Chile
84 Chiloé: wooden churches, Chile
85 Parque Nacional Rapa Nui*, Easter Island

EUROPE† (including Atlantic islands)

86 Pico: vineyard landscape, Azores
87 Angra do Heroísmo: central area, Terceira, Azores
88 San Cristóbal de la Laguna, Tenerife, Canary Is.
89 Thingvellir National Park: site of Althing, Iceland
90 Urnes: stave church, Norway
91 Røros: mining town, Norway
92 Vega Archipelago, Norway
93 Alta: rock drawings, Norway
94 *Lapponian area*, Sweden
95 Luleå: Gammelstad church village, Sweden
96 Rauma: old town, Finland; Sammallahdenmäki: Bronze Age burial site, Finland
97 Petäjävesi: old church, Finland
98 Verla: groundwood and board mill, Finland

RUSSIAN FEDERATION†

99 Solovetskiye Ostrova: cultural and historic ensemble
100 Kizhi Pogost: wooden churches and clock tower
101 Kazan: Kremlin
102 Derbent: citadel, ancient city and fortress

AFRICA†

103 St Catherine (Jebel Musa) area, Egypt
104 Thebes: ancient city and necropolis (incl. Hatshepsut's Temple*, Karnak*, Luxor, Valley of the Kings*, Valley of the Queens*), Egypt
105 Abu Simbel* to Philae: Nubian monuments, Egypt
106 Gebel Barkal: archaeological sites, Sudan
107 Aksum: archaeological site, Ethiopia; Fasil Ghebbi: fortress-city, Ethiopia
108 Lalibela: rock-hewn churches, Ethiopia
109 Awash lower valley, Ethiopia
110 Tiya: carved steles, Ethiopia; Omo lower valley, Ethiopia
111 Tadrart Acacus: rock-art sites, Libya
112 Tassili n'Ajjer, Algeria
113 Chinguetti, Ouadane, Oualata and Tichitt: trading and religious centres, Mauritania
114 Gao: tomb of Askia, Mali
115 Tombouctou (Timbuktu), Mali
116 *Bandiagara Cliffs: Land of the Dogons*, Mali
117 Djenné: trading and religious centre (incl. Grand Mosque*), Mali
118 Île de St-Louis, Senegal
119 Île de Gorée: slave-trading centre, Senegal
120 James Island and related sites, Gambia
121 Ashante traditional buildings, Ghana
122 Accra and Volta areas: forts and castles, Ghana
123 Koutammakou: Land of the Batammariba, Togo
124 **Abomey: royal palaces**, Benin
125 Oshogbo: Osun sacred grove, Nigeria
126 Sukur: cultural landscape, Nigeria
127 Kasubi: tombs of Buganda kings, Uganda
128 Lamu: old town, Kenya
129 Zanzibar: stone town*, Tanzania
130 **Kilwa Kisiwani and Songo Mnara: port ruins**, Tanzania
131 Ilha de Moçambique, Mozambique
132 Great Zimbabwe National Monument*, Zimbabwe
133 Khami Ruins National Monument, Zimbabwe; Matobo Hills: rock paintings, Zimbabwe
134 Tsodilo rock paintings ('Louvre of the Desert'), Botswana
135 Mapungubwe: cultural landscape, South Africa
136 Sterkfontein, Swartkrans, Kromdraai and environs: fossil hominid sites, South Africa
137 *uKhahlamba-Drakensberg Park*, South Africa
138 Robben Island*, South Africa
139 Ambohimanga: Royal Hill, Madagascar

ASIA†

140 **Zabid: historic town**, Yemen
141 Sana'a (Sana): old city*, Yemen
142 Shibam: old walled city, Yemen
143 The Frankincense Trail, Oman
144 Bahla: fort, Oman
145 Bat, Al-Khutm and Al-Ayn: archaeological sites, Oman
146 Qal'at al-Bahrain: archaeological site*, Bahrain
147 **Bam and its cultural landscape**, Iran
148 Persepolis: ancient city*, Iran; Pasargadae: ancient city, Iran
149 Esfahan (Isfahan): Meidan Emam*, Iran

See also… • cont < US National Parks Service (166-167); Latin America Historical/Museums & Galleries (187); World Monuments Fund (198)

The listings above refer to a selection of related themes. For more information, see the Contents (2-7).

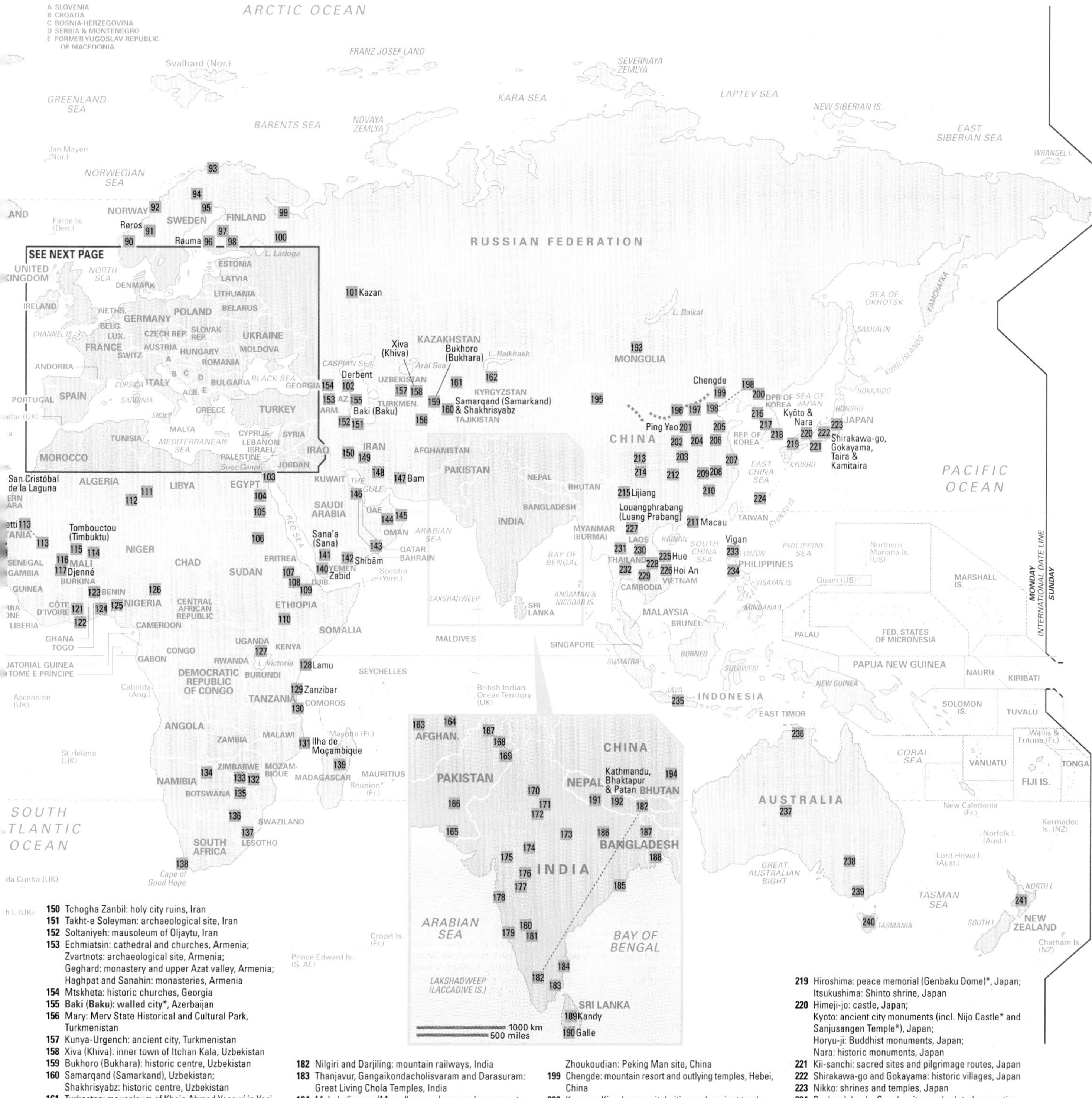
A SLOVENIA
B CROATIA
C BOSNIA-HERZEGOVINA
D SERBIA & MONTENEGRO
E FORMER YUGOSLAV REPUBLIC OF MACEDONIA
ARCTIC OCEAN
FRANZ JOSEF LAND
SEVERNAYA ZEMLYA
Svalbard (Nor.)
GREENLAND SEA
KARA SEA
LAPTEV SEA
NEW SIBERIAN IS.
EAST SIBERIAN SEA
BARENTS SEA
NOVAYA ZEMLYA
WRANGEL I.
Jan Mayen (Nor.)
NORWEGIAN SEA
NORWAY
Røros
SWEDEN
FINLAND
Rauma
RUSSIAN FEDERATION
SEE NEXT PAGE
UNITED KINGDOM
NORTH SEA
DENMARK
ESTONIA
LATVIA
LITHUANIA
L. Ladoga
IRELAND
NETHS.
GERMANY
POLAND
BELARUS
BELG.
LUX.
CZECH REP.
SLOVAK REP.
UKRAINE
FRANCE
SWITZ.
AUSTRIA
HUNGARY
MOLDOVA
ROMANIA
ANDORRA
CORSICA
ITALY
BULGARIA
BLACK SEA
GEORGIA
PORTUGAL
SPAIN
SARDINIA
ALB.
GREECE
TURKEY
SICILY
MALTA
CYPRUS
SYRIA
TUNISIA
MEDITERRANEAN SEA
LEBANON
ISRAEL
IRAQ
PALESTINE
JORDAN
Suez Canal
MOROCCO
101 Kazan
KAZAKHSTAN
Xiva (Khiva)
Bukhoro (Bukhara)
L. Balkhash
Aral Sea
CASPIAN SEA
Derbent
UZBEKISTAN
KYRGYZSTAN
TURKMEN.
Samarqand (Samarkand) & Shakhrisyabz
TAJIKISTAN
Baki (Baku)
AZ.
ARM.
IRAN
AFGHANISTAN
PAKISTAN
NEPAL
BHUTAN
BANGLADESH
INDIA
MONGOLIA
L. Baikal
SEA OF OKHOTSK
KAMCHATKA
SAKHALIN
KURIL ISLANDS
HOKKAIDO
Chengde
DPR OF KOREA
SEA OF JAPAN
HONSHU
JAPAN
Kyōto & Nara
Ping Yao
CHINA
REP. OF KOREA
Shirakawa-go, Gokayama, Taira & Kamitaira
KYUSHU
EAST CHINA SEA
PACIFIC OCEAN
San Cristóbal de la Laguna
ALGERIA
LIBYA
EGYPT
KUWAIT
THE GULF
147 Bam
SAUDI ARABIA
UAE
OMAN
ARABIAN SEA
Sana'a (Sana)
QATAR
BAHRAIN
142 Shibām
Zabid
YEMEN
Socotra (Yem.)
RED SEA
Tombouctou (Timbuktu)
NIGER
MALI
Djenné
BURKINA
SENEGAL
GAMBIA
GUINEA
CHAD
SUDAN
ERITREA
DJIB.
BENIN
NIGERIA
CÔTE D'IVOIRE
LIBERIA
GHANA
TOGO
CAMEROON
CENTRAL AFRICAN REPUBLIC
ETHIOPIA
SOMALIA
UGANDA
KENYA
CONGO
GABON
RWANDA
L. Victoria
128 Lamu
BURUNDI
DEMOCRATIC REPUBLIC OF CONGO
SEYCHELLES
MALDIVES
129 Zanzibar
TANZANIA
COMOROS
Cabinda (Ang.)
Ascension (UK)
ANGOLA
ZAMBIA
MALAWI
Mayotte (Fr.)
131 Ilha de Moçambique
St Helena (UK)
ZIMBABWE
MOZAMBIQUE
MADAGASCAR
MAURITIUS
Réunion (Fr.)
NAMIBIA
BOTSWANA
SWAZILAND
SOUTH ATLANTIC OCEAN
SOUTH AFRICA
LESOTHO
Cape of Good Hope
Tristan da Cunha (UK)
Prince Edward Is. (S. Af.)
Crozet Is. (Fr.)
British Indian Ocean Territory (UK)
LAKSHADWEEP
SRI LANKA
BAY OF BENGAL
ANDAMAN & NICOBAR IS.
SINGAPORE
MYANMAR (BURMA)
215 Lijiang
Louangphrabang (Luang Prabang)
211 Macau
TAIWAN
RYUKYUS
LAOS
HAINAN
SOUTH CHINA SEA
Vigan
LUZON
THAILAND
225 Hue
226 Hoi An
VIETNAM
CAMBODIA
PHILIPPINES
PHILIPPINE SEA
VISAYAN IS.
Northern Mariana Is. (US)
Guam (US)
MARSHALL IS.
MALAYSIA
BRUNEI
MINDANAO
PALAU
FED. STATES OF MICRONESIA
SUMATRA
BORNEO
SULAWESI
PAPUA NEW GUINEA
NEW GUINEA
NAURU
KIRIBATI
JAVA
INDONESIA
EAST TIMOR
SOLOMON IS.
TUVALU
Wallis & Futuna (Fr.)
CORAL SEA
VANUATU
TONGA
FIJI IS.
AUSTRALIA
New Caledonia (Fr.)
Norfolk I. (Aust.)
Kermadec Is. (NZ)
Lord Howe I. (Aust.)
GREAT AUSTRALIAN BIGHT
TASMAN SEA
NORTH I.
SOUTH I.
NEW ZEALAND
TASMANIA
Chatham Is. (NZ)
MONDAY
SUNDAY
INTERNATIONAL DATE LINE
AFGHAN.
PAKISTAN
CHINA
NEPAL
Kathmandu, Bhaktapur & Patan
BHUTAN
BANGLADESH
INDIA
ARABIAN SEA
BAY OF BENGAL
LAKSHADWEEP (LACCADIVE IS.)
SRI LANKA
189 Kandy
190 Galle
1000 km
500 miles

150 Tchogha Zanbil: holy city ruins, Iran
151 Takht-e Soleyman: archaeological site, Iran
152 Soltaniyeh: mausoleum of Oljaytu, Iran
153 Echmiatsin: cathedral and churches, Armenia;
Zvartnots: archaeological site, Armenia;
Geghard: monastery and upper Azat valley, Armenia;
Haghpat and Sanahin: monasteries, Armenia
154 Mtskheta: historic churches, Georgia
155 **Baki (Baku): walled city***, Azerbaijan
156 Mary: Merv State Historical and Cultural Park, Turkmenistan
157 Kunya-Urgench: ancient city, Turkmenistan
158 Xiva (Khiva): inner town of Itchan Kala, Uzbekistan
159 Bukhoro (Bukhara): historic centre, Uzbekistan
160 Samarqand (Samarkand), Uzbekistan;
Shakhrisyabz: historic centre, Uzbekistan
161 Turkestan: mausoleum of Khoja Ahmed Yasawi in Yasi, Kazakhstan
162 Tamgaly Gorge: rock carvings, Kazakhstan
163 **Jam: minaret and archaeological remains**, Afghanistan
164 **Bamiyan valley: cultural landscape and archaeological remains**, Afghanistan
165 Thatta: historical monuments, Pakistan
166 Moenjodaro: archaeological site, Pakistan
167 Takht-i-Bahi: Buddhist monastic complex, and Sahr-i-Bahlol: fortified city ruins, Pakistan;
Taxila: archaeological site, Pakistan
168 Rohtas: fort, Pakistan
169 **Lahore: fort and Shalamar gardens**, Pakistan
170 Delhi: Humayun's tomb, India;
Delhi: Qutb Minar and its monuments, India
171 Agra: Red Fort*, India;
Agra: Taj Mahal*, Agra, India
172 Fatehpur Sikri: Mughal city, India
173 Khajuraho: group of temples*, India
174 Sanchi: Buddhist monuments, India;
Bhimbetka: rock shelters, India
175 Champaner-Pavagadh: archaeological site, India
176 Ajanta Caves, India
177 Ellora Caves*, India
178 Mumbai (Bombay): Chhatrapati Shivaji (Victoria) Terminus Station, India;
Elephanta Caves, India
179 Goa: churches and convents, India
180 Pattadakal: group of monuments, India
181 **Hampi: group of monuments**, India
182 Nilgiri and Darjiling: mountain railways, India
183 Thanjavur, Gangaikondacholisvaram and Darasuram: Great Living Chola Temples, India
184 Mahabalipuram (Mamallapuram): group of monuments, India
185 Konarak: Sun Temple, India
186 Bodhgaya: Mahabodi Temple complex, India
187 Paharpur: ruins of the Buddhist Vihara, Bangladesh
188 Bagerhat: historic city, Bangladesh
189 Anuradhapura: sacred city, Sri Lanka;
Sigiriya: ancient city*, Sri Lanka;
Polonnaruwa: ancient city, Sri Lanka;
Dambulla Golden Temple, Sri Lanka;
Kandy: sacred city (incl. Temple of the Sacred Tooth*), Sri Lanka
190 Galle: old town and its fortifications, Sri Lanka
191 Lumbini: birthplace of Lord Buddha, Nepal
192 **Kathmandu valley** (incl. Kathmandu Durban Square*), Nepal
193 Orkhon valley: cultural landscape, including site of Karakorum, Mongolia
194 Lhasa: Potala Palace*, Norbulinka Summer Palace and Jokhang Monastery, Tibet, China
195 Mogao Caves, Dunhuang, Gansu, China
196 Great Wall of China*
197 Yungang Caves, Shanxi, China
198 Beijing (Peking) and Shenyang: imperial palaces of the Ming and Qing dynasties (incl. Forbidden City*), China;
Beijing (Peking): Summer Palace*, China;
Beijing (Peking): Temple of Heaven, China;
Beijing (Peking) and Liaoning Province: imperial tombs of the Ming and Qing dynasties, China;
Zhoukoudian: Peking Man site, China
199 Chengde: mountain resort and outlying temples, Hebei, China
200 Koguryo Kingdom: capital cities and ancient tombs, China
201 Ping Yao: ancient city, Shanxi, China
202 Xi'an area: mausoleum of Qin Shihuangdi (Terracotta Army)*, Shaanxi, China
203 Wudang Shan: ancient building complex, Hubei, China
204 Longmen Caves, Henan, China
205 *Tai Shan,* Shandong, China
206 Qufu: temple & cemetery of Confucius and Kong family mansion, Shandong, China
207 Suzhou: classical gardens, Jiangsu, China
208 Hongcun and Xidi: ancient villages, Anhui, China;
Huang Shan, Anhui, China
209 Lu Shan National Park, Jiangxi, China
210 *Wuyi Shan,* Fujian, China
211 Macau (Aomen): historic centre, China
212 Dazu: rock carvings, Chongqing, China
213 Qincheng Shan and Dujiangyan irrigation system, Sichuan, China
214 *Emei Shan and Leshan giant buddha,* Sichuan, China
215 Lijiang: old town, Yunnan, China
216 Koguryo Kingdom: tomb complex, DPR of Korea
217 Hwasun, Ganghwa and Gochang: Megalithic cemeteries, Rep. of Korea;
Seoul: Changdeokgung Palace complex, Rep. of Korea;
Seoul: Jongmyo Shrine, Rep. of Korea;
Suwon: Hwaseong Fortress, Rep. of Korea
218 Haeinsa Temple*, Rep. of Korea;
Gyeongju: historic areas*, Rep. of Korea;
Seokguram Grotto and Bulguksa Temple, Rep. of Korea
219 Hiroshima: peace memorial (Genbaku Dome)*, Japan;
Itsukushima: Shinto shrine, Japan
220 Himeji-jo: castle, Japan;
Kyoto: ancient city monuments (incl. Nijo Castle* and Sanjusangen Temple*), Japan;
Horyu-ji: Buddhist monuments, Japan;
Nara: historic monuments, Japan
221 Kii-sanchi: sacred sites and pilgrimage routes, Japan
222 Shirakawa-go and Gokayama: historic villages, Japan
223 Nikko: shrines and temples, Japan
224 Ryukyu Islands: Gusuku sites and related properties, Japan
225 Hue: monuments complex (incl. Imperial Palace*), Vietnam
226 Hoi An: ancient town, Vietnam;
My Son: Hindu sanctuary, Vietnam
227 Louangphrabang (Luang Prabang), Laos
228 Champasak: cultural landscape, including Vat Phou Temple complex, Laos
229 Angkor: Khmer capital cities*, Cambodia
230 Ban Chiang: archaeological site, Thailand
231 Sukhothai and its region: historic towns, Thailand
232 Ayutthaya and its region: historic towns, Thailand
233 Vigan: historic town, the Philippines;
Banaue rice terraces*, the Philippines
234 Manila, Santa Maria, Paoay and Miag-ao: Baroque churches, the Philippines
235 Borobodur: temple compounds, Indonesia;
Prambanan: temple compounds*, Indonesia;
Sangiran: early man site, Indonesia

AUSTRALASIA & OCEANIA

236 *Kakadu National Park*,* Australia
237 *Uluru - Kata Tjuta National Park*,* Australia
238 *Willandra Lakes region,* Australia
239 Melbourne: Royal Exhibition Building and Carlton Gardens, Australia
240 *Tasmanian wilderness,* Australia
241 *Tongariro National Park*,* New Zealand

†See next page for other sites in these areas

See also... Europe Historical (58-59); Europe Museums & Galleries (68)

The listings above refer to a selection of related themes. For more information, see the Contents (2-7).

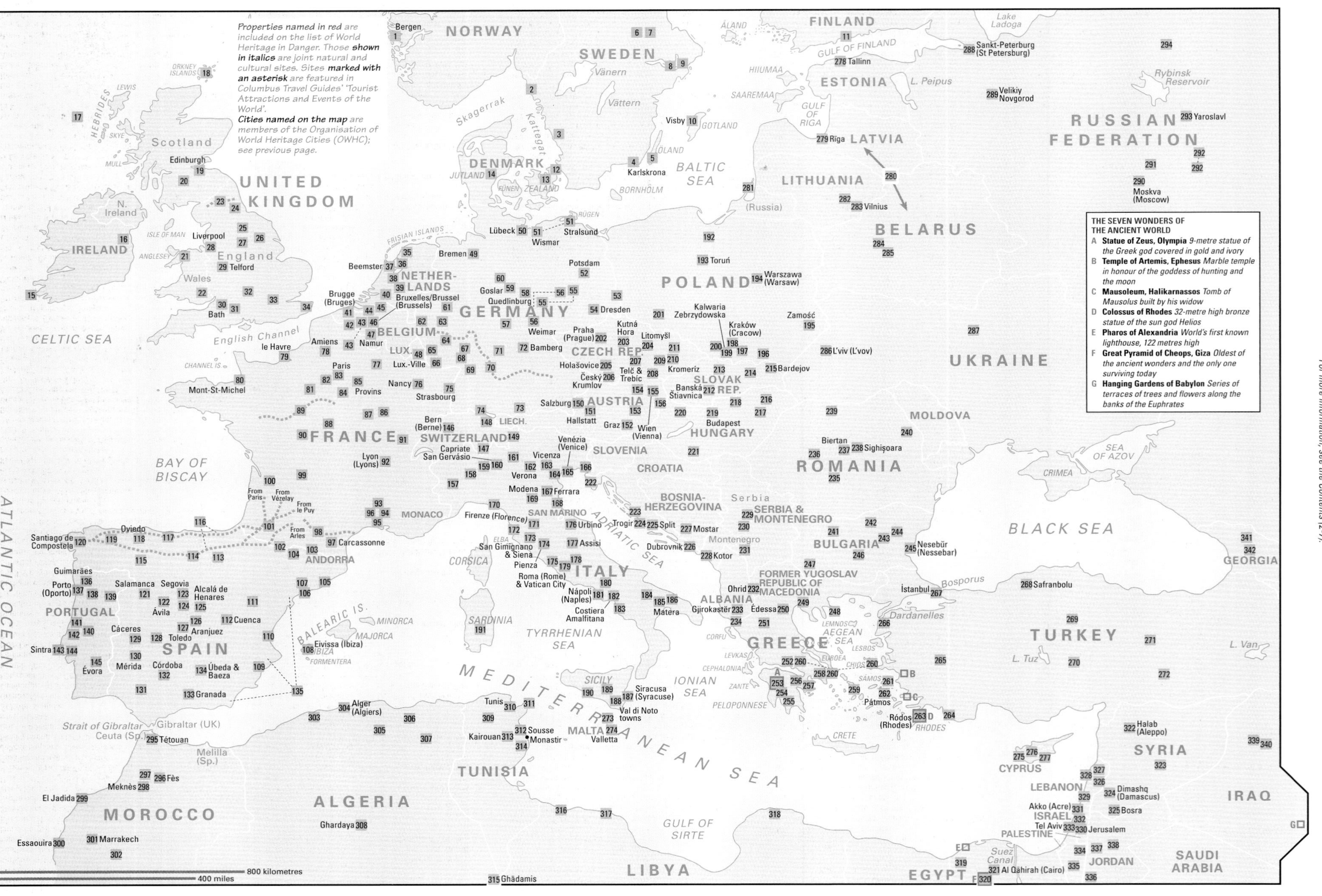
Properties named in red are included on the list of World Heritage in Danger. Those shown in italics are joint natural and cultural sites. Sites marked with an asterisk are featured in Columbus Travel Guides' 'Tourist Attractions and Events of the World'.
Cities named on the map are members of the Organisation of World Heritage Cities (OWHC); see previous page.
THE SEVEN WONDERS OF THE ANCIENT WORLD
A Statue of Zeus, Olympia 9-metre statue of the Greek god covered in gold and ivory
B Temple of Artemis, Ephesus Marble temple in honour of the goddess of hunting and the moon
C Mausoleum, Halikarnassos Tomb of Mausolus built by his widow
D Colossus of Rhodes 32-metre high bronze statue of the sun god Helios
E Pharos of Alexandria World's first known lighthouse, 122 metres high
F Great Pyramid of Cheops, Giza Oldest of the ancient wonders and the only one surviving today
G Hanging Gardens of Babylon Series of terraces of trees and flowers along the banks of the Euphrates
ATLANTIC OCEAN
NORWAY
SWEDEN
FINLAND
ESTONIA
LATVIA
LITHUANIA
BELARUS
RUSSIAN FEDERATION
UNITED KINGDOM
IRELAND
DENMARK
NETHERLANDS
BELGIUM
GERMANY
POLAND
UKRAINE
FRANCE
SWITZERLAND
AUSTRIA
CZECH REP.
SLOVAK REP.
HUNGARY
ROMANIA
MOLDOVA
SLOVENIA
CROATIA
BOSNIA-HERZEGOVINA
SERBIA & MONTENEGRO
BULGARIA
FORMER YUGOSLAV REPUBLIC OF MACEDONIA
ALBANIA
GREECE
ITALY
SPAIN
PORTUGAL
ANDORRA
MONACO
SAN MARINO
MALTA
TURKEY
CYPRUS
SYRIA
LEBANON
ISRAEL
PALESTINE
JORDAN
IRAQ
SAUDI ARABIA
GEORGIA
EGYPT
LIBYA
TUNISIA
ALGERIA
MOROCCO
BLACK SEA
BALTIC SEA
CELTIC SEA
BAY OF BISCAY
MEDITERRANEAN SEA
TYRRHENIAN SEA
IONIAN SEA
AEGEAN SEA
ADRIATIC SEA
GULF OF SIRTE
400 miles
800 kilometres

See also... Europe Historical (58-59); Europe Museums & Galleries (68)

EUROPE (including Turkey & Cyprus)

1 Bergen: Bryggen wharf*, Norway
2 Tanum: rock carvings, Sweden
3 Grimeton: Varberg radio station, Sweden
4 Karlskrona: naval city, Sweden
5 Southern Öland: agricultural landscape, Sweden
6 Falun: mining area of the Great Copper Mountain, Sweden
7 Engelsberg: ironworks, Sweden
8 Birka and Hovgården: archaeological sites, Sweden
9 Stockholm: Skogskyrkogården cemetery, Sweden; Drottningholms Slot (Drottningholm Royal Palace)*, Sweden
10 Visby: Hanseatic town and former Viking site, Sweden
11 Helsinki (Helsingfors): Suomenlinna Sea Fortress*, Finland
12 Helsingør (Elsinore): Kronborg Slot (Kronborg Castle)*, Denmark
13 Roskilde: cathedral, Denmark
14 Jelling: mounds, runic stones and church, Denmark
15 Skellig Michael: monastic complex, Ireland
16 Brú Na Bóinne: Newgrange, Knowth and Dowth prehistoric sites, Ireland
17 *St Kilda*, Scotland
18 Orkney: Neolithic monuments, Scotland
19 Edinburgh: old and new towns (incl. Castle*, Palace of Holyroodhouse*, Royal Museum & Museum of Scotland*, Scotch Whisky Heritage Centre & Royal Mile* and Scottish Parliament Building*), Scotland
20 New Lanark: industrial village*, Scotland
21 Castles and town walls of King Edward (incl. Caernarfon Castle* and Conwy Castle*), northwest Wales
22 Blaenavon: industrial landscape (incl. Big Pit National Mining Museum of Wales*), Wales
23 Frontiers of the Roman Empire (1): Hadrian's Wall*, England
24 Durham: castle and cathedral*, England
25 Studley Royal Park and Fountains Abbey ruins, England
26 Derwent Valley mills, England
27 Saltaire: industrial village, England
28 Liverpool: maritime mercantile city (incl. Albert Dock*), England
29 Ironbridge Gorge, England
30 Bath (incl. Roman baths and pumproom*), England
31 Stonehenge*, Avebury and associated Megalithic sites, England
32 Blenheim Palace, England
33 London: Tower of London*, England; London: Westminster Palace*, Westminster Abbey* and St Margaret's Church, England; Kew: Royal Botanic Gardens, England; Maritime Greenwich*, England
34 Canterbury: cathedral*, St Augustine's Abbey and St Martin's Church, England
35 Wouda steam pumping station, The Netherlands
36 Schokland: prehistoric settlements, The Netherlands
37 Droogmakerij de Beemster (Beemster Polder), The Netherlands
38 Amsterdam: defence line, The Netherlands
39 Utrecht: Rietveld Schröderhuis, The Netherlands
40 Kinderdijk-Elshout: mill network, The Netherlands
41 Brugge (Bruges): historic centre, Belgium
42 Tournai: Cathedrale Notre-Dame, Belgium
43 Belfries of Belgium and France (incl. Onze Lieve Vrouwekathedraal, Antwerpen (Antwerp)*), Belgium/France
44 Antwerpen (Antwerp): Plantin-Moretus Museum, Belgium
45 Flemish Béguinages, Belgium
46 Bruxelles/Brussel (Brussels): Grand-Place*, Belgium; Bruxelles/Brussel (Brussels): four town houses of architect Victor Horta, Belgium
47 Canal du Centre: four boat-lifts and environs, La Louvière and Le Rœulx, Belgium; Mons: Spiennes Neolithic flint mines, Belgium
48 Luxembourg-Ville: old quarters and fortifications
49 Bremen: town hall and statue of Roland, Germany
50 Lübeck: Hanseatic city, Germany
51 Stralsund and Wismar: historic centres, Germany
52 Berlin: Museumsinsel (incl. Pergamonmuseum*), Germany; Potsdam and SW Berlin: palaces and parks (incl. Schloss Sanssouci*), Germany
53 Muskauer Park, Germany, and Park Muzakowski, Poland
54 Dresden Elbe valley: cultural landscape, Germany
55 Eisleben and Wittenberg: Luther memorials, Germany
56 Dessau-Wörlitz: Garden Kingdom, Germany; Dessau and Weimar: Bauhaus buildings, Germany; Weimar: classical city, Germany
57 Schloss Wartburg, Germany
58 Quedlinburg: collegiate church, castle and old town, Germany
59 Goslar: historic town and Rammelsberg mines, Germany
60 Hildesheim: cathedral and St Michaeliskirche, Germany
61 Essen: Zollverein coal mine industrial complex, Germany
62 Aachen (Aix-la-Chapelle): cathedral, Germany
63 Köln (Cologne): cathedral*, Germany; Brühl: Schloss Augustusburg & Jagdschl. Falkenlust, Germany
64 Upper Middle Rhine Valley, Germany
65 Trier: Roman monuments, cathedral and Liebfrauenkirche, Germany
66 Völklingen: ironworks, Germany
67 Lorsch: abbey and Altenmünster, Germany
68 Speyer: cathedral, Germany
69 Maulbronn: Cistercian monastery complex, Germany
70 Frontiers of the Roman Empire (2): Roman Limes, Germany
71 Würzburg: Residenz with gardens and square, Germany
72 Bamberg, Germany
73 Wies: pilgrimage church, Germany
74 Reichenau: monastic island, Germany
75 Strasbourg: Grand Île, France
76 Nancy: Place Stanislas, Place de la Carrière and Place d'Alliance, France
77 Reims: Cathedrale Notre-Dame, Abbaye St-Remi and Palais du Tau, France
78 Amiens: cathedral, France
79 Le Havre: city rebuilt after Second World War, France
80 Mont-St-Michel* and its bay, France
81 Chartres: cathedral, France
82 Versailles: palace and park*, France
83 Paris: banks of the Seine (incl. Tour Eiffel*, Musée du Louvre*, Musée d'Orsay* and Cathédrale de Notre-Dame*), France
84 Fontainebleau: palace and park, France
85 Provins: fortified medieval town, France
86 Fontenay: Cistercian abbey, France
87 Vézelay: church and hill, France
88 Bourges: cathedral, France
89 Loire Valley between Chalonnes & Sully-sur-Loire, including Château de Chambord, France
90 St-Savin-sur-Gartempe: church, France
91 Arc-et-Senans: royal saltworks, France
92 Lyon (Lyons): historic city, France
93 Orange: Roman theatre and its surroundings and the triumphal arch, France
94 Avignon: historic centre (incl. Palais des Papes*), France
95 Arles: Roman and Romanesque monuments (incl. Roman amphitheatre*), France
96 Remoulins: Pont du Gard Roman aqueduct, France
97 Carcassonne: historic fortified city*, France
98 Canal du Midi, France
99 Vallée du Vézère: Lascaux* and other decorated caves, France
100 St-Émilion: vineyard landscape, France
101 Way of St James pilgrimage route: four routes through France
102 *Mont Perdu/Monte Perdido*, France/Spain
103 Madriu-Perafita-Claror valley: cultural landscape, Andorra
104 Vall de Boi: Catalan Romanesque churches, Spain
105 Barcelona: works of Antonio Gaudí (incl. Parque Güell* and Sagrada Familia*), Spain; Barcelona: Palau de la Música Catalaña and the Hospital de Sant Pau: art nouveau buildings, Spain
106 Tarragona: Roman city of Tárraco, Spain
107 Poblet: Cistercian monastery, Spain
108 *Eivissa (Ibiza): biodiversity and culture*, Spain
109 Elx (Elche): Palmeral (date palm) landscape, Spain
110 València: La Lonja de la Seda (Silk Exchange), Spain
111 Aragón: Mudéjar architecture, Spain
112 Cuenca: historic walled town, Spain
113 San Millán de la Cogolla: Suso and Yuso monasteries, Spain
114 Burgos: cathedral, Spain; Cuevas de Atapuerca: archaeological site, Spain
115 Las Médulas: Roman gold workings, Spain
116 Camino de Santiago: Way of St James pilgrimage route*, Spain
117 Cuevas de Altamira: archaeological site, Spain
118 Oviedo: churches of the Asturias Kingdom and La Foncalada hydraulic structure, Spain
119 Lugo: Roman walls, Spain
120 Santiago de Compostela: old town (incl. cathedral*), Spain
121 Salamanca: old city, Spain
122 Ávila: old town with extra-muros churches, Spain
123 Segovia: old town and Roman aqueduct*, Spain
124 El Escorial: monastery*, Spain
125 Alcalá de Henares: university and historic precinct, Spain
126 Aranjuez: cultural landscape, Spain
127 Toledo: historic city, Spain
128 Guadalupe: Real Monasterio de Santa María, Spain
129 Cáceres: old town, Spain
130 Mérida: archaeological ensemble, Spain
131 Sevilla (Seville): cathedral*, Alcazar and Archivo de Indias, Spain
132 Córdoba: mosque and historic centre, Spain
133 Granada: Alhambra*, Generalife & Albaicín quarter, Spain
134 Úbeda and Baeza: Renaissance monumental ensembles, Spain
135 Mediterranean seaboard prehistoric rock-art sites, Spain
136 Guimarães: historic centre, Portugal
137 Porto (Oporto): historic centre, Portugal
138 Alto Douro wine region, Portugal
139 Vale do Côa: prehistoric rock-art sites, Portugal
140 Tomar: Convent of Christ, Portugal
141 Batalha: Dominican monastery, Portugal
142 Alcobaça: Cistercian monastery, Portugal
143 Sintra: cultural landscape, Portugal
144 Lisboa (Lisbon): Mosteiro dos Jerónimos* and Torre de Belém*, Portugal
145 Évora: historic centre, Portugal
146 Bern (Berne): old city, Switzerland
147 Bellinzona: group of fortifications, Switzerland
148 St Gallen (St Gall): convent, Switzerland
149 Müstair: Benedictine convent of St John, Switzerland
150 Salzburg: historic centre (incl. Mozart's birthplace and residence*), Austria
151 Hallstatt-Dachstein-Salzkammergut: cultural landscape, Austria
152 Graz: historic centre, Austria
153 Semmering Railway, Austria
154 Wachau: cultural landscape, Austria
155 Wien (Vienna): historic centre (incl. Belvedere*), Austria; Wien (Vienna): Schloss Schönbrunn and gardens*, Austria
156 Neusiedlersee, Austria / Fertő, Hungary: cultural landscape
157 Torino (Turin) and surrounding area: Residences of the Royal House of Savoy, Italy
158 Sacri Monti ('Sacred Mountains') of Piedmont and Lombardy, Italy
159 Milano (Milan): church and convent of Santa Maria delle Grazie with 'The Last Supper' by Leonardo da Vinci, Italy
160 Crespi d'Adda: industrial workers' town, Italy
161 Val Camónica: rock drawings, Italy
162 Verona: historic city, Italy
163 Vicenza: city and the Palladian villas of the Veneto, Italy
164 Pádova (Padua): botanical garden, Italy
165 Venèzia (Venice) and its lagoon (incl. Basilica di San Marco*, Palazzo Ducale* and Ponte di Rialto*), Italy
166 Aquileia: archaeological site incl. Patriarchal Basilica, Italy
167 Ferrara: Renaissance city and Po delta, Italy
168 Ravenna: early Christian monuments and mosaics, Italy
169 Modena: cathedral, Torre Civica and Piazza Grande, Italy
170 Portovénere, Cinque Terre (Corniglia, Manarola, Monterosso, Riomaggiore, Vernazza) and the islands (Ísola Palmária, Í. del Tino and Í. del Tinetto), Italy
171 Firenze (Florence): historic centre (incl. Duomo Santa Maria del Fiore*, Galleria degli Uffizi*, Ponte Vecchio*), Italy
172 Pisa: Piazza del Duomo (incl. Torre Pendente: The Leaning Tower*), Italy
173 San Gimignano: historic centre, Italy; Siena: historic centre (incl. Piazza del Campo*), Italy
174 Pienza: historic centre, Italy; Val d'Orcia: Renaissance agricultural landscape, Italy
175 Cervéteri and Tarquinia: Etruscan necropolises, Italy
176 Urbino: historic centre, Italy
177 Assisi: Basilica di San Francesco and other Franciscan sites, Italy
178 Tivoli: Villa d'Este, Italy; Tivoli: Villa Adriana (Hadrian's Villa), Italy
179 Vatican City (incl. Basilica di San Pietro*, Musei Vaticani & Capella Sistina*); Roma (Rome): historic centre and extraterritorial properties of the Holy See & San Paolo fuori le Mura (incl. Colosseo*, Fontana di Trevi*, Foro Romano* and Pantheon*), Italy
180 Caserta: Palazzo Reale & gardens, Vanvitelli aqueduct & San Leucio complex, Italy
181 Nápoli (Naples): historic centre, Italy; Herculaneum, Pompeii* and Torre Annunziata: archaeological areas, Italy
182 Costiera Amalfitana, Italy
183 Cilento area: cultural landscape including Parco Nazionale del Cilento e Vallo di Diano, Certosa di San Lorenzo in Padula and the archaeological sites of Paestum and Vélia, Italy
184 Castel del Monte: medieval castle, Italy
185 Matera: I Sassi di Matera troglodyte settlement, Italy
186 Alberobello: Trulli limestone houses, Italy
187 Siracusa (Syracuse) and necropolis of Pantalica, Sicily, Italy
188 Val di Noto: late Baroque towns (Caltagirone, Catánia, Militello in Val di Catánia, Módica, Noto, Palazzolo, Ragusa and Scicli), Sicily, Italy
189 Villa Romana del Casale, Sicily, Italy
190 Agrigento: archaeological area, Sicily, Italy
191 Su Nuraxi di Barúmini, Sardinia, Italy
192 Malbork: Teutonic fortified monastery, Poland
193 Torun: medieval town, Poland
194 Warszawa (Warsaw): historic centre (incl. Warsaw Royal Castle*), Poland
195 Zamosc: Renaissance city, Poland
196 Wooden churches of southern Little Poland
197 Wieliczka: salt mines, Poland
198 Kraków (Cracow): historic centre (incl. Market Square* and Wawel Royal Castle*), Poland
199 Kalwaria Zebrzydowska: Mannerist architectural and park landscape complex and pilgrimage park, Poland
200 Oswiecim (Auschwitz): Auschwitz-Birkenau concentration camp*, Poland
201 Jawor and Swidnica: Churches of Peace, Poland
202 Praha (Prague): historic centre (incl. Charles Bridge*, Castle & St Vitus Cathedral* and Old Town Square*), Czech Rep.
203 Kutná Hora*: historical centre, Church of Santa Barbara and Cathedral of Our Lady at Sedlec, Czech Rep.
204 Litomysl Castle, Czech Rep.
205 Holasovice: historical village reservation, Czech Rep.
206 Cesky Krumlov: historic centre, Czech Rep.
207 Telc: historic centre, Czech Rep.; Trebic: Jewish quarter and St Procopius' Basilica, Czech Rep.
208 Lednice-Valtice: cultural landscape, Czech Rep.
209 Brno: Tugendhat Villa, Czech Rep.
210 Zelená Hora: St John of Nepomuk church, Czech Rep.; Kromeriz: castle and gardens, Czech Rep.
211 Olomouc: Holy Trinity column, Czech Rep.
212 Banská Stiavnica: city and mining landscape, Slovak Rep.
213 Vlkolinec: traditional village, Slovak Rep.
214 Spisské Pohradie: Spissky Hrad* and associated monuments, Slovak Rep.
215 Bardejov: fortified medieval town, Slovak Rep.
216 Tojaki wine region: cultural landscape, Hungary
217 Hortobágyi National Park, Hungary
218 Hollokö: traditional village, Hungary
219 Budapest: banks of the Danube, Buda Castle* area (incl. Fisherman's Bastion*), Andrássy Avenue and the Millennium Underground, Hungary
220 Pannonhalma: millenary Benedictine monastery and its natural environment, Hungary
221 Pécs: early Christian cemetery of Sopianae, Hungary
222 Porec: Episcopal complex, Croatia
223 Sibenik: St James cathedral, Croatia
224 Trogir: historic city, Croatia
225 Split: historic centre with Diocletian's Palace*, Croatia
226 Dubrovnik: old city*, Croatia
227 Mostar: old bridge area, Bosnia-Herzegovina
228 Kotor and its gulf, Serbia & Montenegro
229 Stari Ras: medieval buildings and monuments, Serbia & Mont.; Sopocani Monastery, Serbia & Montenegro
230 Studenica: monastery, Serbia & Montenegro
231 Decani: monastery*, Serbia & Montenegro
232 *Ohrid and its region*, FYR of Macedonia
233 Gjirokastër: Ottoman town, Albania
234 **Butrint (Buthrotum): archaeological site**, Albania
235 Horezu: monastery, Romania
236 Orastie Mountains: Dacian fortresses, Romania
237 Southern Transylvania: fortified churches, Romania
238 Sighisoara: historic centre, Romania
239 Maramures: wooden churches, Romania
240 Moldavian churches, Romania
241 Boyana: church, Bulgaria
242 Sveshtari: Thracian tomb, Bulgaria
243 Ivanovo: rock-hewn churches, Bulgaria
244 Madara Rider: horseman stone relief, Bulgaria
245 Nesebur (Nessebar): ancient city, Bulgaria
246 Kazanluk: Thracian tomb, Bulgaria
247 Rila: monastery*, Bulgaria
248 *Athos ('Holy Mountain')*, Greece
249 Thessaloniki (Salonika): Palaeochristian and Byzantine monuments, Greece
250 Vergina: archaeological site of Aigai, Greece
251 *Metéora: monasteries*, Greece
252 Delfí (Delphi): archaeological site*, Greece
253 Olimbía (Olympia): archaeological site*, Greece
254 Bassae: Temple of Apollo Epicurius, Greece
255 Mistrás: medieval ruins, Greece
256 Mycenae* and Tiryns: archaeological sites, Greece
257 Epídavros (Epidaurus): archaeological site*, Greece
258 Athína (Athens): Acropolis*, Greece
259 Delos: archaeological site, Greece
260 Daphni, Hossios Luckas and Néa Moni monasteries, Greece
261 Sámos: Pythagoreion port and Heraion temple remains, Greece
262 Pátmos: historic centre (chorá) with the monastery of St John the Theologian and Cave of the Apocalypse, Greece
263 Ródos (Rhodes): medieval city, Greece
264 Xanthos-Letoon: archaeological site, Turkey
265 *Hierapolis-Pamukkale*, Turkey
266 Truva (Troy): archaeological site*, Turkey
267 Istanbul: historic areas (incl. Blue Mosque*, Hagia Sophia* and Topkapi Palace*), Turkey
268 Safranbolu: historic city, Turkey
269 Hattusha: Hittite archaeological site, Turkey
270 *Göreme National Park* and Cappadocia rock sites*, Turkey
271 Divrigi: Great Mosque and hospital, Turkey
272 Nemrut Dag: archaeological site, Turkey
273 Megalithic temples: Ggantija, Hagar Qim*, Mnajdra, Tarxien, Ta'Hagrat and Skorba, Malta
274 Valletta: old city, Malta; Hal Saflieni Hypogeum, Malta
275 Pafos (Paphos): historic city*, Cyprus
276 Troodos region: painted churches, Cyprus
277 Choirokoitia: archaeological site, Cyprus
278 Tallinn: historic centre (incl. Town Hall Square*), Estonia
279 Riga: historic centre*, Latvia
280 Struve Geodetic Arc: a chain of survey triangulations stretching from northern Norway to the Black Sea
281 Curonian Spit, Lithuania/Russian Federation
282 Kernavé Cultural Reserve: archaeological site, Lithuania
283 Vilnius: historic centre, Lithuania
284 Mir: castle complex, Belarus
285 Nyasvizh: architectural, residential and cultural complex of the Radziwill family, Belarus
286 L'viv (L'vov): historic centre, Ukraine
287 Kyiv (Kiev): St Sophia Cathedral*, related monastic buildings and Lavra of Kyiv-Pechersk, Ukraine

RUSSIAN FEDERATION

288 Sankt-Peterburg (St Petersburg): historic centre (incl. State Hermitage Museum*)
289 Velikiy Novgorod: historic monuments and surroundings
290 Moskva (Moscow): Kremlin*, Red Square* and St Basil's Cathedral*; Moskva (Moscow): Novodevichy Convent; Kolomenskoye: Church of the Ascension
291 Sergiyev Posad: Trinity Sergius Lavra architectural ensemble
292 Vladimir and Suzdal: White Monuments
293 Yaroslavl: historic centre
294 Ferapontov Monastery

AFRICA

295 Tétouan: medina, Morocco
296 Fès: medina*, Morocco
297 Volubilis: archaeological site, Morocco
298 Meknès: historic city, Morocco
299 El Jadida: Portuguese fortified city of Mazagan, Morocco
300 Essaouira: medina, Morocco
301 Marrakech: medina (incl. Djemaa el Fna square* and Saadian Tombs*), Morocco
302 Aït Benhaddou: fortified village, Morocco
303 **Tipasa: archaeological park**, Algeria
304 Alger (Algiers): kasbah, Algeria
305 Benî Hammâd: Al Qal'a, Algeria
306 Djemila: Roman ruins, Algeria
307 Timgad: Roman ruins, Algeria
308 M'Zab Valley: fortified towns, Algeria
309 Dougga (Thugga): archaeological site, Tunisia
310 Tunis: medina*, Tunisia; Carthage: archaeological site*, Tunisia
311 Kerkouane: Punic town and its necropolis, Tunisia
312 Sousse: medina, Tunisia
313 Kairouan: holy city, Tunisia
314 El Jem: Roman amphitheatre ruins, Tunisia
315 Ghadamis: old town, Libya
316 Sabratha: archaeological site, Libya
317 Leptis Magna: archaeological site, Libya
318 Cyrene: archaeological site, Libya
319 **Abu Mina: Christian ruins**, Egypt
320 Memphis: Pyramid fields from Giza to Dahshur and its necropolis*, Egypt
321 Al Qahirah (Cairo): Islamic city, Egypt

ASIA

322 Halab (Aleppo): ancient city of Aleppo*, Syria
323 Tadmur: archaeological site of Palmyra*, Syria
324 Dimashq (Damascus): ancient city, Syria
325 Bosra: ancient city, Syria
326 Anjar: archaeological site, Lebanon; Baalbek: archaeological site of Heliopolis, Lebanon
327 Holy Valley: early Christian monastic settlements, and Forest of the Cedars of God, Lebanon
328 Byblos: archaeological site, Lebanon
329 Soûr (Tyre): archaeological site of Tyre*, Lebanon
330 **Jerusalem: old city and walls** (incl. Temple Mount*, Western (Wailing) Wall*), site proposed by Jordan
331 Akko: old city of Acre, Israel
332 Biblical tels: Megiddo, Hazor and Beer Sheba, Israel
333 Tel Aviv: White City, Israel
334 Masada: fortress and Roman siege works*, Israel
335 The Incense and Spice Route: desert cities in the Negev, Israel
336 Petra: archaeological site*, Jordan
337 Umm ar Rasas (Kastron Mefa'a): archaeological site, Jordan
338 Qasr Amra: desert castle, Jordan
339 Hatra: fortified city remains, Iraq
340 **Ash Sharqat: ancient city of Ashur**, Iraq
341 Upper Svaneti area, Georgia
342 K'ut'aisi: Bagrati Cathedral and Gelati Monastery, Georgia

▶ See also... World Introduction (8-11); Tourism (24-25); Countries A-Z (202-210)

The listings above refer to a selection of related themes. For more information, see the Contents (2-7).

Europe

EUROPE'S TRAVEL and tourism industry continues to dominate the world and it remains comfortably the world's most visited continent. It has numerous natural and man-made attractions, a generally excellent transport network and a wide range of cities, landscapes and climates. These factors helped draw over 435 million international visitors in 2005, over half the world's total and an increase of some 20 million over 2004. Global recession and the struggle against terrorism depressed the travel industry in 2001 and 2003, but many European travel patterns are well established and impervious to all but the very worst catastrophes. Stability has been vital to this.

That is not to say that Europe has stood still. The political map has altered many times since 1989, as has the membership and influence of the EU (which now rivals the USA as the world's largest economy). Most importantly, these changes have generally been effected peacefully. Given Europe's violent history between 1914 and 1945, this is a considerable achievement.

In general, European states are wealthy, stable, secular, liberal, multi-cultural democracies. Despite linguistic differences, national economies and societies are closely integrated, frontier formalities (for surface travel at any rate) are simple or non-existent and intra-regional trade is high. Apart from some intermittent separatist movements, there is little violent conflict. This inter-dependence, security and stability underpins Europe's vast travel and tourism industry.

Travel overview

Europe's visitor numbers have increased on average by about 2.3% a year since 2000. Although this is below the world average of 3.2%, Europe is a mature market and thus offers less easy opportunities for growth. Intra-regional travel has underpinned Europe's pre-eminence: with so many attractions within easy reach, it is not surprising so many Europeans holiday in their own continent. Nearly nine out of every ten journeys, which start in Europe also finish there. Indeed, trips made by Europeans within Europe account for around half of all international journeys worldwide.

More good news for Europe is that the US market seems to be bouncing back to pre-2001 levels, with an estimated 12.6 million visitors reported in 2005. This is despite the US dollar having lost 6% of its value against the euro in the 12 months up to May 2005, to say nothing of other price increases such as airline fuel and security surcharges.

Whilst the low-cost carriers in Europe continue their seemingly inexorable growth – 100 million passengers in 2005 compared to around 50 million in 2003 – the performance of Europe's airlines overall has been encouraging, with a 6% increase in 2005. All of Europe's 25 busiest airports recorded an increase in passenger numbers in year ending October 2005 compared to the previous 12 months (5.25% on average), led by Istanbul with a rise of over 23%. A further 13 airports with one million-plus passengers saw growth of over 35% in this period. In mature markets, such as the UK, low-cost traffic is expected to continue to grow at around 30% a year, while in newer markets the figure is even higher – 35% in Hungary, for instance. In 2005, low-cost airlines accounted for about 20% of European air travel, as opposed to 5% in 2000. Many observers expect them to account for between a quarter and a third of the continent's market by 2010.

Over 20 European countries now have their own low-cost carriers with more emerging. While not all will survive, the business model has radically changed the face of aviation and has caused major carriers to re-evaluate their pricing, routes and service levels.

Set against this growth is the issue of rising fuel prices which will continue to eat into profitability, particularly for long-haul flights. Fuel surcharges have been imposed by many of the flag-carriers since early 2004 but have so far been resisted by their low-cost rivals. With over half of international journeys in Europe being taken by car, however, the continent's travel industry is much less reliant on air travel than in other parts of the world. With so many countries offering different attractions, history and cultures in such close proximity, touring by rail or road remains popular. Travellers can cover huge swathes of Europe by utilising the continent's integrated transport network.

The seemingly relentless rise of the internet has been another significant feature of the European travel scene. As the preferred booking method for low-cost airlines it has also helped open up many previously under-visited areas of the continent. According to the Centre for Regional and Tourism Research, European online travel sales increased by over 80% between 2003 and 2005 and now accounts for sales of 24 billion euros. This is nearly 10% of the total market: in 1998, online travel was responsible for just 0.1%. The UK, followed by Germany, are the countries with the highest share of internet bookings, although the fastest growth is occurring in the new EU members of Eastern Europe. The internet is increasingly used to research holiday options, even if many may then book through more conventional methods. The continued roll-out of high-speed broadband access across the continent and the increasing willingness of consumers to trust the web for on-line payments are likely to increase this trend. One major hotel chain believes that 50% of all hotel bookings will be online by 2010: at present, the figure is closer to 10%. In the UK, 54% of holidays abroad were pre-paid packages in 2000. By 2004, this had fallen to 45%.

The movement from northern to southern Europe, traditionally in the summer but increasingly at other times, has been happening for decades. Nearly half of all British trips abroad in 2004 were for holidays to the EU15 countries, mainly France and Spain.

Increasingly affordable travel has led to a constant demand for new destinations. Most of the northern Mediterranean coastal region is now seen as a holiday area. To the long-established favourites, one must add Turkey, Croatia, Slovenia and Serbia & Montenegro, all of which saw arrivals increase in 2004 by more than the European average.

To add to the variety, activities such as camping, city-breaks, skiing and rural holidays are also increasing. Many provide separate holiday options, but sometimes are combined with traditional beach holidays: even skiing, which can be enjoyed in Spain's Sierra Nevada only an hour's drive from the Costa del Sol. Many people take more than one holiday a year to experience more of these ever-increasing alternatives. These factors combined to boost the number of beach holidays taken by Europeans within Europe in 2004 compared to 2003 by 5%, an increase of 3.6 million visits.

According to Eurostat, Europe's economy grew by around 2.2% in 2005. This was below the world average, but – as with visitor arrivals – the continent is generally highly developed and thus offers less opportunity for spectacular increases. Mirroring the performance of the travel industry, the largest growth (in most cases exceeding the world average) is to be found in the east of the continent. Rising fuel costs may have an effect on consumer confidence, but there are few signs that the travel business is going to suffer as a result. Even the spectre of terrorism has not tarnished Europe's appeal. In April 2005, the European Travel Commission commented that 'people are growing more accustomed to living in an unsafe world', and many travellers seem to agree: two weeks after the July 2005 attacks in London, the city's hotel occupancy rates were only slightly down

Key facts

Number of Countries	48
Area ('000 sq km)	25,926
Population ('000)	799,763
Population Density (per sq km)	31
Gross National Income (US$m)	13,200,398
Visitor Arrivals ('000)	409,570
Visitor Receipts (US$m)	322,678

GNI figures are for 2004. Population figures are taken from the most recent reliable source. Travel figures (UNWTO) are based on overnight stays, not same-day visitors, and are for 2004. For more information see the Countries A-Z section from page 202.

Big spenders

Expenditure on foreign travel (excluding international transport), 2004 – top ten countries (US$ billions) *Source: WTO*

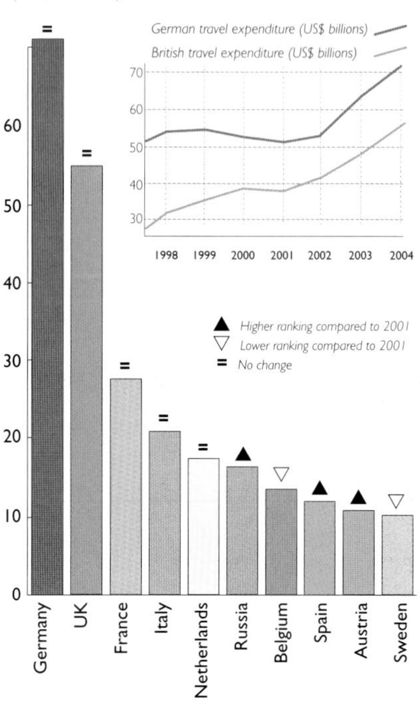
German travel expenditure (US$ billions)
British travel expenditure (US$ billions)
70
60
50
40
30
1998 1999 2000 2001 2002 2003 2004
Higher ranking compared to 2001
Lower ranking compared to 2001
No change
60
50
40
30
20
10
0
Germany
UK
France
Italy
Netherlands
Russia
Belgium
Spain
Austria
Sweden

Economies

The region's 10 largest economies
Source: World Bank/International Monetary Fund

	GNI US$m 2004	GNI/cap US$ 2004	GDP growth 2004	GDP growth av p/a '97-'06
Germany	2,488,974	30,194	1.6	1.2
UK	2,016,393	33,361	2.7	2.3
France	1,858,731	30,644	1.4	1.7
Italy	1,503,562	25,878	0.4	1.2
Spain	875,817	21,710	2.5	3.1
Netherlands	515,148	31,397	1.7	2.3
Russia	487,335	3,398	7.2	4.7
Switzerland	356,052	47,541	1.8	1.5
Belgium	322,837	31,149	2.6	2.2
Sweden	321,401	35,704	3.6	2.7

Heading south

European sunshine destinations ex-UK (000s)
Source: BTA/Visit Britain

	1997	2004
to Spain	8,281	13,833
to France	11,149	11,602
to Greece	1,512	2,709
to Italy	1,801	2,974
to Portugal	1,304	1,804
TOTAL	24,047	32,922
% of all outbound trips	52.3%	51.3%

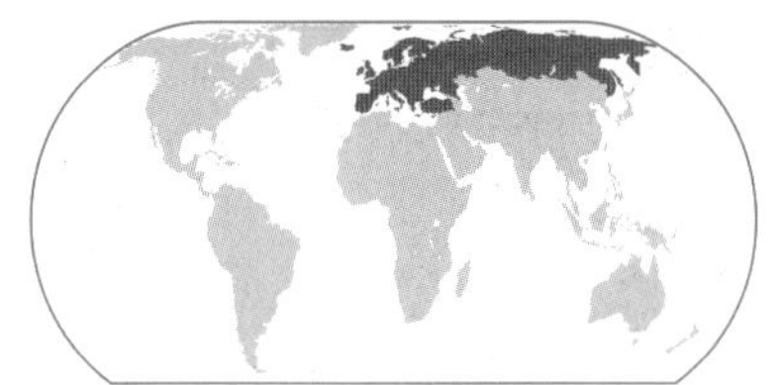

- Europe occupies 18.9% of the world's land area and is home to 12.4% of the world's population. 65% of the area and 18.0% of the population is provided by Russia.
- Europe accounts for 50.3% of global travel departures and 50.0% of arrivals.
- International travel and tourism contributed over US$320 billion to Europe's economy in 2004.
- 17 countries in Europe received more than US$5 billion from travel and tourism in 2004 and ten received more than US$10 billion.
- Europe has six of the ten most visited countries in the world and seven of the top ten travel earners.
- Germans continue to spend more money on foreign travel than any other nationality.
- 12 European countries received more than 10 million visitors in 2004.
- The most popular destination, France, on its own received about one in eleven of the world's international travellers.
- There were 410 million international tourist arrivals in Europe in 2004, an increase of 100 million since 1997.
- The budget of the EU (approx US$135bn) is only slightly less than the GNI of Argentina.
- The most significant growth in tourist arrivals in 2004 compared to 2003 was in Central and Eastern Europe which showed a rise of 13.8%.
- Europe had over 5.5 million hotel rooms in 2003.
- The Leningrad Metro has the world's longest escalator.
- Russia spans 11 time zones.
- Luxembourg has the highest per capita income of any country in the world.
- Italy is the only country that completely surrounds two other countries (the Vatican City and San Marino).
- The Hermitage in St Petersburg has over 3 million works of art.
- Over 100 tons of tomatoes are thrown during the La Tomatina festival in Buñol in Spain.
- Istanbul is the only city which spans two continents.
- Finland has over 81,000 islands and over 187,000 lakes.
- Andorra is the only country with two heads of state.
- Over 24% of Italians are over 60, the highest percentage in the world.
- Switzerland is the only country with a square flag.
- Lake Baikal in Russia is the deepest lake in the world and holds an estimated 20% of the world's liquid fresh water.

on the same period the year before, while Madrid's visitor figures increased in the first nine months of 2004 compared to 2003. In common with other parts of the world, the European travel industry has shown itself to be remarkably resilient. Times are certainly changing; but change is not always for the worse. Certainly, those who value choice, flexibility and value-for-money have never had it so good.

Travel trends

The more extreme tastes in adventure holidays are best satisfied in other continents but, that aside, Europe has something for everyone, from castles to clubs, scuba-diving to ski resorts and golf courses to art galleries. Major patterns or possible future trends, in addition to those discussed above, are as follows.

- In general, people are tending to take more shorter trips rather than one long summer holiday (although this option still remains popular). City breaks are the main examples of this trend, and in 2004 12% more Europeans took city breaks within the continent compared to 2003. Urban fashions come and go, but the main capitals are ever-popular, as are cities such as Bruges, St Petersburg, Istanbul, Tallinn, Dresden, Venice, Barcelona, Munich, Milan, Dubrovnik and Cracow.
- Short breaks to beach destinations such as Majorca, the Côte d'Azur and the Algarve are on the increase.
- Travellers are increasingly looking for holidays that will challenge them and provide new experiences. Adventure holidays fill part of this desire, but educational and foreign-language tourism are growing, as are holidays involving an element of voluntary work.
- The phrases 'responsible tourism' and 'ethical tourism' are in some ways more relevant to other parts of the world than Europe, but numerous resorts across the continent are now taking steps to respond to this increasingly important aspect of travellers' requirements.
- The sun-migration pattern reverses into a dash to the mountains for winter sports. The central Alps remain ever-popular, but Slovenia, Romania and Bulgaria are fast-emerging destinations.
- The recent opening up of Eastern Europe has led to an increase of travel not only between these countries but also from other parts of Europe. Poland, Hungary and the Czech Republic have been in the forefront.
- The states of the former Yugoslavia, particularly Slovenia, Croatia and – increasingly – Serbia & Montenegro have shown solid growth in recent years and are likely to continue to do so.
- Health and spa holidays are also on the increase: again, Eastern Europe is helping to lead the way.
- Golf holidays in Spain and Portugal, have long been popular, while France's uncrowded courses make it a strengthening force in the market.
- The Mediterranean and the Baltic are, after the Caribbean, the most popular cruise areas in the world.
- No-frills hotels are now competing with deluxe brands for the attention of business and leisure travellers who, having invested little in their air fare, are frequenting higher grade hotels and restaurants than in the past.
- EU enlargement is leading to the ten most recent members being further assimilated into Europe's travel patterns. They are also likely to be offer value for money when compared with many traditional destinations.

Destination overview

- **France** – comfortably Europe's, and the world's, most visited country, accounting for nearly one in five of the continent's international arrivals. Paris is the city-break destination *par excellence* and the Côte d'Azur one of the world's most famous playgrounds. From gastronomy to golf and from adventure breaks to fine art, France's highly varied holiday products cater for virtually all tastes.
- **Spain** – the continent's second most popular destination, and the favourite amongst Europeans (with a 13% market share in 2004 compared to France's 12%). The traditional image of beach holidays on the Mediterranean coast is fast changing, spearheaded by the city-breaks to its many magnificent cities, mainly Madrid, Seville and Barcelona.
- **Italy** – Europe's third most visited country has an enviable blend of climate, culture, natural beauty and urban sophistication. *Benessere* (well-being) and *agriturismi* (farm-stay) holidays are increasingly important niche markets. It is hoped the 2006 Winter Olympics in Turin will boost travel to Piedmont.
- **UK** – with estimates from Visit Britain putting growth in tourist arrivals and receipts at about 4.4%, the UK is expected to break the 30 million visitors mark in 2006. The country has long benefitted from its 'heritage' appeal, particularly in the North American market.
- **Germany** – the country's tourism profile has been raised through an effective series of national and regional marketing campaigns emphasising Germany's diversity. It was one of the first countries to be granted Approved Destination Status by China, which has contributed to a growth of nearly 2 million visitors to bring total arrivals up above the 20 million mark. Germany's vibrant cities have also proved popular.
- **Greece** – with around 1,400 islands, Greece can boast a coastline of some 15,000km, and it is upon this, together with its incomparable heritage sites, that its tourism appeal has largely been founded.
- **Turkey** – one of the consistent star performers of the European travel scene in recent years, Turkey's visitor numbers have risen steadily from 9 million in 1997 to nearly 17 million in 2004. Turkey's appeal has been built on the solid foundations of its beaches and cultural sites, as well as value-for-money.
- **Scandinavia** – a mature market with healthy intra-regional trade. Increasing numbers of visitors are drawn by the area's pristine environment and stunning scenery. Short-breaks to the major Scandinavian cities have increased as a result of the rise of the low-cost airlines.
- **Benelux** – these three countries attract around 16 million visitors. Cities such as Amsterdam, Brussels and Bruges are prime short-break destinations.
- **Eastern Europe** – the eight countries in this region that joined the EU in 2004 have benefited from improved air links, reduced border formalities and a favourable rate against the euro. Arrivals to the region grew by 11% in 2004, more than twice the European average. The strong Russian outbound market and well-established patterns of intra-regional travel have also played their part in this increase.

Big earners

Receipts from foreign travel (excluding international transport), 2004 – top ten countries (US$ billions) *Source: WTO*

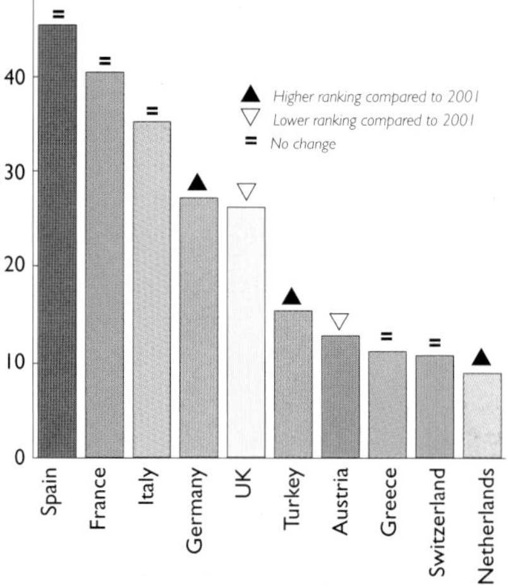

40
30
20
10
0
Higher ranking compared to 2001
Lower ranking compared to 2001
No change
Spain
France
Italy
Germany
UK
Turkey
Austria
Greece
Switzerland
Netherlands

Problem areas

- Further terrorist attacks cannot be ruled out.
- Until the UK adopts the euro (if it does), its imports and exports, including travel, will remain at the mercy of euro/sterling exchange rate fluctuations.
- Although away from the European mainstream, instability is a risk in Russia and some of the former Russian republics. The newly expanded EU's relations with these countries will be of great importance.
- Traffic congestion in some cities has reduced average driving speeds to near walking-pace.
- Air travel has increased more quickly than the investment in air traffic control and airport infrastructure, which can cause delays at peak times, particularly at major hubs: 70% of the air traffic delays in 2004 took place at 30% of Europe's airports.
- Europe's wealth is attracting migrants from poorer parts of the world, which is fuelling social tensions and the growth of right-wing political parties.

Visitors

Visitor arrivals 2004: top ten countries *Source: WTO*

	Visitors (thousands)	Change since 1997
France	75,121	11.4%
Spain	53,599	27.1%
Italy	37,071	6.0%
United Kingdom	27,755	9.1%
Germany	20,137	23.4%
Austria	19,373	14.3%
Turkey	16,826	58.4%
Ukraine	15,629	64.5%
Poland	14,290	-38.1%
Greece	13,787	26.6%

See also... World Physical (12-13); World Political (14-15), World Climate (16)

The listings above refer to a selection of related themes. For more information, see the Contents (2-7).

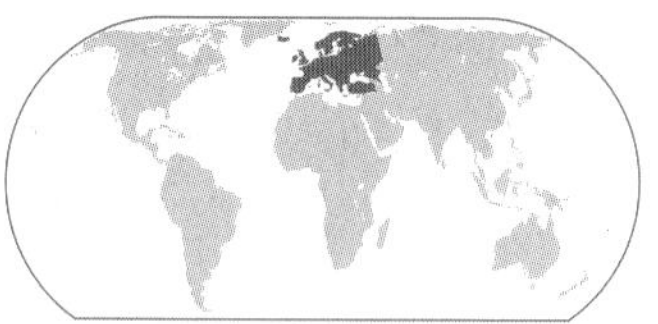

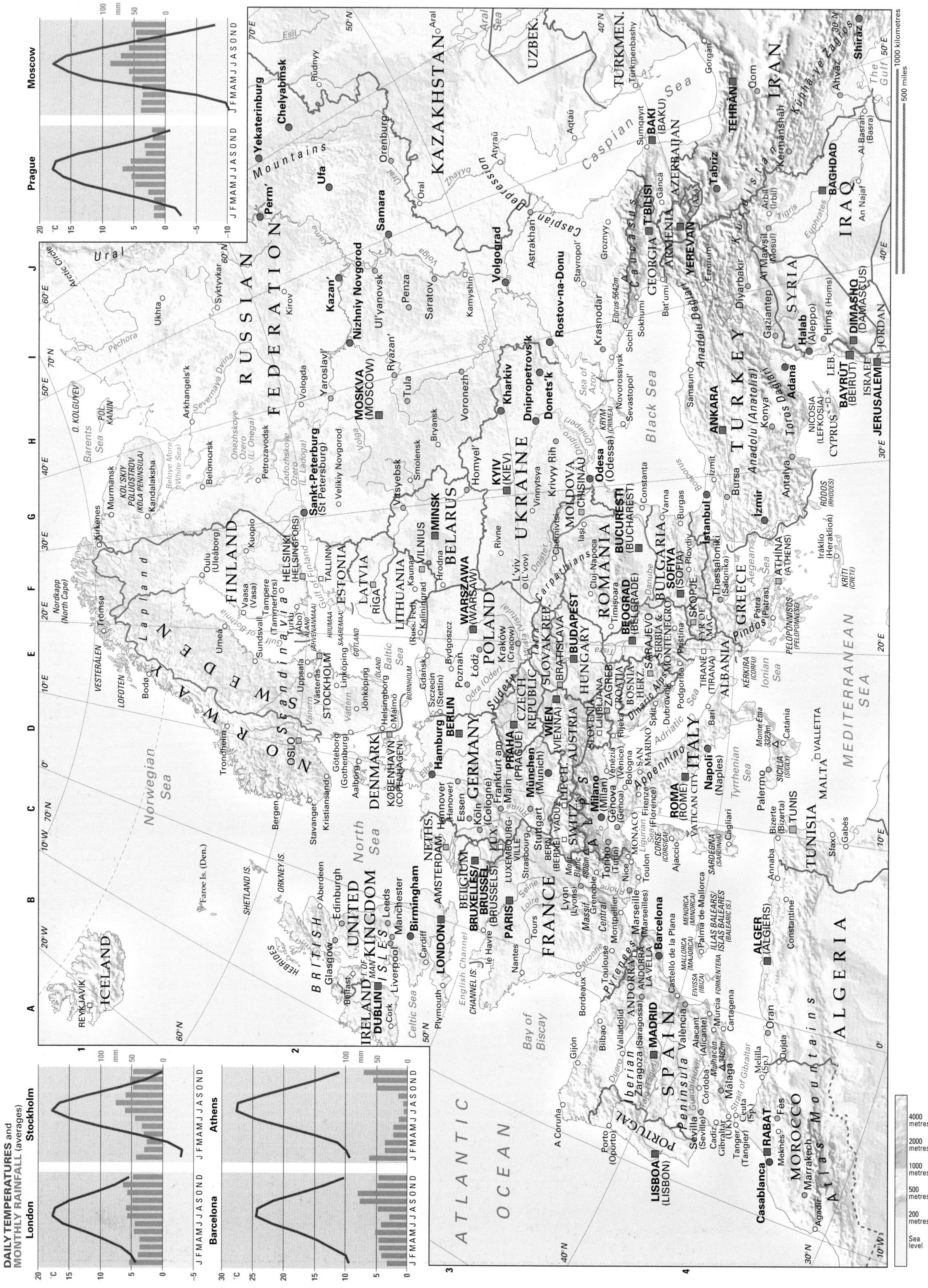

DAILY TEMPERATURES and **MONTHLY RAINFALL** (averages)

London · Stockholm · Barcelona · Athens · Prague · Moscow

°C · mm · J F M A M J J A S O N D

Europe

4000 metres
2000 metres
1000 metres
500 metres
200 metres
Sea level

1000 kilometres
500 miles

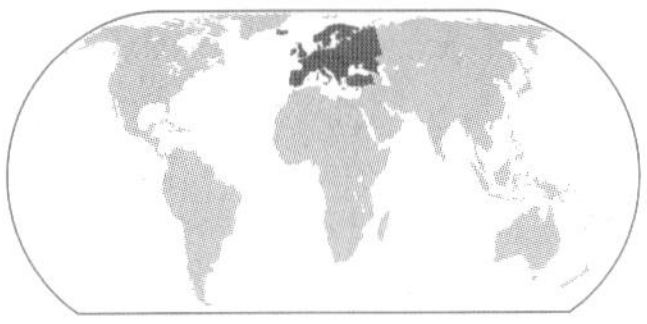

See also... World Climate (16); Regional Climate Terms (196)

The listings above refer to a selection of related themes. For more information, see the Contents (2-7).

WINTER

TEMPERATURE
(January average, degrees Celsius)
- 10° – 19°
- 0° – 9°
- Minus 10° – minus 1°
- Below minus 10°

RAINFALL
(November to April total)
- 500mm and over
- 250 – 499mm
- Less than 250mm

PREVAILING WIND shown as white arrows

TEMPERATURE CONVERSION

°Celsius	–10	0	10	20	30	40
°Fahrenheit	14	32	50	68	86	104

RAINFALL CONVERSION

Millimetres	102	203	305	406	508	610
Inches	4	8	12	16	20	24

NORTH ATLANTIC DRIFT
An extension of the Gulf Stream which helps to maintain relatively mild winters in the British Isles and along the coast of Norway

FÖHN
A wind which blows down Alpine valleys, warming as it descends, and melts snow rapidly

MISTRAL
A strong cold dry wind from the north

BORA
A cold dry wind which blows from the N and NE, affecting the Adriatic coastline

LEVECHE
A hot, dry and dusty wind which blows from the Sahara

Columbus Travel Guides' *World Travel Guide* contains detailed climate charts for every country in the world, including temperature, rainfall, sunshine and humidity

SUMMER

TEMPERATURE
(July average, degrees Celsius)
- 30° and over
- 20° – 29°
- 10° – 19°
- 0° – 9°

RAINFALL
(May to October total)
- 500mm and over
- 250 – 499mm
- Less than 250mm

PREVAILING WIND shown as white arrows

SIROCCO
A hot dusty wind which blows from north Africa; after crossing the Mediterranean the wind is often very humid

ETESIAN WIND / MELTEMI
A wind blowing from the N and NW, often creating rough seas

1000 kilometres
500 miles

See also... Religion (21); UNESCO Cultural Heritage (50-53); Europe Museums & Galleries (68); World War I Battlefields (79); • *cont >*

The listings above refer to a selection of related themes. For more information, see the Contents (2-7).

This map shows selected aspects of European history between the end of the Roman Empire in the 5th century and the Peace of Westphalia in 1648. Modern equivalents of important cities are included in parentheses. No historical boundaries are indicated apart from the maximum extent of Roman and Islamic conquests. The present-day coastline is shown and current international boundaries are marked in grey.

- Northern limit of the Roman Empire at its greatest extent
- Northern limit of Islamic conquests in Europe between the 7th and 11th centuries
- Trieste — Cities and regions which came under Venetian influence in any period prior to 1648
  Venice acquired many trading posts at various times during its period of commercial expansion in the late Middle Ages
- ✕ Sites of major battles in the period 476–1648, with date
  In general, battles have only been marked which had important political consequences
- The Hanseatic League
  A commercial union of northern European cities, designed to create economic security in an age of political chaos, which flourished in the 14th and 15th centuries
  - • Principal cities
  - ◆ Principal foreign trading posts (kontore)
- Principal cities of the Lombard League
  A shifting political alliance of northern Italian cities designed to combat the territorial ambitions of the Holy Roman Emperors (principally Frederick I and Frederick II) between 1153 and 1268
- The Cinque Ports
  A loose confederation of towns in southern England whose defensive obligations were first established in the 11th century and subsequently redefined by many royal charters, principally that of 1278. At one time there were over 30 towns and villages in the Cinque Ports Confederation; the original five are shown here
- ○ Universities founded prior to 1600, with year of foundation
  In some cases, particularly for the oldest universities, precise dates are open to debate
- Major ecclesiastical centres, 16th century:
  - Roman Catholic (Patriarchal and Archiepiscopal Sees)
  - Orthodox (Patriarchal Sees and other major centres)
- Camino de Santiago (the Way of St James)
  A medieval pilgrimage route which developed after the discovery of the tomb of St James the Apostle in Galicia in about 812; the pilgrimage's popularity was at its height in the 11th and 12th centuries, resulting in the legacy of many churches and chapels along its various routes

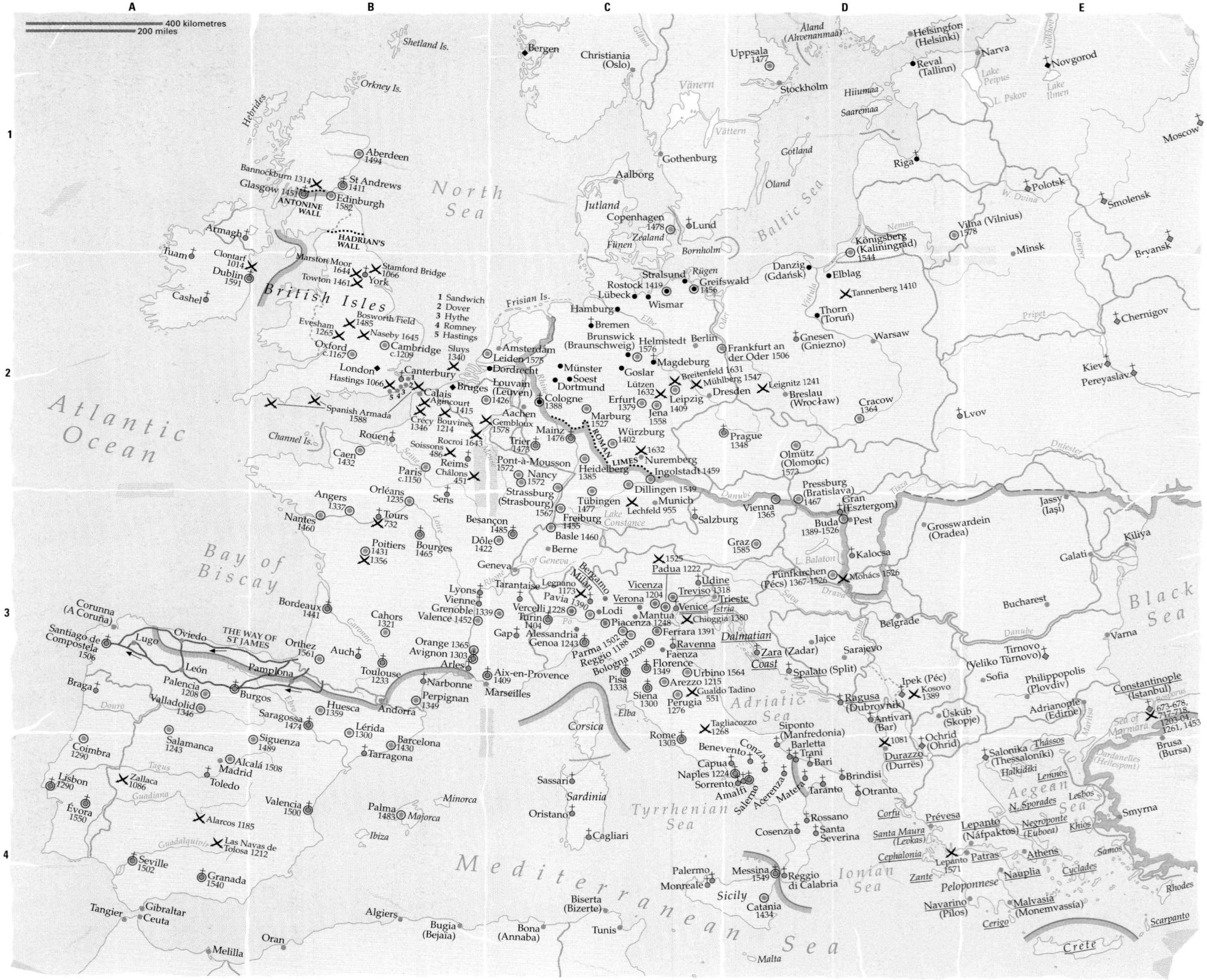

1 Sandwich
2 Dover
3 Hythe
4 Romney
5 Hastings

400 kilometres
200 miles

See also... cont < • Asia Historical (128); North America Historical (156-157); Latin America Historical (187)

The listings above refer to a selection of related themes. For more information, see the Contents (2-7).

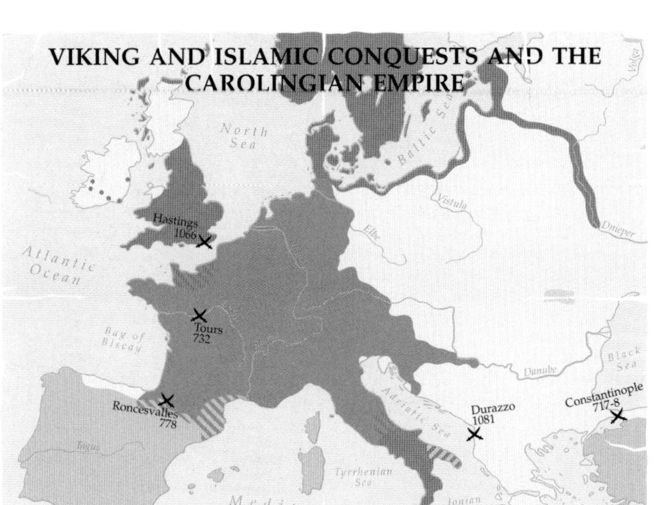
VIKING AND ISLAMIC CONQUESTS AND THE CAROLINGIAN EMPIRE
North Sea
Baltic Sea
Atlantic Ocean
Bay of Biscay
Hastings 1066
Tours 732
Roncesvalles 778
Durazzo 1081
Constantinople 717-8
Adriatic Sea
Tyrrhenian Sea
Ionian Sea
Mediterranean Sea
Black Sea
Danube
Vistula
Elbe
Dnieper
Volga
Tagus

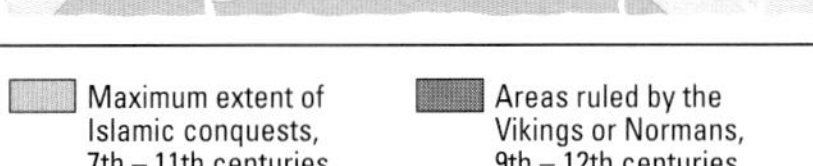
Maximum extent of Islamic conquests, 7th – 11th centuries
Areas ruled by the Vikings or Normans, 9th – 12th centuries
The Carolingian Empire at the death of Charlemagne in 814

THE ANGEVIN AND HOHENSTAUFEN EMPIRES AND THE IBERIAN KINGDOMS
North Sea
Atlantic Ocean
Bay of Biscay
ENGLAND
Tinchbrai 1432
NORMANDY
Bouvines 1214
HOLY ROMAN EMPIRE
ANJOU
AQUITAINE
GASCONY
Legnano 1173
LEON
PORTUGAL
ARAGON
CASTILLE
Las Navas de Tolosa 1212
MUWAHID CALIPHATE
SICILY
Adriatic Sea
Tyrrhenian Sea
Ionian Sea
Black Sea
Danube
Vistula
Dnieper
Volga
Tagus

The Angevin Empire at the death of Henry II in 1189
The Hohenstaufen Empire at the death of Frederick II in 1250
The Christian Kingdoms of Iberia in the mid 13th century

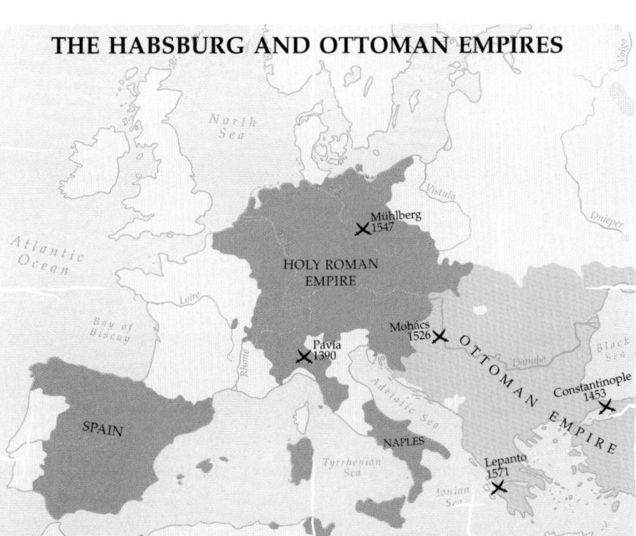
THE HABSBURG AND OTTOMAN EMPIRES
North Sea
Atlantic Ocean
Bay of Biscay
Mühlberg 1547
HOLY ROMAN EMPIRE
Mohács 1526
Pavia 1390
OTTOMAN EMPIRE
Constantinople 1453
SPAIN
NAPLES
Lepanto 1571
Adriatic Sea
Tyrrhenian Sea
Ionian Sea
Black Sea
Danube
Vistula
Loire
Rhone
Dnieper
Volga

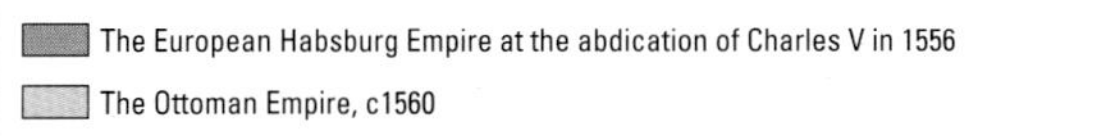
The European Habsburg Empire at the abdication of Charles V in 1556
The Ottoman Empire, c1560

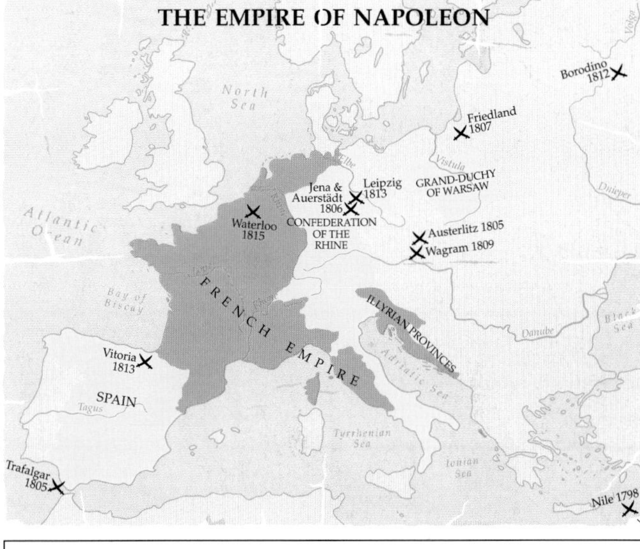
THE EMPIRE OF NAPOLEON
North Sea
Atlantic Ocean
Bay of Biscay
Borodino 1812
Friedland 1807
Jena & Auerstädt 1806
Leipzig 1813
GRAND-DUCHY OF WARSAW
Waterloo 1815
CONFEDERATION OF THE RHINE
Austerlitz 1805
Wagram 1809
FRENCH EMPIRE
ILLYRIAN PROVINCES
Vitoria 1813
SPAIN
Trafalgar 1805
Nile 1798
Adriatic Sea
Tyrrhenian Sea
Ionian Sea
Black Sea
Danube
Vistula
Dnieper
Volga
Tagus

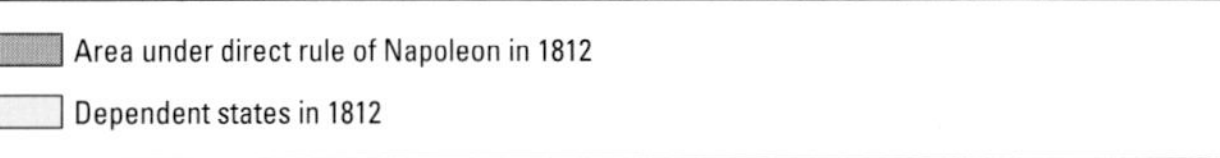
Area under direct rule of Napoleon in 1812
Dependent states in 1812

EVE OF WORLD WAR ONE
NORWAY
SWEDEN
North Sea
DENMARK
RUSSIA
UNITED KINGDOM
Atlantic Ocean
NETHS.
BELG.
LUX.
GERMAN EMPIRE
AUSTRO-HUNGARIAN EMPIRE
FRANCE
SWITZ.
Bay of Biscay
RUMANIA
SERBIA
BULGARIA
MONT.
ITALY
ALBANIA
OTTOMAN EMPIRE
PORTUGAL
SPAIN
GREECE
RHODES
ALGERIA
TUNIS
Adriatic Sea
Tyrrhenian Sea
Ionian Sea
Black Sea
Danube
Tagus

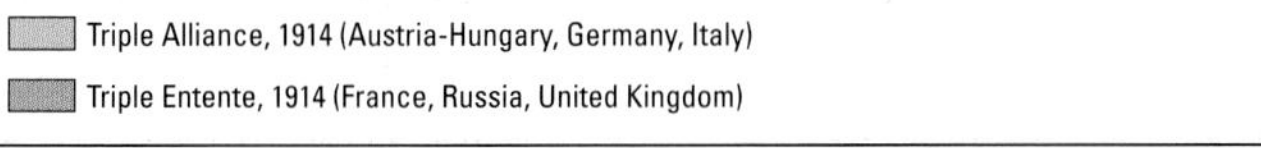
Triple Alliance, 1914 (Austria-Hungary, Germany, Italy)
Triple Entente, 1914 (France, Russia, United Kingdom)

THE COLD WAR
FIN.
NORWAY
SWEDEN
North Sea
DENMARK
UNION OF SOVIET SOCIALIST REPUBLICS
IRELAND
UNITED KINGDOM
GERMAN DEMOCRATIC REP.
POLAND
NETHS.
BELG.
LUX.
FED. REP. OF GERMANY
CZECHOSLOVAKIA
Atlantic Ocean
AUSTRIA
HUNGARY
ROMANIA
FRANCE
SWITZ.
YUGOSLAVIA
BULGARIA
ITALY
PORTUGAL
ALBANIA
TURKEY
SPAIN
GREECE
MOROCCO
ALGERIA
TUNISIA
Bay of Biscay
Adriatic Sea
Tyrrhenian Sea
Ionian Sea
Black Sea
Tagus

North Atlantic Treaty Organisation (NATO), 1964 *[other members: Iceland, Canada, USA]*
Warsaw Pact, 1964
Non-Aligned Movement, 1964

See also... International Organisations (30-31); Europe Historical (59); Countries A-Z (202-210)

The listings above refer to a selection of related themes. For more information, see the Contents (2-7).

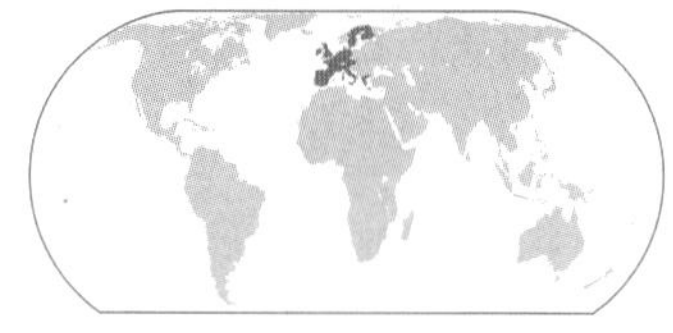

The European Union has its origin in the European Coal and Steel Community, established in 1951. It was originally designed to ensure peace in Europe by combining the essential economic interests of its six member countries. These countries became the founding members of the European Economic Community (EEC) in 1957 under the Treaty of Rome. A gradual process of expansion and economic and political integration led in November 1993 to the creation of the 12-member European Union (EU).

The EU has developed far beyond its original design of a free-trade bloc, embracing not only a single currency and a European Central Bank, but also common measures in justice, policing, immigration, transport, environment, security and foreign policy. The EU is also the world's single largest provider of aid to developing countries. As a result, the EU has a complicated structure, in which both individual national governments and pan-EU bodies play a role. The most important of the latter are: the Council of the EU, which comprises senior representatives of the constituent national governments; the European Commission which operates, in effect, as the 'government' or executive of the EU; and the elected European Parliament which serves as its legislature.

Greenland exercised its autonomy under the Danish Crown and withdrew from the EEC in 1985. The territory now has an Association Agreement with the EU.

Iceland

Iceland and Norway are Associate Members of the Schengen Agreement

The Faroe Islands, a self-governing territory of Denmark, is not part of the EU but has a trading agreement with it

FAROE IS. (Den.)

Norway

SWEDEN

Stockholm

The Åland Is. are exempted from certain EU taxes

FINLAND

Helsinki

Tallinn

ESTONIA

Riga

LATVIA

LITHUANIA

Vilnius

The Baltic port of Kaliningrad and its hinterland form an enclave of the Russian Federation completely surrounded by EU territory. The EU Commission and the Russian government have agreed special arrangements to allow travel between the enclave and Russia proper. There are, at present, no special economic or trade agreements between the enclave and the EU although these may be negotiated at a later date.

SCOTLAND

N. IRE.

UNITED KINGDOM

Dublin

IRELAND

I.o.M.

WALES

ENGLAND

London

The Channel Is. and the Isle of Man are not officially part of the UK, but as dependencies of the British Crown they maintain certain connections with the EU

Ch. Is.

DENMARK

Copenhagen

EUROPEAN ENVIRONMENT AGENCY

Bonn was the capital of the Fed. Rep. of Germany until 2002

(German Dem. Rep.)

Berlin

NETHS.

Amsterdam

GERMANY

Bonn

Warsaw

POLAND

BELG.

Brussels

COUNCIL OF THE EUROPEAN UNION

EUROPEAN COMMISSION

EUROPEAN PARLIAMENT

COMMITTEE OF PERMANENT REPRESENTATIVES

EU ECONOMIC AND SOCIAL COMMITTEE

EU COMMITTEE OF THE REGIONS

LUX.

Frankfurt am Main

EUROPEAN CENTRAL BANK

Prague

CZECH REP.

SLOVAK REP.

Bratislava

Paris

Strasbourg

EUROPEAN PARLIAMENT

Vienna

AUSTRIA

Budapest

HUNGARY

Romania

Bucharest

Liech.

Switzerland

Luxembourg

FRANCE

EUROPEAN COURT OF JUSTICE

EUROPEAN COURT OF AUDITORS

EUROPEAN INVESTMENT BANK

EUROSTAT

SLOVENIA

Ljubljana

Zagreb

Croatia

Switzerland and Liechtenstein are not members of the EU

Monaco

San Marino

Bulgaria

Sofia

Andorra

Andorra is not a member of the EU but has a trading agreement with it

ITALY

Rome

Vatican City

Former Yugoslav Republic of Macedonia

Skopje

Turkey has had an Association Agreement with the then EEC since 1963. A formal application to join was lodged in 1987 but has since been in abeyance until December 2004. This is a result of the attitude of existing EU members towards Turkey's poor human rights record, continuing support of northern Cyprus, perceived lack of democratic credentials and state-controlled economic system.

Ankara

Turkey

PORTUGAL

Lisbon

Madrid

SPAIN

Monaco, San Marino and the Vatican City maintain connections with the EU due to their close relationships with France and Italy respectively

GREECE

Athens

Gibraltar, as a dependency of the UK, is part of the EU

GIBRALTAR (UK)

CEUTA (Sp.)

MELILLA (Sp.)

The Canary Islands, Ceuta and Melilla are integral parts of Spain; The Azores and Madeira are integral parts of Portugal

CANARY IS. (Sp.)

AZORES (Port.)

MADEIRA (Port.)

Valletta

MALTA

REP. OF CYPRUS

Nicosia

Since the 1974 Turkish invasion, Cyprus has been partitioned between the southern, mainly Greek-populated Republic of Cyprus and the Turkish-controlled northern sector. Only the Republic of Cyprus, which enjoys full international recognition, has been admitted to the EU. The 'Turkish Republic of Northern Cyprus' is not recognised by the EU.

The provisions and conditions of EU membership also apply to the following territories which are integral parts of member states: Canary Is., Ceuta and Melilla (Spain); Azores and Madeira (Portugal) and (both not Schengen) French Guiana, Guadeloupe, Martinique and Réunion (France);

1957 Founder members (6)

Subsequent members:

- **1973** (3)
- **1981** (1)
- **1986** (2)
- **1990** Following the reunification of Germany in 1990, the former German Democratic Republic was automatically admitted to the EEC.
- **1995** (3)

EU-15

- **2004** (10)

EU NEW 10

Accession countries (to join in 2007?)

Candidate countries (to join in 2012/13?)

There are no formal limits on the ultimate boundaries of the EU and other nations may apply to join in future. These include countries which have previously opted out (Norway, Iceland, Switzerland), the Balkan countries yet to be candidates (Bosnia-Herzegovina, Serbia and Montenegro, Albania) and perhaps others beyond Europe in the former Soviet Union, the Levant and North Africa.

The process of joining the EU begins with the signing of an Association Agreement, essentially a free trade accord. The next stage is to become a Candidate country by meeting three conditions (The Copenhagen Criteria):

- Democracy, human rights and the rule of law;
- A market economy;
- The adoption of the EU's acquis, which lay down the precepts and standards for all member states and cover almost every aspect of government.

Once a timetable has been agreed for the acquis, the Candidate country is certain to join the EU and becomes an Accession country.

EURO ZONE Members which have adopted monetary union are shown in RED

The single European currency, the euro, came into being in 1999 along with the European Central Bank which supervises the eurozone and sets interest rates. Since 2002, the euro has been the sole legitimate currency in the 12 (out of 25) EU countries which have adopted it. Eurozone membership requires that a country meets various economic criteria covering inflation, interest and exchange rates, and government finances (although these can be somewhat flexible). The UK and Denmark have derogations under the 1992 Maastricht Treaty while Sweden appears to have no intention to join. Of the 10 countries which joined the EU in 2004, all wish to enter the eurozone and all should be admitted by 2012; at present, they have either pegged their currencies to the euro or allow them to float within a fixed range.

Several countries outside the EU, mostly former colonies and associated territories, have linked their currencies to the euro which is now a major force in international finance.

Schengen countries

The Schengen Agreement allows for the removal of most frontier controls and the harmonisation of procedures governing the movement of people and goods between signatory countries. It also provides for co-operation between law enforcement agencies in specified areas including immigration, terrorism and serious crime. Two non-EU countries, Iceland and Norway, are associate members of the Schengen Agreement.

The United Kingdom and Ireland subscribe only to some parts of the Schengen Agreement.

Most of the Schengen conditions have now been incorporated into the acquis which comprise the basic conditions for entry into the EU. As such, all new EU members will necessarily adopt the Schengen measures in due course.

Principal EU institutions

■ **Capital cities**

SUMMARY TABLE

For more country statistics, including tourism, energy and health, see the Countries A-Z section in the Appendices

Country	Exchange rate, 1st Feb 2006 One euro=	Currency	Central Bank interest rate, 1st Feb 2006 (%)	Standard VAT rate 2005 (%)	Inflation, 2005 average (%)	Unemployment, 2005 average (% of workforce)	Gross National Income (GNI), 2004 (US$ billion)	GDP growth, 2003-2004 (%)	Balance of payments, 2004 (m euros)	Government debt, 2004 (% of GDP)	Gov't expenditure, 2004 (% of GDP)
EUROZONE Central Bank interest rate in the Eurozone is set by the European Central Bank, Frankfurt											
Austria	1		3.25	[1] 20	1.6	5.2	262.2	2.4	+573	64.3	49.9
Belgium	1		3.25	21	2.4	8.4	322.8	2.6	+9,513	96.2	49.5
Finland	1		3.25	[2] 22	1.0	8.3	171.0	3.6	+7,667	45.1	51.1
France	1		3.25	[3] 19.6	1.8	9.2	1,858.7	2.3	–6,760	65.1	53.4
Germany	1		3.25	[4] 16	2.3	9.3	2,489.0	1.6	+83,509	66.4	46.9
Greece	1		3.25	[5] 19	3.4	10.5	183.9	4.7	–8,800	109.3	49.8
Ireland	1		3.25	21	2.2	4.3	137.8	4.5	–1,181	29.8	33.7
Italy	1		3.25	[6] 20	2.4	8.0	1,503.6	1.2	–12,054	106.5	48.6
Luxembourg	1		3.25	15	3.6	5.6	25.3	4.5	+2,851	6.6	45.3
Netherlands	1		3.25	19	1.6	4.7	515.1	1.7	+44,163	53.1	46.6
Portugal	1		3.25	[7] 21	2.5	7.5	149.8	1.2	–8,603	59.4	46.1
Spain	1		3.25	[8] 16	3.4	8.5	875.8	3.1	–44,451	46.9	38.8
NON-EUROZONE											
Cyprus, Rep.of	0.57	*Cyprus Pound*	4.25	15	2.0	7.9	13.6	3.8	–716	72.0	43.6
Czech Republic	28.41	*Koruna*	2.00	[9] 19	2.2	7.9	93.2	4.4	–4,518	36.8	44.3
Denmark	7.46	*Krone*	2.40	[10] 25	1.9	4.5	219.4	2.1	4,493	43.2	55.1
Estonia	15.65	*Kroon*	3.80	18	4.0	6.6	9.4	7.8	–1,148	5.5	36.4
Hungary	252.55	*Forint*	6.00	25	3.3	7.3	83.3	4.6	–7,132	57.4	49.7
Latvia	0.70	*Lats*	4.00	18	7.5	8.6	12.6	9.8	–1,445	14.7	35.8
Lithuania	3.45	*Litas*	3.25	18	2.8	7.0	19.7	7.0	–1,393	19.6	33.2
Malta	0.43	*Maltese Lira*	3.25	18	4.3	7.7	4.9	0.1	–431	75.9	48.8
Poland	3.83	*Zloty*	4.50	22	1.1	17.4	232.4	5.3	–8,406	43.6	43.0
Slovak Republic	37.35	*Koruna*	3.00	19	3.6	16.0	34.9	5.5	–1,156	42.5	40.6
Slovenia	239.51	*Tolar*	6.25	20	2.1	5.9	29.6	4.2	–542	29.8	47.4
Sweden	9.24	*Krona*	1.75	25	1.2	6.4	321.4	3.7	+22,594	51.1	56.7
United Kingdom	0.68	*Sterling*	4.50	[11] 17.5	2.1	4.7	2,016.4	3.2	–34,563	41.5	43.7

[1] 16% in Jungholz & Mittelberg. [2] Excluding Åland Is. [3] 8.5% in Guadeloupe, Martinique & Réunion. [4] Excluding Helgoland & Busingen. [5] 13% on many of the Greek islands. No VAT applies to Mount Athos. [6] Excluding Livigno, the Italian enclave of Campione d'Italia & territorial waters of Lake Lugano. [7] 15% in the Azores & Madeira. [8] Excluding Canary Is., Ceuta & Melilla. [9] Including UK Sovereign Base Areas. [10] Excluding Faroe Is. & Greenland. [11] Excluding Channel Is.

Sources: European System of Central Banks; Eurostat; European Commission; World Bank; oanda.com

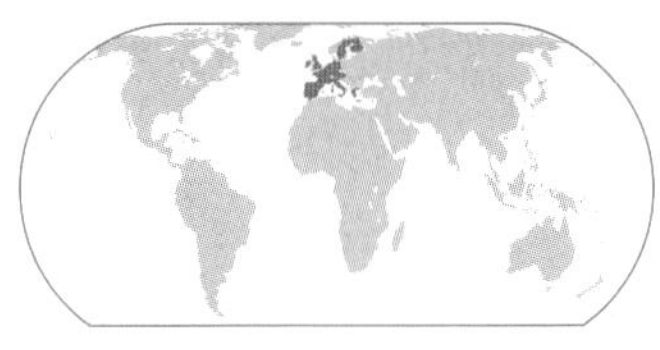

See also... International Organisations (30-31); Europe Historical (59); Countries A-Z (202-210)

The listings above refer to a selection of related themes. For more information, see the Contents (2-7).

POPULATION DENSITY

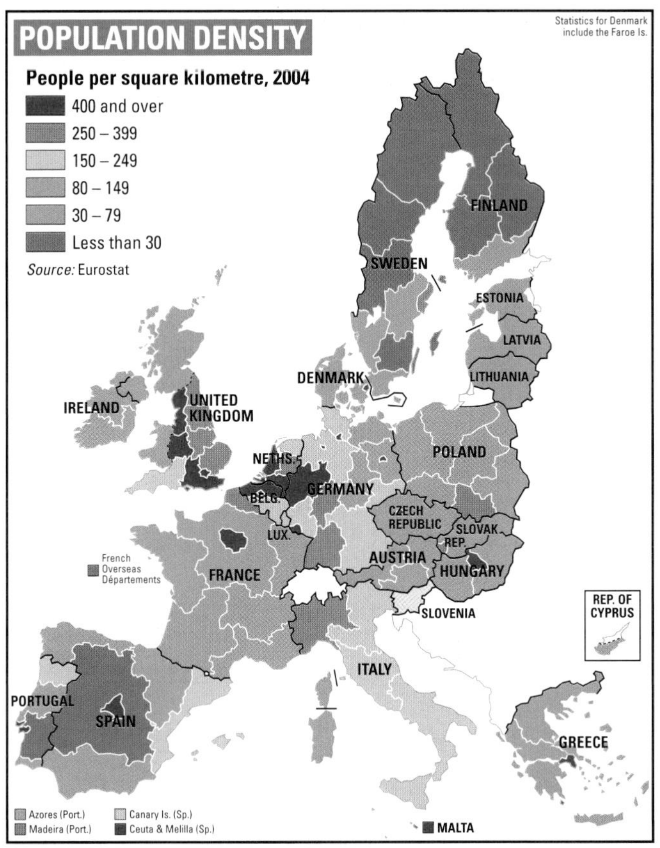
POPULATION DENSITY
Statistics for Denmark include the Faroe Is.
People per square kilometre, 2004
400 and over
250 – 399
150 – 249
80 – 149
30 – 79
Less than 30
Source: Eurostat
FINLAND
SWEDEN
ESTONIA
LATVIA
LITHUANIA
DENMARK
IRELAND
UNITED KINGDOM
POLAND
NETHS.
BELG.
GERMANY
CZECH REPUBLIC
SLOVAK REP.
LUX.
AUSTRIA
HUNGARY
French Overseas Départements
FRANCE
SLOVENIA
REP. OF CYPRUS
ITALY
PORTUGAL
SPAIN
GREECE
Azores (Port.)
Madeira (Port.)
Canary Is. (Sp.)
Ceuta & Melilla (Sp.)
MALTA

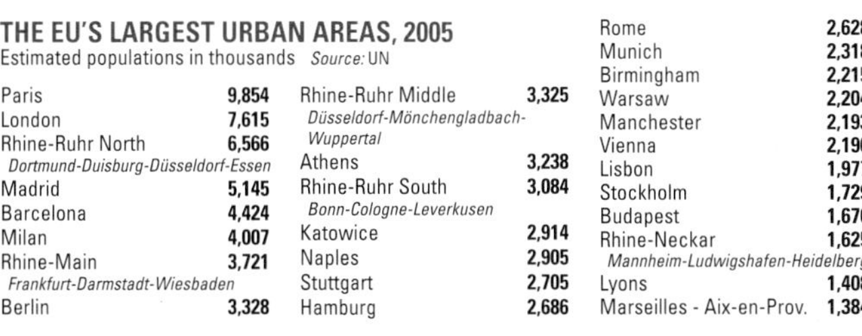

THE EU'S LARGEST URBAN AREAS, 2005

Estimated populations in thousands *Source:* UN

Urban area	Population
Paris	9,854
London	7,615
Rhine-Ruhr North *Dortmund-Duisburg-Düsseldorf-Essen*	6,566
Madrid	5,145
Barcelona	4,424
Milan	4,007
Rhine-Main *Frankfurt-Darmstadt-Wiesbaden*	3,721
Berlin	3,328
Rhine-Ruhr Middle *Düsseldorf-Mönchengladbach-Wuppertal*	3,325
Athens	3,238
Rhine-Ruhr South *Bonn-Cologne-Leverkusen*	3,084
Katowice	2,914
Naples	2,905
Stuttgart	2,705
Hamburg	2,686
Rome	2,628
Munich	2,318
Birmingham	2,215
Warsaw	2,204
Manchester	2,193
Vienna	2,190
Lisbon	1,977
Stockholm	1,729
Budapest	1,670
Rhine-Neckar *Mannheim-Ludwigshafen-Heidelberg*	1,625
Lyons	1,408
Marseilles - Aix-en-Prov.	1,384

THE EU BUDGET

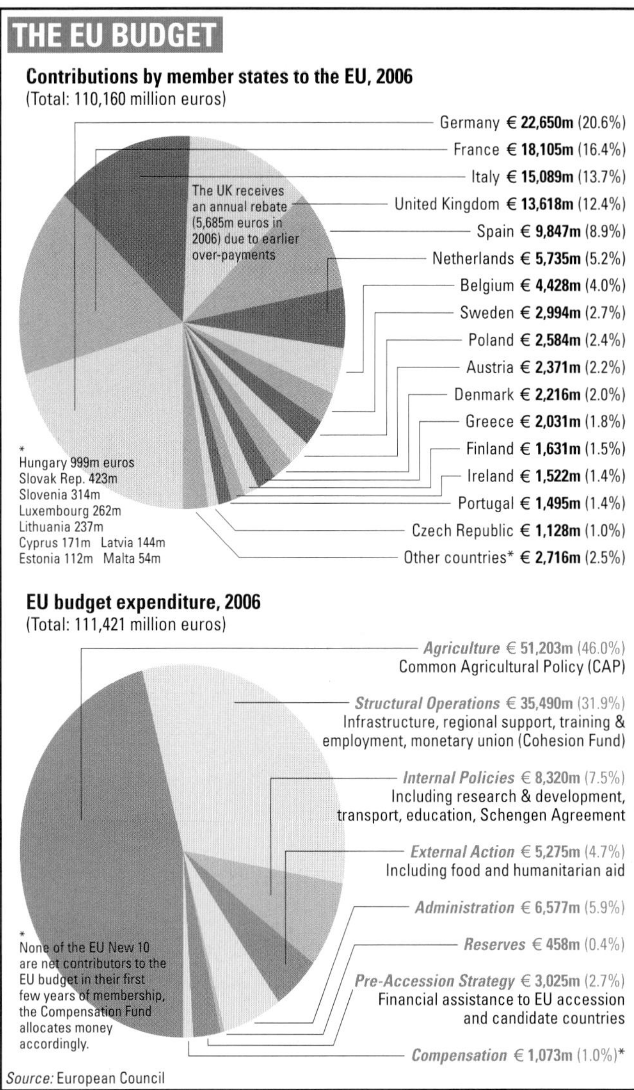
THE EU BUDGET
Contributions by member states to the EU, 2006
(Total: 110,160 million euros)
Germany € 22,650m (20.6%)
France € 18,105m (16.4%)
Italy € 15,089m (13.7%)
United Kingdom € 13,618m (12.4%)
Spain € 9,847m (8.9%)
Netherlands € 5,735m (5.2%)
Belgium € 4,428m (4.0%)
Sweden € 2,994m (2.7%)
Poland € 2,584m (2.4%)
Austria € 2,371m (2.2%)
Denmark € 2,216m (2.0%)
Greece € 2,031m (1.8%)
Finland € 1,631m (1.5%)
Ireland € 1,522m (1.4%)
Portugal € 1,495m (1.4%)
Czech Republic € 1,128m (1.0%)
Other countries* € 2,716m (2.5%)
The UK receives an annual rebate (5,685m euros in 2006) due to earlier over-payments
* Hungary 999m euros
Slovak Rep. 423m
Slovenia 314m
Luxembourg 262m
Lithuania 237m
Cyprus 171m Latvia 144m
Estonia 112m Malta 54m
EU budget expenditure, 2006
(Total: 111,421 million euros)
Agriculture € 51,203m (46.0%)
Common Agricultural Policy (CAP)
Structural Operations € 35,490m (31.9%)
Infrastructure, regional support, training & employment, monetary union (Cohesion Fund)
Internal Policies € 8,320m (7.5%)
Including research & development, transport, education, Schengen Agreement
External Action € 5,275m (4.7%)
Including food and humanitarian aid
Administration € 6,577m (5.9%)
Reserves € 458m (0.4%)
Pre-Accession Strategy € 3,025m (2.7%)
Financial assistance to EU accession and candidate countries
Compensation € 1,073m (1.0%)*
* None of the EU New 10 are net contributors to the EU budget in their first few years of membership, the Compensation Fund allocates money accordingly.
Source: European Council

INCOME

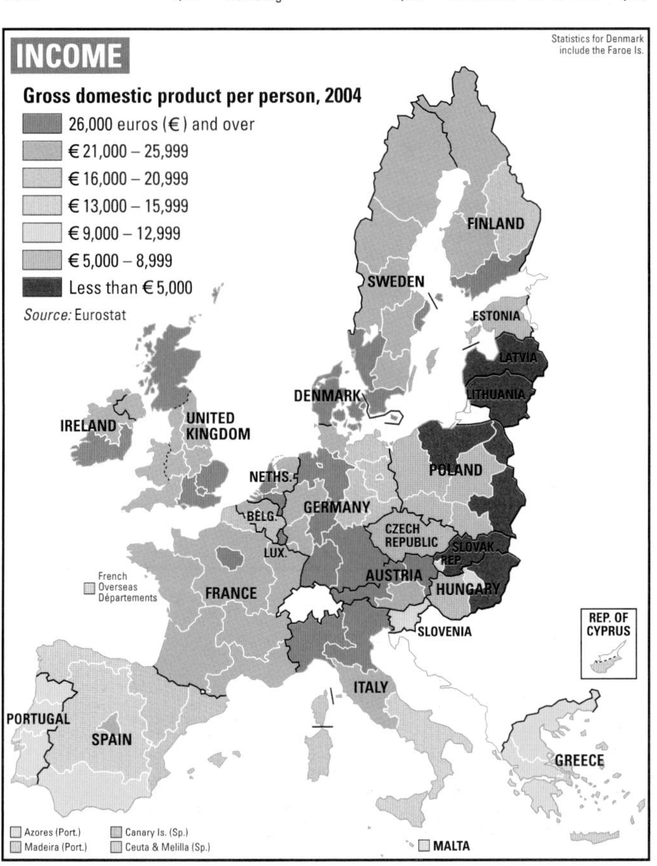
INCOME
Statistics for Denmark include the Faroe Is.
Gross domestic product per person, 2004
26,000 euros (€) and over
€ 21,000 – 25,999
€ 16,000 – 20,999
€ 13,000 – 15,999
€ 9,000 – 12,999
€ 5,000 – 8,999
Less than € 5,000
Source: Eurostat
FINLAND
SWEDEN
ESTONIA
LATVIA
LITHUANIA
DENMARK
IRELAND
UNITED KINGDOM
POLAND
NETHS.
BELG.
GERMANY
CZECH REPUBLIC
SLOVAK REP.
LUX.
AUSTRIA
HUNGARY
French Overseas Départements
FRANCE
SLOVENIA
REP. OF CYPRUS
ITALY
PORTUGAL
SPAIN
GREECE
Azores (Port.)
Madeira (Port.)
Canary Is. (Sp.)
Ceuta & Melilla (Sp.)
MALTA

UNEMPLOYMENT

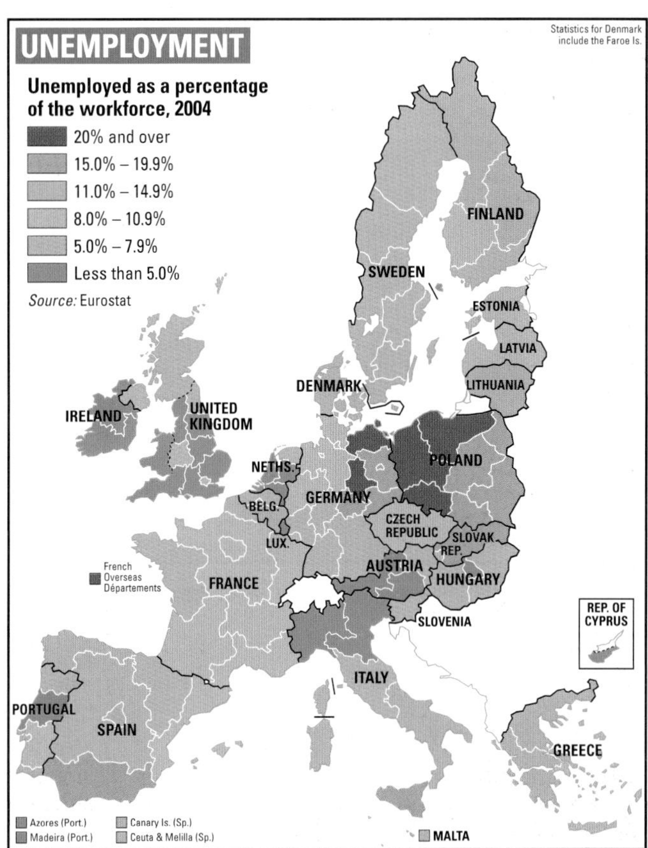
UNEMPLOYMENT
Statistics for Denmark include the Faroe Is.
Unemployed as a percentage of the workforce, 2004
20% and over
15.0% – 19.9%
11.0% – 14.9%
8.0% – 10.9%
5.0% – 7.9%
Less than 5.0%
Source: Eurostat
FINLAND
SWEDEN
ESTONIA
LATVIA
LITHUANIA
DENMARK
IRELAND
UNITED KINGDOM
POLAND
NETHS.
BELG.
GERMANY
CZECH REPUBLIC
SLOVAK REP.
LUX.
AUSTRIA
HUNGARY
French Overseas Départements
FRANCE
SLOVENIA
REP. OF CYPRUS
ITALY
PORTUGAL
SPAIN
GREECE
Azores (Port.)
Madeira (Port.)
Canary Is. (Sp.)
Ceuta & Melilla (Sp.)
MALTA

Airports & High-Speed Rail

See also... World Airports (42-44); World Flight Times (45); Europe Railways & Ferries (64-65); London Airport Connections (75) • cont >

The listings above refer to a selection of related themes. For more information, see the Contents (2-7).

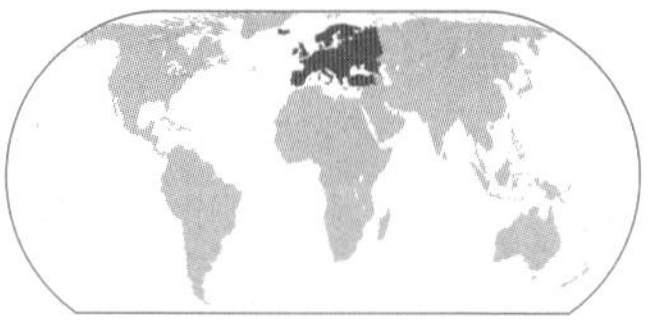

Faced with stern competition from the ever-expanding high-speed rail services and the need to utilise precious runway slots for the more lucrative long-haul routes, several European airlines have been forced into co-operation with rail companies. As a result, many previously prestigious air routes, such as Air France's Paris–Brussels and Lufthansa's Stuttgart–Frankfurt, are now run by, or in conjunction with, high-speed rail operators offering city-centre to city-centre services. As the European rail network expands, as its standards of safety, speed and comfort improve and as the continent's airports become more overcrowded, this development is likely to become more widespread. Increasingly, a consideration of Europe's air routes thus also requires an appreciation of these complementary high-speed rail services.

Note: the airports shown are selected, on the basic of international passenger movements, from those which report to Airports Council International (ACI). Some airports in some countries are therefore not shown.

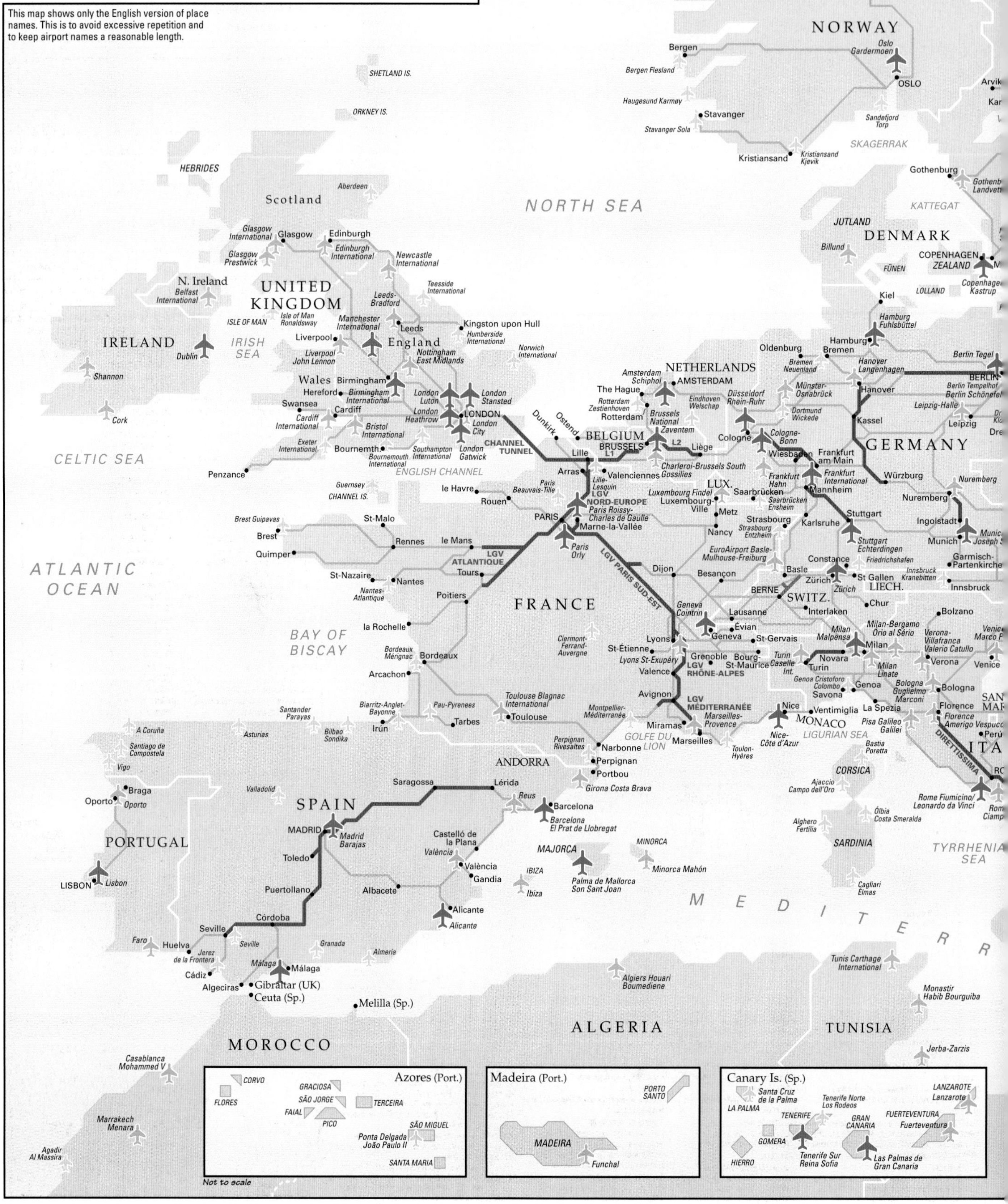

This map shows only the English version of place names. This is to avoid excessive repetition and to keep airport names a reasonable length.

NORWEGIAN SEA
NORTH SEA
CELTIC SEA
ATLANTIC OCEAN
BAY OF BISCAY
ENGLISH CHANNEL
IRISH SEA
SKAGERRAK
KATTEGAT
GOLFE DU LION
LIGURIAN SEA
TYRRHENIAN SEA
MEDITERR

NORWAY
Trondheim
Trondheim Vaernes
Ålesund Vigra
Bergen
Bergen Flesland
Oslo Gardermoen
OSLO
Haugesund Karmøy
Stavanger
Stavanger Sola
Sandefjord Torp
Kristiansand
Kristiansand Kjevik

SHETLAND IS.
ORKNEY IS.
HEBRIDES
Scotland
Aberdeen
Glasgow International
Glasgow
Glasgow Prestwick
Edinburgh
Edinburgh International
Newcastle International
Teesside International
N. Ireland
Belfast International
UNITED KINGDOM
ISLE OF MAN
Isle of Man Ronaldsway
Leeds-Bradford
Leeds
Manchester International
Kingston upon Hull
Humberside International
IRELAND
Dublin
Shannon
Cork
Liverpool
Liverpool John Lennon
England
Nottingham East Midlands
Norwich International
Wales
Birmingham
Birmingham International
Hereford
Swansea
Cardiff
Cardiff International
Bristol International
Exeter International
London Luton
London Stansted
London Heathrow
LONDON
London City
London Gatwick
Southampton International
Bournemouth
Bournemouth International
Penzance
CHANNEL TUNNEL
Guernsey
CHANNEL IS.

NETHERLANDS
Amsterdam Schiphol
AMSTERDAM
The Hague
Rotterdam Zestienhoven
Rotterdam
Eindhoven Welschap
Düsseldorf Rhein-Ruhr
BELGIUM
Dunkirk
Ostend
Brussels National Zaventem
BRUSSELS
L1
L2
Liège
Lille
Charleroi-Brussels South
Gossilies
Valenciennes
LUX.
Luxembourg Findel
Luxembourg Ville

GERMANY
Oldenburg
Bremen Neuenland
Bremen
Hamburg
Hamburg Fuhlsbüttel
Kiel
Hanover Langenhagen
Hanover
Münster-Osnabrück
Dortmund Wickede
Cologne
Cologne-Bonn
Kassel
Berlin Tegel
BERLIN
Berlin Tempelhof
Berlin Schönefeld
Leipzig-Halle
Leipzig
Wiesbaden
Frankfurt am Main
Frankfurt International
Frankfurt Hahn
Saarbrücken
Saarbrücken Ensheim
Mannheim
Würzburg
Nuremberg
Karlsruhe
Stuttgart
Stuttgart Echterdingen
Friedrichshafen
Ingolstadt
Munich
Munich Joseph S
Garmisch-Partenkirchen

DENMARK
JUTLAND
Billund
FÜNEN
ZEALAND
LOLLAND
COPENHAGEN
Copenhagen Kastrup
Gothenburg
Gothenburg Landvetter

FRANCE
Arras
Lille Lesquin
LGV NORD-EUROPE
Paris Roissy-Charles de Gaulle
Paris Beauvais-Tille
le Havre
Rouen
PARIS
Marne-la-Vallée
Paris Orly
Metz
Nancy
Strasbourg
Strasbourg Entzheim
EuroAirport Basle-Mulhouse-Freiburg
Brest Guipavas
Brest
Quimper
St-Malo
Rennes
le Mans
LGV ATLANTIQUE
Tours
St-Nazaire
Nantes
Nantes-Atlantique
Poitiers
la Rochelle
LGV PARIS SUD-EST
Dijon
Besançon
Clermont-Ferrand-Auvergne
Lyons
St-Étienne
Lyons St-Exupéry
LGV RHÔNE-ALPES
Grenoble
Bourg-St-Maurice
Valence
Bordeaux Mérignac
Bordeaux
Arcachon
Avignon
LGV MÉDITERRANÉE
Marseilles-Provence
Miramas
Marseilles
Toulon-Hyères
Nice
Nice-Côte d'Azur
MONACO
Montpellier-Méditerranée
Toulouse Blagnac International
Toulouse
Pau-Pyrenees
Tarbes
Biarritz-Anglet-Bayonne
Irún
Perpignan Rivesaltes
Narbonne
Perpignan
Portbou
ANDORRA

SWITZ.
Basle
Zürich
BERNE
Geneva Cointrin
Lausanne
Évian
Geneva
St-Gervais
Interlaken
Constance
St Gallen
LIECH.
Chur
Innsbruck
Innsbruck Kranebitten

ITA
Milan-Bergamo Orio al Sério
Milan Malpensa
Milan
Milan Linate
Turin
Turin Caselle Int.
Novara
Verona
Verona-Villafranca Valerio Catullo
Venice
Venice Marco P
Bolzano
Genoa
Genoa Cristoforo Colombo
Savona
Ventimiglia
La Spezia
Bologna
Bologna Guglielmo Marconi
Florence
Florence Amerigo Vespucci
Perú
Pisa Galileo Galilei
DIRETTISSIMA
SAN MAR
Rome Fiumicino/ Leonardo da Vinci
Rome Ciamp
CORSICA
Bastia Poretta
Ajaccio Campo dell'Oro
SARDINIA
Olbia Costa Smeralda
Alghero Fertilia
Cagliari Elmas

SPAIN
A Coruña
Santiago de Compostela
Vigo
Asturias
Santander Parayas
Bilbao Sondika
Valladolid
Saragossa
Lérida
Reus
Barcelona
Barcelona El Prat de Llobregat
Girona Costa Brava
MADRID
Madrid Barajas
Toledo
Castelló de la Plana
València
Albacete
Puertollano
Alicante
Gandia
Córdoba
Seville
Granada
Almeria
Málaga
Jerez de la Frontera
Huelva
Cádiz
Algeciras
Gibraltar (UK)
Ceuta (Sp.)
Melilla (Sp.)
MAJORCA
Palma de Mallorca Son Sant Joan
MINORCA
Minorca Mahón
IBIZA
Ibiza

PORTUGAL
Braga
Oporto
LISBON
Lisbon
Faro

MOROCCO
Casablanca Mohammed V
Marrakech Menara
Agadir Al Massira
ALGERIA
Algiers Houari Boumediene
TUNISIA
Tunis Carthage International
Monastir Habib Bourguiba
Jerba-Zarzis

Azores (Port.)
CORVO
FLORES
GRACIOSA
SÃO JORGE
TERCEIRA
FAIAL
PICO
SÃO MIGUEL
Ponta Delgada João Paulo II
SANTA MARIA

Madeira (Port.)
PORTO SANTO
MADEIRA
Funchal

Canary Is. (Sp.)
Santa Cruz de la Palma
LA PALMA
TENERIFE
Tenerife Norte Los Rodeos
GOMERA
HIERRO
Tenerife Sur Reina Sofía
GRAN CANARIA
Las Palmas de Gran Canaria
LANZAROTE
Lanzarote
FUERTEVENTURA
Fuerteventura

Not to scale

See also... cont < • Berlin Airport Connections (83); Paris Airport Connections (87)

The listings above refer to a selection of related themes. For more information, see the Contents (2-7).

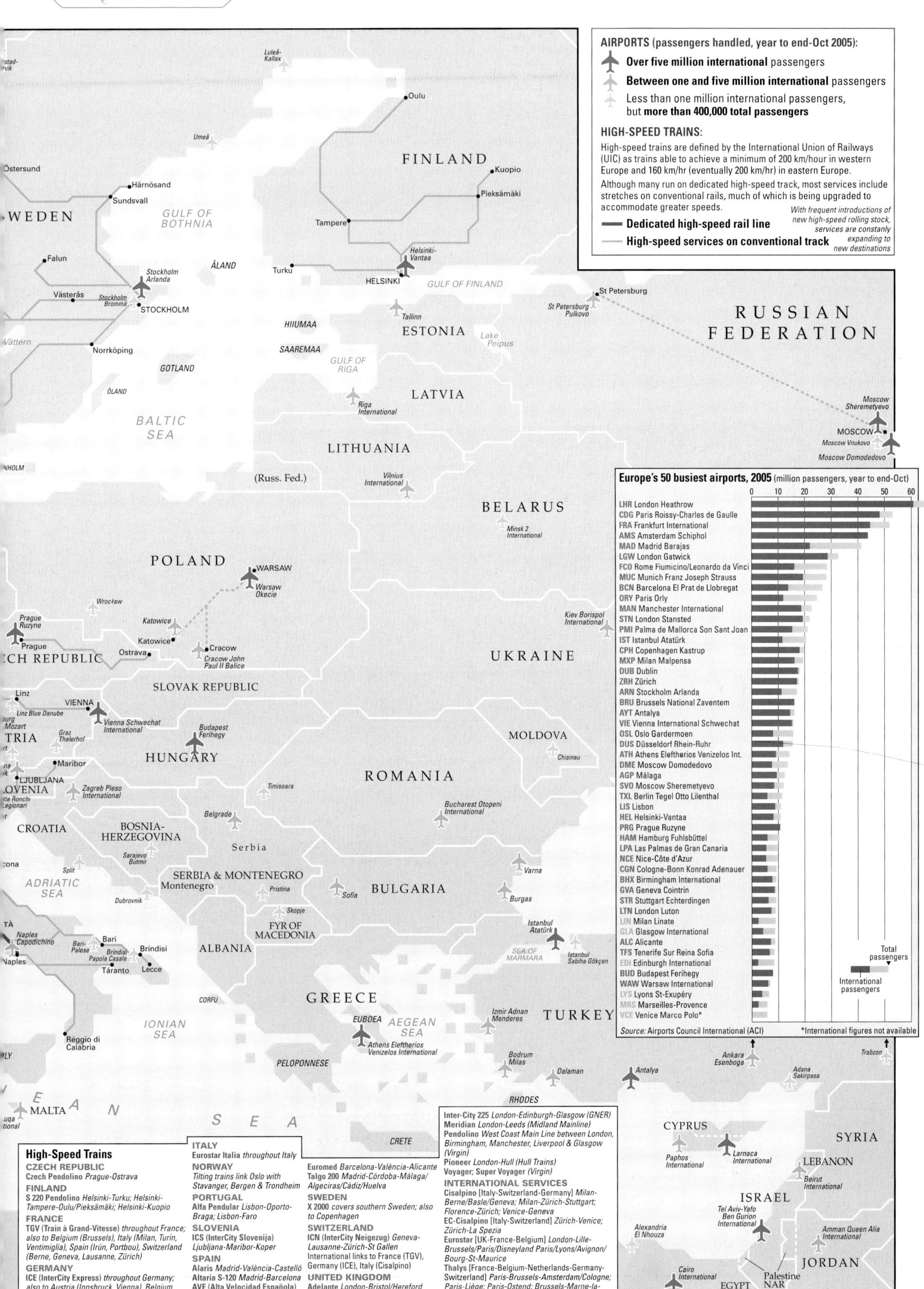
AIRPORTS (passengers handled, year to end-Oct 2005):
Over five million international passengers
Between one and five million international passengers
Less than one million international passengers, but more than 400,000 total passengers
HIGH-SPEED TRAINS:
High-speed trains are defined by the International Union of Railways (UIC) as trains able to achieve a minimum of 200 km/hour in western Europe and 160 km/hr (eventually 200 km/hr) in eastern Europe.
Although many run on dedicated high-speed track, most services include stretches on conventional rails, much of which is being upgraded to accommodate greater speeds.
With frequent introductions of new high-speed rolling stock, services are constanly expanding to new destinations
Dedicated high-speed rail line
High-speed services on conventional track
Europe's 50 busiest airports, 2005 (million passengers, year to end-Oct)
0 10 20 30 40 50 60
LHR London Heathrow
CDG Paris Roissy-Charles de Gaulle
FRA Frankfurt International
AMS Amsterdam Schiphol
MAD Madrid Barajas
LGW London Gatwick
FCO Rome Fiumicino/Leonardo da Vinci
MUC Munich Franz Joseph Strauss
BCN Barcelona El Prat de Llobregat
ORY Paris Orly
MAN Manchester International
STN London Stansted
PMI Palma de Mallorca Son Sant Joan
IST Istanbul Atatürk
CPH Copenhagen Kastrup
MXP Milan Malpensa
DUB Dublin
ZRH Zürich
ARN Stockholm Arlanda
BRU Brussels National Zaventem
AYT Antalya
VIE Vienna International Schwechat
OSL Oslo Gardermoen
DUS Düsseldorf Rhein-Ruhr
ATH Athens Eleftherios Venizelos Int.
DME Moscow Domodedovo
AGP Málaga
SVO Moscow Sheremetyevo
TXL Berlin Tegel Otto Lilenthal
LIS Lisbon
HEL Helsinki-Vantaa
PRG Prague Ruzyne
HAM Hamburg Fuhlsbüttel
LPA Las Palmas de Gran Canaria
NCE Nice-Côte d'Azur
CGN Cologne-Bonn Konrad Adenauer
BHX Birmingham International
GVA Geneva Cointrin
STR Stuttgart Echterdingen
LTN London Luton
LIN Milan Linate
GLA Glasgow International
ALC Alicante
TFS Tenerife Sur Reina Sofia
EDI Edinburgh International
BUD Budapest Ferihegy
WAW Warsaw International
LYS Lyons St-Exupéry
MRS Marseilles-Provence
VCE Venice Marco Polo*
Total passengers
International passengers
Source: Airports Council International (ACI)
*International figures not available
FINLAND
RUSSIAN FEDERATION
ESTONIA
LATVIA
LITHUANIA
(Russ. Fed.)
BELARUS
POLAND
UKRAINE
SLOVAK REPUBLIC
HUNGARY
MOLDOVA
ROMANIA
CROATIA
BOSNIA-HERZEGOVINA
Serbia
SERBIA & MONTENEGRO
Montenegro
BULGARIA
FYR OF MACEDONIA
ALBANIA
GREECE
TURKEY
CYPRUS
SYRIA
LEBANON
ISRAEL
JORDAN
EGYPT
Palestine NAR
MALTA
GULF OF BOTHNIA
GULF OF FINLAND
GULF OF RIGA
BALTIC SEA
ADRIATIC SEA
IONIAN SEA
AEGEAN SEA
SEA OF MARMARA
ÅLAND
HIIUMAA
SAAREMAA
GOTLAND
ÖLAND
CORFU
EUBOEA
PELOPONNESE
RHODES
CRETE
Lake Peipus
Oulu
Kuopio
Pieksämäki
Tampere
Turku
Helsinki-Vantaa
HELSINKI
Luleå-Kallax
Umeå
Östersund
Härnösand
Sundsvall
Falun
Stockholm Arlanda
Västerås
Stockholm Bromma
STOCKHOLM
Norrköping
St Petersburg
St Petersburg Pulkovo
Tallinn
Riga International
Vilnius International
Minsk 2 International
Moscow Sheremetyevo
MOSCOW
Moscow Vnukovo
Moscow Domodedovo
WARSAW
Warsaw Okecie
Wrocław
Katowice
Cracow
Cracow John Paul II Balice
Ostrava
Prague Ruzyne
Prague
Kiev Borispol International
Linz
VIENNA
Linz Blue Danube
Vienna Schwechat International
Graz Thalerhof
Budapest Ferihegy
Maribor
LJUBLJANA
Zagreb Pleso International
Timisoara
Chisinau
Belgrade
Bucharest Otopeni International
Sarajevo Butmir
Split
Dubrovnik
Pristina
Sofia
Varna
Burgas
Skopje
Naples Capodichino
Naples
Bari
Bari-Palese
Brindisi
Brindisi-Papola Casale
Táranto
Lecce
Réggio di Calábria
Istanbul Atatürk
Istanbul Sabiha Gökçen
Izmir Adnan Menderes
Athens Eleftherios Venizelos International
Bodrum Milas
Dalaman
Antalya
Ankara Esenboga
Adana Sakirpasa
Trabzon
Paphos International
Larnaca International
Beirut International
Tel Aviv-Yafo Ben Gurion International
Alexandria El Nhouza
Amman Queen Alia International
Cairo International
High-Speed Trains
CZECH REPUBLIC
Czech Pendolino Prague-Ostrava
FINLAND
S 220 Pendolino Helsinki-Turku; Helsinki-Tampere-Oulu/Pieksämäki; Helsinki-Kuopio
FRANCE
TGV (Train à Grand-Vitesse) throughout France; also to Belgium (Brussels), Italy (Milan, Turin, Ventimiglia), Spain (Irún, Portbou), Switzerland (Berne, Geneva, Lausanne, Zürich)
GERMANY
ICE (InterCity Express) throughout Germany; also to Austria (Innsbruck, Vienna), Belgium (Brussels), Netherlands (Amsterdam), Switzerland (Basle, Interlaken, Zürich)
ITALY
Eurostar Italia throughout Italy
NORWAY
Tilting trains link Oslo with Stavanger, Bergen & Trondheim
PORTUGAL
Alfa Pendular Lisbon-Oporto-Braga; Lisbon-Faro
SLOVENIA
ICS (InterCity Slovenija) Ljubljana-Maribor-Koper
SPAIN
Alaris Madrid-València-Castelló
Altaria S-120 Madrid-Barcelona
AVE (Alta Velocidad Española) Madrid-Puertollano-Córdoba-Seville; Madrid-Lérida
Euromed Barcelona-València-Alicante
Talgo 200 Madrid-Córdoba-Málaga/Algeciras/Cádiz/Huelva
SWEDEN
X 2000 covers southern Sweden; also to Copenhagen
SWITZERLAND
ICN (InterCity Neigezug) Geneva-Lausanne-Zürich-St Gallen
International links to France (TGV), Germany (ICE), Italy (Cisalpino)
UNITED KINGDOM
Adelante London-Bristol/Hereford (First Great Western)
Inter-City 125 throughout Great Britain
Inter-City 225 London-Edinburgh-Glasgow (GNER)
Meridian London-Leeds (Midland Mainline)
Pendolino West Coast Main Line between London, Birmingham, Manchester, Liverpool & Glasgow (Virgin)
Pioneer London-Hull (Hull Trains)
Voyager; Super Voyager (Virgin)
INTERNATIONAL SERVICES
Cisalpino [Italy-Switzerland-Germany] Milan-Berne/Basle/Geneva; Milan-Zürich-Stuttgart; Florence-Zürich; Venice-Geneva
EC-Cisalpino [Italy-Switzerland] Zürich-Venice; Zürich-La Spezia
Eurostar [UK-France-Belgium] London-Lille-Brussels/Paris/Disneyland Paris/Lyons/Avignon/Bourg-St-Maurice
Thalys [France-Belgium-Netherlands-Germany-Switzerland] Paris-Brussels-Amsterdam/Cologne; Paris-Liège; Paris-Ostend; Brussels-Marne-la-Vallée; Brussels-Geneva; summer services to south of France, winter services to French Alps

See also... Europe Airports & High-Speed Rail (62-63); UK Airports, Motorways & Ferries (74)

The listings above refer to a selection of related themes. For more information, see the Contents (2-7).

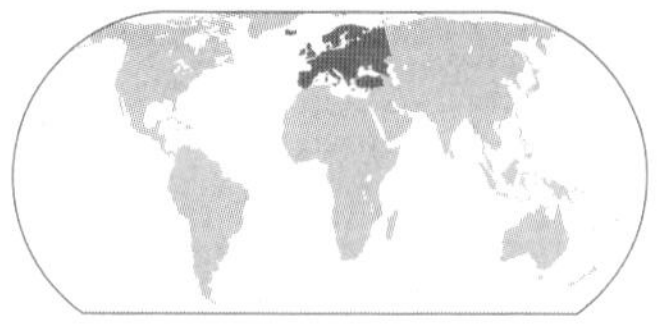

This map shows principal passenger rail and shipping routes in Europe. Some of the railways marked have limited services but are included because of their significance (such as connection to resort or international crossing).

A number of European rail passes are available, offering free travel on many rail and ferry services.

The Eurailpass is valid for first-class rail travel in the countries shown on the map. For those under 26, the Eurailpass Youth is valid in the same countries for second-class rail travel. The pass is not available to European residents or to visitors from Algeria, Morocco, Tunisia, Turkey or the Russian Federation.

European residents are eligible for the Inter-Rail pass, offering train travel in the area shown on the map, excluding the country of purchase.

Passes are available for one or more zones within the validity area.

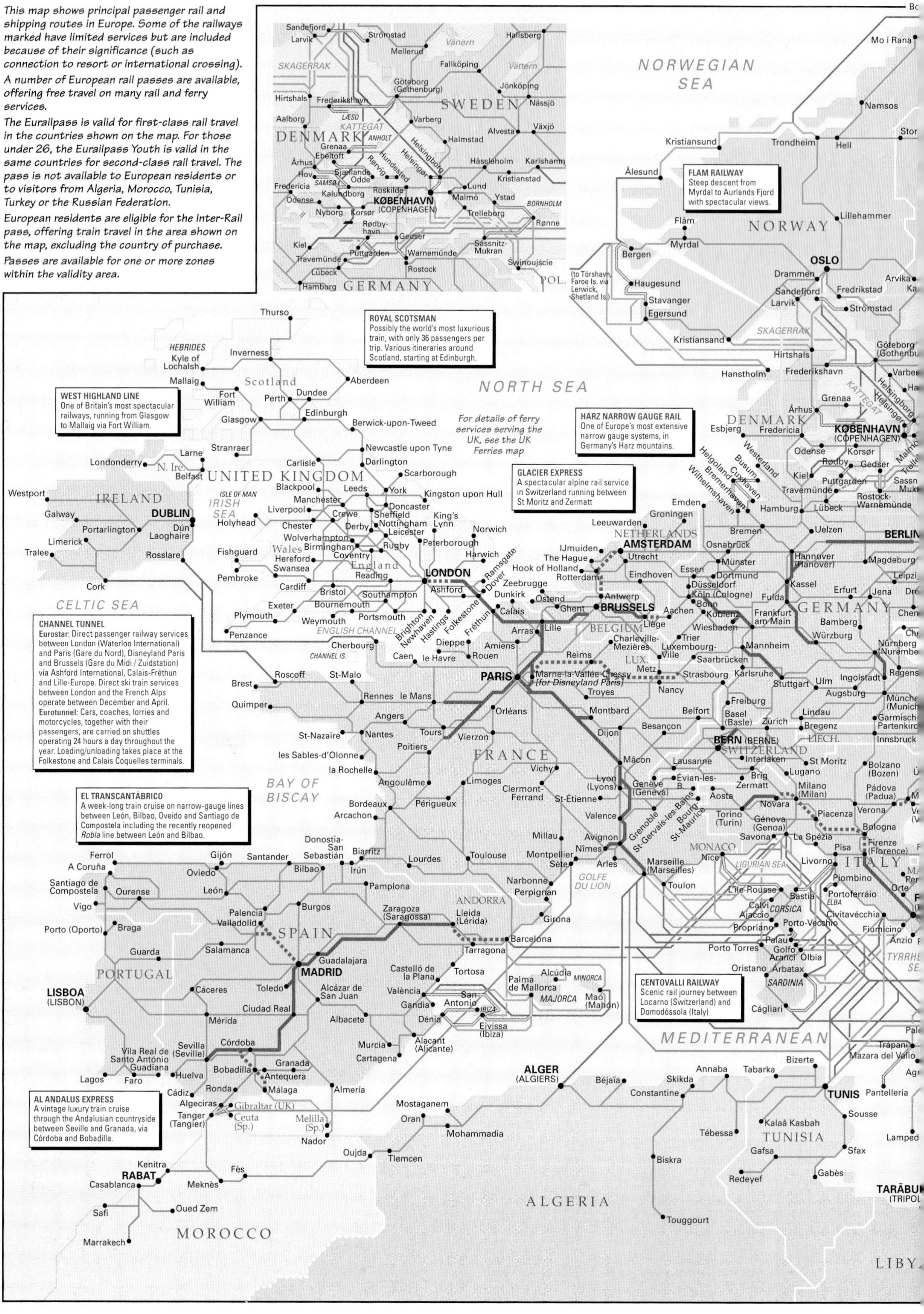

FLAM RAILWAY
Steep descent from Myrdal to Aurlands Fjord with spectacular views.

ROYAL SCOTSMAN
Possibly the world's most luxurious train, with only 36 passengers per trip. Various itineraries around Scotland, starting at Edinburgh.

WEST HIGHLAND LINE
One of Britain's most spectacular railways, running from Glasgow to Mallaig via Fort William.

For details of ferry services serving the UK, see the UK Ferries map

HARZ NARROW GAUGE RAIL
One of Europe's most extensive narrow gauge systems, in Germany's Harz mountains.

GLACIER EXPRESS
A spectacular alpine rail service in Switzerland running between St Moritz and Zermatt

CHANNEL TUNNEL
Eurostar: Direct passenger railway services between London (Waterloo International) and Paris (Gare du Nord), Disneyland Paris and Brussels (Gare du Midi / Zuidstation) via Ashford International, Calais-Fréthun and Lille-Europe. Direct ski train services between London and the French Alps operate between December and April.
Eurotunnel: Cars, coaches, lorries and motorcycles, together with their passengers, are carried on shuttles operating 24 hours a day throughout the year. Loading/unloading takes place at the Folkestone and Calais Coquelles terminals.

EL TRANSCANTÁBRICO
A week-long train cruise on narrow-gauge lines between León, Bilbao, Oveido and Santiago de Compostela including the recently reopened *Robla* line between León and Bilbao.

CENTOVALLI RAILWAY
Scenic rail journey between Locarno (Switzerland) and Domodóssola (Italy)

AL ANDALUS EXPRESS
A vintage luxury train cruise through the Andalusian countryside between Seville and Granada, via Córdoba and Bobadilla.

See also... Europe Airports & High-speed Rail (62-63); UK Airports, Motorways & Ferries (74)

The listings above refer to a selection of related themes. For more information, see the Contents (2-7).

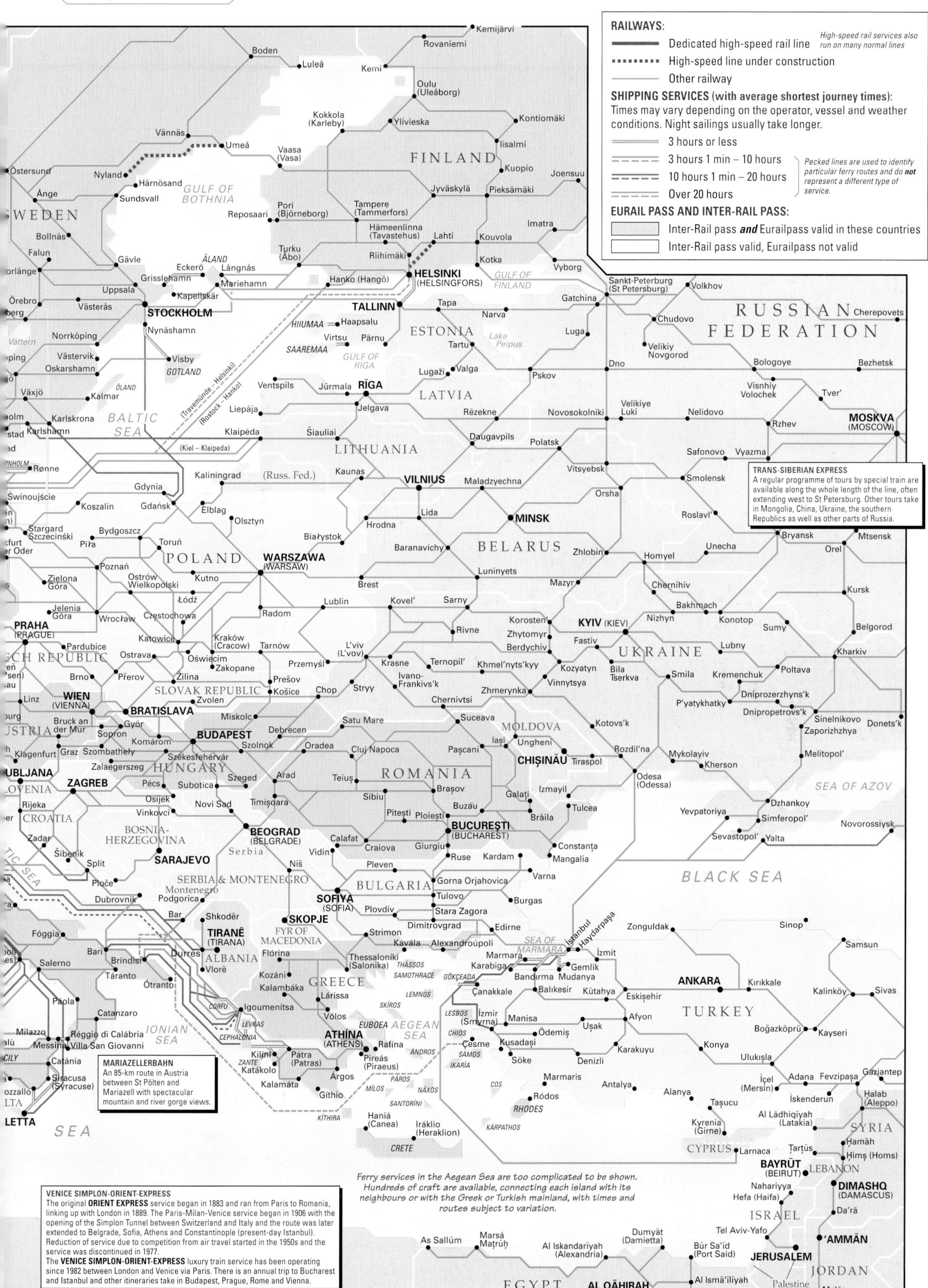
RAILWAYS:
Dedicated high-speed rail line
High-speed line under construction
Other railway
High-speed rail services also run on many normal lines
SHIPPING SERVICES (with average shortest journey times):
Times may vary depending on the operator, vessel and weather conditions. Night sailings usually take longer.
3 hours or less
3 hours 1 min – 10 hours
10 hours 1 min – 20 hours
Over 20 hours
Pecked lines are used to identify particular ferry routes and do not represent a different type of service.
EURAIL PASS AND INTER-RAIL PASS:
Inter-Rail pass and Eurailpass valid in these countries
Inter-Rail pass valid, Eurailpass not valid
TRANS-SIBERIAN EXPRESS
A regular programme of tours by special train are available along the whole length of the line, often extending west to St Petersburg. Other tours take in Mongolia, China, Ukraine, the southern Republics as well as other parts of Russia.
MARIAZELLERBAHN
An 85-km route in Austria between St Pölten and Mariazell with spectacular mountain and river gorge views.
VENICE SIMPLON-ORIENT-EXPRESS
The original ORIENT EXPRESS service began in 1883 and ran from Paris to Romania, linking up with London in 1889. The Paris-Milan-Venice service began in 1906 with the opening of the Simplon Tunnel between Switzerland and Italy and the route was later extended to Beograd, Sofia, Athens and Constantinople (present-day Istanbul). Reduction of service due to competition from air travel started in the 1950s and the service was discontinued in 1977.
The VENICE SIMPLON-ORIENT-EXPRESS luxury train service has been operating since 1982 between London and Venice via Paris. There is an annual trip to Bucharest and Istanbul and other itineraries take in Budapest, Prague, Rome and Vienna.
Ferry services in the Aegean Sea are too complicated to be shown. Hundreds of craft are available, connecting each island with its neighbours or with the Greek or Turkish mainland, with times and routes subject to variation.
FINLAND
RUSSIAN FEDERATION
ESTONIA
LATVIA
LITHUANIA
BELARUS
POLAND
UKRAINE
MOLDOVA
ROMANIA
HUNGARY
SLOVAK REPUBLIC
BULGARIA
SERBIA & MONTENEGRO
BOSNIA-HERZEGOVINA
CROATIA
ALBANIA
GREECE
TURKEY
CYPRUS
SYRIA
LEBANON
ISRAEL
JORDAN
EGYPT
GULF OF BOTHNIA
GULF OF FINLAND
GULF OF RIGA
BALTIC SEA
BLACK SEA
SEA OF AZOV
SEA OF MARMARA
AEGEAN SEA
IONIAN SEA
HELSINKI (HELSINGFORS)
STOCKHOLM
TALLINN
RĪGA
VILNIUS
MINSK
MOSKVA (MOSCOW)
WARSZAWA (WARSAW)
KYIV (KIEV)
CHIȘINĂU
BUCUREȘTI (BUCHAREST)
BUDAPEST
BRATISLAVA
WIEN (VIENNA)
PRAHA (PRAGUE)
BEOGRAD (BELGRADE)
SARAJEVO
ZAGREB
SOFIYA (SOFIA)
SKOPJE
TIRANË (TIRANA)
ATHÍNA (ATHENS)
ANKARA
BAYRŪT (BEIRUT)
DIMASHQ (DAMASCUS)
'AMMĀN
JERUSALEM
AL QĀHIRAH (CAIRO)

National Parks

See also... UNESCO Natural Heritage (48-49); US National Parks Service (166-167); Canadian National Parks (175)

The listings above refer to a selection of related themes. For more information, see the Contents (2-7).

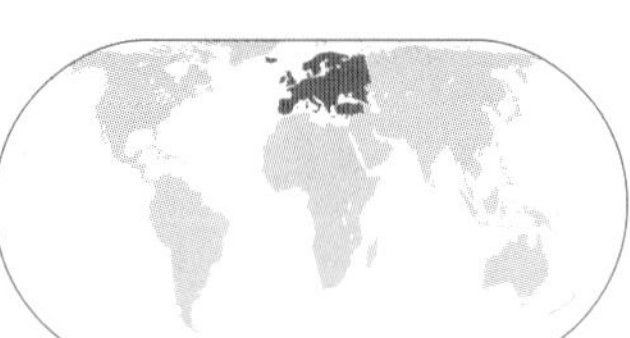

This map shows the most important areas that have been designated as National Parks throughout Western and Central Europe.

Sites marked with an asterisk (*) are featured in Columbus Travel Guides' *Tourist Attractions and Events of the World*

ICELAND
Arctic Circle
NORWEGIAN SEA
NORTH SEA
CELTIC SEA
ATLANTIC OCEAN
BAY OF BISCAY
NORWAY
SWEDEN
FINLAND
ESTONIA
LATVIA
LITHUANIA
BELARUS
UKRAINE
MOLDOVA
POLAND
GERMANY
CZECH REPUBLIC
SLOVAK REP.
AUSTRIA
HUNGARY
ROMANIA
BULGARIA
TURKEY
GREECE
ALBANIA
FYR OF MAC.
SERBIA & MONTENEGRO
BOSNIA-HERZEGOVINA
CROATIA
SLOVENIA
ITALY
SWITZ.
LIECH.
LUX.
BELGIUM
NETHS.
FRANCE
ANDORRA
MONACO
SPAIN
PORTUGAL
MOROCCO
UNITED KINGDOM
IRELAND
N. Ireland
Scotland
Wales
England
DENMARK
SENJA
VESTERÅLEN
LOFOTEN
FAROE ISLANDS (Den.)
SHETLAND ISLANDS
ORKNEY ISLANDS
HEBRIDES
ISLE OF MAN
CHANNEL IS.
English Channel
Skagerrak
Kattegat
Vänern
Vättern
GULF OF BOTHNIA
ÅLAND
GULF OF FINLAND
HIIUMAA
SAAREMAA
GOTLAND
ÖLAND
BORNHOLM
BALTIC SEA
(Russia)
BALEARIC IS.
MINORCA
MAJORCA
IBIZA
FORMENTERA
CORSICA
SARDINIA
SICILY
MALTA
TYRRHENIAN SEA
ADRIATIC SEA
IONIAN SEA
AEGEAN SEA
CORFU
PELOPONNESE
CRETE
RHODES
Gibraltar (UK)
Strait of Gibraltar
Ceuta (Sp.)
Melilla (Sp.)
Azores (Port.)
FLORES
FAIAL
PICO
TERCEIRA
SÃO JORGE
SÃO MIGUEL
SANTA MARIA
Madeira (Port.)
Canary Is. (Sp.)
LA PALMA
TENERIFE
GOMERA
HIERRO
GRAN CANARIA
LANZ.
FUERT.
800 kilometres
400 miles

Iceland
- **1 Jökulsárgljúfur** Spectacular glacial canyon landscape
- **2 Skaftafell** Example of active glacial landscape
- **3 Thingvellir** Broad forested plain, home of historic Iceland parliam't

Norway
- **4 Øvre Pasvik** Forest & tundra
- **5 Stabbursdalen** Arctic landscape: tundra, lakes, gravel plains & forest
- **6 Øvre Anarjokka** Undulating tundra with woodland & lakes
- **7 Reisa** Mixed mountain country
- **8 Øvre Dividal** Mountainous country with tundra & woodland
- **9 Ånderdalen** Mixed mountain country
- **10 Saltfjellet-Svartisen** Varied landscape; fjords, mountains & glacier
- **11 Børgefjell** Remote mountain area with varied habitats
- **12 Gressåmoen** Mountainous country & spruce forest
- **13 Dovrefjell** Mountainous tundra & snowfields; famous for its flora
- **14 Rondane** Mixed mountain country
- **15 Jostedalsbreen** Europe's largest mainland glacier
- **16 Jotunheimen** Mountainous area with tundra, bogs & forest
- **17 Hardangervidda** Large mountain plateau, a popular walking area

Sweden
- **18 Vadvetjåkka** Wild terrain with karst caves
- **19 Abisko** Mountain & forest with tundra, lakes & rivers
- **20 Muddus** Forest, tundra & bog
- **21 Padjelanta, Sarek and Stora Sjöfallet** 3 parks protect Europe's largest wilderness area; mixed landscape
- **22 Pieljekaise** Wooded mountain country with tundra, open water & bogs
- **23 Skuleskogen** Coastal forest landscape
- **24 Töfsingdalen** Woodland, tundra & bog
- **25 Sånfjället** Woodland, tundra & bog
- **26 Hamra** Woodland, tundra & bog, noted for its insects
- **27 Garphyttan** Forest & meadows
- **28 Tiveden** Hilly forest, lakes & bogs
- **29 Store Mosse** Predominantly boggy, with lakes & forest
- **30 Gotska Sandön** Sand & gravel island

Finland
- **31 Pallas-ja-Ounastunturin** Upland plateau & taiga, with lakes, tundra, gorges & forest
- **32 Lemmenjoen** Wilderness mountain area; gold rush in 1940's
- **33 Urho Kekkosen** Large wilderness area with fells, forest & peatlands
- **34 Pyhätunturin** Mountainous area with tundra, bogs & forest
- **35 Oulangen** Varied tundra landscape
- **36 Petkeljärven** Typical Finnish lakeland scenery
- **37 Linnansaaren** Lake & islands
- **38 Pyhä-Häkin** Mainly forest & bog
- **39 Seitsemisen** Typical S Finland landscape with forest & bog
- **40 Liesjärven** Lakes, previously cultivated land & forest
- **41 Saaristomeren** Extensive island group with mixed habitats

Denmark
- **42 Rebild Bakker** Glacial valleys, hills & woodland; home to largest 4th July celebrations outside US

Ireland
- **43 Glenveagh** Mixed upland area
- **44 Connemara** Typical W Ireland mountain area
- **45 Killarney*** Ancient woodland with moorland, lakes, bogs, wetland & mountains
- **46 Wicklow Mountains** Partly wooded mountains with upland moorland & grassland

United Kingdom
- **47 Cairngorms** Mountain region with ski resorts
- **48 Loch Lomond & The Trossachs** Lakes & wooded valley with literary associations
- **49 Northumberland** Mainly upland grassy moorland; Hadrian's Wall in S
- **50 Lake District** Mountain & lakeland; very popular all year
- **51 Yorkshire Dales** Varied upland country
- **52 North York Moors** Hilly uplands with heather moorland
- **53 Peak District** Limestone in the south, with many caves; high peat moors in the north
- **54 Snowdonia*** Mountain country with lakes, moorland, grassland & woodland
- **55 Pembrokeshire Coast** Scenic coastline; varied seabird habitats
- **56 Brecon Beacons*** Mainly grass-covered mountain area
- **57 Exmoor** High heather moorland & wooded valleys, with dramatic coastline
- **58 Dartmoor** Granite uplands with heather & grassland
- **59 New Forest** Woodland & heath; famous for wild ponies

Netherlands
- **60 Dwingelderveld** Heathland, fen & woodland with lakes
- **61 De Hoge Veluwe** Variety of habitats: heathland, dunes, fens, wet heath & woodland
- **Veluwezoom** Heath & mixed woodland
- **62 De Biesbosch** Confluence of Maas & Waal

Germany
- **63 Niedersächsisches Wattenmeer** East Frisian Islands; mudflats & saltmarsh
- **64 Hamburgisches W'meer & Schleswig-Holsteinisches W'meer** Mudflats & saltmarsh
- **65 Vorpommersche Boddenlandschaft** Mudflats & saltmarsh with dunes, lagoons, lakes & woodland
- **66 Jasmund** Varied landscape with cliffs, lakes & woodland
- **67 Müritz** Woodland & lakes with heath, marsh & pasture
- **68 Unteres Odertal** Floodplain of the Oder; park shared with Poland
- **69 Sächsische Schweiz** Numerous rock towers; lower slopes wooded; deep valleys
- **70 Hoch Harz** Wooded mountains with moorland, bogs & lakes
- **71 Bayerischer Wald** Wooded mountain area
- **72 Berchtesgaden** Mountain landscape with Alpine pastures, small glaciers, cliffs, lakes & varied woodland

France
- **73 Vanoise & Écrins** High mountain scenery
- **74 Mercantour** Some of the best parts of the Maritime Alps
- **75 Port-Cros** Small wooded island
- **76 Cévennes** Varied mountain & forest
- **77 Pyrénées-Occidentales** Diverse mountain landscape; snowfields, pastures & woodland

Spain
- **78 Aigües Tortes-Sant Maurici** Characteristic glacial landscape of high Pyrenees
- **79 Ordesa** Spectacular mountain & gorge scenery; forests & Alpine pastures
- **80 Covadonga** Mountain area with mixed woodlands, pasture & glacial lakes
- **81 Tablas de Daimiel** Small wetland
- **82 Doñana** Guadalquivir delta; important wildlife site
- **83 Caldera de Taburiente** Volcanic landscape
- **84 Garajonay** Sub-tropical forests
- **85 Cañadas del Teide** Volcanic landscapes
- **86 Timanfaya** Volcanic landscapes

Portugal
- **87 Peneda-Gerês** Mountain & forest area; cliffs & rock formations

Switzerland
- **88 The Swiss National Park** Strictly controlled mountainous area; forests, pastures, lakes, cliffs & snowfields

Austria
- **89 Hohe Tauern** High Alpine scenery; forests in lower areas
- **90 Nockberge** Forested mountain area with bogs & moors
- **91 Donau-auen** Danube flood plain E of Vienna
- **Neusiedler See** Europe's largest steppe lake, over half is thick reedbeds

Italy
- **92 Stelvio** Typical Alpine scenery & large glacier
- **93 Gran Paradiso** High Alpine country; famous for the Ibex
- **94 Monti Sibillini** Upspoilt mountain area with folklore connections
- **95 Gran Sasso e Monti della Laga** Varied landscape of mountains, rivers & lakes
- **96 Abruzzo** Wooded mountainous area
- **Maiella** Group of high peaks with karst plains
- **97 Circeo** Coastal marsh & rocky promontory
- **98 Calàbria** Three areas of wooded mountainous landscape

Poland
- **99 Wolinski** Woodland, lakes and sea cliffs; white-tailed sea eagle the main attraction
- **100 Slowinski** Coastal landscape with shifting sand dunes
- **101 Kampinoski** Varied landscape nr. Warsaw
- **102 Mazurski & Wigierski** Numerous lakes and extensive forests
- **103 Biebrzanski** Central Europe's largest area of natural peat bogs
- **104 Bialowieski** Europe's largest original lowland forest; principal attraction the European bison
- **105 Bieszczadzki** Remote wooded mountain area in E Carpathians
- **106 Babiogórski, Tatrzanski, Gorczanski & Pieninski** Four parks in the spectacular High Tatra mountains
- **107 Ojcówski** Hilly landscape with many rock pinnacles
- **108 Gory Stolowe & Karkonoski** Dramatic mountain scenery of the Sudety Mountains

Czech Republic
- **109 Krkonose** Wooded mountain area with Alpine pastures, meadows, bogs & lakes
- **110 Sumava** Forested slopes, ancient mountains & peat bogs

Slovak Republic
- **111 Vysoké Tatry*** (High Tatras) **Nizke Tatry*** (Low Tatras) Spectacular mtn area: forests, lakes, grassland & bogs
- **112 Pieninsky** Limestone mountains with mixed forests
- **113 Slovenská raj** Karst plateau with extensive caves

Hungary
- **114 Aggtelek** Important karst scenery
- **Bukk** Hilly forested region
- **115 Hortobágyi** Varied steppe landscape with rich birdlife
- **116 Kiskunság** Wide range of lowland habitats

Slovenia
- **117 Triglav** Limestone mountain scenery & mixed forest

Croatia
- **118 Risnjak** Limestone mountain scenery & mixed forest
- **119 Plitvice Lakes*** Scenic lakes linked by waterfalls formed by limestone deposition
- **Paklenica** Limestone peaks, gorges & mixed forest
- **120 Kornati** Limestone islands, karst scenery
- **121 Krka** Park follows the route of the Krka river; lakes, dams, gorges, falls & woodland
- **122 Mljet** Western part of island

Bosnia-Herzegovina
- **123 Sutjeska** Wooded mountainous area; mixed landscape & reserve of virgin forest

Serbia & Montenegro
- **124 Fruska Gora** Wooded hilly valley
- **125 Djerdap** Gorge of the Danube; dam has created a long thin lake
- **126 Tara** Mixed upland scenery
- **127 Durmitor** Mountain area in the west, Tara Gorge in east; mixed landscape & karst
- **Biogradska Gora** Mountain area with high grasslands & five lakes
- **128 Lovcen** Wooded limestone mountains
- **Skadarsko jezero** Montenegran part of Lake Scutari

Former Yugoslav Rep. of Macedonia
- **129 Mavrovo** Mountain area, partly wooded
- **130 Galicica** S end of Dinaric Alps; mostly natural forest
- **Pelister** Wooded mountain area with Alpine pastures

Albania
- **131 Divjaka** Dunes & coastal woodland with rich birdlife on neighbouring lagoon

Romania
- **132 Retezat** Mountain country with extensive forests

Bulgaria
- **133 Rusenski Lom** Deciduous woodland
- **134 Central Balkan** Widely varied landscape; thick forests
- **135 Vitosa** Varied mountain area
- **136 Pirin** High mountains; forest & mixed landscape
- **Rila** Alpine peaks & many small lakes: the 'Eyes of the Rila'

Greece
- **137 Préspa** Shallow lakes with reed- & sedge-beds
- **138 Olimbos (Olympus)** Mountain area with maquis & forest; home of the gods in ancient Greek mythology
- **139 Pindos** Wooded mountain area
- **Vikos-Aóos** Wooded mountain area; Vikos & Aóos gorges
- **140 Aínos** Area around Mt Aínos
- **141 Iti Óros** Wooded mountain area
- **Parnassós** Wilderness mountain area; mixed habitats
- **142 Párnitha** Limestone area; maquis
- **Soúnion** Typical Greek coastline

Turkey
- **143 Manyas-Kuscenneti** Bird reserve, part of large lake
- **144 Sipil Dagi** Home of the famous 'crying rock' of Niobe

Estonia
- **145 Lahemaa** Wooded area & scenic coast
- **146 Soomaa** Marsh & forest, severe annual flooding
- **147 Karula** Forested area with glacial debris

Latvia
- **148 Gauja** River & gorge scenery; the 'Switzerland of Latvia'

Lithuania
- **149 Kursiv Nerija** Long sand spit with popular beaches; ice fishing in winter
- **150 Zemaitija** Forest with popular Lake Plateliai
- **151 Aukstaitija (Ignalina)** Forest & lakes; great diversity of wildlife
- **152 Trakai** 5 lakes; Trakai Castle as centrepiece
- **153 Dzukija** Confluence of Nemunas & Merkys rivers

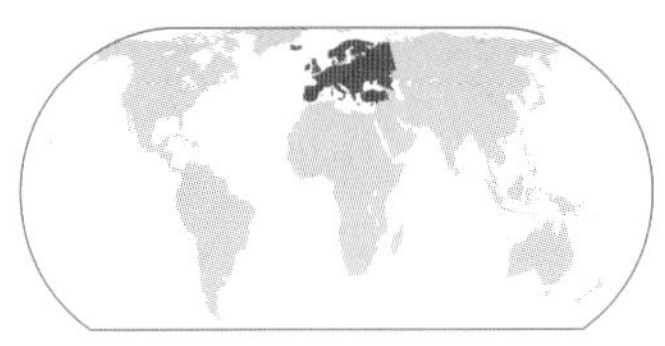

▶ *See also...* Attractions in UK (76), Belgium (79), Netherlands (81), Germany (85), France (89), Iberia (91) and Italy (98); US Theme Parks (171)

The listings above refer to a selection of related themes. For more information, see the Contents (2-7).

This map shows a selection of theme and amusement parks in Europe. Most of these are members of either the International Association of Amusement Parks and Attractions (IAAPA) or the various national associations of amusement parks. For more information see www.ticketforfun.com

Parks marked with an asterisk (*) are featured in Columbus Travel Guides' *Tourist Attractions and Events of the World.*

Thanks to Jeff Bertus Leisure for help in compiling this section.

NORWEGIAN SEA
SWEDEN
FINLAND
NORWAY
GULF OF BOTHNIA
ÅLAND
GULF OF FINLAND
HIIUMAA
SAAREMAA
ESTONIA
Vänern
Vättern
Skagerrak
Kattegat
ORKNEY ISLANDS
HEBRIDES
NORTH SEA
Scotland
DENMARK
BALTIC SEA
BORNHOLM
UNITED KINGDOM
N. Ireland
IRELAND
ISLE OF MAN
England
Wales
NETHS.
POLAND
CELTIC SEA
English Channel
CHANNEL IS.
BELG.
LUX.
GERMANY
CZECH REPUBLIC
SLOVAK REPUBLIC
UKRAINE
MOLDOVA
FRANCE
LIECH.
AUSTRIA
HUNGARY
SWITZERLAND
SLOVENIA
CROATIA
ROMANIA
BAY OF BISCAY
ATLANTIC OCEAN
MONACO
BOSNIA-HERZEGOVINA
Serbia
SERBIA & MONTENEGRO
Montenegro
BULGARIA
ITALY
ADRIATIC SEA
CORSICA
ANDORRA
SPAIN
PORTUGAL
FORMER YUGO. REP. OF MACEDONIA
ALBANIA
BALEARIC IS.
MINORCA
MAJORCA
IBIZA
FORMENTERA
SARDINIA
TYRRHENIAN SEA
CORFU
AEGEAN SEA
GREECE
TURKEY
IONIAN SEA
SICILY
PELOPONNESE
CRETE
RHODES
MALTA
Madeira (Port.)
Azores (Port.)
FLORES
FAIAL
PICO
TERCEIRA
SÃO JORGE
SÃO MIGUEL
SANTA MARIA
Canary Is. (Sp.)
LA PALMA
TENERIFE
LANZ.
FUERT.
GOMERA
HIERRO
GRAN CANARIA
Gibraltar (UK)
Strait of Gibraltar
Ceuta (Sp.)
Melilla (Sp.)
MOROCCO
800 kilometres
400 miles

EUROPE'S MOST POPULAR PARKS IN 2005
Number of visitors (world ranking in brackets)
Disneyland Paris France: 10.2 million (5th)
Blackpool Pleasure Beach UK: 6.0m (13th)
Tivoli Gardens Denmark: 4.1m (=21st)
Europa-Park Germany: 4.0m (24th)
Port Aventura Spain: 3.4m (28th)
De Efteling The Netherlands: 3.3m (30th)
Liseberg Sweden: 3.2m (31st)
Gardaland Italy: 3.1m (34th)
Bakken Denmark: 2.6m (=40th)
Alton Towers UK: 2.4m (44th)
Source: Amusement Business & Economics Research Associates

Norway

1 **Lunds Tivoli**, Ålgård
Amusement park

2 **Kristiansand Dyrepark**
Norway's largest zoo and amusement park

3 **Bo Sommarland**, Bø
Combined waterpark and theme park

4 **TusenFryd & VikingLandet**, Vinterbro
Theme park and a small water park; VikingLandet is a re-enactment of the Viking Age

Sweden

5 **Liseberg**, Gothenburg
Large theme park with convention facilities and harbour

6 **Astrid Lindgren's World**, Vimmerby
Park dedicated to the world-famous childrens' author

7 **Parken Zoo i Eskilstuna**
Zoo, amusement park and waterpark

8 **Gröna Lunds Tivoli**, Stockholm
Amusement park in the centre of Stockholm, founded 1883

9 **Furuviksparken**, Gavle
Amusement park and zoo

10 **Jamtli Historieland**, Östersund
Combined indoor and outdoor museum

Finland

11 **Wasalandia**, Vaasa
Family theme park with Tropical Spa Tropiclandia

12 **Lillbacka Powerpark**, Alahärmä
Family theme park with Tropical Spa Tropiclandia

13 **Tampereen Sarkanniemi Oy**, Tampere
City-centre amusement park and entertainment centre; includes an art museum, dolphinarium and planetarium

14 **Linnanmäki***, Helsinki
Finland's most popular amusement park with live stage shows and a Sea Life Centre

15 **Tykkimäki**, Kouvola
Large amusement park with reptile zoo and dance pavilion

Denmark

16 **Jesperhus Blomstherpark**, Nykøbing, Mors
Animal and flower parks; family entertainment centre

17 **Fårup Aquapark & Sommerland**, Saltum
Amusement park with more than 30 activities and Scandinavia's largest waterpark

18 **Tivoliland**, Aalborg
Large amusement park

19 **Djurs Sommerland**, Nimtofte
Amusement park with more than 60 attractions and shows and a waterpark

20 **LEGOLAND Billund***
Theme park based on LEGO toy products; interactive attractions, building challenges, *Driving School* & *Miniland*

21 **BonBon-Land**, Holme-Olstrup
Fourth-largest amusement park in Denmark with over 60 attractions and activities

22 **Dyrehavsbakken ('Bakken')**, Klampenborg
The world's oldest amusement park, over 100 attractions
Tivoli Gardens*, Copenhagen
Large amusement park in the centre of Copenhagen, opened in 1843; a mixture of new and old rides; the famous Copenhagen Christmas Market is held here in Nov & Dec

Ireland

23 **Perks Pleasure Park**, Youghal
Seaside amusement park with neighbouring wildlife park

24 **Clara Lara Fun Park**, Wicklow
Park and amusement centre plus a junior playground

United Kingdom

25 **Barry's Amusement Park**, Portrush
Family amusement park with rides for all ages

26 **The New Metroland**, Gateshead
Europe's largest indoor funfair with many rides

27 **Blackpool Pleasure Beach***
Opened in 1896, over 145 attractions and rides classified according to their 'terror factor'; one of the biggest collections of white-knuckle rides in the world, plus spectacular shows & Ripley's Believe It or Not! Odditorium
Camelot Theme Park, Chorley, Lancashire
A medieval world with over 100 attractions and rides

28 **Flamingo Land and Holiday Village***, Malton
Amusement park and zoo with eight coaster rides and many extreme rides in White Knuckle Valley
Lightwater Valley, Ripon
Theme park with unique attractions including the world's first suspended hang-glider ride

29 **Alton Towers***, near Stoke-on-Trent
One of the UK's most popular theme parks with 125 rides and attractions in a number of different kingdoms: *Ugland, Forbidden Valley, Towers Street* and *Cred Street*
Gullivers Kingdom, Matlock Bath
Theme park with over 35 rides and hot-air balloon flights

30 **American Adventure World**, Ilkeston
Adventure park with a American theme

31 **West Midland Safari Park**, Bewdley
Drive-around safari park; leisure area with over 25 rides

32 **Drayton Manor Park***, Tamworth
Theme park with over 100 rides and attractions, plus a zoo, parkland, lakes and walks

33 **Wicksteed Park**, Kettering
UK's oldest theme park, opened in 1921

34 **Pleasurewood Hills**, Lowestoft
50 rides, sea lion and parrot shows, a castle and theatre

35 **Oakwood***, Narberth
Theme park with over 40 attractions including stage shows

36 **LEGOLAND Windsor***
Over 50 interactive rides, building workshops and driving schools in beautiful parkland

37 **Chessington World of Adventures***
Zoo includes gorillas and large cats; amusement park with many rides
Thorpe Park, Chertsey
The UK's fastest changing thrill park with many white-knuckle rides

38 **Harbour Park**, Littlehampton
Seaside amusement park with extensive undercover facilities and arcades

39 **Crealy Adventure Park**, Exeter
A re-creation of a country childhood; with six different realms combining magic, adventure, action, animals, farming and nature

The Netherlands

40 **Attractiepark Slagharen**, Slagharen
Theme park with Wild West shows and over 40 rides
Avonturenpark Hellendoorn
Amusement park with many rides and animal attractions

41 **Dolfinarium Harderwijk**
Europe's largest marine theme park featuring six different shows with animals plus a dolphin rehabilitation centre, an open-air dolphin lagoon and a research centre
Walibi World, Dronten
Family amusement park famous for its rollercoasters

42 **Drievliet**, Rijswijk
Family park with over 30 major attractions, shows and playgrounds
Duinrell, Wassenaar
Family park with educational exhibitions; over 50 rides and water attractions

43 **De Efteling**, Kaatsheuvel
One of Europe's leading family leisure parks; a full range of attractions includes spectacular shows and PandaVision, an educational 3D journey through the world of nature

44 **BillyBird Park Hemelrijk**, Volkel
Artificial lake with nature area, beaches, restaurants, pools and interactive playground
Toverland, Sevenum
Large indoor and outdoor amusement park

Belgium

45 **Bellewaerde Park**, Ypres
Mix of attractions and exotic animals in a natural setting
Boudewijn Seapark, Bruges
Family park, famous for its dolphinarium; with rides, skating, boating, Seal Island and other animals
Plopsaland, De Panne
Theme park for families with children up to 12 years old

46 **Bobbejaanland**, Lichtaart
Amusement and theme park with 45 major rides, including *The Revolution* and *Arcade 2000*; also includes *Kinderland*, a covered children's play area with 20 rides

47 **Bruparck**, Brussels
Includes Mini-Europe, cinemas and IMAX, tropical swimming pool and saunaland
Walibi Belgium, Wavre
Over 50 attractions and shows; includes Aqualibi, a tropical waterpark

Germany

48 **Familien-Freizeitpark Tolk-Schau**, Tolk
Amusement park situated in a scenic landscape

49 **Hansapark**, Sierksdorf
Theme park with many rides and attractions including water circus and 3,000-seat Hansapark Theatre

50 **Ferienzentrum Schloss Dankern**, Haren
Family entertainment centre with many water facilities

51 **Movie Park Germany**, Bottrop
Movie theme park with over 40 attractions and shows including stunt shows and a free-fall tower

52 **Kernwasser Wunderland**, Kalkar
Unique amusement park for children up to 12 years old on the site of a former nuclear power station

53 **Phantasialand**, Brühl
Theme park divided into six areas: *China Town, Old Berlin, Fantasy, Mystery, Mexico* and *Silver City*; attractions include shows and culinary delicacies

54 **Eifelpark**, Gondorf bei Bitburg
Wild animal park and amusement park with open-air theatre

55 **Panoramapark Sauerland**, Kirchhundem
Wild animal park and amusement park with its own 500-kilowatt windpower station

56 **Fort Fun Abenteuerland**, Bestwig
Indoor and outdoor children's amusement park; offers facilities for corporate events

57 **Safari & Hollywood-Park**, Schloss Holte-Stukenbrock
Combined safari park and amusement park

58 **Dinosaurier Park Münchehagen**, Rehburg-Loccum
Dinosaur park

59 **Heide-Park**, Soltau
Amusement park with shows and 40 major rides
Serengeti Safaripark, Hodenhagen
Animal park with over 1,000 animals and three themed areas: *Monkey Land, Leisure Land* and *Water Land*

60 **Autostadt**, Wolfsburg
Theme park of the automobile: Volkswagen distribution centre combined with car museum, displays, go-kart track and rides

61 **BELANTIS**, Leipzig
Attractions and live shows in six BELANTIS Worlds: *Castle BELANTIS, Beach of the Gods, Valley of the Pharoahs, Country of the Counts, Island of the Knights* and *Coast of the Discoverers*

62 **Freizeit-Land**, Geiselwind
Theme park and zoo, including four rollercoasters

63 **Holiday-Park**, Hassloch
Theme park with many attractions and rides including a 180-degree cinema and a live show parade

64 **Erlebnispark Tripsdrill**, Cleebronn
Germany's oldest amusement park with rides and animals

65 **LEGOLAND Deutschland**, Günzburg
Unique blend of entertainment and learning by play for families with children up to 13 years old

66 **Ravensberger Spieleland**, Meckenbeuren
Largest playground in the world with over 40 attractions

67 **Europa-Park**, Rust
One of Europe's major parks, close to France & Switzerland

France

68 **Walibi Lorraine**, Maizières-les-Metz
Amusement park with over 30 attractions and shows

69 **Disneyland Resort Paris***, Marne-la-Vallée
Disneyland Paris is divided into five areas: *Main Street USA, Frontierland, Adventure-land, Fantasyland* and *Discoveryland*. ***Walt Disney Studios Park***, opened in 2002, takes visitors back to the golden age of Hollywood and also behind the scenes of movie-making. ***Disney Village*** is Europe's largest entertainment complex.
La Mer de Sable, Ermenonville
Amusement park developed into themed areas: *China, Wild West* and *Morocco*; includes *Babagattau Village*
Parc Astérix*, Plailly
Theme park offering visitors a 3D trip into comic strip Asterix's universe, spread out over six neighbourhoods

70 **Le Jardin d'Acclimatation**, Paris
Amusement park with family rides and a zoo

71 **Grand Parc du Puy du Fou**, Les Espesses
Historical park with live shows and other attractions

72 **Futuroscope**, Jaunay-Clan, near Poitiers
Space-age park with advanced visual-image technology including an IMAX screen, virtual reality and Cyberspace

73 **Walibi Aquitaine**, Roquefort
With an 18th century castle and 20 attractions and shows

74 **Le Pal**, Dompierre sur Besbre
Animal and amusement park; shows feature sea lions, parrots and birds

75 **Walibi Rhône-Alpes**, Les Avenières
Regional amusement park with more than 30 rides and a waterpark area

Spain

76 **Parc d'Atraccions Tibidabo**, Barcelona
Urban amusement park, founded 1899, renovated 1988

77 **Port Aventura***, Salou
Includes Costa Caribe waterpark and Zona de Playa beach

78 **Terra Mitica***, Benidorm
Five areas: *Egypt, Iberia, Greece, Rome* and *The Islands*, illustrate the past, present and future of Mediterranean culture

79 **Txiki Park**, Pamplona
Family entertainment centre designed for children

80 **Parque de Atracciones Casa de Campo**, Madrid
Urban amusement park, Madrid's main entertainment centre
Warner Brothers Movie World, Madrid
Movie theme park with live shows and numerous attractions including Superman and Batman rides

81 **Parque Isla Mágica**, Seville
Theme park based upon exploration of the New World by 16th century Spanish adventurers

82 **Sioux City**, San Agustín, Gran Canaria
Western-themed park with stage shows and concerts

Portugal

83 **Bracalândia**, Braga
Theme park with various themed areas and attractions

84 **Zoomarine**, Albufeira
Zoo and marine park taking its theme from the Algarve's links with the sea

Switzerland

85 **Mystery Park**, Interlaken
Theme parks presenting unexplained mysteries of the world

86 **Conny-Land**, Lipperswil
Amusement park with underwater and animal shows

Austria

87 **Freizeitpark Familienland**, St Jakob in Haus
Amusement park with over 40 attractions

88 **Wiener Prater**, Vienna
Amusement park for over 100 years

Italy

89 **Gardaland**, Castelnuovo del Garda
Huge multifunctional amusement park with many attractions; four themed villages; profusion of plants and flowers

90 **Mirabilandia**, Ravenna
Amusement park with rides, stage shows and concerts

91 **Fiabilandia**, Rimini
Amusement park and funfair

92 **Luneur**, Rome
Traditional amusement park and funfair, 30 years old

93 **Edenlandia**, Naples
One of Italy's largest amusement parks

Hungary

94 **Budapesti Vidam Park**, Budapest
Amusement park with 33 games and rides; more than one million visitors per year

Greece

95 **Luna Park 'Ta Aidonakia'**, Athens
20 family and children's rides

Turkey

96 **Tatilya Turizm**, Avcilar, Istanbul
Largest indoor entertainment centre in Europe and the Middle East, Tatilya is a holiday and amusement republic with its own president, citizens and constitution

97 **Aqua Fantasy**, Selçuk
Turkey's largest water park

Cyprus

98 **WaterWorld**, Ayia Napa
Cyprus' largest waterpark and most popular attraction

Musuems & Art Galleries

See also... UNESCO Cultural Heritage (50-53); Europe Historical (58-59); Museums & Galleries in Asia (129), USA & Canada (159) and Latin America (182, 184, 187)

The listings above refer to a selection of related themes. For more information, see the Contents (2-7).

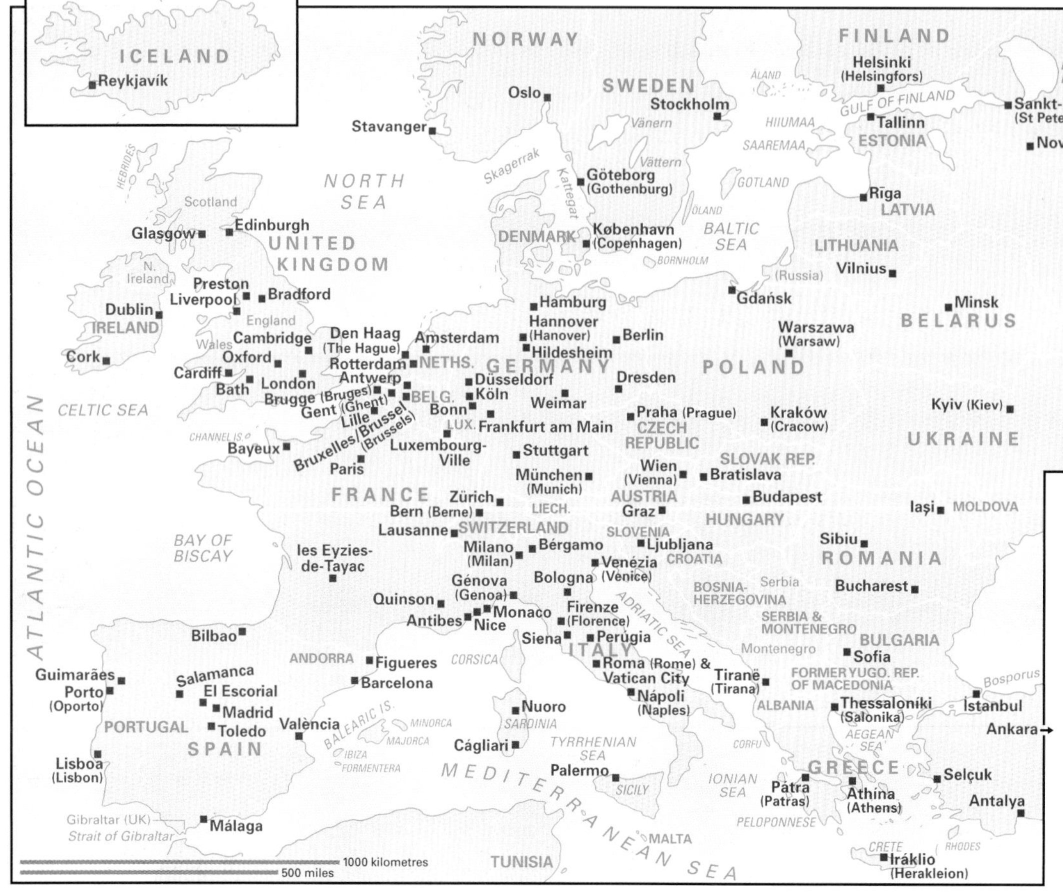
ICELAND
Reykjavík
NORWAY
Oslo
Stavanger
SWEDEN
Stockholm
FINLAND
Helsinki (Helsingfors)
GULF OF FINLAND
Tallinn
ESTONIA
Sankt-Peterburg (St Petersburg)
Novgorod
Lake Onega
Lake Ladoga
Principal museums and art galleries in the Russian Federation east of Moscow are included on the Asian map, p.129
RUSSIAN FEDERATION
Moskva (Moscow)
NORTH SEA
Skagerrak
Kattegat
Göteborg (Gothenburg)
Vänern
Vättern
GOTLAND
ÖLAND
Rïga
LATVIA
HIIUMAA
SAAREMAA
ÅLAND
Scotland
Glasgow
Edinburgh
UNITED KINGDOM
DENMARK
København (Copenhagen)
BORNHOLM
BALTIC SEA
LITHUANIA
Vilnius
(Russia)
N. Ireland
Preston
Bradford
Liverpool
Dublin
IRELAND
England
Wales
Cambridge
Oxford
Cork
Cardiff
Bath
London
Hamburg
Hannover (Hanover)
Hildesheim
Berlin
Gdańsk
Warszawa (Warsaw)
Minsk
BELARUS
Den Haag (The Hague)
Amsterdam
Rotterdam
NETHS.
GERMANY
Düsseldorf
Dresden
POLAND
Antwerp
Brugge (Bruges)
Gent (Ghent)
BELG.
Köln
Bonn
Weimar
Lille
Bruxelles/Brussel (Brussels)
Praha (Prague)
Kraków (Cracow)
Kyiv (Kiev)
UKRAINE
CELTIC SEA
CHANNEL IS.
Bayeux
LUX.
Frankfurt am Main
CZECH REPUBLIC
Luxembourg-Ville
Stuttgart
SLOVAK REP.
Paris
Wien (Vienna)
Bratislava
München (Munich)
FRANCE
Zürich
LIECH.
AUSTRIA
Budapest
Bern (Berne)
Graz
HUNGARY
Iaşi
MOLDOVA
Lausanne
SWITZERLAND
SLOVENIA
Sibiu
ATLANTIC OCEAN
BAY OF BISCAY
les Eyzies-de-Tayac
Milano (Milan)
Bérgamo
Ljubljana
Venézia (Venice)
CROATIA
ROMANIA
Génova (Genoa)
Bologna
BOSNIA-HERZEGOVINA
Serbia
Bucharest
Quinson
Monaco
Firenze (Florence)
ADRIATIC SEA
SERBIA & MONTENEGRO
Antibes
Nice
Siena
Perúgia
Montenegro
BULGARIA
Sofia
Bilbao
ITALY
ANDORRA
Figueres
CORSICA
Roma (Rome) & Vatican City
Tiranë (Tirana)
FORMER YUGO. REP. OF MACEDONIA
Bosporus
Guimarães
Salamanca
Barcelona
Nápoli (Naples)
ALBANIA
Thessaloníki (Salonika)
Istanbul
Porto (Oporto)
El Escorial
Madrid
BALEARIC IS.
MINORCA
Nuoro
SARDINIA
AEGEAN SEA
Ankara
PORTUGAL
Toledo
València
MAJORCA
Cágliari
TYRRHENIAN SEA
CORFU
SPAIN
IBIZA
FORMENTERA
GREECE
Selçuk
Lisboa (Lisbon)
MEDITERRANEAN SEA
Palermo
SICILY
IONIAN SEA
Pátra (Patras)
Athína (Athens)
Antalya
Gibraltar (UK)
Strait of Gibraltar
Málaga
PELOPONNESE
MALTA
CRETE
RHODES
Iráklio (Herakleion)
TUNISIA
1000 kilometres
500 miles

EUROPEAN CAPITALS/CITIES OF CULTURE

1985	Athens	1999	Weimar
1986	Florence	2000	Avignon, Bergen, Bologna, Brussels, Cracow, Helsinki, Prague, Reykjavik, Santiago de Compostela
1987	Amsterdam		
1988	Berlin		
1989	Paris		
1990	Glasgow		
1991	Dublin	2001	Oporto, Rotterdam
1992	Madrid	2002	Bruges, Salamanca
1993	Antwerp	2003	Graz
1994	Lisbon	2004	Genoa, Lille
1995	Luxembourg	2005	Cork
1996	Copenhagen	2006	Patras
1997	Thessaloniki	2007	Luxembourg-Ville, Sibiu
1998	Stockholm	2008	Liverpool, Stavanger

Europe's most important museums and art galleries are listed here. Selection is based on importance and depth of the collection and its cultural diversity within a geographic spread.
Most cities named will also offer the visitor a number of smaller museums of specialist interest. Many single great works of art may also be housed in local cathedrals and churches.

Compiled by Jon A. Gillaspie
email: let@sarastro.com

Principal contents of institution:

- AA Applied & decorative art
- AR Archaeology / ancient art
- FA Fine art (paintings, sculpture)
- FO Folk art & culture / ethnography
- H History / historical site / reconstruction
- NH Natural history
- ST Science / technology
- W Wide range of subjects

Amsterdam THE NETHERLANDS
AA FA Hermitage ann de Amstel
W Rijksmuseum
FA Stedelijk Museum; Van Gogh Museum
Ankara TURKEY
AR Museum of Anatolian Civilizations
Antalya TURKEY
AR Archaeological Museum
Antibes FRANCE
FA Musée Picasso
Antwerpen (Antwerp) BELGIUM
FA Museum voor Schone Kunsten
Athína (Athens) GREECE
AR Acropolis Museum; National Archaeological Museum
W Benáki Museum
AR Museum of Cycladic and Ancient Greek Art
Barcelona SPAIN
AR Museu Arqueològic
FA Museu d'Art Contemporani; Museu Nacional d'Art de Catalunya; Museu Picasso
Bath ENGLAND
AA Museum of Costume
AR Roman Baths and Museum
Bayeux FRANCE
AA Bayeux Tapestry
Bérgamo ITALY
FA Accademia Carrara
Berlin GERMANY
AR Ägyptisches Museum; Antiken Museum
W Dahlem museums
ST Deutsches Teknikmuseum
W Kulturforum *includes:*
FA Gemäldegalerie
AA Kunstgewerbemuseum
NH Museum für Naturkunde
W Museumsinsel *includes:*
FA Alte Nationalgalerie
AR Bodemuseum; Pergamonmuseum
Bern (Berne) SWITZERLAND
FA Kunstmuseum
Bilbao SPAIN
FA Museo de Bellas Arte; Museo Guggenheim
Bologna ITALY
AR Museo Civico Archeologico
Bonn GERMANY
NH Alexander-Koenig-Museum
FA Kunstmuseum
Bradford UNITED KINGDOM
ST National Museum of Photography, Film & TV
Bratislava SLOVAK REPUBLIC
FA National Gallery
W National Museum
Brugge (Bruges) BELGIUM
FA Groeningemuseum
Bruxelles/Brussel (Brussels) BELGIUM
FA Musées Royaux des Beaux-Arts
Bucharest ROMANIA
FA National Art Museum
AR H National History Museum
Budapest HUNGARY
H Holocaust Museum
FA Museum of Fine Arts; National Gallery
AA National Jewish Museum
W National Museum
Cágliari SARDINIA, ITALY
AR Museo Nazionale Archeologico
Cambridge ENGLAND
W Fitzwilliam Museum
Cardiff WALES
FO Museum of Welsh Life [St Fagans]
W National Museum and Gallery of Wales
Cork IRELAND
AA FA Crawford Municipal Art Gallery
Den Haag (The Hague) THE NETHERLANDS
W Gemeentemuseum
FA Mauritshuis
Dresden GERMANY
FA Gemäldegalerie Alte Meister
Dublin IRELAND
FA National Gallery
AR National Museum
Düsseldorf GERMANY
W Kunstmuseum
FA Kunstsammlung Nordrhein-Westfalen
Edinburgh SCOTLAND
W Royal Museum and Museum of Scotland
FA Scottish National Portrait Gallery
El Escorial SPAIN
FA Monasterio de El Escorial
Les Eyzies-de-Tayac FRANCE
AR Musée national de Préhistoire
Figueres SPAIN
FA Teatre-Museu Dalí
Firenze (Florence) ITALY
FA Bargello; Uffizi
AR Museo Archeologico
Frankfurt am Main GERMANY
FA Museum für Moderne Kunst
W Museumsufer *includes:*
AA FA Städel; Museum für Kunsthandwerk
Gdansk POLAND
W National Art Museum
Génova (Genoa) ITALY
FA Galleria Nazionale di Palazzo Spinola; Palazzo Bianco; Palazzo Rosso
Gent (Ghent) BELGIUM
FA Museum voor Schone Kunsten
Glasgow SCOTLAND
W Burrell Collection
FA Gallery of Modern Art (GOMA); Hunterian Art Gallery and Museum
Göteborg (Gothenburg) SWEDEN
FA Konstmuseet
AA Röhsska Konstlöjdmuseet
Graz AUSTRIA
FA Alte Galerie; Kunsthaus
W Landesmuseum Joanneum
Guimarães PORTUGAL
AA Museu Alberto Sampaio
AR Museu Martins Sarmiento
AA Sé (Cathedral museum) [Braga]
Hamburg GERMANY
FA Kunsthalle
AA Museum für Kunst und Gewerbe
Hannover (Hanover) GERMANY
FA Sprengel Museum
Helsinki (Helsingfors) FINLAND
FA Helsinki kaupingin museo
W Kansallismuseo; Kiasma
Hildesheim GERMANY
AR Roemer-Pelizaeus Museum
Iasi ROMANIA
W Palace of Culture
Iráklio (Herakleion) CRETE, GREECE
AR Archaeological Museum
Istanbul TURKEY
W Museum of Turkish and Islamic Art
København (Copenhagen) DENMARK
AR Nationalmuseet
W Ny Carlsberg Glyptotek
FA Statens Museum for Kunst
Köln (Cologne) GERMANY
FA Ludwig Museum; Wallraf-Richartz Museum
AR Römisch-Germanisches Museum
Kraków (Cracow) POLAND
W Czartoryski Museum
FO Museum of Ethnography
Kyiv (Kiev) UKRAINE
W Historical Treasures Museum
FA Russian Art Museum
Lausanne SWITZERLAND
H Musée Olympique
Lille FRANCE
FA Musée des Beaux-Arts
Lisboa (Lisbon) PORTUGAL
FA Museu Nacional de Arte Antiga
W Museu Calouste Gulbenkian
Liverpool ENGLAND
FA Walker Art Gallery
W World Museum
Ljubljana SLOVENIA
FA National Gallery
W National Museum
London ENGLAND
W British Museum; Museum of London
FA National Gallery; National Portrait Gallery; Tate Britain; Tate Modern
NH Natural History Museum
ST Science Museum
AA Victoria and Albert Museum
Luxembourg-Ville LUXEMBOURG
W Musée national d'Histoire et d'Art
NH Musée national d'Histoire naturelle
Madrid SPAIN
FA Centro de Arte Reina Sofia; Museo del Prado; Museo Thyssen-Bornemisza
AR Museo Arqueológico Nacional
W Museo de América
Málaga SPAIN
FA Museo Picasso
Milano (Milan) ITALY
FA Civico Museo di Arte Contemporanea; Pinacoteca Ambrosiana; Pinacoteca di Brera
AR Museo Civico di Archeologico
Minsk BELARUS
FA Belarusian State Art Museum
W National Museum of History and Culture
Monaco
NH ST Musée Océanographique
Moskva (Moscow) RUSSIAN FEDERATION
AA Kremlin
FA Mus. of Private Collections; Tretyakov Gallery
W Pushkin Museum of Fine Arts
München (Munich) GERMANY
FA Alte Pinakothek; Neue Pinakothek; Pinakothek der Moderne
AA Bayerisches Nationalmuseum
ST Deutsches Museum
AR Glyptothek und Antikensammlungen
Nápoli (Naples) ITALY
AR Museo Archeologico Nazionale
Nice FRANCE
FA Fondation Maeght [St-Paul-de-Vence]
FA Musée Marc-Chagall; Musée Matisse
Novgorod RUSSIAN FEDERATION
AA Museum of History, Architecture and Art
Nuoro SARDINIA, ITALY
FO Museo Etnografico
Oslo NORWAY
FA Nasjonalgalleriet
FO Norsk Folkemuseum
AR Vikingskiphuset
Oxford ENGLAND
W Ashmolean Museum
FA Museum of Modern Art (MOMA)
Palermo SICILY, ITALY
AR Museo Archeologico Regionale
FO Museo Etnografico Pitrè
Paris FRANCE
ST Cité des Sciences et de l'Industrie
W Institut du Monde Arabe; Louvre
FA Musée d'Orsay; Musée Marmottan; Musée national d'art moderne (Centre Georges Pompidou); Musée national du Moyen-Âge; Musée national Picasso; Musée Rodin
Pátra (Patras) GREECE
AR Archaeological Museum of Patras
Perúgia ITALY
AR Museu Archeologico Nazionale dell'Umbria
Porto (Oporto) PORTUGAL
AA FA Museu Nacional Soares dos Reis
Praha (Prague) CZECH REPUBLIC
AA Jewish Museum; Museum of Decorative Arts (UPM)
FA Museum of Modern and Contemporary Czech Art; Mucha Museum; Museum of Modern Czech Sculpture (Zbraslav); National Gallery of Old Bohemian Art (St George Convent)
NH National Museum
ST National Museum of Technology
Preston ENGLAND
H National Football Museum
Quinson FRANCE
AR Musée de Préhistoire
Reykjavík ICELAND
W Thjódminjasafn Íslands (National Museum)
Riga LATVIA
AA Museum of Decorative and Applied Arts
Roma (Rome) ITALY **& Vatican City**
W Capitoline museums *includes:*
AR Museo Capitolino
W Museo del Palazzo del Conservatori
AR Museo Nazionale di Villa Giulia; Museo Naz. Romano
FA Galleria Borghese; Gall. Doria Pamphili; Pal. Barberini
W Musei Vaticani
Rotterdam THE NETHERLANDS
FA Museum Boymans-van Beuningen
Salamanca SPAIN
AA Museo Art Nouveau y Art Deco
Sankt-Peterburg (St Petersburg) RUSSIAN FED.
W State Hermitage Museum
FO Museum of Anthropology and Ethnography
FA Russian Museum
Selçuk TURKEY
AR Archaeological Museum
Sibiu ROMANIA
FO ASTRA museums
AA FA The Brukenthal Museum
Siena ITALY
W Ospedale di Santa Maria della Scala
Sofia BULGARIA
FO Ethnographic Museum
FA National Art Gallery
AR H National Historical Museum
Stavanger NORWAY
AR Arkeologist Museum
W Stavanger Museum and Maritime Museum
Stockholm SWEDEN
FA Modernamuséet
AA Nationalmuseum
H Statens Historiska Museum
AR Vasamuseet
Stuttgart GERMANY
FA Staatsgalerie
Tallinn ESTONIA
FA National Art Museum
Thessaloníki (Salonika) GREECE
AR Archaeological Museum
FO Folklore Museum
Tiranë (Tirana) ALBANIA
AR National Archaeology Museum
FA National Art Gallery
W National Historical Museum
Toledo SPAIN
AR Museo de Arte Visigótico
FA Museo de Santa Cruz
València SPAIN
ST Ciutat de las Arts i les Ciències
FA Museo de Bellas Artes San Pio V
Venézia (Venice) ITALY
FA Collezione Guggenheim; Galleria dell'Accademia
W Museo Correr
AA Museo Vitrario di Murano
Vilnius LITHUANIA
AA Lithuanian History and Ethnographic Museum
Warszawa (Warsaw) POLAND
W National Museum
Weimar GERMANY
FA Schlossmuseum
Wien (Vienna) AUSTRIA
FA Albertina; Kunsthistorisches Museum Österrischische Galerie, Belvedere
W MuseumsQuartier *includes:*
FA MUMOK (Museum moderner Kunst); Leopold Mus.
Zürich SWITZERLAND
FA Kunsthaus
W Schweizerisches Landesmuseum

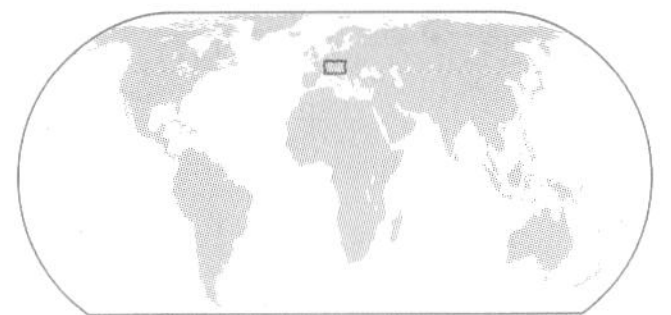

See also... USA & Canada Winter Sports (160)

The listings above refer to a selection of related themes. For more information, see the Contents (2-7).

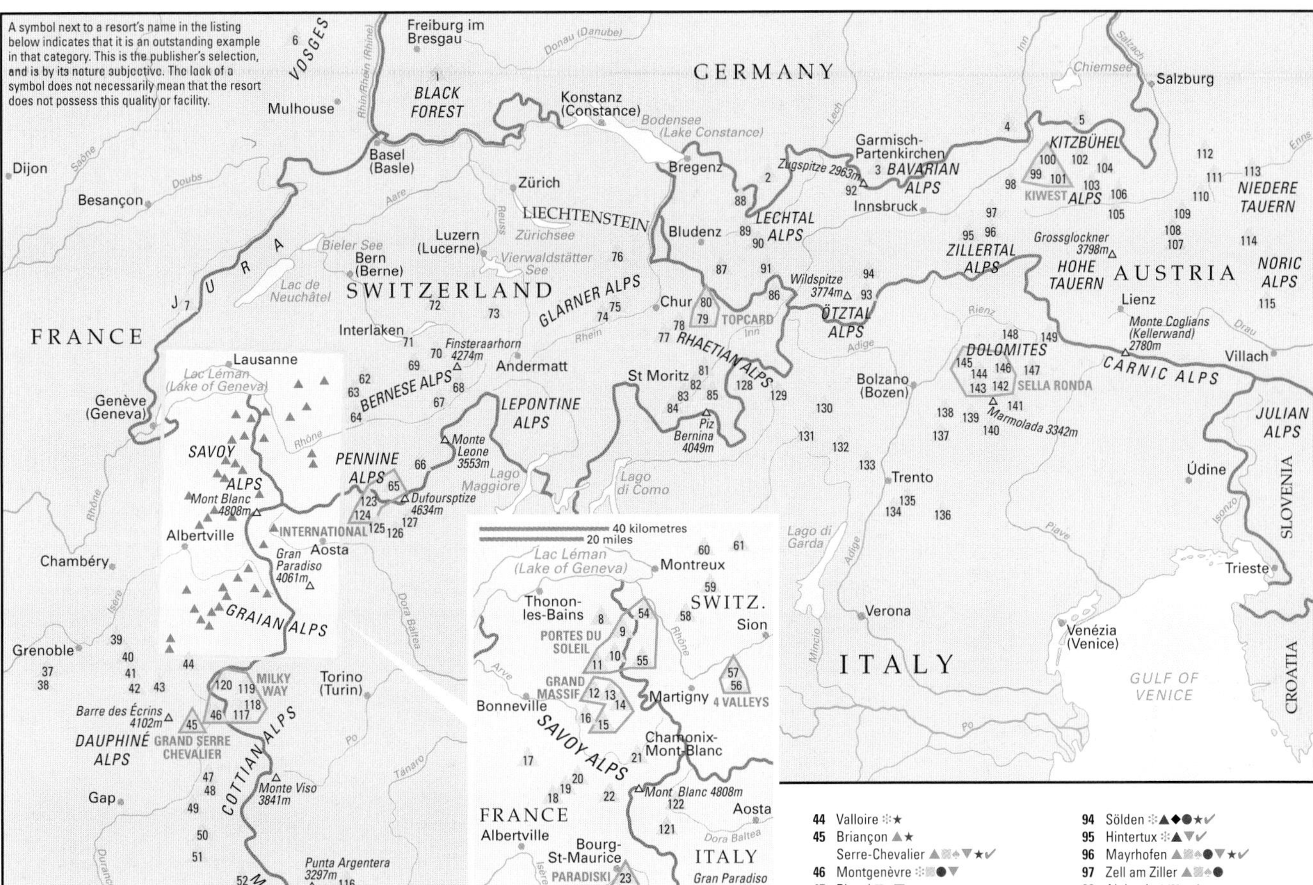

A symbol next to a resort's name in the listing below indicates that it is an outstanding example in that category. This is the publisher's selection, and is by its nature subjective. The lack of a symbol does not necessarily mean that the resort does not possess this quality or facility.
GERMANY
FRANCE
SWITZERLAND
AUSTRIA
ITALY
SLOVENIA
CROATIA
LIECHTENSTEIN
MONACO
Freiburg im Bresgau
BLACK FOREST
VOSGES
Mulhouse
Basel (Basle)
Konstanz (Constance)
Bodensee (Lake Constance)
Zürich
Bregenz
Garmisch-Partenkirchen
Zugspitze 2963m
BAVARIAN ALPS
Innsbruck
Salzburg
KITZBÜHEL ALPS
KIWEST
NIEDERE TAUERN
Dijon
Besançon
JURA
Bieler See
Lac de Neuchâtel
Bern (Berne)
Luzern (Lucerne)
Zürichsee
Vierwaldstätter See
Bludenz
LECHTAL ALPS
ZILLERTAL ALPS
Grossglockner 3798m
HOHE TAUERN
NORIC ALPS
GLARNER ALPS
Chur
TOPCARD
Wildspitze 3774m
ÖTZTAL ALPS
Lienz
Monte Coglians (Kellerwand) 2780m
Interlaken
Finsteraarhorn 4274m
Andermatt
RHAETIAN ALPS
St Moritz
DOLOMITES
SELLA RONDA
CARNIC ALPS
Villach
Lausanne
Lac Léman (Lake of Geneva)
BERNESE ALPS
LEPONTINE ALPS
Piz Bernina 4049m
Bolzano (Bozen)
Marmolada 3342m
JULIAN ALPS
Genève (Geneva)
Monte Leone 3553m
Lago Maggiore
Lago di Como
Trento
Údine
SAVOY ALPS
PENNINE ALPS
Mont Blanc 4808m
Dufourspitze 4634m
INTERNATIONAL
Lago di Garda
Albertville
Aosta
Gran Paradiso 4061m
Trieste
Chambéry
GRAIAN ALPS
Verona
Venézia (Venice)
Grenoble
MILKY WAY
Torino (Turin)
GULF OF VENICE
Barre des Écrins 4102m
DAUPHINÉ ALPS
GRAND SERRE CHEVALIER
COTTIAN ALPS
Gap
Monte Viso 3841m
Punta Argentera 3297m
MARITIME ALPS
Nice
100 km
50 miles
40 kilometres
20 miles
Montreux
SWITZ.
Thonon-les-Bains
Sion
PORTES DU SOLEIL
GRAND MASSIF
Martigny
4 VALLEYS
Bonneville
Chamonix-Mont-Blanc
Mont Blanc 4808m
Aosta
FRANCE
Albertville
Bourg-St-Maurice
ITALY
PARADISKI
Gran Paradiso 4061m
Moûtiers
ESPACE KILLY
VANOISE
TROIS VALLEES
LES SYBELLES
St-Jean-de-Maurienne

- ▲ **THE MOST BEAUTIFUL RESORTS** *Ski areas with spectacular scenery*
- ❄ **SNOWSURE** *The best reputations for season-long snow cover*
- ▲ **SUMMER SKIING DESTINATIONS** *Resorts where lifts stay open for skiing or boarding during the summer*
- ◆ **EXPERT** *Best of the black diamond destinations*
- ■ **BEGINNER SKI AREAS** *Best choices for first timers*
- ♠ **FAMILY FRIENDLY** *Ideal choices for family ski holidays*
- ● **PARTY TOWNS** *Après ski centres*
- ▼ **SNOWBOARDER HEAVEN** *Best bets for boarders*
- ★ **NOT JUST SKIING** *Plenty to do if you don't want to slide*
- ✓ **ECO-FRIENDLY REPUTATION** *(not all resorts have been graded in this category)*

Information supplied by Snow24 plc www.snow24.com

THE LARGEST LINKED RESORT AREAS △

Portes du Soleil (650 km of ski piste) *France/Switz.*
9 Châtel
10 Avoriaz
11 les Gets
11 Morzine
54 Torgon
55 Champéry-Planachaux / Val-d'Illiez / Les Crosets

Grand Massif (265 km) *France*
12 Morillon les Essert
13 Samoëns
14 Sixt
15 Flaine

Paradiski (425 km) *France*
23 les Arcs
24 Peisey / Nancroix-Vallandry
27 la Plagne / les Coches / Montchavin / Plagne Montalbert
28 Champagny-en-Vanoise

Espace Killy (300 km) *France*
25 Tignes
26 Val d'Isère

Trois Vallées (600 km) *France*
29 Courchevel
29 la Tania
30 Méribel
31 Val Thorens
32 les Menuires
33 St-Martin-de-Belleville

Les Sybelles (350 km) *France*
35 le Corbier
35 la Toussuire
36 St-Jean d'Arves

Grand Serre-Chevalier (250 km) *France*
45 Briançon
45 Serre-Chevalier

Milky Way (400 km) *France/Italy*
46 Montgenèvre
117 Clavière
117 San Sicário / Cesana
118 Sestriere
119 Sàuze d'Oulx

4 Valleys (412 km) *Switzerland*
56 Verbier
57 la Tzoumas (Mayens-de-Riddes)

International (350 km) *Italy/Switzerland*
65 Zermatt
123 Breuil-Cervinia
124 Valtournenche

TopCard (308 km) *Switzerland*
79 Davos
80 Klosters / Fideris

KiWest (400 km) *Austria*
99 Hopfgarten im Brixental
99 Westendorf
100 Söll
101 Kitzbühel

Sella Ronda (510 km) *Italy*
142 Arabba
143 Campitello di Fassa
143 Canazei
144 Santa Cristina / Pranauron
144 Selva Gardena (Wolkenstein)
145 Ortisei (St Ulrich)
146 Alta Badia [Colfosco / Corvara / La Villa (Stern) / San Cassiano (St Kassian) / Pedráces / San Leonardo (St Leonhard)]

Germany
1 Feldberg ■★
2 Oberstdorf ▲◆■●
3 Garmisch-Partenkirchen ▲❄▲◆●★▼
4 Bayrischzell ▲■
5 Reit im Winkl ▲■★

France
6 la Bresse-Hohneck ■▼
7 Métabief / le Mont d'Or ♠★
8 Abondance / la Chapelle d'Abondance ▲■♠
9 Châtel ▲■♠
10 Avoriaz ❄◆■♠●▼
11 les Gets ▲■♠✓
Morzine ▲◆♠●★✓
12 Morillon les Essert ▲■
13 Samoëns ▲■♠
15 Flaine ❄◆■♠▼✓
16 les Carroz ▼
17 la Clusaz ●▼
18 Notre-Dame-de-Bellecombe ■
19 Praz-sur-Arly ♠
20 Megève ▲■●★
21 Chamonix-Mont-Blanc ▲❄◆●▼
22 les Contamines-Montjoie ▲❄◆■
St-Nicolas-de-Véroce ▲■
23 les Arcs ❄◆■♠●▼
25 Tignes ❄▲◆●▼
26 Val d'Isère ❄▲◆●▼✓
27 la Plagne / les Coches / Montchavin / Plagne Montalbert ❄▼★
28 Champagny-en-Vanoise ▲▼
29 Courchevel ❄◆●▼
la Tania ❄♠✓
30 Méribel / Brides-les-Bains ▲◆●▼★
31 Val Thorens ❄▲◆■▼
32 les Menuires ◆■♠▼
33 St-Martin-de-Belleville ▲■♠
34 Valmorel ■♠▼
35 le Corbier ■
la Toussuire ▼
36 St-Jean d'Arves ▲
37 Villard-de-Lans / Cote 2000 ■♠
38 Corrençon-en-Vercors ▲
39 les Sept Laux (le Pleiney / Prapoutel) ▲■
40 Vaujany / Oz-en-Oisans ▲◆
41 Alpe d'Huez / Auris-en-Oisans / Villard-Reculas ▲❄▲◆♠●▼★
42 les Deux-Alpes ❄▲◆■♠●▼★
43 la Grave ▲❄▲◆
44 Valloire ❄★
45 Briançon ▲★
Serre-Chevalier ▲■♠▼★✓
46 Montgenèvre ❄■●▼
47 Risoul ■♠▼
48 Vars ♠
49 les Orres ■♠▼
50 Pra-Loup ■♠★
51 Val d'Allos-la Foux ♠
52 Auron / St-Étienne-de-Tinée ♠●
53 Beuil-les-Launes ▲
Valberg ■

Switzerland
55 Champéry-Planachaux / Val-d'Illiez / Les Crosets ▲■♠
56 Verbier ❄◆■♠●▼★
57 la Tzoumas (Mayens-de-Riddes) ❄◆
58 Villars-sur-Ollon / Gryon ❄▲◆■▼
59 les Diablerets ▲❄▲◆♠▼✓
60 Château-d'Oex ▲■♠▼
61 Gstaad-Saanenland ▲▲●▼★✓
62 Adelboden ▲♠●
63 Lenk ▲■♠●▼★
64 Crans-Montana ❄▲◆▼★✓
65 Zermatt ▲❄▲◆●▼★✓
66 Saas-Fee ▲❄▲◆■♠●▼★✓
67 Bettmeralp ▲♠
Fiesch ★
Mörel-Breiten ■
68 Sörenberg ▲
69 Mürren / Stechelberg ▲◆■♠✓
Wengen ▲◆♠●▼✓
70 Riederalp ♠
71 Interlaken / Wilderswil bei Interlaken ▲■●★
72 Grindelwald ▲❄◆♠★✓
73 Engelberg ❄▲◆♠●▼★
74 Laax ▲❄◆♠▼
75 Flims ❄◆▼✓
76 Flumserberg ■♠
77 Lenzerheide-Valbella ❄◆♠●▼
Parpan ▲■
78 Arosa ▲❄♠★
79 Davos ▲❄◆♠●▼★✓
80 Klosters / Fideris ▲◆■▼
81 Celerina ❄
Samedan ❄■
82 St Moritz ❄◆♠●▼★✓
83 Sils-Maria ▲❄
84 Maloja ■
85 Pontresina ❄▼
86 Samnaun ●★

Austria
87 St Gallenkirch ■▼
88 Kleinwalsertal [Hirschegg /Mittelberg / Riezlern] ■
89 Lech / Oberlech ❄◆■●▼✓
Zürs ❄◆
90 St Anton am Arlberg / St Jakob am Arlberg ▲❄◆●✓
St Christoph am Arlberg ❄◆
91 Ischgl / Silvretta ❄◆●▼★✓
92 Ehrwald ❄■
Lermoos ▲■
93 Obergurgl / Hochgurgl ▲❄♠
94 Sölden ❄▲◆●★✓
95 Hintertux ❄▲▼✓
96 Mayrhofen ▲■♠●▼★✓
97 Zell am Ziller ▲■♠●
98 Alpbach ▲■♠✓
99 Hopfgarten im Brixental ■♠▼
Westendorf ▲■♠●▼
100 Söll ■●▼
101 Kitzbühel ▲◆♠●▼★
102 Fieberbrunn ◆●▼
St Johann im Tirol ▲■♠●▼
103 Saalbach Hinterglemm ◆■●▼✓
104 Leogang ▲■♠▼
105 Kaprun ▲❄▲■▼✓
106 Zell am See ■♠●★✓
107 Badgastein ❄■♠★
108 Bad Hofgastein ■♠●★
109 Grossarl ▼
110 Flachau ◆●▼
111 Altenmarkt-Zauchensee ★
112 Annaberg im Lammertal ▲
113 Ramsau am Dachstein ▲❄▲▼
Schladming ▲▲♠●▼★✓
114 St Michael im Lungau ▲★
115 Bad Kleinkirchheim ▲◆▼★

Italy
116 Limone Piemonte ■●
117 Clavière ❄■
118 Sestriere ❄◆●▼
119 Sàuze d'Oulx ■♠●
120 Bardonécchia ❄■●
121 la Thuile ❄◆■♠
122 Courmayeur ◆●★
123 Breuil-Cervínia ❄▲◆●
124 Valtournenche ❄
125 Champoluc / Antagnod ❄■
126 Gressoney-la-Trinité / Gressoney-St Jean ❄◆■
127 Alagna-Valsésia ❄◆
128 Livigno ❄■●▼
129 Bormio ♠●★
130 Folgárida ▼
131 Passo Tonale ❄▲■♠★
132 Madonna di Campíglio ▲●▼★✓
133 Andalo ●
134 Folgaría ★
135 Lavarone / Luserna ▲
136 Asiago / Canove ★
137 Cavalese ♠★
138 Obereggen ▼
139 Bellamonte ■
140 San Martino di Castrozza ▲●▼★
141 Alleghe ■♠
142 Arabba ❄▲◆■▼
143 Campitello di Fassa ▲
Canazei ♠●
144 Santa Cristina / Pranauron ▲■♠
Selva Gardena (Wolkenstein) ▲◆●
146 **Alta Badia** [Colfosco / Corvara / La Villa (Stern) / San Cassiano (St Kassian) / Pedráces / San Leonardo (St Leonhard)] ▲■●★
147 Cortina ▲❄▲◆■●★
148 San Vigilio di Marebbe ■
149 Versciaco (Vierschach) ❄♠

See also... 72-76 for more on the United Kingdom

The listings above refer to a selection of related themes. For more information, see the Contents (2-7).

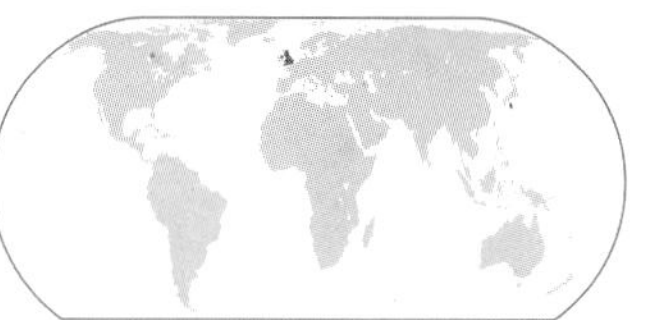

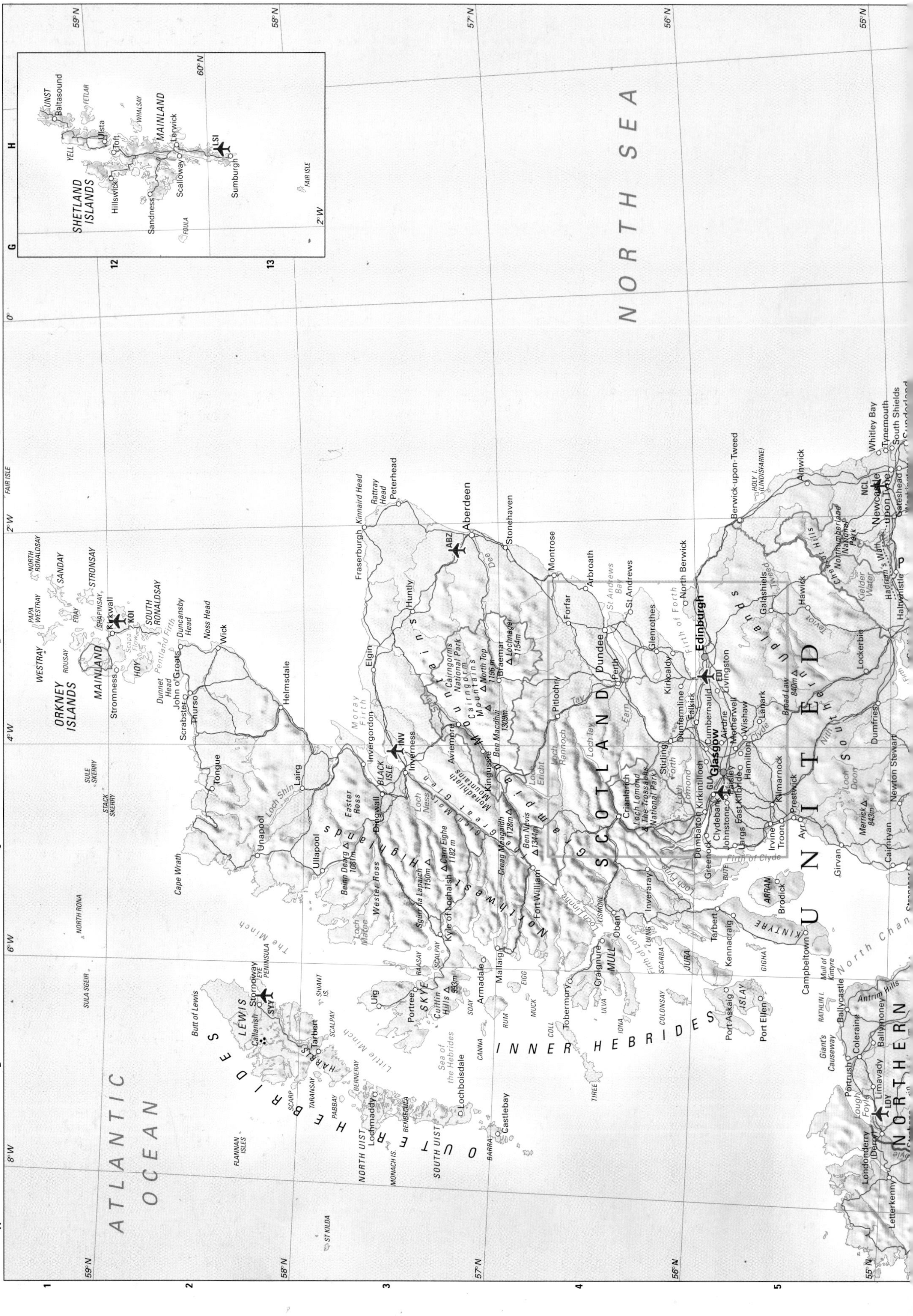

SHETLAND ISLANDS
UNST
Baltasound
FETLAR
YELL
Ulsta
WHALSAY
MAINLAND
Lerwick
Toft
Hillswick
Sandness
Scalloway
LSI
Sumburgh
FOULA
FAIR ISLE

ORKNEY ISLANDS
NORTH RONALDSAY
SANDAY
PAPA WESTRAY
WESTRAY
STRONSAY
EDAY
SHAPINSAY
ROUSAY
MAINLAND
Kirkwall
KOI
Stromness
HOY
SOUTH RONALDSAY
Scapa Flow
Pentland Firth
Dunnet Head
Duncansby Head
John o'Groats
Noss Head
Wick
Thurso
Scrabster
Helmsdale
SULE SKERRY
STACK SKERRY
NORTH RONA
SULA SGEIR
Cape Wrath
Tongue
Lairg
Loch Shin
Ullapool
Ullapool
Easter Ross
Wester Ross
Beinn Dearg 1081m
Loch Maree
Dingwall
BLACK ISLE
Inverness
INV
Invergordon
Moray Firth
Elgin
Fraserburgh
Kinnaird Head
Rattray Head
Peterhead
Huntly
Aberdeen
ABZ
Stonehaven
Dee
Braemar
Lochnagar 1154m
Cairngorms National Park
Cairngorm Mountains
North Top 1196m
Ben Macdhui 1309m
Aviemore
Kingussie
Monadhliath Mountains
Loch Ness
Glen Mor
Great Glen
North West Highlands
Grampian Mountains
Creag Meagaidh 1128m
Ben Nevis 1344m
Fort William
Sgurr na Lapaich 1150m
Carn Eighe 1182m
Kyle of Lochalsh
Mallaig
Loch Ericht
Loch Rannoch
Loch Tay
Tay
Pitlochry
Forfar
Montrose
Arbroath
Dundee
Perth
Earn
St Andrews Bay
St Andrews
Glenrothes
Kirkcaldy
Firth of Forth
North Berwick
Edinburgh
EDI
Livingston
Dunfermline
Falkirk
Stirling
Forth
Crianlarich
Loch Lomond & The Trossachs National Park
Loch Lomond
Kirkintilloch
Cumbernauld
Airdrie
Motherwell
Wishaw
Glasgow
GLA
Clydebank
Paisley
Johnstone
East Kilbride
Hamilton
Lanark
Clyde
Dumbarton
Greenock
Largs
Firth of Clyde
BUTE
Inveraray
Loch Fyne
Oban
Loch Linnhe
LISMORE
Craignure
MULL
ULVA
IONA
Tobermory
COLL
TIREE
Firth of Lorn
LUING
SCARBA
COLONSAY
JURA
ISLAY
Port Askaig
Port Ellen
GIGHA
Tarbert
Kennacraig
KINTYRE
Campbeltown
Mull of Kintyre
ARRAN
Brodick
Irvine
Troon
Kilmarnock
Prestwick
Ayr
Girvan
Merrick 843m
Loch Doon
Cairnryan
Newton Stewart
Dumfries
Nith
Broad Law 840m
Southern Uplands
Galashiels
Tweed
Lockerbie
Hawick
Teviot
Cheviot Hills
Kielder Water
Northumberland National Park
Haltwhistle
Hadrian's Wall
Alnwick
HOLY I. (LINDISFARNE)
Berwick-upon-Tweed
Newcastle-upon-Tyne
NCL
Gateshead
Whitley Bay
Tynemouth
South Shields
Sunderland
SCOTLAND
NORTH SEA
ATLANTIC OCEAN
OUTER HEBRIDES
INNER HEBRIDES
The Minch
Little Minch
Sea of the Hebrides
Butt of Lewis
LEWIS
Stornoway
SYY
EYE PENINSULA
Callanish
Tarbert
HARRIS
SHIANT IS.
SCALPAY
TARANSAY
SCARP
BERNERAY
PABBAY
FLANNAN ISLES
NORTH UIST
Lochmaddy
BENBECULA
MONACH IS.
SOUTH UIST
Lochboisdale
BARRA
Castlebay
ST KILDA
SKYE
Uig
Portree
RAASAY
SCALPAY
Cuillin Hills 993m
SOAY
Armadale
CANNA
RUM
EGG
MUCK
UNITED
NORTHERN
North Channel
Antrim Hills
Mull of Kintyre
RATHLIN I.
Giant's Causeway
Ballycastle
Ballymoney
Coleraine
Portrush
Limavady
LDY
Lough Foyle
Londonderry (Derry)
Letterkenny

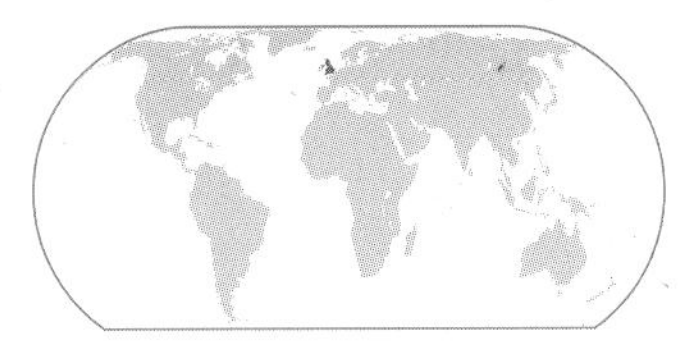

See also... 72-76 for more on the United Kingdom

Lambert Conformal Conic Projection

Blue boxes indicate focus map coverage

0 50 miles
0 100 kilometres

UK: Beaches & National Parks

See also... Europe National Parks (66); UK Attractions (76)

The listings above refer to a selection of related themes. For more information, see the Contents (2-7).

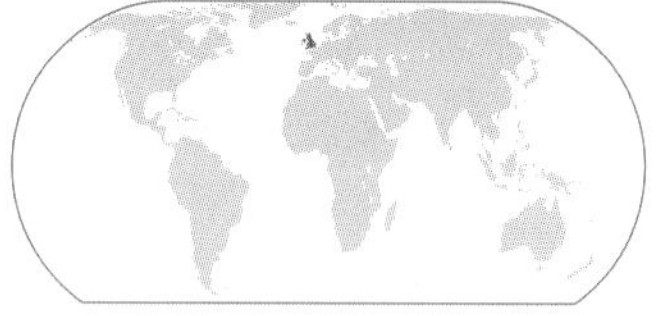

The European Blue Flag Campaign is an environmental awareness raising activity by the Foundation for Environmental Education in Europe (FEEE).

To qualify for a Blue Flag, a beach has to fulfil a number of strict criteria regarding water quality (compliance with the EU Bathing Water Directive), environmental education and information, environmental management and safety and services. The Blue Flag is awarded annually and is valid for one year. The map shows beaches awarded the Blue Flag in 2005. For more information visit: www.seasideawards.org.uk

The UK maps show geographical counties, and not the administrative counties and unitary authorities which have, for administrative purposes, replaced them. Geographical counties give a more familiar picture of the divisions of the UK: they are also of a more consistent size, as they do not reflect the growth of urban populations over the last 200 years. For more information on geographical countries, visit: www.abcounties.co.uk

Scotland
1 Montrose Seafront
2 Broughty Ferry
3 St Andrews: East Sands
St Andrews: West Sands
4 Elie Harbour
5 Burntisland
6 Aberdour: Silver Sands

Northumbria
7 Whitley Bay South
Tynemouth: King Edward's Bay
Tynemouth: Longsands South
8 South Shields: Sandhaven
Whitburn North: Seaburn

Yorkshire
9 Whitby
10 Scarborough: North Bay
11 Bridlington North
12 Hornsea
13 Cleethorpes Central

Heart of England
14 Mablethorpe Central
Sutton on Sea Central
15 Skegness: Tower Esplanade

East of England
16 Sheringham
17 Cromer
18 Mundesley
19 Sea Palling
20 Great Yarmouth: Gorleston on Sea
21 Lowestoft North
Lowestoft South
22 Southwold Pier
23 Felixstowe South
24 Dovercourt
25 Brightlingsea
26 Shoeburyness East
Shoebury Common
Southend-on-Sea: Jubilee Beach

South East England
27 Birchington: Minnis Bay
Westgate-on-Sea: West Bay
28 Margate: Westbrook Bay
29 Eastbourne: Pier to Wish Tower
30 Littlehampton: Coastguards
31 Bognor Regis: East of Pier
32 West Wittering

Southern England
33 Hayling Island: Beachlands Central
Hayling Island: Beachlands West
34 Bournemouth: Alum Chine
Bournemouth: Durley Chine
Bournemouth: Fisherman's Walk
Bournemouth: Southbourne
35 Poole: Branksome Chine
Poole: Canford Cliffs Chine
Poole: Sandbanks
Poole: Shore Road
36 Swanage Central

Isle of Wight
37 Ryde East
38 Sandown
Shanklin

South West
39 Dawlish Warren
40 Torquay: Oddicombe
Torquay: Meadfoot
41 Brixham: Shoalstone Breakwater
42 Blackpool Sands
43 Bigbury-on-Sea North
Challaborough
44 Falmouth: Gyllyngvase
45 Sennen Cove
46 St Ives: Porthmeor
St Ives: Porthminster
47 Porthtowan
48 Polzeath
49 Westward Ho!
50 Croyde Bay
Woolacombe
51 Ilfracombe: Tunnels Beaches

Wales
52 Southerndown
Porthcawl: Rest Bay
53 Swansea: Bracelet Bay
Swansea: Caswell Bay
Swansea: Langland Bay
54 Port-Eynon
55 Pembrey Country Park: Cefn Sidan
56 Amroth
Saundersfoot
57 Tenby Castle
Tenby North
Tenby South
58 Lydstep
59 Dale
60 Broad Haven North
61 Newgale
62 St David's: Whitesands
63 Cardigan: Poppit Sands
64 Aberporth
65 New Quay: Traeth y Harbwr
66 Aberystwyth North
67 Borth
68 Tywyn
69 Fairbourne: Ffriog
70 Barmouth: Abermaw
71 Criccieth
72 Pwllheli: Marian y De
73 Abersoch
74 Dinas Dinlle
75 Penmaenmawr
76 Rhos-on-Sea
77 Prestatyn Central

Anglesey
78 Newborough: Llanddwyn
79 Holy Island: Porth Dafarch
Holy Island: Trearddur Bay
80 Benllech
81 Llanddona

Northern Ireland
82 Magilligan: Benone Strand
Downhill Strand
83 Portstewart Strand
Portrush: East Strand
Portrush: West Strand
Portrush: White Rocks
84 Tyrella
85 Cranfield West

International arrivals (millions)

1980 1985 1990 1995 2000 2005

Source: World Tourism Organisation

[0] Blue Flag beach 2005
Geographical county boundary
English Tourist Board boundary
National Park
100 kilometres
50 miles

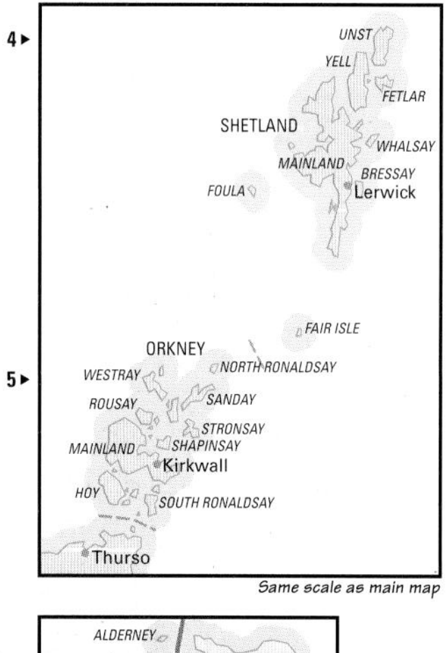
UNST
YELL
FETLAR
SHETLAND
WHALSAY
MAINLAND
BRESSAY
Lerwick
FOULA
FAIR ISLE
ORKNEY
NORTH RONALDSAY
WESTRAY
ROUSAY
SANDAY
STRONSAY
MAINLAND
SHAPINSAY
Kirkwall
HOY
SOUTH RONALDSAY
Thurso

Same scale as main map

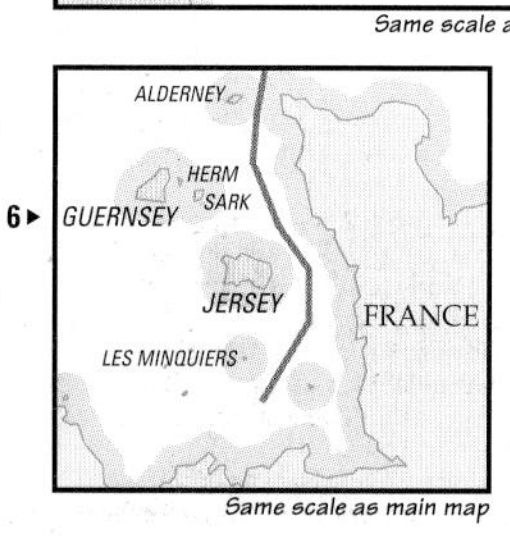
ALDERNEY
HERM
SARK
GUERNSEY
JERSEY
FRANCE
LES MINQUIERS

Same scale as main map

BELGIUM
FRANCE

Blue boxes indicate focus map coverage

See also... Contents (2-7) – this country features in many thematic and regional maps throughout the *World Travel Atlas*.

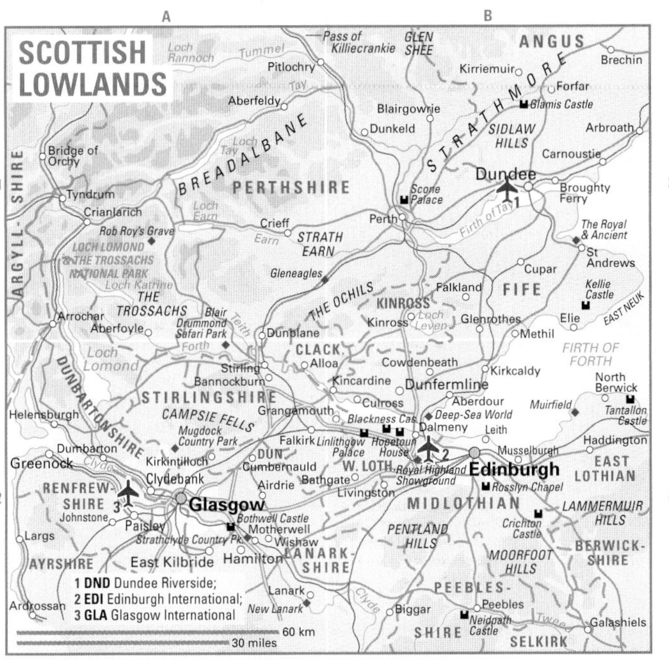
SCOTTISH LOWLANDS
ANGUS
PERTHSHIRE
BREADALBANE
STRATHMORE
FIFE
KINROSS
THE OCHILS
THE TROSSACHS
STIRLINGSHIRE
CAMPSIE FELLS
DUNBARTONSHIRE
RENFREWSHIRE
AYRSHIRE
LANARKSHIRE
MIDLOTHIAN
W. LOTH.
EAST LOTHIAN
LAMMERMUIR HILLS
PENTLAND HILLS
MOORFOOT HILLS
BERWICKSHIRE
PEEBLESSHIRE
SELKIRK
ARGYLL-SHIRE
Pitlochry
Aberfeldy
Kirriemuir
Brechin
Forfar
Glamis Castle
Blairgowrie
Dunkeld
Arbroath
Carnoustie
Dundee
Broughty Ferry
Scone Palace
Perth
Crieff
Gleneagles
St Andrews
Cupar
Falkland
Kinross
Glenrothes
Methil
Elie
Dunblane
Stirling
Bannockburn
Alloa
Cowdenbeath
Kirkcaldy
Kincardine
Dunfermline
North Berwick
Grangemouth
Falkirk
Linlithgow Palace
Hopetoun House
Dalmeny
Leith
Musselburgh
Haddington
Edinburgh
Rosslyn Chapel
Livingston
Bathgate
Cumbernauld
Airdrie
Kirkintilloch
Clydebank
Glasgow
Paisley
Johnstone
Motherwell
Wishaw
Hamilton
East Kilbride
Largs
Greenock
Dumbarton
Helensburgh
Arrochar
Aberfoyle
Crianlarich
Tyndrum
Bridge of Orchy
Loch Lomond
Ardrossan
Lanark
New Lanark
Biggar
Peebles
Galashiels
Neidpath Castle
1 DND Dundee Riverside;
2 EDI Edinburgh International;
3 GLA Glasgow International
60 km
30 miles

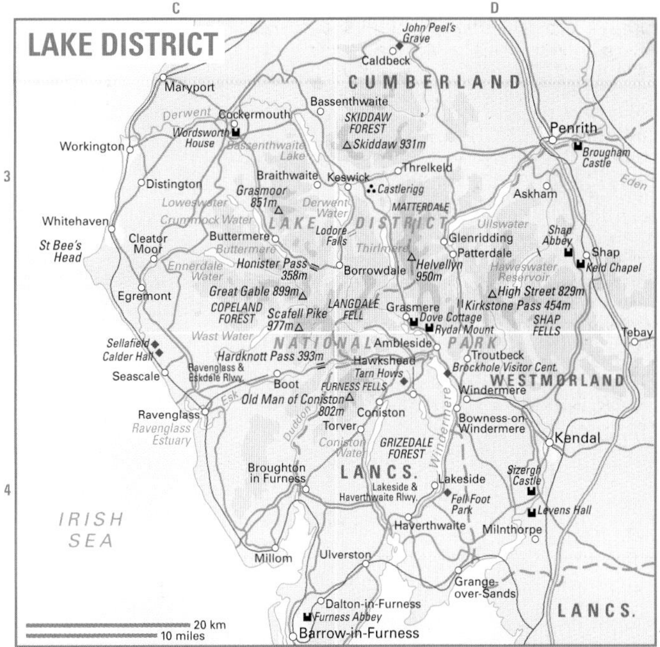
LAKE DISTRICT
CUMBERLAND
WESTMORLAND
LANCS.
LAKE DISTRICT NATIONAL PARK
IRISH SEA
John Peel's Grave
Caldbeck
Maryport
Bassenthwaite
Cockermouth
Skiddaw 931m
Penrith
Workington
Wordsworth House
Keswick
Castlerigg
Threlkeld
Brougham Castle
Askham
Distington
Whitehaven
St Bee's Head
Cleator Moor
Egremont
Buttermere
Honister Pass 358m
Borrowdale
Helvellyn 950m
Glenridding
Patterdale
Shap
Shap Abbey
Keld Chapel
High Street 829m
Kirkstone Pass 454m
Great Gable 899m
Scafell Pike 977m
Grasmere
Dove Cottage
Rydal Mount
Ambleside
Tebay
Sellafield
Calder Hall
Seascale
Hardknott Pass 393m
Hawkshead
Troutbeck
Brockhole Visitor Cent.
Windermere
Boot
Ravenglass
Old Man of Coniston 802m
Coniston
Torver
Bowness-on-Windermere
Kendal
Grizedale Forest
Broughton in Furness
Lakeside
Sizergh Castle
Levens Hall
Haverthwaite
Milnthorpe
Millom
Ulverston
Grange-over-Sands
Dalton-in-Furness
Furness Abbey
Barrow-in-Furness
20 km
10 miles

HEART OF ENGLAND
STAFFORDSHIRE
LEICESTERSHIRE
SHROPSHIRE
WORCESTERSHIRE
WARWICKSHIRE
HEREFORDSHIRE
GLOUCESTERSHIRE
MONMOUTHSHIRE
RADNORSHIRE
NORTHANTS.
OXFORDSHIRE
BERKS.
GLAM.
THE MARCHES
VALE OF EVESHAM
COTSWOLD HILLS
Shrewsbury
Telford
Lichfield
Tamworth
Leicester
Welshpool
Wolverhampton
Walsall
Sutton Coldfield
West Bromwich
Dudley
Birmingham
Nuneaton
Coventry
Rugby
Ludlow
Kidderminster
Royal Leamington Spa
Redditch
Warwick
Worcester
Stratford-upon-Avon
Great Malvern
Evesham
Hereford
Ledbury
Tewkesbury
Cheltenham
Gloucester
Ross-on-Wye
Monmouth
Abergavenny
Stroud
Cirencester
Bourton-on-the-Water
Moreton-in-Marsh
Banbury
Bicester
Oxford
Chepstow
Newport
Malmesbury
Abingdon
1 BHX Birmingham Int.; 2 CVT Coventry Baginton;
3 BZZ Brize Norton; 4 GLO Gloucester Staverton
50 km
25 miles

SOUTHEAST ENGLAND
ESSEX
HERTFORDSHIRE
BUCKS.
SURREY
KENT
SUSSEX
NORTH DOWNS
SOUTH DOWNS
THE WEALD
NORTH SEA
ENGLISH CHANNEL
STRAIT OF DOVER
FRANCE
Felixstowe
Harwich
Colchester
Luton
Clacton-on-Sea
St Albans
Harlow
Chelmsford
Watford
Enfield
Brentwood
Southend-on-Sea
Slough
LONDON
Windsor
Gravesend
Chatham
Margate
Kingston-upon-Thames
Croydon
Woking
Guildford
Maidstone
Canterbury
Ramsgate
Deal
Ashford
Dover
Folkestone
Crawley
Horsham
Royal Tunbridge Wells
Rye
Hastings
Brighton
Worthing
Chichester
Eastbourne
Boulogne-sur-Mer
Cap Gris-Nez
1 LTN London Luton; 2 STN London Stansted;
3 SEN Southend; 4 LCY London City;
5 LHR London Heathrow; 6 BQH London Biggin Hill;
7 LGW London Gatwick; 8 LYX Lydd
60 kilometres
30 miles
600 metres
300 metres
Sea level

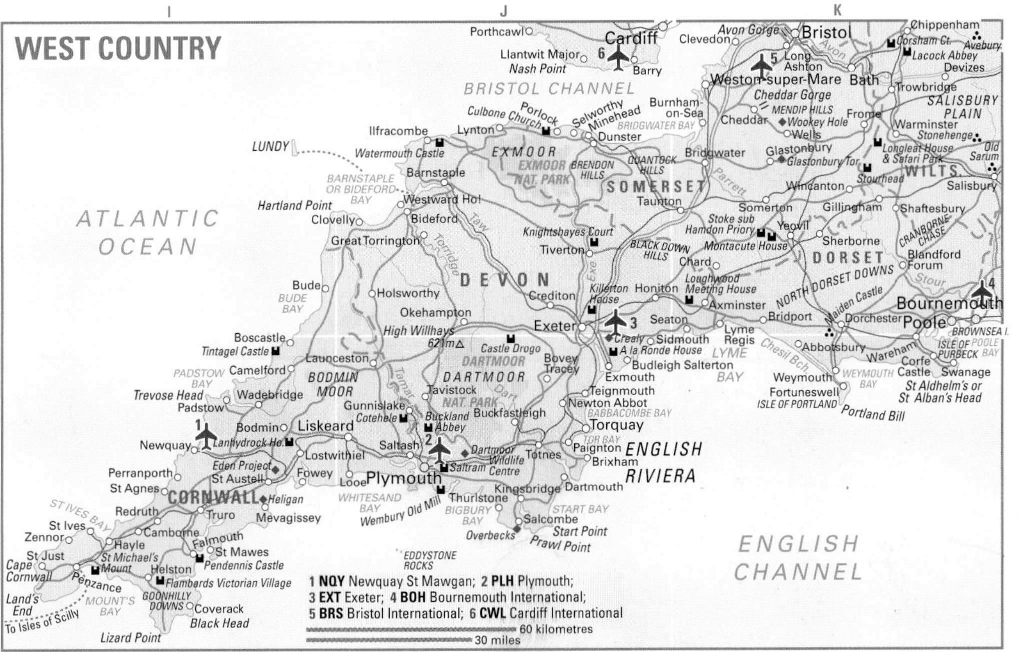
WEST COUNTRY
ATLANTIC OCEAN
BRISTOL CHANNEL
ENGLISH CHANNEL
EXMOOR
SOMERSET
DEVON
DORSET
WILTS.
CORNWALL
DARTMOOR
BODMIN MOOR
ENGLISH RIVIERA
Cardiff
Bristol
Bath
Weston-super-Mare
Minehead
Barnstaple
Ilfracombe
Bideford
Taunton
Wells
Glastonbury
Yeovil
Salisbury
Tiverton
Exeter
Sidmouth
Exmouth
Bournemouth
Poole
Weymouth
Torquay
Paignton
Brixham
Plymouth
Newquay
Bodmin
Liskeard
St Austell
Truro
Falmouth
Penzance
St Ives
Land's End
Lizard Point
1 NQY Newquay St Mawgan; 2 PLH Plymouth;
3 EXT Exeter; 4 BOH Bournemouth International;
5 BRS Bristol International; 6 CWL Cardiff International
60 kilometres
30 miles

NEW YEAR Hogmanay **(Edinburgh)**
JAN 1st New Year's Day Parade **(London)**
JAN Celtic Connections **(Glasgow)**
JAN 25th Burns Night **(Scotland)**
late JAN Up Helly Aa **(Lerwick, Shetland)**
MAR-APR Ideal Home Show **(London)**
APR **London** Marathon
APR Oxford-Cambridge Boat Race **(London)**
APR **Edinburgh** International Science Festival
APR 30th Beltane: Celtic Fire Festival
MAY 1st Hobby Horse **(Minehead & Padstow)**
MAY Furry Dance **(Helston)** MAY Mayfest **(Glasgow)**
end MAY Chelsea Flower Show **(London)**
MAY-JUN **Bath** International Festival
MAY-AUG **Glyndebourne** Opera Festival
early JUN Queen's Birthday parade: Trooping The Colour **(London)**
JUN Royal Highland Show **(Ingliston)**
JUN **Aldeburgh** Festival late JUN **Glastonbury** Festival
JUN-JUL **York** Mystery Plays; 2004 and every four years
JUN-JUL Lawn Tennis Championships **(Wimbledon)**
JUN-AUG Riding of the Marches **(England-Scotland borders)**
JUN-AUG **Cardiff** Festival JUL **Henley** Royal Regatta
JUL **Llangollen** International Music Eisteddfod
JUL/AUG WOMAD World Music Festival **(Reading)**
JUL/AUG Highland Games (various places in **Scotland**)
JUL-SEP Promenade Concerts 'Proms' **(London)**
early AUG Royal National Eisteddfod **(Wales**: venue changes**)**
AUG Three Choirs Festival **(Gloucester/Hereford/Worcester)**
AUG **Edinburgh** International Festival & Fringe; Military Tattoo
AUG **Brecon** Jazz Festival
AUG Great British Beer Festival **(London)**
AUG **Bank Holiday** Notting Hill Carnival **(London)**
SEP Royal Highland Gathering **(Braemar)**
SEP-NOV **Blackpool** Illuminations
NOV 5th Guy Fawkes Night
early NOV **London-Brighton** Veteran Car Rally
NOV **London** Film Festival; **London** Jazz Festival
NOV **Cardiff** Screen Festival
NOV State Opening of Parliament **(London)**
NOV Lord Mayor's Procession and Show **(London)**

UK: Airports, Motorways & Ferries

See also... Flight Times (45); Europe Airports & High-Speed Rail (62-63); Europe Railways & Ferries (64-65); London Airport Connections (75)

The listings above refer to a selection of related themes. For more information, see the Contents (2-7).

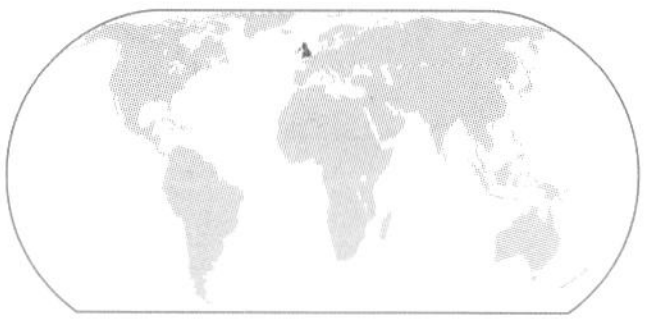

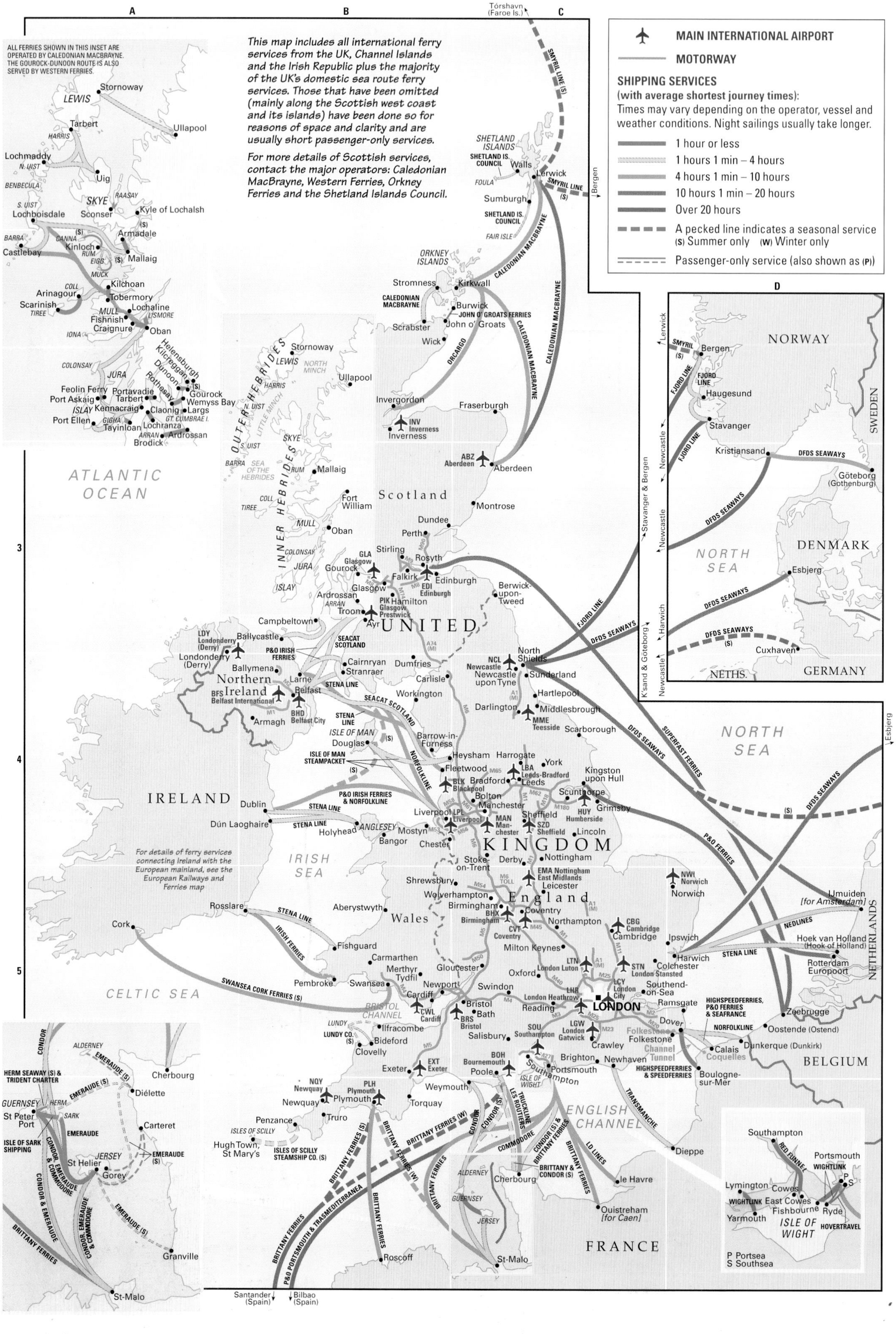

This map includes all international ferry services from the UK, Channel Islands and the Irish Republic plus the majority of the UK's domestic sea route ferry services. Those that have been omitted (mainly along the Scottish west coast and its islands) have been done so for reasons of space and clarity and are usually short passenger-only services.

For more details of Scottish services, contact the major operators: Caledonian MacBrayne, Western Ferries, Orkney Ferries and the Shetland Islands Council.

ALL FERRIES SHOWN IN THIS INSET ARE OPERATED BY CALEDONIAN MACBRAYNE. THE GOUROCK-DUNOON ROUTE IS ALSO SERVED BY WESTERN FERRIES.

For details of ferry services connecting Ireland with the European mainland, see the European Railways and Ferries map

MAIN INTERNATIONAL AIRPORT

MOTORWAY

SHIPPING SERVICES
(with average shortest journey times):
Times may vary depending on the operator, vessel and weather conditions. Night sailings usually take longer.

- 1 hour or less
- 1 hours 1 min – 4 hours
- 4 hours 1 min – 10 hours
- 10 hours 1 min – 20 hours
- Over 20 hours
- A pecked line indicates a seasonal service (S) Summer only (W) Winter only
- Passenger-only service (also shown as (P))

P Portsea
S Southsea

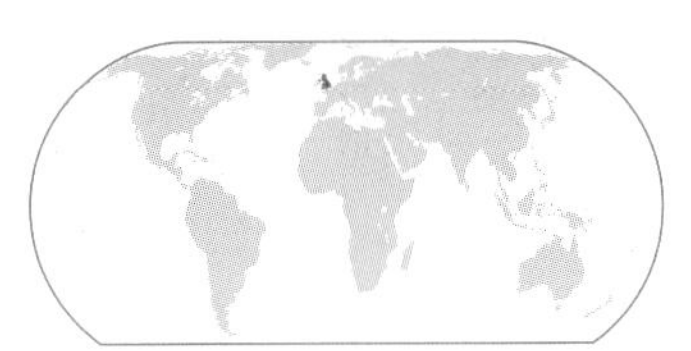

See also... Flight Times (45); Europe Airports & High-Speed Rail (62-63); Europe Railways & Ferries (64-65); UK Airports, Motorways & Ferries (74)

UK: London Airport Connections

The listings above refer to a selection of related themes. For more information, see the Contents (2-7).

This diagram shows the main public transport connections to London's airports from central London and the links between the airports. It is not drawn to scale and many incidental transport links – including the vast majority of the London Underground – have been omitted to improve legibility. Note that all information (particularly bus routes) is subject to change.

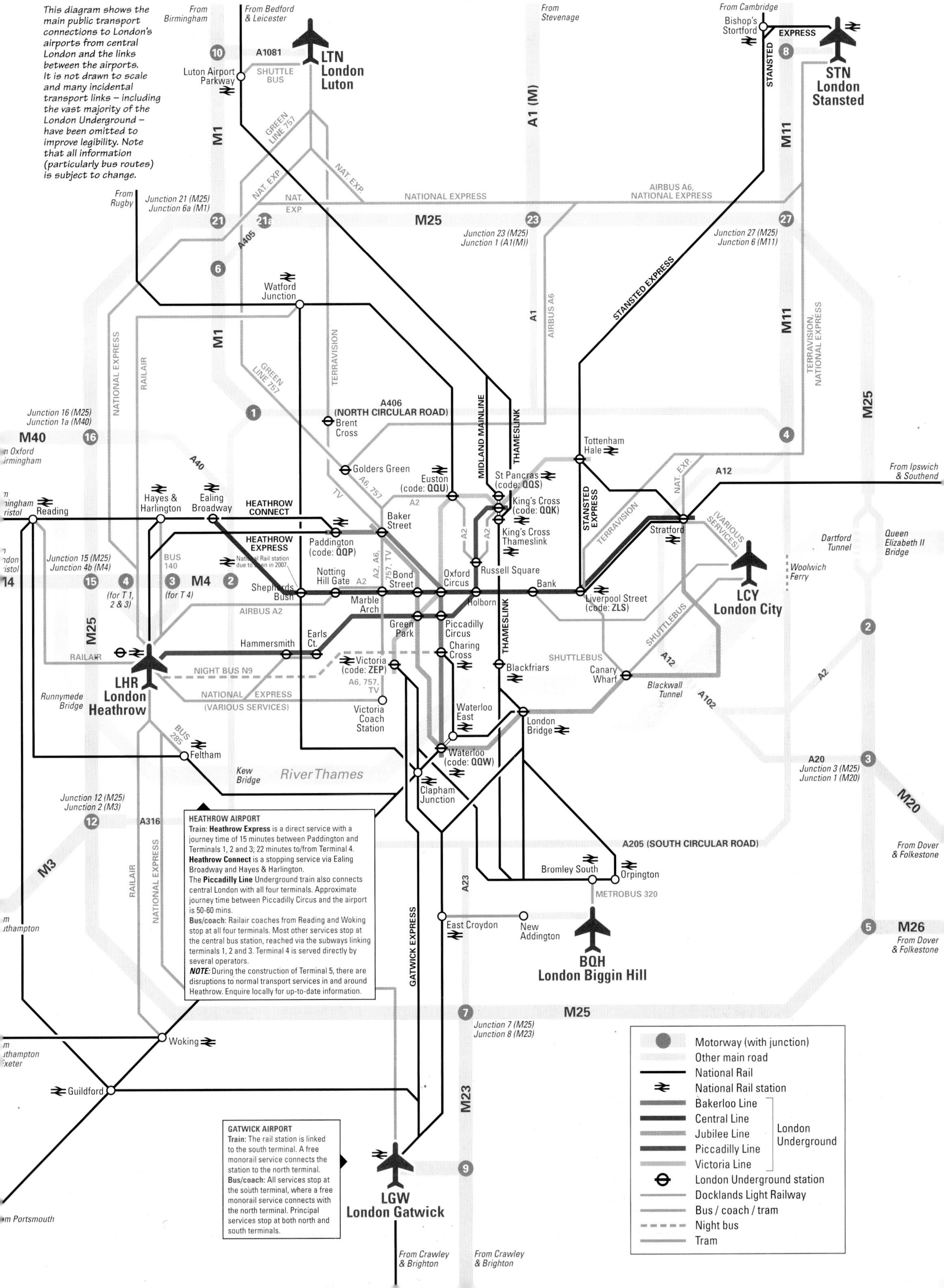

From Birmingham
From Bedford & Leicester
A1081
LTN London Luton
Luton Airport Parkway
SHUTTLE BUS
GREEN LINE 757
NAT. EXP.
From Stevenage
A1 (M)
From Cambridge
Bishop's Stortford
EXPRESS
STANSTED
STN London Stansted
M11
M1
From Rugby
Junction 21 (M25) Junction 6a (M1)
NATIONAL EXPRESS
AIRBUS A6, NATIONAL EXPRESS
M25
Junction 23 (M25) Junction 1 (A1(M))
Junction 27 (M25) Junction 6 (M11)
A405
Watford Junction
STANSTED EXPRESS
TERRAVISION
RAILAIR
A1
AIRBUS A6
TERRAVISION, NATIONAL EXPRESS
MIDLAND MAINLINE
THAMESLINK
A406 (NORTH CIRCULAR ROAD)
Brent Cross
Junction 16 (M25) Junction 1a (M40)
M40
From Oxford & Birmingham
A40
Golders Green
Tottenham Hale
Euston (code: QQU)
St Pancras (code: QQS)
King's Cross (code: QQK)
King's Cross Thameslink
From Ipswich & Southend
A12
Hayes & Harlington
Ealing Broadway
HEATHROW CONNECT
Reading
Baker Street
Paddington (code: QQP)
HEATHROW EXPRESS
Stratford
(VARIOUS SERVICES)
Dartford Tunnel
Queen Elizabeth II Bridge
Junction 15 (M25) Junction 4b (M4)
BUS 140
National Rail station due to open in 2007
Notting Hill Gate
Bond Street
Oxford Circus
Russell Square
Woolwich Ferry
M4
(for T 1, 2 & 3)
(for T 4)
Shepherds Bush
Marble Arch
Bank
Liverpool Street (code: ZLS)
LCY London City
AIRBUS A2
Holborn
Green Park
Piccadilly Circus
SHUTTLEBUS
Hammersmith
Earls Ct.
Charing Cross
Victoria (code: ZEP)
Blackfriars
Canary Wharf
RAILAIR
NIGHT BUS N9
A6, 757, TV
Blackwall Tunnel
A102
LHR London Heathrow
NATIONAL EXPRESS (VARIOUS SERVICES)
Victoria Coach Station
Waterloo East
London Bridge
Runnymede Bridge
BUS 285
Feltham
Waterloo (code: QQW)
Kew Bridge
River Thames
Clapham Junction
A20
Junction 3 (M25) Junction 1 (M20)
M20
Junction 12 (M25) Junction 2 (M3)
A316
M3
A205 (SOUTH CIRCULAR ROAD)
From Dover & Folkestone
Bromley South
Orpington
A23
METROBUS 320
East Croydon
New Addington
M26
From Dover & Folkestone
From Southampton
BQH London Biggin Hill
GATWICK EXPRESS
M25
Junction 7 (M25) Junction 8 (M23)
Woking
From Southampton & Exeter
Guildford
M23
LGW London Gatwick
From Portsmouth
From Crawley & Brighton
From Crawley & Brighton

HEATHROW AIRPORT
Train: Heathrow Express is a direct service with a journey time of 15 minutes between Paddington and Terminals 1, 2 and 3; 22 minutes to/from Terminal 4.
Heathrow Connect is a stopping service via Ealing Broadway and Hayes & Harlington.
The **Piccadilly Line** Underground train also connects central London with all four terminals. Approximate journey time between Piccadilly Circus and the airport is 50-60 mins.
Bus/coach: Railair coaches from Reading and Woking stop at all four terminals. Most other services stop at the central bus station, reached via the subways linking terminals 1, 2 and 3. Terminal 4 is served directly by several operators.
NOTE: During the construction of Terminal 5, there are disruptions to normal transport services in and around Heathrow. Enquire locally for up-to-date information.

GATWICK AIRPORT
Train: The rail station is linked to the south terminal. A free monorail service connects the station to the north terminal.
Bus/coach: All services stop at the south terminal, where a free monorail service connects with the north terminal. Principal services stop at both north and south terminals.

Motorway (with junction)
Other main road
National Rail
National Rail station
Bakerloo Line
Central Line
Jubilee Line
Piccadilly Line
Victoria Line
London Underground
London Underground station
Docklands Light Railway
Bus / coach / tram
Night bus
Tram

UK: Attractions

See also... Europe Historical (58-59)

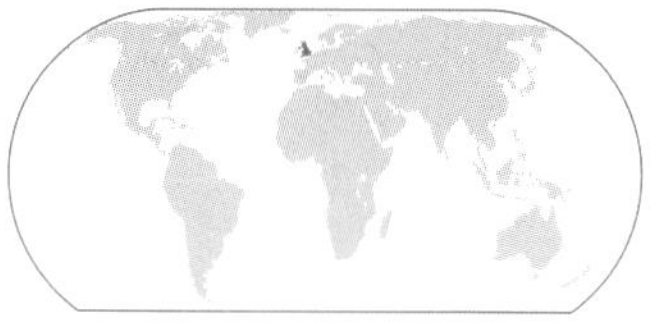

The listings above refer to a selection of related themes. For more information, see the Contents (2-7). See also the Columbus Tourist Attractions & Events of the World.

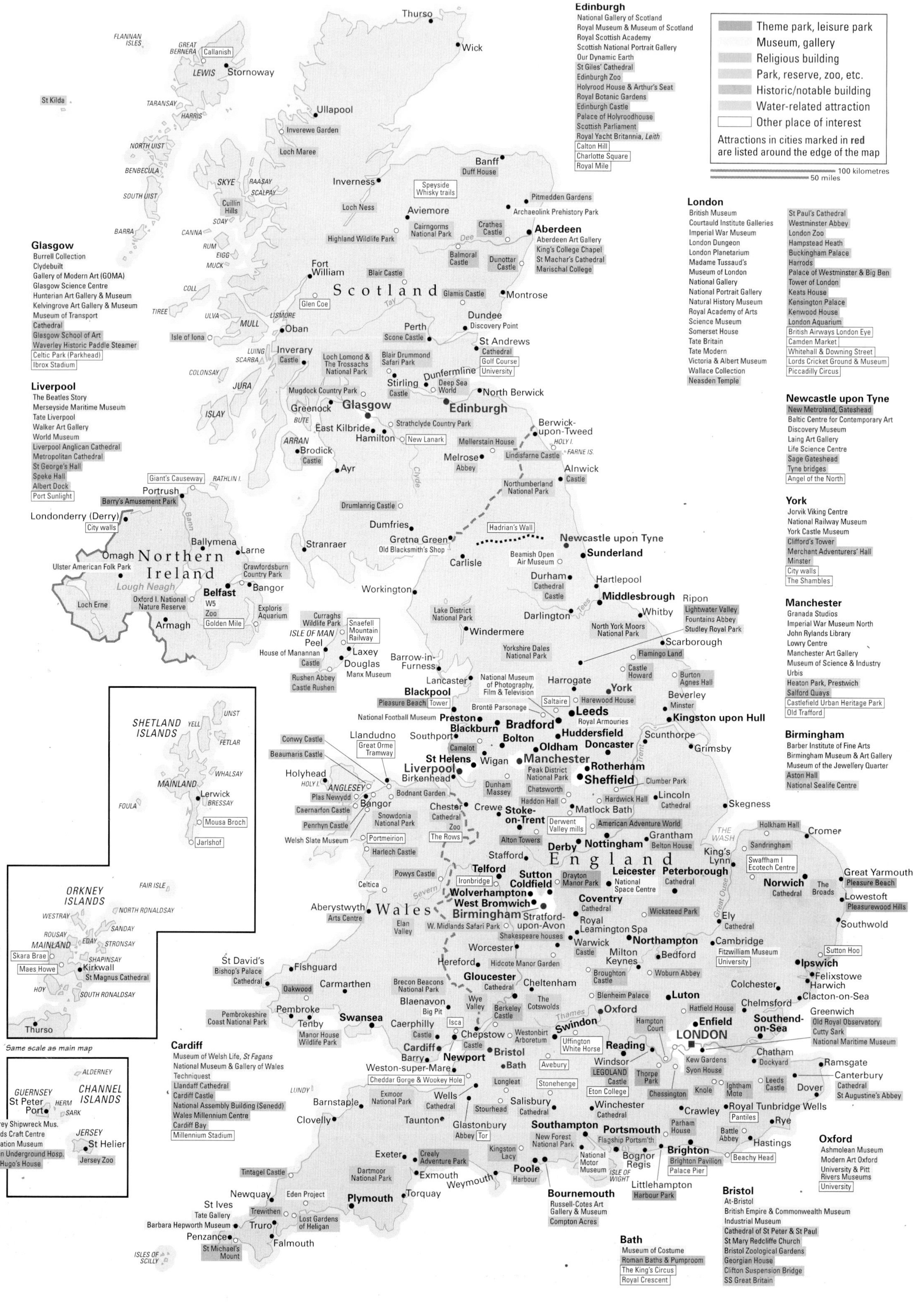
Theme park, leisure park
Museum, gallery
Religious building
Park, reserve, zoo, etc.
Historic/notable building
Water-related attraction
Other place of interest
Attractions in cities marked in red are listed around the edge of the map
100 kilometres
50 miles
Scotland
Northern Ireland
England
Wales
Thurso
Wick
FLANNAN ISLES
GREAT BERNERA
Callanish
LEWIS
Stornoway
St Kilda
TARANSAY
HARRIS
Ullapool
Inverewe Garden
NORTH UIST
Loch Maree
BENBECULA
Banff
Duff House
SKYE
RAASAY
SCALPAY
Inverness
Speyside Whisky trails
SOUTH UIST
Cuillin Hills
Loch Ness
Pitmedden Gardens
Archaeolink Prehistory Park
SOAY
Aviemore
BARRA
CANNA
Cairngorms National Park
Crathes Castle
Aberdeen
Highland Wildlife Park
Dee
Aberdeen Art Gallery
King's College Chapel
St Machar's Cathedral
Marischal College
RUM
EIGG
MUCK
Balmoral Castle
Dunottar Castle
Fort William
Blair Castle
COLL
Glamis Castle
Montrose
Glen Coe
TIREE
ULVA
LISMORE
Tay
MULL
Dundee
Discovery Point
Perth
Scone Castle
Isle of Iona
Oban
St Andrews
Cathedral
Golf Course
University
LUING
SCARBA
Inverary Castle
Loch Lomond & The Trossachs National Park
Blair Drummond Safari Park
COLONSAY
Dunfermline
JURA
Stirling Castle
Deep Sea World
Mugdock Country Park
North Berwick
ISLAY
Greenock
Glasgow
Edinburgh
BUTE
Strathclyde Country Park
East Kilbride
Berwick-upon-Tweed
ARRAN
Hamilton
New Lanark
Mellerstain House
HOLY I.
Brodick Castle
Melrose Abbey
Lindisfarne Castle
FARNE IS.
Ayr
Clyde
Alnwick Castle
Giant's Causeway
RATHLIN I.
Northumberland National Park
Portrush
Barry's Amusement Park
Drumlanrig Castle
Londonderry (Derry)
City walls
Bann
Dumfries
Hadrian's Wall
Ballymena
Gretna Green
Stranraer
Old Blacksmith's Shop
Newcastle upon Tyne
Larne
Omagh
Sunderland
Beamish Open Air Museum
Carlisle
Ulster American Folk Park
Crawfordsburn Country Park
Durham Cathedral Castle
Hartlepool
Lough Neagh
Bangor
Belfast
Workington
Middlesbrough
Ripon
Loch Erne
Oxford I. National Nature Reserve
W5
Zoo
Golden Mile
Exploris Aquarium
Lake District National Park
Darlington
Tees
Whitby
Lightwater Valley
Fountains Abbey
Studley Royal Park
Armagh
Curraghs Wildlife Park
Snaefell Mountain Railway
North York Moors National Park
ISLE OF MAN
Windermere
Scarborough
Peel
House of Manannan Castle
Laxey
Yorkshire Dales National Park
Flamingo Land
Douglas
Manx Museum
Barrow-in-Furness
Castle Howard
Rushen Abbey
Castle Rushen
Lancaster
National Museum of Photography, Film & Television
Harrogate
Burton Agnes Hall
York
Blackpool
Pleasure Beach
Tower
Saltaire
Harewood House
Beverley Minster
Brontë Parsonage
Leeds
National Football Museum
Preston
Royal Armouries
Kingston upon Hull
Blackburn
Bradford
Huddersfield
Conwy Castle
Llandudno
Great Orme Tramway
Southport
Bolton
Scunthorpe
Grimsby
Beaumaris Castle
Camelot
Oldham
Doncaster
Trent
St Helens
Wigan
Manchester
Holyhead
Liverpool
Birkenhead
Peak District National Park
Rotherham
HOLY I.
ANGLESEY
Sheffield
Clumber Park
Plas Newydd
Bodnant Garden
Dunham Massey
Chatsworth
Lincoln Cathedral
Bangor
Haddon Hall
Hardwick Hall
Skegness
Caernarfon Castle
Snowdonia National Park
Chester Cathedral Zoo
Crewe
Stoke-on-Trent
Matlock Bath
Penrhyn Castle
Derwent Valley mills
American Adventure World
Holkham Hall
Cromer
Portmeirion
The Rows
THE WASH
Welsh Slate Museum
Alton Towers
Grantham
Belton House
Sandringham
Harlech Castle
Derby
Nottingham
King's Lynn
Stafford
Swaffham Ecotech Centre
Powys Castle
Telford
Sutton Coldfield
Leicester
Peterborough Cathedral
Great Yarmouth
Pleasure Beach
Ironbridge
Drayton Manor Park
National Space Centre
Norwich Cathedral
The Broads
Celtica
Severn
Wolverhampton
Great Ouse
West Bromwich
Coventry Cathedral
Lowestoft
Pleasurewood Hills
Aberystwyth
Arts Centre
Birmingham
Wicksteed Park
Ely Cathedral
Southwold
Elan Valley
W. Midlands Safari Park
Stratford-upon-Avon
Royal Leamington Spa
Shakespeare houses
Warwick Castle
Northampton
Cambridge
Fitzwilliam Museum
University
Sutton Hoo
Worcester
Milton Keynes
Bedford
Ipswich
St David's
Bishop's Palace
Cathedral
Fishguard
Hereford
Hidcote Manor Garden
Broughton Castle
Woburn Abbey
Felixstowe
Harwich
Gloucester Cathedral
Oakwood
Carmarthen
Brecon Beacons National Park
Cheltenham
Colchester
Clacton-on-Sea
Blenheim Palace
Luton
Blaenavon Big Pit
Wye Valley
Berkeley Castle
The Cotswolds
Pembrokeshire Coast National Park
Pembroke
Chelmsford
Oxford
Hatfield House
Tenby
Swansea
Thames
Greenwich
Old Royal Observatory
Cutty Sark
National Maritime Museum
Manor House Wildlife Park
Caerphilly Castle
Isca
Swindon
Hampton Court
Enfield
Southend-on-Sea
Chepstow Castle
Westonbirt Arboretum
LONDON
Cardiff
Uffington White Horse
Reading
Bristol
Chatham Dockyard
Newport
Barry
Windsor
LEGOLAND
Castle
Thorpe Park
Kew Gardens
Syon House
Ramsgate
Weston-super-Mare
Bath
Avebury
Canterbury Cathedral
St Augustine's Abbey
Cheddar Gorge & Wookey Hole
Longleat
Stonehenge
Eton College
Chessington
Knole
Ightham Mote
Leeds Castle
Dover
LUNDY
Exmoor National Park
Wells Cathedral
Barnstaple
Salisbury Cathedral
Winchester Cathedral
Crawley
Royal Tunbridge Wells
Stourhead
Pantiles
Clovelly
Taunton
Glastonbury Abbey
Tor
Southampton
Parham House
Rye
Portsmouth
Flagship Portsm'th
Battle Abbey
Hastings
New Forest National Park
Exeter
Crealy Adventure Park
Kingston Lacy
National Motor Museum
Bognor Regis
Brighton
Brighton Pavilion
Palace Pier
Beachy Head
Tintagel Castle
Dartmoor National Park
Exmouth
Poole Harbour
ISLE OF WIGHT
Weymouth
Littlehampton
Harbour Park
Newquay
Eden Project
Torquay
Bournemouth
Plymouth
St Ives
Tate Gallery
Trewithen
Barbara Hepworth Museum
Truro
Lost Gardens of Heligan
Penzance
Falmouth
St Michael's Mount
ISLES OF SCILLY
SHETLAND ISLANDS
YELL
UNST
FETLAR
WHALSAY
MAINLAND
Lerwick
BRESSAY
FOULA
Mousa Broch
Jarlshof
ORKNEY ISLANDS
FAIR ISLE
WESTRAY
NORTH RONALDSAY
SANDAY
ROUSAY
EDAY
STRONSAY
MAINLAND
Skara Brae
SHAPINSAY
Maes Howe
Kirkwall
St Magnus Cathedral
HOY
SOUTH RONALDSAY
Thurso
Same scale as main map
ALDERNEY
CHANNEL ISLANDS
GUERNSEY
St Peter Port
HERM
SARK
Fort Grey Shipwreck Mus.
Oatlands Craft Centre
Occupation Museum
German Underground Hosp.
Victor Hugo's House
JERSEY
St Helier
Jersey Zoo

Edinburgh
- National Gallery of Scotland
- Royal Museum & Museum of Scotland
- Royal Scottish Academy
- Scottish National Portrait Gallery
- Our Dynamic Earth
- St Giles' Cathedral
- Edinburgh Zoo
- Holyrood House & Arthur's Seat
- Royal Botanic Gardens
- Edinburgh Castle
- Palace of Holyroodhouse
- Scottish Parliament
- Royal Yacht Britannia, *Leith*
- Calton Hill
- Charlotte Square
- Royal Mile

Glasgow
- Burrell Collection
- Clydebuilt
- Gallery of Modern Art (GOMA)
- Glasgow Science Centre
- Hunterian Art Gallery & Museum
- Kelvingrove Art Gallery & Museum
- Museum of Transport
- Cathedral
- Glasgow School of Art
- Waverley Historic Paddle Steamer
- Celtic Park (Parkhead)
- Ibrox Stadium

Liverpool
- The Beatles Story
- Merseyside Maritime Museum
- Tate Liverpool
- Walker Art Gallery
- World Museum
- Liverpool Anglican Cathedral
- Metropolitan Cathedral
- St George's Hall
- Speke Hall
- Albert Dock
- Port Sunlight

London
- British Museum
- Courtauld Institute Galleries
- Imperial War Museum
- London Dungeon
- London Planetarium
- Madame Tussaud's
- Museum of London
- National Gallery
- National Portrait Gallery
- Natural History Museum
- Royal Academy of Arts
- Science Museum
- Somerset House
- Tate Britain
- Tate Modern
- Victoria & Albert Museum
- Wallace Collection
- Neasden Temple
- St Paul's Cathedral
- Westminster Abbey
- London Zoo
- Hampstead Heath
- Buckingham Palace
- Harrods
- Palace of Westminster & Big Ben
- Tower of London
- Keats House
- Kensington Palace
- Kenwood House
- London Aquarium
- British Airways London Eye
- Camden Market
- Whitehall & Downing Street
- Lords Cricket Ground & Museum
- Piccadilly Circus

Newcastle upon Tyne
- New Metroland, Gateshead
- Baltic Centre for Contemporary Art
- Discovery Museum
- Laing Art Gallery
- Life Science Centre
- Sage Gateshead
- Tyne bridges
- Angel of the North

York
- Jorvik Viking Centre
- National Railway Museum
- York Castle Museum
- Clifford's Tower
- Merchant Adventurers' Hall
- Minster
- City walls
- The Shambles

Manchester
- Granada Studios
- Imperial War Museum North
- John Rylands Library
- Lowry Centre
- Manchester Art Gallery
- Museum of Science & Industry
- Urbis
- Heaton Park, Prestwich
- Salford Quays
- Castlefield Urban Heritage Park
- Old Trafford

Birmingham
- Barber Institute of Fine Arts
- Birmingham Museum & Art Gallery
- Museum of the Jewellery Quarter
- Aston Hall
- National Sealife Centre

Cardiff
- Museum of Welsh Life, *St Fagans*
- National Museum & Gallery of Wales
- Techniquest
- Llandaff Cathedral
- Cardiff Castle
- National Assembly Building (Senedd)
- Wales Millennium Centre
- Cardiff Bay
- Millennium Stadium

Oxford
- Ashmolean Museum
- Modern Art Oxford
- University & Pitt Rivers Museums
- University

Bournemouth
- Russell-Cotes Art Gallery & Museum
- Compton Acres

Bath
- Museum of Costume
- Roman Baths & Pumproom
- The King's Circus
- Royal Crescent

Bristol
- At-Bristol
- British Empire & Commonwealth Museum
- Industrial Museum
- Cathedral of St Peter & St Paul
- St Mary Redcliffe Church
- Bristol Zoological Gardens
- Georgian House
- Clifton Suspension Bridge
- SS Great Britain

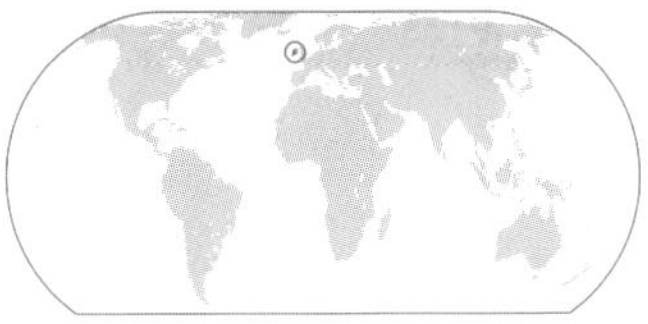

See also... Contents (2-7) – this country features in many thematic and regional maps throughout the *World Travel Atlas*.

ATLANTIC OCEAN
NORTHERN IRELAND
UNITED KINGDOM
IRELAND
ULSTER
CONNACHT (CONNAUGHT)
LEINSTER
MUNSTER
IRISH SEA
CELTIC SEA
North Channel
St George's Channel
Malin Head
Cardonagh
Londonderry (Derry)
Coleraine
Letterkenny
Lifford
Strabane
Larne
Ballymena
Antrim
Newtownabbey
Bangor
Belfast
Donegal
Omagh
Ballyshannon
Bundoran
Lisburn
Portadown
Enniskillen
Armagh
Sligo
Newry
Monaghan
Bangor
Ballina
Charlestown
Boyle
Cavan
Dundalk (Dún Dealgan)
Castlebar
Westport
Carrick-on-Shannon
Ardee
Drogheda (Droichead Átha)
Longford
Mostrim
Navan
Roscommon
Clifden
Tuam
Mullingar
DUBLIN (BAILE ÁTHA CLIATH)
Athlone
Dún Laoghaire
Ballinasloe
Galway (Gaillimh)
Bray
Slieve Bloom Mountains
Portlaoise
Wicklow Mountains
Wicklow
Roscrea
Ennis
Nenagh
Carlow
Arklow
Kilkee
Thurles
Kilkenny
Limerick (Luimneach)
Tarbert
Cashel
Enniscorthy
Listowel
Tipperary
Cahir
New Ross
Wexford
Tralee (Traighli)
Clonmel
Rosslare
Killarney
Mallow
Waterford (Port Láirge)
Dungarvan
Cork (Corcaigh)
Youghal
Bantry
Mizen Head
IVERAGH PENINSULA
DINGLE PENINSULA
BEARA PENINSULA
ARAN ISLANDS
ACHILL I.
NOC
SNN
ORK
DUB

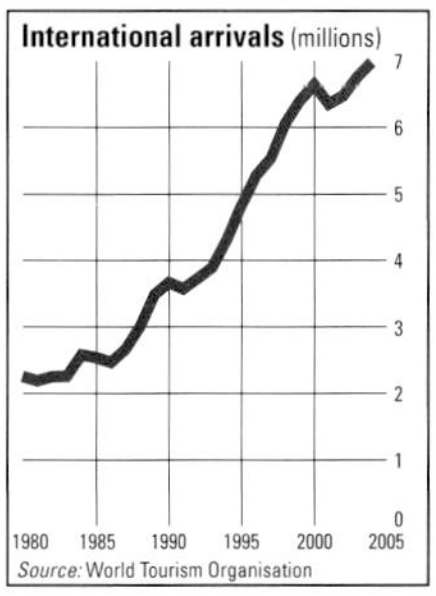
International arrivals (millions)
Source: World Tourism Organisation

MAR 17th St Patrick's Day
APR-MAY **Cork** International Choral Festival
MAY Heineken Green Energy Festival **(Dublin)**
JUN 16th Bloomsday Festival **(Dublin)**
JUL **Galway** Arts Festival
JUL Fleadh Cheoil na Éireann (different venue each year)
AUG Rose of **Tralee** International Festival
AUG Puck Fair **(Killorglin)**
AUG Royal **Dublin** Society's Horse Show
AUG **Kilkenny** International Arts Week
SEP **Lisdoonvarna** Matchmaking Festival
SEP-OCT **Dublin** Fringe Festival
OCT **Cork** Film Festival
OCT **Cork** Jazz Festival
OCT-NOV **Wexford** Opera Festival

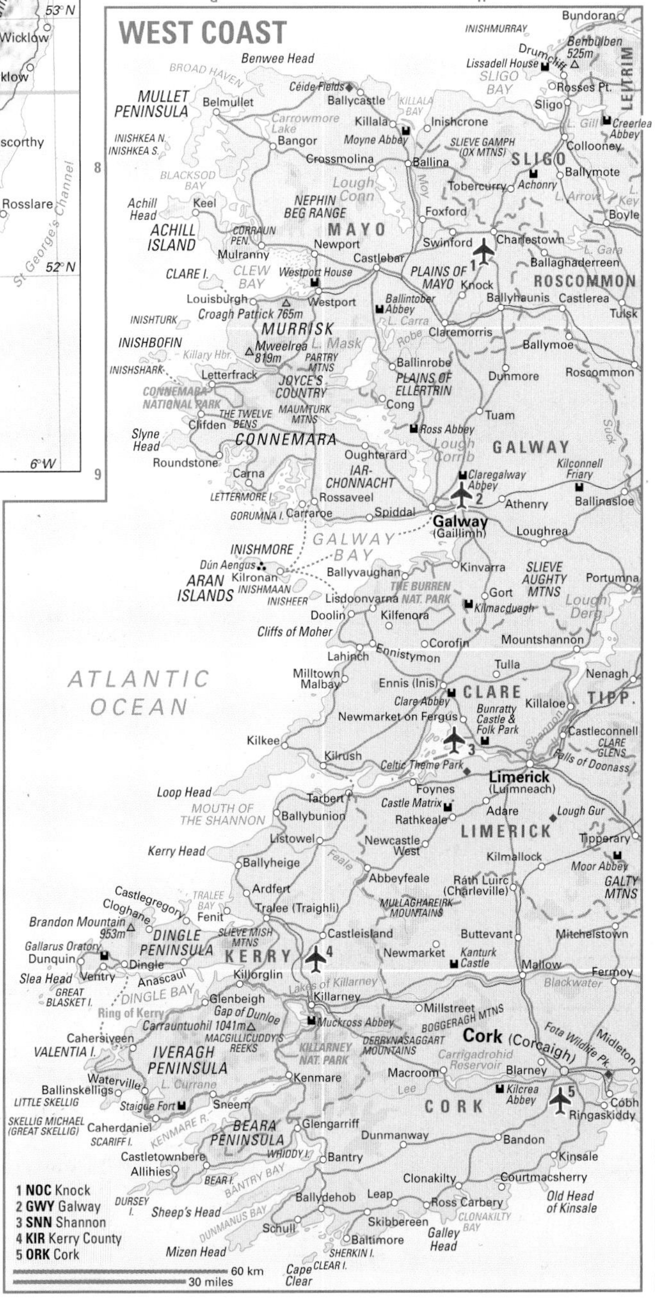
WEST COAST
ATLANTIC OCEAN
MAYO
SLIGO
ROSCOMMON
GALWAY
CLARE
LIMERICK
KERRY
CORK
Galway (Gaillimh)
Limerick (Luimneach)
Cork (Corcaigh)
Killarney
Westport
Castlebar
Ennis
Tralee (Traighli)
ARAN ISLANDS
CONNEMARA
DINGLE PENINSULA
IVERAGH PENINSULA
BEARA PENINSULA
1 NOC Knock
2 GWY Galway
3 SNN Shannon
4 KIR Kerry County
5 ORK Cork
60 km
30 miles
600 metres
300 metres
Sea level

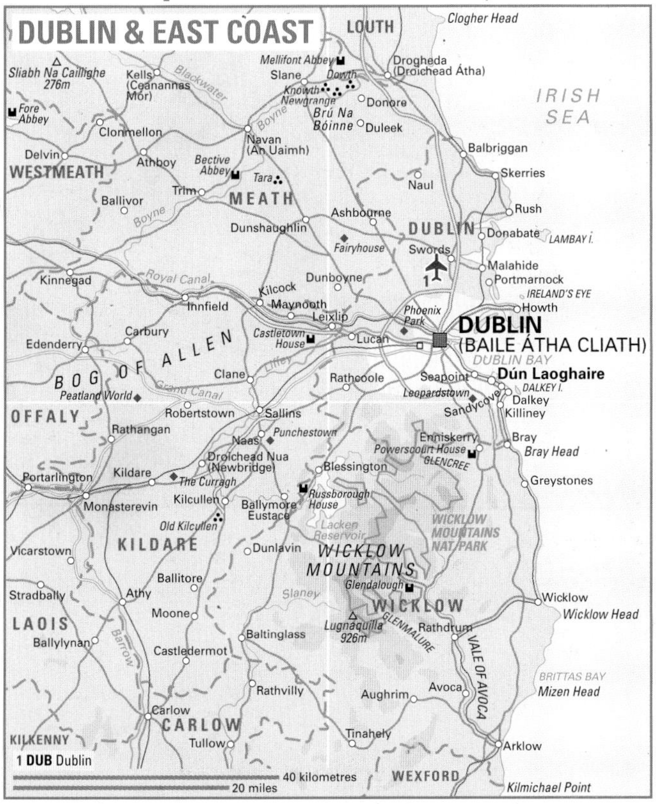
DUBLIN & EAST COAST
IRISH SEA
LOUTH
MEATH
DUBLIN
WESTMEATH
OFFALY
KILDARE
LAOIS
CARLOW
WICKLOW
WEXFORD
KILKENNY
DUBLIN (BAILE ÁTHA CLIATH)
Dún Laoghaire
Drogheda (Droichead Átha)
Navan (An Uaimh)
BOG OF ALLEN
WICKLOW MOUNTAINS
Wicklow
Arklow
1 DUB Dublin
40 kilometres
20 miles

Benelux

See also... Belgium (79); Netherlands (80-81)

The listings above refer to a selection of related themes. For more information, see the Contents (2-7).

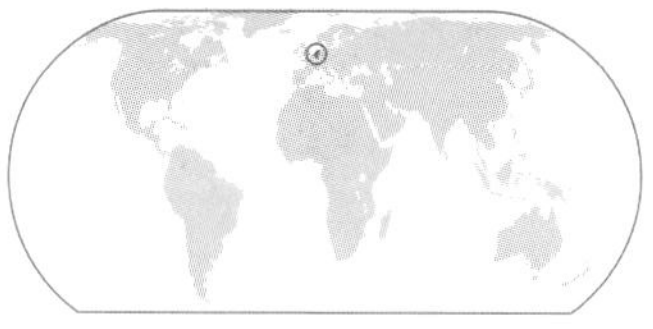

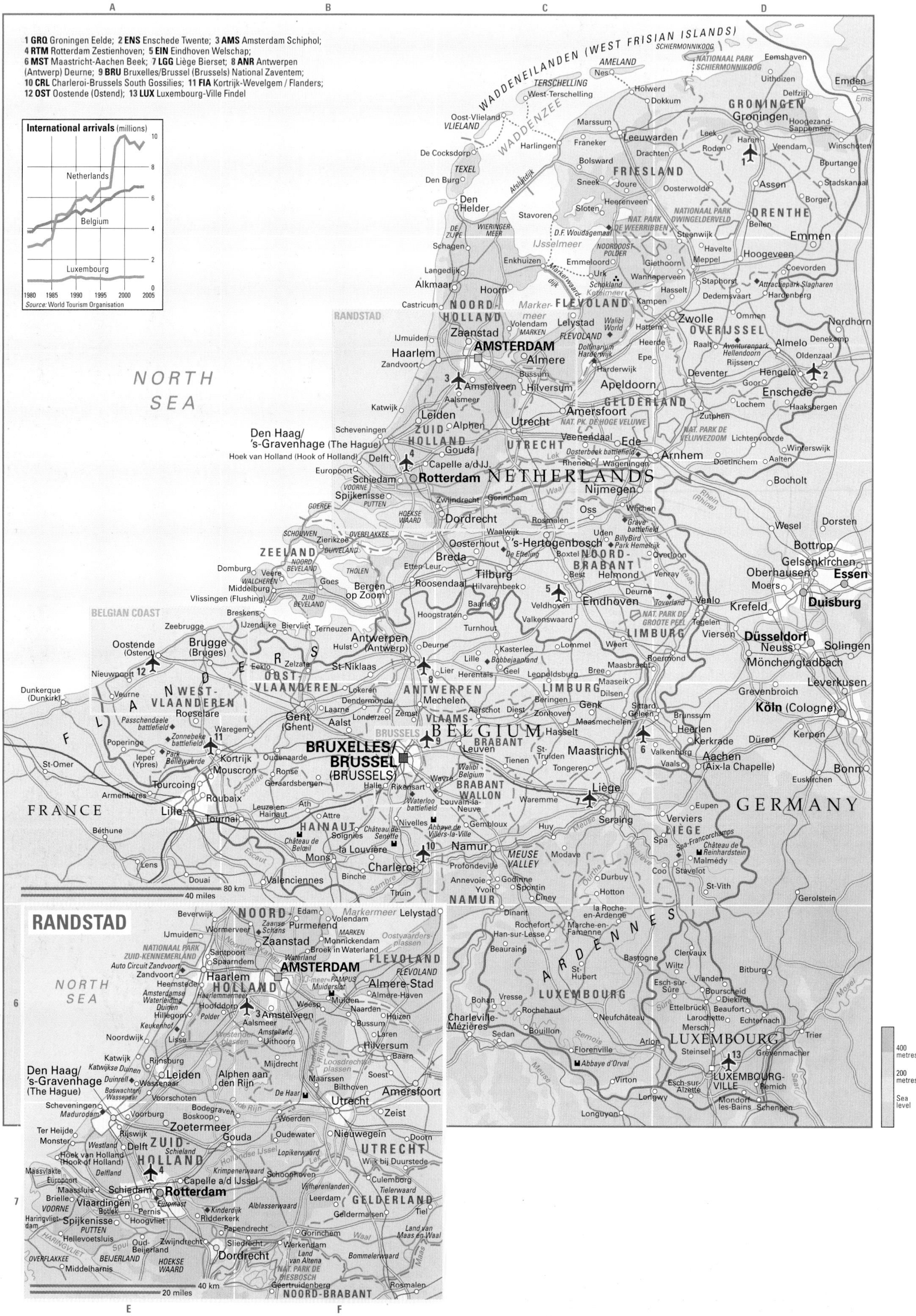

1 GRQ Groningen Eelde; **2 ENS** Enschede Twente; **3 AMS** Amsterdam Schiphol; **4 RTM** Rotterdam Zestienhoven; **5 EIN** Eindhoven Welschap; **6 MST** Maastricht-Aachen Beek; **7 LGG** Liège Bierset; **8 ANR** Antwerpen (Antwerp) Deurne; **9 BRU** Bruxelles/Brussel (Brussels) National Zaventem; **10 CRL** Charleroi-Brussels South Gossilies; **11 FIA** Kortrijk-Wevelgem / Flanders; **12 OST** Oostende (Ostend); **13 LUX** Luxembourg-Ville Findel

International arrivals (millions)

Netherlands
Belgium
Luxembourg

10, 8, 6, 4, 2, 0

1980, 1985, 1990, 1995, 2000, 2005

Source: World Tourism Organisation

NORTH SEA

NETHERLANDS

BELGIUM

LUXEMBOURG

FRANCE

GERMANY

80 km
40 miles

RANDSTAD

40 km
20 miles

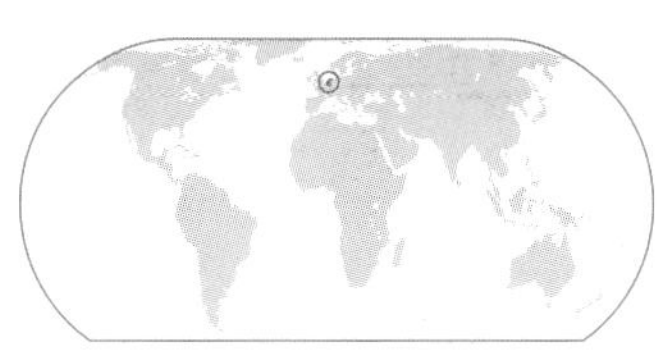

See also... Europe Historical (58-59); European Union (60-61); Benelux (78)

The listings above refer to a selection of related themes. For more information, see the Contents (2-7).

Brugge (Bruges)
OOST-VLAANDEREN
Gent (Ghent)
WEST-VLAANDEREN
VLAANDEREN
ANTWERPEN
Antwerpen (Antwerp)
LIMBURG
Hasselt
VLAAMS-BRABANT
Leuven
BRUXELLES/BRUSSEL (BRUSSELS)
Wavre
BRABANT WALLON
Liège
LIÈGE
HAINAUT
Mons
Namur
WALLONIE
NAMUR
LUXEMBOURG
Arlon
Region boundary
Province boundary
Province capital
Language areas:
Flemish
French
German
Bilingual (Flemish-French)
80 km
40 miles

BELGIAN COAST
Het Zwin
Knokke-Heist
Zeebrugge
Blankenberge
Wenduine
De Haan
Bredene-aan-Zee
Oostende (Ostend)
OST Ostend
Middelkirke-Bad
Westende-Bad
Lombardsijde-Bad
Nieuwpoort-aan-Zee
Nieuwpoort
Oostduinkerke-Bad
De Panne
Koksijde-Bad
St-Idesbald
Veurne
Plopsaland
Damme
Brugge (Bruges)
Boudewijn Seapark
Kanaal van Gent naar Oostende
Jabbeke
Gistel
Loppem
WEST-VLAANDEREN
Ruddervoorde
Torhout
Aalter
Wingene
Lichtervelde
Ruiselede
Kortemark
Diksmuide
Tielt
FR.
NETHS.
20 kilometres
10 miles

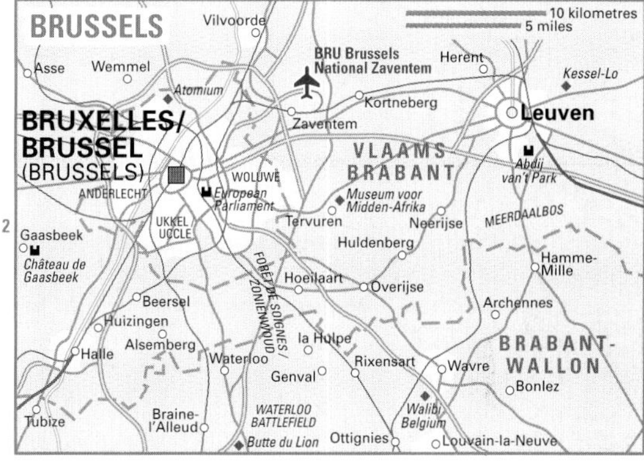
BRUSSELS
Vilvoorde
BRU Brussels National Zaventem
Herent
Kessel-Lo
Asse
Wemmel
Atomium
Kortneberg
Leuven
Zaventem
BRUXELLES/BRUSSEL (BRUSSELS)
VLAAMS BRABANT
Abdij van 't Park
ANDERLECHT
WOLUWE
European Parliament
Museum voor Midden-Afrika
Tervuren
Neerijse
MEERDAALBOS
Gaasbeek
Château de Gaasbeek
UKKEL UCCLE
Huldenberg
Hamme-Mille
FORÊT DE SOIGNES ZONIËNWOUD
Hoeilaart
Overijse
Beersel
Archennes
Huizingen
la Hulpe
Alsemberg
Waterloo
Rixensart
Halle
Genval
Wavre
BRABANT-WALLON
Bonlez
Tubize
Braine-l'Alleud
WATERLOO BATTLEFIELD
Butte du Lion
Ottignies
Walibi Belgium
Louvain-la-Neuve
10 kilometres
5 miles

FEB Bruges Festival Musica Antiqua
MAR Bal des Rats Morts: Dead Rats Ball **(Ostend)**
before LENT Carnival **(Binche, Eupen, Malmédy,** and **countrywide)**
LENT Laetare: street parade **(Stavelot)**
APR Festival van Vlaanderen **(Flanders)**
MAY Kattenfestival: cat festival **(Ypres)**, with a parade of giant cats every 3 years
MAY KunstenFESTIVALdesArts: international cultural festival **(Brussels)**
MAY Brussels Jazz Marathon
MAY Hanswijkprocessie: Procession of Our Lady **(Mechelin)**
MAY Heilig-Bloedprocessie: Holy Blood Procession **(Bruges)**
TRINITY SUNDAY Ducasse: Chariot of Gold procession; and Combat de Lumeçon: St George killing the dragon **(Mons)**
JUN-OCT Festival de Wallonie **(Wallonia)**
JUN Couleur Café: world music event **(Brussels)**
JUN/JUL Ommegang: medieval-style procession **(Brussels)**
JUL Rock Werchter: rock festival **(Leuven)**
JUL De Gentse Feesten: multicultural festival **(Ghent)**
JUL Kroningsfeesten: Virgin Mary procession **(Tongeren)**; 2009 and every seven years
JUL 21st Belgian National Day
JUL Boetprocessie: penitents' procession **(Veurne)**
AUG Tapis des Fleurs: floral carpet (Grand Place, **Brussels**); even years
AUG Ducasse: parade of giants **(Ath)**
AUG Breugel Festival **(Wingene)**
SEP Belgian Beer Weekend **(Brussels)**
SEP Combat de l'Échasse d'Or: Fight for the Golden Stilt **(Namur)**
OCT Hasseltse Jeneverfeesten **(Hasselt)**
DEC Marché de Noël: Christmas market (Grand Place, **Brussels**)

Brugge (Bruges)
Boudewijn Seapark
Groeningemuseum
Memlingmuseum
Onze Lieve Vrouwekerk
Begijnhof
Belfort
Canals
Markt

Gent (Ghent)
Museum voor Schone Kunsten
Stedelijk Museum voor Actuele Kunst Gent (SMAK)
St-Baafskathedraal
Belfort & Lakenhalle
Gravensteen
Graslei
St-Michielsbrug

Liège
Musée Curtius
Musée de la Vie Wallonne
Cathédrale St-Paul
Église St-Barthélemy
Église St-Jacques
Palais des Princes-Évêques

40 km
20 miles

Theme park, leisure park
Museum, gallery
Religious building
Park, reserve, zoo, etc.
Historic/notable building
Water-related attraction
Other place of interest

Attractions in cities marked in red are listed around the map

Antwerpen (Antwerp)
Etnografisch Museum
Koninklijk Museum voor Schone Kunsten
Modemuseum (MOMU)
Museum Mayer van den Bergh
Museum Plantin-Moretus
Rubenshuis
Onze Lieve Vrouwkathedraal
St-Pauluskerk
Dierentuin van Antwerpen
Stadhuis
Grote Markt
Wijk Zurenborg

Mechelen
Speelgoedmuseum
Technopolis
St-Romboutskathedraal
Parc Zoologique de Planckendael
Stadhuis

Bruxelles/Brussel (Brussels)
Bruparck
Autoworld
Centre Belge de la Bande Dessinée
Musées Bellevue
Musée David et Alice van Buuren
Musée Horta
Musée des Instruments de Musique (MIM)
Musée Magritte
Musées Royaux des Beaux-Arts
Musées Royaux d'Art et d'Histoire
Musée des Sciences Naturelles
Abbaye Notre-Dame-de-la-Cambre
Basilique nationale du Sacré-Cœur
Cathédrale des Sts-Michel-et-Gudule
Palais Royale
Stadhuis
Serres royales de Laeken
Atomium
Grand Place
Mannekin Pis

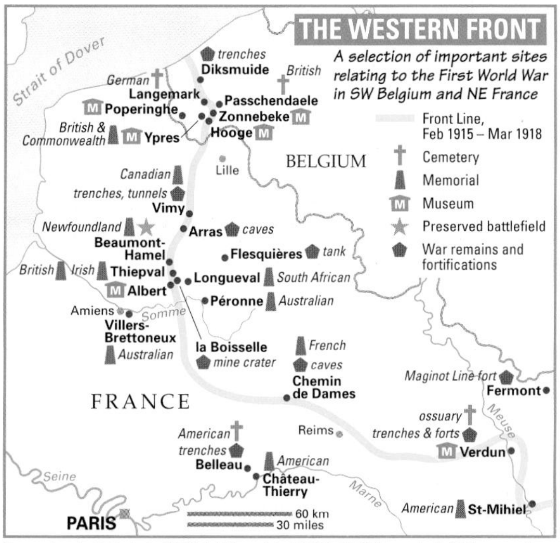

THE WESTERN FRONT

A selection of important sites relating to the First World War in SW Belgium and NE France

Front Line, Feb 1915 – Mar 1918
Cemetery
Memorial
Museum
Preserved battlefield
War remains and fortifications

60 km
30 miles

Map produced with the help of Battlefield Tours, tel +44 (0)121 430 5348, www.battlefieldtours.co.uk

See also... UNESCO Cultural Heritage (52-53); Benelux (78)

The listings above refer to a selection of related themes. For more information, see the Contents (2-7).

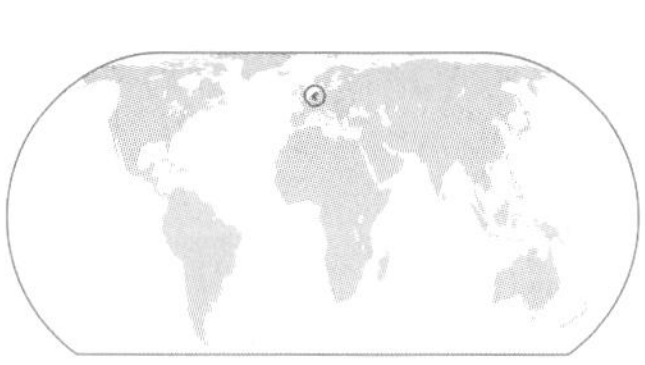

Province boundary
Province capital
60 km
30 miles
WADDENEILANDEN (WEST FRISIAN ISLANDS)
Waddenzee
Leeuwarden
FRIESLAND
GRONINGEN
Groningen
GRQ Groningen
Assen
DRENTHE
Emmen
Den Helder
IJsselmeer
Alkmaar
NOORD-HOLLAND
FLEVOLAND
Lelystad
Zwolle
OVERIJSSEL
AMSTERDAM
Haarlem
AMS Amsterdam
ENS Enschede
Enschede
Apeldoorn
RANDSTAD
Amersfoort
IJssel
Den Haag/ 's-Gravenhage (The Hague)
Leiden
ZUID-HOLLAND
Utrecht
UTRECHT
GELDERLAND
Hoek van Holland (Hook of Holland)
RTM Rotterdam
Lek
Arnhem
Rotterdam
Waal
Nijmegen
THE DELTA
Dordrecht
's-Hertogenbosch
NOORD-BRABANT
Breda
Tilburg
Middelburg
ZEELAND
Vlissingen (Flushing)
Eindhoven
EIN Eindhoven
Maas
Schelde
LIMBURG
MST Maastricht
Heerlen
Maastricht

FEB/MAR Carnaval (**Breda, Maastricht** & **'s-Hertogenbosch**)
MAR Stille Ommegang: silent procession (**Amsterdam**)
MAR-MAY National Floral Exhibition (**Keukenhof**)
APR Floral Procession (**Haarlem** to **Noordwijk**)
APR Rotterdam Marathon
APR 30th Koninginnedag: Queen's Birthday
MAY National Windmill & Pumping Station Day
MAY-SEP Passion Plays (**Tegelen**); 2005 and every five years
JUN Holland Festival & Amsterdam Roots Festival (**Amsterdam**)
JUL North Sea Jazz Festival (**Rotterdam**)
AUG International Fireworks Festival (**Scheveningen**)
AUG Boekenmarkt (**Deventer**)
AUG Amsterdam Gay Pride
AUG-SEP Festival of Ancient Music (**Utrecht**)
SEP Bloemen Corso: floral procession (**Aalsmeer** to **Amsterdam**)
SEP Jordaan Festival (**Amsterdam**)
OCT 3rd Leidens Ontzet: historical procession (**Leiden**)
mid NOV St Nicholas' official entrance (**Amsterdam**)
DEC Candle Festival (**Gouda**)

THE DUTCH vs THE SEA

Without damming or dyking:
Altitude (metres)
20
5
0
Safe from flooding
Subject to river flooding
Subject to almost continual sea flooding
Totally submerged
60 km
30 miles
Waddenzee
Leeuwarden
Groningen
Assen
Den Helder
IJsselmeer
Emmen
Alkmaar
LOW NETHERLANDS
HIGH NETHERLANDS
Zwolle
Lelystad
AMSTERDAM
Haarlem
VELUWE
IJssel
Enschede
Apeldoorn
Den Haag/ 's-Gravenhage (The Hague)
Leiden
Amersfoort
Utrecht
Lek
Arnhem
Hoek van Holland (Hook of Holland)
Lowest point: Nieuwerkerk aan den IJssel –6.7m
Rotterdam
Waal
Nijmegen
Dordrecht
's-Hertogenbosch
Breda
Tilburg
DE PEEL
Middelburg
Eindhoven
Vlissingen (Flushing)
Maas
Schelde
Heerlen
Maastricht
Highest point: Vaalserberg 321m

The Dutch have waged a constant battle against the waters of the North Sea. Nearly one third of The Netherlands is below sea level and every major storm and flood has redrawn the landscape. Dyke building and reclamation has continued for centuries and the two major projects undertaken in the 20th century have provided some degree of security as well as increasing the land area. The engineering achievement is staggering – 'God created the world but the Dutch created the Netherlands' – but opinion is divided as to how long these defences will be able to last without serious modification.

The **IJSSELMEER** scheme was begun in 1918, following the1916 floods. Its aims were to provide protection against flooding in the Zuiderzee, create more land for agriculture and help combat soil salinity in the area by the creation of a freshwater lake, the IJsselmeer.

1 Amsteldiep Dyke, 1919-24 & **Wieringermeer**, 1927-30
2 Afsluitdijk (enclosing dam), 1927-32
3 **Noordoostpoider**, 1937-42
4 **Oostelijk Flevoland**, 1950-57
5 **Zuidelijk Flevoland**, 1959-68
6 Markerwaard, 1963- *(abandoned 1986)*

The sand islands enclosing the Waddenzee provide an important barrier against North Sea storms.

NORTH SEA
Zuiderzee
Amsterdam
IJssel
The Hague
Rotterdam
Maas
Rhine
Schelde

1650

The 17th century: the Dutch 'Golden Age'. Coastal dykes protected low-lying land; windmills used to drain inland lakes.

Present-day international boundary shown

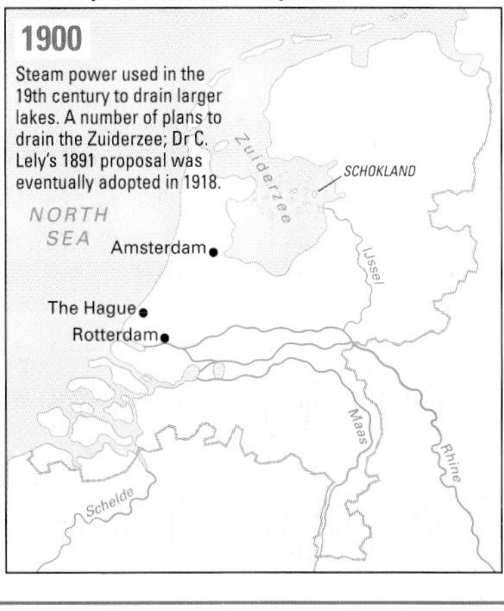
SCHOKLAND
NORTH SEA
Zuiderzee
Amsterdam
IJssel
The Hague
Rotterdam
Maas
Rhine
Schelde

1900

Steam power used in the 19th century to drain larger lakes. A number of plans to drain the Zuiderzee; Dr C. Lely's 1891 proposal was eventually adopted in 1918.

SCHIERMONNIKOOG
AMELAND
TERSCHELLING
VLIELAND
TEXEL
Waddenzee
Leeuwarden
GRONINGEN
Groningen
FRIESLAND
Assen
Wouda Steam Pumping Station 1920
DRENTHE
Den Helder
IJsselmeer
Emmeloord
Emmen
Hoogeveen
Zuiderzee Museum
Schokland Former island in the Zuiderzee
NOORD-HOLLAND
Alkmaar
Hoorn
Beemster Polder Drained 1612
Markermeer
FLEVOLAND
Zwolle
Lelystad
OVERIJSSEL
Noordzee Kanaal
Zaanstad
Almere
Haarlem
AMSTERDAM
IJssel
Hengelo
Cruquius Steam Pumping Station 1849
Deventer
Enschede
Apeldoorn
Hilversum
Amersfoort
Leiden
UTRECHT
GELDERLAND
Den Haag/ 's-Gravenhage (The Hague)
Hoek van Holland (Hook of Holland)
Utrecht
Ede
ZUID-HOLLAND
Delft
Lek
Arnhem
Rotterdam
Kinderdijk 1738-1761
Waal
Nijmegen
Haringvliet
Dordrecht
Grevelingen
's-Hertogenbosch
Delta Expo
Oosterschelde
Breda
NOORD-BRABANT
Tilburg
Middelburg
ZEELAND
Bergen op Zoom
Helmond
Vlissingen (Flushing)
Eindhoven
Venlo
Maas
Westerschelde
Breskens
LIMBURG
Terneuzen
Schelde
60 km
30 miles

DYKES have been built on the coast and along many rivers to prevent flooding. In creating polders (land reclaimed from the sea, a lake or marshland), a dyke is first built to enclose the area before the water is pumped out. Principal sea dykes are shown here.

Coastal **SAND DUNES**, planted with marram grass to increase stability, provide an important defence against high tides.

Principal places of interest connected with land reclamation

The Dutch have utilised wind power for many purposes and in the low-lying coastal areas **WINDMILLS** have become synonymous with the draining of the land. No typical Dutch landscape is complete without the inclusion of a windmill – at one time there were over 9,000 in the country. Today there are still approximately 1,000 windmills; the most famous being at Kinderdijk, where a group of 19 drained the Alblasserwaard until 1950.

The **DELTA WORKS** were undertaken after flooding on 1st February 1953 killed nearly 2,000 people. The dams and barriers provide security from inundation and improve the infrastructure of the region. The Delta Works and Afsluitdijk (IJsselmeer dam) together are considered one of the 'seven wonders of the modern world'.

A Maeslantkering: Nieuwe Waterweg Storm Surge Barrier (S.S.B)
B Haringvlietdam
C Brouwersdam
D Oosterschelde S.S.B.
E Veerse Gatdam
F Zandkreekdam
G Oesterdam
H Grevelingendam & Philipsdam
I Volkerakdam & Haringvlietbrug
J Hartelkering
K Hollandse IJssel S.S.B.

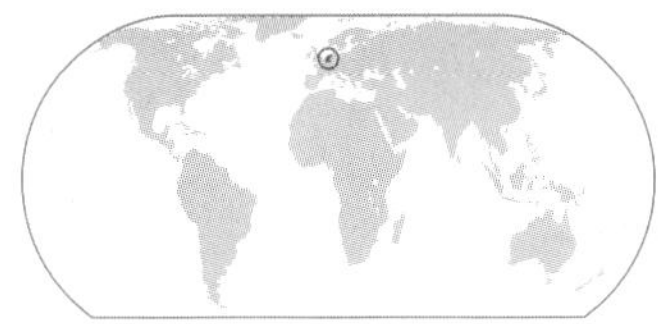

▶ *See also...* Europe Historical (58-59); Benelux (78)

The listings above refer to a selection of related themes. For more information, see the Contents (2-7). See also the Columbus Tourist Attractions and Events of the World.

- Theme park, leisure park
- Museum, gallery
- Religious building
- Park, reserve, zoo, etc.
- Historic/notable building
- Water-related attraction
- Other place of interest

Attractions in cities marked in **red** are listed on the left of the map

Amsterdam
Museum Amstelkring
Amsterdams Historisch Museum
Anne Frankhuis
Hermitage aan de Amstel
Joods Historisch Museum
Madame Tussaud Scenerama
Museum Het Rembrandthuis
Nederlands Scheepvaart Museum
NeMo (New Metropolis)
Rijksmuseum
Stedelijk Museum
Tropenmuseum
Van Gogh Museum
Esnoga Synagogue
Nieuwe Kerk
Westerkerk
Artis
Bloemenmarkt
Begijnhof
Koninklijk Paleis
Amsterdam canals (grachten)

Haarlem
Frans Halsmuseum
Teylers Museum
St Bavokerk
Vleeshal
Grote Markt

Leiden
Museum Boerhaave
Molenmuseum De Valk
Naturalis
Stedelijk Museum De Lakenhal
Rijksmuseum van Oudheden
Rijksmuseum voor Volkenkunde
De Burcht

Den Haag (The Hague)
Madurodam
Museum voor Communicatie
Gemeentemuseum
Mauritshuis
Museum Mesdag; Panorama Mesdag
Museon
Schilderijengalerij Prins Willem V
Binnenhof
Paleis Noordeinde

Delft
Koninklijk Nederlands Leger- en Wapenmuseum
Prinsenhof
Nieuwe Kerk
Oude Kerk

Rotterdam
Kunsthal
Historisch Museum Het Schielandshuis
Museum Boymans-Van Beuningen
Museum De Dubbelde Palmboom
Nederlands Architectuurinstituut
Diergaarde Blijdorp
Boat trips to the port
Erasmusbrug
Maritiem Museum
Euromast

Gouda
Stedelijk Museum Het Catharina Gasthuis
Sint Jan
Stadhuis

Utrecht
Centraal Museum
Museum Het Catharijneconvent
Nationaal Museum van Speelklok Tot Pierement
Nederlands Spoorwegmuseum
Domkirk; Domtoren
Pieterskerk
Rietveld Schröderhuis

NORTH

30 km
15 miles

See also... 83-85 for more on Germany

For more information, see the Contents (2-7).

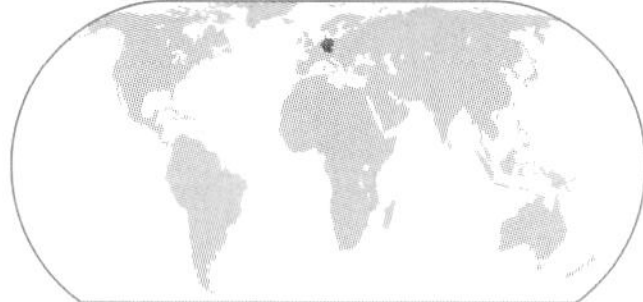

A B C D E F

1 2 3 4 5

Lambert Equal Area Projection Blue boxes indicate focus map coverage

200 kilometres
100 miles

See also... Europe Airports & High-Speed Rail (62-63); Europe Railways & Ferries (64-65)

The listings above refer to a selection of related themes. For more information, see the Contents (2-7).

JAN-FEB Fasching: Carnival (**Munich**)
FEB Berliner Filmfestspiele: **Berlin** International Film Festival
APR Walpurgisnacht: witches' sabbath festival (**Harz** region)
MAY-SEP Rattenfängerspiele: Ratcatcher's Play (**Hameln**)
MAY-SEP Passionspiele: Passion Play (**Oberammergau**); 2010 and every ten years
JUN Karneval der Kulturen: Carnival of the Cultures (**Berlin**)
JUN 14th City Foundation Day (**Munich**)
JUN Christopher Street Day (**Berlin**)
JUN Corpus Christi Procession (**Hüfingen; Cologne** & **Munich**)
JUN Kieler Woche: regatta (**Kiel**)
JUN-JUL Fürstenhochzeit: royal marriage (**Landshut**); 2005 and every four years
JUN-AUG Meistertrunk: 'Long Drink' history play (**Rothenburg ob der Tauber**)
JUL Love Parade (**Berlin**)
JUL-AUG Bayreuther Festspiele: Wagner opera festival (**Bayreuth**)
AUG Der Rhein in Flammen: The Rhine in Flames (**Braubach to Koblenz**)
AUG Schlossfest: castle festival (**Heidelberg**)
SEP Dürkheimer Wurstmarkt: sausage & wine festival (**Bad Dürkheim**)
SEP **Berlin** Marathon
SEP-OCT Oktoberfest (**Munich**); Cannstatter Volksfest (**Stuttgart**)
OCT Weinlesefest: wine fair & Queen of Wine (**Neustadt an der Weinstrasse**)
OCT **Frankfurt** Book Fair
NOV Hamburger Dom: festival (**Hamburg**)
NOV-DEC Weihnachtsmarkt: Christmas markets (**Munich, Nuremberg** & countrywide)

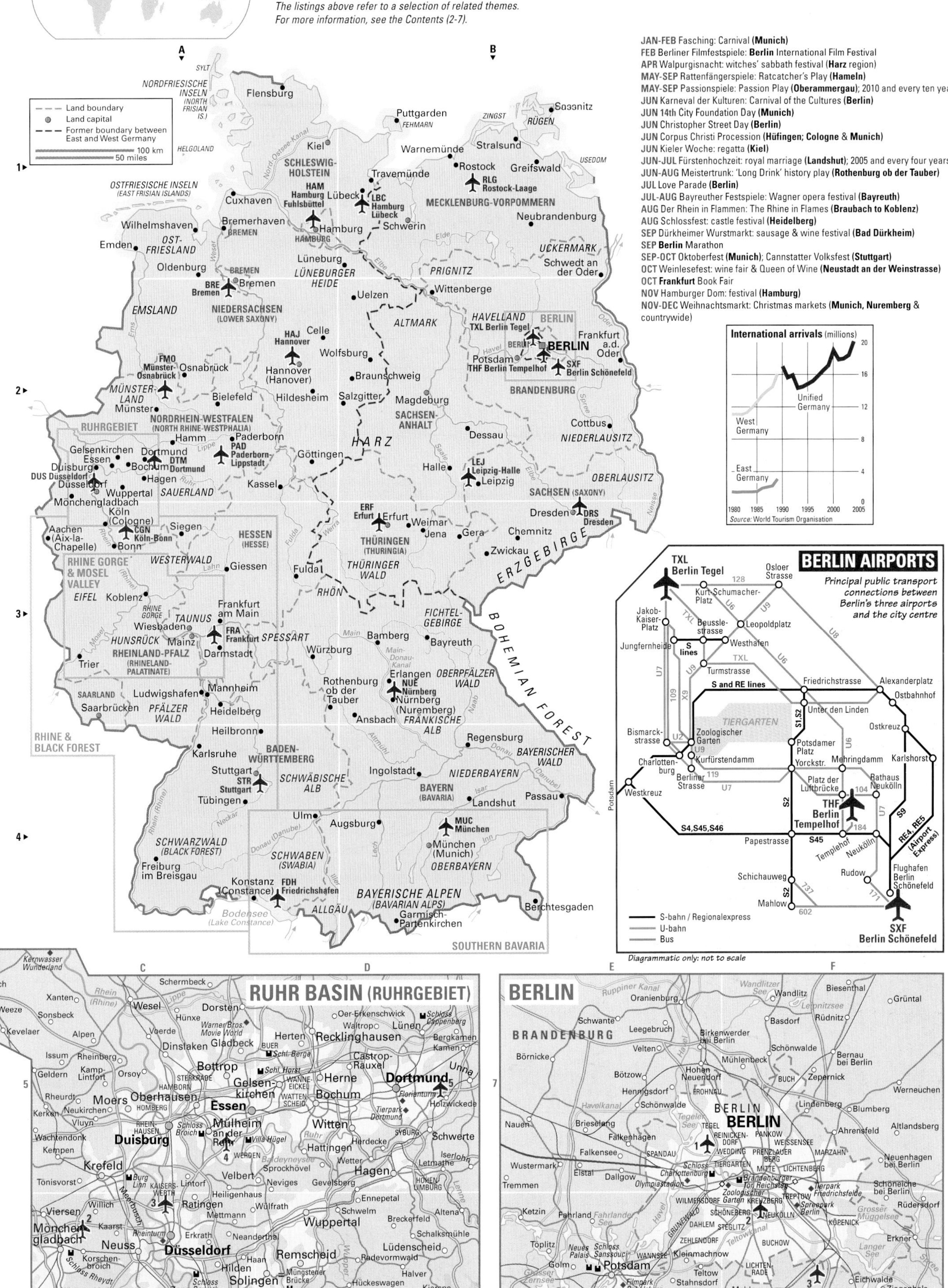
Land boundary
Land capital
Former boundary between East and West Germany
100 km
50 miles
International arrivals (millions)
West Germany
East Germany
Unified Germany
Source: World Tourism Organisation
BERLIN AIRPORTS
Principal public transport connections between Berlin's three airports and the city centre
TXL Berlin Tegel
THF Berlin Tempelhof
SXF Berlin Schönefeld
S-bahn / Regionalexpress
U-bahn
Bus
Diagrammatic only: not to scale
RUHR BASIN (RUHRGEBIET)
1 NRN Niederrhein; 2 MGL Düsseldorf Mönchengladbach 3 DUS Düsseldorf Rhein-Ruhr; 4 ESS Essen; 5 DTM Dortmund Wickede
30 km
15 miles
BERLIN
1 TXL Berlin Tegel; 2 THF Berlin Tempelhof; 3 SXF Berlin Schönefeld
20 km
10 miles
RUHRGEBIET
RHINE GORGE & MOSEL VALLEY
RHINE & BLACK FOREST
SOUTHERN BAVARIA
BOHEMIAN FOREST
ERZGEBIRGE
HARZ
1000 metres
500 metres
Sea level

See also... Germany Attractions (85)

The listings above refer to a selection of related themes. For more information, see the Contents (2-7).

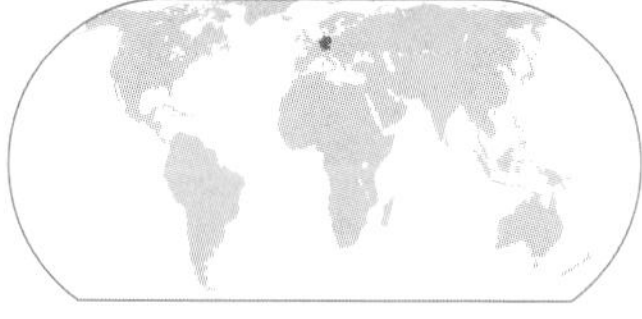

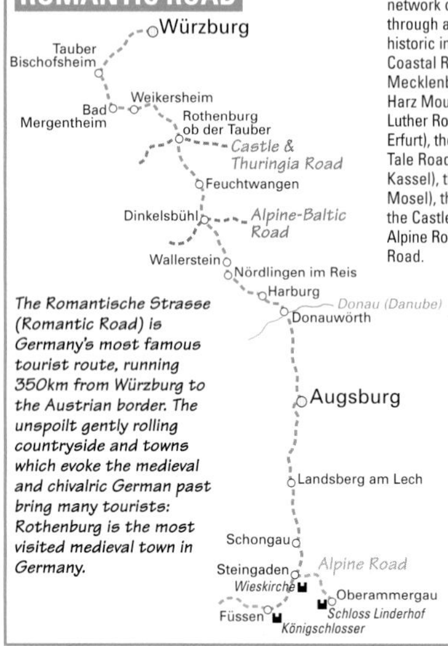

ROMANTIC ROAD

Würzburg
Tauber Bischofsheim
Weikersheim
Bad Mergentheim
Rothenburg ob der Tauber
Castle & Thuringia Road
Feuchtwangen
Dinkelsbühl
Alpine-Baltic Road
Wallerstein
Nördlingen im Reis
Harburg
Donau (Danube)
Donauwörth
Augsburg
Landsberg am Lech
Schongau
Steingaden
Alpine Road
Wieskirche
Oberammergau
Schloss Linderhof
Füssen
Königschlosser

Germany has a well-developed network of tourist routes passing through areas of scenic or historic interest. They include the Coastal Road, the Lakes Road (in Mecklenburg-Vorpommern), the Harz Mountains Road, the Martin Luther Road (Leipzig, Magdeburg, Erfurt), the Saxon Road, the Fairy-Tale Road (Bremen, Hameln, Kassel), the River Road (Rhine & Mosel), the Black Forest Road, the Castle & Thuringia Road, the Alpine Road and the Alpine-Baltic Road.

The Romantische Strasse (Romantic Road) is Germany's most famous tourist route, running 350km from Würzburg to the Austrian border. The unspoilt gently rolling countryside and towns which evoke the medieval and chivalric German past bring many tourists: Rothenburg is the most visited medieval town in Germany.

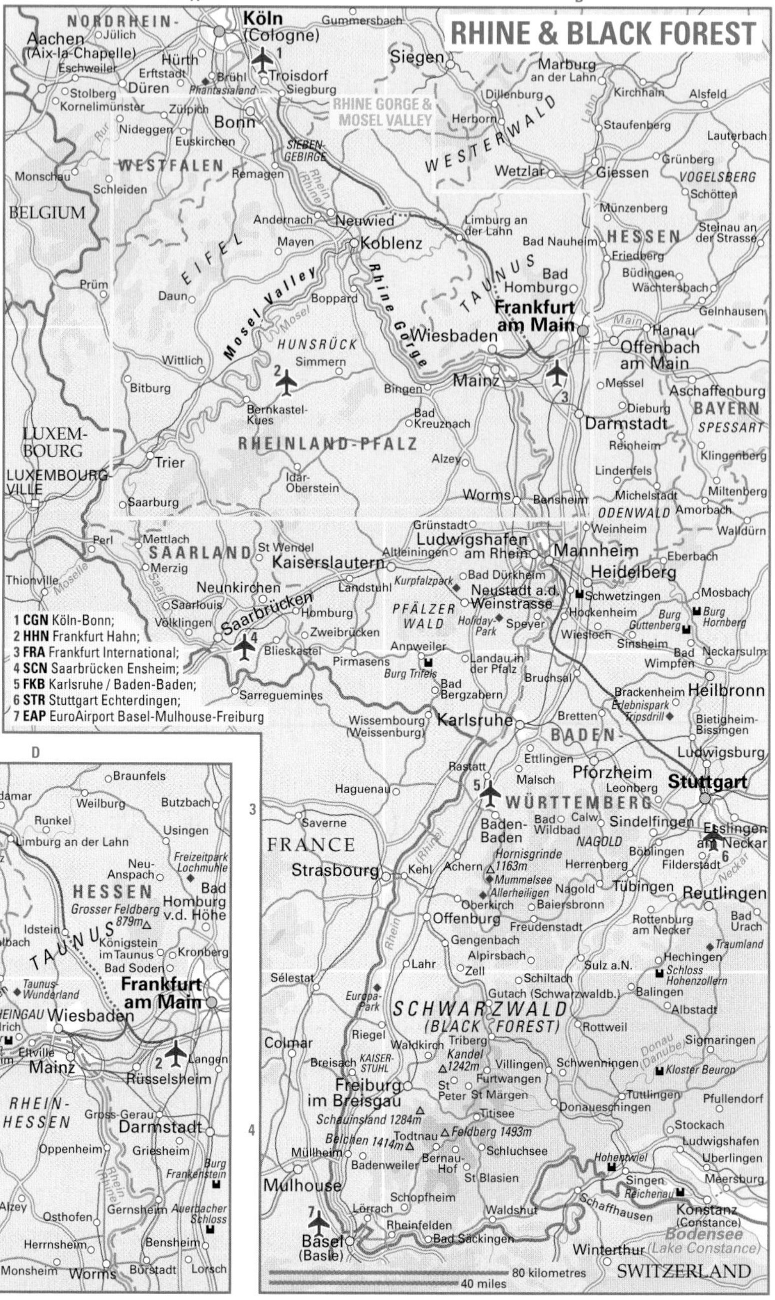

RHINE & BLACK FOREST

NORDRHEIN-WESTFALEN
Köln (Cologne)
Aachen (Aix-la-Chapelle)
Bonn
Koblenz
Siegen
Marburg an der Lahn
Giessen
HESSEN
BELGIUM
LUXEMBOURG
Trier
Saarbrücken
Kaiserslautern
Mainz
Wiesbaden
Frankfurt am Main
Darmstadt
Ludwigshafen am Rhein
Mannheim
Heidelberg
Heilbronn
Karlsruhe
Pforzheim
Stuttgart
BADEN-WÜRTTEMBERG
FRANCE
Strasbourg
Tübingen
Reutlingen
Offenburg
SCHWARZWALD (BLACK FOREST)
Freiburg im Breisgau
Mulhouse
Basel (Basle)
Konstanz (Constance)
Bodensee (Lake Constance)
SWITZERLAND

1 CGN Köln-Bonn;
2 HHN Frankfurt Hahn;
3 FRA Frankfurt International;
4 SCN Saarbrücken Ensheim;
5 FKB Karlsruhe / Baden-Baden;
6 STR Stuttgart Echterdingen;
7 EAP EuroAirport Basel-Mulhouse-Freiburg

80 kilometres
40 miles

RHINE GORGE & MOSEL VALLEY

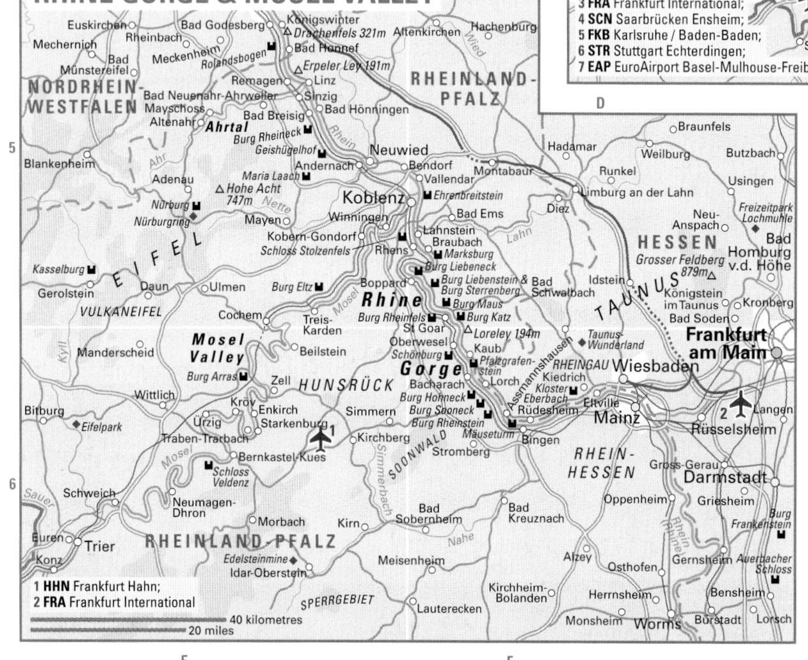
NORDRHEIN-WESTFALEN
RHEINLAND-PFALZ
Koblenz
Neuwied
EIFEL
Mosel Valley
HUNSRÜCK
Rhine Gorge
TAUNUS
HESSEN
Wiesbaden
Frankfurt am Main
Mainz
Darmstadt
Trier
Bingen
1 HHN Frankfurt Hahn;
2 FRA Frankfurt International
40 kilometres
20 miles

SOUTHERN BAVARIA

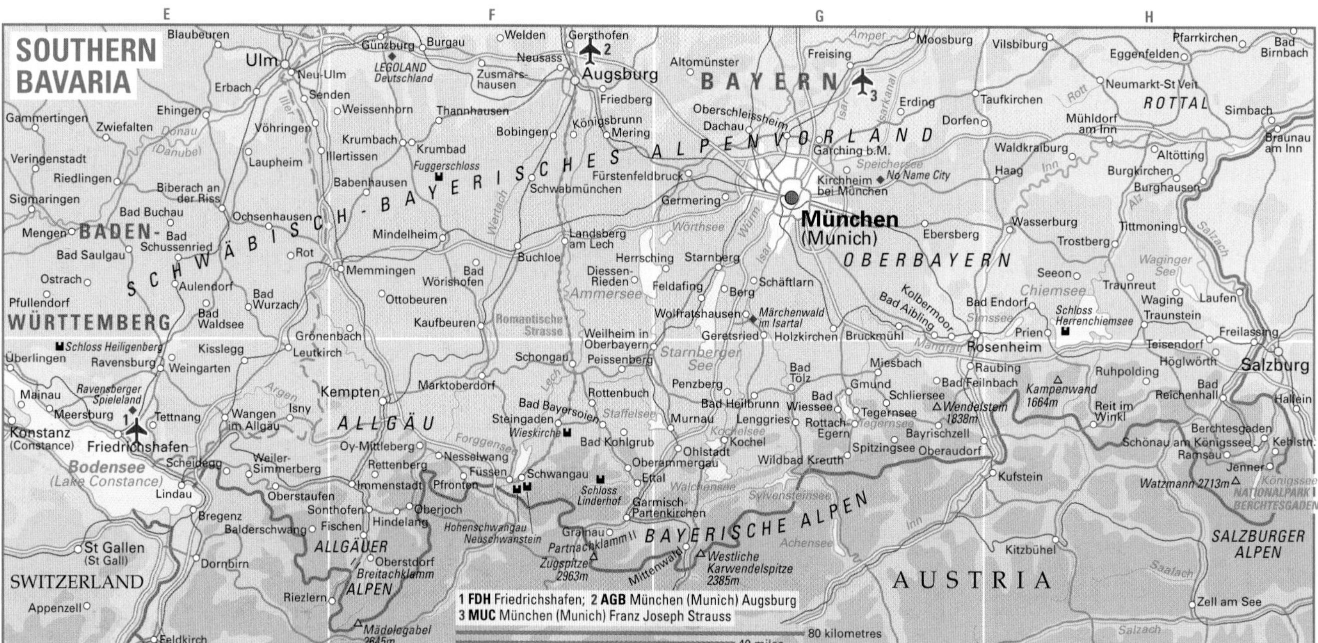
Ulm
Augsburg
BAYERN
ALPENVORLAND
München (Munich)
OBERBAYERN
BADEN-WÜRTTEMBERG
SCHWÄBISCH-BAYERISCHES
ALLGÄU
Kempten
Friedrichshafen
Bodensee (Lake Constance)
BAYERISCHE ALPEN
Zugspitze 2963m
Rosenheim
Salzburg
AUSTRIA
SWITZERLAND
1 FDH Friedrichshafen; 2 AGB München (Munich) Augsburg
3 MUC München (Munich) Franz Joseph Strauss
80 kilometres
40 miles
1000 metres
500 metres
Sea level

The listings above refer to a selection of related themes. For more information, see the Contents (2-7). See also the Columbus Tourist Attractions and Events of the World.

Theme park, leisure park
Museum, gallery
Religious building
Park, reserve, zoo, etc.
Historic/notable building
Water-related attraction
Other place of interest
Attractions in cities marked in red are listed around the edge of the map
100 kilometres
50 miles
Recklinghausen
Ikonenmuseum
Bochum
Deutsches Bergbau Museum
Gelsenkirchen
Schloss Horst
Essen
Museum Folkwang
Villa Hügel
Berlin
Ägyptisches Museum
Antiken Museum
Bauhaus Archiv
Dahlem Museums
Deutsches Teknikmuseum
Dokumentationzentrum der Berliner Mauer
Hamburger Bahnhof-Museum für Gegenwart
Haus am Checkpoint Charlie
Jüdisches Museum
Kulturforum
Kunstgewerbemuseum
Museum für Naturkunde
Museumsinsel
Berliner Dom
Botanischer Garten
Zoologischer Garten
Brandenburger Tor
Bundestag (Reichstag)
Philharmonie
Schloss Charlottenburg
Sony Center
AquaDom & Sea Life Centre
Fernsehturm
Gendarmenmarkt
Kurfürstendamm
Nikolaiviertal
Potsdamer Platz
Unter den Linden
Hamburg
Altonaer Museum
Kunsthalle
Museum für Kunst & Gewerbe
Hauptkirche St Michaelis
Planten un Blomen
Tierpark Hagenpark (zoo)
Aussenalster
Hafen (port)
Altstadt
Fernsehturm
Reeperbahn
Düsseldorf
Hetjens Museum
Kunstmuseum
Kunstsammlung Nordrhein-Westfalen
EKO-House
Schloss Jägerhof
Altstadt
Königsallee (Kö)
Dresden
Albertinum
Zwinger Museums
Dom
Frauenkirche
Dresdner Schloss
Japanisches Palais
Semperoper
Schloss Pillnitz
Zwinger
Blaues Wunder
Köln (Cologne)
Agfa Foto-Historama
Ludwig Museum
Museum für Ostasiatische Kunst
Römisch-Germanisches Museum
Schnütgen Museum
Wallraf-Richartz Museum
Dom
St Gereonskirche
Fernsehturm
Bonn
Haus der Geschichte
Kunstmuseum Bonn
Museum Alexander Koenig
Rheinisches Landesmuseum
Münster
Beethovenhaus
Frankfurt am Main
Goethe-Haus
Jüdisches Museum
Museum für Moderne Kunst
Museumsufer
Palmengarten
Zoo
Römerberg
Stuttgart
Linden Museum
Mercedes-Benz Museum
Staatsgalerie
Württembergischer Landesmuseum
Schlossgarten
München (Munich)
Alte & Neue Pinakothek
Antikensammlungen
Bayerisches Nationalmuseum
Deutsches Museum
Glyptothek
Pinakothek der Moderne
Dom
Englischer Garten
Residenz
Schloss Nymphenburg
Marienplatz
Olympiaturm
Leipzig
BELANTIS
Grassimuseum
Museum der Bildenen Kunst
Museum in der "Runden Ecke"
Nikolaikirche
Altes Rathaus
Völkerschlachtdenkmal

See also... 87-89 for more on France

For more information, see the Contents (2-7).

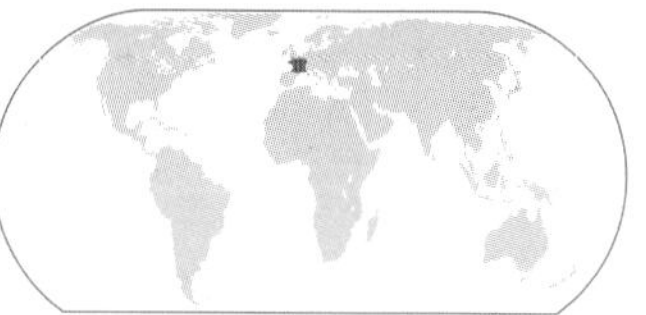

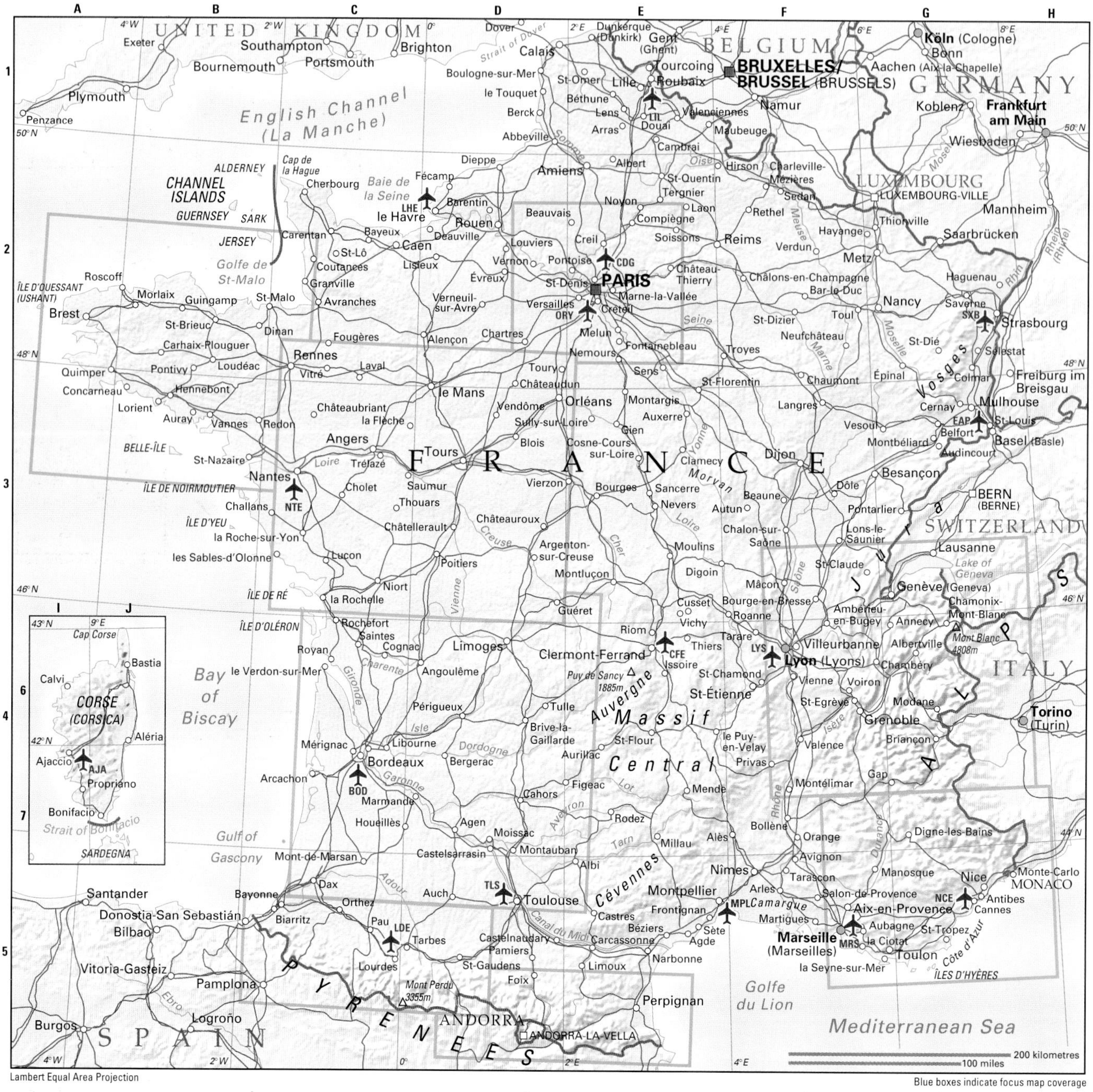

Lambert Equal Area Projection

200 kilometres
100 miles

Blue boxes indicate focus map coverage

WINE REGIONS

Some of the more important vin de pays areas are shown in BLUE TYPE. Numbers indicate the month when important wine festivals occur in each region (1=Jan., 12=Dec., E=Easter)

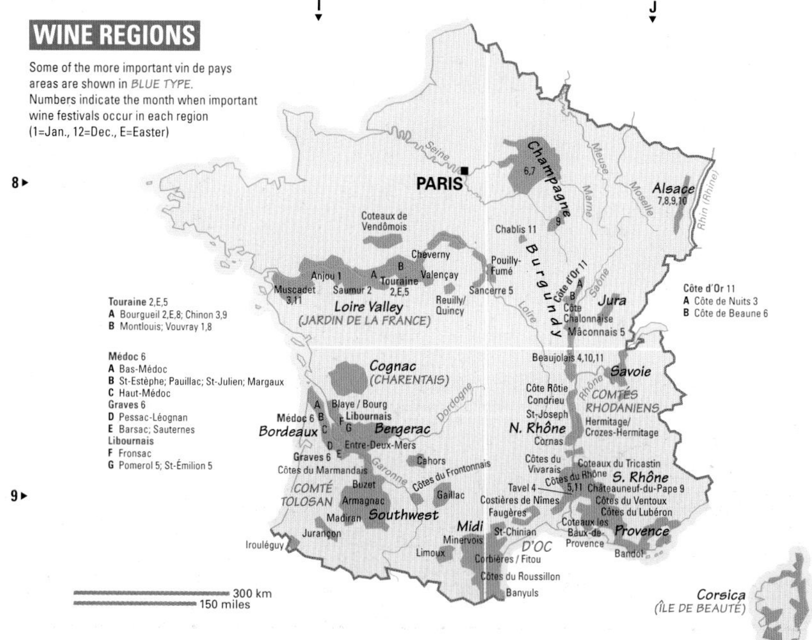
PARIS
Champagne 6,7
Alsace 7,8,9,10
Coteaux de Vendômois
Chablis 11
Cheverny
Pouilly-Fumé
Anjou 1
Valençay
Touraine 2,E,5
Muscadet 3,11
Saumur 2
Reuilly/Quincy
Sancerre 5
Loire Valley
(JARDIN DE LA FRANCE)
Burgundy
Côte d'Or 11
Côte Chalonnaise
Mâconnais 5
Jura
Touraine 2,E,5
A Bourgueil 2,E,8; Chinon 3,9
B Montlouis; Vouvray 1,8
Côte d'Or 11
A Côte de Nuits 3
B Côte de Beaune 6
Beaujolais 4,10,11
Savoie
Cognac
(CHARENTAIS)
Médoc 6
A Bas-Médoc
B St-Estèphe; Pauillac; St-Julien; Margaux
C Haut-Médoc
Graves 6
D Pessac-Léognan
E Barsac; Sauternes
Libournais
F Fronsac
G Pomerol 5; St-Émilion 5
Blaye / Bourg
Libournais
Bordeaux
Bergerac
Entre-Deux-Mers
Côte Rôtie
Condrieu
St-Joseph
COMTÉS RHODANIENS
N. Rhône
Hermitage/Crozes-Hermitage
Cornas
Côtes du Vivarais
Coteaux du Tricastin
Côtes du Rhône 5,11
Châteauneuf-du-Pape 9
S. Rhône
Tavel 4
Côtes du Ventoux
Côtes du Lubéron
Costières de Nîmes
Cahors
Côtes du Frontonnais
Côtes du Marmandais
Buzet
COMTÉ TOLOSAN
Armagnac
Gaillac
Southwest
Madiran
Jurançon
Irouléguy
Midi
Fougères
St-Chinian
Minervois
Limoux
Corbières / Fitou
Côtes du Roussillon
Banyuls
Coteaux les Baux-de-Provence
Provence
Bandol
D'OC
Corsica
(ÎLE DE BEAUTÉ)
300 km
150 miles

JAN 1st La Grande Parade de Montmartre **(Paris)**
JAN International Circus Festival **(Monaco)**
JAN 22nd St Vincent Festival: patron saint of wine **(Burgundy)**
FEB Fête des Citrons: Lemon Festival **(Menton)**
before LENT Carnaval de **Nice**
MAY La Fête des Mais: The Feasts of May **(Nice)**
MAY **Cannes** Film Festival
MAY Annual Gypsy gathering **(les Saintes-Maries-de-la-Mer)**
MAY/JUN French Tennis Open (Roland Garros) **(Paris)**
WHIT MONDAY Procession of the Giants of France and Belgium **(Lille)**
JUN **Paris** Air Show
JUN Fête de la Musique: Festival of Music (**Paris** and countrywide)
JUN 24th Fête de St-Jean
JUN-JUL Festival International d'Art Lyrique **(Aix-en-Provence)**
JUL Gypsy and World Music Festival **(Arles)**
JUL Festival of the Giants **(Douai)**
JUL **Nantes** Quinzaine Celtique
JUL 14th Bastille Day, Fête Nationale
JUL La Festival de Cornouaille: folklore festival **(Quimper)**
JUL Festival du **Marseille**
JUL Tour de France (finishes in **Paris**)
JUL **Nice** Jazz Festival
JUL-AUG Quartier d'Été: Summer Arts Festival **(Paris)**
JUL-AUG International Fireworks Festival **(Monaco)**
JUL-AUG Festival d'**Avignon**
AUG Basque festivals **(Bayonne** & **Biarritz)**
AUG Festival Inter-Celtique **(Lorient)**
AUG Haute-Provence Festival **(Forcalquier)**
AUG 15th Assumption of the Blessed Virgin Mary
SEP Festival du Livre Vivant: historical pageant **(Fougères)**
SEP Côtes du Rhône Grape Harvest **(Avignon)**
SEP German-French Festival **(Strasbourg** and Germany)
SEP Coupe Icarus: unpowered flight festival **(St-Hilaire-du-Touvet)**
SEP-DEC Festival d'Automne: Autumn Festival **(Paris)**
OCT Festival des Chants Sacrés en Méditerranée; Fiesta des Suds **(Marseille)**
NOV Mondial du Snowboard **(les Deux Alpes)**
NOV Les Trois Glorieuses: wine festival **(Cote d'Or)**
NOV Les Sarmentelles: Beaujolais Nouveau
DEC Festival of Lights **(Lyons)**
DEC Marché de Noël: Christmas market **(Strasbourg)**

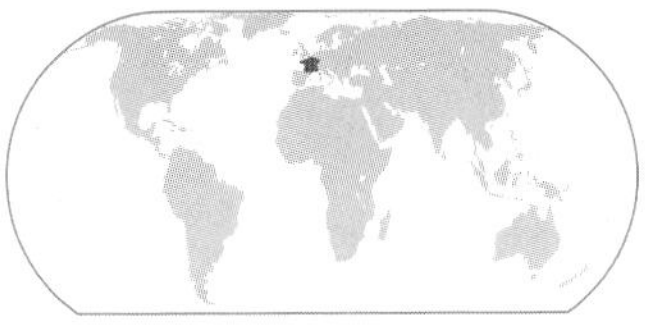

See also... Europe Airports & High-Speed Rail (62-63); Europe Railways & Ferries (64-65)

The listings above refer to a selection of related themes. For more information, see the Contents (2-7).

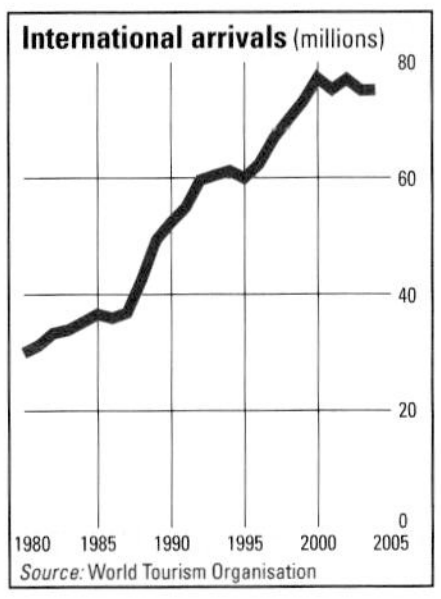
International arrivals (millions)
80
60
40
20
0
1980
1985
1990
1995
2000
2005
Source: World Tourism Organisation

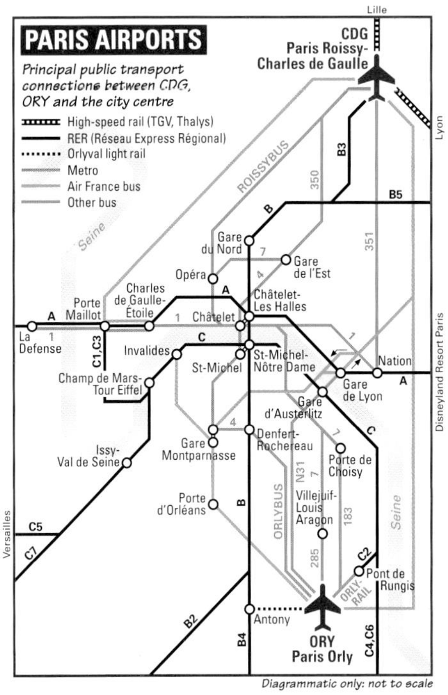
PARIS AIRPORTS
Principal public transport connections between CDG, ORY and the city centre
High-speed rail (TGV, Thalys)
RER (Réseau Express Régional)
Orlyval light rail
Metro
Air France bus
Other bus
CDG
Paris Roissy-Charles de Gaulle
ORY
Paris Orly
Lille
Lyon
ROISSYBUS
ORLYBUS
ORLY-RAIL
Gare du Nord
Gare de l'Est
Opéra
Châtelet-Les Halles
Châtelet
Charles de Gaulle-Étoile
Porte Maillot
La Defense
Invalides
St-Michel
St-Michel-Nôtre Dame
Champ de Mars-Tour Eiffel
Nation
Gare de Lyon
Gare d'Austerlitz
Denfert-Rochereau
Gare Montparnasse
Issy-Val de Seine
Porte de Choisy
Porte d'Orléans
Villejuif-Louis Aragon
Pont de Rungis
Antony
Versailles
Disneyland Resort Paris
Seine
Diagrammatic only: not to scale

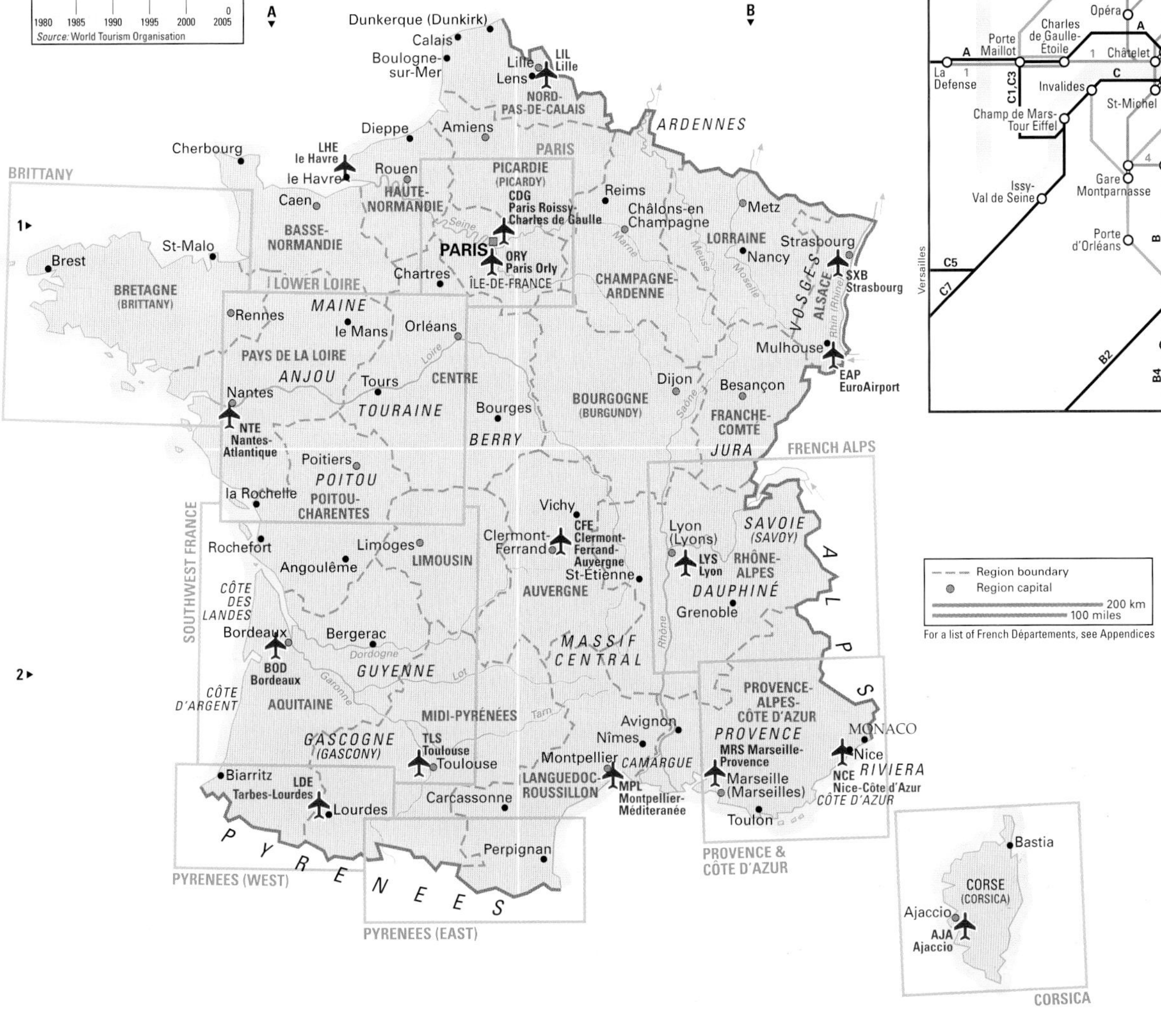
Dunkerque (Dunkirk)
Calais
Boulogne-sur-Mer
Lille
LIL Lille
Lens
NORD-PAS-DE-CALAIS
ARDENNES
Dieppe
Amiens
Cherbourg
LHE le Havre
le Havre
Rouen
HAUTE-NORMANDIE
PICARDIE (PICARDY)
CDG Paris Roissy-Charles de Gaulle
Reims
Châlons-en Champagne
Metz
Caen
BASSE-NORMANDIE
St-Malo
Brest
BRETAGNE (BRITTANY)
PARIS
ORY Paris Orly
ÎLE-DE-FRANCE
Chartres
LORRAINE
Nancy
Strasbourg
SXB Strasbourg
VOSGES
ALSACE
CHAMPAGNE-ARDENNE
MAINE
Rennes
le Mans
Orléans
PAYS DE LA LOIRE
ANJOU
Tours
CENTRE
Nantes
NTE Nantes-Atlantique
TOURAINE
Bourges
BERRY
BOURGOGNE (BURGUNDY)
Dijon
Besançon
FRANCHE-COMTE
JURA
Mulhouse
EAP EuroAirport
FRENCH ALPS
Poitiers
POITOU
la Rochelle
POITOU-CHARENTES
Vichy
CFE Clermont-Ferrand-Auvergne
Clermont-Ferrand
Lyon (Lyons)
LYS Lyon
SAVOIE (SAVOY)
RHÔNE-ALPES
Rochefort
Limoges
LIMOUSIN
Angoulême
St-Étienne
AUVERGNE
DAUPHINÉ
Grenoble
ALPS
CÔTE DES LANDES
SOUTHWEST FRANCE
Bordeaux
BOD Bordeaux
Bergerac
MASSIF CENTRAL
GUYENNE
CÔTE D'ARGENT
AQUITAINE
MIDI-PYRÉNÉES
PROVENCE-ALPES-CÔTE D'AZUR
PROVENCE
Avignon
Nîmes
MONACO
GASCOGNE (GASCONY)
TLS Toulouse
Toulouse
Montpellier
CAMARGUE
MRS Marseille-Provence
Marseille (Marseilles)
Nice
NCE Nice-Côte d'Azur
RIVIERA
CÔTE D'AZUR
Biarritz
LDE Tarbes-Lourdes
Lourdes
LANGUEDOC-ROUSSILLON
Carcassonne
MPL Montpellier-Méditeranée
Toulon
Perpignan
PYRENEES
PYRENEES (WEST)
PYRENEES (EAST)
PROVENCE & CÔTE D'AZUR
Bastia
CORSE (CORSICA)
Ajaccio
AJA Ajaccio
CORSICA
BRITTANY
LOWER LOIRE
Region boundary
Region capital
200 km
100 miles
For a list of French Départements, see Appendices

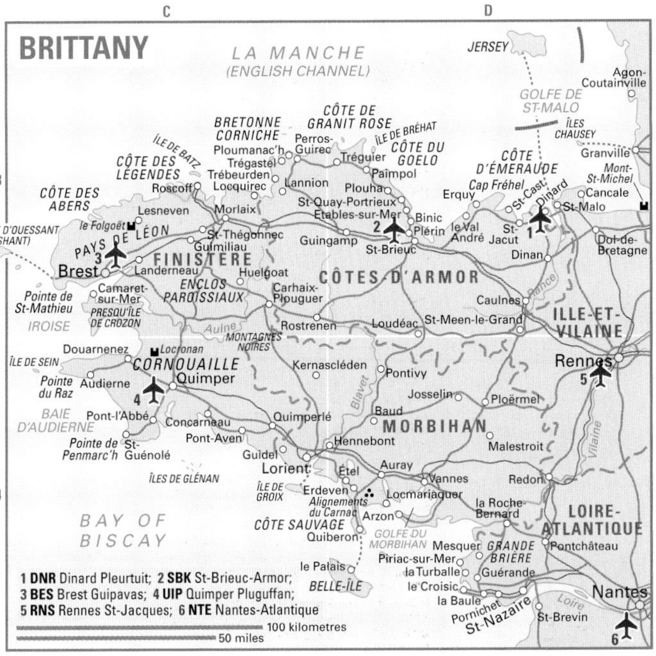
BRITTANY
LA MANCHE (ENGLISH CHANNEL)
JERSEY
GOLFE DE ST-MALO
ÎLES CHAUSEY
Granville
CÔTE DE GRANIT ROSE
BRETONNE CORNICHE
CÔTE DES LÉGENDES
CÔTE DES ABERS
CÔTE DU GOELO
CÔTE D'ÉMERAUDE
Roscoff
Morlaix
Lannion
Paimpol
St-Malo
Dinard
Brest
PAYS DE LÉON
FINISTÈRE
CÔTES D'ARMOR
St-Brieuc
Guingamp
Dinan
ILLE-ET-VILAINE
Rennes
CORNOUAILLE
Quimper
Douarnenez
Pointe du Raz
Concarneau
MORBIHAN
Lorient
Vannes
Auray
Quiberon
CÔTE SAUVAGE
BELLE-ÎLE
BAY OF BISCAY
LOIRE-ATLANTIQUE
la Baule
St-Nazaire
Nantes
1 DNR Dinard Pleurtuit; 2 SBK St-Brieuc-Armor; 3 BES Brest Guipavas; 4 UIP Quimper Pluguffan; 5 RNS Rennes St-Jacques; 6 NTE Nantes-Atlantique
100 kilometres
50 miles

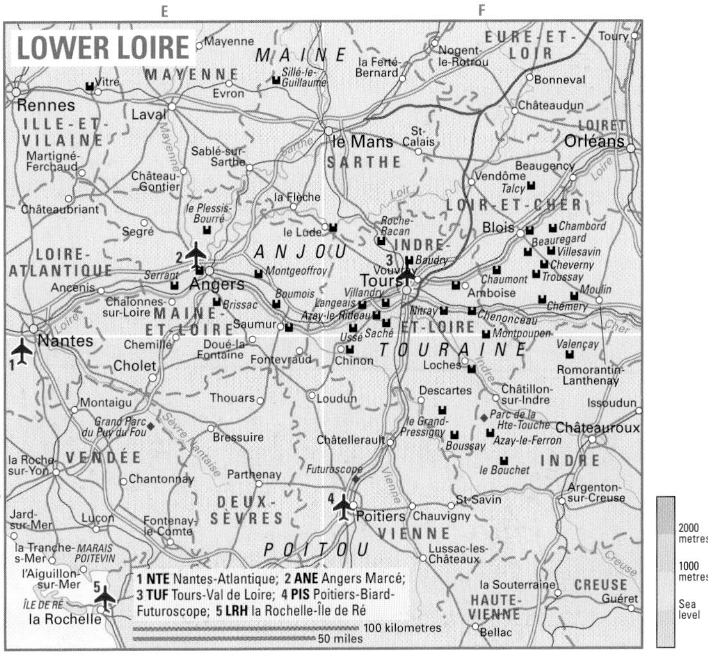
LOWER LOIRE
Mayenne
MAINE
MAYENNE
EURE-ET-LOIR
Rennes
ILLE-ET-VILAINE
Laval
le Mans
SARTHE
Orléans
LOIRET
Vendôme
Blois
LOIR-ET-CHER
Chambord
Châteaubriant
LOIRE-ATLANTIQUE
Angers
ANJOU
Tours
INDRE-ET-LOIRE
Amboise
Chenonceau
Nantes
MAINE-ET-LOIRE
Saumur
TOURAINE
Cholet
Chinon
Loches
VENDÉE
Châteauroux
INDRE
Futuroscope
Poitiers
DEUX-SÈVRES
VIENNE
POITOU
la Rochelle
HAUTE-VIENNE
CREUSE
1 NTE Nantes-Atlantique; 2 ANE Angers Marcé; 3 TUF Tours-Val de Loire; 4 PIS Poitiers-Biard-Futuroscope; 5 LRH la Rochelle-Île de Ré
100 kilometres
50 miles
2000 metres
1000 metres
Sea level

See also... Contents (2-7) – this country features in many thematic and regional maps throughout the *World Travel Atlas.*

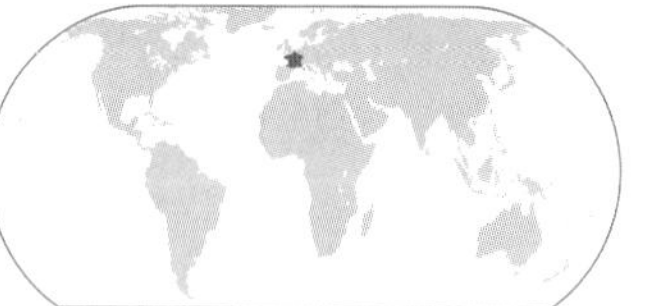

PARIS
A
B
1
2
OISE
EURE
VEXIN
VAL D'OISE
YVELINES
EURE-ET-LOIR
ESSONNE
SEINE-ET-MARNE
AISNE
VALOIS
THELLE
BRIE
VAL DE SEINE
YONNE
Beauvais
Compiègne
Soissons
Pierrefonds
Senlis
Chantilly
Pontoise
Cergy
Mantes-la-Jolie
Dreux
St-Denis
PARIS
Versailles
Marne-la-Vallée
Meaux
Evry
Melun
Fontainebleau
Étampes
Chartres
Rambouillet
Provins
Nemours
1 CDG Paris Roissy-Charles de Gaulle;
2 LBG Paris Le Bourget; 3 ORY Paris Orly
4 BVA Paris Beauvais-Tillé
60 kilometres
30 miles

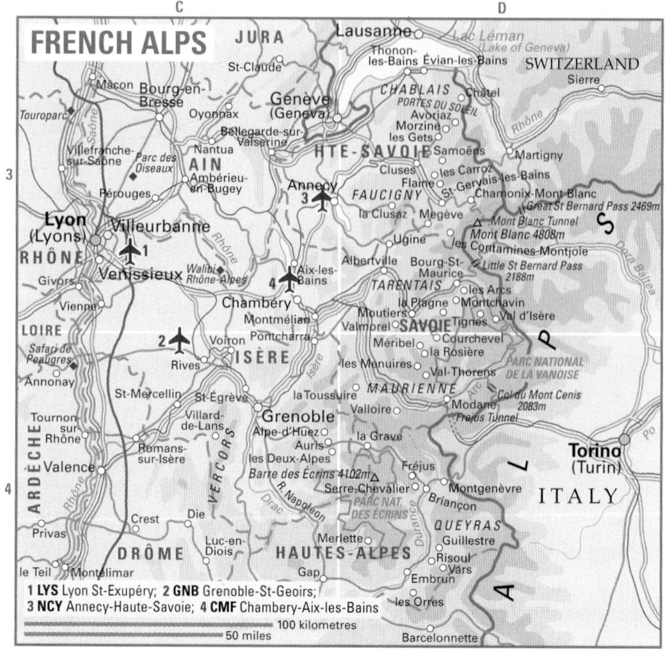
FRENCH ALPS
C
D
3
4
JURA
Lausanne
Lac Léman (Lake of Geneva)
SWITZERLAND
Genève (Geneva)
Bourg-en-Bresse
Mâcon
AIN
HTE-SAVOIE
CHABLAIS
FAUCIGNY
Annecy
Chamonix-Mont-Blanc
Mont Blanc 4808m
Lyon (Lyons)
Villeurbanne
Vénissieux
RHÔNE
LOIRE
Chambéry
Aix-les-Bains
SAVOIE
TARENTAISE
ISÈRE
Grenoble
MAURIENNE
PARC NATIONAL DE LA VANOISE
Valence
ARDÈCHE
VERCORS
DRÔME
HAUTES-ALPES
Barre des Écrins 4102m
Briançon
QUEYRAS
Torino (Turin)
ITALY
ALPS
Barcelonnette
1 LYS Lyon St-Exupéry; 2 GNB Grenoble-St-Geoirs;
3 NCY Annecy-Haute-Savoie; 4 CMF Chambery-Aix-les-Bains
100 kilometres
50 miles

SOUTHWEST FRANCE
E
F
5
6
VIENNE
HAUTE-VIENNE
CREUSE
Rochefort
ÎLE D'OLÉRON
CHARENTE
Limoges
CHAR-MARITIME
SAINTONGE
Angoulême
Royan
Périgueux
DORDOGNE
CORRÈZE
Brive-la-Gaillarde
MÉDOC
Bordeaux
St-Émilion
Bergerac
Sarlat-la-Canéda
CÔTE D'ARGENT
CÔTE DES LANDES
Arcachon
GIRONDE
GUYENNE
LOT
LANDES
LOT-ET-GARONNE
Agen
Cahors
Mont-de-Marsan
Montauban
TARN-ET-GARONNE
GASCOGNE
GERS
TARN
Toulouse
HTE-GARONNE
1 LIG Limoges; 2 BOD Bordeaux Mérignac;
3 EGC Bergerac; 4 TLS Toulouse Blagnac
100 kilometres
50 miles

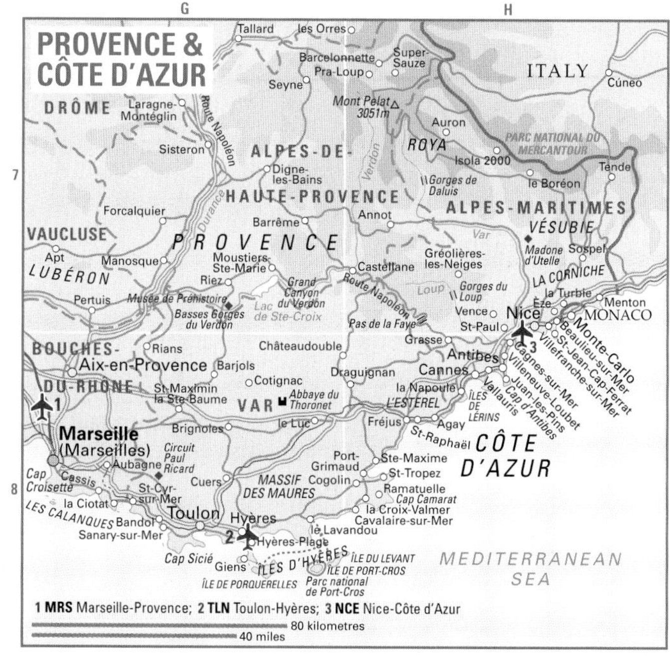
PROVENCE & CÔTE D'AZUR
G
H
7
8
DRÔME
ITALY
Mont Pelat 3051m
PARC NATIONAL DU MERCANTOUR
ALPES-DE-HAUTE-PROVENCE
ALPES-MARITIMES
VAUCLUSE
LUBÉRON
PROVENCE
Grand Canyon du Verdon
BOUCHES-DU-RHÔNE
Aix-en-Provence
Marseille (Marseilles)
VAR
Toulon
Hyères
Nice
Monte-Carlo
MONACO
Cannes
Antibes
St-Tropez
CÔTE D'AZUR
MASSIF DES MAURES
L'ESTÉREL
ÎLES D'HYÈRES
MEDITERRANEAN SEA
1 MRS Marseille-Provence; 2 TLN Toulon-Hyères; 3 NCE Nice-Côte d'Azur
80 kilometres
40 miles

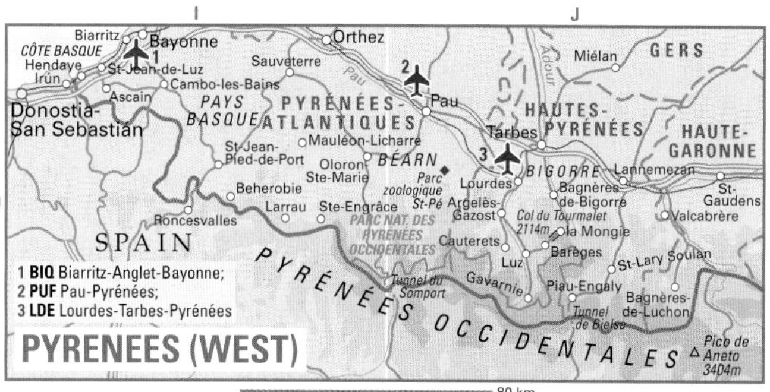
I
J
9
Biarritz
Bayonne
CÔTE BASQUE
Donostia-San Sebastián
PAYS BASQUE
PYRÉNÉES-ATLANTIQUES
BÉARN
Pau
HAUTES-PYRÉNÉES
Tarbes
Lourdes
BIGORRE
HAUTE-GARONNE
GERS
SPAIN
PARC NAT. DES PYRÉNÉES OCCIDENTALES
PYRÉNÉES OCCIDENTALES
Pico de Aneto 3404m
1 BIQ Biarritz-Anglet-Bayonne;
2 PUF Pau-Pyrénées;
3 LDE Lourdes-Tarbes-Pyrénées
PYRENEES (WEST)
80 km
40 miles

CORSICA
M
N
11
12
Cap Corse
MEDITERRANEAN SEA
Bastia
Calvi
NEBBIO
BALAGNE
HAUTE CORSE
Monte Cinto 2706m
Corte
PLAINE ORIENTALE
Mte. Renoso 2352m
Ajaccio
CORSE-DU-SUD
TYRRHENIAN SEA
Propriano
Porto-Vecchio
Bonifacio
STRAIT OF BONIFACIO
1 BIA Bastia Poretta;
2 CLY Calvi Ste-Catherine;
3 AJA Ajaccio Campo dell'Oro;
4 FSC Figari-Sud Corse
80 km
40 miles
2000 metres
1000 metres
Sea level

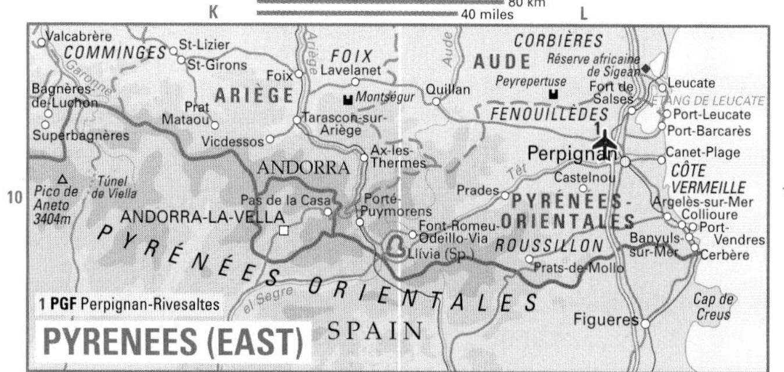
K
L
10
COMMINGES
ARIÈGE
FOIX
AUDE
CORBIÈRES
FENOUILLÈDES
ANDORRA
ANDORRA-LA-VELLA
Perpignan
CÔTE VERMEILLE
PYRÉNÉES-ORIENTALES
ROUSSILLON
PYRÉNÉES ORIENTALES
Pico de Aneto 3404m
SPAIN
Figueres
Cap de Creus
1 PGF Perpignan-Rivesaltes
PYRENEES (EAST)

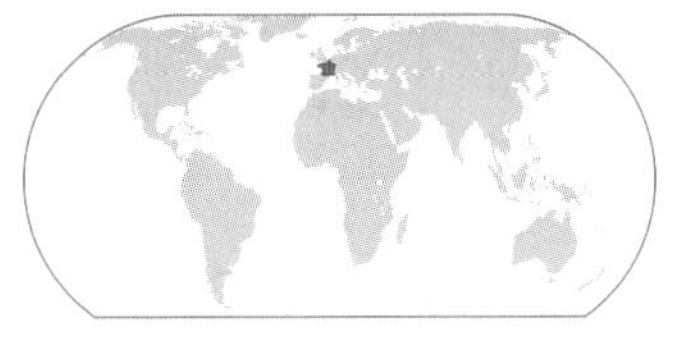

See also... Europe Historical (58-59)

The listings above refer to a selection of related themes. For more information, see the Contents (2-7). See also the Columbus Tourist Attractions & Events of the World.

Theme park, leisure park
Museum, gallery
Religious building
Park, reserve, zoo, etc.
Historic/notable building
Water-related attraction
Other place of interest
Attractions in cities marked in **red** are listed above and below the map

200 kilometres
100 miles

Paris
Le Jardin d'Acclimatation
Centre Georges-Pompidou
Cité des Sciences et de l'Industrie
Institut du Monde Arabe
Louvre
Musée d'Orsay
Musée Marmottan Monet
Musée national du Jeu de Paume
Musée national du Moyen-Âge
Musée national de l'Orangerie
Musée national Picasso
Musée Rodin
Basilique Royale de St-Denis
Cathédrale de Notre-Dame
Eglise du Dôme
Panthéon
Sacré-Cœur
Ste-Chapelle
Jardin de Luxembourg
La Grande Arche de la Défense
Hôtel des Invalides
Opéra Garnier
Palais de Chaillot
Arc de Triomphe de l'Étoile
Champs-Élysées
Cimetière de Montmartre
Cimetère du Père-Lachaise
Le Marais
Montmartre
Place de la Concorde
Place des Vosges
Tour Eiffel

Dunkerque (Dunkirk)
Calais
Boulogne-sur-Mer
NORD-PAS-DE-CALAIS
le Touquet-Paris-Plage
Roubaix La Piscine Musée d'Art et d'Industrie
Lille Palais des Beaux-Arts, Vieux Bourse
Arras
Valenciennes
Amiens Musée de Picardie, Cathédrale
Étretat Falaise d'Amont, Falaise d'Aval
Honfleur Vieux Bassin
Dieppe
St-Quentin
Rouen Cathédrale, Musée des Beaux-Arts, Place du Vieux-Marché
HAUTE-NORMANDIE
PICARDIE (PICARDY)
Laon Cathédrale
Charleville-Mezières
Beauvais Cathédrale
Compiegne Palace national
le Havre Musée des Beaux-Arts André Malraux
Cherbourg La Cité de la Mer
D-Day beaches
Bayeux Tapisserie de la Reine Mathilde
Deauville
Abbaye de Jumièges
Château Gaillard
Château de Chantilly
La Mer de Sable
Parc Astérix
Caen Le Mémorial, Église St-Étienne
Pont de Normandie
NORMANDIE
Évreux
Giverny Maison de Claude Monet
Reims Cathédrale, Basilique St-Rémi
Battlefields of Verdun
Walibi Lorraine
Metz Cathédrale
Strasbourg Musée d'Art moderne et contemporain, Cathédrale, La Petite France
Marne
Châlons-en-Champagne
Épernay Maison Moët et Chandon
PARIS
Disneyland Resort Paris
Château de Versailles
ÎLE-DE-FRANCE
Seine
Meuse
LORRAINE
Nancy Place Stanislas
Moselle
ALSACE
Rhin (Rhine)
St-Malo Les Remparts
Vire
BASSE-NORMANDIE
Île d'Ouessant
Morlaix
Brest Oceanopolis
Mont-St-Michel
Dinan Église St-Sauveur
Fougères Château
Alençon
Chartres Cathédrale
Château de Vaux-le-Vicomte
Provins Ville Haute
CHAMPAGNE-ARDENNE
St-Dizier
Colmar Musée d'Unterlinden, La Petite Venise
Pointe du Raz
Quimper
BRETAGNE (BRITTANY)
Rennes
Laval
le Mans Musée de l'Automobile, Cathédrale
Château de Fontainebleu
Troyes Musée d'Art moderne, Cathédrale
Chaumont
Épinal
Grand Ballon
Concarneau Ville Close
Lorient
Orléans Musée des Beaux-Arts, Maison Jeanne d'Arc
Château de Ancy-le-Franc
Abbaye de Fontenay
Chapelle de Ronchamp
Mulhouse Musée national de l'Automobile, Cité du Train
Île de Groix
Carnac Menhirs
PAYS DE LA LOIRE
Angers Château
Tours Musée des Beaux-Arts, Cathédrale
Blois Château
CENTRE
Château de Chambord
Château de Cheverny
Auxerre
BOURGOGNE (BURGUNDY)
Vézelay Basilique Ste-Madeleine
Vesoul
FRANCHE-COMTE
Besançon Citadelle
Belle-Île
la Baule
St-Nazaire
Loire
Château de Villandry
Château d'Azay-le-Rideau
Château de Chenonceau
Nantes Château des Ducs de Bretagne
Dijon Musée des Beaux-Arts, Quartier Notre-Dame
Île de Noirmoutier
Cholet
Loches Citadelle
Vierzon
Bourges Cathédrale, Palais Jacques-Cœur
Nevers
Beaune Hôtel-Dieu
Saône
Arc-et-Senans Saline Royale
Grand Parc du Puy du Fou
Futuroscope
Châteauroux
Chalon-sur-Saône
Cascades du Hérisson
Lac Léman (Lake of Geneva)
Île d'Yeu
la Roche-sur-Yon
Poitiers Église Notre-Dame-le-Grand, Église St-Hilaire-le-Grand
Vienne
St-Savin-sur-Gartempe Église Abbatiale
Montluçon
Le Pal
Abbaye de Cluny
Mâcon
Bourg-en-Bresse
Chamonix-Mont-Blanc Aiguille du Midi, Mer de Glace
Île de Ré
la Rochelle Vieux Port, Rue du Palais
POITOU-CHARENTES
Gueret
Vichy Spa buildings
Île d'Oléron
Rochefort
Limoges Musée national Adrien-Dubouché
AUVERGNE
Roanne
Annecy Lac d'Annecy, Vieux Annecy
Funivie Mont-Blanc
Angoulême
LIMOUSIN
Puy de Dôme
Clermont Ferrand
Lyon (Lyons)
Villeurbanne
Walibi Rhône-Alpes
Rhône
Chambéry
Brantôme Église abbatiale
Puy de Sancy
St-Étienne
Parc national de la Vanoise
Parc natural régional des Volcans d'Auvergne
RHÔNE-ALPES
Pauillac Château Mouton-Rothschild
Périgueux
Grotte du Grand-Roc
Brive-la Gaillard
Grotte de Lascaux
Grenoble Musée de Grenoble, Fort de la Bastille
Bordeaux Musée d'Aquitaine, Musée des Beaux-Arts, Grand Théâtre
les Eyzies-de-Tayac Musée national de Préhistoire
Grotte de Font-de-Gaume
Aurillac
le Puy-en-Velay Musée Crozatier, Cathédrale, Rocher Corneille
Valence
Parc national des Écrins
Sarlat Vieille Ville
Bergerac
Dordogne
Garonne
Bastide de Monpazier
Rocamadour
Arcachon Dune du Pilat
Conques Église Ste-Foy
Montélimar
Gap
Durance
Bastide de Monflanquin
Lot
Cahors
Mende
Parc national des Cévennes
Gorges de l'Ardèche
AQUITAINE
Rodez
Gorges du Tarn
Alès
Mont Ventoux
Orange
PROVENCE-ALPES-CÔTE D'AZUR
Parc national du Mercantour
Walibi Aquitaine
Agen
Viaduc de Tarn
Grasse Musée international de la Parfumerie
Mont-de-Marsan
Montauban
Tarn
Pont du Gard
Avignon
Fontaine-de-Vaucluse
MIDI-PYRÉNÉES
Albi Cathédrale
Nîmes
Les Baux de Provence
Gorges du Verdon
Menton Jardins
Auch
Arles Arènes
Musée de Préhistoire
Cannes Boulevard de la Croisette
Biarritz
Bayonne Musée Basque
Toulouse Musée des Augustins, Basilique St-Sernin
Montpellier
Parc natural régional de Camargue
Fréjus Cité Episcopal
Pau
Canal du Midi
Béziers
LANGUEDOC-ROUSSILLON
Tarbes
Narbonne
Aigues-Mortes Les Remparts
Toulon
Hyères
Lourdes Cité religieuse
Carcassonne La Cité
Foix
Château de Peyrepertuse
Château de Quéribus
Aix-en-Provence Musée Granet, Cours Mirabeau
Marseille (Marseilles) Vieux-Port
Parc national de Port-Cros
MONACO Musée Océanographique
Parc national des Pyrénées-Occidentales
Château de Montségur
Château de Puilaurens
Perpignan
Antibes Parc de la Mer, Musée Picasso
Nice Fondation Maeght, *St-Paul-de-Vence*, Musée d'Art moderne et d'Art contemporain, Musée Marc Chagall, Musée Matisse, Promenade des Anglais, *Riviera Corniche roads*

Calvi Cathédrale
Golf de Girolata, Golf de Porto
CORSE (CORSICA)
Ajaccio Musée Fesch
Bonifacio Ville Haute

Orange
Théâtre Antique
Arc de Triomphe

Avignon
Musée Calvet
Musée du Petit Palais
Palais des Papes
Pont St-Bénézet

Nîmes
Jardin de la Fontaine
Les Arènes
Maison Carée

Lyon (Lyons)
Musée d'Art contemporain
Musée des Beaux-Arts
Musée de la Civilisation Gallo-Romaine
Musée Henri-Malartre
Centre d'histoire de la Résistance
Musée historique des Tissus
Basilique du Fourvière
Maison des Canuts
Quartier St-Jean

See also... 91-94 for more on Iberia

For more information, see the Contents (2-7).

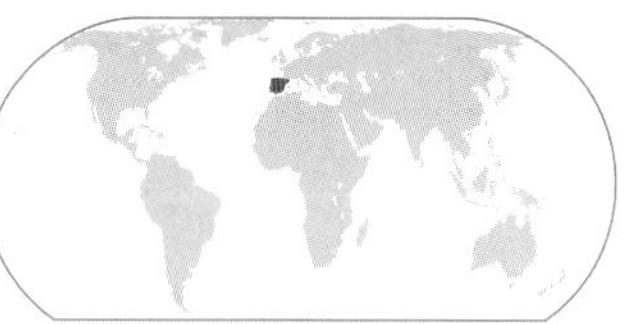

Blue boxes indicate focus map coverage

Lambert Equal Area Projection

200 kilometres
100 miles

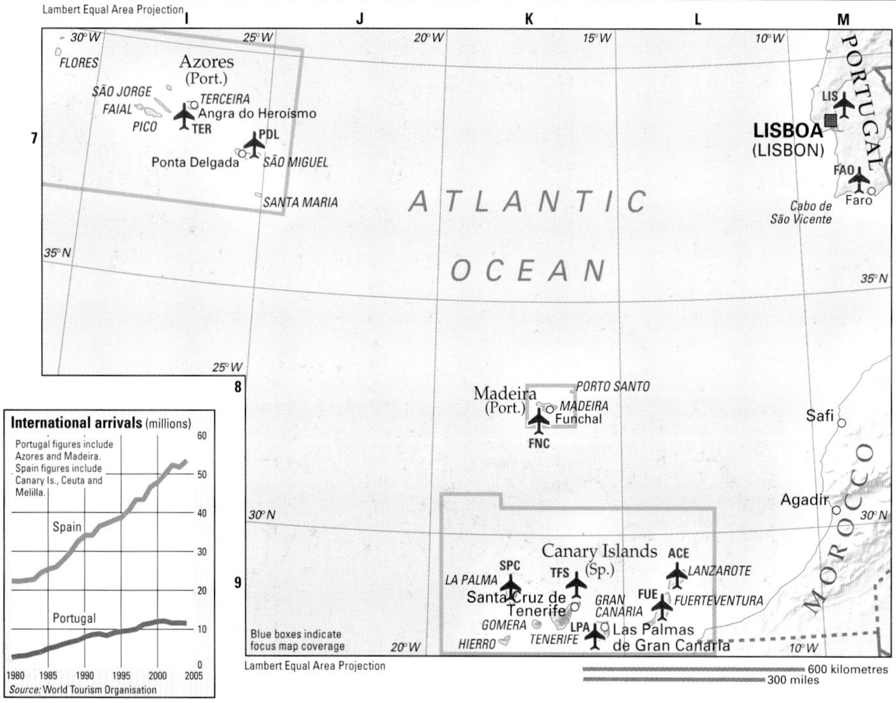

Blue boxes indicate focus map coverage

Lambert Equal Area Projection

600 kilometres
300 miles

International arrivals (millions)

Portugal figures include Azores and Madeira. Spain figures include Canary Is., Ceuta and Melilla.

Spain

Portugal

Source: World Tourism Organisation

SPAIN

JAN 5th Cabalgata de los Reyes Magos: Three Kings Parade **(Barcelona)**
JAN Festividad de **San Sebastián**: drum parades
before Lent Carnaval (**Cádiz, Madrid** and countrywide)
MAR Las Fallas de **València**
EASTER Semana Santa: Holy Week (**Seville** and countrywide)
APR La Feria de **Sevilla**
APR Moros y Cristanos mock battle: St George's Festival **(Alcoy)**
APR 23rd La Diada de Sant Jordi: Day of St George 'Day of Lovers' **(Barcelona)**
MAY Cruces de Mayo and national flamenco competition **(Córdoba)**
MAY Feria del Caballo: horse fair **(Jeréz de la Frontera)**
MAY Festimad Alternative Music Festival **(Madrid)**
MAY-JUN Fiestas de San Isidro **(Madrid)**
WHIT SUNDAY Romería del Rocić: pilgrimage (near **Huelva**)
JUN Sonar: electronic music festival **(Barcelona)**
JUN Haro: Wine war **(La Rioja)**
JUN 23-24th Festes de Sant Joan (**Barcelona** and Catalonia)
JUN 24th Xiquets de Valls: human towers **(Valls)**
JUN-JUL GREC: **Barcelona** Summer Festival
JUN-JUL International Festival of Music and Dance **(Granada)**
JUL Los Sanfermines: running of the bulls **(Pamplona)**
JUL Jazzaldia: Festival de Jazz de **San Sebastián**
JUL Santa Marta de Ribarteme: 'near-death' pilgrimage **(Las Nieves, Pontevadra)**
JUL 22nd Cuesta de los Danzadores: stilt dancers (**Anguiano**, La Rioja)
JUL 25th Feast of St James **(Santiago de Compostela)**
AUG Semana Grande, includes Basque Herri Kilorak: traditional sports **(Bilbao)**
AUG Moros y Cristanos mock battle and mystery play **(Elx)**
AUG La Tomatina: Tomato Battle **(Buñol)**
SEP San Sebastián International Film Festival
SEP 19th Americas Day **(Oviedo)**
SEP 24th Festa de la Mercé: Our Lady of Mercy Festival **(Barcelona)**
OCT-NOV Madrid Autumn Festival

PORTUGAL

before Lent Lisbon Carnival **APR Lisbon** Half Marathon
MAY 13th Pilgrimage to the Shrine of Our Lady of **Fátima**
MAY Queimade Fitas: academic celebrations **(Coimbra)**
JUN Festas de Lisboa: festivities in honour of three saints **(Lisbon)**
JUL Festa do Colete Encarnado: Festival of the Red Waistcoat **(Vila Franca de Xira)**
AUG Romaria de Nossa Senhora de Agonía: fair & pilgrimage **(Viana do Castelo)**
OCT Fiera de Outabro: October Festival **(Vila Franca de Xira)**
OCT 13th Pilgrimage to the Shrine of Our Lady of **Fátima**
NOV Feira Nacional de Cavalo: National Horse Fair **(Golegã)**
NEW YEAR'S EVE Noite Mágica: Magic Night **(Lisbon)**

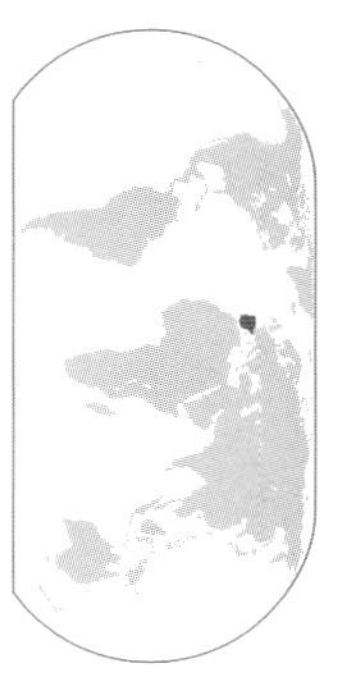

See also... Europe Historical (58-59)

Iberia: Attractions

The listings above refer to a selection of related themes. For more information, see the Contents (2-7). See also the Columbus Tourist Attractions & Events of the World.

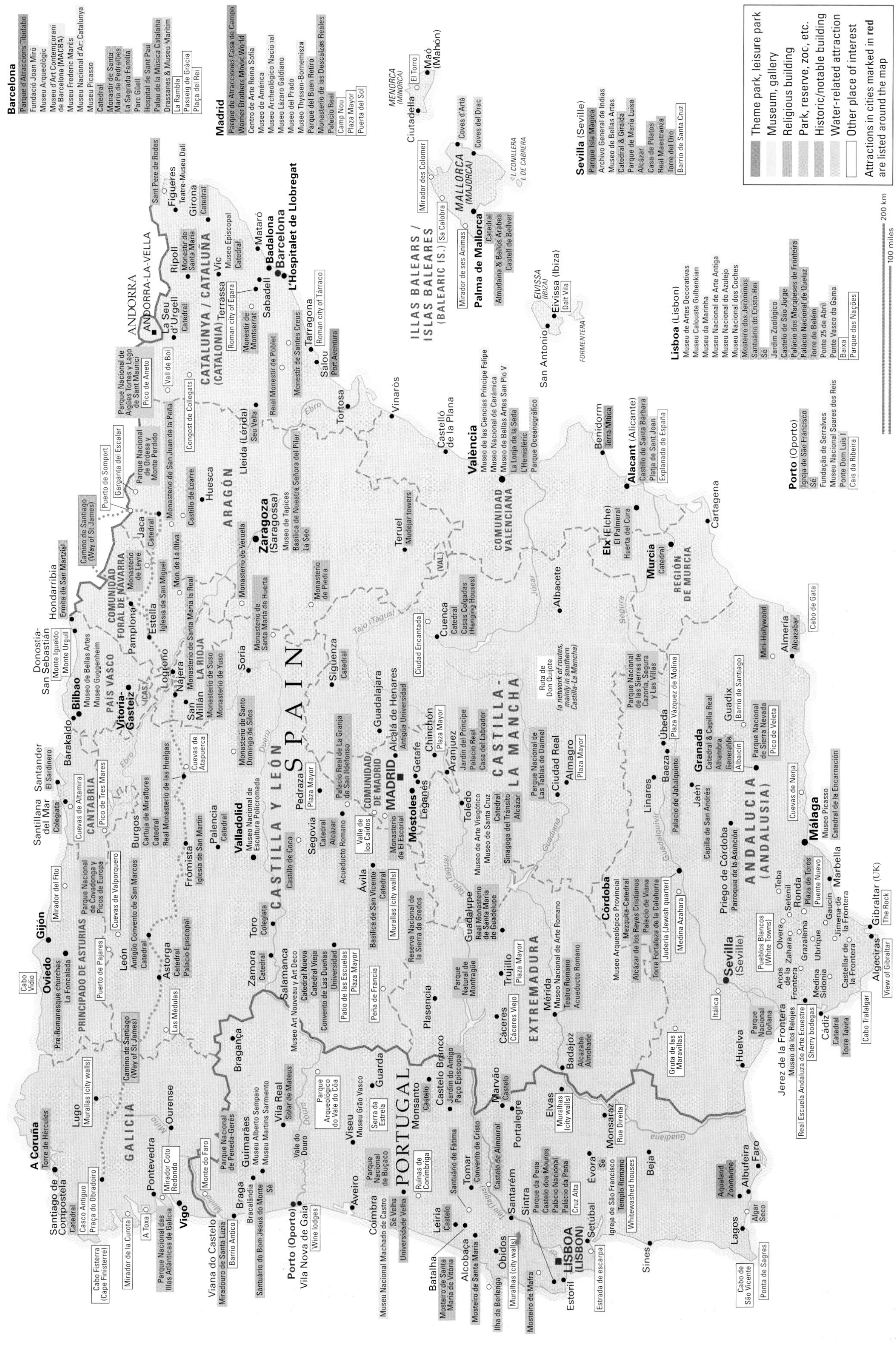

Theme park, leisure park
Museum, gallery
Religious building
Park, reserve, zoo, etc.
Historic/notable building
Water-related attraction
Other place of interest
Attractions in cities marked in red are listed around the map
200 km
100 miles
Barcelona
Parque d'Atracciones Tibidabo
Fundació Joan Miró
Museu Arqueològic
Museu d'Art Contemporani de Barcelona (MACBA)
Museu Frederic Marès
Museu Nacional d'Art de Catalunya
Museu Picasso
Catedral
Monastir de Santa Maria de Pedralbes
La Sagrada Família
Parc Güell
Hospital de Sant Pau
Palau de la Música Catalana
Drassanes & Museu Marítim
La Rambla
Passeig de Gràcia
Plaça del Rei
Madrid
Parque de Atracciones Casa de Campo
Warner Brothers Movie World
Centro de Arte Reina Sofía
Museo de América
Museo Archeológico Nacional
Museo Lázaro Galdiano
Museo del Prado
Museo Thyssen-Bornemisza
Parque del Buen Retiro
Monasterio de las Descalzas Reales
Palacio Real
Camp Nou
Plaza Mayor
Puerta del Sol
Sevilla (Seville)
Parque Isla Mágica
Archivo General de Indias
Museo de Bellas Artes
Catedral & Giralda
Parque de María Luisa
Alcázar
Casa de Pilatos
Real Maestranza
Torre del Oro
Barrio de Santa Cruz
Lisboa (Lisbon)
Museu de Artes Decorativas
Museu Calouste Gulbenkian
Museu da Marinha
Museu Nacional de Arte Antiga
Museu Nacional do Azulejo
Museu Nacional dos Coches
Mosteiro dos Jerónimos
Santuário do Cristo-Rei
Sé
Jardim Zoológico
Castelo de São Jorge
Palácio dos Marqueses de Fronteira
Palácio Nacional de Queluz
Torre de Belém
Ponte 25 de Abril
Ponte Vasco da Gama
Baixa
Parque das Nações
Porto (Oporto)
Igreja de São Francisco
Sé
Fundação de Serralves
Museu Nacional Soares dos Reis
Ponte Dom Luís I
Cais da Ribeira
SPAIN
PORTUGAL
ANDORRA
GALICIA
PRINCIPADO DE ASTURIAS
CANTABRIA
PAIS VASCO
COMUNIDAD FORAL DE NAVARRA
LA RIOJA
ARAGÓN
CATALUNYA / CATALUÑA (CATALONIA)
CASTILLA Y LEÓN
COMUNIDAD DE MADRID
CASTILLA - LA MANCHA
EXTREMADURA
COMUNIDAD VALENCIANA
REGIÓN DE MURCIA
ANDALUCIA (ANDALUSIA)
ILLAS BALEARS / ISLAS BALEARES (BALEARIC IS.)

Spain, Andorra & Gibraltar

See also... Contents (2-7) – These countries feature in many thematic and regional maps throughout the *World Travel Atlas*.

The listings above refer to a selection of related themes. For more information, see the Contents (2-7). See also the Columbus Tourist Attractions & Events of the World.

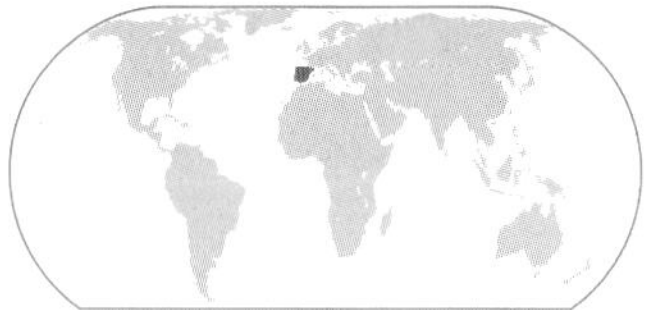

- – – Autonomous community boundary
- ● Autonomous community capital

Languages spoken in **Spain**:
- Castilian Spanish

Bilingual areas of Spain:
- Basque (spoken by a significant & increasing minority)
- Catalan* (spoken by 50-70% of people)
- Galician (spoken by over 90% of people)

Languages spoken in the **rest of Iberia**:
- Portuguese
- English
- Catalan is the official language in Andorra

300 km / 150 miles

*Catalan, an official EU language since 1990, is often called Valencian in Comunidad Valenciana

Local spellings are used in bilingual areas. Where more than one version is shown, the Castilian spelling appears after the local spelling.

(Not shown on map):
- CANARIAS (CANARY IS.) (Capital: Santa Cruz de Tenerife)
- CEUTA AND MELILLA

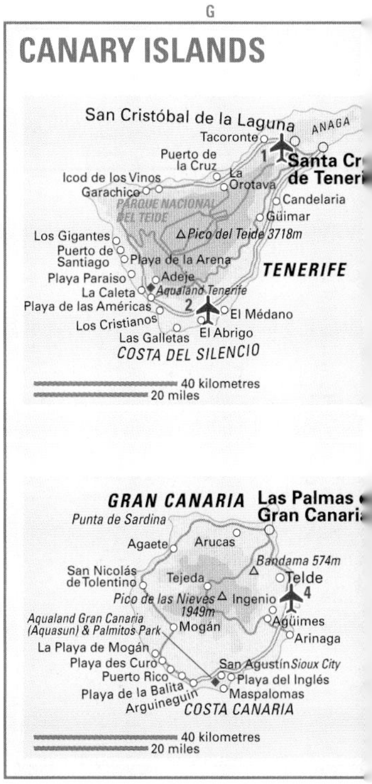

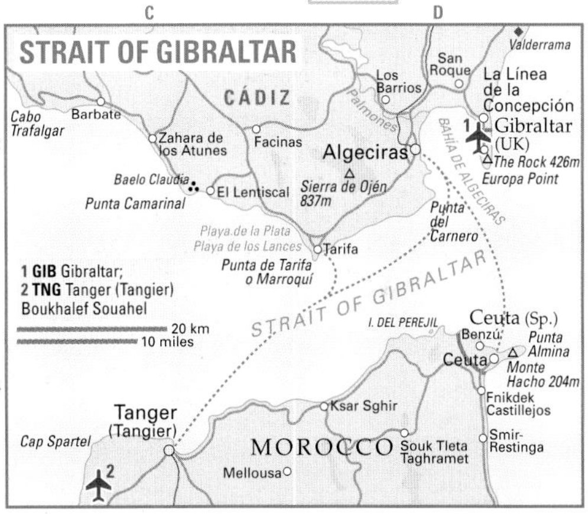

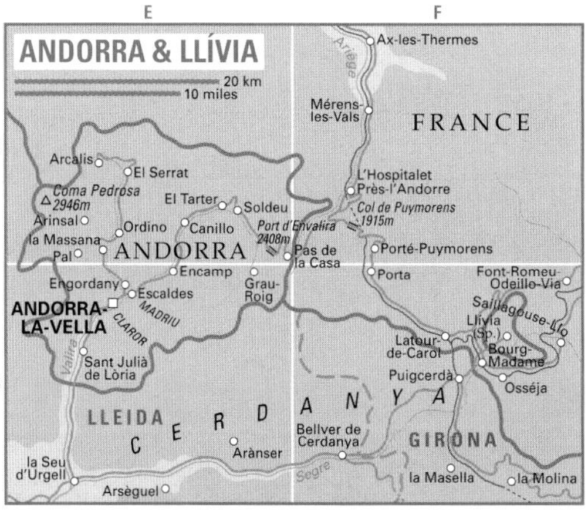

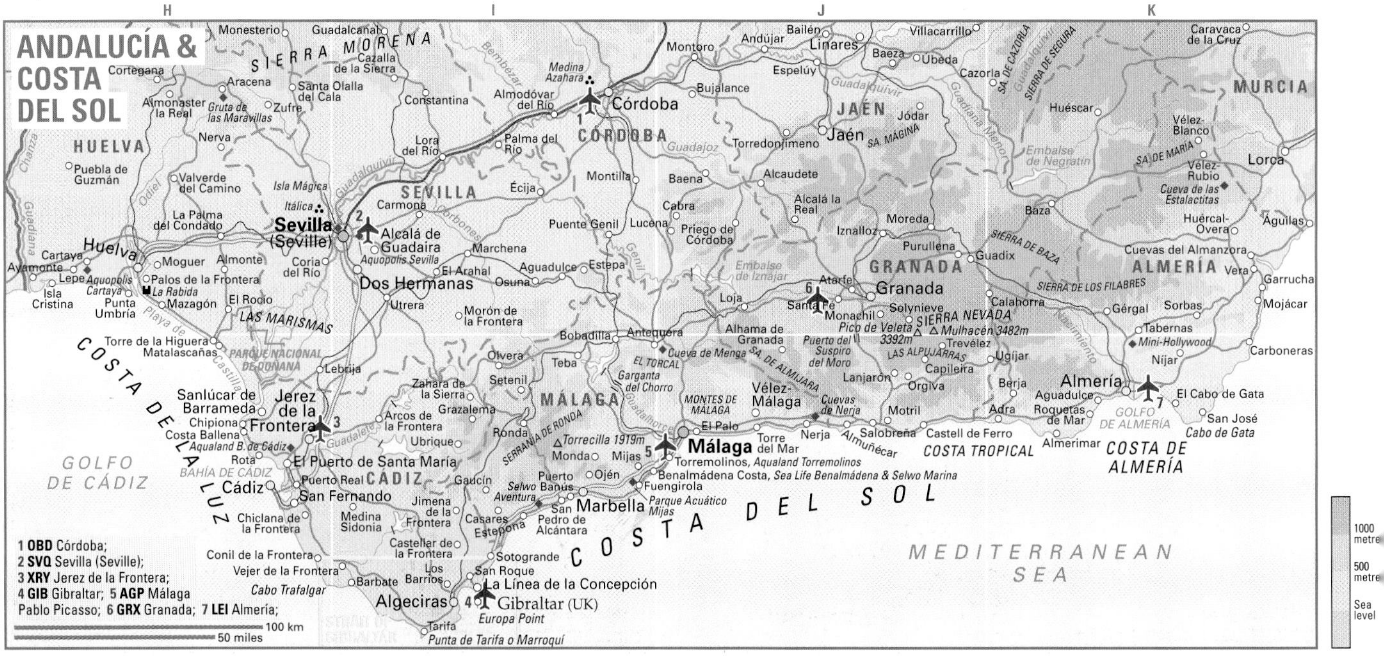

CANARY ISLANDS

40 kilometres / 20 miles

STRAIT OF GIBRALTAR

1 GIB Gibraltar;
2 TNG Tanger (Tangier) Boukhalef Souahel

20 km / 10 miles

ANDORRA & LLÍVIA

20 km / 10 miles

ANDALUCÍA & COSTA DEL SOL

1 OBD Córdoba;
2 SVQ Sevilla (Seville);
3 XRY Jerez de la Frontera;
4 GIB Gibraltar; **5 AGP** Málaga Pablo Picasso; **6 GRX** Granada; **7 LEI** Almería;

100 km / 50 miles

1000 metres / 500 metres / Sea level

See also... Contents (2-7) – this country features in many thematic and regional maps throughout the *World Travel Atlas*.

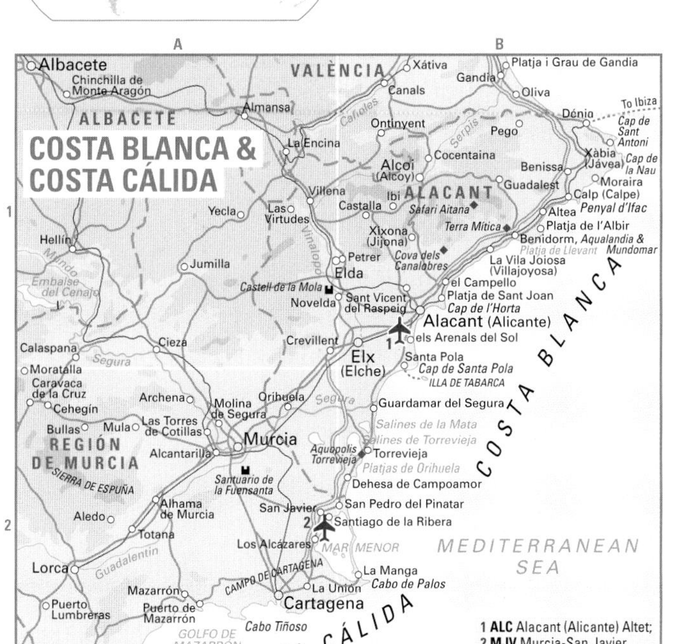
COSTA BLANCA & COSTA CÁLIDA
VALÈNCIA
ALBACETE
Albacete
Chinchilla de Monte-Aragón
Almansa
La Encina
Xàtiva
Canals
Gandia
Platja i Grau de Gandia
Oliva
Dénia
Cap de Sant Antoni
Ontinyent
Pego
Xàbia (Jávea)
Cap de la Nau
Moraira
Calp (Calpe)
Penyal d'Ifac
Altea
Platja de l'Albir
Benidorm, Aqualandia & Mundomar
Cocentaina
Alcoi (Alcoy)
Benissa
Guadalest
Ibi
ALACANT
Safari Aitana
Terra Mítica
Villena
Castalla
Xixona (Jijona)
La Vila Joiosa (Villajoyosa)
el Campello
Platja de Sant Joan
Cap de l'Horta
Alacant (Alicante)
els Arenals del Sol
Yecla
Las Virtudes
Hellín
Jumilla
Petrer
Elda
Cova dels Canalobres
Castell de la Mola
Novelda
Sant Vicent del Raspeig
Embalse del Cenajo
Calasparra
Cieza
Crevillent
Elx (Elche)
Santa Pola
Cap de Santa Pola
ILLA DE TABARCA
Moratalla
Caravaca de la Cruz
Cehegín
Archena
Molina de Segura
Orihuela
Segura
Guardamar del Segura
Bullas
Mula
Las Torres de Cotillas
Murcia
Salines de la Mata
Salines de Torrevieja
Aquopolis Torrevieja
Torrevieja
Platjas de Orihuela
REGIÓN DE MURCIA
Alcantarilla
Santuario de la Fuensanta
SIERRA DE ESPUÑA
Dehesa de Campoamor
San Pedro del Pinatar
Santiago de la Ribera
Aledo
Alhama de Murcia
Totana
San Javier
Los Alcázares
MAR MENOR
Guadalentín
Lorca
La Manga
Cabo de Palos
CAMPO DE CARTAGENA
La Unión
Cartagena
Mazarrón
Puerto Lumbreras
Puerto de Mazarrón
GOLFO DE MAZARRÓN
Cabo Tiñoso
Cabo Cope
Águilas
COSTA BLANCA
COSTA CÁLIDA
MEDITERRANEAN SEA
To Ibiza
1 ALC Alacant (Alicante) Altet;
2 MJV Murcia-San Javier
80 km
40 miles

COSTA BRAVA & COSTA DORADA
Sant Joan d'Isil
Espot
PYRENEES
ANDORRA
ANDORRA LA VELLA
FRANCE
Llavorsí
Sort
la Seu d'Urgell
CERDANYA
Puigcerdà
Llívia (Sp.)
La Molina
Núria
Camprodon
Port-Vendres
Cerbère
Portbou
la Jonquera
Sant Pere de Rodes
Llançà
Cap de Creus
Aquabrava
Cadaquès
Roses
Empuriabrava
GOLF DE ROSES
Ampurias
l'Escala
Congost de Collegats
la Pobla de Segur
Organyà
SERRA DEL CADÍ
Pedraforca 2497m
Ribes de Freser
Sant Joan de les Abadesses
Castellfollit de la Roca
Bagà
Sant Jaume de Frontanyà
Ripoll
Figueres
Besalú
Castelló d'Empúries
Olot
GIRONA
Banyoles
Santa Pau
Port del Comte
Rasos de Peguera
Berga
LLEIDA
Solsona
Torroella de Montgrí
l'Estartit
COSTA DE LA MORT
Girona (Gerona)
Ullastret
Pals
Begur
la Bispal
Palafrugell
Aiguablava
Llafranc
Calella de Pala.
Calonge
Cap Roig
Palamós
S'Agaró
Sant Feliu de Guíxols
Segre
Ponts
Cardona
Artesa de Segre
Agramunt
l'Estany
Vic
Sant Hilari Sacalm
Cova d'en Daina
Aquadiver, la Platja d'Aro
SERRA DEL MONTSENY
Breda
Maçanet
Water World Lloret
Tossa de Mar
Lloret de Mar
Marineland Cataluña
Blanes
Malgrat de Mar
Sant Pol de Mar
Canet de Mar
COSTA MARESME
Mataró
Arenys de Mar
BARCELONA
Calaf
Manresa
Tàrrega
Monestir de Montserrat
Terrassa (Tarrasa)
Granollers
Vallbona de les Monges
Igualada
Illa Fantasia
Sabadell
Rubí
Santa Coloma de Gramenet
Badalona
Barcelona
l'Hospitalet de Llobregat
Cornellà de Llobregat
Martorell
Tibidabo
Reial Monestir de Poblet
Montblanc
Monestir de Santes Creus
Vilafranca del Penedès
TARRAGONA
Aqualand
Safari-Aqualeón
Castelldefels
Garraf
COSTAS DE GARRAF
Sitges
Valls
el Vendrell
Sant Vicenç
Calafell
Vilanova i la Geltrú
Torredembarra
Reus
Salou
Tarragona
COSTA DE PONENT
Cambrils
Aquopolis Costa Daurada
Port Aventura
COSTA DAURADA (COSTA DORADA)
COSTA BRAVA
MEDITERRANEAN SEA
To Balearic Is.
1 REU Reus; 2 BCN Barcelona El Prat de Llobregat;
3 GRO Girona Costa Brava
80 km
40 miles

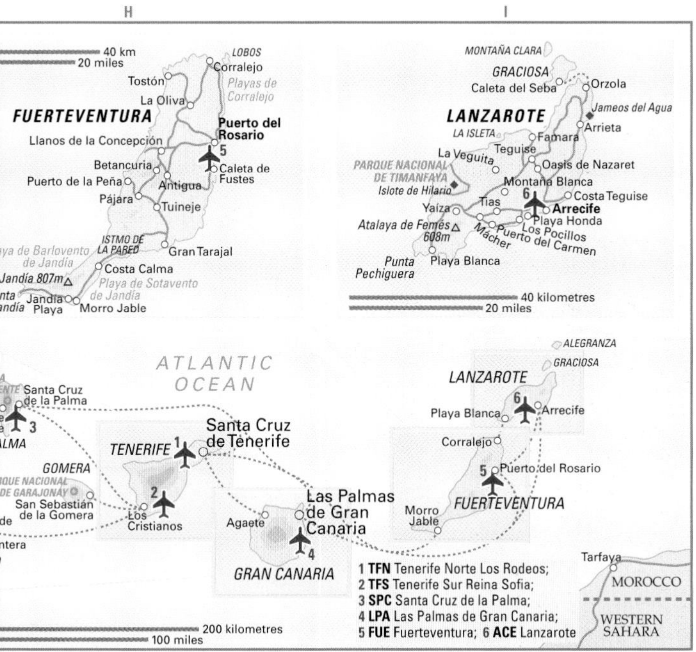
40 km
20 miles
LOBOS
Corralejo
Playas de Corralejo
Tostón
La Oliva
FUERTEVENTURA
Puerto del Rosario
Llanos de la Concepción
Betancuria
Caleta de Fustes
Puerto de la Peña
Antigua
Pájara
Tuineje
ISTMO DE LA PARED
Gran Tarajal
Playa de Barlovento de Jandía
Costa Calma
Playa de Sotavento de Jandía
Jandía 807m
Jandía Playa
Morro Jable
MONTAÑA CLARA
GRACIOSA
Caleta del Sebo
Orzola
LANZAROTE
Jameos del Agua
LA ISLETA
Arrieta
Famara
Teguise
La Vegueta
Oasis de Nazaret
PARQUE NACIONAL DE TIMANFAYA
Islote de Hilario
Montaña Blanca
Costa Teguise
Tías
Arrecife
Yaiza
Playa Honda
Atalaya de Femés 608m
Los Pocillos
Puerto del Carmen
Mácher
Punta Pechiguera
Playa Blanca
40 kilometres
20 miles
ATLANTIC OCEAN
ALEGRANZA
GRACIOSA
LANZAROTE
Playa Blanca
Arrecife
Corralejo
Puerto del Rosario
FUERTEVENTURA
Santa Cruz de la Palma
PALMA
GOMERA
PARQUE NACIONAL DE GARAJONAY
San Sebastián de la Gomera
TENERIFE
Santa Cruz de Tenerife
Los Cristianos
Las Palmas de Gran Canaria
Agaete
Morro Jable
GRAN CANARIA
Tarfaya
MOROCCO
WESTERN SAHARA
1 TFN Tenerife Norte Los Rodeos;
2 TFS Tenerife Sur Reina Sofía;
3 SPC Santa Cruz de la Palma;
4 LPA Las Palmas de Gran Canaria;
5 FUE Fuerteventura; 6 ACE Lanzarote
200 kilometres
100 miles

MINORCA
MEDITERRANEAN SEA
Cala Pregonda
Cap de Cavalleria
Cala Morell
Es Delfins
Cala Forcat
Cala Blanes
Cala Tirant
Fornells
Son Parc
Arenal d'en Castell
Port d'Addaia
S'Albufera
Ciutadella
Naveta d'Es Tudóns
Cala de Santandria
Cala Blanca
Es Mercadal
El Toro 357m
Ferreries
Cap de Favàritx
ILLA D'EN COLOM
Es Migjorn Gran
Es Migjorn Redones
Sant Cristòbal
Santa Galdana
Es Grau
Shangri-La
Alaior
Tamarinda
Cap d'Artrutx
Cala En Bosc
San Xoriguer
Cala Turqueta
Platja de Son Bou
Sant Tomàs
Sant Jaume Mediterrani
Son Bou de Baix
Talatí de Dalt
Maó (Mahón)
Cala Llonga
Villa Carlos
Trepucó
Sant Climent
Cala En Porter
Cales Coves
Es Canutells
Trebaluger
Sant Lluís
Binissafúller
Binibequer Vell
Cala Torret
S'Algar
Punta Prima
Biniancolla
ILLA DE L'AIRE
1 MAH Maó (Mahón)
20 km
10 miles

IBIZA
Portinatx
Port de Sant Miquel
Sant Joan de Labritja
Cova d'es Cuilleram
Cala de Sant Vicenç
Sant Miquel de Balansat
Santa Agnès de Corona
Cova de las Fontanelles
Sant Carles de Peralta
ILLA DE TAGOMAGO
EIVISSA (IBIZA)
Cala Salada
Cala Llenya
SA CONILLERA
Cala Gració
San Antonio (Sant Antoni de Portmany)
Es Canyar
S'Argamassa
ILLES BLEDES
Cala Bassa
Port d'es Torrent
Sant Rafael de Forca
Fantasylandia
Santa Eulària del Riu
Cala Conta
Cala Tarida
Cala Llonga
Sant Josép
Platja Talamanca
Cala Vadella
Sa Talaiassa de Sant Josep 475m
Eivissa (Ibiza)
Cala d'Hort
Ses Figueretes
Cova Santa
Cubells
Platja d'En Bossa
ILLA ES VEDRÁ
Sa Canal
Punta de ses Portes
ILLA DES PENJAT
ILLA ESPARDELL
ILLA ESPALMADOR
MEDITERRANEAN SEA
Sa Savina
Estany Pudent
Es Pujols
FORMENTERA
Sant Fransesc de Formentera
Sant Ferran
Cala Sahona
Torre des Pi des Català
Platja de Migjorn
El Pilar
Punta de sa Ruda
1 IBZ Eivissa (Ibiza)
20 km
10 miles

MAJORCA
Cap de Formentor
Cala Sant Vicenç
Formentor
Port de Pollença
S'Horta
Cap d'es Pinar
Pollença
MEDITERRANEAN SEA
Sa Calobra
Monestir de Lluc
Alcúdia
Port d'Alcúdia
BADIA D'ALCÚDIA
Puig Major 1445m
SERRA DE TRAMUNTANA
Platja de Muro
Sa Mesquida de Baix
Port de Sóller
Sóller
Lluc Alcari
Sa Pobla
S'ALBUFERA
Ca'n Picafort
PENINSULA DE LLEVANT
Cala Rajada
Capdepera
Deià
Orient
Inca
Muro
Artà
Son Moll
Valldemossa
Santa Margalida
Coves d'Artà
Banyalbufar
Mirador de ses Animes
Cala Bona
COSTA DE LOS PINOS
Estellencs
Sineu
Sant Llorenç des Cardassar
SERRA DE LLEVANT
Cala Millor
Reserva Africana
ES PLA
Petra
S'Illot; Sa Coma
ILLA DRAGONERA
Sant Elm
Palma de Mallorca
Manacor
Portocristo
Andratx
Calvià
Castell de Bendinat
Santuari de Nostra Senyora de Cura
Cala Estany
Coves del Drac
Randa
Llucmajor
Felanitx
Cales de Mallorca
Playa de Palma
Santuari de Sant Salvador
Cala Antena
Cala Murada
COSTA DE LA CALMA
BADIA DE PALMA
Portocolom
Cap de Cala Figuera
Campos
Cas Concos
Cala Marçal
Bahía Grande
Alquería Blanca
Cala d'Or
La Rapita
Santanyí
Cala Llonga; Cala Egos
Portopetro
Cala Pi
Ses Salines
Cala Mondragó
Colònia de Sant Jordi
Platja dels Dols
Cala Figuera
Cala Santanyí
Cala Llombarts
Cap de ses Salines
ILLA CONILLERA
ILLA DE CABRERA
1 Cala Blava
2 Cala Egos
3 Cala Fornells
4 Cala Major; Sant Agusti
5 Cala Vinyes
6 Camp de Mar
7 Ca'n Pastilla
8 Costa d'en Blanes Marineland Mallorca
9 El Molinar
10 Illetes
11 Magalluf Aqualand Mallorca
12 Palma Nova
13 Peguera
14 Portals Nous; Puerto Portals
15 Portals Vells
16 Port de Andratx
17 Santa Ponça
18 S'Arenal Aquacity de Mallorca
1 PMI Palma de Mallorca Son Sant Joan
40 km
20 miles
1000 metres
500 metres
Sea level

See also... Contents (2-7) – this country features in many thematic and regional maps throughout the *World Travel Atlas*.

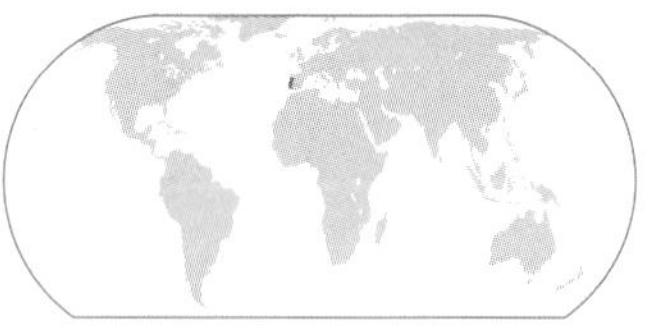

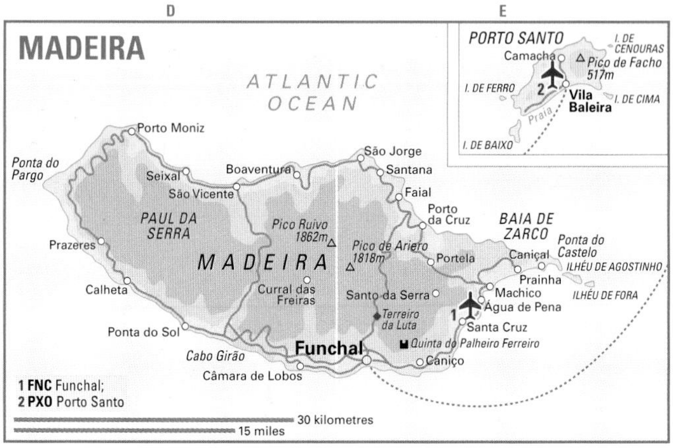

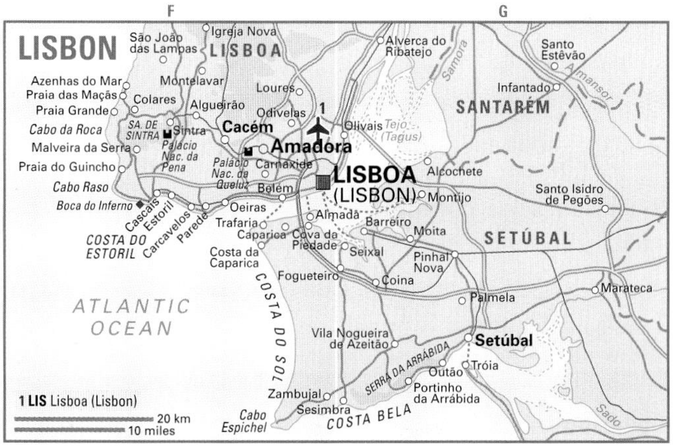

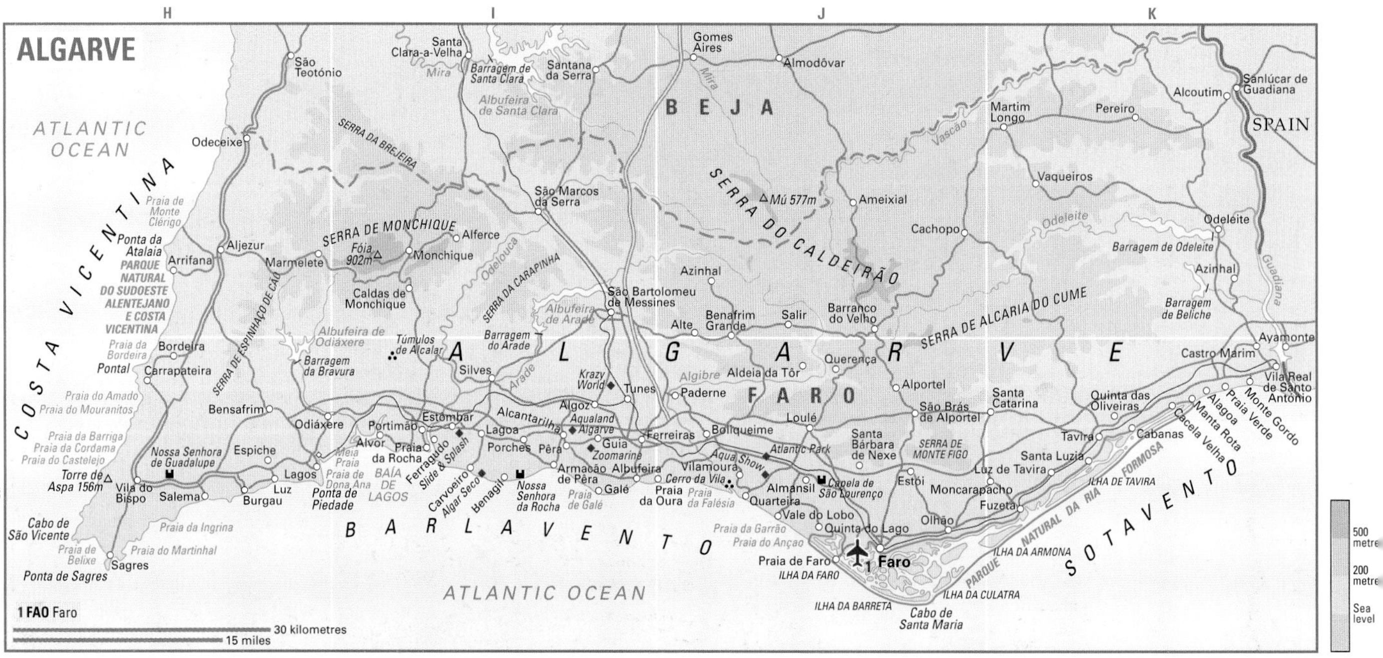

Portugal

- - - District boundary
● District capital

100 km
50 miles

(Not shown on map) AUTONOMOUS REGIONS OF:
AÇORES (AZORES) (Capital: Ponta Delgada)
MADEIRA (Capital: Funchal)

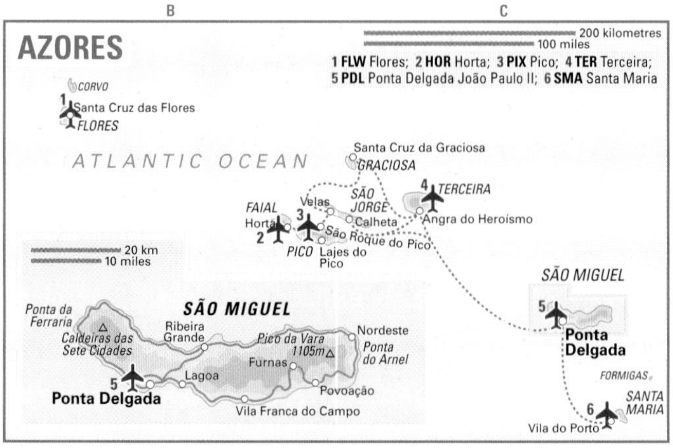

AZORES

200 kilometres
100 miles

1 FLW Flores; **2 HOR** Horta; **3 PIX** Pico; **4 TER** Terceira; **5 PDL** Ponta Delgada João Paulo II; **6 SMA** Santa Maria

20 km
10 miles

MADEIRA

1 FNC Funchal;
2 PXO Porto Santo

30 kilometres
15 miles

LISBON

1 LIS Lisboa (Lisbon)

20 km
10 miles

ALGARVE

1 FAO Faro

30 kilometres
15 miles

500 metres
200 metres
Sea level

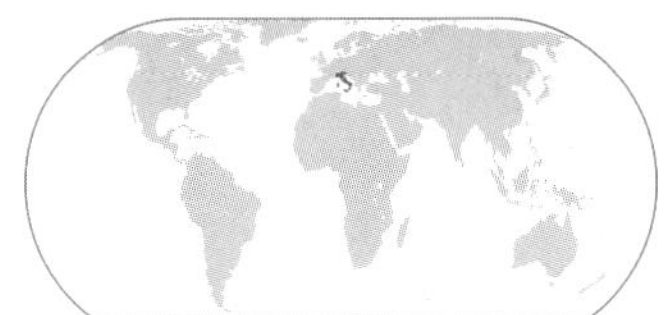

See also... 91-94 for more on Italy
For more information, see the Contents (2-7).

A B C D E F G

1 2 3 4 5 6 7

8°E 10°E 12°E 14°E 16°E 18°E
46°N 44°N 42°N 40°N 38°N 36°N

SWITZERLAND
LIECHTENSTEIN
AUSTRIA
HUNGARY
SLOVENIA
CROATIA
BOSNIA-HERZEGOVINA
FRANCE
MONACO
SAN MARINO
VATICAN CITY
ITALY
MALTA
TUNISIA
ALGERIA

ALPS
APPENNINO (APENNINES)
Dolomiti
Appennino Abruzzese
Appennino Lucano
Dalmatia
ISTRA

Ligurian Sea
Adriatic Sea
Tyrrhenian Sea
MEDITERRANEAN SEA
Ionian Sea
Gulf of Venice
Golfo di Génova
Golfo di Gaeta
Golfo di Salerno
Golfo di Manfredónia
Golfo di Táranto
Golfo di Squillace
Golfo di Catánia
Golfe de Hammamet
Canale di Sicilia
Malta Channel
Strait of Bonifacio
Stretto di Messina

Zürich
Innsbruck
Graz
Székesfehérvár
BERN (BERNE)
VADUZ
Bressanone
Merano
Bolzano (Bozen)
Ortles 3905m
Marmolada 3342m
Tolmezzo
Villach
Maribor
Pécs
Domodossola
Lago Maggiore
Sóndrio
Morbegno
Lago di Como
Riva del Garda
Trento
Belluno
Údine
Gemona del Friuli
Gorizia
LJUBLJANA
ZAGREB
Osijek
Mont Blanc 4808m
Monte Rosa 4634m
Aosta
Varese
Lecco
Como
Bérgamo
Biella
Legnano
Monza
Bréscia
Gran Paradiso 4061m
Novara
Milano (Milan)
Vicenza
Verona
Lago di Garda
Mestre
Treviso
Pordenone
Trieste
Rijeka
Slavonski Brod
Vercelli
Mantova (Mantua)
Pádova (Padua)
Venézia (Venice)
Laguna Veneta
Susa
Torino (Turin)
Pavia
Cremona
Legnago
Chióggia
Rivoli
Moncalieri
Voghera
Piacenza
Rovigo
Pinerolo
Tortona
Mirándola
Ferrara
Porto Tolle
Pula
CRES
KRK
Banja Luka
Asti
Alessandria
Carpi
Parma
Reggio nell' Emília
Módena
Valli di Comácchio
Alba
Saluzzo
Cúneo
Mondovì
Génova (Genoa)
Rapallo
Chiávari
Savona
Lugo
Ravenna
Bologna
Imola
Faenza
Forlì
Pavullo nel Frignano
La Spezia
Cesena
Rímini
Riccione
Pésaro
Fano
Zadar
Albenga
Impéria
San Remo
Nice
Carrara
Massa
Pietrasanta
Viaréggio
Pistóia
Prato
Lucca
Émpoli
Pisa
Cascina
Firenze (Florence)
Urbino
Falconara Marittimo
Ancona
Split
Livorno (Leghorn)
Cécina
Arezzo
Citta di Castello
Jesi
Civitanova Marche
BRAČ
HVAR
KORČULA
Siena
Cortona
Gúbbio
Fermo
Lago Trasimeno
Perúgia
Assisi
Foligno
Í. DI CAPRÁIA
Piombino
Í. D'ELBA
Follónica
San Benedetto del Tronto
Ascoli Piceno
Teramo
Dubrovnik
Bastia
Grosseto
Orvieto
Lago di Bolsena
Spoleto
Terni
Rieti
Corno Grande 2912m
Pescara
Chieti
PALAGRUŽA
Í. PIANOSA
Í. DEL GÍGLIO
Í. DI MONTECRISTO
Í. DI GIANNUTRI
Orbetello
Viterbo
L'Áquila
Lanciano
Vasto
ÍSOLE TRÉMITI
Lago di Lesina
Lago di Varano
Vieste
CORSE (CORSICA) (Fr.)
Ajaccio
Civitavécchia
Avezzano
Sulmona
Térmoli
PROMONTÓRIO DEL GARGANO
San Severo
Tívoli
ROMA (ROME)
Lido di Óstia
Sora
Isérnia
Manfredónia
Cassino
Campobasso
Fóggia
Barletta
Anzio
Latina
Terracina
Fórmia
Gaeta
Cerignola
Ándria
Molfetta
Bari
Bitonto
Caserta
Benevento
Nápoli (Naples)
Vesuvio 1279m
Avellino
Rionero in Vulture
Altamura
Gióia del Colle
Ostuni
Bríndisi
ÍSOLE PONZIANE
Í. VENTOTÉNE
Í. D'ISCHIA
Í. DI CAPRI
Torre del Greco
Salerno
Éboli
Potenza
Matera
Alberobello
Táranto
Lecce
Battipáglia
Agrópoli
Nardò
Ótranto
Policoro
Gallípoli
Sapri
Maratea
Capo Santa Maria di Leuca
Castrovillari
Corigliano Cálabro
Cetraro
Rossano
Cosenza
Cirò Marina
Crotone
Capo Colonna
Lamézia Terme
Catanzaro
Vibo Valentia
Rosarno
Í. ASINARA
ARC. DE LA MADDALENA
Golfo Aranci
Ólbia
Porto Tórres
Sassari
Ozieri
Alghero
Siniscóla
Nuoro
Macomér
Punta La Marmora 1834m
SARDEGNA (SARDINIA)
Oristano
Tortolì
Terralba
Gúspini
Villaputzu
Iglésias
Cágliari
Quartu Sant'Élena
Í. DI SAN PIETRO
Carbónia
Í. DI SANT' ANTIOCO
Capo Carbonara
Capo Spartivento
Í. STRÓMBOLI
ÍSOLE EÓLIE
Í. SALINA
(LIPARI)
Í. LIPARI
Í. VULCANO
Í. DI ÚSTICA
Capo San Vito
Partinico
Palermo
Capo d'Orlando
Milazzo
Messina
Réggio di Calábria
Capo Spartivento
ÍSOLE ÉGADI
Trápani
Castellammare del Golfo
Bagheria
Cefalù
Monte Etna 3350m
Taormina
Adrano
Marsala
Castelvetrano
SICILIA (SICILY)
Paternò
Mazara del Vallo
Enna
Catánia
Sciacca
Caltanissetta
Canicattì
Agrigento
Licata
Gela
Ragusa
Siracusa (Syracuse)
Vittoria
Módica
Ávola
Pachino
Capo Pássaro
Bizerte (Bizerta)
Annaba
Ras el Tib (Cap Bon)
TUNIS
Í. DI PANTELLERIA
GOZO
VALLETTA
Í. DI LINOSA
ÍSOLE PELAGIE
Í. DI LAMPEDUSA
Kairouan
Sousse

TRN MXP LIN BGY VRN VCE TRS GOA BLQ FLR PSA AOI CIA FCO NAP BRI BDS OLB CAG PMO CTA

See also... Contents (2-7) – this country features in many thematic and regional maps throughout the *World Travel Atlas*.

For more information, see the Contents (2-7).

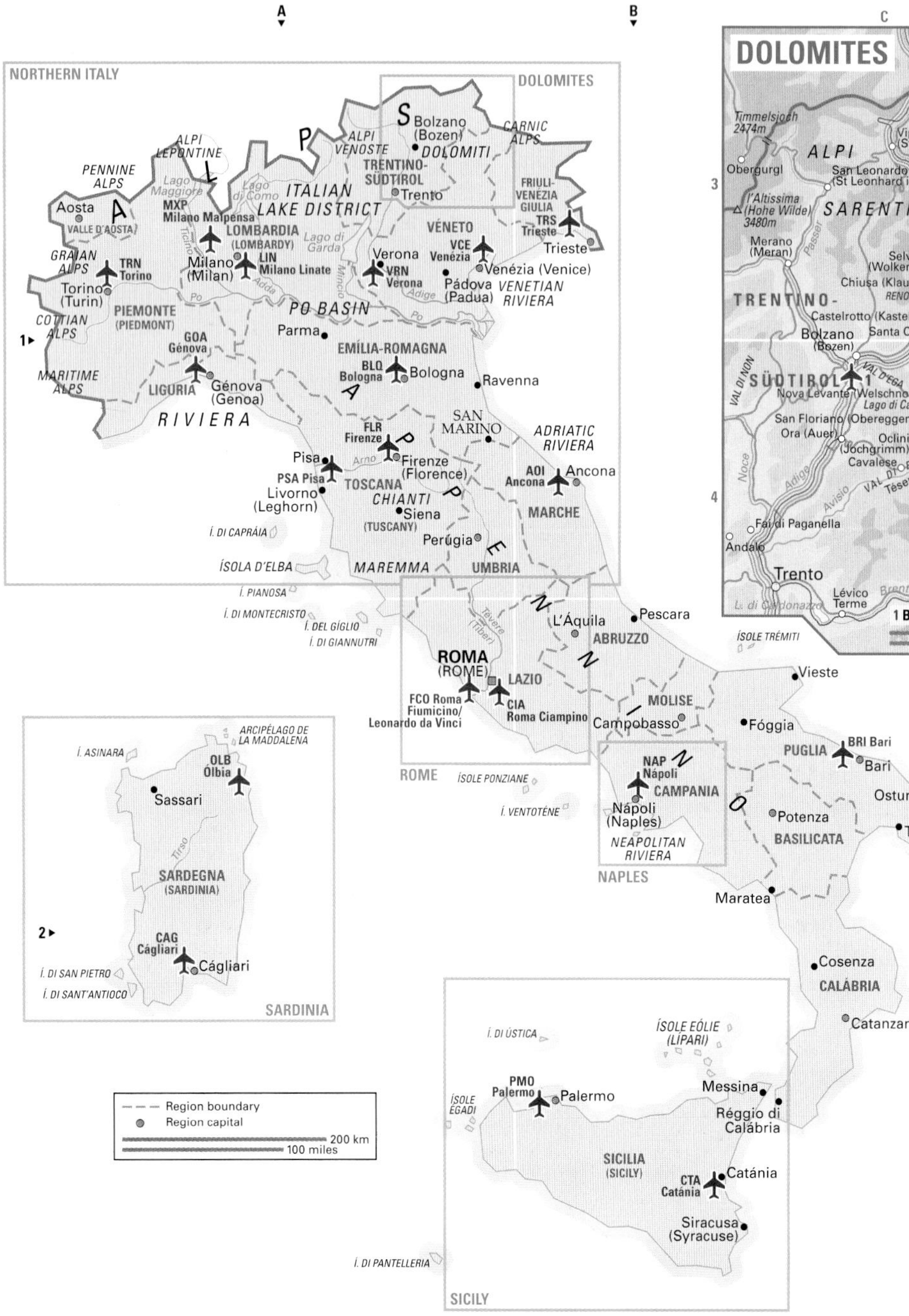
NORTHERN ITALY
DOLOMITES
ALPS
APENNINO
PENNINE ALPS
ALPI LEPONTINE
ALPI VENOSTE
CARNIC ALPS
GRAIAN ALPS
COTTIAN ALPS
MARITIME ALPS
ITALIAN LAKE DISTRICT
PO BASIN
RIVIERA
ADRIATIC RIVIERA
VENETIAN RIVIERA
Aosta
VALLE D'AOSTA
MXP Milano Malpensa
LOMBARDIA (LOMBARDY)
LIN Milano Linate
Milano (Milan)
TRN Torino
Torino (Turin)
PIEMONTE (PIEDMONT)
GOA Génova
Génova (Genoa)
LIGURIA
Bolzano (Bozen)
DOLOMITI
TRENTINO-SÜDTIROL
Trento
FRIULI-VENEZIA GIULIA
TRS Trieste
Trieste
VÉNETO
VCE Venézia
Venézia (Venice)
Verona
VRN Verona
Pádova (Padua)
Parma
EMÍLIA-ROMAGNA
BLQ Bologna
Bologna
Ravenna
SAN MARINO
FLR Firenze
Firenze (Florence)
Pisa
PSA Pisa
Livorno (Leghorn)
TOSCANA (TUSCANY)
CHIANTI
Siena
MARCHE
AOI Ancona
Ancona
Perúgia
UMBRIA
MAREMMA
Í. DI CAPRÁIA
ÍSOLA D'ELBA
Í. PIANOSA
Í. DI MONTECRISTO
Í. DEL GÍGLIO
Í. DI GIANNUTRI
L'Áquila
Pescara
ABRUZZO
ROMA (ROME)
LAZIO
FCO Roma Fiumicino/ Leonardo da Vinci
CIA Roma Ciampino
ROME
MOLISE
Campobasso
ÍSOLE TRÉMITI
Vieste
Fóggia
PUGLIA
BRI Bari
Bari
ÍSOLE PONZIANE
Í. VENTOTÉNE
NAP Nápoli
CAMPANIA
Nápoli (Naples)
NEAPOLITAN RIVIERA
NAPLES
Ostuni
BDS Brindisi
Bríndisi
Potenza
BASILICATA
Táranto
Lecce
Maratea
Cosenza
CALÁBRIA
Catanzaro
Í. ASINARA
ARCIPÉLAGO DE LA MADDALENA
OLB Ólbia
Sassari
SARDEGNA (SARDINIA)
CAG Cágliari
Cágliari
Í. DI SAN PIETRO
Í. DI SANT'ANTIOCO
SARDINIA
Í. DI ÚSTICA
ÍSOLE EÓLIE (LIPARI)
ÍSOLE EGADI
PMO Palermo
Palermo
Messina
Réggio di Calábria
SICILIA (SICILY)
CTA Catánia
Catánia
Siracusa (Syracuse)
Í. DI PANTELLERIA
SICILY
Region boundary
Region capital
200 km
100 miles

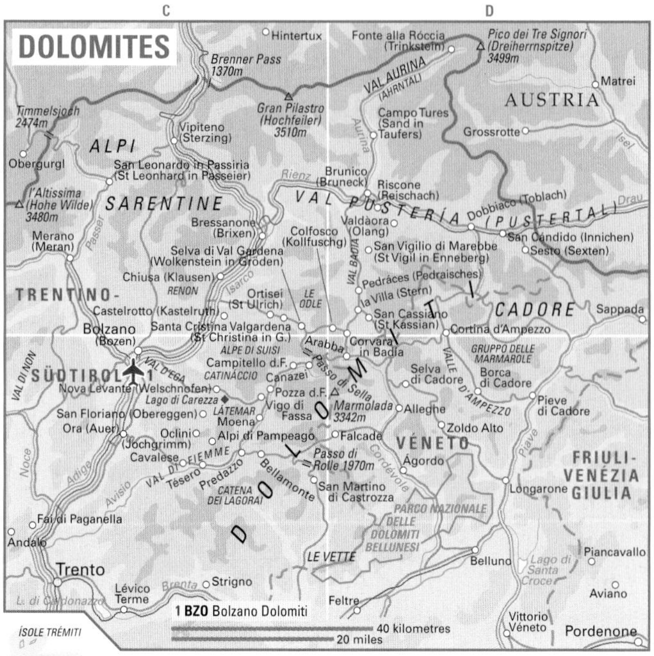
DOLOMITES
Hintertux
Fonte alla Róccia (Trinkstein)
Pico dei Tre Signori (Dreiherrnspitze) 3499m
Brenner Pass 1370m
Matrei
AUSTRIA
Timmelsjoch 2474m
Gran Pilastro (Hochfeiler) 3510m
VAL AURINA (AHRNTAL)
Campo Tures (Sand in Taufers)
Grossrotte
Vipiteno (Sterzing)
ALPI SARENTINE
Obergurgl
San Leonardo in Passiria (St Leonhard in Passeier)
Brunico (Bruneck)
Riscone (Reischach)
VAL PUSTERÍA (PUSTERTAL)
Dobbiaco (Toblach)
l'Altissima (Hohe Wilde) 3480m
Bressanone (Brixen)
Valdaora (Olang)
San Cándido (Innichen)
Sesto (Sexten)
Merano (Meran)
Colfosco (Kolfuschg)
San Vigilio di Marebbe (St Vigil in Enneberg)
Selva di Val Gardena (Wolkenstein in Gröden)
Chiusa (Klausen)
Pedráces (Pedraisches)
TRENTINO-SÜDTIROL
Castelrotto (Kastelruth)
Ortisei (St Ulrich)
la Villa (Stern)
CADORE
Sappada
San Cassiano (St Kassian)
Bolzano (Bozen)
Santa Cristina Valgardena (St Christina in G.)
Corvara in Badia
Cortina d'Ampezzo
ALPE DI SUISI
Arabba
Campitello d.F.
GRUPPO DELLE MARMAROLE
CATINÁCCIO
Canazei
Selva di Cadore
Borca di Cadore
Nova Levante (Welschnofen)
Pozza d.F.
Lago di Carezza
Marmolada 3342m
Alleghe
San Floriano (Obereggen)
Vigo di Fassa
Pieve di Cadore
Ora (Auer)
Moena
Zoldo Alto
Alpi di Pampeago
DOLOMITI
Oclini (Jochgrimm)
Falcade
VÉNETO
Cavalese
Passo di Rolle 1970m
Ágordo
FRIULI-VENÉZIA GIULIA
VAL DI FIEMME
Tésero
Predazzo
Bellamonte
San Martino di Castrozza
Longarone
CATENA DEI LAGORAI
PARCO NAZIONALE DELLE DOLOMITI BELLUNESI
Fai di Paganella
Andalo
Piancavallo
LE VETTE
Belluno
Trento
Strigno
Aviano
Lévico Terme
Feltre
Vittorio Véneto
Pordenone
1 BZO Bolzano Dolomiti
40 kilometres
20 miles

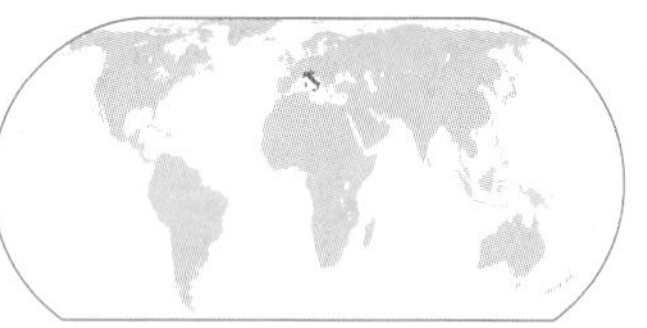

- **JAN 31st** Fiera di Sant'Orso **(Aosta)**
- **FEB** Festa del Mandorlo in fiore: almond blossom festival **(Agrigento)**
- before Lent Carnevale **(Venice** and countrywide)
- **ASH WEDNESDAY** Il Pranzo del Purgatori: Purgatory Dinner **(Grádoli**, Lazio)
- **GOOD FRIDAY** Processions (Southern Italy and Sicily)
- **EASTER SUNDAY** Il Scoppio del Carro: fireworks **(Florence)**
- **MAR-APR** La Festa di Primavera: Spring Festival **(Rome)**
- **MAY 1st** Festa di Sant'Efisio **(Cágliari)**
- **MAY** Festa di San Domenico Abate **(Cocullo, L'Aquila)**
- **MAY** Festa di San Gennaro **(Naples)**; also Sep 19th and Dec 16th
- **MAY** Sagra di San Nicola **(Bari)**
- **MAY 15th** Corso dei Ceri: 'candle' race **(Gúbbio)**
- **MAY** Cavalcata Sarda: Sardinian Cavalcade **(Sassari)**
- **MAY** La Festa della Sensa: Wedding to the Sea **(Venice)**
- **JUN** Luminaria: Festival of Lights; Gioco del Ponte: tug-of-war; historical regatta **(Pisa)**
- **JUN** Corpus Christi Procession **(Orvieto)**
- **JUN** La Festa di San Giovanni and Gioco di Calcio Storico: football match in medieval costume **(Florence)**
- **JUN-JUL** Festival dei Due Mondi: arts festival **(Spoleto)**
- **JUN-SEP** Biennale **(Venice)**; every two (odd) years
- **JUL 2nd** Palio delle Contrade: horse races **(Siena)**; also **AUG 16th**
- **JUL** La Festa del Redentore: Feast of the Redeemer **(Venice)**
- **JUL-AUG** International Opera Festival **(Verona)**
- **JUL-SEP** Estate Romana: Roman Summer arts festival **(Rome)**
- **AUG** La Festa del Redentore: Feast of the Redeemer **(Nuoro)**
- **AUG-SEP** International Film Festival **(Venice Lido)**
- **SEP** La Giostra del Saracine: jousting tournament **(Arezzo)**
- **SEP** La Regatta Storico: historical regatta **(Venice)**
- **SEP** Douja d'Or: wine festival; Festival delle Sagre; Palio **(Asti)**
- **SEP** La Partita a Scacchi: living chess **(Maróstica)**; every two (even) years
- **SEP 19th** La Festa di San Gennaro **(Naples)**
- **OCT** Festa dell'uva: Grape Festival **(Merano)**
- **OCT-DEC Rome** Jazz Festival
- **NOV** La Festa della Madonna della Salute **(Venice)**

SARDINIA
STRAIT OF BONIFACIO
Capo Testa
la Maddalena
Santa Teresa di Gallura
ÍSOLA MADDALENA
Porto Rafael
ÍSOLA CAPRERA
Palau
Porto Cervo
ÍSOLA ASINARA
GOLFO DELL' ASINARA
Arzachena
GOLFO DI MARINELLA
Báia Sardinia
Golfo Aranci
Capo del Falcone
Stintino
Porto Rotondo
COSTA SMERALDA
Castelsardo
ÍSOLA TAVOLARA
Ólbia
ÍSOLA MOLARA
Porto Tórres
LA NURRA
Sassari
ANGLONA
Santissima Trinità di Saccargia
Posada
Porto Conte
la Caletta
Grotta di Nettuno
LOGUDORO
Ozieri
Siniscóla
Alghero
Necropoli di S. Andria Priu
Capo Comino
RIVIERA DEL CORALLO
BARONIA
Orosei
Cala Liberotto
Nùoro
Villaggio nuragico di Serra Órrios
Bosa
Dorgali
Monte Ferru 1050m
Macomér
Oliena
GOLFO DI OROSEI
Santa Caterina di Pittinuri
MONTI DEL GENNARGENTU
Punta La Mármora 1834m
MEDITERRANEAN SEA
SINIS
SARDEGNA
Árbatax
Thárros
Oristano
Tortolì
GOLFO DI ORISTANO
Su Nuraxi di Barúmini
Ulassai
Terralba
Barúmini
TYRRHENIAN SEA
COSTA VERDE
Gúspini
CAMPIDANO
Sanluri
Villacidro
Villaputzu
Muravera
IGLESIENTE
Iglésias
Quartu Sant'Elena
COSTA REI
Portoscuso
Carbónia
Carloforte
Cágliari
ÍSOLA DI SAN PIETRO
Capo Boi
Villasimíus
Calasetta
Sant' Antioco
GOLFO DI CÁGLIARI
Capo Carbonara
ÍSOLA DI SANT'ANTIOCO
Pula
PINETA
Nora
GOLFO DI PÁLMAS
Chia
Santa Margherita di Pula
Bithia
Forte Village Resort
Capo Spartivento
COSTA DEL SUD
1 AHO Alghero Fertília;
2 OLB Ólbia Costa Smeralda;
3 CAG Cágliari Élmas
100 km
50 miles

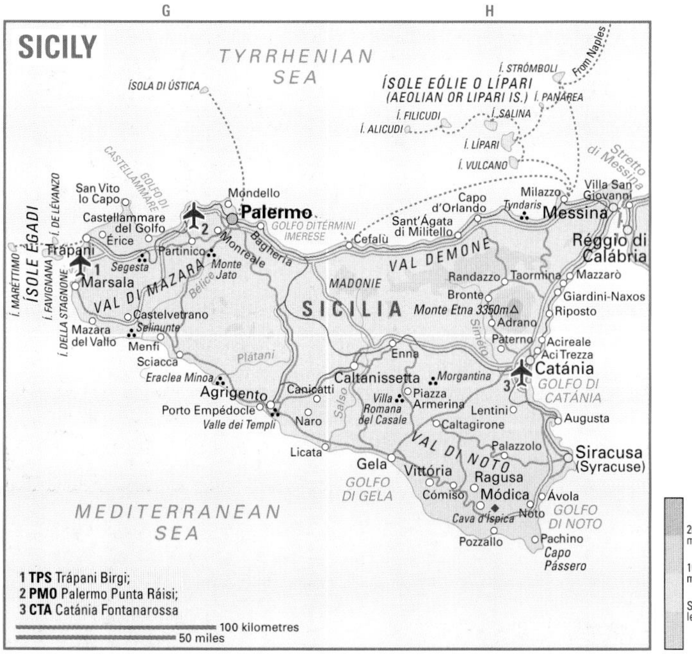
SICILY
TYRRHENIAN SEA
Í. STRÓMBOLI
From Naples
ÍSOLE EÓLIE O LÍPARI (AEOLIAN OR LIPARI IS.)
Í. PANAREA
ÍSOLA DI ÚSTICA
Í. FILICUDI
Í. SALINA
Í. ALICUDI
Í. LÍPARI
Í. VULCANO
Stretto di Messina
GOLFO DI CASTELLAMMARE
Mondello
Milazzo
Villa San Giovanni
San Vito lo Capo
Capo d'Orlando
Tyndaris
Palermo
Messina
Í. DI LEVANZO
Castellammare del Golfo
GOLFO DI TÉRMINI IMERESE
Sant'Ágata di Militello
ÍSOLE ÉGADI
Érice
Monreale
Cefalù
Réggio di Calábria
Trápani
Segesta
Partinico
Bagheria
VAL DEMONE
Í. MARÉTTIMO
Í. FAVIGNANA
Monte Jato
Taormina
Mazzarò
Marsala
VAL DI MAZARA
MADONIE
Randazzo
Giardini-Naxos
Bronte
Í. DELLA STAGNONE
SICILIA
Monte Etna 3350m
Riposto
Castelvetrano
Mazara del Vallo
Selinunte
Adrano
Menfi
Paterno
Acireale
Aci Trezza
Sciacca
Plátani
Enna
Catánia
Eraclea Minoa
Morgantina
Agrigento
Canicatti
Caltanissetta
GOLFO DI CATÁNIA
Villa Romana del Casale
Piazza Armerina
Porto Empédocle
Naro
Lentini
Valle dei Templi
Caltagirone
Augusta
Licata
VAL DI NOTO
Palazzolo
Siracusa (Syracuse)
Gela
Vittória
GOLFO DI GELA
Ragusa
Cómiso
Módica
Ávola
MEDITERRANEAN SEA
Cava d'Íspica
Noto
GOLFO DI NOTO
Pozzallo
Pachino
Capo Pássero
1 TPS Trápani Birgi;
2 PMO Palermo Punta Ráisi;
3 CTA Catánia Fontanarossa
100 kilometres
50 miles
2000 metres
1000 metres
Sea level

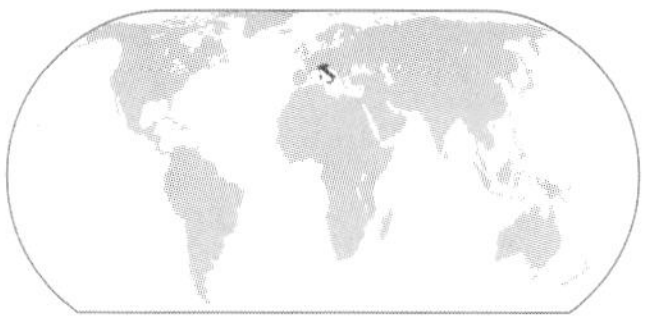

See also... Contents (2-7) – this country features in many thematic and regional maps throughout the *World Travel Atlas*.

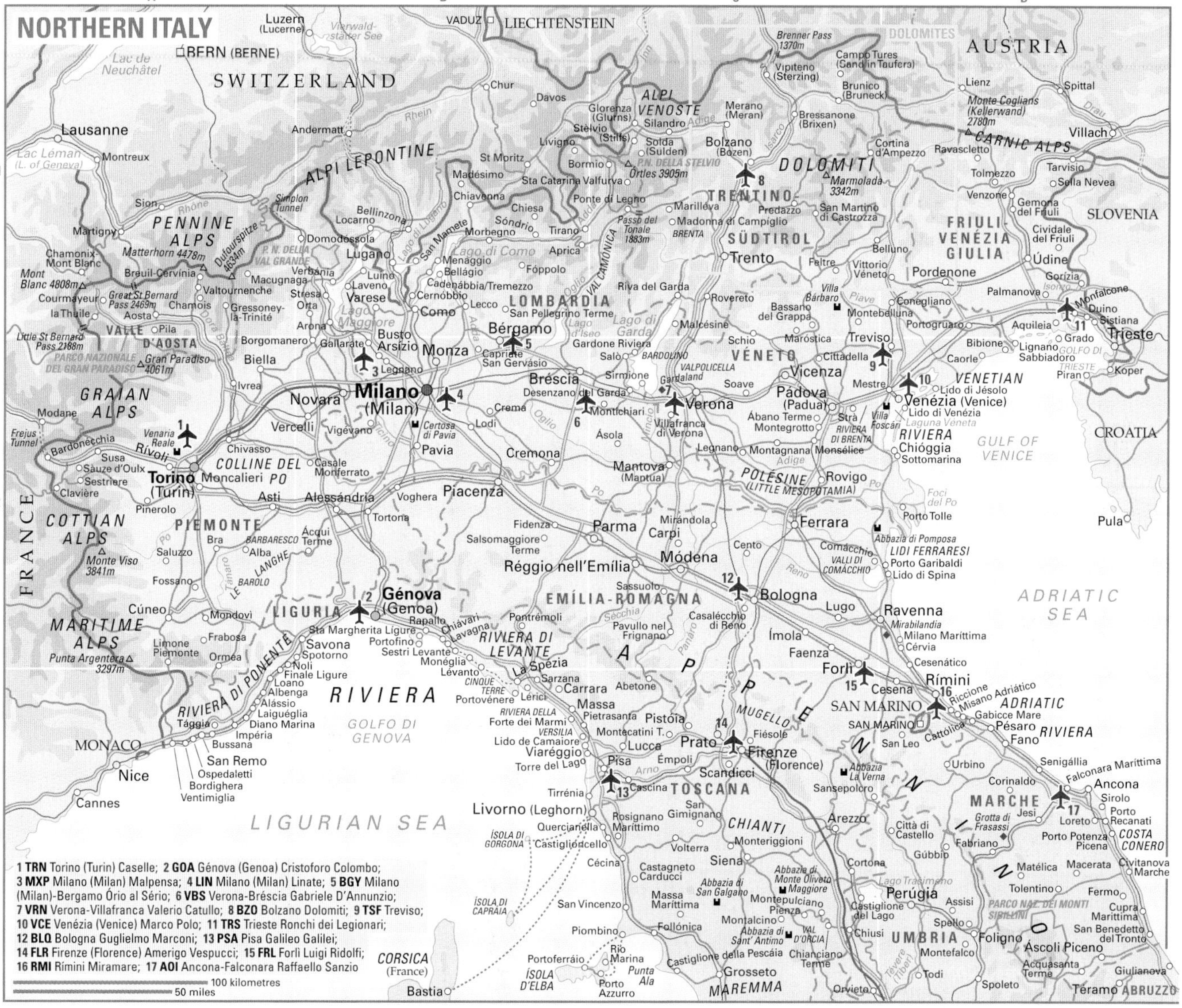
NORTHERN ITALY
SWITZERLAND
AUSTRIA
SLOVENIA
CROATIA
FRANCE
LIECHTENSTEIN
VADUZ
BERN (BERNE)
ALPI LEPONTINE
PENNINE ALPS
GRAIAN ALPS
COTTIAN ALPS
MARITIME ALPS
DOLOMITI
CARNIC ALPS
Matterhorn 4478m
Mont Blanc 4808m
Gran Paradiso 4061m
Monte Viso 3841m
Marmolada 3342m
Ortles 3905m
LOMBARDIA
PIEMONTE
VALLE D'AOSTA
TRENTINO-SÜDTIROL
FRIULI-VENÉZIA GIULIA
VÉNETO
LIGURIA
EMÍLIA-ROMAGNA
TOSCANA
UMBRIA
MARCHE
SAN MARINO
APPENNINO
RIVIERA
RIVIERA DI PONENTE
RIVIERA DI LEVANTE
LIGURIAN SEA
GOLFO DI GENOVA
GULF OF VENICE
ADRIATIC SEA
VENETIAN RIVIERA
ADRIATIC RIVIERA
Milano (Milan)
Torino (Turin)
Génova (Genoa)
Venézia (Venice)
Bologna
Firenze (Florence)
Verona
Pádova (Padua)
Trieste
Pisa
Livorno (Leghorn)
Perugia
Ancona
Rímini
Nice
MONACO
CORSICA (France)
1 TRN Torino (Turin) Caselle; 2 GOA Génova (Genoa) Cristoforo Colombo;
3 MXP Milano (Milan) Malpensa; 4 LIN Milano (Milan) Linate; 5 BGY Milano (Milan)-Bergamo Ório al Sério; 6 VBS Verona-Bréscia Gabriele D'Annunzio;
7 VRN Verona-Villafranca Valerio Catullo; 8 BZO Bolzano Dolomiti; 9 TSF Treviso;
10 VCE Venézia (Venice) Marco Polo; 11 TRS Trieste Ronchi dei Legionari;
12 BLQ Bologna Guglielmo Marconi; 13 PSA Pisa Galileo Galilei;
14 FLR Firenze (Florence) Amerigo Vespucci; 15 FRL Forlì Luigi Ridolfi;
16 RMI Rímini Miramare; 17 AOI Ancona-Falconara Raffaello Sanzio
100 kilometres
50 miles

ROME
ROMA (ROME)
VATICAN CITY
LAZIO
UMBRIA
ABRUZZO
APPENNINO ABRUZZESE
TYRRHENIAN SEA
Tívoli
Ostia Antica
Latina
L'Aquila
Viterbo
Civitavecchia
1 FCO Roma (Rome) Fiumicino/ Leonardo da Vinci;
2 CIA Roma (Rome) Ciampino
60 km
30 miles

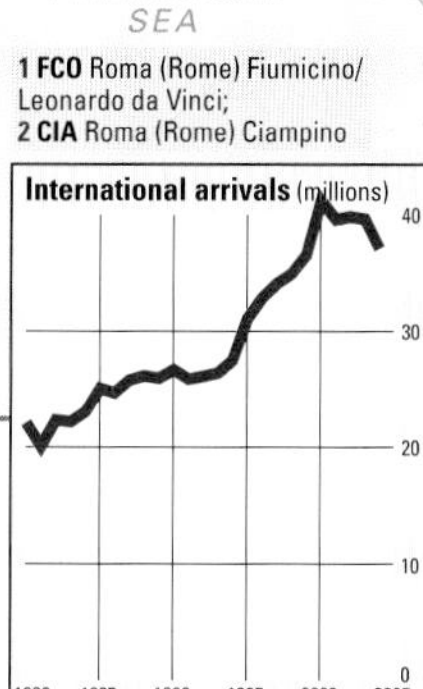
International arrivals (millions)
40
30
20
10
0
1980 1985 1990 1995 2000 2005
Source: World Tourism Organisation

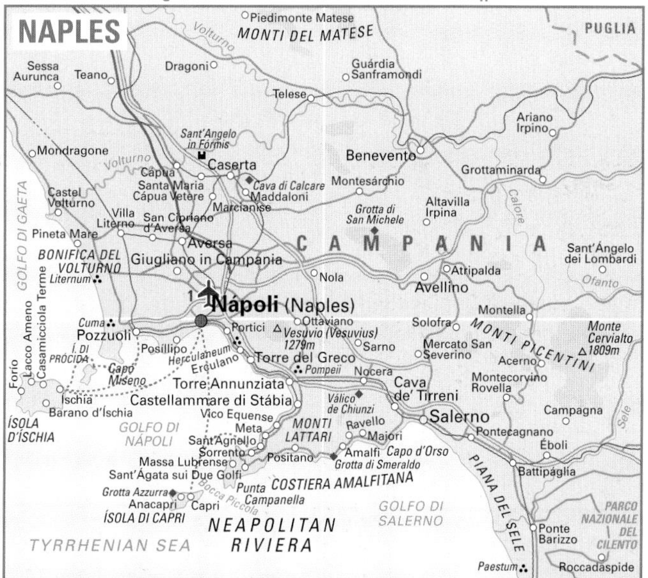
NAPLES
Nápoli (Naples)
CAMPANIA
PUGLIA
MONTI DEL MATESE
MONTI PICENTINI
Vesuvio (Vesuvius) 1279m
Pompeii
Caserta
Benevento
Salerno
Sorrento
Amalfi
Capri
ÍSOLA DI CAPRI
ÍSOLA D'ÍSCHIA
GOLFO DI NÁPOLI
GOLFO DI SALERNO
TYRRHENIAN SEA
NEAPOLITAN RIVIERA
COSTIERA AMALFITANA
1 NAP Nápoli (Naples) Capodichino
40 kilometres
20 miles

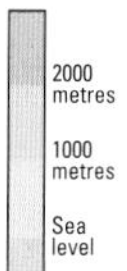
2000 metres
1000 metres
Sea level

Italy: Attractions

See also... Europe Historical (58-59)

The listings above refer to a selection of related themes. For more information, see the Contents (2-7). See also the Columbus Tourist Attractions and Events of the World.

Theme park, leisure park
Museum, gallery
Religious building
Park, reserve, zoo, etc.
Historic/notable building
Water-related attraction
Other place of interest
Attractions in cities marked in **red** are listed around the map

200 km
100 miles

Milano (Milan)
- Il Cenacolo (Last Supper)
- Civico Museo di Arte Contemporanea
- Museo Civico di Archeologico
- Museo Nazionale della Scienza e Tecnica Leonardo da Vinci
- Museo Poldi-Pezzoli
- Pinacoteca Ambrosiana
- Pinacoteca di Brera
- Duomo
- Santa Maria presso San Satiro
- Giardini Pubblici
- Castello Sforzesco
- Galleria Vittorio Emanuele II
- Teatro alla Scala
- Quadrilatero d'Oro
- Stadio Meazza (San Siro)

Torino (Turin)
- Galleria Civica d'Arte Moderna e Contemporanea
- Galleria Sabauda
- Museo dell'Automobile
- Museo Egizio
- Museo Nazionale del Cinema
- Pinacoteca Giovanni e Marella Agnelli
- Palazzo Reale
- Basilica di Superga
- Duomo di San Giovanni
- Piazza San Carlo

Verona
- Arche Scaligiari
- Basilica di San Zeno Maggiore
- Chiesa di Sant'Anastasia
- Arena
- Casa di Giuletta
- Castelvecchio
- Piazza delle Erbe
- Piazza dei Signori

Bologna
- Museo Civico Archeologico
- Museo Civico Medievale e del Rinascimento
- Pinacoteca Nazionale
- Basilica di San Petronio
- Piazzale Maggiore e del Nettuno
- Torre Pendenti

Venézia (Venice)
- Ca d'Oro
- Collezione Peggy Guggenheim
- Galleria dell'Accademia
- Museo Correr
- Museo Diocesano
- Museo Vitrario di Murano
- Basilica di San Marco
- Chiesa di Santa Maria della Salute
- Chiesa di Santa Maria Gloriosa dei Frari
- Chiesa di San Zaccaria
- Palazzo Ducale
- Scuola di San Giorgio degli Schiavoni
- Scuola di San Rocco
- Villa Fóscari (at Malcontenta)
- Canal Grande
- Museo Storico Navale
- Ponte di Rialto
- Ponte dei Sospiri (Bridge of Sighs)
- Arsenale
- Burano
- Ghetto
- Murano
- Piazza San Marco

Firenze (Florence)
- Galleria degli Uffizi
- Galleria dell'Accademia
- Museo Archeologico
- Museo dell'Opera del Duomo
- Museo di Storia della Scienza
- Palazzo e Museo Nazionale del Bargello
- Palazzo Medici-Riccardi
- Palazzo Pitti
- Chiesa di San Lorenzo
- Chiesa di Santa Croce
- Chiesa di Santa Maria del Carmine
- Chiesa di Santa Maria Novella
- Chiesa di Santo Spirito
- Piazza del Duomo
- Giardino di Boboli
- Orsanmichele
- Palazzo Vecchio
- Ponte Vecchio

Génova (Genoa)
- Galleria Nazionale di Palazzo Spinola
- Museo di Arte Orientale
- Palazzo Bianco
- Palazzo Rosso
- Cattedrale di San Lorenzo
- Casa Mazzini
- Acquario di Génova
- Centro Storico
- Gran Bigo
- Lanterna

Roma (Rome) & **Vatican City**
- Luneur
- Galleria Borghese
- Galleria Doria Pamphili
- Museo Capitolino
- Museo del Palazzo dei Conservatori
- Museo Nazionale di Villa Giulia
- Museo Nazionale Romano
- Musei Vaticani e Cappella Sistina
- Palazzo Barberini
- Basilica di San Giovanni in Laterano
- Basilica di San Paolo Fuori le Mura
- Basilica di San Pietro
- Chiesa del Gesù
- Chiesa di Santa Maria Maggiore
- Chiesa di Santa Maria della Vittoria
- Giardini Vaticani
- Castel Sant'Angelo
- Colosseo
- Keats-Shelley Memorial House
- Pantheon
- Fontana di Trevi
- Campidoglio
- Catacombe
- Fori Imperiali
- Foro Romano
- Palatino
- Piazza Navona
- Piazza del Popolo
- Piazza di San Pietro
- Piazza del Spagna & Spanish Steps
- Terme di Caracalla

Nápoli (Naples)
- Edenlandia
- Museo Archeologico Nazionale
- Palazzo e Galleria Nazionale di Capodimonte
- Certosa di San Martino
- Castel Nuovo
- Catacombe di San Gennaro
- Porto di Santa Lucia

Aosta: Isole Borromee
VALLE D'AOSTA
Funivie Mont-Blanc
Parco Nazionale del Gran Paradiso
Sacri Monti
Parco Naz. della Val Grande
Tremezzo: Villa Carlotta
Bellágio: Villa Serbelloni, Villa Melzi
Villa Táranto
Varallo
Lago Maggiore
Como: Duomo
Lago di Como
LOMBARDIA (LOMBARDY)
Sondrio
Val Camónica
Monza
Bérgamo: Accademia Carrara, Città Alta
Novara
Vercelli: Basilica di Sant'Andrea
Certosa di Pavia
Pavia
Venaria Reale
Sacra di San Michele
Torino (Turin)
Abbazia di Vezzolano
Cremona: Piazza del Commune
Piacenza: Palazzo del Commune
Alessándria
PIEMONTE (PIEDMONT)
Cuneo
Génova (Genoa)
LIGURIA
Savona
Parco Naturale di Portofino
Albenga: Cattedrale
San Remo
La Spézia
Cinque Terre
Merano (Meran): Passeggiate
Bressanone (Brixen): Abbazia di Novacella, Plose
Bolzano (Bozen)
Parco Nazionale Dello Stelvio
TRENTINO-SÜDTIROL
Trento
Cortina: Tofana di Mezzo, Tondi di Faloria
FRIULI-VENÉZIA GIULIA
Údine: Piazza della Libertà
Cividale del Friuli: Museo Archeologico Nazionale, Tempietto
Pordenone
VÉNETO
Trieste: Castello di Miramare, Colle di San Giusto, Piazza dell'Unità d'Italia
Aquiléia: Museo Archeologico, Basilica
Treviso
Vicenza: La Rotonda, Piazza dei Signori
Lago di Garda
Gardaland
Verona
Venézia (Venice)
Riviera del Brenta
Mantova (Mantua): Palazzo Ducale, Palazzo Tè
Pádova (Padua): Basilica di Sant'Antonio, Capella degli Scrovegni, Chiesa degli Eremitani, Villa Pisani, Strà, Orto Botanico
Parma: Galleria Nazionale, Centro Episcopale
Réggio nell'Emília
Módena: Galleria Estense, Duomo
Ferrara: Duomo, Palazzo dei Diamanti
Abbazia di Pomposa
Bologna
ÉMILIA-ROMAGNA
Ravenna: Basilica di Sant'Apollinare in Classe, Basilica di San Vitale, Mausoleo di Galla Placidia, Domus dei Tappeti di Pietra
Mirabilandia
Forlì
Rímini: Fiabilandia
SAN MARINO: Rocca Gualta
San Leo: Forte
Úrbino: Galleria Nazionale delle Marche, Palazzo Ducale
Gúbbio: Palazzo dei Consoli, Città Vecchia
Ancona: Conero Riviera
MARCHE
Loreto: Santuario della Santa Casa
Pistoia: Piazza del Duomo
Prato: Duomo
Lucca: Museo Nazionale Guinigi, Chiesa di San Michele in Foro, Duomo
Firenze (Florence)
Pisa: Museo Nazionale di San Matteo, Campo dei Miracoli, Chiesa di Santa Maria della Spina
Livorno (Leghorn)
TOSCANA (TUSCANY)
Arezzo: Chiesa di San Francisco
Volterra: Piazza dei Priori
San Gimignano: Piazza della Cisterna, Piazza del Duomo
Í. DI CAPRÁIA
Siena: Ospedale di Santa Maria della Scala, Pinacoteca, Duomo, Palazzo Pubblico, Piazza del Campo
ÍSOLA D'ELBA: Monte Capanne
Í. PIANOSA
Massa Maríttima: Piazza Garibaldi
Grosseto
Abbazia di Monte Oliveto Maggiore
Í. DEL GIGLIO
Í. DI MONTECRISTO
Cortona: Piazza del Duomo
Pienza
Montepulciano: Madonna di San Biagio
Piazza Grande
Parco Nazionale dei Monti Sibillini
Tolentino: Basilica di San Nicola
Perúgia: Galleria Nazionale dell'Umbria, Museo Archeologico Nazionale dell'Umbria, Chiesa di San Pietro, Piazza 4 Novembre
Assisi: Basilica di San Francesco, Chiesa di Santa Chiara, Eremo delle Carceri, Rocca Maggiore
Áscoli Piceno: Piazza del Popolo
Orvieto: Duomo
Todi: Piazza del Popolo
UMBRIA
Parco dei Mostri
Parco Nazionale del Gran Sasso
L'Áquila: Basilica di San Bernadino, Fontane delle 99 Cannelle
Tarquínia: Necropoli Etrusca
Villa Farnese
Cervéteri: Necropoli della Banditacaccia
LAZIO
Civitavécchia
VATICAN CITY
ROMA (ROME)
Ostia Antica
Tívoli: Villa Adriana, Villa d'Este
Castelli Romani
Abbazia di San Clemente a Casauria
ABRUZZO
Parco Nazionale della Maiella
Parco Nazionale d'Abruzzo
ÍSOLE TRÉMITI
Vieste
Parco Nazionale del Gargano
Monte Sant'Angelo: Santuario di San Michele
MOLISE
Campobasso
Abbazia di Casamari
Abbazia di Fossanova
Abbazia di Montecassino
Parco Nazionale del Circeo
Fóggia
Trani: Cattedrale
Bari: Basilica di San Nicola
Benevento: Museo Sannio, Arco di Traiano
Castel del Monte
Caserta: La Reggia
CAMPANIA
PUGLIA
Grotte di Castellana
Alberobello: Trulli
Bríndisi
ÍSOLE PONZIANE
Nápoli (Naples)
Vesuvio
Ísola d'Ischia
Pompeii
Ercolano: Herculaneum
Sorrento
Ísola di Capri
Salerno: Duomo
Paestum
Potenza
Matera: Sassi
BASILICATA
Táranto: Museo Nazionale
Lecce: Museo Sigismundo Castromediano, Basilica di Santa Croce, Piazza del Duomo
Amalfi: Grotta dello Smeraldo, Costiera Amalfitana
Ravello: Villa Cimbrone, Villa Rufolo
Maratea
CALÁBRIA
Cosenza: La Sila
Parco Nazionale della Calábria
Crotone
Lamézia
Catanzaro
Strómboli
ÍSOLE EÓLIE (LÍPARI)
Í. DI ÚSTICA
Aspromonte
Messina
Réggio di Calábria: Museo Nazionale
ARCIPÉLAGO DE LA MADDALENA
Í. ASINARA
Costa Smeralda
Porto Tórres
Ólbia
Sassari
Santissima Trinità di Saccargia
Alghero
Grotta di Nettuno
Nuoro: Museo Etnografico
SARDEGNA (SARDINIA)
Oristano
Su Nuraxi du Barúmini
Cágliari: Museo Nazionale Archeologico
Strada di Muravera
Í. DI SAN PIETRO
Í. DI SANT'ANTIOCO
Palermo: Museo Archeologico Regionale, Museo Etnografico Pitrè, La Martorana, Palazzo dei Normanni
ÍSOLE EGADI
Monreale: Duomo
Trápani
Segesta
Cefalù: Cattedrale
SICILIA (SICILY)
Enna: Castello di Lombardia
Taormina: Teatro Greco
Monte Etna
Caltanissetta
Catánia
Militello in Val di Catánia
Late Baroque towns of the Val di Noto
Agrigento: Valli dei Templi
Caltagirone
Palazzolo
Siracusa (Syracuse): Museo Archeologico Regionale, Zona Archeologica
Ragusa
Noto
Scicli
Módica
Í. DI PANTELLERIA

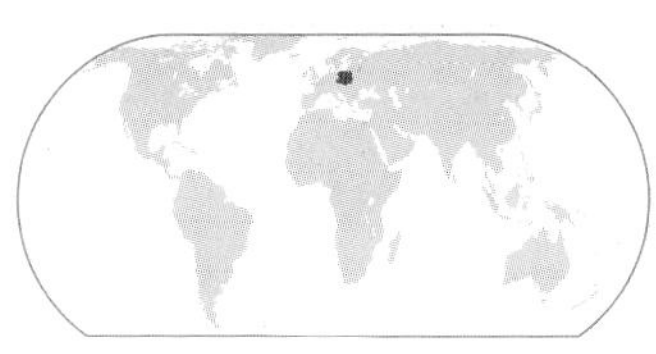

▶ *See also...* Contents (2-7) – these countries feature in many thematic and regional maps throughout the *World Travel Atlas*.

A B C
1 2 3 4 5

12° E 16° E 20° E 24° E
54° N 52° N 50° N 48° N

DENMARK
Baltic Sea
RUSSIAN FEDERATION
LITHUANIA
BELARUS
GERMANY
POLAND
CZECH REPUBLIC
SLOVAK REPUBLIC
AUSTRIA
HUNGARY
UKRAINE
ROMANIA

POMERANIA
MAZURIA
SILESIA
BOHEMIA
MORAVIA
Carpathians
Sudety
Krušné Hory
Šumava
Tatry

Sassnitz
Stralsund
RÜGEN
Pomeranian Bay
USEDOM
WOLIN
Rostock
Kołobrzeg
Świnoujście
Wolin
Schwerin
Płoty
SZZ
Goleniów
Szczecin (Stettin)
Stargard Szczeciński
Chojna
Barlinek
Myślibórz
Gorzów Wielkopolski
BERLIN
Kostrzyn
Słubice
Potsdam
Magdeburg
Halle
Cottbus
Leipzig
Dresden
Zwickau
Chemnitz
Elbe
Odra (Oder)
Nysa Łużycka
Łeba
Władysławowo
Gulf of Gdańsk
Ustka
Słupsk
Lębork
Gdynia
Sopot
Gdańsk
GDN
Tczew
Koszalin
Bytów
Miastko
Starogard Gdański
Malbork
Elbląg
Braniewo
Kaliningrad
Bartoszyce
Kętrzyn
Giżycko
Suwałki
Biskupiec
Ełk
Augustów
Olsztyn
Ostróda
Iława
Pisz
Grajewo
Hrodna
Olsztynek
Nidzica
Łomża
Ostrołęka
Zambrów
Białystok
Bielsk Podlaski
Kaunas
Nemunas
Szczecinek
Człuchów
Kalisz Pomorski
Jastrowie
Chełmno
Grudziądz
Wisła (Vistula)
Piła
Bydgoszcz
Toruń
Rypin
Narew
Ciechanów
Pułtusk
Noteć
Krzyż
Inowrocław
Włocławek
Płońsk
Wyszków
Płock
Warta
Oborniki
Gniezno
Poznań
POZ
Września
Kutno
Sochaczew
WARSZAWA (WARSAW)
WAW
Bug
Siedlce
Brest
Świebodzin
Konin
Łowicz
Skierniewice
Garwolin
Biała Podlaska
Zielona Góra
Jarocin
Prosna
Zgierz
Łódź
Grójec
Radzyń Podlaski
Leszno
Kalisz
Ryki
Żary
Ostrów Wielkopolski
Głogów
Tomaszów Mazowiecki
Włodawa
Sieradz
Zduńska Wola
Puławy
Rawicz
Bolesławiec
Kępno
Piotrków Trybunalski
Radom
Lublin
Chełm
Legnica
Zgorzelec
Oleśnica
WRO
Wrocław
Wieluń
Starachowice
Děčín
Śnieżka 1602m
Jelenia Góra
Brzeg
Kluczbork
Kielce
Kraśnik
Teplice
Liberec
Wałbrzych
Częstochowa
Opatów
Zamość
Most
Ústí nad Labem
Litoměřice
Opole
Lubliniec
Jędrzejów
Stalowa Wola
Chomutov
Jičín
Náchod
Nysa
Kędzierzyn-Koźle
KTW
Bytom
Zawiercie
Tarnobrzeg
Karlovy Vary
Kladno
Mladá Boleslav
Hradec Králové
Kłodzko
Zabrze
Chorzów
Sosnowiec
San
Cheb
PRG
PRAHA (PRAGUE)
Gliwice
Rybnik
Katowice
KRK
Kraków (Cracow)
Rzeszów
Jarosław
L'viv (L'vov)
Beroun
Pardubice
Wodzisław Śląski
Tychy
Jastrzębie-Zdrój
Tarnów
Plzeň
Benešov
Litomyšl
Opava
Ostrava
Przemyśl
Příbram
Vltava
Svitavy
Havlíčkův Brod
Olomouc
Bielsko-Biała
Frýdek-Místek
Jasło
Krosno
Klatovy
Hranice
Żywiec
Nowy Sącz
Sanok
Rabka
Gorlice
Lesko
Písek
Tábor
Jihlava
Prostějov
Přerov
Zakopane
Nowy Targ
Ustrzyki Dolne
Strakonice
Třebíč
Brno
Zlín
Žilina
Gerlachovský štít 2666m
Bardejov
Svidník
BRQ
Jindřichův Hradec
Bučovice
Uherské Hradiště
Martin
Ružomberok
Levoča
Regensburg
České Budějovice
Poprad
Prešov
Nová Ves
Trenčín
Břeclav
Prievidza
Banská Bystrica
KSC
Košice
Michalovce
Piešťany
Zvolen
Rožňava
Uzhhorod
Morava
Váh
Trnava
Rimavská Sobota
Linz
Donau (Danube)
Pezinok
WIEN (VIENNA)
Senec
Nitra
Lučenec
BTS
BRATISLAVA
Šala
Levice
Ipeľ
Tisza
Salzburg
Dunaj (Danube)
Miskolc
Nyíregyháza
Satu Mare
Komárno
Győr

200 kilometres
100 miles

Lambert Equal Area Projection

D E F G
6 7 8 9

BOHEMIA
Dresden
POLAND
Jelenia Góra
Zwickau
Chemnitz
ČESKÉ ŠVÝCARSKO (BOHEMIAN SWITZERLAND)
Děčín
Liberec
Sněžka 1602m
KRUŠNÉ HORY
Teplice
Ústí nad Labem
Plauen
Klínovec 1244m
Most
Chomutov
Litoměřice
Mělník
Mladá Boleslav
Jáchymov
Karlovy Vary (Karlsbad)
Žatec
CZECH
Kladno
PRAHA (PRAGUE)
Kolín
Hradec Králové
Františkovy Lázně
Cheb
Sokolov
Křivoklát
Karlštejn
Kutná Hora
Pardubice
Mariánské Lázně (Marienbad)
Plasy
Beroun
Benešov
Konopiště
Čáslav
Lichnice
Rokycany
Hořovice
Český Šternberk
Plzeň
Příbram
REPUBLIC
Havlíčkův Brod
Kladruby
Přibyslav
ČESKÝ LES
Orlík
Zvíkov
Milevsko
Chýnovská jeskyně
Kaliště
Lipnice nad Sázavou
Domažlice
Blatná
Švihov
Klatovy
Tábor
Kámen
Pelhřimov
Jihlava
GERMANY
Cham
Sušice
Rabí
Strakonice
Písek
Bechyně
Červená Lhota
Telč
Třebíč
Kratochvíle
Hluboká
Jindřichův Hradec
Regensburg
Vimperk
Prachatice
Třeboň
Slavonice
SUMAVA NAT. PARK
České Budějovice
Straubing
Deggendorf
Holašovice
Volary
Zlatá Koruna
Raabs
Znojmo
Plechý 1378m
Český Krumlov
Gmünd
Retz
Rožmberk
Passau
Vyšší Brod
AUSTRIA
Krems an der Donau
Freistadt
1 KLV Karlovy Vary (Karlsbad); 2 PRG Praha (Prague) Ruzyne
100 kilometres
50 miles

CENTRAL SOUTHERN POLAND
ŚWIĘTOKRZYSKI NAT. PARK
Częstochowa
Kielce
Olsztyn
Zamek Krzyżtopór
Lubliniec
Jędrzejów
Jura Krakowska
Myszków
Staszów
Tarnowskie Góry
Zawiercie
POLAND
Piekary Śląskie
Busko-Zdrój
Kędzierzyn-Koźle
Zamek Bonerów
Działoszyce
Zabrze
Bytom
Dąbrowa Górnicza
Wiślica
Gliwice
Chorzów
Miechów
Ruda Śląska
Sosnowiec
Olkusz
Pieskowa Skała
Katowice
Jaworzno
OJCOWSKI NAT. PARK
Rybnik
Tychy
Chrzanów
Racibórz
Wodzisław Śląski
Auschwitz-Birkenau
Oświęcim (Auschwitz)
Kraków (Cracow)
Jastrzębie Zdrój
Bochnia
Tarnów
Skawina
Wieliczka
Zamek Lubomirskich
Czechowice-Dziedzice
Wadowice
Kalwaria Zebrzydowska
Nowy Wiśnicz
Ostrava
Karviná
Bielsko-Biała
Myślenice
Havířov
Cieszyn
CARPATHIANS
Kościół drewniany
Frýdek-Místek
Český Těšín
Żywiec
Nowy Sącz
ŚLĄSKI BESKIDY ZACHODNIE
Gorlice
CZECH REPUBLIC
Wisła
Rabka-Zdrój
Szymbark
BABIOGÓRSKI NAT. PARK
Stary Sącz
GORCZAŃSKI NAT. PK.
PIENIŃSKI NAT. PARK
Nowy Targ
Szczawnica
Krynica
Čadca
PODHALE
SLOVAK
TATRZAŃSKI NAT. PARK
VYSOKÉ TATRY NAT. PARK
Bardejov
Zakopane
Bytča
MALÁ FATRA NAT. PK.
TATRY (TATRA)
Rysy 2499m
Gerlachovský štít 2666m
1 KTW Katowice; 2 KRK Kraków (Cracow) John Paul II Balice
Žilina
Dolný Kubín
Považská Bystrica
Martin
Ružomberok
REPUBLIC
60 km
30 miles

1000 metres
500 metres
Sea level

The Alps

See also... Europe Winter Sports (69); Germany (82-85); France (86-89); Italy (95-98); Central Europe: South (102)

The listings above refer to a selection of related themes. For more information, see the Contents (2-7).

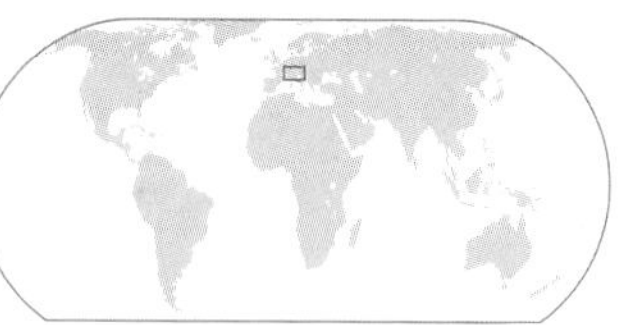

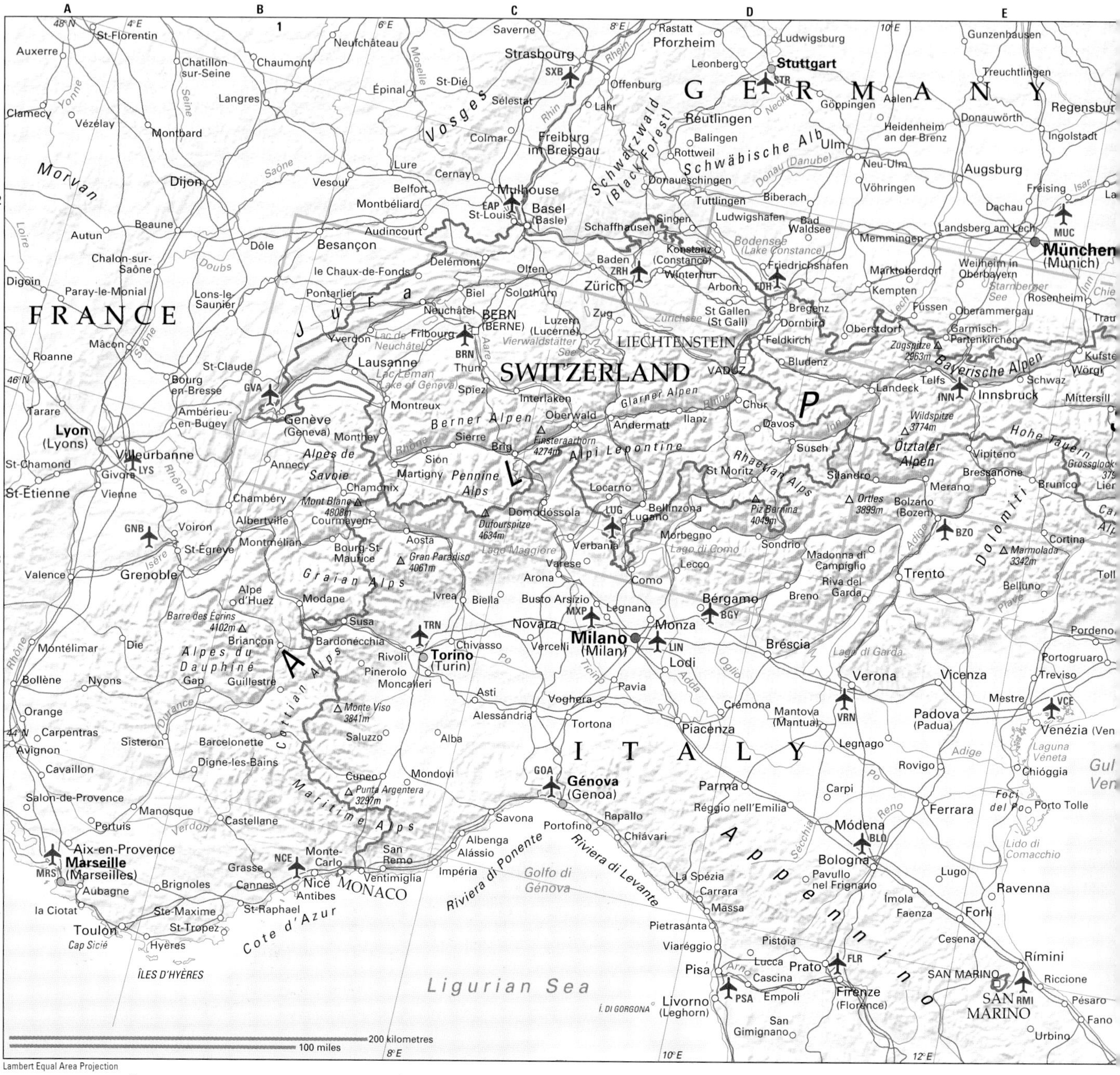

FRANCE · SWITZERLAND · GERMANY · ITALY · LIECHTENSTEIN · MONACO · SAN MARINO · ALPS

Ligurian Sea

200 kilometres
100 miles

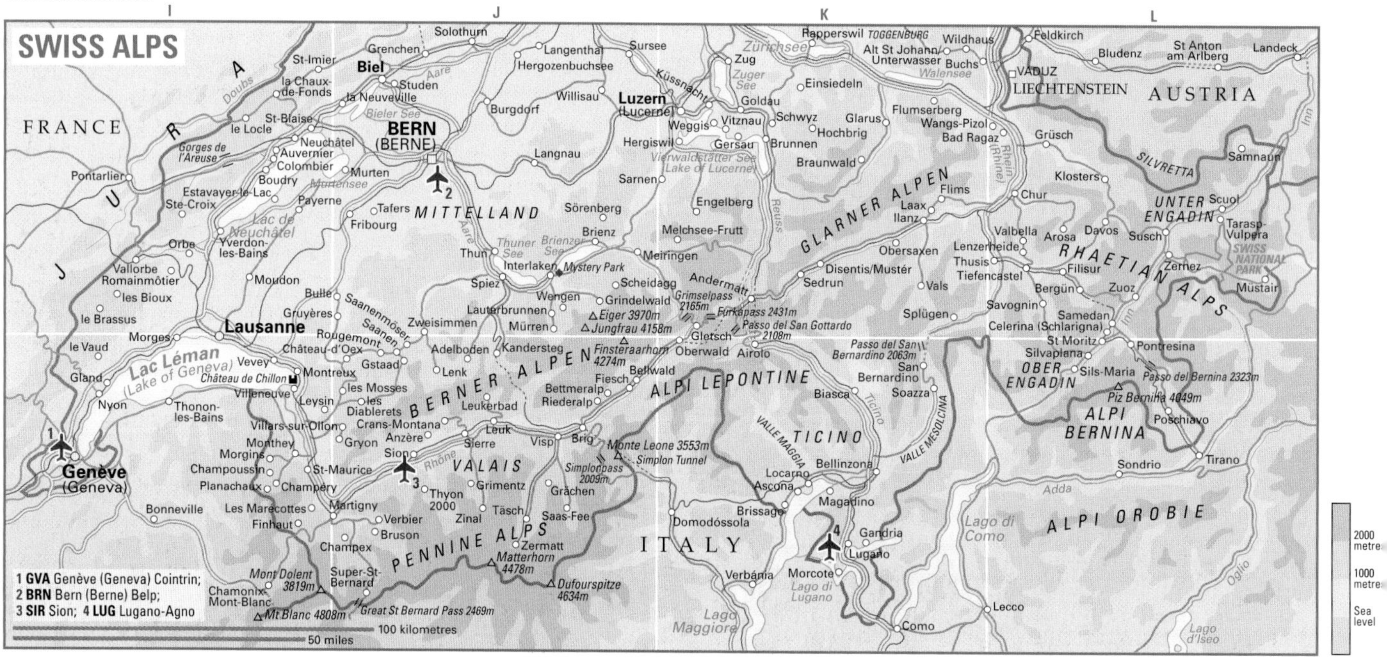

Lambert Equal Area Projection

SWISS ALPS

FRANCE · ITALY · AUSTRIA · LIECHTENSTEIN · JURA · MITTELLAND · BERNER ALPEN · GLARNER ALPEN · ALPI LEPONTINE · PENNINE ALPS · RHAETIAN ALPS · ALPI BERNINA · ALPI OROBIE · TICINO · VALAIS

1 **GVA** Genève (Geneva) Cointrin;
2 **BRN** Bern (Berne) Belp;
3 **SIR** Sion; 4 **LUG** Lugano-Agno

100 kilometres
50 miles

2000 metres
1000 metres
Sea level

See also... Europe Winter Sports (69); Germany (82-85); France (86-89); Italy (95-98); Central Europe: South (102)

The listings above refer to a selection of related themes. For more information, see the Contents (2-7).

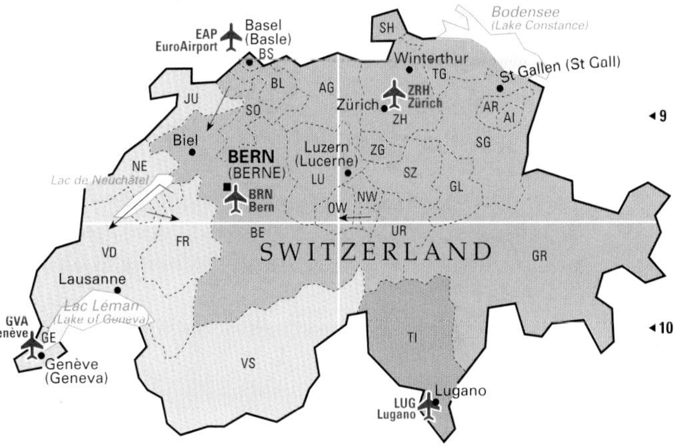

CZECH REPUBLIC
Bohemian Forest
Cham
Strakonice
Písek
Tábor
Vltava
Jindřichuv Hradec
Olomouc
Třebíč
Brno
BRQ
Prachatice
České Budějovice
Český Krumlov
Znojmo
Regen
Deggendorf
Vilshofen
Passau
Gmünd
Dyje
Morava
Břeclav
Pocking
Braunau am Inn
Freistadt
Krems an der Donau
Hollabrunn
Mistelbach
Linz
LNZ
Tulln
WIEN (VIENNA)
SLOVAK REP.
Malacky
Trnava
Vöcklabruck
Wels
Melk
Donau (Danube)
Gmunden
Steyr
Amstetten
St Pölten
Pezinok
Senec
Salzburg
SZG
Traunsee
Attersee
Waidhofen an der Ybbs
Mödling
Baden
BRATISLAVA
BTS
VIE
Šamorín
Bad Ischl
Hallein
Wiener Neustadt
Neusiedler See
Mariazell
Bischofshofen
Enns
Rottenmann
Neunkirchen
Eisenstadt
Mosonmagyaróvár
48° N
AUSTRIA
Niedere Tauern
Leoben
Mürzzuschlag
Sopron
Csorna
Győr
Knittelfeld
Bruck an der Mur
Kőszeg
Pápa
St Michael im Langau
Mur
Judenburg
Raba
Szombathely
Sárvár
Köflach
Graz
GRZ
Fürstenfeld
St Veit an der Glan
Raab
Wolfsberg
Wildon
Körmend
HUNGARY
Villach
KLU
Völkermarkt
Velden
Klagenfurt
Leibnitz
Zalaegerszeg
Tapolca
Balaton
Jesenice
Pesnica
Murska Sobota
Keszthely
Fonyód
Julijske Alpe
Kranj
LJU
Maribor
Drava
LJUBLJANA
Trbovlje
Celje
Varaždin
Nagykanizsa
Kaposvár
SLOVENIA
Koprivnica
46° N
Ribnica
Novo Mesto
ZAGREB
ZAG
Sava
Poreč
Opatija
Rijeka
Karlovac
ISTRA
Sisak
Ogulin
Crikvenica
KRK
CROATIA
Bosanski Novi
CRES
Senj
RAB
Bosanska Krupa
PUY
Bihać
BOSNIA-HERZ.
PAG
Velebit
Gospić
Dinara
Adriatic Sea
Bosanski Petrovak
Gračac
Zadar
DUGI OTOK
Knin
14° E
16° E

SWITZERLAND
Bodensee (Lake Constance)
SH
EAP EuroAirport
Basel (Basle)
BS
Winterthur
TG
St Gallen (St Gall)
JU
BL
AG
ZRH Zürich
Zürich
ZH
AR
AI
SO
Biel
Luzern (Lucerne)
ZG
SG
NE
BERN (BERNE)
BRN Bern
LU
SZ
GL
Lac de Neuchâtel
NW
OW
UR
VD
FR
BE
GR
Lausanne
Lac Léman (Lake of Geneva)
GVA Genève
GE
Genève (Geneva)
TI
VS
LUG Lugano
Lugano

Cantons where the majority of the population speak:
French
German
Italian

AG	AARGAU	NW	NIDWALDEN
AI	APPENZELL-INNER RHODEN	OW	OBWALDEN
AR	APPENZELL-AUSSER RHODEN	SG	ST GALLEN
BE	BERN	SH	SCHAFFHAUSEN
BL	BASEL-LAND	SO	SOLOTHURN
BS	BASEL-STADT	SZ	SCHWYZ
FR	FRIBOURG	TG	THURGAU
GE	GENÈVE	TI	TICINO
GL	GLARUS	UR	URI
GR	GRAUBÜNDEN	VD	VAUD
JU	JURA	VS	VALAIS
LU	LUZERN	ZG	ZUG
NE	NEUCHÂTEL	ZH	ZÜRICH

International arrivals (millions) 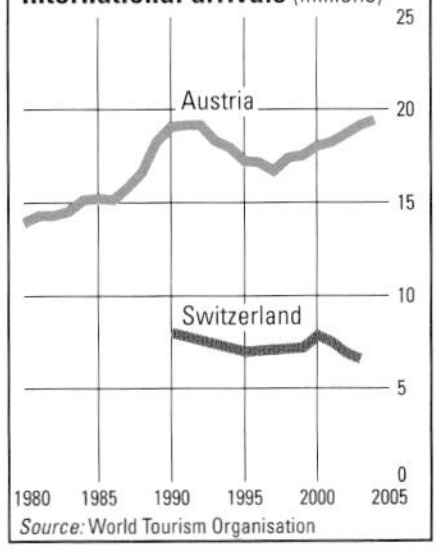
Austria
Switzerland
25
20
15
10
5
0
1980
1985
1990
1995
2000
2005
Source: World Tourism Organisation

Gmünd
Krems an der Donau
Donau (Danube)
Wachau
WIEN (VIENNA)
WIEN
LNZ Linz
Linz
St Pölten
OBERÖSTERREICH (UPPER AUSTRIA)
NIEDERÖSTERREICH (LOWER AUSTRIA)
VIE Wien
Eisenstadt
Neusiedler See
Bodensee (Lake Constance)
Salzburg
SZG Salzburg
BAYERISCHE ALPEN
Bregenz
INN Innsbruck
Innsbruck
VORARLBERG
LIECHTENSTEIN
TIROL
AUSTRIA
Bruck an der Mur
SALZBURG
NIEDERE TAUERN
STEIERMARK (STYRIA)
BURGENLAND
HOHE TAUERN
Mur
Graz
GRZ Graz
ÖTZTALER ALPEN
TIROL
KÄRNTEN (CARINTHIA)
KLU Klagenfurt
Klagenfurt
Drau
Villach
KARAWANKEN

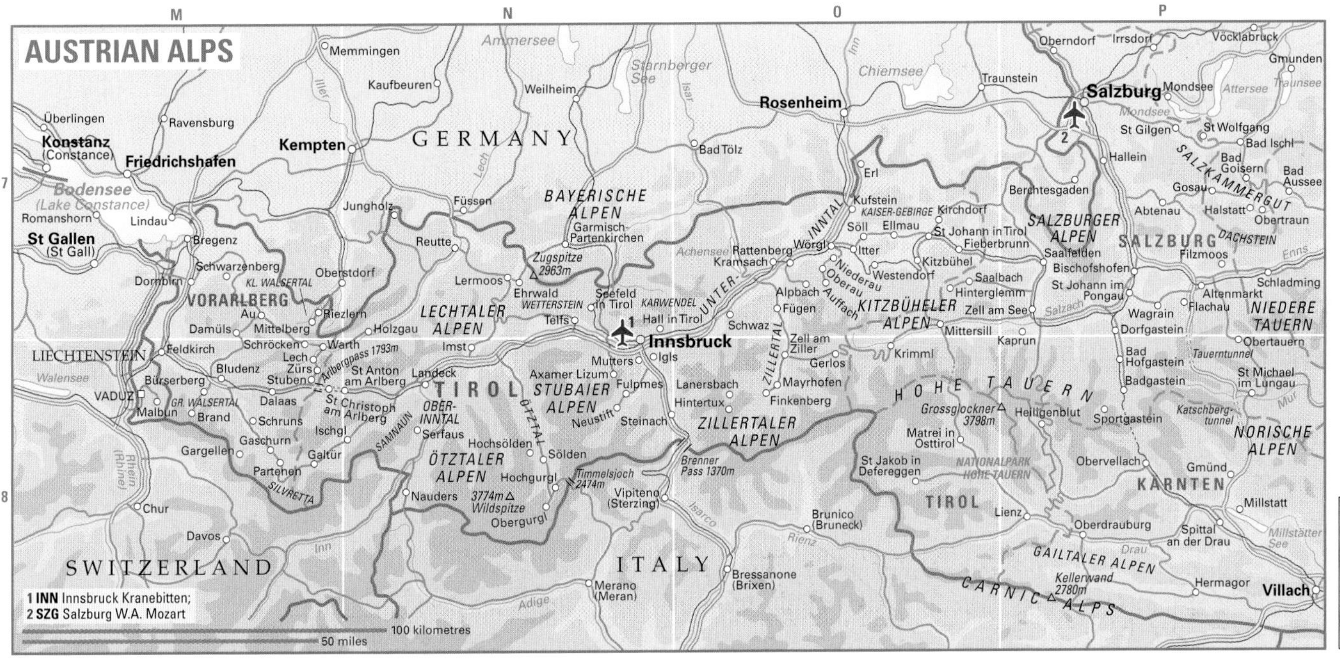
AUSTRIAN ALPS
GERMANY
Memmingen
Ammersee
Kaufbeuren
Starnberger See
Weilheim
Rosenheim
Chiemsee
Traunstein
Oberndorf
Irrsdorf
Vöcklabruck
Gmunden
Salzburg
Mondsee
Attersee
Traunsee
Überlingen
Ravensburg
Konstanz (Constance)
Friedrichshafen
Kempten
Bad Tölz
St Gilgen
St Wolfgang
Bad Ischl
Bodensee (Lake Constance)
Romanshorn
Lindau
Jungholz
Füssen
BAYERISCHE ALPEN
Garmisch-Partenkirchen
Kufstein
Erl
Berchtesgaden
Hallein
Bad Goisern
Bad Aussee
St Gallen (St Gall)
Bregenz
Reutte
Söll
Ellmau
St Johann in Tirol
Fieberbrunn
SALZBURGER ALPEN
SALZBURG
Abtenau
Halstatt
Obertraun
Gosau
DACHSTEIN
Dornbirn
Schwarzenberg
Oberstdorf
Zugspitze 2963m
Lermoos
Rattenberg
Wörgl
Kramsach
Itter
Kitzbühel
Saalfelden
Filzmoos
VORARLBERG
Riezlern
Ehrwald
Seefeld in Tirol
KARWENDEL
Saalbach
Hinterglemm
Bischofshofen
Schladming
Au
Mittelberg
LECHTALER ALPEN
WETTERSTEIN
Alpbach
Fügen
KITZBÜHELER ALPEN
Zell am See
St Johann im Pongau
Altenmarkt
Flachau
NIEDERE TAUERN
Damüls
Holzgau
Telfs
Hall in Tirol
Schwaz
Mittersill
Wagrain
Dorfgastein
LIECHTENSTEIN
Feldkirch
Schröcken
Warth
Imst
Innsbruck
Zell am Ziller
Kaprun
Obertauern
Lech
Zürs
Arlbergpass 1793m
Axamer Lizum
Mutters
Igls
Gerlos
Krimml
Bad Hofgastein
St Michael im Lungau
Walensee
Bludenz
St Anton am Arlberg
Landeck
Mayrhofen
Bürserberg
Stuben
TIROL
STUBAIER ALPEN
Fulpmes
Lanersbach
HOHE TAUERN
Badgastein
VADUZ
Malbun
Dalaas
St Christoph am Arlberg
OBER-INNTAL
Neustift
Hintertux
Finkenberg
Grossglockner 3798m
Heiligenblut
Katschberg-tunnel
Brand
Schruns
Ischgl
Serfaus
Steinach
ZILLERTALER ALPEN
Sportgastein
NORISCHE ALPEN
Gaschurn
SAMNAUN
Hochsölden
Matrei in Osttirol
Gargellen
Galtür
Sölden
ÖTZTALER ALPEN
Brenner Pass 1370m
St Jakob in Defereggen
Obervellach
Gmünd
Partenen
SILVRETTA
Hochgurgl
Timmelsjoch 2474m
NATIONALPARK HOHE TAUERN
KÄRNTEN
Rhein (Rhine)
Nauders
3774m Wildspitze
Vipiteno (Sterzing)
TIROL
Millstatt
Chur
Obergurgl
Isarco
Lienz
Oberdrauburg
Spittal an der Drau
Millstätter See
Davos
Inn
Brunico (Bruneck)
Rienz
Drau
GAILTALER ALPEN
SWITZERLAND
ITALY
Bressanone (Brixen)
Kellerwand 2780m
Hermagor
Villach
Merano (Meran)
Adige
CARNIC ALPS
1 INN Innsbruck Kranebitten;
2 SZG Salzburg W.A. Mozart
100 kilometres
50 miles
2000 metres
1000 metres
Sea level

See also... Contents (2-7) – these countries feature in many thematic and regional maps throughout the *World Travel Atlas*.

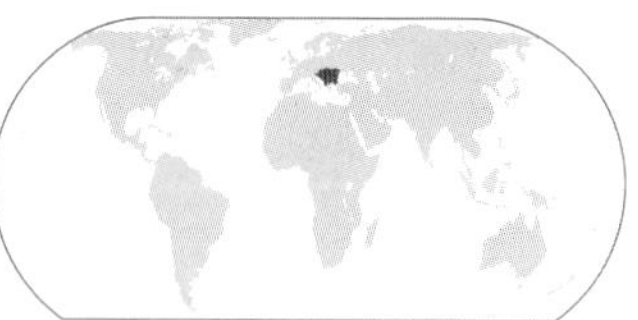

Coverage of Croatia continues on previous page

300 kilometres
150 miles

Lambert Equal Area Projection

SLOVENIA AND THE CROATIAN COAST
1 LJU Ljubljana Brnik; 2 ZAG Zagreb Pleso;
3 PUY Pula; 4 ZAD Zadar; 5 SPU Split;
6 DBV Dubrovnik; 7 SJJ Sarajevo Butmir
100 kilometres
50 miles

ROMANIAN AND BULGARIAN COAST
1 OTP Bucharest Otopeni;
2 BBU Bucharest Baneasa;
3 CND Constanta Mihail Kogalniceanu;
4 VAR Varna; 5 BOJ Burgas
200 kilometres
100 miles
1000 metres
500 metres
Sea level

For more information, see the Contents (2-7).

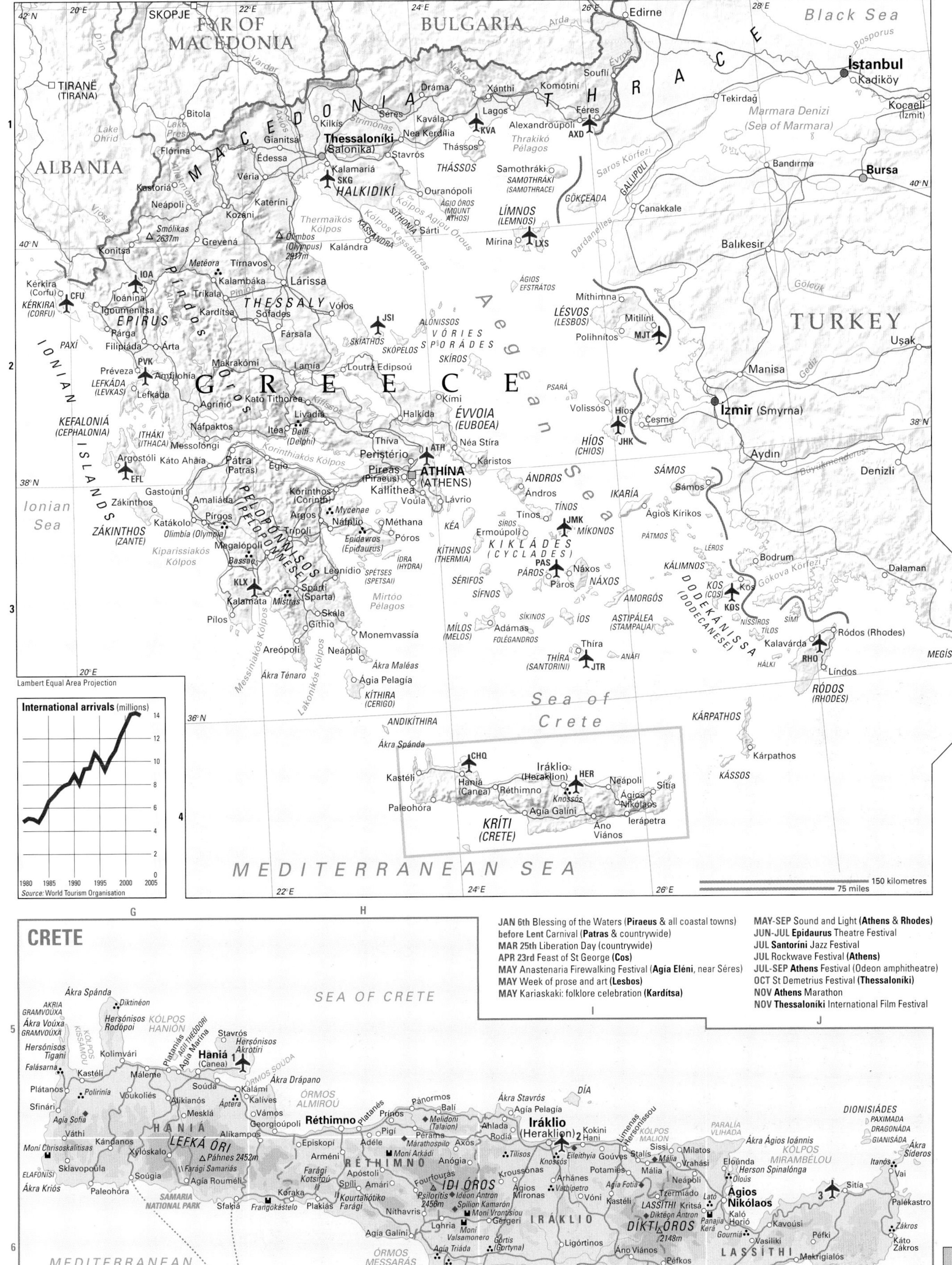

BULGARIA
FYR OF MACEDONIA
SKOPJE
ALBANIA
TIRANË (TIRANA)
TURKEY
GREECE
MACEDONIA
THRACE
THESSALY
EPIRUS
Black Sea
Aegean Sea
Ionian Sea
Sea of Crete
MEDITERRANEAN SEA
IONIAN ISLANDS
Edirne
İstanbul
Kadiköy
Kocaeli (İzmit)
Tekirdağ
Marmara Denizi (Sea of Marmara)
Bandırma
Bursa
Çanakkale
Balıkesir
Manisa
İzmir (Smyrna)
Çeşme
Aydın
Denizli
Uşak
Bodrum
Dalaman
Bitola
Flórina
Kastoriá
Neápoli
Kónitsa
Ioánina
Igoumenítsa
Párga
Filipiáda
Árta
Préveza
Lefkáda
Agrínio
Messolóngi
Náfpaktos
Kato Ahaïa
Pátra (Patras)
Égio
Gastoúni
Amaliáda
Pírgos
Katákolo
Olimbía (Olympia)
Megalópoli
Kalamáta
Pílos
Areópoli
Ákra Ténaro
Spárti (Sparta)
Mistrás
Skála
Gíthio
Monemvassía
Neápoli
Ákra Maléas
Ágia Pelagía
KÍTHIRA (CERIGO)
ANDIKÍTHIRA
Trípoli
Árgos
Náfplio
Mycenae
Kórinthos (Corinth)
Epídavros (Epidaurus)
Méthana
Póros
Leonídio
Athína (Athens)
Pireás (Piraeus)
Peristério
Kallithea
Voúla
Lávrio
Thíva
Halkída
Livadiá
Delfí (Delphi)
Itéa
Lamía
Loutrá Edipsoú
Kími
ÉVVOIA (EUBOEA)
Néa Stíra
Káristos
Lárissa
Vólos
Kalambáka
Metéora
Tríkala
Kardítsa
Sofádes
Fársala
Tírnavos
Grevená
Kozáni
Kateríni
Véria
Édessa
Gianitsá
Kilkís
Thessaloníki (Salonika)
Kalamariá
Stavrós
Sérres
Dráma
Kavála
Xánthi
Komotiní
Alexandroúpoli
Féres
Soufli
Néa Kerdília
Ouranópoli
Kalándra
Sárti
HALKIDIKÍ
THÁSSOS
Thássos
SAMOTHRÁKI (SAMOTHRACE)
Samothráki
GÖKÇEADA
LÍMNOS (LEMNOS)
Mírina
ÁGIOS EFSTRÁTIOS
LÉSVOS (LESBOS)
Míthimna
Mitilíni
Polihnítos
PSARÁ
HÍOS (CHIOS)
Híos
Volissós
SÁMOS
Sámos
IKARÍA
Ágios Kírikos
PÁTMOS
LÉROS
KÁLIMNOS
KOS (COS)
Kos
DODEKÁNISSA (DODECANESE)
NÍSSIROS
TÍLOS
SÍMI
HÁLKI
RÓDOS (RHODES)
Ródos (Rhodes)
Kalavárda
Líndos
MEGÍSTI
KÁRPATHOS
Kárpathos
KÁSSOS
ÁNDROS
Ándros
TÍNOS
Tínos
SÍROS
Ermoúpoli
MÍKONOS
KIKLÁDES (CYCLADES)
PÁROS
Páros
NÁXOS
Náxos
AMORGÓS
ÍOS
ASTIPÁLEA (STAMPALIA)
THÍRA (SANTORINI)
Thíra
ANÁFI
SÍKINOS
FOLÉGANDROS
MÍLOS (MELOS)
Adámas
SÍFNOS
SÉRIFOS
KÍTHNOS (THERMIA)
KÉA
ÍDRA (HYDRA)
SPÉTSES (SPETSAI)
Mirtóo Pélagos
VÓRIES SPORÁDES
ALÓNISSOS
SKÍATHOS
SKÓPELOS
SKÍROS
KÉRKIRA (CORFU)
Kérkira (Corfu)
PAXÍ
LEFKÁDA (LEVKAS)
ITHÁKI (ITHACA)
KEFALONIÁ (CEPHALONIA)
Argostóli
ZÁKINTHOS (ZANTE)
Zákinthos
Kiparissiakós Kólpos
Messiniakós Kólpos
Lakonikós Kólpos
Korinthiakós Kólpos
Thermaïkós Kólpos
Thrakikó Pélagos
Saros Körfezi
Gökova Körfezi
Smólikas 2637m
Ólimbos (Olympus) 2917m
PELOPÓNNISOS (PELOPONNESE)
KRÍTI (CRETE)
Kastéli
Haniá (Canea)
Réthimno
Iráklio (Heraklion)
Knossós
Ágios Nikólaos
Sitía
Neápoli
Ierápetra
Áno Viános
Agía Galíni
Paleohóra
Ákra Spánda
Lambert Equal Area Projection
150 kilometres
75 miles
International arrivals (millions)
Source: World Tourism Organisation
CRETE
SEA OF CRETE
MEDITERRANEAN SEA
HANIÁ
RÉTHIMNO
IRÁKLIO
LASSÍTHI
LEFKÁ ÓRI
Páhnes 2452m
IDI ÓROS 2456m
DÍKTI ÓROS 2148m
SAMARIA NATIONAL PARK
GÁVDOS
GAVDOPOÚLA
DÍA
DIONISIÁDES
KOUFONÍSI
HRISSÍ
PAXIMÁDIA
ELAFONÍSI
1 CHQ Haniá (Canea);
2 HER Iráklio (Herakleion);
3 JSH Sitia
1000 metres
500 metres
Sea level
60 kilometres
30 miles

JAN 6th Blessing of the Waters (**Piraeus** & all coastal towns)
before Lent Carnival (**Patras** & countrywide)
MAR 25th Liberation Day (countrywide)
APR 23rd Feast of St George (**Cos**)
MAY Anastenaria Firewalking Festival (**Agía Eléni**, near Séres)
MAY Week of prose and art (**Lesbos**)
MAY Kariaskaki: folklore celebration (**Kardítsa**)
MAY-SEP Sound and Light (**Athens & Rhodes**)
JUN-JUL **Epidaurus** Theatre Festival
JUL **Santorini** Jazz Festival
JUL Rockwave Festival (**Athens**)
JUL-SEP **Athens** Festival (Odeon amphitheatre)
OCT St Demetrius Festival (**Thessaloníki**)
NOV **Athens** Marathon
NOV **Thessaloníki** International Film Festival

Greece

See also... Contents (2-7) – this country features in many thematic and regional maps throughout the *World Travel Atlas*.

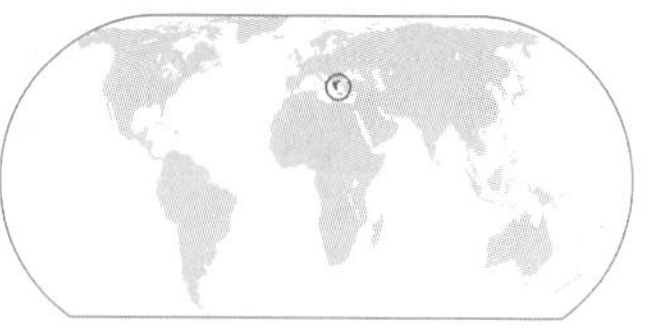

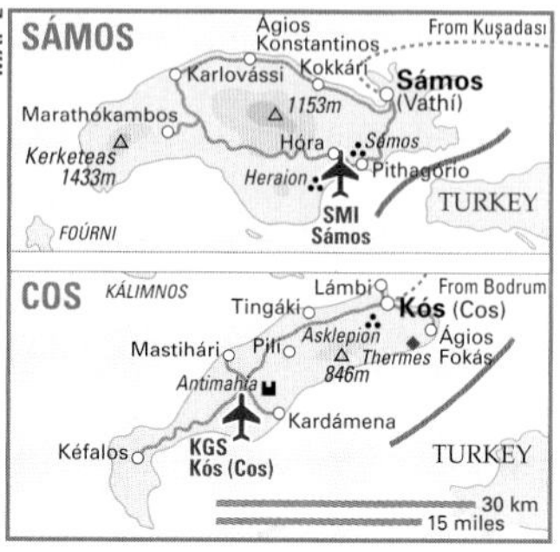

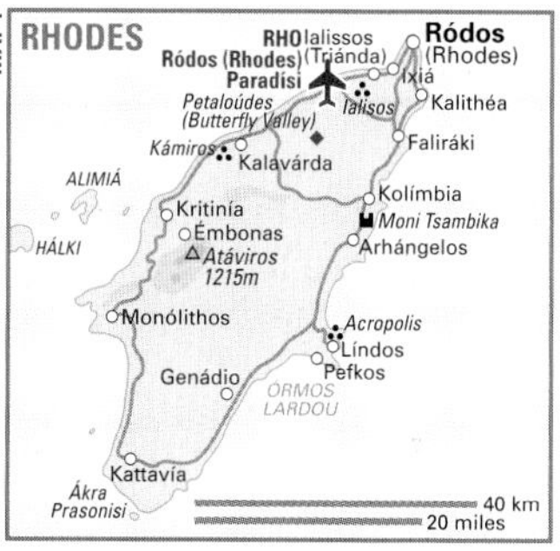

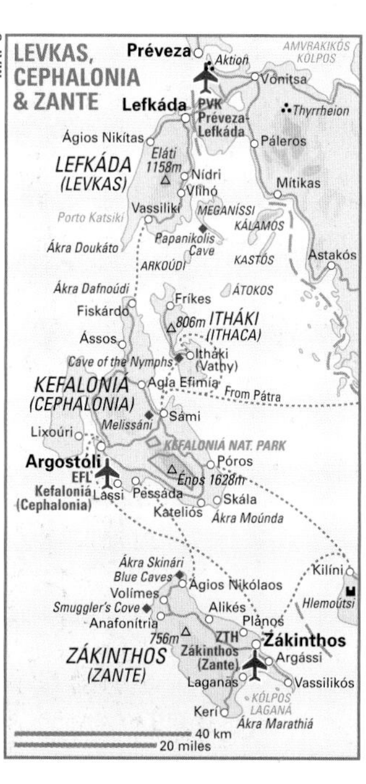

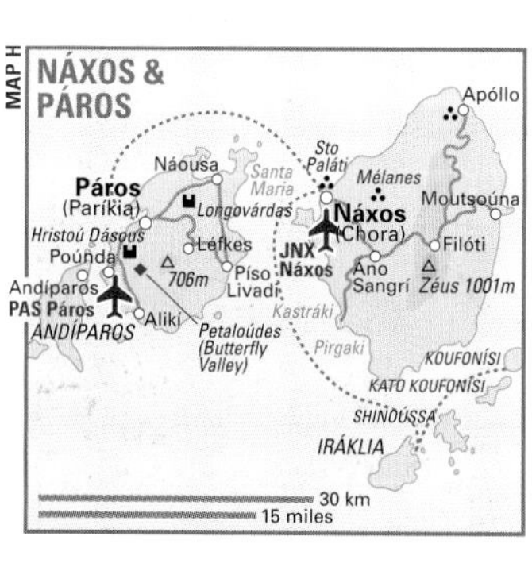

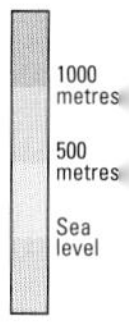

See also... Contents (2-7) – this country features in many thematic and regional maps throughout the *World Travel Atlas*.

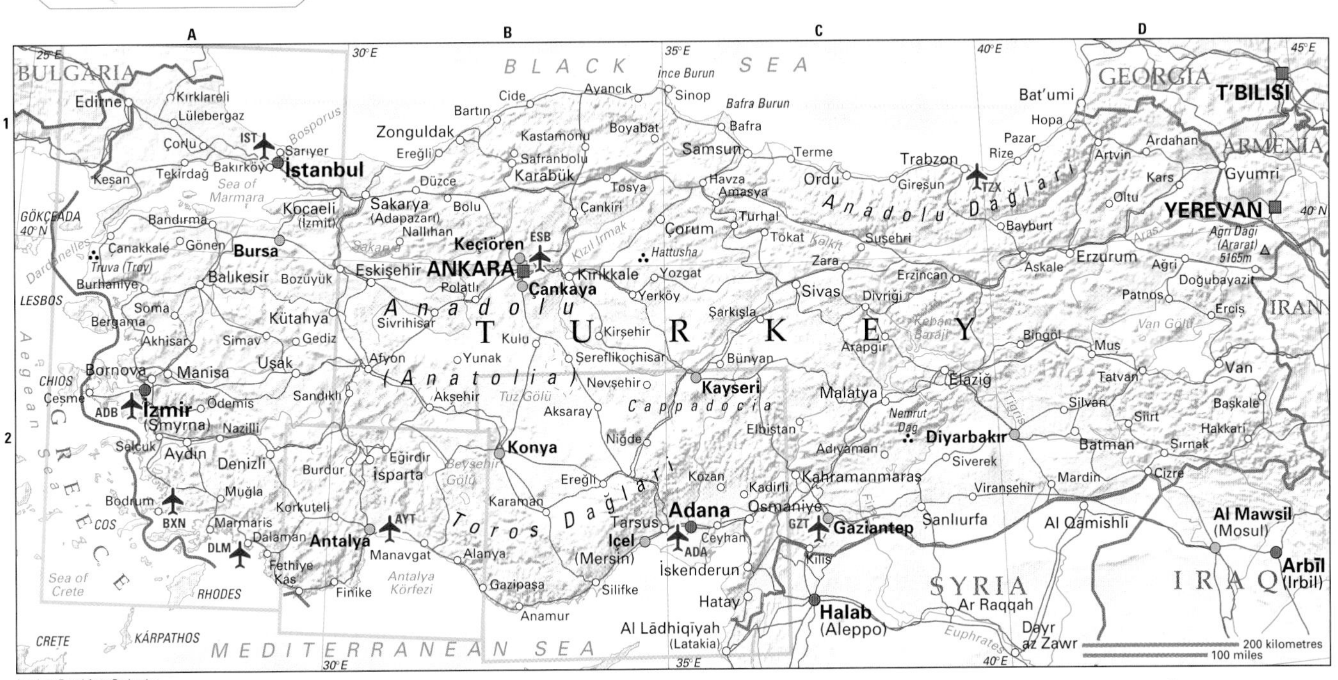
BLACK SEA
MEDITERRANEAN SEA
BULGARIA
GEORGIA
T'BILISI
ARMENIA
YEREVAN
IRAN
IRAQ
SYRIA
GREECE
TURKEY
Anadolu (Anatolia)
Anadolu Dağlari
Toros Dağlari
Cappadocia
Aegean Sea
Sea of Marmara
Sea of Crete
ANKARA
İstanbul
İzmir (Smyrna)
Bursa
Adana
Konya
Antalya
Kayseri
Gaziantep
Diyarbakır
Trabzon
Samsun
Erzurum
Eskişehir
Halab (Aleppo)
Al Mawsil (Mosul)
Arbīl (Irbil)
Al Lādhiqīyah (Latakia)
Lambert Equal Area Projection
200 kilometres
100 miles

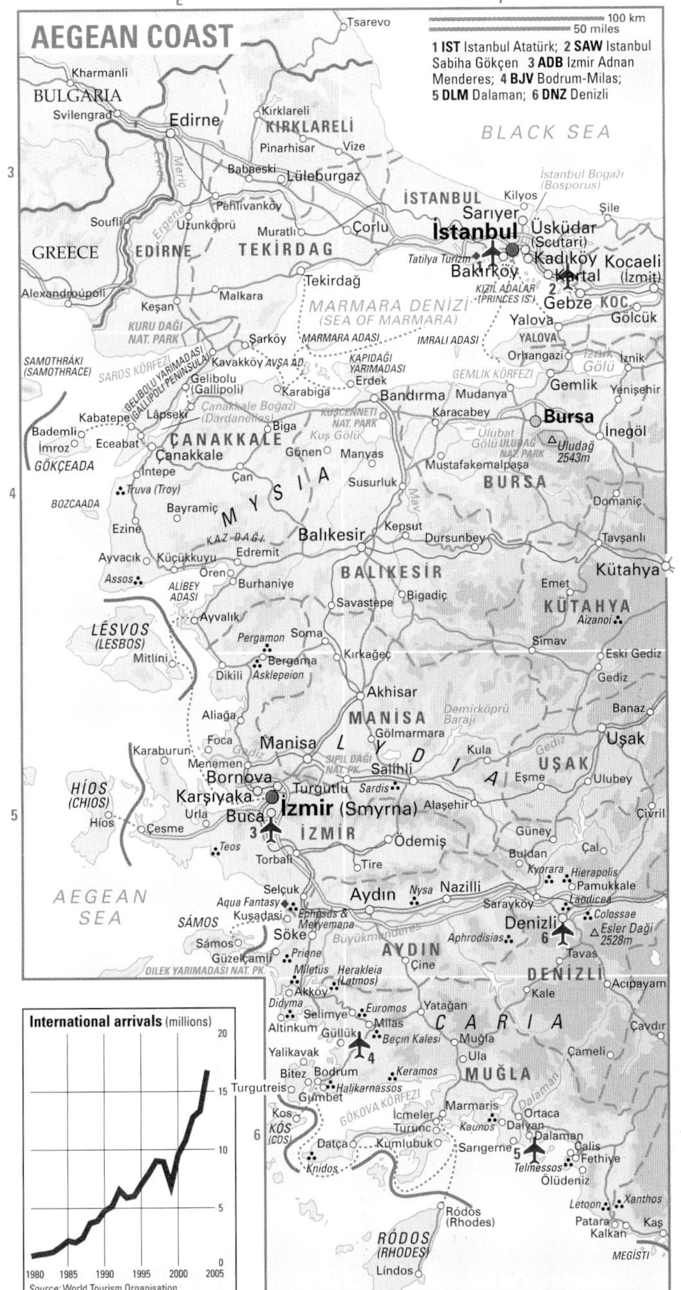
AEGEAN COAST
100 km
50 miles
1 IST Istanbul Atatürk; 2 SAW Istanbul Sabiha Gökçen 3 ADB Izmir Adnan Menderes; 4 BJV Bodrum-Milas; 5 DLM Dalaman; 6 DNZ Denizli
BLACK SEA
AEGEAN SEA
BULGARIA
GREECE
MARMARA DENİZİ (SEA OF MARMARA)
İstanbul
Edirne
Tekirdağ
Bursa
Çanakkale
Balıkesir
Kütahya
Manisa
İzmir (Smyrna)
Aydın
Denizli
Muğla
Bodrum
Marmaris
MYSIA
LYDIA
CARIA
LÉSVOS (LESBOS)
HÍOS (CHIOS)
SÁMOS
KÓS (COS)
RÓDOS (RHODES)
International arrivals (millions)
Source: World Tourism Organisation

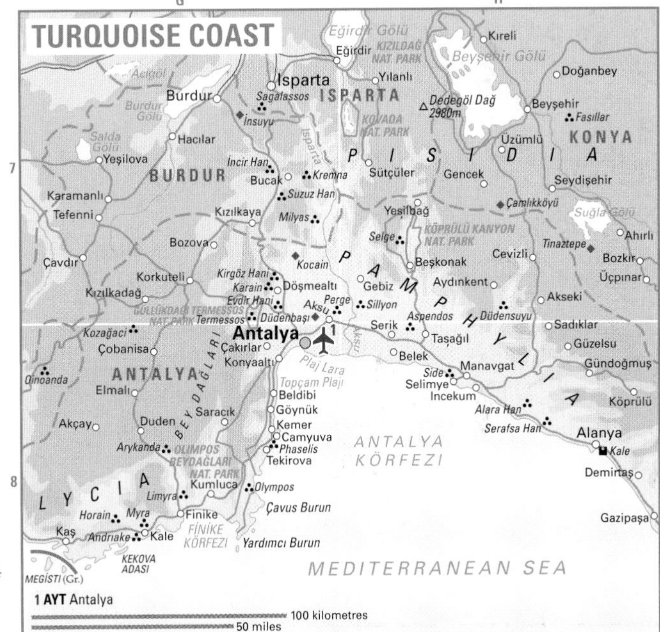
TURQUOISE COAST
Eğirdir Gölü
Beyşehir Gölü
Isparta
Burdur
ISPARTA
BURDUR
PISIDIA
PAMPHYLIA
KONYA
ANTALYA
LYCIA
Antalya
Alanya
Manavgat
Side
Aspendos
Termessos
Kaş
Kemer
Finike
ANTALYA KÖRFEZİ
MEDITERRANEAN SEA
1 AYT Antalya
100 kilometres
50 miles

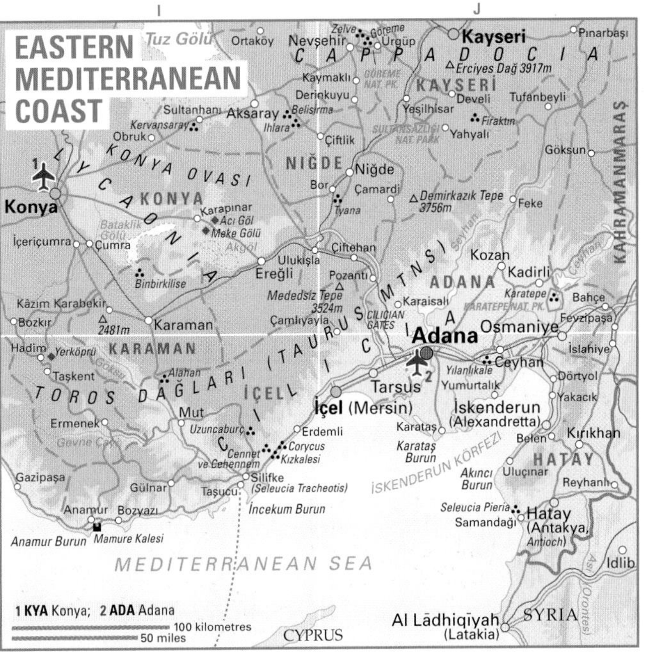
EASTERN MEDITERRANEAN COAST
Tuz Gölü
CAPPADOCIA
Kayseri
Nevşehir
Göreme
Ürgüp
Erciyes Dağ 3917m
KAYSERİ
NİĞDE
Niğde
Aksaray
KONYA
Konya
LYCAONIA
KONYA OVASI
KARAMAN
Karaman
TOROS DAĞLARI (TAURUS MTNS)
CILICIA
ADANA
Adana
İÇEL
İçel (Mersin)
Tarsus
İskenderun (Alexandretta)
HATAY
Hatay (Antakya, Antioch)
KAHRAMANMARAŞ
MEDITERRANEAN SEA
CYPRUS
SYRIA
Al Lādhiqīyah (Latakia)
1 KYA Konya; 2 ADA Adana
100 kilometres
50 miles
1000 metres
500 metres
Sea level

See also... Europe Railways & Ferries (64-65); Red Sea Diving (119); Pacific Diving (150-151); Caribbean Diving (180-181)

The listings above refer to a selection of related themes. For more information, see the Contents (2-7).

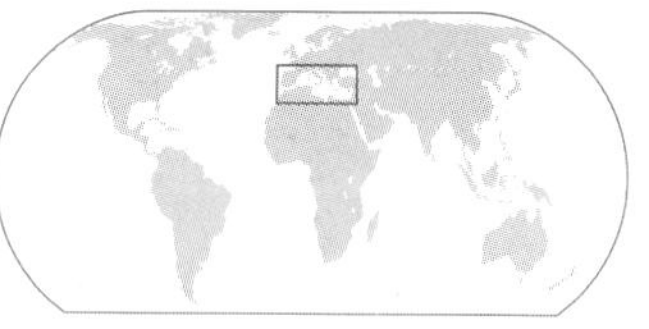

This map shows the principal diving destinations in the Mediterranean Sea and the main underwater attractions including the existence of soft corals or sea fans, cliffs and caves and shipwrecks (including submerged aircraft). The diver may encounter turtle and dolphin at any time, shark and rays less often, but only those places where regular sightings occur are indicated here. Whales are now exceedingly rare.

Diving facilities for each destination, including availability of scuba diving equipment and related support services, are graded as limited, good or excellent. It must be emphasised that these grades are a general reflection on the overall availability of everything required by the visiting scuba diver and are not an interpretation of the standards found within any one facility or organisation.

Each diving destination provides every level of depth from the very shallow to the extremely deep.

FRANCE: SOUTH COAST
1 2 3 4 D S T W ★
Dive sites all along the coast; main facilities in Marseilles, Nice and Toulon
Shipwreck 'Liban' off Cap Croisette and submarine 'Rubis' off Cap Camarat are outstanding; the diving infrastructure on mainland France is rather limited, largely because French divers favour the club system for diving; PADI is, however, opening up new shops and facilities all the time and it is worth requesting a PADI Centre List before departure

FRANCE: CORSICA
1 2 3 4 D S T W ★
Dive sites all around the island; main facilities in Ajaccio, Calvi and Sagone
British Vickers Viking, Canadian CL215 and US B17 bomber provide three very unusual aircraft wrecks off the west coast

ITALY: MAINLAND
1 2 3 4 D S T W ★★★
Dive sites all around the coast; facilities in all major towns, especially Genoa and Portofino
Diving is very popular in Italy; there are numerous shipwrecks, both ancient and modern, although many lie in very deep waters; cave systems on the Adriatic coast and steep underwater cliffs everywhere; away from the busy industrial ports, water clarity is very good

ITALY: SARDINIA
1 2 3 4 D S T W ★½
Dive sites all around the island; facilities centred on Bosa, Cágliari, Orosei and Palau
Several shipwrecks including 'Romagna'; at least one aircraft plus several cave systems including the Nereo Caves off Cape Caccia

ITALY: WESTERN ISLANDS (Caprâia, Elba, Giannutri, Giglio, Montecristo)
1 2 3 4 D S T W ★
Dive sites all around the islands; some facilities on Elba but generally very limited on the islands – best nearby mainland facilities at Portofino
Spectacular vertical cliffs with outstanding seafans, red coral and large shoals of tuna; a few very exciting shipwrecks, such as the vehicle ferry 'Nasim II' off Giannutri

ITALY: SICILY
1 2 3 4 D S T W ★★
Dive sites all around the island; facilities centred on Catánia, Messina and Palermo
Shipwreck 'Amerique' on the northern tip of the island; Sicily attracts large pelagics and large shoals of tuna at certain times of the year

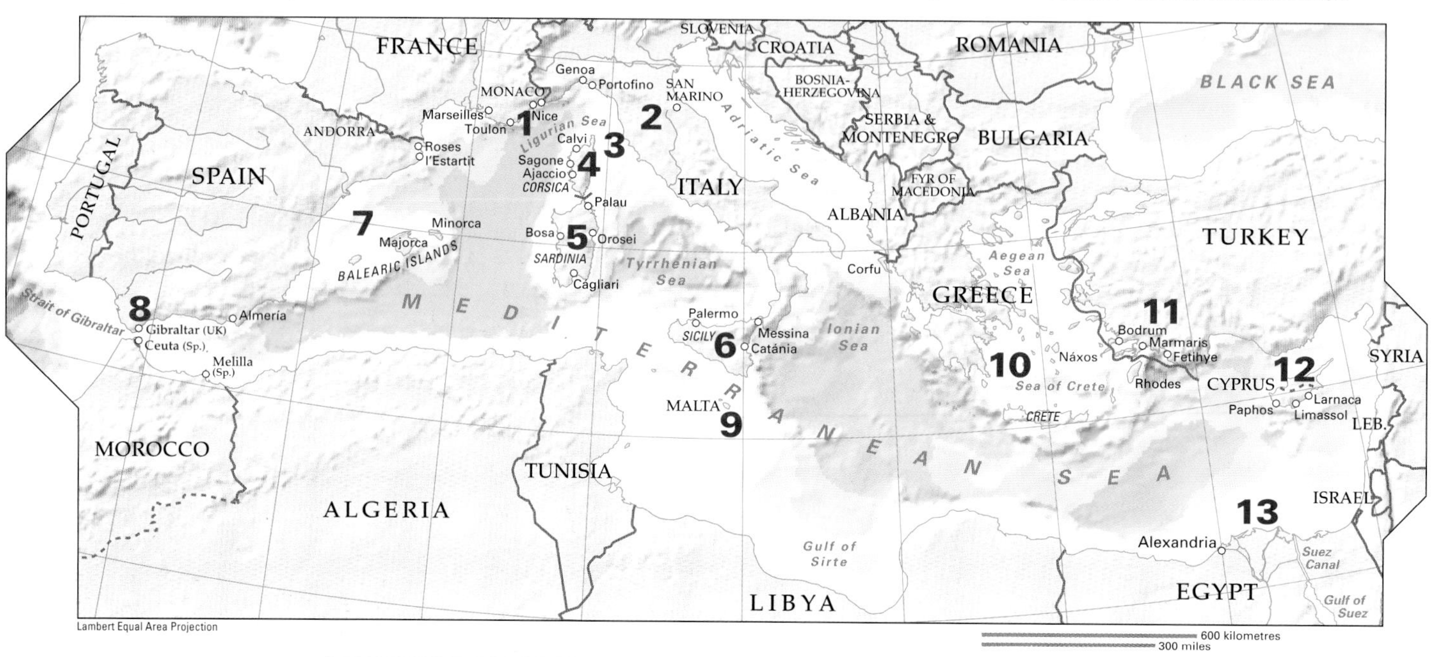
FRANCE
SLOVENIA
CROATIA
ROMANIA
BLACK SEA
BOSNIA-HERZEGOVINA
SAN MARINO
MONACO
Genoa
Portofino
Marseilles
Nice
Toulon
Ligurian Sea
Calvi
Roses
l'Estartit
ANDORRA
SPAIN
PORTUGAL
Sagone
Ajaccio
CORSICA
ITALY
Adriatic Sea
SERBIA & MONTENEGRO
BULGARIA
FYR OF MACEDONIA
ALBANIA
Palau
Minorca
Majorca
BALEARIC ISLANDS
Bosa
Orosei
SARDINIA
Tyrrhenian Sea
Cágliari
Corfu
Aegean Sea
GREECE
TURKEY
Strait of Gibraltar
Gibraltar (UK)
Ceuta (Sp.)
Almeria
Melilla (Sp.)
MEDITERRANEAN SEA
Palermo
SICILY
Messina
Catánia
Ionian Sea
Náxos
Sea of Crete
CRETE
Bodrum
Marmaris
Fethiye
Rhodes
CYPRUS
Larnaca
Paphos
Limassol
SYRIA
LEB.
MALTA
MOROCCO
TUNISIA
ALGERIA
ISRAEL
Alexandria
Suez Canal
Gulf of Sirte
LIBYA
EGYPT
Gulf of Suez
1 2 3 4 5 6 7 8 9 10 11 12 13
Lambert Equal Area Projection
600 kilometres
300 miles

SPAIN
1 2 3 4 D S T W ★★½
Main dive areas Balearic Islands and Costa Brava; best facilities at l'Estartit and Roses (Costa Brava), Almeria, Majorca, Minorca
Submarine cave system 'Pont en Gill' holds outstanding examples of submerged stalactites and stalagmites; the Medes Islands (off l'Estartit) are a protected marine reserve where the flora and fauna is quite prolific

GIBRALTAR
1 2 3 4 D S T W ★★★
Main dive sites off the western and southern coastlines; facilities in Gibraltar town
Shipwrecks 'Excellent' and 'Rosslyn' just outside Gibraltar Harbour are outstanding; there is also ongoing artificial reef programme which involves the sinking of small vessels near Rosia Bay

Dive sites:	Regular sightings of:
1 Soft corals / sea fans	D Dolphins
2 Steep underwater cliffs	S Sharks / rays / pelagics
3 Cave diving	T Turtles
4 Shipwrecks	W Whales
White square: not present	White square: not regularly seen

Facilities for the diver:
★ Limited ★★ Good ★★★ Excellent

MALTA
1 2 3 4 D S T W ★★★
Dive sites all around the islands; facilities in all resort towns
Diving is very popular here although a valid medical certificate and proof of diving experience/qualifications are required; outstanding submarine arches, walls, reefs, tunnels and caves plus some new and very exciting shipwrecks deliberately sunk for divers

GREECE
1 2 3 4 D S T W ★★
Main dive areas Corfu, Crete, Náxos and Rhodes; best facilities on Crete
Until recently, Greece frowned upon scuba divers; today, however, new centres are opening all the time and there are several sites of ancient amphora where the diver is allowed to look but not touch; there are also spectacular submarine cave systems

CYPRUS
1 2 3 4 D S T W ★★★
Main dive sites off the southern and western coastlines; facilities centred on Larnaca, Limassol and Paphos
12,000 tonne ro-ro ferry 'Zenobia' sank off Larnaca in 1980 and is the largest shipwreck in the Mediterranean; the seas are very warm but Cyprus suffers from severe over-fishing
The Turkish Republic of Northern Cyprus has less opportunities for divers and limited facilities

TURKEY
1 2 3 4 D S T W ★★½
Dive sites all along the coast; facilities centred on the southwest coast, in particular at Bodrum, Fethiye and Marmaris
Many ancient amphora wrecks available for inspection and new diving areas are being explored all the time before being opened to visitors

EGYPT: NORTH COAST
1 2 3 4 D S T W ★
Main dive sites and facilities at Alexandria
Not as popular as Egypt's Red Sea coast and often overlooked; the remains of Cleopatra's Palace were recently found in Alexandria Harbour
For Egypt's Red Sea dive sites, see page 109

Sea level
-200 metres
-1000 metres
-2000 metres

Data compiled by Ned Middleton, all rights reserved
email: ned@nedmiddleton.demon.co.uk

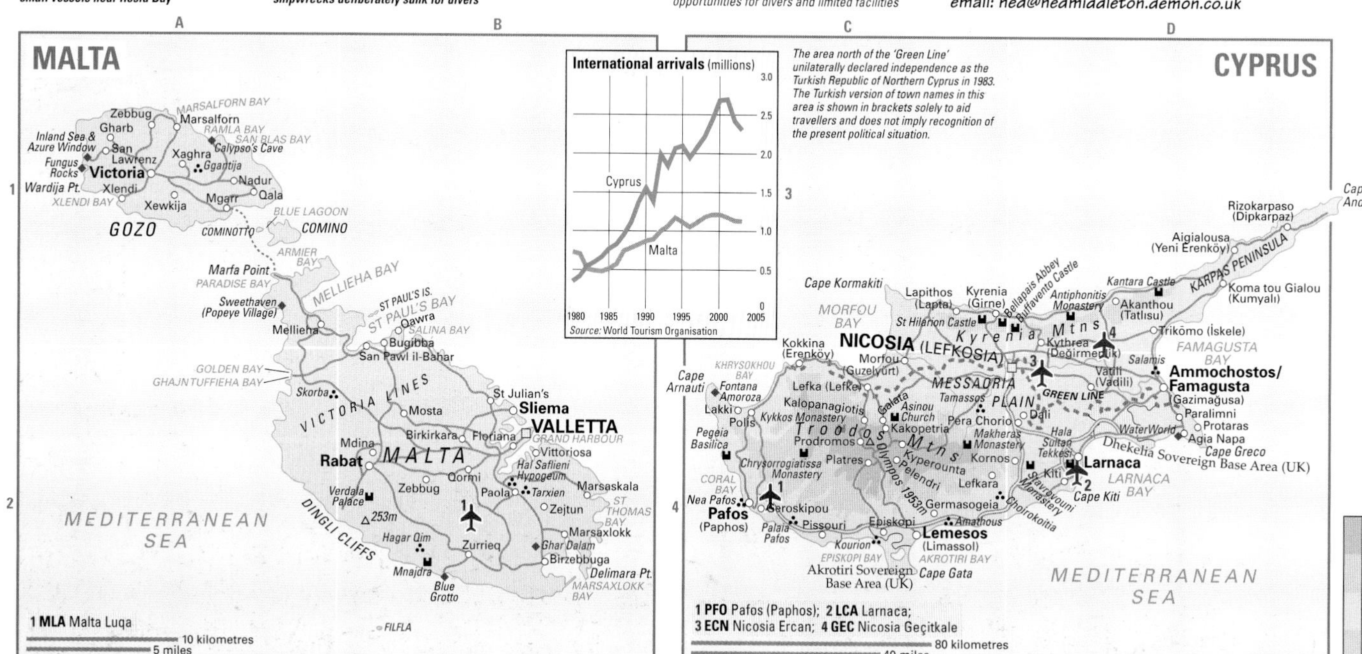
A
B
C
D
1
2
3
4
MALTA
Zebbug
MARSALFORN BAY
Marsalforn
Gharb
RAMLA BAY
SAN BLAS BAY
Inland Sea & Azure Window
San Lawrenz
Xaghra
Calypso's Cave
Fungus Rocks
Victoria
Ggantija
Nadur
Wardija Pt.
Xlendi
Qala
XLENDI BAY
Xewkija
Mgarr
BLUE LAGOON
GOZO
COMINOTTO
COMINO
ARMIER BAY
Marfa Point
PARADISE BAY
MELLIEHA BAY
Sweethaven (Popeye Village)
ST PAUL'S IS.
ST PAUL'S BAY
Qawra
Mellieha
SALINA BAY
Bugibba
San Pawl il-Bahar
GOLDEN BAY
GHAJN TUFFIEHA BAY
Skorba
VICTORIA LINES
St Julian's
Mosta
Sliema
Birkirkara
VALLETTA
Floriana
GRAND HARBOUR
Mdina
MALTA
Vittoriosa
Rabat
Hal Saflieni Hypogeum
Qormi
Tarxien
Marsaskala
Verdala Palace
Zebbug
Paola
ST THOMAS BAY
Zejtun
253m
Marsaxlokk
DINGLI CLIFFS
Hagar Qim
Zurrieq
Ghar Dalam
Birzebbuga
Mnajdra
Delimara Pt.
Blue Grotto
MARSAXLOKK BAY
MEDITERRANEAN SEA
FILFLA
1 MLA Malta Luqa
10 kilometres
5 miles
International arrivals (millions)
3.0
2.5
2.0
1.5
1.0
0.5
0
Cyprus
Malta
1980 1985 1990 1995 2000 2005
Source: World Tourism Organisation
The area north of the 'Green Line' unilaterally declared independence as the Turkish Republic of Northern Cyprus in 1983. The Turkish version of town names in this area is shown in brackets solely to aid travellers and does not imply recognition of the present political situation.
CYPRUS
Cape Andreas
Rizokarpaso (Dipkarpaz)
Aigialousa (Yeni Erenköy)
KARPAS PENINSULA
Kantara Castle
Koma tou Gialou (Kumyalı)
Cape Kormakiti
Lapithos (Lapta)
Kyrenia (Girne)
Bellapais Abbey
Buffavento Castle
Antiphonitis Monastery
Akanthou (Tatlısu)
MORFOU BAY
St Hilarion Castle
Kyrenia Mtns
Trikómo (İskele)
Kokkina (Erenköy)
Morfou (Guzelyurt)
NICOSIA (LEFKOSIA)
Kythrea (Değirmenlik)
FAMAGUSTA BAY
Salamis
KHRYSOKHOU BAY
Vadili (Vadili)
Ammochostos/ Famagusta
Cape Arnauti
Fontana Amoroza
Lefka (Lefke)
MESSAORIA PLAIN
Tamassos
GREEN LINE
Gazimağusa)
Lakki
Kalopanagiotis
Galata
Asinou Church
Dáli
Paralimni
Polis
Kykkos Monastery
Kakopetria
Pera Chorio
Protaras
Pegeia
Basilica
Prodromos
Troodos Mtns
Makheras Monastery
Hala Sultan Tekke
WaterWorld
Agia Napa
Cape Greco
Olympus 1953m
Dhekelia Sovereign Base Area (UK)
Chrysorrogiatissa Monastery
Platres
Kyperounta
Kornos
Larnaca
Pelendri
Lefkara
Kiti
CORAL BAY
Stavrovouni Monastery
LARNACA BAY
Cape Kiti
Nea Pafos
Pafos (Paphos)
Geroskipou
Germasogeia
Choirokoitia
Palaia Pafos
Pissouri
Episkopi
Amathous
Kourion
Lemesos (Limassol)
EPISKOPI BAY
AKROTIRI BAY
Akrotiri Sovereign Base Area (UK)
Cape Gata
MEDITERRANEAN SEA
1 PFO Pafos (Paphos); 2 LCA Larnaca;
3 ECN Nicosia Ercan; 4 GEC Nicosia Geçitkale
80 kilometres
40 miles
1000 metres
500 metres
Sea level

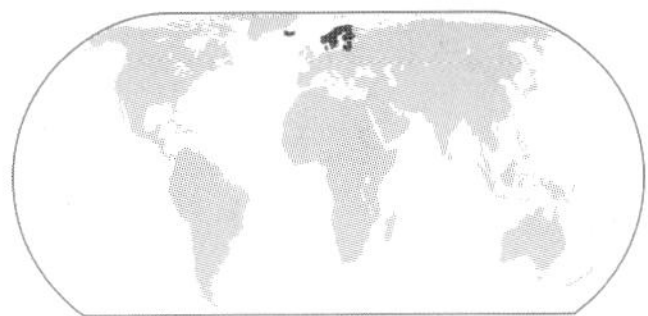

See also... 108-109 for more on Scandinavia; 110 for more on the Baltic States

Scandinavia, Iceland & the Baltic States

The listings above refer to a selection of related themes. For more information, see the Contents (2-7).

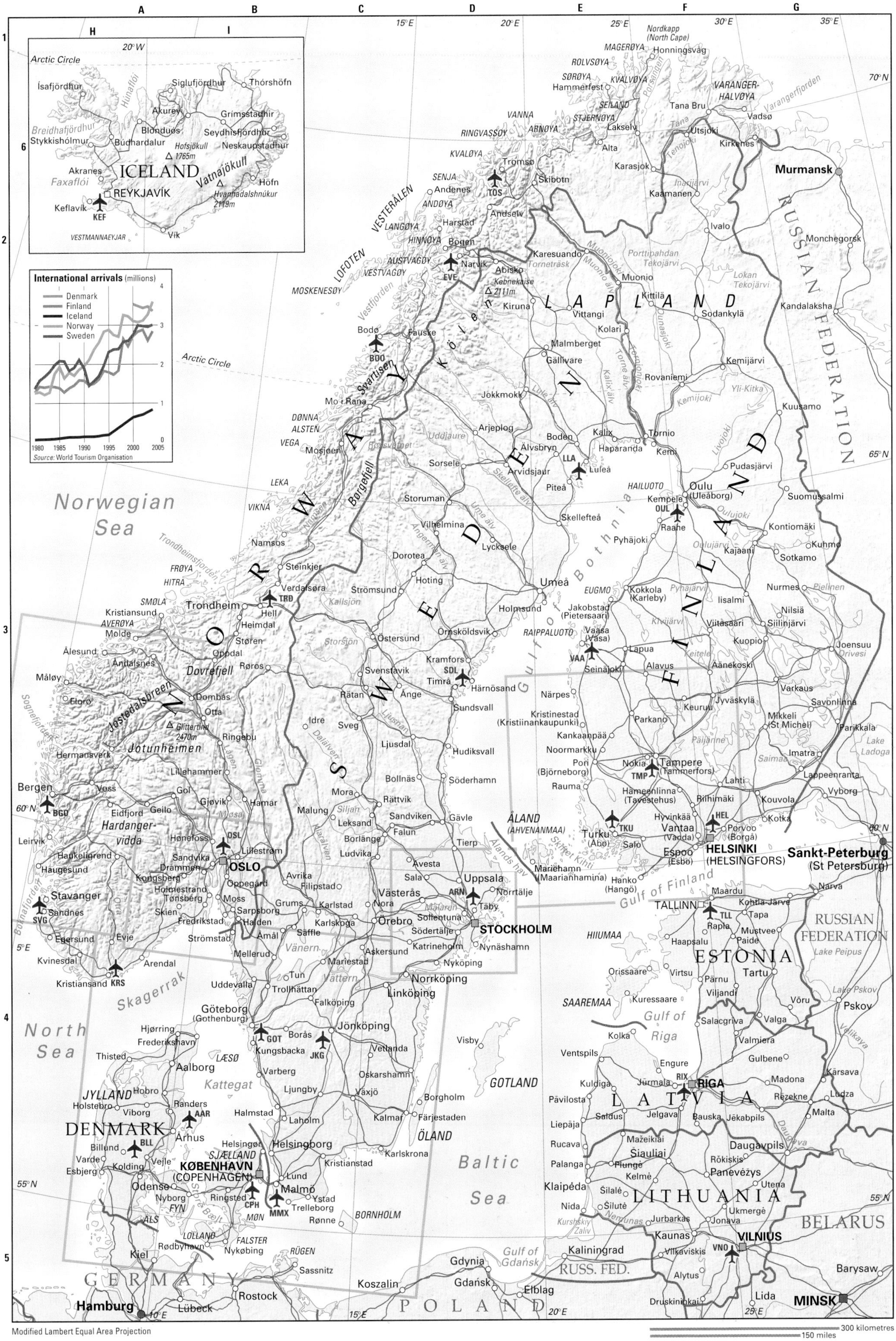

ICELAND
NORWAY
SWEDEN
FINLAND
DENMARK
ESTONIA
LATVIA
LITHUANIA
RUSSIAN FEDERATION
BELARUS
POLAND
GERMANY
RUSS. FED.
LAPLAND

Norwegian Sea
North Sea
Baltic Sea
Gulf of Bothnia
Gulf of Finland
Gulf of Riga
Skagerrak
Kattegat

International arrivals (millions)

- Denmark
- Finland
- Iceland
- Norway
- Sweden

0 1 2 3 4

1980 1985 1990 1995 2000 2005

Source: World Tourism Organisation

Modified Lambert Equal Area Projection

300 kilometres
150 miles

See also... Contents (2-7) – These countries feature in many thematic and regional maps throughout the *World Travel Atlas*.

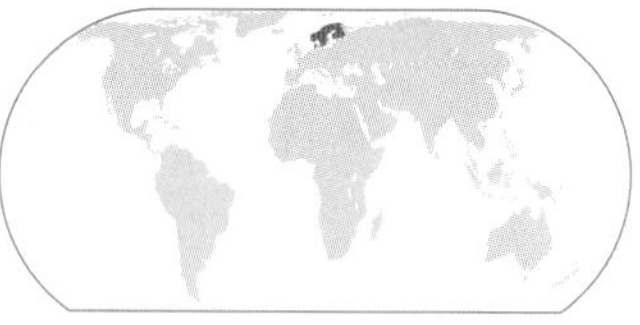

NORWAY
FEB Holmenkollen Ski Festival
MAY-JUN Bergen International Festival
MAY-JUN Bergen Night Jazz Festival ('Nattjazz')
JUN Midsummer Eve
JUL Forde Folk Music Festival
JUL Molde International Jazz Festival
JUL Riddu Riddu Festival **(Kåfjord, nr Alta)**
JUL-AUG Notodden International Blues Festival
AUG Elvefestivalen **(Vormsund)**
AUG Oslo Jazz Festival
AUG International Chamber Music Festival **(Stavanger)**
AUG Norwegian International Film Festival **(Haugesund)**

DENMARK
MAY 21st Aalborg Carnival
JUN Skagen Festival
JUN Midsummer Eve
JUN-JUL Viking Festival **(Frederikssund)**
JUN-JUL Roskilde Festival
JUL Copenhagen Jazz Festival
JUL 4th US Independence Festival **(Rebild)**
AUG Fire Festival Regatta **(Silkeborg)**
AUG Denmark Tattoo **(Varde**, every 3 years**)**
AUG Copenhagen International Ballet Festival
AUG Baltic Sail **(Helsingør)**
AUG Esbjerg International Chamber Music Festival
AUG European Medieval Festival **(Horsens)**
AUG-SEP Århus Festival

SWEDEN
JAN-FEB Kiruna Snow Festival
APR 30th Walpurgis Night (countrywide)
MAY Drottningholm Court Theatre
JUN 6th Swedish National Day **(Stockholm** & countrywide**)**
JUN Midsummer Eve
JUN-JUL Musik van Siljan **(Lake Siljan)**
JUN-JUL Östhammar Music Week
JUL Falun Folkmusik Festival ('Ethno')
JUL Trästock Festival ('Woodstock') **(Skellefteå)**
AUG Stockholm Water Festival
AUG Göteborgskalaseti: **Gothenburg** Party
AUG Medieval Week **(Gotland)**
SEP Stockholm Beer & Whisky Festival
NOV Stockholm International Film Festival
DEC 10th Nobel Prize ceremony **(Stockholm)**
Peace Prize awarded in Oslo
DEC 13th St Lucia Day (countrywide)

FINLAND
MAR Tar Skiing Race **(Oulu)**
JUN Midsummer Eve
JUN Midnight Sun Film Festival **(Sodankylä)**
JUN-JUL Kuopio Dance & Music Festival
JUL Savonlinna Opera Festival
JUL Pori Jazz Festival
JUL Tammerfest **(Tampere)**
JUL Kotka Maritime Festival
AUG-SEP Helsinki Festival
DEC 6th Finland Independence Day

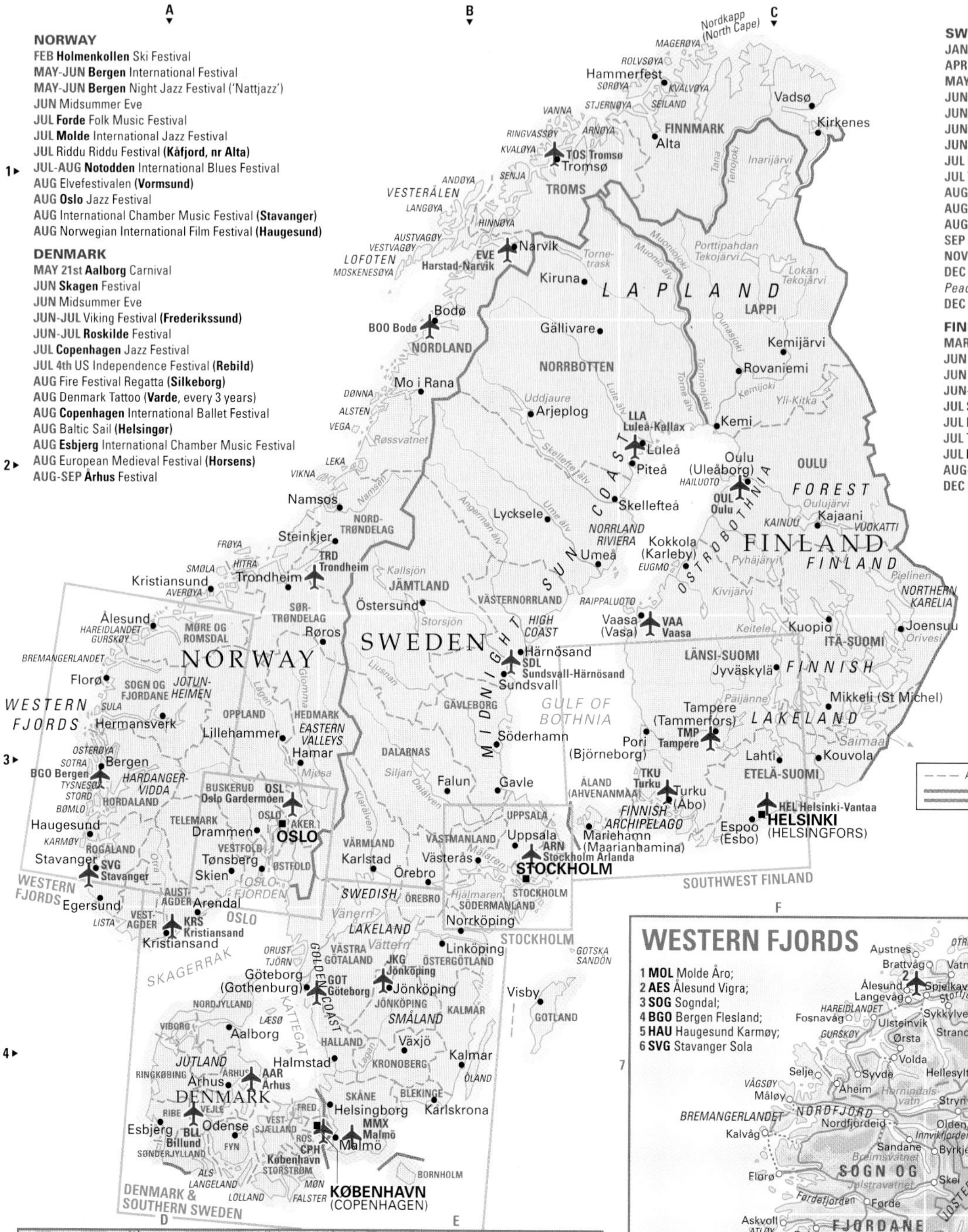

— — Administrative boundary
400 km
200 miles

WESTERN FJORDS

1 **MOL** Molde Åro;
2 **AES** Ålesund Vigra;
3 **SOG** Sogndal;
4 **BGO** Bergen Flesland;
5 **HAU** Haugesund Karmøy;
6 **SVG** Stavanger Sola

100 kilometres
50 miles

1000 metres
500 metres
Sea level

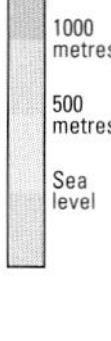

OSLO

1 **OSL** Oslo Gardermoen; 2 **TRF** Sandefjord Torp

80 kilometres
40 miles

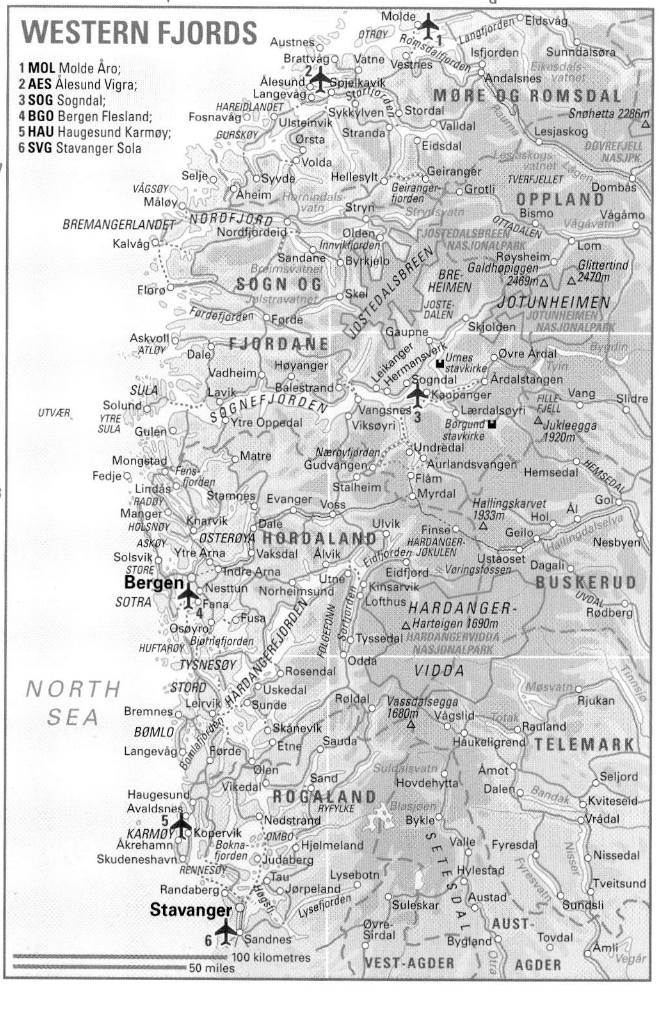

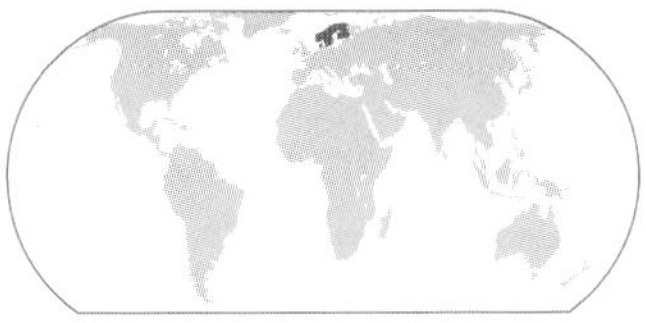

See also... Contents (2-7) – These countries feature in many thematic and regional maps throughout the *World Travel Atlas*.

STOCKHOLM
UPPSALA
Uppsala
VÄSTMANLAND
Västerås
Mälaren
Eskilstuna
STOCKHOLM
Nacka
Huddinge
Södertälje
SÖDERMANLAND
ROSLAGEN
ÅLANDS HAV
GULF OF BOTHNIA
1 VST Stockholm Västerås;
2 ARN Stockholm Arlanda;
3 BMA Stockholm Bromma
80 km
40 miles

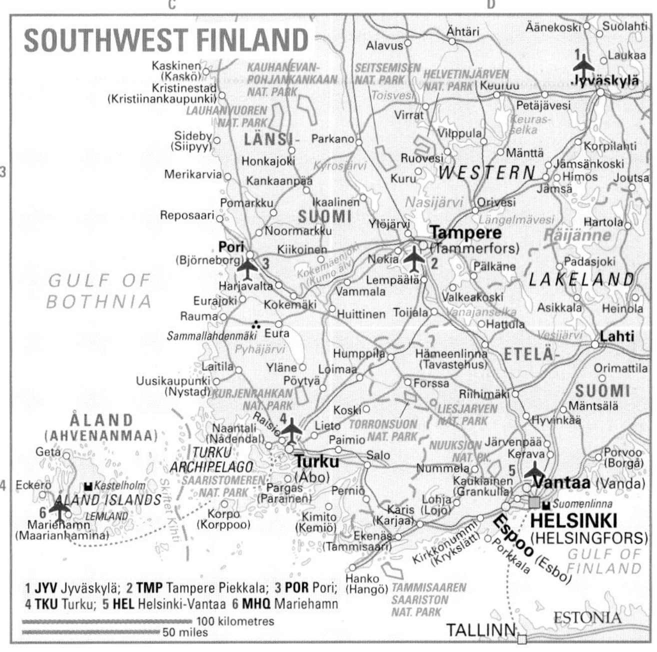
SOUTHWEST FINLAND
Jyväskylä
Tampere (Tammerfors)
Pori (Björneborg)
Turku (Åbo)
Vantaa (Vanda)
HELSINKI (HELSINGFORS)
Espoo (Esbo)
ÅLAND (AHVENANMAA)
Mariehamn (Maarianhamina)
GULF OF BOTHNIA
GULF OF FINLAND
WESTERN LAKELAND
TALLINN
ESTONIA
1 JYV Jyväskylä; 2 TMP Tampere Piekkala; 3 POR Pori;
4 TKU Turku; 5 HEL Helsinki-Vantaa 6 MHQ Mariehamn
100 kilometres
50 miles

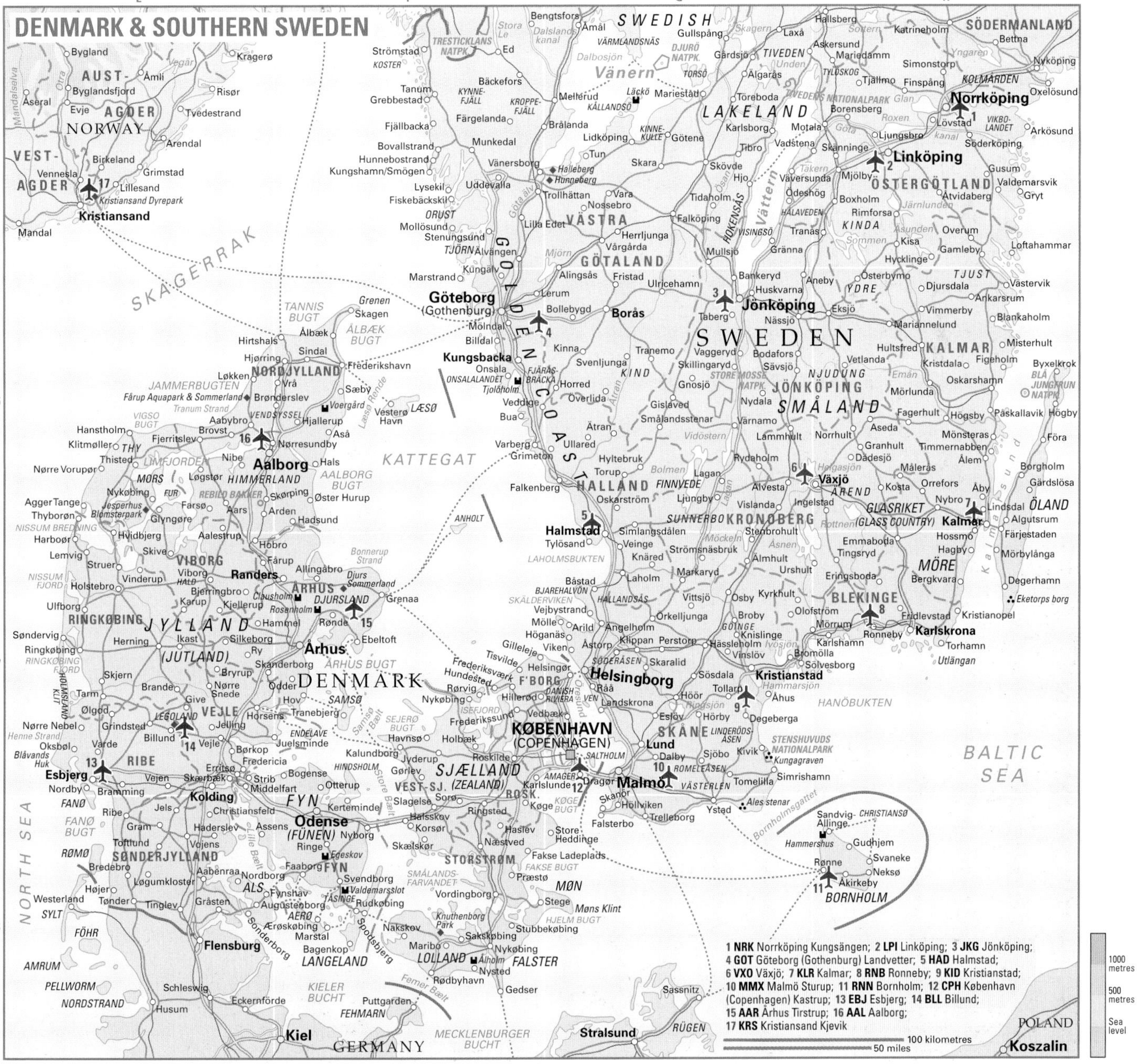

DENMARK & SOUTHERN SWEDEN

NORWAY
SWEDEN
DENMARK
GERMANY
POLAND
SKAGERRAK
KATTEGAT
NORTH SEA
BALTIC SEA

1 NRK Norrköping Kungsängen; 2 LPI Linköping; 3 JKG Jönköping;
4 GOT Göteborg (Gothenburg) Landvetter; 5 HAD Halmstad;
6 VXO Växjö; 7 KLR Kalmar; 8 RNB Ronneby; 9 KID Kristianstad;
10 MMX Malmö Sturup; 11 RNN Bornholm; 12 CPH København (Copenhagen) Kastrup; 13 EBJ Esbjerg; 14 BLL Billund;
15 AAR Århus Tirstrup; 16 AAL Aalborg;
17 KRS Kristiansand Kjevik

100 kilometres
50 miles

1000 metres
500 metres
Sea level

See also... Contents (2-7) – These countries feature in many thematic and regional maps throughout the *World Travel Atlas*.

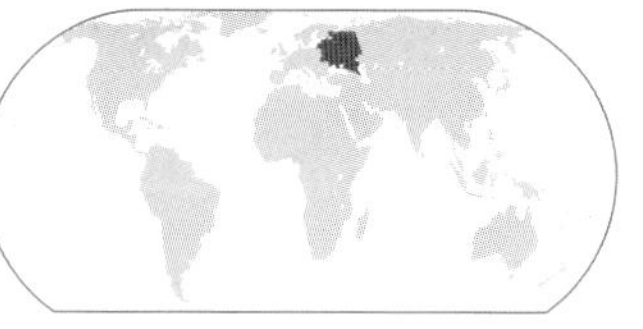

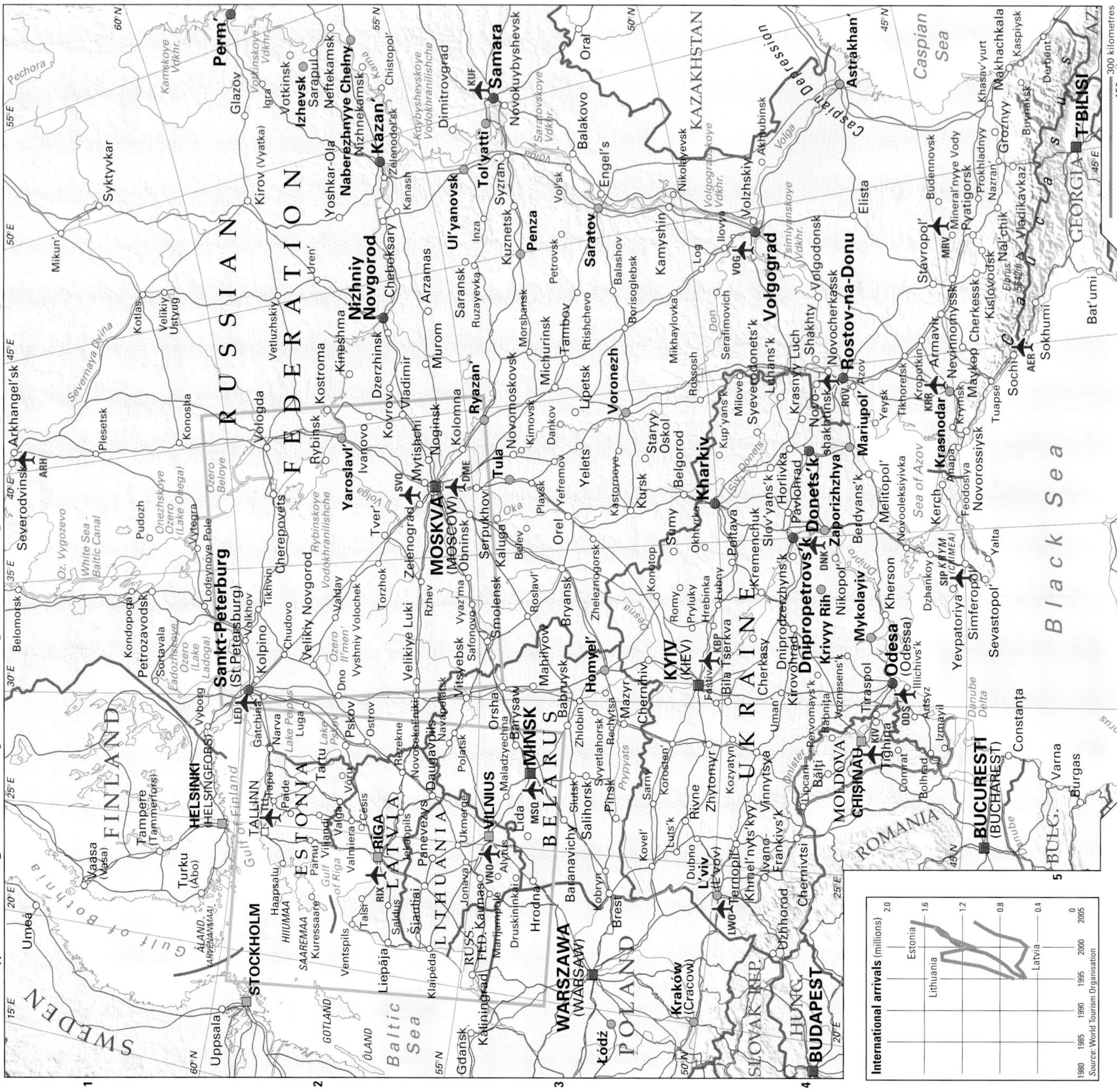

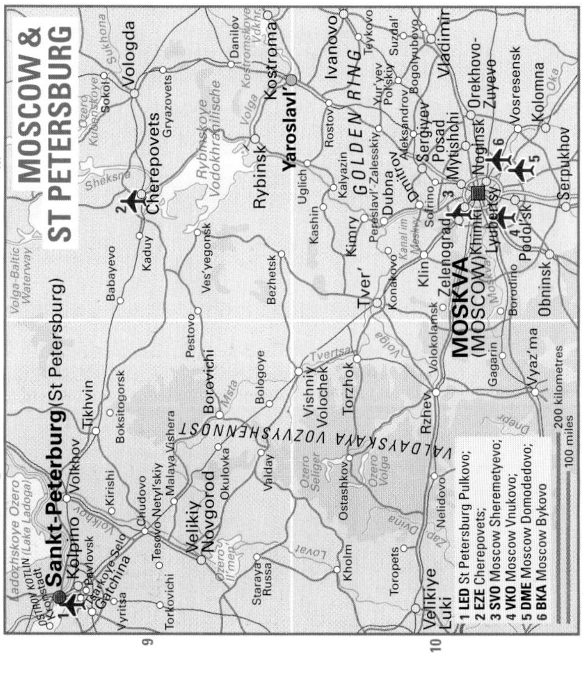

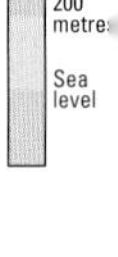

BALTIC REPUBLICS

1 TLL Tallinn; 2 RIX Riga; 3 LPX Liepaja; 4 PLQ Palanga; 5 KGD Kaliningrad; 6 KUN Kaunas; 7 VNO Vilnius

MOSCOW & ST PETERSBURG

1 LED St Petersburg Pulkovo; 2 EZE Cherepovets; 3 SVO Moscow Sheremetyevo; 4 VKO Moscow Vnukovo; 5 DME Moscow Domodedovo; 6 BKA Moscow Bykovo

International arrivals (millions)

Estonia, Lithuania, Latvia

Source: World Tourism Organisation

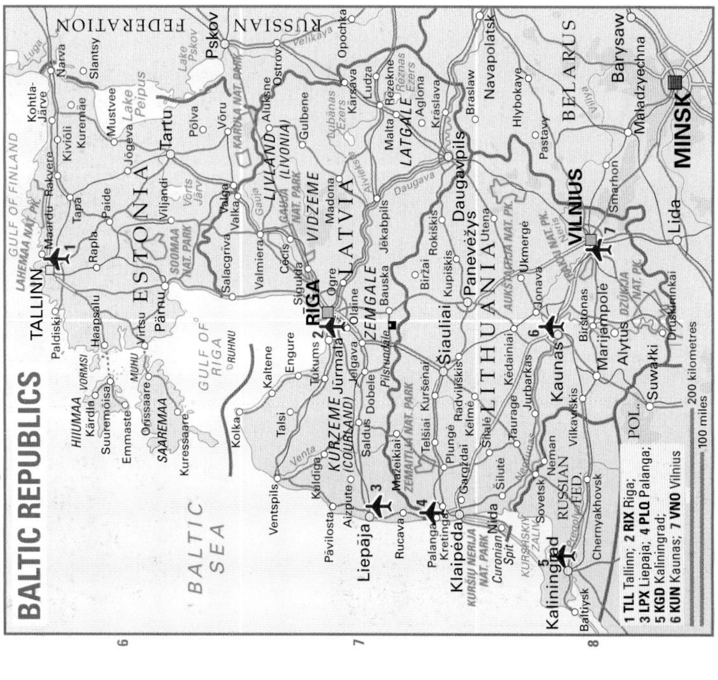

Focus map

500 metres
200 metres
Sea level

See also... Contents (2-7) – this country features in many thematic and regional maps throughout the *World Travel Atlas*.

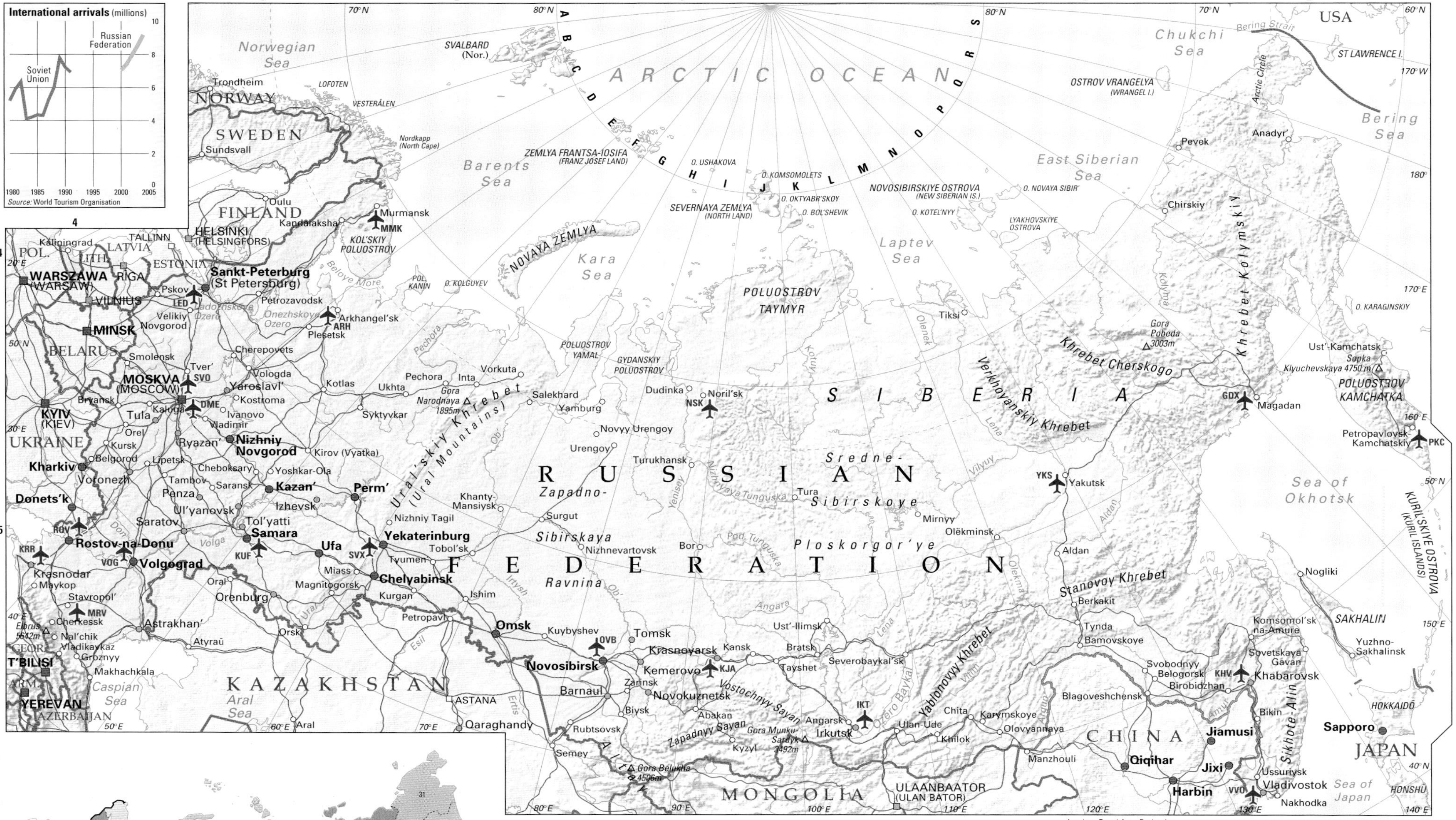

International arrivals (millions)

Soviet Union
Russian Federation
10, 8, 6, 4, 2, 0
1980 1985 1990 1995 2000 2005
Source: World Tourism Organisation

ARCTIC OCEAN
RUSSIAN FEDERATION
SIBERIA
KAZAKHSTAN
CHINA
MONGOLIA
JAPAN

Lambert Equal Area Projection
1000 kilometres
500 miles

REPUBLIC	Autonomous Area or Region	
1 ADYGEYA	12 MARI-EL	23 ALTAY
2 KARACHAY-CHERKESSIA	13 TATARSTAN	24 KHAKASSIA
3 KABARDINO-BALKARIA	14 BASHKORTOSTAN	25 TUVA
4 NORTH OSSETIA (ALANIA)	15 UDMURTIA	26 Ust'-Ordyn-Buryat
5 INGUSHETIA	16 Komi-Permyak	27 BURYATIA
6 CHECHNYA	17 KOMI	28 Agin-Buryat
7 DAGESTAN	18 Nenets	29 Jewish Autonomous Region
8 KALMYKIA	19 Yamalo-Nenets	30 SAKHA (YAKUTIA)
9 KARELIA	20 Khanty-Mansi	31 Chukot
10 MORDOVIA	21 Taymyr	32 Koryak
11 CHUVASHIA	22 Evenki	

MOSKVA (MOSCOW)

TRANS-SIBERIAN RAILWAY

	Moscow	Vladimir	Nizhniy Novgorod	Kirov	Perm'	Yekaterinburg	Omsk	Novosibirsk	Krasnoyarsk	Irkutsk	Ulan-Ude	Ulan Bator	Beijing	Chita	Karymskoye	Harbin	Belogorsk	Khabarovsk	Ussuriysk	Nakhodka	Vladivostok
Km		210	461	917	1,397	1,778	2,676	3,303	4,065	5,152	5,608	6,266	7,622	6,165	6,261	7,613	7,834	8,492	9,146	9,402	9,258
Miles		130	286	570	868	1,105	1,663	2,052	2,526	3,201	3,485	3,894	4,736	3,831	3,890	4,730	4,868	5,277	5,683	5,842	5,753

Distances from Moscow ▲

See also... World Introduction (8-11); Tourism (24-25); Countries A-Z (202-210)

The listings above refer to a selection of related themes. For more information, see the Contents (2-7).

Africa

Africa is the birthplace of mankind and one of the cradles of civilization. It contains the world's largest desert, longest river and biggest rift valley. It occupies 25% of the world's landmass and is home to 13% of its people, who are spread across nearly 60 countries. It has the world's most accessible wild-life, managed and protected in parks larger than many European countries. The superlatives and diversity are breathtaking although, sadly, so are many of the problems the continent faces. Travel and tourism, however, has been one of the areas of solid achievement.

Africa was the only WTO region to have performed better in 2005 than in 2004, with an increase of over 10%, nearly double the world average. Sub-Saharan Africa saw particularly strong growth (12.6% increase in visitor arrivals). It is also the only continent not to have experienced any year-on-year fall in visitor numbers since 1999. Tourism receipts have performed even more impressively, up from US$15.8bn in 2003 to US$18.9bn in 2004, a rise of nearly 20%, with the north African states in the forefront. African airlines also prospered in 2005, with passenger numbers up by 10%. More people, therefore, are travelling; and each person is spending more money. Although these figures are from a comparatively low base, the increases are encouraging for all those who have directed, promoted and serviced Africa as an attractive travel destination. Tourism is already reckoned to be the continent's third largest industry and the potential for future growth remains vast.

Problems & opportunities

The travel industry, both in Africa and elsewhere, has taken many positive steps to increase respect both for the natural environment and the human social and economic communities. Travel companies are ever-more aware of the need to strike the delicate balance between demand and responsibility. Many are also becoming involved in projects whereby local organisations, such as schools and hospitals, benefit from local tourism expenditure. Co-operation between the public and private sectors is on the increase and numerous key infrastructure projects are under way as a result. New properties throughout Africa are increasingly built with local materials and operated by local staff, with the subsequent revenue more likely to be enjoyed by the local population. Many parts of the continent are thus at the forefront of a radical change in the travel business, with individual visitors helping to act as catalysts for positive change.

These achievements, however, exist against a backdrop of deep-rooted and divisive problems that have hampered Africa's development for decades. 2005 witnessed many energetic attempts, such as the 'Make Poverty History' campaign and Live8, to draw attention to these, but opinions differ widely as to whether the year's key event, the World Trade Organization meeting in Hong Kong, will produce the hoped-for benefits. It certainly seems that the issues of debt relief and EU and US farm subsidies will rumble on for some time.

One of the key tenets of capitalism is the 'trickle-down effect', by which wealth created by the richest members of society will, in time and with many deductions, filter down to everyone else. This, however, works better in economies founded on manufacturing and services, which are more efficient at creating and distributing prosperity, than in agricultural and commodity-based economies, as are common in Africa. Such economies also tend to have small GNIs and are vulnerable to international market prices, the distorting effects of subsidies and, in the case of agriculture, the weather. They also tend towards concentration of power in the hands of a few people, which can lead to a number of other misfortunes including corruption, poor government and divisive inequalities of opportunity and wealth.

In Africa, these problems operate against a further background of numerous complex ethnic conflicts, which colonialism obscured or complicated but rarely solved, and an often acrimonious religious divide, broadly between a Muslim north and a Christian south. Over 30 wars since 1970 and countless million refugees are the result. Global terrorism has also left its mark, both as an alleged base (Somalia) and as a target (Kenya).

Africa also suffers heavily from two of the world's most serious diseases, HIV/AIDS and malaria. HIV has been described as a demographic time-bomb. 75% of global AIDS deaths are in Africa, and in some countries 25% of the population is believed to be infected. Malaria – which by some estimates has caused half of all human deaths since the Stone Age and which wastes perhaps 5% of the Africa's GDP through lost work and disease control – is becoming more prevalent due to the mosquitoes' immunity to drugs, inadequate precautions and global warming. These and other diseases are more likely to be fatal amongst populations already weakened by war, malnutrition, poverty and poor water supplies. All are clearly also risks for foreign visitors.

None of these problems are conducive to either internal or external investment on a scale necessary to cure them. As a result, governments mortgage assets or borrow money, leading to increased poverty and debt. Deforestation, whether for timber sales or to create land for growing cash crops, has been one solution. This briefly solves some problems, but creates others by threatening the delicate eco-systems on which both Africa's agriculture and tourism products depend. Steps are now being taken to redress this, such as the proposed 'Great Green Wall' of trees between Dakar and Djibouti to hold back the previously relentless advance of the Sahel.

All these challenges lead to several travel-safety concerns for foreign visitors. These include gun-related crime, particularly on public transport, at border crossings and in urban areas and exposure to dangerous and unfamiliar diseases. Specialist advice should be sought before travelling, and local advice followed once arrived.

Economies

The region's 10 largest economies
Source: World Bank/International Monetary Fund

	GNI US$m 2004	GNI/cap US$ 2004	GDP growth 2004	GDP growth av p/a '97-'06
South Africa	165,326	3,728	3.7	3.1
Egypt	90,129	1,163	4.1	4.9
Algeria	73,676	2,265	5.2	4.1
Nigeria	53,983	419	6.0	4.1
Morocco	46,518	1,421	4.2	3.3
Tunisia	26,301	2,611	5.8	5.0
Libya	25,257	4,381	4.4	3.5
Sudan	18,152	452	6.9	8.7
Kenya	14,987	443	4.3	2.8
Angola	14,441	1,221	11.1	9.5

Key facts

Number of Countries	57
Area ('000 sq km)	30,211
Population ('000)	891,430
Population Density (per sq km)	30
Gross National Income (US$m)	698.026
Visitor Arrivals ('000)	36,643
Visitor Receipts (US$m)	24,460

GNI figures are for 2004. Population figures are taken from the most recent reliable source. Travel figures (UNWTO) are based on overnight stays, not same-day visitors, and are for 2005. For more information see the Countries A-Z section from page 202.

Big earners

Receipts from foreign travel (excluding international transport), 2004 – top ten countries (US$ billions) *Source: WTO*

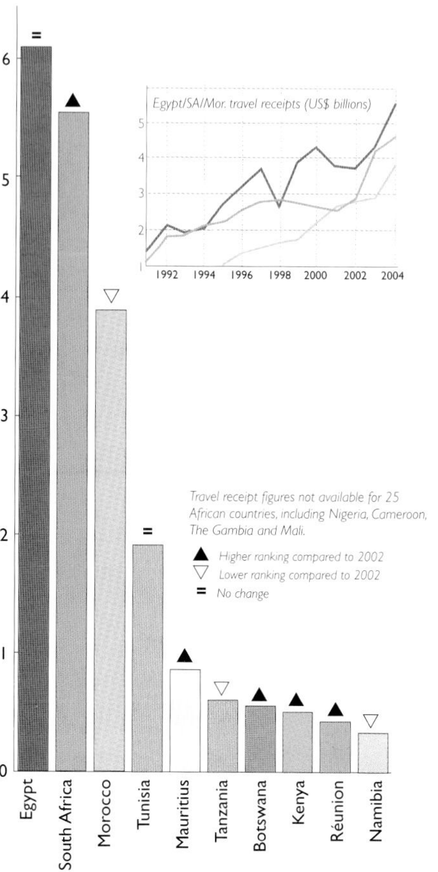
0
1
2
3
4
5
6
Egypt
South Africa
Morocco
Tunisia
Mauritius
Tanzania
Botswana
Kenya
Réunion
Namibia
Egypt/SA/Mor. travel receipts (US$ billions)
1992 1994 1996 1998 2000 2002 2004
Travel receipt figures not available for 25 African countries, including Nigeria, Cameroon, The Gambia and Mali.
▲ Higher ranking compared to 2002
▽ Lower ranking compared to 2002
= No change

Travel overview

In travel terms, Africa possesses numerous advantages. It is a vast, largely pristine and staggeringly beautiful continent, rich in wildlife, teeming with a vibrant cultural diversity, and utterly different from Europe or North America. From the dramatic struggle for survival on the African plains to the stunning panorama of mountains, deserts and waterfalls, from sun-washed beaches to the steaming jungles of the interior, the variety is truly awesome.

Africa's inequalities persist in its travel patterns. More than half of all visitors to the country go to either South Africa, Egypt, Morocco or Tunisia, and these are the only countries in Africa which appear in world's top 50 by visitor numbers. Only eight African countries attracted more than one million visitors in 2004, but the WTO figures for one of these, Zimbabwe, are something of an anomoly and reflect short-term local land-border crossings rather than evidence of the thriving tourist industry the country once enjoyed. Indeed, Zimbabwe is one of only two states in the world to have experienced negative GDP growth between 1997 and 2006. For those who believe that education holds the key to prosperity, however, there are encouraging signs, for Zimbabwe has comfortably the highest adult literacy rate in Africa.

Adventure is a key feature of African holidays. Although many safaris concentrate on luxury, an increasing number of overland and adventure operators offer packages for those on lower budgets.

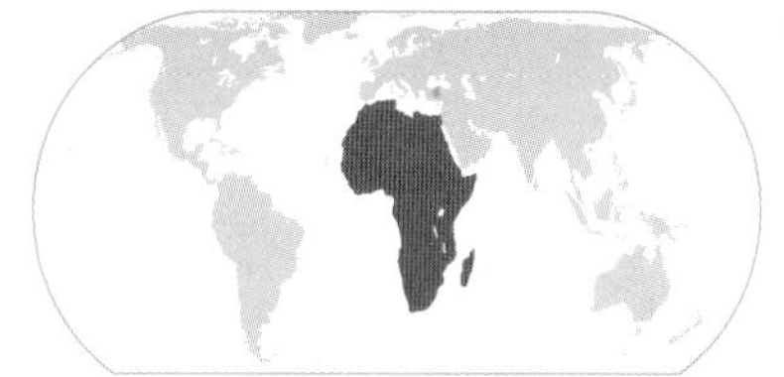

- Africa occupies 18% of the world's land area and is home to 13.7% of the world's population.
- Africa accounts for 4.5% of global travel arrivals.
- International travel and tourism contributed over US$21 billion to Africa's economy in 2004.
- The most-visited country in Africa, South Africa, ranked 28th in the world in 2004, compared to 26th in 2003. The country also accounts for about one-third of Africa's travel receipts.
- Botswana is the world's third largest producer of diamonds, from which it derives 80% of its earnings.
- South Africans are Africa's most frequent travellers, accounting for over 40% of Africa's total recorded international departures.
- 14 of the world's 40 largest countries are in Africa.
- Esmeralda, a Giant Tortoise living on Aldabra, in the Seychelles, is at least 200 years old and regarded as being the world's oldest living creature.
- The Great Rift Valley is over 3,000 miles long.
- Libya is the only country with a single-coloured flag.
- Lest anyone doubt the economic, as well as the zoological, importance of the species, the research institute Panos Media has calculated that a Kenyan elephant is worth $900,000 in tourism revenue if it is allowed to realise its full lifespan.
- The *Cathédrale Notre-Dame de la Paix* in Yamoussoukro in the Côte d'Ivoire is only fractionally smaller than St Peter's in Rome and has more stained glass than in all the churches in France combined.
- The remains of what is believed to be the world's earliest human being, dating back perhaps 200,000 years, was discovered in 1967 in Kibish, Ethiopia.
- The UK is slightly larger than Uganda and slightly smaller than Guinea.
- Lake Malawi contains more different species of fish than any other lake in the world.
- The world's largest diamond, weighing 0.62kg, was mined in South Africa in 1905.
- South Africa has three capital cities – Pretoria, Cape Town and Bloemfontein.
- The Great Pyramid at Giza is the only one of the seven wonders of the ancient world still standing.
- Namibia's Fish River Canyon is the second largest in the world, after the Grand Canyon in the USA
- At the height of the flood season, up to 550 million litres of water plummet over the edge of the Victoria Falls every minute.
- Egypt won the African Cup of Nations in 2006: this was their fifth success, making them the most successful country in the tournament's history.

Many countries such as South Africa, Tanzania and Kenya have well-administered game parks which enable them to count safari holidays as a major foreign currency earner. Africa's rivers, waterfalls, mountains, deserts, reefs and jungles provide other nature-related experiences.

Luxury holidays are an established niche. Options include small, intimate lodges in game parks as well as secure country club accommodation and the luxury train journeys offered by the Blue Train and Rovos Rail through southern Africa. Beach holidays, often combined with diving opportunities or spectacular safaris, are ever-popular. The standard of the roads is often poor, and many companies have stepped in to provide internal flight services aimed particularly at the top end of the market.

Destination overview

- **South Africa** – The main destination in the sub-Saharan market. It has stunning natural attractions (including some of the continent's most celebrated national parks), a range of products (such as beach holidays, luxury train journeys, touring and golf), an excellent infrastructure and vibrant cities. This combination has long supported a thriving travel industry. Around 60% of the South Africa's visitors come from neighbouring countries. The UK is South Africa's strongest non-African market, providing some 450,000 visitors in 2004; Germany and the USA contribute about the same again between them. The country will be hosting the football world cup in 2010 and considerable infrastructure investment is expected in the run- up to the event.

African adventures

Wildlife parks in Sub-Saharan Africa, 2005
Source: Safari Consultants Ltd

Enduring favourites...	
Kruger, SA	Ngorongoro, Tanz.
Hluhluwe-Umfolozi, SA	Etosha, Nam.
Tsavo, Ken.	Amboseli, Ken
Masai Mara, Ken.	Luangwa, Zam.
Samburu, Ken.	Moremi (Okavango), Bots.
Serengeti, Tanz.	Chobe, Bots.
Up-and-coming...	
Selous, Tanz.	Limpopo Valley, Bots.
Ruaha, Tanz.	Katavi, Tanz.
Tarangire, Tanz.	Parc des Volcans, Rwa.
Kafue, Zam.	Lower Zambezi, Zam.

- **Egypt** saw 2005 visitor numbers from the UK increase by over 50% to 838,000 compared to 2004. In addition to the perennially popular Nile region tours, recent promotion has, with great success, focussed on the Red Sea Riviera. The Mediterranean coast is likely to be the next growth area in the country.
- **Morocco** – The closest African country to Europe. Attractions include golf, the Sahara, fine Atlantic beaches and its historic imperial cities.
- **Tunisia** – Several developed resorts to suit European tastes and a growing inventory of excellent golf courses. 65% of international visitors are from Europe.
- **Kenya** – Safaris and beach holidays are the dominant travel themes with, respectively, Nairobi and Mombasa being the main gateways. The wildebeest migration (July to October) is still proving an exceptional attraction.
- **Gambia** – Long popular with the British market, this small West African state has maintained its position as a beach destination, with opportunities for visits inland along the River Gambia.
- **Nigeria** – Africa's giant in terms of population, Nigeria has benefitted from the recent considerable increase in direct flights from Europe. This has fuelled the growth in package holiday opportunities, incentive travel and the fast-growing family visiting and 'genealogy travel' market.
- **Ghana** – Tourism is still comparatively under-developed, but steps are being taken to redress this. Various events in 2007 will commemorate the 200th anniversary of the abolition of the slave trade. Ghana's hosting of the 2008 African Cup of Nations is also likely to boost vistor numbers.
- **Botswana** – A long period of prosperity and stability has helped establish this southern African state as a stop-over and dual-centre destination with neighbouring South Africa. The contrasting splendours of the Kalahari Desert and the Okavango Delta are two of the main attractions.
- **Tanzania** – A combination of safaris and beach holidays has allowed Tanzania to build a strong package-holiday and tailor-made appeal, particularly in the mid-price market. The offshore islands lend themselves to more up-market dual-centre holidays and cruise-and-stay options.
- **Malawi** – The number of foreign visitors has more than doubled since 1997. The north of the country has been a major growth area, often in combination with Zambia's Luangwa National Park. The Scotland-Malawi Partnership is one of many bi-lateral programmes designed to boost tourism and sustainable development programmes.
- The Indian Ocean islands of the **Seychelles, Réunion** and **Mauritius** are in different ways stunningly beautiful and ecologically unique and have used these advantages to create a powerful tourism industry. Their combined travel receipts are exceeded in Africa only by South Africa, Morocco, Egypt and Tunisia. Traditionally appealing to the luxury market, these islands are increasingly marketing themselves to a wider audience.

Big spenders

Expenditure on foreign travel (excluding international transport), 2003 – top ten countries (US$ billions) *Source: WTO*

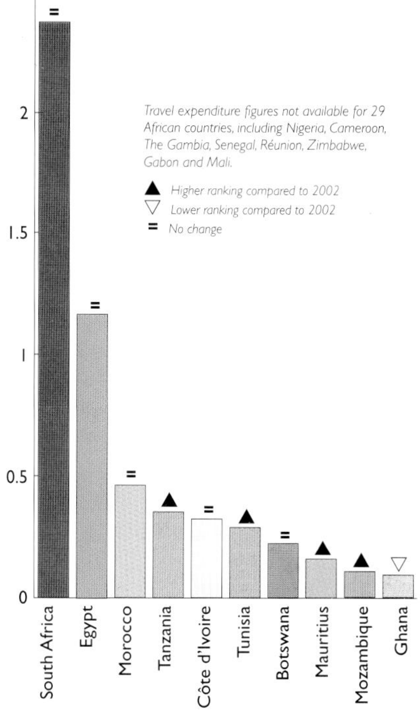
2
1.5
1
0.5
0
Travel expenditure figures not available for 29 African countries, including Nigeria, Cameroon, The Gambia, Senegal, Réunion, Zimbabwe, Gabon and Mali.
▲ Higher ranking compared to 2002
▽ Lower ranking compared to 2002
= No change
South Africa
Egypt
Morocco
Tanzania
Côte d'Ivoire
Tunisia
Botswana
Mauritius
Mozambique
Ghana

Developing areas

Africa is still developing its travel and tourism potential, and even the countries leading the way still have much to do to realise their ambitions. The challenges of climate, geography, politics and economics are, however, vast.

An encouraging recent trend has been the extent to which countries emerging from long periods of conflict, such as Ethiopia, Angola and Mozambique have been quick to develop a tourist industry.

Several other countries, including Namibia, Zambia, Botswana, Ghana, Cape Verde, Lesotho, Gabon, Rwanda, Malawi and (perhaps surprisingly) Libya offer, in different ways and for different reasons, hopes for future travel and tourism growth. Political stability and international perceptions will remain key to progress here, and elsewhere in the continent. Bodies such as the Peace Parks Foundation (see page 122) also have a valuable role to play.

Africa remains a uniquely fascinating and rewarding continent for all kinds of travellers, particularly those seeking adventure and close encounters with nature. All connected with the industry hope that responsible tourism policies, both by suppliers and consumers, can help the continent's travel and tourism product reach its full potential.

Visitors

Visitor arrivals 2004: top ten countries *Source: WTO*

	Visitors (thousands)	Change since 1997
Egypt	7,051	92.9%
South Africa	6,678	29.2%
Tunisia	5,998	40.7%
Morocco	5,501	79.1%
Zimbabwe	1,853	-11.3%
Algeria	1,234	94.3%
Botswana	1,202	96.7%
Kenya	1,132	24.8%
Mauritius	719	34.1%
Tanzania	566	63.1%

Physical

See also... World Physical (12-13); World Political (14-15), World Climate (16)

The listings above refer to a selection of related themes. For more information, see the Contents (2-7).

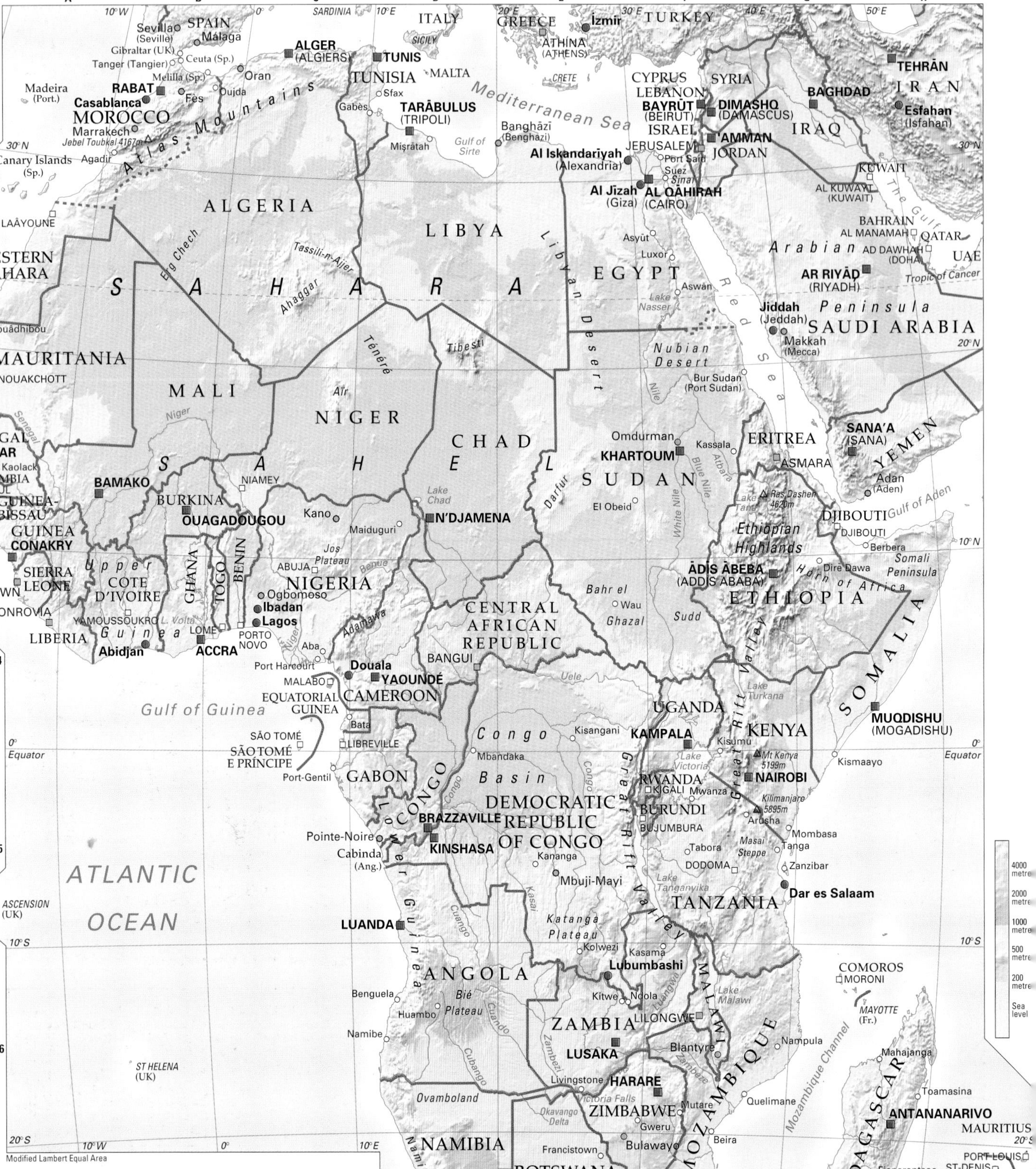

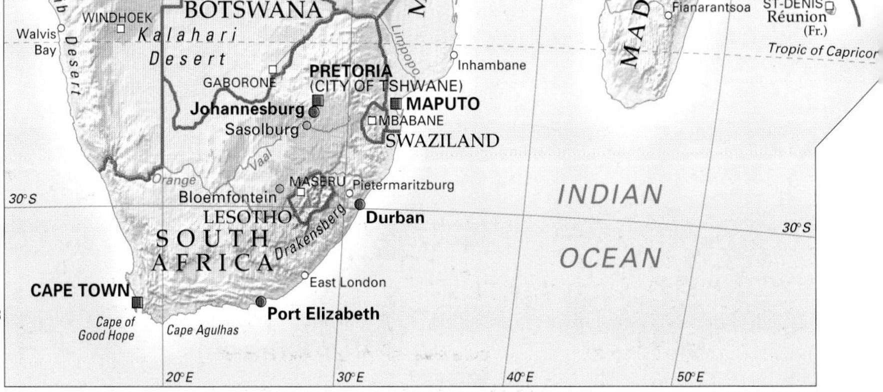

Modified Lambert Equal Area

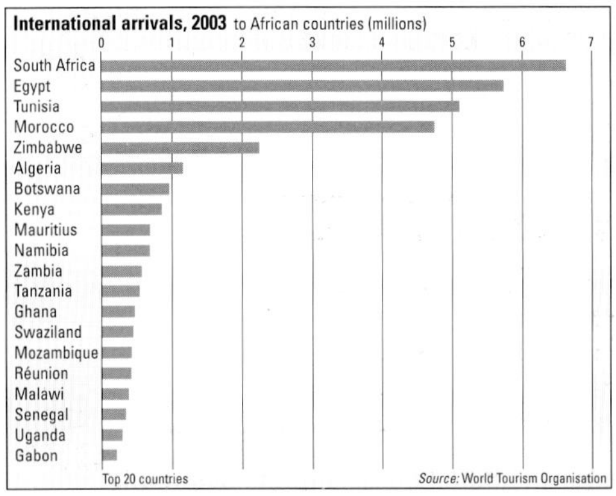

International arrivals, 2003 to African countries (millions)

0 1 2 3 4 5 6 7

South Africa
Egypt
Tunisia
Morocco
Zimbabwe
Algeria
Botswana
Kenya
Mauritius
Namibia
Zambia
Tanzania
Ghana
Swaziland
Mozambique
Réunion
Malawi
Senegal
Uganda
Gabon

Top 20 countries

Source: World Tourism Organisation

4000 metres
2000 metres
1000 metres
500 metres
200 metres
Sea level

2000 kilometres
1000 miles

See also... World Climate (16); Regional Climate Terms (196)

The listings above refer to a selection of related themes.
For more information, see the Contents (2-7).

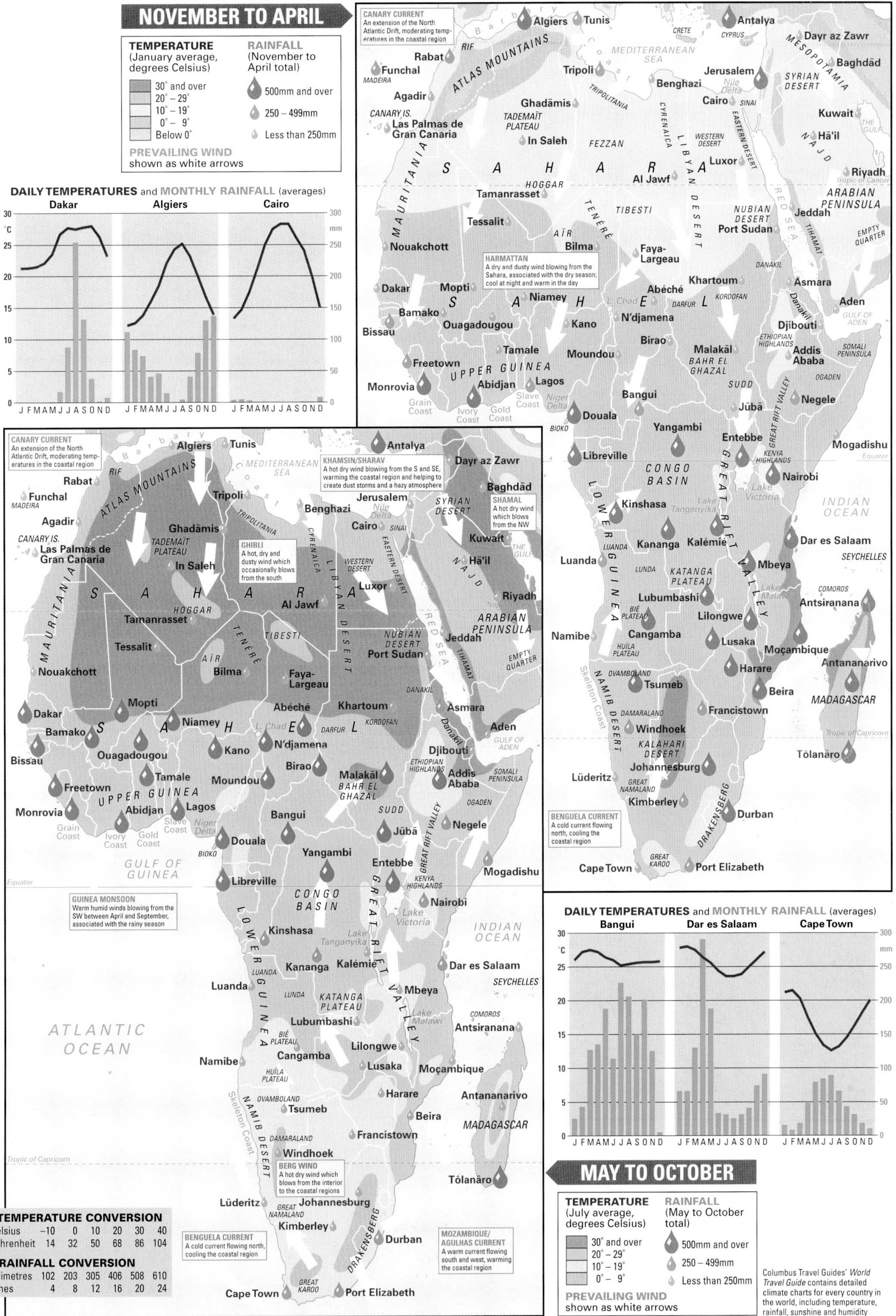
NOVEMBER TO APRIL
TEMPERATURE (January average, degrees Celsius)
30° and over
20° – 29°
10° – 19°
0° – 9°
Below 0°
RAINFALL (November to April total)
500mm and over
250 – 499mm
Less than 250mm
PREVAILING WIND shown as white arrows
DAILY TEMPERATURES and MONTHLY RAINFALL (averages)
Dakar
Algiers
Cairo
°C
mm
J F M A M J J A S O N D
CANARY CURRENT An extension of the North Atlantic Drift, moderating temperatures in the coastal region
HARMATTAN A dry and dusty wind blowing from the Sahara, associated with the dry season; cool at night and warm in the day
KHAMSIN/SHARAV A hot dry wind blowing from the S and SE, warming the coastal region and helping to create dust storms and a hazy atmosphere
SHAMAL A hot dry wind which blows from the NW
GHIBLI A hot, dry and dusty wind which occasionally blows from the south
GUINEA MONSOON Warm humid winds blowing from the SW between April and September, associated with the rainy season
BENGUELA CURRENT A cold current flowing north, cooling the coastal region
BERG WIND A hot dry wind which blows from the interior to the coastal regions
MOZAMBIQUE/AGULHAS CURRENT A warm current flowing south and west, warming the coastal region
ATLANTIC OCEAN
INDIAN OCEAN
MEDITERRANEAN SEA
S A H A R A
S A H E L
ATLAS MOUNTAINS
CONGO BASIN
GREAT RIFT VALLEY
NAMIB DESERT
KALAHARI DESERT
ARABIAN PENINSULA
MADAGASCAR
TEMPERATURE CONVERSION
°Celsius −10 0 10 20 30 40
°Fahrenheit 14 32 50 68 86 104
RAINFALL CONVERSION
Millimetres 102 203 305 406 508 610
Inches 4 8 12 16 20 24
DAILY TEMPERATURES and MONTHLY RAINFALL (averages)
Bangui
Dar es Salaam
Cape Town
MAY TO OCTOBER
TEMPERATURE (July average, degrees Celsius)
30° and over
20° – 29°
10° – 19°
0° – 9°
RAINFALL (May to October total)
500mm and over
250 – 499mm
Less than 250mm
PREVAILING WIND shown as white arrows
Columbus Travel Guides' World Travel Guide contains detailed climate charts for every country in the world, including temperature, rainfall, sunshine and humidity

See also... Contents (2-7) – these countries feature in many thematic and regional maps throughout the *World Travel Atlas*.

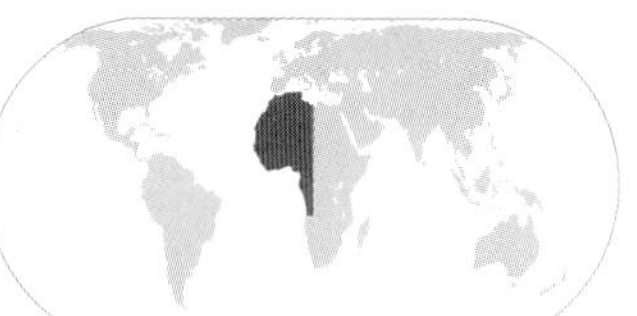

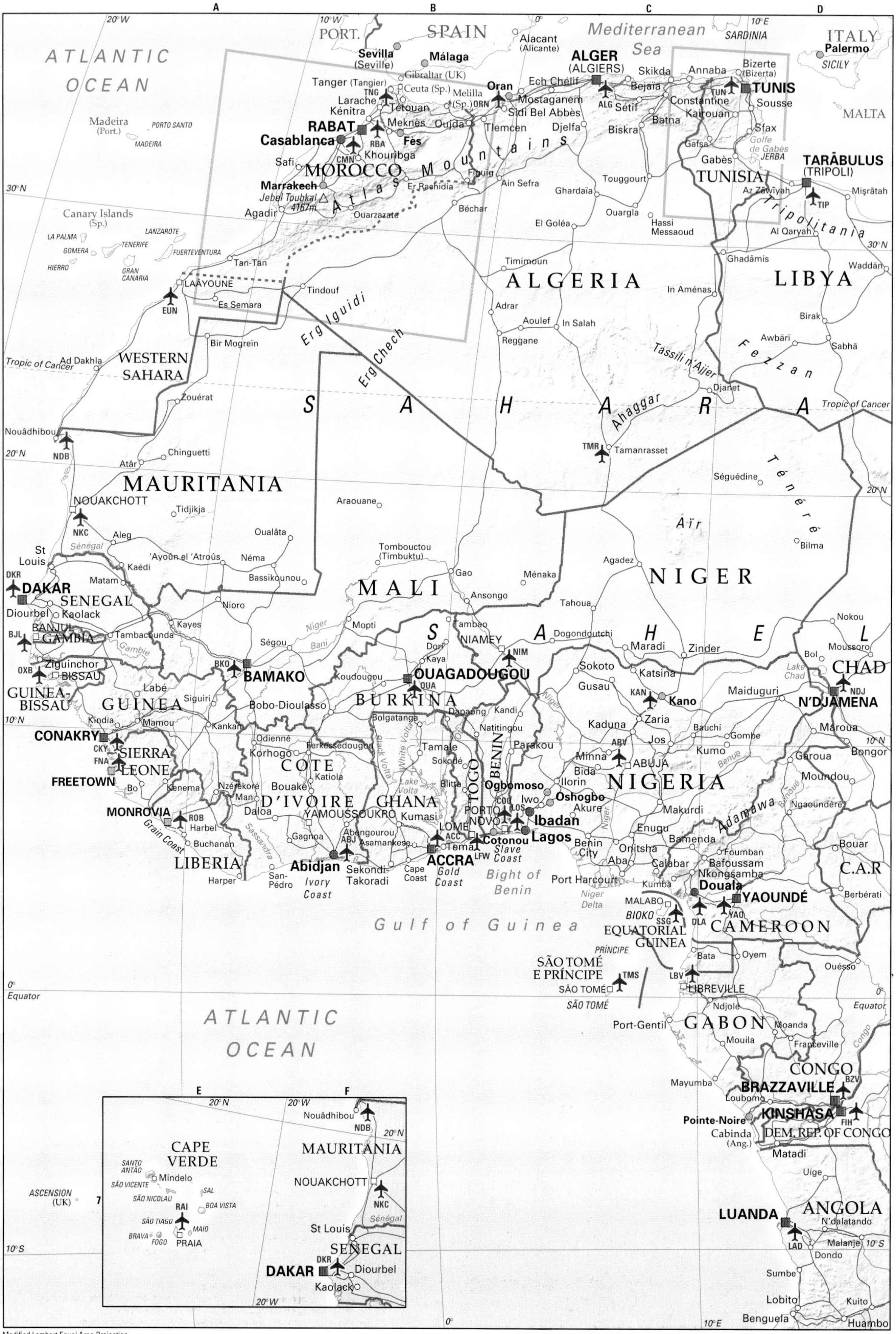

A B C D
1 2 3 4 5 6

20°W 10°W 0° 10°E
ATLANTIC OCEAN
PORT.
SPAIN
Mediterranean Sea
SARDINIA
ITALY
Palermo
SICILY
MALTA
Sevilla (Seville)
Málaga
Gibraltar (UK)
Alacant (Alicante)
ALGER (ALGIERS)
Skikda
Annaba
Bizerte (Bizerta)
TUN
TUNIS
Tanger (Tangier)
TNG
Ceuta (Sp.)
Melilla (Sp.)
ORN
Oran
Ech Chélif
ALG
Bejaïa
Constantine
Sousse
Larache
Kénitra
Tétouan
Mostaganem
Sidi Bel Abbès
Sétif
Kairouan
Madeira (Port.)
PORTO SANTO
MADEIRA
RABAT
Meknès
Oujda
Tlemcen
Djelfa
Biskra
Batna
Sfax
Casablanca
RBA
Fès
CMN
Khouribga
Gafsa
Golfe de Gabès
JERBA
Gabès
TARĀBULUS (TRIPOLI)
Safi
MOROCCO
Atlas Mountains
Figuig
Touggourt
TUNISIA
Az Zāwiyah
Mişrātah
TIP
Marrakech
Jebel Toubkal △ 4167m
Er Rachidia
Ain Sefra
Ghardaïa
30°N
Agadir
Ouarzazate
Béchar
Ouargla
Hassi Messaoud
Tripolitania
Canary Islands (Sp.)
LA PALMA
GOMERA
HIERRO
LANZAROTE
TENERIFE
FUERTEVENTURA
GRAN CANARIA
El Goléa
Al Qaryah
30°N
Tan-Tan
Timimoun
Ghadāmis
Waddān
LAÂYOUNE
EUN
Tindouf
Es Semara
ALGERIA
In Aménas
LIBYA
Erg Iguidi
Adrar
Aoulef
In Salah
Birak
Erg Chech
Reggane
Awbārī
Sabhā
Bir Mogreïn
Tassili n'Ajjer
Fezzan
Tropic of Cancer
Ad Dakhla
WESTERN SAHARA
Djanet
Zouérat
S A H A R A
Ahaggar
Tropic of Cancer
Nouâdhibou
NDB
TMR
Tamanrasset
20°N
Chinguetti
Atâr
Ténéré
Séguédine
MAURITANIA
20°N
NOUAKCHOTT
Araouane
NKC
Tidjikja
Aïr
Aleg
Oualâta
Bilma
Sénégal
St Louis
'Ayoûn el 'Atroûs
Néma
Tombouctou (Timbuktu)
Kaédi
Agadez
DKR
Matam
Bassikounou
Gao
Ménaka
NIGER
DAKAR
MALI
SENEGAL
Ansongo
Tahoua
Diourbel
Kaolack
Nioro
Nokou
BANJUL
GAMBIA
Kayes
Tambacounda
Mopti
Tambao
Dogondoutchi
BJL
Niger
S A H E L
Gambie
Ségou
Bani
Dori
NIAMEY
Maradi
Zinder
Moussoro
Ziguinchor
NIM
OXB
BISSAU
Kaya
Bol
BKO
BAMAKO
OUAGADOUGOU
Sokoto
Katsina
Lake Chad
CHAD
GUINEA-BISSAU
Labé
Koudougou
QUA
GUINEA
Siguiri
Bobo-Dioulasso
BURKINA
Gusau
KAN
Kano
Maiduguri
NDJ
N'DJAMENA
10°N
Kindia
Mamou
Kankan
Bolgatanga
Dapaong
Kandi
Kaduna
Zaria
CONAKRY
Odienné
Natitingou
Bauchi
Gombe
Maroua
10°N
CKY
SIERRA LEONE
FNA
Korhogo
Ferkessédougou
Tamale
BENIN
Parakou
Jos
ABV
ABUJA
Minna
Kumo
Garoua
Bongor
FREETOWN
COTE D'IVOIRE
Katiola
Sokodé
Bida
Benue
Moundou
Bo
Kenema
Nzérékoré
Bouaké
Black Volta
White Volta
Lake Volta
TOGO
Ogbomoso
Ilorin
NIGERIA
Man
Daloa
GHANA
Blitta
Oshogbo
Iwo
Adamawa
Bénoué
MONROVIA
ROB
YAMOUSSOUKRO
Kumasi
PORTO NOVO
COO
LOS
Akure
Makurdi
Ngaoundéré
Harbel
Sassandra
Gagnoa
Abengourou
LOME
ACC
Ibadan
Enugu
Bamenda
Foumban
Bouar
Grain Coast
Buchanan
ABJ
Asamankese
Tema
Cotonou
Lagos
Benin City
Onitsha
Bafoussam
LIBERIA
Abidjan
Sekondi-Takoradi
ACCRA
LFW
Slave Coast
Aba
Calabar
Nkongsamba
Harper
San-Pédro
Ivory Coast
Cape Coast
Gold Coast
Bight of Benin
Port Harcourt
Kumba
Douala
C.A.R
Niger Delta
MALABO
SSG
DLA
YAOUNDÉ
Berbérati
BIOKO
YAO
Gulf of Guinea
EQUATORIAL GUINEA
CAMEROON
PRÍNCIPE
Bata
Oyem
SÃO TOMÉ E PRÍNCIPE
TMS
LBV
Ouésso
0°
SÃO TOMÉ
LIBREVILLE
0°
Equator
SÃO TOMÉ
Equator
Ndjolé
ATLANTIC OCEAN
Port-Gentil
GABON
Moanda
Mouila
Franceville
Congo
CONGO
Mayumba
BZV
BRAZZAVILLE
Loubomo
Pointe-Noire
KINSHASA
FIH
Cabinda (Ang.)
DEM. REP. OF CONGO
Matadi
Uige
LUANDA
ANGOLA
N'dalatando
LAD
Malanje
10°S
Dondo
Sumbe
10°S
Lobito
Kuito
Benguela
Huambo
0°
10°E

E F
20°N 20°W
Nouâdhibou
NDB
20°N
CAPE VERDE
MAURITANIA
SANTO ANTÃO
Mindelo
SÃO VICENTE
SAL
NOUAKCHOTT
ASCENSION (UK)
7
SÃO NICOLAU
RAI
BOA VISTA
NKC
SÃO TIAGO
MAIO
Sénégal
BRAVA
FOGO
PRAIA
St Louis
SENEGAL
DKR
DAKAR
Diourbel
Kaolack
20°W

Modified Lambert Equal Area Projection
1000 kilometres
500 miles

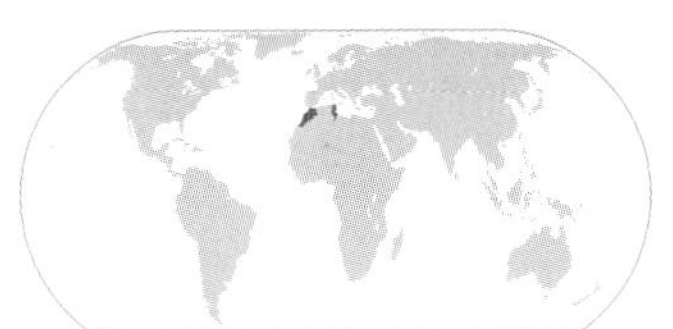

See also... Contents (2-7) – these countries feature in many thematic and regional maps throughout the *World Travel Atlas*.

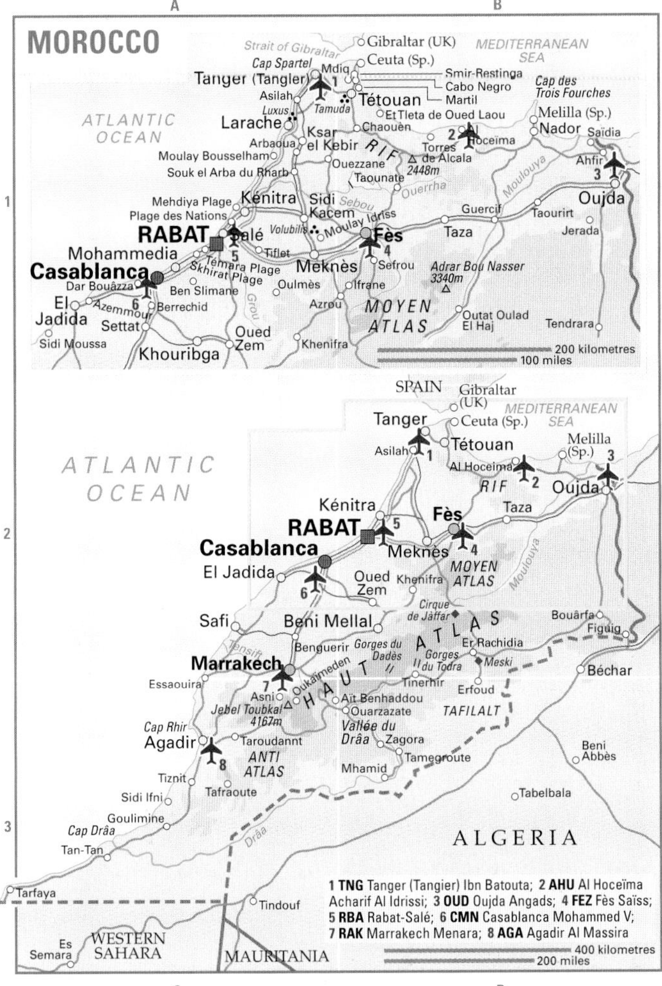
MOROCCO
A
B
1
2
3
Strait of Gibraltar
Gibraltar (UK)
Ceuta (Sp.)
MEDITERRANEAN SEA
Cap Spartel
Mdiq
Tanger (Tangier)
Smir-Restinga
Cabo Negro
Martil
Cap des Trois Fourches
Asilah
Tétouan
Luxus
Tamuda
Et Tleta de Oued Laou
Melilla (Sp.)
ATLANTIC OCEAN
Larache
Chaouèn
Nador
Saïdia
Ksar el Kebir
Al Hoceima
Torres de Alcala
Moulay Bousselham
Arbaoua
Ouezzane
RIF
Ahfir
Souk el Arba du Rharb
Taounate
2448m
Ouerrha
Moulouya
Mehdiya Plage
Kénitra
Sidi Kacem
Sebou
Guercif
Taourirt
Oujda
Plage des Nations
Moulay Idriss
Volubilis
RABAT
Salé
Fès
Taza
Jerada
Mohammedia
Tiflet
Casablanca
Temara Plage
Skhirat Plage
Meknès
Sefrou
Adrar Bou Nasser
3340m
Dar Bouâzza
Ben Slimane
Oulmès
Ifrane
Azemmour
Berrechid
Azrou
MOYEN ATLAS
El Jadida
Settat
Grou
Outat Oulad El Haj
Tendrara
Sidi Moussa
Khouribga
Oued Zem
Khenifra
200 kilometres
100 miles
SPAIN
Gibraltar (UK)
MEDITERRANEAN SEA
Tanger
Ceuta (Sp.)
Melilla (Sp.)
Asilah
Tétouan
Al Hoceima
RIF
Oujda
ATLANTIC OCEAN
Kénitra
Taza
RABAT
Fès
Casablanca
Meknès
El Jadida
MOYEN ATLAS
Oued Zem
Khenifra
Cirque de Jaffar
Safi
Beni Mellal
Bouârfa
Figuig
Benguerir
Gorges du Dadès
Er Rachidia
Tensift
Gorges du Todra
Meski
Marrakech
HAUT ATLAS
Béchar
Essaouira
Oukaimeden
Tinerhir
Asni
Erfoud
Aït Benhaddou
Jebel Toubkal 4167m
Ouarzazate
TAFILALT
Cap Rhir
Vallée du Drâa
Agadir
Taroudannt
Zagora
Beni Abbès
ANTI ATLAS
Tamegroute
Tiznit
Mhamid
Sidi Ifni
Tafraoute
Tabelbala
Goulimine
Cap Drâa
Drâa
Tan-Tan
ALGERIA
Tarfaya
Tindouf
Es Semara
WESTERN SAHARA
MAURITANIA
1 TNG Tanger (Tangier) Ibn Batouta; 2 AHU Al Hoceïma Acharif Al Idrissi; 3 OUD Oujda Angads; 4 FEZ Fès Saïss; 5 RBA Rabat-Salé; 6 CMN Casablanca Mohammed V; 7 RAK Marrakech Menara; 8 AGA Agadir Al Massira
400 kilometres
200 miles

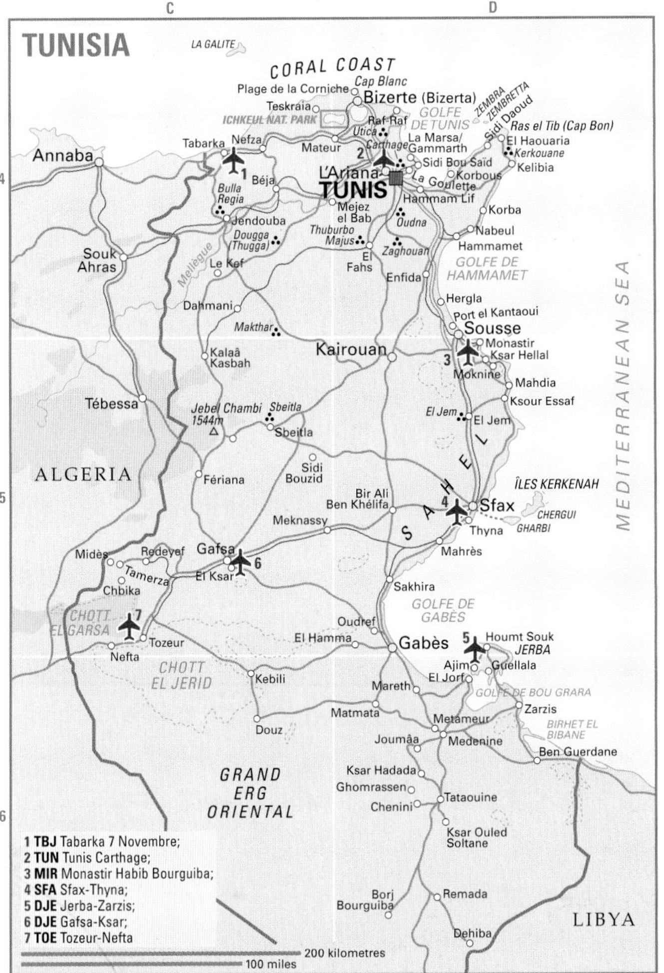
TUNISIA
C
D
4
5
6
LA GALITE
CORAL COAST
Cap Blanc
Plage de la Corniche
Bizerte (Bizerta)
Teskraia
ICHKEUL NAT. PARK
Raf Raf
GOLFE DE TUNIS
ZEMBRA
ZEMBRETTA
Sidi Daoud
Ras el Tib (Cap Bon)
Tabarka
Nefza
Utica
La Marsa
Carthage
Gammarth
Mateur
El Haouaria
Kerkouane
Annaba
Sidi Bou Saïd
Kelibia
Béja
L'Ariana
TUNIS
Korbous
La Goulette
Bulla Regia
Hammam Lif
Mejez el Bab
Oudna
Korba
Jendouba
Thuburbo Majus
Nabeul
Dougga (Thugga)
Hammamet
Souk Ahras
Le Kef
Zaghouan
El Fahs
GOLFE DE HAMMAMET
Mellègue
Enfida
Hergla
Port el Kantaoui
Dahmani
Makthar
Sousse
Monastir
Kalaâ Kasbah
Kairouan
Ksar Hellal
Moknine
Mahdia
Tébessa
Ksour Essaf
Jebel Chambi 1544m
Sbeitla
El Jem
ALGERIA
Sidi Bouzid
Fériana
ÎLES KERKENAH
Bir Ali Ben Khélifa
SAHEL
Sfax
CHERGUI
GHARBI
Meknassy
Thyna
Midès
Redeyef
Gafsa
Mahrès
Tamerza
El Ksar
Chbika
Sakhira
CHOTT EL GARSA
GOLFE DE GABÈS
Tozeur
Oudref
El Hamma
Gabès
Houmt Souk
JERBA
Nefta
CHOTT EL JERID
Ajim
Guellala
Kebili
Mareth
El Jorf
GOLFE DE BOU GRARA
Zarzis
Matmata
Metameur
BIRHET EL BIBANE
Douz
Medenine
Ben Guerdane
Joumâa
Ksar Hadada
GRAND ERG ORIENTAL
Ghomrassen
Chenini
Tataouine
Ksar Ouled Soltane
Remada
Borj Bourguiba
LIBYA
Dehiba
MEDITERRANEAN SEA
1 TBJ Tabarka 7 Novembre;
2 TUN Tunis Carthage;
3 MIR Monastir Habib Bourguiba;
4 SFA Sfax-Thyna;
5 DJE Jerba-Zarzis;
6 DJE Gafsa-Ksar;
7 TOE Tozeur-Nefta
200 kilometres
100 miles
2000 metres
1000 metres
Sea level

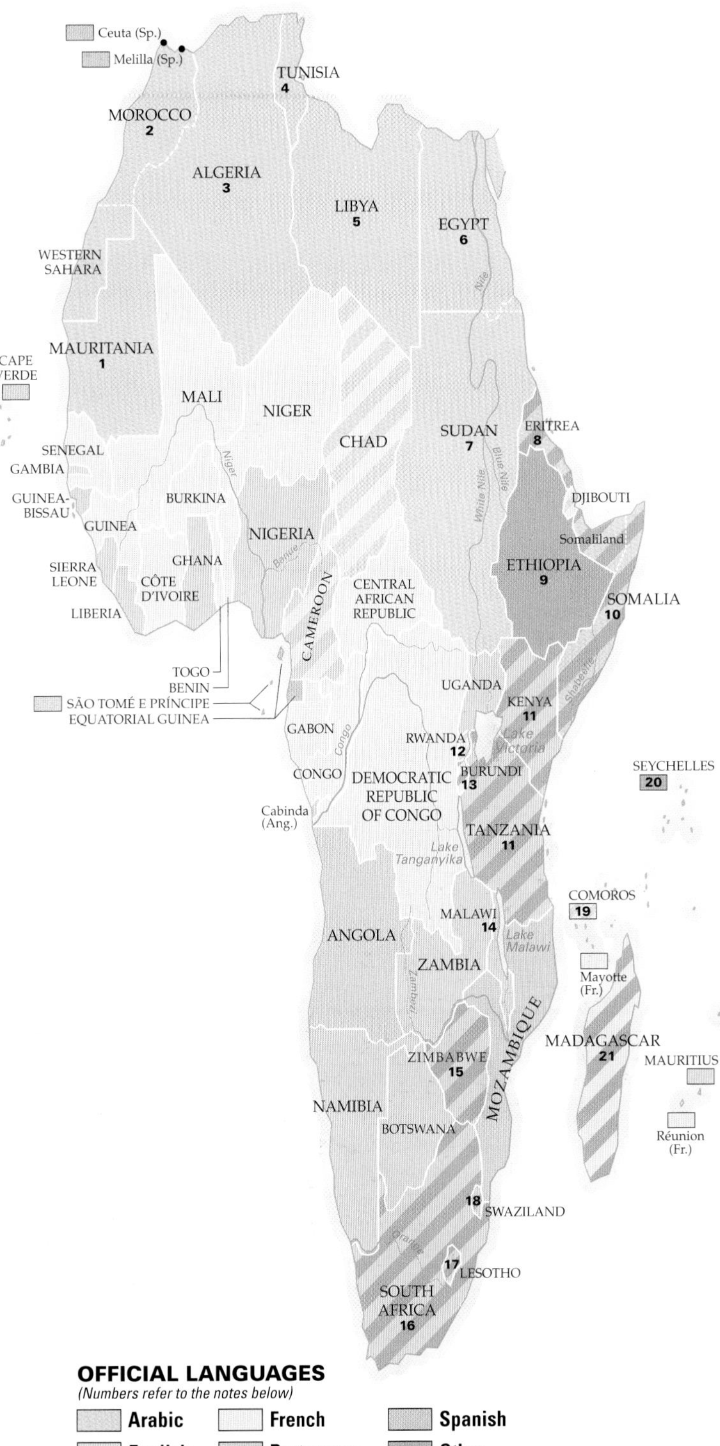
Ceuta (Sp.)
Melilla (Sp.)
TUNISIA 4
MOROCCO 2
ALGERIA 3
LIBYA 5
EGYPT 6
WESTERN SAHARA
Nile
MAURITANIA 1
CAPE VERDE
MALI
NIGER
CHAD
SUDAN 7
ERITREA 8
SENEGAL
GAMBIA
GUINEA-BISSAU
GUINEA
BURKINA
Niger
Blue Nile
White Nile
DJIBOUTI
Somaliland
NIGERIA
Benue
ETHIOPIA 9
SIERRA LEONE
GHANA
CÔTE D'IVOIRE
LIBERIA
CAMEROON
CENTRAL AFRICAN REPUBLIC
SOMALIA 10
TOGO
BENIN
SÃO TOMÉ E PRÍNCIPE
EQUATORIAL GUINEA
UGANDA
KENYA 11
Shabeelle
GABON
Congo
RWANDA 12
Lake Victoria
CONGO
DEMOCRATIC REPUBLIC OF CONGO
BURUNDI 13
SEYCHELLES 20
Cabinda (Ang.)
TANZANIA 11
Lake Tanganyika
COMOROS 19
MALAWI 14
ANGOLA
Lake Malawi
ZAMBIA
Zambezi
Mayotte (Fr.)
MOZAMBIQUE
MADAGASCAR 21
MAURITIUS
ZIMBABWE 15
NAMIBIA
BOTSWANA
Réunion (Fr.)
18
SWAZILAND
Orange
17
LESOTHO
SOUTH AFRICA 16

OFFICIAL LANGUAGES

(Numbers refer to the notes below)

Arabic
French
Spanish
English
Portuguese
Other

1 French is widely spoken by black communities in the south.
2 French is widely spoken throughout the country, except in the north where Spanish is more predominant. Berber is spoken by a large minority.
3 Arabic is compulsory for all official business. English has replaced French as the official second language. Berber is spoken by a large minority.
4 French is used for most business transactions. English is spoken in major cities and resorts. Berber is spoken by a large minority.
5 English is normally understood in hotels, restaurants and shops.
6 English and French are widely spoken in urban centres.
7 English is widely spoken throughout the country.
8 The official languages are Arabic and Tigrinya. English and Italian are the most common foreign languages.
9 The official language is Ahmaric, and English is widely understood. Italian and French are still widely spoken.
10 The official languages are Arabic and Somali. Some English and Italian are also spoken.
11 The official languages are English and Kiswahili.
12 The official languages are English, French and Kinyarwanda.
13 The official languages are French and Kirundi.
14 Chichewa is widely spoken and is regarded as the national language by Malawi's largest ethnic group, the Chewa.
15 The official languages are English, Ndebele and Shona.
16 The official languages are Afrikaans, English, Ndebele, Pedi, Sesotho, Siswati, Tsonga, Tswana, Venda, Xhosa and Zulu.
17 The official languages are English and Sesotho.
18 The official languages are English and Siswati.
19 The official languages are English, French and Comorian (a blend of Arabic and Swahili).
20 The official language is Creole, but English and French are widely spoken.
21 The official languages are French and Malagasy. Very little English is spoken.

See also... Contents (2-7) – these countries feature in many thematic and regional maps throughout the *World Travel Atlas*.

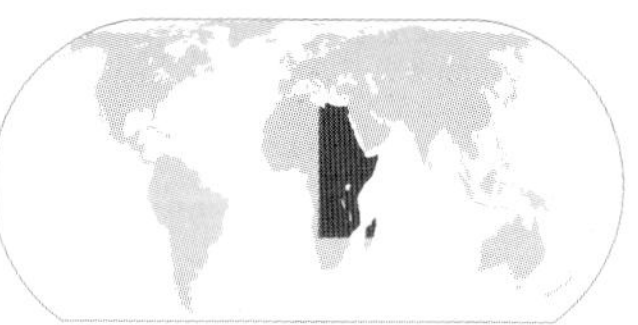

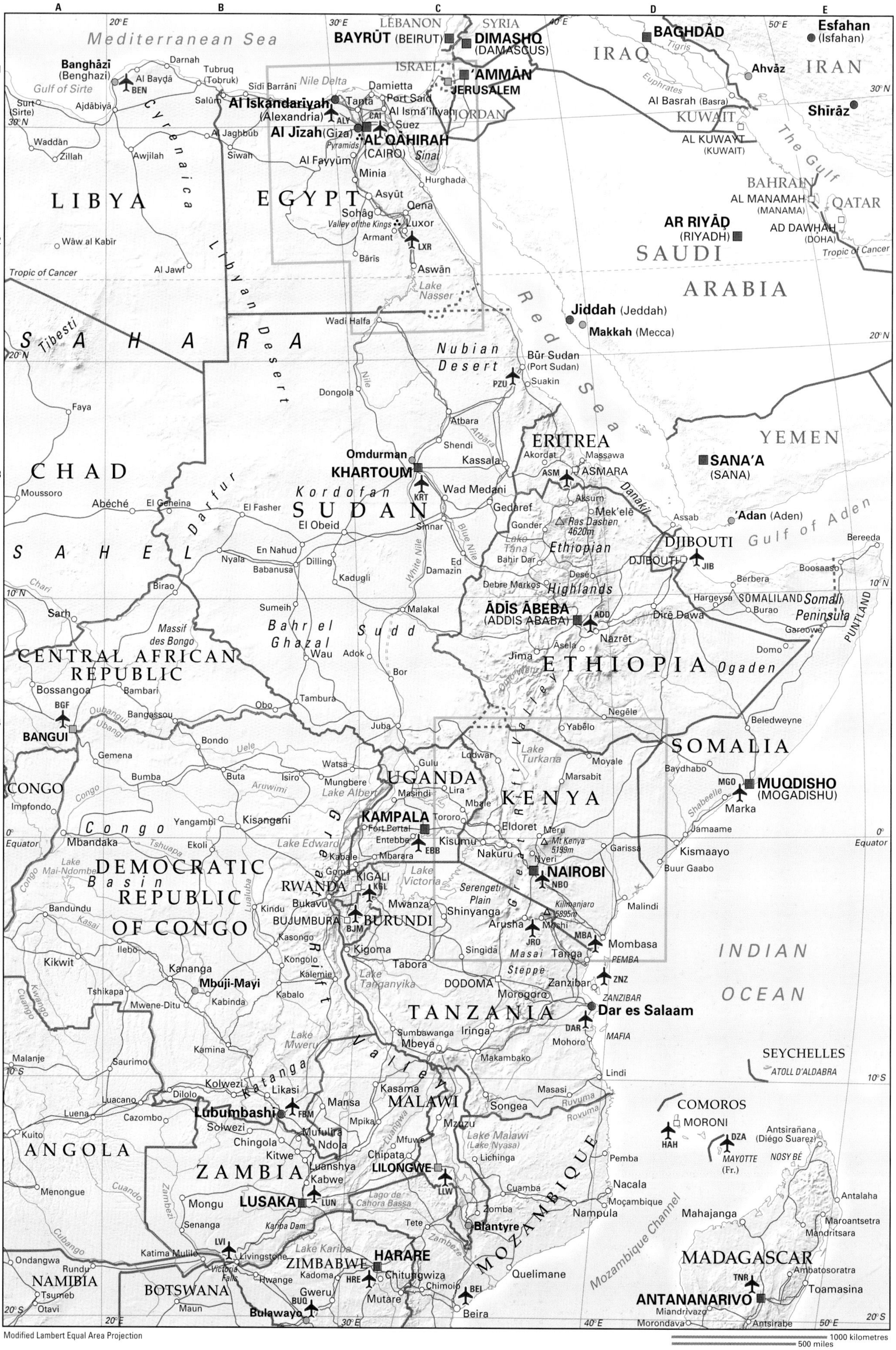

A B C D E
20°E 30°E 40°E 50°E

Mediterranean Sea
LEBANON SYRIA
BAYRŪT (BEIRUT) DIMASHQ (DAMASCUS)
BAGHDĀD IRAQ Esfahan (Isfahan) IRAN Ahvāz Shīrāz
Banghāzī (Benghazi) BEN Darnah Al Baydā Tubruq (Tobruk) Gulf of Sirte Surt (Sirte) Ajdābiyā
ISRAEL 'AMMĀN JERUSALEM JORDAN
Nile Delta Sīdī Barrānī Salūm Al Iskandarīyah (Alexandria) ALY Tanta Damietta Port Said Al Ismā'īlīyah Suez
Al Jīzah (Giza) Pyramids AL QĀHIRAH (CAIRO) CAI Sinai
Al Jaghbūb Siwah Waddān Zillah Awjilah Al Fayyūm Minia
Tigris Euphrates Al Basrah (Basra) KUWAIT AL KUWAYT (KUWAIT) The Gulf
LIBYA Cyrenaica EGYPT Asyūt Hurghada Qena Sohâg Valley of the Kings Luxor Armant LXR Bāris Aswān
Wāw al Kabīr Al Jawf Libyan Desert Tropic of Cancer Lake Nasser
BAHRAIN AL MANAMAH (MANAMA) QATAR AR RIYĀD (RIYADH) AD DAWHAH (DOHA) SAUDI ARABIA
Wadi Halfa Red Sea Jiddah (Jeddah) Makkah (Mecca)
Tibesti SAHARA Nubian Desert Būr Sudan (Port Sudan) PZU Suakin
Faya Dongola Nile Atbara Artbara Shendi
CHAD Omdurman KHARTOUM KRT Kassala ERITREA Akordat Massawa ASM ASMARA YEMEN SANA'A (SANA)
Moussoro Abéché El Geneina Darfur El Fasher Kordofan SUDAN El Obeid Wad Medani Gedaref Aksum Mek'elē Danakil Assab 'Adan (Aden) Gulf of Aden
SAHEL En Nahud Nyala Dilling Babanusa Sinnar Blue Nile White Nile Ed Damazin Gonder Ras Dashen 4620m Lake Tana Bahir Dar Ethiopian Highlands DJIBOUTI DJIBOUTI JIB Bereeda Bosaaso
Chari Birao Kadugli Debre Markos Desē Berbera Hargeysa SOMALILAND Somali Peninsula Burao PUNTLAND
Sarh Massif des Bongo Sumeih Malakal Bahr el Ghazal Sudd ĀDĪS ĀBEBA (ADDIS ABABA) ADD Nazrēt Dirē Dawa Garoowe
CENTRAL AFRICAN REPUBLIC Wau Adok Bor Āsela Jīma Domo ETHIOPIA Ogaden
Bossangoa Bambari Tambura Omo Wenz Great Rift Valley
BGF BANGUI Oubangui Ubangi Bangassou Obo Juba Yabēlo Negēle Beledweyne SOMALIA
Bondo Uele Gemena Gulu Lodwar Lake Turkana Moyale Baydhabo
CONGO Impfondo Bumba Buta Isiro Watsa Mungbere Lake Albert Masindi Lira UGANDA KENYA Marsabit MGO MUQDISHO (MOGADISHU) Marka Shabeelle
Congo Aruwimi Yangambi Kisangani KAMPALA Fort Portal Entebbe EBB Tororo Mbale Eldoret Meru Mt Kenya 5199m
0° Equator Mbandaka Congo Basin Tshuapa Ekoli Lake Edward Kabale Mbarara Kisumu Nakuru Nyeri Garissa Jamaame Kismaayo
Lake Mai-Ndombe DEMOCRATIC REPUBLIC OF CONGO Lualaba Goma KIGALI KGL RWANDA Lake Victoria Serengeti Plain NAIROBI NBO Buur Gaabo
Bandundu Kasai Kindu Bukavu Mwanza BUJUMBURA BJM BURUNDI Shinyanga Arusha JRO Moshi Kilimanjaro 5895m Malindi
Kikwit Ilebo Kasongo Kigoma Kongolo Tabora Singida Masai Steppe Tanga MBA Mombasa PEMBA INDIAN OCEAN
Kananga Tshikapa Kalemie Lake Tanganyika DODOMA Morogoro Zanzibar ZNZ ZANZIBAR
Kwango Cuango Mwene-Ditu Mbuji-Mayi Kabinda Kabalo TANZANIA Dar es Salaam DAR MAFIA
Kamina Lake Mweru Sumbawanga Mbeya Iringa Mohoro
Malanje Saurimo Makambako SEYCHELLES ATOLL D'ALDABRA 10°S Lindi
Katanga Kolwezi Likasi Dilolo Kasama Mansa Masasi Ruvuma
Luacano Luena Cazombo Lubumbashi FBM MALAWI Songea Rovuma COMOROS MORONI HAH
Kuito Solwezi Mpika Mzuzu Mufulira Ndola Lake Malawi (Lake Nyasa) DZA Antsiranana (Diégo Suarez)
ANGOLA Chingola Kitwe Luangwa Mfuwe Lichinga Pemba MAYOTTE (Fr.) NOSY BÉ
ZAMBIA Luanshya Chipata Kabwe LILONGWE LLW
Menongue Cuando Zambezi Mongu LUSAKA LUN Lago de Cahora Bassa Cuamba Nacala Moçambique Nampula Antalaha
Senanga Kariba Dam Tete Zomba Blantyre Mahajanga Maroantsetra Mandritsara
LVI Katima Mulilo Livingstone Lake Kariba Zambezi MOZAMBIQUE Mozambique Channel
Ondangwa Rundu Cubango NAMIBIA Victoria Falls Hwange ZIMBABWE HARARE Kadoma HRE Chitungwiza Quelimane MADAGASCAR Ambatosoratra
Tsumeb BOTSWANA Gweru BUQ Mutare Chimoio BEI TNR Toamasina
20°S Otavi Maun Bulawayo Beira ANTANANARIVO Miandrivazo Morondava Antsirabe

Modified Lambert Equal Area Projection
1000 kilometres
500 miles

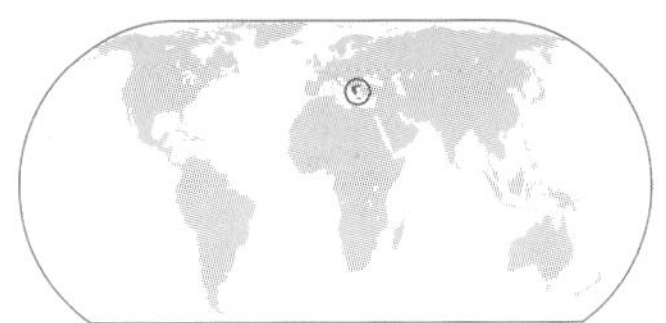

See also... Mediterranean Diving (106); Wildlife Parks (122-123); Pacific Diving (150-151); Caribbean Diving (180-181)

The listings above refer to a selection of related themes. For more information, see the Contents (2-7).

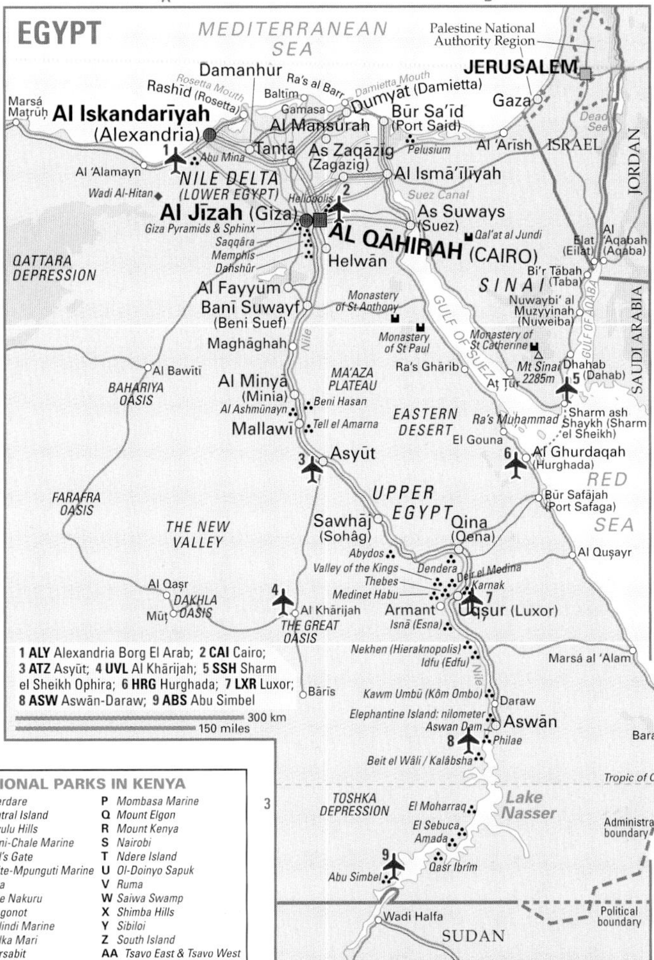

EGYPT

1 **ALY** Alexandria Borg El Arab; 2 **CAI** Cairo; 3 **ATZ** Asyūt; 4 **UVL** Al Khārijah; 5 **SSH** Sharm el Sheikh Ophira; 6 **HRG** Hurghada; 7 **LXR** Luxor; 8 **ASW** Aswān-Daraw; 9 **ABS** Abu Simbel

300 km / 150 miles

NATIONAL PARKS IN KENYA

A	*Aberdare*	P	*Mombasa Marine*
B	*Central Island*	Q	*Mount Elgon*
C	*Chyulu Hills*	R	*Mount Kenya*
D	*Diani-Chale Marine*	S	*Nairobi*
E	*Hell's Gate*	T	*Ndere Island*
F	*Kisite-Mpunguti Marine*	U	*Ol-Doinyo Sapuk*
G	*Kora*	V	*Ruma*
H	*Lake Nakuru*	W	*Saiwa Swamp*
J	*Longonot*	X	*Shimba Hills*
K	*Malindi Marine*	Y	*Sibiloi*
L	*Malka Mari*	Z	*South Island*
M	*Marsabit*	AA	*Tsavo East & Tsavo West*
N	*Meru*	BB	*Watumu Marine*

KENYA

1 **EDL** Eldoret; 2 **KIS** Kisumu; 3 **NBO** Nairobi Jomo Kenyatta; 4 **LAU** Lamu; 5 **MYD** Malindi; 6 **MBA** Mombasa Moi

400 km / 200 miles

80 km / 40 miles

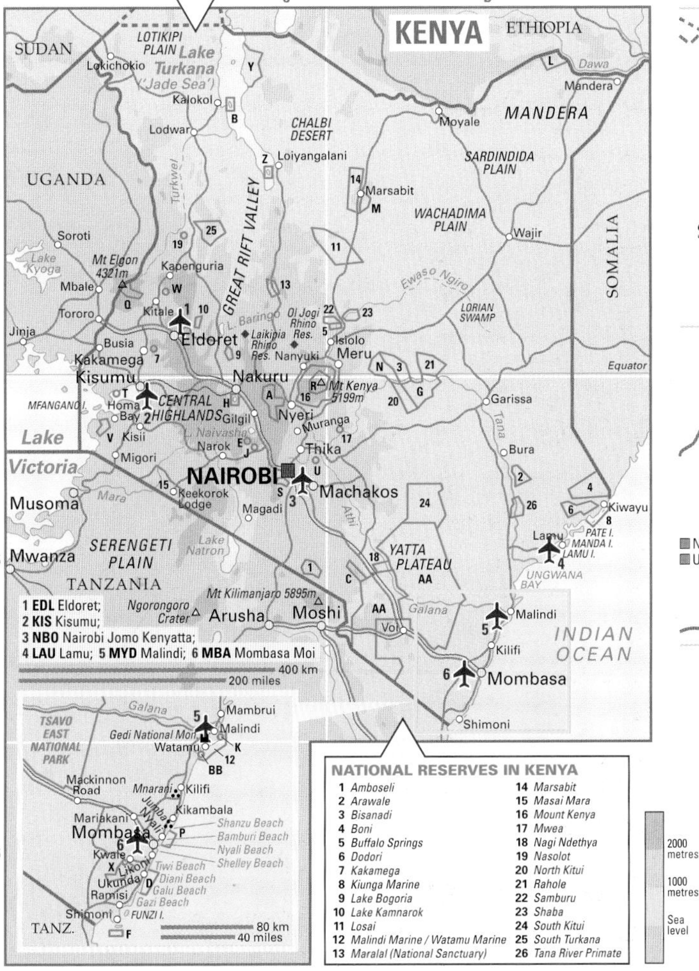

NATIONAL RESERVES IN KENYA

1	*Amboseli*	14	*Marsabit*
2	*Arawale*	15	*Masai Mara*
3	*Bisanadi*	16	*Mount Kenya*
4	*Boni*	17	*Mwea*
5	*Buffalo Springs*	18	*Nagi Ndethya*
6	*Dodori*	19	*Nasolot*
7	*Kakamega*	20	*North Kitui*
8	*Kiunga Marine*	21	*Rahole*
9	*Lake Bogoria*	22	*Samburu*
10	*Lake Kamnarok*	23	*Shaba*
11	*Losai*	24	*South Kitui*
12	*Malindi Marine / Watamu Marine*	25	*South Turkana*
13	*Maralal (National Sanctuary)*	26	*Tana River Primate*

2000 metres / 1000 metres / Sea level

*The map below shows the top dive sites in the Red Sea and highlights the main diving resort towns. The three sites close to Eilat are shore dives: all other sites can be visited from the many day boats or 'live-aboard' boats which regularly ply these waters. Sites marked with * are also accessible from the shore. All the resort towns marked act as bases for these boats and have equipment for hire, but most have few specialist facilities at present.*

The dives are divided into those which feature an underwater wreck and those where the main focus is on the prolific marine life and the reef.

The sharks of Ra's Muhammad are legendary; professional photographers and film makers travel to this site just to photograph them. Hammerheads, Reef Sharks and Oceanic White Tip Sharks are regularly sighted in the Red Sea. Manta Ray, Eagle Ray and various species of dolphin and turtle are also quite common. Whilst any of these may be seen at any time, the sites where this is a regular occurrence have been marked.

The table below gives the depths that divers must reach to achieve a reasonable exploration of each site: this will determine the equipment and level of experience required.

email: ned@nedmiddleton.demon.co.uk

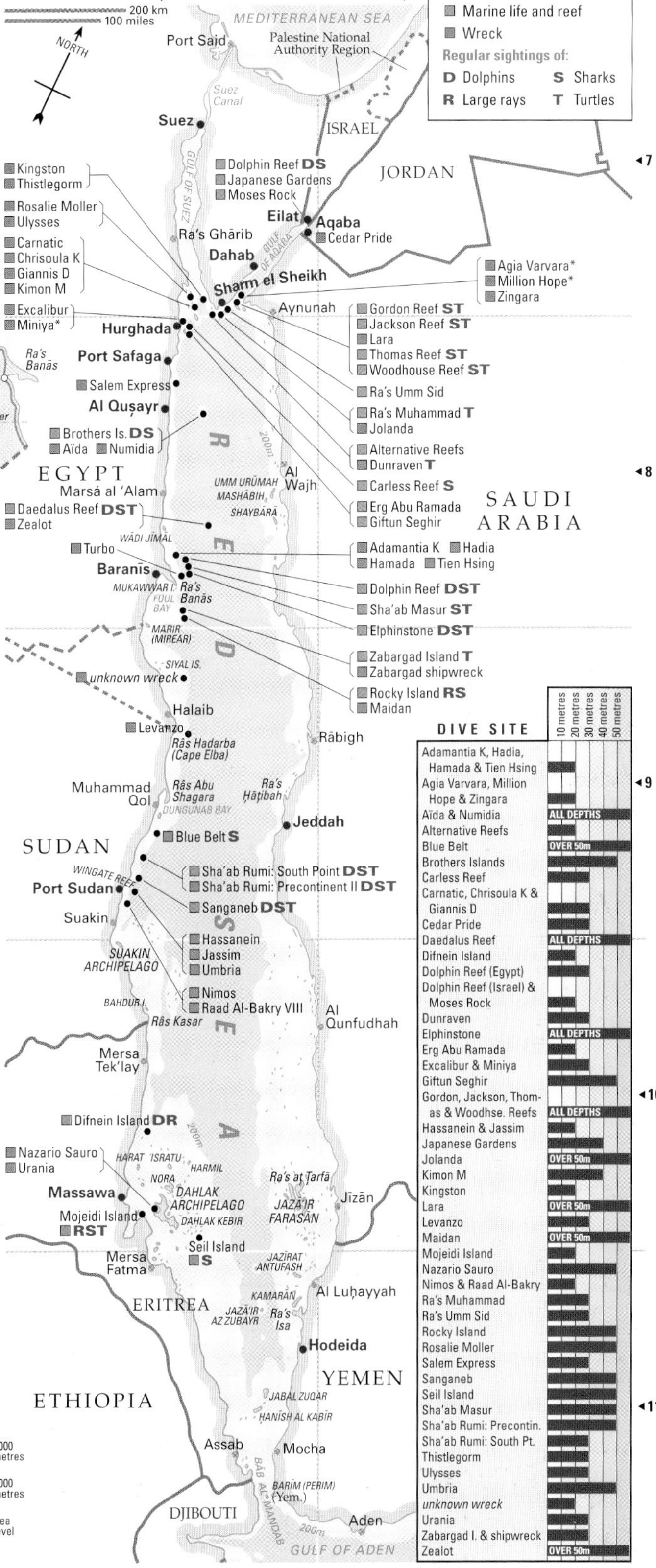

● Diving resort town

Dive sites:
- Marine life and reef
- Wreck

Regular sightings of:
- **D** Dolphins
- **S** Sharks
- **R** Large rays
- **T** Turtles

200 km / 100 miles

DIVE SITE	10 metres	20 metres	30 metres	40 metres	50 metres
Adamantia K, Hadia, Hamada & Tien Hsing	■	■			
Agia Varvara, Million Hope & Zingara	■	■			
Aïda & Numidia	ALL DEPTHS				
Alternative Reefs	■	■			
Blue Belt	OVER 50m				
Brothers Islands	■	■	■	■	
Carless Reef	■	■	■		
Carnatic, Chrisoula K & Giannis D	■	■	■		
Cedar Pride	■	■	■		
Daedalus Reef	ALL DEPTHS				
Difnein Island	■	■			
Dolphin Reef (Egypt)	■	■	■		
Dolphin Reef (Israel) & Moses Rock	■	■			
Dunraven	■	■	■		
Elphinstone	ALL DEPTHS				
Erg Abu Ramada	■	■			
Excalibur & Miniya	■	■	■		
Giftun Seghir	■	■	■	■	
Gordon, Jackson, Thomas & Woodhse. Reefs	ALL DEPTHS				
Hassanein & Jassim	■	■			
Japanese Gardens	■	■	■	■	
Jolanda	OVER 50m				
Kimon M	■	■	■	■	
Kingston	■	■			
Lara	OVER 50m				
Levanzo	■	■	■		
Maidan	OVER 50m				
Mojeidi Island	■	■			
Nazario Sauro	■	■	■	■	
Nimos & Raad Al-Bakry	■	■			
Ra's Muhammad	■	■	■		
Ra's Umm Sid	■	■	■		
Rocky Island	■	■	■	■	
Rosalie Moller	■	■	■	■	
Salem Express	■	■	■		
Sanganeb	■	■	■	■	
Seil Island	■	■	■	■	
Sha'ab Masur	■	■	■	■	
Sha'ab Rumi: Precontin.	■	■	■	■	
Sha'ab Rumi: South Pt.	■	■	■		
Thistlegorm	■	■	■		
Ulysses	■	■	■		
Umbria	■	■	■	■	
unknown wreck	■	■			
Urania	■	■	■		
Zabargad I. & shipwreck	■	■	■		
Zealot	OVER 50m				

Africa: Southern

See also... Kenya (119); South Africa (121); Wildlife Parks (122-123); Indian Ocean Islands (123)

The listings above refer to a selection of related themes. For more information, see the Contents (2-7).

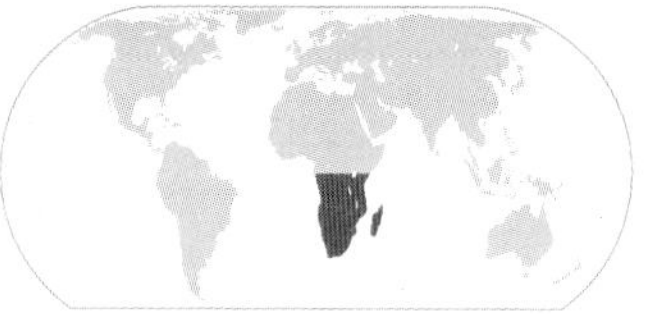

Lambert Equal Area Projection

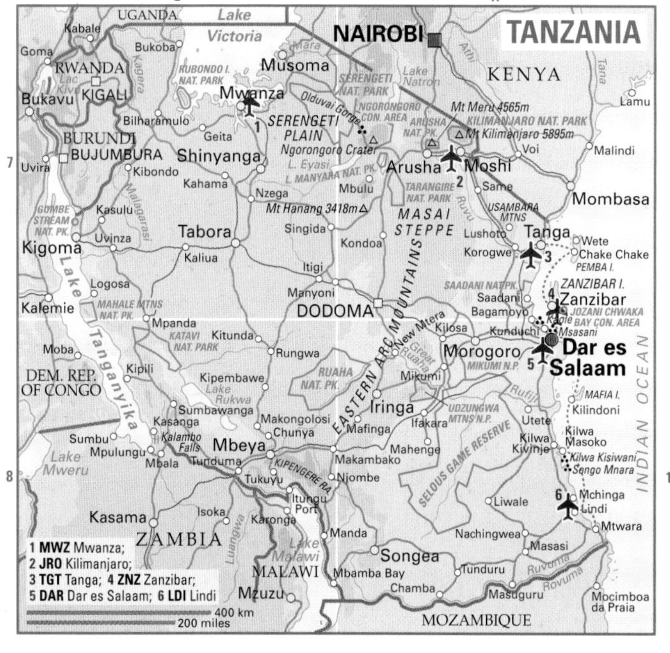
TANZANIA
NAIROBI
KENYA
UGANDA
RWANDA
KIGALI
BURUNDI
BUJUMBURA
Mwanza
Musoma
Shinyanga
Arusha
Moshi
Mt Kilimanjaro 5895m
Mt Meru 4565m
Mombasa
Malindi
Lamu
Tabora
Kigoma
Singida
DODOMA
Tanga
Zanzibar
Dar es Salaam
Morogoro
Iringa
Mbeya
Songea
Lindi
Mtwara
Kilwa Masoko
Mafia I.
Pemba I.
DEM. REP. OF CONGO
ZAMBIA
MALAWI
MOZAMBIQUE
INDIAN OCEAN
EASTERN ARC MOUNTAINS
SELOUS GAME RESERVE
SERENGETI PLAIN
MASAI STEPPE
1 MWZ Mwanza; 2 JRO Kilimanjaro; 3 TGT Tanga; 4 ZNZ Zanzibar; 5 DAR Dar es Salaam; 6 LDI Lindi
400 km
200 miles

BOTSWANA
ANGOLA
ZAM.
NAMIBIA
ZIMBABWE
SOUTH AFRICA
Kasane
Livingstone
Victoria Falls
Hwange
Shakawe
Okavango Delta
Maun
Nata
Gweta
Bulawayo
Francistown
Selebi-Phikwe
Ghanzi
CENTRAL KALAHARI GAME RESERVE
KALAHARI DESERT
Tropic of Capricorn
GABORONE
Molepolole
Mochudi
Kanye
Lobatse
Tshabong
Bokspits
PRETORIA (CITY OF TSHWANE)
Johannesburg
Soweto
Sasolburg
Kempton Park
Mamelodi
1 BBK Kasane; 2 MUB Maun; 3 FRW Francistown; 4 GBE Gaborone Seretse Khama
300 km
150 miles
2000 metres
1000 metres
Sea level

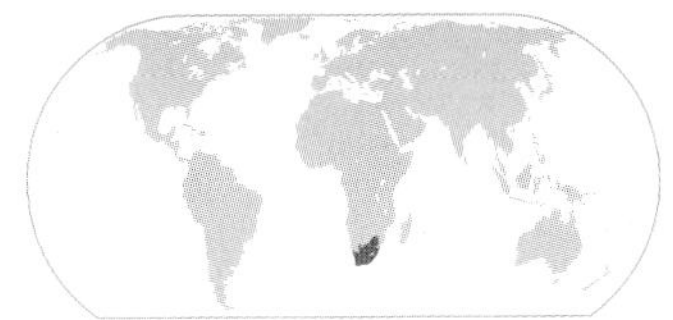

See also... Wildlife Parks (122-123)

The listings above refer to a selection of related themes. For more information, see the Contents (2-7).

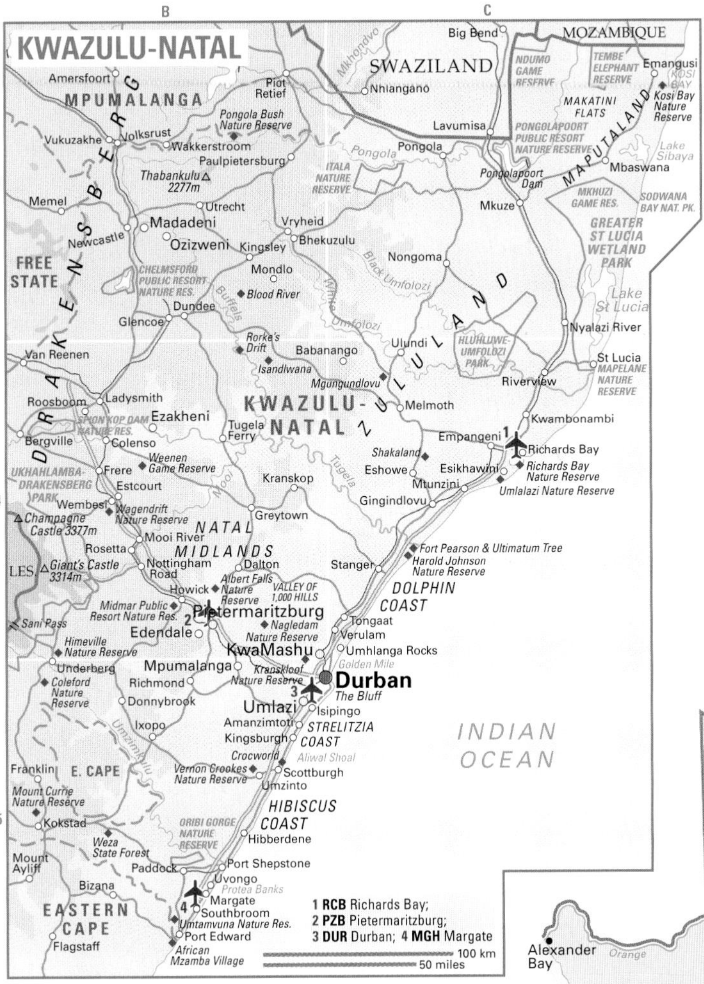

KWAZULU-NATAL

1 **RCB** Richards Bay; 2 **PZB** Pietermaritzburg; 3 **DUR** Durban; 4 **MGH** Margate

100 km
50 miles

The *Blue Train* is a luxury train service which runs scheduled trips between Cape Town and Pretoria and charter journeys to Victoria Falls and Hoedspruit.

Rovos Rail provide a variety of journeys on what is claimed to be the most luxurious train in the world including Pretoria-Cape Town, Pretoria-Durban, Pretoria-Victoria Falls and Cape Town-George. The company also operates annual rail safaris within South Africa, to Namibia and to Dar es Salaam via Zimbabwe and Zambia.

Shongololo Express offers long and short excursions throughout Southern Africa, including a number of itineraries within South Africa such as The Good Hope Adventure and Garden Route.

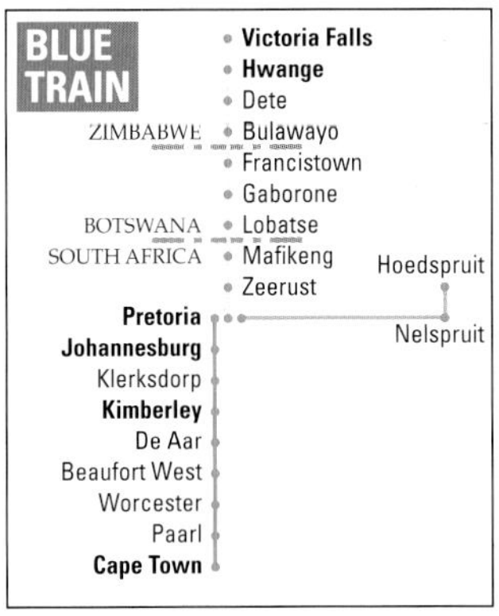

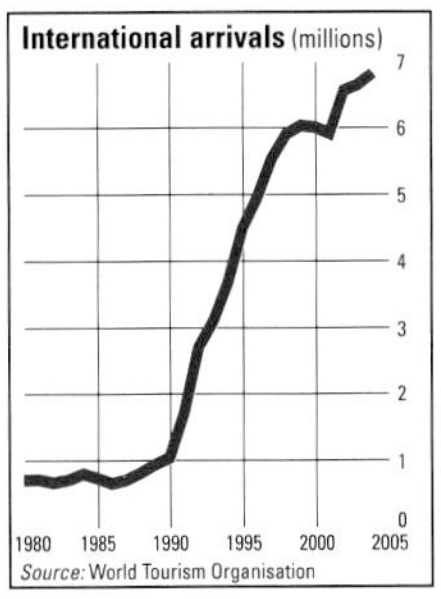

BLUE TRAIN

Victoria Falls, **Hwange**, Dete, Bulawayo (ZIMBABWE), Francistown, Gaborone, Lobatse (BOTSWANA), Mafikeng (SOUTH AFRICA), Zeerust, **Pretoria**, **Johannesburg**, Klerksdorp, **Kimberley**, De Aar, Beaufort West, Worcester, Paarl, **Cape Town**; Hoedspruit, Nelspruit

International arrivals (millions)

1980, 1985, 1990, 1995, 2000, 2005

Source: World Tourism Organisation

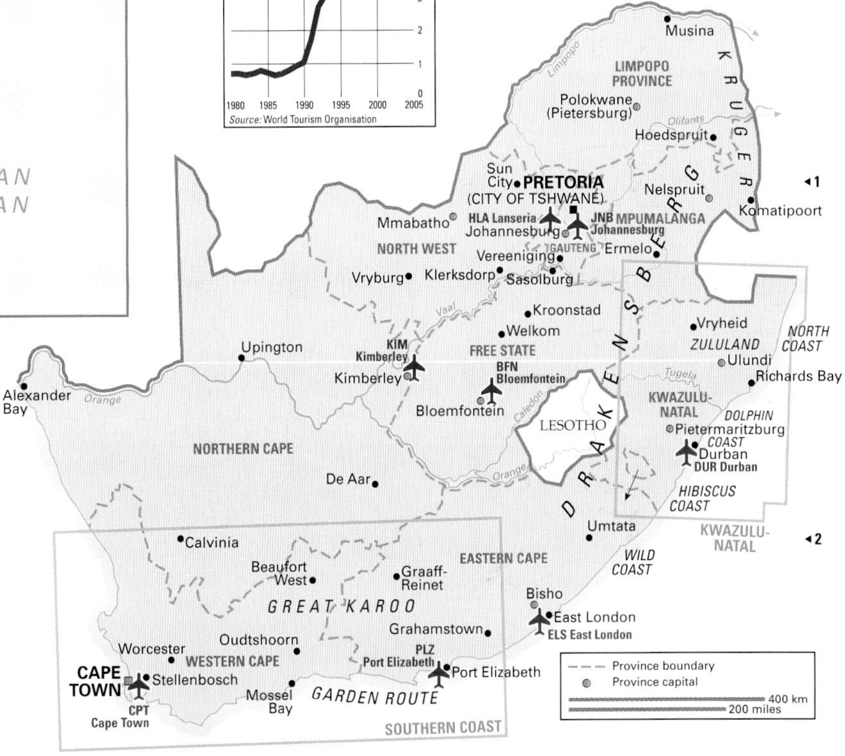

Province boundary
Province capital
400 km
200 miles

- JAN 1st New Year's Parade **(Cape Town)**
- MAR One City Festival **(Cape Town)**
- EASTER Rand Easter Show **(Johannesburg)**
- EASTER Rustlers Valley Easter Festival **(eastern Free State)**
- MAY Cape Gourmet Festival **(Cape Town)**
- MAY Pink Loerie Festival **(Knysna)**
- JUN **Durban** International Film Festival
- JUL Youth Arts Festival **(Montagu)**
- JUL National Arts Festival **(Grahamstown)**
- AUG Oppi Koppi Music Festival **(Northam)**
- AUG **Stellenbosch** Wine Festival
- SEP Arts Alive International Festival **(Johannesburg)**
- SEP **Hermanus** Whale Festival
- SEP **Stellenbosch** Music Festival
- OCT Poetry Africa Festival **(Durban)**
- DEC16th Reconciliation Day (countrywide)

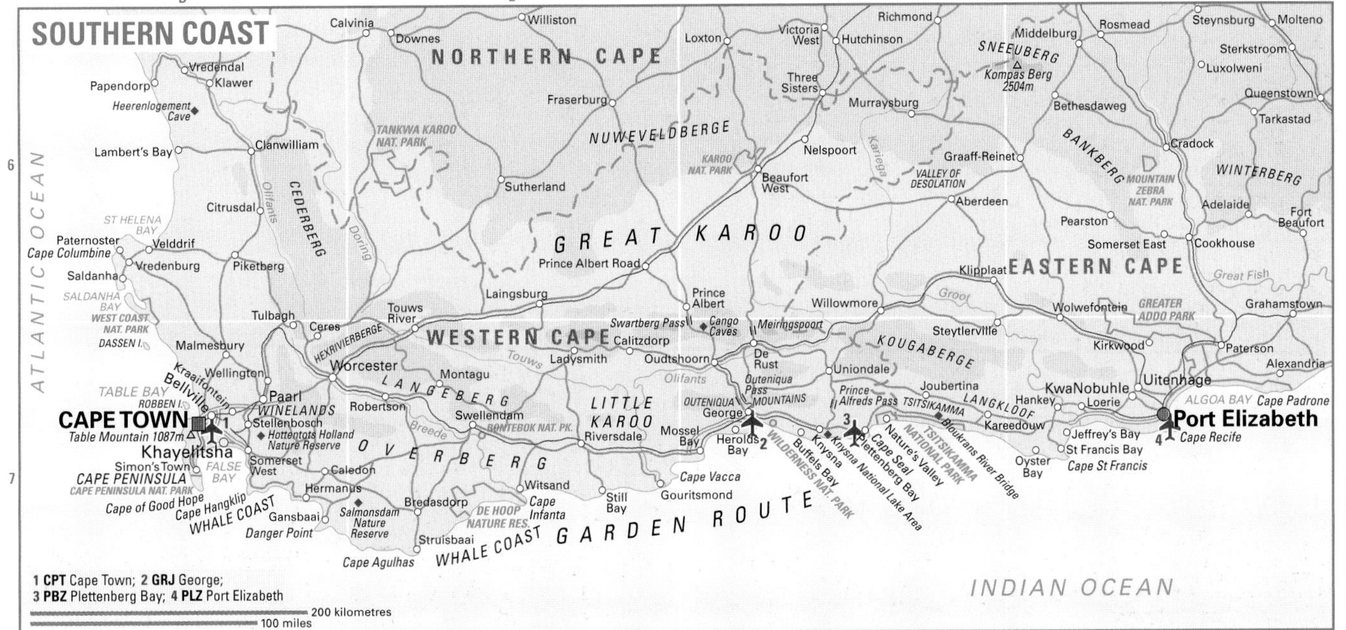
SOUTHERN COAST
NORTHERN CAPE
GREAT KAROO
EASTERN CAPE
WESTERN CAPE
GARDEN ROUTE
WHALE COAST
ATLANTIC OCEAN
INDIAN OCEAN
CAPE TOWN
Port Elizabeth
1 CPT Cape Town; 2 GRJ George;
3 PBZ Plettenberg Bay; 4 PLZ Port Elizabeth
200 kilometres
100 miles
2000 metres
1000 metres
Sea level

Wildlife Parks

See also... Kenya (119); Tanzania (120); Botswana (120); South Africa (121); Indian Ocean Islands (123)

The listings above refer to a selection of related themes. For more information, see the Contents (2-7).

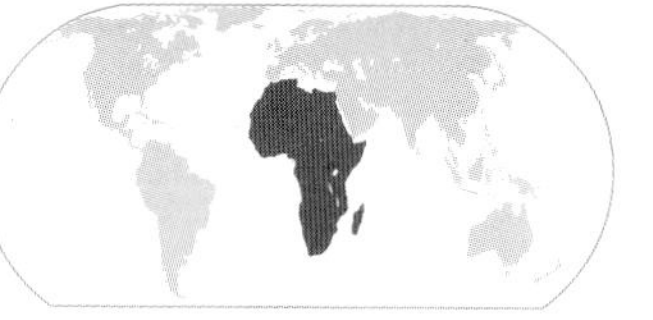

Parks and reserves marked with an asterisk (*) are featured in Columbus Travel Guides' *Tourist Attractions and Events of the World*

Thanks to the following for their help in compiling this section:

Bill Adams of Safari Consultants: bill@safariconsultantuk.com
John Knighton of African Pride: info@African-pride.co.uk
John Douglas of Malawi Tourism: enquiries@malawitourism.com

Any errors or omissions remain the responsibility of the publishers

Africa is a prime destination for wildlife holidays: its national parks, game reserves and wildlife sanctuaries feature prominently in package holidays and tourist itineraries. Many parks, such as the Masai Mara, Serengeti and Kruger, are well-known throughout the world and a number of ther have been recognised by both UNESCO and the WWF for their unique and important character.

The area of Africa south of the Sahara is featured here. Although there are areas of wildlife intere in northern Africa, particularly on the Mediterranean coast, these are generally on a much smalle scale and do not usually provide the primary motivation for travel to these countries.

The map and table features the major parks and reserves used by tour operators and visited by overseas tourists. Some lesser-known parks are also included to give a broader geographical spread; access to many of these may be difficult due to poor infrastructure or political problems

The table lists the major species most likely to be seen while visiting each park or those animals f which the park is famous, according to government literature and independent reports. Quality of information varies considerably from country to country and the following table should be regard as a rough guide only. Poaching is a serious problem in some countries, particularly where wildlife tourism is less developed or where wars or civil unrest have diverted resources and personnel awa from park administration.

The Peace Parks Foundation, established in 1997, is helping to develop transfrontier conservation areas (peace parks) in southern Africa, allowing wildlife greater freedom of movement. The remova of physical barriers between countries helps to restore traditional animal migration routes, as we as encouraging tourism and economic development.

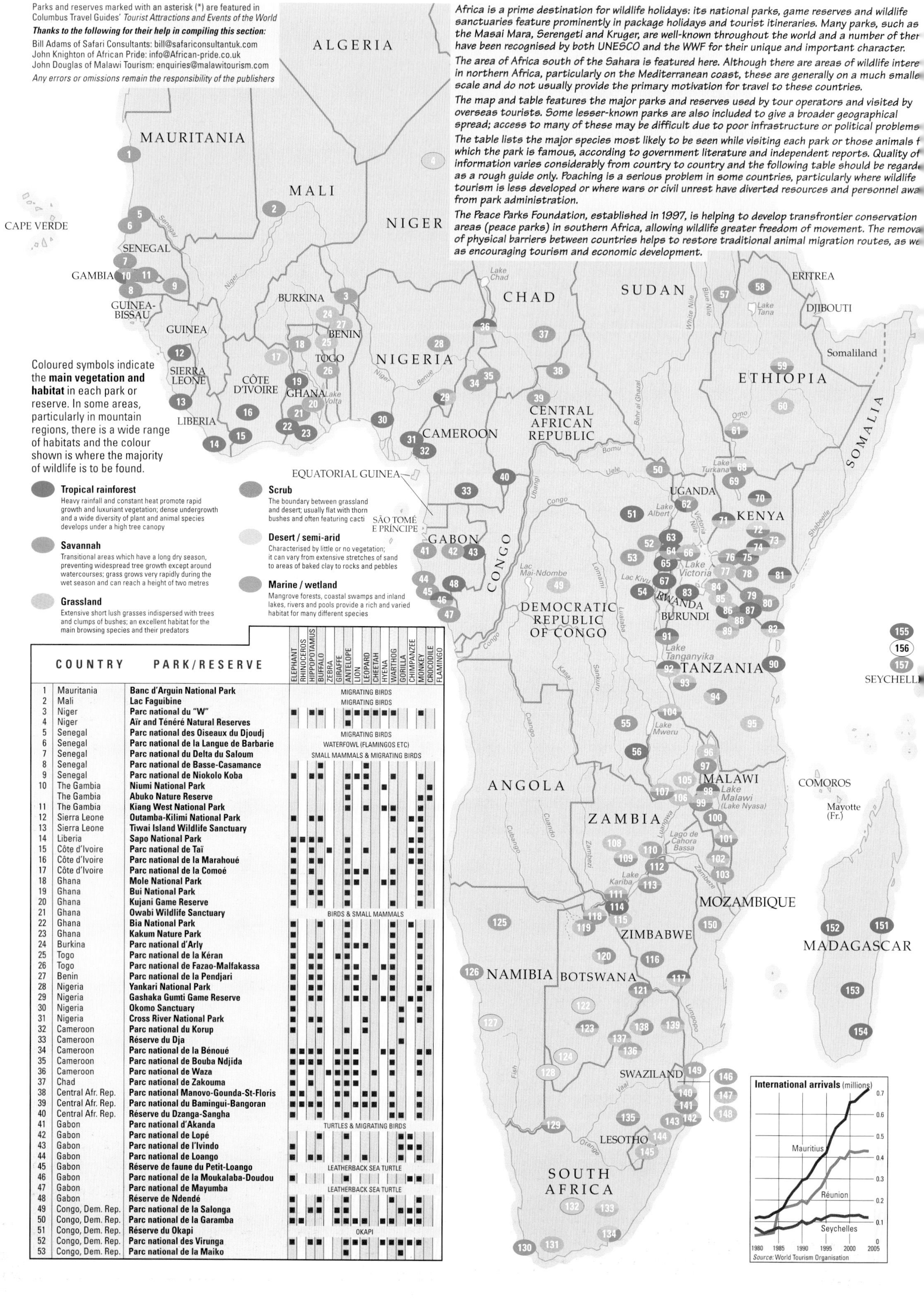

ALGERIA
MAURITANIA
MALI
NIGER
CAPE VERDE
SENEGAL
GAMBIA
GUINEA-BISSAU
GUINEA
SIERRA LEONE
LIBERIA
CÔTE D'IVOIRE
BURKINA
GHANA
TOGO
BENIN
NIGERIA
CHAD
SUDAN
ERITREA
DJIBOUTI
Somaliland
ETHIOPIA
SOMALIA
CAMEROON
CENTRAL AFRICAN REPUBLIC
EQUATORIAL GUINEA
SÃO TOMÉ E PRÍNCIPE
GABON
CONGO
DEMOCRATIC REPUBLIC OF CONGO
UGANDA
KENYA
RWANDA
BURUNDI
TANZANIA
SEYCHELLES
ANGOLA
ZAMBIA
MALAWI
COMOROS
Mayotte (Fr.)
MOZAMBIQUE
ZIMBABWE
MADAGASCAR
NAMIBIA
BOTSWANA
SWAZILAND
LESOTHO
SOUTH AFRICA
Senegal, Niger, Benue, Lake Chad, Lake Volta, Blue Nile, White Nile, Lake Tana, Bahr al Ghazal, Omo, Lake Turkana, Bomu, Uele, Ubangi, Congo, Lac Mai-Ndombe, Lake Albert, Victoria Nile, Lake Victoria, Lac Kivu, Lomami, Lualaba, Kasai, Sankuru, Lake Tanganyika, Shabeelle, Cuango, Lake Mweru, Lake Malawi (Lake Nyasa), Luangwa, Lago de Cahora Bassa, Zambezi, Cuando, Cubango, Lake Kariba, Limpopo, Fish, Vaal, Orange

Coloured symbols indicate the **main vegetation and habitat** in each park or reserve. In some areas, particularly in mountain regions, there is a wide range of habitats and the colour shown is where the majority of wildlife is to be found.

Tropical rainforest
Heavy rainfall and constant heat promote rapid growth and luxuriant vegetation; dense undergrowth and a wide diversity of plant and animal species develops under a high tree canopy

Savannah
Transitional areas which have a long dry season, preventing widespread tree growth except around watercourses; grass grows very rapidly during the wet season and can reach a height of two metres

Grassland
Extensive short lush grasses indispersed with trees and clumps of bushes; an excellent habitat for the main browsing species and their predators

Scrub
The boundary between grassland and desert; usually flat with thorn bushes and often featuring cacti

Desert / semi-arid
Characterised by little or no vegetation; it can vary from extensive stretches of sand to areas of baked clay to rocks and pebbles

Marine / wetland
Mangrove forests, coastal swamps and inland lakes, rivers and pools provide a rich and varied habitat for many different species

	COUNTRY	PARK/RESERVE	ELEPHANT	RHINOCEROS	HIPPOPOTAMUS	BUFFALO	ZEBRA	GIRAFFE	ANTELOPE	LION	LEOPARD	CHEETAH	HYENA	WARTHOG	GORILLA	CHIMPANZEE	MONKEY	CROCODILE	FLAMINGO
1	Mauritania	Banc d'Arguin National Park	MIGRATING BIRDS																
2	Mali	Lac Faguibine	MIGRATING BIRDS																
3	Niger	Parc national du "W"	■		■	■			■	■	■	■	■	■			■		
4	Niger	Aïr and Ténéré Natural Reserves							■										
5	Senegal	Parc national des Oiseaux du Djoudj	MIGRATING BIRDS																
6	Senegal	Parc national de la Langue de Barbarie	WATERFOWL (FLAMINGOS ETC)																
7	Senegal	Parc national du Delta du Saloum	SMALL MAMMALS & MIGRATING BIRDS																
8	Senegal	Parc national de Basse-Casamance				■					■								
9	Senegal	Parc national de Niokolo Koba	■		■	■			■	■	■			■			■		
10	The Gambia	Niumi National Park							■		■		■					■	
	The Gambia	Abuko Nature Reserve							■								■	■	
11	The Gambia	Kiang West National Park							■		■		■	■			■		
12	Sierra Leone	Outamba-Kilimi National Park	■		■	■								■		■	■		
13	Sierra Leone	Tiwai Island Wildlife Sanctuary															■		
14	Liberia	Sapo National Park	■	■	■	■			■							■	■		
15	Côte d'Ivoire	Parc national de Taï	■		■		■		■		■			■		■	■		
16	Côte d'Ivoire	Parc national de la Marahoué	■		■	■			■							■	■		
17	Côte d'Ivoire	Parc national de la Comoé	■		■				■	■	■			■			■		
18	Ghana	Mole National Park	■			■			■	■			■	■			■		
19	Ghana	Bui National Park	■		■	■			■								■		
20	Ghana	Kujani Game Reserve	■			■			■					■			■		
21	Ghana	Owabi Wildlife Sanctuary	BIRDS & SMALL MAMMALS																
22	Ghana	Bia National Park	■			■			■					■		■			
23	Ghana	Kakum Nature Park	■						■					■			■		
24	Burkina	Parc national d'Arly	■			■			■	■	■			■			■		
25	Togo	Parc national de la Kéran	■		■	■		■	■					■			■		
26	Togo	Parc national de Fazao-Malfakassa	■		■	■			■	■			■	■			■		
27	Benin	Parc national de la Pendjari	■		■	■			■	■		■		■			■		
28	Nigeria	Yankari National Park	■		■	■				■				■			■	■	
29	Nigeria	Gashaka Gumti Game Reserve	■		■	■			■	■	■		■	■		■	■		
30	Nigeria	Okomo Sanctuary	■												■		■		
31	Nigeria	Cross River National Park	■		■	■					■				■		■		
32	Cameroon	Parc national du Korup	■			■			■		■								
33	Cameroon	Réserve du Dja													■				
34	Cameroon	Parc national de la Bénoué	■	■	■	■		■	■	■			■	■			■	■	
35	Cameroon	Parc national de Bouba Ndjida	■	■	■	■		■	■	■				■			■		
36	Cameroon	Parc national de Waza	■		■		■	■	■	■		■		■			■		
37	Chad	Parc national de Zakouma	■		■			■	■	■									
38	Central Afr. Rep.	Parc national Manovo-Gounda-St-Floris	■	■		■		■	■		■	■		■			■		
39	Central Afr. Rep.	Parc national du Bamingui-Bangoran	■	■	■	■		■		■	■	■		■			■		
40	Central Afr. Rep.	Réserve du Dzanga-Sangha	■			■			■					■	■		■		
41	Gabon	Parc national d'Akanda	TURTLES & MIGRATING BIRDS																
42	Gabon	Parc national de Lopé				■			■						■	■			
43	Gabon	Parc national de l'Ivindo	■												■	■	■		
44	Gabon	Parc national de Loango	■		■	■			■		■				■		■		
45	Gabon	Réserve de faune du Petit-Loango	LEATHERBACK SEA TURTLE																
46	Gabon	Parc national de la Moukalaba-Doudou	■						■							■	■		
47	Gabon	Parc national de Mayumba	LEATHERBACK SEA TURTLE																
48	Gabon	Réserve de Ndendé	■			■			■					■			■		
49	Congo, Dem. Rep.	Parc national de la Salonga	■		■	■		■	■						■	■	■		
50	Congo, Dem. Rep.	Parc national de la Garamba	■	■				■	■	■	■		■	■		■	■		
51	Congo, Dem. Rep.	Réserve du Okapi	OKAPI																
52	Congo, Dem. Rep.	Parc national des Virunga	■		■	■			■	■	■		■	■	■	■	■		
53	Congo, Dem. Rep.	Parc national de la Maiko							■						■				

International arrivals (millions)

0.7
0.6
0.5
0.4
0.3
0.2
0.1
0
Mauritius
Réunion
Seychelles
1980 1985 1990 1995 2000 2005

Source: World Tourism Organisation

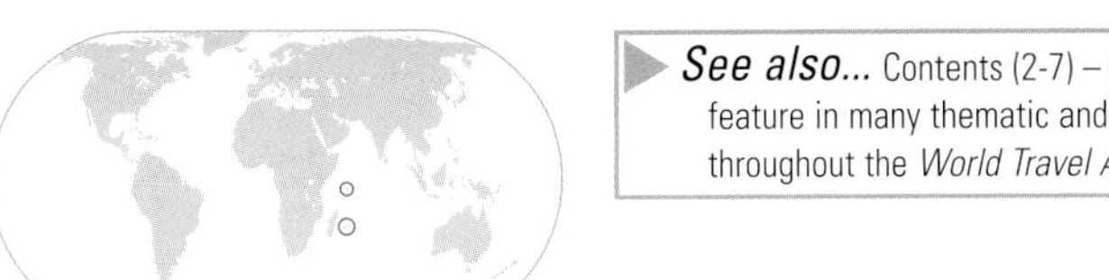

See also... Contents (2-7) – these countries feature in many thematic and regional maps throughout the *World Travel Atlas*.

Wildlife Parks: Indian Ocean Islands

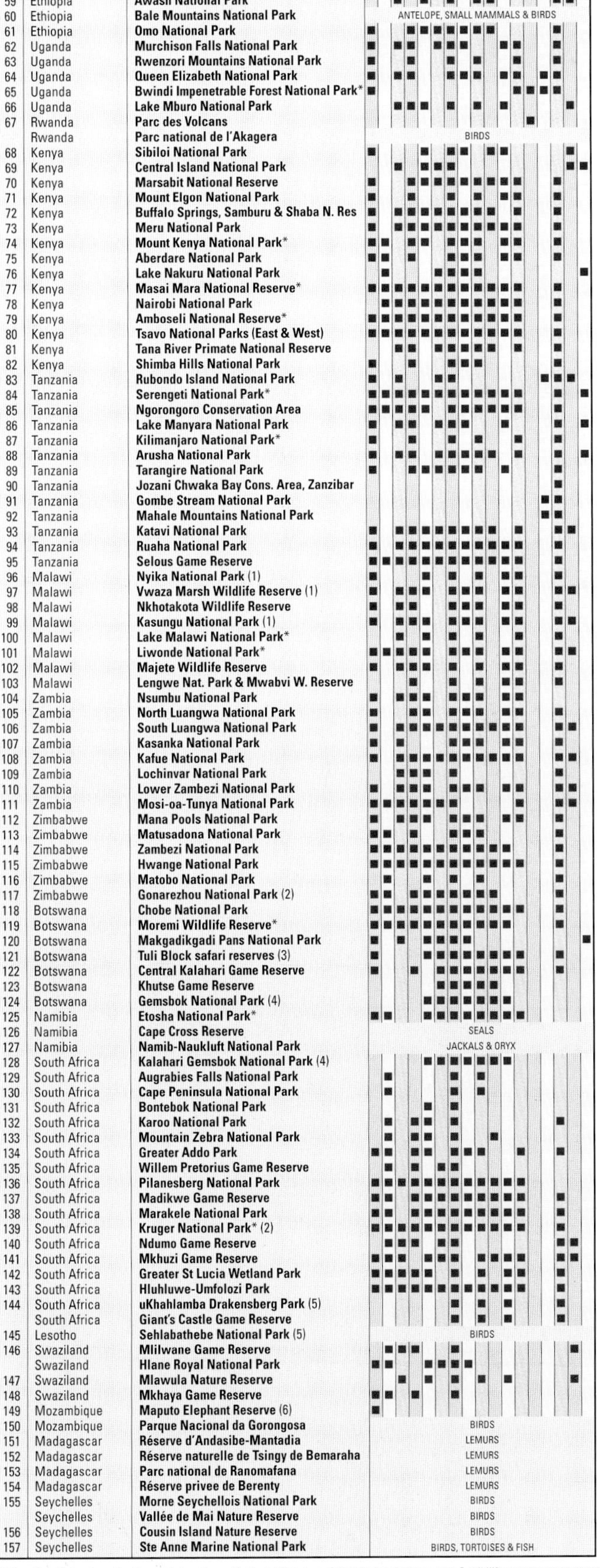

	COUNTRY	PARK/RESERVE	ELEPHANT	RHINOCEROS	HIPPOPOTAMUS	BUFFALO	ZEBRA	GIRAFFE	ANTELOPE	LION	LEOPARD	CHEETAH	HYENA	WARTHOG	GORILLA	CHIMPANZEE	MONKEY	CROCODILE	FLAMINGO
54	Congo, Dem. Rep.	**Parc national du Kahuzi-Biega**													■	■	■		
55	Congo, Dem. Rep.	**Parc national de l'Upemba**	■			■	■						■		■	■	■		
56	Congo, Dem. Rep.	**Parc national de Kundelungu**			■		■		■			■					■		
57	Sudan	**Dinder National Park**	■					■	■	■	■	■							
58	Ethiopia	**Simien Mountains National Park**	BABOONS & SMALL ANIMALS																
59	Ethiopia	**Awash National Park**			■		■		■		■	■					■	■	
60	Ethiopia	**Bale Mountains National Park**	ANTELOPE, SMALL MAMMALS & BIRDS																
61	Ethiopia	**Omo National Park**	■			■	■	■	■	■	■	■					■		
62	Uganda	**Murchison Falls National Park**	■		■	■		■	■	■			■	■			■		
63	Uganda	**Rwenzori Mountains National Park**	■			■			■		■			■			■		
64	Uganda	**Queen Elizabeth National Park**	■		■	■			■	■	■		■	■		■	■		
65	Uganda	**Bwindi Impenetrable Forest National Park***	■											■	■	■	■		
66	Uganda	**Lake Mburo National Park**			■	■	■		■		■		■					■	
67	Rwanda	**Parc des Volcans**													■				
	Rwanda	**Parc national de l'Akagera**	BIRDS																
68	Kenya	**Sibiloi National Park**	■				■		■	■		■	■					■	
69	Kenya	**Central Island National Park**			■		■	■	■									■	■
70	Kenya	**Marsabit National Reserve**	■			■	■	■	■	■	■	■	■	■			■		
71	Kenya	**Mount Elgon National Park**	■			■			■		■		■	■			■		
72	Kenya	**Buffalo Springs, Samburu & Shaba N. Res**	■		■	■	■	■	■	■	■	■		■			■		
73	Kenya	**Meru National Park**	■		■	■	■	■	■	■	■	■	■	■			■		
74	Kenya	**Mount Kenya National Park***	■	■		■	■		■	■	■		■	■			■		
75	Kenya	**Aberdare National Park**	■	■		■			■	■	■		■	■			■		
76	Kenya	**Lake Nakuru National Park**		■				■	■	■	■								■
77	Kenya	**Masai Mara National Reserve***	■	■	■	■	■	■	■	■	■	■	■	■			■		
78	Kenya	**Nairobi National Park**		■	■	■	■	■	■	■	■	■	■	■			■		
79	Kenya	**Amboseli National Reserve***	■	■	■	■	■	■	■	■	■	■	■	■			■		
80	Kenya	**Tsavo National Parks (East & West)**	■	■	■	■	■	■	■	■	■	■	■	■			■		
81	Kenya	**Tana River Primate National Reserve**			■	■		■	■	■	■	■		■			■		
82	Kenya	**Shimba Hills National Park**	■			■			■	■	■						■		
83	Tanzania	**Rubondo Island National Park**	■		■			■	■							■	■	■	
84	Tanzania	**Serengeti National Park***	■	■	■	■	■	■	■	■	■	■	■	■			■		■
85	Tanzania	**Ngorongoro Conservation Area**	■	■	■	■	■		■	■	■	■	■	■			■		
86	Tanzania	**Lake Manyara National Park**	■		■	■		■	■	■			■				■		■
87	Tanzania	**Kilimanjaro National Park***	■			■			■		■			■			■		
88	Tanzania	**Arusha National Park**	■		■	■		■	■	■	■	■		■			■		■
89	Tanzania	**Tarangire National Park**	■			■	■	■	■	■	■		■				■		
90	Tanzania	**Jozani Chwaka Bay Cons. Area, Zanzibar**															■		
91	Tanzania	**Gombe Stream National Park**														■	■		
92	Tanzania	**Mahale Mountains National Park**														■	■		
93	Tanzania	**Katavi National Park**	■		■	■	■	■	■	■	■	■		■			■	■	
94	Tanzania	**Ruaha National Park**	■		■	■	■	■	■	■	■	■	■	■			■		
95	Tanzania	**Selous Game Reserve**	■	■	■	■	■	■	■	■	■	■	■	■			■		
96	Malawi	**Nyika National Park** (1)	■				■		■		■		■	■			■		
97	Malawi	**Vwaza Marsh Wildlife Reserve** (1)	■		■	■	■		■	■	■		■	■			■	■	
98	Malawi	**Nkhotakota Wildlife Reserve**	■		■	■			■	■	■		■	■			■		
99	Malawi	**Kasungu National Park** (1)	■		■	■	■		■	■	■		■	■			■	■	
100	Malawi	**Lake Malawi National Park***			■		■		■		■			■			■		
101	Malawi	**Liwonde National Park***	■	■	■	■	■		■	■	■		■	■			■	■	
102	Malawi	**Majete Wildlife Reserve**	■		■	■	■		■		■		■	■			■		
103	Malawi	**Lengwe Nat. Park & Mwabvi W. Reserve**				■			■		■		■	■			■		
104	Zambia	**Nsumbu National Park**	■		■	■	■		■	■	■		■	■					
105	Zambia	**North Luangwa National Park**	■			■	■		■	■	■		■	■			■		
106	Zambia	**South Luangwa National Park**	■		■	■	■	■	■	■	■	■	■	■			■	■	
107	Zambia	**Kasanka National Park**	■		■				■	■	■		■	■			■		
108	Zambia	**Kafue National Park**	■		■	■	■	■	■	■	■	■	■	■			■	■	
109	Zambia	**Lochinvar National Park**			■	■	■		■								■		
110	Zambia	**Lower Zambezi National Park**	■		■	■	■		■	■	■		■	■			■	■	
111	Zambia	**Mosi-oa-Tunya National Park**	■	■	■	■	■	■	■					■			■	■	
112	Zimbabwe	**Mana Pools National Park**	■		■	■	■		■	■	■		■	■			■		
113	Zimbabwe	**Matusadona National Park**	■	■		■			■	■	■						■		
114	Zimbabwe	**Zambezi National Park**	■	■	■	■	■	■	■	■	■	■	■				■		
115	Zimbabwe	**Hwange National Park**	■	■	■	■	■	■	■	■	■	■	■	■			■		
116	Zimbabwe	**Matobo National Park**		■			■		■		■						■		
117	Zimbabwe	**Gonarezhou National Park** (2)	■	■		■	■	■	■	■	■	■					■		
118	Botswana	**Chobe National Park**	■	■	■	■	■	■	■	■	■	■	■	■			■		
119	Botswana	**Moremi Wildlife Reserve***	■	■	■	■	■	■	■	■	■	■	■				■		
120	Botswana	**Makgadikgadi Pans National Park**	■		■		■	■	■	■									■
121	Botswana	**Tuli Block safari reserves** (3)	■				■	■	■	■	■	■	■	■			■		
122	Botswana	**Central Kalahari Game Reserve**	■			■		■	■	■	■	■	■	■			■		
123	Botswana	**Khutse Game Reserve**						■	■	■	■	■							
124	Botswana	**Gemsbok National Park** (4)					■	■	■	■	■	■	■						
125	Namibia	**Etosha National Park***	■	■			■	■	■	■	■	■	■	■					
126	Namibia	**Cape Cross Reserve**	SEALS																
127	Namibia	**Namib-Naukluft National Park**	JACKALS & ORYX																
128	South Africa	**Kalahari Gemsbok National Park** (4)					■	■	■	■	■	■	■						
129	South Africa	**Augrabies Falls National Park**		■					■		■								
130	South Africa	**Cape Peninsula National Park**		■					■		■								
131	South Africa	**Bontebok National Park**					■		■										
132	South Africa	**Karoo National Park**		■		■	■		■								■		
133	South Africa	**Mountain Zebra National Park**		■		■	■		■			■							
134	South Africa	**Greater Addo Park**	■	■		■	■		■	■	■			■			■		
135	South Africa	**Willem Pretorius Game Reserve**		■		■		■	■										
136	South Africa	**Pilanesberg National Park**	■	■	■	■	■	■	■	■	■	■	■	■					
137	South Africa	**Madikwe Game Reserve**	■	■		■	■	■	■	■	■	■	■	■			■		
138	South Africa	**Marakele National Park**	■	■		■	■	■	■	■	■	■	■	■			■		
139	South Africa	**Kruger National Park*** (2)	■	■	■	■	■	■	■	■	■	■	■	■			■		
140	South Africa	**Ndumo Game Reserve**		■	■	■		■	■								■	■	
141	South Africa	**Mkhuzi Game Reserve**	■	■	■		■	■	■		■	■	■	■			■	■	
142	South Africa	**Greater St Lucia Wetland Park**	■	■	■	■	■		■		■		■	■			■		
143	South Africa	**Hluhluwe-Umfolozi Park**	■	■	■	■	■	■	■	■	■	■	■	■			■		
144	South Africa	**uKhahlamba Drakensberg Park** (5)							■		■		■				■		
	South Africa	**Giant's Castle Game Reserve**							■		■		■				■		
145	Lesotho	**Sehlabathebe National Park** (5)	BIRDS																
146	Swaziland	**Mlilwane Game Reserve**		■	■	■			■									■	
	Swaziland	**Hlane Royal National Park**	■	■			■	■	■	■									
147	Swaziland	**Mlawula Nature Reserve**			■		■		■		■		■					■	
148	Swaziland	**Mkhaya Game Reserve**	■	■		■			■										
149	Mozambique	**Maputo Elephant Reserve** (6)	■																
150	Mozambique	**Parque Nacional da Gorongosa**	BIRDS																
151	Madagascar	**Réserve d'Andasibe-Mantadia**	LEMURS																
152	Madagascar	**Réserve naturelle de Tsingy de Bemaraha**	LEMURS																
153	Madagascar	**Parc national de Ranomafana**	LEMURS																
154	Madagascar	**Réserve privee de Berenty**	LEMURS																
155	Seychelles	**Morne Seychellois National Park**	BIRDS																
	Seychelles	**Vallée de Mai Nature Reserve**	BIRDS																
156	Seychelles	**Cousin Island Nature Reserve**	BIRDS																
157	Seychelles	**Ste Anne Marine National Park**	BIRDS, TORTOISES & FISH																

(1) Combined into a transfrontier park, together with Zambia's Lukusuzi Nat. Park, other reserves & wildlife management areas.
(2) Linked via the Sengwe Corridor to form **Great Limpopo Transfrontier Park** (together with Limpopo Nat. Park in Mozambique).
(3) Part of **Limpopo-Shashe Transfrontier Conservation Area**, together with other areas in Botswana and reserves in South Africa and Zimbabwe. **(4)** Combined to form **Kgalagadi Transfrontier Park**.
(5) Linked, together with other areas in Lesotho, to form **Maloti-Drakensberg Transfrontier Conservation Area**.
(6) Linked to South Africa's Tembe Elephant Park in via the Lubombo Conservancy in Swaziland to form **Lubombo Transfrontier Conservation Area**.

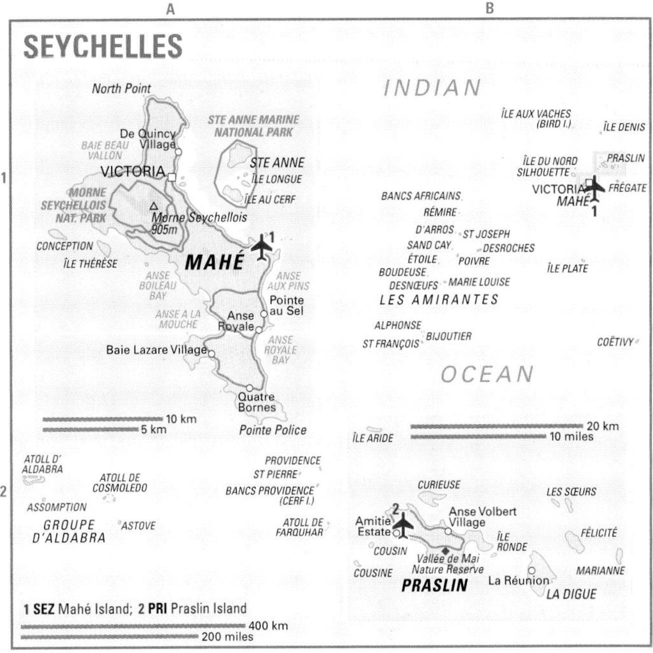

SEYCHELLES
INDIAN
OCEAN
North Point
De Quincy Village
VICTORIA
STE ANNE MARINE NATIONAL PARK
STE ANNE
ÎLE LONGUE
ÎLE AU CERF
MORNE SEYCHELLOIS NAT. PARK
Morne Seychellois 905m
CONCEPTION
ÎLE THÉRÈSE
MAHÉ
ANSE BOILEAU BAY
ANSE AUX PINS
Pointe au Sel
Anse Royale
Baie Lazare Village
Quatre Bornes
Pointe Police
ÎLE AUX VACHES (BIRD I.)
ÎLE DENIS
ÎLE DU NORD
SILHOUETTE
PRASLIN
VICTORIA
MAHÉ
FRÉGATE
BANCS AFRICAINS
RÉMIRE
D'ARROS
ST JOSEPH
SAND CAY
DESROCHES
ÉTOILE
POIVRE
BOUDEUSE
DESNŒUFS
MARIE LOUISE
LES AMIRANTES
ÎLE PLATE
ALPHONSE
ST FRANÇOIS
BIJOUTIER
COËTIVY
ÎLE ARIDE
ATOLL D'ALDABRA
ATOLL DE COSMOLEDO
ASSOMPTION
GROUPE D'ALDABRA
ASTOVE
PROVIDENCE
ST PIERRE
BANCS PROVIDENCE (CERF I.)
ATOLL DE FARQUHAR
CURIEUSE
LES SŒURS
Amitié Estate
Anse Volbert Village
ÎLE RONDE
FÉLICITÉ
COUSIN
Vallée de Mai Nature Reserve
COUSINE
PRASLIN
La Réunion
MARIANNE
LA DIGUE
10 km
5 km
20 km
10 miles
1 SEZ Mahé Island; 2 PRI Praslin Island
400 km
200 miles

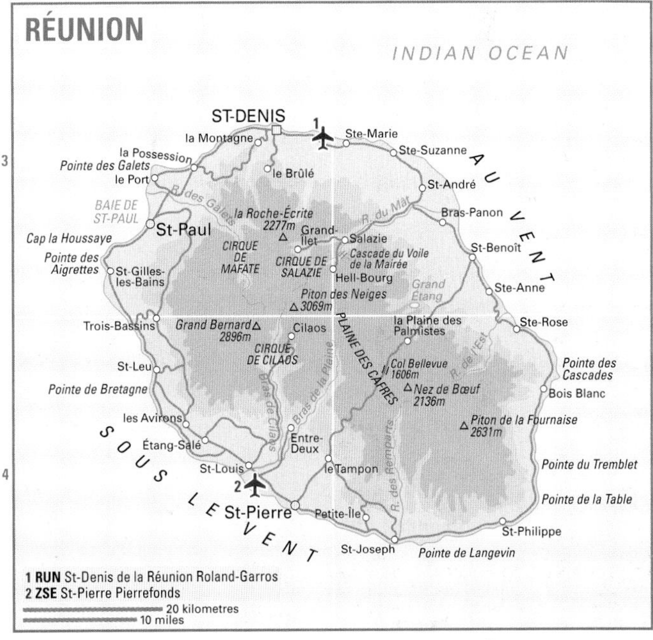

RÉUNION
INDIAN OCEAN
ST-DENIS
la Montagne
Ste-Marie
Ste-Suzanne
la Possession
Pointe des Galets
le Port
le Brûlé
St-André
BAIE DE ST-PAUL
St-Paul
la Roche-Écrite 2277m
Grand Ilet
Salazie
Bras-Panon
Cap la Houssaye
Pointe des Aigrettes
St-Gilles-les-Bains
CIRQUE DE MAFATE
CIRQUE DE SALAZIE
Cascade du Voile de la Mariée
Hell-Bourg
St-Benoît
Piton des Neiges 3069m
Ste-Anne
Trois-Bassins
Grand Bernard 2896m
Cilaos
CIRQUE DE CILAOS
PLAINE DES CAFRES
la Plaine des Palmistes
Ste-Rose
St-Leu
Col Bellevue 1606m
Nez de Bœuf 2136m
Pointe des Cascades
Pointe de Bretagne
Bois Blanc
les Avirons
Piton de la Fournaise 2631m
Étang-Salé
Entre-Deux
St-Louis
le Tampon
Pointe du Tremblet
St-Pierre
Petite-Île
Pointe de la Table
St-Philippe
St-Joseph
Pointe de Langevin
AU VENT
SOUS LE VENT
1 RUN St-Denis de la Réunion Roland-Garros
2 ZSE St-Pierre Pierrefonds
20 kilometres
10 miles

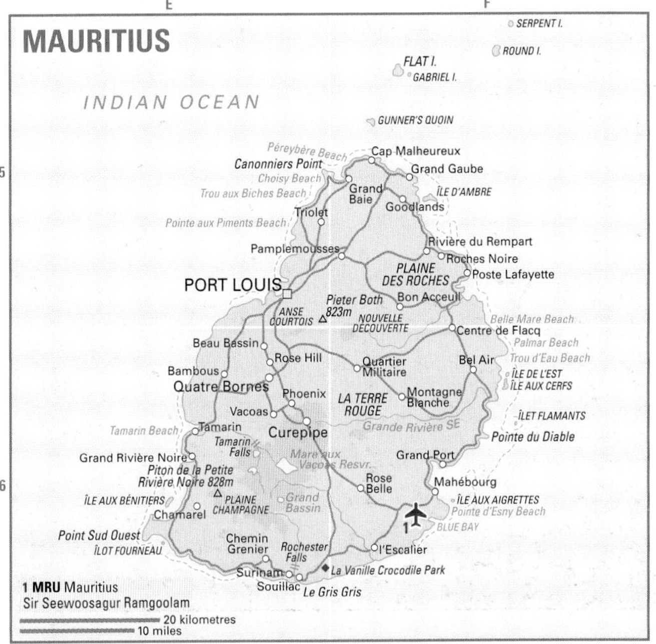

MAURITIUS
INDIAN OCEAN
SERPENT I.
ROUND I.
FLAT I.
GABRIEL I.
GUNNER'S QUOIN
Péreybère Beach
Cap Malheureux
Canonniers Point
Grand Gaube
Choisy Beach
Trou aux Biches Beach
Grand Baie
ÎLE D'AMBRE
Goodlands
Pointe aux Piments Beach
Triolet
Pamplemousses
Rivière du Rempart
Roches Noire
PLAINE DES ROCHES
Poste Lafayette
PORT LOUIS
Pieter Both 823m
Bon Acceuil
ANSE COURTOIS
NOUVELLE DÉCOUVERTE
Belle Mare Beach
Centre de Flacq
Palmar Beach
Beau Bassin
Rose Hill
Quartier Militaire
Bel Air
Trou d'Eau Beach
ÎLE DE L'EST
ÎLE AUX CERFS
Bambous
Quatre Bornes
Phoenix
LA TERRE ROUGE
Montagne Blanche
Vacoas
ÎLET FLAMANTS
Tamarin Beach
Tamarin
Curepipe
Grande Rivière SE
Pointe du Diable
Tamarin Falls
Mare aux Vacoas Resvr.
Grand Rivière Noire
Grand Port
Piton de la Petite Rivière Noire 828m
Rose Belle
Mahébourg
ÎLE AUX BÉNITIERS
PLAINE CHAMPAGNE
Grand Bassin
ÎLE AUX AIGRETTES
Chamarel
Pointe d'Esny Beach
BLUE BAY
Point Sud Ouest
Chemin Grenier
ÎLOT FOURNEAU
Rochester Falls
l'Escalier
Surinam
La Vanille Crocodile Park
Souillac
Le Gris Gris
1 MRU Mauritius Sir Seewoosagur Ramgoolam
20 kilometres
10 miles
1000 metres
500 metres
Sea level

See also... World Introduction (8-11); Tourism (24-25); Countries A-Z (202-210)

Key facts	
Number of Countries	49
Area ('000 sq km)	30,211
Population ('000)	3,843,201
Population Density (per sq km)	124
Gross National Income (US$m)	10,074,406
Visitor Arrivals ('000)	184,105
Visitor Receipts (US$m)	115,872

GNI figures are for 2004. Population figures are taken from the most recent reliable source. Travel figures (UNWTO) are based on overnight stays, not same-day visitors, and are for 2005. For more information see the Countries A-Z section from page 202.

Asia

Asia is a continent of superlatives. The most populous country, the largest city, the fastest growing major economy, the tallest mountain (and building), the longest tunnel (and bridge), the largest oil reserves – all are to be found here. Nor are its achievements recent. It has given the world its most important civilizations, its five main religions and three of its most potent inventions: paper, gunpowder and Arabic numerals. It stretches from the Mediterranean to the Pacific, from the exotic cultures of the Middle East to the mysteries of China, and from the Gobi Desert to the rain forests of New Guinea. There are other contrasts, too: command economies and free-market capitalism, dictatorships and well-established democracies. Although this sophistication, vibrancy and diversity has brought its share of problems as well as advantages, most observers now agree that Asia (and China in particular) in many ways represents 'the future'.

Support for this idea is certainly provided by Asia's travel and tourism industry. Visitors to Asian countries increased by about 7% in 2005 as against 2004, above the global average of 5.5%, despite various areas of regional instability and the devastating Indian Ocean tsunami. North-East Asia (including China, Japan and Korea) has seen the most impressive growth. Indeed, China has now overtaken Italy as the fourth most visited country in the world and overtaken the UK as the world's fourth largest economy.

Influences

Any view of Asia is almost meaningless without an awareness of the influence of the three main faiths, Buddhism, Hinduism and Islam. Each provides distinct solutions for human problems, and not all are compatible with the Christian separation between church and state that is the bedrock of most western societies. Islam – the dominant religion in around half of Asia's countries – has recently become increasingly politicised, challenging existing conceptions of governance and, partly as a consequence, polarising views of Islam globally. Whether these developments have been a cause or a result of problems in Asia and elsewhere is debateable: what is not, is that Islam's relationship with the non-Islamic world (Christian or otherwise) is now the one of the central issues in global affairs.

Another is Asia's increasing economic power. Japan has long been the world's second-largest economy, but recent decades have seen spectacular growth, initially in the so-called 'tiger economies' of East Asia but, most recently and spectacularly, in China, where average GDP growth in 1997 to 2006 has exceeded 8%. The disparity of wealth between the affluent Pacific rim and the poorer western provinces is rapidly widening, prompting Prime Minister Wen Jiabao to issue a warning in March 2006 about unsustainable growth and the dangers of social and economic inequality. Elsewhere, the country's increased wealth is seen as both a threat and an opportunity. For example, the Chinese bought over three million cars in 2005 compared to 635,000 in 2000: good news for the auto industry but less good for those hoping for a reduction in fossil-fuel emissions.

Economies

The region's 10 largest economies
Source: World Bank/International Monetary Fund

	GNI US$m 2004	GNI/cap US$ 2004	GDP growth 2004	GDP growth av p/a '97-'06
Japan	4,749,910	37,278	2.6	0.9
China	1,676,846	1,284	9.5	8.4
India	674,580	624	7.3	6.0
Korea, Rep.	673,036	13,837	4.6	4.7
Taiwan	317,070	13,849	6.0	4.3
Indonesia	248,007	1,025	5.1	2.7
Saudi Arabia	242,180	9,167	5.2	3.4
China: HK	183,516	26,602	7.9	3.1
Thailand	158,703	2,473	6.1	2.6
Iran	153,984	2,264	5.6	4.8

Many Asian adaptations of Western capitalism have been achieved without political liberalisation, the pursuit of which is often seen as a prerequisite of economic transformation. As the global economy moves into a services- and information-based phase the underlying contradictions are likely to become more acute. States such as China which seek to maintain control over media and internet access are unlikely to reap the full benefits of this revolution.

Travel overview

The emergence of China, both as a tourist destination and, increasingly, as a source of tourists, is one of the most significant trends in the global travel industry. Considerable economic growth (over 9% in 2005, more than twice the world's average) and some liberalisation of policies for both inbound and outbound travel, such as an increase in the countries accorded Approved Destination Status, have combined to create increases of 27% in visitor arrivals and 48% in tourism receipts in 2004 compared to 2003. Air traffic to and from China increased by over 50% in this period. The Beijing Olympics in 2008 is likely to further boost China's travel and tourism industry.

Asia has had its share of problems to contend with. The conflicts in Iraq and Palestine, terrorism and the perhaps even more menacing spread of avian flu show few signs of a rapid solution. Most deadly of all was the tsunami which struck the Indian Ocean on 26 December 2004 with the loss of over 200,000 lives, some as far away as South Africa. The initial impact on the travel and tourism industry, on which many of the affected countries heavily rely, was initially catastrophic: but within six months there were signs of remarkable resilience and recovery. Sri Lanka and Thailand both showed increases in visitor numbers within six months, partly due to effective marketing campaigns. The Maldives, which derives over 55% of its GDP from tourism, has been hardest hit, with visitor numbers down by a third in this period. "We cannot help these communities to get back on their feet by staying away," PATA's CEO Peter de Jong remarked in August 2005. Many countries, the Maldives in particular, will echo this sentiment.

As in Europe and North America, low-cost airlines in South and East Asia have become increasingly significant in recent years. The first such service was only launched in January 2002: in March 2006 there were over 40, with more scheduled to start operating in India and elsewhere during 2006. The large flag-carriers may be looking anxiously over their shoulders, but they certainly have a long-established and well-deserved reputation for quality on their side: in Skytrax's 2005 Airline of the Year Awards, five of the top seven were from Asia. In the Middle East, however, the picture is rather different. Following the lead of Dubai's Emirates – which was only created in 1985 and now has a fleet of 77 aircraft and regularly tops travellers' polls for service and facilities – the other states in the region have created or revitalised their own airlines to the highest standards. Travellers between Europe and the Far East are being wooed with some enticing deals, often with a stopover in the Gulf as part of the package.

Another aviation development is producing benefits for the Middle East's Mediterranean seaboard. With so many European travellers now making their own arrangements with low-cost airlines to visit Spain, France and Italy, capacity on charter flights is being redeployed further east.

Big earners

Receipts from foreign travel (excluding international transport), 2004 – top ten countries (US$ billions) *Source: WTO*

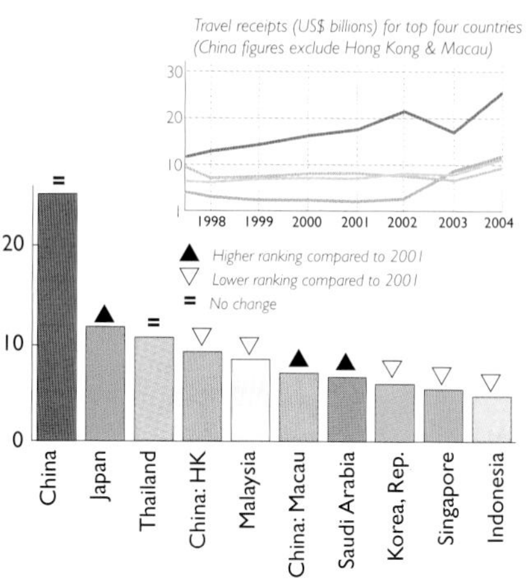
Travel receipts (US$ billions) for top four countries (China figures exclude Hong Kong & Macau)
30
20
10
1998 1999 2000 2001 2002 2003 2004
Higher ranking compared to 2001
Lower ranking compared to 2001
No change
20
10
0
China
Japan
Thailand
China: HK
Malaysia
China: Macau
Saudi Arabia
Korea, Rep.
Singapore
Indonesia

Destination overview

- **China** – the country retains great mystique but the 'Bamboo Curtain' is now parting. Beijing will host the 2008 Olympics, and a US$22 billion infrastructure programme is well under way. As the completion of the Three Gorges Dam approaches, Yangtze River cruises are selling fast. The Terracotta Army in Xi'an and the Great Wall are hugely popular attractions.
- **Hong Kong** – visitor figures have recovered well post-SARS. US$2.3 billion will have been spent by 2007 on upgrading tourist attractions and facilities.
- **Malaysia** – the main attractions are the beaches in Penang and Langkawi, but efforts are being made to promote dual-centre trips that also take in the country's vibrant cultural heritage, particularly in Malacca. Areas with future potential include Sabah, Sarawak, Tioman and Redang.
- **Thailand** – the country has made a remarkable recovery from the tsunami, although capacity (both of hotels and airlines) will take time to return to 2004 levels. Its exceptional beaches have enjoyed an environmental clean-up and current marketing activity is stressing the country's eco-tourism credentials. The northeast of the country has been identified as the next area for tourism development.
- **Singapore** – an established city-break, stopover and business/convention destination, and a major

Asian leaders

Top 10 Asian destinations (Kuoni holidays, ex-UK), 2005 *Source: Kuoni*

	'05	'04		'05	'04
Maldives	1	2	Singapore	5	6
Thailand	2	1	Malaysia	6	5
Dubai (UAE)	3	4	Hong Kong	7	7
Sri Lanka	4	3	Indonesia	8	8

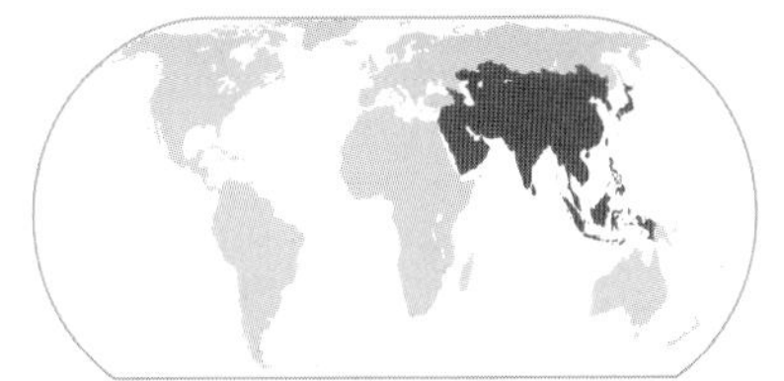

- Asia occupies 22.8% of the world's land area and is home to 60% of the world's population.
- Asia accounts for 23% of global travel arrivals.
- International travel and tourism contributed over US$115 billion to Asia's economy 2004.
- The most visited country in Asia in 2004 was China, which (not including Hong Kong or Macau) received nearly 42 million visitors: worldwide, only France, the USA and Spain received more.
- 20 countries in Asia received over one million visitors in 2004.
- There were 184 million international tourist arrivals in Asia in 2005, an increase of 7.5% over 2004.
- Visitors to countries in North East Asia increased by 10.2% in 2005 compared to 2004, nearly twice the world average.
- The fastest growing Asian destination in the first half of 2005 compared to 2004 was Cambodia, with an increase in international visitors of over 52%.
- In Skytrax's 2005 'Best of the Best' awards, Asian airlines filled seven of the top ten places in the 'Best Airline' category and six out of the top ten places in 'Best Airport'.
- 14 countries (including Hong Kong and Macau) received in excess of US$1 billion from travel and tourism in 2003.
- Asia had over 3.7 million hotel rooms in 2003.
- The Japanese continue to top the Asian big spenders' league. Their expenditure on travel in 2005 was US$38 billion. Worldwide, only the Americans, the Germans and the British spent more.
- With 22,460 people per sq km, Macau is the most densely populated state in the world.
- India has 108,700km (67,550 miles) of railway track.
- 60% of the world's population increase between 2000 and 2003 was in Asian countries.
- The Republic of Korea finished fourth in the 2002 World Cup, the best ever performance by an Asian country.
- The Chinese government has set a target of all police officers in Beijing being conversant in Russian, Japanese, Arabic and English by the time of the 2008 Olympics.
- Nine of the 14 tallest mountains in the world can be reached via Nepal.
- The deepest point in the ocean is the Mariana trench off the Philippines at 10,025 metres (35,843 feet).
- China produces an estimated 60% of the world's bicycles.
- Three of the world's five longest five tunnels are in Japan, with a combined length of over 100km. Japan also has the world's longest suspension bridge.
- China's Three Gorges Dam will contain 1.39 trillion cubic feet of water.
- More people work in factories in China than live in the UK, France and Spain combined.
- Nepal is the only country in the world that does not have a rectangular flag.

boarding point for Asian cruises. It is looking to attract a younger clientele and to increase lengths of stay. The islands south-west of Sentosa are being developed as eco-tourism destinations.

- **Japan** and the **Republic of Korea** – the successful joint-hosting of the 2002 Football World Cup helped to increase visitors and shake off their 'business-only' tags. Japan has begun an ambitious plan to double overseas arrivals by 2007, while Seoul's new airport should cement its position as a regional hub and encourage stop-over and dual-centre business. Five of the world's 11 most visited theme parks in 2005 are in Korea or Japan.
- **Indonesia** – the country's tourism industry has been rocked in recent years by the tsunami and the terrorist attacks in its premier resort of Bali. Visitor numbers for 2004 are below those for 1997 but its many attractions make it perennially popular, particularly in the Australasian market .
- **The Maldives** – this nation of low-lying islands suffered heavily from the tsunami but is re-establishing its position as a leading diving and water-sports destination as well as a wedding and honeymoon favourite. Bookings with British operators in the first quarter of 2006 were close to 2004 levels. Many resort islands have recently been renovated to the highest standards of luxury, and several others are projected to open.
- **India** – a country of staggering diversity, with one of the world's oldest civilizations. The Golden Triangle, Goa and the major cities have long been popular. Growth areas include Ayurveda and spa resorts in Kerala, wildlife sanctuaries and heritage tourism. Visitor numbers have increased by over 35% between 2001 and 2005.
- **Sri Lanka** – the island is recovering after the tsunami and political troubles, and is keen to advance from being an add-on destination as part of longer trips. Most holidays combine temple and hill-country tours with time on the island's magnificent beaches.
- **Vietnam** and **Cambodia** – both states have seen increased stability, rapidly normalising relations with the USA and co-ordinated marketing activities with neighbouring countries. All have helped combined visitor arrivals grow by 80% between 2001 and 2004.
- **Macau** – the former Portuguese colony has taken steps to reform and modernise its gambling businesses on which so much of its revenue depends. It is currently a stopover for travellers between Taiwan and China and may thus suffer if direct links are restored. There are plans to build up to 60,000 additional hotel rooms on the Cotai Strip between the two islands.
- **Taiwan** – the long-running dispute with China shows some signs of relenting with a relaxation of trade and transport restrictions which may increase stability and encourage more leisure travellers to this traditionally business destination.
- **The Gulf** – from being little more than a staging-post between Europe and Asia ten years ago, the UAE, and in particular Dubai, has reinvented itself in spectacular style as an up-market tourist destination. Infrastructure investment has been nothing short of staggering. Recent projects include the world's most expensively-built hotel, a US$3 billion theme park and 250 artificial offshore islands designed to resemble a map of the world. Visitor figures have grown at more than twice the global average since 1997 and official predictions are for a further three-fold increase by 2010. Other states in the area, such as Bahrain and Qatar, have similar ambitions to become more than just a shopping stopover. At the southern tip of the Arabian peninsula, Oman has a quite different appeal. Excellent dive sites, varied scenery, ancient forts and bustling markets offer the romance of Arabia with the advantages of 21st-century facilities.
- **Jordan**, despite its proximity to Israel and Palestine, has a successful tourism industry, built mainly around seven-night tours, with a cultural theme, most of which take in the incomparable Petra. Many hotels have recently been opened or upgraded. Dual-centre holidays with Egypt's Red Sea are growing in popularity.
- Two nearby countries which will hope to emulate Jordan's long-established success, and which have the capacity to offer a similar tourism package, are **Syria** and **Lebanon**. Both have had their share of problems in recent decades but their combined number of visitors has doubled between 2001 and 2004. Syria has several cultural attractions, including Damascus, the oldest continuously inhabited city on earth, numerous archaeological remains and some imposing Crusader castles. A programme is under way to increase the number of bed places and to simplify entry formalities for foreign visitors. Lebanon's upheavals have now mainly been resolved and the economy and infrastructure largely rebuilt, and Beirut is fast reclaiming its 1970's tag of 'the Paris of the Middle East'.
- **Israel** – the continuing tensions in the region resulted in 2004 visitor arrival figures falling to 75% of their 1997 level. Recognising the attraction of almost year-round favourable weather on the Mediterranean coast, a number of luxury orientated hotel and apartment complexes have opened to provide an alternative to the already established Red Sea resort of Eilat.
- The **Central Asian** economies rely heavily on their oil and gas reserves, and many visitors are connected with these industries. The WTO's Silk Road project may in time encourage more leisure travellers. Political stability will be another key factor.

Problem areas

- The aftermaths of the wars in Afghanistan and Iraq are currently highly uncertain.
- Several countries including the Philippines, Yemen and Nepal have experienced considerable security problems in recent years.
- Long-running disputes in Kashmir, Taiwan and Korea have generally produced only localised stand-offs, but all have the capacity to escalate. Iran's complex relations with the USA could provide another regional flashpoint.
- Avian flu may well become a serious problem, in Asia and elsewhere.
- Burma (Myanmar) stands accused of widespread human rights abuses and attracts little international tourism or investment as a result. China's human rights record is also a concern to many.
- Israel's tourism industry, once thriving, is in crisis as a result of the ongoing Palestinian conflict.
- Some countries are major sources of illegal drugs, which can contribute to social, political and economic instability.

Big spenders

Expenditure on foreign travel (excluding international transport), 2003 – top ten countries (US$ billions) *Source: WTO*

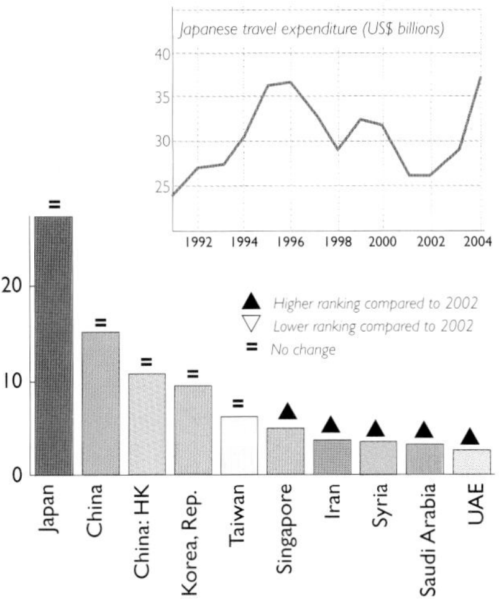
Japanese travel expenditure (US$ billions)
40
35
30
25
1992
1994
1996
1998
2000
2002
2004
Higher ranking compared to 2002
Lower ranking compared to 2002
No change
20
10
0
Japan
China
China: HK
Korea, Rep.
Taiwan
Singapore
Iran
Syria
Saudi Arabia
UAE

Visitors

Visitor arrivals 2004: top ten countries *Source: WTO*

	Visitors (thousands)	Change since 1997
China	41,761	75.7%
China: HK	21,811	93.5%
Malaysia	15,703	152.8%
Thailand	11,651	59.7%
Saudi Arabia	8,580	n/a
Singapore	8,328	27.5%
China: Macau	8,323	117.0%
UAE	6,394	158.2%
Japan	6,138	45.5%
Korea, Rep.	5,818	48.9%

See also... World Physical (12-13); World Political (14-15), World Climate (16)

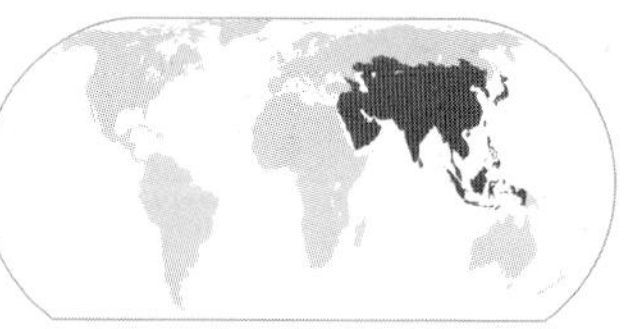

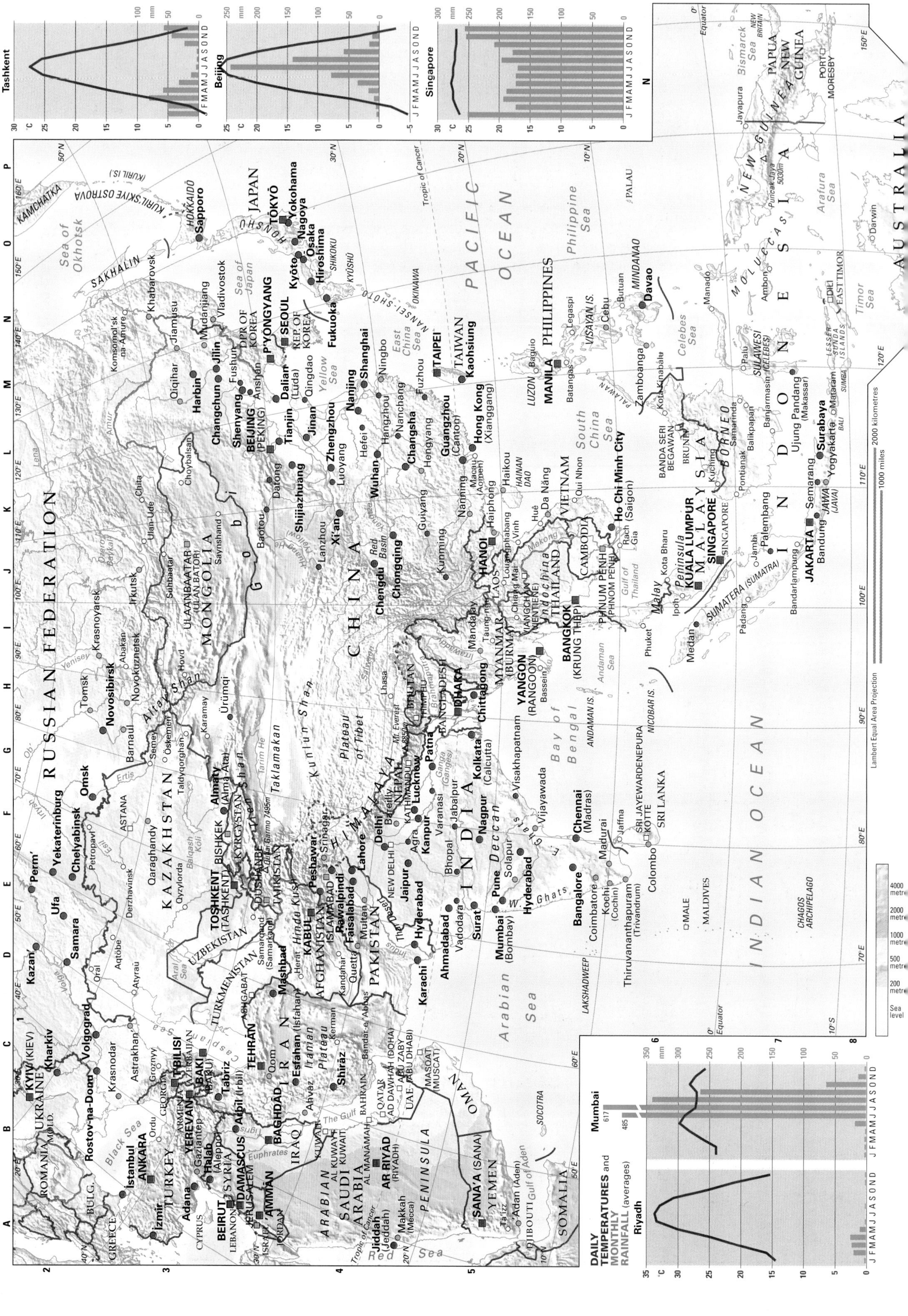

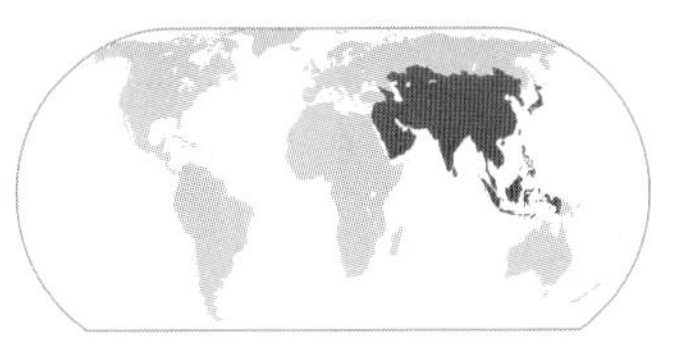

See also... World Climate (16); Regional Climate Terms (196)

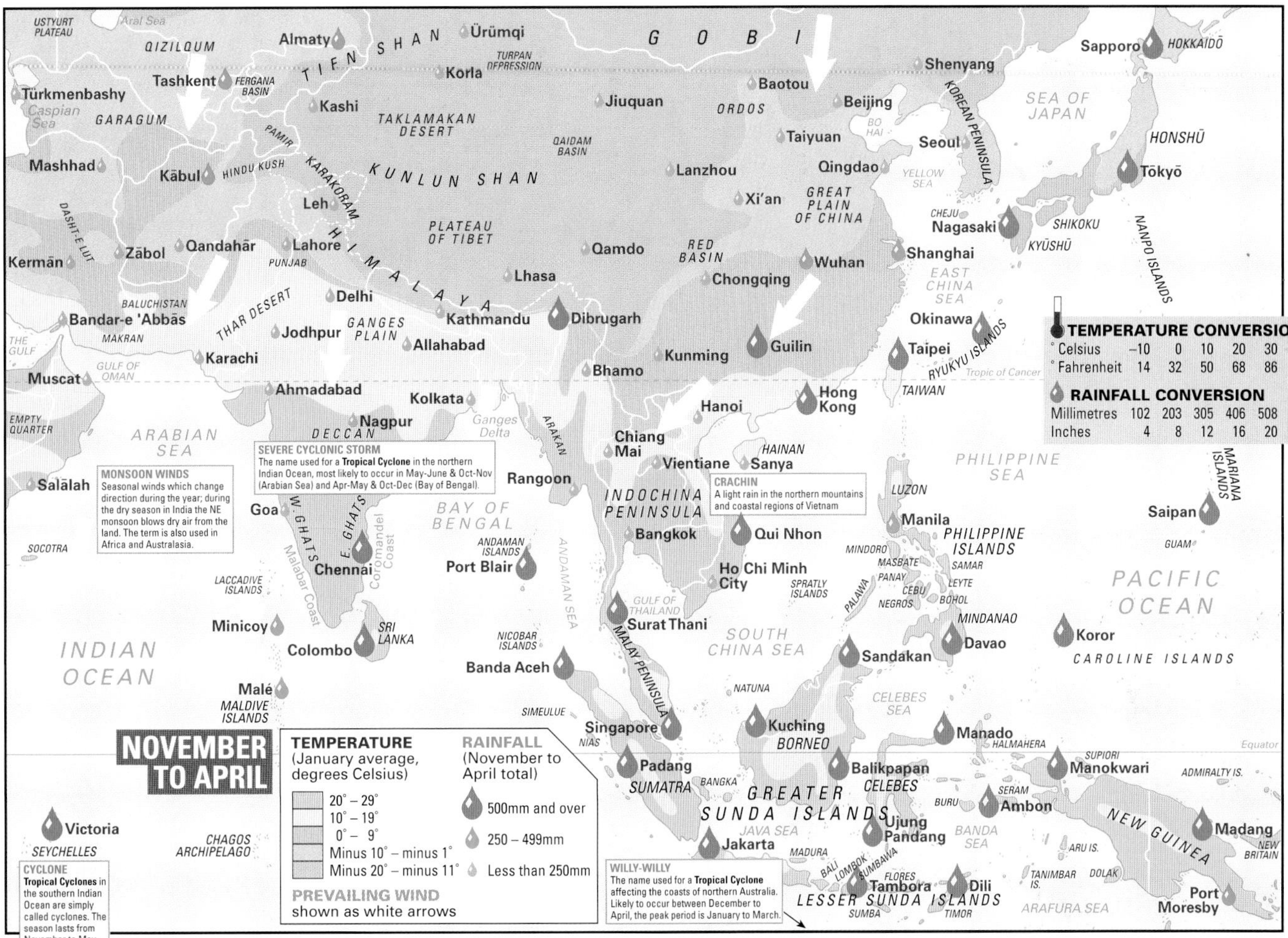

NOVEMBER TO APRIL

TEMPERATURE CONVERSION

Celsius	−10	0	10	20	30	40
Fahrenheit	14	32	50	68	86	104

RAINFALL CONVERSION

Millimetres	102	203	305	406	508	610
Inches	4	8	12	16	20	24

MONSOON WINDS
Seasonal winds which change direction during the year; during the dry season in India the NE monsoon blows dry air from the land. The term is also used in Africa and Australasia.

SEVERE CYCLONIC STORM
The name used for a **Tropical Cyclone** in the northern Indian Ocean, most likely to occur in May-June & Oct-Nov (Arabian Sea) and Apr-May & Oct-Dec (Bay of Bengal).

CRACHIN
A light rain in the northern mountains and coastal regions of Vietnam

TEMPERATURE (January average, degrees Celsius)
- 20° – 29°
- 10° – 19°
- 0° – 9°
- Minus 10° – minus 1°
- Minus 20° – minus 11°

RAINFALL (November to April total)
- 500mm and over
- 250 – 499mm
- Less than 250mm

PREVAILING WIND shown as white arrows

CYCLONE
Tropical Cyclones in the southern Indian Ocean are simply called cyclones. The season lasts from November to May.

WILLY-WILLY
The name used for a **Tropical Cyclone** affecting the coasts of northern Australia. Likely to occur between December to April, the peak period is January to March.

Columbus Travel Guides' *World Travel Guide* contains detailed climate charts for every country in the world, including temperature, rainfall, sunshine and humidity

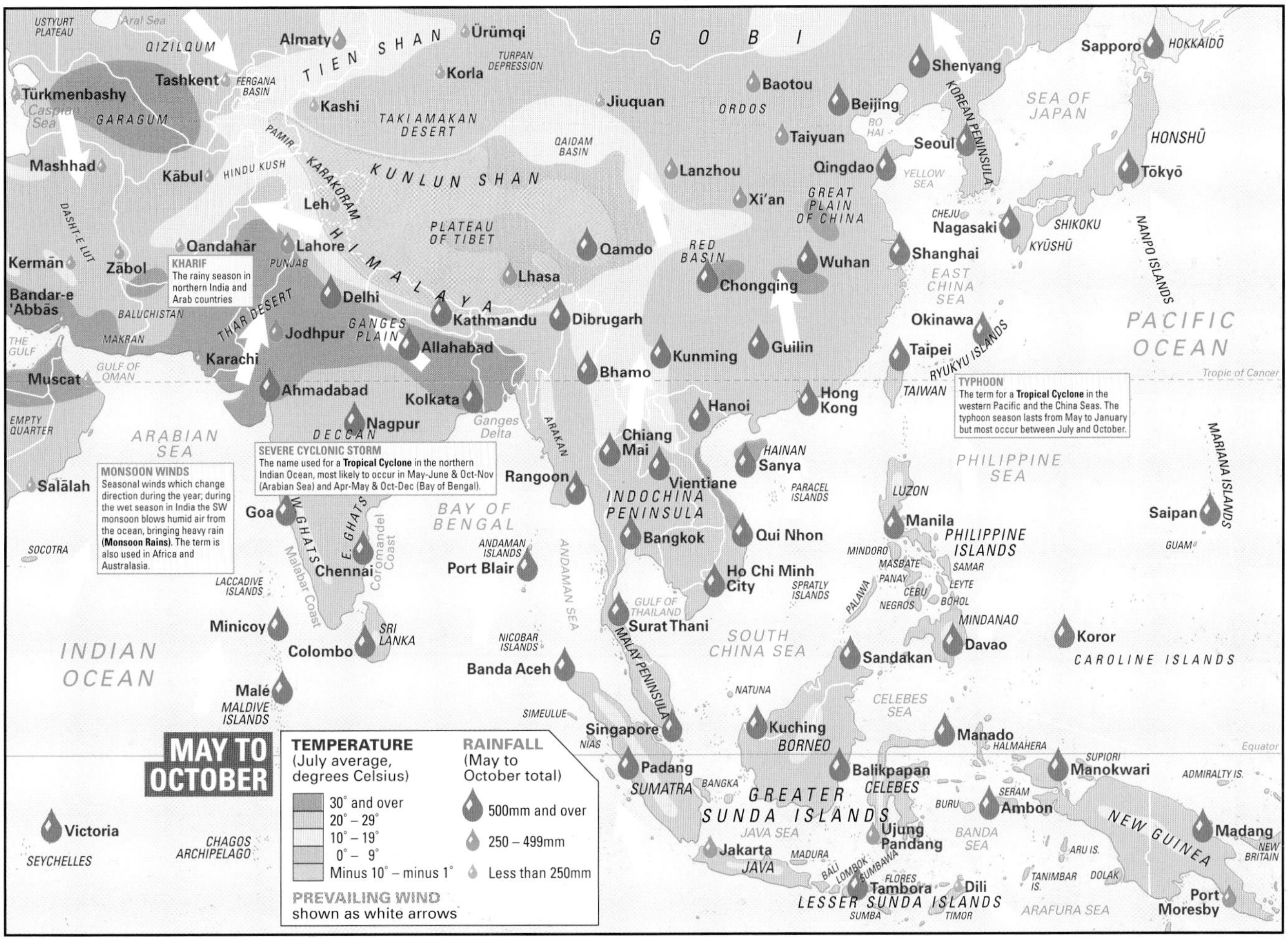

MAY TO OCTOBER

KHARIF
The rainy season in northern India and Arab countries

MONSOON WINDS
Seasonal winds which change direction during the year; during the wet season in India the SW monsoon blows humid air from the ocean, bringing heavy rain (**Monsoon Rains**). The term is also used in Africa and Australasia.

SEVERE CYCLONIC STORM
The name used for a **Tropical Cyclone** in the northern Indian Ocean, most likely to occur in May-June & Oct-Nov (Arabian Sea) and Apr-May & Oct-Dec (Bay of Bengal).

TYPHOON
The term for a **Tropical Cyclone** in the western Pacific and the China Seas. The typhoon season lasts from May to January but most occur between July and October.

TEMPERATURE (July average, degrees Celsius)
- 30° and over
- 20° – 29°
- 10° – 19°
- 0° – 9°
- Minus 10° – minus 1°

RAINFALL (May to October total)
- 500mm and over
- 250 – 499mm
- Less than 250mm

PREVAILING WIND shown as white arrows

See also... Religion (21); Europe Historical (58-59); Asia Musuems & Galleries (129); Silk Road (132); N. America Historical (156-157); Latin America Historical (187)

The listings above refer to a selection of related themes. For more information, see the Contents (2-7).

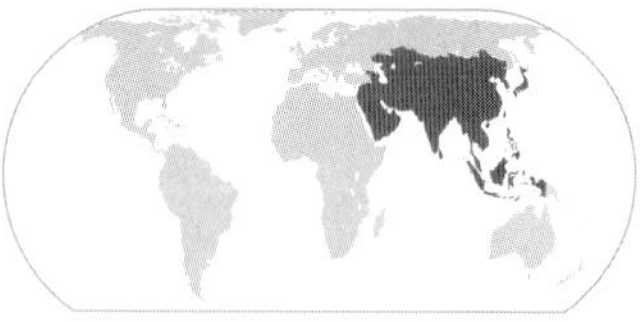

4th & 3rd CENTURIES BC

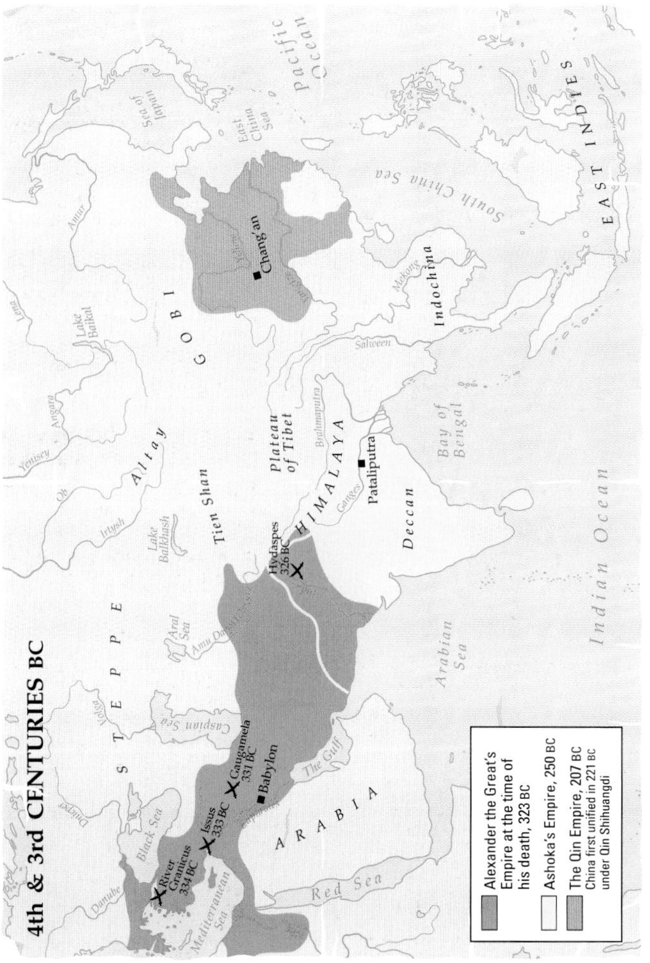
Alexander the Great's Empire at the time of his death, 323 BC
Ashoka's Empire, 250 BC
The Qin Empire, 207 BC
China first unified in 221 BC under Qin Shihuangdi
River Granicus 334 BC
Issus 333 BC
Gaugamela 331 BC
Babylon
Hydaspes 326 BC
Pataliputra
Chang'an
STEPPE
ARABIA
Tien Shan
Altay
GOBI
Plateau of Tibet
HIMALAYA
Deccan
Indochina
EAST INDIES
Indian Ocean
Pacific Ocean
Arabian Sea
Bay of Bengal
South China Sea
East China Sea
Sea of Japan
Red Sea
Black Sea
Caspian Sea
Aral Sea
Mediterranean Sea
The Gulf

7th – 10th CENTURIES

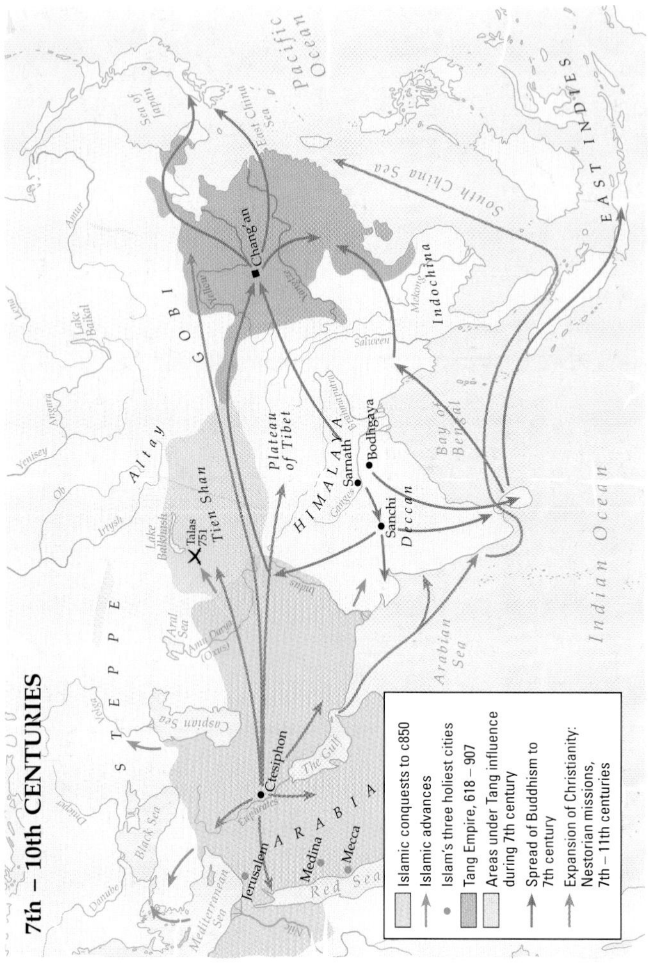
Islamic conquests to c850
Islamic advances
Islam's three holiest cities
Tang Empire, 618 – 907
Areas under Tang influence during 7th century
Spread of Buddhism to 7th century
Expansion of Christianity: Nestorian missions, 7th – 11th centuries
Jerusalem
Medina
Mecca
Ctesiphon
Talas 751
Sarnath
Bodhgaya
Sanchi
Chang'an
STEPPE
ARABIA
Tien Shan
Altay
GOBI
Plateau of Tibet
HIMALAYA
Deccan
Indochina
EAST INDIES
Indian Ocean
Pacific Ocean
Arabian Sea
Bay of Bengal
South China Sea
East China Sea
Sea of Japan
Red Sea
Black Sea
Caspian Sea
Mediterranean Sea
The Gulf

13th & 14th CENTURIES

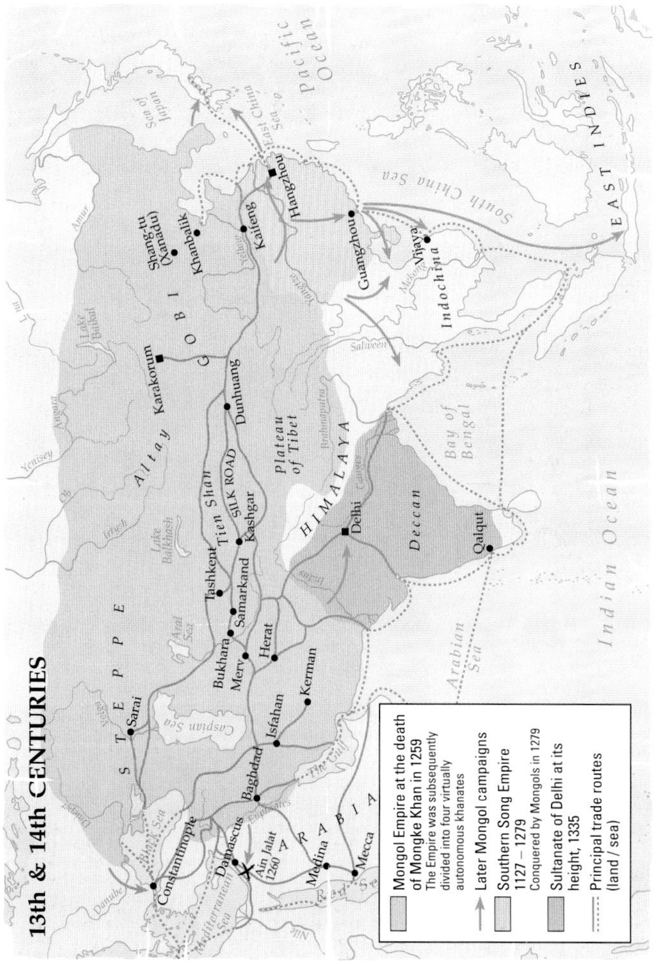
Mongol Empire at the death of Mongke Khan in 1259
The Empire was subsequently divided into four virtually autonomous khanates
Later Mongol campaigns
Southern Song Empire 1127 – 1279
Conquered by Mongols in 1279
Sultanate of Delhi at its height, 1335
Principal trade routes (land / sea)
Constantinople
Sarai
Damascus
Ain Jalut 1260
Baghdad
Medina
Mecca
Isfahan
Kerman
Bukhara
Merv
Herat
Samarkand
Tashkent
Kashgar
SILK ROAD
Dunhuang
Karakorum
Shang-tu (Xanadu)
Khanbalik
Kaifeng
Hangzhou
Guangzhou
Vijaya
Delhi
Qalqut
STEPPE
ARABIA
Tien Shan
Altay
GOBI
Plateau of Tibet
HIMALAYA
Deccan
Indochina
EAST INDIES
Indian Ocean
Pacific Ocean
Arabian Sea
Bay of Bengal
South China Sea
East China Sea
Sea of Japan

17th – 19th CENTURIES

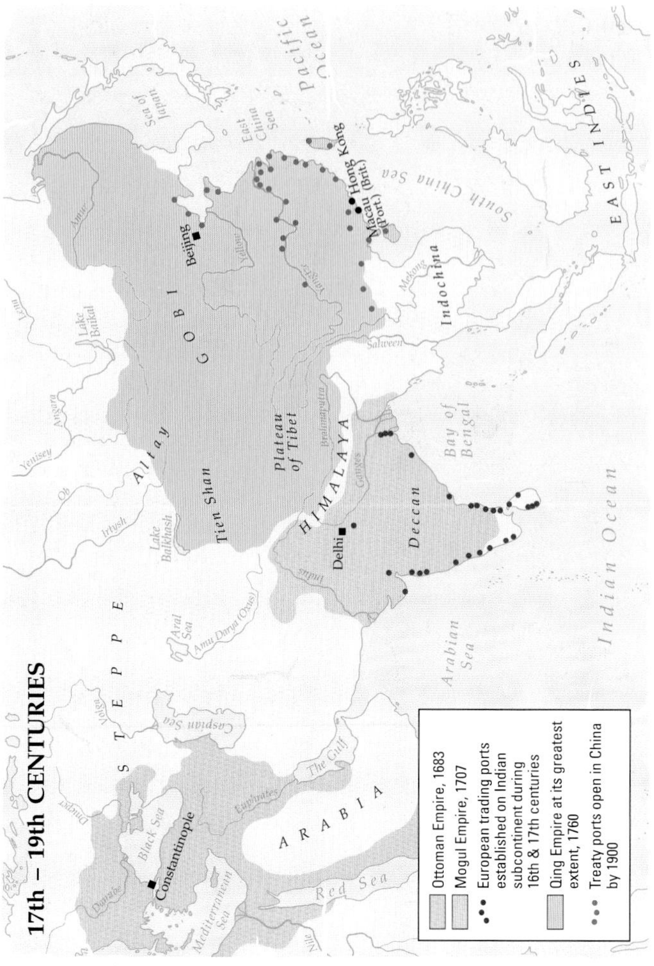
Ottoman Empire, 1683
Mogul Empire, 1707
European trading ports established on Indian subcontinent during 16th & 17th centuries
Qing Empire at its greatest extent, 1760
Treaty ports open in China by 1900
Constantinople
Delhi
Beijing
Hong Kong (Brit.)
Macau (Port.)
STEPPE
ARABIA
Tien Shan
Altay
GOBI
Plateau of Tibet
HIMALAYA
Deccan
Indochina
EAST INDIES
Indian Ocean
Pacific Ocean
Arabian Sea
Bay of Bengal
South China Sea
East China Sea
Sea of Japan
Red Sea
Black Sea
Caspian Sea
The Gulf

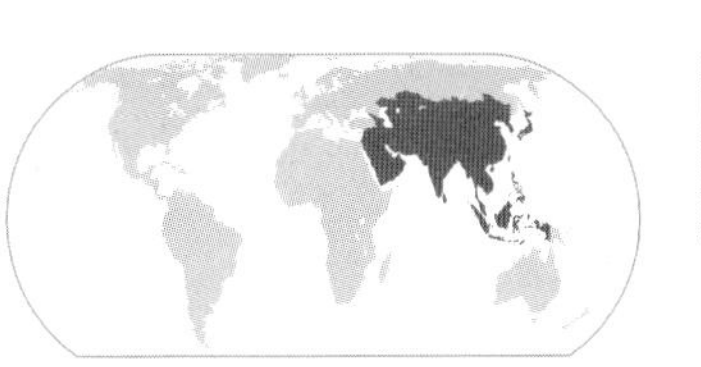

See also... UNESCO Cultural Heritage (50-53); Asia Historical (128); Museums & Galleries in Europe (68), USA & Canada (159) and Latin America (182, 184, 187)

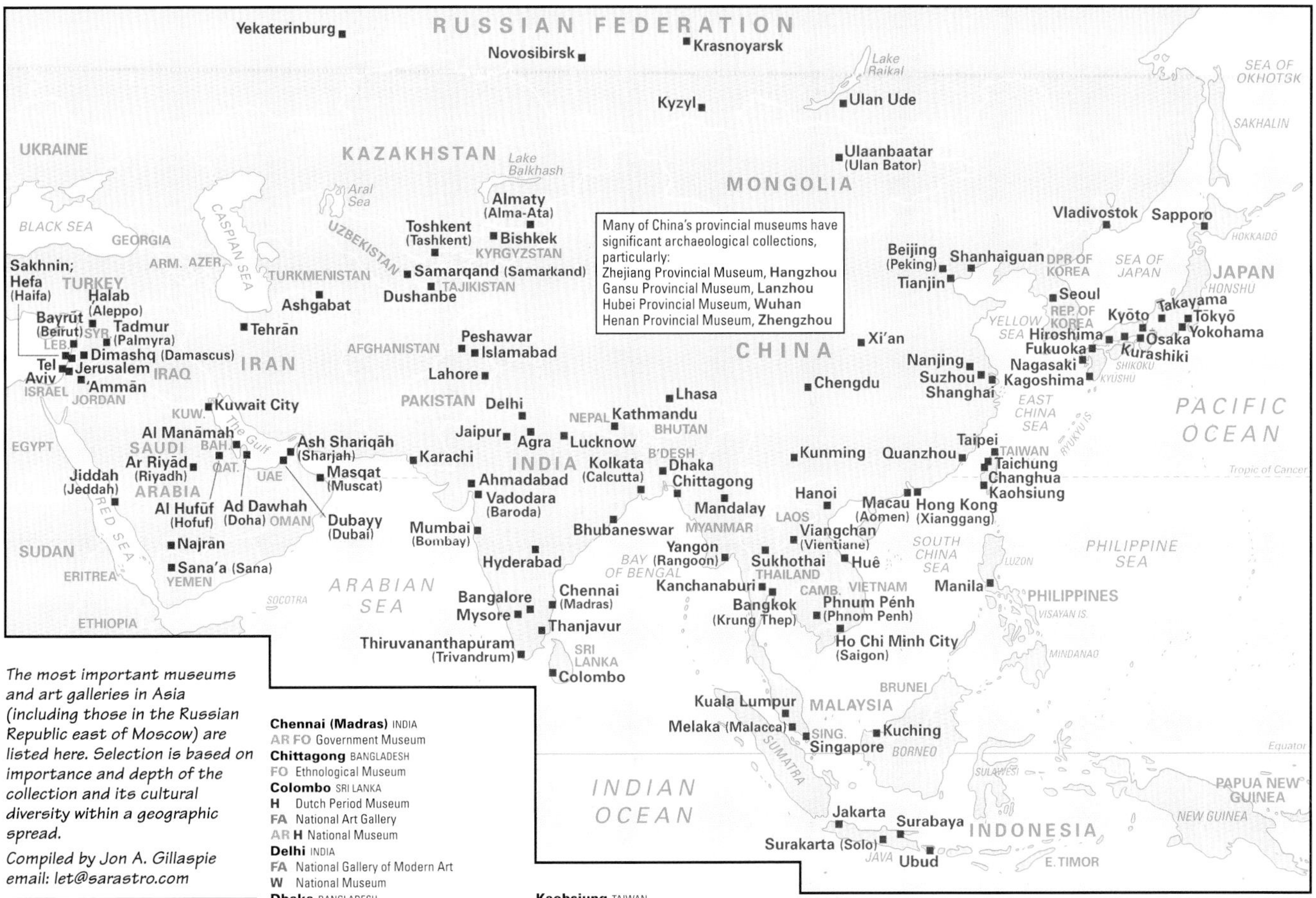
RUSSIAN FEDERATION
Yekaterinburg
Novosibirsk
Krasnoyarsk
Lake Baikal
SEA OF OKHOTSK
Kyzyl
Ulan Ude
SAKHALIN
UKRAINE
KAZAKHSTAN
Lake Balkhash
Ulaanbaatar (Ulan Bator)
MONGOLIA
Aral Sea
Almaty (Alma-Ata)
BLACK SEA
GEORGIA
CASPIAN SEA
UZBEKISTAN
Toshkent (Tashkent)
Bishkek
KYRGYZSTAN
Many of China's provincial museums have significant archaeological collections, particularly:
Zhejiang Provincial Museum, Hangzhou
Gansu Provincial Museum, Lanzhou
Hubei Provincial Museum, Wuhan
Henan Provincial Museum, Zhengzhou
Vladivostok
Sapporo
HOKKAIDO
Sakhnin;
Hefa (Haifa)
TURKEY
ARM.
AZER.
TURKMENISTAN
Samarqand (Samarkand)
TAJIKISTAN
Dushanbe
Beijing (Peking)
Shanhaiguan
DPR OF KOREA
SEA OF JAPAN
JAPAN
Tianjin
HONSHU
Halab (Aleppo)
Ashgabat
Seoul
REP. OF KOREA
Bayrut (Beirut)
SYR.
Tadmur (Palmyra)
Tehran
YELLOW SEA
Kyoto
Takayama
Tokyo
Yokohama
LEB.
Dimashq (Damascus)
AFGHANISTAN
Peshawar
Islamabad
CHINA
Xi'an
Hiroshima
Osaka
Tel Aviv
Jerusalem
IRAQ
IRAN
Fukuoka
Kurashiki
ISRAEL
'Amman
JORDAN
Lahore
Nanjing
Nagasaki
SHIKOKU
Suzhou
Kagoshima
KYUSHU
Chengdu
Shanghai
Lhasa
EAST CHINA SEA
PACIFIC OCEAN
KUW.
Kuwait City
PAKISTAN
Delhi
NEPAL
Kathmandu
BHUTAN
Al Manamah
The Gulf
EGYPT
SAUDI ARABIA
BAH.
Ash Shariqah (Sharjah)
Jaipur
Agra
Lucknow
RYUKYU IS.
Ar Riyad (Riyadh)
QAT.
Karachi
INDIA
B'DESH
Kolkata (Calcutta)
Dhaka
Kunming
Quanzhou
Taipei
TAIWAN
Tropic of Cancer
Jiddah (Jeddah)
UAE
Masqat (Muscat)
Ahmadabad
Chittagong
Taichung
Changhua
Kaohsiung
Vadodara (Baroda)
Hanoi
Macau (Aomen)
Hong Kong (Xianggang)
RED SEA
Al Hufuf (Hofuf)
Ad Dawhah (Doha)
OMAN
Dubayy (Dubai)
Mumbai (Bombay)
Mandalay
LAOS
Bhubaneswar
MYANMAR
Viangchan (Vientiane)
SUDAN
Najran
Yangon (Rangoon)
SOUTH CHINA SEA
PHILIPPINE SEA
Hyderabad
BAY OF BENGAL
Sukhothai
Huê
LUZON
ERITREA
Sana'a (Sana)
YEMEN
ARABIAN SEA
THAILAND
Chennai (Madras)
Kanchanaburi
CAMB.
VIETNAM
Manila
PHILIPPINES
SOCOTRA
Bangalore
Mysore
Bangkok (Krung Thep)
Phnum Pénh (Phnom Penh)
VISAYAN IS.
ETHIOPIA
Thanjavur
Thiruvananthapuram (Trivandrum)
SRI LANKA
Ho Chi Minh City (Saigon)
MINDANAO
Colombo
BRUNEI
Kuala Lumpur
MALAYSIA
Melaka (Malacca)
SING.
Kuching
Singapore
BORNEO
Equator
SUMATRA
SULAWESI
INDIAN OCEAN
PAPUA NEW GUINEA
Jakarta
Surabaya
INDONESIA
NEW GUINEA
Surakarta (Solo)
JAVA
Ubud
E. TIMOR

The most important museums and art galleries in Asia (including those in the Russian Republic east of Moscow) are listed here. Selection is based on importance and depth of the collection and its cultural diversity within a geographic spread.

Compiled by Jon A. Gillaspie
email: let@sarastro.com

Principal contents of institution:

- AA Applied & decorative art
- AR Archaeology / ancient art
- FA Fine art (paintings, sculpture)
- FO Folk art & culture / ethnography
- H History / historical site / reconstruction
- NH Natural history
- ST Science / technology
- W Wide range of subjects

Ad Dawhah (Doha) QATAR
FO Heritage Centre
W Qatar National Museum

Agra INDIA
H Taj Mahal Museum

Ahmadabad INDIA
FA N.C. Mehta Gallery (Indology Institute)
FO Tribal Art Museum

Al Hufuf (Hofuf) SAUDI ARABIA
AR Hofuf Museum

Al Manamah BAHRAIN
W National Museum

Almaty KAZAKHSTAN
AR H Central State Museum
FA Kasteyev Museum of Fine Arts

Amman JORDAN
FO Jordanian Museum of Popular Traditions
AR National Archaeological Museum
FA National Gallery of Fine Art

Ar Riyad (Riyadh) SAUDI ARABIA
AR FO National Museum

Ashgabat TURKMENISTAN
FO NH Brunei Museum
FO Malay Technology Museum

Ash Shariqah (Sharjah) UNITED ARAB EM.
AR Sharjah Archaeology Museum
FA Sharjah Art Museum
ST Sharjah Science Museum

Bangalore INDIA
W Government Museum

Bangkok (Krung Thep) THAILAND
AR National Museum
AA FA Thai Houses of Jim Thompson

Bayrut (Beirut) LEBANON
AR American University of Beirut (AUB) Museum; National Museum of Beirut

Beijing (Peking) CHINA
FA China Art Gallery; Xu Beihong Museum
FO Cultural Palace of National Minorities
AR FO Museum of Chinese History
NH Natural History Museum
H Military Museum; Palace Museum

Bhubaneshwar INDIA
FO Museum of Man
W Orissa State Museum

Bishkek KYRGYZSTAN
AR H State Historical Museum

Changhua TAIWAN
FO Taiwanese Cultural Village

Chengdu CHINA
H Three Kingdoms Museum

Chennai (Madras) INDIA
AR FO Government Museum

Chittagong BANGLADESH
FO Ethnological Museum

Colombo SRI LANKA
H Dutch Period Museum
FA National Art Gallery
AR H National Museum

Delhi INDIA
FA National Gallery of Modern Art
W National Museum

Dhaka BANGLADESH
W National Museum

Dimashq (Damascus) SYRIA
W National Museum

Dubayy (Dubai) UNITED ARAB EMIRATES
W Dubai Museum

Dushanbe TAJIKISTAN
AA FO Museum of Ethnography
W Tajikistan Unified Museum

Fukuoka JAPAN
FA Fukuoka Art Museum

Halab (Aleppo) SYRIA
FO Museum of Popular Tradition
W National Museum of Aleppo

Hanoi VIETNAM
AR H History Museum
H Ho Chi Minh Museum; Museum of the Vietnamese Revolution
FA FO National Fine Arts Museum

Hefa (Haifa) ISRAEL
W Haifa Art Museum
ST National Museum of Science, Planning and Technology

Hiroshima JAPAN
H Hiroshima Peace Memorial Museum

Ho Chi Minh City (Saigon) VIETNAM
W History Museum
H Revolutionary Museum; War Crimes Museum

Hong Kong (Xianggang) CHINA
ST Hong Kong Space Museum
AR FA Museum of Art
H HK Museum of History; Sam Tung Uk Museum; Sha Tin Heritage Museum

Huê VIETNAM
AA AR Hue Museum of Antique Objects

Hyderabad INDIA
AR Archaeology Museum
W Salar Jung Museum

Islamabad PAKISTAN
W Lok Virsa Museum
FO Islamabad Museum

Jaipur INDIA
W Central Museum; Museum of Indology

Jakarta INDONESIA
AA FA Adam Malik Museum; Balai Seni Rupa
W National Museum
W Taman Mini Indonesia Indah *includes:* Asmat Museum; Museum Indonesia; Komodo Museum; Science Museum

Jerusalem ISRAEL/PALESTINE NAR
ST Bloomfield Science Museum
H Holocaust Museum (Yad Vashem)
AR Islamic Museum; Museum of the History of Jeruslaem; Wohl Archaeology Museum (and Burnt House)
W Israel Museum
FA L.A. Mayer Memorial Museum of Islamic Art
AR H Rockefeller Museum

Jiddah (Jeddah) SAUDI ARABIA
AR FO Regional Museum of Archaeology and Ethnography

Kagoshima JAPAN
FA Museum of Fine Arts
W Reimeikan – Prefectural Museum of Culture

Kanchanaburi THAILAND
H JEATH War Museum (River Kwai Bridge)

Kaohsiung TAIWAN
FA Fine Arts Museum
ST Science and Technology Museum

Karachi PAKISTAN
W National Museum

Kathmandu NEPAL
W Biheswari – National Museum

Kolkata (Calcutta) INDIA
FA Academy of Fine Arts
H Ashutosh Museum of Indian History
FA FO Birla Academy of Art and Culture
ST Birla Industrial and Technological Museum
AR H Indian Museum

Krasnoyarsk RUSSIAN FEDERATION
FA Surikov Art Museum

Kuala Lumpur MALAYSIA
AR FA Muzium Negara
FA National Art Gallery
W National Museum of Islamic Arts

Kuching MALAYSIA
W Islamic Museum; Sarawak Museum

Kunming CHINA
W Kunming City Museum

Kurashiki JAPAN
FA Ohara New Art Museum

Kuwait City KUWAIT
NH ST Scientific Centre
FA Tareq Rajab Museum

Kyoto JAPAN
AR Archaeological Museum
AA FA Kyoto Municipal Museum of Art
FA Kyoto National Museum; National Museum of Modern Art

Kyzyl RUSSIAN FEDERATION
W Tuva National Museum

Lahore PAKISTAN
W Lahore Central Museum

Lhasa CHINA
AR H Potala Palace

Lucknow INDIA
FO Kaisarbagh's Folk Art Museum
FA Muhammad Ali Shah Art Gallery
AR State Museum

Macau (Aomen) CHINA
AA Macau Museum of Art
H Maritime Museum; Musee de Macau

Mandalay MYANMAR
W National Museum and Library

Manila THE PHILIPPINES
AR FA Metropolitan Museum
ST Museo Pambata
AR Museum of the Filipino People
W Nayong Pilipino, includes: Museum of Ethnology; Museo ng Buhag; Torogan House

Masqat (Muscat) OMAN
W Oman Museum

Melaka (Malacca) MALAYSIA
W Istana Ke Sultanan
FO Museum of Ethnology

Mumbai (Bombay) INDIA
AA FA Jehangir Art Gallery
W Prince of Wales Museum of Western India

Mysore INDIA
FA Jayachamarahendra Art Gallery

Nagasaki JAPAN
H Atomic Bomb Museum

Najran SAUDI ARABIA
W Najran Museum

Nanjing CHINA
W Nanjing Museum
H Taiping Heavenly Kingdom History Museum

Novosibirsk RUSSIAN FEDERATION
AR FO Russian Institute of Archaeology and Ethnography

Osaka JAPAN
FO Japanese Folk Art Museum; National Ethnology Museum
FA National International Art Museum
AR FA Osaka Municipal Art Museum

Pengosekan INDONESIA
FA Agung Rai Museum of Art (ARRIA)

Peshawar PAKISTAN
AR FO Peshawar Museum

Phnom Pénh (Phnom Penh) CAMBODIA
W National Museum

Quanzhou CHINA
H Maritime Museum

Sakhnin ISRAEL
FO Museum of Palestinian Folk Heritage

Samarqand (Samarkand) UZBEKISTAN
AR Historical Museum of Uzbek Culture and Art

Sana'a (Sana) YEMEN
AA FA Museum of Arts and Crafts
W National Museum

Sapporo JAPAN
FA Hokkaido Museum of Modern Art; National Migishi Kotaro Museum of Art

Seoul REP. OF KOREA
FO National Folk Museum
W National Museum
FA National Museum of Contemporary Art

Shanghai CHINA
FA Art Museum
W Shanghai Museum

Shanhaiguan CHINA
AR H Great Wall Museum

Singapore
AR H Asian Civilization Museum
H Changi Prison Museum
FA Singapore Art Museum
ST Singapore Science Centre

Sukhothai THAILAND
AR Ramkhamhaeng Museum

Surabaya INDONESIA
FO H Museum Negiri Propinsi Jawa Timur

Surakarta (Solo) INDONESIA
W Radya Pustaka Museum

Suzhou CHINA
FO Museum of Opera and Theatre
AA Suzhou Silk Museum

Tadmur (Palmyra) SYRIA
AR Palmyra Archaeological Museum

Taichung TAIWAN
FA Taiwan Museum of Art
ST National Science Museum

Taipei TAIWAN
AA Chang Foundation Museum
FA Fine Arts Museum
W National Palace Museum
FO Taiwan Folk Arts Museum

Takayama JAPAN
AA AR Hida Minzuko Kukuokan
FA Hida Minzuko Mura

Tehran IRAN
AA FO Golestan Palace
AA Carpet Museum; Malek Museum; National Jewels Museum
AR National Museum of Iran
FA Tehran Museum of Contemporary Art

Tel Aviv ISRAEL
AR Eretz Israel Museum (HaAretz Museum)
H Nahum Goldman Museum of the Jewish Diaspora
FA Tel Aviv Museum of Art

Thanjavur INDIA
FA Nayak Durbar Hall Art Museum
AR Rajaraja Cholan Museum

Tokyo JAPAN
FA National Museum of Modern Art; National Museum of Western Art; Tokyo Central Museum of Arts; Tokyo Metropolitan Fine Art Museum
NH Natural Science Museum
ST Science and Technology Museum
H Shitamachi History Museum
AA FA Suntory Bijutsukan
AR FA Tokyo National Museum

Toshkent (Tashkent) UZBEKISTAN
AR H Amur Timur Museum
AA Museum of Applied Arts
AA AR Museum of the History of the People of Uzbekistan
FA State Fine Arts Museum

Thiruvananthapuram (Trivandrum) INDIA
FO Government (Napier) Museum
FA Shri Chitra Art Gallery

Tianjin CHINA
ST Science and Technology Museum

Ubud BALI, INDONESIA
FA Neka Museum

Ulaanbaatar (Ulan Bator) MONGOLIA
FA Mongolian National Modern Art Gallery; Zanabazar Museum of Fine Arts
AR H National Museum of Mongolian History

Ulan Ude RUSSIAN FEDERATION
AR FO Ethnographical Museum
FA Fine Arts Museum
AR Museum of Oriental Art and Buryat History

Vadodara (Baroda) INDIA
W Baroda Museum and Picture Gallery

Viangchan (Vientiane) LAOS
AR FA Haw Pha Kaew

Vladivostok RUSSIAN FEDERATION
W Arsenev Regional Museum
FA Primorsky Art Museum

Xi'an CHINA
AR Banpo Museum; Shaanxi History Museum
W Tang Dynasty Arts Museum

Yangon (Rangoon) MYANMAR
AR FO National Museum

Yekaterinburg RUSSIAN FEDERATION
AA FA Fine Arts Museum
AR H History and Local Studies Museum

Yokohama JAPAN
W Kanagawa Kenritsu Hakubutsukan
AA Silk Centre Museum

See also... Red Sea Diving (119); the Holy Land (131)

The listings above refer to a selection of related themes.
For more information, see the Contents (2-7).

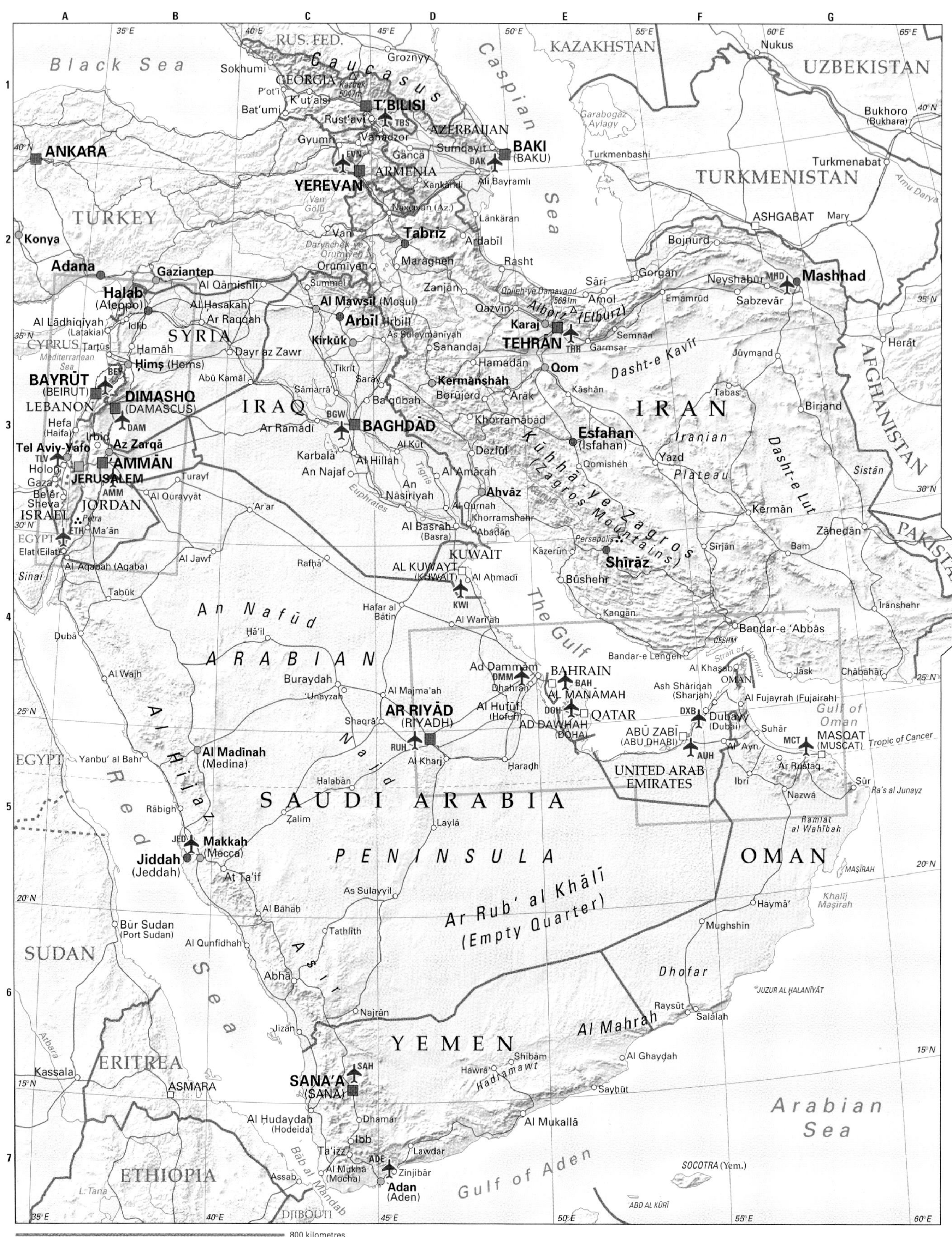
A
B
C
D
E
F
G
1
2
3
4
5
6
7
Black Sea
RUS. FED.
Caucasus
Groznyy
KAZAKHSTAN
UZBEKISTAN
Nukus
Sokhumi
GEORGIA
P'ot'i
K'ut'aisi
Bat'umi
T'BILISI
TBS
Rust'avi
AZERBAIJAN
Gyumri
Vanadzor
Sumqayit
BAKI
(BAKU)
BAK
ARMENIA
EVN
YEREVAN
Xankändi
Äli Bayramlı
ANKARA
Caspian Sea
Garabogaz Aylagy
Turkmenbashi
Bukhoro
(Bukhara)
Turkmenabat
TURKMENISTAN
Amu Darya
ASHGABAT
Mary
TURKEY
Konya
Van
Van Gölü
Naxçıvan (Az.)
Tabrīz
Ardabīl
Länkäran
Daryācheh-ye Orūmīyeh
Orūmīyeh
Marāgheh
Rasht
Adana
Gaziantep
Al Qāmishlī
Summel
Zanjān
Sārī
Gorgān
Bojnūrd
Neyshābūr
MHD
Mashhad
Halab
(Aleppo)
Al Ḩasakah
Ar Raqqah
Al Mawşil (Mosul)
Arbīl (Irbil)
Kirkūk
As Sulaymānīyah
Qazvīn
Qolleh-ye Damavand 5681m
Alborz (Elburz)
Āmol
Emāmrūd
Sabzevār
Karaj
TEHRĀN
THR
Semnān
Garmsar
Al Lādhiqīyah
(Latakia)
Idlib
SYRIA
CYPRUS
Tartūs
Ḩamāh
Dayr az Zawr
Sanandaj
Hamadān
Qom
Dasht-e Kavīr
Jūymand
Herāt
Mediterranean Sea
Ḩimş (Homs)
Abū Kamāl
Tikrīt
Sāmarrā'
Sarāy
Kermānshāh
Borūjerd
Arāk
Kāshān
Tabas
AFGHANISTAN
BAYRŪT
(BEIRUT)
BEY
LEBANON
DIMASHQ
(DAMASCUS)
DAM
IRAQ
Ba'qūbah
BGW
BAGHDĀD
Khorramābād
IRAN
Birjand
Hefa
(Haifa)
Irbid
Az Zarqā
Ar Ramādī
Al Kūt
Dezfūl
Esfahan
(Isfahan)
Iranian
Plateau
Dasht-e Lut
Tel Aviv-Yafo
TLV
Holon
'AMMĀN
Karbalā'
Al Ḩillah
An Najaf
Tigris
Euphrates
Al 'Amārah
Qomishëh
Yazd
Sīstān
Gaza
JERUSALEM
AMM
Turayf
Be'er Sheva
JORDAN
Al Qurayyāt
An Nāşirīyah
Ahvāz
Kūhhā-ye Zagros
Zagros Mountains
Kermān
ISRAEL
Petra
'Ar'ar
Al Qurnah
Khorramshahr
Ābādān
Al Başrah
(Basra)
Zāhedān
PAKISTAN
EGYPT
ETH
Ma'ān
Elat (Eilat)
Al 'Aqabah (Aqaba)
Al Jawf
Rafḩā'
KUWAIT
AL KUWAYT
(KUWAIT)
Al Aḩmadī
Kāzerūn
Persepolis
Shīrāz
Sīrjān
Bam
Sinai
Būshehr
The Gulf
Tabūk
KWI
Hafar al Bātin
Kangān
Īrānshahr
An Nafūd
Ḩā'il
Al Wari'ah
Bandar-e 'Abbās
QESHM
Strait of Hormuz
Ḑubā
ARABIAN
Bandar-e Lengeh
Al Khaşab
Jāsk
Chābahār
Al Wajh
Buraydah
'Unayzah
Ad Dammām
DMM
Dhahran
BAHRAIN
BAH
AL MANĀMAH
OMAN
Al Majma'ah
Ash Shāriqah
(Sharjah)
Al Fujayrah (Fujairah)
AR RIYĀD
(RIYADH)
Shaqrā'
Al Hufūf
(Hofuf)
DOH
QATAR
AD DAWḨAH
(DOHA)
DXB
Dubayy
(Dubai)
Gulf of Oman
Al Ḩijāz
Najd
RUH
Al Kharj
ABŪ ZABĪ
(ABU DHABI)
AUH
Şuḩār
MCT
MASQAT
(MUSCAT)
Tropic of Cancer
Al Madīnah
(Medina)
Yanbu' al Bahr
Ḩaraḑh
UNITED ARAB EMIRATES
Al 'Ayn
Ar Rustāq
Ḩalabān
Ibrī
Şūr
Ra's al Junayz
SAUDI ARABIA
Nazwá
Rābigh
Red Sea
Ẓalim
Laylá
Ramlat al Wahībah
JED
Makkah
(Mecca)
Jiddah
(Jeddah)
PENINSULA
OMAN
MAŞĪRAH
At Ta'if
As Sulayyil
Ar Rub' al Khālī
(Empty Quarter)
Ḩaymā'
Khalīj Maşīrah
Al Bāḩah
Būr Sudan
(Port Sudan)
Tathlīth
Mughshin
SUDAN
Al Qunfidhah
'Asīr
Dhofar
Abhā
JUZUR AL ḨALANĪYĀT
Najrān
Raysūt
Şalālah
Jīzān
Al Mahrah
Atbara
YEMEN
ERITREA
Shibām
Al Ghayḑah
Kassala
Hawrā'
Hadramawt
ASMARA
SAH
SANA'A
(SANA)
Sayḩūt
Arabian Sea
Al Ḩudaydah
(Hodeida)
Dhamār
Al Mukallā
Ibb
Ta'izz
Lawdar
ADE
SOCOTRA (Yem.)
ETHIOPIA
Assab
Bāb al Mandab
Al Mukhā
(Mocha)
Zinjibār
Adan
(Aden)
Gulf of Aden
L. Tana
DJIBOUTI
'ABD AL KŪRĪ
35°E
40°E
45°E
50°E
55°E
60°E
65°E
40°N
35°N
30°N
25°N
20°N
15°N

800 kilometres
400 miles

Lambert Equal Area Projection
Blue boxes indicate focus map coverage

Crucible of ancient civilizations, harsh landscape of the Prophets of the Old Testament revered by Jew, Muslim and Christian alike, and dramatic setting for the story of Christ from his birth in Bethlehem to his crucifixion outside Jerusalem, the HOLY LAND is a region of monumental and complex significance – as Promised Land, place of pilgrimage and miracles and the setting for the rise and fall of empires and kingdoms.

No city symbolises this rich heritage more than Jerusalem. As the site of the ancient Temples of Judaism, so central to the ancient Jewish state, Jerusalem is the region's spiritual heart. For Christians, Jerusalem is the site of the Crucifixion, the culmination of the life of Christ. The city is also an integral part of the sacred geography of Islam, which also reveres the Old Testament Patriarchs, and is the third most sacred site in Islam after Mecca and Medina. In addition to sites of spiritual significance, the Holy Land contains archaeological and architectural sites of immense importance.

Since the proclamation of the state of Israel in 1948, the politics of the area have been dominated by conflict between Israel and surrounding Arab states. Despite many false dawns, fragile ceasefires and internationally backed mediation processes, a lasting peace still seems a long way off.

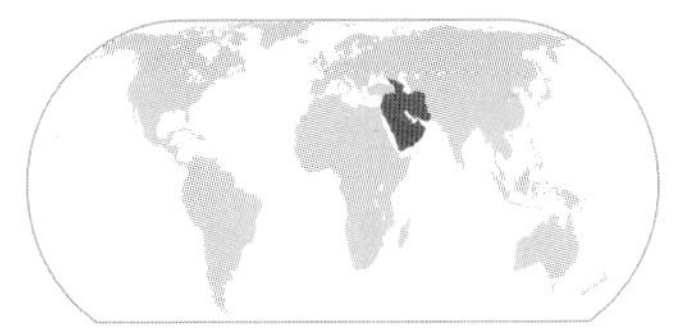

See also... Religion (21); Asia Historical (128); West Asia (130)

The listings above refer to a selection of related themes. For more information, see the Contents (2-7).

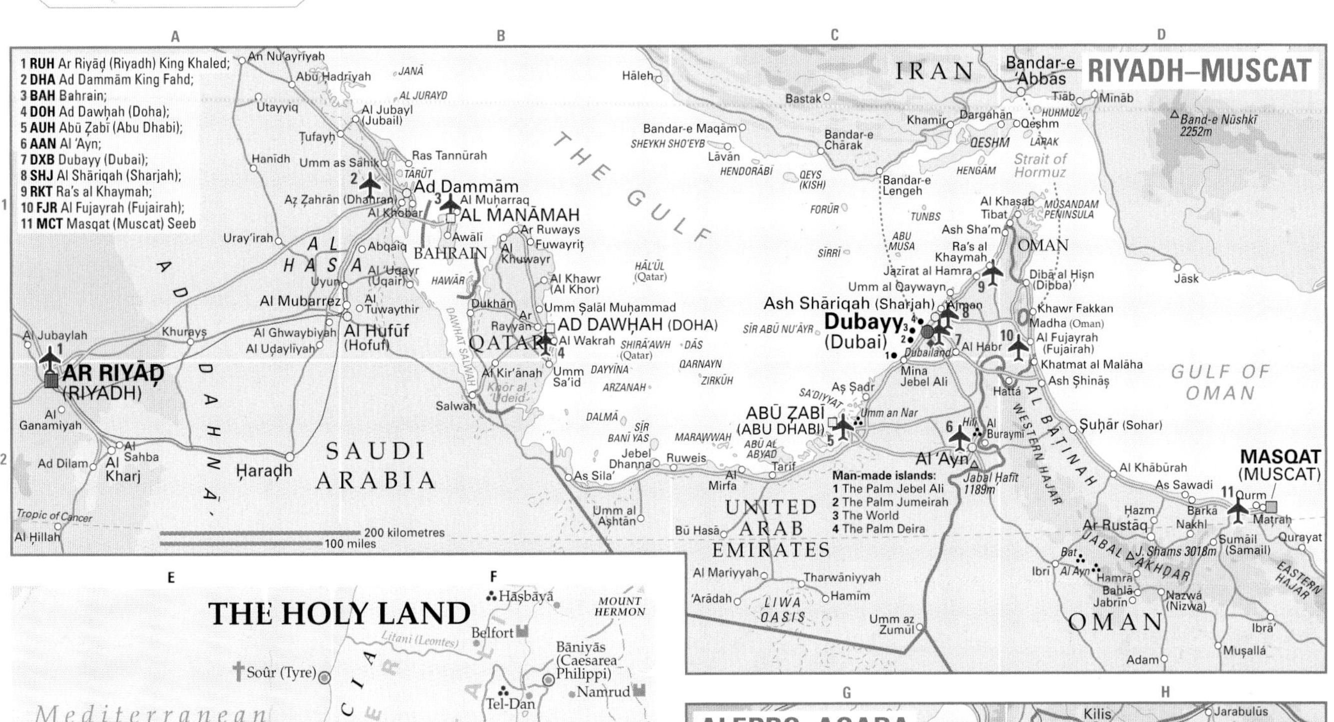
RIYADH–MUSCAT
1 RUH Ar Riyāḑ (Riyadh) King Khaled;
2 DHA Ad Dammām King Fahd;
3 BAH Bahrain;
4 DOH Ad Dawḩah (Doha);
5 AUH Abū Z̧abī (Abu Dhabi);
6 AAN Al 'Ayn;
7 DXB Dubayy (Dubai);
8 SHJ Al Shāriqah (Sharjah);
9 RKT Ra's al Khaymah;
10 FJR Al Fujayrah (Fujairah);
11 MCT Masqat (Muscat) Seeb
Man-made islands:
1 The Palm Jebel Ali
2 The Palm Jumeirah
3 The World
4 The Palm Deira
IRAN
THE GULF
SAUDI ARABIA
AR RIYĀḐ (RIYADH)
AD DAWḨAH (DOHA)
QATAR
BAHRAIN
AL MANĀMAH
Ad Dammām
Al Hufūf (Hofuf)
ABŪ Z̧ABĪ (ABU DHABI)
Dubayy (Dubai)
UNITED ARAB EMIRATES
OMAN
MASQAT (MUSCAT)
GULF OF OMAN
Strait of Hormuz
Bandar-e 'Abbās
200 kilometres
100 miles
Tropic of Cancer

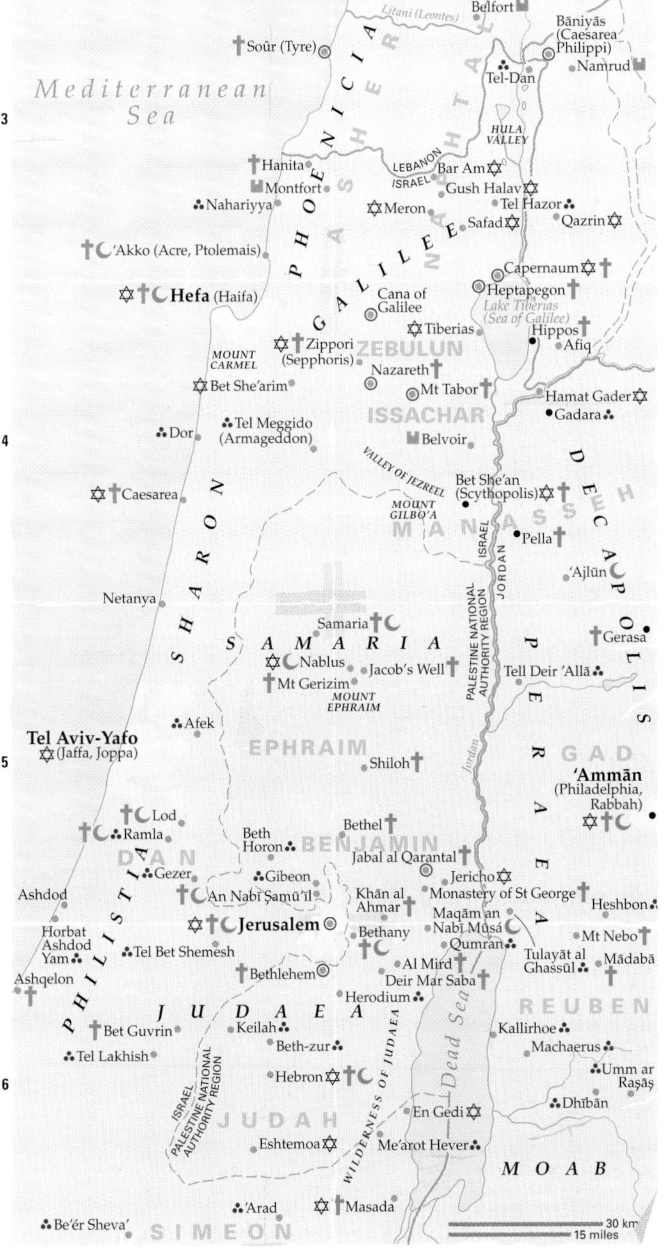
THE HOLY LAND
Mediterranean Sea
Site significant in Judaism
Site significant in Islam
Site significant in Christianity
Important location relating to the life of Jesus
Crusader castle or fortifications
Other important historical site
City of the Decapolis
DAN The Twelve Tribes of Israel
Present-day boundaries are shown as grey lines
PHOENICIA
GALILEE
ZEBULUN
ISSACHAR
MANASSEH
SAMARIA
EPHRAIM
BENJAMIN
JUDAEA
JUDAH
SIMEON
REUBEN
GAD
DECAPOLIS
PERAEA
MOAB
SHARON
PHILISTIA
Jerusalem
Tel Aviv-Yafo (Jaffa, Joppa)
Hefa (Haifa)
Nazareth
Bethlehem
Jericho
Dead Sea
Jordan
Lake Tiberias (Sea of Galilee)
'Ammān (Philadelphia, Rabbah)
Masada
30 km
15 miles

ALEPPO–AQABA
1 ALP Halab (Aleppo) Nejrab;
2 LTK Al Lādhiqīyah (Latakia);
3 DAM Dimashq (Damascus);
4 BEY Bayrūt (Beirut) Khalden;
5 HFA Hefa (Haifa) U. Michaeli;
6 TLV Tel Aviv Ben Gurion;
7 GZA Gaza;
8 ETH Elat (Eilat) J. Hozman;
9 AQJ Al 'Aqabah (Aqaba) King Hussein;
10 AMM 'Ammān Queen Alia
TURKEY
SYRIA
LEBANON
ISRAEL
JORDAN
EGYPT
SAUDI ARABIA
CYPRUS
MEDITERRANEAN SEA
Halab (Aleppo)
BAYRŪT (BEIRUT)
DIMASHQ (DAMASCUS)
JERUSALEM
'AMMĀN
BĀDIYAT ASH SHĀM (SYRIAN DESERT)
NEGEV
GULF OF AQABA
150 kilometres
75 miles
1000 metres
500 metres
Sea level

Central Asia & the Silk Road

See also... Asia Historical (128)

The listings above refer to a selection of related themes. For more information, see the Contents (2-7).

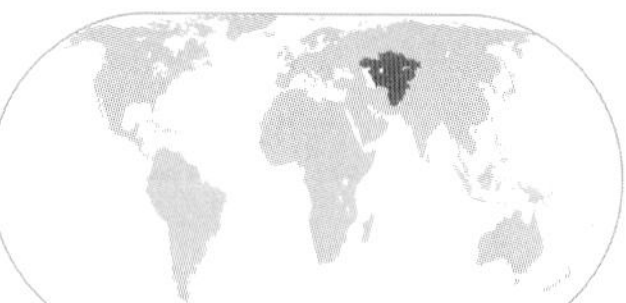

600 kilometres

300 miles

Lambert Equal Area Projection

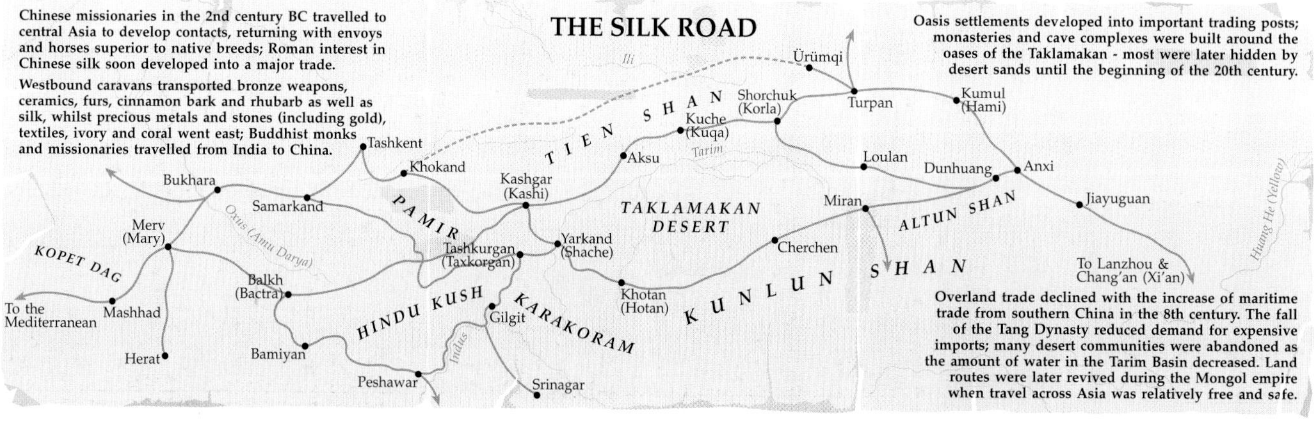

THE SILK ROAD

Chinese missionaries in the 2nd century BC travelled to central Asia to develop contacts, returning with envoys and horses superior to native breeds; Roman interest in Chinese silk soon developed into a major trade.

Westbound caravans transported bronze weapons, ceramics, furs, cinnamon bark and rhubarb as well as silk, whilst precious metals and stones (including gold), textiles, ivory and coral went east; Buddhist monks and missionaries travelled from India to China.

Oasis settlements developed into important trading posts; monasteries and cave complexes were built around the oases of the Taklamakan - most were later hidden by desert sands until the beginning of the 20th century.

Overland trade declined with the increase of maritime trade from southern China in the 8th century. The fall of the Tang Dynasty reduced demand for expensive imports; many desert communities were abandoned as the amount of water in the Tarim Basin decreased. Land routes were later revived during the Mongol empire when travel across Asia was relatively free and safe.

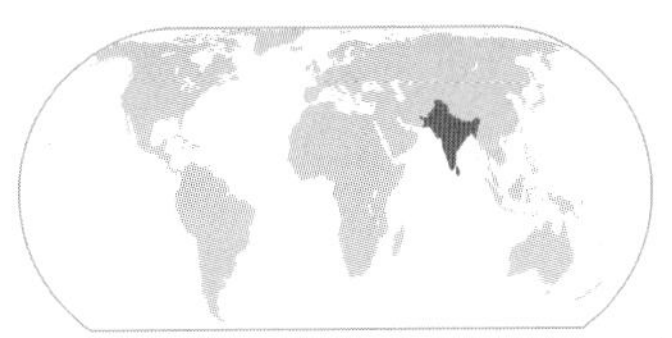

See also... Contents (2-7) – These countries feature in many thematic and regional maps throughout the *World Travel Atlas*.

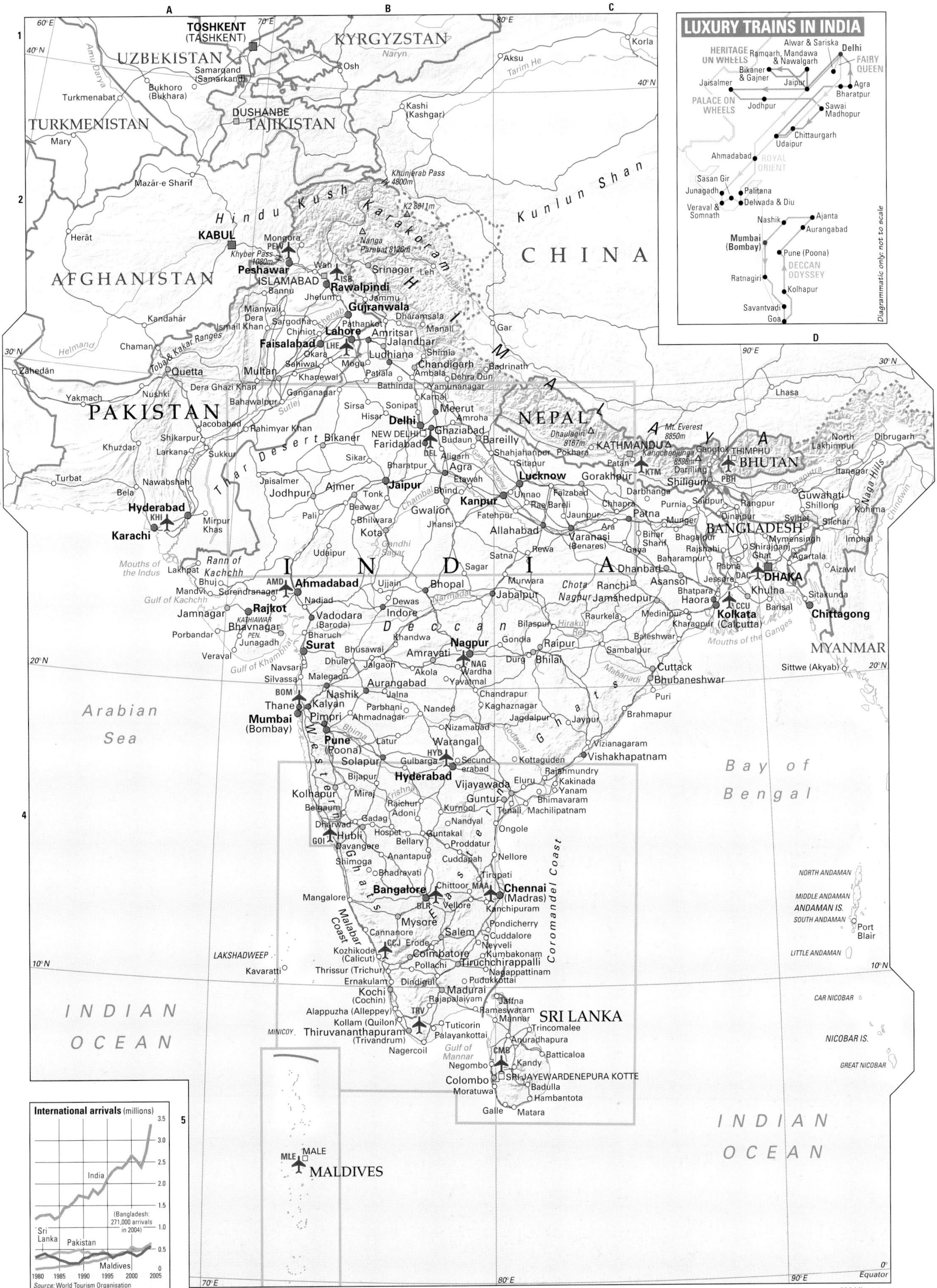

LUXURY TRAINS IN INDIA

HERITAGE ON WHEELS
PALACE ON WHEELS
FAIRY QUEEN
ROYAL ORIENT
DECCAN ODYSSEY
Delhi
Alwar & Sariska
Ramgarh, Mandawa & Nawalgarh
Bikaner & Gajner
Jaisalmer
Jaipur
Agra
Bharatpur
Jodhpur
Sawai Madhopur
Chittaurgarh
Udaipur
Ahmadabad
Sasan Gir
Junagadh
Palitana
Veraval & Somnath
Delwada & Diu
Nashik
Ajanta
Aurangabad
Mumbai (Bombay)
Pune (Poona)
Ratnagiri
Kolhapur
Savantvadi
Goa
Diagrammatic only: not to scale

AFGHANISTAN
PAKISTAN
INDIA
CHINA
NEPAL
BHUTAN
BANGLADESH
MYANMAR
SRI LANKA
MALDIVES
UZBEKISTAN
TURKMENISTAN
TAJIKISTAN
KYRGYZSTAN
Arabian Sea
Bay of Bengal
INDIAN OCEAN

International arrivals (millions)

3.5
3.0
2.5
2.0
1.5
1.0
0.5
0
India
(Bangladesh: 271,000 arrivals in 2004)
Sri Lanka
Pakistan
Maldives
1980 1985 1990 1995 2000 2005

Source: World Tourism Organisation

Lambert Equal Area Projection

Blue boxes indicate focus map coverage

800 kilometres
400 miles

See also... page 135 for more on India

For more information, see the Contents (2-7).

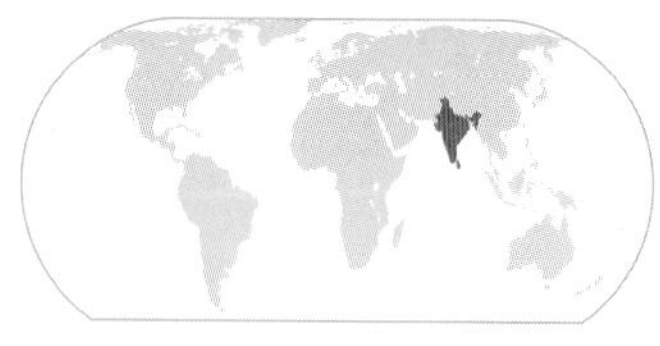

EVERY THREE YEARS Kumbh Mela (**Allahabad:** *Ganges & Yamuna* / **Haridwar:** *Ganges* / **Nashik:** *Godavari* / **Ujjain:** *Shipra*)
mid JAN Pongal: harvest festival (**Tamil Nadu**)
mid JAN Makar Sankranti: harvest festival (**E India**)
JAN 26th Republic Day (countrywide)
JAN/FEB Vasant Panchami: spring festival (**N India**)
JAN/FEB International Kite Festival (**Aurangabad**)
JAN/FEB Teppa Floating Festival (**Madurai**)
FEB Tibetan New Year (**Dharamsala**)
FEB/MAR Shivrati: Shiva's creation and wedding (countrywide)
FEB/MAR Holi: water festival to celebrate Spring (**N India**)
FEB/MAR **Khajuraho** Dance Festival
before Lent Carnival/Mardi Gras (**Goa**)
MAR/APR Gangaur: Parvati festival (**Rajasthan**)
MAR/APR Ramanavami: Rama's birthday (countrywide)
MAR/APR Pateti: Parsi New Year (**Mumbai**)
MAR/APR Khorvad Sal: birthday of Zarathustra (**Mumbai**)
MAR/APR Id uz-Zuha: Muslim pilgrimage festival
APR/MAY Chittirai: festival in celebration of Meenakshi (**Madurai**)
APR/MAY Baisakhi: Hindu New Year (countrywide); also anniversary of foundation of Sikh brotherhood (**Punjab**)
APR/MAY Mahavir Jayanti: birthday of Mahavira (**Gujarat**)
APR/MAY Puram: drumming and elephant parades (**Thrissur**)
APR/MAY Buddha Jayanti: Buddha's birthday (**Sarnath** & **Bodhgaya**)
MAY/JUN Ganga Dussehra: bathing festival
JUN/JUL Rath Yatra: Krishna's journey to Mathura (**Puri** & **S India**)
JUN/JUL Teej: monsoon festival (**Rajasthan**)
JUN/JUL Hemis: Buddhist festival (**Leh**)
JUL/AUG Naag Panchami: snake festival (**Rajasthan** & **Maharashtra**)
JUL/AUG Raksha Bandhan/Narial Purnima: festival to honour Varuna (countrywide)
AUG 15th Independence Day (countrywide)
AUG/SEP Avani Mula: Shiva's coronation festival (**Madurai**)
AUG/SEP Ganesh Chaturthi (**Mumbai** & **Maharashtra**)
AUG/SEP Onam: harvest festival (**Alappuzha**)
AUG/SEP Janmashtami: Krishna's birthday (countrywide)
SEP/OCT Dussehra: to celebrate Rama's victory over Ravana (**Mysore**, **Ahmadabad** & **Kullu**)
OCT 2nd Gandhi's birthday (countrywide)
OCT/NOV Diwali: festival of lights (countrywide); also Jain New Year
OCT/NOV Nanak Jayanti: Sikh processions (**Punjab** & **Patna**)
NOV **Pushkar** Camel Fair

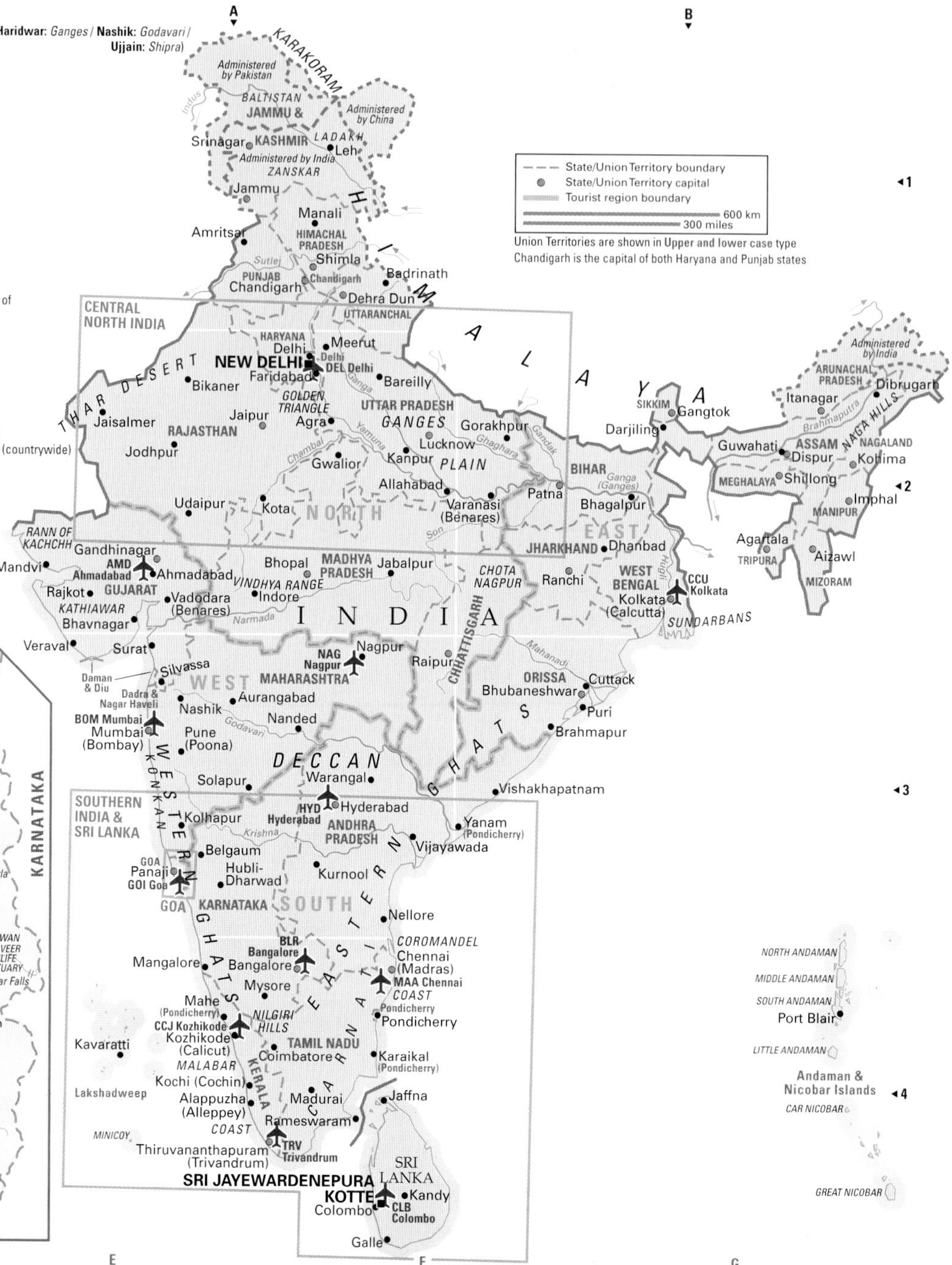

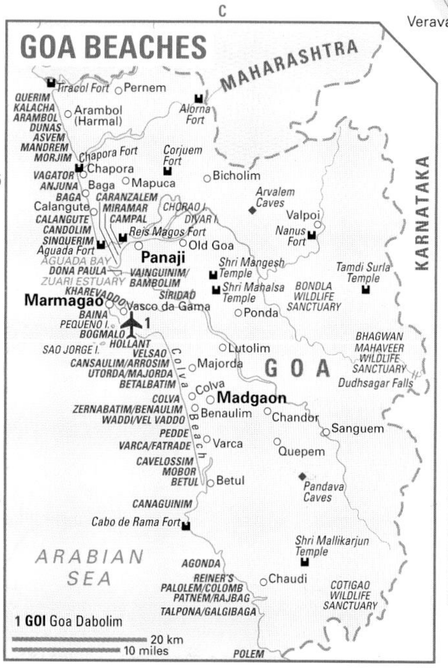

State/Union Territory boundary
State/Union Territory capital
Tourist region boundary
600 km
300 miles

Union Territories are shown in Upper and lower case type
Chandigarh is the capital of both Haryana and Punjab states

GOA BEACHES

1 GOI Goa Dabolim
20 km
10 miles

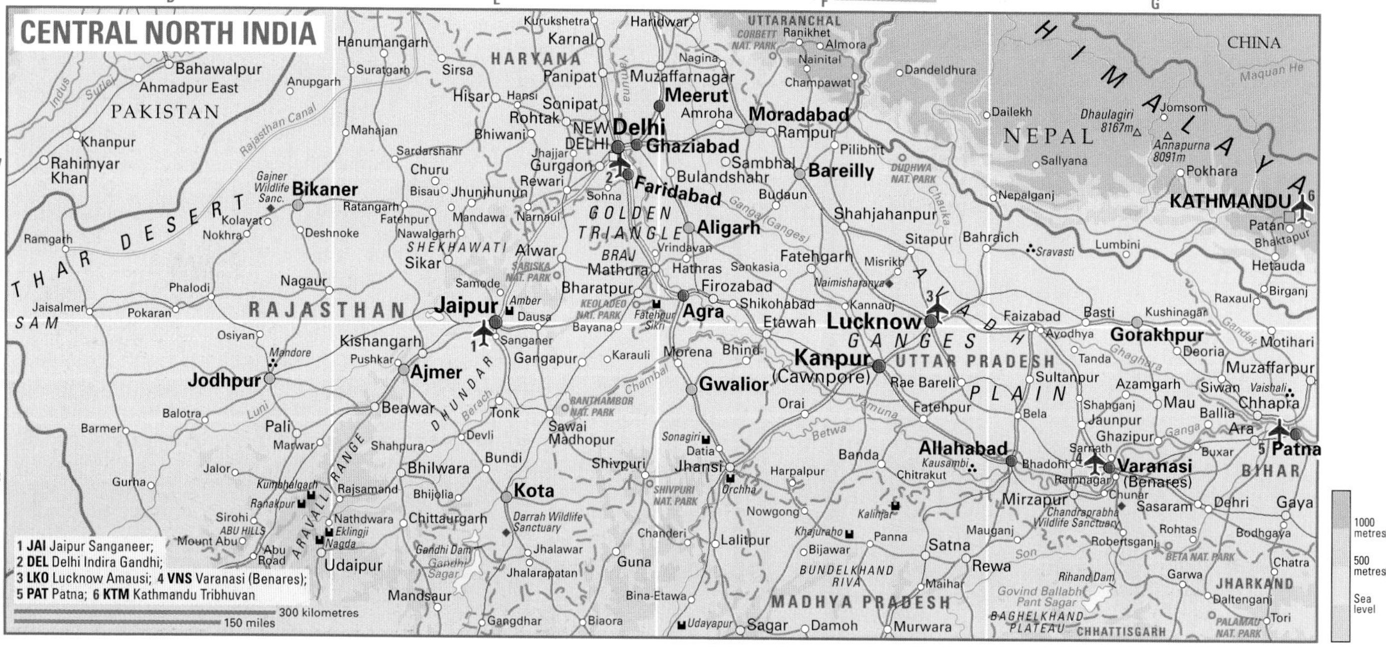

CENTRAL NORTH INDIA

1 JAI Jaipur Sanganeer; 2 DEL Delhi Indira Gandhi; 3 LKO Lucknow Amausi; 4 VNS Varanasi (Benares); 5 PAT Patna; 6 KTM Kathmandu Tribhuvan

300 kilometres
150 miles

1000 metres
500 metres
Sea level

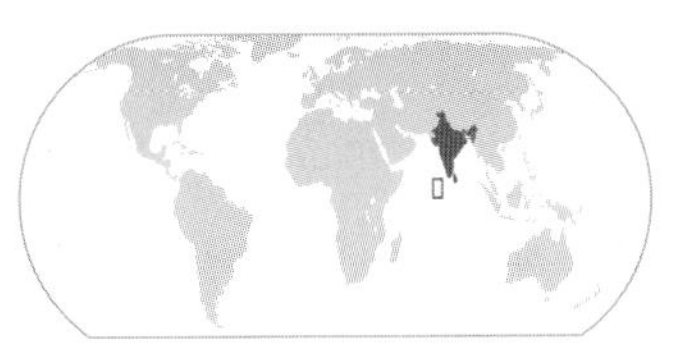

See also... Contents (2-7) – These countries feature in many thematic and regional maps throughout the *World Travel Atlas*.

SOUTHERN INDIA & SRI LANKA

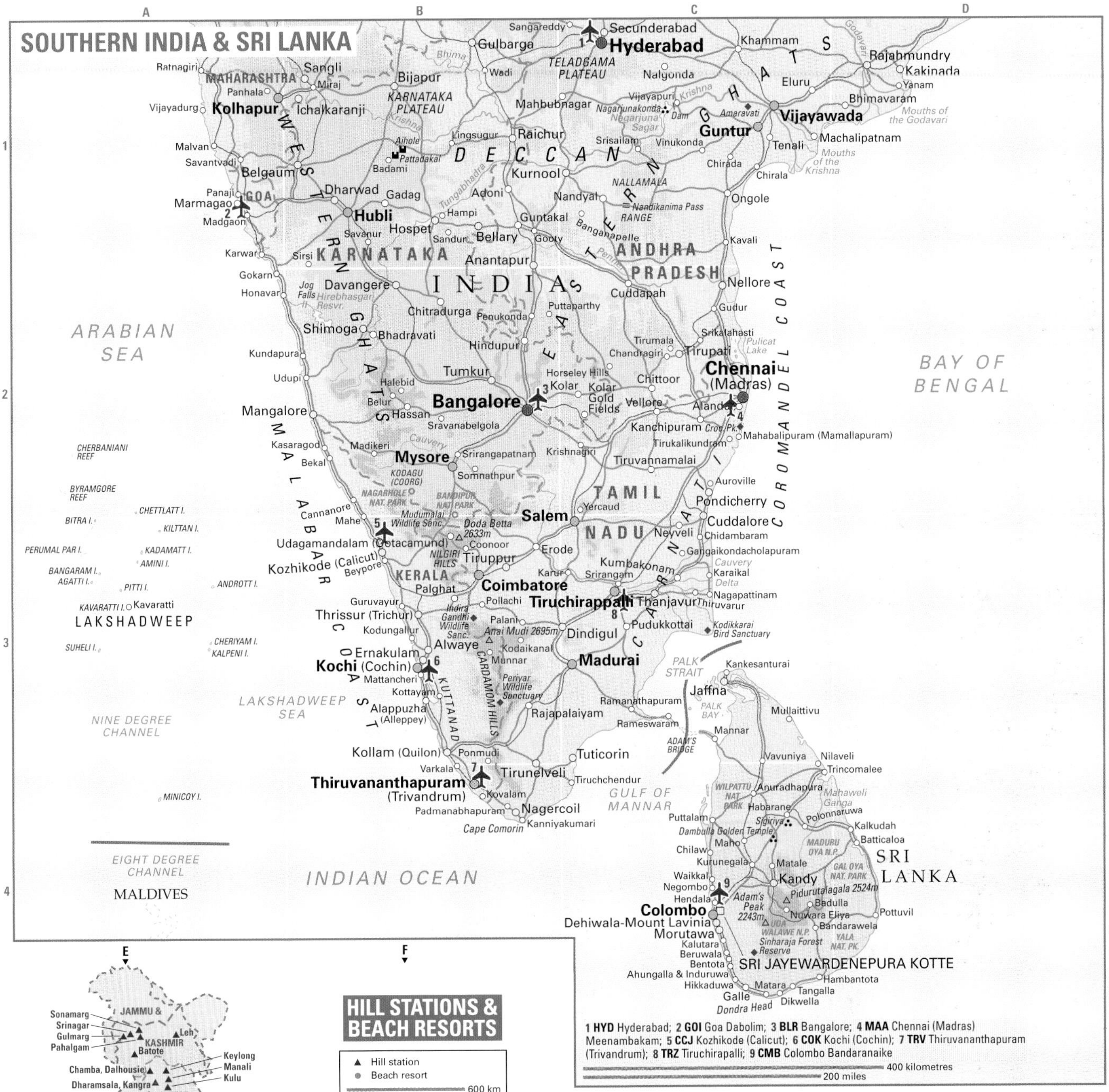

ARABIAN SEA
BAY OF BENGAL
INDIAN OCEAN
LAKSHADWEEP SEA
NINE DEGREE CHANNEL
EIGHT DEGREE CHANNEL
GULF OF MANNAR
PALK STRAIT
PALK BAY
ADAM'S BRIDGE
INDIA
SRI LANKA
MALDIVES
LAKSHADWEEP
MAHARASHTRA
KARNATAKA
ANDHRA PRADESH
TAMIL NADU
KERALA
GOA
DECCAN
WESTERN GHATS
EASTERN GHATS
MALABAR COAST
COROMANDEL COAST
CARNATIC
TELANGANA PLATEAU
KARNATAKA PLATEAU
NALLAMALA RANGE
CARDAMOM HILLS
NILGIRI HILLS
KUTTANAD

Hyderabad, Secunderabad, Sangareddy, Gulbarga, Wadi, Nalgonda, Khammam, Rajahmundry, Kakinada, Yanam, Eluru, Bhimavaram, Vijayawada, Guntur, Tenali, Machalipatnam, Amaravati, Nagarjunakonda, Nagarjuna Sagar, Vijayapuri, Mahbubnagar, Raichur, Lingsugur, Srisailam, Vinukonda, Chirala, Ongole, Kurnool, Nandyal, Nandikanima Pass, Banganapalle, Guntakal, Gooty, Bellary, Hospet, Hampi, Adoni, Gadag, Dharwad, Hubli, Savanur, Sandur, Anantapur, Kavali, Nellore, Gudur, Srikalahasti, Pulicat Lake, Tirupati, Tirumala, Chandragiri, Cuddapah, Puttaparthy, Penukonda, Hindupur, Chittoor, Chennai (Madras), Alandur, Mahabalipuram (Mamallapuram), Kanchipuram, Vellore, Kolar, Kolar Gold Fields, Horseley Hills, Bangalore, Tumkur, Chitradurga, Davangere, Shimoga, Bhadravati, Jog Falls, Hirebhasgar Resvr., Sirsi, Karwar, Gokarn, Honavar, Kundapura, Udupi, Mangalore, Kasaragod, Bekal, Madikeri, Kodagu (Coorg), Mysore, Srirangapatnam, Somnathpur, Hassan, Halebid, Belur, Sravanabelgola, Krishnagiri, Tiruvannamalai, Tirukalikundram, Auroville, Pondicherry, Cuddalore, Chidambaram, Neyveli, Salem, Yercaud, Erode, Coonoor, Udagamandalam (Ootacamund), Doda Betta 2633m, Mudumalai Wildlife Sanc., Bandipur Nat. Park, Nagarhole Nat. Park, Mahe, Cannanore, Kozhikode (Calicut), Beypore, Tiruppur, Coimbatore, Palghat, Pollachi, Palani, Indira Gandhi Wildlife Sanc., Anai Mudi 2695m, Kodaikanal, Munnar, Dindigul, Madurai, Tiruchirappalli, Srirangam, Thanjavur, Kumbakonam, Gangaikondacholapuram, Karaikal, Nagapattinam, Thiruvarur, Pudukkottai, Kodikkarai Bird Sanctuary, Karur, Guruvayur, Thrissur (Trichur), Kodungallur, Alwaye, Ernakulam, Kochi (Cochin), Mattancheri, Kottayam, Alappuzha (Alleppey), Periyar Wildlife Sanctuary, Rajapalaiyam, Ramanathapuram, Rameswaram, Kollam (Quilon), Ponmudi, Varkala, Thiruvananthapuram (Trivandrum), Kovalam, Tirunelveli, Tuticorin, Tiruchchendur, Nagercoil, Padmanabhapuram, Kanniyakumari, Cape Comorin, Ratnagiri, Sangli, Miraj, Bijapur, Panhala, Kolhapur, Ichalkaranji, Vijayadurg, Malvan, Savantvadi, Belgaum, Aihole, Pattadakal, Badami, Panaji, Marmagao, Madgaon

Cherbaniani Reef, Byramgore Reef, Bitra I., Chetlatt I., Kiltan I., Perumal Par I., Kadamatt I., Amini I., Bangaram I., Agatti I., Pitti I., Androtti I., Kavaratti I., Kavaratti, Suheli I., Cheriyam I., Kalpeni I., Minicoy I.

Kankesanturai, Jaffna, Mullaittivu, Mannar, Vavuniya, Nilaveli, Trincomalee, Wilpattu Nat. Park, Anuradhapura, Mahaweli Ganga, Habarane, Polonnaruwa, Sigiriya, Dambulla Golden Temple, Kalkudah, Batticaloa, Puttalam, Chilaw, Maho, Kurunegala, Maduru Oya N.P., Matale, Gal Oya Nat. Park, Waikkal, Negombo, Kandy, Hendala, Colombo, Adam's Peak 2243m, Pidurutalagala 2524m, Badulla, Nuwara Eliya, Pottuvil, Bandarawela, Dehiwala-Mount Lavinia, Moratuwa, Kalutara, Beruwala, Uda Walawe N.P., Sinharaja Forest Reserve, Yala Nat. Pk., Bentota, Sri Jayewardenepura Kotte, Ahungalla & Induruwa, Hikkaduwa, Matara, Hambantota, Tangalla, Galle, Dikwella, Dondra Head

1 HYD Hyderabad; **2 GOI** Goa Dabolim; **3 BLR** Bangalore; **4 MAA** Chennai (Madras) Meenambakam; **5 CCJ** Kozhikode (Calicut); **6 COK** Kochi (Cochin); **7 TRV** Thiruvananthapuram (Trivandrum); **8 TRZ** Tiruchirapalli; **9 CMB** Colombo Bandaranaike

400 kilometres
200 miles

HILL STATIONS & BEACH RESORTS

▲ Hill station
● Beach resort

600 km
300 miles

Jammu & Kashmir: Sonamarg, Srinagar, Gulmarg, Pahalgam, Leh, Batote
H. Prad.: Chamba, Dalhousie, Dharamsala, Kangra, Keylong, Manali, Kulu, Kufri, Shimla
Punjab; Nahan, Paonta Sahib; Dehra Dun, Mussoorie
Uttaranchal: Lansdowne, Almora, Nainital, Ranikhet
Haryana, Delhi, Rajasthan: Mount Abu
Uttar Pradesh, Bihar
Sikkim: Darjiling, Kalimpong, Mirik, Gangtok
Arunachal Pradesh, Assam, Shillong, Meghalaya, Nagaland, Manipur, Tripura, Mizoram
Gujarat: Champaner, Dwarka, Porbandar, Somnath, Veraval, Ahmedpur-Mandvi, Dumas, Hajira, Ubarat, Tithal, Daman, Umbargaon
Madhya Pradesh: Pachmarhi
Jharkhand: Netarhat
West Bengal: Digha
Chhattisgarh, Orissa: Puri, Gopalpur-on-Sea
Maharashtra: Saputura, Juhu Beach, Manori, Marve, Matheran, Lonavala, Murud, Mahabaleshwar, Panchgani, Panhala
Andhra Pradesh: Bheemunipatnam, Machilipatnam, Manginipudi, Horseley Hills, Maipadu
Goa
Karnataka: Udupi, Mangalore, Ullal, Mercara
Lakshadweep, Cannanore, Mahe, Ugadamandalam (Otacamund 'Ooty'), Coonoor, Kotagiri, Yercaud
Tamil Nadu: Covelong, Mahabalipuram (Mamallapuram), Pondicherry, Karaikal, Kodaikanal, Rameswaram, Tiruchendur, Kanniyakumari
Kerala: Munnar, Kollam (Quilon), Varkala, Ponmudi, Kovalam
Andaman & Nicobar Is.

MALDIVES

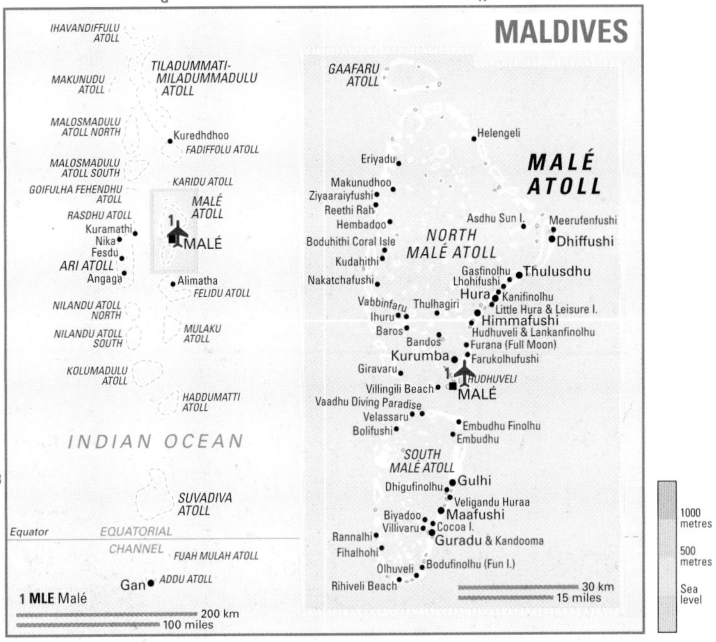

Ihavandiffulu Atoll, Tiladummati-Miladummadulu Atoll, Makunudu Atoll, Malosmadulu Atoll North, Malosmadulu Atoll South, Kuredhdhoo, Fadiffolu Atoll, Karidu Atoll, Goifulha Fehendhu Atoll, Rasdhu Atoll, Male Atoll, Kuramathi, Nika, Fesdu, Ari Atoll, Angaga, Alimatha, Felidu Atoll, Nilandu Atoll North, Nilandu Atoll South, Mulaku Atoll, Kolumadulu Atoll, Haddummati Atoll, Indian Ocean, Suvadiva Atoll, Equator, Equatorial Channel, Fuah Mulah Atoll, Addu Atoll, Gan

Gaafaru Atoll, Helengeli, Eriyadu, Makunudhoo, Ziyaaraiyfushi, Reethi Rah, Hembadoo, Boduhithi Coral Isle, Kudahithi, Nakatchafushi, North Malé Atoll, Asdhu Sun I., Meerufenfushi, Dhiffushi, Gasfinolhu, Thulusdhu, Lhohifushi, Hura, Kanifinolhu, Vabbinfaru, Thulhagiri, Little Hura & Leisure I., Ihuru, Himmafushi, Baros, Hudhuveli & Lankanfinolhu, Bandos, Furana (Full Moon), Kurumba, Farukolhufushi, Giravaru, Hudhuveli, Villingili Beach, Malé, Vaadhu Diving Paradise, Velassaru, Bolifushi, Embudhu Finolhu, Embudhu, South Malé Atoll, Dhigufinolhu, Gulhi, Veligandu Huraa, Biyadoo, Maafushi, Villivaru, Cocoa I., Rannalhi, Guradu & Kandooma, Fihalhohi, Olhuveli, Bodufinolhu (Fun I.), Rihiveli Beach

MALÉ ATOLL

1 MLE Malé

200 km
100 miles

30 km
15 miles

1000 metres
500 metres
Sea level

China, Mongolia & Korea

See also... Contents (2-7) – These countries feature in many thematic and regional maps throughout the *World Travel Atlas*.

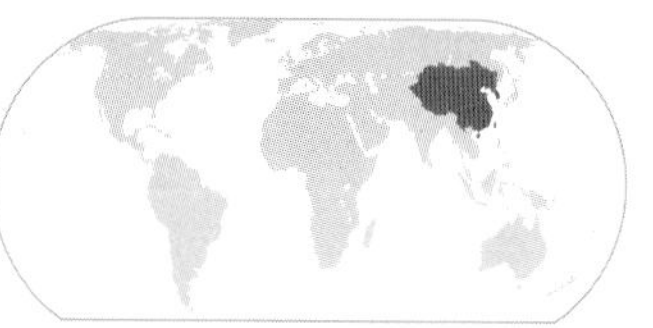

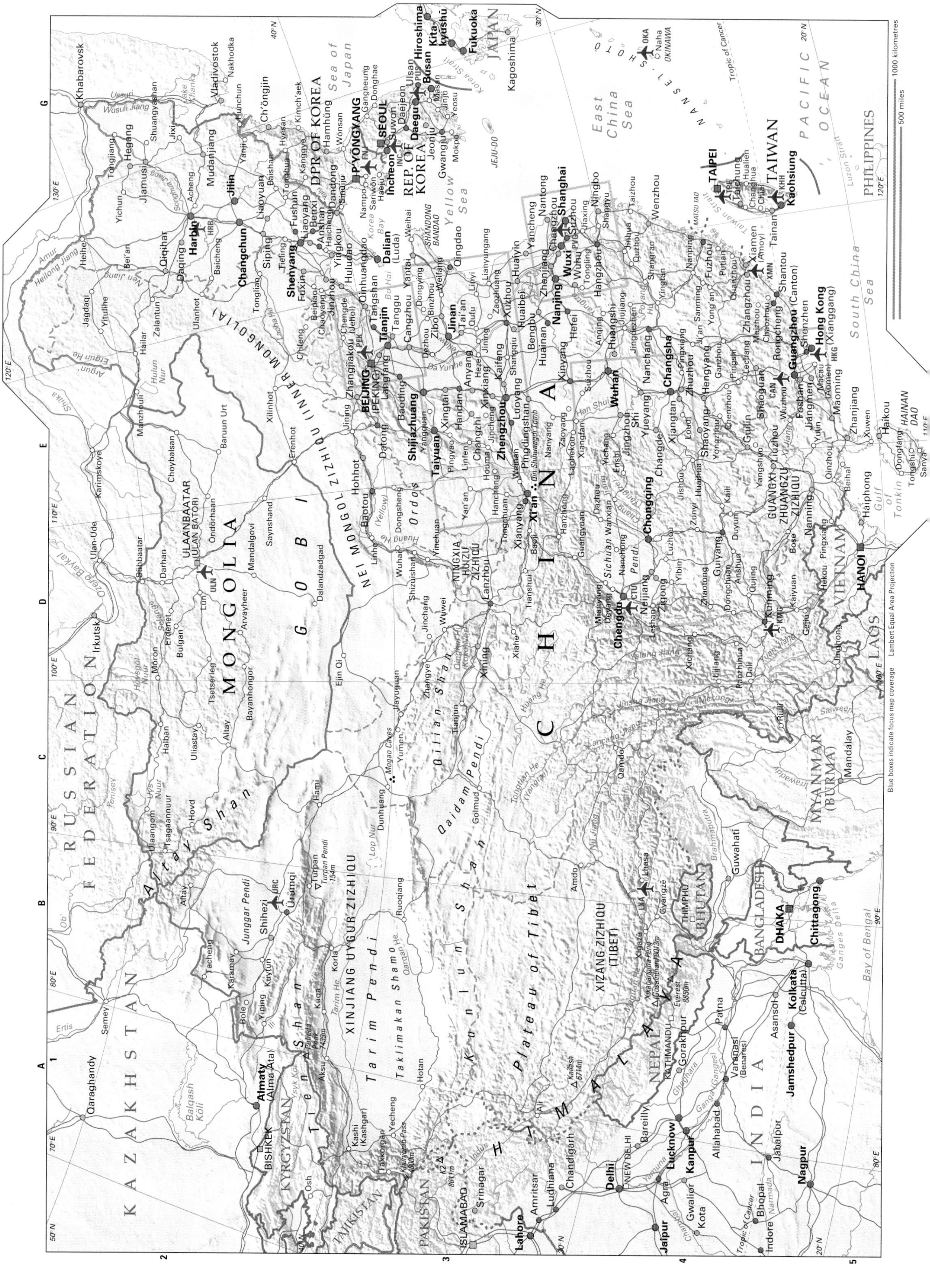

Blue boxes indicate focus map coverage

Lambert Equal Area Projection

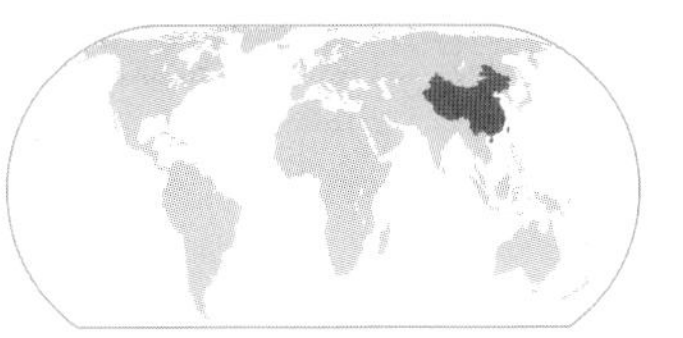

See also... page 138 for more on China

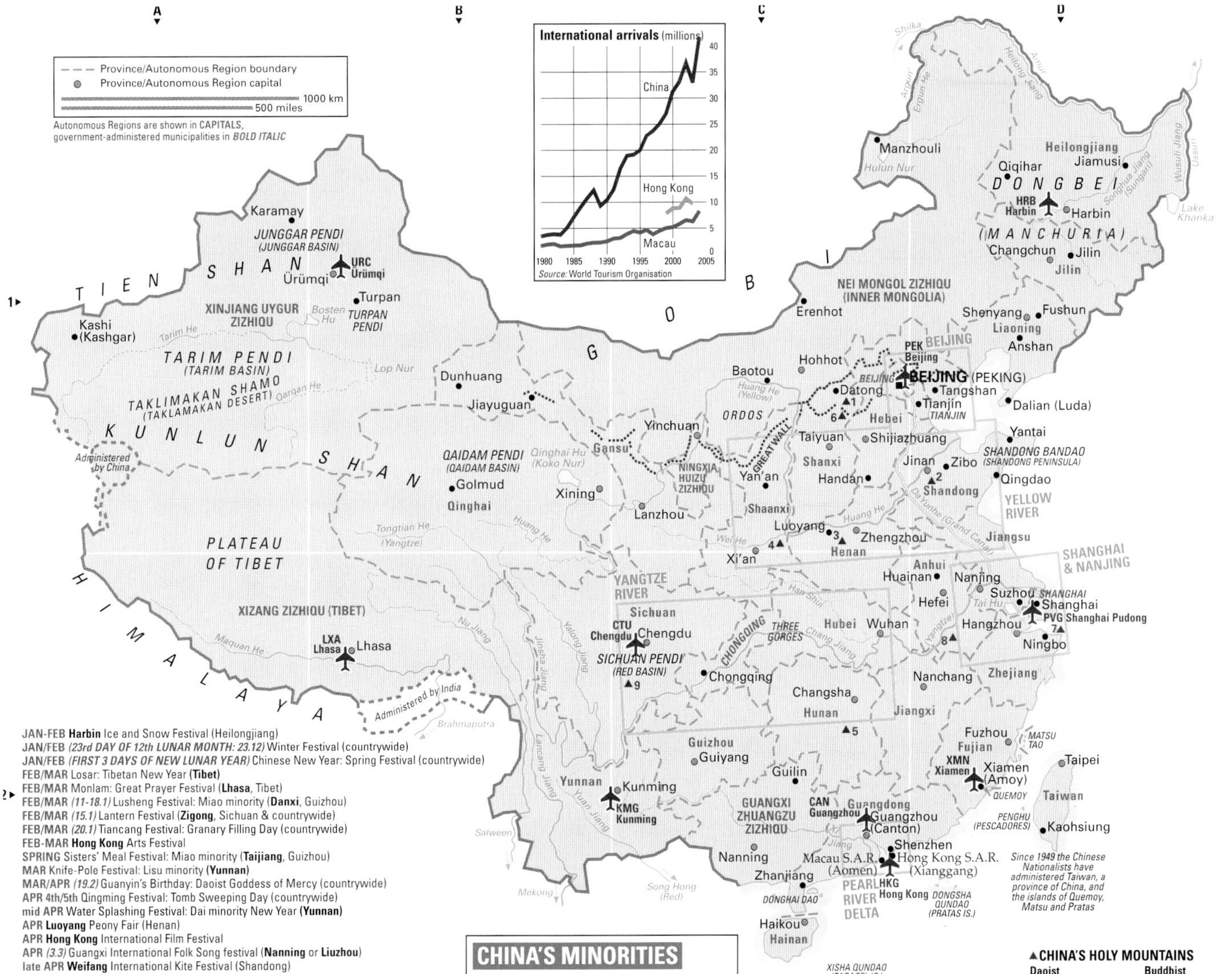
A
B
C
D
1
2
Province/Autonomous Region boundary
Province/Autonomous Region capital
1000 km
500 miles
Autonomous Regions are shown in CAPITALS, government-administered municipalities in BOLD ITALIC
Karamay
JUNGGAR PENDI
(JUNGGAR BASIN)
TIEN SHAN
URC Ürümqi
Ürümqi
Turpan
TURPAN PENDI
XINJIANG UYGUR ZIZHIQU
Bosten Hu
Kashi (Kashgar)
Tarim He
TARIM PENDI (TARIM BASIN)
TAKLIMAKAN SHAMO (TAKLAMAKAN DESERT)
Lop Nur
Qarqan He
KUNLUN SHAN
Administered by China
PLATEAU OF TIBET
HIMALAYA
XIZANG ZIZHIQU (TIBET)
Maquan He
LXA Lhasa
Lhasa
Administered by India
Brahmaputra
Dunhuang
Jiayuguan
GOBI
QAIDAM PENDI (QAIDAM BASIN)
Golmud
Qinghai
Qinghai Hu (Koko Nur)
Xining
Gansu
Lanzhou
Tongtian He (Yangtze)
Huang He
Yinchuan
NINGXIA HUIZU ZIZHIQU
GREAT WALL
ORDOS
Baotou
Hohhot
Erenhot
NEI MONGOL ZIZHIQU (INNER MONGOLIA)
Manzhouli
Hulun Nur
Argun
Ergun He
Shilka
Amur
Heilong Jiang
Heilongjiang
Qiqihar
Jiamusi
DONGBEI (MANCHURIA)
HRB Harbin
Harbin
Songhua Jiang (Sungari)
Wusuli Jiang
Ussuri
Lake Khanka
Changchun
Jilin
Shenyang
Fushun
Liaoning
Anshan
Dalian (Luda)
PEK Beijing
BEIJING (PEKING)
Tangshan
Tianjin
TIANJIN
Datong
Hebei
Taiyuan
Shijiazhuang
Shanxi
Yan'an
Shaanxi
Handan
Jinan
Zibo
Shandong
Yantai
SHANDONG BANDAO (SHANDONG PENINSULA)
Qingdao
YELLOW RIVER
Da Yunhe (Grand Canal)
Luoyang
Zhengzhou
Henan
Wei He
Xi'an
Jiangsu
SHANGHAI & NANJING
Anhui
Huainan
Nanjing
Hefei
Suzhou
SHANGHAI
Shanghai
PVG Shanghai Pudong
Tai Hu
Hangzhou
Ningbo
Zhejiang
YANGTZE RIVER
Sichuan
CTU Chengdu
Chengdu
SICHUAN PENDI (RED BASIN)
CHONGQING
Chongqing
THREE GORGES
Chang Jiang
Han Shui
Hubei
Wuhan
Nanchang
Changsha
Hunan
Jiangxi
Guizhou
Guiyang
Guilin
Fuzhou
Fujian
MATSU TAO
XMN Xiamen
Xiamen (Amoy)
QUEMOY
Taipei
Taiwan
PENGHU (PESCADORES)
Kaohsiung
Yunnan
Kunming
KMG Kunming
Jinsha Jiang
Yalong Jiang
Nu Jiang
Lancang Jiang
Salween
Mekong
Yuan Jiang
Song Hong (Red)
GUANGXI ZHUANGZU ZIZHIQU
CAN Guangzhou
Guangdong
Guangzhou (Canton)
Nanning
Zhanjiang
Macau S.A.R. (Aomen)
Shenzhen
Hong Kong S.A.R. (Xianggang)
HKG Hong Kong
PEARL RIVER DELTA
DONGSHA QUNDAO (PRATAS IS.)
DONGHAI DAO
Haikou
Hainan
Since 1949 the Chinese Nationalists have administered Taiwan, a province of China, and the islands of Quemoy, Matsu and Pratas
XISHA QUNDAO (PARACEL IS.)
ZHONGSHA QUNDAO (MACCLESFIELD BANK)
Administered by China, claimed by Vietnam
SPRATLY IS.
Claimed by China, Malaysia, the Philippines and Vietnam
International arrivals (millions)
40
35
30
25
20
15
10
5
0
China
Hong Kong
Macau
1980
1985
1990
1995
2000
2005
Source: World Tourism Organisation

▲CHINA'S HOLY MOUNTAINS

Daoist	Buddhist
1 *Heng Shan* (Shanxi)	6 *Wutai Shan*
2 *Tai Shan*	7 *Putuo Shan*
3 *Song Shan*	8 *Jiuhua Shan*
4 *Hua Shan*	9 *Emei Shan*
5 *Heng Shan* (Hunan)	

JAN-FEB **Harbin** Ice and Snow Festival (Heilongjiang)
JAN/FEB *(23rd DAY OF 12th LUNAR MONTH: 23.12)* Winter Festival (countrywide)
JAN/FEB *(FIRST 3 DAYS OF NEW LUNAR YEAR)* Chinese New Year: Spring Festival (countrywide)
FEB/MAR Losar: Tibetan New Year (**Tibet**)
FEB/MAR Monlam: Great Prayer Festival (**Lhasa**, Tibet)
FEB/MAR *(11-18.1)* Lusheng Festival: Miao minority (**Danxi**, Guizhou)
FEB/MAR *(15.1)* Lantern Festival (**Zigong**, Sichuan & countrywide)
FEB/MAR *(20.1)* Tiancang Festival: Granary Filling Day (countrywide)
FEB-MAR **Hong Kong** Arts Festival
SPRING Sisters' Meal Festival: Miao minority (**Taijiang**, Guizhou)
MAR Knife-Pole Festival: Lisu minority (**Yunnan**)
MAR/APR *(19.2)* Guanyin's Birthday: Daoist Goddess of Mercy (countrywide)
APR 4th/5th Qingming Festival: Tomb Sweeping Day (countrywide)
mid APR Water Splashing Festival: Dai minority New Year (**Yunnan**)
APR **Luoyang** Peony Fair (Henan)
APR **Hong Kong** International Film Festival
APR *(3.3)* Guangxi International Folk Song festival (**Nanning** or **Liuzhou**)
late APR **Weifang** International Kite Festival (Shandong)
MAY 4th Youth Day (countrywide)
MAY/JUN *(23.3)* Mazu's Birthday: Sea Goddess [Tianhou in Guangdong, Tin Hau in HK] **(southern coastal regions)**
JUN 1st Children's Day (countrywide)
JUN/JUL *(5.5)* Dragon Boat Festival (**Hong Kong** & **Yueyang**, Hunan)
mid JUL **Jiayuguan Pass** International Glider Festival (Gansu)
late JUL **Harbin** Music Festival (Heilongjiang)
late JUL Torch Festival: Yi minority (**Liangshan**, Sichuan)
JUL/AUG Nadam Fair: traditional Mongol games (**Inner Mongolia**)
AUG Shotun / Yogurt Banquet Festival (**Lhasa**, Tibet)
mid AUG **Qingdo** International Beer Festival (Shandong)
late AUG Xinjiang Grape Festival: Uygur minority (**Turpan**)
AUG-SEP *(FIRST 15 DAYS OF 7th LUNAR MONTH)* Ghost Month (countrywide)
SEP **Xi'an** Ancient Culture Festival (Shaanxi)
SEP **Zhengzhou** International Shaolin Martial Arts Festival (Henan)
late SEP **Shanghai** Huangpu Tourist Festival
late SEP **Suzhou** Silk Tourist Festival (Jiangsu)
SEP-OCT **Qufu** International Confucius Culture Festival (Shandong)
SEP/OCT *(15.8)* Mid-Autumn (Moon) Festival (countrywide)
SEP/OCT *(18.8)* Qiantang River Tide-Observing Festival (**Yanguan**, nr Hangzhou, Zhejiang)
SEP/OCT *(9.9)* Double Ninth Festival (countrywide)
OCT 1st National Day (countrywide)
mid OCT **Jingdezhen** International Pottery and Porcelain Festival (Jiangxi)
DEC 22nd/23rd Winter Solstice Festival (countrywide)

CHINA'S MINORITIES

The Chinese population consists of 56 officially recognised nationalities. 92% of the total are Han Chinese. The largest of the 55 ethnic minorities are:*

ZHUANG *Guangxi, also Guangdong, Guizhou, Yunnan*

MANCHU *scattered throughout NE China*

HUI *Ningxia & throughout C & SW China*

MIAO *Guizhou, Yunnan & throughout C & SW China*

UYGUR *Xinjiang*

YI *Yunnan, also Guangxi, Guizhou, Sichuan*

TUJIA *Hunan, Hubei*

MONGOLIAN *mainly N & NW China, also Yunnan (Jiluhu Lake)*

TIBETAN *Tibet & W China*

*Population of over four million in 1990

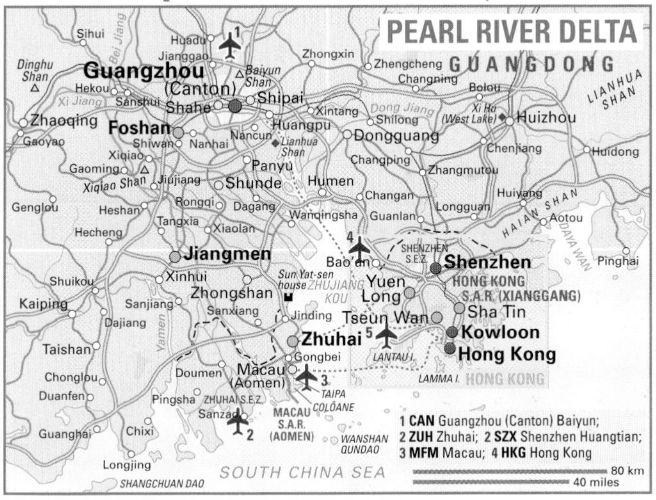
PEARL RIVER DELTA
E
F
3
4
GUANGDONG
Guangzhou (Canton)
Huadu
Sihui
Dinghu Shan
Jianggao
Baiyun Shan
Zhongxin
Zhengcheng
Changning
Bolou
LIANHUA SHAN
Hekou
Xi Jiang
Sanshui
Shahe
Shipai
Xintang
Dong Jiang
Xi Hu (West Lake)
Huizhou
Zhaoqing
Foshan
Huangpu
Shilong
Dongguang
Gaoyao
Shiwan
Nanhai
Nancun
Lianhua Shan
Chenjiang
Huidong
Xiqiao
Gaoming
Panyu
Changping
Zhangmutou
Xiqiao Shan
Jiujiang
Shunde
Humen
Genglou
Heshan
Rongqi
Dagang
Changan
Huiyang
Wanqingsha
Guanlan
Longgang
Aotou
HAIAN SHAN
DAYA WAN
Hecheng
Tangxia
Xiaolan
Jiangmen
Bao'an
SHENZHEN S.E.Z.
Shenzhen
Pinghai
Shuikou
Xinhui
Sun Yat-sen house
ZHUJIANG KOU
Yuen Long
HONG KONG S.A.R. (XIANGGANG)
Kaiping
Sanjiang
Zhongshan
Sanxiang
Tseun Wan
Sha Tin
Dajiang
Jinding
Kowloon
Taishan
Zhuhai
LANTAU I.
Hong Kong
Gongbei
LAMMA I.
HONG KONG
Chonglou
Doumen
Macau (Aomen)
Duanfen
Pingsha
ZHUHAI S.E.Z.
TAIPA
COLOANE
Sanzao
MACAU S.A.R. (AOMEN)
Guanghai
Chixi
WANSHAN QUNDAO
Longjing
SHANGCHUAN DAO
SOUTH CHINA SEA
1 CAN Guangzhou (Canton) Baiyun; 2 ZUH Zhuhai; 2 SZX Shenzhen Huangtian; 3 MFM Macau; 4 HKG Hong Kong
80 km
40 miles

HONG KONG
G
H
5
6
Longhua
SHENZHEN SPECIAL ECONOMIC ZONE
Henggang
Xili Lake Resort
Wutong Shan 943m
Silver Lake Resort
Yantian
Xiaomeisha Beach Resort
Dapeng
Bao'an
Honey Lake Resort
Shenzhen
Shatoujiao
China Folk Culture Villages
Splendid China
CROOKED I.
MIRS BAY
PING CHAU
Nantou
Window on the World
Shau Tau Kok
CRESCENT I.
DEEP BAY
Shek Wu Hui
PAT SIN LENG
PLOVER COVE
DOUBLE I.
Seaworld
Shekou
Mai Po Marsh
San Tin
Luen Wo Hui
PORT I.
Mawan
Fairview Park
LAM TSUEN
Plover Cove Reservoir
TAP MUN CHAU (GRASS I.)
Chiwan
Tin Shui Wai
NEW TERRITORIES
Shek Kong
Tai Po
Shagang
Yuen Long
NEILINGDING I.
Pat Heung
TAI MO SHAN
HONG KONG SPECIAL ADMINISTRATIVE REGION
Tsing Shan (Castle Peak) 583m
Tai Mo Shan 957m
10,000 Buddhas Mon.
SAI KUNG
LUNG KWU CHAU
Tuen Mun
Tsuen Wan
Sha Tin
KIU TSUI CHAU (SHARP I.)
High Island Reservoir
MA WAN
TSING YI
LION ROCK
Sai Kung
KAU SAI CHAU
Port Shelter
JIN I.
CHEK LAP KOK
HK Disneyland
Kowloon
Tseung Kwan O
Tung Chung
PENG CHAU
Victoria Hbr
Quarry Bay
CLEAR WATER BAY
Clear Water Bay
Po Lin Monastery
LANTAU I.
Mui Wo
Victoria Peak 552m
Hong Kong
Tai O
HEI LING CHAU
POK FU LAM
Aberdeen
AP LEI CHAU
TAI TAM
Repulse Bay
TUNG LING CHAU
Fung Wong Shan (Lantau Peak) 934m
CHEUNG CHAU
Ocean Park
ABERDEEN
HONG KONG ISLAND
Shek O
Stanley
LAMMA I.
SOKO IS.
SHEK KWU CHAU
BEAUFORT I.
PO TOI
GUISHAN I.
1 Causeway Bay
2 Central
3 Kowloon City
4 Mong Kok
5 Sheung Wan
6 Tsim Sha Tsui
7 Wan Chai
8 Yau Ma Tei
1 SZX Shenzhen Huangtian; 2 HKG Hong Kong
20 km
10 miles
Country Parks are shown in GREEN TYPE
1000 metres
500 metres
Sea level

See also... Contents (2-7) – this country features in many thematic and regional maps throughout the *World Travel Atlas*.

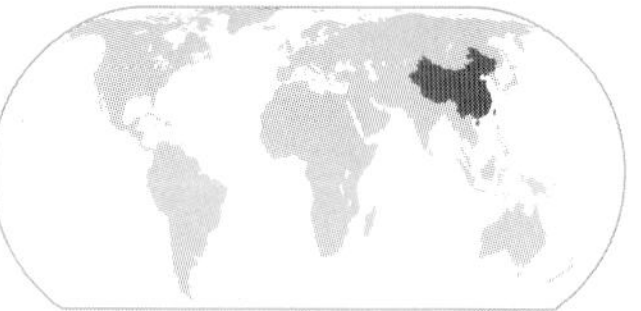

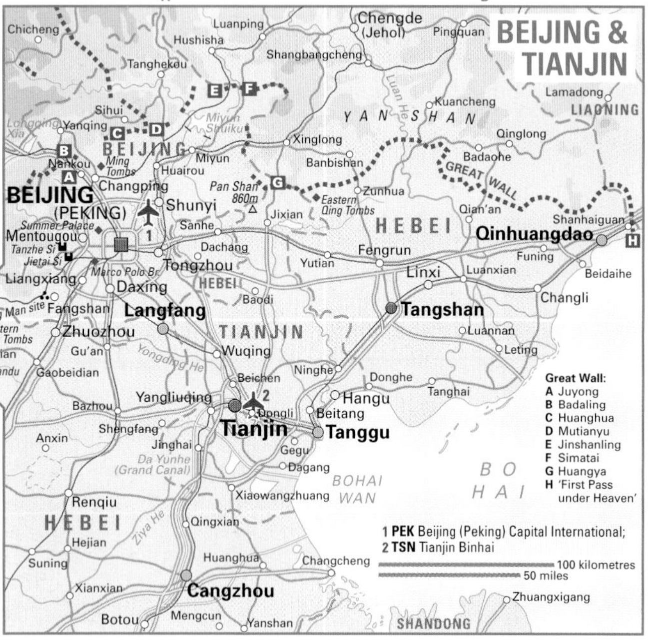

BEIJING & TIANJIN

Great Wall:
A Juyong
B Badaling
C Huanghua
D Mutianyu
E Jinshanling
F Simatai
G Huangya
H 'First Pass under Heaven'

1 PEK Beijing (Peking) Capital International;
2 TSN Tianjin Binhai

100 kilometres
50 miles

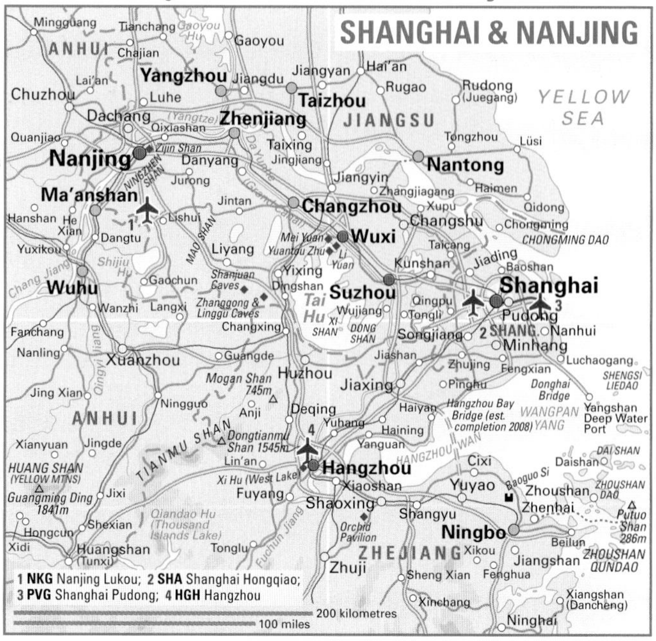

SHANGHAI & NANJING

1 NKG Nanjing Lukou; 2 SHA Shanghai Hongqiao;
3 PVG Shanghai Pudong; 4 HGH Hangzhou

200 kilometres
100 miles

YELLOW RIVER
1 XIY Xi'an-Xianyang; 2 TAO Qingdao
200 km
100 miles

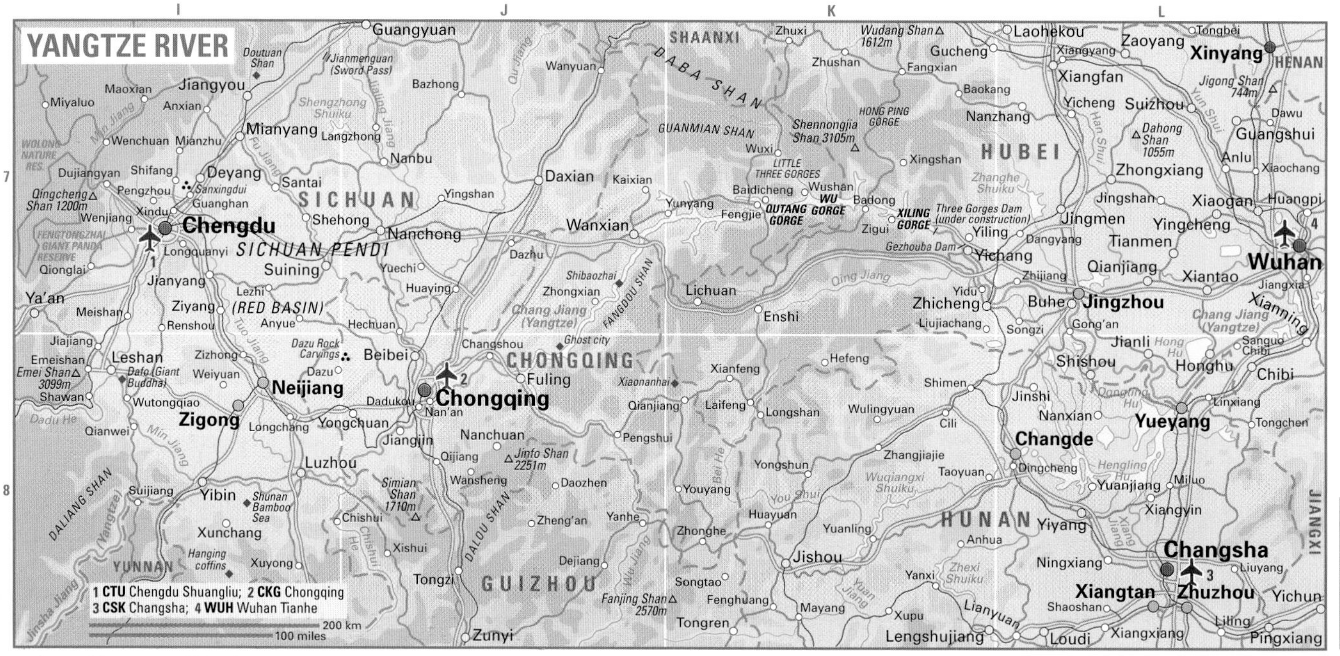
YANGTZE RIVER
1 CTU Chengdu Shuangliu; 2 CKG Chongqing
3 CSK Changsha; 4 WUH Wuhan Tianhe
200 km
100 miles
1000 metres
500 metres
Sea level

See also... Top US Theme Parks (171)

The listings above refer to a selection of related themes. For more information, see the Contents (2-7).

ŌSAKA–KYŌTO–KŌBE
1 ITM Ōsaka Itami; 2 KIX Ōsaka Kansai
40 km
20 miles
TOP JAPANESE THEME PARKS IN 2005
Number of visitors (world ranking in brackets)
Tokyo Disneyland Chiba: 13.0 million (3rd)
Tokyo Disney Sea Chiba: 12.0m (4th)
Universal Studios Japan (USJ) Ōsaka: 8.0m (9th)
Yokohama-Hakkeijima Sea Paradise Kanagawa: 5.3m (17th)
Nagashima Spa Land Mie: 3.8m (25th)
Suzuka Circuit Mie: 2.6m (=40th)
Source: Amusement Business & Economics Research Assocs.
JAPAN
RUSSIAN FEDERATION
Sea of Okhotsk
KURIL ISLANDS (administered by Russ. Fed.)
Sea of Japan
REP. OF KOREA
PACIFIC OCEAN
HOKKAIDŌ
HONSHŪ
SHIKOKU
KYŪSHŪ
International arrivals (millions)
1980 1985 1990 1995 2000 2005
Source: World Tourism Organisation
JAN 7th Hadaka Mairi: naked festival (Fukushima)
JAN Wakakusa Yamayaki: bonfire & fireworks (Nara)
FEB Sapporo Yuki Matsuri: snow festival
FEB Kamakura: 'igloo' festival (Yokote)
MAR 12th Omizutori: well & torch festival (Nara)
MAR-APR Ueno Cherry Blossom Festival (Tokyo)
APR 14-15th Takayama Matsuri: parade of floats
MAY 2nd-4th Hakata Dontaku: costume parade (Fukuoka)
MAY 15th Aoi Matsuri: costume parade (Kyoto)
MAY 17-18th Toshogu Haru-no-Taisai: costume parade (Nikko)
MAY Kanda* & Sanja Matsuri: shrine parades (Tokyo)
JUN Sanno* Matsuri: parade of shrines (Tokyo)
JUN 15th Chagu-Chagu Umakko: horse fest. (Morioka)
JUL Gion Matsuri: parade of floats (Kyoto)
JUL Gion Yamagasa: parade of floats (Fukuoka)
late JUL Sumidagawa Hanabi Taikai: fireworks festival (Tokyo)
JUL 24-25th Tenjin Matsuri: parade of boats (Osaka)
AUG 1st-7th Hirosaki Neputa: parade of floats
AUG 2nd-7th Aomori Nebuta: parade of floats
AUG 5-7th Kanto: lantern festival (Akita)
AUG 6-8th Hanagasa Odori: dancing (Yamagata)
AUG 6-8th Tanabata: star festival (Sendai)
AUG 12-15th Awa Odori: dancing (Tokushima)
AUG 15th Daimonji Okuribi: fire festival (Kyoto)
SEP 14-16th Yabusamé: horseback archery (Kamakura)
OCT 7-9th Nagasaki Kunchi: parade & dancing
OCT 9-10th Takayama Matsuri: parade of floats
OCT 22nd Jidai Matsuri: costume parade (Kyoto)
OCT 22nd Kurama-no-Himatsuri: fire festival (Kyoto)
DEC 2nd-3rd Chichibu Yomatsuri: parade of floats
DEC 31st Namahage: demon festival (Oga)
* Alternate years (i.e. Kanda one year, then Sanno next)
Focus maps:
1000 metres
500 metres
Sea level
TŌKYŌ
1 NRT Tōkyō Narita; 2 HND Tōkyō Haneda
60 kilometres
30 miles
SHINKANSEN
The 'Bullet Train' network
Japan Railpass is accepted on all routes except ultra high-speed 'Nozomi' service between Tōkyō and Hakata
Diagrammatic only: not to scale

See also... pages 141-142 for more on South-East Asia

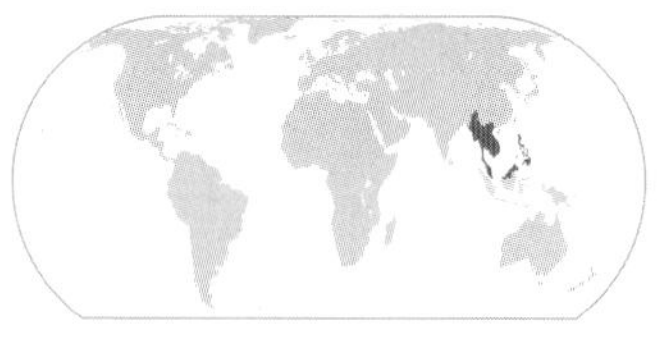

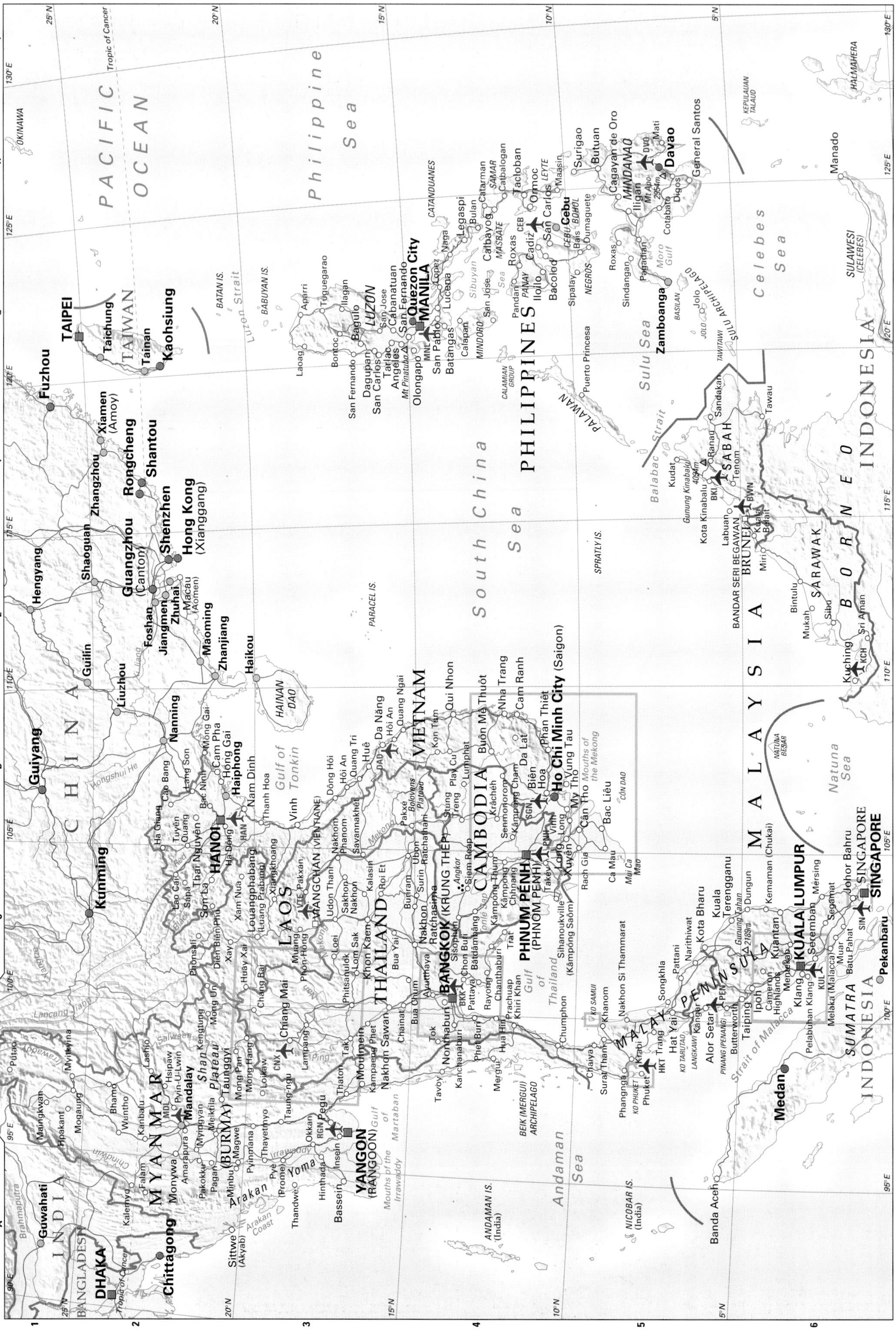

Lambert Equal Area Projection

Blue boxes indicate focus map coverage

600 kilometres
300 miles

▶ *See also...* Contents (2-7) – These countries feature in many thematic and regional maps throughout the *World Travel Atlas*.

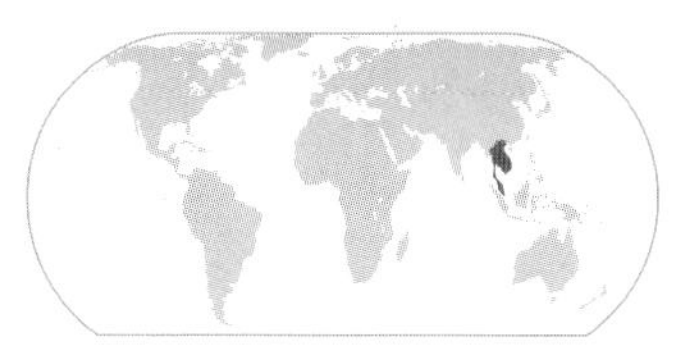

A
1▸
2▸
3▸
4▸
GOLDEN TRIANGLE
TONGKING
Phôngsali
Diên Biên Phu
HANOI
HAN Hanoi
HALONG BAY
Haiphong
Nam Dinh
Thanh Hoa
Louangphabang (Luang Prabang)
Mekong
LAOS
Vinh
VIANGCHAN (VIENTIANE)
VTE Viangchan
Dông Hôi
Savannakhét
Huê
Da Năng
Hôi An
THAILAND
SEE NEXT PAGE
Pakxé (Pakse)
BOLOVENS PLATEAU
VIETNAM
Quang Ngai
Champasak
BANGKOK (KRUNG THEP)
Chao Phraya
REP Siem Reap
Angkor
Stung Treng
KONTUM PLATEAU
Qui Nhon
Bătdâmbâng
Tonle Sap
CAMBODIA
Buôn Mê Thuôt
Nha Trang
PHNUM PÉNH (PHNOM PENH)
PNH Phnom Penh
Kâmpóng Cham
Da Lat
SGN Ho Chi Minh City
Ho Chi Minh City (Saigon)
Sihanoukville (Kâmpóng Saôm)
PHU QUÔC
Vung Tau
COCHIN CHINA
Cân Tho
Mouths of the Mekong
CON DAO
HO CHI MINH CITY & PHNOM PENH
Mui Ca Mau
MALAY PENINSULA
LANGKAWI
Kota Bharu
PERHENTIAN
REDANG
George Town
PENANG
PEN Pinang
Kuala Terengganu
KUALA LUMPUR
Ipoh
TAMAN NEGARA NATIONAL PARK
Kemaman (Chukai)
MALAYSIA
Kuantan
KUALA LUMPUR
KUL Kuala Lumpur
TIOMAN
Melaka (Malacca)
Muar
JHB Johor Bahru
Johor Bahru
Desaru
SINGAPORE
SIN Singapore
300 km
150 miles
International arrivals (millions)
16
14
12
10
8
6
4
2
0
1980
1985
1990
1995
2000
2005
Malaysia
Singapore
Vietnam
Cambodia
Laos
Source: World Tourism Organisation

HO CHI MINH CITY & PHNOM PENH
B
C
5
6
Krâchéh
Senmonorom
Buôn Mê Thuôt
Chu Yang Sin 2405m
Ninh Hoa
HON LON
Kâmpóng Chhnăng
Kâmpóng Cham
Mekong
CAMBODIA
Snuŏl
DA LAT PLATEAU
Nha Trang
Da Lat
Prenn Falls
Ngoan Muc Pass
HON TRE
Cam Ranh
CAM RANH BAY
Udong
PHNUM PÉNH (PHNOM PENH)
Lôc Ninh
Xom An Lôc
Dong Nai
Duc Trong
Nui Ba Den (Black Lady Mtn) 986m
Chon Thanh
NAM CAT TIEN NAT. PARK
Bao Lôc
Phan Rang
Tonle Bati
Tây Ninh
VIETNAM
Ca Na
Phnom Chisor
Cu Chi Tunnels
Biên Hoa
Xuân Lôc
Hoa Da
Takév
Thu Dâu Môt
Mui Ne
Phan Thiêt
Kâmpôt
Chau Dôc
Ho Chi Minh City (Saigon)
Nui Sam
Long Xuyên
PLAIN OF REEDS
Tân An
Thuy Duong
Long Hai
CU LAO HON
Ha Tiên
My Tho
Vung Tau
Vinh Long
Ben Tre
Hon Chong
Rach Gia
COCHIN CHINA
Cân Tho
Mouths of the Mekong
To Phu Quoc
Tra Vinh
Soc Trăng
Bac Liêu
SOUTH CHINA SEA
Ca Mau (Quan Long)
CÔN DAO
Mui Ca Mau
HON KHOAI
1 PNH Phnum Pénh (Phnom Penh) Pochentong;
2 SGN Ho Chi Minh City (Saigon) Tan Son Nhat
200 kilometres
100 miles

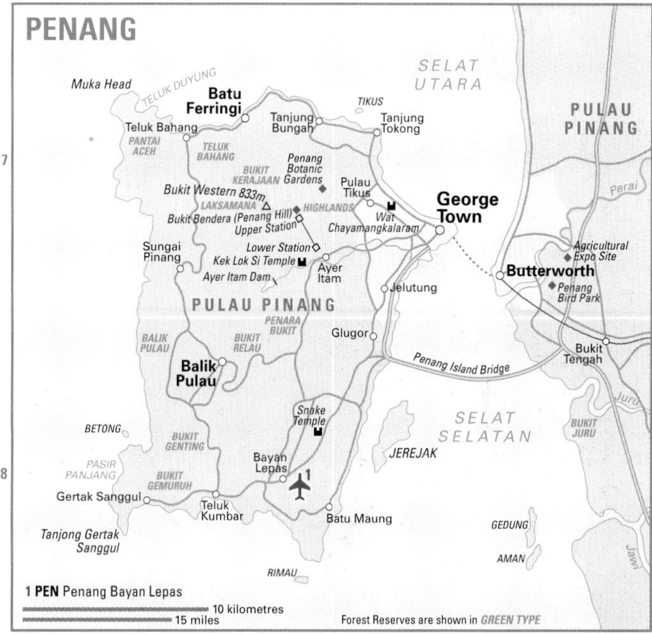
PENANG
D
E
7
8
Muka Head
TELUK DUYUNG
Batu Ferringi
TIKUS
SELAT UTARA
Tanjung Bungah
Tanjung Tokong
PULAU PINANG
Teluk Bahang
PANTAI ACEH
TELUK BAHANG
BUKIT KERAJAAN
Penang Botanic Gardens
Pulau Tikus
Bukit Western 833m
LAKSAMANA
HIGHLANDS
Wat Chayamangkalaram
George Town
Perai
Bukit Bendera (Penang Hill)
Upper Station
Sungai Pinang
Lower Station
Kek Lok Si Temple
Ayer Itam
Ayer Itam Dam
Agricultural Expo Site
Butterworth
Jelutung
Penang Bird Park
PULAU PINANG
PENARA BUKIT
BALIK PULAU
BUKIT RELAU
Glugor
Bukit Tengah
Balik Pulau
Penang Island Bridge
Juru
Snake Temple
SELAT SELATAN
BETONG
BUKIT GENTING
BUKIT JURU
JEREJAK
PASIR PANJANG
BUKIT GEMURUH
Bayan Lepas
Gertak Sanggul
Teluk Kumbar
Batu Maung
Tanjong Gertak Sanggul
GEDUNG
AMAN
RIMAU
Jawi
1 PEN Penang Bayan Lepas
10 kilometres
15 miles
Forest Reserves are shown in GREEN TYPE

KUALA LUMPUR
F
G
9
10
Ipoh
Kellie's Castle
Gunung Batu Berinchang 2031m
Beruas
Batu Gajah
Cameron Highlands
Cegar Perah
Bota Kanan
Tanah Rata
PERAK
Kampar
Padang Tengku
Tembeling
PANGKOR
Lumut
Gunung Batu Putih 2130m
Tapah
Tapah Road
BANJARAN TITIWANGSA
Kuala Lipis
Jelai
KUALA PERAK
Perak
Bidor
Kuala Tembeling
Benta
Seberang
Bagan Datuk
Teluk Intan (Teluk Anson)
Jerantut
PAHANG
Bernam
Bukit Fraser
Raub
Benom 2107m
Pahang
Sabak
Tanjung Malim
Sungai Besar
Bentung
Kuala Kubu Baharu
Sekinchan
Genting Highlands
Mentekab
Temerloh
SELANGOR
Templer Park
Rawang
Orang Asli Centre
Kuala Selangor
Selayang Baru
Batu Caves
Jinjang
STRAIT OF MALACCA
Petaling Jaya
KUALA LUMPUR
Shah Alam
Pelabuhan Klang (Port Kelang)
KLANG
Klang
Seri Kembangan
PINTU GEDONG
LUMUT
Kajang
Kuala Klawang
Ayer Hitam
Teluk Datok
NEGERI SEMBILAN
Bahau
Morib
Seremban
Kuala Pilah
Sepang
Rembau
Gemas
1 KUL Kuala Lumpur KLIA
Port Dickson
Tampin
50 kilometres
25 miles

SINGAPORE
H
I
11
12
Johor Bahru
Masai
MALAYSIA
JOHOR STRAIT
Sungei Buloh Wetland Reserve
Woodlands
Yishun
Seletar Reservoirs
Mandai Orchid Gardens
Singapore Zoological Gardens
UBIN
Punggol
Bukit Panjang
Pierce Reservoirs
Ang Mo Kio
Seletar
Pasir Ris
Hougang
Changi
Changi Prison Museum & Chapel
Serangoon
Bukit Batok
Bukit Timah Nature Reserve
Crocodile farm
Paya Lebar
Tampines
Jurong
Singapore Science Centre
Chinese & Japanese Gardens
Tang Dynasty Village
Toa Payoh
Tuas
Bedok
Jurong Bird Park & Crocodile Paradise
Katong
Tanglin
National Stadium
East Coast Park
Ming Village
Queenstown
Raffles
Singapore Crocodilarium
JURONG ISLAND
Haw Par Villa
Tiger Balm Gardens
SINGAPORE CITY
Station
Marina Bay
Cable car
Fort Siloso
BRANI
Underwater World
Images of Singapore
STRAITS OF SINGAPORE
BUSING
BUKUM
SENTOSA
HANTU
SEMAKAU
SAKIJANG
SUDONG
SEBAROK
PAWAI
SENANG
Raffles Lighthouse
INDONESIA
1 SIN Singapore Changi
20 kilometres
10 miles
1000 metres
500 metres
Sea level

See also... Contents (2-7) – this country features in many thematic and regional maps throughout the *World Travel Atlas*.

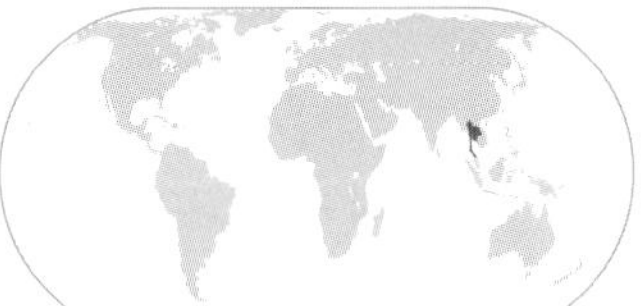

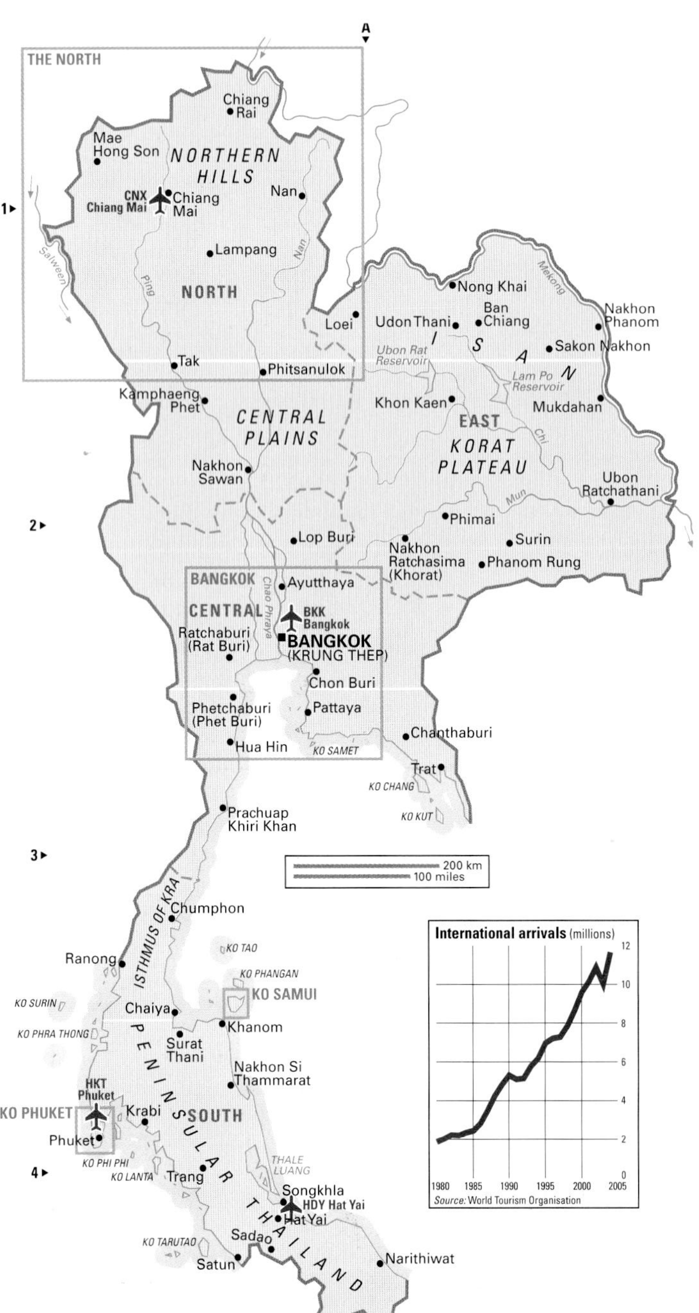
THE NORTH
Chiang Rai
Mae Hong Son
NORTHERN HILLS
CNX Chiang Mai
Chiang Mai
Nan
Lampang
NORTH
Loei
Tak
Phitsanulok
Udon Thani
Nong Khai
Ban Chiang
Nakhon Phanom
Sakon Nakhon
ISAN
Udon Rat Reservoir
Lam Po Reservoir
Khon Kaen
Mukdahan
Kamphaeng Phet
CENTRAL PLAINS
EAST
KORAT PLATEAU
Nakhon Sawan
Ubon Ratchathani
Phimai
Lop Buri
Nakhon Ratchasima (Khorat)
Surin
Phanom Rung
BANGKOK
Ayutthaya
CENTRAL
BKK Bangkok
Ratchaburi (Rat Buri)
BANGKOK (KRUNG THEP)
Chon Buri
Phetchaburi (Phet Buri)
Pattaya
Hua Hin
KO SAMET
Chanthaburi
Trat
KO CHANG
KO KUT
Prachuap Khiri Khan
200 km
100 miles
ISTHMUS OF KRA
Chumphon
Ranong
KO TAO
KO PHANGAN
KO SAMUI
KO SURIN
Chaiya
Khanom
KO PHRA THONG
Surat Thani
PENINSULAR
Nakhon Si Thammarat
SOUTH
HKT Phuket
KO PHUKET
Krabi
Phuket
KO PHI PHI
KO LANTA
Trang
THALE LUANG
Songkhla
HDY Hat Yai
Hat Yai
KO TARUTAO
Sadao
Satun
THAILAND
Narathiwat
International arrivals (millions)
1980 1985 1990 1995 2000 2005
Source: World Tourism Organisation

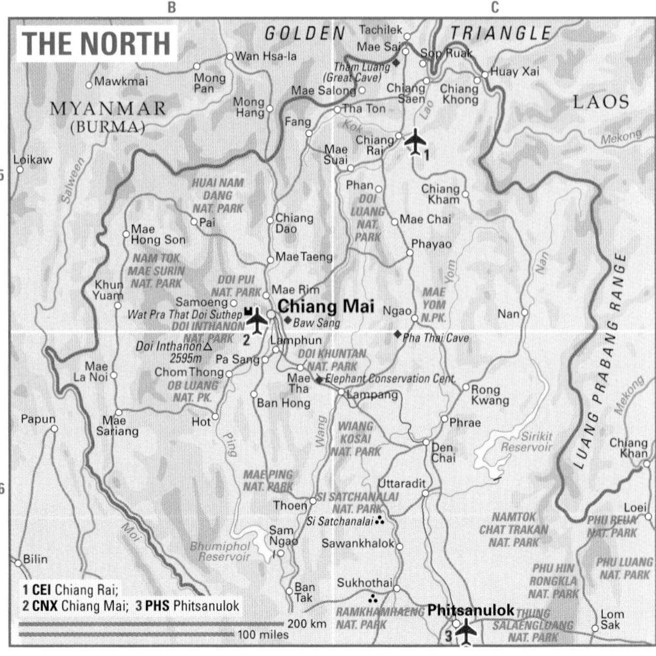
THE NORTH
GOLDEN TRIANGLE
Tachilek
Mae Sai
Sop Ruak
Wan Hsa-la
Tham Luang (Great Cave)
Huay Xai
Mawkmai
Mong Pan
Mae Salong
Chiang Saen
Chiang Khong
MYANMAR (BURMA)
Tha Ton
LAOS
Mong Hang
Fang
Chiang Rai
Loikaw
Mae Suai
HUAI NAM DANG NAT. PARK
Phan
DOI LUANG NAT. PARK
Chiang Kham
Pai
Chiang Dao
Mae Chai
Mae Hong Son
Phayao
NAM TOK MAE SURIN NAT. PARK
Mae Taeng
DOI PUI NAT. PARK
Mae Rim
Khun Yuam
Chiang Mai
Baw Sang
Ngao
MAE YOM N.PK.
Nan
Samoeng
Wat Pra That Doi Suthep
DOI INTHANON NAT. PARK
Lamphun
Pha Thai Cave
Doi Inthanon 2595m
Pa Sang
DOI KHUNTAN NAT. PARK
LUANG PRABANG RANGE
Mae La Noi
Chom Thong
Mae Tha
Elephant Conservation Cent.
OB LUANG NAT. PK.
Lampang
Rong Kwang
Ban Hong
Papun
Mae Sariang
Hot
Phrae
WIANG KOSAI NAT. PARK
Sirikit Reservoir
Den Chai
Chiang Khan
MAE PING NAT. PARK
Uttaradit
SI SATCHANALAI NAT. PARK
Thoen
Si Satchanalai
Loei
Sam Ngao
NAMTOK CHAT TRAKAN NAT. PARK
PHU REUA NAT. PARK
Sawankhalok
Bhumiphol Reservoir
PHU HIN RONGKLA NAT. PARK
PHU LUANG NAT. PARK
Bilin
Ban Tak
Sukhothai
RAMKHAMHAENG NAT. PARK
Phitsanulok
THUNG SALAENGLUANG NAT. PARK
Lom Sak
1 CEI Chiang Rai;
2 CNX Chiang Mai; 3 PHS Phitsanulok
200 km
100 miles

BANGKOK
Phra Phutthabat
Suphan Buri
Phachi
Sara Buri
Khao Khiaw 1351m
Ayutthaya
KHAO YAI NATIONAL PARK
Wat Phai Rong Wua
Aisawan Tippaya Asna
Bang Pa-In
Nakhon Nayok
River Kwai Bridge
Wang Takhrai Gardens
Prachantakham
Kanchanaburi
Prachin Buri
Ban Kao
Phra Pathom Chedi
Safari World
Kabin Buri
Nonthaburi
Khok Pip
Ban Pong
Nakhon Pathom
BANGKOK (KRUNG THEP)
Thon Buri
Rose garden
Floating market
Phra Buddha Sothorp
Chachoengsao
Ratchaburi (Rat Buri)
Damnoan Saduak floating market
Samut Prakan
Muang Boran
Samut Sakhon
Phanat Nikhom
Samut Songkhram
Chon Buri
Pak Tho
Bang Saen
Khao Khiew Zoo
Luang Po Ban Laem
Ban Laem
Ocean World Water Park
KO SICHANG
Si Racha
Wat Phra Sriratana Mahathat
BIGHT OF BANGKOK
Wang Phetburi Mountain
Phetchaburi (Phet Buri)
Laem Chabang
Bang Lamung
Hat Chao Samran
Pattaya
KHAO CHAMAO-KHAO WONG NAT. PARK
KO PHAI
KO LARN
Wang Chan
Ban Tah
KAENG KRACHAN NATIONAL PARK
Jomtien
Klaeng
Cha-Am
KO KHRAM
Nong Nooch Garden
Rayong
Soontornpoo Monument
Sattahip
Ban Klaeng
Hua Hin
KO SAMAE SAN
Chong Samae San
Ban Phe
KO CHUANG
KO SAMET
1 BKK Bangkok Don Muang;
2 Bangkok Suvarnabhumi (open in 2006)
100 kilometres
50 miles

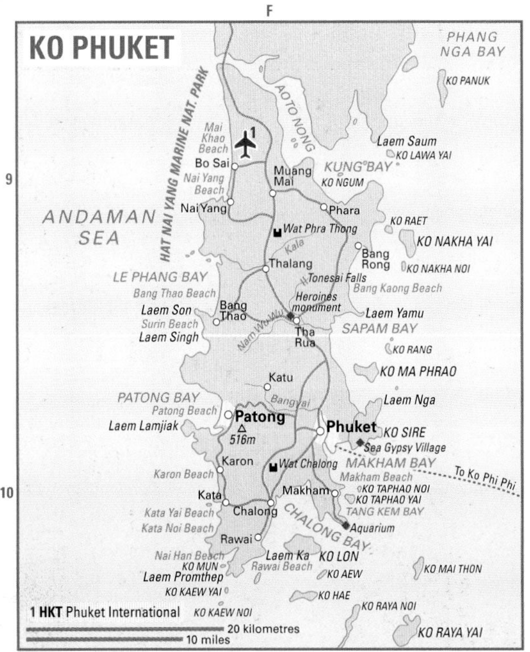
KO PHUKET
PHANG NGA BAY
KO PANUK
HAT NAI YANG MARINE NAT. PARK
Mai Khao Beach
Laem Saum
KO LAWA YAI
Bo Sai
Muang Mai
KUNG BAY
KO NGUM
Nai Yang Beach
ANDAMAN SEA
Nai Yang
Phara
KO RAET
Wat Phra Thong
KO NAKHA YAI
Bang Rong
KO NAKHA NOI
Thalang
LE PHANG BAY
Tonesai Falls
Bang Thao Beach
Bang Kaong Beach
Laem Son
Bang Thao
Heroines monument
Laem Yamu
Surin Beach
SAPAM BAY
Laem Singh
Tha Rua
KO RANG
KO MA PHRAO
Katu
PATONG BAY
Laem Nga
Patong Beach
Patong
Laem Lamjiak
516m
Phuket
KO SIRE
Sea Gypsy Village
Karon
Wat Chalong
MAKHAM BAY
To Ko Phi Phi
Karon Beach
Makham Beach
Kata
Makham
KO TAPHAO NOI
KO TAPHAO YAI
Kata Yai Beach
Chalong
TANG KEM BAY
Kata Noi Beach
CHALONG BAY
Aquarium
Rawai
Nai Han Beach
Laem Ka
KO LON
KO MUN
Rawai Beach
KO AEW
KO MAI THON
Laem Promthep
KO KAEW YAI
KO HAE
KO RAYA NOI
1 HKT Phuket International
KO KAEW NOI
KO RAYA YAI
20 kilometres
10 miles

EASTERN & ORIENTAL EXPRESS

	Distance from Bangkok Kilometres	Miles
Chiang Mai	751	467
Lampang	642	390
Phitsanulok	389	242
Ayutthaya	71	44
Bangkok	0	0
Kanchanaburi	(138)	(86)
Hua Hin	229	142
Hat Yai	945	587
Butterworth	1161	721
Kuala Lumpur	1552	964
Singapore	1946	1209

The Eastern & Oriental Express is a luxury train service operating between Chiang Mai, Bangkok and Singapore. Various itineraries are offered, with excursions to Ayutthaya, River Kwai and Penang scheduled.

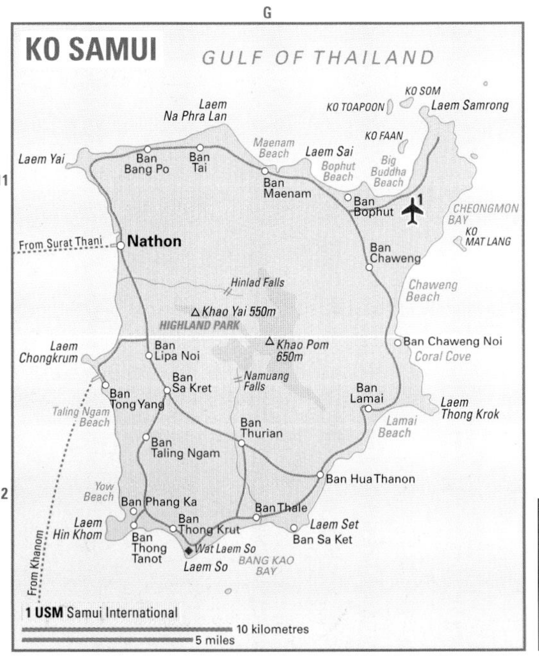
KO SAMUI
GULF OF THAILAND
KO SOM
KO TOAPOON
Laem Samrong
Laem Na Phra Lan
KO FAAN
Laem Yai
Ban Bang Po
Ban Tai
Maenam Beach
Laem Sai
Bophut Beach
Big Buddha Beach
Ban Maenam
Ban Bophut
CHEONGMON BAY
KO MAT LANG
From Surat Thani
Nathon
Ban Chaweng
Chaweng Beach
Hinlad Falls
Khao Yai 550m
HIGHLAND PARK
Laem Chongkrum
Ban Lipa Noi
Khao Pom 650m
Ban Chaweng Noi
Coral Cove
Ban Sa Kret
Namuang Falls
Ban Tong Yang
Ban Lamai
Laem Thong Krok
Taling Ngam Beach
Ban Thurian
Lamai Beach
Ban Taling Ngam
Ban Hua Thanon
Yow Beach
Ban Phang Ka
Ban Thale
Laem Hin Khom
Ban Thong Krut
Laem Set
Ban Thong Tanot
Wat Laem So
Ban Sa Ket
Laem So
BANG KAO BAY
From Khanom
1 USM Samui International
10 kilometres
5 miles
1000 metres
500 metres
Sea level

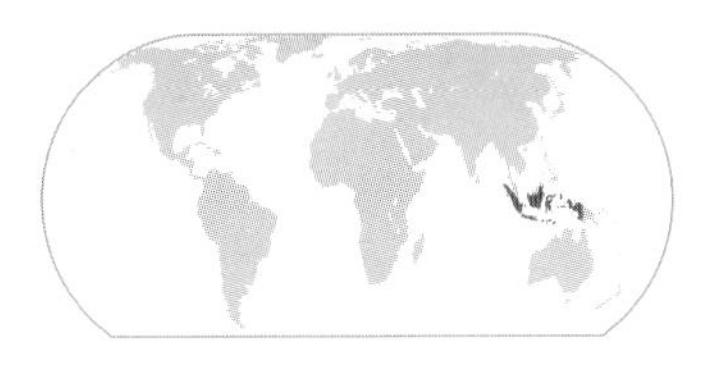

See also... Contents (2-7) – this country features in many thematic and regional maps throughout the *World Travel Atlas*.

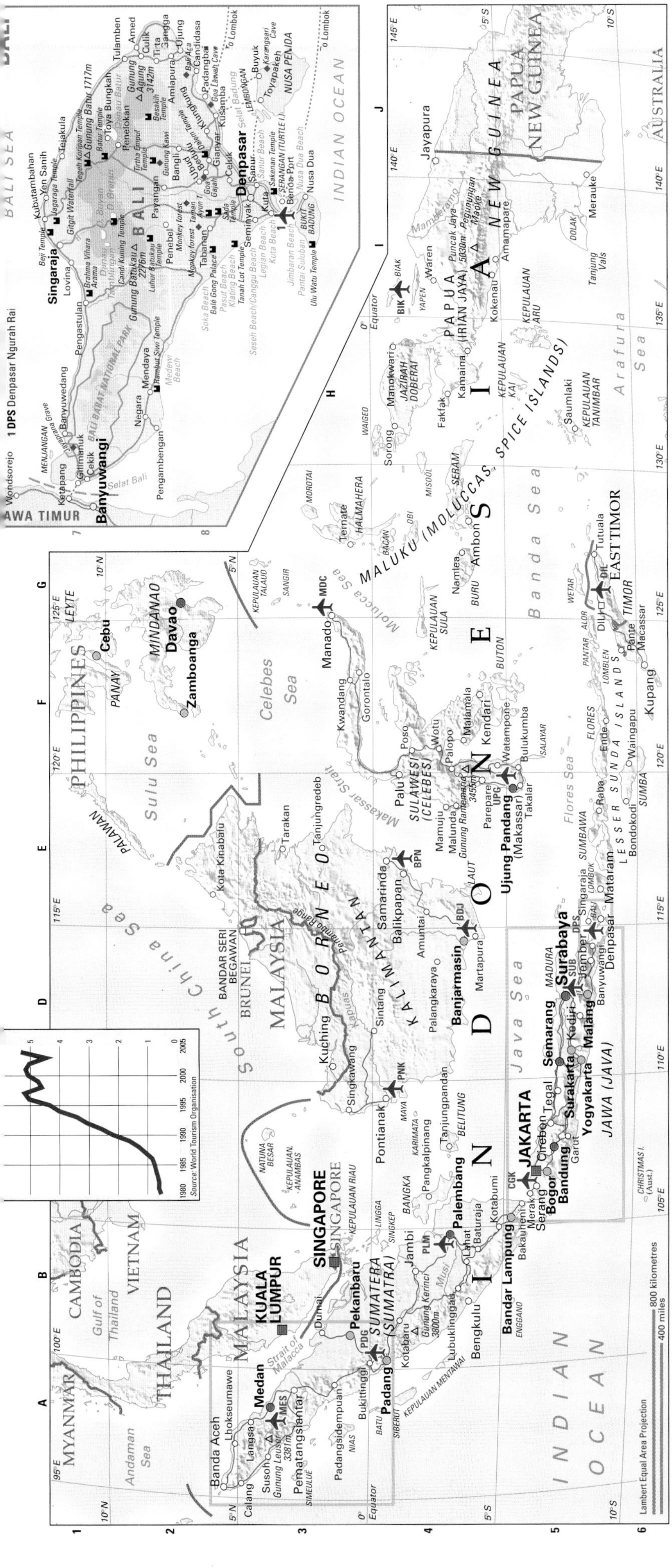

Source: World Tourism Organisation

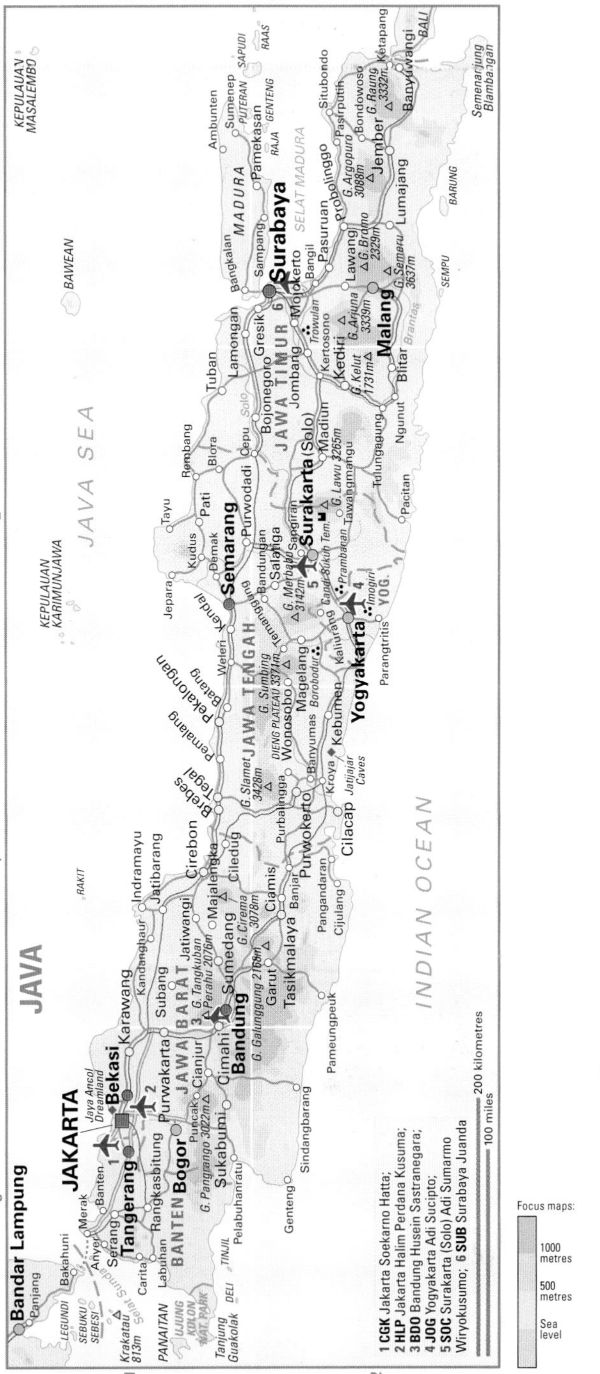

Lambert Equal Area Projection

BALI

1 DPS Denpasar Ngurah Rai

JAVA

1 CGK Jakarta Soekarno Hatta; 2 HLP Jakarta Halim Perdana Kusuma; 3 BDO Bandung Husein Sastranegara; 4 JOG Yogyakarta Adi Sucipto; 5 SOC Surakarta (Solo) Adi Sumarmo Wiryokusumo; 6 SUB Surabaya Juanda

NORTHERN SUMATRA

1 BTJ Banda Aceh Sultan Iskandarmuda; 2 MES Medan Polonia; 3 PKU Pekanbaru Sultan Syarif Kasim II; 4 PDG Padang Minangkabau

Focus maps:
1000 metres
500 metres
Sea level

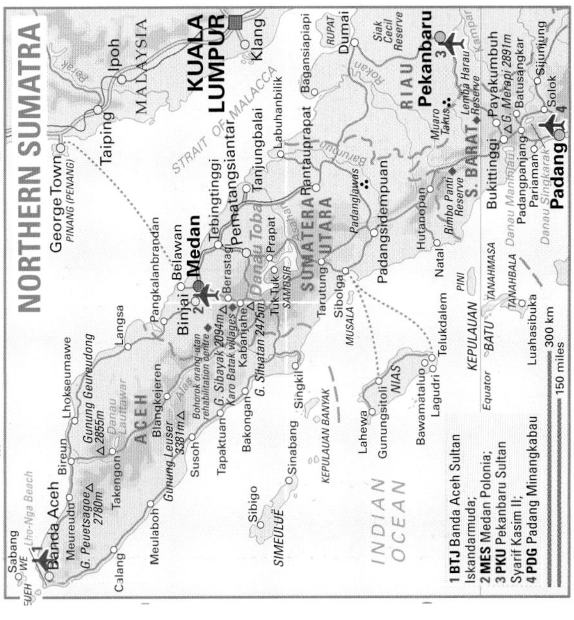

See also... World Introduction (8-11); Tourism (24-25); Countries A-Z (202-210)

The listings above refer to a selection of related themes. For more information, see the Contents (2-7).

Australasia & Oceania

Distance is probably what best characterises Australasia & Oceania: vast distances must be covered to get there and, once arrived, intra-regional distances are often formidable too. This obvious point explains both the region's strengths and its weaknesses economically and, particularly, as a travel destination. A major advantage is that many global problems tend to pass the region by. Modern communications have made Australasia & Oceania a seamless part of the 21st century, but physical distance helps protect it from the world's worst problems.

The regional power-house is Australia, a country over 30 times the size of the UK but with less than one-third of its population. New Zealand, more European in scale, runs it a respectable second by most travel indicators. Together they account for 97% of the region's GNI and 73% of its visitors (Guam, with a mainly American clientele, receives 11%). In 2005, the region saw a 3.9% growth in international visitors. This was rather below the world average of 5.5%, but both major countries confidently predict strong growth during the rest of the decade.

Travel overview

Of all the many factors which influence travel, three perhaps predominate – cost, safety and the desire for new or exciting experiences. On all three measures, Australasia and Oceania scores highly. For new and exciting experiences, the region can hardly be matched. From cosmopolitan cities to sun-drenched Pacific beaches, from the awesome emptiness of the Outback to the staggering landscapes of New Zealand or the wonders of the Great Barrier Reef, there truly is something for everyone. Unspoiled quality is also a major selling point. '100% Pure' has been Tourism New Zealand's slogan for some years, and it could justly be applied to most of the other countries in the region.

Although travel costs are high, there are an increasing number of bargains available. The 'holiday of a lifetime' appeal is still strong, but it is no longer necessary to write out the cheque of a lifetime to pay for it. Most travellers agree: the repeat-visitor figure is on the increase, with 60% of 2004 visitors to Australia making at least their second trip. Once arrived, many visitors are, despite the size of the country, prepared to go the extra mile, and over a quarter spend at least one night away from the key attractions of the six main cities, the Gold Coast and Tropical North Queensland. Many also take in a visit to New Zealand or the Pacific islands, particularly if on a round-the-world trip.

Just as importantly, the region is regarded as being safe in a way that large parts of the world are currently not. Crime levels are lower than those in most of the countries from which visitors come. Now that Fiji's recent tensions have eased, there are no wars. As for terrorism, the countries have neither the internal problems to encourage it, nor the external policies to attract it from elsewhere. Most foreign interventions, such as Australia's in East Timor, have been uncontroversial. Australia and New Zealand have had an uneasy relationship with their pasts, but generally equitable settlements with the Aborigine and Maori communities have been achieved without serious conflict. In general, Australasian influence on world affairs has been conciliatory rather than aggressive.

The positive perceptions of Australia generated by the 2000 Sydney Olympics and the 2003 Rugby World Cup helped boost visitor arrivals and spending. The 2006 Melbourne Commonwealth Games stimulated further growth. Across the Tasman Sea, the stunning cinematography of *The Lord of the Rings* films (which used over 150 locations around the country) has given a significant boost to New Zealand's tourism, and the *Chronicles of Narnia* is having a similar effect.

Both countries are supportive of each other's travel product, with Australia supplying 37% of New Zealand's visitors and New Zealand 21% of Australia's. Both countries see themselves as being part of the Asian region, as well as members of the far-flung English-speaking world, and both have been quick to develop travel links with the vast and fast-growing Chinese market. Varied travel products, in each case a unique blend of the exotic, the untamed and the familiar, are clearly and effectively marketed worldwide – both tourist boards, for example, have particularly good web sites.

Australia and New Zealand's other major markets – mainly the USA, the UK and Japan – are spread widely across the world. While this reduces the effects of regional downturns, all these journeys involve air travel, and usually long-haul. Australia is, apart from Japan, the only country in the world's top 40 by visitor numbers which receives all its arrivals (cruise and ferry passengers aside) by air. This clearly makes it vulnerable to fuel costs, which rose by over 30% in 2005. As Australasia & Oceania is entirely composed of islands, this is a problem across the region and perhaps helps to explain why the growth in tourist arrivals in 2005 was less than a third of 2004's 12.4%. The relative strengths of the Australian and New Zealand dollars in this period have also been a factor.

Low-cost airlines have not established themselves in Australasia and the Pacific to anything like the same extent as in Europe, North America or, increasingly, Asia. Those that have, tend to operate mainly trans-Tasman services. In the coming years, some Asian low-cost operators may offer regular services to Australia. Airline capacity across the whole region is currently limited. The delivery of the new A340s in 2007 will help solve this problem for the major carriers at least.

Adventure holidays have long been popular in Australia and New Zealand. The back-packing market has traditionally been strong and nearly half a million people (130,000 from the UK) visited Australia for this reason in 2004, some 75,000 more than in 1999. There is a wide range of landscapes, many comparatively close to major centres. Touring is also a major growth area in the form of self-drive cars, coach tours and, increasingly, motorhomes. Rail travel is also increasing, particularly on the scenic routes. The cities are among the most cosmopolitan in the world, each with a unique blend of Asian, European, American and native ingredients.

The region features on an increasing number of world cruises. With longer cruises becoming more attractive, many ports in the area are visited by ships originating from South-East Asia.

Visits to the country's many superb wineries by international travellers rose by over 35% between 1999 and 2004. Nearly a quarter of wine tourists were from the UK. Indigenous tourism and gastro-tourism are also increasing in popularity.

Key facts

Number of Countries	22
Area ('000 sq km)	8,505
Population ('000)	32,746
Population Density (per sq km)	4
Gross National Income (US$m)	642,174
Visitor Arrivals ('000)	10,561
Visitor Receipts (US$m)	17,925

GNI figures are for 2004. Population figures are taken from the most recent reliable source. Travel figures (UNWTO) are based on overnight stays, not same-day visitors, and are for 2005. For more information see the Countries A-Z section from page 202.

Visitors, state-by-state

International visitors to Australian states and other countries, 2005 (millions)

Sources: WTO/Tourism Australia

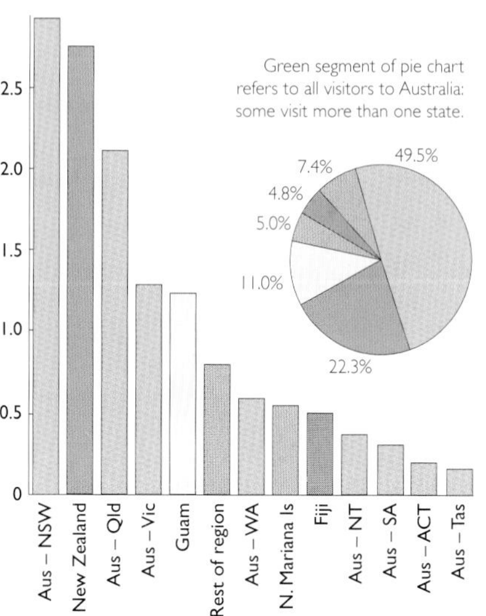
2.5
2.0
1.5
1.0
0.5
0
Green segment of pie chart refers to all visitors to Australia: some visit more than one state.
7.4%
49.5%
4.8%
5.0%
11.0%
22.3%
Aus – NSW
New Zealand
Aus – Qld
Aus – Vic
Guam
Rest of region
Aus – WA
N. Mariana Is
Fiji
Aus – NT
Aus – SA
Aus – ACT
Aus – Tas

Major markets

Top four markets for visitors to Australia and New Zealand, 2005; UK visitors to Australian states and New Zealand, 2005 (000s)

Source: WTO/Tourism Australia/New Zealand Tourism

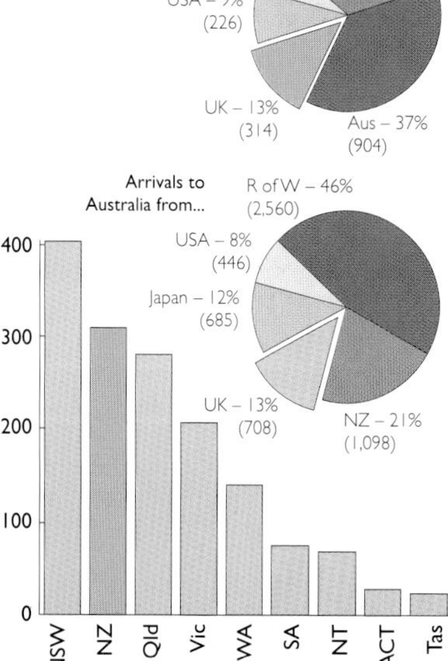
Arrivals to New Zealand from...
R of W – 34% (839)
Japan – 7% (165)
USA – 9% (226)
UK – 13% (314)
Aus – 37% (904)
Arrivals to Australia from...
R of W – 46% (2,560)
USA – 8% (446)
Japan – 12% (685)
UK – 13% (708)
NZ – 21% (1,098)
400
300
200
100
0
NSW
NZ
Qld
Vic
WA
SA
NT
ACT
Tas

Economies

The region's two main economies

Source: World Bank/International Monetary Fund

	GNI US$m 2004	GNI/cap US$ 2004	GDP growth 2004	GDP growth av p/a '97-'06
Australia	541,173	26,937	3.5	3.6
New Zealand	82,465	20,435	4.8	3.1

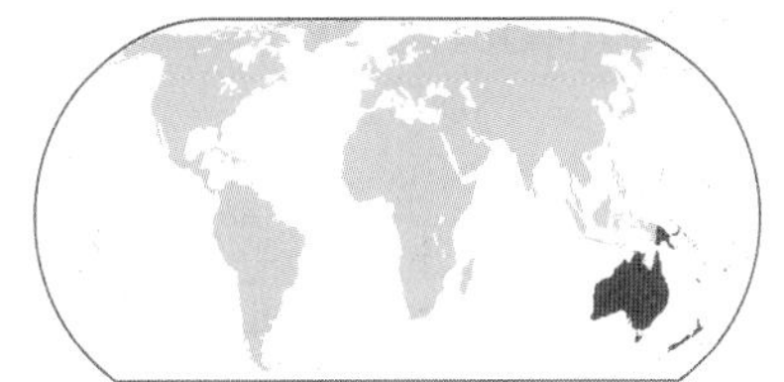

- Australasia & Oceania (A&O) occupies 6.3% of the world's land area and is home to 0.5% of the world's population.
- A&O's combined GDI is US$642.2 billion.
- A&O accounts for 1.3% of global travel arrivals.
- International travel and tourism contributed almost US$18 billion to A&O's economy in 2004.
- Australia dominates the travel economy of the region, accounting for about 50% of all international visitors.
- If the UK had the same population density as Australia it would have about 600,000 people, rather than about 59 million.
- If Western Australia were a country, it would be the tenth largest in the world.
- Sydney spent over A$3.3 billion of public and private money on infrastructure and facilities prior to hosting the 2000 Olympics. Over 35 new hotels opened in the run-up to the event.
- New Zealand's receipts from international travel and tourism doubled between 2001 and 2004.
- Australia's volcanoes have not erupted for at least 5,000 years.
- The longest straight stretch of rail track in the world – 478 kilometres – is between Nurina in Western Australia and Ooldea in South Australia.
- Australia has won the Cricket World Cup three times (1987, 1999 & 2003), more than any other country.
- In 1893, New Zealand became the first country in the world to extend the vote to women.
- 482,000 backpackers visited Australia in 2004.
- Caroline Island in Kiribati (pronounced 'Kiribass') was renamed Millennium Island after it became the first place on earth to see the sun rise on the 21st century. To do this, that part of the island republic redefined its time as being 14 hours ahead of GMT.
- The islands of French Polynesia are spread over an area of ocean about the size of Western Europe; yet, put together, they would comfortably fit inside the US state of Connecticut.
- New Zealand produces more ice cream per capita than any other country.
- Qantas was originally an acronym for Queensland And Northern Territories Air Service.
- A tortoise given to the King of Tonga by Captain Cook in the 1770s lived to be 172 years old.

The UK is Australia's most important source of visitors outside New Zealand, and the one that is of most economic value (see chart above right). Britons spent 21.6m nights in Australia in 2005, a slight decline from 2004 despite a slight increase in the actual number of visitors. In 2004, 57% of UK visitors were repeats, as against 50% in 1999. Visiting friends and relations is still an important reason for travel (for 35% of British arrivals in 2004 it was the main purpose of the visit), but is now less dominant a motive than in 1980, when about 80% of ex-UK trips were for that reason. Over 40% of first-time visitors from the UK used the internet to research their trip. UK visitor numbers are predicted to grow at about 3.8% a year until 2014.

Destination overview – Australia

- **New South Wales** – Australia's most visited state and the capital, Sydney, is Australia's main gateway. The state has superb surfing as well as skiing in the Blue Mountains. Travel and tourism is worth over A$20 billion to the state economy and employs an estimated one in 12 people.
- **Queensland** – the main attractions are its state capital of Brisbane, the Gold Coast, the Great Barrier Reef and the tropical north. The Whitsunday Islands are becoming popular, as is the area around Cape Tribulation. The state currently has a ten-year sustainable tourism strategy in place.
- **Western Australia** – this state occupies the western third of the country, with cosmopolitan Perth as its capital. It is famed for the unique Wave Rock and Pinnacles geological formations.
- **Victoria** – home to Australia's second largest city, Melbourne, and many national parks. The Great Southern Touring Route is growing in popularity, as is the Sydney to Melbourne coastal route, the Gippsland Lakes and Jervis Bay. Visitor figures have increased by an average of 8.5% a year since 1994, more than the national average.
- **Northern Territory** – this state was made famous by the *Crocodile Dundee* films. Main attractions are the Outback, the town of Alice Springs and Australia's greatest icon, Uluru (Ayers Rock). The rail extension of the Ghan from Alice Springs to Darwin has already boosted travel to the region.
- **South Australia** – the least visited of Australia's mainland states (around 320,000 international arrivals in 2005) with Adelaide as its capital. The state is currently promoting itself as 'a brilliant blend', focussing on its diversity.
- **Tasmania** – the island state is perceived as being good value for money and is currently promoting itself as a walking, cycling and eco-tourism destination.

Destination overview – New Zealand

New Zealand's scenery is exceptional, as *The Lord of the Rings* proved, and includes some of the best wilderness walking itineraries in the world. The major cities, though small by European and American standards, are cosmopolitan and sophisticated. Christchurch is being developed as a second gateway that will offer easier access to the South Island.

Geo-thermal sites remain a popular attraction, closely followed by beaches. Luxury lodge-style accommodation is attracting an increasing number of guests. Themed highways, such as the Southern Scenic Route, the Thermal Explorer and the Twin Coast Discovery Highway are also being promoted. The current government tourism forecast predicts that international visitor arrivals will increase by about 38% by 2011, although the average length of stay is projected to fall slightly to 18.5 nights.

Destination overview – Pacific islands

These islands offer some of the most idyllic and unspoiled beaches in the world and provide a welcome break on many long-haul and round-the-world trips. The addition of a South Pacific leg to trips to Australia and New Zealand is a feature of some tour operators' packages, and is helping the region to lose its high-price perception. Top island destinations include:

- **Fiji Islands** – watersports and hiking are the main attractions. The country is recovering from recent unrest, and benefitted as a post-Bali replacement destination. Remoter islands such as Treasure Island and Castaway Island are increasing in popularity, particularly amongst eco-minded tourists.
- **French Polynesia** – a tropical taste of France, although in 1999 American visitors exceeded French ones for the first time. Tourist arrivals have fallen in recent years but new tax incentives for cruise lines and a programme of investment should reverse the trend. The economy is heavily reliant on tourism: a French-backed plan is currently in place to address this.
- **Guam** – the island has long been both a popular travel destination, particularly from the American and Asian markets, and is the site of an important US military base. A combination of a fall in visitors from Japan (Guam's biggest market) and US military cutbacks has led to some decline in its fortunes. None the less, the island is making significant investment in its tourism facilities and general infrastructure.
- **New Caledonia** – this former French colony, mid-way between Fiji and Brisbane, currently has a ten-year strategic plan funded by France in place to avoid over-reliance on its nickel mining industry, which currently accounts for 90% of the country's exports. Tourism has been identified as a growth area and many infrastructure and ecological projects are under way.
- **Northern Mariana Islands** – a compact group roughly half-way between Australia and Japan, and popular with the American market. There are many shipwrecks accessible to divers. The country is promoting itself to Australians as an alternative to Bali
- **Cook Islands** – perceived for some time as being slightly more affordable than other Pacific destinations, the islands offer pristine beaches and a relaxed atmosphere.

Economic impact

Receipts from international visitors (Total Inbound Economic Value method), 2005 – top ten countries (US$ billions)
Source: Tourism Australia

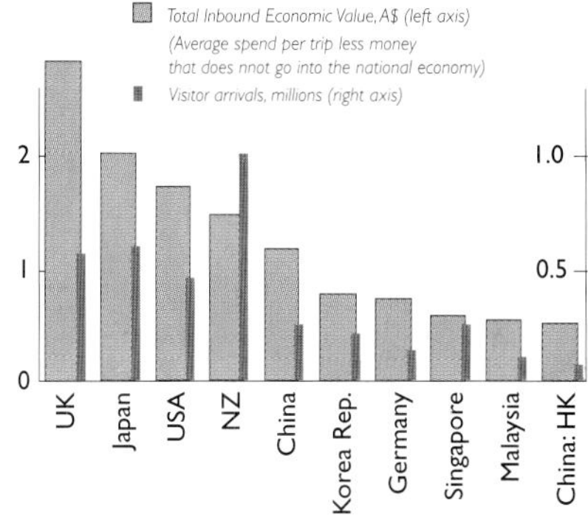
Total Inbound Economic Value, A$ (left axis)
(Average spend per trip less money that does nnot go into the national economy)
Visitor arrivals, millions (right axis)
0
1
2
0.5
1.0
UK
Japan
USA
NZ
China
Korea Rep.
Germany
Singapore
Malaysia
China: HK

Problem areas

- The biggest challenge for the Pacific island states is that of developing sustainable and diverse economies. There is currently some debate as to whether those countries that still have their own currencies should adandon them in favour of the Australian or New Zealand dollar.
- Many of these countries are very low-lying and are thus particularly vulnerable to the threat of rising sea levels.
- From most of the world, the flying times to the region are considerable. Much of the publicity surrounding deep vein thrombosis (DVT) has centred on ultra-long haul flights as experienced by travellers to the Antipodes.
- Australia has many species of highly venomous plant, reptile, insect and marine life.
- For water-sports enthusiasts and divers, sea-rescue facilities in some of the Pacific islands may not be comprehensive. Medical facilities may also be basic.
- The return of political problems in Fiji cannot be ruled out. Sporadic unrest, often due to ethnic conflicts, is also a risk in the Solomon Islands.

Visitors

Visitor arrivals 2004: top ten countries *Source: WTO*

	Visitors (thousands)	Change since 1997
Australia	5,200	20.4%
New Zealand	2,348	56.8%
Guam	1,160	-16.1%
Northern Mariana Is.	525	-23.4%
Fiji Is.	507	41.2%
French Polynesia	212	17.8%
New Caledonia	100	-4.8%
Samoa	98	44.1%
Palau	89	20.3%
Cook Is.	83	66.0%

Oceania

See also... World Physical (12-13); World Political (14-15); World Climate (16)

The listings above refer to a selection of related themes. For more information, see the Contents (2-7).

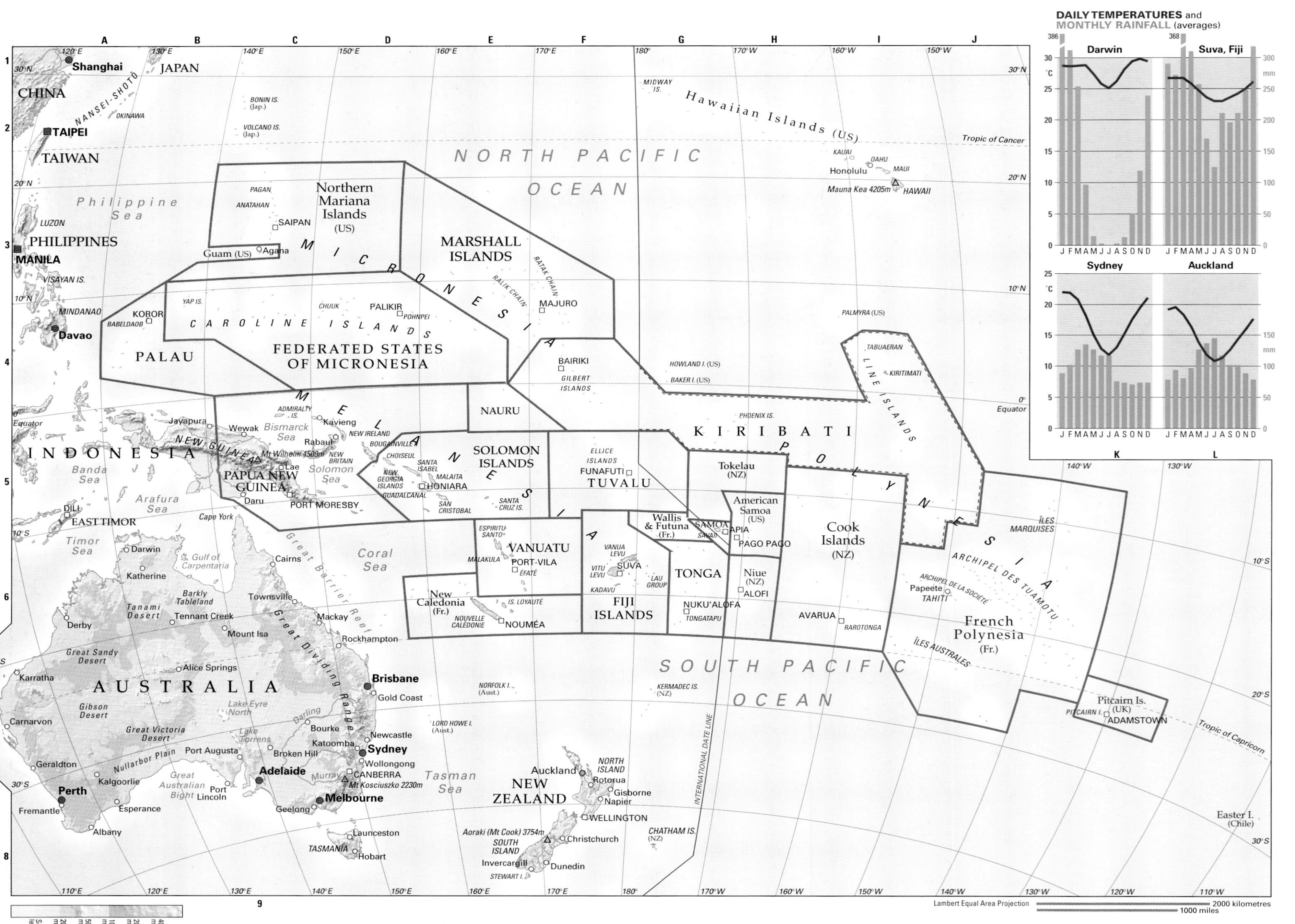
DAILY TEMPERATURES and MONTHLY RAINFALL (averages)
Darwin
Suva, Fiji
Sydney
Auckland
NORTH PACIFIC OCEAN
SOUTH PACIFIC OCEAN
Hawaiian Islands (US)
Honolulu
Mauna Kea 4205m
MARSHALL ISLANDS
MAJURO
Northern Mariana Islands (US)
SAIPAN
Guam (US)
Agana
FEDERATED STATES OF MICRONESIA
PALIKIR
CAROLINE ISLANDS
PALAU
KOROR
NAURU
KIRIBATI
BAIRIKI
LINE ISLANDS
TUVALU
FUNAFUTI
SOLOMON ISLANDS
HONIARA
PAPUA NEW GUINEA
PORT MORESBY
VANUATU
PORT-VILA
New Caledonia (Fr.)
NOUMÉA
FIJI ISLANDS
SUVA
TONGA
NUKU'ALOFA
SAMOA
APIA
American Samoa (US)
PAGO PAGO
Tokelau (NZ)
Wallis & Futuna (Fr.)
Niue (NZ)
ALOFI
Cook Islands (NZ)
AVARUA
French Polynesia (Fr.)
Papeete
Pitcairn Is. (UK)
ADAMSTOWN
MICRONESIA
MELANESIA
POLYNESIA
INTERNATIONAL DATE LINE
Tropic of Capricorn
Tropic of Cancer
Equator
AUSTRALIA
CANBERRA
Sydney
Melbourne
Brisbane
Adelaide
Perth
Darwin
Hobart
TASMANIA
NEW ZEALAND
WELLINGTON
Auckland
Christchurch
Dunedin
Tasman Sea
Coral Sea
INDONESIA
PHILIPPINES
MANILA
JAPAN
CHINA
TAIWAN
TAIPEI
Easter I. (Chile)
Lambert Equal Area Projection
2000 kilometres
1000 miles

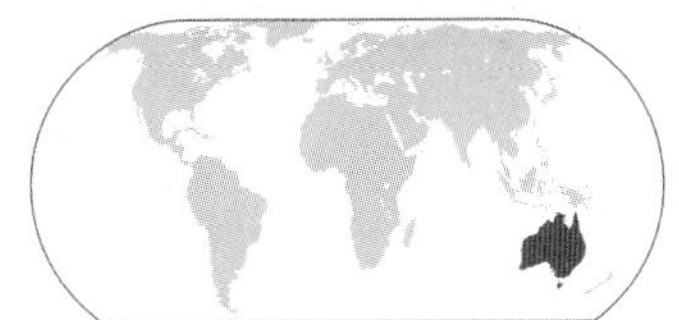

See also... page 148 for more on Australia

For more information, see the Contents (2-7).

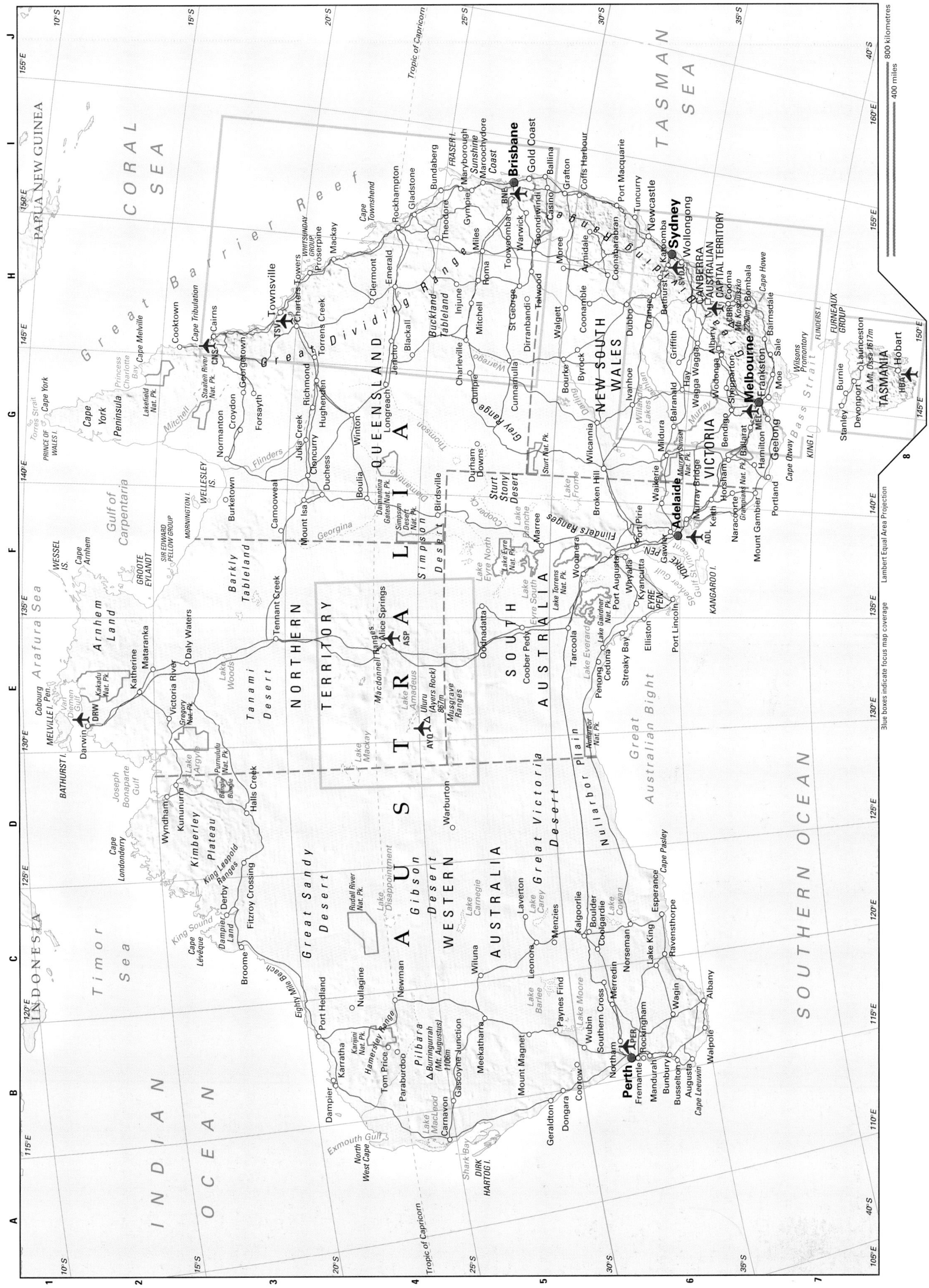

AUSTRALIA

WESTERN AUSTRALIA
NORTHERN TERRITORY
SOUTH AUSTRALIA
QUEENSLAND
NEW SOUTH WALES
VICTORIA
AUSTRALIAN CAPITAL TERRITORY
TASMANIA

INDIAN OCEAN
SOUTHERN OCEAN
CORAL SEA
TASMAN SEA
Timor Sea
Arafura Sea
Gulf of Carpentaria
Great Australian Bight
Bass Strait
INDONESIA
PAPUA NEW GUINEA

Great Barrier Reef
Great Dividing Range
Great Sandy Desert
Gibson Desert
Great Victoria Desert
Tanami Desert
Simpson Desert
Sturt Stony Desert
Nullarbor Plain
Kimberley Plateau
Barkly Tableland
Arnhem Land
Cape York Peninsula
Pilbara
Macdonnell Ranges
Musgrave Ranges
Flinders Ranges
Grey Range
Uluru (Ayers Rock) 867m
Lake Eyre North
Lake Eyre South
Lake Torrens
Lake Gairdner
Lake Frome
Lake Amadeus
Lake Mackay
Lake Disappointment
Lake Carnegie
KANGAROO I.
MELVILLE I.
BATHURST I.
GROOTE EYLANDT
FRASER I.
FURNEAUX GROUP
KING I.

Perth
Fremantle
Adelaide
Melbourne
Sydney
Brisbane
Canberra
Darwin
Hobart
Alice Springs
Cairns
Townsville
Mackay
Rockhampton
Newcastle
Wollongong
Gold Coast
Geelong
Ballarat
Bendigo
Launceston
Kalgoorlie
Broome
Port Hedland
Carnarvon
Geraldton
Albany
Esperance
Port Augusta
Port Lincoln
Mount Isa
Katherine
Tennant Creek
Broken Hill
Mildura
Wagga Wagga
Dubbo
Toowoomba
Bundaberg
Longreach
Charleville
Birdsville
Coober Pedy
Ceduna

Tropic of Capricorn

400 miles
800 kilometres
Blue boxes indicate focus map coverage
Lambert Equal Area Projection

▶ See also... Contents (2-7) – this country features in many thematic and regional maps throughout the World Travel Atlas.

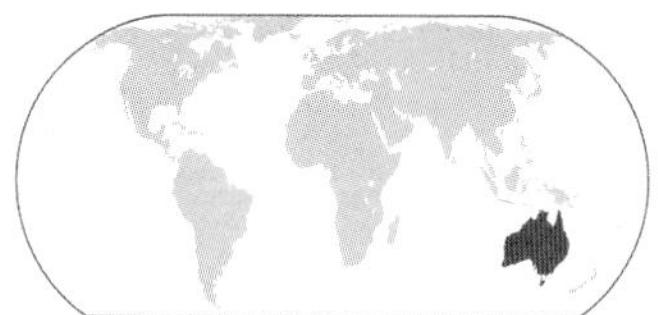

JAN Australian Tennis Open (**Melbourne**)
JAN Sydney Festival
JAN Montsalvet Jazz Festival (**Eltham** *NE Melbourne*)
JAN 26th Australia Day (**Sydney** & countrywide)
JAN-FEB Perth International Arts Festival
FEB/MAR Sydney Gay and Lesbian Mardi Gras
MAR Adelaide Arts Festival; biennial, even years
APR Barossa Valley Vintage Festival; biennial, odd years (**SA**)
APR 25th ANZAC Day
JUN Melbourne International Film Festival
JUN Barunga Sports Festival (**Beswick Aboriginal Land NT** *near Katherine*)
JUL Camel Cup: camel racing (**Alice Springs NT**)
AUG Shinju Matsuri: oriental festival (**Broome WA**)
AUG Mount Isa Rodeo (**QL**)
SEP Bathurst 1,000 Road Races (**NS**)
SEP Birdsville Races (**QL**)
SEP Warana Arts Festival (**Brisbane**)
OCT-NOV Melbourne Festival
NOV Melbourne Cup: horse race
DEC 26th **Sydney-Hobart** Yacht Race

International arrivals (millions)
5, 4, 3, 2, 1, 0
1980 1985 1990 1995 2000 2005
Source: World Tourism Organisation

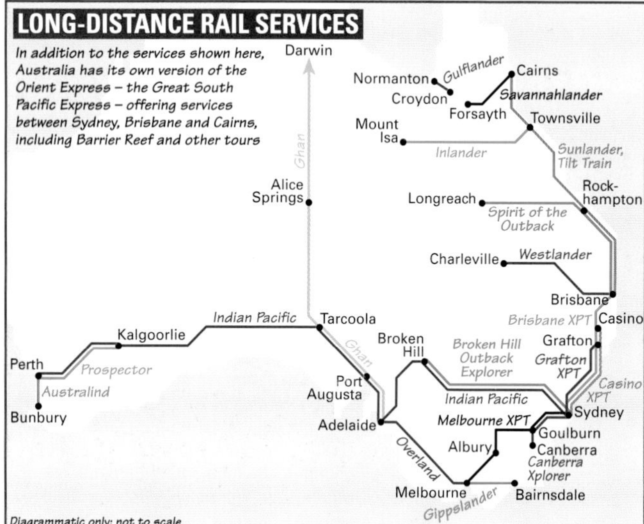
LONG-DISTANCE RAIL SERVICES
In addition to the services shown here, Australia has its own version of the Orient Express – the Great South Pacific Express – offering services between Sydney, Brisbane and Cairns, including Barrier Reef and other tours
Darwin
Normanton
Gulflander
Cairns
Croydon
Savannahlander
Forsayth
Townsville
Mount Isa
Inlander
Sunlander, Tilt Train
Ghan
Alice Springs
Rock-hampton
Longreach
Spirit of the Outback
Charleville
Westlander
Brisbane
Brisbane XPT
Casino
Indian Pacific
Tarcoola
Kalgoorlie
Broken Hill
Broken Hill Outback Explorer
Grafton
Grafton XPT
Perth
Prospector
Port Augusta
Casino XPT
Australind
Indian Pacific
Bunbury
Sydney
Adelaide
Melbourne XPT
Goulburn
Albury
Canberra
Overland
Canberra Xplorer
Melbourne
Bairnsdale
Gippslander
Diagrammatic only: not to scale

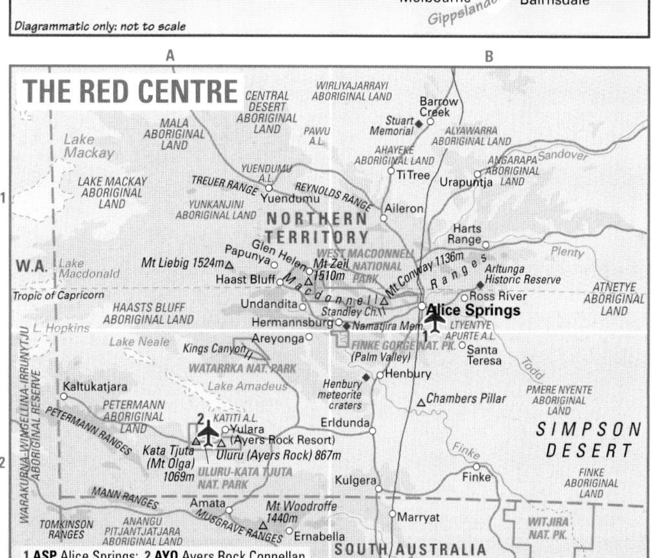
THE RED CENTRE
NORTHERN TERRITORY
W.A.
SOUTH AUSTRALIA
SIMPSON DESERT
Alice Springs
Yulara
Uluru (Ayers Rock) 867m
Kata Tjuta (Mt Olga) 1069m
Tropic of Capricorn
1 ASP Alice Springs; 2 AYQ Ayers Rock Connellan
300 kilometres
150 miles

CAIRNS TO BRISBANE
CORAL SEA
CORAL SEA ISLANDS TERRITORY
GREAT BARRIER REEF
QUEENSLAND
GREAT DIVIDING RANGE
Cairns
Townsville
Mackay
Rockhampton
Brisbane
Toowoomba
GOLD COAST
SUNSHINE COAST
Tropic of Capricorn
1 CNS Cairns; 2 TSV Townsville; 3 MKY Mackay;
4 ROK Rockhampton; 5 MCY Sunshine Coast-Maroochydore;
6 BNE Brisbane Eagle Farm; 7 OOL Gold Coast-Coolangatta
400 km
200 miles

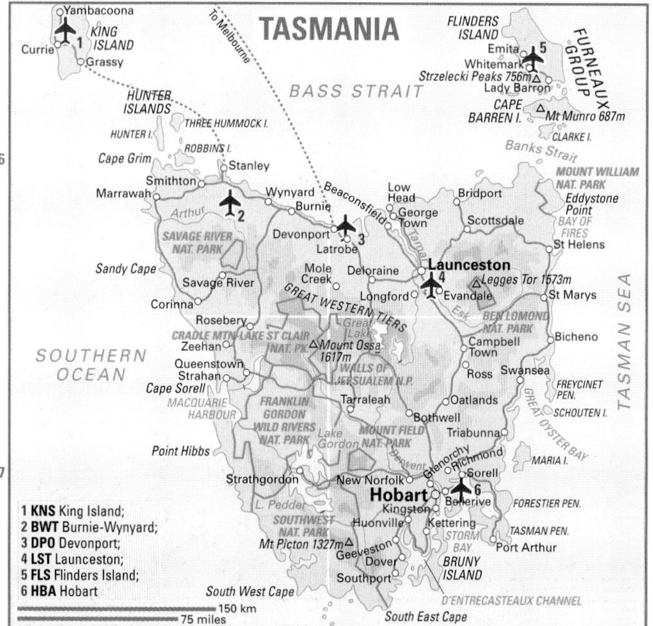
TASMANIA
BASS STRAIT
TASMAN SEA
SOUTHERN OCEAN
FURNEAUX GROUP
KING ISLAND
FLINDERS ISLAND
Launceston
Hobart
Devonport
1 KNS King Island;
2 BWT Burnie-Wynyard;
3 DPO Devonport;
4 LST Launceston;
5 FLS Flinders Island;
6 HBA Hobart
150 km
75 miles

SYDNEY TO MELBOURNE
NEW SOUTH WALES
VICTORIA
A.C.T.
CANBERRA
Sydney
Melbourne
Newcastle
Wollongong
Parramatta
Campbelltown
Geelong
Frankston
Albury
Bendigo
TASMAN SEA
BASS STRAIT
1 SYD Sydney Kingsford Smith; 2 CBR Canberra;
3 ABX Albury; 4 MEL Melbourne Tullamarine
300 kilometres
150 miles
1000 metres
500 metres
Sea level

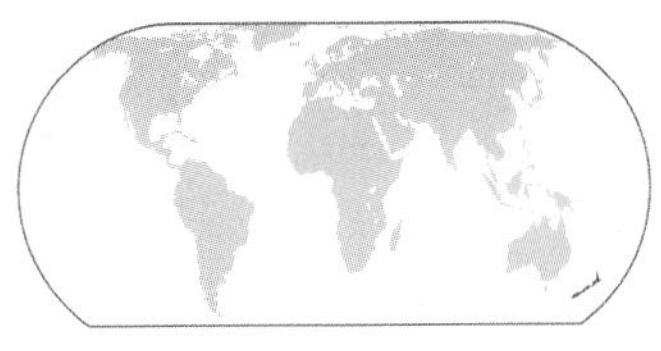

See also... Contents (2-7) – this country features in many thematic and regional maps throughout the *World Travel Atlas*.

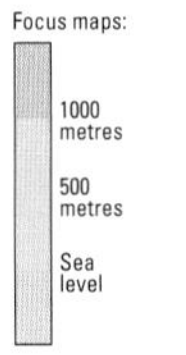

CENTRAL NORTH ISLAND

1 HLZ Hamilton;
2 NPE Napier-Hastings

80 kilometres
40 miles

JAN Yachting Regatta **(Auckland)**
JAN World Buskers Festival **(Christchurch)**
JAN-FEB Summer City Programme **(Wellington)**
FEB 6th Waitangi/New Zealand Day
FEB International Festival of the Arts **(Wellington)**; even-numbered years
FEB Marlborough Food and Wine festival **(Blenheim)**
FEB Art Deco weekend **(Napier)**
MAR Pasifika Festival **(Auckland)**
MAR Golden Shears Sheep Shearing Contest **(Masterton)**
EASTER Royal Easter Show **(Auckland)**
APR Highland Games **(Hastings)**
APR 25th ANZAC Day
NOV Ellerslie Flower Show **(Auckland)**
NOV Canterbury Show Week

International arrivals (millions)

2.4, 2.0, 1.6, 1.2, 0.8, 0.4, 0
1980, 1985, 1990, 1995, 2000, 2005

Source: World Tourism Organisation

NEW ZEALAND

NORTH ISLAND

SOUTH ISLAND

TASMAN SEA

PACIFIC OCEAN

SOUTHLAND

1 ZQN Queenstown

80 kilometres
40 miles

Focus maps:
1000 metres
500 metres
Sea level

Lambert Equal Area Projection

200 kilometres
100 miles

See also... Contents (2-7) – these countries feature in many thematic and regional maps throughout the *World Travel Atlas*.

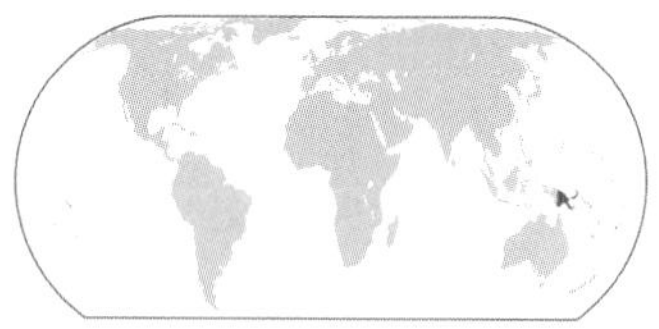

MAP A
OKINAWA
JAPAN
Hedo-misaki
Hedo
Okuma
IE-JIMA
Nakijin
Ogimi
Ocean Expo Park
Yonaha-dake 498m
Motobu
NAGO-WAN
Nago
Ryukyu-mura
Onna
Kin
Moon Beach
Nakadomari
Ishikawa
Kadena
(US Air Force base)
KIN-WAN
Gushikawa
Koza (Okinawa City)
MIYAGUSUKU-JIMA
Katsuren-zaki
NAHA
Shuri
NAKAGUSUKU-WAN
MAE-JIMA
OKA
Naha
Yonabaru
NANBU
Itoman
Gyokusendo Okoku mura
Arasaki
40 km
20 miles

MAP B
SAIPAN & TINIAN
N. MARIANA IS.
Puntan Sabaneta
MAÑAGAHA I.
Tanapag
American Memorial Park
CAPITOL HILL
Garapan
Okso' Takpochao 466m
SAIPAN
Magpi Susupe
Chalan Kanoa
BAHIA LAULAU
Puntan Hagman
Ushi Point
SPN Saipan
Saipan Channel
Puntan I Naftan
TINIAN
TIQ Tinian
SUNBARAN ROADS
San Jose
187m
Puntan Carolina
20 km
10 miles

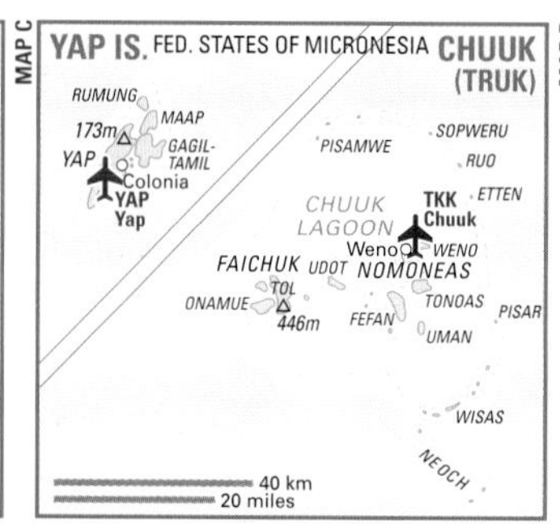
MAP C
YAP IS.
FED. STATES OF MICRONESIA
CHUUK (TRUK)
RUMUNG
173m
MAAP
YAP
GAGIL-TAMIL
Colonia
YAP Yap
PISAMWE
SOPWERU
RUO
CHUUK LAGOON
TKK Chuuk
ETTEN
Weno
WENO
FAICHUK
UDOT
NOMONEAS
TOL
ONAMUE
446m
FEFAN
TONOAS
PISAR
UMAN
WISAS
NEOCH
40 km
20 miles

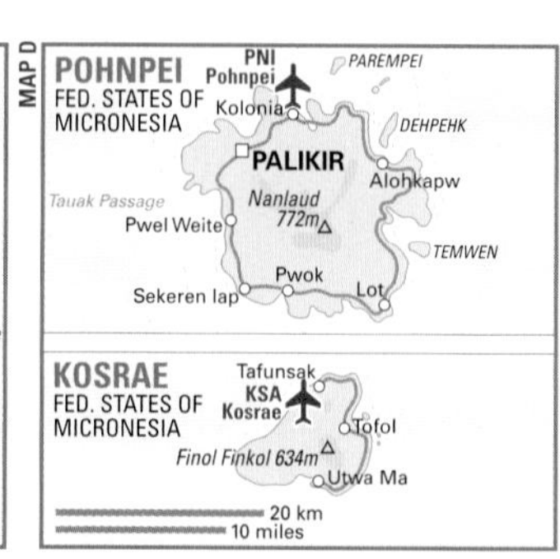
MAP D
POHNPEI
FED. STATES OF MICRONESIA
PNI Pohnpei
PAREMPEI
Kolonia
DEHPEHK
PALIKIR
Tauak Passage
Alohkapw
Pwel Weite
Nanlaud 772m
TEMWEN
Pwok
Sekeren Iap
Lot
KOSRAE
FED. STATES OF MICRONESIA
Tafunsak
KSA Kosrae
Tofol
Finol Finkol 634m
Utwa Ma
20 km
10 miles

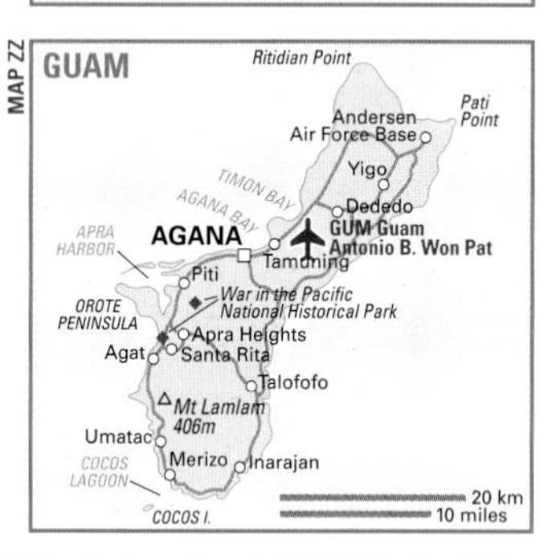
MAP ZZ
GUAM
Ritidian Point
Andersen Air Force Base
Pati Point
Yigo
TIMON BAY
AGANA BAY
Dededo
APRA HARBOR
AGANA
GUM Guam Antonio B. Won Pat
Tamuning
Piti
OROTE PENINSULA
War in the Pacific National Historical Park
Agat
Apra Heights
Santa Rita
Talofofo
Mt Lamlam 406m
Umatac
COCOS LAGOON
Merizo
Inarajan
COCOS I.
20 km
10 miles

MAP Z
PALAU
Konrei
AREKALONG PENINSULA
Ngamegei Passage
West Passage
Mt Makelulu 240m
Melekeiok
BABELDAOB
Mukeru
ROR Koror Babeldaob
Garusuun
KOMEBAIL LAGOON
KOROR
Malakal
AULUPTAGEL
URUKTHAPEL
FLOATING GARDEN ISLANDS
EIL MALIK
Koulklubed
PELELIU
Saipan
ANGAUR
50 km
25 miles

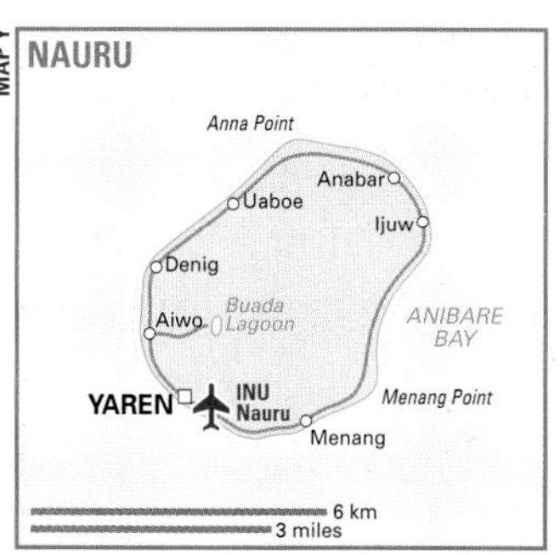
MAP Y
NAURU
Anna Point
Anabar
Uaboe
Ijuw
Denig
Buada Lagoon
Aiwo
ANIBARE BAY
YAREN
INU Nauru
Menang Point
Menang
6 km
3 miles

AA
BB
CC
REP. OF KOREA
Busan
JAPAN
HONSHŪ
TŌKYŌ
Nagoya
Hiroshima
Ōsaka
SHIKOKU
IZU-SHOTŌ
CHEJU-DO
KYŪSHŪ
ŌSUMI-SHOTŌ
NANSEI-SHOTŌ
NANPO-SHOTŌ
AMAMI-SHOTŌ
OGASAWARA-SHOTŌ (BONIN IS.)
OKINAWA
MAP A
DAITŌ-SHOTŌ
KAZAN-SHOTŌ (VOLCANO IS.)
MINAMI TORI SHIMA (MARCUS, Japan)
Tropic of Cancer
KURE ATOLL (OCEAN I.)
MIDWAY IS.
PEARL & HERMES ATOLL
LISIANSKI I.
LAYSAN
NORTH PACIFIC OCEAN
OKINO TORI SHIMA (PARECE VELA)
PHILIPPINE SEA
AGRIHAN
PAGAN
Northern Mariana Islands (US)
WAKE I. (US)
ANATAHAN
SAIPAN
TINIAN
MAP B
ROTA
3
MAP ZZ Guam (US)
INTERNATIONAL DATE LINE
MONDAY
SUNDAY
TAONGI
5
BIKINI
RONGELAP
MARSHALL ISLANDS
ENEWETAK
MICRONESIA
2
YAP IS.
ULITHI ATOLL
UJELANG
PHILIPPINES
MAP C
MAP E
KWAJALEIN
RATAK CHAIN
RALIK CHAIN
WOTJE
MINDANAO
MAP Z
BABELDAOB
NGULU ATOLL
HALL IS.
MALOELAP
Davao
KOROR
PULUWAT ATOLL
4
MAP C
NAMU
MAJURO
MAP E
ANGAUR
1
CHUUK
AILINGLAPLAP
ARNO
PALAU
CAROLINE ISLANDS
POHNPEI
PALIKIR
MAP D
JALUIT
MILI
SONSOROL IS.
MORTLOCK IS.
KOSRAE
EBON
FEDERATED STATES OF MICRONESIA
KEP. TALAUD
MOROTAI
HELEN REEF
MAKIN
ABAIANG
TARAWA
MAP F
BAIRIKI
HALMAHERA
KAPINGAMARANGI ATOLL
GILBERT ISLANDS (TUNGARU)
HOWLAND I. (US)
BAKER I. (US)
Equator
WAIGEO
BIAK
NINIGO GROUP
ST MATTHIAS GROUP
ADMIRALTY IS.
NAURU
MAP Y
BANABA (OCEAN I.)
KINGSMILL GROUP
KANTON
SERAM
YAPEN
NEW HANOVER
BISMARCK ARCHIPELAGO
NEW IRELAND
MELANESIA
KIRIBATI
BURU
Jayapura
NEW GUINEA
INDONESIA
KEP. ARU
PAPUA NEW GUINEA
BOUGAINVILLE I.
ONTONG JAVA ATOLL
NANUMEA
NEW BRITAIN
CHOISEUL
SOLOMON ISLANDS
TUVALU
VAITUPU
KEP. TANIMBAR
TROBRIAND IS.
SANTA ISABEL
ELLICE ISLANDS
VAIAKU
EAST TIMOR
ARAFURA SEA
Torres Strait
PORT MORESBY
WOODLARK I.
NEW GEORGIA IS.
MALAITA
MAP X
FUNAFUTI
MAP S
SWAINS I. (Am. Sam.)
ATAFU
NUKUNONO
FAKAOFO
MELVILLE I.
BATHURST I.
Cape York
D'ENTRECASTEAUX IS.
HONIARA
6
GUADALCANAL
SAN CRISTOBAL
SANTA CRUZ IS.
RENNELL
MAP G
SAMOA
LOUISIADE ARCHIPELAGO
Great Barrier Reef
Wallis & Futuna (Fr.)
ÎLES DE HOORN
ÎLES WALLIS
MAP R
TORRES IS.
BANKS IS.
VANUATU
ESPÍRITU SANTO
MAP W
7
MAP T
VANUA LEVU
CORAL SEA
WILLIS GROUP
MALAKULA
SHEPHERD IS.
TAVEUNI
LIHOU REEF
YASAWA GROUP
PORT-VILA
ÉFATÉ
MAP U
VITI LEVU
SUVA
TONGA
MARION REEF
ERROMANGO
LAU GROUP
VAVA'U GROUP
Townsville
ÎLES CHESTERFIELD
ÎLES BÉLEP
TANNA
ANATOM
KADAVU
FIJI ISLANDS
8
9
HA'APAI GROUP
NUKU'ALOFA
TONGATAPU GROUP
MAP Q
KENN REEF
WRECK REEF
NOUVELLE CALÉDONIE
ÎLES LOYAUTÉ
NOUMÉA
Tropic of Capricorn
New Caledonia (Fr.)
MAP V
AUSTRALIA
FRASER I.
Brisbane
Gold Coast
SOUTH

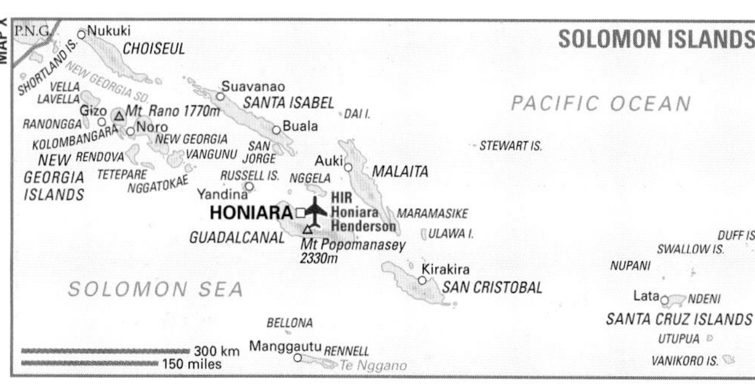
MAP X
SOLOMON ISLANDS
P.N.G.
Nukuki
CHOISEUL
SHORTLAND IS.
NEW GEORGIA SD
VELLA LAVELLA
Suavanao
SANTA ISABEL
PACIFIC OCEAN
Gizo
Mt Rano 1770m
DAI I.
RANONGGA
KOLOMBANGARA
Noro
NEW GEORGIA
VANGUNU
Buala
SAN JORGE
NEW GEORGIA ISLANDS
RENDOVA
TETEPARE
NGGATOKAE
RUSSELL IS.
NGGELA
Auki
MALAITA
STEWART IS.
Yandina
HIR Honiara Henderson
HONIARA
MARAMASIKE
GUADALCANAL
Mt Popomanasey 2330m
ULAWA I.
DUFF IS.
SWALLOW IS.
NUPANI
Kirakira
SAN CRISTOBAL
SOLOMON SEA
Lata
NDENI
SANTA CRUZ ISLANDS
BELLONA
Manggautu
RENNELL
UTUPUA
Te Nggano
VANIKORO IS.
300 km
150 miles

MAP W
VANUATU
TORRES IS.
VANUA LAVA
BANKS IS.
SANTA MARÍA I.
ESPÍRITU SANTO
Mt Tabwémasana 1879m
AOBA
MAÉWO
Luganville
PENTECOST I.
Norsup
AMBRYM
MALAKULA
Lamen
ÉPI
SHEPHERD IS.
VLI Port-Vila Bauerfield
ÉFATÉ
PORT-VILA
CORAL SEA
ERROMANGO
Potnarvon
TANNA
Yasur
300 km
150 miles
ANATOM

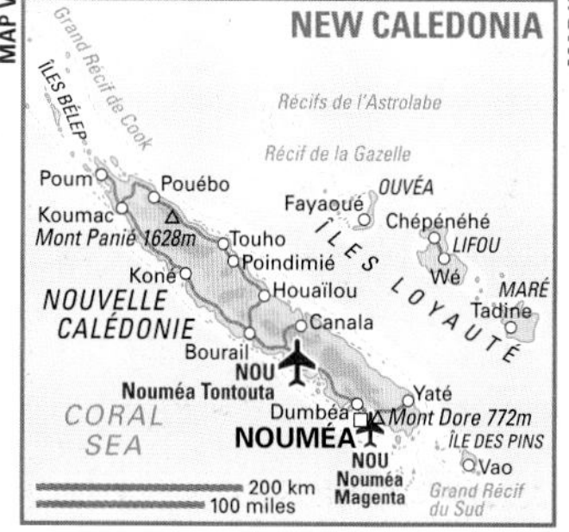
MAP V
NEW CALEDONIA
Grand Récif de Cook
ÎLES BÉLEP
Récifs de l'Astrolabe
Récif de la Gazelle
Poum
Pouébo
OUVÉA
Fayaoué
Koumac
Chépénéhé
Mont Panié 1628m
Touho
LIFOU
Poindimié
ÎLES LOYAUTÉ
Wé
MARÉ
Koné
Houaïlou
Tadine
NOUVELLE CALÉDONIE
Canala
Bourail
NOU
Nouméa Tontouta
Yaté
CORAL SEA
Dumbéa
Mont Dore 772m
NOUMÉA
ÎLE DES PINS
NOU Nouméa Magenta
Vao
Grand Récif du Sud
200 km
100 miles

MAP U
NAVITI
YASAWA GROUP
BLIGH WATER
VITI LEVU
FIJI ISLANDS
Vatu-i-Ra Channel
WAYA
Rakiraki
Tavura
Ba
Vatukoula
MAMANUCA GROUP
Lautoka
Tomanivi 1323m
OVALAU
Levuka
MOTURIKI
NAN Nadi
Nadi
Korovou
Malolo Barrier Reef
Nausori
Sigatoka
Korotogo
Navua
SUVA
SUV Suva Nausori
BEQA
VATULELE
BEQA LAGOON
1 TOKORIKI
2 MONU; MONURIKI; YANUYA
3 MATAMANOA
4 TAVUA
5 MANA
6 LUVUKA; TAI
7 KADAVU
8 NAVINI
9 MALOLO LAILAI
10 MALOLO; QALITO
11 NAMOTU; TAVARUA
100 km
50 miles

MAP T
VANUA LEVU
FIJI ISLANDS
Great Sea Reef
LBS Labasa
Nubu
Naduri
Labasa
RABI
YAQAGA
NATEWA BAY
Nasorolevu 1032m
Votua
Natua
Buca
YADUA
SVU Savusavu
Savusavu
Somosomo
Bua
SAVUSAVU BAY
Bouma
Dama
TAVEUNI
1241m
Vatu-i-Ra Channel
KORO SEA
KORO
Nasau
MAKOGAI
KXF Koro
VITI LEVU
100 km
50 miles

See also... Mediterranean Diving (106); Red Sea Diving (119); Caribbean Diving (180-181)

For more information, see the Contents (2-7).

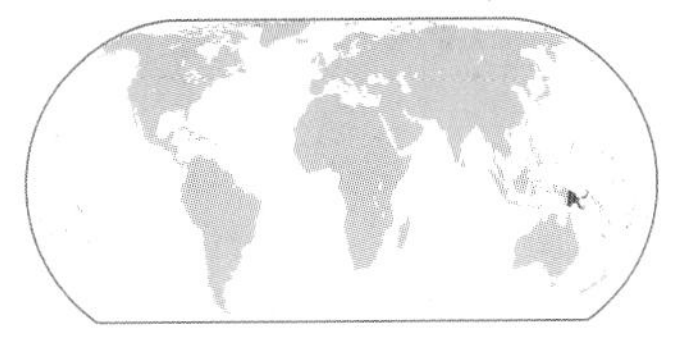

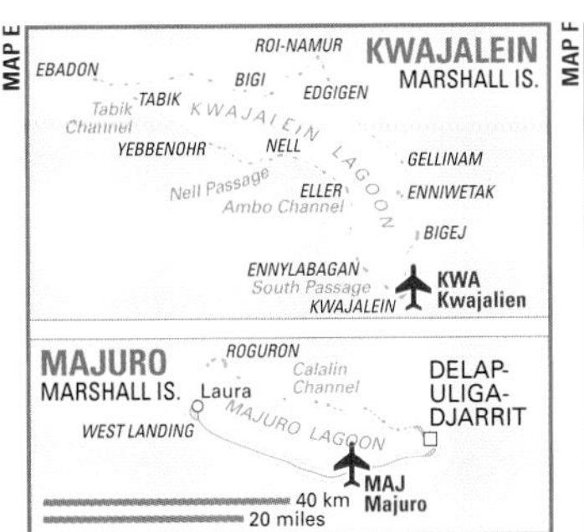
MAP E
KWAJALEIN
MARSHALL IS.
ROI-NAMUR
EBADON
BIGI
EDIGGEN
TABIK
Tabik Channel
YEBBENOHR
NELL
GELLINAM
Nell Passage
ELLER
Ambo Channel
ENNIWETAK
BIGEJ
ENNYLABAGAN
South Passage
KWAJALEIN
KWA
Kwajalien
MAJURO
MARSHALL IS.
ROGURON
Calalin Channel
Laura
DELAP-
ULIGA-
DJARRIT
WEST LANDING
MAJURO LAGOON
MAJ
Majuro
40 km
20 miles

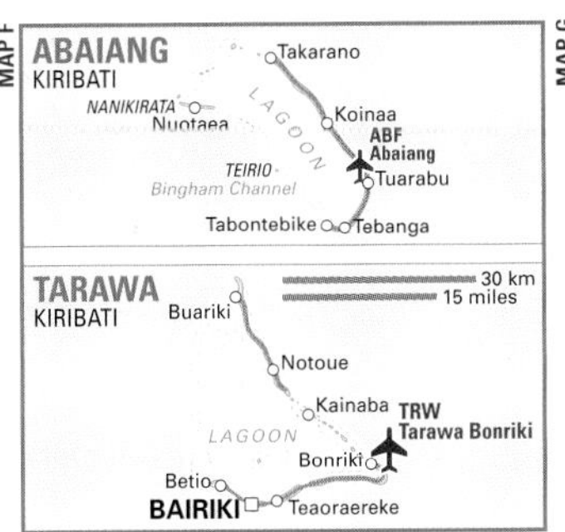
MAP F
ABAIANG
KIRIBATI
Takarano
NANIKIRATA
Nuotaea
Koinaa
ABF
Abaiang
TEIRIO
Bingham Channel
Tuarabu
Tabontebike
Tebanga
TARAWA
KIRIBATI
Buariki
30 km
15 miles
Notoue
Kainaba
TRW
Tarawa Bonriki
LAGOON
Bonriki
Betio
BAIRIKI
Teaoraereke

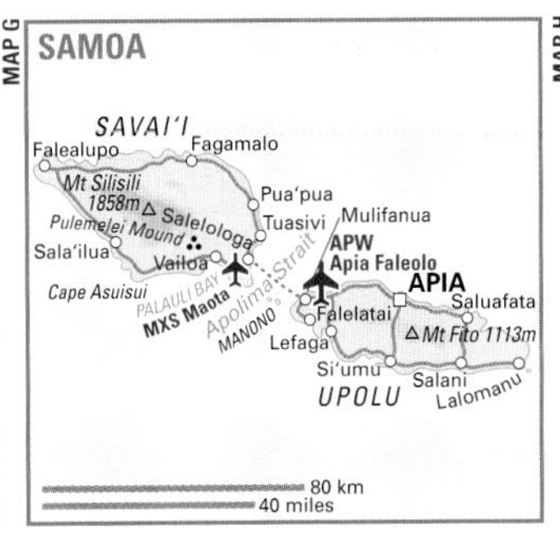
MAP G
SAMOA
SAVAI'I
Falealupo
Fagamalo
Mt Silisili 1858m
Pulemelei Mound
Salelologa
Pua'pua
Tuasivi
Mulifanua
Sala'ilua
Vailoa
APW
Apia Faleolo
Cape Asuisui
MXS Maota
Apolima Strait
MANONO
APIA
Saluafata
Falelatai
Lefaga
Mt Fito 1113m
Si'umu
Salani
UPOLU
Lalomanu
80 km
40 miles

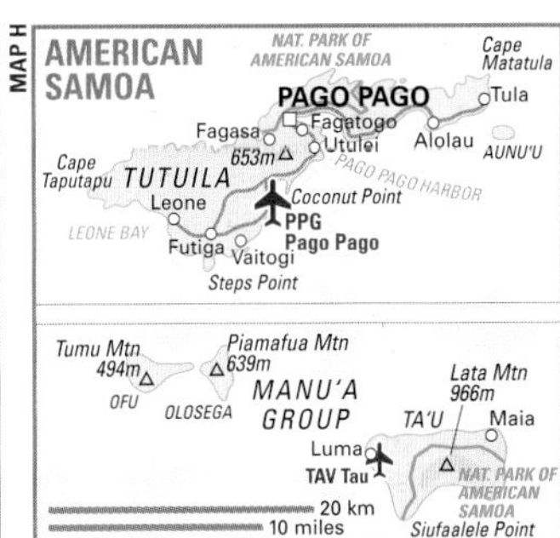
MAP H
AMERICAN SAMOA
NAT. PARK OF AMERICAN SAMOA
Cape Matatula
PAGO PAGO
Tula
Fagatogo
Fagasa
653m
Utulei
Alolau
AUNU'U
Cape Taputapu
TUTUILA
Leone
Coconut Point
PAGO PAGO HARBOR
PPG
Pago Pago
LEONE BAY
Futiga
Vaitogi
Steps Point
Tumu Mtn 494m
Piamafua Mtn 639m
OFU
OLOSEGA
MANU'A GROUP
Lata Mtn 966m
TA'U
Maia
Luma
TAV Tau
NAT. PARK OF AMERICAN SAMOA
Siufaalele Point
20 km
10 miles

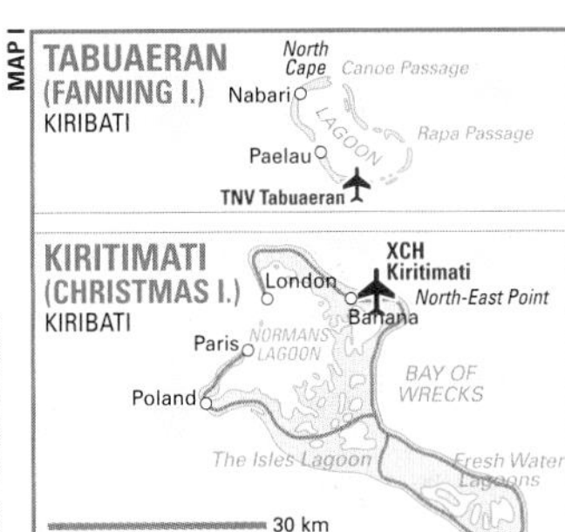
MAP I
TABUAERAN
(FANNING I.)
KIRIBATI
North Cape
Canoe Passage
Nabari
Rapa Passage
Paelau
TNV Tabuaeran
KIRITIMATI
(CHRISTMAS I.)
KIRIBATI
XCH
Kiritimati
London
North-East Point
Banana
Paris
BAY OF WRECKS
Poland
The Isles Lagoon
Fresh Water Lagoons
30 km
15 miles

The names of some South Pacific islands have become synonymous with unspoilt, pristine coral reefs and an exciting, vibrant fish life whereas others have become the very byword for shipwrecks. Many of these destinations already have a well-established diving infrastructure.

The Pacific's premier diving sites:

PALAU (1)
Information is limited but Palau claims one of Micronesia's largest collections of WW2 shipwrecks. Reef walls, coral gardens and stunning drop-offs all teeming with marine life and an abundance of large pelagics

YAP (2)
Famous amongst divers for its large population of resident manta rays, Yap also boasts more than 200 species of coral in addition to some exciting underwater cave systems. The outer coral reefs teem with tropical fish and invertebrates where shark and turtle are common.

GUAM (3)
In addition to numerous wrecks from WW2, Guam has a reputation for drift dives along a wide choice of reefs with outstanding marine life. Two historic shipwrecks lie together: Japanese *Tokai Maru* & German *SMS Cormoran*.

CHUUK LAGOON (4) (formerly Truk Lagoon)
World-famous ship graveyard of approx. 70 Japanese support vessels sunk in 1944 by US forces. Probably the world's no. 1 shipwreck destination for scuba divers.

BIKINI ATOLL (5)
Outstanding wreck diving; a US aircraft carrier, US submarine and Japanese battleship were used in 1946 when the US detonated an atomic bomb to test the effects of a nuclear explosion on a naval fleet. The resultant radioactive fallout left Bikini untouched for almost 50 years. With marine life virtually untouched during that time, there are outstanding examples of shark, manta ray, marlin, tuna and turtle.

GUADALCANAL (6)
The scene of fierce WW2 naval battles and today, 'Iron Bottom Sound' contains hundreds of wrecked aeroplanes and ships, providing an exciting selection of dive sites. The rest of the Islands have excellent natural underwater terrain & marine life.

VANUATU (7)
The many ship and aeroplane wrecks from WW2 include the 22,288 tonne *President Coolidge* - one of the largest accessible shipwrecks in the Pacific. Elsewhere there are spectacular coral reefs, prolific marine life, cave diving and a genuine 'blue hole'

FIJI ISLANDS (8)
Hundreds of small islands where the underwater environment is largely unvisited and unspoilt. Well known for abundant 'soft corals', there are also a number of historic shipwrecks in addition to spectacular walls, caves and large pelagics such as shark, manta ray, turtle, pilot whale and dolphin.

TONGA (9)
Known for its caves, drop-offs and pinnacles, as well as opportunities for diving with whales at certain times of the year, but facilities are limited.

HAWAII (10)
Known for passing migratory whales, Hawaii boasts an almost unique underwater terrain formed by volcanic action with lava formations, walls, caves, archways and lava-tubes - all with abundant marine life. Night diving with manta rays.

Hawaiian Islands
(US)
SEE USA SECTION
NECKER I.
Tropic of Cancer
NIHOA
KAUAI
NIIHAU
OAHU
MOLOKAI
MAUI
Honolulu
10
HAWAII

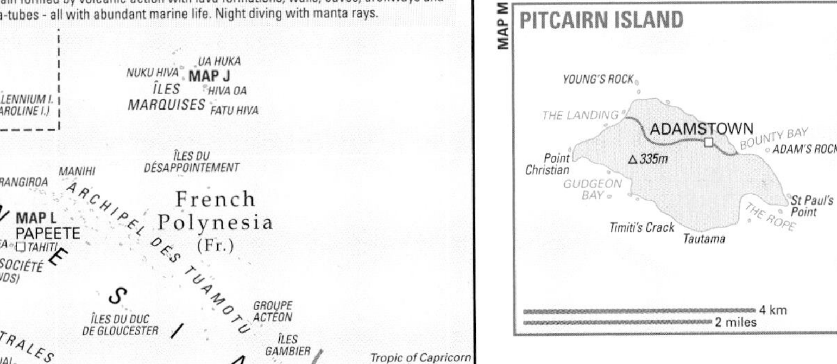
PENRHYN
RAKAHANGA
PUKAPUKA ATOLL
MANIHIKI
NASSAU
SUWARROW
Cook Islands (NZ)
AITUTAKI ATOLL
MAP O
RAROTONGA
AVARUA
MAUKE
MANGAIA
MAP K
BORA BORA
MAP L
PAPEETE
RAIATEA
MOOREA
TAHITI
ARCHIPEL DE LA SOCIÉTÉ (SOCIETY ISLANDS)
ARCHIPEL DES TUAMOTU
French Polynesia (Fr.)
ÎLES AUSTRALES
RURUTU
RIMATARA
TUBUAI
RAIVAVAE
ÎLES DU DUC DE GLOUCESTER
GROUPE ACTÉON
ÎLES GAMBIER
Tropic of Capricorn
OENO I.
HENDERSON I.
DUCIE I.
PITCAIRN I.
ADAMSTOWN
Pitcairn Is. (UK)
MAP M
Easter I. (Chile)
MAP N
SALA-Y-GÓMEZ (Chile)
ÎLOTS DE BASS
PACIFIC OCEAN
Scale at Equator:
3000 kilometres
1500 miles

MAP J
NUKU HIVA
FRENCH POLYNESIA
Cap Matautoa
Aakapa
NHV Nuku Hiva
Hatiheu
Mont Tekao 1224m
TERRE DÉSERTE
Hooumi
Taiohae
Cap Tikapo
Hakaui
HIVA OA
FR. POLY.
Hanaiapa
Cap Balguerie
Hanamenu
AUQ Atuona
Puamau
Pointe Kiukiu
Mont Temetiu 1276m
Atuona
Hekeani
Taaoa
BAIE TAAOA
Pointe Teaehoa
30 km
15 miles

MAP N
EASTER ISLAND
(RAPA NUI / ISLA DE PASCUA)
Cabo Norte
Anakena
Ovahe
Terevaka 510m
Te Pito Kura
Puakatiki 400m
MOTU TAUTARA
Rano Raraku quarry
POIKE
Cabo Roggeveen
Puna Pau quarry
Tongariki
Hanga Piko
Hanga Roa
Punta Cuidado
Mataveri
Vaihu
Orongo
IPC Easter I. Mataveri
Vinapu
Cabo Sur
MOTU NUI
Rano Kau 410m
10 km
5 miles

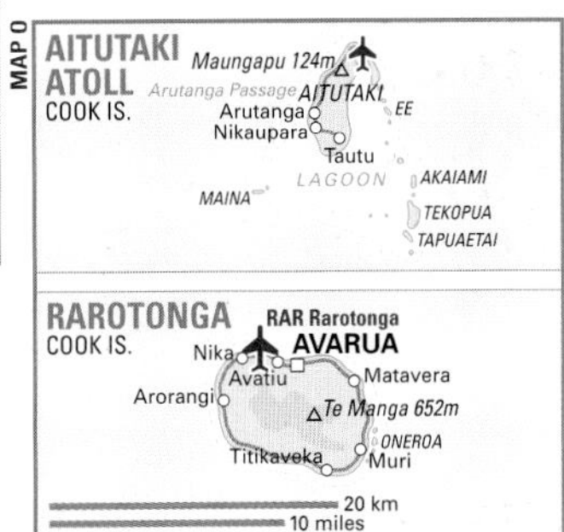
MAP O
AITUTAKI ATOLL
COOK IS.
Maungapu 124m
AITUTAKI
Arutanga Passage
Arutanga
Nikaupara
Tautu
LAGOON
AKAIAMI
MAINA
TEKOPUA
TAPUAETAI
RAROTONGA
COOK IS.
RAR Rarotonga
AVARUA
Nikao
Avatiu
Matavera
Arorangi
Te Manga 652m
ONEROA
Titikaveka
Muri
20 km
10 miles

SOCIETY ISLANDS: LEEWARD GROUP FRENCH POLYNESIA — MAP K; TAHITI & MOOREA FRENCH POLYNESIA — MAP L; PITCAIRN ISLAND — MAP M

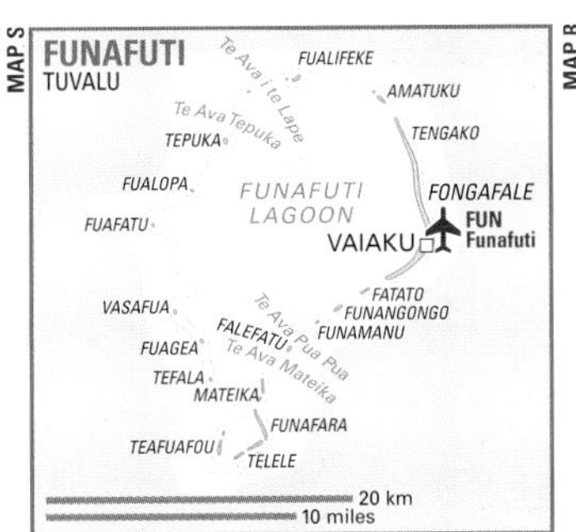
MAP S
FUNAFUTI
TUVALU
FUALIFEKE
Te Ava i te Lape
AMATUKU
Te Ava Tepuka
TEPUKA
TENGAKO
FUALOPA
FUNAFUTI LAGOON
FONGAFALE
FUAFATU
VAIAKU
FUN
Funafuti
FATATO
VASAFUA
FUNANGONGO
FUNAMANU
FUAGEA
FALEFATU
TEFALA
MATEIKA
FUNAFARA
TEAFUAFOU
TELELE
20 km
10 miles

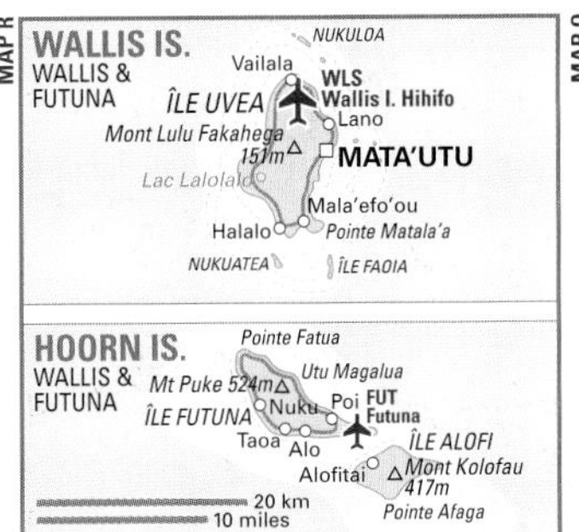
MAP R
WALLIS IS.
WALLIS & FUTUNA
NUKULOA
Vailala
ÎLE UVEA
WLS
Wallis I. Hihifo
Lano
Mont Lulu Fakahega 151m
MATA'UTU
Lac Lalolalo
Mala'efo'ou
Halalo
Pointe Matala'a
NUKUATEA
ÎLE FAOIA
HOORN IS.
WALLIS & FUTUNA
Pointe Fatua
Utu Magalua
Mt Puke 524m
Poi
FUT Futuna
ÎLE FUTUNA
Nuku
Taoa
Alo
ÎLE ALOFI
Alofitai
Mont Kolofau 417m
Pointe Afaga
20 km
10 miles

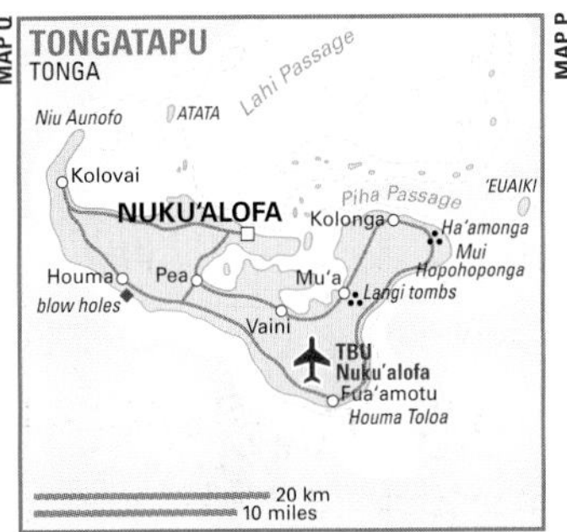
MAP Q
TONGATAPU
TONGA
Lahi Passage
Niu Aunofo
ATATA
Kolovai
Piha Passage
'EUAIKI
NUKU'ALOFA
Kolonga
Ha'amonga
Mui Hopohoponga
Houma
Pea
Mu'a
blow holes
Langi tombs
Vaini
TBU
Nuku'alofa
Fua'amotu
Houma Toloa
20 km
10 miles

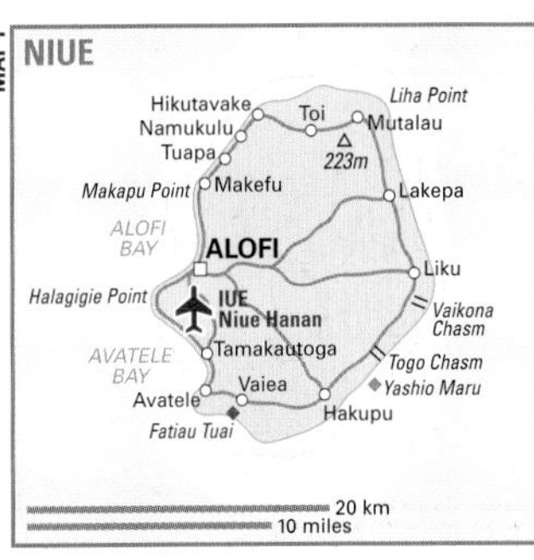
MAP P
NIUE
Liha Point
Hikutavake
Toi
Namukulu
Mutalau
Tuapa
223m
Makapu Point
Makefu
Lakepa
ALOFI BAY
ALOFI
Liku
Halagigie Point
IUE
Niue Hanan
Vaikona Chasm
AVATELE BAY
Tamakautoga
Togo Chasm
Vaiea
Yashio Maru
Avatele
Hakupu
Fatiau Tuai
20 km
10 miles
1000 metres
500 metres
Sea level
200 metres

See also... World Introduction (8-11); Tourism (24-25); Countries A-Z (202-210)

USA & Canada

Key facts	
Number of Countries	2
Area ('000 sq km)	19,343
Population ('000)	328,546
Population Density (per sq km)	17
Gross National Income (US$m)	13,056,668
Visitor Arrivals ('000)	67,907
Visitor Receipts (US$m)	87,324

GNI figures are for 2004. Population figures are taken from the most recent reliable source. Travel figures (UNWTO) are based on overnight stays, not same-day visitors, and are for 2005. For more information see the Countries A-Z section from page 202.

It is almost impossible to overstate North America's staggering achievements over the last fifty or so years. The USA is the richest and most powerful country the world has ever seen, accounting for around a third of the world's GNI, while Canada has long been the standard by which the world's quality of life is judged. The two countries rank third and eleventh respectively in terms of visitor arrivals, accounting for nearly 10% of the world's total. Their combined expenditure on foreign travel is 12% more than Germany's and their combined travel and tourism receipts nearly twice those of Spain. Recent surveys indicate an increasing desire to travel and, now that the regional economy has recovered from the darker days of the early 2000s, an increasing ability to do so. The travel business has without doubt been through a time of flux in recent years, but few industries, and few parts of the world, have a better record of adapting to change.

Travel overview

Travel to the USA and Canada in 2005 increased by 4.1% compared to 2004, rather less than the world average but respectable for such a mature market. Prospects for 2006 and beyond are encouraging and involve what the WTO describes as 'the release of pent-up demand' for the destination, particularly from Europe and Asia. In 2006, visitors to the US are expected to top the 50 million mark, a figure not reached since 2000. In the outbound market, many surveys suggest that Americans' desire to travel abroad is also on the increase, and this may also reach a six-year high in 2006.

The UK remains the USA's largest overseas market, with over 4.3 million British visitors in 2004, an increase of 9% over 2003. This comes on top of smaller growth in 2003 which none the less bucked the general trend in a year when overall visitors to the US dropped by 4%. Japan and Germany are the only other markets above the one-million mark. About 43% of American's 18.1 million overseas (non-Canada or Mexico) outbound trips in 2004 were to Western Europe, with the UK accounting for about one in three. (For more information on the various travel patterns between the USA and UK, see page 25.)

The growth in international air traffic from North America in 2005 was strong, with increases of 7% on trans-Atlantic services and 10% to and from Asia. Taken together with a 7% increase in US outbound travel in 2005, this suggests a revival of American's fondness for air travel. In an unofficial survey conducted among US retail travel agents in September 2005 by tours.com, an overwhelming majority felt that Americans were now more willing to travel abroad than two years previously. Given the size and wealth of the US market, this is likely to be good news for the travel business worldwide.

Some major ('legacy') airlines such as United and US Airways, having survived bankruptcy protections and other turmoils, expect to be posting profits for 2006. By contrast, some of the low-cost airlines are finding life rather tougher than previously, with rising fuel costs and fierce competition generally getting the blame. JetBlue, the USA's fastest-growing airline, showed a quarterly loss for the first time in December 2005, while even Southwest Airlines – the original low-cost carrier – reported in mid-2005 that it needed to save 'hundreds of millions' to maintain its position. Good news for all is the prediction that 2006-7 seems set to see high load factors of up to 90%, 10% better than 2005. This is partly due to a fall in capacity resulting from cutbacks by the majors and partly to a general economic upturn. Fares are so far reflecting this trend: in April 2006, prices were about 10% more than 12 months previously although still some way short of their high-water mark before the events of September 2001.

One important feature of the travel industry worldwide, but which applies particularly strongly to the USA, is the seemingly relentless rise of the internet. Online sales are expected to account for 40% of US travel bookings by the end of 2007. On the face of it, this looks like bad news for the conventional travel agents. In fact, they have been adapting to changed industry circumstances ever since the mid 1990s when airlines began cutting sales commission, and many have since re-invented themselves as niche-market specialists. The most successful agents are not fighting the internet, but seeing it as another way to attract customers and to remain, in the words of ASTA's CEO Kathy Sudeikis, 'an invaluable link between travellers and their destinations.' The North American public, moreover, retains a fondness for agents, with over two thirds still preferring to book that way, particularly with complex or expensive products: 87% of cruises but only 45% of car rentals, for example, are booked offline. Nor is adaptation and change limited to the traditional suppliers: many major US online companies are engaged in mergers and acquisitions or are looking to target business bookings and foreign markets, all with a view of increasing market share and boosting profitability.

Economies

The region's two main economies
Source: World Bank/International Monetary Fund

	GNI US$m 2004	GNI/cap US$ 2004	GDP growth 2004	GDP growth av p/a '97-'06
USA	12,150,931	41,087	3.2	2.2
Canada	905,629	32,805	2.0	2.5

Comings & goings

Visitor arrivals and international departures to and from the USA & Canada, 2004: top ten countries (000s) – colour codings refer to WTA sections
Sources: Office of Travel & Tourism Statistics/CTC

	Visitors to the USA *from*			US outbound *to*	
1	Canada	13,849	1	Mexico	19,369
2	Mexico	11,906	2	Canada	15,056
3	UK	4,303	3	UK	3,692
4	Japan	3,748	4	France	2,407
5	Germany	1,320	5	Italy	1,915
6	France	775	6	Germany	1,750
7	Korea Rep.	627	7	Jamaica	1,258
8	Australia	520	8	China	1,067
9	Italy	471	9	Japan	1,067
10	Netherlands	425	10	Bahamas	1,067

	Visitors to Canada *from*			Canadian outbound *to*	
1	USA	15,088	1	USA	15,127
2	UK	801	2	UK	754
3	Japan	391	3	Mexico	705
4	France	337	4	France	590
5	Germany	296	5	Cuba	570
6	Australia	174	6	Dom. Rep.	527
7	Mexico	169	7	Germany	328
8	Korea Rep	164	8	Italy	255
9	China: HK	115	9	Netherlands	188
10	Netherlands	114	10	China	162

Visitors, state-by-state

Overseas visitors to US states and Canadian provinces 2004, top ten (millions)
Sources: Office of Travel & Tourism Statistics/CTC

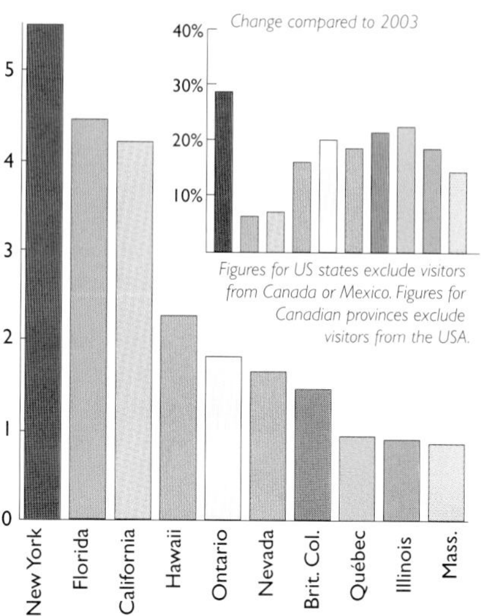
5
4
3
2
1
0
New York
Florida
California
Hawaii
Ontario
Nevada
Brit. Col.
Québec
Illinois
Mass.
Change compared to 2003
40%
30%
20%
10%
Figures for US states exclude visitors from Canada or Mexico. Figures for Canadian provinces exclude visitors from the USA.

Canada

In Canada, the last two years have seen a slow recovery from the havoc caused by the 2003 SARS outbreak in Toronto, although not helped by the recently strong Canadian dollar. Air Canada is certainly prospering, reporting in March 2006 a load factor of nearly 82%, its 24th consecutive month of record-breaking increases, and other carriers like WestJet have posted similar figures.

Canada greatly depends on the US market, which provides around four-fifths of its arrivals. A recent fall-off in this source of visitors has led to Canada recently slipping out of the top ten of the world's most visited countries. The Canadian Tourism Commission has identified several areas for growth, including sharpening Canada's marketing message, positioning it as a alternative destination to the USA, pushing the hard-adventure market and attracting more Chinese and Mexican visitors. It is also seeking to encourage more Canadians to take holidays at home.

The UK is by far Canada's most important overseas market, supplying about 25% of its non-US visitors. It is also the most popular overseas destination for Canadians (754,000 visits in 2004), just ahead of Mexico. Canadians are now more likely to travel outside North America than ten years ago: in 2005, 70% of their trips were to the USA compared to 81% in 1994.

Travel trends

Most travel promotion in the USA (and to a lesser extent in Canada) is conducted at state or regional, rather than national, level, so creating the often confusing illusion of over 60 separate destinations. This is perhaps justified, given the size of some states – 70% of visitors to the USA take in just one and only 13% visit three or more. Whichever state, province or territory is chosen, however, virtually all tastes are catered for. The appeal lingers, too: 76% of 2004 visits to the USA were repeats, only slightly down compared to 1999.

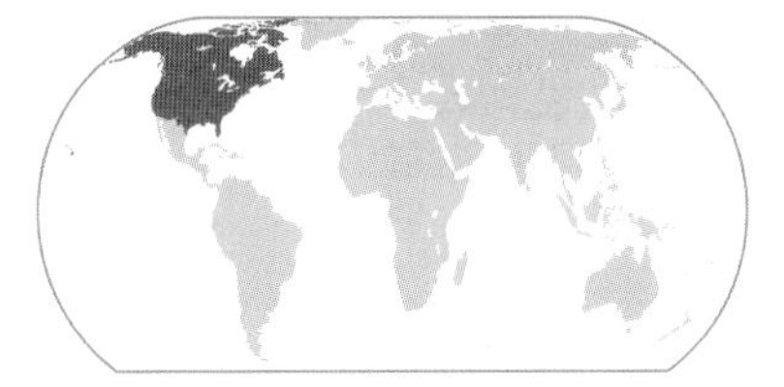

- The US & Canada occupies 14.3% of the world's land area and is home to 5.1% of the world's population.
- The US & Canada accounted for 8.4% of global travel arrivals in 2005.
- International travel and tourism contributed US$87.3 billion to the economies of the US & Canada in 2004.
- The combined GNI of the US & Canada is US$13,056,668 million, 33% of the world's total.
- One in four visitors to the USA in 2004 visited New York City.
- The average traveller to the USA in 2004 spent 16 nights in the country and was visiting for the sixth time since 1999.
- The average American travelling abroad in 2004 spent 16 nights away and was travelling abroad for the 11th time since 1999
- Travel and tourism is responsible directly or indirectly for over 12% of jobs in the USA.
- 44% of overseas visitors to the USA in 2004 entered via New York, Miami or Los Angeles.
- 40% of all US overseas (non-Mexico or Canada) trips in 2004 were to Western Europe.
- 59% of overseas (non-US) visitors to Canada in 2004 were visiting friends or relatives.
- The cost of aviation fuel per gallon was about four times higher in 2005 than in 1977.
- The USA receives more from international travel than any other country. Only the Germans spent more money in 2004, only France received more foreign visitors and only the Germans and the British made more foreign trips.
- In February 2006, only 75% of flight operated by the USA's 19 largest carriers were on time.
- Canada has nearly 29% of the world's coastline. If stretched out, it would go six times round the equator.
- If Manhatten had the same population density as Alaska, 14 people would live there.
- The Statue of Liberty's index finger is eight feet long.
- Mount Rushmore National Memorial took 400 workers over 14 years to create.
- The USA received nearly 14 million visitors from Canada in 2004, more than from any other country. At the other end of the scale, there were 7 visitors from the Vatican City, 6 from the Comoros, 4 from the Pitcairn Islands and 3 from Niue.
- More than five times as many US and Canadian residents went on a cruise in 2004 than in 1980.
- The Buffalo Bills reached four consecutive Super Bowls between 1991 and 1994 (XXV to XXVIII) and lost each time.
- America's first parking meter was installed in Oklahoma City in July 1935.
- Over a third of US residents who travel abroad are from New York or California.
- New Yorkers are at least three times more likely to travel abroad than the inhabitants of any other US city.
- West Edmonton Mall in Alberta, Canada is the largest shopping map in the world.
- Mount Rainier in Washington state received over 1,224 inches of snow during a twelve-month period in 1972-3, making it the world's snowiest place.

North America has some of the most diverse and dynamic cities in the world, including New York, Las Vegas, Chicago, Miami, New Orleans, San Francisco, Los Angeles, Toronto, Québec and Vancouver.

Over a third of international leisure travellers to the USA in 2004 made a visit to an amusement or theme park, and this trend is increasing. 26 of the of the 50 most visited theme parks in the world are in the USA: eight of these are in Florida and between them attracted in 2005 a total of some 60 million visitors – roughly the population of the UK. The cruise market, in- and out-bound, continues to thrive, particularly in Alaska and Hawaii.

New York, Florida and California dominate the US inbound travel market. Nearly 70% of international tourists visit at least one, and the USA's five most-frequented cities are all in these states. Florida and California are also major beach destinations, although every state with a coastline has something to offer. A quarter of all international visitors spend at least part of their holiday in, on or by the ocean. 'Soft adventure' opportunities include skiing, white-water rafting, canoeing and national park trekking in the wilderness areas that both the USA and Canada have diligently preserved. There were over 60 million domestic and international visitors to US national parks in 2004: nearly one in four international tourists went to at least one. Shopping, though, is the number one attraction for foreign visitors, with nearly 90% specifying this as a major leisure activity during their stay. Given the variety and quality of goods available, this is perhaps not surprising and underlines the fact that international visitors benefit a country's economy as a whole, not just its travel and tourism sector.

Destination overview – USA

- **California** – the USA's most populous state has myriad attractions, including not only beaches and theme parks but also city visits and touring. It also offers excellent adventure holiday options.
- **Florida** – the image is mainly one of sun-drenched pleasure centring on beaches and theme parks. Another strength is golf: the state has over 1,000 courses. Florida received nearly 80 million visitors (domestic and international) in 2004, and the industry directly supports over 900,000 jobs.
- **New York** – the state offers probably the world's most intense urban experience, as well as spectacular up-state countryside. Neighbouring New Jersey includes the famous gaming resort of Atlantic City. A quarter of all overseas visitors spend at least some time in New York City.
- **Hawaii** – a firm favourite with the USA's Far East market. Tourism is the state's main industry, and its tourism promotion budget is traditionally the highest in the country. There is a growing trend for cruise ships to be based in Honolulu.
- **Nevada** – a state where tourism accounts for over a third of all state employment and home to the comparison-defying city of Las Vegas.
- **Washington DC, Virginia** and **Maryland** – all are strongly associated with some of the country's historic events and have a strong 'heritage' appeal.
- The **New England** states of Vermont, Connecticut, Rhode Island, New Hampshire, Massachusetts and Maine – popular for family touring and skiing.
- The **Deep South** – the region is attracting ever-increasing interest, particularly New Orleans for its Cajun culture and jazz (although the city and surrounding area will take some time to recover from the devastation of Hurricane Katrina in August 2005); and Georgia, one of the country's fastest growing economies.
- The **Rocky Mountain** states – these offer a range of adventure activities including rafting and trekking to mountain climbing and cycling..
- **Texas** – this vast and diverse state has recently been targeting overseas markets.

For more information on visitor numbers to each state, please see page 163.

Market share

US international arrivals and tourism receipts as a percentage of global totals, and annual changes in US international arrivals, 1991-2004

Source: Office of Travel & Tourism Statistics

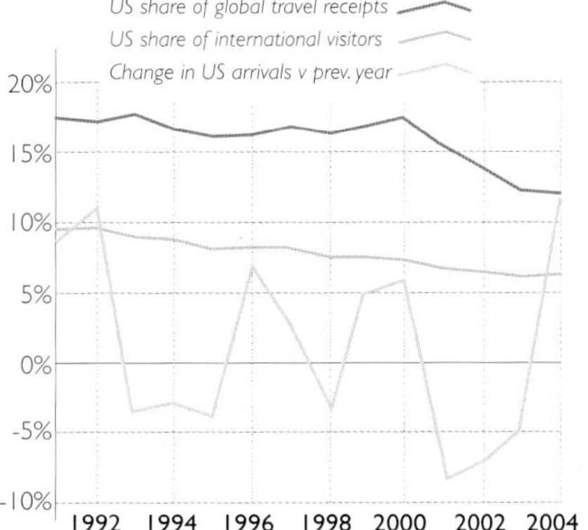

US share of global travel receipts
US share of international visitors
Change in US arrivals v prev. year
20%
15%
10%
5%
0%
-5%
-10%
1992
1994
1996
1998
2000
2002
2004

Visitors, city-by-city

Overseas visitors to US and Canadian cities 2004, top ten (millions)

Sources: Office of Travel & Tourism Statistics/CTC

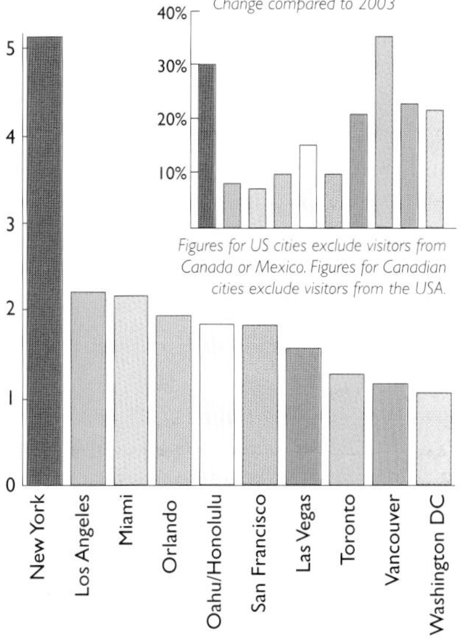

Change compared to 2003
40%
30%
20%
10%
5
4
3
2
1
0
Figures for US cities exclude visitors from Canada or Mexico. Figures for Canadian cities exclude visitors from the USA.
New York
Los Angeles
Miami
Orlando
Oahu/Honolulu
San Francisco
Las Vegas
Toronto
Vancouver
Washington DC

Destination overview – Canada

- Traditionally, tours took in the east or the west and skipped the wilderness in-between. This imbalance is now being redressed, and an increasing number of visits now take in one of Canada's many national parks or, for those with a taste for the even wider outdoors, the Western and Northern wilderness regions. Skiing has long been a popular attraction.
- Eastern Canada's highlights include the Niagara Falls, and Ontario and Québec, large provinces with excellent variety for touring and city visiting. The Atlantic coast provinces are attracting increased interest, particularly with the US short-break market.
- Many visitors to Vancouver combine a self-drive tour of British Columbia with Alberta on the eastern side of the Rockies, or with the Pacific states of the USA.
- Theme-based holidays, such as cultural heritage, wildlife, adventure and gastronomy, are becoming more popular.

Problem areas

US involvement in Iraq and Afghanistan may contribute to security problems that could discourage travel to or from North America. Fluctuations in the value of the US dollar, airline bankruptcies, further oil price rises and any economic downturn may lead to similar results.

Visitors

Visitor arrivals 2004 *Source: WTO*

	Visitors (thousands)	Change since 1997
USA	46,082	-3.5%
Canada	19,150	8.4%

North America: Physical

See also... World Physical (12-13); World Political (14-15); World Climate (16); Caribbean (178-181); Mexico (182-183); Central America (184)

The listings above refer to a selection of related themes. For more information, see the Contents (2-7).

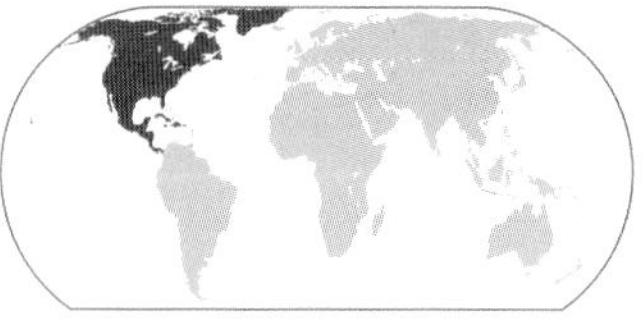

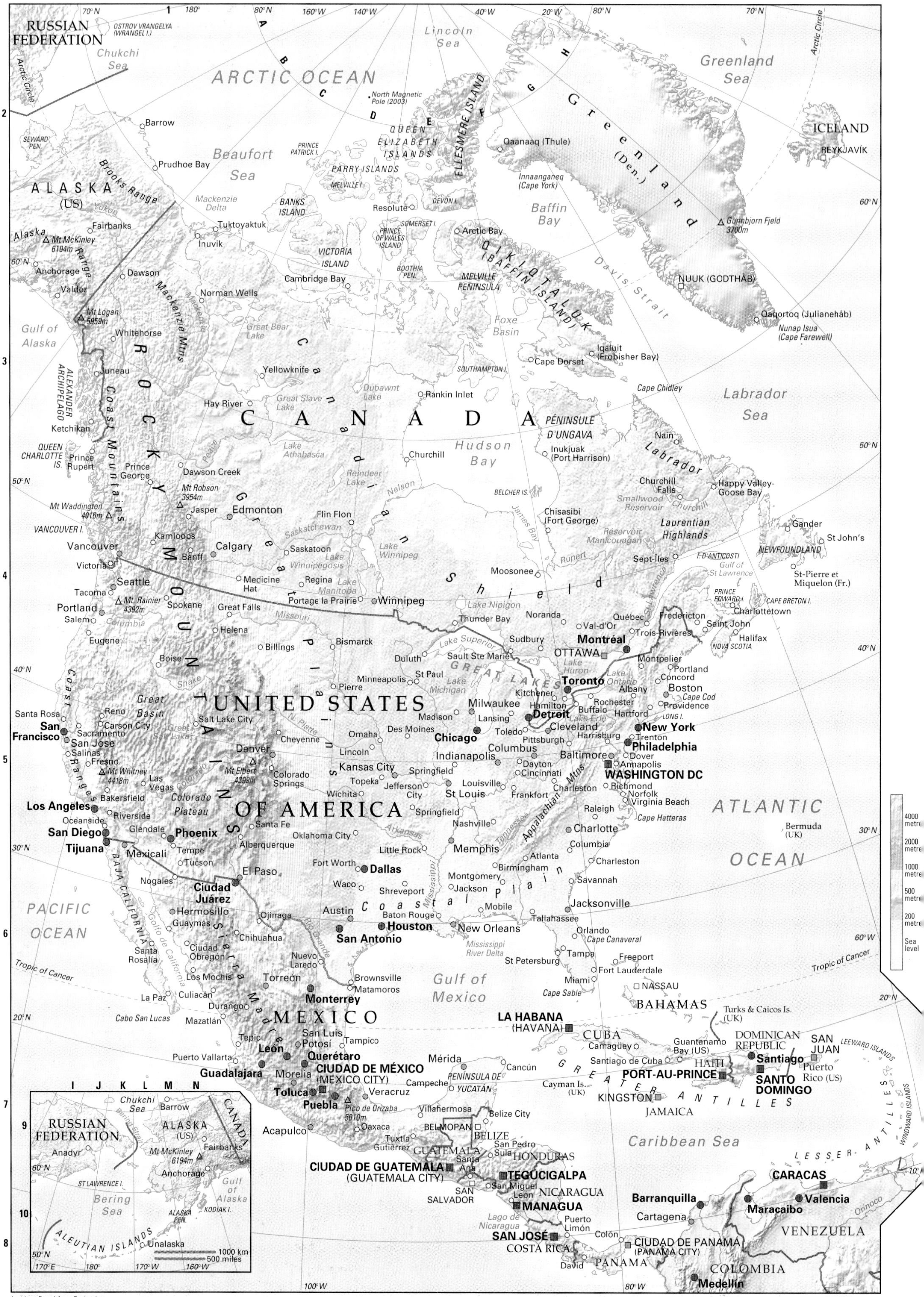

RUSSIAN FEDERATION
OSTROV VRANGELYA (WRANGEL I.)
Chukchi Sea
Arctic Circle
ARCTIC OCEAN
Lincoln Sea
Greenland Sea
North Magnetic Pole (2003)
QUEEN ELIZABETH ISLANDS
ELLESMERE ISLAND
Greenland (Den.)
ICELAND
REYKJAVÍK
Barrow
SEWARD PEN.
Beaufort Sea
PRINCE PATRICK I.
PARRY ISLANDS
MELVILLE I.
Qaanaaq (Thule)
Innaanganeq (Cape York)
Prudhoe Bay
Brooks Range
ALASKA (US)
Mackenzie Delta
BANKS ISLAND
Resolute
DEVON I.
Baffin Bay
Yukon
Fairbanks
Tuktoyaktuk
Inuvik
SOMERSET I.
PRINCE OF WALES ISLAND
Arctic Bay
Gunnbjorn Fjeld 3700m
Alaska Range
Mt McKinley 6194m
VICTORIA ISLAND
QIKIQTALUK (BAFFIN ISLAND)
Anchorage
Dawson
Cambridge Bay
BOOTHIA PEN.
MELVILLE PENINSULA
Davis Strait
NUUK (GODTHÅB)
Valdez
Mackenzie Mtns
Norman Wells
Qaqortoq (Julianehåb)
Nunap Isua (Cape Farewell)
Mt Logan 5959m
Gulf of Alaska
Whitehorse
Great Bear Lake
Foxe Basin
Iqaluit (Frobisher Bay)
Cape Dorset
Juneau
ALEXANDER ARCHIPELAGO
ROCKY MOUNTAINS
Yellowknife
SOUTHAMPTON I.
Cape Chidley
Labrador Sea
Coast Mountains
Hay River
Great Slave Lake
Dubawnt Lake
Rankin Inlet
CANADA
Canadian Shield
PÉNINSULE D'UNGAVA
Ketchikan
Nain
QUEEN CHARLOTTE IS.
Prince Rupert
Lake Athabasca
Churchill
Hudson Bay
Inukjuak (Port Harrison)
Labrador
Prince George
Dawson Creek
Reindeer Lake
Nelson
Churchill Falls
Happy Valley-Goose Bay
Mt Robson 3954m
BELCHER IS.
Smallwood Reservoir
Churchill
Mt Waddington 4016m
Jasper
Edmonton
Great Plains
Flin Flon
Chisasibi (Fort George)
James Bay
Laurentian Highlands
Gander
VANCOUVER I.
Saskatchewan
Réservoir Manicouagan
St John's
Kamloops
Vancouver
Calgary
Saskatoon
Lake Winnipeg
NEWFOUNDLAND
Banff
Lake Winnipegosis
Rupert
Sept-Îles
Victoria
Medicine Hat
Regina
Lake Manitoba
Moosonee
Î. D'ANTICOSTI
Gulf of St Lawrence
St-Pierre et Miquelon (Fr.)
Seattle
Tacoma
Mt Rainier 4392m
Spokane
Portage la Prairie
Winnipeg
Lake Nipigon
St Lawrence
PRINCE EDWARD I.
CAPE BRETON I.
Portland
Salem
Columbia
Great Falls
Missouri
Thunder Bay
Noranda
Québec
Charlottetown
Fredericton
Helena
Val-d'Or
Trois-Rivières
Saint John
Halifax
NOVA SCOTIA
Eugene
Billings
Bismarck
Lake Superior
Sudbury
Montréal
Duluth
Sault Ste Marie
OTTAWA
Montpelier
Boise
Snake
GREAT LAKES
Lake Huron
Lake Ontario
Portland
Concord
Minneapolis
St Paul
Lake Michigan
Toronto
Albany
Boston
Cape Cod
Coast Ranges
Pierre
Kitchener
Hamilton
Rochester
Providence
Great Basin
UNITED STATES OF AMERICA
Milwaukee
Buffalo
Hartford
LONG I.
Santa Rosa
Reno
Salt Lake City
Madison
Lansing
Detroit
Lake Erie
San Francisco
Carson City
Great Salt Lake
N. Platte
Des Moines
Cleveland
New York
Sacramento
Cheyenne
Omaha
Chicago
Toledo
Pittsburgh
Harrisburg
Trenton
Philadelphia
San Jose
Salinas
Denver
Lincoln
Indianapolis
Columbus
Baltimore
Dover
Fresno
Mt Elbert 4399m
Kansas City
Springfield
Dayton
Annapolis
WASHINGTON DC
Mt Whitney 4418m
Las Vegas
Colorado
Colorado Springs
Topeka
Jefferson City
Louisville
Cincinnati
Charleston
Richmond
Norfolk
Virginia Beach
Bakersfield
Colorado Plateau
Wichita
St Louis
Frankfort
Appalachian Mtns
Los Angeles
Riverside
Springfield
Raleigh
ATLANTIC OCEAN
Oceanside
Santa Fe
Nashville
Cape Hatteras
Glendale
Arkansas
Bermuda (UK)
San Diego
Phoenix
Tennessee
Charlotte
Tijuana
Tempe
Oklahoma City
Albuquerque
Little Rock
Memphis
Columbia
Mexicali
Tucson
Atlanta
Charleston
BAJA CALIFORNIA
Fort Worth
Dallas
Birmingham
El Paso
Mississippi
Montgomery
Nogales
Ciudad Juárez
Waco
Shreveport
Jackson
Savannah
Coastal Plain
PACIFIC OCEAN
Hermosillo
Austin
Baton Rouge
Mobile
Jacksonville
Ojinaga
Tallahassee
Guaymas
Golfo de California
Chihuahua
Rio Grande
San Antonio
Houston
New Orleans
Orlando
Cape Canaveral
Sierra Madre
Santa Rosalía
Ciudad Obregón
Mississippi River Delta
Tampa
St Petersburg
Freeport
Nuevo Laredo
Fort Lauderdale
Tropic of Cancer
Los Mochis
Torreón
Brownsville
Matamoros
Gulf of Mexico
Miami
NASSAU
La Paz
Culiacán
Monterrey
Cape Sable
BAHAMAS
Durango
Turks & Caicos Is. (UK)
Cabo San Lucas
Mazatlán
MEXICO
LA HABANA (HAVANA)
CUBA
Tepic
San Luis Potosí
Tampico
Camagüey
Guantanamo Bay (US)
DOMINICAN REPUBLIC
SAN JUAN
LEEWARD ISLANDS
Puerto Vallarta
León
Querétaro
Mérida
Santiago de Cuba
HAITI
Santiago
Guadalajara
Morelia
CIUDAD DE MÉXICO (MEXICO CITY)
PENÍNSULA DE YUCATÁN
Cancún
GREATER ANTILLES
PORT-AU-PRINCE
SANTO DOMINGO
Puerto Rico (US)
Toluca
Puebla
Veracruz
Campeche
Cayman Is. (UK)
KINGSTON
JAMAICA
Pico de Orizaba 5610m
Villahermosa
Belize City
WINDWARD ISLANDS
Acapulco
Oaxaca
BELMOPAN
BELIZE
Tuxtla Gutiérrez
GUATEMALA
San Pedro Sula
HONDURAS
Caribbean Sea
LESSER ANTILLES
CIUDAD DE GUATEMALA (GUATEMALA CITY)
Santa Ana
TEGUCIGALPA
CARACAS
SAN SALVADOR
San Miguel
León
NICARAGUA
Barranquilla
Maracaibo
Valencia
MANAGUA
Cartagena
Lago de Nicaragua
Puerto Limón
Orinoco
SAN JOSÉ
Colón
CIUDAD DE PANAMÁ (PANAMA CITY)
VENEZUELA
COSTA RICA
David
PANAMA
COLOMBIA
Medellín

4000 metres
2000 metres
1000 metres
500 metres
200 metres
Sea level

RUSSIAN FEDERATION
Chukchi Sea
Barrow
ALASKA (US)
CANADA
Bering Strait
Anadyr
Fairbanks
Mt McKinley 6194m
Anchorage
ST LAWRENCE I.
Gulf of Alaska
Bering Sea
ALASKA PEN.
KODIAK I.
ALEUTIAN ISLANDS
Unalaska
1000 km
500 miles

Lambert Equal Area Projection

2000 kilometres
1000 miles

See also... World Climate (16); Regional Climate Terms (196); Caribbean (178-181); Mexico (182-183); Central America (184)

The listings above refer to a selection of related themes. For more information, see the Contents (2-7).

TEMPERATURE CONVERSION

°Celsius	–10	0	10	20	30	40
°Fahrenheit	14	32	50	68	86	104

RAINFALL CONVERSION

Millimetres	102	203	305	406	508	610
Inches	4	8	12	16	20	24

WINTER

TEMPERATURE (January average, degrees Celsius)
- 20° and over
- 10° – 19°
- 0° – 9°
- Minus 10° – minus 1°
- Minus 20° – minus 11°
- Below minus 20°

RAINFALL (November to April total)
- 500mm and over
- 250 – 499mm
- Less than 250mm

PREVAILING WIND shown as white arrows

CHINOOK
A warm dry wind which blows down the eastern slopes of the Rockies, rapidly melting lying snow

NORTH SLOPE, BROOKS RANGE, Kaktovik, Mackenzie Delta, Aklavik, Arctic Circle, Fairbanks, ALASKA RANGE, Anchorage, YUKON PLATEAU, MACKENZIE MOUNTAINS, Norman Wells, Whitehorse, Juneau, KODIAK I., ALEXANDER ARCHIPELAGO, GULF OF ALASKA, Prince Rupert, QUEEN CHARLOTTE IS., COAST MOUNTAINS, Prince George, Yellowknife, Great Slave Lake, Fort Nelson, Lake Athabasca, Reindeer Lake, Edmonton, The Pas, VANCOUVER I., Vancouver, ROCKY MOUNTAINS, CANADIAN SHIELD, KING WILLIAM I., BOOTHIA PENINSULA, Garry Lake, Dubawnt Lake, Baker Lake, SOUTHAMPTON I., FOXE BASIN, COATS I., MANSEL I., HUDSON BAY, Churchill, BELCHER IS., Inukjuak, JAMES BAY, AKIMISKI I., LABRADOR, Goose Bay, LAURENTIDE SCARP, ANTICOSTI I., NEWFOUNDLAND, Gulf of St Lawrence, St John's, PRINCE EDWARD I., CAPE BRETON I., Halifax, NOVA SCOTIA, Regina, Winnipeg, Lake Winnipeg, Lake of the Woods, Lake Superior, Lake Huron, Lake Michigan, Lake Ontario, L. Erie, GREAT PLAINS, Bismarck, Minneapolis, Montréal, Toronto, Portland, CASCADE RANGE, Billings, Boise, COLUMBIA PLATEAU, Great Salt Lake, Cheyenne, Chicago, Detroit, Boston, Eureka, COAST RANGES, SIERRA NEVADA, GREAT BASIN, Salt Lake City, Omaha, Cincinnati, APPALACHIAN MOUNTAINS, New York, Washington DC, San Francisco, COLORADO PLATEAU, Dodge City, St Louis, OZARK PLATEAU, Los Angeles, Albuquerque, Little Rock, Nashville, COASTAL PLAIN, Charleston, Phoenix, LLANO ESTACADO, El Paso, Abilene, EDWARDS PLATEAU, Houston, New Orleans, Jacksonville, BERMUDA, Hamilton, ATLANTIC OCEAN, BAJA CALIFORNIA, Guaymas, SIERRA MADRE OCCIDENTAL, SIERRA MADRE ORIENTAL, Monterrey, GULF OF MEXICO, FLORIDA, Miami, Nassau, BAHAMA IS., Tropic of Cancer, La Paz, Mazatlán, Mérida, Havana, CUBA, YUCATAN PENINSULA, Santo Domingo, HISPANIOLA, GREATER ANTILLES, San Juan, Mexico City, PACIFIC OCEAN, Kingston, Belize City, SIERRA MADRE DEL SUR, Acapulco, CARIBBEAN SEA, Roseau, Guatemala City, LESSER ANTILLES, Willemstad, Bridgetown, Managua, Barranquilla, Caracas, Port of Spain

DAILY TEMPERATURES and **MONTHLY RAINFALL** (averages)

Winnipeg | New York

°C: 25, 20, 15, 10, 5, 0, –5, –10, –15
mm: 150, 100, 50, 0

J F M A M J J A S O N D | J F M A M J J A S O N D

Columbus Travel Guides' *World Travel Guide* contains detailed climate charts for every country in the world, including temperature, rainfall, sunshine and humidity

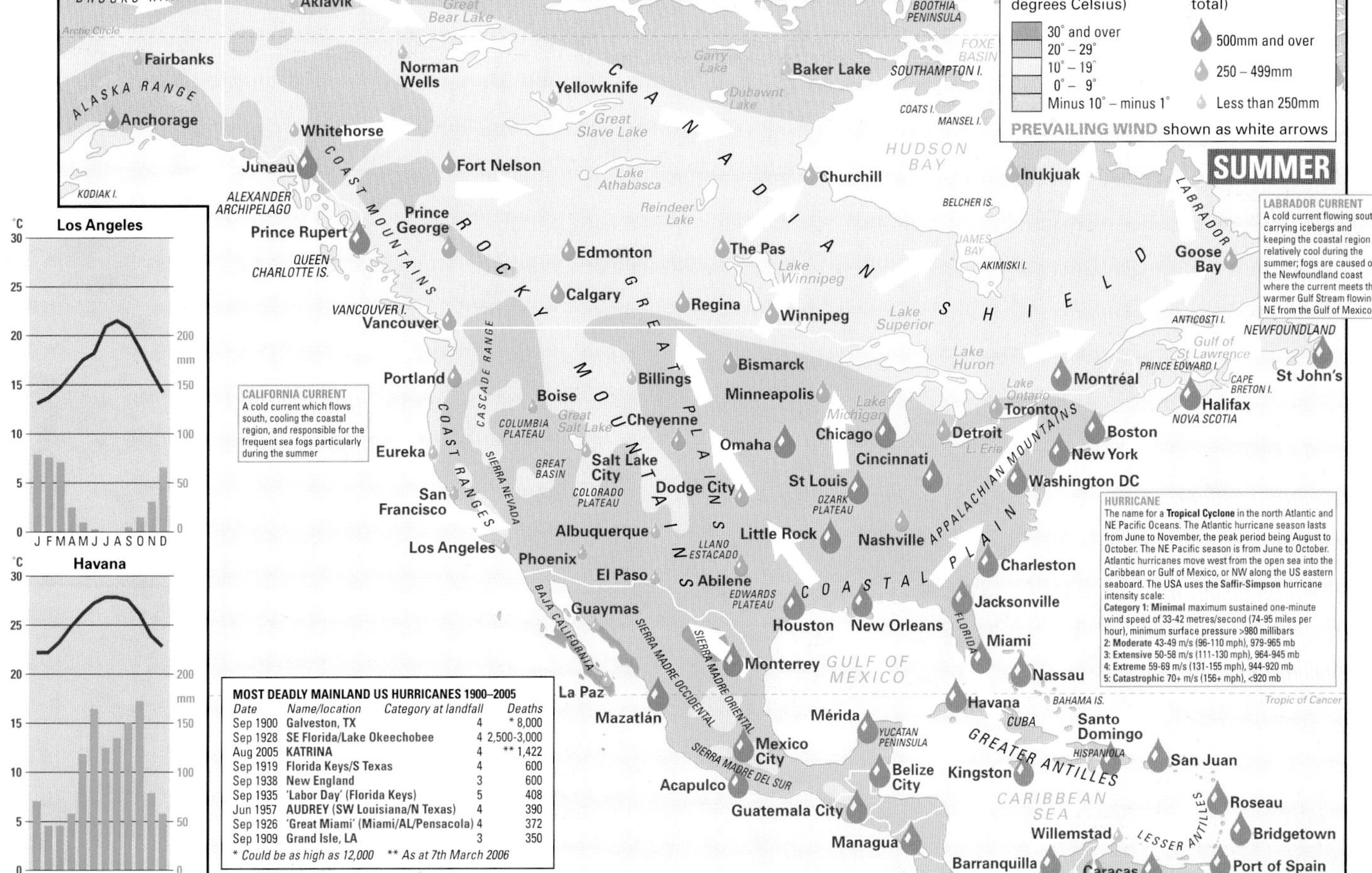
SUMMER
TEMPERATURE (July average, degrees Celsius)
30° and over
20° – 29°
10° – 19°
0° – 9°
Minus 10° – minus 1°
RAINFALL (May to October total)
500mm and over
250 – 499mm
Less than 250mm
PREVAILING WIND shown as white arrows
LABRADOR CURRENT
A cold current flowing south, carrying icebergs and keeping the coastal region relatively cool during the summer; fogs are caused off the Newfoundland coast where the current meets the warmer Gulf Stream flowing NE from the Gulf of Mexico
CALIFORNIA CURRENT
A cold current which flows south, cooling the coastal region, and responsible for the frequent sea fogs particularly during the summer
HURRICANE
The name for a Tropical Cyclone in the north Atlantic and NE Pacific Oceans. The Atlantic hurricane season lasts from June to November, the peak period being August to October. The NE Pacific season is from June to October. Atlantic hurricanes move west from the open sea into the Caribbean or Gulf of Mexico, or NW along the US eastern seaboard. The USA uses the Saffir-Simpson hurricane intensity scale:
Category 1: Minimal maximum sustained one-minute wind speed of 33-42 metres/second (74-95 miles per hour), minimum surface pressure >980 millibars
2: Moderate 43-49 m/s (96-110 mph), 979-965 mb
3: Extensive 50-58 m/s (111-130 mph), 964-945 mb
4: Extreme 59-69 m/s (131-155 mph), 944-920 mb
5: Catastrophic 70+ m/s (156+ mph), <920 mb
Los Angeles
Havana
°C
mm
J F M A M J J A S O N D
VICTORIA ISLAND
Great Bear Lake
Calgary
Tropic of Cancer

MOST DEADLY MAINLAND US HURRICANES 1900–2005

Date	Name/location	Category at landfall	Deaths
Sep 1900	Galveston, TX	4	* 8,000
Sep 1928	SE Florida/Lake Okeechobee	4	2,500-3,000
Aug 2005	KATRINA	4	** 1,422
Sep 1919	Florida Keys/S Texas	4	600
Sep 1938	New England	3	600
Sep 1935	'Labor Day' (Florida Keys)	5	408
Jun 1957	AUDREY (SW Louisiana/N Texas)	4	390
Sep 1926	'Great Miami' (Miami/AL/Pensacola)	4	372
Sep 1909	Grand Isle, LA	3	350

* Could be as high as 12,000 ** As at 7th March 2006

See also... UNESCO Cultural Heritage (52-53); Europe Historical (58-59), Asia Historical (128); USA & Canada Museums & Art Galleries (159) • cont >

The listings above refer to a selection of related themes. For more information, see the Contents (2-7).

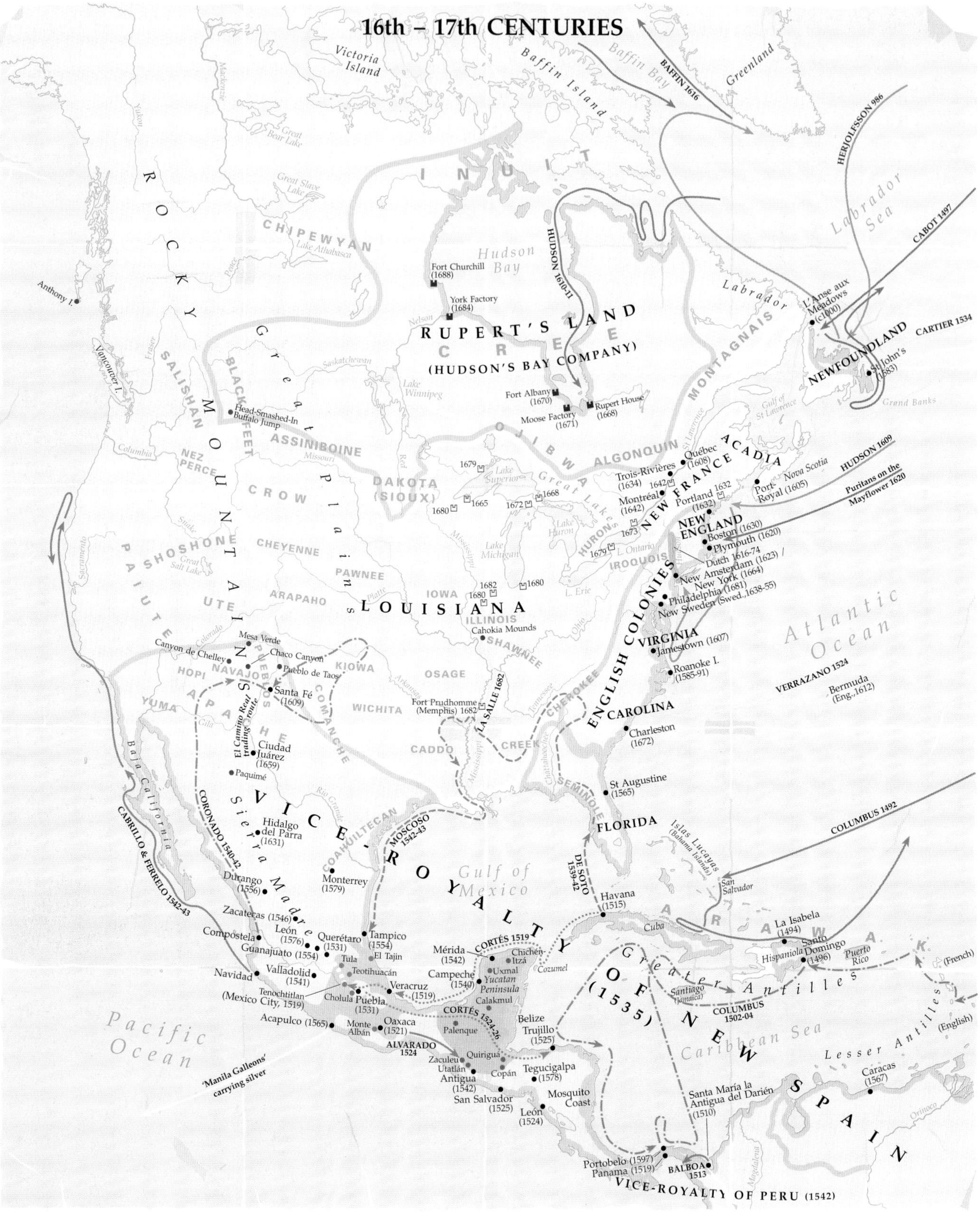

16th – 17th CENTURIES

Victoria Island
Baffin Island
Baffin Bay
BAFFIN 1616
Greenland
HERJOLFSSON 986
Labrador Sea
CABOT 1497
Great Bear Lake
Great Slave Lake
Lake Athabasca
INUIT
CHIPEWYAN
Hudson Bay
HUDSON 1610-11
Fort Churchill (1688)
York Factory (1684)
Labrador
L'Anse aux Meadows (c.1000)
NEWFOUNDLAND
CARTIER 1534
St John's (1583)
Grand Banks
RUPERT'S LAND (HUDSON'S BAY COMPANY)
CREE
MONTAGNAIS
Fort Albany (1670)
Moose Factory (1671)
Rupert House (1668)
Lake Winnipeg
Saskatchewan
Anthony I.
Vancouver I.
ROCKY MOUNTAINS
Great Plains
SALISHAN
BLACKFEET
Head-Smashed-In Buffalo Jump
ASSINIBOINE
NEZ PERCE
CROW
DAKOTA (SIOUX)
OJIBWA
ALGONQUIN
Gulf of St Lawrence
Québec (1608)
Trois-Rivières (1634)
Montréal (1642)
ACADIA
NEW FRANCE
Nova Scotia
Port-Royal (1605)
HUDSON 1609
Puritans on the Mayflower 1620
Portland 1632 (1632)
NEW ENGLAND
Boston (1630)
Plymouth (1620)
Dutch 1616-74
New Amsterdam (1623) / New York (1664)
Philadelphia (1681)
New Sweden (Swed.,1638-55)
HURONS
IROQUOIS
Lake Superior
Lake Huron
Lake Michigan
L. Ontario
L. Erie
Great Lakes
SHOSHONE
CHEYENNE
PAWNEE
ARAPAHO
UTE
PAIUTE
IOWA
LOUISIANA
ILLINOIS
Cahokia Mounds
SHAWNEE
ENGLISH COLONIES
VIRGINIA
Jamestown (1607)
Roanoke I. (1585-91)
Atlantic Ocean
VERRAZANO 1524
Bermuda (Eng.,1612)
Mesa Verde
Canyon de Chelly
Chaco Canyon
Pueblo de Taos
HOPI
NAVAJO
PUEBLOS
Santa Fé (1609)
KIOWA
OSAGE
COMANCHE
WICHITA
YUMA
APACHE
El Camino Real trading route
Ciudad Juárez (1659)
Paquimé
Fort Prudhomme (Memphis) 1682
LA SALLE 1682
CADDO
CREEK
CHEROKEE
CAROLINA
Charleston (1672)
SEMINOLE
St Augustine (1565)
FLORIDA
Islas Lucayas (Bahama Islands)
COLUMBUS 1492
San Salvador
CORONADO 1540-42
CABRILLO & FERRELO 1542-43
Baja California
VICE-ROYALTY OF NEW SPAIN (1535)
Hidalgo del Parra (1631)
Sierra Madre
COAHUILTECAN
MOSCOSO 1542-43
DE SOTO 1539-42
Monterrey (1579)
Gulf of Mexico
Durango (1556)
Zacatecas (1546)
Havana (1515)
Cuba
La Isabela (1494)
Santo Domingo (1496)
Hispaniola
Puerto Rico
(French)
(English)
Compostela
León (1576)
Querétaro (1531)
Tampico (1554)
Guanajuato (1554)
Tula
El Tajín
Mérida (1542)
CORTÉS 1519
Chichén-Itzá
Cozumel
Uxmal
Yucatan Peninsula
Navidad
Valladolid (1541)
Teotihuacán
Campeche (1540)
Tenochtitlan (Mexico City, 1519)
Cholula
Puebla (1531)
Veracruz (1519)
Calakmul
CORTÉS 1524-26
Greater Antilles
Santiago (Jamaica)
COLUMBUS 1502-04
Pacific Ocean
Acapulco (1565)
Monte Albán
Oaxaca (1521)
Palenque
Belize
Trujillo (1525)
Caribbean Sea
Lesser Antilles
ALVARADO 1524
Quiriguá
Zaculeu
Utatlán
Antigua (1542)
Copán
Tegucigalpa (1578)
'Manila Galleons' carrying silver
San Salvador (1525)
León (1524)
Mosquito Coast
Santa María la Antigua del Darién (1510)
Caracas (1567)
Orinoco
Magdalena
Portobelo (1597)
Panama (1519)
BALBOA 1513
VICE-ROYALTY OF PERU (1542)

ALGONQUIN
Major North American Indian tribes at the time of the first European settlement
Hundreds of different tribes with different languages populated the continent. Woodlands Indians (E of the Mississippi) developed a settled lifestyle with farming; Plains Indians followed and hunted bison; in the South-West irrigation was developed to farm the desert and the houses built of thick stone or adobe; on the Pacific coast the sea and rivers provided much of the food.

•
Some important archaeological and historic North American Indian sites

Aztec Empire under Montezuma II, 1509-19

Maya civilisation to 1524

Spanish explorers/ conquistadors
Columbus, a Genoan in the service of Spain's Ferdinand and Isabella, believed he had reached Asia. He undertook four journeys of discovery and exploration around the Caribbean, the first and fourth voyages are shown here.

Herjolfsson (Norse trader), 986
First discover of North America, settlements such as L'Anse aux Meadows lasted until the early 11th century

English explorers
John Cabot, a Venetian in the service of England, intended to reach Asia by a northern route.

French explorers

Dutch explorers

European powers in the New World, 1682
In Central America settlement was boosted by discovery of silver deposits. In the Caribbean, sugar plantations became valuable assets and the focus for imperial rivalry. Further north, settlers in search of land and freedom of religion populated the eastern seaboard, whilst traders explored inland, supported by fortified trading posts. The rich fishing grounds off Newfoundland spurred early exploration; later around the Great Lakes and Hudson Bay a valuable trade in fur developed.

Limit of territory controlled by:

Spain
England
France
The Netherlands

English fort or trading post
French fort or trading post
( ) Year of foundation

See also... cont < • US National Parks Service (166-167); Mexico (182); Central America (184); Latin America Historical (187)

The listings above refer to a selection of related themes. For more information, see the Contents (2-7).

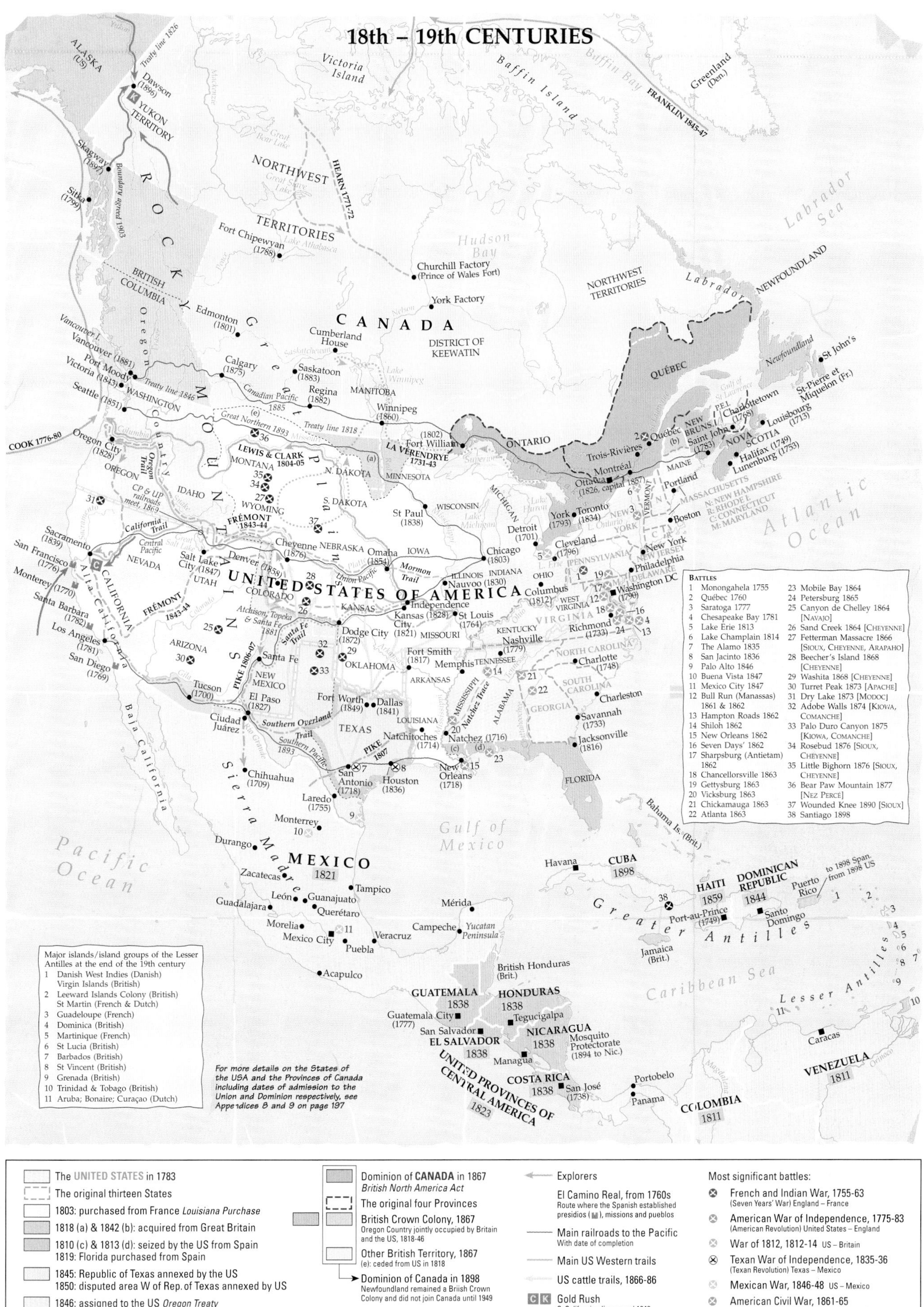
18th – 19th CENTURIES
ALASKA (US)
Treaty line 1826
Dawson (1896)
YUKON TERRITORY
Skagway (1897)
Sitka (1799)
Boundary agreed 1903
ROCKY MOUNTAINS
Victoria Island
Baffin Island
Baffin Bay
Greenland (Den.)
FRANKLIN 1845-47
NORTHWEST TERRITORIES
HEARN 1771-72
Great Bear Lake
Great Slave Lake
Fort Chipewyan (1788)
Lake Athabasca
Hudson Bay
Churchill Factory (Prince of Wales Fort)
York Factory
Labrador Sea
Labrador
NEWFOUNDLAND
NORTHWEST TERRITORIES
BRITISH COLUMBIA
Edmonton (1801)
CANADA
Cumberland House
DISTRICT OF KEEWATIN
Great Plains
Oregon
Vancouver I.
Vancouver (1881)
Port Moody
Victoria (1843)
Calgary (1875)
Saskatoon (1883)
Lake Winnipeg
Regina (1882)
MANITOBA
Canadian Pacific 1885
Treaty line 1846
WASHINGTON
Seattle (1851)
Great Northern 1893
Treaty line 1818
Winnipeg (1860)
Fort William (1802)
LA VERENDRYE 1731-43
ONTARIO
QUÉBEC
Newfoundland
St John's
St-Pierre et Miquelon (Fr.)
P.E.I.
Charlottetown (1768)
Louisbourg (1713)
NEW BRUNS.
Saint John (1783)
NOVA SCOTIA
Halifax (1749)
Lunenburg (1753)
Québec
Trois-Rivières
Montréal
Ottawa (1826, capital 1857)
MAINE
Portland
VERMONT
NEW YORK
MASSACHUSETTS
N: NEW HAMPSHIRE
R: RHODE I.
C: CONNECTICUT
M: MARYLAND
Boston
Atlantic Ocean
COOK 1776-80
Oregon City (1828)
Oregon Trail
OREGON
LEWIS & CLARK 1804-05
MONTANA
N. DAKOTA
MINNESOTA
IDAHO
CP & UP railroads meet, 1869
WYOMING
S. DAKOTA
WISCONSIN
St Paul (1838)
MICHIGAN
Lake Huron
Lake Michigan
FRÉMONT 1843-44
California Trail
Sacramento (1839)
San Francisco (1776)
Central Pacific
NEVADA
Salt Lake City (1847)
UTAH
Denver (1858)
Cheyenne (1876)
NEBRASKA
Omaha (1854)
IOWA
Mormon Trail
Union Pacific
Chicago (1803)
Detroit (1701)
York (1793)
Toronto (1834)
L. Ontario
Cleveland (1796)
L. Erie
PENNSYLVANIA
NEW JERSEY
New York
Philadelphia
DELAWARE
OHIO
Columbus (1812)
Washington DC (1790)
WEST VIRGINIA
VIRGINIA
Richmond (1733)
ILLINOIS
INDIANA
Nauvoo (1830)
UNITED STATES OF AMERICA
COLORADO
KANSAS
Independence
Kansas City (1821)
St Louis (1764)
MISSOURI
KENTUCKY
Nashville (1779)
NORTH CAROLINA
Charlotte (1748)
Monterey (1770)
CALIFORNIA
Alta California
Santa Barbara (1782)
Los Angeles (1781)
San Diego (1769)
FRÉMONT 1843-44
Atchison, Topeka & Santa Fe 1881
Santa Fe Trail
Dodge City (1872)
ARIZONA
Santa Fe
NEW MEXICO
PIKE 1806-07
OKLAHOMA
Fort Smith (1817)
Memphis
TENNESSEE
ARKANSAS
MISSISSIPPI
ALABAMA
Natchez Trace
SOUTH CAROLINA
Charleston
GEORGIA
Savannah (1733)
Jacksonville (1816)
FLORIDA
Tucson (1700)
El Paso (1827)
Ciudad Juárez
Southern Overland Trail
Southern Pacific 1893
Fort Worth (1849)
Dallas (1841)
TEXAS
LOUISIANA
Natchitoches (1714)
Natchez (1716)
PIKE 1807
San Antonio (1718)
Houston (1836)
New Orleans (1718)
Chihuahua (1709)
Laredo (1755)
Baja California
Sierra Madre
Monterrey
Durango
Pacific Ocean
MEXICO 1821
Zacatecas
Tampico
León
Guanajuato
Querétaro
Guadalajara
Morelia
Mexico City
Puebla
Veracruz
Campeche
Yucatan Peninsula
Mérida
Acapulco
Gulf of Mexico
Bahama Is. (Brit.)
Havana
CUBA 1898
HAITI 1859
DOMINICAN REPUBLIC 1844
Port-au-Prince (1749)
Santo Domingo
Puerto Rico
to 1898 Span. from 1898 US
Greater Antilles
Jamaica (Brit.)
Caribbean Sea
Lesser Antilles
British Honduras (Brit.)
GUATEMALA 1838
Guatemala City (1777)
HONDURAS 1838
Tegucigalpa
San Salvador
EL SALVADOR 1838
NICARAGUA 1838
Managua
Mosquito Protectorate (1894 to Nic.)
COSTA RICA 1838
San José (1738)
UNITED PROVINCES OF CENTRAL AMERICA 1823
Portobelo
Panama
COLOMBIA 1811
Caracas
VENEZUELA 1811
BATTLES
1 Monongahela 1755
2 Québec 1760
3 Saratoga 1777
4 Chesapeake Bay 1781
5 Lake Erie 1813
6 Lake Champlain 1814
7 The Alamo 1835
8 San Jacinto 1836
9 Palo Alto 1846
10 Buena Vista 1847
11 Mexico City 1847
12 Bull Run (Manassas) 1861 & 1862
13 Hampton Roads 1862
14 Shiloh 1862
15 New Orleans 1862
16 Seven Days' 1862
17 Sharpsburg (Antietam) 1862
18 Chancellorsville 1863
19 Gettysburg 1863
20 Vicksburg 1863
21 Chickamauga 1863
22 Atlanta 1863
23 Mobile Bay 1864
24 Petersburg 1865
25 Canyon de Chelley 1864 [NAVAJO]
26 Sand Creek 1864 [CHEYENNE]
27 Fetterman Massacre 1866 [SIOUX, CHEYENNE, ARAPAHO]
28 Beecher's Island 1868 [CHEYENNE]
29 Washita 1868 [CHEYENNE]
30 Turret Peak 1873 [APACHE]
31 Dry Lake 1873 [MODOC]
32 Adobe Walls 1874 [KIOWA, COMANCHE]
33 Palo Duro Canyon 1875 [KIOWA, COMANCHE]
34 Rosebud 1876 [SIOUX, CHEYENNE]
35 Little Bighorn 1876 [SIOUX, CHEYENNE]
36 Bear Paw Mountain 1877 [NEZ PERCÉ]
37 Wounded Knee 1890 [SIOUX]
38 Santiago 1898
Major islands/island groups of the Lesser Antilles at the end of the 19th century
1 Danish West Indies (Danish) Virgin Islands (British)
2 Leeward Islands Colony (British) St Martin (French & Dutch)
3 Guadeloupe (French)
4 Dominica (British)
5 Martinique (French)
6 St Lucia (British)
7 Barbados (British)
8 St Vincent (British)
9 Grenada (British)
10 Trinidad & Tobago (British)
11 Aruba; Bonaire; Curaçao (Dutch)
For more details on the States of the USA and the Provinces of Canada including dates of admission to the Union and Dominion respectively, see Appendices 8 and 9 on page 197

The UNITED STATES in 1783
The original thirteen States
1803: purchased from France *Louisiana Purchase*
1818 (a) & 1842 (b): acquired from Great Britain
1810 (c) & 1813 (d): seized by the US from Spain
1819: Florida purchased from Spain
1845: Republic of Texas annexed by the US
1850: disputed area W of Rep. of Texas annexed by US
1846: assigned to the US *Oregon Treaty*
1848: ceded by Mexico *Treaty of Guadalupe Hidalgo*
1853: purchased from Mexico *Gadsden Purchase*
1867: Alaska purchased from Russia

Dominion of **CANADA** in 1867
British North America Act
The original four Provinces
British Crown Colony, 1867
Oregon Country jointly occupied by Britain and the US, 1818-46
Other British Territory, 1867
(e): ceded from US in 1818
Dominion of Canada in 1898
Newfoundland remained a Briish Crown Colony and did not join Canada until 1949
Spanish Treaty line, 1819
Republic of Texas
Independent from Mexico in 1836; annexed by the US in 1845

Explorers
El Camino Real, from 1760s
Route where the Spanish established presidios, missions and pueblos
Main railroads to the Pacific
With date of completion
Main US Western trails
US cattle trails, 1866-86
C K Gold Rush
C: California, discovered 1848
K: Klondike, discovered 1897
( ) Year of foundation
1800 Year of independence

Most significant battles:
French and Indian War, 1755-63
(Seven Years' War) England – France
American War of Independence, 1775-83
(American Revolution) United States – England
War of 1812, 1812-14 US – Britain
Texan War of Independence, 1835-36
(Texan Revolution) Texas – Mexico
Mexican War, 1846-48 US – Mexico
American Civil War, 1861-65
US North (Union) – US South (Confederacy)
Northern boundary of Confederacy, 1861
Indian Wars, 1864-90
Spanish-American War, 1898

Railways & Airports

See also... World Airports (42-44); World Flight Times (45)

The listings above refer to a selection of related themes. For more information, see the Contents (2-7).

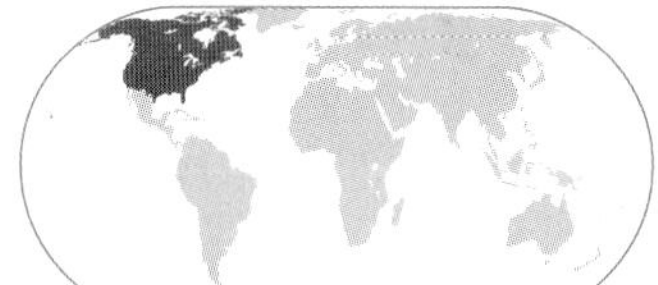

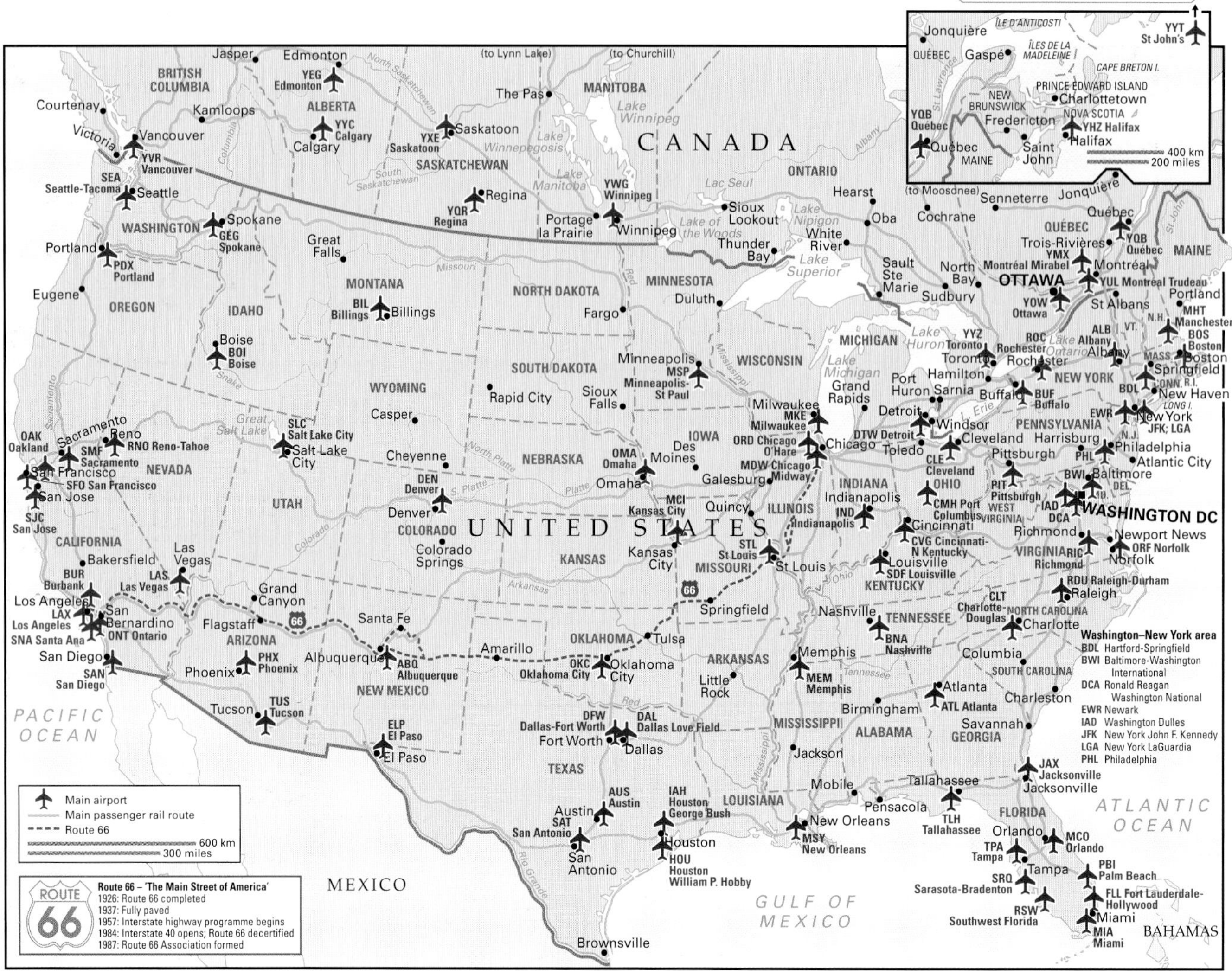

Main airport
Main passenger rail route
Route 66
600 km
300 miles

ROUTE 66

Route 66 – 'The Main Street of America'
1926: Route 66 completed
1937: Fully paved
1957: Interstate highway programme begins
1984: Interstate 40 opens; Route 66 decertified
1987: Route 66 Association formed

Washington–New York area
BDL Hartford-Springfield
BWI Baltimore-Washington International
DCA Ronald Reagan Washington National
EWR Newark
IAD Washington Dulles
JFK New York John F. Kennedy
LGA New York LaGuardia
PHL Philadelphia

PACIFIC OCEAN

ATLANTIC OCEAN

GULF OF MEXICO

MEXICO

CANADA

UNITED STATES

BAHAMAS

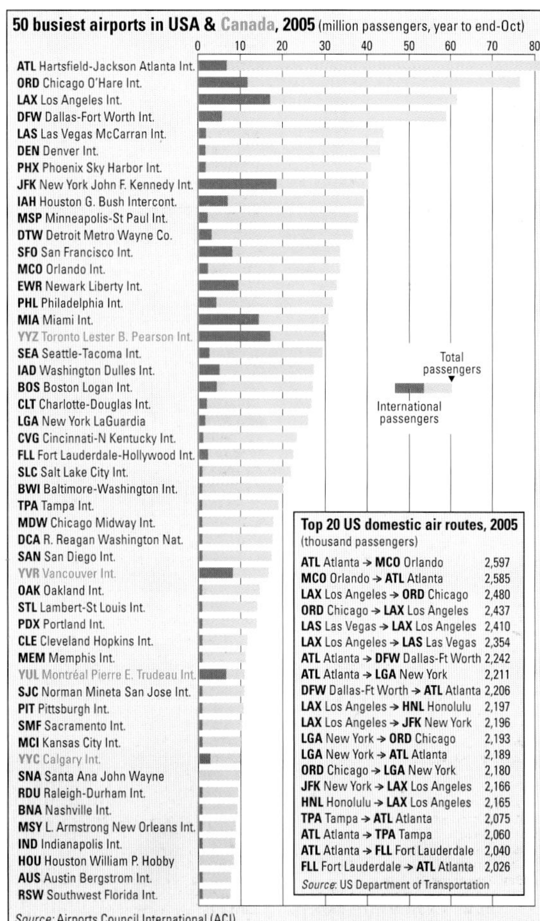
50 busiest airports in USA & Canada, 2005 (million passengers, year to end-Oct)
0
10
20
30
40
50
60
70
80
ATL Hartsfield-Jackson Atlanta Int.
ORD Chicago O'Hare Int.
LAX Los Angeles Int.
DFW Dallas-Fort Worth Int.
LAS Las Vegas McCarran Int.
DEN Denver Int.
PHX Phoenix Sky Harbor Int.
JFK New York John F. Kennedy Int.
IAH Houston G. Bush Intercont.
MSP Minneapolis-St Paul Int.
DTW Detroit Metro Wayne Co.
SFO San Francisco Int.
MCO Orlando Int.
EWR Newark Liberty Int.
PHL Philadelphia Int.
MIA Miami Int.
YYZ Toronto Lester B. Pearson Int.
SEA Seattle-Tacoma Int.
IAD Washington Dulles Int.
BOS Boston Logan Int.
CLT Charlotte-Douglas Int.
LGA New York LaGuardia
CVG Cincinnati-N Kentucky Int.
FLL Fort Lauderdale-Hollywood Int.
SLC Salt Lake City Int.
BWI Baltimore-Washington Int.
TPA Tampa Int.
MDW Chicago Midway Int.
DCA R. Reagan Washington Nat.
SAN San Diego Int.
YVR Vancouver Int.
OAK Oakland Int.
STL Lambert-St Louis Int.
PDX Portland Int.
CLE Cleveland Hopkins Int.
MEM Memphis Int.
YUL Montréal Pierre E. Trudeau Int.
SJC Norman Mineta San Jose Int.
PIT Pittsburgh Int.
SMF Sacramento Int.
MCI Kansas City Int.
YYC Calgary Int.
SNA Santa Ana John Wayne
RDU Raleigh-Durham Int.
BNA Nashville Int.
MSY L. Armstrong New Orleans Int.
IND Indianapolis Int.
HOU Houston William P. Hobby
AUS Austin Bergstrom Int.
RSW Southwest Florida Int.
Total passengers
International passengers
Source: Airports Council International (ACI)

Top 20 US domestic air routes, 2005 (thousand passengers)

Route	
ATL Atlanta → MCO Orlando	2,597
MCO Orlando → ATL Atlanta	2,585
LAX Los Angeles → ORD Chicago	2,480
ORD Chicago → LAX Los Angeles	2,437
LAS Las Vegas → LAX Los Angeles	2,410
LAX Los Angeles → LAS Las Vegas	2,354
ATL Atlanta → DFW Dallas-Ft Worth	2,242
ATL Atlanta → LGA New York	2,211
DFW Dallas-Ft Worth → ATL Atlanta	2,206
LAX Los Angeles → HNL Honolulu	2,197
LAX Los Angeles → JFK New York	2,196
LGA New York → ORD Chicago	2,193
LGA New York → ATL Atlanta	2,189
ORD Chicago → LGA New York	2,180
JFK New York → LAX Los Angeles	2,166
HNL Honolulu → LAX Los Angeles	2,165
TPA Tampa → ATL Atlanta	2,075
ATL Atlanta → TPA Tampa	2,060
ATL Atlanta → FLL Fort Lauderdale	2,040
FLL Fort Lauderdale → ATL Atlanta	2,026

Source: US Department of Transportation

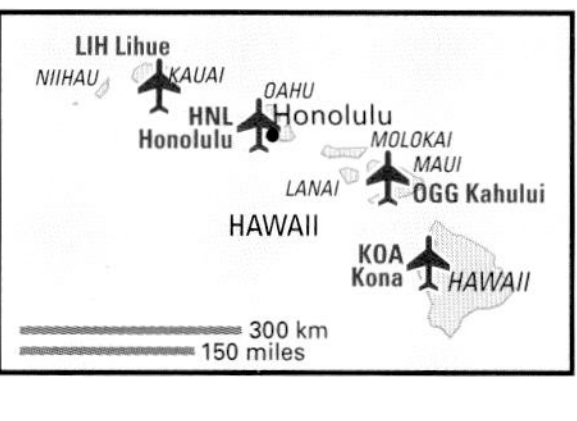
LIH Lihue
NIIHAU
KAUAI
OAHU
HNL Honolulu
Honolulu
MOLOKAI
MAUI
LANAI
OGG Kahului
HAWAII
KOA Kona
HAWAII
300 km
150 miles

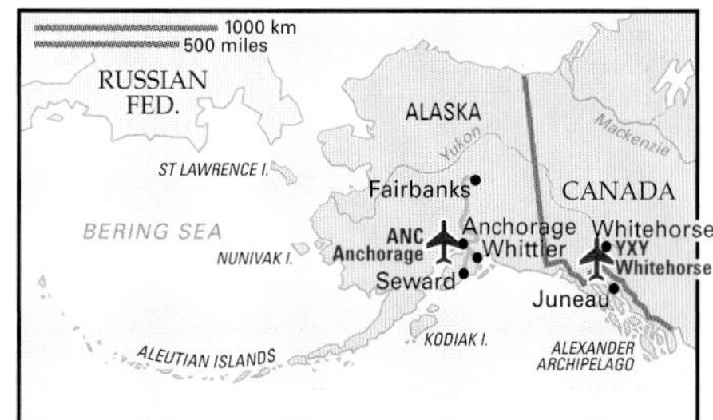
1000 km
500 miles
RUSSIAN FED.
ALASKA
CANADA
ST LAWRENCE I.
Fairbanks
BERING SEA
NUNIVAK I.
ANC Anchorage
Anchorage
Whittier
Whitehorse
YXY Whitehorse
Seward
Juneau
KODIAK I.
ALEUTIAN ISLANDS
ALEXANDER ARCHIPELAGO

LONG-DISTANCE RAIL SERVICES

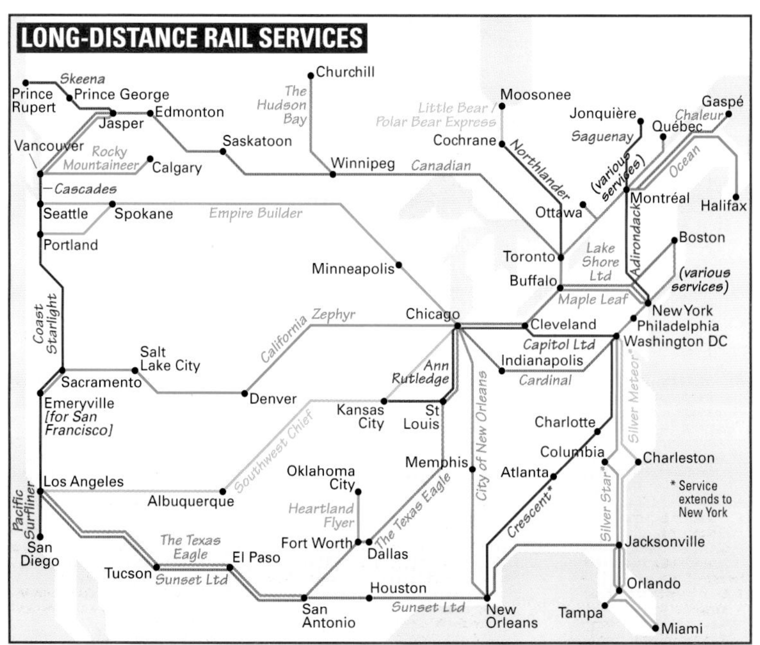
Skeena
Prince Rupert
Prince George
Edmonton
Jasper
Churchill
The Hudson Bay
Little Bear / Polar Bear Express
Moosonee
Cochrane
Northlander
Jonquière
Saguenay
Gaspé
Chaleur
Québec
Ocean
(various services)
Saskatoon
Winnipeg
Canadian
Vancouver
Rocky Mountaineer
Calgary
Cascades
Seattle
Spokane
Empire Builder
Ottawa
Montréal
Halifax
Adirondack
Portland
Minneapolis
Toronto
Lake Shore Ltd
Boston
Buffalo
Maple Leaf
(various services)
Coast Starlight
California Zephyr
Chicago
New York
Philadelphia
Washington DC
Cleveland
Capitol Ltd
Salt Lake City
Indianapolis
Cardinal
Ann Rutledge
Sacramento
Denver
Emeryville [for San Francisco]
Kansas City
St Louis
City of New Orleans
Southwest Chief
Charlotte
Memphis
Columbia
Silver Meteor
Charleston
Oklahoma City
Atlanta
Crescent
Silver Star
Los Angeles
Albuquerque
Heartland Flyer
The Texas Eagle
Pacific Surfliner
San Diego
The Texas Eagle
El Paso
Fort Worth
Dallas
Jacksonville
Tucson
Sunset Ltd
Houston
Sunset Ltd
Orlando
San Antonio
New Orleans
Tampa
Miami
* Service extends to New York

Diagrammatic only: not to scale

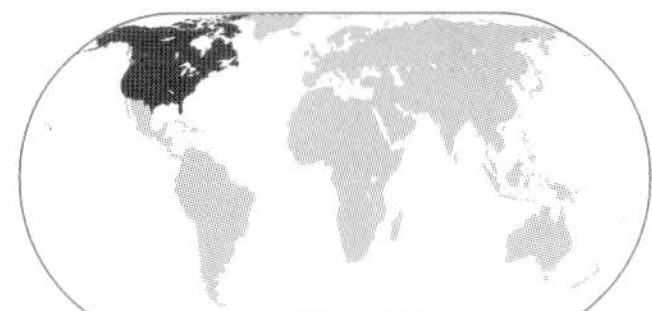

See also... UNESCO Cultural Heritage (50-53); North American Historical (156-157); Museums & Galleries in Europe (68), Asia (129) and Latin America (182, 184, 187)

Museums & Art Galleries

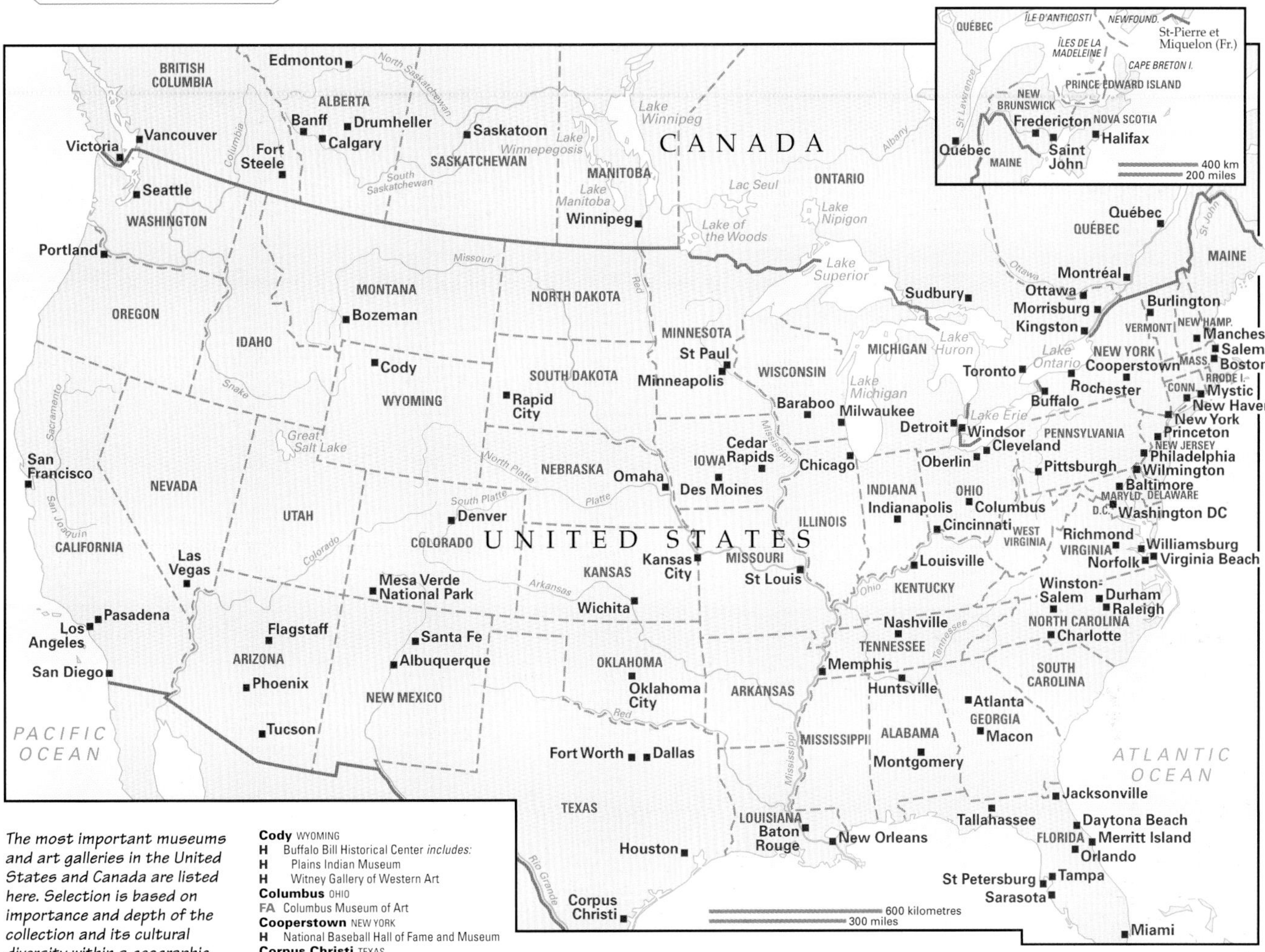

CANADA
UNITED STATES
BRITISH COLUMBIA
ALBERTA
SASKATCHEWAN
MANITOBA
ONTARIO
QUÉBEC
Edmonton
Banff
Drumheller
Calgary
Fort Steele
Saskatoon
Vancouver
Victoria
Seattle
WASHINGTON
Portland
OREGON
IDAHO
MONTANA
Bozeman
NORTH DAKOTA
SOUTH DAKOTA
WYOMING
Cody
Rapid City
Winnipeg
Lake Winnipeg
Lake Winnipegosis
Lake Manitoba
Lac Seul
Lake Nipigon
Lake of the Woods
Lake Superior
Lake Huron
Lake Michigan
Lake Ontario
Lake Erie
Great Salt Lake
Sudbury
Ottawa
Montréal
Québec
Morrisburg
Kingston
Toronto
Burlington
Manchester
Salem
Boston
Cooperstown
Rochester
Buffalo
Mystic
New Haven
New York
Princeton
Philadelphia
Wilmington
Baltimore
Washington DC
Richmond
Williamsburg
Norfolk
Virginia Beach
MAINE
VERMONT
NEW HAMP.
NEW YORK
MASS.
RHODE I.
CONN.
NEW JERSEY
MARYLD.
DELAWARE
D.C.
PENNSYLVANIA
WEST VIRGINIA
VIRGINIA
MINNESOTA
St Paul
Minneapolis
WISCONSIN
Baraboo
Milwaukee
MICHIGAN
Detroit
Windsor
Cleveland
Oberlin
Pittsburgh
OHIO
Columbus
Cincinnati
INDIANA
Indianapolis
ILLINOIS
Chicago
IOWA
Cedar Rapids
Des Moines
NEBRASKA
Omaha
San Francisco
NEVADA
UTAH
COLORADO
Denver
CALIFORNIA
Las Vegas
Mesa Verde National Park
KANSAS
Kansas City
MISSOURI
St Louis
Louisville
KENTUCKY
Wichita
Pasadena
Los Angeles
San Diego
Flagstaff
ARIZONA
Phoenix
Tucson
Santa Fe
Albuquerque
NEW MEXICO
OKLAHOMA
Oklahoma City
ARKANSAS
Memphis
Nashville
TENNESSEE
Huntsville
Winston-Salem
Durham
Raleigh
NORTH CAROLINA
Charlotte
SOUTH CAROLINA
Atlanta
GEORGIA
Macon
ALABAMA
Montgomery
MISSISSIPPI
Fort Worth
Dallas
TEXAS
LOUISIANA
Baton Rouge
New Orleans
Houston
Corpus Christi
Tallahassee
Jacksonville
Daytona Beach
FLORIDA
Merritt Island
Orlando
Tampa
St Petersburg
Sarasota
Miami
PACIFIC OCEAN
ATLANTIC OCEAN
Missouri
Red
Snake
Columbia
Sacramento
San Joaquin
Colorado
North Platte
South Platte
Platte
Arkansas
Mississippi
Ohio
Tennessee
Rio Grande
South Saskatchewan
North Saskatchewan
Albany
Ottawa
St Lawrence
St John
600 kilometres
300 miles
ÎLE D'ANTICOSTI
NEWFOUND.
St-Pierre et Miquelon (Fr.)
ÎLES DE LA MADELEINE
CAPE BRETON I.
PRINCE EDWARD ISLAND
NEW BRUNSWICK
Fredericton
NOVA SCOTIA
Halifax
Québec
MAINE
Saint John
400 km
200 miles

The most important museums and art galleries in the United States and Canada are listed here. Selection is based on importance and depth of the collection and its cultural diversity within a geographic spread.

Compiled by Jon A. Gillaspie
email: let@sarastro.com

Principal contents of institution:

AA	Applied & decorative art
AR	Archaeology / ancient art
FA	Fine art (paintings, sculpture)
FO	Folk art & culture / ethnography
H	History / historical site / reconstruction
NH	Natural history
ST	Science / technology
W	Wide range of subjects

Albuquerque NEW MEXICO
W Indian Pueblo Cultural Center
Atlanta GEORGIA
FA High Museum of Art
W Michael C. Carlos Museum (Emory Univ.)
Baltimore MARYLAND
FA Baltimore Museum of Art
W Walters Art Gallery
Banff ALBERTA
NH Whyte Museum of Rockies
Baraboo WISCONSIN
H Circus World Museum
Baton Rouge LOUISIANA
W LSU Rural Life Museum
Boston MASSACHUSETTS
W Children's Museum; Museum of Fine Arts
FA Isabella Stewart Gardner Museum
ST Museum of Science
Bozeman MONTANA
W Museum of the Rockies
Buffalo NEW YORK
FA Albright-Knox Art Gallery
Burlington VERMONT
W Shelburne Museum
Calgary ALBERTA
W Glenbow Museum
Cedar Rapids IOWA
FA Museum of Art
Charlotte NORTH CAROLINA
ST Discovery Place
W Mint Museum of Art
Chicago ILLINOIS
FA Art Institute of Chicago; Museum of Contemporary Art
W Field Museum of Chicago
ST Museum of Science and Technology
Cincinnati OHIO
FA Cincinnati Art Museum; Contemporary Arts Center; Taft Museum
Cleveland OHIO
ST Great Lakes Science Center
FA Museum of Art
NH Museum of Natural History
H Rock and Roll Hall of Fame
Cody WYOMING
H Buffalo Bill Historical Center *includes:*
H Plains Indian Museum
H Witney Gallery of Western Art
Columbus OHIO
FA Columbus Museum of Art
Cooperstown NEW YORK
H National Baseball Hall of Fame and Museum
Corpus Christi TEXAS
FA Art Museum of South Texas
Dallas TEXAS
FO African-American Museum
AR FA Dallas Museum of Art
NH Dallas Museum of Natural History
H Sixth Floor Museum (School Book Depository)
Daytona Beach FLORIDA
W Museum of Arts and Sciences
Denver COLORADO
H Black American West Museum
W Art Museum; Museum of Natural History
Des Moines IOWA
FA Des Moines Art Center
Detroit MICHIGAN
W Detroit Institute of Art
H Henry Ford Museum; Motown Museum; Museum of Afro-American History
Drumheller ALBERTA
NH Royal Tyrrell Museum of Paleontology
Durham NORTH CAROLINA
W Duke University Museum of Art
Edmonton ALBERTA
ST Edmonton Space and Science Center
Flagstaff ARIZONA
FO Museum of Northern Arizona
Fort Steele BRITISH COLUMBIA
H Fort Steele Heritage Town
Fort Worth TEXAS
FA Amon Carter Museum; Kimbell Art Museum; Modern Art Museum; Sid Richardson Collection of Western Art
W Museum of Science and History
Fredericton NEW BRUNSWICK
FA Beaverbrook Art Gallery
Halifax NOVA SCOTIA
H Atlantic Maritime Museum
NH Nova Scotia Natural History Museum
Houston TEXAS
FA Museum of Fine Arts
NH Museum of Natural Science
ST Space Center Houston
Huntsville ALABAMA
ST Space and Rocket Center
Indianapolis INDIANA
FO Eiteljorg Museum
FA Indianapolis Museum of Art
W Children's Museum of Indianapolis
Jacksonville FLORIDA
FA Cummer Gallery; Museum of Contemporary Art
Kansas City MISSOURI
W Nelson-Atkins Museum of Art
Kingston ONTARIO
W Agnes Ethrington Art Center
Las Vegas NEVADA
FA Bellagio Gallery of Fine Art
Los Angeles CALIFORNIA
AA FA Getty Center
FA Armand Hammer Museum of Art; Museum of Contemporary Art (MOCA)
AR FA LA County Museum of Art (LACMA)
W Natural History Museum of L.A. County
H Museum of Tolerance
Louisville KENTUCKY
FA J.B. Speed Art Museum
Macon GEORGIA
W Tubman African-American Museum
Manchester NEW HAMPSHIRE
AA FA Currier Gallery of Art
Memphis TENNESSEE
W National Civil Rights Museum
Merritt Island FLORIDA
ST Kennedy Space Center
Mesa Verde National Park COLORADO
AR Archaeological Museum
Miami FLORIDA
FA Bass Museum; Miami Art Museum
W Lowe Art Museum (University of Miami)
ST Miami Museum of Science and Space Transit Planetarium
AA FA Vizcaya Museum
H Weeks Air Museum
AA Wolfsonian Museum
Milwaukee WISCONSIN
FA Milwaukee Art Gallery
W Museum Center
Minneapolis and St Paul MINNESOTA
W Minneapolis Institute of Arts; Minnesota Children's Museum
ST Science Museum of Minnesota
FA Walker Art Center and Sculpture Garden
Montgomery ALABAMA
FA Montgomery Museum of Fine Art
Montréal QUÉBEC
NH Montréal Biodôme
AA Cent. Canadien d'Architecture; Chât. Ramezay
AR Musée d'archélogie et d'histoire de Montréal
FA Musée des beaux-arts de Montréal; Musée d'art contemporain de Montréal
H Musée McCord d'histoire Canadienne
Morrisburg ONTARIO
FO Upper Canada Village
Mystic CONNECTICUT
H Mystic Seaport
Nashville TENNESSEE
H Country Museum Hall of Fame
W Tennessee State Museum
New Haven CONNECTICUT
FA Center for British Art; Yale University Library
NH Peabody Museum of Natural History
New Orleans LOUISIANA
W Louisiana State Museum *includes:* Cabildo; Presbytere; 1850 House; Jazz Mus.
H New Orleans Historic Voodoo Museum
FA New Orleans Museum of Art
New York NEW YORK
W American Museum of Natural History; Brooklyn Museum of Art; Jewish Museum; Metropolitan Museum of Art; New York Historical Society
ST American Museum of the Moving Image; New York Hall of Science
AA Cooper-Hewitt National Design Museum
FA Frick Collection; Guggenheim Museum; Studio Museum in Harlem; Whitney Museum of American Art
AA FA Museum of Modern Art (MoMA)
FO National Museum of the American Indian
Norfolk VIRGINIA
FA Chrysler Museum
Oberlin OHIO
W Allen Memorial Art Museum
Oklahoma City OKLAHOMA
FA FO National Cowboy Hall of Fame
Omaha NEBRASKA
H Great Plains Black Museum
Orlando FLORIDA
ST EPCOT Center
Ottawa QUÉBEC
NH Canadian Museum of Nature
W Canadian Museum of Civilization
FA FO National Gallery
ST National Aviation Museum
ST National Museum of Science
Pasadena CALIFORNIA
FA Huntington Museum and Library; Norton Simon Museum
Philadelphia PENNSYLVANIA
H Afro-American Historical & Cultural Museum
FA Barnes Foundation; Philadelphia Museum of Art; Rodin Museum
AR FO Museum of Archaeology and Anthropology (University of Pennsylvania)
Phoenix ARIZONA
FO Heard Museum
Pittsburgh PENNSYLVANIA
FA Andy Warhol Museum; Museum of Art (Carnegie Center)
AA FA Frick Art Museum
Portland OREGON
ST Oregon Museum of Science and Industry
W Portland Art Museum
Princeton NEW JERSEY
ST Carnegie Science Center
NH Natural History Museum
FA University Art Museum
Québec QUÉBEC
W Musée de la civilisation
FA Musée du Québec
Raleigh NORTH CAROLINA
FA North Carolina Museum of Art
ST North Carolina Museum of Natural Sciences
Rapid City SOUTH DAKOTA
H Sioux Indian Museum
Richmond VIRGINIA
W Virginia Museum of Fine Arts
Rochester NEW YORK
AA International Museum of Photography
Saint John NEW BRUNSWICK
W New Brunswick Museum
St Louis MISSOURI
H Museum of Western Expansion
W St Louis Art Museum
St Petersburg FLORIDA
W Museum of Fine Arts
FA Salvador Dali Museum
Salem MASSACHUSETTS
W Peabody Essex Museum
H Plimoth Plantation
San Diego CALIFORNIA
FA Museum of Contemporary Art [La Jolla]
San Francisco CALIFORNIA
FA California Palace of the Legion of Honor; Yerba Buena Gardens; San Francisco Art Institute; S.F. Museum of Modern Art
Santa Fe NEW MEXICO
W Museum of New Mexico *includes:*
FA Georgia O'Keeffe Museum; Museum of Fine Arts
FO Museum of Indian Arts; Museum of International Folk Art
Sarasota FLORIDA
FA Ringling Museum Complex
Saskatoon SASKATCHEWAN
FA Mendel Art Gallery
Seattle WASHINGTON
FA Henry Art Gallery
ST Interactive Music Museum; Museum of Flight; Pacific Science Center
AA Science Fiction Museum and Hall of Fame
FO Thomas Burke Memorial Museum
Sudbury ONTARIO
ST Science North
Tallahassee FLORIDA
W Black Archives Research Center
Tampa FLORIDA
ST Museum of Science and Industry
W Tampa Museum of Art
Toronto ONTARIO
FA Art Gallery of Ontario (AGO); McMichael Canadian Art Collection; Thomson Gallery
FO Toronto Dominion Gallery of Inuit Art
ST Ontario Science Centre
W Royal Ontario Museum (ROM)
Tucson ARIZONA
NH Arizona-Sonora Desert Museum
FO Arizona State Museum
AR FA Tucson Museum of Art
Vancouver BRITISH COLUMBIA
FO UBC Museum of Anthropology
Victoria BRITISH COLUMBIA
W Royal British Columbia Museum
Virginia Beach VIRGINIA
ST Virginia Marine Museum
Washington DC
FA Corcoran Gallery; National Gallery of Art; National Museum of Women in the Arts; Phillips Collection
H US Holocaust Memorial Museum
W Smithsonian Institution *includes:*
AA FA Freer Gallery of Art
FA Hirshhorn Museum; National Museum of American Art; National Portrait Gallery
ST National Air and Space Museum
FO National Museum of African Art; Sackler Gallery
H National Museum of American History
NH National Museum of Natural History
Wichita KANSAS
FA Wichita Art Museum
Williamsburg VIRGINIA
H Colonial Williamsburg; Jamestown Settlement
Wilmington DELAWARE
AA Nemours Mansion
AA FO Winterthur Museum [Winterthur]
Windsor ONTARIO
FA Art Gallery of Windsor
Winnipeg MANITOBA
NH Manitoba Museum of Man and Nature
W Winnipeg Art Gallery
Winston-Salem NORTH CAROLINA
FA Reynolda House Museum of American Art

See also... Europe Winter Sports (69)

The listings above refer to a selection of related themes. For more information, see the Contents (2-7).

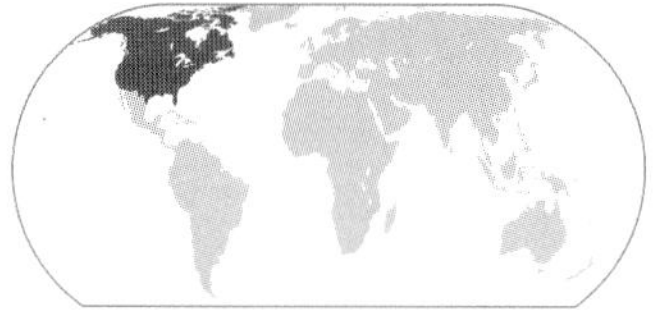

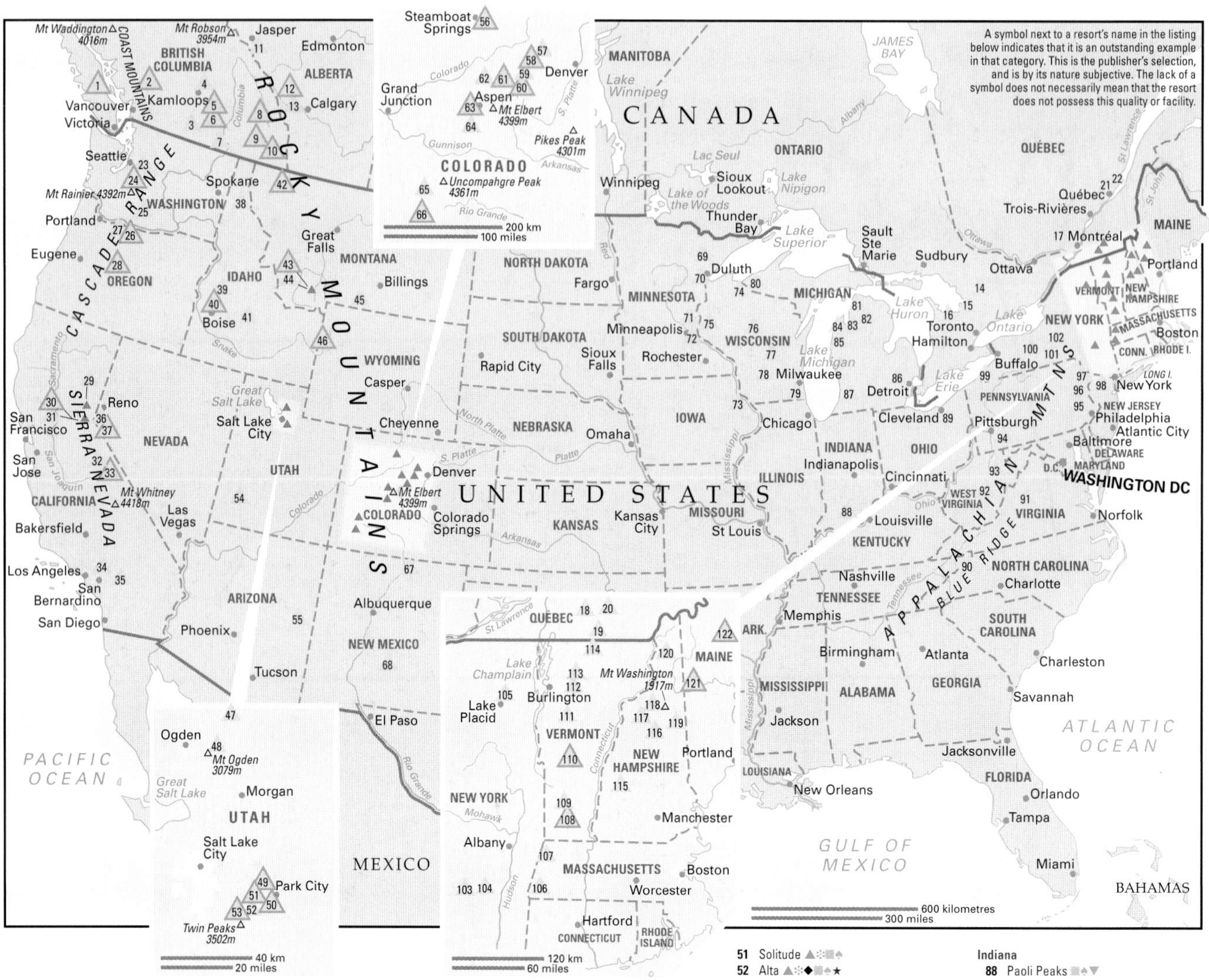

A symbol next to a resort's name in the listing below indicates that it is an outstanding example in that category. This is the publisher's selection, and is by its nature subjective. The lack of a symbol does not necessarily mean that the resort does not possess this quality or facility.

▲ **THE MOST BEAUTIFUL RESORTS**
Ski areas with spectacular scenery

❄ **SNOWSURE**
The best reputations for season-long snow cover

◆ **EXPERT**
Best of the black diamond destinations

■ **BEGINNER SKI AREAS**
Best choices for first timers

♠ **FAMILY FRIENDLY**
Ideal choices for family ski holidays

● **PARTY TOWNS**
Après ski centres

▼ **SNOWBOARDER HEAVEN**
Best bets for boarders

★ **NOT JUST SKIING**
Plenty to do if you don't want to slide

✓ **ECO-FRIENDLY REPUTATION**
(not all resorts have been graded in this category)

Information supplied by Snow24 plc
www.snow24.com

THE LARGEST SKI AREAS ▲

1 Mount Washington, BC
2 Whistler & Blackcomb, BC
5 Silver Star, BC
6 Big White, BC
8 Panorama, BC
9 Kimberley, BC
10 Fernie Snow Valley, BC
12 Lake Louise (Banff), AL
12 Sunshine Village (Banff), AL
24 Crystal Mountain, WA
26 Mount Hood Meadows, OR
28 Mount Bachelor, OR
30 Squaw Valley, CA
33 Mammoth Mountain, CA
37 Heavenly, NV
40 Bogus Basin, ID
42 Big Mountain, MT
43 Big Sky, MT
46 Jackson Hole, WY
49 The Canyons, UT
50 Deer Valley, UT
50 Park City, UT
51 Solitude, UT
53 Snowbird, UT
56 Steamboat, CO
58 Keystone, CO
58 Loveland, CO
58 Winter Park (Mary Jane), CO
60 Breckenridge, CO
61 Copper Mountain, CO
61 Vail, CO
63 Aspen, CO
63 Snowmass, CO
66 Durango Mountain Resort, CO
108 Mount Snow (Haystack / Carinthia), VT
110 Killington, VT
121 Sunday River, ME
122 Sugarloaf USA, ME

Canada

British Columbia
1 Mount Washington ❄▼
2 Whistler & Blackcomb ❄◆♠●▼★✓
3 Apex ❄◆■♠▼
4 Sun Peaks ❄◆■♠▼
5 Silver Star ❄◆■♠▼
6 Big White ❄◆♠●▼
7 Red Mountain ❄◆♠▼
8 Panorama ▲❄◆■♠▼
9 Kimberley ❄■♠●▼
10 Fernie Snow Valley ❄◆▼

Alberta
11 Marmot Basin (Jasper) ▲❄■♠●▼★
12 Lake Louise (Banff) ▲❄◆♠✓
Sunshine Village (Banff) ❄■♠●▼★✓
13 Fortress Mountain ▲❄■
Nakiska ▲❄▼

Ontario
14 Sir Sam's ■♠★
15 Mount St Louis / Moonstone ■♠▼
16 Blue Mountain ❄■♠▼

Québec
17 Mont Blanc ■♠▼★
Mont Gabriel ■♠
Mont Ste-Sauveur ■♠▼★
Ski Morin Heights ■
Tremblant ■♠●▼★✓
18 Bromont ■♠▼
19 Owl's Head ■♠
20 Mont Orford ❄■♠▼
21 Mont Ste-Anne ▲❄■♠●▼★
22 Stoneham ❄■♠▼★

United States

Washington
23 Stevens Pass ♠
24 Crystal Mountain ▲❄◆▼
25 White Pass Village ❄◆■

Oregon
26 Mount Hood Meadows ▲❄◆▼
27 Timberline ▲❄◆■●▼
28 Mount Bachelor ▲❄◆▼

California
29 Boreal ■▼
Donner Ski Area Tahoe ▲▼
30 Squaw Valley ❄◆■♠▼★
31 Alpine Meadows ▲❄♠▼✓
Kirkwood ▲❄■♠▼
Sierra-at-Tahoe ▲❄■♠▼
Northstar-at-Tahoe ◆■♠▼✓
32 Dodge Ridge ▼
June Mountain ▲■♠▼
33 Mammoth Mountain ▲❄◆♠●▼✓
34 Mountain High ❄▼
35 Snow Summit ■▼

Nevada
36 Diamond Peak ▲♠
Mount Rose ◆▼
37 Heavenly ▲❄◆■♠●▼★✓

Idaho
38 Silver Mountain ❄■♠▼
39 Tamarack ❄◆♠
41 Sun Valley ▲❄◆■▼★

Montana
42 Big Mountain ◆■♠▼★
43 Big Sky ▲◆■♠●
44 Moonlight Basin ▲❄◆♠✓
45 Red Lodge Mountain ▲◆♠●▼

Wyoming
46 Jackson Hole ▲❄◆■♠●▼★✓

Utah
47 Powder Mountain ❄◆■
48 Snowbasin ▲❄◆♠
49 The Canyons ❄◆■♠▼★
50 Deer Valley ❄◆■♠●★
Park City ❄◆■●▼★✓
51 Solitude ▲❄■♠
52 Alta ▲❄◆■♠★
53 Snowbird ▲❄◆■♠●▼★
54 Brian Head ❄◆■

Arizona
55 Sunrise Park ❄■

Colorado
56 Steamboat ▲❄■♠●▼★✓
57 Eldora Mountain ▼
58 Keystone ❄■♠●▼✓
Loveland ▲❄◆
Winter Park (Mary Jane) ❄◆■♠●▼★✓
59 Arapahoe Basin ❄◆
60 Breckenridge ❄◆■♠●▼★
61 Copper Mountain ▲❄◆■♠●▼★
Vail ❄◆●★
62 Beaver Creek ▲◆■♠▼★✓
63 Aspen ▲❄◆■♠●▼★✓
Snowmass ❄◆■♠●▼★✓
64 Crested Butte ▲❄◆■♠●▼★
65 Telluride ▲❄◆■♠●▼★✓
66 Durango Mountain Resort ▲❄◆■♠●▼★

New Mexico
67 Taos ▲◆■
68 Ski Apache ◆●▼★

Minnesota
69 Giants Ridge ■★
70 Spirit Mountain ■▼
71 Afton Alps ■▼
72 Buck Hill ■▼

Iowa
73 Sundown Mountain ▼★

Wisconsin
74 Whitecap Mountains ■▼★
75 Trollhaugen ■♠▼
76 Granite Peak ❄■♠●▼
77 Nordic Mountain ■♠▼
78 Cascade Mountain ◆■▼
Devils Head ❄◆■●★
79 Wilmot Mountain ■▼

Michigan
80 Big Powderhorn Mountain ❄♠▼
Indianhead Mountain & Bear Creek ◆★
81 Boyne Highlands ■♠▼★
Boyne Mountain ■♠★
Nub's Nob ◆■▼
82 Treetops / Sylvan ♠
83 Shanty Creek / Schuss Mountain ■
84 Caberfae Peaks ■★
85 Sugar Loaf ▼
86 Alpine Valley ■
87 Timber Ridge ■

Indiana
88 Paoli Peaks ■♠▼

Ohio
89 Boston Mills / Brandywine ■★

North Carolina
90 Ski Beech Mountain ■♠★
Sugar Mountain ■♠▼

Virginia
91 Wintergreen ▲■★

West Virginia
92 Snowshoe ▲■♠▼★
93 Canaan Valley ▲■♠★

Pennsylvania
94 Hidden Valley ▲■♠★
Seven Springs ■♠▼★
95 Bear Creek ■▼
96 Big Boulder ❄■♠▼
Camelback ❄■
97 Shawnee Mountain ■▼

New Jersey
98 Mountain Creek ■♠▼★

New York
99 Holiday Valley ■♠●★
100 Bristol Mountain ■♠★
101 Greek Peak ■♠
102 Labrador Mountain ■▼
103 Belleayre ■♠
104 Hunter Mountain ❄◆■▼
105 Whiteface Mountain ◆▼★

Massachusetts
106 Butternut Basin ■♠
107 Jiminy Peak ■♠

Vermont
108 Mount Snow (Haystack / Carinthia) ■♠▼
109 Stratton ▲❄◆■♠▼★
110 Killington ❄◆■♠●▼
111 Sugarbush ■♠▼
112 Stowe (Mount Mansfield) ▲❄◆■●▼★
113 Smugglers' Notch ▲❄◆■♠●★
114 Jay Peak ▲❄▼

New Hampshire
115 Mount Sunapee ▲
116 Waterville Valley ▲▼★
117 Cannon ◆▼
Loon ▲♠
118 Bretton Woods ♠
119 Attitash-Bear Peak ▼★
120 The Balsams ▲♠●★

Maine
121 Sunday River ❄◆■♠▼✓
122 Sugarloaf USA ❄◆■♠●▼

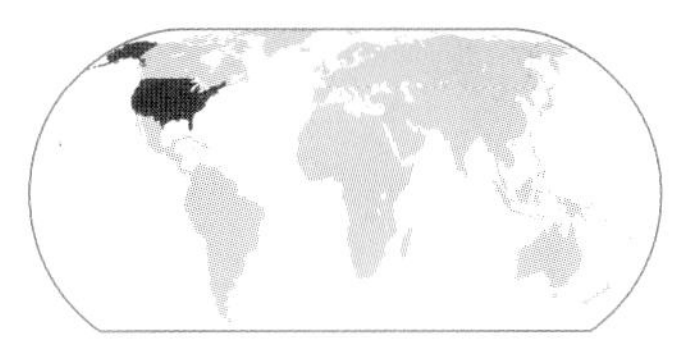

See also... 155-160 and 162-171 for more on the United States

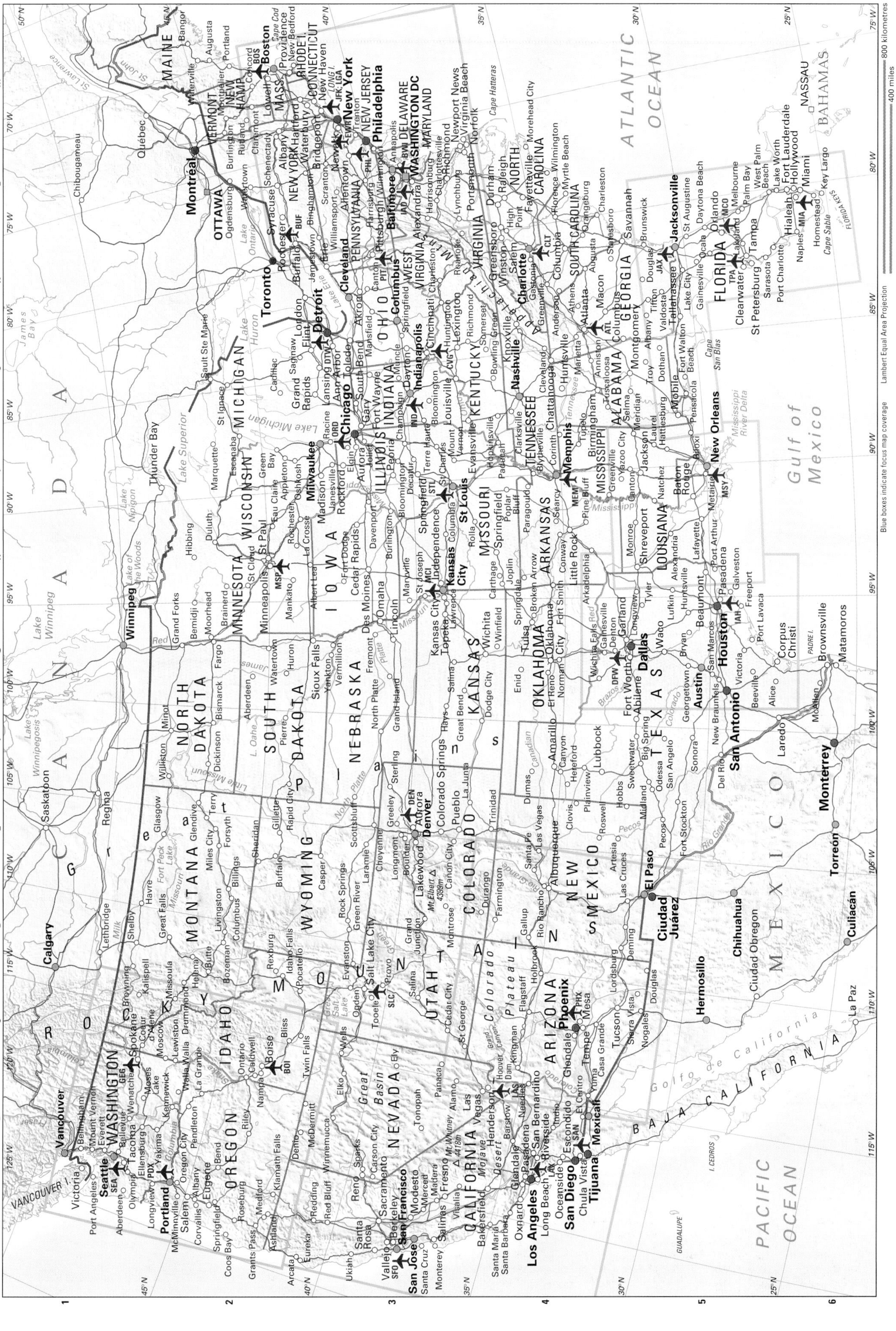

United States of America

Blue boxes indicate focus map coverage

Lambert Equal Area Projection

400 miles

800 kilometres

See also... Tourism UK & USA (25); N. America Climate (155); N. America Historical (156-157); USA & Canada Transport (158); • *cont>*

The listings above refer to a selection of related themes. For more information, see the Contents (2-7).

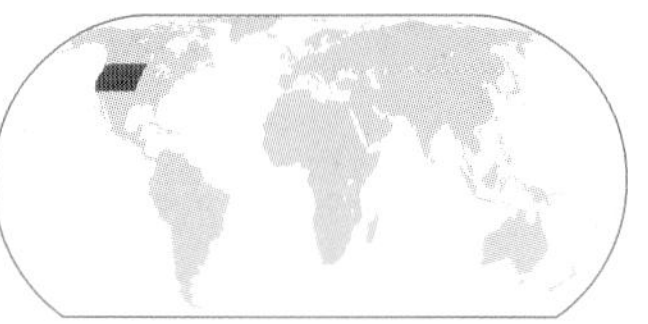

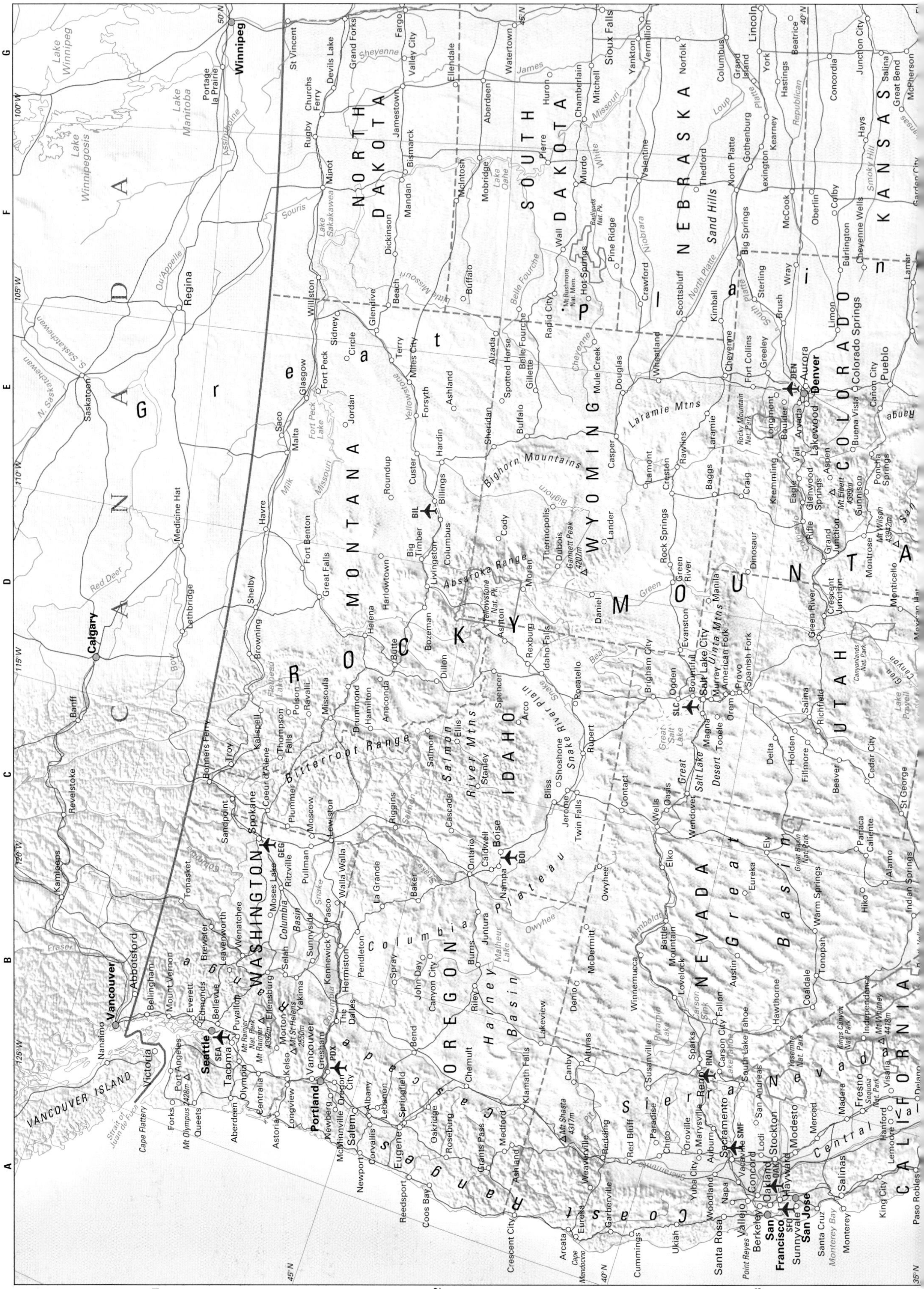

See also... cont< • USA & Canada Museums & Galleries (159); USA & Canada Winter Sports (160); US National Parks Service (166-167); US Theme Parks (165)

400 kilometres
200 miles

Lambert Equal Area Projection

MOST VISITED STATES

First intended address by non-resident visitors to the USA, 2003

ALL INTERNATIONAL VISITORS

VISITORS FROM WESTERN EUROPE

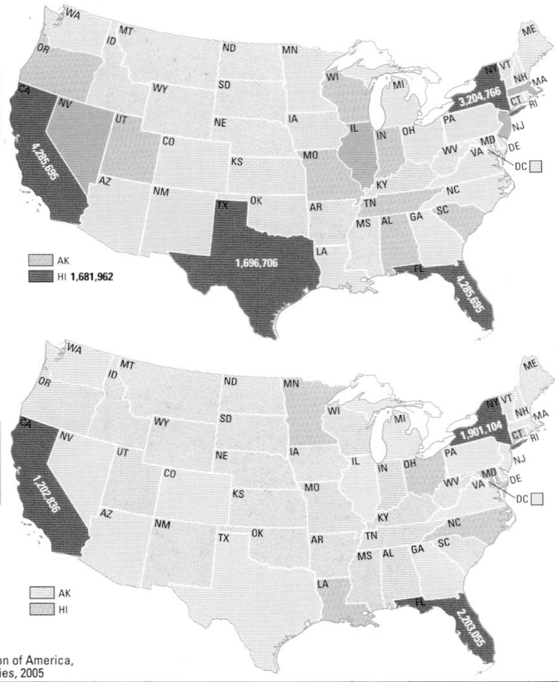

- 1 million and over
- 500,000 – 999,999
- 100,000 – 499,999
- 50,000 – 99,999
- 20,000 – 49,999
- Less than 20,000

Source: Travel Industry Association of America, Impact of Travel on State Economies, 2005

JAN 1st Tournament of Roses Parade **(Pasadena CA)**
JAN 1st Mummers Parade **(Philadelphia PA)**
JAN National Western Stock Show and Rodeo **(Denver CO)**
FEB-MAR Cajun Mardi Gras **(Lafayette LA** & surrounding area)
MAR 17th St Patrick's Day Parade **(Chicago IL** & **New York NY)**
MAR Ice Festival **(Fairbanks AK)**
MAR South by SW Music Conference & Festival **(Austin TX)**
before **LENT** Mardi Gras **(New Orleans LA)**
EASTER SUNDAY Easter Parade **(New York NY)**
APR French Quarter Festival **(New Orleans LA)**
APR Festival International de Louisiane **(Lafayette LA)**
APR-MAY JazzFest Jazz & Heritage Fest. **(New Orleans** & LA)
APR-MAY Kentucky Derby Festival **(Louisville KY)**
MAY 5th Cinco de Mayo **(Los Angeles CA)**
MAY Atlanta Jazz Festival **(GA)** **MAY Boston** Marathon **(MA)**
MAY Folk Festival **(Black Mountain NC)**
MAY Fiesta **San Antonio** & International Conjunto Festival
MAY Zuni Crafts Show **(Flagstaff AZ)**
MEMORIAL DAY WEEKEND Vandalia Festival **(Charleston WV)**
JUN Chicago Blues Festival **(IL)**
JUN Fan Fair: concerts and meeting the stars **(Nashville TN)**
JUN Little Bighorn Days **(Hardin MT)**
JUL 4th Independence Day **(Philadelphia** & countrywide)
JUN-AUG Grant Park Music Festival **(Chicago IL)**
JUL Festival of American Folklife **(Washington DC)**
JUL World Eskimo-Indian Olympics **(Fairbanks AK)**
JUL Cheyenne Frontier Days **(WY)**
JUL Freedom Fest and Riverblues festivals **(Philadelphia PA)**
JUL-AUG Hopi and Navajo Crafts Shows **(Flagstaff AZ)**
JUL-AUG Newport Folk and Jazz Festivals **(RI)**
AUG 4th Corn Dance Festival **(Santo Domingo NM)**
AUG Elvis Week **(Memphis TN)**
AUG Inter-Tribal Indian Ceremonial **(Gallup NM)**
AUG Texas Folklife Festival **(San Antonio TX)**
LABOR DAY WEEKEND Bumbershoot Festival **(Seattle WA)**
SEP Fiestas de **Santa Fe (NM)** **SEP Pendleton** Round-Up **(OR)**
SEP Monterey Jazz Festival **(CA)**
SEP Festivals Acadiens **(Lafayette LA)**
SEP Los Angeles County Fair **(Pomona CA)**
OCT Texas State Fair **(Dallas TX)** **OCT Chicago** Marathon **(IL)**
OCT 31st Greenwich Village Hallowe'en Parade **(New York NY)**
NOV Macy's Thanksgiving Day Parade **(New York NY)**
NOV New York City Marathon **(NY)**
DEC National Rodeo Finals **(Las Vegas NV)**
DEC Boston Tea-Party Re-enactment **(MA)**

SPEED LIMITS

Maximum **rural interstate** speed limits

- 75mph / 120kph
- 70mph / 112kph
- 65mph / 105kph
- 60mph / 97kph

States named in red have an **urban interstate** speed limit of 55mph (50mph in Hawaii). All other states have an urban interstate limit of between 60 and 70 mph.

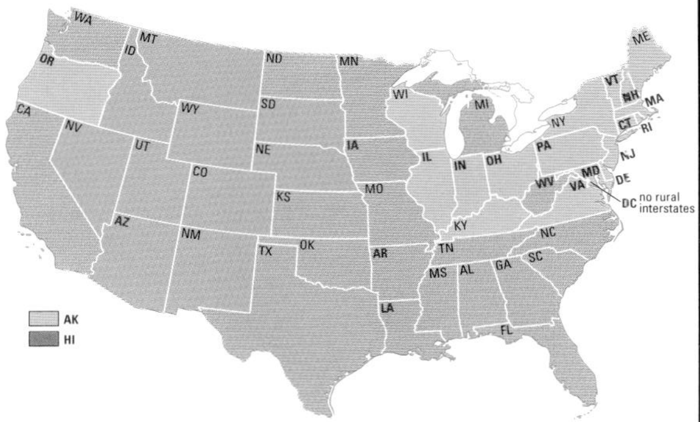

DC no rural interstates

United States: Northeast

See also... Time (18-19); Tourism UK & USA (25); N. America Climate (155); N. America Historical (156-157); USA & Canada Transport (158); • cont >

The listings above refer to a selection of related themes. For more information, see the Contents (2-7).

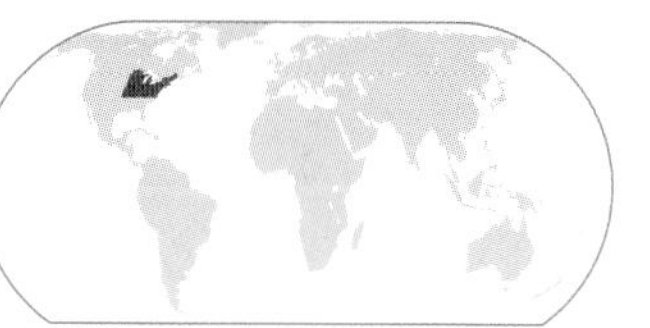

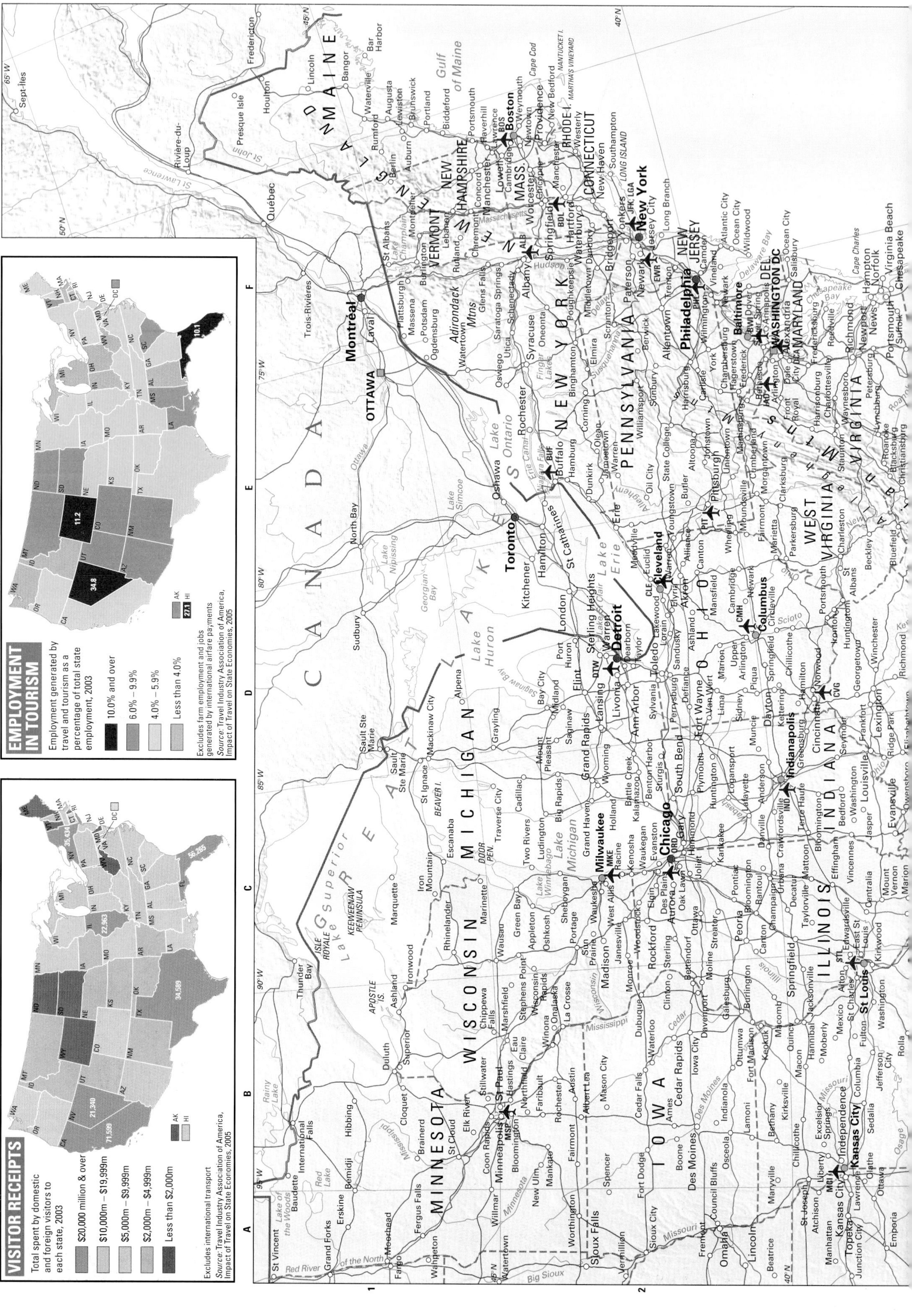

VISITOR RECEIPTS

Total spent by domestic and foreign visitors to each state, 2003

- $20,000 million & over
- $10,000m – $19,999m
- $5,000m – $9,999m
- $2,000m – $4,999m
- Less than $2,000m

Excludes international transport
Source: Travel Industry Association of America, Impact of Travel on State Economies, 2005

EMPLOYMENT IN TOURISM

Employment generated by travel and tourism as a percentage of total state employment, 2003

- 10.0% and over
- 6.0% – 9.9%
- 4.0% – 5.9%
- Less than 4.0%

Excludes farm employment and jobs generated by international airfare payments
Source: Travel Industry Association of America, Impact of Travel on State Economies, 2005

See also... *cont<* • USA & Canada Museums & Galleries (159); USA & Canada Winter Sports (160); US National Parks Service (166-167); US Theme Parks (165)

The listings above refer to a selection of related themes. For more information, see the Contents (2-7).

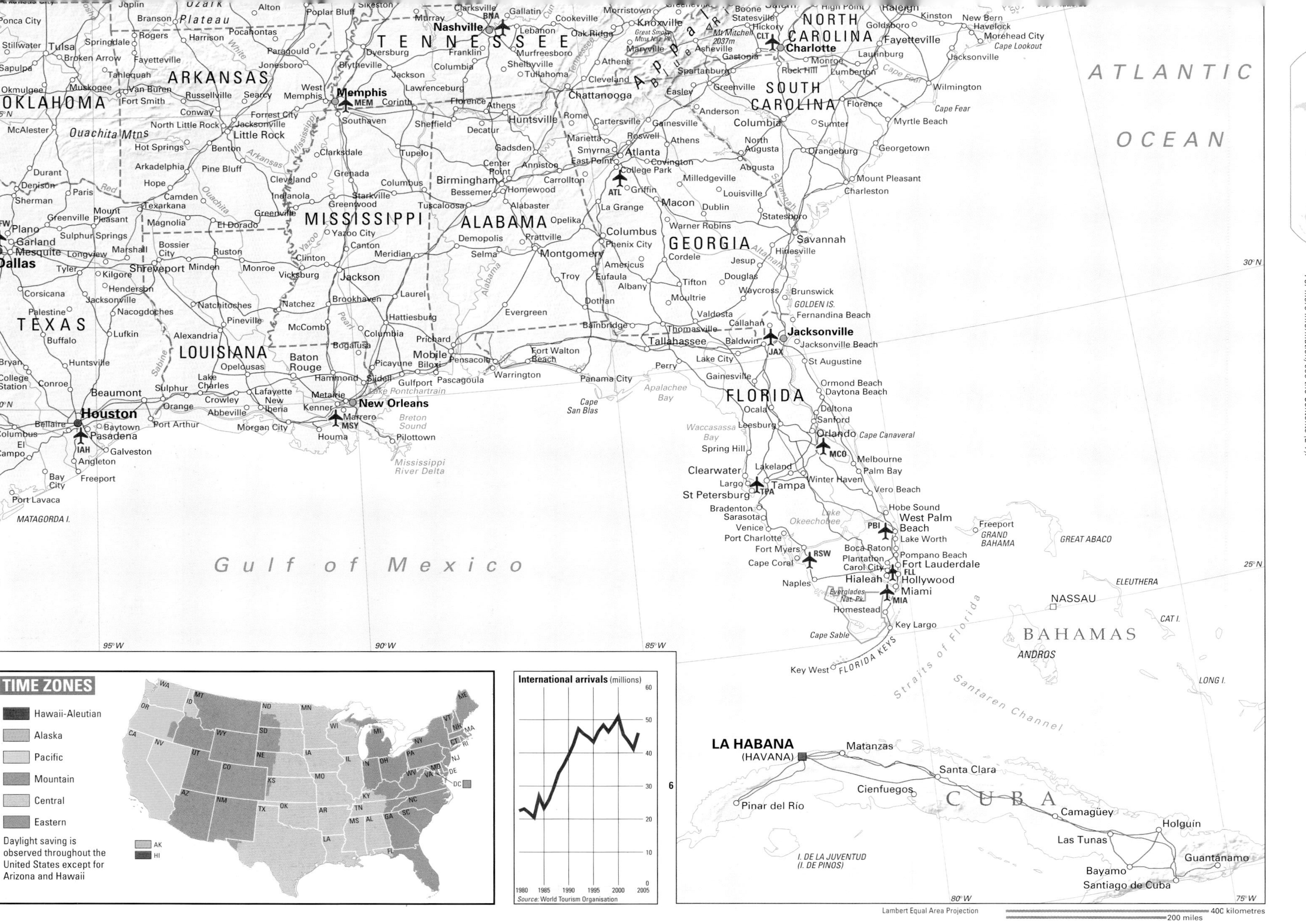
ATLANTIC OCEAN
Gulf of Mexico
OKLAHOMA
ARKANSAS
TENNESSEE
NORTH CAROLINA
SOUTH CAROLINA
MISSISSIPPI
ALABAMA
GEORGIA
TEXAS
LOUISIANA
FLORIDA
BAHAMAS
CUBA
LA HABANA (HAVANA)
NASSAU
Straits of Florida
Santaren Channel
Dallas
Houston
New Orleans
Memphis
Nashville
Atlanta
Charlotte
Jacksonville
Tampa
Orlando
Miami
TIME ZONES
Hawaii-Aleutian
Alaska
Pacific
Mountain
Central
Eastern
Daylight saving is observed throughout the United States except for Arizona and Hawaii
International arrivals (millions)
1980 1985 1990 1995 2000 2005
0 10 20 30 40 50 60
Source: World Tourism Organisation
Lambert Equal Area Projection
200 miles
400 kilometres

US National Parks Service

See also... UNESCO Natural & Cultural Heritage (48-53); North America Historical (156-157); Canadian National Parks (175)

The listings above refer to a selection of related themes. For more information, see the Contents (2-7).

■ **National Park / Preserve**
NATIONAL PARKS contain a variety of resources protected by large areas of land or water; National Preserves permit activities not permitted in National Parks, such as hunting, fishing and mineral extraction

● **National Monument**
Landmarks, structures and other objects of historic or scientific interest

▼ **National Historic Site / Historical Park**
National Historic Sites contain a single historical feature; National Historical Parks are similar but extend beyond single properties or buildings

▲ **National Memorial**
Commemorate a historic person or episode

◆ **National Battlefield / Battlefield Park / Battlefield Site / Military Park**
All associated with US military history; many sites include a National Cemetery

♣ **National Recreation Area / Seashore / Lakeshore**
National Recreation Areas are set aside for purely recreational use and are often near major cities; National Seashores and Lakeshores provide water-oriented recreation whilst preserving shorelines and islands

✪ **National Parkway**
Roadways preserved for their scenic value, often connecting cultural sites

National Reserves *are areas of nationally significant resources protected through local land-use management supported by federal assistance.* **Other protected areas** *managed by the National Park Service include National Rivers (designations: National River & Recreation Area, National Scenic River, Wild River, etc.), National Heritage Corridors, National Scenic Trails and National Historic Trails.* **Affiliated areas** *include National Heritage Areas, managed by government-private partnerships.*

THE TEN MOST VISITED NATIONAL PARKS [■] IN THE USA IN 2004	In list
1 **Great Smoky Mountains** Tenn/N Carolina: 9,167,046 recreational visitors	226
2 **Grand Canyon** Arizona: 4,326,234	97
3 **Cuyahoga Valley** Ohio: 3,306,175	184
4 **Yosemite** California: 3,280,911	46
5 **Olympic** Washington: 3,073,722	25
6 **Yellowstone** Wyoming/Idaho/Montana: 2,868,317	70
7 **Rocky Mountain** Colorado: 2,781,899	85
8 **Zion** Utah: 2,677,342	75
9 **Grand Teton** Wyoming: 2,360,373	71
10 **Acadia** Maine: 2,207,847	296

Source: National Park Service (www.nps.gov)

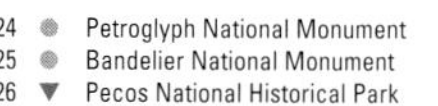

Sites marked with an asterisk (*) are featured in Columbus Travel Guides' *Tourist Attractions and Events of the World*

Alaska
1 ▼ Aleutian World War II National Historic Area
Western Arctic National Parklands:
2 ■ Bering Land Bridge National Preserve
3 ● Cape Krusenstern National Monument
4 ■ KOBUK VALLEY NATIONAL PARK
5 ■ Noatak National Preserve
6 ■ GATES OF THE ARCTIC NATIONAL PARK and Preserve
7 ■ Yukon-Charley Rivers National Preserve
8 ■ DENALI NATIONAL PARK and Preserve
9 ■ LAKE CLARK NATIONAL PARK and Preserve
10 ■ KATMAI NATIONAL PARK and Preserve
11 ● Aniakchak National Monument and Preserve
12 ■ KENAI FJORDS NATIONAL PARK
13 ■ WRANGELL-ST ELIAS NATIONAL PARK and Preserve
14 ▼ Klondike Gold Rush National Historical Park (also in Seattle, WA)
15 ■ GLACIER BAY NATIONAL PARK and Preserve
16 ▼ Sitka National Historical Park

Hawaii
17 ▲ USS Arizona Memorial
18 ▼ Kalaupapa National Historical Park
19 ■ HALEAKALA NATIONAL PARK
20 ▼ Puukohola Heiau National Historic Site
21 ▼ Kaloko-Honokohau National Historical Park
22 ▼ Pu'uhonua o Honaunau National Historical Park
23 ■ HAWAII VOLCANOES NATIONAL PARK*

Washington
24 ▼ San Juan Island National Historical Park
25 ■ OLYMPIC NATIONAL PARK
26 ■ Ebey's Landing National Historical Reserve
27 ■ NORTH CASCADES NATIONAL PARK, including:
♣ Lake Chelan National Recreation Area;
♣ Ross Lake National Recreation Area
28 ♣ Lake Roosevelt National Recreation Area
29 ▼ Whitman Mission National Historic Site
30 ■ MOUNT RAINIER NATIONAL PARK
31 ▼ Fort Vancouver National Historic Site (also in OR), including McLoughlin House

Oregon
32 ▼ Lewis and Clark National Historical Park, including Fort Clatsop
33 ● John Day Fossil Beds National Monument
34 ■ CRATER LAKE NATIONAL PARK
35 ● Oregon Caves National Monument

California
36 ■ REDWOOD NATIONAL PARK
37 ● Lava Beds National Monument
38 ♣ Whiskeytown National Recreation Area
39 ■ LASSEN VOLCANIC NATIONAL PARK
40 ♣ Point Reyes National Seashore
41 ♣ Golden Gate National Recreation Area, including Alcatraz Island*, the Presidio, and:
▼ Fort Point National Historic Site;
● Muir Woods National Monument
▼ San Francisco Maritime National Historical Park
42 ▼ Rosie the Riveter WWII Home Front National Historical Park
43 ▲ Port Chicago Naval Magazine National Memorial;
▼ John Muir National Historic Site
44 ▼ Eugene O'Neill National Historic Site
45 ● Pinnacles National Monument
46 ■ YOSEMITE NATIONAL PARK*
47 ● Devils Postpile National Monument
48 ■ SEQUOIA AND KINGS CANYON NATIONAL PARKS
49 ▼ Manzanar National Historic Site
50 ■ DEATH VALLEY NATIONAL PARK* (also in NV)
51 ■ CHANNEL ISLANDS NATIONAL PARK
52 ♣ Santa Monica Mountains National Recreation Area
53 ● Cabrillo National Monument
54 ■ JOSHUA TREE NATIONAL PARK
55 ■ Mojave National Preserve

Nevada
56 ♣ Lake Mead National Recreation Area (also in AZ), including Hoover Dam*
57 ■ GREAT BASIN NATIONAL PARK

Idaho
58 City of Rocks National Reserve
59 ● Minidoka Internment National Monument
60 ● Hagerman Fossil Beds National Monument
61 ● Craters of the Moon National Monument and Preserve
62 ▼ Nez Perce National Historical Park (also in MT, OR & WA)

Montana
63 ■ GLACIER NATIONAL PARK
64 ▼ Grant-Kohrs Ranch National Historic Site
65 ◆ Big Hole National Battlefield
66 ● Little Bighorn Battlefield National Monument

Wyoming
67 ♣ Bighorn Canyon National Recreation Area (also in MT)
68 ● Devils Tower National Monument
69 ▼ Fort Laramie National Historic Site
70 ■ YELLOWSTONE NATIONAL PARK* (also in ID & MT)
71 ✪ John D. Rockefeller, Jr. Memorial Parkway;
■ GRAND TETON NATIONAL PARK
72 ■ Fossil Butte National Monument

Utah
73 ▼ Golden Spike National Historic Site
74 ● Timpanogos Cave National Monument
75 ■ ZION NATIONAL PARK
76 ● Cedar Breaks National Monument
77 ■ BRYCE CANYON NATIONAL PARK
78 ■ CAPITOL REEF NATIONAL PARK
79 ● Rainbow Bridge National Monument
80 ● Natural Bridges National Monument
81 ■ CANYONLANDS NATIONAL PARK
82 ■ ARCHES NATIONAL PARK
83 ● Hovenweep National Monument (also in CO)

Colorado
84 ● Dinosaur National Monument (also in UT)
85 ■ ROCKY MOUNTAIN NATIONAL PARK
86 ● Colorado National Monument
87 ■ BLACK CANYON OF THE GUNNISON NATIONAL PARK
88 ♣ Curecanti National Recreation Area
89 ● Yucca House National Monument
90 ■ MESA VERDE NATIONAL PARK
91 ■ GREAT SAND DUNES NATIONAL PARK and Preserve
92 ● Florissant Fossil Beds National Monument
93 ▼ Bent's Old Fort National Historic Site
94 ▼ Sand Creek Massacre National Historic Site

Arizona
95 ● Parashant National Monument
96 ● Pipe Spring National Monument
97 ■ GRAND CANYON NATIONAL PARK*
98 ♣ Glen Canyon National Recreation Area (also in UT)
99 ● Navajo National Monument
100 ● Canyon de Chelly National Monument
101 ▼ Hubbell Trading Post National Historic Site
102 ■ PETRIFIED FOREST NATIONAL PARK
103 ● Wupatki National Monument;
● Sunset Crater Volcano National Monument
104 ● Walnut Canyon National Monument
105 ● Tuzigoot National Monument
106 ● Montezuma Castle National Monument
107 ● Tonto National Monument
108 ● Hohokam Pima National Monument
109 ● Casa Grande Ruins National Monument
110 ● Organ Pipe Cactus National Monument
111 ▼ Tumacácori National Historical Park
112 ▲ Coronado National Memorial
113 ■ SAGUARO NATIONAL PARK
114 ▼ Fort Bowie National Historic Site
115 ● Chiricahua National Monument

New Mexico
116 ● Gila Cliff Dwellings National Monument
117 ● White Sands National Monument
118 ■ CARLSBAD CAVERNS NATIONAL PARK
119 ● Salinas Pueblo Missions National Monument
120 ● Aztec Ruins National Monument
121 ▼ Chaco Culture National Historical Park
122 ● El Morro National Monument
123 ● El Malpais National Monument
124 ● Petroglyph National Monument
125 ● Bandelier National Monument
126 ▼ Pecos National Historical Park
127 ● Fort Union National Monument
128 ● Capulin Volcano National Monument

Texas
129 ♣ Lake Meredith National Recreation Area, including:
● Alibates Flint Quarries National Monument
130 ▲ Chamizal National Memorial
131 ■ GUADALUPE MOUNTAINS NATIONAL PARK
132 ▼ Fort Davis National Historic Site
133 ■ BIG BEND NATIONAL PARK
134 ♣ Amistad National Recreation Area
135 ▼ Lyndon B. Johnson National Historical Park
136 ▼ San Antonio Missions National Historical Park
137 ▼ Palo Alto Battlefield National Historic Site
138 ♣ Padre Island National Seashore
139 ■ Big Thicket National Preserve

Oklahoma
140 ♣ Chickasaw National Recreation Area
141 ▲ Oklahoma City National Memorial
142 ▼ Washita Battlefield National Historic Site

North Dakota
143 ▼ Fort Union Trading Post National Historic Site
144 ■ THEODORE ROOSEVELT NATIONAL PARK
145 ▼ Knife River Indian Villages National Historic Site

South Dakota
146 ● Jewel Cave National Monument;
▲ Mount Rushmore National Memorial*
147 ■ WIND CAVE NATIONAL PARK
148 ■ BADLANDS NATIONAL PARK
149 ▼ Minuteman Missile National Historic Site

Minnesota
150 ● Pipestone National Monument
151 ■ VOYAGEURS NATIONAL PARK
152 ● Grand Portage National Monument

Wisconsin
153 ♣ Apostle Islands National Lakeshore

Michigan
154 ■ ISLE ROYALE NATIONAL PARK
155 ▼ Keweenaw National Historical Park
156 ♣ Pictured Rocks National Lakeshore
157 ▲ Father Marquette National Memorial
158 ♣ Sleeping Bear Dunes National Lakeshore

Nebraska
159 ● Agate Fossil Beds National Monument

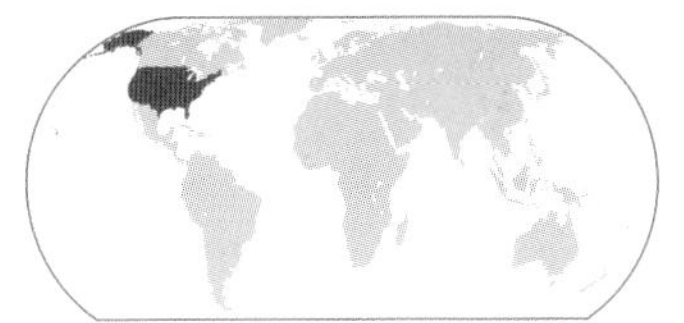

▶ *See also...* UNESCO Natural & Cultural Heritage (48-53); North America Historical (156-157); Canadian National Parks (175)

The listings above refer to a selection of related themes. For more information, see the Contents (2-7).

US National Parks Service

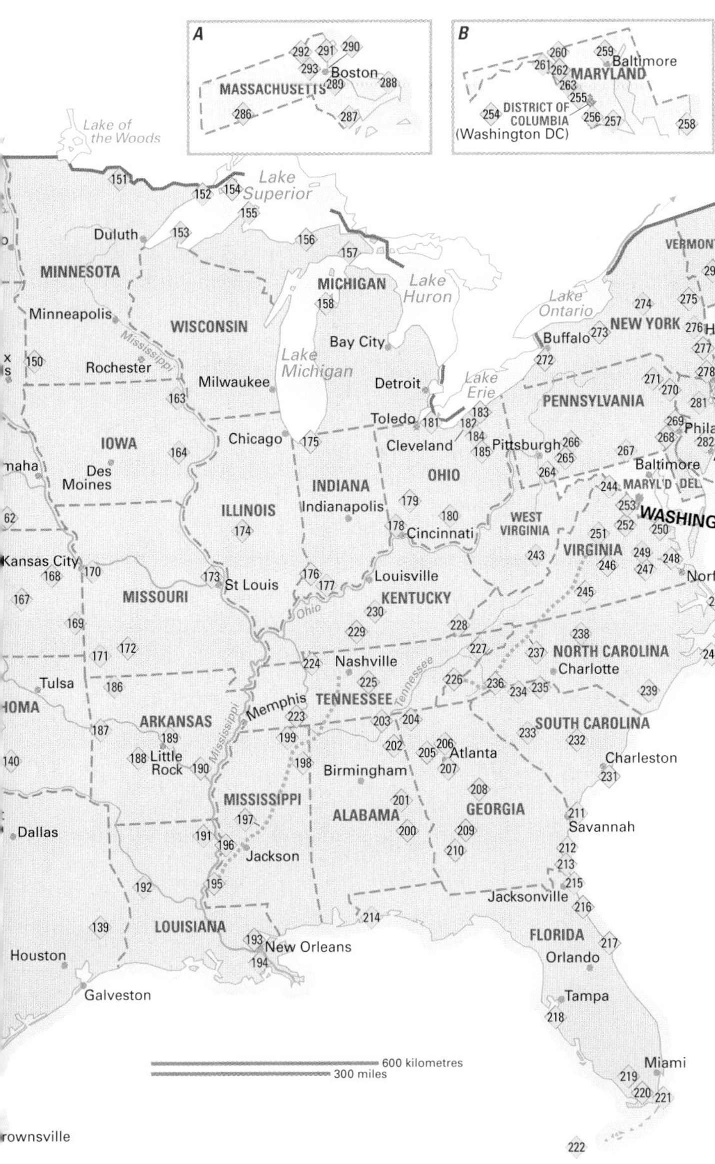
A
MASSACHUSETTS
Boston
B
MARYLAND
Baltimore
DISTRICT OF COLUMBIA
(Washington DC)
Lake of the Woods
Lake Superior
Duluth
MINNESOTA
Minneapolis
Rochester
WISCONSIN
Milwaukee
MICHIGAN
Lake Huron
Lake Michigan
Bay City
Detroit
IOWA
Des Moines
Chicago
ILLINOIS
INDIANA
Indianapolis
OHIO
Toledo
Cleveland
Lake Erie
Lake Ontario
Buffalo
NEW YORK
PENNSYLVANIA
Pittsburgh
Philadelphia
Atlantic City
NEW JERSEY
New York
VERMONT
NEW HAMPSHIRE
MAINE
Portland
MASSACHUSETTS: SEE ENLARGEMENT A ABOVE
Boston
Hartford
Providence
CONN.
RHODE I.
MARYLAND & DC: SEE ENLARGEMENT B ABOVE
WASHINGTON DC
MARYL'D
DEL.
WEST VIRGINIA
VIRGINIA
Norfolk
Cincinnati
Louisville
KENTUCKY
Kansas City
MISSOURI
St Louis
Nashville
TENNESSEE
NORTH CAROLINA
Charlotte
Memphis
ARKANSAS
Little Rock
Tulsa
SOUTH CAROLINA
Charleston
Atlanta
Birmingham
MISSISSIPPI
ALABAMA
GEORGIA
Savannah
Jackson
Dallas
LOUISIANA
New Orleans
Houston
Galveston
Jacksonville
FLORIDA
Orlando
Tampa
Miami
Brownsville
600 kilometres
300 miles

160 ● Scotts Bluff National Monument
161 ▼ Chimney Rock National Historic Site
162 ● Homestead National Monument of America

Iowa
163 ● Effigy Mounds National Monument
164 ▼ Herbert Hoover National Historic Site

Kansas
165 ▼ Nicodemus National Historic Site
166 ▼ Fort Larned National Historic Site
167 ■ Tallgrass Prairie National Preserve
168 ▼ Brown v. Board of Education National Historic Site
169 ▼ Fort Scott National Historic Site

Missouri
170 ▼ Harry S. Truman National Historic Site
171 ● George Washington Carver National Monument
172 ◆ Wilson's Creek National Battlefield
173 ▼ Ulysses S. Grant National Historic Site;
▲ Jefferson National Expansion Memorial

Illinois
174 ▼ Lincoln Home National Historic Site

Indiana
175 ♣ Indiana Dunes National Lakeshore
176 ▼ George Rogers Clark National Historical Park
177 ▲ Lincoln Boyhood National Memorial

Ohio
178 ▼ William Howard Taft National Historic Site
179 ▼ Dayton Aviation Heritage National Historical Park
180 ▼ Hopewell Culture National Historical Park
181 ▲ Perry's Victory and International Peace Memorial
182 ▲ David Berger National Memorial
183 ▼ James A. Garfield National Historic Site
184 ■ CUYAHOGA VALLEY NATIONAL PARK
185 ▼ First Ladies National Historic Site

Arkansas
186 ◆ Pea Ridge National Military Park
187 ▼ Fort Smith National Historic Site (also in OK)
188 ■ HOT SPRINGS NATIONAL PARK
189 ▼ Central High School National Historic Site
190 ▲ Arkansas Post National Memorial

Louisiana
191 ● Poverty Point National Monument
192 ▼ Cane River Creole National Historical Park
193 ▼ New Orleans Jazz National Historical Park*
194 ▼ Jean Lafitte National Historical Park and Preserve

Mississippi
195 ▼ Natchez National Historical Park
196 ◆ Vicksburg National Military Park (and Cemetery)
197 ○ Natchez Trace Parkway (also in AL & TN), including:
198 ◆ Tupelo National Battlefield
199 ◆ Brices Cross Roads National Battlefield Site

Alabama
200 ▼ Tuskegee Airmen National Historic Site;
▼ Tuskegee Institute National Historic Site
201 ◆ Horseshoe Bend National Military Park
202 ■ Little River Canyon National Preserve
203 ● Russell Cave National Monument

Georgia
204 ◆ Chickamauga & Chattanooga National Military Park
205 ◆ Kennesaw Mountain National Battlefield Park
206 ♣ Chattahoochee River National Recreation Area
207 ▼ Martin Luther King Jr. National Historic Site
208 ● Ocmulgee National Monument
209 ● Andersonville National Historic Site
210 ▼ Jimmy Carter National Historic Site
211 ● Fort Pulaski National Monument
212 ● Fort Frederica National Monument
213 ♣ Cumberland Island National Seashore

Florida
214 ♣ Gulf Islands National Seashore (also in MS)
215 Timucuan Ecological and Historic Preserve;
▲ Fort Caroline National Memorial
216 ● Castillo de San Marcos National Monument;
● Fort Matanzas National Monument
217 ♣ Canaveral National Seashore
218 ▲ De Soto National Memorial
219 ■ Big Cypress National Preserve
220 ■ EVERGLADES NATIONAL PARK*
221 ■ BISCAYNE NATIONAL PARK
222 ■ DRY TORTUGAS NATIONAL PARK, including Fort Jefferson

Tennessee
223 ◆ Shiloh National Military Park (and Cemetery)
224 ◆ Fort Donelson National Battlefield (and Cemetery)
225 ◆ Stones River National Battlefield (and Cemetery)
226 ■ GREAT SMOKY MOUNTAINS NATIONAL PARK (also in NC)
227 ▼ Andrew Johnson National Historic Site

Kentucky
228 ▼ Cumberland Gap National Historical Park (also in TN & VA)
229 ■ MAMMOTH CAVE NATIONAL PARK
230 ▼ Abraham Lincoln Birthplace National Historic Site

South Carolina
231 ● Fort Sumter National Monument;
● Fort Moultrie National Monument;
▼ Charles Pinckney National Historic Site
232 ■ CONGAREE NATIONAL PARK
233 ▼ Ninety Six National Historic Site
234 ◆ Kings Mountain National Military Park
235 ◆ Cowpens National Battlefield

North Carolina
236 ▼ Carl Sandburg Home National Historic Site
237 ○ Blue Ridge Parkway (also in VA)
238 ◆ Guilford Courthouse National Military Park
239 ◆ Moores Creek National Battlefield
240 ♣ Cape Lookout National Seashore
241 ♣ Cape Hatteras National Seashore
242 ▼ Fort Raleigh National Historic Site;
▲ Wright Brothers National Memorial

West Virginia
243 ♣ Gauley River National Recreation Area
244 ▼ Harpers Ferry National Historical Park

Virginia–DC–Maryland
○ George Washington Memorial Parkway, including:
253 ▲ Arlington House, The Robert E. Lee Memorial, VA;
Claude Moore Colonial Farm, VA;
Great Falls Park, VA
254 ▲ Lyndon Baines Johnson Memorial Grove on the Potomac, DC;
▲ Theodore Roosevelt Island, DC
255 ▼ Clara Barton National Historic Site, MD;
Glen Echo Park, MD

Virginia
245 ● Booker T. Washington National Monument
246 ▼ Appomattox Court House National Historical Park
247 ◆ Petersburg National Battlefield, including Poplar Grove National Cemetery
248 ▼ Colonial National Historical Park, including Cape Henry Memorial, Jamestown National Historic Site, Yorktown Battlefield and National Cemetery
249 ▼ Maggie L. Walker National Historic Site;
◆ Richmond National Battlefield Park
250 ● George Washington Birthplace National Monument
251 ■ SHENANDOAH NATIONAL PARK;
▼ Cedar Creek and Belle Grove National Historical Park
252 ◆ Fredericksburg and Spotsylvania National Military Park, including Fredericksburg National Cemetery;
Green Springs National Historic Landmark District;
Prince William Forest Park
253 ◆ Manassas National Battlefield Park;
Wolf Trap National Park for the Performing Arts

District of Columbia and Maryland
254 ▼ Ford's Theatre National Historic Site
National Capital Parks, Central:
▲ African-American Civil War Memorial;
Constitution Gardens;
▲ Franklin Delano Roosevelt Memorial;
▲ George Mason Memorial;
▲ John Ericsson National Memorial;
▲ Korean War Veterans Memorial;
▲ Lincoln Memorial*;
Old Post Office Tower;
▲ Thomas Jefferson Memorial;
▲ Vietnam Veterans Memorial;
▲ Washington Monument
National Capital Parks, East:
Anacostia Park;
Baltimore–Washington Parkway;
Capitol Hill Parks;
Fort Dupont Park;
Fort Washington Park;
▼ Frederick Douglass National Historic Site;
Greenbelt Park;
Harmony Hall;
Kenilworth Park and Aquatic Gardens;
▼ Mary McLeod Bethune Council House National Historic Site;
Oxon Cove Park and Oxon Hill Farm;
Piscataway Park;
▼ Sewall-Belmont National Historic Site;
Suitland Parkway
National Mall and Memorial Parkway
▼ Pennsylvania Avenue National Historic Site
Presidents Park and The White House*
Rock Creek Park, including Battleground National Cemetery, The Old Stone House and Peirce Mill
256 Fort Foote Park
257 ▼ Thomas Stone National Historic Site
258 ♣ Assateague Island National Seashore (also in VA)
259 ● Fort McHenry National Monument and Historic Shrine;
▼ Hampton National Historic Site
260 Catoctin Mountain Park
261 ◆ Antietam National Battlefield (and Cemetery)
262 ◆ Monocacy National Battlefield
263 ▼ Chesapeake and Ohio Canal National Historical Park (also in DC & VA)

Pennsylvania
264 ▼ Friendship Hill National Historic Site;
◆ Fort Necessity National Battlefield
265 ▲ Flight 93 National Memorial
266 ▲ Johnstown Flood National Memorial;
▼ Allegheny Portage Railroad National Historic Site
267 ▼ Eisenhower National Historic Site;
◆ Gettysburg National Military Park (and Cemetery)
268 ▼ Hopewell Furnace National Historic Site;
▼ Valley Forge National Historical Park
269 ▼ Edgar Allen Poe National Historic Site;
▼ Independence National Historical Park, including Deshler-Morris House and Gloria Dei Church National Historic Site;
▲ Thaddeus Kosciuszko National Memorial
270 ♣ Delaware Water Gap National Recreation Area (also in NJ)
271 ▼ Steamtown National Historic Site

New York
272 ▼ Theodore Roosevelt Inaugural National Historic Site
273 ▼ Women's Rights National Historical Park
274 ● Fort Stanwix National Monument
275 ▼ Saratoga National Historical Park
276 ▼ Martin Van Buren National Historic Site
277 ▼ Eleanor Roosevelt National Historic Site;
▼ Vanderbilt Mansion National Historic Site;
▼ Home of Franklin Delano Roosevelt National Historic Site
278 National Parks of New York Harbor:
♣ Gateway National Recreation Area (also in NJ);
● Governors Island National Monument;
▼ Lower East Side Tenement Museum National Historic Site;
Manhattan Sites:
● Castle Clinton National Monument;
▲ Federal Hall National Memorial;
▲ General Grant National Memorial;
▲ Hamilton Grange National Memorial;
▼ St Paul's Church National Historic Site;
▼ Theodore Roosevelt Birthplace National Historic Site;
● Statue of Liberty National Monument*, incl. Ellis Island National Monument
279 ▼ Sagamore Hill National Historic Site
280 ♣ Fire Island National Seashore

New Jersey
281 ▼ Edison National Historic Site;
▼ Morristown National Historical Park
282 New Jersey Pinelands National Reserve

Connecticut
283 ▼ Weir Farm National Historic Site

Rhode Island
284 ▲ Roger Williams National Memorial
285 ▼ Touro Synagogue National Historic Site

Massachusetts
286 ▼ Springfield Armory National Historic Site
287 ▼ New Bedford Whaling National Historical Park
288 ♣ Cape Cod National Seashore
289 ▼ Adams National Historical Park
290 ▼ Boston African American National Historical Site;
♣ Boston Harbor Islands National Recreation Area;
▼ Boston National Historical Park (The Freedom Trail)*;
▼ Frederick Law Olmsted National Historic Site;
▼ John F. Kennedy National Historic Site;
▼ Longfellow National Historic Site
291 ▼ Saugus Iron Works National Historic Site;
▼ Salem Maritime National Historic Site
292 ▼ Lowell National Historical Park
293 ▼ Minute Man National Historical Park

Vermont
294 ▼ Marsh-Billings-Rockefeller National Historical Park

New Hampshire
295 ▼ St-Gaudens National Historic Site

Maine
296 ■ ACADIA NATIONAL PARK
297 ▼ St Croix Island International Historic Site

The following are not shown on the map:

Puerto Rico
▼ San Juan National Historic Site

US Virgin Islands
● Buck Island Reef National Monument
▼ Christiansted National Historic Site
▼ Salt River Bay National Historical Park and Ecological Preserve
● Virgin Islands Coral Reef National Monument
■ VIRGIN ISLANDS NATIONAL PARK

American Samoa
■ NATIONAL PARK OF AMERICAN SAMOA

Guam
▼ War in the Pacific National Historical Park

Northern Mariana Islands
American Memorial Park

United States of America

See also... Contents (2-7) – this country features in many thematic and regional maps throughout the *World Travel Atlas*.

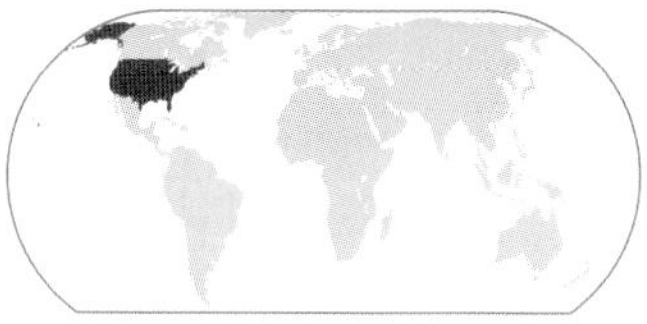

WASHINGTON & OREGON
CALIFORNIA & NEVADA
WEST OF THE RIO GRANDE
EAST TEXAS
LOUISIANA
FLORIDA
BOSTON-NEW YORK-WASHINGTON
Seattle
Olympia
Spokane
WASHINGTON
Portland
Salem
Eugene
OREGON
IDAHO
Boise
CASCADE RANGE
Great Falls
Helena
MONTANA
Billings
ROCKY MOUNTAINS
HIGH PLAINS
GREAT PLAINS
PRAIRIES
NORTH DAKOTA
Bismarck
Fargo
SOUTH DAKOTA
Pierre
Rapid City
BADLANDS
Sioux Falls
WYOMING
Casper
Cheyenne
NEBRASKA
Omaha
Lincoln
MINNESOTA
St Paul
Minneapolis
Duluth
Rochester
WISCONSIN
Madison
Milwaukee
MICHIGAN
Lansing
Detroit
Bay City
Lake Superior
Lake Michigan
Lake Huron
Lake Erie
Lake Ontario
Great Lakes
Lake of the Woods
MAINE
Augusta
Portland
NEW ENGLAND
Montpelier
VERMONT
NEW HAMPSHIRE
Concord
MASSACHUSETTS
Boston
RHODE ISLAND
Providence
CONNECTICUT
Hartford
Albany
NEW YORK
Rochester
Buffalo
New York
LONG I.
Trenton
NEW JERSEY
Philadelphia
Atlantic City
PENNSYLVANIA
Harrisburg
Pittsburgh
Baltimore
Dover
DELAWARE
Annapolis
MARYLAND
WASHINGTON DC
WEST VIRGINIA
Charleston
VIRGINIA
Richmond
Norfolk
APPALACHIAN MTS
BLUE RIDGE
Sacramento
San Francisco
San Jose
Reno
Carson City
GREAT BASIN
NEVADA
CALIFORNIA
SIERRA NEVADA
Salt Lake City
UTAH
Great Salt Lake
Denver
COLORADO
Colorado Springs
Las Vegas
COLORADO PLATEAU
GRAND CANYON
Bakersfield
Los Angeles
San Bernardino
CHANNEL IS.
San Diego
ARIZONA
Phoenix
Tucson
Albuquerque
Santa Fe
NEW MEXICO
IOWA
Des Moines
KANSAS
Topeka
Kansas City
MISSOURI
Jefferson City
St Louis
OZARK PLATEAU
Branson
ILLINOIS
Chicago
Springfield
INDIANA
Indianapolis
OHIO
Columbus
Cleveland
Toledo
Cincinnati
KENTUCKY
Louisville
Frankfort
TENNESSEE
Nashville
Memphis
NORTH CAROLINA
Raleigh
Charlotte
SOUTH CAROLINA
Columbia
Charleston
GEORGIA
Atlanta
Savannah
ALABAMA
Birmingham
Montgomery
MISSISSIPPI
Jackson
LOUISIANA
Baton Rouge
New Orleans
MISSISSIPPI RIVER DELTA
ARKANSAS
Little Rock
OKLAHOMA
Oklahoma City
Tulsa
Amarillo
Lubbock
LLANO ESTACADO
El Paso
TEXAS
Fort Worth
Dallas
EDWARDS PLATEAU
Austin
San Antonio
Houston
Galveston
Brownsville
FLORIDA
Jacksonville
Tallahassee
Orlando
Tampa
Miami
FLORIDA KEYS
State boundary
State capital
800 km
400 miles

For an alphabetical list of US states, see Appendices

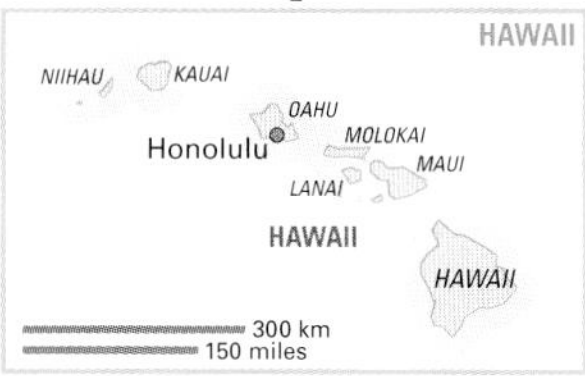
HAWAII
NIIHAU
KAUAI
OAHU
MOLOKAI
MAUI
LANAI
Honolulu
HAWAII
300 km
150 miles

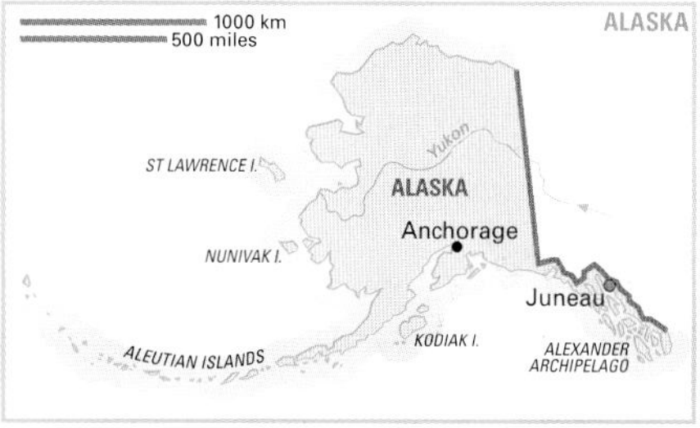
1000 km
500 miles
ALASKA
ST LAWRENCE I.
ALASKA
Anchorage
NUNIVAK I.
Juneau
KODIAK I.
ALEUTIAN ISLANDS
ALEXANDER ARCHIPELAGO

1 **SMF** Sacramento
2 **OAK** Oakland
3 **SFO** San Francisco
4 **SJO** San Jose Norman Mineta
5 **MRY** Monterey Peninsula
6 **FCH** Fresno-Yosemite
7 **BUR** Burbank-Glendale-Pasadena
8 **LAX** Los Angeles
9 **SNA** Santa Ana John Wayne
10 **ONT** Ontario
11 **SAN** San Diego Lindbergh Field
12 **PSP** Palm Springs
13 **LAS** Las Vegas McCarran
14 **RNO** Reno-Tahoe Cannon

1 **SEA** Seattle-Tacoma
2 **GEG** Spokane
3 **PDX** Portland
4 **EUG** Eugene
5 **BOI** Boise

WASHINGTON & OREGON
CANADA
VANCOUVER ISLAND
Victoria
Bellingham
Mt Baker 3285m
Cape Flattery
Port Angeles
Forks
Mt Olympus 2428m
OLYMPIC NAT. PARK
Queets
Everett
Seattle
Bellevue
Tacoma
Olympia
Aberdeen
GRAYS HARBOR
WILLAPA BAY
Mt Rainier 4392m
Centralia
Mt St Helens 2550m
Astoria
Seaside
Cannon Beach
Longview
Vancouver
Portland
Gresham
Mt Hood 3425m
The Dalles
Salem
Corvallis
Albany
Eugene
Newport
Lincoln City
McMinnville
Florence
Coos Bay
Bandon
Cape Blanco
Gold Beach
Grants Pass
Medford
Ashland
Klamath Falls
Bend
Mt Batchelor 2763m
CASCADE RANGE
WASHINGTON
Wenatchee
Ellensburg
Yakima
COLUMBIA BASIN
Richland
Pasco
Walla Walla
Spokane
Coeur d'Alene
Pullman
Moscow
Lewiston
Grand Coulee Dam
OREGON
PACIFIC OCEAN
Pendleton
La Grande
Baker City
BLUE MTNS
COLUMBIA PLATEAU
John Day
HARNEY BASIN
Burns
GREAT SANDY DESERT
Ontario
Nampa
Boise
Caldwell
Idaho City
IDAHO
SALMON RIVER MOUNTAINS
BITTERROOT RA.
Missoula
Kalispell
Polson
MT
Twin Falls
Shoshone
NEVADA
300 kilometres
150 miles

*Combined as the Waterton-Glacier International Peace Park

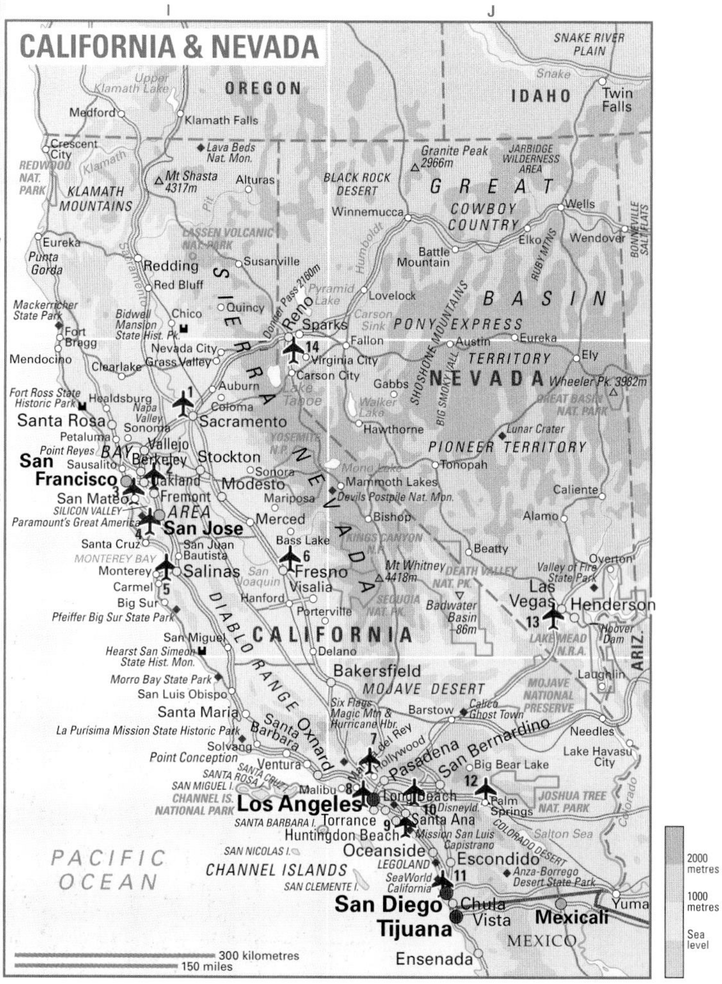
CALIFORNIA & NEVADA
OREGON
IDAHO
Twin Falls
Klamath Falls
Medford
Crescent City
Eureka
Redding
Red Bluff
Mt Shasta 4317m
KLAMATH MOUNTAINS
Chico
Mendocino
Fort Bragg
Santa Rosa
Sacramento
Stockton
San Francisco
Oakland
San Mateo
Fremont
San Jose
Santa Cruz
Monterey
Salinas
Carmel
Big Sur
Modesto
Merced
Fresno
Visalia
Hanford
Porterville
Bakersfield
San Luis Obispo
Santa Maria
Santa Barbara
Ventura
Oxnard
Los Angeles
Pasadena
Long Beach
Santa Ana
Huntington Beach
Oceanside
Escondido
San Diego
Tijuana
Chula Vista
Ensenada
Mexicali
Yuma
MEXICO
San Bernardino
Palm Springs
Big Bear Lake
Reno
Sparks
Carson City
Virginia City
Lake Tahoe
SIERRA NEVADA
CALIFORNIA
DIABLO RANGE
MOJAVE DESERT
Barstow
Needles
Mt Whitney 4418m
Bishop
Mammoth Lakes
Tonopah
Beatty
Las Vegas
Henderson
NEVADA
GREAT BASIN
Winnemucca
Elko
Wells
Ely
Austin
Eureka
Fallon
Lovelock
Hawthorne
PACIFIC OCEAN
CHANNEL ISLANDS
300 kilometres
150 miles
2000 metres
1000 metres
Sea level

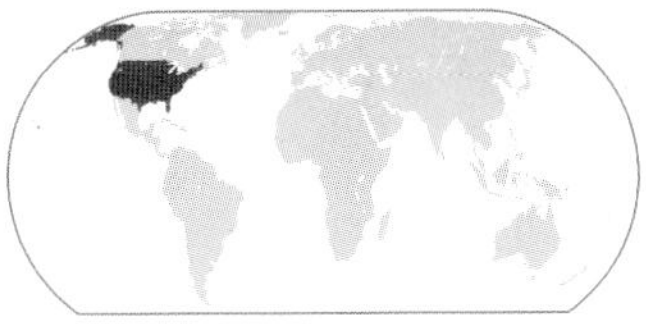

See also... Contents (2-7) – this country features in many thematic and regional maps throughout the *World Travel Atlas*.

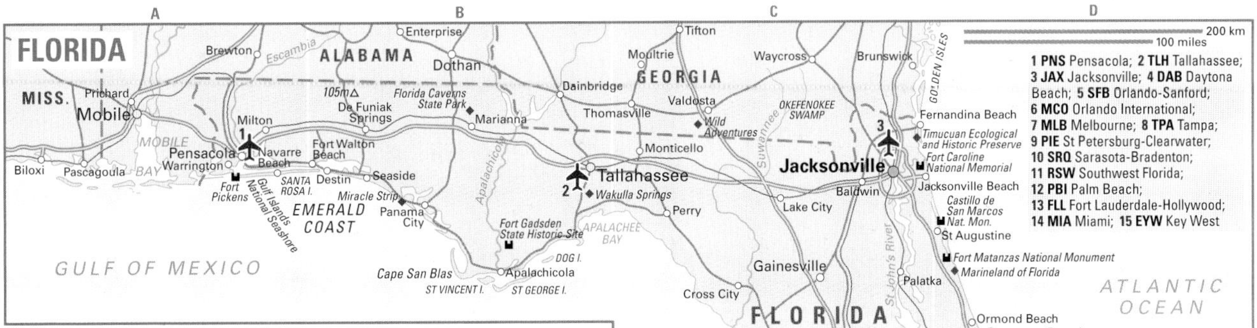
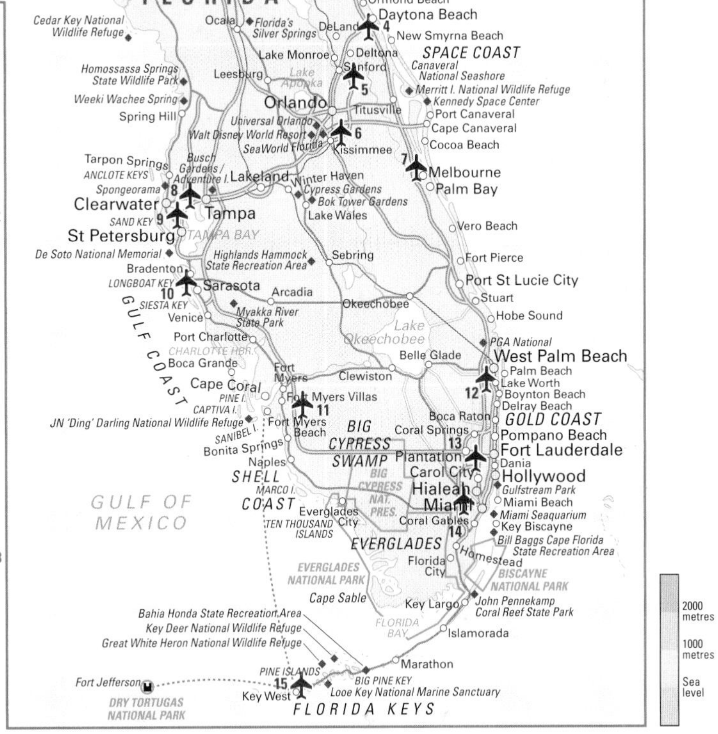
FLORIDA
ALABAMA
GEORGIA
MISS.
Mobile
Pensacola
Tallahassee
Jacksonville
Dothan
Panama City
EMERALD COAST
GULF OF MEXICO
ATLANTIC OCEAN
FLORIDA
Gainesville
Daytona Beach
SPACE COAST
Orlando
Titusville
Kissimmee
Melbourne
Palm Bay
Lakeland
Clearwater
Tampa
St Petersburg
Sarasota
GULF COAST
Fort Myers
Naples
Vero Beach
Port St Lucie City
West Palm Beach
Boca Raton
GOLD COAST
Fort Lauderdale
Hollywood
Hialeah
Miami
BIG CYPRESS SWAMP
SHELL COAST
EVERGLADES
EVERGLADES NATIONAL PARK
Key Largo
Marathon
Key West
FLORIDA KEYS
DRY TORTUGAS NATIONAL PARK
GULF OF MEXICO
200 km
100 miles
2000 metres
1000 metres
Sea level

1 **PNS** Pensacola; 2 **TLH** Tallahassee; 3 **JAX** Jacksonville; 4 **DAB** Daytona Beach; 5 **SFB** Orlando-Sanford; 6 **MCO** Orlando International; 7 **MLB** Melbourne; 8 **TPA** Tampa; 9 **PIE** St Petersburg-Clearwater; 10 **SRQ** Sarasota-Bradenton; 11 **RSW** Southwest Florida; 12 **PBI** Palm Beach; 13 **FLL** Fort Lauderdale-Hollywood; 14 **MIA** Miami; 15 **EYW** Key West

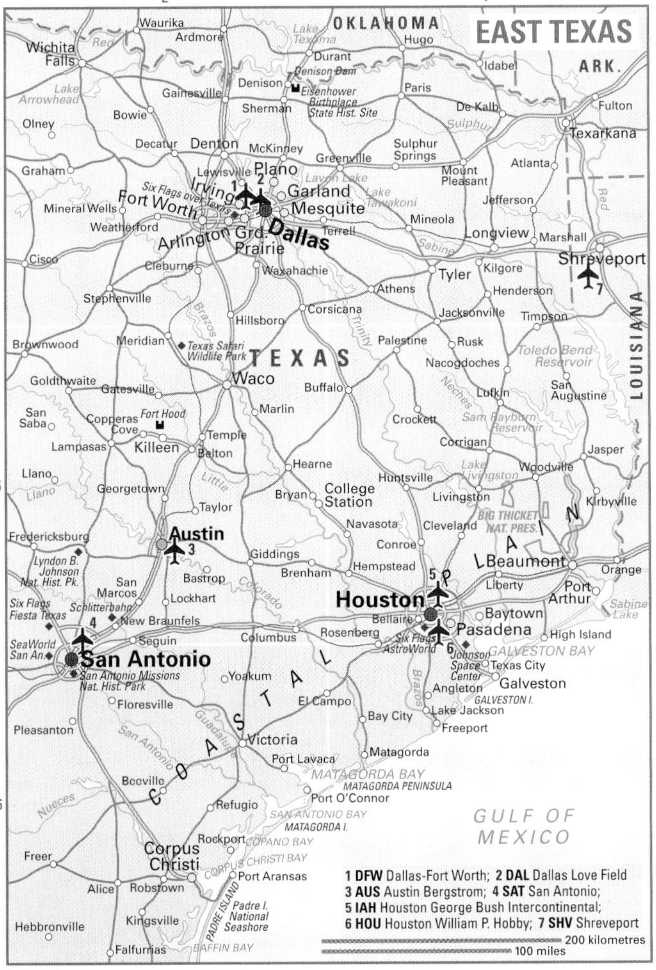
EAST TEXAS
OKLAHOMA
ARK.
LOUISIANA
TEXAS
Wichita Falls
Denton
Fort Worth
Dallas
Arlington
Irving
Plano
Garland
Mesquite
Waco
Texarkana
Shreveport
Tyler
Longview
Killeen
College Station
Austin
San Antonio
Houston
Pasadena
Beaumont
Port Arthur
Galveston
Corpus Christi
COASTAL PLAIN
GULF OF MEXICO
200 kilometres
100 miles

1 **DFW** Dallas-Fort Worth; 2 **DAL** Dallas Love Field
3 **AUS** Austin Bergstrom; 4 **SAT** San Antonio;
5 **IAH** Houston George Bush Intercontinental;
6 **HOU** Houston William P. Hobby; 7 **SHV** Shreveport

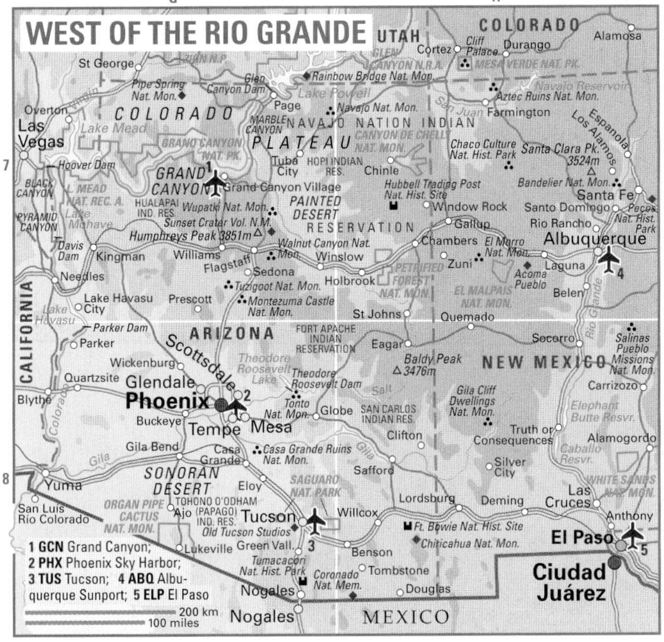
WEST OF THE RIO GRANDE
UTAH
COLORADO
COLORADO PLATEAU
NAVAJO NATION INDIAN RESERVATION
GRAND CANYON
Las Vegas
CALIFORNIA
ARIZONA
NEW MEXICO
Flagstaff
Sedona
Santa Fe
Albuquerque
Phoenix
Scottsdale
Tempe
Mesa
Glendale
SONORAN DESERT
Yuma
Tucson
Las Cruces
El Paso
Ciudad Juárez
Nogales
MEXICO
200 km
100 miles

1 **GCN** Grand Canyon;
2 **PHX** Phoenix Sky Harbor;
3 **TUS** Tucson; 4 **ABQ** Albuquerque Sunport; 5 **ELP** El Paso

INDIAN RESERVATIONS

Principal reservations in the 48 states. Navajo Nation, the largest, covers over 65,000 sq km (25,000 sq miles) in three states and completely surrounds the Hopi Indian Reservation.
A large number of smaller reservations are distributed in Arizona, California, Nevada, New Mexico and Washington states.

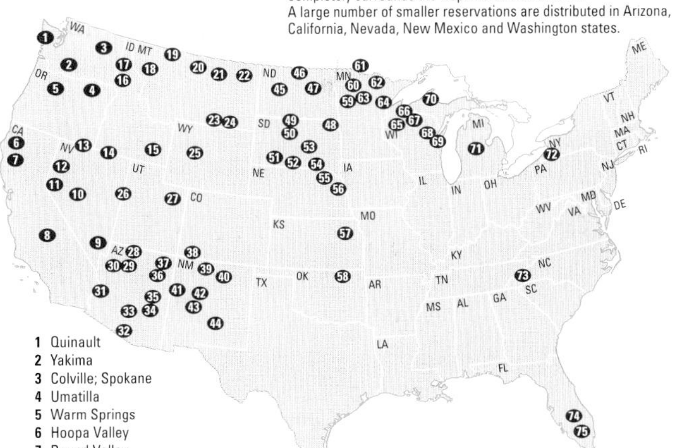

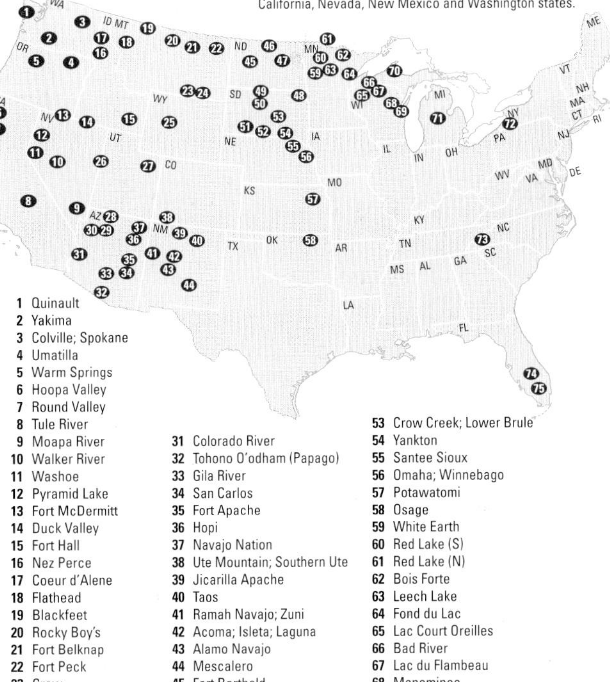

1 Quinault
2 Yakima
3 Colville; Spokane
4 Umatilla
5 Warm Springs
6 Hoopa Valley
7 Round Valley
8 Tule River
9 Moapa River
10 Walker River
11 Washoe
12 Pyramid Lake
13 Fort McDermitt
14 Duck Valley
15 Fort Hall
16 Nez Perce
17 Coeur d'Alene
18 Flathead
19 Blackfeet
20 Rocky Boy's
21 Fort Belknap
22 Fort Peck
23 Crow
24 Northern Cheyenne
25 Wind River
26 Goshute
27 Uintah & Ouray
28 Kaibab
29 Havasupai
230 Hualapai
31 Colorado River
32 Tohono O'odham (Papago)
33 Gila River
34 San Carlos
35 Fort Apache
36 Hopi
37 Navajo Nation
38 Ute Mountain; Southern Ute
39 Jicarilla Apache
40 Taos
41 Ramah Navajo; Zuni
42 Acoma; Isleta; Laguna
43 Alamo Navajo
44 Mescalero
45 Fort Berthold
46 Turtle Mountain
47 Spirit Lake
48 Lake Traverse
49 Standing Rock
50 Cheyenne River
51 Pine Ridge
52 Rosebud
53 Crow Creek; Lower Brule
54 Yankton
55 Santee Sioux
56 Omaha; Winnebago
57 Potawatomi
58 Osage
59 White Earth
60 Red Lake (S)
61 Red Lake (N)
62 Bois Forte
63 Leech Lake
64 Fond du Lac
65 Lac Court Oreilles
66 Bad River
67 Lac du Flambeau
68 Menominee
69 Oneida
70 L'Anse
71 Isabella
72 Cattaraugus
73 Cherokee
74 Brighton
75 Big Cypress; Miccosukee

See also... USA & Canada Transport (158)
The listings above refer to a selection of related themes. For more information, see the Contents (2-7).

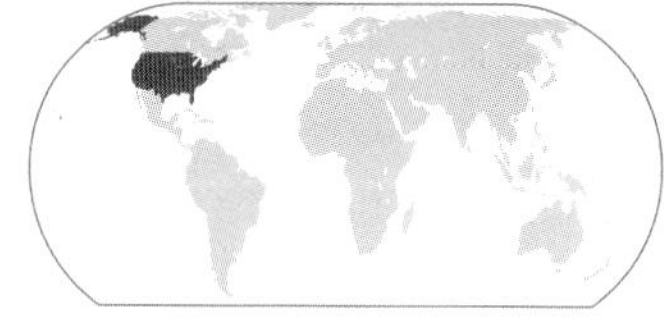

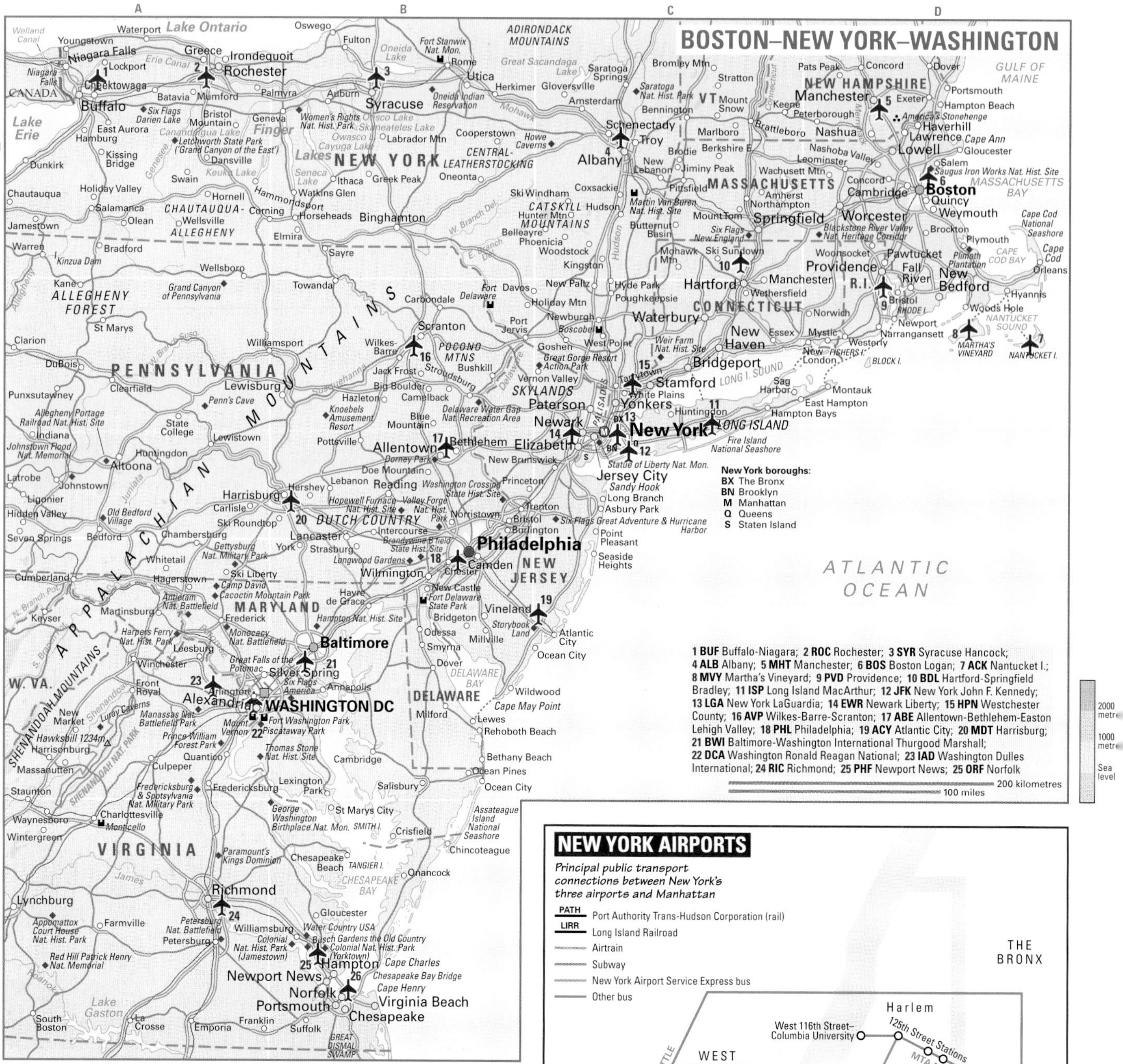

BOSTON–NEW YORK–WASHINGTON

New York boroughs:
BX The Bronx
BN Brooklyn
M Manhattan
Q Queens
S Staten Island

ATLANTIC OCEAN

1 BUF Buffalo-Niagara; **2 ROC** Rochester; **3 SYR** Syracuse Hancock; **4 ALB** Albany; **5 MHT** Manchester; **6 BOS** Boston Logan; **7 ACK** Nantucket I.; **8 MVY** Martha's Vineyard; **9 PVD** Providence; **10 BDL** Hartford-Springfield Bradley; **11 ISP** Long Island MacArthur; **12 JFK** New York John F. Kennedy; **13 LGA** New York LaGuardia; **14 EWR** Newark Liberty; **15 HPN** Westchester County; **16 AVP** Wilkes-Barre-Scranton; **17 ABE** Allentown-Bethlehem-Easton Lehigh Valley; **18 PHL** Philadelphia; **19 ACY** Atlantic City; **20 MDT** Harrisburg; **21 BWI** Baltimore-Washington International Thurgood Marshall; **22 DCA** Washington Ronald Reagan National; **23 IAD** Washington Dulles International; **24 RIC** Richmond; **25 PHF** Newport News; **25 ORF** Norfolk

200 kilometres
100 miles

2000 metres
1000 metres
Sea level

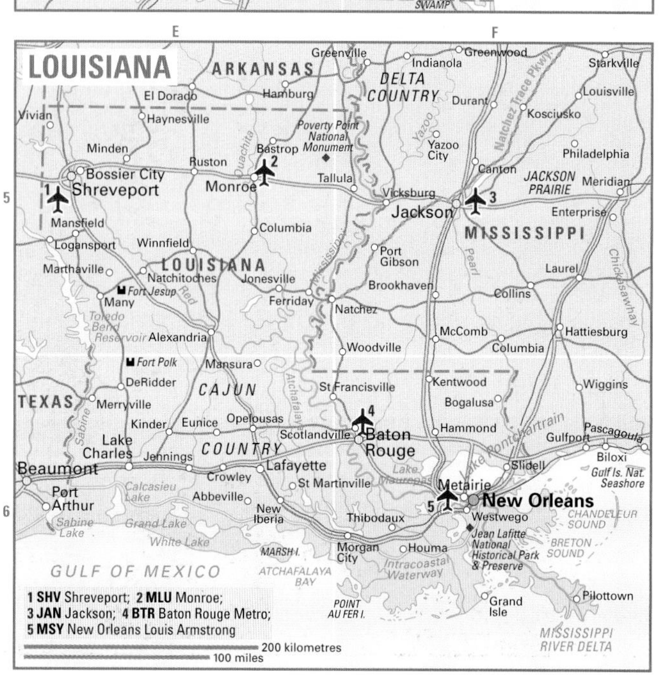
LOUISIANA
ARKANSAS
DELTA COUNTRY
MISSISSIPPI
LOUISIANA
CAJUN COUNTRY
TEXAS
GULF OF MEXICO
New Orleans
Baton Rouge
Jackson
Shreveport
1 SHV Shreveport; 2 MLU Monroe;
3 JAN Jackson; 4 BTR Baton Rouge Metro;
5 MSY New Orleans Louis Armstrong
200 kilometres
100 miles

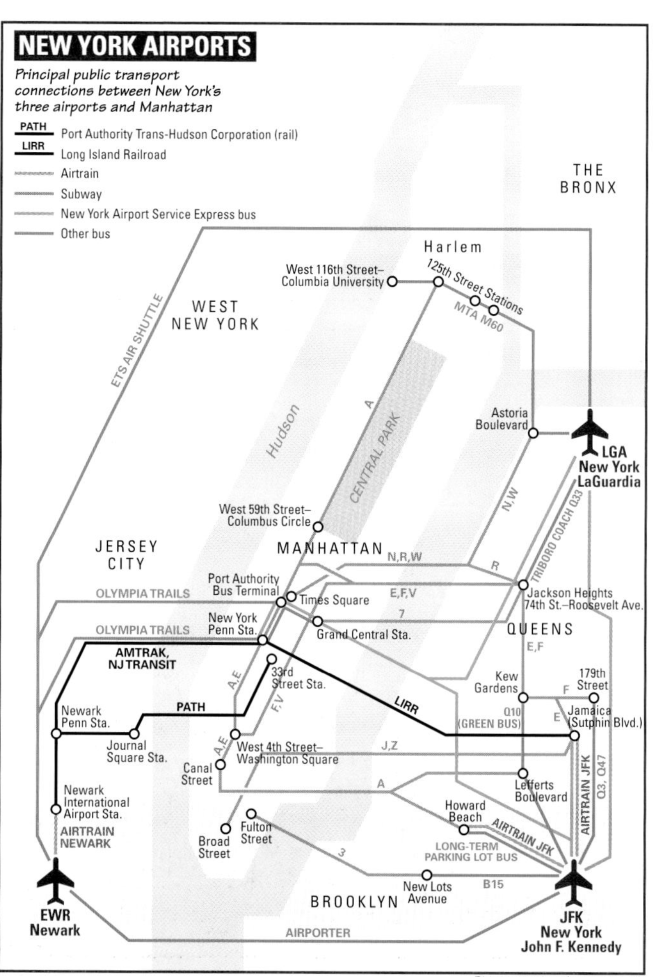
NEW YORK AIRPORTS
Principal public transport connections between New York's three airports and Manhattan
PATH Port Authority Trans-Hudson Corporation (rail)
LIRR Long Island Railroad
Airtrain
Subway
New York Airport Service Express bus
Other bus
THE BRONX
Harlem
WEST NEW YORK
JERSEY CITY
MANHATTAN
QUEENS
BROOKLYN
EWR Newark
LGA New York LaGuardia
JFK New York John F. Kennedy
Diagrammatic only: not to scale

See also... Europe Leisure Parks (67); Top Japanese Theme Parks (139)

The listings above refer to a selection of related themes. For more information, see the Contents (2-7).

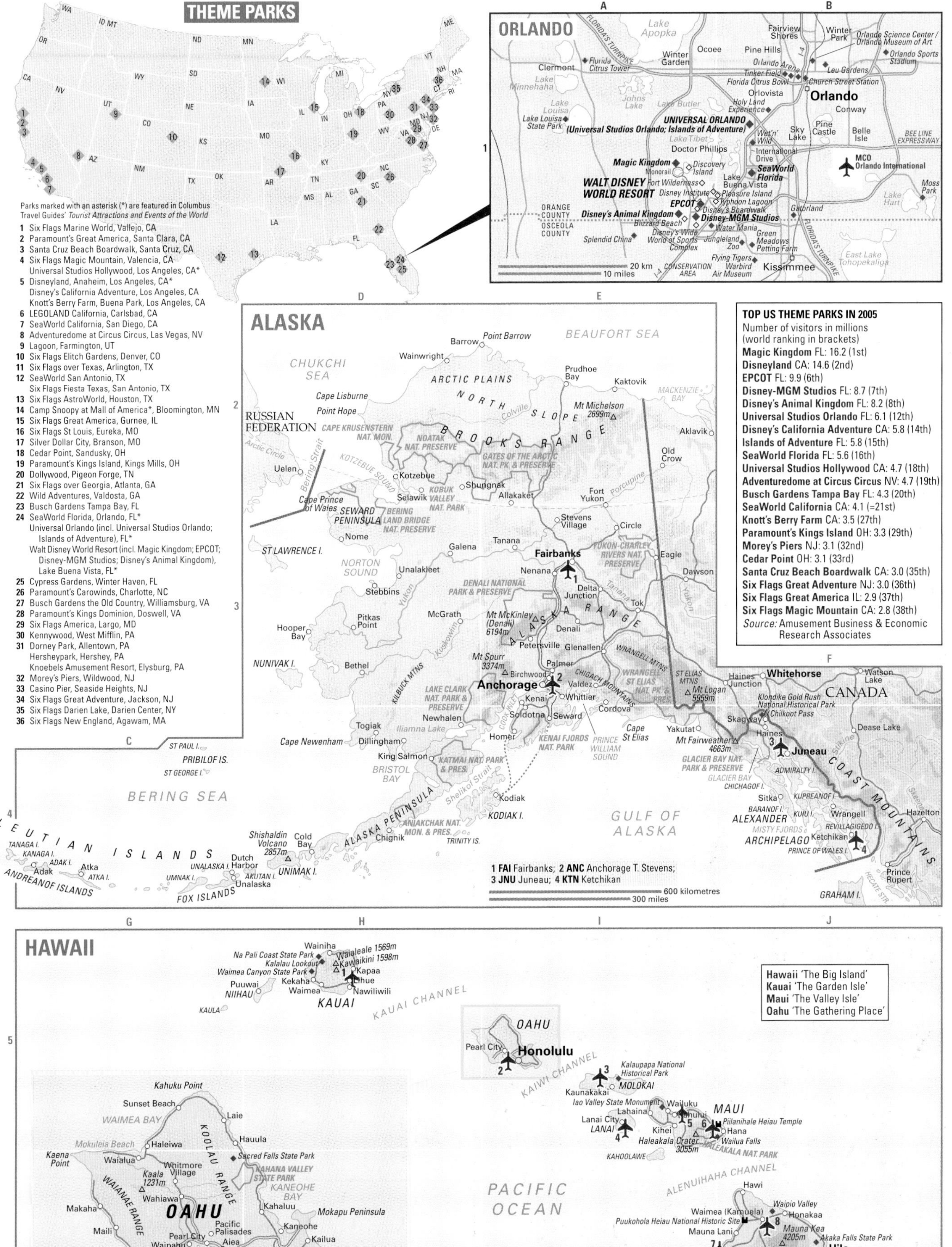
THEME PARKS
ORLANDO
ALASKA
HAWAII
1 FAI Fairbanks; 2 ANC Anchorage T. Stevens; 3 JNU Juneau; 4 KTN Ketchikan
1 LIH Lihue; 2 HNL Honolulu; 3 MKK Molokai; 4 LNY Lanai; 5 OGG Kahului; 6 HNM Hana; 7 KOA Kona; 8 MUE Waimea-Kohala; 9 ITO Hilo
Hawaii 'The Big Island'
Kauai 'The Garden Isle'
Maui 'The Valley Isle'
Oahu 'The Gathering Place'
UNIVERSAL ORLANDO (Universal Studios Orlando; Islands of Adventure)
WALT DISNEY WORLD RESORT
Magic Kingdom
EPCOT
Disney's Animal Kingdom
Disney-MGM Studios
SeaWorld Florida
MCO Orlando International
PACIFIC OCEAN
GULF OF ALASKA
BERING SEA
BEAUFORT SEA
CHUKCHI SEA
ALEUTIAN ISLANDS
RUSSIAN FEDERATION
CANADA

THEME PARKS

Parks marked with an asterisk (*) are featured in Columbus Travel Guides' *Tourist Attractions and Events of the World*

1 Six Flags Marine World, Vallejo, CA
2 Paramount's Great America, Santa Clara, CA
3 Santa Cruz Beach Boardwalk, Santa Cruz, CA
4 Six Flags Magic Mountain, Valencia, CA
Universal Studios Hollywood, Los Angeles, CA*
5 Disneyland, Anaheim, Los Angeles, CA*
Disney's California Adventure, Los Angeles, CA
Knott's Berry Farm, Buena Park, Los Angeles, CA
6 LEGOLAND California, Carlsbad, CA
7 SeaWorld California, San Diego, CA
8 Adventuredome at Circus Circus, Las Vegas, NV
9 Lagoon, Farmington, UT
10 Six Flags Elitch Gardens, Denver, CO
11 Six Flags over Texas, Arlington, TX
12 SeaWorld San Antonio, TX
Six Flags Fiesta Texas, San Antonio, TX
13 Six Flags AstroWorld, Houston, TX
14 Camp Snoopy at Mall of America*, Bloomington, MN
15 Six Flags Great America, Gurnee, IL
16 Six Flags St Louis, Eureka, MO
17 Silver Dollar City, Branson, MO
18 Cedar Point, Sandusky, OH
19 Paramount's Kings Island, Kings Mills, OH
20 Dollywood, Pigeon Forge, TN
21 Six Flags over Georgia, Atlanta, GA
22 Wild Adventures, Valdosta, GA
23 Busch Gardens Tampa Bay, FL
24 SeaWorld Florida, Orlando, FL*
Universal Orlando (incl. Universal Studios Orlando; Islands of Adventure), FL*
Walt Disney World Resort (incl. Magic Kingdom; EPCOT; Disney-MGM Studios; Disney's Animal Kingdom), Lake Buena Vista, FL*
25 Cypress Gardens, Winter Haven, FL
26 Paramount's Carowinds, Charlotte, NC
27 Busch Gardens the Old Country, Williamsburg, VA
28 Paramount's Kings Dominion, Doswell, VA
29 Six Flags America, Largo, MD
30 Kennywood, West Mifflin, PA
31 Dorney Park, Allentown, PA
Hersheypark, Hershey, PA
Knoebels Amusement Resort, Elysburg, PA
32 Morey's Piers, Wildwood, NJ
33 Casino Pier, Seaside Heights, NJ
34 Six Flags Great Adventure, Jackson, NJ
35 Six Flags Darien Lake, Darien Center, NY
36 Six Flags New England, Agawam, MA

TOP US THEME PARKS IN 2005

Number of visitors in millions (world ranking in brackets)

Magic Kingdom FL: 16.2 (1st)
Disneyland CA: 14.6 (2nd)
EPCOT FL: 9.9 (6th)
Disney-MGM Studios FL: 8.7 (7th)
Disney's Animal Kingdom FL: 8.2 (8th)
Universal Studios Orlando FL: 6.1 (12th)
Disney's California Adventure CA: 5.8 (14th)
Islands of Adventure FL: 5.8 (15th)
SeaWorld Florida FL: 5.6 (16th)
Universal Studios Hollywood CA: 4.7 (18th)
Adventuredome at Circus Circus NV: 4.7 (19th)
Busch Gardens Tampa Bay FL: 4.3 (20th)
SeaWorld California CA: 4.1 (=21st)
Knott's Berry Farm CA: 3.5 (27th)
Paramount's Kings Island OH: 3.3 (29th)
Morey's Piers NJ: 3.1 (32nd)
Cedar Point OH: 3.1 (33rd)
Santa Cruz Beach Boardwalk CA: 3.0 (35th)
Six Flags Great Adventure NJ: 3.0 (36th)
Six Flags Great America IL: 2.9 (37th)
Six Flags Magic Mountain CA: 2.8 (38th)

Source: Amusement Business & Economic Research Associates

Canada

See also... 155-160 and 174-175 for more on Canada

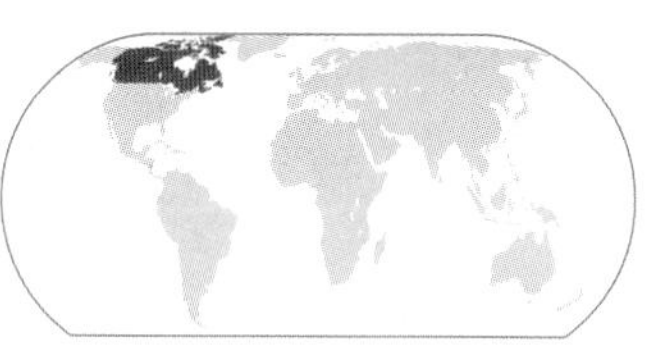

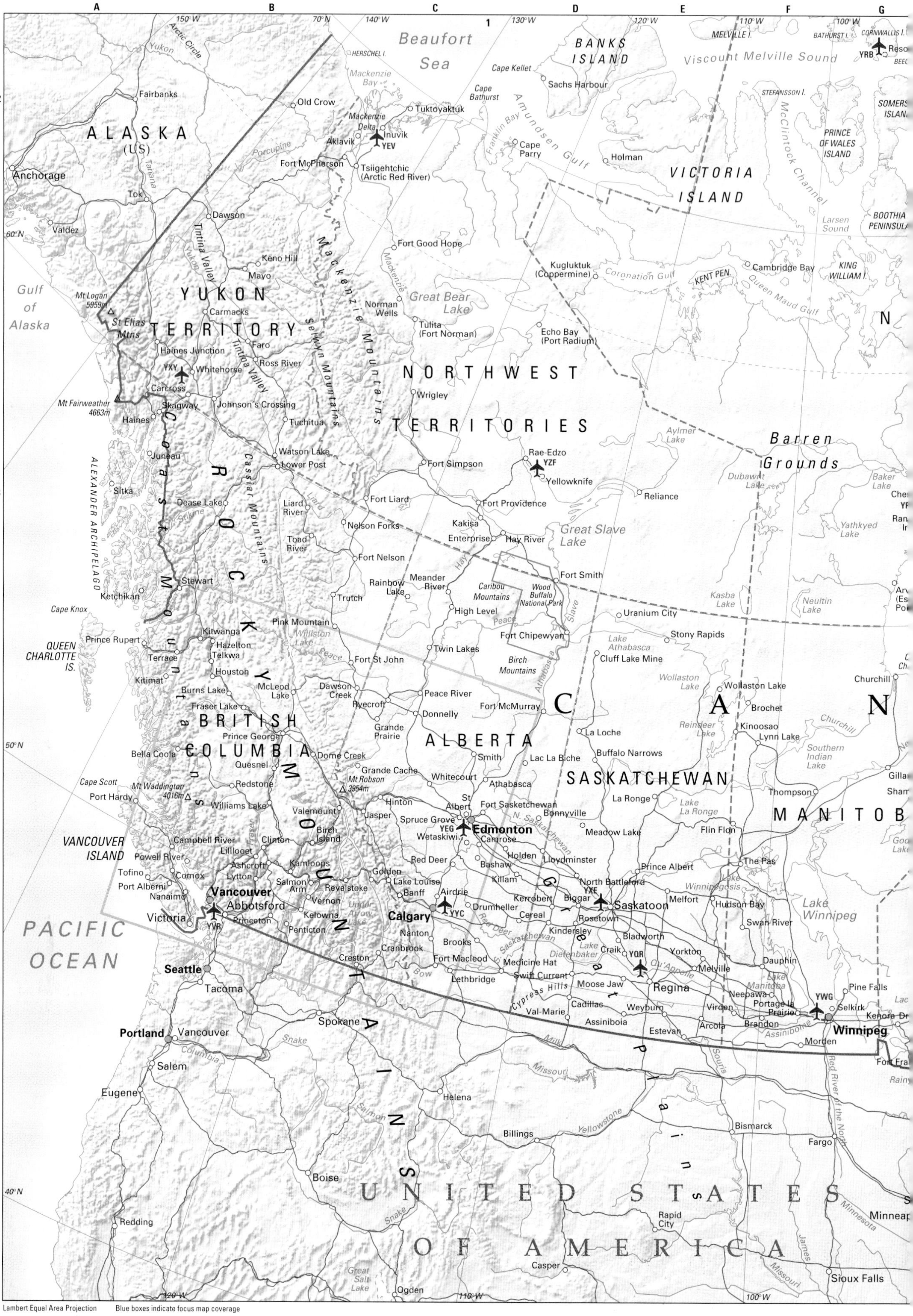

A B C D E F G

1 2 3 4

150°W 140°W 130°W 120°W 110°W 100°W 70°N 60°N 50°N 40°N

Beaufort Sea
BANKS ISLAND
Viscount Melville Sound
MELVILLE I.
BATHURST I.
CORNWALLIS I.
YRB
HERSCHEL I.
Mackenzie Bay
Cape Kellet
Sachs Harbour
Cape Bathurst
Amundsen Gulf
Franklin Bay
Cape Parry
STEFANSSON I.
M'Clintock Channel
PRINCE OF WALES ISLAND
SOMERSET ISLAND
Holman
VICTORIA ISLAND
Larsen Sound
BOOTHIA PENINSULA
Arctic Circle
Yukon
Fairbanks
ALASKA (US)
Old Crow
Mackenzie Delta
Inuvik
YEV
Aklavik
Tuktoyaktuk
Porcupine
Fort McPherson
Tsiigehtchic (Arctic Red River)
Anchorage
Tanana
Tok
Dawson
Valdez
Tintina Valley
Keno Hill
Mayo
Mackenzie Mountains
Fort Good Hope
Kugluktuk (Coppermine)
Coronation Gulf
KENT PEN.
Cambridge Bay
Queen Maud Gulf
KING WILLIAM I.
Gulf of Alaska
Mt Logan 5959m
YUKON TERRITORY
Carmacks
St Elias Mtns
Faro
Haines Junction
Ross River
Selwyn Mountains
Norman Wells
Great Bear Lake
Tulita (Fort Norman)
Echo Bay (Port Radium)
YXY
Whitehorse
NORTHWEST TERRITORIES
Carcross
Wrigley
Mt Fairweather 4663m
Skagway
Johnson's Crossing
Haines
Tuchitua
Coast Mountains
Juneau
Watson Lake
Lower Post
Cassiar Mountains
Fort Simpson
Rae-Edzo
YZF
Yellowknife
Aylmer Lake
Barren Grounds
Dubawnt Lake
Baker Lake
ALEXANDER ARCHIPELAGO
Sitka
Dease Lake
Stikine
Liard River
Fort Liard
Fort Providence
Reliance
Nelson Forks
Kakisa
Enterprise
Hay River
Great Slave Lake
Yathkyed Lake
ROCKY MOUNTAINS
Toad River
Fort Nelson
Stewart
Meander River
Rainbow Lake
Fort Smith
Ketchikan
Caribou Mountains
Wood Buffalo National Park
Cape Knox
Truth
High Level
Uranium City
Kasba Lake
Neultin Lake
Pink Mountain
Williston Lake
Peace
Slave
Fort Chipewyan
Stony Rapids
Kitwanga
Hazelton
Prince Rupert
Telkwa
QUEEN CHARLOTTE IS.
Terrace
Fort St John
Twin Lakes
Lake Athabasca
Cliff Lake Mine
Houston
Birch Mountains
Athabasca
Kitimat
Wollaston Lake
Churchill
Burns Lake
McLeod Lake
Dawson Creek
Peace River
Fraser Lake
Rycroft
Fort McMurray
CANADA
Brochet
Donnelly
BRITISH COLUMBIA
Grande Prairie
Reindeer Lake
Kinoosao
Prince George
ALBERTA
La Loche
Lynn Lake
Southern Indian Lake
Bella Coola
Quesnel
Dome Creek
Smith
Lac La Biche
Buffalo Narrows
Grande Cache
Cape Scott
Mt Waddington 4016m
Redstone
Mt Robson 3954m
Whitecourt
Athabasca
SASKATCHEWAN
Port Hardy
Williams Lake
Hinton
St Albert
Fort Saskatchewan
La Ronge
Lake La Ronge
Thompson
Valemount
Jasper
Spruce Grove
Bonnyville
N. Saskatchewan
MANITOBA
YEG
Edmonton
Wetaskiwin
Meadow Lake
Flin Flon
VANCOUVER ISLAND
Campbell River
Clinton
Birch Island
Camrose
Lillooet
Powell River
Holden
Lloydminster
Ashcroft
Kamloops
Red Deer
Bashaw
Prince Albert
The Pas
Tofino
Comox
Lytton
Golden
Killam
Port Alberni
Salmon Arm
Revelstoke
Lake Louise
North Battleford
Winnipegosis
Nanaimo
Vancouver
Banff
Airdrie
YXE
Melfort
Hudson Bay
Lake Winnipeg
Abbotsford
Vernon
Upper Arrow Lake
Drumheller
Kerrobert
Biggar
Saskatoon
Victoria
YVR
Princeton
Kelowna
Calgary
YYC
Rosetown
Swan River
PACIFIC OCEAN
Penticton
Red Deer
Cereal
Kindersley
Great Plains
Nanton
Saskatchewan
Bladworth
Brooks
Lake Diefenbaker
Cranbrook
Craik
YQR
Yorkton
Creston
Fort Macleod
Medicine Hat
Qu'Appelle
Dauphin
Seattle
Bow
Swift Current
Melville
Lethbridge
Lake Manitoba
Tacoma
Cypress Hills
Moose Jaw
Regina
Neepawa
Pine Falls
Val-Marie
Cadillac
Weyburn
Virden
Portage la Prairie
YWG
Selkirk
Kenora
Spokane
Assiniboia
Brandon
Arcola
Winnipeg
Portland
Vancouver
Snake
Estevan
Assiniboine
Morden
Milk
Columbia
Souris
Salem
Missouri
Red River of the North
Eugene
Helena
Salmon
Yellowstone
Bismarck
Billings
Fargo
Boise
UNITED STATES OF AMERICA
Snake
Rapid City
Minnesota
Minneapolis
Redding
Casper
James
Missouri
Great Salt Lake
Ogden
Sioux Falls

Lambert Equal Area Projection
Blue boxes indicate focus map coverage

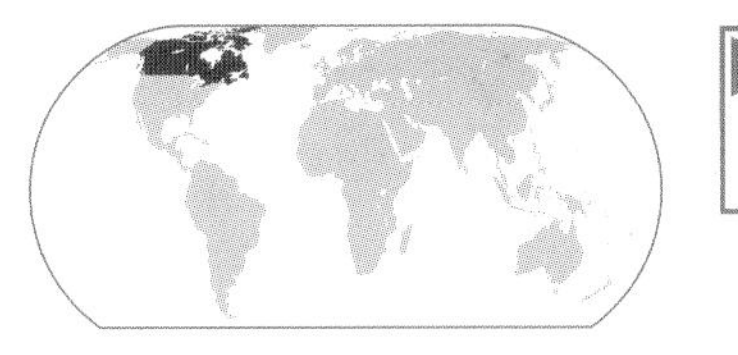

See also... Contents (2-7) – This country features in many thematic and regional maps throughout the *World Travel Atlas*.

I J K L M

80° W
70° W
60° W
50° W
70° N
40° W
60° N
50° N
40° N
90° W
80° W
70° W

Baffin Bay
Uummannaq
QEQERTARSUAQ (DISKO)
Qeqertarsuaq (Godhavn)
Greenland (Den.)
Arctic Circle
Kangerlussuaq (Søndre Strømfjord)
Sisimiut
Davis Strait
NUUK (GODTHÅB)
Narsarsuaq
Qaqortoq (Julianehåb)
Nunap Isua (Cape Farewell)
Paamiut (Frederikshåb)
ON ISLAND
caster Sound
BYLOT I.
Pond Inlet
Arctic Bay
BORDEN PENINSULA
Clyde River
QIKIQTALUK (BAFFIN ISLAND)
CUMBERLAND PENINSULA
Pangnirtung
Cumberland Sound
Hall Beach
PRINCE CHARLES I.
MELVILLE PENINSULA
mittee Bay
NAVUT
Foxe Basin
se Bay
Amadjuak Lake
HALL PENINSULA
Iqaluit (Frobisher Bay)
YFB
Frobisher Bay
META INCOGNITA PENINSULA
FOXE PENINSULA
Cape Dorset
Foxe Channel
SOUTHAMPTON I.
Roes Welcome Sound
Coral Harbour
SALISBURY I.
NOTTINGHAM I.
Hudson Strait
RESOLUTION I.
Labrador Sea
ATLANTIC OCEAN
Cape Chidley
Evans Strait
Fisher Strait
COATS I.
MANSEL I.
Ivujivik
Salliut
Quaqtaq
AKPATOK I.
Mont d'Iberville (Mt Caubvick) 1652m
Hebron
Ungava Bay
Aupaluk
PÉNINSULE D'UNGAVA
Koksoak
YVP
Kuujjuaq (Fort Chimo)
Nain
Labrador
Cape Harrison
Makkovik
Rigolet
Hudson Bay
Inukjuak (Port Harrison)
NEWFOUNDLAND AND LABRADOR
Port Hope Simpson
Battle Harbour
BELLE ISLE
Cape Bauld
L'Anse aux Meadows
Smallwood Reservoir
Schefferville
Happy Valley-Goose Bay
Churchill Falls
Blanc-Sablon
CANADA
Churchill
Esker
Port Saunders
BELCHER IS.
Kuujjuarapik (Poste de la Baleine)
Réservoir Caniapiscau
Springdale
Gander
Harrington Harbour
Strait of Belle Isle
Grand Falls
St John's
Labrador City
Fermont
Deer Lake
NEWFOUNDLAND
YYT
Cape Henrietta Maria
QUÉBEC
Laurentides
Natashquan
Corner Brook
Winisk
Réservoir La Grande 2
Sakami
Gagnon
Stephenville
Cape Race
Réservoir La Grande 3
Radisson
Havre-St-Pierre
Fortune
Chisasibi (Fort George)
Réservoir Manicouagan
ÎLE D'ANTICOSTI
Channel-Port-aux-Basques
St-Pierre et Miquelon (Fr.)
St-Pierre
Gulf of St Lawrence
Eastmain
Sept-Îles
Attawapiskat
AKIMISKI I.
James Bay
Eastmain
Rupert
St-Laurent (St Lawrence)
Cap Gaspé
Gaspé
Cabot Strait
ÎLES DE LA MADELEINE
Cape North
Lake Mistassini
Fort Albany
Albany
Baie-Comeau
Notre Dame
Sydney
Glace Bay
TARIO
Moosonee
Matane
PRINCE EDWARD ISLAND
CAPE BRETON I.
Pickle Lake
Chibougamau
Rimouski
Bathurst
Campbellton
Charlottetown
Jonquière
Chicoutimi
Miramichi
Savant Lake
Armstrong
Pagwa River
Matagami
Miquelon
Roberval
Alma
Rivière-du-Loup
Edmundston
YQM
Moncton
New Glasgow
Nakina
Hearst
Fraserdale
Kapuskasing
NEW BRUNSWICK
Riverview
Truro
YHZ
SABLE I.
Grand Falls
St John
Dartmouth
Fredericton
Lake Nipigon
Senneterre
La Tuque
Québec
YQB
Montmagny
Lévis
Saint John
NOVA SCOTIA
Halifax
Cochrane
Noranda
Monts Notre Dame
Bay of Fundy
Terrace Bay
Timmins
Rouyn
Val-d'Or
Trois-Rivières
Thetford Mines
Red Rock
White River
Kirkland Lake
Victoriaville
St-Georges
Lunenburg
Thunder Bay
Wawa
Mont-Laurier
Joliette
Drummondville
Shelburne
Gogama
New Liskeard
Maniwaki
St-Jérôme
Sorel
YMX
Lachute
YUL
Laval
Sherbrooke
Yarmouth
Cape Sable
Chapleau
Montréal
Lake Superior
Sudbury
North Bay
Ottawa
Hull
Gatineau
Pembroke
Sault Ste Marie
Nepean
OTTAWA
St Albans
YOW
Parry Sound
Huntsville
Portland
MANITOULIN I.
Georgian Bay
Bancroft
Brockville
Kingston
GREAT LAKES
Owen Sound
Orillia
Lindsay
Manchester
Trenton
Lake Ontario
Hudson
Boston
Lake Huron
Collingwood
YYZ
Oshawa
Cape Cod
Brampton
Toronto
Albany
Providence
Green Bay
Lake Michigan
Kitchener
St Catharines
Syracuse
Springfield
Hamilton
Niagara Falls
Buffalo
Hartford
Grand Rapids
Sarnia
London
Lake Erie
New Haven
Lansing
Lake St Clair
LONG I.
Madison
Milwaukee
Detroit
Windsor
Erie
New York
Cleveland
Chicago
Toledo
ATLANTIC OCEAN

600 kilometres
300 miles

See also... Contents (2-7) – This country features in many thematic and regional maps throughout the *World Travel Atlas*.

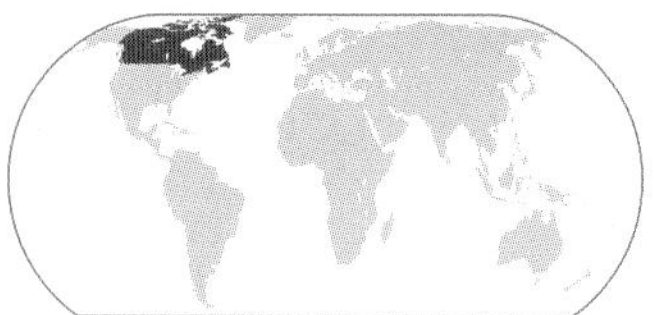

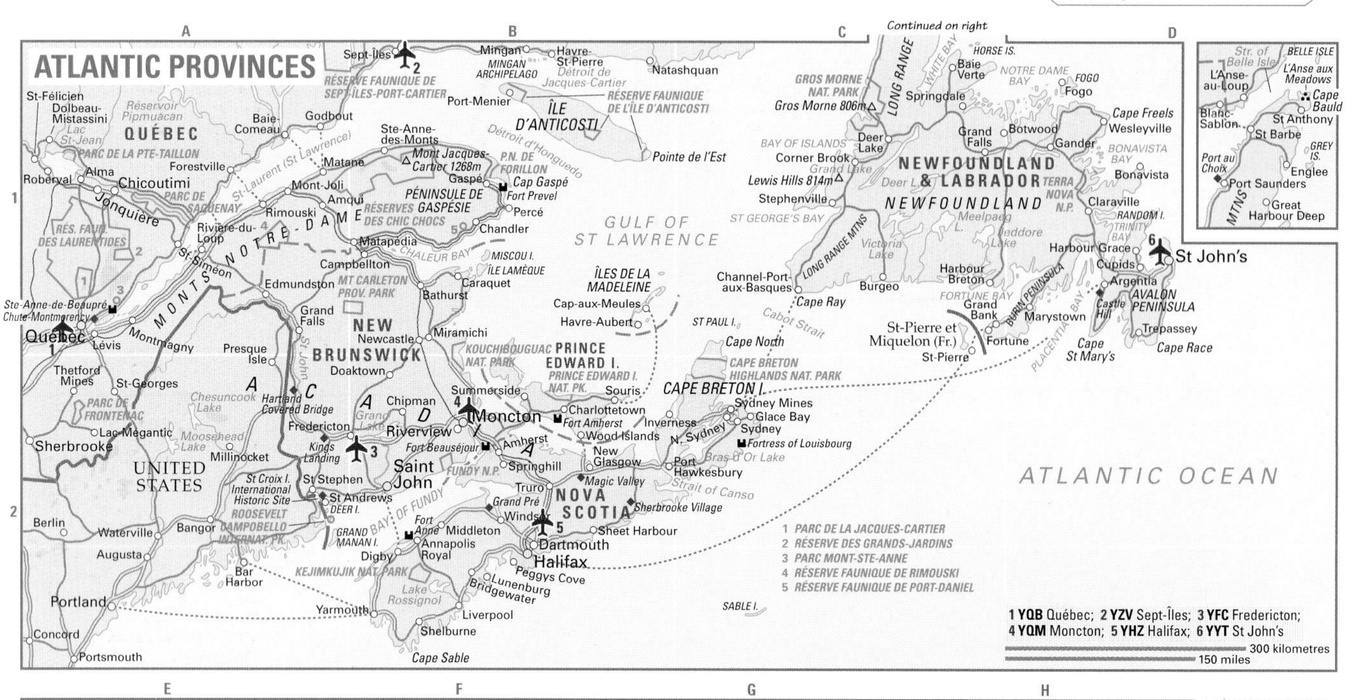
ATLANTIC PROVINCES
Continued on right
GULF OF ST LAWRENCE
ATLANTIC OCEAN
1 PARC DE LA JACQUES-CARTIER
2 RÉSERVE DES GRANDS-JARDINS
3 PARC MONT-STE-ANNE
4 RÉSERVE FAUNIQUE DE RIMOUSKI
5 RÉSERVE FAUNIQUE DE PORT-DANIEL
1 YQB Québec; 2 YZV Sept-Îles; 3 YFC Fredericton;
4 YQM Moncton; 5 YHZ Halifax; 6 YYT St John's
300 kilometres
150 miles

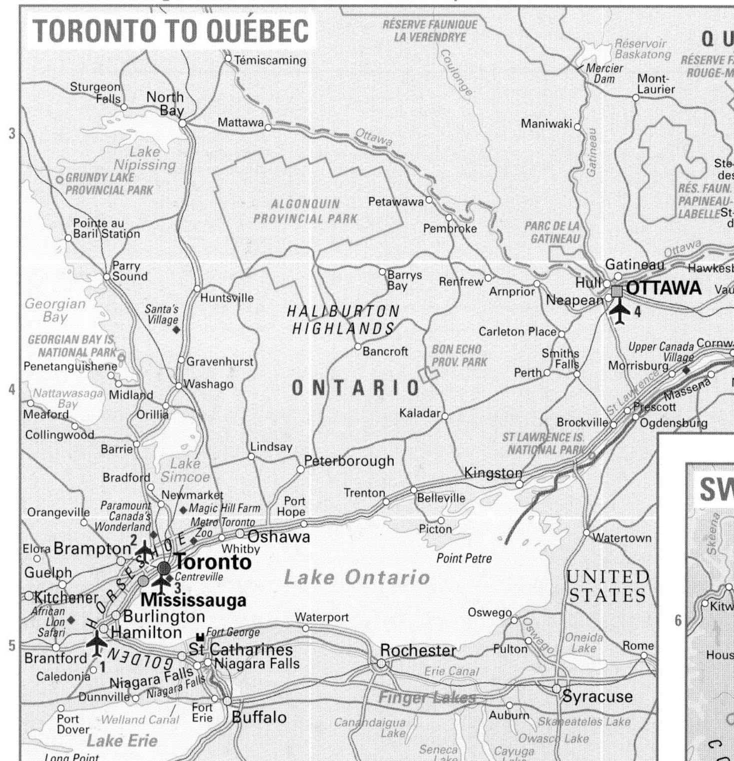
TORONTO TO QUÉBEC
1 RÉSERVE FAUNIQUE DU ST-MAURICE
2 RÉSERVE FAUNIQUE MASTIGOUCHE
3 PARC NATIONAL DE LA MAURICIE
1 YHM Hamilton John C. Munro; 2 YYZ Toronto Lester B. Pearson;
3 YTZ Toronto City Centre; 4 YOW Ottawa Uplands; 5 YMX Montréal Mirabel; 6 YUL Montréal Pierre Elliott Trudeau; 7 YQB Québec
200 kilometres
100 miles

SW CANADA

400 kilometres
200 miles

1 YYJ Victoria; 2 YVR Vancouver; 3 YLW Kelowna; 4 YXS Prince George; 5 YQU Grande Prairie; 6 YEG Edmonton; 7 YYC Calgary

1 MT ROBSON PROVINCIAL PARK
2 HAMBER PROVINCIAL PARK
3 YOHO NATIONAL PARK
4 KOOTENAY NATIONAL PARK
5 MT ASSINIBOINE PROVINCIAL PARK
6 Lake Louise
7 Banff
8 Canmore

*Combined as the Waterton-Glacier International Peace Park

2000 metres
1000 metres
Sea level

FEB Carnaval de **Québec (QC)**
FEB Winterlude (**Ottawa ON**)
FEB Toronto Wintercity Festival (**ON**)
FEB Sourdough Rendezvous (**Whitehorse YT**)
MAY Canadian Tulip Festival (**Ottawa ON**)
MAY-JUN Vancouver International Children's Festival (**BC**)
MAY-OCT Shakespeare Festival (**Stratford ON**)
JUN Festival d'Été (**Québec City QC**)
JUN Metro International Caravan (**Toronto ON**)
JUN Nova Scotia International Tattoo (**Halifax NS**)
JUN 24th St-Jean Baptiste Day (**Québec City QC**)
JUN-JUL Montréal International Jazz Festival (**ON**)
JUN-SEP Harbourfront Centre Summerfete (**Toronto ON**)
JUL 1st Canada Day (**Ottawa ON** & countrywide)
JUL International Freedom Festival (**Windsor ON**)
JUL Stampede (**Williams Lake BC**)
JUL Marine Festival (**Nanaimo BC**)
JUL Celebration of Light: Fireworks Festival (**Vancouver BC**)
JUL Loyalist Days Festival (**Saint John NB**)
JUL Klondike Days (**Edmonton AB**)
JUL Calgary Stampede (**AB**)
JUL Folklorama (**Winnipeg MB**)
JUL Manitoba Stampede & Exhibition (**Morris MB**)
JUL Manitoba Threshermen's Reunion (**Austin MB**)
JUL New Brunswick Highland Games & Scottish Festival (**Fredericton NB**)
JUL-AUG Caribana (**Toronto ON**)
AUG Regatta Day (**St John's NL**)
AUG Abbotsford International Air Show (**BC**)
AUG Folklorama (**Winnipeg MB**)
AUG Gaelic Mod: Scottish festival (**St Ann's NS**)
AUG Fringe Festival (**Edmonton AB**)
AUG Six Nations Native Pageant (**Brantford ON**)
AUG Nova Scotia Fisheries Exhibition & Fishermen's Reunion (**Lunenburg NS**)
AUG Discovery Day (**Dawson City YT**)
AUG-SEP Canadian National Exhibition (**Toronto ON**)
OCT Oktoberfest (**Kitchener-Waterloo ON**)
OCT Vancouver International Film Festival (**BC**)
NOV Canadian Rodeo Finals (**Edmonton AB**)

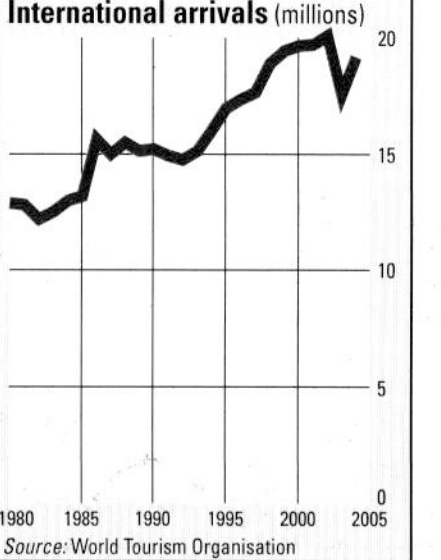
International arrivals (millions)
20
15
10
5
0
1980 1985 1990 1995 2000 2005
Source: World Tourism Organisation

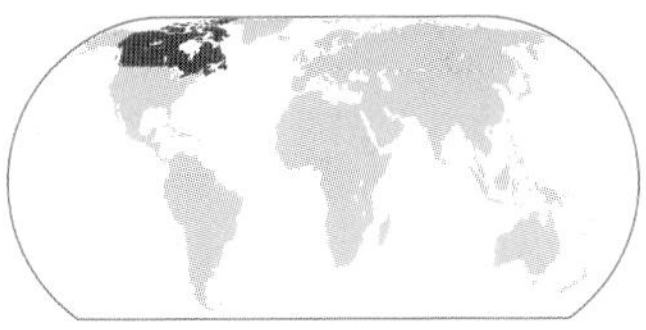

See also... UNESCO Natural Heritage (48-49); US National Parks Service (166-167)

Parks Canada administers Canada's National Parks and marine conservation areas. Parks Canada also administers a large number of the country's many National Historic Sites.

Parks marked with an asterisk (*) are featured in Columbus Travel Guides' *Tourist Attractions and Events of the World*

Province boundary
National Park of Canada
1000 km
500 miles

Yukon Territory
1 Ivvavik National Park
2 Vuntut National Park
3 Kluane National Park & Reserve*
Northwest Territories
4 Nahanni National Park
5 Tuktut Nogait National Park (also in NU)
6 Aulavik National Park
Nunavut
7 Quttinirpaaq (Ellesmere Island) National Park
8 Sirmilik National Park
9 Auyuittuq National Park
British Columbia
10 Gwaii Haanas National Park Reserve and Haida Heritage Site
11 Pacific Rim National Park Reserve
12 Gulf Islands National Park Reserve
13 Mount Revelstoke National Park; Glacier National Park
14 Yoho National Park
15 Kootenay National Park
Alberta
16 Wood Buffalo National Park (also in NT)
17 Elk Island National Park
18 Jasper National Park*
19 Banff National Park*
20 Waterton Lakes National Park
Saskatchewan
21 Prince Albert National Park
22 Grasslands National Park
Manitoba
23 Wapusk National Park
24 Riding Mountain National Park
Ontario
25 Pukaskwa National Park
26 Bruce Peninsula National Park; Fathom Five National Marine Park
27 Georgian Bay Islands National Park
28 Point Pelee National Park
29 St Lawrence Islands National Park
Québec
30 Parc national de la Mauricie
31 Parc marin du Saguenay-St-Laurent
32 Réserve du Parc national de l'Archipel-de-Mingan
33 Parc national de Forillon
New Brunswick
34 Kouchibouguac National Park
35 Fundy National Park
Prince Edward Island
36 Prince Edward Island National Park
Nova Scotia
37 Kejimkujik National Park
38 Cape Breton Highlands National Park
Newfoundland and Labrador
39 Gros Morne National Park
40 Terra Nova National Park

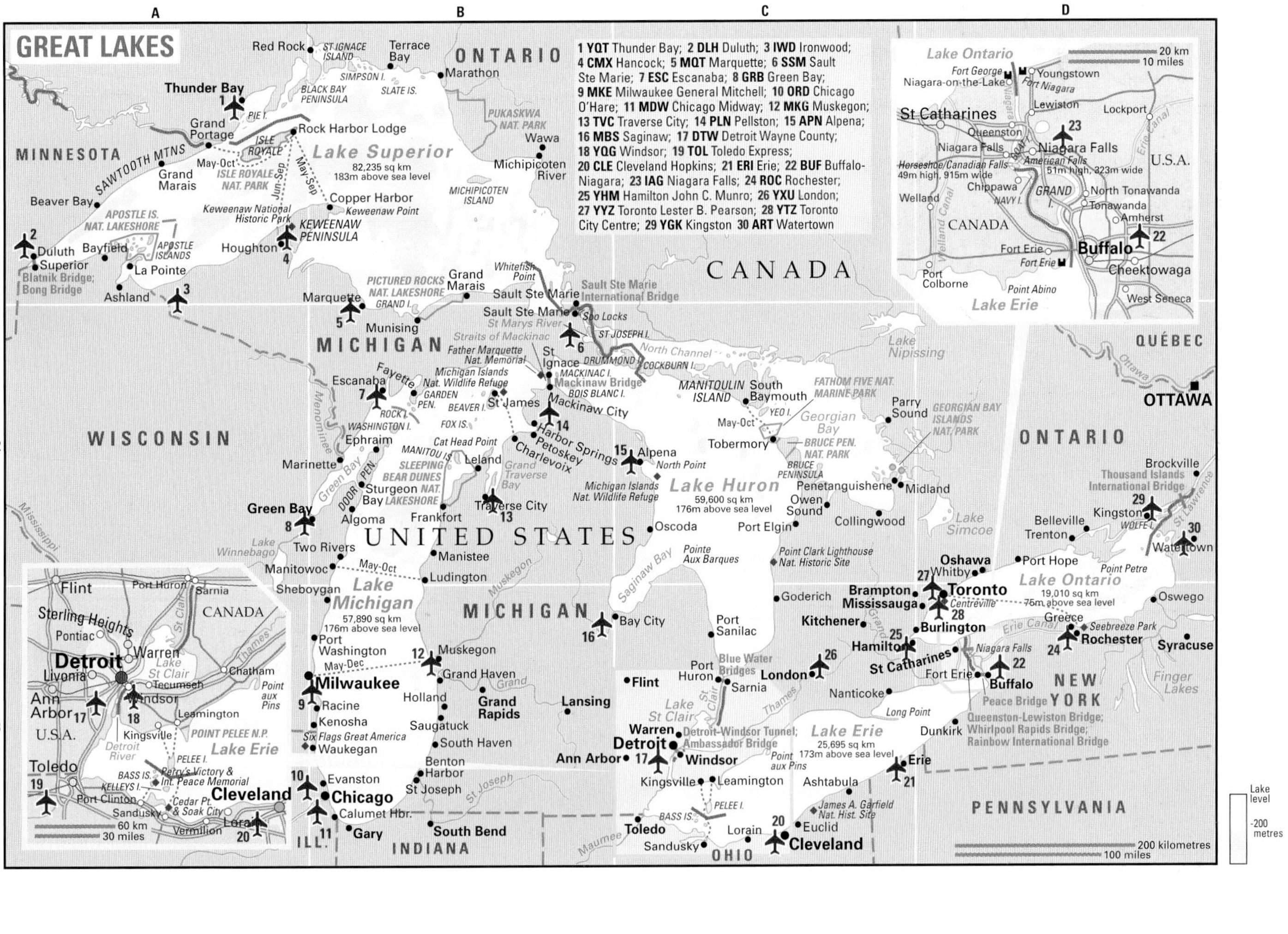

GREAT LAKES

1 **YQT** Thunder Bay; 2 **DLH** Duluth; 3 **IWD** Ironwood; 4 **CMX** Hancock; 5 **MQT** Marquette; 6 **SSM** Sault Ste Marie; 7 **ESC** Escanaba; 8 **GRB** Green Bay; 9 **MKE** Milwaukee General Mitchell; 10 **ORD** Chicago O'Hare; 11 **MDW** Chicago Midway; 12 **MKG** Muskegon; 13 **TVC** Traverse City; 14 **PLN** Pellston; 15 **APN** Alpena; 16 **MBS** Saginaw; 17 **DTW** Detroit Wayne County; 18 **YQG** Windsor; 19 **TOL** Toledo Express; 20 **CLE** Cleveland Hopkins; 21 **ERI** Erie; 22 **BUF** Buffalo-Niagara; 23 **IAG** Niagara Falls; 24 **ROC** Rochester; 25 **YHM** Hamilton John C. Munro; 26 **YXU** London; 27 **YYZ** Toronto Lester B. Pearson; 28 **YTZ** Toronto City Centre; 29 **YGK** Kingston 30 **ART** Watertown

Lake Superior 82,235 sq km 183m above sea level
Lake Michigan 57,890 sq km 176m above sea level
Lake Huron 59,600 sq km 176m above sea level
Lake Erie 25,695 sq km 173m above sea level
Lake Ontario 19,010 sq km 75m above sea level

200 kilometres
100 miles
Lake level
-200 metres

See also... World Introduction (8-11); Tourism (24-25); Countries A-Z (202-210)

The listings above refer to a selection of related themes. For more information, see the Contents (2-7).

Latin America & The Caribbean

Latin America has, more than perhaps any other part of the world, succeeded in re-inventing itself in recent times. Political and economic change has brought stability few would have predicted fifteen years ago. This has helped increase awareness of a region that, despite occupying only 15% of the world's land area, has a greater latitudinal range than any other continent. It stretches from the southern temperate zone of the northern hemisphere to the edge of the Antarctic and offers a similarly broad range of activities and attractions. Although many areas have recently become accessible – and not just to the adventurous traveller – much remains to be explored. The Caribbean, by contrast, is firmly established as a sunshine holiday destination. Many of the islands are heavily dependent on visitors from North America and on the cruise market.

Travel overview

Recent years have witnessed a considerable increase in visitor numbers for virtually the entire region. 20 countries recorded double-digit growth in 2004, and 2005 regional figures show increases of between 4.1% (Mexico) and 13.9% (Central America). Airline capacity across Latin America increased by 10% in this period. In the Caribbean area, this is in the context of some particularly damaging hurricanes in 2004 and 2005. The favourable US dollar/euro exchange rate has also helped make the many dollar-pegged economies in the region more attractive. Most indicators suggest that Latin America and the Caribbean is experiencing solid and stable growth in developing its massive tourism potential. It remains, however, heavily reliant on travel from within the Americas, a market that, in the case of countries like Mexico and Puerto Rico, provides around nine out of every ten visitors.

South and Central America's biggest opportunity may be the growing perception – unforeseeable just a decade ago – that they are relatively safe destinations. This is likely to appeal particularly to the US market, which currently accounts for around one in three of Central America's arrivals but only around one in seven of South America's. Aware, perhaps, of this positive perception, efforts are being made by several national tourist offices to attract more visitors.

If the tourist offices of the Caribbean sometimes seem to present a more emphatic marketing message than those of Latin America, it is perhaps because they are longer-established as tourism destinations; perhaps also that their message as predominantly sunshine destinations is more straightforward. It is also true that they need the tourism business more. Many Caribbean islands derive more than 20% of their GDP from travel and tourism. In Central and South America, the figures are generally far lower.

One encouraging factor across the region – indeed, one echoed in many parts of the world – is the extent to which responsible, ethical and sustainable tourism is taking root. Many operators are organising trips that involve some element of voluntary work. More of the revenue from travel and tourism activities is staying in the local economies. Much progress is being made towards ensuring that the presence of foreign visitors helps preserve, rather than destroy, the wide range of natural and man-made attractions on which so much of the region's appeal depends. The Association of Caribbean States (ACS) is but one body that is using various initiatives to encourange the sustainable development of travel and tourism in the region.

The typical visitor to Latin America might once have been a backpacker, prepared to rough it on a low budget, but the picture is now more diverse. The growth in the 1990s was fuelled partly by an increase in family package holidays, such as to beach destinations in Brazil; partly by a growth in intra-regional travel; and partly by the appetite for adventure holidays, a taste Latin America is well able to satisfy. This has helped open up many new destinations, especially around the Amazon river and in the Andes.

Traditional low-budget destinations such as the Mayan trail from Mexico to Honduras and the Inca paths through Peru are seeking a more upmarket and ecologically-minded clientele. Interest in all aspects of local culture, indigenous and Iberian, is on the rise, and holiday options increasingly try to satisfy this. South America's major cities are amongst the most vibrant on earth and events such as the Rio Carnival are celebrated with a verve that draws visitors from all over the world. Throughout the mainland region, overland travel and tailor-made holidays are proving enduringly popular, and specialist operators are offering an ever-increasing range of options.

Central America has capitalised on its indigenous culture, beaches, diving destinations and colonial heritage. Its Caribbean coastline, comparative proximity to the USA and recent political stability help explain why the area has experienced solid growth in visitor numbers for several years.

The Caribbean islands, with high average temperatures, year-round warm waters of around 24°C and idyllic palm-fringed coastlines, are principally beach and water-sports destinations. They pioneered the 'all-inclusive holiday' and are very popular stop-off points for cruises. Improved inter-island air services are assisting the development of island-hopping and multi-centre holidays, as is the expansion of direct air services for the USA. The Cricket World Cup in March and April 2007 will take place in seven islands (and Guyana) and is expected to provide increased airline capacity and a general boost to the economy of the whole region. Despite all these encouraging signs, many states are taking prudent steps to diversify their economies to avoid over-reliance on tourism.

Cruise passengers provide a vital part of the tourism industry in the Caribbean and a major source of income for the Panama Canal. Some countries receive more than twice as many cruise passengers on shore trips as they do arrivals by air. Hoteliers can take comfort from this, for such day-trip visitors often return for a longer holiday. Newer ships in the Caribbean are amongst the world's largest, carrying up to 4,000 passengers. Operators are now forced to be more environmentally friendly and there is strict control on the number of vessels entering each port each day. Cruise lines provide valuable employment for many Latin Americans.

Many tour operators are featuring Spanish and Portuguese language courses throughout the region. Several countries are also promoting themselves as wedding & honeymoon destinations, offering a mixture of adventure and traditional beach holiday.

Economic and political change

The long-term economic prospects for the region are largely encouraging, again in contrast to the picture a decade or so ago. Helped by high oil prices (benefiting Mexico and Venezuela in particular), free-trade agreements with the USA and growing demand from China (up a third from the year before), Latin America's economy grew by 5.5% in 2004, its best performance for 24 years, while exports were at a 20-year high. The last fifteen years have seen a general shift from dictatorships, protectionism and state control to democracy, free trade and privatisation, and reflect in part the changing preoccupations of US foreign policy since the end of the Cold War. These changes have often been painful, as recent problems and in Brazil, Venezuela and Argentina have shown, but and many would argue that they are largely for the better. The transition has generally been smoother in Central America. Inter-regional ties are also being strengthened, with three regional associations working towards the eventual formation of the South American Community of Nations. Many industries require economic and political stability in order to thrive, travel and tourism industry perhaps more than most. As long as these factors remain in place, the future looks bright for the region.

Some areas of concern remain, however. Trade disputes periodically threaten to undermine moves towards integration, particularly when they involve the large economies of Mexico, Argentina or Brazil. Falling infrastructure standards, affecting everything from

Economies

The region's 10 largest economies
Source: World Bank/International Monetary Fund

	GNI US$m 2004	GNI/cap US$ 2004	GDP growth 2004	av p/a '97-'06
Mexico	703,080	6,620	4.4	3.5
Brazil	552,096	2,966	4.9	2.4
Argentina	142,338	3,600	9.0	2.2
Venezuela	104,958	4,136	17.9	2.1
Colombia	90,626	2,110	4.1	2.2
Chile	78,407	4,906	6.1	4.1
Peru	65,043	2,329	4.8	3.4
Ecuador	28,783	2,154	6.9	2.6
Guatemala	26,945	2,243	2.7	3.3
Cuba	25,501	2,247	3.0	*3.7

*'96-'06

Key facts

Number of Countries	48
Area ('000 sq km)	20,567
Population ('000)	555,101
Population Density (per sq km)	27
Gross National Income (US$m)	1,988,093
Visitor Arrivals ('000)	65,196
Visitor Receipts (US$m)	44,357

GNI figures are for 2004. Population figures are taken from the most recent reliable source. Travel figures (UNWTO) are based on overnight stays, not same-day visitors, and are for 2005. For more information see the Countries A-Z section from page 202.

Big earners

Receipts from foreign travel (excluding international transport), 2004 – top 11 countries (US$ billions) *Source: WTO*

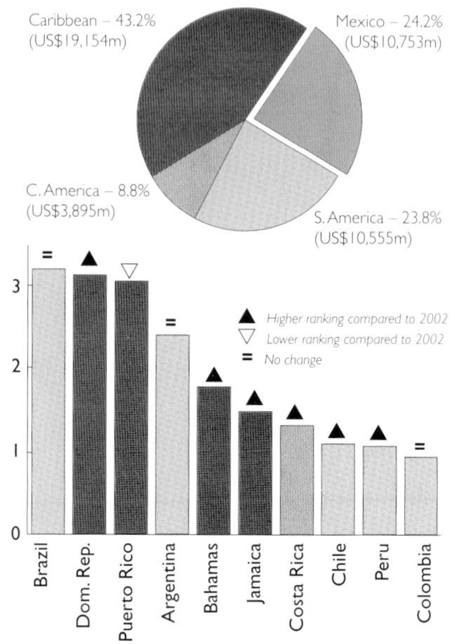
Caribbean – 43.2% (US$19,154m)
Mexico – 24.2% (US$10,753m)
C. America – 8.8% (US$3,895m)
S. America – 23.8% (US$10,555m)
Higher ranking compared to 2002
Lower ranking compared to 2002
No change
0
1
2
3
Brazil
Dom. Rep.
Puerto Rico
Argentina
Bahamas
Jamaica
Costa Rica
Chile
Peru
Colombia

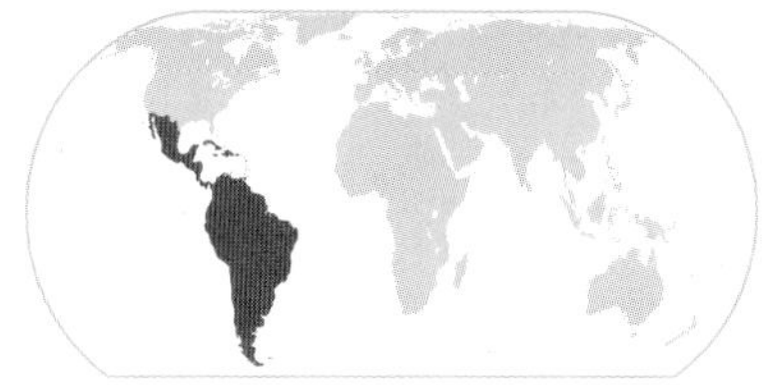

- Latin America and the Caribbean (LA&C) occupies 15.2% of the world's land area and is home to 8.6% of the world's population.
- LA&C's combined GDI is US$1,988,093 million, 5.1% of the world's total.
- LA&C accounts for 8.1% of global travel arrivals.
- The Caribbean accounts for 43% of the region's receipts from travel and tourism.
- 13 LA&C countries – five in South America, five in the Caribbean, two in Central America, and Mexico – received over one million visitors in 2004. Mexico alone accounted for over 30% of all regional international arrivals.
- The Bahamas received 1.73 million cruise visitors in 2005, a fall of 5.7% over 2004.
- The most-visited country in LA&C, Mexico, ranked 8th in the world in 2004 with 19 million visitors: over 90% of these were from the USA.
- There were 65.2 million international tourist arrivals in LA&C in 2005, an increase of 8.1% over 2004. 46 million of these were to the mainland and 19.2 million to the Caribbean.
- Visitors to the US Virgin Islands in 2003 each spent an average of over US$2,300.
- Central America's European visitors have more than doubled since 1990.
- Citizens of the USA accounted for 21% of all arrivals to the region (not including Mexico) in 2005.
- Many experts believe that south-eastern Peru has more diversity of birdlife than any place on earth.
- The Amazon and its various tributaries contain more water than the world's next eight largest river systems combined.
- The largest pyramid in the world is the Cholulu de Rivadahia in Mexico.
- Brazil has the world's longest continuous coastline.
- The Atlantic opening of the Panama Canal is further west than the Pacific one.
- The Atacama Desert in Chile is the driest place on earth, receiving no measurable rainfall during a typical year.

roads to telecommunications, is another problem, and the World Bank warned in August 2005 that investment here needs to be tripled to match that of the East Asian states. Despite recent growth, living standards in many areas have not recovered from the financial crises of the last decade. As recent election results in Venezuela and Bolivia have shown, there is discontent about the distribution of wealth and some aspects of US policy, notably the coca farming issue in Bolivia and the military intervention in Colombia.

Destination overview

- **Mexico** – one of the world's major travel destinations, especially for other North Americans. Despite the effects of Hurricane Wilma on the Caribbean coast in October 2005, the country reported a 4.1% growth in visitor arrivals for the year, only slightly below the world average. Puerto Vallarta is one of the world's major cruising ports, and the number of ships calling there increased by over 25% in 2005 compared to 2004. Attractions range from Mayan sites to beach resorts such as Cancún and Acapulco, and the Baja California. Hacienda (farm) holidays have long been popular.
- **Brazil** – despite its being the second largest economy in Latin America after Mexico and the fifth largest country in the world, the tourism industry is comparatively small. Beach holidays around Salvador de Bahia, Recife and Natal have benefited from the introduction of charter flights from Europe. Brazil accommodates the majority of the vast Amazon rainforest. Rio de Janeiro's attractions include the carnival, Corcovado Mountain with its statue of Christ the Redeemer and the world-famous Ipanema and Copacabana beaches.
- **Peru** – ever-popular with adventure-seeking travellers, its attractions include dramatic mountains and jungles, Lake Titicaca and Inca sites such as Machu Picchu, the Nasca Lines and Cusco. International visitor arrivals have doubled since 1997.
- **Argentina** – the second-most visited South American country after Brazil, Argentina has recorded double-digit annual increases in visitors for several years. Buenos Aires is one of the continent's most vibrant and sophisticated cities. Since the Peso devaluations of 2001, the country has represented particularly good value for money. Activity and estancia (ranch) holidays are increasing in popularity, as are wine holidays.
- **Venezuela** – an oil-rich state with a long Caribbean coastline and, in the hinterland, the spectacular Guiana Highlands and the northern tip of the Andes. The Angel Falls, the world's tallest waterfall, and the offshore islands are popular attractions. The country has experienced some political and economic unrest in recent years but recent economic growth may well underpin a period of stability.
- **Chile** – after a particularly divisive period of dictatorship ending in 1990, the country is slowly building up a varied tourism portfolio reflecting its extraordinarily diverse geography. The Patagonian region is proving increasingly popular, while skiing holidays are starting to feature on operators' programmes.
- **Galapagos Islands (Ecuador)** – featured on many expedition cruise itineraries and popular with those interested in wildlife. They have benefited from improved transport connections with Europe and USA via Ecuador.
- **Puerto Rico** and **the US Virgin Islands** – long popular in the US, the islands have undergone revitalisation and are now attracting Europeans for pre- and post-cruise stays. They received 3.2 million day visitors from cruise ships in 2004.
- **Dominican Republic** – this country offers some of the Caribbean's best beaches. Hotel standards have improved in recent years and each season sees an increase in the number of charter flights from Europe. Tourism accounts for about 25% of the country's GDP.
- **Jamaica** – one of the most varied destinations in the Caribbean and with a strong US and European market. 2005 saw over 2,000 hotel rooms added, with a further 1,200 in 2006. A programme of road and airport improvements is also under way.
- **Cayman Islands** – one of the world's top diving locations and in the forefront of recent international efforts to protect coral reefs.
- **Lesser Antilles** – islands such as Antigua, Barbados and St Lucia are established as holiday destinations from Europe and North America, but in some cases growth has slowed in recent years. Many are promoting niche markets such as weddings, honeymoons, diving and golf.
- **The Bahamas** – a country of over 700 islands, Grand Bahama and New Providence being the most important. Nassau is the main cruise port. The country attracts nearly three times as many cruise-ship stopovers as overnight visitors and has long relied on visitors from the nearby USA.
- **Cuba** – tourism has developed rapidly in this communist outpost, with a 12.9% growth in arrivals in 2005. 'Tour and Stay' options are popular, with visits to historical and cultural sites, especially Havana, being followed by time spent in beach resorts such as Varadero.
- **Central America** – in visitor-arrival terms, the region's success story: no sub-region in the world posted a larger 2005 increase compared to 2004, and this despite severe floods caused by Hurricane Stan. Increased air capacity and joint marketing campaigns, such as between Honduras and Nicaragua and the Ruta Maya initiative, have contributed to this, as has the region's political stability. Lush jungles, ancient monuments and spectacular diving (Belize, for instance, has the world's second largest reef) all form part of a successful and varied eco-tourism product.
- **Guyana** – The only English-speaking country in South America, Guyana has traditionally promoted itself as being a blend of Latin America and the Caribbean. Three new carriers began offering services from Trinidad and North America in 2006 which should help increase visitor arrivals.

Latin leapers

Fastest growing destinations and holiday types, 2005
Source: Journey Latin America

Fastest growing destinations...

1 Peru	3 Chile	5 Mexico
2 Brazil	4 Argentina	6 Guyana

Fastest growing holiday types...

1 Honeymoons	3 Family holidays
2 Active holidays	4 Wildlife holidays

Big spenders

Expenditure on foreign travel (excluding international transport), 2003 – top ten countries (US$ billions) *Source: WTO*

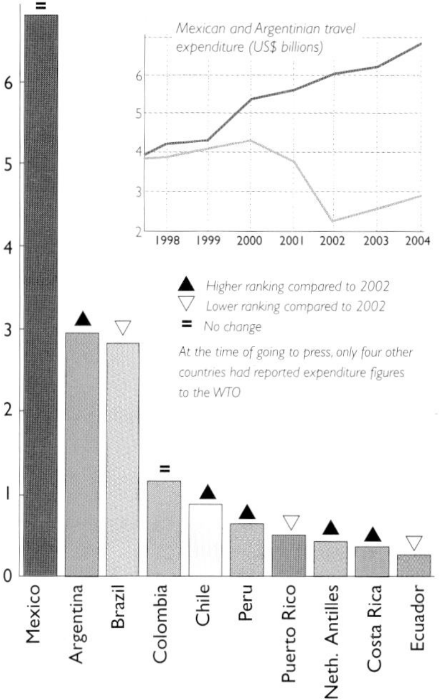

Mexican and Argentinian travel expenditure (US$ billions)
1998 1999 2000 2001 2002 2003 2004
Higher ranking compared to 2002
Lower ranking compared to 2002
No change
At the time of going to press, only four other countries had reported expenditure figures to the WTO
0 1 2 3 4 5 6
Mexico
Argentina
Brazil
Colombia
Chile
Peru
Puerto Rico
Neth. Antilles
Costa Rica
Ecuador

Problem areas

- Seasonal hurricanes occur in parts of Central America and the Caribbean, and have done so increasingly in recent years.
- The rain forests continue to be depleted, affecting the local and global environment.
- Street crime and kidnapping has increased in South America in recent years, as it has worldwide, and continues to be a risk for travellers.
- Colombia remains a trading post for illegal drugs.
- Further industrial and social unrest, such as have affected Venezuela and Bolivia in recent years, can disrupt many aspects of life including travel plans.

Visitors

Visitor arrivals 2004: top ten countries *Source: WTO*

	Visitors (thousands)	Change since 1997
Mexico	20,618	6.5%
Brazil	4,725	65.8%
Puerto Rico	3,541	9.2%
Dominican Rep.	3,450	56.0%
Argentina	3,353	21.3%
Cuba	2,017	74.9%
Chile	1,785	8.6%
Uruguay	1,756	-24.2%
Bahamas	1,561	-3.5%
Costa Rica	1,453	79.2%

Caribbean: Languages & the Greater Antilles

See also... North America Climate (155); Caribbean Diving (180-181); the Lesser Antilles (180-181)

The listings above refer to a selection of related themes. For more information, see the Contents (2-7).

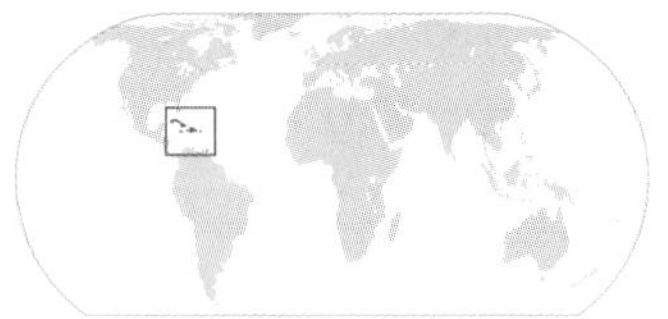

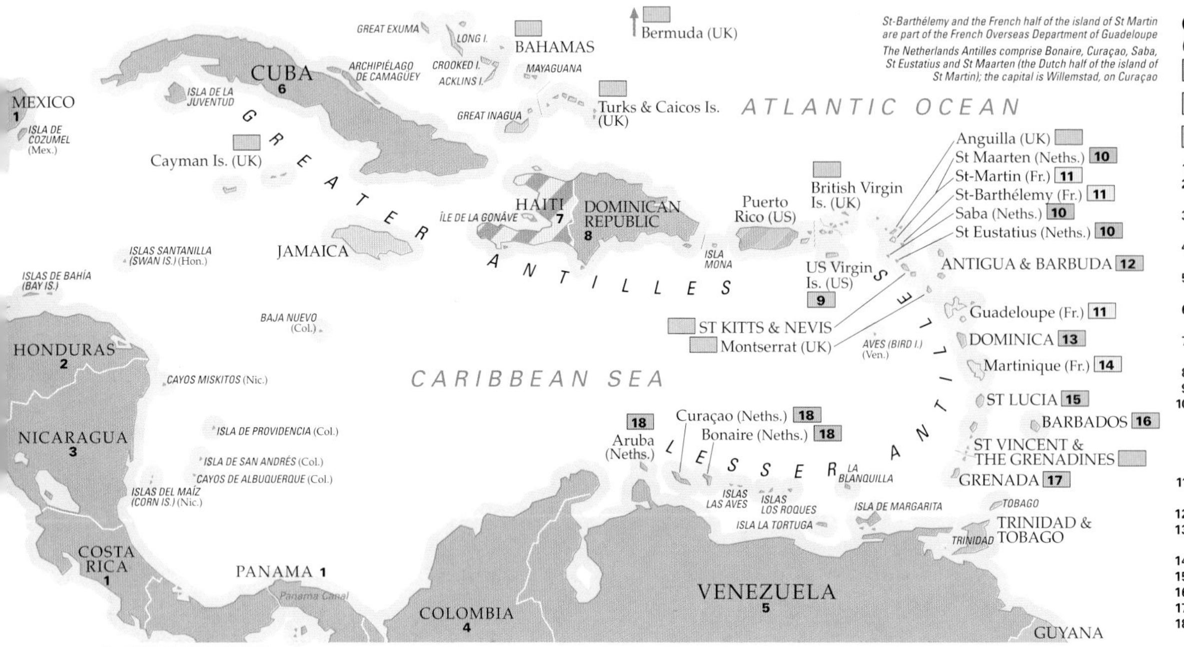

St-Barthélemy and the French half of the island of St Martin are part of the French Overseas Department of Guadeloupe

The Netherlands Antilles comprise Bonaire, Curaçao, Saba, St Eustatius and St Maarten (the Dutch half of the island of St Martin); the capital is Willemstad, on Curaçao

GREAT EXUMA · LONG I. · BAHAMAS · Bermuda (UK) · CROOKED I. · MAYAGUANA · ACKLINS I. · ARCHIPIÉLAGO DE CAMAGUEY · CUBA 6 · ISLA DE LA JUVENTUD · MEXICO 1 · ISLA DE COZUMEL (Mex.) · GREAT INAGUA · Turks & Caicos Is. (UK) · ATLANTIC OCEAN · Cayman Is. (UK) · GREATER ANTILLES · HAITI 7 · ÎLE DE LA GONÂVE · DOMINICAN REPUBLIC 8 · Puerto Rico (US) · British Virgin Is. (UK) · ISLA MONA · JAMAICA · ISLAS SANTANILLA (SWAN IS.) (Hon.) · ISLAS DE BAHÍA (BAY IS.) · US Virgin Is. (US) 9 · Anguilla (UK) · St Maarten (Neths.) 10 · St-Martin (Fr.) 11 · St-Barthélemy (Fr.) 11 · Saba (Neths.) 10 · St Eustatius (Neths.) 10 · ANTIGUA & BARBUDA 12 · ST KITTS & NEVIS · Montserrat (UK) · Guadeloupe (Fr.) 11 · DOMINICA 13 · AVES (BIRD I.) (Ven.) · Martinique (Fr.) 14 · BAJA NUEVO (Col.) · HONDURAS 2 · CAYOS MISKITOS (Nic.) · CARIBBEAN SEA · ST LUCIA 15 · BARBADOS 16 · ISLA DE PROVIDENCIA (Col.) · NICARAGUA 3 · ISLA DE SAN ANDRÉS (Col.) · CAYOS DE ALBUQUERQUE (Col.) · ISLAS DEL MAÍZ (CORN IS.) (Nic.) · Aruba (Neths.) 18 · Curaçao (Neths.) 18 · Bonaire (Neths.) 18 · LESSER ANTILLES · ST VINCENT & THE GRENADINES · LA BLANQUILLA · GRENADA 17 · ISLAS LAS AVES · ISLAS LOS ROQUES · ISLA LA TORTUGA · ISLA DE MARGARITA · TOBAGO · TRINIDAD · TRINIDAD & TOBAGO · COSTA RICA 1 · PANAMA 1 · Panama Canal · COLOMBIA 4 · VENEZUELA 5 · GUYANA

OFFICIAL LANGUAGES

(Numbers refer to the notes below)

English · Dutch · French · Other · Spanish

1. English is widely spoken.
2. English is widely spoken by the West Indian settlers in the north and on the Bay Islands.
3. English-speaking communities are found on the Caribbean coast.
4. Local Indian dialects and some English, French, German and Italian are spoken
5. English, French, German and Portuguese are spoken by some sections of the community.
6. Some English and French are spoken. Some German, Italian and Russian are also spoken.
7. The official languages are French and Creole. English is widely spoken in tourist areas.
8. Some English and French is spoken.
9. Spanish and Creole are widely spoken.
10. The official language is Dutch. Papiamento (a combination of Dutch, English, Portuguese, Spanish and African languages) is the commonly used *lingua franca*. English and Spanish are also widely spoken.
11. The islanders speak Creole. *Patois* and English are also widely spoken.
12. English *patois* is widely spoken.
13. Creole French is the national language and is spoken by most of the population.
14. The main local dialect is Creole.
15. Local French *patois* is also spoken.
16. Local Bajan dialect is also spoken.
17. A French *patois* is spoken by a minority.
18. English and Spanish are also spoken. The islanders speak Papiamento (see 10).

BAHAMAS

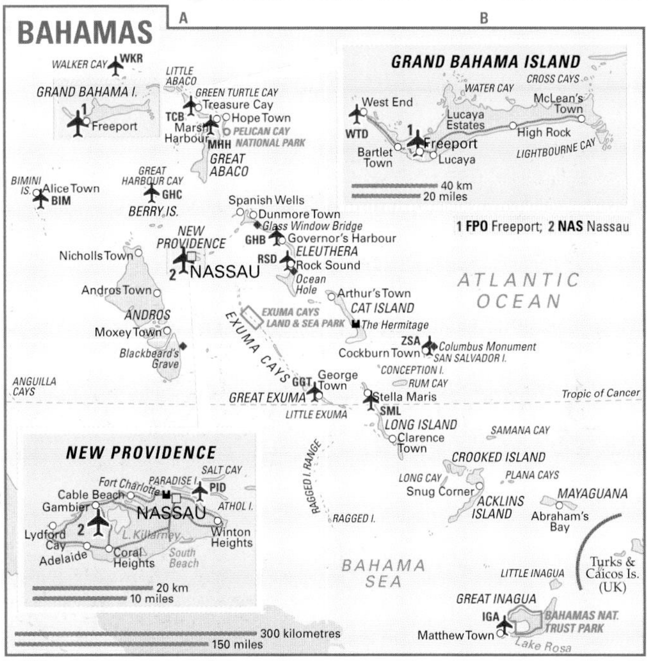

WALKER CAY WKR · LITTLE ABACO · GRAND BAHAMA I. · 1 Freeport · GREEN TURTLE CAY · Treasure Cay · TCB · Hope Town · Marsh Harbour · MHH · PELICAN CAY NATIONAL PARK · GREAT ABACO · GREAT HARBOUR CAY · BIMINI IS. · Alice Town · BIM · GHC · BERRY IS. · Spanish Wells · Dunmore Town · Glass Window Bridge · GHB · Governor's Harbour · NEW PROVIDENCE · Nicholls Town · 2 NASSAU · RSD · ELEUTHERA · Rock Sound · Ocean Hole · Andros Town · Arthur's Town · CAT ISLAND · ANDROS · EXUMA CAYS LAND & SEA PARK · The Hermitage · Moxey Town · ZSA · Columbus Monument · SAN SALVADOR I. · Blackbeard's Grave · Cockburn Town · EXUMA CAYS · CONCEPTION I. · ANGUILLA CAYS · GGT · George Town · RUM CAY · GREAT EXUMA · Stella Maris · SML · Tropic of Cancer · LITTLE EXUMA · LONG ISLAND · SAMANA CAY · Clarence Town · CROOKED ISLAND · RAGGED I. RANGE · LONG CAY · PLANA CAYS · Snug Corner · ACKLINS ISLAND · MAYAGUANA · RAGGED I. · Abraham's Bay · BAHAMA SEA · LITTLE INAGUA · Turks & Caicos Is. (UK) · GREAT INAGUA · IGA · BAHAMAS NAT. TRUST PARK · Matthew Town · Lake Rosa · ATLANTIC OCEAN

GRAND BAHAMA ISLAND: WATER CAY · CROSS CAYS · West End · McLean's Town · WTD · Lucaya Estates · 1 Freeport · High Rock · Bartlet Town · Lucaya · LIGHTBOURNE CAY · 40 km · 20 miles

1 **FPO** Freeport; 2 **NAS** Nassau

NEW PROVIDENCE: SALT CAY · PARADISE I. · Fort Charlotte · PID · Cable Beach · Gambier · NASSAU · ATHOL I. · Lydford Cay · 2 · L. Killarney · Winton Heights · Adelaide · Coral Heights · South Beach · 20 km · 10 miles

300 kilometres · 150 miles

International arrivals, 2004 to Caribbean* destinations (millions) *Venezuelan islands not included*

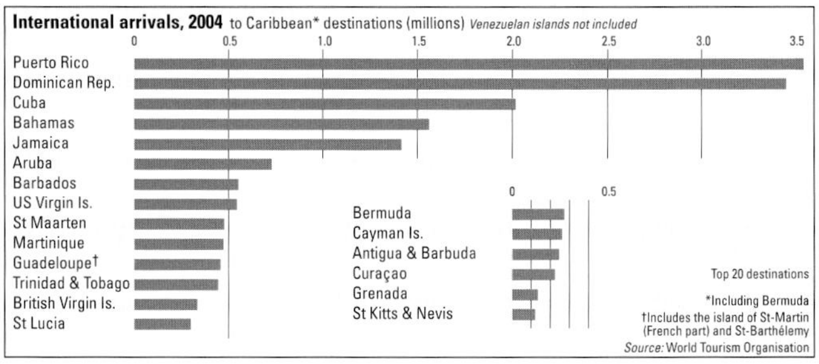

Scale: 0 · 0.5 · 1.0 · 1.5 · 2.0 · 2.5 · 3.0 · 3.5

Puerto Rico · Dominican Rep. · Cuba · Bahamas · Jamaica · Aruba · Barbados · US Virgin Is. · St Maarten · Martinique · Guadeloupe† · Trinidad & Tobago · British Virgin Is. · St Lucia

Scale: 0 · 0.5

Bermuda · Cayman Is. · Antigua & Barbuda · Curaçao · Grenada · St Kitts & Nevis

Top 20 destinations

*Including Bermuda

†Includes the island of St-Martin (French part) and St-Barthélemy

Source: World Tourism Organisation

TURKS & CAICOS ISLANDS

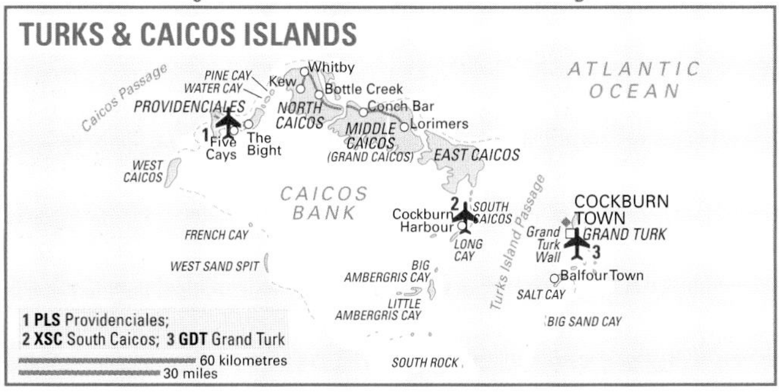

Caicos Passage · PINE CAY · WATER CAY · Kew · Whitby · Bottle Creek · PROVIDENCIALES · NORTH CAICOS · Conch Bar · 1 Five Cays · The Bight · MIDDLE CAICOS (GRAND CAICOS) · Lorimers · EAST CAICOS · WEST CAICOS · CAICOS BANK · 2 SOUTH CAICOS · Cockburn Harbour · LONG CAY · COCKBURN TOWN · Grand Turk Wall · GRAND TURK · 3 · FRENCH CAY · WEST SAND SPIT · BIG AMBERGRIS CAY · LITTLE AMBERGRIS CAY · Balfour Town · SALT CAY · Turks Island Passage · BIG SAND CAY · SOUTH ROCK · ATLANTIC OCEAN

1 **PLS** Providenciales; 2 **XSC** South Caicos; 3 **GDT** Grand Turk

60 kilometres · 30 miles

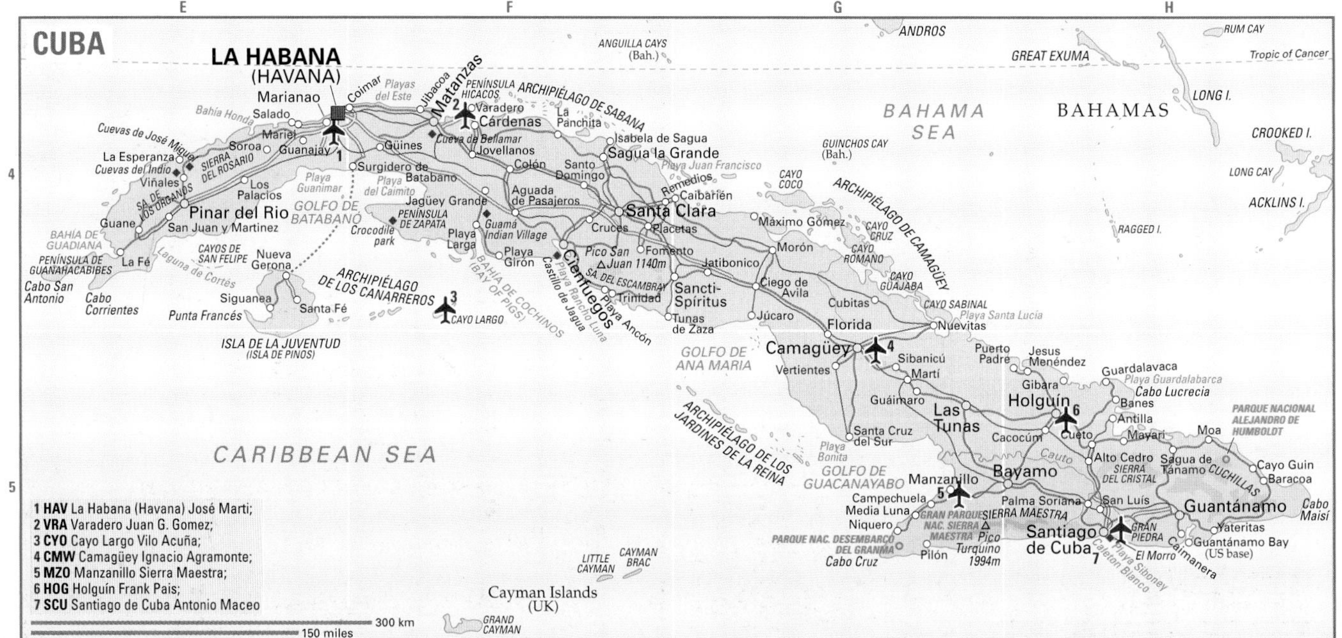
CUBA
LA HABANA (HAVANA)
BAHAMA SEA
BAHAMAS
CARIBBEAN SEA
Tropic of Cancer
Pinar del Rio
Matanzas
Cárdenas
Varadero
Santa Clara
Cienfuegos
Sancti-Spíritus
Camagüey
Las Tunas
Holguín
Bayamo
Manzanillo
Santiago de Cuba
Guantánamo
ISLA DE LA JUVENTUD (ISLA DE PINOS)
ARCHIPIÉLAGO DE LOS CANARREOS
ARCHIPIÉLAGO DE CAMAGÜEY
ARCHIPIÉLAGO DE SABANA
ARCHIPIÉLAGO DE LOS JARDINES DE LA REINA
GOLFO DE BATABANÓ
GOLFO DE ANA MARIA
GOLFO DE GUACANAYABO
Cayman Islands (UK)
1000 metres
500 metres
Sea level
1 HAV La Habana (Havana) José Marti;
2 VRA Varadero Juan G. Gomez;
3 CYO Cayo Largo Vilo Acuña;
4 CMW Camagüey Ignacio Agramonte;
5 MZO Manzanillo Sierra Maestra;
6 HOG Holguín Frank Pais;
7 SCU Santiago de Cuba Antonio Maceo
300 km
150 miles

See also... Contents (2-7) – these countries feature in many thematic and regional maps throughout the *World Travel Atlas*.

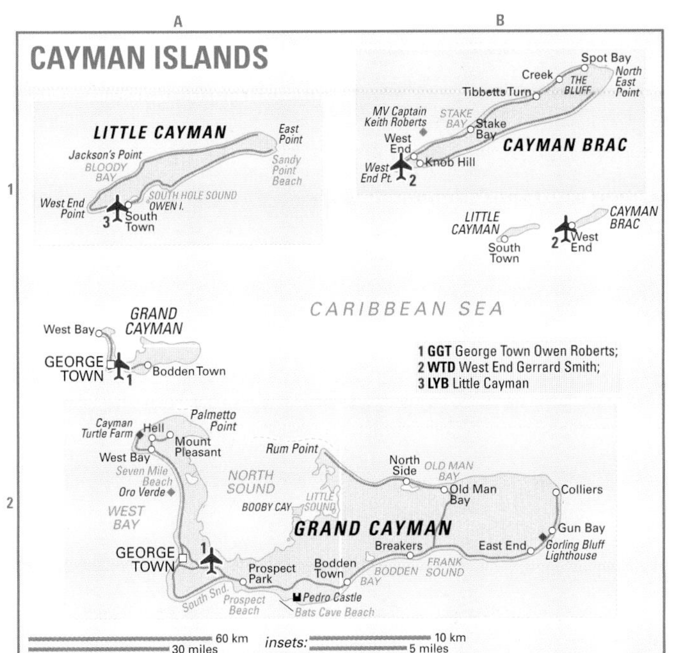
CAYMAN ISLANDS
LITTLE CAYMAN
East Point
Jackson's Point
BLOODY BAY
Sandy Point Beach
SOUTH HOLE SOUND
OWEN I.
West End Point
3
South Town
Spot Bay
Creek
Tibbetts Turn
THE BLUFF
North East Point
MV Captain Keith Roberts
STAKE BAY
Stake Bay
West End
CAYMAN BRAC
West End Pt.
2
Knob Hill
LITTLE CAYMAN
South Town
CAYMAN BRAC
West End
CARIBBEAN SEA
West Bay
GRAND CAYMAN
GEORGE TOWN
Bodden Town
1 GGT George Town Owen Roberts;
2 WTD West End Gerrard Smith;
3 LYB Little Cayman
Cayman Turtle Farm
Hell
Palmetto Point
Mount Pleasant
Rum Point
West Bay
Seven Mile Beach
Oro Verde
NORTH SOUND
North Side
OLD MAN BAY
Old Man Bay
Colliers
WEST BAY
BOOBY CAY
LITTLE SOUND
GRAND CAYMAN
Breakers
East End
Gun Bay
Gorling Bluff Lighthouse
GEORGE TOWN
Prospect Park
Bodden Town
BODDEN BAY
FRANK SOUND
South Snd.
Prospect Beach
Pedro Castle
Bats Cave Beach
60 km
30 miles
insets:
10 km
5 miles

JAMAICA
CARIBBEAN SEA
Rose Hall
Greenwood Great House
Falmouth
Martha Brae
Rio Bueno
Columbus Park
Discovery Bay
Runaway Bay
Seville Nueva
St Ann's Bay
Dunn's River Falls
Ocho Rios
Oracabessa
Galina Point
Annotto Bay
Buff Bay
Hope Bay
Port Antonio
Blue Hole
Boston Bay
Montego Bay
Lucea
North Negril Point
Sandy Bay
QUEEN OF SPAINS VALLEY
THE COCKPIT COUNTRY
Albert Town
Claremont
FERN GULLY
Firefly
Port Maria
Negril
DRY HARBOUR MOUNTAINS
Goshen
South Negril Point
Savanna-la-Mar
Seaford Town
Ipswich
Christiana
Highgate
Castleton
Bluefields
BLUEFIELDS BAY
SURINAM QUARTER
Appleton
Linstead
BLUE MOUNTAINS
Long Bay
Whitehouse
Luana Point
Mandeville
Spanish Town
Newcastle
Blue Mtn Peak 2256m
Reach Falls
Black River
SANTA CRUZ MTNS
MAY DAY MTNS
May Pen
Colbeck Castle
Portmore
HELLSHIRE HILLS
KINGSTON
PALISADOES
Morant Bay
Bath
Treasure Beach
Great Pedro Bluff
Lover's Leap
Milk River Spa
Old Harbour
LONG BAY
Rocky Point
PORTLAND BIGHT
Port Royal
Port Morant
Morant Point
Portland Point
1 MBJ Montego Bay Sir Donald Sangster;
2 KIN Kingston Norman Manley
80 kilometres
40 miles

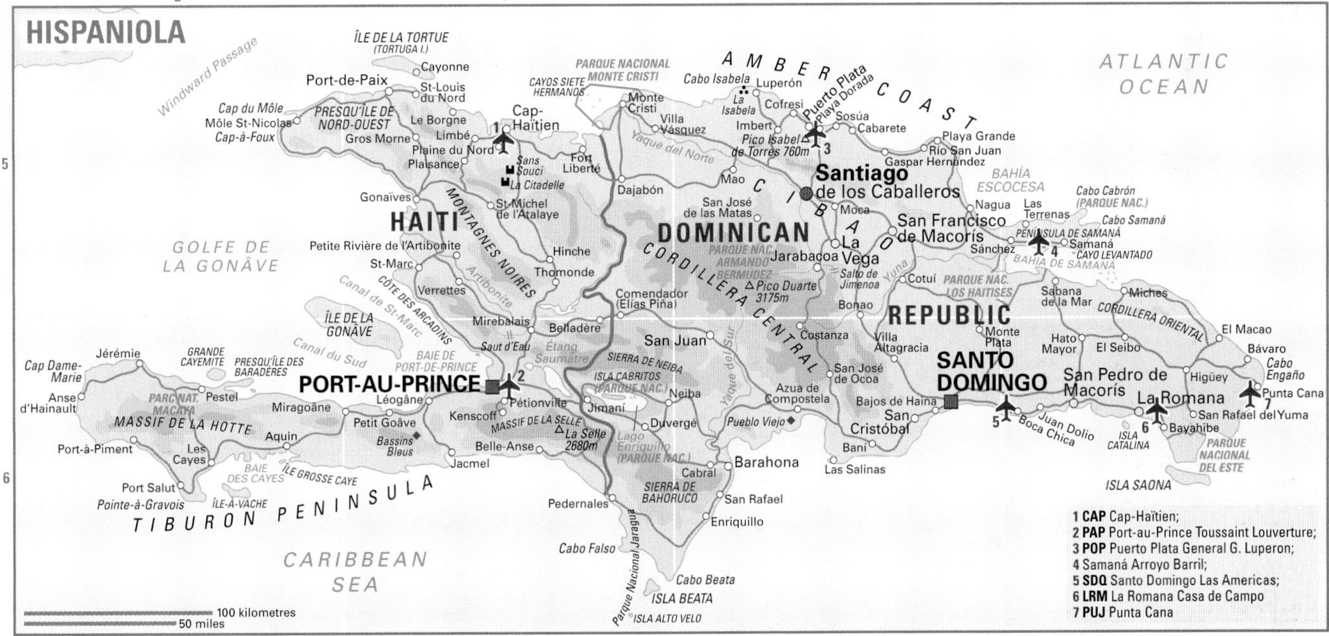
HISPANIOLA
ÎLE DE LA TORTUE (TORTUGA I.)
Cayonne
Windward Passage
Port-de-Paix
St-Louis du Nord
PARQUE NACIONAL MONTE CRISTI
CAYOS SIETE HERMANOS
AMBER COAST
Cabo Isabela
Luperón
Puerto Plata
Playa Dorada
ATLANTIC OCEAN
Cap du Môle
Môle St-Nicolas
Cap-à-Foux
PRESQU'ÎLE DE NORD-OUEST
Gros Morne
Le Borgne
Limbé
Cap-Haïtien
Monte Cristi
Villa Vásquez
La Isabela
Imbert
Cofresí
Sosúa
Cabarete
Playa Grande
Río San Juan
Plaine du Nord
Plaisance
Sans Souci
La Citadelle
Fort Liberté
Yaque del Norte
Pico Isabel de Torres 760m
Gaspar Hernández
Mao
Santiago de los Caballeros
BAHÍA ESCOCESA
Gonaïves
MONTAGNES NOIRES
St-Michel de l'Atalaye
Dajabón
San José de las Matas
CIBAO
Moca
Nagua
Las Terrenas
Cabo Cabrón (PARQUE NAC.)
Cabo Samaná
HAITI
DOMINICAN
San Francisco de Macorís
PENÍNSULA DE SAMANÁ
Samaná
CAYO LEVANTADO
Sánchez
BAHÍA DE SAMANÁ
GOLFE DE LA GONÂVE
Petite Rivière de l'Artibonite
St-Marc
Hinche
Thomonde
Artibonite
CORDILLERA CENTRAL
PARQUE NAC. ARMANDO BERMÚDEZ
Jarabacoa
La Vega
Salto de Jimenoa
Pico Duarte 3175m
Cotuí
PARQUE NAC. LOS HAITISES
Sabana de la Mar
Miches
CORDILLERA ORIENTAL
El Macao
Canal de St-Marc
CÔTE DES ARCADINS
Verrettes
Mirebalais
Comendador (Elías Piña)
Bonao
REPUBLIC
Monte Plata
Hato Mayor
El Seibo
Bávaro
Cabo Engaño
ÎLE DE LA GONÂVE
Belladère
San Juan
Costanza
Villa Altagracia
Canal du Sud
Saut d'Eau
Étang Saumâtre
SIERRA DE NEIBA
ISLA CABRITOS (PARQUE NAC.)
Neiba
Yaque del Sur
SANTO DOMINGO
San Pedro de Macorís
Higüey
Punta Cana
Jérémie
GRANDE CAYEMITE
PRESQU'ÎLE DES BARADÈRES
BAIE DE PORT-AU-PRINCE
PORT-AU-PRINCE
Pétionville
San José de Ocoa
Cap Dame-Marie
Anse d'Hainault
PARC NAT. MACAYA
Pestel
Léogâne
Kenscoff
Jimaní
Azua de Compostela
Bajos de Haina
La Romana
San Rafael del Yuma
MASSIF DE LA HOTTE
Miragoâne
Petit Goâve
MASSIF DE LA SELLE
La Selle 2680m
Duvergé
Pueblo Viejo
San Cristóbal
Juan Dolio
Boca Chica
Bayahíbe
Port-à-Piment
Aquin
Bassins Bleus
Belle-Anse
Lago Enriquillo (PARQUE NAC.)
Baní
ISLA CATALINA
PARQUE NACIONAL DEL ESTE
Les Cayes
BAIE DES CAYES
ÎLE GROSSE CAYE
Jacmel
Cabral
Barahona
Las Salinas
Port Salut
Pointe-à-Gravois
ÎLE-À-VACHE
TIBURON PENINSULA
SIERRA DE BAHORUCO
San Rafael
ISLA SAONA
Pedernales
Enriquillo
CARIBBEAN SEA
Cabo Falso
Parque Nacional Jaragua
Cabo Beata
ISLA BEATA
ISLA ALTO VELO
1 CAP Cap-Haïtien;
2 PAP Port-au-Prince Toussaint Louverture;
3 POP Puerto Plata General G. Luperon;
4 Samaná Arroyo Barril;
5 SDQ Santo Domingo Las Americas;
6 LRM La Romana Casa de Campo
7 PUJ Punta Cana
100 kilometres
50 miles

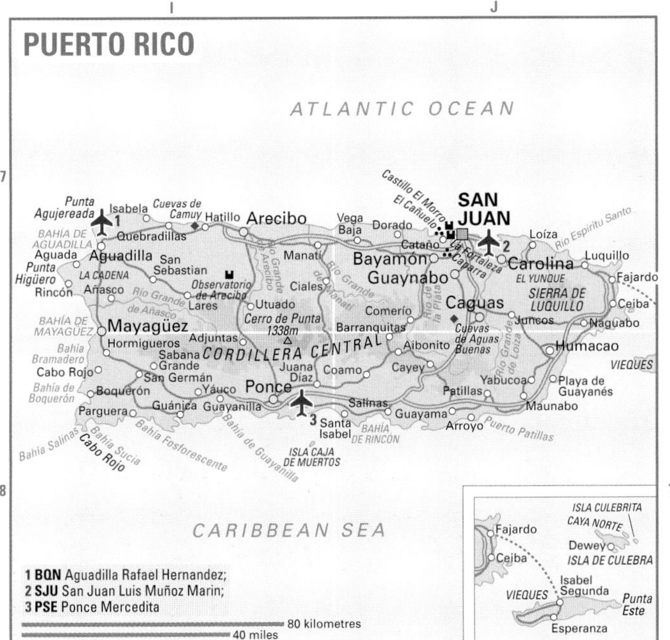
PUERTO RICO
ATLANTIC OCEAN
Castillo El Morro
El Cañuelo
SAN JUAN
Punta Agujereada
Isabela
Cuevas de Camuy
Hatillo
Arecibo
Vega Baja
Dorado
La Fortaleza
Río Espíritu Santo
BAHÍA DE AGUADILLA
Quebradillas
Cataño
Loíza
Aguada
Aguadilla
San Sebastián
Manatí
Bayamón
Carolina
Luquillo
Punta Higüero
LA CADENA
Observatorio de Arecibo
Guaynabo
EL YUNQUE
Fajardo
Rincón
Añasco
Río Grande de Añasco
Ciales
SIERRA DE LUQUILLO
Lares
Utuado
Comerío
Caguas
Ceiba
BAHÍA DE MAYAGÜEZ
Mayagüez
Cerro de Punta 1338m
Barranquitas
Cuevas de Aguas Buenas
Juncos
Naguabo
Bahía Bramadero
Hormigueros
Adjuntas
Aibonito
Humacao
Sabana Grande
CORDILLERA CENTRAL
VIEQUES
Cabo Rojo
San Germán
Coamo
Cayey
Yabucoa
Bahía de Boquerón
Boquerón
Yauco
Ponce
Juana Díaz
Patillas
Playa de Guayanés
Parguera
Guánica
Guayanilla
Salinas
Guayama
Maunabo
Arroyo
Puerto Patillas
Bahía Salinas
Cabo Rojo
Bahía Sucia
Bahía Fosforescente
Bahía de Guayanilla
Santa Isabel
BAHÍA DE RINCÓN
ISLA CAJA DE MUERTOS
CARIBBEAN SEA
ISLA CULEBRITA
Fajardo
CAYA NORTE
Ceiba
Dewey
ISLA DE CULEBRA
VIEQUES
Isabel Segunda
Punta Este
Esperanza
1 BQN Aguadilla Rafael Hernandez;
2 SJU San Juan Luis Muñoz Marin;
3 PSE Ponce Mercedita
80 kilometres
40 miles

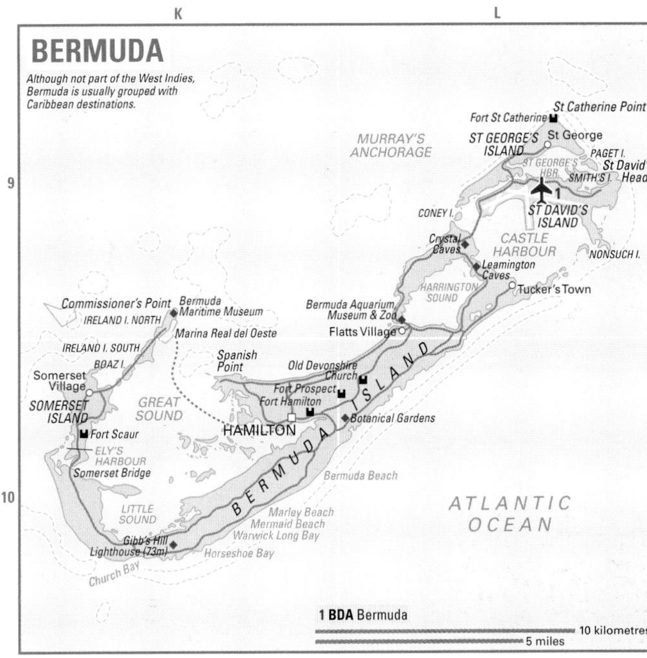
BERMUDA
Although not part of the West Indies, Bermuda is usually grouped with Caribbean destinations.
St Catherine Point
Fort St Catherine
MURRAY'S ANCHORAGE
ST GEORGE'S ISLAND
St George
PAGET I.
St David's Head
SMITH'S I.
ST GEORGE'S HBR
ST DAVID'S ISLAND
CONEY I.
Crystal Caves
CASTLE HARBOUR
NONSUCH I.
Leamington Caves
HARRINGTON SOUND
Tucker's Town
Commissioner's Point
Bermuda Maritime Museum
IRELAND I. NORTH
Bermuda Aquarium, Museum & Zoo
Flatts Village
Marina Real del Oeste
IRELAND I. SOUTH
BOAZ I.
Spanish Point
Old Devonshire Church
Somerset Village
Fort Prospect
Fort Hamilton
SOMERSET ISLAND
GREAT SOUND
Botanical Gardens
HAMILTON
BERMUDA ISLAND
Fort Scaur
ELY'S HARBOUR
Somerset Bridge
Bermuda Beach
LITTLE SOUND
Marley Beach
Mermaid Beach
Warwick Long Bay
ATLANTIC OCEAN
Gibb's Hill Lighthouse (73m)
Horseshoe Bay
Church Bay
1 BDA Bermuda
10 kilometres
5 miles
1000 metres
500 metres
Sea level

Caribbean: Dive Sites & the Lesser Antilles

See also... Mediterranean Diving (106); Red Sea Diving (119); Pacific Diving (150-151); North America Climate (155); the Greater Antilles (178-179)

The listings above refer to a selection of related themes. For more information, see the Contents (2-7).

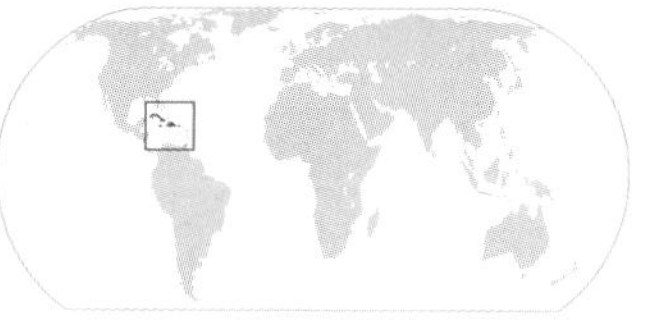

MAP A
BRITISH VIRGIN ISLANDS
30 km
15 miles
The Settlement
ANEGADA
HORSESHOE REEF
PRICKLY PEAR I.
GREAT CAMANOE
TUP
THE DOGS
GUANA I.
Beef Island
Terrance B. Lettsome
VIRGIN GORDA
GT. TOBAGO
ROAD TOWN
TORTOLA
Spanish Town
JOST VAN DYKE
Mt Sage 521m
The Baths
Sir Francis Drake Ch.
GINGER I.
COOPER I.
SALT I.
RMS Rhone
PETER I.
NORMAN I.
US Virgin Is.

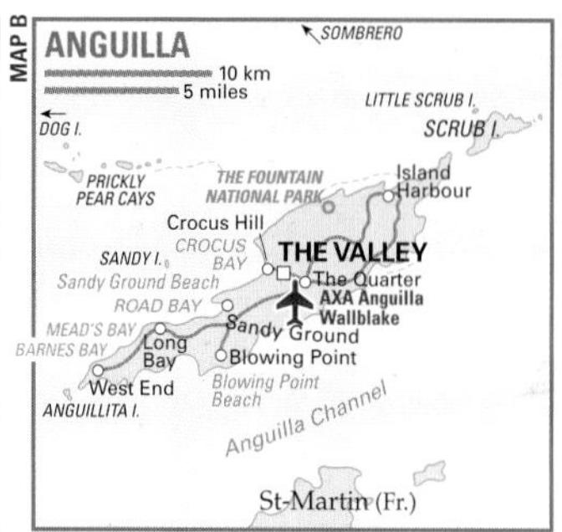
MAP B
ANGUILLA
SOMBRERO
10 km
5 miles
DOG I.
LITTLE SCRUB I.
SCRUB I.
PRICKLY PEAR CAYS
THE FOUNTAIN NATIONAL PARK
Island Harbour
Crocus Hill
CROCUS BAY
SANDY I.
THE VALLEY
Sandy Ground Beach
The Quarter
AXA Anguilla Wallblake
ROAD BAY
Sandy Ground
MEAD'S BAY
BARNES BAY
Long Bay
Blowing Point
West End
ANGUILLITA I.
Blowing Point Beach
Anguilla Channel
St-Martin (Fr.)

MAP C
ST MARTIN
ÎLE DE TINTAMARRE
SFG St-Martin Espérance
ÎLET PINEL
Grand Case
Cul-de-Sac
St-Martin (Fr.)
CAYE VERTE
SIMPSON BAY LAGOON
Colombier
TERRES BASSES
BAIE NETTLE
Marigot
Orléans
Mt Flagstaff 392m
SXM St Maarten Princess Juliana
Benenden Prinsen
Boven Prinsen
Great Salt Pond
SIMSON BAAI
Philipsburg
St Maarten (Neths.)
GROOT BAAI
Fort Amsterdam
10 km
5 miles

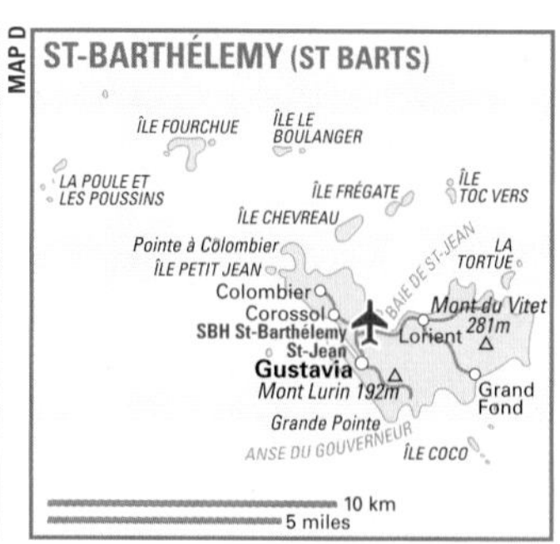
MAP D
ST-BARTHÉLEMY (ST BARTS)
ÎLE FOURCHUE
ÎLE LE BOULANGER
LA POULE ET LES POUSSINS
ÎLE FRÉGATE
ÎLE TOC VERS
ÎLE CHEVREAU
Pointe à Colombier
LA TORTUE
ÎLE PETIT JEAN
BAIE DE ST-JEAN
Colombier
Corossol
Mont du Vitet 281m
SBH St-Barthélemy
Lorient
St-Jean
Gustavia
Mont Lurin 192m
Grand Fond
Grande Pointe
ANSE DU GOUVERNEUR
ÎLE COCO
10 km
5 miles

MAP X
US VIRGIN ISLANDS
HANS LOLLIK I.
British Virgin Is.
CHARLOTTE AMALIE
MAGENS BAY
ST THOMAS
Coral Bay
ST JOHN
Mai Gen. Rodgers
Bordeaux Mtn 389m
STT St Thomas Cyril E. King
HASSEL I.
Pillsbury Sound
Cruz Bay
VIRGIN ISLANDS NAT. PARK
WATER I.
GREAT ST JAMES I.
CAPELLA I.
DAVIS BAY
BUCK I. REEF NAT. MON.
BUCK I.
East Point
ST CROIX
Christiansted
Rainbow Beach
Frederiksted
Whim Greathouse Museum
Sandy Point
STX St Croix Henry E. Rohlsen
20 km
10 miles

MAP W
ARUBA
Kudarebe
California Lighthouse
Arashi Beach
Antilla
Malmok Beach
Palm Beach
Alto Vista Chapel
Noord
Eagle Beach
Natural Bridge
Druif Beach
Diorite boulders
Santa Cruz
ORANJESTAD
Fontein Cave
Guadirikiri Caves
AUA Aruba Queen Beatrix
Jamanota 188m
Spaans Lagoen
Huliba Cave
Savaneta
Commandeursbaai
Seroe Colorado
San Nicolas
Rodgers Beach
Colorado Point Lighthouse
10 km
5 miles

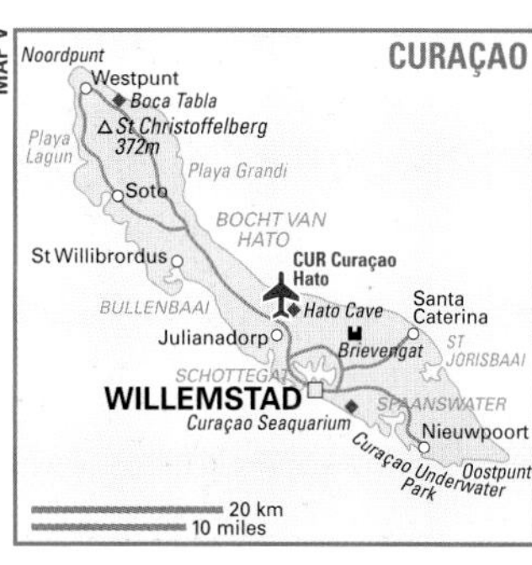
MAP V
CURAÇAO
Noordpunt
Westpunt
Boca Tabla
St Christoffelberg 372m
Playa Lagun
Playa Grandi
Soto
BOCHT VAN HATO
St Willibrordus
CUR Curaçao Hato
BULLENBAAI
Hato Cave
Santa Caterina
Julianadorp
Brievengat
ST JORISBAAI
SCHOTTEGAT
WILLEMSTAD
SPAANSWATER
Curaçao Seaquarium
Nieuwpoort
Oostpunt
Curaçao Underwater Park
20 km
10 miles

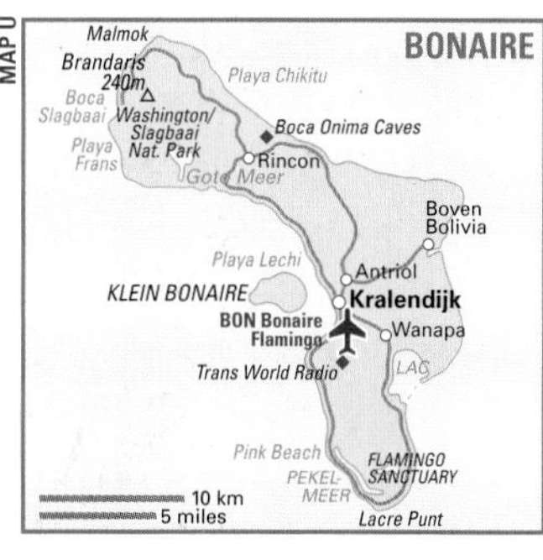
MAP U
BONAIRE
Malmok
Brandaris 240m
Playa Chikitu
Boca Slagbaai
Washington/Slagbaai Nat. Park
Playa Frans
Boca Onima Caves
Rincon
Gotomeer
Boven Bolivia
Playa Lechi
Antriol
KLEIN BONAIRE
Kralendijk
BON Bonaire Flamingo
Wanapa
Trans World Radio
LAC
Pink Beach
PEKELMEER
FLAMINGO SANCTUARY
Lacre Punt
10 km
5 miles

MAIN MAP

GULF OF MEXICO
UNITED STATES
GRAND BAHAMA I.
GREAT ABACO
BIMINI IS.
BERRY IS.
NEW PROVIDENCE
ELEUTHERA
DRY TORTUGAS
FLORIDA KEYS
ANDROS
BAHAMAS
CAT I.
STRAITS OF FLORIDA
GREAT BAHAMA BANK
CAY SAL BANK
SAN SALVADOR
RUM CAY
GREAT EXUMA
LONG I.
Tropic of Cancer
Varadero
ARCH. DE SABANA
GUINCHOS CAY
CROOKED I.
ACKLINS I.
ARCH. DE CAMAGÜEY
RAGGED I.
GOLFO DE BATABANÓ
María la Gorda
Isla de la Juventud (Isla de Pinos)
Cayo Largo
Cienfuegos/ Rancho Luna
CUBA
Santa Lucía
LITTLE INAGUA
GREAT INAGUA
YUCATAN CHANNEL
ISLA CANCÚN
ARCHIPIÉLAGO DE LOS JARDINES DE LA REINA
Guardalavaca
MEXICO
ISLA COZUMEL
YUCATAN BASIN
Santiago de Cuba
Windward Passage
LITTLE CAYMAN
CAYMAN BRAC
GRAND CAYMAN
Cayman Is. (UK)
CAYMAN TRENCH
ÎLE DE LA GONÂVE
BANCO CHINCHORRO
NAVASSA I. (US)
AMBERGRIS CAYE
JAMAICA
Jamaica Channel
BELIZE
TURNEFFE IS.
LIGHTHOUSE REEF
ISLAS SANTANILLA (SWAN IS.) (Hon.)
PEDRO BANK
BARRIER REEF
GLOVER REEF
ISLAS DE LA BAHÍA (BAY IS.)
GUANAJA
ROATÁN
UTILA
BANCO GORDA
CAYOS CAJONES
ARRECIFE DE LA MEDIA LUNA
CARIBBEAN
HONDURAS
CAYOS MISKITOS (Nic.)
QUITA SUEÑO BANK (Col.)
SERRANA BANK (Col.)
COLOMBIAN BASIN
EL SALVADOR
CAYO DE RONCADOR (Col.)
ISLA DE PROVIDENCIA (Col.)
NICARAGUA
ISLA DE SAN ANDRÉS (Col.)
CAYOS DE ALBUQUERQUE (Col.)
ISLAS DEL MAÍZ (CORN IS.) (Nic.)
PACIFIC OCEAN
COSTA RICA
COLOMBI

BAHAMAS 1 2 3 4 D S T W ★★★
Dive sites off western (lee) shores of most islar and all around Andros and New Providence; facilities at Nassau and on individual islands
Blue Hole diving; 700 islands; shark feeding

CANCÚN 1 2 3 4 D S T W ★★
Main dive sites off eastern shore; facilities centred at Cancún
Eight main reef dives to 10m; more popular is a boat trip to Cozumel

COZUMEL 1 2 3 4 D S T W ★★★
Main dive sites off western (lee) shore; facilities centred at San Miguel
Dramatic underwater vertical cliffs; diving with manatee and cave diving

CUBA 1 2 3 4 D S T W ★
Several designated diving regions around the country (shown in red); limited facilities in most major coastal towns
96m frigate recently sunk off Varadero as a diving attraction

BANCO CHINCHORRO 1 2 3 4 D S T W ★
Main dive sites off east coast of atoll; no facilities on atoll or nearby mainland
Atoll reef with numerous shipwrecks on east coast; large unidentified/intact freighter in north

CAYMAN ISLANDS 1 2 3 4 D S T W ★★★
Dive sites all around the islands due to their sheltered location within the Caribbean; facilities at George Town and West Bay (Grand Cayman) and West End (Cayman Brac)
Grand Cayman: Stingray City, where many stingrays congregate and are fed by divers, and shipwreck Oro Verde – a 56m ship in 25m of water; Cayman Brac: wreck of Russian frigate – a 100m ship in 25m of water, renamed MV Captain Keith Tibbetts

BELIZE 1 2 3 4 D S T W ★★★
Main dive sites Lighthouse and Turneffe atoll reefs; facilities centred at San Pedro (Ambergris Caye) and on all three atoll reefs
World's second largest barrier reef; three atoll reefs; the Great Blue Hole; exceptional corals and marine life; regular whale shark sightings

JAMAICA 1 2 3 4 D S T W ★
Main dive sites off north coast (Negril, Montego Bay, Ocho Rios, Runaway Bay and Port Antonio), and Kingston (Port Royal); facilities centred at Ocho Rios, Port Royal and Montego Bay
Spectacular canyons and deep walls off the north coast; sunken city of Port Royal

BAY ISLANDS 1 2 3 4 D S T W ★★
Main dive sites mostly off southern shores; facilities centred at Roatán
Roatán: exceptional wall diving on north coast when sea is calm; Guanaja: 55m shipwreck 'Jado Trader' in 30m of water

ARUBA 1 2 3 4 D S T W ★★★
Main dive sites off western (lee) shore facilities centred at Oranjestad
121m shipwreck 'Antilla' – a large Ge freighter scuttled at the outbreak of W

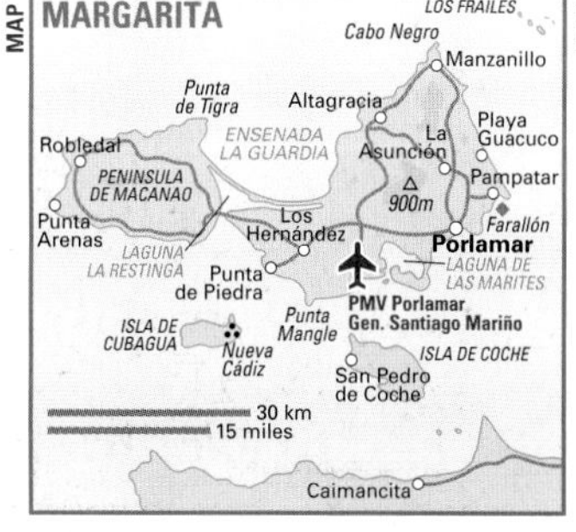
MAP T
MARGARITA
LOS FRAILES
Cabo Negro
Manzanillo
Punta de Tigra
Altagracia
Playa Guacuco
Robledal
ENSENADA LA GUARDIA
Asunción
PENINSULA DE MACANAO
900m
Pampatar
Punta Arenas
Los Hernández
Farallón
Porlamar
LAGUNA LA RESTINGA
LAGUNA DE LAS MARITES
Punta de Piedra
PMV Porlamar Gen. Santiago Mariño
ISLA DE CUBAGUA
Nueva Cádiz
Punta Mangle
ISLA DE COCHE
San Pedro de Coche
30 km
15 miles
Caimancita

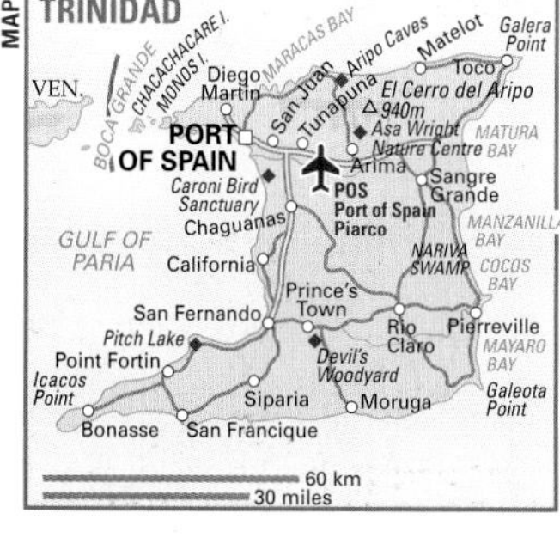
MAP S
TRINIDAD
MARACAS BAY
Aripo Caves
Matelot
Galera Point
VEN.
Toco
Diego Martin
El Cerro del Aripo 940m
PORT OF SPAIN
Asa Wright Nature Centre
MATURA BAY
Arima
Sangre Grande
Caroni Bird Sanctuary
POS Port of Spain Piarco
MANZANILLA BAY
GULF OF PARIA
Chaguanas
NARIVA SWAMP
California
COCOS BAY
Prince's Town
San Fernando
Rio Claro
Pierreville
Pitch Lake
MAYARO BAY
Point Fortin
Devil's Woodyard
Icacos Point
Galeota Point
Siparia
Moruga
Bonasse
San Francique
60 km
30 miles

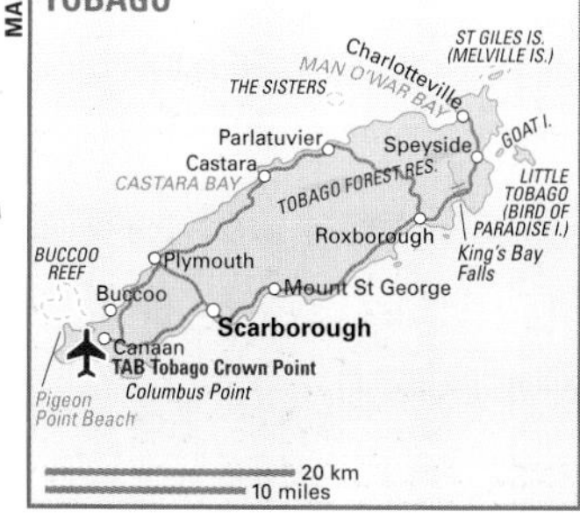
MAP R
TOBAGO
ST GILES IS. (MELVILLE IS.)
Charlotteville
MAN O'WAR BAY
THE SISTERS
GOAT I.
Parlatuvier
Speyside
Castara
CASTARA BAY
TOBAGO FOREST RES.
LITTLE TOBAGO (BIRD OF PARADISE I.)
BUCCOO REEF
Plymouth
Roxborough
King's Bay Falls
Buccoo
Mount St George
Scarborough
Canaan
TAB Tobago Crown Point
Columbus Point
Pigeon Point Beach
20 km
10 miles

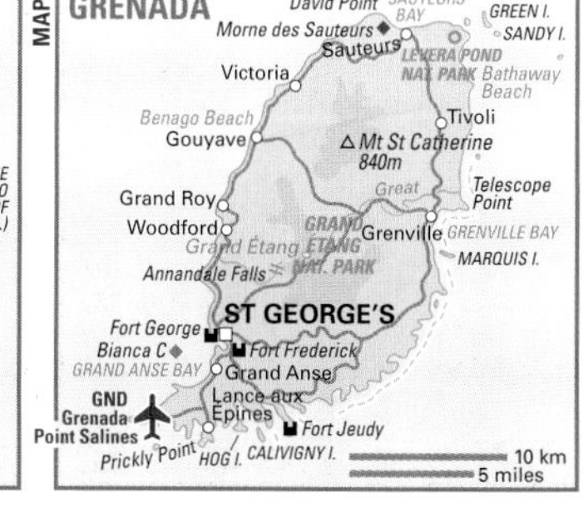
MAP Q
GRENADA
David Point
SAUTEURS BAY
GREEN I.
Morne des Sauteurs
SANDY I.
Sauteurs
LEVERA POND NAT. PARK
Victoria
Bathaway Beach
Tivoli
Benago Beach
Gouyave
Mt St Catherine 840m
Grand Roy
Telescope Point
Woodford
GRAND ETANG
Grenville
GRENVILLE BAY
Grand Étang Nat. Park
Annandale Falls
MARQUIS I.
Fort George
ST GEORGE'S
Bianca C
Fort Frederick
GRAND ANSE BAY
Grand Anse
GND Grenada Point Salines
Lance-aux-Epines
Fort Jeudy
Prickly Point
HOG I.
CALIVIGNY I.
10 km
5 miles

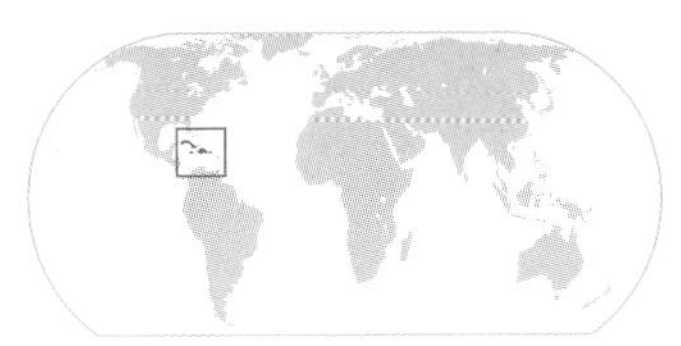

See also... Contents (2-7) – these countries feature in many thematic and regional maps throughout the *World Travel Atlas*.

Caribbean: Dive Sites & the Lesser Antilles

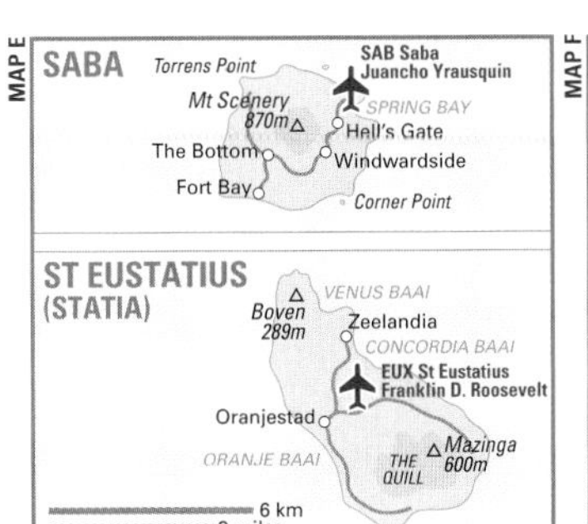

MAP E
SABA
SAB Saba Juancho Yrausquin
Mt Scenery 870m
Hell's Gate
Windwardside
The Bottom
Fort Bay
Corner Point
ST EUSTATIUS (STATIA)
Boven 289m
Zeelandia
EUX St Eustatius Franklin D. Roosevelt
Oranjestad
The Quill
Mazinga 600m
6 km
3 miles

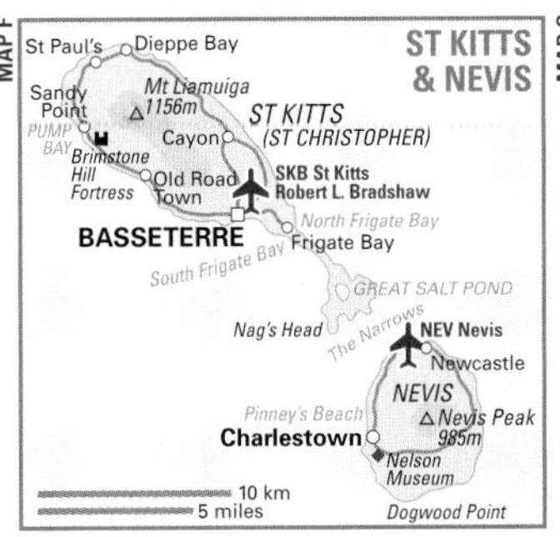

MAP F
ST KITTS & NEVIS
St Paul's
Dieppe Bay
Sandy Point
Mt Liamuiga 1156m
ST KITTS (ST CHRISTOPHER)
Cayon
Brimstone Hill Fortress
Old Road Town
SKB St Kitts Robert L. Bradshaw
BASSETERRE
Frigate Bay
Nag's Head
NEV Nevis
Newcastle
NEVIS
Nevis Peak 985m
Charlestown
Nelson Museum
Dogwood Point
10 km
5 miles

MAP G
MONTSERRAT
North West Bluff
Silver Hill
Gerald's
St John's
Recent volcanic activity has destroyed the former capital, Plymouth. An exclusion zone operates in the southern half of the island.
Katy Hill
CENTRE HILLS
MNI Montserrat William H. Bramble (closed)
Olveston
Salem
SOUFRIÈRE HILLS
Long Ground
Bransby Point
Soufrière Hills Volcano
Galway's Soufrière
Plymouth
Fort Barrington
Exclusion zone
Morris
Old Fort Point
10 km
5 miles

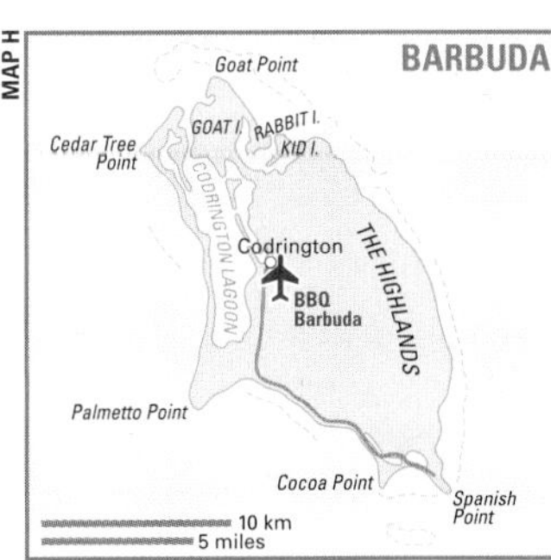

MAP H
BARBUDA
Goat Point
Cedar Tree Point
Codrington
BBQ Barbuda
THE HIGHLANDS
Palmetto Point
Cocoa Point
Spanish Point
10 km
5 miles

Dive sites:	Regular sightings of:
1 Coral reefs	D Dolphins
2 Atoll reefs	S Sharks / rays / pelagics
3 Blue holes / cave diving	T Turtles
4 Shipwrecks	W Whales
White square: not present	White square: not regularly seen

Facilities for the diver: ★ Limited ★★ Good ★★★ Excellent

This map shows the Caribbean's principal diving destinations and the main underwater attractions they have to offer. Details include the existence of coral reefs; atoll reefs (of which there are only four in the entire Caribbean); blue hole and cave diving plus the existence of shipwrecks (including wrecked aircraft). Whilst the diver may encounter turtle, shark, large rays and dolphin at any time – and whales occasionally – only those places where these are featured and regular sightings occur are indicated here.

Diving facilities for each destination, including availability of scuba diving equipment and related support services, are graded as limited, good or excellent. It must be emphasised that these grades are a general reflection on the overall availability of everything required by the visiting scuba diver and are not an interpretation of the standards found within any one facility or organisation.

Each diving destination provides every level of depth from the very shallow to the extremely deep.

Data compiled by Ned Middleton, all rights reserved. email: ned@nedmiddleton.demon.co.uk

TURKS AND CAICOS ISLANDS ★★★
Main dive sites off western shores of Providenciales, West Caicos and Grand Turk, and north coast of French Cay; facilities on all above except for French Cay
West of Grand Turk is Grand Turk Wall with outstanding vertical walls from 6m to over 2000m

DOMINICAN REPUBLIC ★★
Main dive sites off Samaná Peninsula in north, and off southern shore; facilities centred at Samaná and Santo Domingo
Cave diving in Islas Ballenas (north coast) and Humpback Whales from Jan-Mar; coral reefs in south

BRITISH VIRGIN ISLANDS ★★★
Main dive sites off the eastern islands; facilities on all main islands
Royal Mail Packet Ship (RMS) Rhone which sank in the hurricane of 1867; many other shipwrecks to be found off Anegada

US VIRGIN ISLANDS ★★★
Main dive sites mainly between St Thomas and St John; facilities centred on St Thomas and St Croix
Outstanding coral formations in relatively shallow water; 'Major General Rodgers' is an exciting shipwreck – 49m long in 25m of water

ANGUILLA ★
Main dive sites between Crocus Valley and West End; facilities centred at Crocus Hill
A number of small shipwrecks along an unspoilt reef

PUERTO RICO ★
Main dive sites off west and south coasts; facilities centred at Ponce, Mayagüez and Guayama
Outstanding marine life, especially seahorses, octopus and sardines

ST KITTS & NEVIS ★
Main dive sites off west/southwest (lee) shores; facilities centred at Basseterre
Devil's Caves – a series of coral grottoes and caves with underwater lava tubes in less than 15m of water; virgin and unspoilt reefs; large shoals of fish everywhere

ANTIGUA ★★
Main dive sites off English Harbour; facilities centred at Falmouth and English Harbour Town
Coral reefs and marine life

GUADELOUPE ★
Main dive sites off western (lee) shore; facilities centred at Basse-Terre
Excellent and unspoilt coral reefs in relatively shallow waters; one 49m shipwreck

DOMINICA ★★
Main dive sites off western (lee) shore; facilities centred at Portsmouth and Roseau
Sperm Whales, Pilot Whales and Spinner Dolphins seen off east coast; majority of scuba diving off west coast

CURAÇAO ★★
Main dive sites off northwest and southwest shores; facilities centred at Willemstad
Exceptional coral reef diving with outstanding visibility

ST LUCIA ★★
Main dive sites off northwest shore; facilities centred at Castries
Shipwreck 'Lesleen M'; outstanding coral reefs

ST VINCENT & THE GRENADINES ★
Main dive sites off southwest shore of St Vincent and west shore of Bequia; facilities centred at Kingstown and Port Elizabeth (Bequia)
One of the largest shipwrecks in the Caribbean – 19,878 tonne, 190m cruise liner 'Antilles' which struck a reef off Mustique and sank in 1971

MARTINIQUE ★★
Main dive sites off west (lee) shore; facilities centred at Fort-de-France
Outstanding coral formations at every depth; two good wrecks – 'Roraima' and 'Nahoon'

BONAIRE ★★
Main dive sites off western (lee) shore; facilities centred at Kralendijk
Exceptional coral reef diving with outstanding visibility

GRENADA ★★★
Main dive sites off southwest shore; facilities centred at Grande Anse Beach
One of the largest shipwrecks in the Caribbean – 18,000 tonne, 200m cruise liner 'Bianca C' which caught fire and sank in 1961

BARBADOS ★★
Main dive sites off west and southwest (lee) shores; facilities centred at Bridgetown
Over 500 ships are known to be lost off Barbados; the most outstanding is the 'Stavronikita' which sank in 1978 – a 111m Greek cargo ship sitting upright in 40m of water

LOS ROQUES ★
Dive sites all around the archipelago; facilities centred at Gran Roque
Coral reefs and marine life in excellent condition

MARGARITA ★
Main dive sites Farallón, off Cubagua and Los Frailes; facilities centred at Porlamar
Unspoilt coral reefs, prolific marine life plus two shipwrecks off Cubagua

TOBAGO ★★
Main dive sites off northeast and northwest shores; facilities centred at Charlotteville and Canaan
Large Atlantic Manta Ray with wingspans over 6m every Apr-Sept

St-Barthélemy and the French half of the island of St Martin are part of the French Overseas Department of Guadeloupe

The Netherlands Antilles comprise Bonaire, Curaçao, Saba, St Eustatius and St Maarten (the Dutch half of the island of St Martin); the capital is Willemstad, on Curaçao

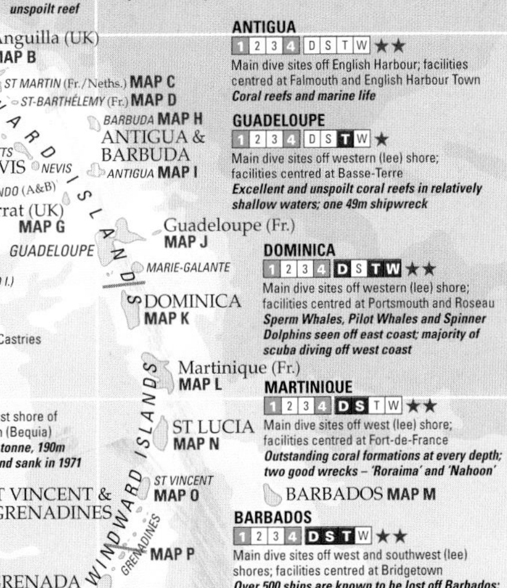

LEEWARD ISLANDS
Anguilla (UK) MAP B
ST MARTIN (Fr./Neths.) MAP C
ST-BARTHÉLEMY (Fr.) MAP D
BARBUDA MAP H
ANTIGUA & BARBUDA
ANTIGUA MAP I
SABA (Neths.)
ST EUSTATIUS (Neths.)
MAP E
ST KITTS & NEVIS MAP F
REDONDO (A&B)
Montserrat (UK) MAP G
Guadeloupe (Fr.) MAP J
GUADELOUPE
MARIE-GALANTE
DOMINICA MAP K
AVES (BIRD I.) (Ven.)

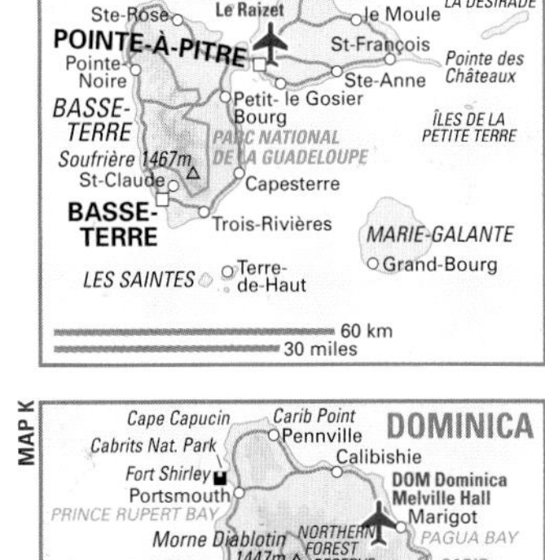

MAP I
ANTIGUA
Cedar Grove
ANU Antigua V.C. Bird
Fort James
ST JOHN'S
Parham
Indian Town Point
Bolans
All Saints
Boggy Peak 402m
Freetown
Falmouth
English Harbour Town
Nelson's Dockyard
Shirley Heights
Cape Shirley
10 km
5 miles

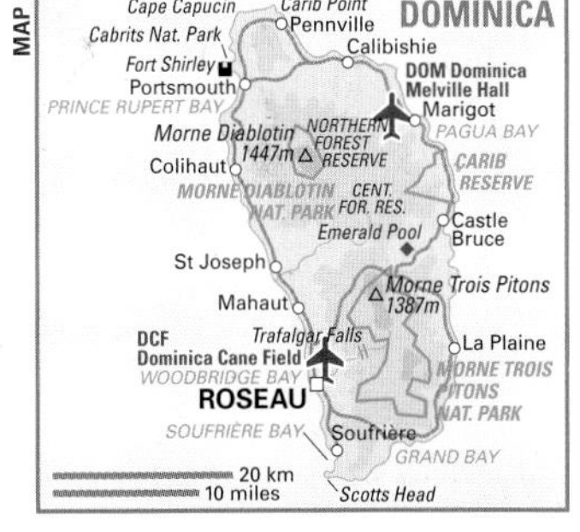

MAP J
GUADELOUPE
Anse-Bertrand
Port-Louis
GRANDE-TERRE
PTP Point-à-Pitre Le Raizet
POINTE-À-PITRE
Le Moule
St-François
Ste-Anne
BASSE-TERRE
Soufrière 1467m
BASSE-TERRE
Trois-Rivières
MARIE-GALANTE
Grand-Bourg
LES SAINTES
60 km
30 miles

MAP K
DOMINICA
Cape Capucin
Pennville
Calibishie
DOM Dominica Melville Hall
Portsmouth
Marigot
Morne Diablotin 1447m
Colihaut
Castle Bruce
St Joseph
Morne Trois Pitons 1387m
DCF Dominica Cane Field
La Plaine
ROSEAU
Soufrière
Scotts Head
20 km
10 miles

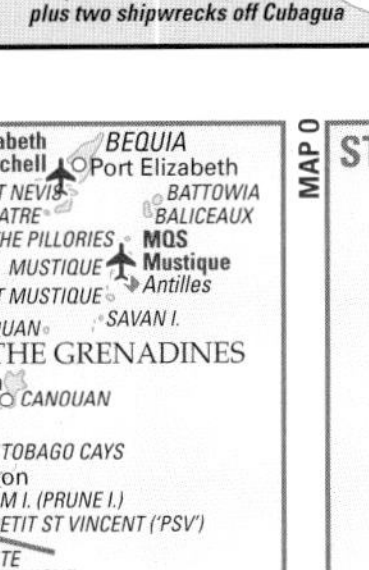

MAP P
THE GRENADINES
BQU Port Elizabeth J.F. Mitchell
BEQUIA
MQS Mustique
ST VINCENT & THE GRENADINES
UNI Union Island
Ashton
CRU Carriacou
Hillsborough
GRENADA
30 km
15 miles

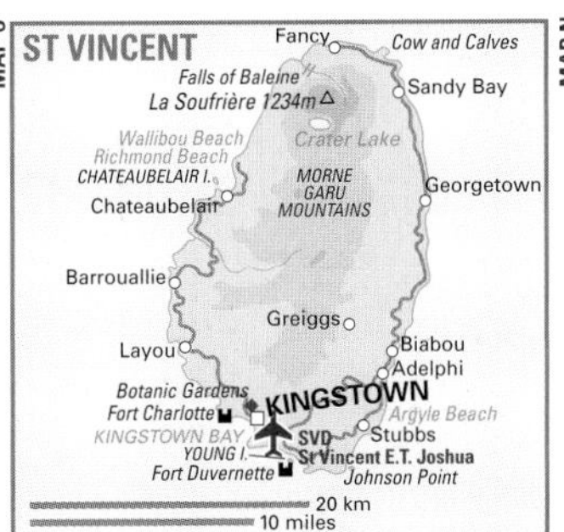

MAP O
ST VINCENT
Fancy
La Soufrière 1234m
Sandy Bay
Georgetown
Chateaubelair
Barrouallie
Greiggs
Biabou
Layou
KINGSTOWN
SVD St Vincent E.T. Joshua
Stubbs
20 km
10 miles

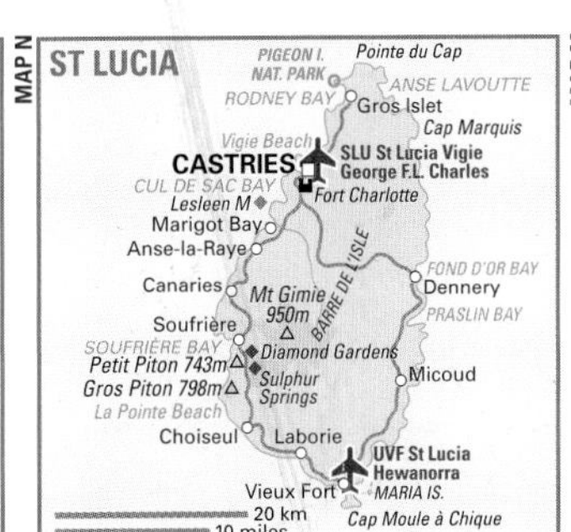

MAP N
ST LUCIA
Pointe du Cap
Gros Islet
CASTRIES
SLU St Lucia Vigie George F.L. Charles
Marigot Bay
Anse-la-Raye
Canaries
Mt Gimie 950m
Dennery
Soufrière
Petit Piton 743m
Gros Piton 798m
Micoud
Choiseul
Laborie
UVF St Lucia Hewanorra
Vieux Fort
20 km
10 miles

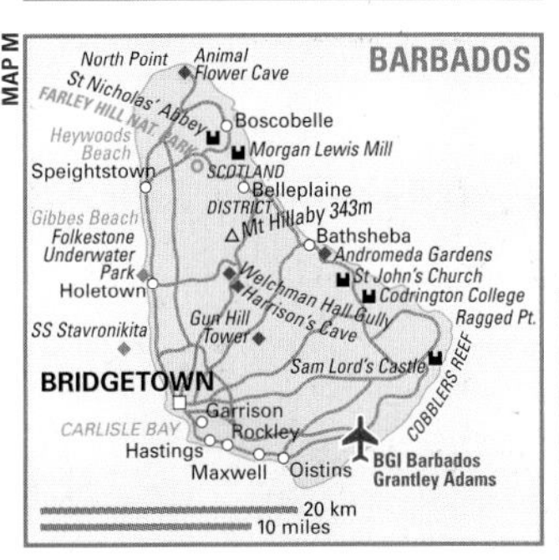

MAP M
BARBADOS
North Point
Speightstown
Mt Hillaby 343m
Bathsheba
Holetown
BRIDGETOWN
Oistins
BGI Barbados Grantley Adams
20 km
10 miles

MAP L
MARTINIQUE
Grand' Rivière
Basse-Pointe
Montagne Pelée 1397m
Ste-Marie
Le Prêcheur
St-Pierre
la Trinité
Le Carbet
Le Robert
FORT-DE-FRANCE
FDF Fort-de-France Lamentin
Le Vauclin
les Trois-Ilets
Rivière-Pilote
les Anses-d'Arlets
le Diamant
Ste-Luce
Ste-Anne
30 km
15 miles

Mexico

See also... North America Climate (155); The Caribbean (178-181); Central America (184); Latin America Museums & Galleries (187)

The listings above refer to a selection of related themes. For more information, see the Contents (2-7).

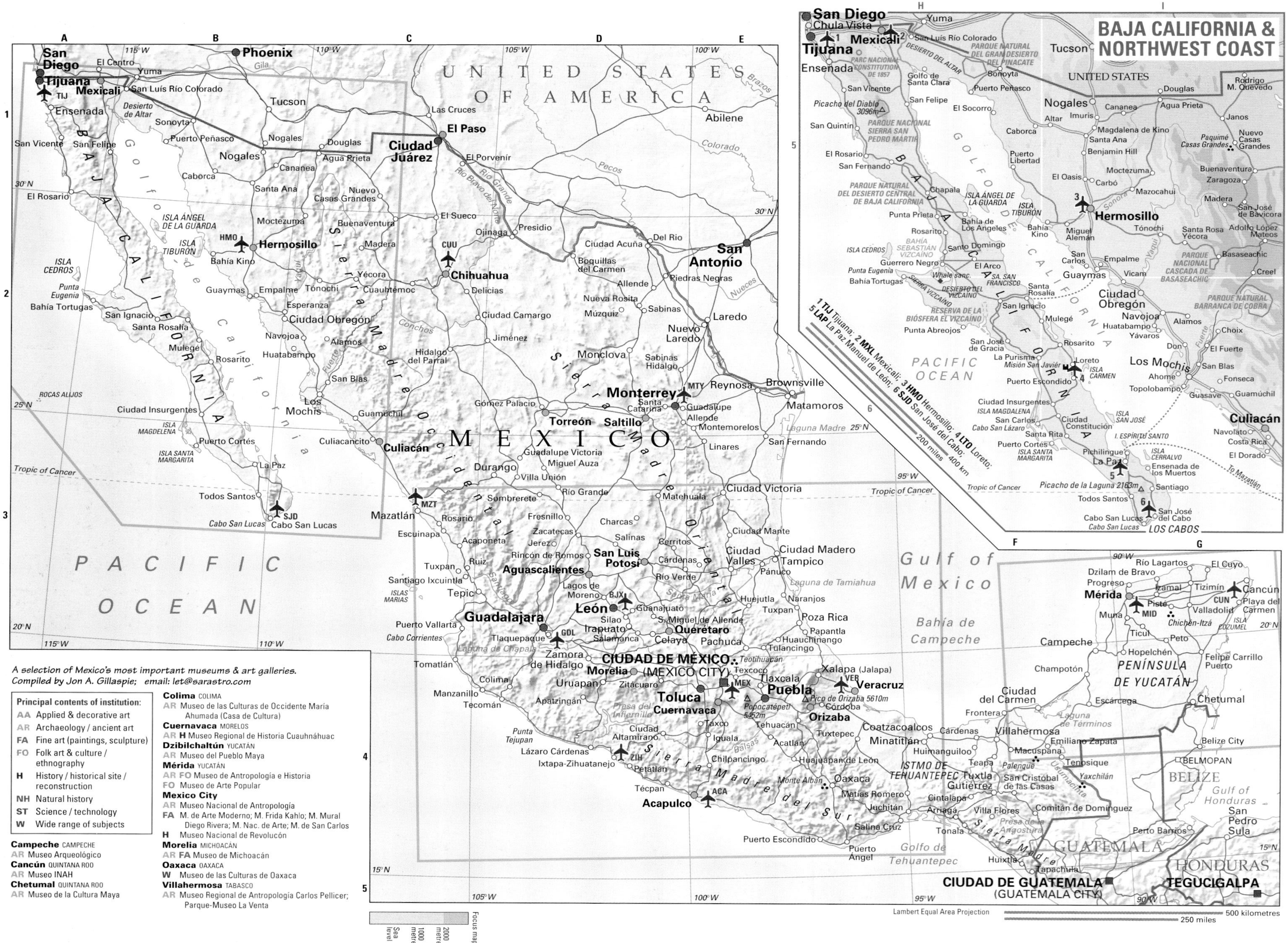

BAJA CALIFORNIA & NORTHWEST COAST

1 TIJ Tijuana; **2 MXL** Mexicali; **3 HMO** Hermosillo; **4 LTO** Loreto; **5 LAP** La Paz Manuel de León; **6 SJD** San José del Cabo;

A selection of Mexico's most important museums & art galleries.
Compiled by Jon A. Gillaspie; email: let@sarastro.com

Principal contents of institution:

- **AA** Applied & decorative art
- **AR** Archaeology / ancient art
- **FA** Fine art (paintings, sculpture)
- **FO** Folk art & culture / ethnography
- **H** History / historical site / reconstruction
- **NH** Natural history
- **ST** Science / technology
- **W** Wide range of subjects

Campeche CAMPECHE
AR Museo Arqueológico
Cancún QUINTANA ROO
AR Museo INAH
Chetumal QUINTANA ROO
AR Museo de la Cultura Maya
Colima COLIMA
AR Museo de las Culturas de Occidente María Ahumada (Casa de Cultura)
Cuernavaca MORELOS
AR H Museo Regional de Historia Cuauhnáhuac
Dzibilchaltún YUCATÁN
AR Museo del Pueblo Maya
Mérida YUCATÁN
AR FO Museo de Antropología e Historia
FO Museo de Arte Popular
Mexico City
AR Museo Nacional de Antropología
FA M. de Arte Moderno; M. Frida Kahlo; M. Mural Diego Rivera; M. Nac. de Arte; M. de San Carlos
H Museo Nacional de Revolucón
Morelia MICHOACÁN
AR FA Museo de Michoacán
Oaxaca OAXACA
W Museo de las Culturas de Oaxaca
Villahermosa TABASCO
AR Museo Regional de Antropología Carlos Pellicer; Parque-Museo La Venta

Focus map: 2000 metres, 1000 metres, Sea level

Lambert Equal Area Projection

500 kilometres / 250 miles

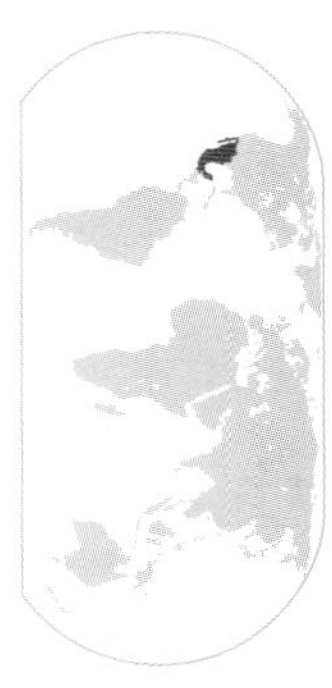

See also... Contents (2-7) – this country features in many thematic and regional maps throughout the *World Travel Atlas*.

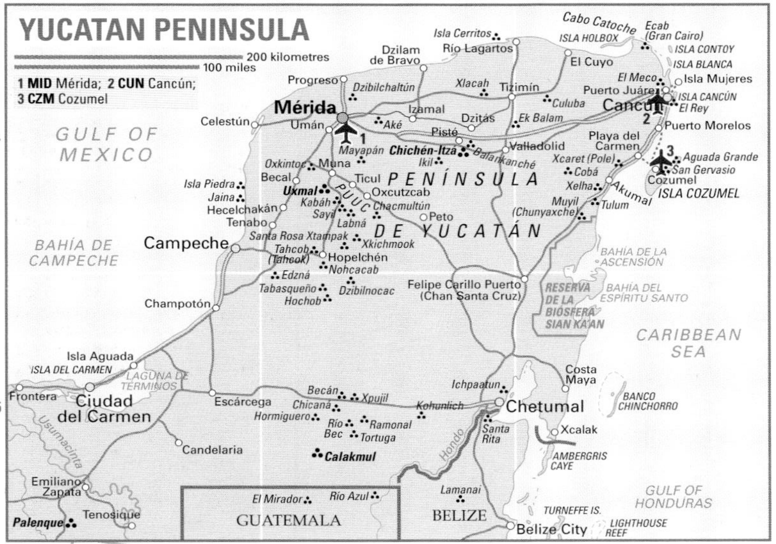

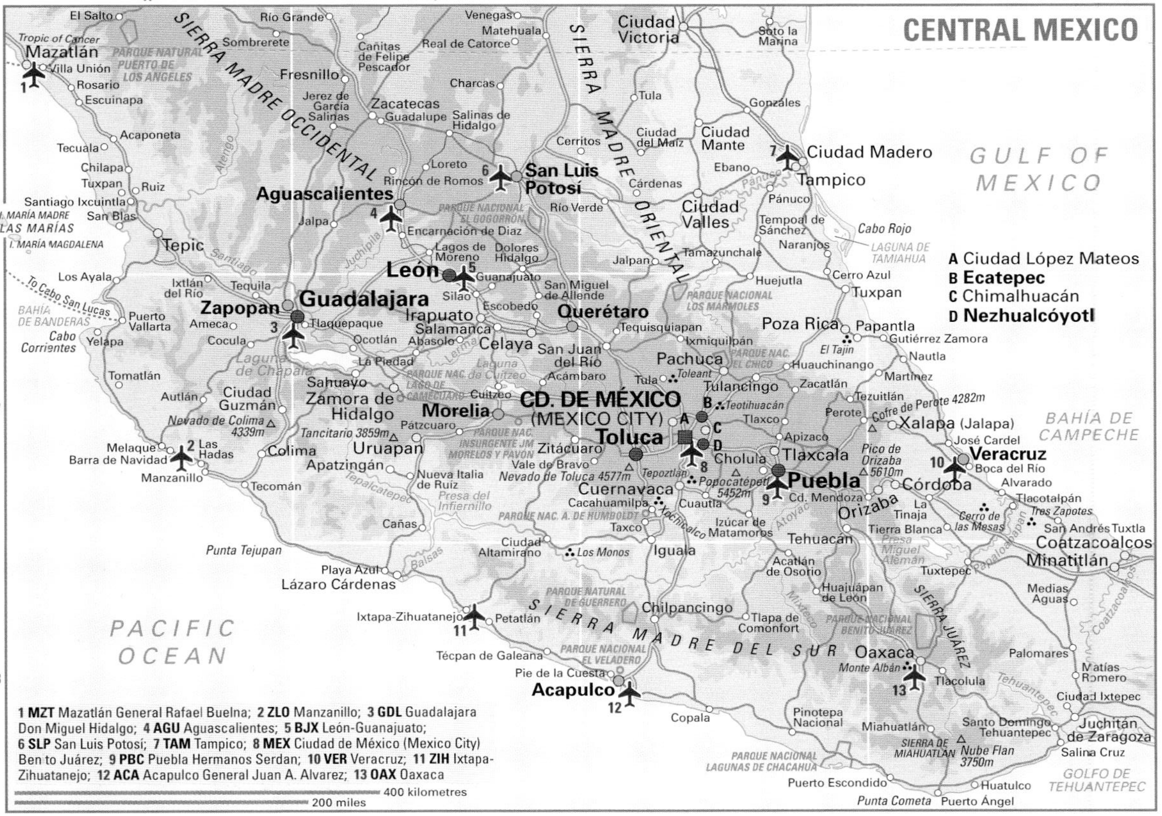

YUCATAN PENINSULA
200 kilometres
100 miles
1 MID Mérida; 2 CUN Cancún; 3 CZM Cozumel
GULF OF MEXICO
BAHÍA DE CAMPECHE
CARIBBEAN SEA
GULF OF HONDURAS
PENÍNSULA DE YUCATÁN
Mérida
Cancún
Campeche
Chetumal
Ciudad del Carmen
Chichén-Itzá
Cozumel
GUATEMALA
BELIZE
Belize City

CENTRAL MEXICO
A Ciudad López Mateos
B Ecatepec
C Chimalhuacán
D Nezhualcóyotl
GULF OF MEXICO
PACIFIC OCEAN
BAHÍA DE CAMPECHE
SIERRA MADRE OCCIDENTAL
SIERRA MADRE ORIENTAL
SIERRA MADRE DEL SUR
CD. DE MÉXICO (MEXICO CITY)
Guadalajara
Puebla
Veracruz
Acapulco
Oaxaca
1 MZT Mazatlán General Rafael Buelna; 2 ZLO Manzanillo; 3 GDL Guadalajara Don Miguel Hidalgo; 4 AGU Aguascalientes; 5 BJX León-Guanajuato; 6 SLP San Luis Potosí; 7 TAM Tampico; 8 MEX Ciudad de México (Mexico City) Ben to Juárez; 9 PBC Puebla Hermanos Serdan; 10 VER Veracruz; 11 ZIH Ixtapa-Zihuatanejo; 12 ACA Acapulco General Juan A. Alvarez; 13 OAX Oaxaca
400 kilometres
200 miles

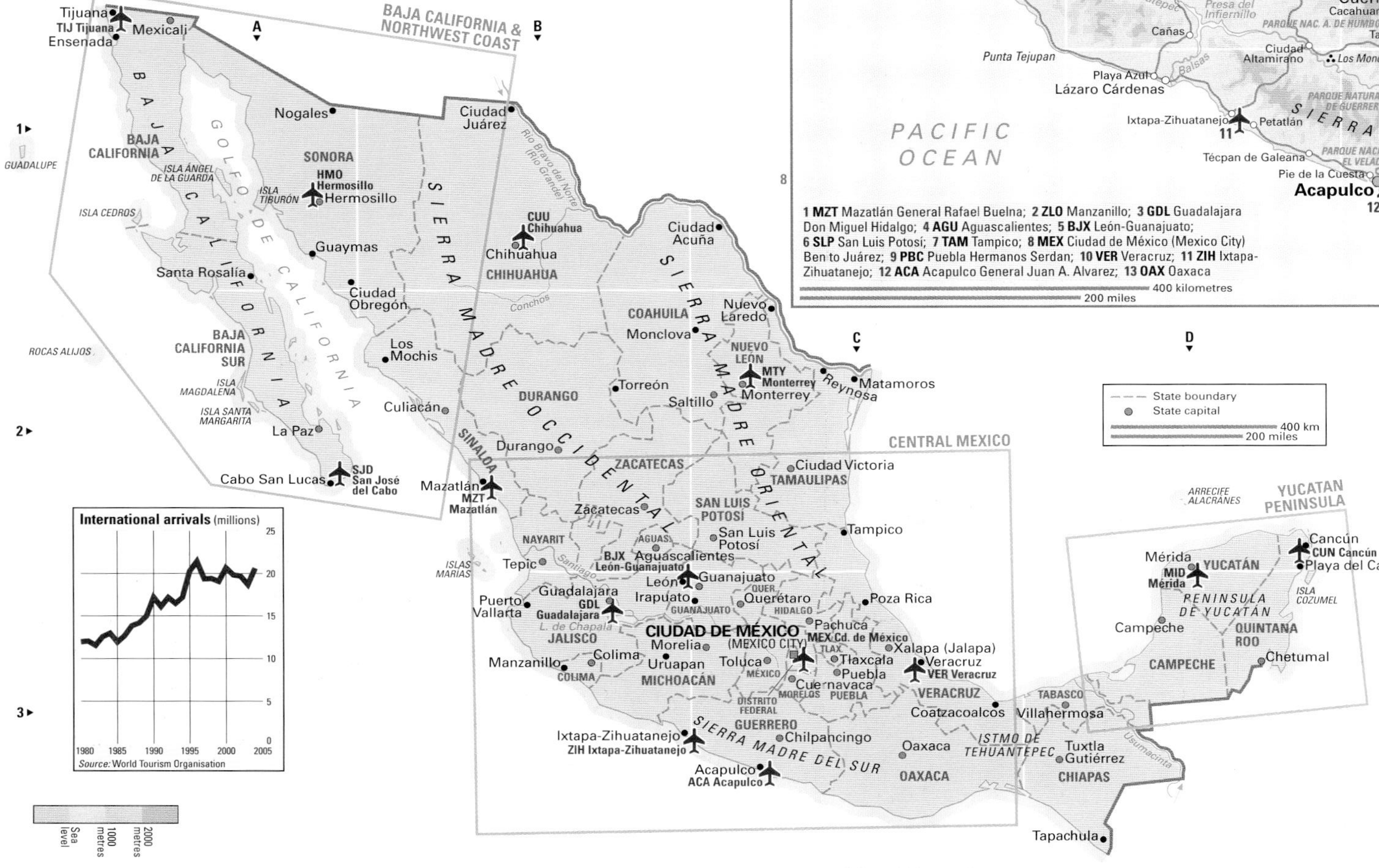

BAJA CALIFORNIA & NORTHWEST COAST
CENTRAL MEXICO
YUCATAN PENINSULA
GOLFO DE CALIFORNIA
SIERRA MADRE OCCIDENTAL
SIERRA MADRE ORIENTAL
SIERRA MADRE DEL SUR
CIUDAD DE MÉXICO
State boundary
State capital
400 km
200 miles
TIJ Tijuana
HMO Hermosillo
CUU Chihuahua
MTY Monterrey
SJD San José del Cabo
MZT Mazatlán
BJX León-Guanajuato
GDL Guadalajara
MEX Cd. de México
VER Veracruz
ZIH Ixtapa-Zihuatanejo
ACA Acapulco
MID Mérida
CUN Cancún
International arrivals (millions)
25
20
15
10
5
0
1980
1985
1990
1995
2000
2005
Source: World Tourism Organisation
Sea level
1000 metres
2000 metres

JAN Fiesta of San Sebastian the Martyr (**Chiapa de Corzo**)
JAN 17th San Antonio de Abad: Blessing of the Animals (**Mexico City**)
FEB 5th Constitution Day (countrywide)
FEB Blessing of the Sea (**San Blas**)
MAR 6th Day of Our Lord of Xalpa (**Taxco**)
before Lent Carnaval (countrywide)
MAR 20th Vernal Equinox (**Chichén-Itzá**)
MAR/APR Festival del Centro Histórico (**Mexico City**)
early APR Flower Fiar (**Cuernavaca**)
APR-MAY San Marcos National Fair (**Aguascalientes**)
MAY Fiesta of St Isador the Farmer (**Tepic**)
JUN 1st Mexican Navy Day (**Guaymas**)
late JUL Guelaguetza/Lunes del Cerro (**Oaxaca**)
JUL 25th Day of St James the Apostle (**Santiago Tuxtla**)
AUG 2nd Cuauhtémoc Day (**Mexico City**)
AUG Celebration for the Day of the Virgin of Charity and Assumption Day: processions & bull-running (**Huamantia**)
early SEP National Fair (**Zacatecas**)
SEP Independence Day Fair & Regional Exposition (**Dolores Hidalgo**)
NOV 1st & 2nd Dia de los Muertos: Day of the Dead (countrywide)
early DEC Fiesta de Inmaculada Concepcion (**Isla Mujeres**)
DEC 12th Day of the Virgin of Guadalupe (**Mexico City, San Cristobal las Casas** & countrywide)
DEC 23rd Noche de los Rabanos: Festival of the Radishes (**Oaxaca**)
DEC-JAN Feria del Bastón: Walking Cane Fair (**Tlaxcala**)

See also... North America Climate (155); The Caribbean (178-181); Mexico (182); Latin America Museums & Galleries (187)

Central America
MEXICO
GUATEMALA
BELIZE
HONDURAS
EL SALVADOR
NICARAGUA
COSTA RICA
PANAMA
COLOMBIA
Caribbean Sea
PACIFIC OCEAN
CIUDAD DE GUATEMALA (GUATEMALA CITY)
TEGUCIGALPA
SAN SALVADOR
MANAGUA
SAN JOSÉ
CIUDAD DE PANAMÁ (PANAMA CITY)
BELMOPAN
Lambert Equal Area Projection
300 kilometres
150 miles
PANAMA CANAL
20 kilometres
10 miles
1 ONX Colón;
2 PTY Panama City Tocumen;
3 PAC Panama City Paitilla
CARIBBEAN SEA
COLÓN
PANAMÁ
CIUDAD DE PANAMÁ (PANAMA CITY)
Lago Gatún
PARQUE NACIONAL CHAGRES
GOLFO DE PANAMÁ

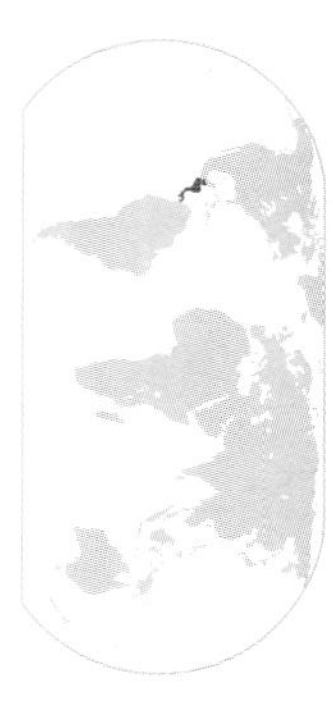

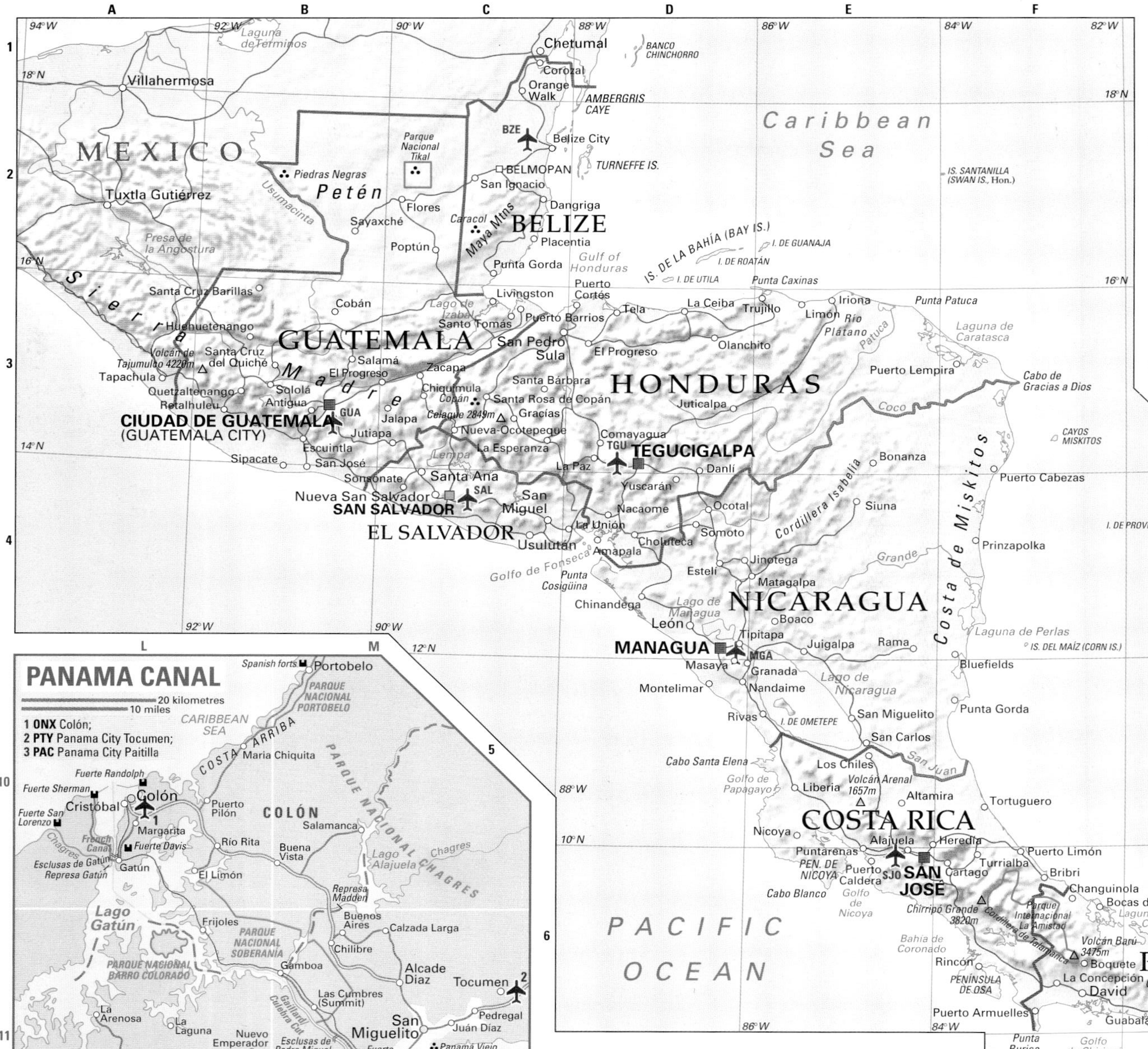

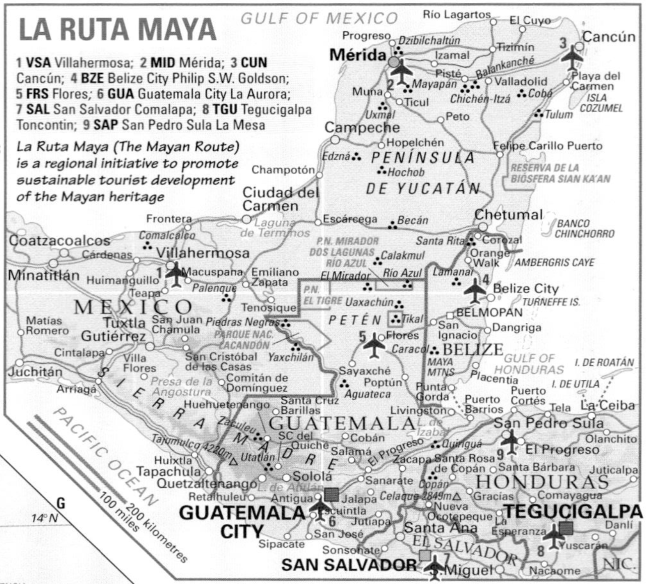

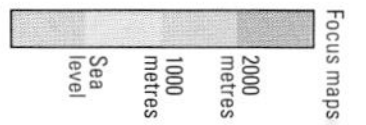

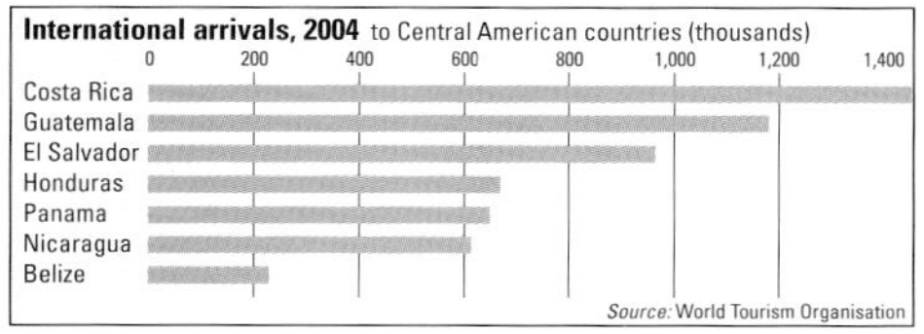

LA RUTA MAYA
1 VSA Villahermosa; 2 MID Mérida; 3 CUN Cancún; 4 BZE Belize City Philip S.W. Goldson; 5 FRS Flores; 6 GUA Guatemala City La Aurora; 7 SAL San Salvador Comalapa; 8 TGU Tegucigalpa Toncontín; 9 SAP San Pedro Sula La Mesa
La Ruta Maya (The Mayan Route) is a regional initiative to promote sustainable tourist development of the Mayan heritage
GULF OF MEXICO
PACIFIC OCEAN
200 kilometres
100 miles

Focus maps
2000 metres
1000 metres
Sea level

International arrivals, 2004 to Central American countries (thousands)
0
200
400
600
800
1,000
1,200
1,400
Costa Rica
Guatemala
El Salvador
Honduras
Panama
Nicaragua
Belize
Source: World Tourism Organisation

A selection of Central America's most important museums & art galleries. See Mexico page for key to abbreviations.

Antigua GUATEMALA
FA Museo de Arte Colonial

Belize City BELIZE
AR H Museum of Belize

Guatemala City GUATEMALA
AR Museo Popul Vuh de Arquelogia
AR FO Museo National de Antropologia y Etonologia

Managua NICARUGA
AR NH Museo Nacional de Nicaragua

Panama City PANAMA
AR Museo Antropológico Reina Torres de Araúz
FA Museo de Arte Religioso Colonial
H Museo del Canal Interoceánico

San José COSTA RICA
AR Museo del Oro Precolombino
FA Museo de Arte Costarricense; Museo del Jade Fidel Tristán
NH Museo de Ciencias Naturales
ST Museo de Formas, Espacios y Sonidos
W Museo Nacional

San Salvador EL SALVADOR
AR Museo Antropológico David J. Guzmán

Tegucigalpa HONDURAS
FA Galeria Nacional de Arte

See also... World Physical (12-13); World Political (14-15), World Climate (16)

The listings above refer to a selection of related themes. For more information, see the Contents (2-7).

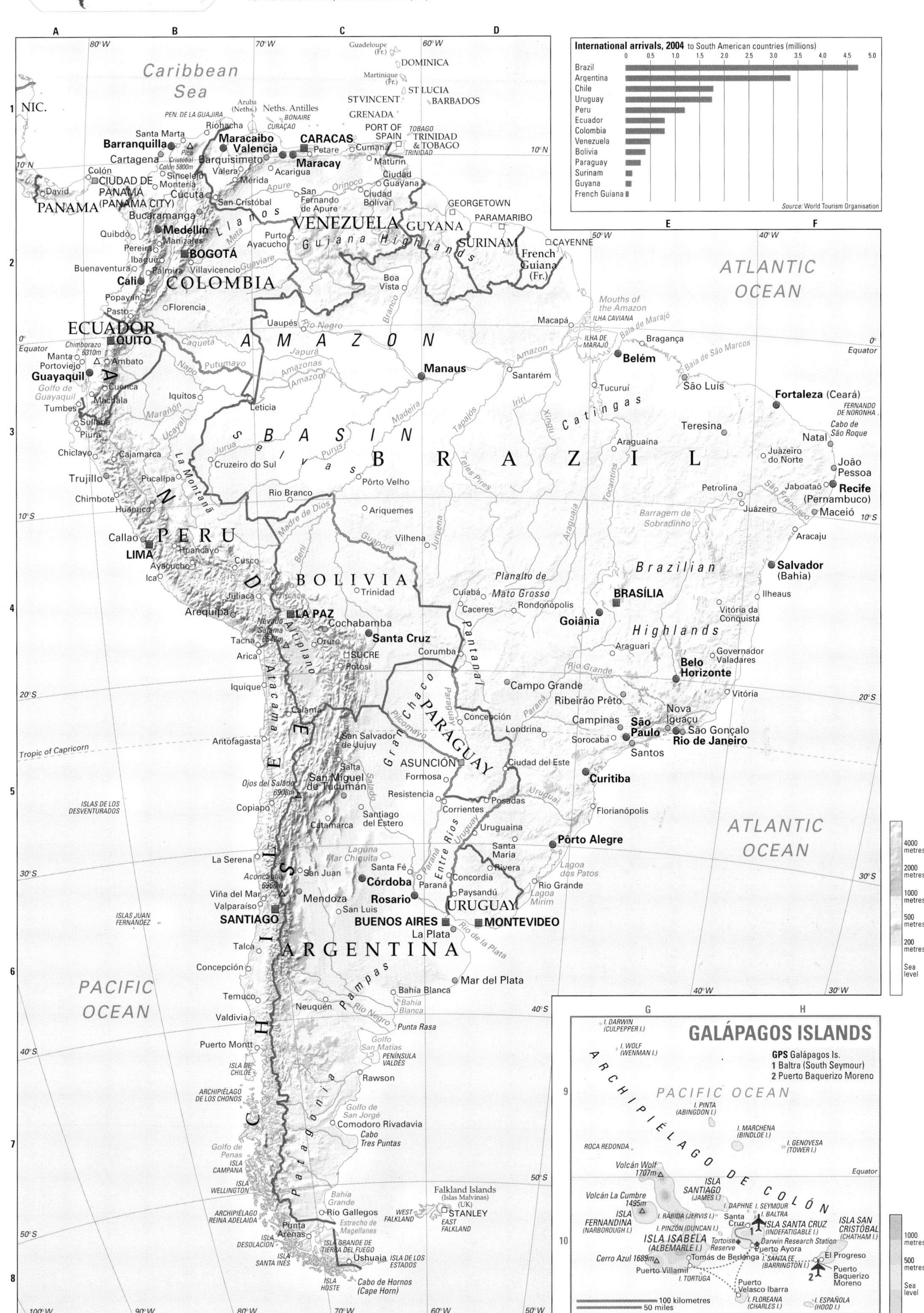
International arrivals, 2004 to South American countries (millions)
0 0.5 1.0 1.5 2.0 2.5 3.0 3.5 4.0 4.5 5.0
Brazil
Argentina
Chile
Uruguay
Peru
Ecuador
Colombia
Venezuela
Bolivia
Paraguay
Surinam
Guyana
French Guiana
Source: World Tourism Organisation
Caribbean Sea
ATLANTIC OCEAN
PACIFIC OCEAN
NIC.
PANAMA
COLOMBIA
VENEZUELA
GUYANA
SURINAM
French Guiana (Fr.)
ECUADOR
PERU
BOLIVIA
BRAZIL
PARAGUAY
URUGUAY
ARGENTINA
CHILE
AMAZON BASIN
Brazilian Highlands
Guiana Highlands
Llanos
Catingas
Selvas
Mato Grosso
Planalto de
Gran Chaco
Pampas
Patagonia
Atacama
Altiplano
ANDES
La Montaña
Pantanal
Barranquilla
Maracaibo
CARACAS
Valencia
Maracay
Barquisimeto
Cartagena
Santa Marta
Medellín
BOGOTÁ
Cali
QUITO
Guayaquil
LIMA
LA PAZ
Santa Cruz
SUCRE
Manaus
Belém
Fortaleza (Ceará)
Recife (Pernambuco)
Salvador (Bahia)
BRASÍLIA
Goiânia
Belo Horizonte
São Paulo
Rio de Janeiro
Curitiba
Pôrto Alegre
ASUNCIÓN
MONTEVIDEO
BUENOS AIRES
Córdoba
Rosario
SANTIAGO
Falkland Islands (Islas Malvinas) (UK)
STANLEY
Cabo de Hornos (Cape Horn)
Tropic of Capricorn
Equator
4000 metres
2000 metres
1000 metres
500 metres
200 metres
Sea level
Lambert Equal Area Projection
1000 kilometres
500 miles
GALÁPAGOS ISLANDS
GPS Galápagos Is.
1 Baltra (South Seymour)
2 Puerto Baquerizo Moreno
ARCHIPIÉLAGO DE COLÓN
PACIFIC OCEAN
ISLA ISABELA (ALBEMARLE I.)
ISLA SANTA CRUZ (INDEFATIGABLE I.)
ISLA SAN CRISTÓBAL (CHATHAM I.)
ISLA FERNANDINA (NARBOROUGH I.)
ISLA SANTIAGO (JAMES I.)
100 kilometres
50 miles

See also... World Climate (16); Regional Climate Terms (196)

The listings above refer to a selection of related themes. For more information, see the Contents (2-7).

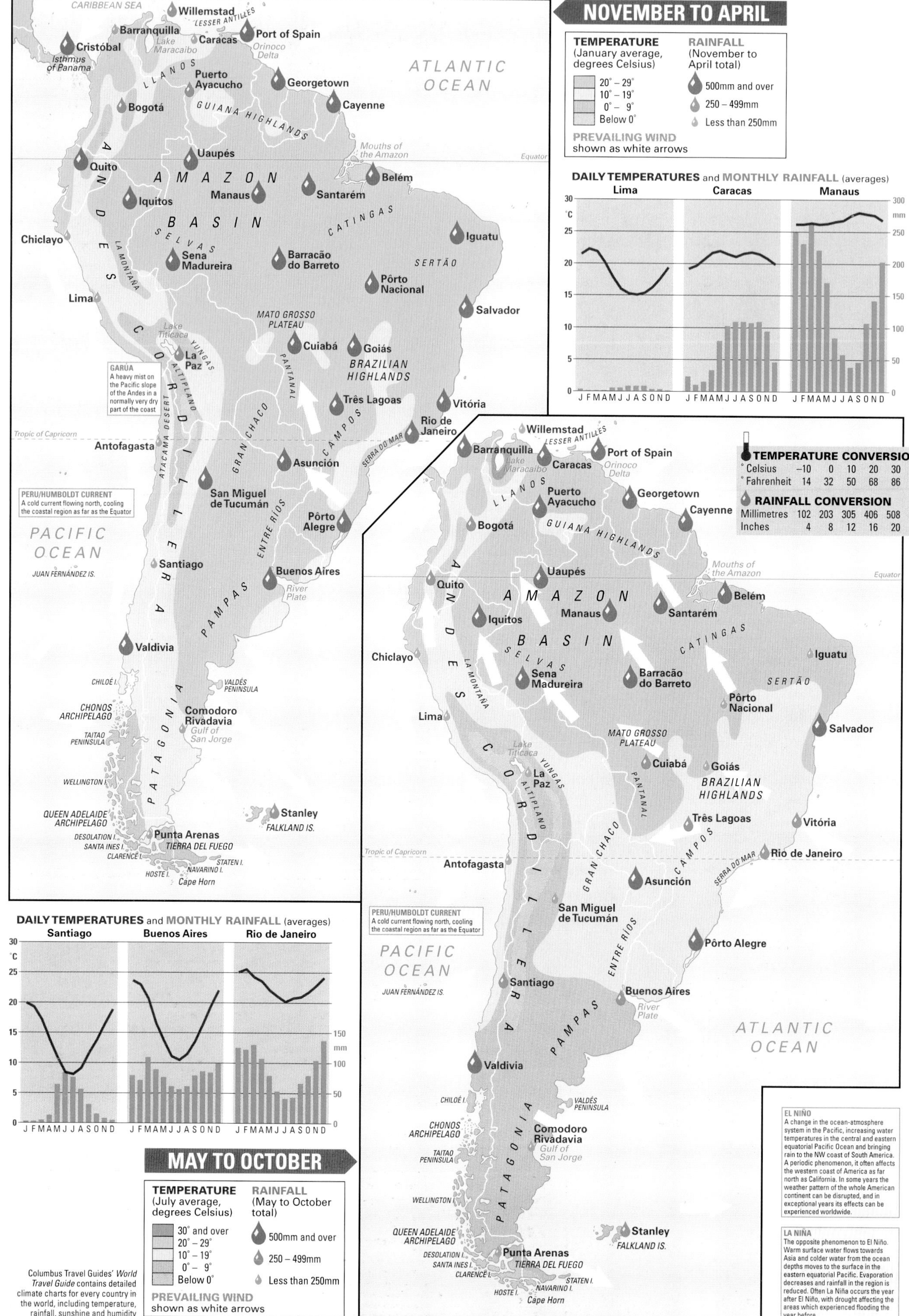
NOVEMBER TO APRIL
TEMPERATURE (January average, degrees Celsius)
20° – 29°
10° – 19°
0° – 9°
Below 0°
RAINFALL (November to April total)
500mm and over
250 – 499mm
Less than 250mm
PREVAILING WIND shown as white arrows
DAILY TEMPERATURES and MONTHLY RAINFALL (averages)
Lima
Caracas
Manaus
°C
mm
J F M A M J J A S O N D
TEMPERATURE CONVERSION
°Celsius –10 0 10 20 30 40
°Fahrenheit 14 32 50 68 86 104
RAINFALL CONVERSION
Millimetres 102 203 305 406 508 610
Inches 4 8 12 16 20 24
MAY TO OCTOBER
TEMPERATURE (July average, degrees Celsius)
30° and over
20° – 29°
10° – 19°
0° – 9°
Below 0°
RAINFALL (May to October total)
500mm and over
250 – 499mm
Less than 250mm
PREVAILING WIND shown as white arrows
DAILY TEMPERATURES and MONTHLY RAINFALL (averages)
Santiago
Buenos Aires
Rio de Janeiro
Columbus Travel Guides' *World Travel Guide* contains detailed climate charts for every country in the world, including temperature, rainfall, sunshine and humidity
GARUA
A heavy mist on the Pacific slope of the Andes in a normally very dry part of the coast
PERU/HUMBOLDT CURRENT
A cold current flowing north, cooling the coastal region as far as the Equator
EL NIÑO
A change in the ocean-atmosphere system in the Pacific, increasing water temperatures in the central and eastern equatorial Pacific Ocean and bringing rain to the NW coast of South America. A periodic phenomenon, it often affects the western coast of America as far north as California. In some years the weather pattern of the whole American continent can be disrupted, and in exceptional years its effects can be experienced worldwide.
LA NIÑA
The opposite phenomenon to El Niño. Warm surface water flows towards Asia and colder water from the ocean depths moves to the surface in the eastern equatorial Pacific. Evaporation decreases and rainfall in the region is reduced. Often La Niña occurs the year after El Niño, with drought affecting the areas which experienced flooding the year before.
CARIBBEAN SEA
Willemstad
LESSER ANTILLES
Barranquilla
Caracas
Port of Spain
Cristóbal
Isthmus of Panama
Lake Maracaibo
Orinoco Delta
LLANOS
Puerto Ayacucho
Georgetown
Cayenne
Bogotá
GUIANA HIGHLANDS
ATLANTIC OCEAN
Mouths of the Amazon
Equator
Quito
Uaupés
AMAZON BASIN
Manaus
Santarém
Belém
Iquitos
SELVAS
CATINGAS
Iguatu
Chiclayo
ANDES
LA MONTAÑA
Sena Madureira
Barracão do Barreto
SERTÃO
Pôrto Nacional
Lima
Salvador
MATO GROSSO PLATEAU
Lake Titicaca
YUNGAS
Cuiabá
Goiás
La Paz
ALTIPLANO
PANTANAL
BRAZILIAN HIGHLANDS
Três Lagoas
Vitória
CORDILLERA
ATACAMA DESERT
GRAN CHACO
CAMPOS
Rio de Janeiro
Tropic of Capricorn
Antofagasta
SERRA DO MAR
Asunción
San Miguel de Tucumán
ENTRE RÍOS
Pôrto Alegre
PACIFIC OCEAN
Santiago
JUAN FERNÁNDEZ IS.
Buenos Aires
River Plate
PAMPAS
Valdivia
CHILOÉ I.
VALDÉS PENINSULA
CHONOS ARCHIPELAGO
Comodoro Rivadavia
Gulf of San Jorge
TAITAO PENINSULA
PATAGONIA
WELLINGTON I.
QUEEN ADELAIDE ARCHIPELAGO
Stanley
FALKLAND IS.
DESOLATION I.
Punta Arenas
SANTA INES I.
TIERRA DEL FUEGO
CLARENCE I.
STATEN I.
HOSTE I.
NAVARINO I.
Cape Horn

See also... UNESCO Heritage (48-53); Europe Historical (58-59); Asia Historical (128); N. America Historical (156-157); Mexico (182); C. America (184)

The listings above refer to a selection of related themes. For more information, see the Contents (2-7).

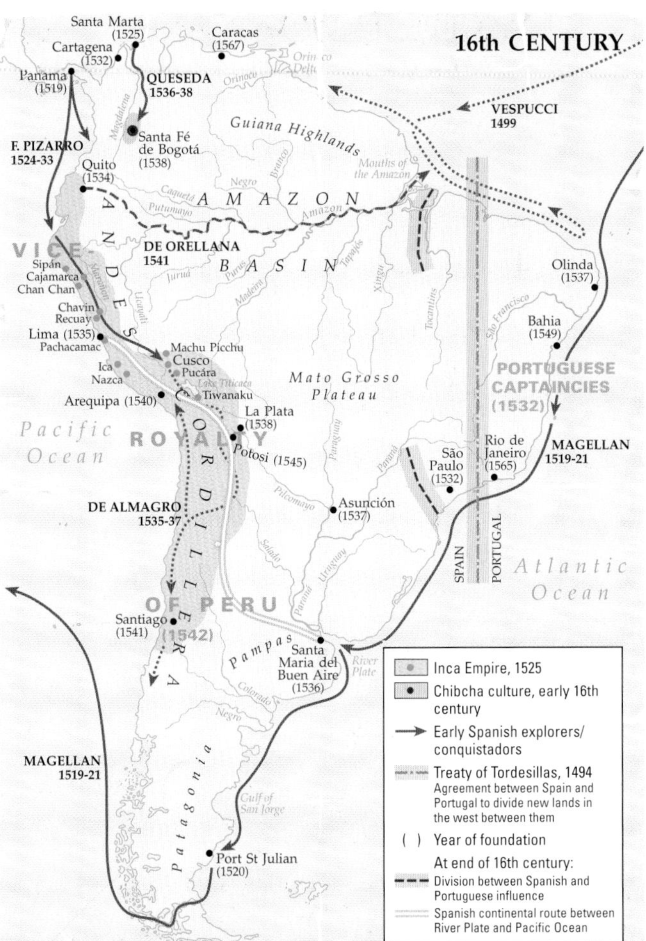
16th CENTURY
Santa Marta (1525)
Cartagena (1532)
Caracas (1567)
Panama (1519)
QUESEDA 1536-38
VESPUCCI 1499
Santa Fé de Bogotá (1538)
Guiana Highlands
F. PIZARRO 1524-33
Quito (1534)
Mouths of the Amazon
AMAZON
DE ORELLANA 1541
BASIN
VICE-ROYALTY OF PERU (1542)
Sipán
Cajamarca
Chan Chan
Chavin
Recuay
Lima (1535)
Pachacamac
Machu Picchu
Cusco
Pucára
Lake Titicaca
Tiwanaku
Ica
Nazca
Arequipa (1540)
Olinda (1537)
Bahia (1549)
PORTUGUESE CAPTAINCIES (1532)
Mato Grosso Plateau
La Plata (1538)
Potosí (1545)
Pacific Ocean
ANDES CORDILLERA
Rio de Janeiro (1565)
São Paulo (1532)
MAGELLAN 1519-21
DE ALMAGRO 1535-37
Asunción (1537)
SPAIN
PORTUGAL
Atlantic Ocean
Santiago (1541)
Pampas
Santa Maria del Buen Aire (1536)
River Plate
Patagonia
Gulf of San Jorge
MAGELLAN 1519-21
Port St Julian (1520)
Inca Empire, 1525
Chibcha culture, early 16th century
Early Spanish explorers/ conquistadors
Treaty of Tordesillas, 1494
Agreement between Spain and Portugal to divide new lands in the west between them
( ) Year of foundation
At end of 16th century:
Division between Spanish and Portuguese influence
Spanish continental route between River Plate and Pacific Ocean

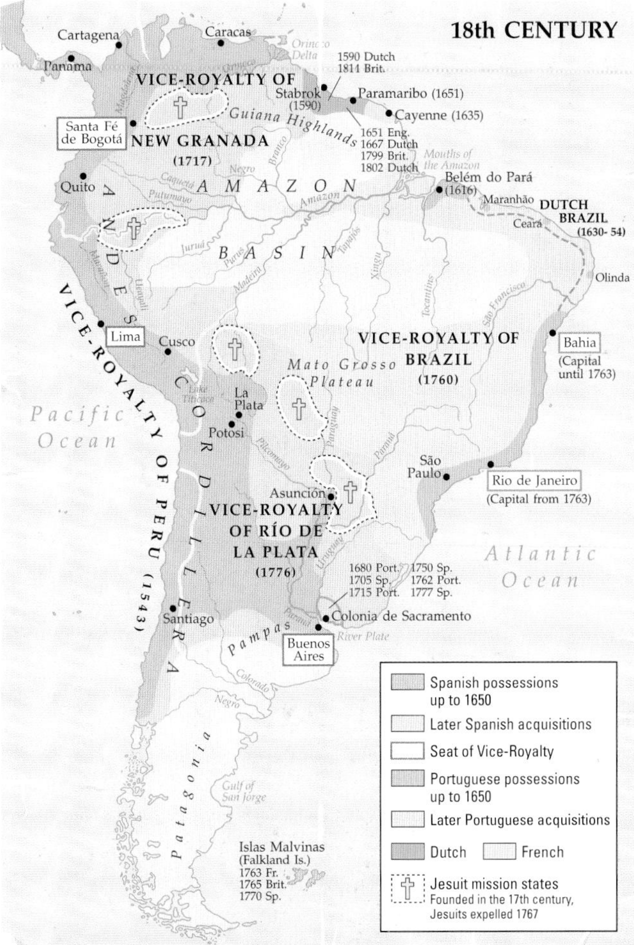
18th CENTURY
Cartagena
Caracas
Panama
1590 Dutch
1814 Brit.
VICE-ROYALTY OF NEW GRANADA (1717)
Stabrok (1590)
Paramaribo (1651)
Santa Fé de Bogotá
Guiana Highlands
Cayenne (1635)
1651 Eng.
1667 Dutch
1799 Brit.
1802 Dutch
Mouths of the Amazon
Quito
AMAZON
Belém do Pará (1616)
Maranhão
Ceará
DUTCH BRAZIL (1630-54)
BASIN
Olinda
VICE-ROYALTY OF PERU (1543)
Lima
Cusco
VICE-ROYALTY OF BRAZIL (1760)
Bahia (Capital until 1763)
Mato Grosso Plateau
La Plata
Potosí
Pacific Ocean
ANDES CORDILLERA
São Paulo
Rio de Janeiro (Capital from 1763)
Asunción
VICE-ROYALTY OF RÍO DE LA PLATA (1776)
Atlantic Ocean
1680 Port.
1705 Sp.
1715 Port.
1750 Sp.
1762 Port.
1777 Sp.
Colonia de Sacramento
Santiago
Pampas
Buenos Aires
River Plate
Patagonia
Gulf of San Jorge
Islas Malvinas (Falkland Is.)
1763 Fr.
1765 Brit.
1770 Sp.
Spanish possessions up to 1650
Later Spanish acquisitions
Seat of Vice-Royalty
Portuguese possessions up to 1650
Later Portuguese acquisitions
Dutch
French
Jesuit mission states
Founded in the 17th century, Jesuits expelled 1767

PANAMA 13
Caracas
TRINIDAD & TOBAGO
Orinoco Delta
VENEZUELA 5
GUYANA 4
SURINAM 3
French Guiana (Fr.) 2
Medellín
Bogotá
COLOMBIA 6
Mouths of the Amazon
Equator
Quito
ECUADOR 7
Lambayeque
Lima
PERU 8
Cusco
BRAZIL 1
Salvador
Arequipa
La Paz
BOLIVIA 9
Oruro
Potosí
PACIFIC OCEAN
San Pedro de Atacama
PARAGUAY 10
Asunción
Rio de Janeiro
São Paulo
Tropic of Capricorn
CHILE 13
ATLANTIC OCEAN
JUAN FERNÁNDEZ IS.
Santiago
URUGUAY 11
Montevideo
Santa Cruz
Buenos Aires
La Plata
ARGENTINA 12
River Plate
CHONOS ARCHIPELAGO
VALDÉS PENINSULA
TAITAO PENINSULA
Gulf of San Jorge
QUEEN ADELAIDE ARCHIPELAGO
Falkland Is. (UK)
TIERRA DEL FUEGO
Cape Horn

OFFICIAL LANGUAGES

(Numbers refer to the notes on right)

- Spanish
- Portuguese
- English
- French
- Dutch

South America's most important museums and art galleries are listed here. Selection is based on importance and depth of the collection and its cultural diversity within a geographic spread. Compiled by Jon A. Gillaspie. email: let@sarastro.com

Principal contents of institution:

AA	Applied & decorative art
AR	Archaeology / ancient art
FA	Fine art (paintings, sculpture)
FO	Folk art & culture / ethnography
H	History / historical site / reconstruction
NH	Natural history
ST	Science / technology
W	Wide range of subjects

Arequipa PERU
AR Museo Santuarios Andinos

Asunción PARAGUAY
FA FO Museo de Arte Indigeno; Museo del Barro

Bogotá COLOMBIA
AR Museo Arqueológico; Museo del Oro
AR FA Museo Nacional
FA Donación Botero; Museo de Arte Colonial; Museo de Arte Moderno
FO Museo de Trajes Regionales

Buenos Aires ARGENTINA
FA Museo de Arte Hispanoamericano Isaac Fernández Blanco; Museo de Arte Latinamericano de Buenos Aires (MALBA); Museo de Bellas Artes Benito Quinquela; Museo Nacional de Bellas Artes
H Casa de Carlos Gardel; Museo de la Pasión Boquense; Museo Evita; World Tango Museum

Caracas VENEZUELA
FA Galería de Arte Nacional; Mus. de Arte Colonial; Mus. de Arte Contemporáneo; Mus. Sacro de Caracas

Cusco PERU
AR Museo de Arte Precolombino; Museo Inka
FA Museo de Arte Religioso

La Paz BOLIVIA
AR Museo Nacional de Arquelogia; Museo Tiahuanaco
FA Museo Nacional de Arte; Museo Tambo Quirquincho
FO Museo Nacional de Etnografía y Folklore
ST Museo Kusillo

La Plata ARGENTINA
AR NH Museo de La Plata

Lambayeque PERU
AR Museo Arqueológico Nacional Brüning; Museo de las Tumbes Reales de Sipán

Lima PERU
AR Museo de Oro del Perú; Museo Arqueológico Rafael Larco Herrera
FO Museo de Arte
W Museo de la Nación

Medellín COLOMBIA
FA Museo de Antioquia

Montevideo URUGUAY
AA Museo Romántico
H Museo del Gaucho y de la Moneda
W Casa Rivera

Oruro BOLIVIA
AR FO Museo Sacro, Folklórico y Arqueológico

Potosí BOLIVIA
AR FA Casa Nacional de Moneda

Quito ECUADOR
AR FA Museo Nacional del Banco Central del Ecuador
FA Museo Nacional de Arte Colonial
H Museo de la Ciudad
W Casa de la Culture

Rio de Janeiro BRAZIL
FA Museu Nacional de Belas Artes
FO Museu do Folclore Edison Carneiro; Museu Internacional de Arte Naif do Brasil
W Museu Nacional

Salvador BRAZIL
FA Museu de Arte Sacra; Museu de Arte de Bahia
W Museu Afro-Brasileiro

Santiago CHILE
AR Museo Chileno de Arte Precolombino
FA Palacio de Bellas Artes
H Museo de Santiago

San Pedro de Atacama CHILE
AR Museo Archeológico Padre Paige

Santa Cruz CHILE
H Museo de Colchagua

São Paulo BRAZIL
FA Museu de Arte de São Paulo (MASP); Museu de Arte Moderna (MAM); Museu de Arte Sacra

1 Spanish, English, Italian, French and German are widely spoken, especially in tourist areas.
2 Most of the population speak a Creole *patois.*
3 *Sranan Tongo*, originating in Creole, is the popular language. The other main languages are Hindi and Javanese. English, Chinese, French and Spanish are also spoken.
4 Creole, Hindi, Urdu and Amerindian are also spoken.
5 English, French, German and Portuguese are spoken by some sections of the community.
6 Local Indian dialects and some English, French, German and Italian are spoken.
7 Quechua, the Inca tongue, and other indigenous languages are common. Some English is spoken.
8 Quechua is the most important native language and is spoken in the majority of the Andean cities. Aymará is spoken in some areas of Puno Department. Many other dialects exist in the jungle regions. English is spoken in major tourist areas.
9 The Indians of the Altiplano speak Aymará and elsewhere Quechua is spoken. English is also spoken by a small number of officials and businessmen in commercial centres.
10 Guaraní is widely spoken. Most Paraguayans are bilingual, but prefer to speak Guaraní outside Asunción.
11 Some English is spoken in tourist resorts.
12 English, German, French and Italian are sometimes spoken.
13 English is widely spoken.

See also... Contents (2-7) – these countries feature in many thematic and regional maps throughout the *World Travel Atlas*.

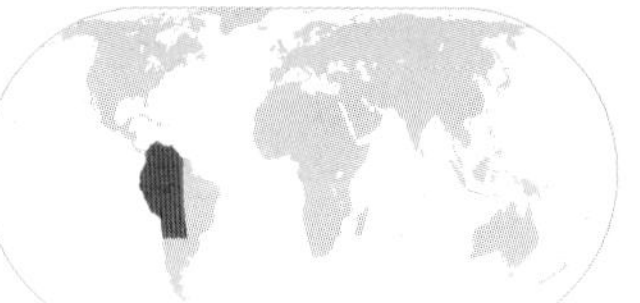

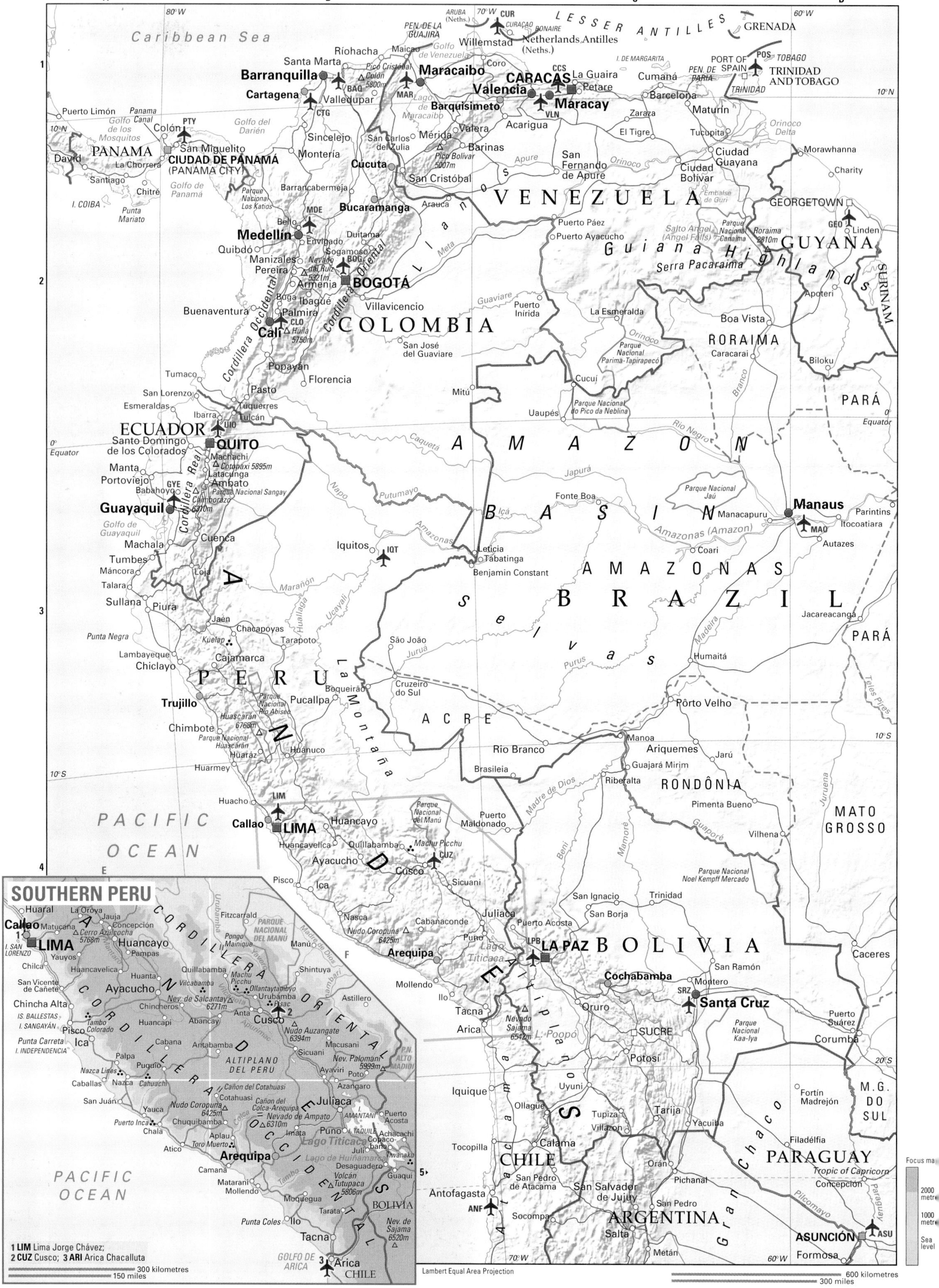

A B C D

1 2 3 4 5 6 7

80° W 70° W 60° W 10° N 0° Equator 10° S 20° S

Caribbean Sea
LESSER ANTILLES
ARUBA (Neths.)
CUR CURAÇAO BONAIRE
Netherlands Antilles (Neths.)
Willemstad
GRENADA
I. DE MARGARITA
PORT OF SPAIN
POS TOBAGO
TRINIDAD AND TOBAGO
PEN. DE PARIA
TRINIDAD
PEN. DE LA GUAJIRA
Golfo de Venezuela
Ríohacha
Maicao
Santa Marta
Barranquilla
BAQ
Pico Cristóbal Colón 5800m
Cartagena
CTG
Valledupar
Maracaibo
MAR
Lago de Maracaibo
Coro
CCS
CARACAS
La Guaira
Valencia
Petare
Maracay
VLN
Barquisimeto
Cumaná
Barcelona
Maturín
Zaraza
Orinoco Delta
Tucupita
El Tigre
Ciudad Guayana
Ciudad Bolívar
Morawhanna
Charity
Puerto Limón
Panama Canal
Golfo de los Mosquitos
PTY
Colón
Golfo del Darién
San Miguelito
PANAMA
David
La Chorrera
CIUDAD DE PANAMÁ (PANAMA CITY)
Santiago
Chitré
Golfo de Panamá
I. COIBA
Punta Mariato
Sincelejo
Montería
San Carlos del Zulia
Mérida
Valera
Acarigua
Pico Bolívar 5007m
Barinas
Apure
San Fernando de Apure
Cúcuta
San Cristóbal
Barrancabermeja
Parque Nacional Los Katíos
MDE
Bucaramanga
Arauca
VENEZUELA
Embalse de Guri
GEORGETOWN
GEO
Linden
Salto Angel (Angel Falls)
Parque Nacional Canaima
Roraima 2810m
GUYANA
Puerto Páez
Puerto Ayacucho
Guiana Highlands
Serra Pacaraima
SURINAM
Apoteri
Bello
Medellín
Envigado
Duitama
Quibdó
Sogamoso
Manizales
BOG
Pereira
Nevado del Ruiz 5321m
Armenia
BOGOTÁ
Llanos
Meta
Buga
Ibagué
Villavicencio
Cordillera Oriental
Guaviare
Puerto Inírida
La Esmeralda
Boa Vista
Buenaventura
Palmira
CLO
Cali
Huila 5750m
Cordillera Occidental
COLOMBIA
San José del Guaviare
Orinoco
Parque Nacional Parima-Tapirapecó
RORAIMA
Caracaraí
Biloku
Popayán
Tumaco
Florencia
Pasto
San Lorenzo
Mitú
Cucuí
Branco
PARÁ
Esmeraldas
Ipiales
Túquerres
Parque Nacional do Pico da Neblina
Uaupés
Ibarra
Tulcán
UIO
ECUADOR
QUITO
Santo Domingo de los Colorados
Machachi
Cotopaxi 5895m
Manta
Latacunga
Portoviejo
Ambato
GYE
Babahoyo
Parque Nacional Sangay
Chimborazo 6310m
Cordillera Real
Guayaquil
Golfo de Guayaquil
Machala
Cuenca
Tumbes
Máncora
Loja
Talara
Sullana
Piura
Caquetá
AMAZON BASIN
Rio Negro
Japurá
Napo
Putumayo
Parque Nacional Jaú
Fonte Boa
Içá
Manaus
Manacapuru
MAO
Parintins
Itacoatiara
Autazes
Amazonas (Amazon)
Coari
Iquitos
IQT
Amazonas
Leticia
Tabatinga
Benjamin Constant
AMAZONAS
Marañón
BRAZIL
Selvas
Jacareacanga
Huallaga
Ucayali
Jaén
Chacapoyas
Kuelap
Tarapoto
São João
Juruá
Madeira
Humaitá
Punta Negra
Lambayeque
Chiclayo
Cajamarca
PERU
Purus
Boqueirão
Cruzeiro do Sul
Pucallpa
Parque Nacional Río Abiseo
Trujillo
La Montaña
ACRE
Pôrto Velho
Teles Pires
Chimbote
Huascarán 6768m
Parque Nacional Huascarán
Huaráz
Huánuco
Rio Branco
Manoa
Ariquemes
Jarú
Huarmey
Brasileia
Guajará Mirim
Riberalta
Madre de Dios
RONDÔNIA
Juruena
Huacho
LIM
Parque Nacional del Manú
Puerto Maldonado
Pimenta Bueno
PACIFIC OCEAN
Callao
LIMA
Huancayo
Huancavelica
Quillabamba
Machu Picchu
MATO GROSSO
Guaporé
Mamoré
Vilhena
Ayacucho
CUZ
Cusco
Beni
ANDES
Pisco
Sicuani
Parque Nacional Noel Kempff Mercado
Ica
San Ignacio
Trinidad
Nasca
San Borja
Juliaca
Nudo Coropuna 6425m
Cabanaconde
Puerto Acosta
Puno
LPB
LA PAZ
BOLIVIA
Lago Titicaca
Arequipa
Altiplano
Caceres
San Ramón
Mollendo
Cochabamba
Montero
Ilo
SRZ
Santa Cruz
Tacna
Oruro
Nevado Sajama 6542m
Arica
L. Poopó
SUCRE
Puerto Suárez
Parque Nacional Kaa-Iya
Corumbá
Potosí
Iquique
Uyuni
Fortín Madrejón
M.G. DO SUL
Ollagüe
Tupiza
Tarija
Villazón
Yacuiba
Gran Chaco
Filadélfia
Atacama
Tocopilla
Calama
CHILE
PARAGUAY
Orán
Tropic of Capricorn
San Pedro de Atacama
Pichanal
Concepción
Antofagasta
San Salvador de Jujuy
San Pedro
Pilcomayo
Paraguay
ANF
Socompa
ARGENTINA
Salta
ASUNCIÓN
ASU
Metán
Formosa

Lambert Equal Area Projection

600 kilometres
300 miles

Focus map
2000 metres
1000 metres
Sea level

E F

SOUTHERN PERU

Huaral
La Oroya
Jauja
Callao
Matucana
Concepción
Cerro Azulcocha 5768m
I. SAN LORENZO
LIMA
Huancayo
Yauyos
Pampas
Chilca
Huancavelica
Fitzcarrald
PARQUE NACIONAL DEL MANÚ
Pongo de Mainique
Urubamba
Manú
Madre de Dios
CORDILLERA ORIENTAL
Quillabamba
Machu Picchu
Shintuya
Huanta
Vilcabamba
San Vicente de Cañete
Ayacucho
Ollantaytambo
Urubamba
Pisac
Nev. de Salcantay 6271m
Astillero
Chincha Alta
Chincheros
Anta
Cusco
IS. BALLESTAS
I. SANGAYÁN
Tambo Colorado
Abancay
Huancapi
Nudo Auzangate 6394m
Pisco
Punta Carreta
Ica
Cabana
Macusani
I. INDEPENDENCIA
Antabamba
Sicuani
ANDES
P.N. ALTO MADIDI
Palpa
ALTIPLANO DEL PERU
Nev. Palomani 5999m
Nazca Lines
Puquio
Ayaviri
Poto
Caballas
Nazca
Cahuachi
Cañon del Cotahuasi
Azángaro
CORDILLERA
Cotahuasi
San Juan
Nudo Coropuna 6425m
Yauca
Cañon del Colca-Arequipa
Juliaca
I. AMANTANÍ
Puerto Acosta
Nevado de Ampato 6310m
Puerto Inca
Chuquibamba
Chala
Colca
Imata
Puno
I. TAQUILE
Achacachi
Aplao
Copacabana
Atico
Toro Muerto
Lago Titicaca
Juli
Tiwanaku
Arequipa
Lago de Huiñamarca
Desaguadero
CORDILLERA OCCIDENTAL
Camaná
Tambo
Vulcán Tutupaca 5806m
Guaqui
Matarani
PACIFIC OCEAN
Mollendo
Moquegua
BOLIVIA
Tarata
Punta Coles
Ilo
Nev. de Sajama 6520m
Tacna
GOLFO DE ARICA
Arica
CHILE

1 LIM Lima Jorge Chávez; **2 CUZ** Cusco; **3 ARI** Arica Chacalluta

300 kilometres
150 miles

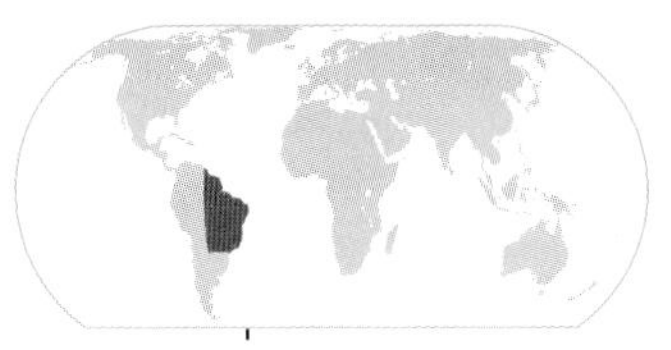

See also... Contents (2-7) – these countries feature in many thematic and regional maps throughout the *World Travel Atlas*.

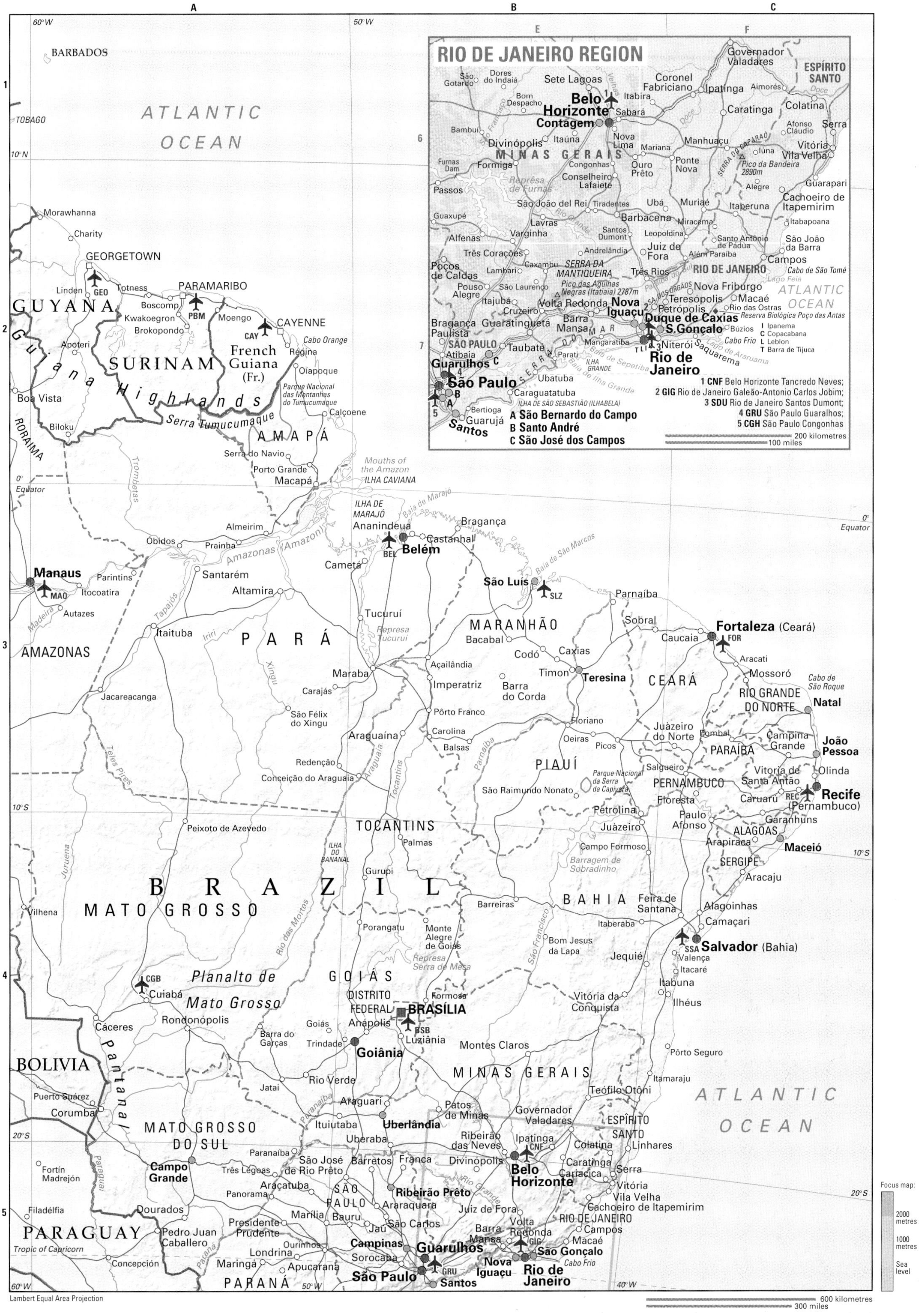

RIO DE JANEIRO REGION

São Gotardo
Dores do Indaiá
Sete Lagoas
Governador Valadares
ESPÍRITO SANTO
Coronel Fabriciano
Ipatinga
Aimorés
Doce
Bom Despacho
Belo Horizonte
Itabira
Sabará
Caratinga
Colatina
Contagem
Bambuí
Afonso Cláudio
Serra
Divinópolis
Itaúna
Nova Lima
Mariana
Manhuaçu
Vitória
Vila Velha
MINAS GERAIS
Furnas Dam
Formiga
Congonhas
Ouro Prêto
Ponte Nova
SERRA DO CAPARAÓ
Iúna
Pico da Bandeira 2890m
Represa de Furnas
Conselheiro Lafaiete
Guarapari
Passos
Alegre
Cachoeiro de Itapemirim
São João del Rei
Tiradentes
Ubá
Muriaé
Itaperuna
Guaxupé
Lavras
Barbacena
Miracema
Itabapoana
Santos Dumont
Leopoldina
Alfenas
Varginha
Rio Grande
Santo Antônio de Padua
São João da Barra
Três Corações
Andrelândia
Juiz de Fora
Além Paraíba
Campos
Poços de Caldas
Lambari
Caxambu
SERRA DA MANTIQUEIRA
Três Rios
RIO DE JANEIRO
Cabo de São Tomé
Lago Feia
Pouso Alegre
São Lourenço
Pico das Agulhas Negras (Itatiaia) 2787m
SERRA DOS ÓRGÃOS
Nova Friburgo
ATLANTIC OCEAN
Itajubá
Volta Redonda
Nova Iguaçu
Teresópolis
Macaé
Cruzeiro
Petrópolis
Rio das Ostras
Bragança Paulista
Guaratinguetá
Barra Mansa
Duque de Caxias
Reserva Biológica Poço das Antas
SÃO PAULO
Taubaté
MAR
Mangaratiba
S.Gonçalo
Búzios
I Ipanema
C Copacabana
L Leblon
T Barra de Tijuca
Atibaia
SERRA DO MAR
Parati
Baía de Sepetiba
Niterói
Saquarema
Cabo Frio
Lago de Araruama
Guarulhos
ILHA GRANDE
Rio de Janeiro
São Paulo
Ubatuba
Baía de Ilha Grande
Caraguatatuba
ILHA DE SÃO SEBASTIÃO (ILHABELA)
Bertioga
Guarujá
Santos
A São Bernardo do Campo
B Santo André
C São José dos Campos

1 CNF Belo Horizonte Tancredo Neves;
2 GIG Rio de Janeiro Galeão-Antonio Carlos Jobim;
3 SDU Rio de Janeiro Santos Dumont;
4 GRU São Paulo Guaralhos;
5 CGH São Paulo Congonhas

200 kilometres
100 miles

BARBADOS
TOBAGO
ATLANTIC OCEAN
Morawhanna
Charity
GEORGETOWN
GEO
Linden
Totness
PARAMARIBO
GUYANA
Boscomp
PBM
Kwakoegron
Moengo
CAYENNE
Brokopondo
CAY
Cabo Orange
Apoteri
French Guiana (Fr.)
Régina
SURINAM
Oiapoque
Guiana Highlands
Parque Nacional das Montanhas do Tumucumaque
Boa Vista
Calçoene
Serra Tumucumaque
Biloku
AMAPÁ
RORAIMA
Serra do Navio
Mouths of the Amazon
Porto Grande
ILHA CAVIANA
Macapá
Equator
Trombetas
ILHA DE MARAJÓ
Baía de Marajó
Bragança
Almeirim
Ananindeua
Óbidos
Prainha
Castanhal
Amazonas (Amazon)
BEL
Belém
Baía de São Marcos
Manaus
Parintins
Cametá
Santarém
MAO
Itacoatiara
São Luís
SLZ
Altamira
Parnaíba
Autazes
Madeira
Tapajós
Tucuruí
Sobral
Represa Tucuruí
Fortaleza (Ceará)
FOR
MARANHÃO
Caucaia
Itaituba
Iriri
PARÁ
Bacabal
Codó
Caxias
AMAZONAS
Aracati
Açailândia
Mossoró
Xingu
Marabá
Timon
Teresina
CEARÁ
Cabo de São Roque
Carajás
Imperatriz
Barra do Corda
RIO GRANDE DO NORTE
Natal
Jacareacanga
Pôrto Franco
São Félix do Xingu
Floriano
Juazeiro do Norte
Carolina
Campina Grande
Pombal
Araguaína
Oeiras
João Pessoa
Balsas
Picos
PARAÍBA
Teles Pires
Redenção
Araguaia
Tocantins
Parnaíba
PIAUÍ
Salgueiro
Olinda
Conceição do Araguaia
Parque Nacional da Serra da Capivara
Vitória de Santa Antão
PERNAMBUCO
São Raimundo Nonato
REC
Recife (Pernambuco)
Caruaru
Floresta
Petrolina
Paulo Afonso
Garanhuns
Peixoto de Azevedo
TOCANTINS
Juazeiro
ALAGOAS
Palmas
Arapiraca
Maceió
ILHA DO BANANAL
Campo Formoso
Barragem de Sobradinho
SERGIPE
Juruena
Gurupi
Aracaju
BRAZIL
BAHIA
Feira de Santana
Barreiras
Alagoinhas
Vilhena
MATO GROSSO
Camaçari
Itaberaba
Porangatu
Monte Alegre de Goiás
Rio das Mortes
São Francisco
Bom Jesus da Lapa
SSA
Salvador (Bahia)
Represa Serra da Mesa
Jequié
Valença
Itacaré
CGB
Planalto de Mato Grosso
GOIÁS
Itabuna
Cuiabá
DISTRITO FEDERAL
Formosa
Vitória da Conquista
Ilhéus
BRASÍLIA
Cáceres
Rondonópolis
Goiás
Anápolis
BSB
Luziânia
Barra do Garças
Trindade
Goiânia
Montes Claros
Pôrto Seguro
BOLIVIA
Pantanal
MINAS GERAIS
Itamaraju
Rio Verde
Jataí
Teófilo Otôni
Puerto Suárez
Araguari
Patos de Minas
ATLANTIC OCEAN
Corumbá
Governador Valadares
MATO GROSSO DO SUL
Ituiutaba
Uberlândia
ESPÍRITO SANTO
Paranaíba
Uberaba
Ribeirão das Neves
Ipatinga
CNF
Colatina
Linhares
Paranaíba
São José de Rio Prêto
Barretos
Franca
Divinópolis
Fortín Madrejón
Paraguai
Campo Grande
Três Lagoas
Belo Horizonte
Caratinga
Cariacica
Serra
Araçatuba
Rio Grande
Vitória
Panorama
SÃO PAULO
Ribeirão Prêto
Vila Velha
Filadélfia
Dourados
Marília
Bauru
Araraquara
Juiz de Fora
Cachoeiro de Itapemirim
RIO DE JANEIRO
PARAGUAY
Presidente Prudente
São Carlos
Jaú
Volta Redonda
Campos
Pedro Juan Caballero
Barra Mansa
Macaé
Tropic of Capricorn
Ourinhos
Campinas
Guarulhos
GIG
Londrina
Sorocaba
Nova Iguaçu
São Gonçalo
Concepción
Paraná
Maringá
Apucarana
Cabo Frio
GRU
Rio de Janeiro
São Paulo
PARANÁ
Santos

Lambert Equal Area Projection

600 kilometres
300 miles

Focus map:
2000 metres
1000 metres
Sea level

South America: Southern

See also... Contents (2-7) – these countries feature in many thematic and regional maps throughout the *World Travel Atlas*.

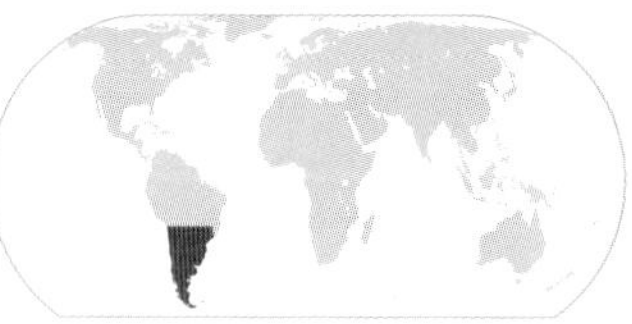

SANTIAGO–MENDOZA

1 SCL Santiago Comodoro Arturo Merino Benítez;
2 MDZ Mendoza El Plumerillo

200 km
100 miles

Focus map
2000 metres
1000 metres
Sea level

RIVER PLATE REGION

1 ROS Rosario; 2 AEP Buenos Aires Jorge Newbery;
3 EZE Buenos Aires Ezeiza-Ministro Pistarini;
4 MVD Montevideo Carrasco

200 km
100 miles

Lambert Equal Area Projection

600 kilometres
300 miles

See also... Weather Extremes (16); Cruising (46-47)

The listings above refer to a selection of related themes. For more information, see the Contents (2-7).

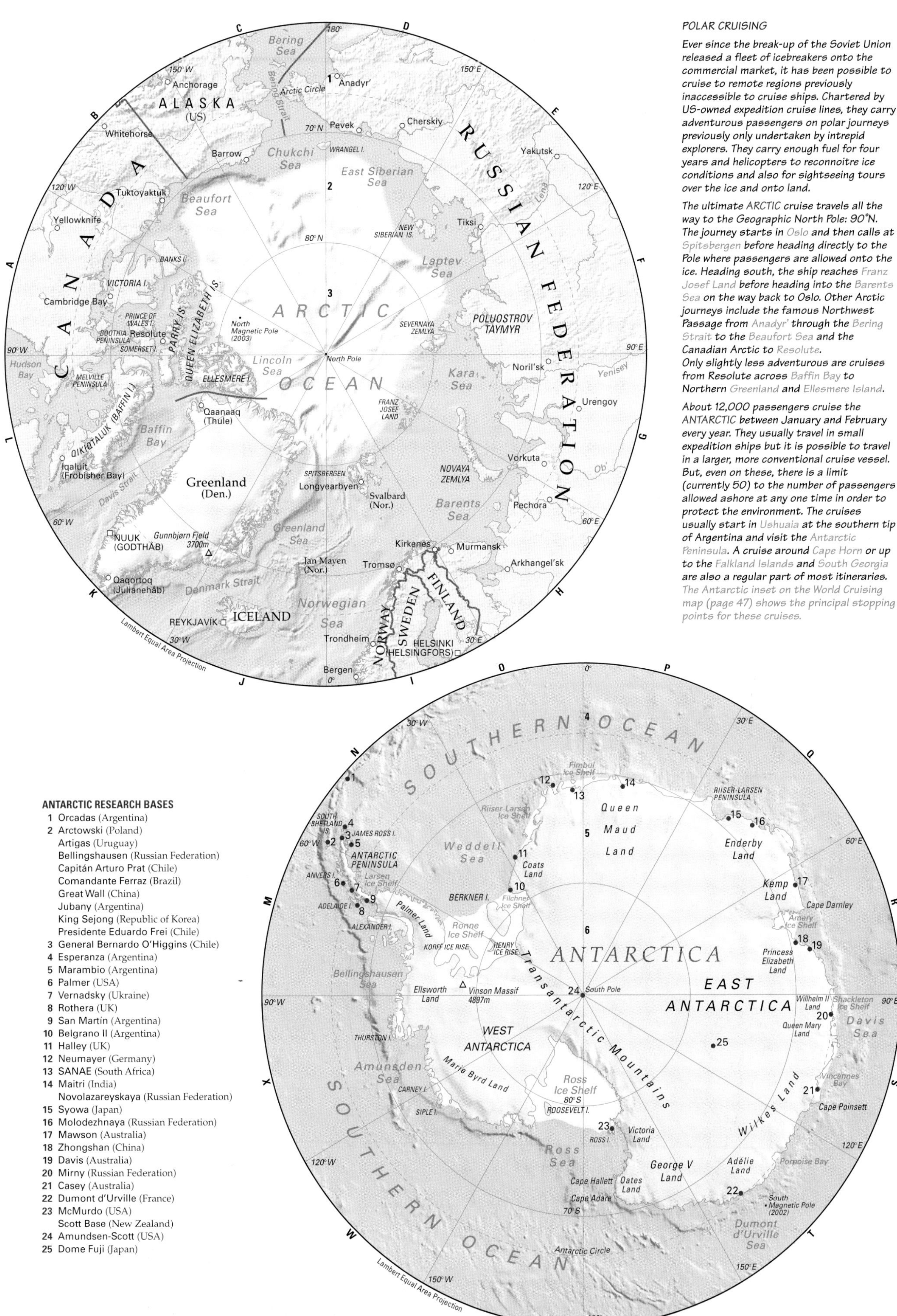
Bering Sea
Anchorage
Anadyr'
Arctic Circle
ALASKA (US)
Whitehorse
Pevek
Cherskiy
Barrow
Chukchi Sea
WRANGEL I.
East Siberian Sea
RUSSIAN FEDERATION
Yakutsk
Tuktoyaktuk
Beaufort Sea
Yellowknife
CANADA
Tiksi
NEW SIBERIAN IS.
BANKS I.
Laptev Sea
VICTORIA I.
Cambridge Bay
PARRY IS.
QUEEN ELIZABETH IS.
ARCTIC OCEAN
North Magnetic Pole (2003)
PRINCE OF WALES I.
BOOTHIA PENINSULA
Resolute
SOMERSET I.
SEVERNAYA ZEMLYA
POLUOSTROV TAYMYR
North Pole
Lincoln Sea
Hudson Bay
MELVILLE PENINSULA
ELLESMERE I.
Kara Sea
Noril'sk
Yenisey
FRANZ JOSEF LAND
Urengoy
Qaanaaq (Thule)
QIKIQTALUK (BAFFIN I.)
Baffin Bay
Iqaluit (Frobisher Bay)
Vorkuta
Ob'
Davis Strait
Greenland (Den.)
SPITSBERGEN
Longyearbyen
Svalbard (Nor.)
NOVAYA ZEMLYA
Barents Sea
Pechora
NUUK (GODTHÅB)
Gunnbjørn Fjeld 3700m
Greenland Sea
Kirkenes
Murmansk
Jan Mayen (Nor.)
Tromsø
Arkhangel'sk
Qaqortoq (Julianehåb)
Denmark Strait
FINLAND
SWEDEN
NORWAY
Norwegian Sea
REYKJAVÍK
ICELAND
Trondheim
HELSINKI (HELSINGFORS)
Bergen
Lambert Equal Area Projection
SOUTHERN OCEAN
Fimbul Ice Shelf
Queen Maud Land
RIISER-LARSEN PENINSULA
Riiser-Larsen Ice Shelf
SOUTH SHETLAND IS.
JAMES ROSS I.
Weddell Sea
Coats Land
Enderby Land
ANTARCTIC PENINSULA
ANVERS I.
Larsen Ice Shelf
Kemp Land
BERKNER I.
Filchner Ice Shelf
ADELAIDE I.
Cape Darnley
Palmer Land
Amery Ice Shelf
ALEXANDER I.
Ronne Ice Shelf
KORFF ICE RISE
HENRY ICE RISE
ANTARCTICA
Princess Elizabeth Land
Bellingshausen Sea
Ellsworth Land
Vinson Massif 4897m
South Pole
EAST ANTARCTICA
Wilhelm II Land
Shackleton Ice Shelf
Queen Mary Land
Davis Sea
WEST ANTARCTICA
THURSTON I.
Transantarctic Mountains
Amundsen Sea
Marie Byrd Land
Ross Ice Shelf
Vincennes Bay
CARNEY I.
ROOSEVELT I.
Cape Poinsett
SIPLE I.
Wilkes Land
ROSS I.
Victoria Land
Ross Sea
George V Land
Adélie Land
Porpoise Bay
Cape Hallett
Oates Land
Cape Adare
South Magnetic Pole (2002)
Dumont d'Urville Sea
Antarctic Circle
1600 kilometres
800 miles

POLAR CRUISING

Ever since the break-up of the Soviet Union released a fleet of icebreakers onto the commercial market, it has been possible to cruise to remote regions previously inaccessible to cruise ships. Chartered by US-owned expedition cruise lines, they carry adventurous passengers on polar journeys previously only undertaken by intrepid explorers. They carry enough fuel for four years and helicopters to reconnoitre ice conditions and also for sightseeing tours over the ice and onto land.

The ultimate ARCTIC cruise travels all the way to the Geographic North Pole: 90°N. The journey starts in Oslo and then calls at Spitsbergen before heading directly to the Pole where passengers are allowed onto the ice. Heading south, the ship reaches Franz Josef Land before heading into the Barents Sea on the way back to Oslo. Other Arctic journeys include the famous Northwest Passage from Anadyr' through the Bering Strait to the Beaufort Sea and the Canadian Arctic to Resolute. Only slightly less adventurous are cruises from Resolute across Baffin Bay to Northern Greenland and Ellesmere Island.

About 12,000 passengers cruise the ANTARCTIC between January and February every year. They usually travel in small expedition ships but it is possible to travel in a larger, more conventional cruise vessel. But, even on these, there is a limit (currently 50) to the number of passengers allowed ashore at any one time in order to protect the environment. The cruises usually start in Ushuaia at the southern tip of Argentina and visit the Antarctic Peninsula. A cruise around Cape Horn or up to the Falkland Islands and South Georgia are also a regular part of most itineraries. The Antarctic inset on the World Cruising map (page 47) shows the principal stopping points for these cruises.

ANTARCTIC RESEARCH BASES

1 Orcadas (Argentina)
2 Arctowski (Poland)
Artigas (Uruguay)
Bellingshausen (Russian Federation)
Capitán Arturo Prat (Chile)
Comandante Ferraz (Brazil)
Great Wall (China)
Jubany (Argentina)
King Sejong (Republic of Korea)
Presidente Eduardo Frei (Chile)
3 General Bernardo O'Higgins (Chile)
4 Esperanza (Argentina)
5 Marambio (Argentina)
6 Palmer (USA)
7 Vernadsky (Ukraine)
8 Rothera (UK)
9 San Martín (Argentina)
10 Belgrano II (Argentina)
11 Halley (UK)
12 Neumayer (Germany)
13 SANAE (South Africa)
14 Maitri (India)
Novolazareyskaya (Russian Federation)
15 Syowa (Japan)
16 Molodezhnaya (Russian Federation)
17 Mawson (Australia)
18 Zhongshan (China)
19 Davis (Australia)
20 Mirny (Russian Federation)
21 Casey (Australia)
22 Dumont d'Urville (France)
23 McMurdo (USA)
Scott Base (New Zealand)
24 Amundsen-Scott (USA)
25 Dome Fuji (Japan)

▶ *See also...* World Physical (12-13); Regions Used in this Atlas (14); World Political (14-15); International Organisations (24-25)

The listings above refer to a selection of related themes. For more information, see the Contents (2-7).

1: Geographical Definitions

The following list covers a number of the main geographical terms which are used to describe areas of the world. In many cases there is no officially adopted definition. Different industries, cultures and international bodies will use their own definitions which are, if consistently applied, as valid of those used by any other. The definitions of the continents, for example, are often not those which have been used in this atlas. Some of these ambiguities are referred to here.

Arabian Peninsula
Geographical region comprising: Bahrain, Kuwait, Oman, Qatar, Saudi Arabia, United Arab Emirates, Yemen.

Australasia
Geographical region comprising: Australia, New Caledonia, New Zealand, Solomon Islands, Vanuatu and the island of New Guinea including all of Papua New Guinea. Often described as equivalent to all of Oceania between the Equator and 47°S. The term is not commonly used in Australia and New Zealand because of confusion with Australia itself.

Bahama Islands
Group of islands in the Atlantic Ocean comprising the Commonwealth of The Bahamas and the Turks and Caicos Islands.

Balkans, The
The Balkan Peninsula, which is bordered by the Adriatic and Ionian Seas to the west, the Aegean and Black Seas to the east and the Mediterranean Sea to the south. The countries occupying this peninsula are described as Balkan states: Albania, Bosnia-Herzegovina, Bulgaria, Croatia, Greece, Former Yugoslav Republic of Macedonia, Romania, Slovenia, Serbia & Montenegro and the European part of Turkey.

Borneo
Island in the Malay Archipelago (qv) divided between Brunei, Indonesia (the provinces of Central, East, South and West Kalimantan) and Malaysia (the states of Sabah and Sarawak).

British Isles
Geographical region comprising: United Kingdom (qv), Republic of Ireland, Isle of Man, Channel Islands.

Caribbean
General tourist destination term used to describe the West Indies (qv) and sometimes the countries with coastlines on the Caribbean Sea (such as Venezuela and Eastern Mexico).

Caroline Islands
Archipelago in the west Pacific Ocean. Islands comprise the Federated States of Micronesia and Palau.

Celebes
Island in the Malay Archipelago (qv), Sulawesi in Indonesian.

Central America
Geographical region comprising: Belize, Costa Rica, El Salvador, Guatemala, Honduras, Nicaragua, Panama. Sometimes considered part of the North American (qv) continent.

Ceylon
Island off the southeast coast of India, officially Sri Lanka.

Channel Islands
Group of islands comprising Jersey, Guernsey, Alderney, Sark and Herm, situated off the northwest coast of France. They are possessions of the British Crown and not officially part of the United Kingdom (qv).

East Indies
General geographical term sometimes applied loosely to India, Indochina and the Malay Archipelago (qv). Often used as alternative to the Malay Archipelago or the Republic of Indonesia itself. The term is now rarely used.

Europe
Continent. Northern boundary formed by Arctic Ocean. Eastern boundary formed by Ural Mountains, Ural River and Caspian Sea. Southern boundary formed by Caucasus Mountains, Black Sea, Bosporus, Aegean Sea and Mediterranean Sea. Western boundary formed by Atlantic Ocean. Includes Iceland, Svalbard and area of Turkey west of the Bosporus.

Far East
General geographical term describing east and South-East Asia: Brunei, Cambodia, China, Indonesia, Japan, Democratic People's Republic of Korea (North Korea), Republic of Korea (South Korea), Laos, Malaysia, Myanmar (Burma), the Philippines, Singapore, Taiwan, Thailand, Vietnam. Sometimes extended to include Mongolia and eastern Siberian region of the Russian Federation.

Formosa
Island off the southeast coast of the People's Republic of China, known variously as Taiwan, the Republic of China, Taiwan (RoC) or China (Taiwan) .

Great Britain
Geographical region comprising: England, Scotland, Wales.

Greater Antilles
Group of Caribbean islands comprising: Cayman Islands, Cuba, Hispaniola, Jamaica, Puerto Rico.

Hispaniola
Island in the Greater Antilles (qv) divided between the Dominican Republic and Haiti.

Iberia
Peninsula in southwest Europe occupied by Spain, Portugal, Andorra and Gibraltar.

Indochina
Geographical region comprising: Cambodia, Laos, Peninsular Malaysia, Myanmar, Singapore, Thailand, Vietnam.

Isle of Man
An island in the Irish Sea between Great Britain (qv) and Ireland. It is a possession of the British Crown and not officially part of the United Kingdom (qv).

Latin America
Defined either as: the Spanish- and Portuguese-speaking countries of the Americas (sometimes also including French-speaking Haiti); or all of the Americas south of the United States. This latter, more general, definition is the one used in this atlas.

Lesser Antilles
Group of Caribbean islands comprising: Leeward Islands (qv), Windward Islands (qv), Aruba, Barbados, Bonaire, Curaçao, Trinidad and Tobago. Also includes the chain of small Venezuelan islands east of Bonaire.

Leeward Islands
Group of Caribbean islands comprising: Anguilla, Antigua and Barbuda, Dominica, Guadeloupe, Montserrat, Saba, St Eustatius, St Kitts and Nevis, St Maarten/St Martin, Virgin Islands.

Low Countries
Geographical region comprising: Belgium, Luxembourg, The Netherlands.

Maghreb
Arabic name for northwest Africa and, in the Moorish period, Spain. Algeria, Morocco and Tunisia are described as Maghreb countries.

Malay Archipelago
The largest island group in the world, off the southeast coast of Asia and between the Indian and Pacific Oceans. Major islands include Borneo (qv), Sulawesi (Celebes, qv), Jawa (Java), New Guinea and Sumatera (Sumatra). Countries within this archipelago: Brunei, Indonesia, East Malaysia, Papua New Guinea, the Philippines.

Mediterranean
General tourist destination term used to describe the islands of the Mediterranean Sea and the countries bordering it.

Melanesia
Collective name for the islands in the southwest Pacific Ocean, south of the Equator and northeast of Australia. Includes: Fiji Islands, Nauru, New Caledonia, Papua New Guinea (excluding New Guinea mainland), Solomon Islands, Vanuatu.

Micronesia
Collective name for the islands in the west Pacific Ocean, north of the Equator and east of the Philippines. Includes: Guam, Kiribati (west), Marshall Islands, Federated States of Micronesia, Northern Mariana Islands, Palau.

Middle East
General geographical term describing a loosely defined area comprising: countries of the Arabian Peninsula (qv), Egypt, Iran, Iraq, Israel, Jordan, Lebanon, Syria. Sometimes extended to include Algeria, Cyprus, Libya, Morocco, Sudan, Tunisia and Turkey

Near East
Rarely used general geographical term describing an area of SW Asia: the Arabian Peninsula, Cyprus, Israel, Jordan, Lebanon, Syria, Turkey. Often extended to Egypt and Sudan.

Netherlands Antilles
Islands of the West Indies administered by The Netherlands, comprising: Bonaire, Curaçao, Saba, St Eustatius, St Maarten. Aruba, formerly part of the Netherlands Antilles, is a separate part of the Kingdom of the Netherlands.

New Guinea
Island in the Malay Archipelago (qv) divided between Papua New Guinea and the Indonesian province of Irian Jaya.

North America
Continent comprising: USA, Canada, Mexico, Bermuda, West Indies (qv). Usually considered to also include Greenland and (less commonly) Central America.

Oceania
General geographical term describing the islands of the central and south Pacific Ocean, including Melanesia, Micronesia and Polynesia. Sometimes extended to include Australia, New Zealand and the Malay Archipelago (qv).

Polynesia
Collective name for the islands of the central and south Pacific Ocean. Includes: American Samoa, Cook Islands, Easter Island, French Polynesia, Hawaii, Kiribati (east), New Zealand, Niue, Pitcairn Islands, Samoa, Tokelau, Tonga, Tuvalu, Wallis & Futuna.

Scandinavia
Geographical region comprising: Denmark, Norway, Sweden. Generally extended to include Finland and (less commonly) Iceland.

South America
Continent comprising: countries on mainland south of Panama, Falkland Islands, Galapagos Islands.

South-East Asia
Geographic region comprising Maynmar, Laos, Thailand, Vietnam, Cambodia, Malaysia, Singapore, Brunei and the Philippines. Sometimes taken to include Indonesia, Taiwan, Macau, Hong Kong and the southern coastal areas of China.

Ulster
Geographical region comprising Northern Ireland plus the counties of Cavan, Donegal and Monaghan in the Republic of Ireland. It is often used (incorrectly) as an unofficial term to describe Northern Ireland.

United Kingdom
Country comprising Great Britain (qv) and Northern Ireland. The Isle of Man and the Channel Islands are Crown dependencies and not officially part of the UK.

West Indies
Islands enclosing the Caribbean Sea, comprising: Bahama Islands (qv), Greater Antilles (qv), Lesser Antilles (qv).

Windward Islands
Group of Caribbean islands comprising: Grenada, Martinique, St Lucia, St Vincent and The Grenadines.

2: Highest & Lowest

Name	*Metres*	*Feet*	*Country*
AFRICA			
▲ **Kilimanjaro (Kibo)**	5,895	19,340	Tanzania
▼ **Lake Assal**	–155	–509	Djibouti
ANTARCTICA			
▲ **Vinson Massif**	4,897	16,066	Antarctica
▼ **(ice covered)**	–2,538	–8,327	Antarctica
ASIA			
▲ **Everest (Qomolangma Feng/ Sagarmatha)**	8,850	29,035	China-Nepal
▼ **Dead Sea**	–411	–1,349	Israel-Jordan-Palestine
AUSTRALASIA & OCEANIA			
▲ **Aoraki (Cook)**	3,754	12,315	New Zealand
▼ **Lake Eyre**	–16	–52	Australia
EUROPE & RUSSIAN FEDERATION			
▲ **Elbrus**	5,642	18,510	Russian Fed.
▼ **Caspian Sea**	–28	–92	Russia-C. Asia-Caucasus
NORTH AMERICA			
▲ **McKinley (Denali)**	6,194	20,321	Alaska, USA
▼ **Death Valley**	–86	–282	California, USA
SOUTH AMERICA			
▲ **Aconcagua**	6,960	22,834	Argentina
▼ **G. Bajo de S. Julián**	–105	–344	Argentina

Name	*Metres*	*Feet*	*Country*
SOME OTHER NOTABLE MOUNTAINS			
K2 (Chogori/ Qogir Feng)	8,611	28,250	China-Kashmir
Kangchenjunga	8,586	28,170	India-Nepal
Makalu	8,463	27,766	China-Nepal
Dhaulagiri	8,167	26,795	Nepal
Nanga Parbat	8,126	26,660	Kashmir
Annapurna	8,091	26,545	Nepal
Gosainthan (Xixabangma Feng)	8,013	26,289	China
Qullai Garmo	7,495	24,590	Tajikistan
Ojos del Salado	6,908	22,664	Argentina-Chile
Huascarán	6,768	22,205	Peru
Logan	5,959	19,550	Yukon, Canada
Damavand	5,681	18,638	Iran
Citlaltépetl (Orizaba)	5,610	18,405	Mexico
Kenya (Kirinyaga)	5,199	17,057	Kenya
Ararat	5,165	16,946	Turkey
Mont Blanc	4,808	15,774	France-Italy
Ras Dashen	4,533	14,872	Ethiopia
Whitney	4,418	14,495	California, USA
Kinabalu	4,094	13,432	Malaysia
Fuji	3,776	12,388	Japan

3: The World's Longest Rivers

Local names are shown in square brackets.

River	*Length: (km)*	*(miles)*	*Source(s) and outflow*
Nile Luvironza-Ruvuvu-Kagera-White Nile	6,825	4,240	Lake Victoria region – Mediterranean Sea
Amazon Apurimac-Ene-Tambo-Ucayali	6,516	4,049	Peruvian Andes – Atlantic Ocean
Chang Jiang (Yangtze) [Tuotuo-Tongtian-Jinsha]	6,380	3,964	Tanggula Shan, China – East China Sea
Mississippi-Missouri Red Rock-Beaverhead	5,969	3,709	SW Montana – Gulf of Mexico
Ob-Irtysh [Ertix]	5,568	3,459	Altay Mountains, China – Kara Sea
Yenisey Selenga-Angara	5,550	3,448	Western Mongolia – Kara Sea
Huang He (Yellow)	5,464	3,395	Bayan Har Shan, China – Yellow Sea
Congo Lualaba	4,667	2,900	Katanga Plateau, Congo D.R. – Atlantic Ocean
Paraná Río de la Plata	4,500	2,796	Serra da Mantiquera, Brazil – Atlantic Ocean
Mekong [Za-Lancang]	4,425	2,749	Tanggula Shan, China – South China Sea
Amur Kerulen-Argun	4,416	2,744	Eastern Mongolia – Sea of Japan
Lena Kirenga	4,400	2,734	Baikal Mtns, Russian Fed., – Laptev Sea
Mackenzie Finlay-Peace-Slave	4,241	2,635	Omineca Mtns, BC, Canada – Beaufort Sea
Niger [Joliba/Kworra]	4,184	2,599	Guinea/Sierra Leone border – Gulf of Guinea
Murray-Darling	3,750	2,330	Gt. Dividing Range, Australia – Southern Ocean

4: Conversions (Kilometres/ Miles; Metres/Feet; Centimetres/Inches; Centigrade/Fahrenheit)

Kms	**10**	**20**	**30**	**40**	**50**	**60**	**70**	**80**	**90**	**100**
Mi	6.2	12.4	18.6	24.9	31.1	37.3	43.5	49.7	55.9	62.1
M	**10**	**20**	**30**	**40**	**50**	**60**	**70**	**80**	**90**	**100**
Ft	33	66	98	131	164	197	230	262	295	328

Cms	**10**	**20**	**30**	**40**	**50**	**60**	**70**	**80**	**90**	**100**
Ins	3.9	7.9	11.8	15.7	19.7	23.6	27.6	31.5	35.4	39.4
°C	**-10**	**-5**	**0**	**5**	**10**	**15**	**20**	**25**	**30**	**35**
°F	14	23	32	41	50	59	68	77	86	95

See also... Appendix 6: Glossary of Climate Terms (196)

*The listings above refer to a selection of related themes.
For more information, see the Contents (2-7).*

5: Glossary of Foreign Geographical Terms

The following list provides the English equivalents for some of the most common foreign geographical terms used in this atlas and other international atlases.

Term	Language	English
Å, -å	Danish, Norwegian	Stream
Abar, Abyar	Arabic	Wells
Açude	Portuguese	Reservoir
Adalar	Turkish	Islands
Adasi	Turkish	Island
Agía, Ágios	Greek	Saint
Aiguille(s)	French	Peak(s)
Ain, Aïn	Arabic	Spring, well
-air	Indonesian	Stream
Ákra, Akrotírion	Greek	Cape, point
Ala-	Finnish	Lower
A'lá	Arabic	Upper
Alt-	German	Old
Alta, Alto	Italian, Portug., Spanish	Upper
Altiplanicie	Spain	High plain, mesa
Älv, -älven	Swedish	River
am, an	German	On, upon
Áno	Greek	Upper
Anse	French	Bay
Ao	Chinese, Thai	Bay
'Aqabat	Arabic	Pass
Arrecife	Spanish	Reef
Arroio/Arroyo	Portuguese/Spanish	Watercourse
Archipiélago	Spanish	Archipelago
Aust-	Norwegian	East, eastern
Austral	Spanish	Southern
'Ayn	Arabic	Spring, well
Baai	Afrikaans	Bay
Bab	Arabic	Strait
Bach	German	Stream
Bad	German	Spa
Badiyat	Arabic	Desert
Bælt	Danish	Strait
Baharu	Malay	New
Bahia	Spanish	Bay
Bahiret	Arabic	Lagoon
Bahr	Arabic	Bay, canal, lake
Bahra/Bahrat	Arabic	Lagoon/Lake
Baía/Baie	Portuguese/French	Bay
Baixo	Portuguese	Lower
Baja, Bajo	Spanish	Lower
Bala	Persian	Upper
Ban	Cambodian, Laotian, Thai	Village
-bana	Japanese	Cape, point
Bañado	Spanish	Marshy land
Banc/Banco	French/Spanish	Sandbank
Bandao	Chinese	Peninsula
Bandar	Arabian, Malay, Persian	Inlet, port
-bando	Korean	Peninsula
Baraj, Baraji	Turkish	Dam
Barat	Indonesian, Malay	West, western
Barqa	Arabic	Hill
Barra	Portuguese	Sandbank
Barracão	Portuguese	Dam, weir
Barragem	Portuguese	Reservoir
Baruun	Mongolian	Western
Bas, Basse	French	Lower
Bassin	French	Basin
Batin, Batn	Arabic	Depression
Becken	German	Basin
Beek	Flemish	Stream
bei	German	At, near
Bei	Chinese	North, northern
Beinn, Ben	Gaelic	Mountain
Belogor'ye	Russian	Mountain
Bereg	Russian	Bank, shore
-berg	Norwegian, Swedish	Mountain
Berg(e)	German	Mountain(s)
Besar	Indonesian, Malay	Big, great
Bir, Bîr/Bi'ar	Arabic	Well/Wells
Birkat, Birket	Arabic	Pool, well
-bjerg	Danish	Hill
Boca	Portuguese, Spanish	Mouth
Bocche	Italian	Estuary, mouths
Bodden	German	Bay, gulf
Bogazi	Turkish	Strait
Bogen	Norwegian	Bay
Bois	French	Woods
Boloto	Russian	Bog, marsh
Bol'sh-aya, -iye, -oy, -oye	Russian	Big
-bong	Korean	Mountain
Boquerón	Spanish	Pass
Bor	Polish	Forest
-botn/-botten	Norwegian/Swedish	Valley floor
Bouche	French	Estuary, mouth
-bre, -breen	Norwegian	Glacier
Bredning	Danish	Bay
Bron	Afrikaans	Spring, well
-brønn	Norwegian	Spring, well
Bucht/Bugt	German/Danish	Bay
Buhayrat, Buheirat	Arabic	Lake
Bukhta	Russian	Bay
Bukit	Malay	Hill
Bukt, Bukten	Norwegian, Swedish	Bay
Bulag	Mongolian	Spring
Bulak	Russian, Uighur	Spring
Burg	German	Castle
Burun, Burnu	Turkish	Cape, point
Büyük	Turkish	Big
Cabeço	Portuguese	Summit
Cabeza	Spanish	Summit
Cabo	Portuguese, Spanish	Cape, headland
Cachoeira	Portuguese	Waterfall
Cala/Caleta	Catalan/Spanish	Inlet
Cañada	Spanish	Ravine
Cañadón	Spanish	Gorge
Canal	Portuguese, Spanish	Channel
Caño	Spanish	Stream
Cañon	Spanish	Canyon
Cap/Capo	Catalan, French/Italian	Cape, headland
Catarata	Spanish	Waterfall
Cayo(s)	Spanish	Islet(s), rock(s)
Cerro	Spanish	Hill, peak
Chaco	Spanish	Plain
Chaîne	French	Mountain chain
Chalb	Arabic	Watercourse
Chapada	Portuguese	Hills, uplands
Chebka	Arabic	Hill
-chedo	Korean	Archipelago
Chenal	French	Channel
Chiang	Thai	Town
-ch'on	Korean	River
Chong	Thai	Bay
Chott	Arabic	Marsh, salt lake
Chuluu	Mongolian	Mountain
Chute	French	Waterfall
Ci	Indonesian	Stream
Ciénaga	Spanish	Marshy lake
Cima/Cime	Italian/French	Summit
Città/Ciudad	Italian/Spanish	City, town
Co	Tibetan	Lake
Col	French	High pass
Collado	Spanish	Hill, saddle
Colle	Italian	Pass
Collina	Italian	Hill
Colline(s)	French	Hill(s)
Combe	French	Valley
Conca	Italian	Hollow
Cordillera	Spanish	Mountain chain
Corne/Corno	French/Italian	Peak
Costa	Italian, Portug., Spanish	Coast, shore
Côte	French	Coast, slope
Coteau(x)	French	Hill(s)
Cove	Catalan	Cave
Cuchilla	Spanish	Mountain chain
Cuenca	Spanish	River basin
Cueva	Spanish	Cave
Cun	Chinese	Village
Da	Chinese	Big
Dag/Dagh	Turkish/Persian	Mountain
Daglar	Turkish	Mountain
-dake	Japanese	Peak
-dal	Afrikaans, Danish, Norwegian, Swedish	Valley
Danau	Indonesian	Lake
Dao	Chinese	Island
Darreh	Persian	Valley
Daryacheh	Persian	Lake
Dasht	Persian, Urdu	Desert
Davaa	Mongolian	Pass
Denizi	Turkish	Sea
Dhar	Arabic	Hills, mountain
-diep	Flemish	Channel
Djebel/Djibâl	Arabic	Mountain/Mtns.
-do	Korean	Island
Dolina	Russian	Valley
Dolna/Dolní	Bulgarian/Czech	Lower
Dolny	Polish	Lower
Dong	Chinese	East, eastern
Dong	Thai	Mountain
-dong	Korean	Village
Donja, Donji	Serbo-Croat	Lower
Dorf	German	Village
-dorp	Afrikaans	Village
Dür	Arabic	Mountains
Dzüün	Mongolian	East, eastern
Eiland(en)	Afrikaans, Flemish	Island(s)
-elv, -elva	Norwegian	River
Embalse	Spanish	Reservoir
Embouchure	French	Estuary
Ensenada	Spanish	Bay
Erg	Arabian	Desert & dunes
Eski	Turkish	Old
Estero	Spanish	Inlet, estuary, swamp
Estrecho	Spanish	Strait
Estreito	Portuguese	Strait
Étang	French	Lake, lagoon
Fajj	Arabic	Watercourse
Fels	German	Rock
Feng	Chinese	Peak
Fiume	Italian	River
-fjäll, -fjället	Swedish	Mountain
-fjärden	Swedish	Fjord
-fjell, -fjellet	Norwegian	Mountain
-fjord, -fjorden	Danish, Norwegian	Fjord, lagoon
Fleuve	French	River
Foce	Italian	River-mouth
-fonn	Norwegian	Glacier
Förde	German	Inlet
Forêt/Forst	French/German	Forest
-foss	Norwegian	Waterfall
Fuente	Spanish	Source, well
-gan	Japanese	Rock
Gang	Chinese	Harbour
Garet	Arabic	Hill
Gardaneh	Persian	Pass
Gat	Flemish	Channel
-gata	Japanese	Inlet, lagoon
Gau	German	District
Gave	French	Torrent
-gawa	Japanese	River
Gebel	Arabic	Mountain
Gebergte	Afrikaans	Mountain range
Gebiet	German	District, region
Gebirge	German	Mountains
Gedigi	Turkish	Pass
Geziret/Gezâir	Arabic	Island/Islands
Ghadfat	Arabic	Watercourse
Ghadir	Arabic	Well
Ghard	Arabic	Sand dunes
Ghubbat	Arabic	Bay
Gipfel	German	Peak
Gletscher	German	Glacier
Gobi	Mongolian	Desert
Gol	Mongolian	River
Göl, Gölü	Turkish	Lake
Golfe	French	Bay, gulf
Golfete	Spanish	Bay
Golfo	Italian, Spanish	Bay, gulf
Gora	Bulgarian	Forest
Gora/Góra	Russian, Serbo-Croat/ Polish	Mountain
Górka	Polish	Hill
Gornja, Gornji	Serbo-Croat	Upper
Gory/Góry	Russian/Polish	Mountains
Goulet	French	Narrow entrance
Grabean	German	Ditch, trench
-grad	Bulgarian, Russian, Serbo-Croat	Town, castle
Grand, Grands	French	Big
Grat	German	Crest, ridge
Greben'	Russian	Ridge
-gród	Polish	Town, castle
Groot	Afrikaans	Big
Gross, -e, -en, -er	German	Big
Grotta/Grotte	Italian/French	Cave, grotto
Grund	German	Ground, valley
Gryada	Russian	Ridge
Guan	Chinese	Pass
Guba	Russian	Bay
Guelta	Arabic	Well
-gunto	Japanese	Island group
Gunung	Indonesian, Malay	Mountain
Hadabat	Arabic	Plain
Hadh, Hadhat	Arabic	Sand dunes
-haehyop	Korean	Strait
Hafar	Arabic	Wells
Hafen	German	Harbour, port
Haff	German	Bay
Hai	Chinese	Sea
Halbinsel	German	Peninsula
-halvøya	Norwegian	Peninsula
Hamad-a, -et	Arabic	Plateau
Hammad-ah, -at	Arabic	Plain, rocky plateau
-hamn	Norwegian, Swedish	Harbour
Hamun	Persian	Marsh
-hanto	Japanese	Peninsula
Hardt	German	Wooded hills
Harrat	Arabic	Lava fields
Hassi, Hasy	Arabic	Well
-haug	Norwegian	Hill
Haut, -e	French	Upper
Hawr	Arabic	Lake
-havn	Danish, Norwegian	Harbour
Hazm	Arabic	Plateau
He	Chinese	River
-hede	Danish, Norwegian	Heath
-hegység	Hungarian	Mountains
-hei/Heide	Norwegian/German	Heath, moor
Hersónisos	Greek	Peninsula
Higashi-	Japanese	East, eastern
-hisar	Turkish	Castle
Hisn	Arabic	Fort
-hø	Norwegian	Peak
Hoch/Hoë	German/Afrikaans	High
Hoek	Flemish	Cape, point
Hög/-høg(d)	Swedish/Norwegian	High, height
Höhe, Hohen-	German	Height

▶ *See also...* Appendix 6: Glossary of Climate Terms (196)

The listings above refer to a selection of related themes. For more information, see the Contents (2-7).

Hoog	Flemish	High
-høj	Danish	Hill
Hora/Hory	Czech	Mountain/Mtns
Horn	German	Peak, summit
Horní	Czech	Upper
Hot	Mongolian	Town
-høy	Norwegian	Height
-hrad	Czech	Castle
Hu	Chinese	Lake
Hügel	German	Hill
Idd	Arabic	Well
Idhan	Arabic	Sand dunes
'Idwet	Arabic	Mountain
Île(s)/Ilha(s)	French/Portuguese	Island(s)
Illa, Illes	Catalan	Island, islands
im, in	German	In
Inférieur, -e	French	Lower
Insel(n)	German	Island(s)
Irmak	Turkish	Large river
'Irq	Arabic	Sand dunes
Isla(s)/Isle	Spanish/French	Island(s)
Islote	Spanish	Small island
Iso	Finnish	Big
Ìsola, Isole	Italian	Island, islands
Istmo	Spanish	Isthmus
Jabal	Arabic	Mountain
-järvi	Finnish	Lake
-jaure, -javrre	Lappish	Lake
Jazirat/Jaza'ir	Arabic	Island/Islands
Jbel, Jebel	Arabic	Mountain
Jezero/Jezioro	Serbo-Croat/Polish	Lake
Jiang	Chinese	River
Jiao	Chinese	Point, reef
Jibal	Arabic	Mountains
-jima	Japanese	Island
-joki/-jokka	Finnish/Lappish	River
-jøkulen	Norwegian	Glacier
-jökull	Icelandic	Glacier
Jun	Arabic	Bay
Kaap	Afrikaans	Cape
-kai	Japanese	Sea, bay, inlet
Kali	Indonesian	River
Kamm	German	Crest, ridge
Kampung	Indonesian, Malay	Village
Kanaal/Kanal	Flemish/German, Russian	Canal
-kapp	Norwegian	Cape
Karif	Arabic	Well
Kathib	Arabic	Sand dunes
Káto	Greek	Lower
-kawa	Japanese	River
Kecil	Indonesian, Malay	Small
Kepulauan	Indonesian	Archipelago
Kereb	Arabic	Hill, ridge
Keski-	Finnish	Central, middle
Khalīg, Khalij	Arabic	Bay, gulf
Khao	Thai	Peak
Khashm	Arabic	Mountain
Khawr, Khor/Khowr	Arabic/Persian	Inlet
Khrebet	Russian	Mountain range
Kis-	Hungarian	Small
Kita-	Japanese	North, northern
Klamm	German	Ravine
Klein	Afrikaans, German	Small
Klint/Klit	Danish	Cliff/Dunes
Klong	Thai	Canal, creek
Kloof	Afrikaans	Gorge
Ko/Koh	Thai/Cambodian	Island
-ko	Japanese	Lake, inlet
Kólpos	Greek	Gulf
Koog	German	Polder
Kop/Kopf	Afrikaans/German	Hill
Körfezi	Turkish	Bay, gulf
Kotlina	Czech, Polish	Basin, depression
Kotlovina	Russian	Depression
-köy	Turkish	Village
Kraj	Czech, Polish, Serbo-Croat	Region
Kray	Russian	Region
Kreis	German	District
Kryazh	Russian	Ridge
Kuala	Malay	Estuary
Küçük	Turkish	Small
Kuduk	Russian	Spring, well
Kuh	Persian	Mountain
Kul'	Russian	Lake
Kület	Arabic	Hill
Kum	Russian	Sandy desert
-kundo	Korean	Island group
-kylä	Finnish	Village
Lac	French	Lake
Laem	Thai	Point
Lago	Italian, Portug., Spanish	Lake
Lagoa	Portuguese	Lagoon
Laguna	Spanish	Lagoon, lake
Lam	Thai	Stream
Län	Swedish	Province
Land	German	Province, area
Lande	French	Heath, sandy moor
Las/Les	Polish/Czech, Russian	Forest, wood
Laut	Indonesia	Sea
Lednik	Russian	Glacier
lès, lez	French	Beside, near
Liedao	Chinese	Island group
Lille	Danish, Norwegian	Small
Liman	Russian	Bay, gulf
Liman, Limani	Turkish	Harbour, port
Limni	Greek	Lake, lagoon
Ling	Chinese	Mountain range
Llano	Spanish	Plain, prairie
Loma	Spanish	Hill
-luoto	Finnish	Rocky island
-lyng	Danish	Heath
Macizo	Spanish	Massif
Madinat	Arabic	City, town
Mae Nam	Thai	River
Mala/Malé	Serbo-Croat/Czech	Small
Malaya, -oye, -yy	Russian	Small
-man	Korean	Bay
Manâqir	Arabic	Hills
Mar	Portuguese, Spanish	Sea
Marais	French	Marsh, swamp
Mare	Italian/Romanian	Sea/Big
Marsá	Arabic	Anchorage, inlet
Marsch	German	Fen, marsh
Masabb	Arabic	Estuary
Mashâsh	Arabic	Well
Massif	French	Mountains, upland
Mayor	Spanish	Higher, larger
Meer	Afrikaans, Flemish, German	Lake, sea
Méga, Megál-a, -i, -o	Greek	Big
Menor	Portuguese, Spanish	Lesser, smaller
Mer	French	Sea
Mersa	Arabic	Anchorage, inlet
Mesa, Meseta	Spanish	Tableland
Mesto	Czech, Serbo-Croat	Town
Mezzo	Italian	Middle, mid-
Miasto	Polish	Town
Mic/Mikr-í, ón	Romanian/Greek	Small
Mina'	Arabic	Harbour, port
Minami-	Japanese	South, southern
Minqâr	Arabic	Hill
-misaki	Japanese	Cape, point
Mishâsh, Mushâsh	Arabic	Well
Miti	Greek	Cape
Mittel-, Mitten-	German	Central, middle
Mjesto	Serbo-Croat	Town
Monasterio/Moni	Spanish/Greek	Monastery
Mont/Monte	French/Italian, Portuguese, Spanish	Mountain
Montagne(s)	French	Mountain(s)
Monti	Italian	Mountains
Moor	German	Bog, moor, swamp
Moos	German	Bog, moss
More	Russian	Sea
Mörön	Mongolian	River
Morro	Portuguese	Hill, mountain
-mose	Danish	Bog, moor
Moyen, -ne	French	Middle, mid-
Muara	Indonesian	Estuary
Mudiriyat	Arabic	Province
Muntii	Romanian	Mountains
-myr	Norwegian, Swedish	Moor, swamp
Mys	Russian	Cape
na	Bulgarian, Russian, Serbo-Croat	On
nad	Czech, Polish, Russian	Above, over
-nada	Japanese	Gulf, sea
Nádrz	Czech	Reservoir
-naes	Danish	Cape, point
Nafud	Arabic	Desert, dune
Nagor'ye	Russian	Highland, uplands
Nagy-	Hungarian	Big, great
Nahr	Arabic	River
Nakhon	Thai	Town
Nam	Korean, Vietnamese	South, southern
Nam	Burmese, Thai, Vietnamese	River
Nan	Chinese	South, southern
Naqb	Arabic	Pass
Nasb	Arabic	Hill, mountain
Né-a, -on, -os	Greek	New
Neder-	Flemish	Lower
Nehri	Turkish	River
Nei	Chinese	Inner
-nes	Icelandic, Norwegian	Cape, point
Neu-/Neuf, Neuve	German/French	New
Nevado	Spanish	Peak
-ni	Korean	Village
Nieder-	German	Lower
Nieu	Afrikaans	New
Nieuw, -e, -en, -er	Flemish	New
Nishi	Japanese	West, western
-nísi	Greek	Island
Nizhn-eye, -iy, -iye, -yaya	Russian	Lower
Nizina/Nizni	Czech	Lowland/Lower
Nizmennost'	Russian	Lowland
Noord-	Flemish	North, northern
Nord	Danish, French, German	North, northern
Nordre, Nørre	Danish	Northern
Norra	Swedish	Northern
Norte	Portuguese, Spanish	North
Nos	Bulgarian, Russian	Point, spit
Nótios	Greek	Southern
Nou	Romanian	New
Nouv-eau, -elle	French	New
Nova	Italian	New
Nova, Novi	Bulgarian, Serbo-Croat	New
Nova, Novo	Portuguese	New
Nová, Nové, Novy	Czech	New
Nov-aya, -o, -oye, -yy, -yye	Russian	New
Nowa, Nowe, Nowy	Polish	New
Nudo	Spanish	Mountain
Nueva, Nuevo	Spanish	New
Nuruu	Mongolian	Mountains
Nusa	Indonesian	Island
Nuur	Mongolian	Lake
Ny-	Danish, Norwegian, Swedish	New
-ö, -ön/-ø	Swedish/Danish	Island
-oaivi, -oaivve	Lappish	Hill, mountain
Ober-	German	Upper
Oblast'	Russian	Province
Occidental	Spanish	Western
-odde	Danish, Norwegian	Cape, point
Ogla, Oglet	Arabic	Well
Okrug	Russian	District
Ömnö-	Mongolian	South, southern
Onder	Flemish	Lower
Öndör-	Mongolian	Upper
-oog	German	Island
Oost, -er, -elijk	Flemish	East, eastern
Orasu	Romanian	Town
Oriental, -e	French, Romanian, Spanish	Eastern
Ormani	Turkish	Forest
Órmos	Greek	Bay
Óros/Óri	Greek	Mountain/Mtns.
Ost-/Øster-	German/Danish, Norweg.	East, eastern
Ostan	Persian	Province
Östra-	Swedish	East, eastern
Ostrov(a)	Russian	Island(s)
Otok/Otoci	Serbo-Croat	Island/Islands
Oud, -e, -en, -er	Flemish	Old
Oued	Arabic	Dry river-bed
Ovasi	Turkish	Plain
Over-	Danish, Flemish	Upper
Över-, Övre-	Norwegian, Swedish	Upper
-øy, -a	Norwegian	Island
Ozero, Ozera	Russian	Lake, lakes
-pää	Finnish	Hill
Palai-á, -ó, Palió	Greek	Old
Parbat	Urdu	Mountain
Parc	French	Park
Pas	French	Low pass, strait
Paso	Spanish	Pass, strait
Pass/Passo	Spanish/Italian	Pass
Pays	French	Region
Pegunungan	Indonesian	Mountain range
Pélagos	Greek	Sea
Peña(s)	Spanish	Cliff(s), rocks(s)
Pendi	Chinese	Basin
Penisola	Italian	Peninsula
Peñon	Spanish	Cliff
Pereval	Russian	Pass
Perv-o, -yy	Russian	First
Peski	Russian	Sands, desert
Petit, -e, -es	French	Little
Pic	French, Spanish	Peak, summit
Pico/Picacho	Portuguese, Spanish	Peak, summit
Pik	Russian	Peak, summit
Pingyuan	Chinese	Plain
Pizzo	Italian	Peak, summit
-plaat	Dutch	Sandbank, shoal
Plage	French	Beach
Plaine/Planicie	French/Spanish	Plain
Plaj(i)	Turkish	Beach(es)
Planalto	Portuguese	Plateau
Planina	Bulgarian, Serbo-Croat	Mountains
Platja/Playa	Catalan/Spanish	Beach
Plato	Afrikaans, Bulg., Russian	Plateau
Platte	German	Plateau, plain
Plosina	Czech	Tableland
Ploskogor'ye	Russian	Plateau
pod	Czech, Russian	Under
Pohor-í, -ie	Czech	Mountain range
Pointe	French	Cape, point
Poluostrov	Russian	Peninsula
Pólwysep	Polish	Peninsula
Pongo	Spanish	Water gap
Ponta, Pontal	Portuguese	Point
Portile	Romanian	Gate
Portillo	Spanish	Gap, pass
Porto	Catalan, Italian, Portug.	Harbour, port
Pradesh	Hindi	State
Praia	Portuguese	Beach, shore
près	French	Near
Presqu'île	French	Peninsula
Pri-	Russian	Near
Proliv	Russian	Strait

See also... Appendix 6: Glossary of Climate Terms (196)

*The listings above refer to a selection of related themes.
For more information, see the Contents (2-7).*

Protoka	Russian	Channel
Prusmyk	Czech	Pass
Przelecz	Polish	Pass
Pubu	Chinese	Waterfall
Pueblo	Spanish	Village
Puente	Spanish	Bridge
Puerta	Spanish	Narrow pass
Puerto	Spanish	Harbour, port
Puk-	Korean	North, northern
Pulau	Indonesian, Malay	Island
Puna	Spanish	Desert plateau
Punta	Catalan, Italian, Spanish	Cape, point
Puntjak	Indonesian	Mountain
Puy	French	Peak
Qa	Arabic	Depression
Qalamat, Qalib	Arabic	Well
Qanat	Arabic, Persian	U'ground conduit
Qararat	Arabic	Depression
Qâret	Arabic	Hill
Qiao	Chinese	Bridge
Qiuling	Chinese	Hills
Qoz	Arabic	Hill
Qu	Tibetan	Stream
Quan	Chinese	Spring
Quedas	Portuguese	Rapids
Qulban	Arabic	Wells
Qum	Persian	Sand
Qundao	Chinese	Archipelago
Qûr, Qurayyat	Arabic	Hills
Qurnat	Arabic	Peak
Quwayrat/Qurûn	Arabic	Hill/Hills
Ramlat	Arabic	Sands
Râs/Ra's	Arabic/Arabic, Persian	Cape, point
Raso	Portuguese	Upland
Ravnina/Razlivy	Russian	Plain
Região	Portuguese	Region
Reprêsa	Portuguese	Dam
Reshteh	Persian	Mountain range
-retto	Japanese	Island chain
-rev	Norwegian	Cliff, reef
Ri	Tibetan	Mountain
-ri	Korean	Village
Ria/Ría	Portuguese/Spanish	River-mouth
Ribeirão	Portuguese	River
Ribeiro	Portuguese	Stream
Rio/Río	Portuguese/Spanish	River
Rivier/Rivière	Afrikaans/French	River
Rocher	French	Cliff, rock
Rocque	French	Rock
Rt	Serbo-Croat	Cape, point
Rücken	German	Ridge
Rud, Rudkhaneh	Persian	River
Rudohorie	Czech	Mountains
-saari	Finnish	Island
Sabkhat	Arabic	Salt-flat
Sagar, Sagara	Hindi	Lake
Sahl	Arabic	Plain
Sahra	Arabic	Desert
-saki	Japanese	Cape, point
Salada/Salar, Salina	Spanish	Salt lake/Salt pan
Salto	Portuguese, Spanish	Waterfall
-san	Japanese, Korean	Mountain
-sanchi	Japanese	Mountainous area
Saniyat	Arabic	Well
Sanmaek	Korean	Mountain range
-sanmyaku	Japanese	Mountain range
San	Italian, Portug., Spanish	Saint
Sankt/Sant	German/Catalan	Saint
Santa, Santo	Italian, Portug., Spanish	Saint
São	Portuguese	Saint
Satu	Romanian	Village
Schloss	German	Castle, mansion
Schutzgebeit	German	Reserve
Sebkra	Arabic	Salt-flat
See	German	Lake
-sehir	Turkish	Town
Selat	Indonesian	Channel, strait
Selatan	Indonesian, Malay	South, southern
-selkä	Finnish	Open water, ridge
Selo	Russian, Serbo-Croat	Village
Selva	Spanish	Forest, wood
-sen	Japanese	Mountain
Serra/Serrania	Catalan, Portug./Span.	Mountain range
-seto	Japanese	Channel, strait
Sever-naya, -noye, -nyy, -o	Russian	North, northern
Sfîntu	Romanian	Saint
Shahr	Persian	Town
Sha'ib, -an	Arabic	Watercourse
Shamo	Chinese	Desert
Shan	Chinese	Mountain(s)
Shandi	Chinese	Mountainous area
Shang	Chinese	Upper
Shankou	Chinese	Pass
Shanmai	Chinese	Mountain range
Sharm	Arabic	Cove, inlet
Shatt	Arabic	River, river-mouth

-shima/-shoto	Japanese	Island/Island group
Shuiku	Chinese	Reservoir
Sierra	Spanish	Mountain range
Silsilesi	Turkish	Mountain range
Sint	Afrikaans, Flemish	Saint
-sjø/sjön	Norwegian/Swedish	Lake
Skala, Skaly	Czech	Cliff, rock
-skog	Norwegian	Woods
-slette	Norwegian	Plain
Sliabh, Slieve	Gaelic	Mountain, upland
Sloboda	Russian	Suburb, large village
Sø	Danish, Norwegian	Lake
Söder-, Södra	Swedish	Southern
Solonchak	Russian	Salt lake
Sommet	French	Peak, summit
Sønder-	Danish	Southern
Søndre	Danish, Norwegian	Southern
Sopka	Russian	Hill
Sør	Norwegian	Southern
sous	French	Under
Spitze	German	Peak
Sredn-a, -i	Bulgarian	Central, middle
Sredn-e, -eye, -iy, -yaya	Russian	Central, middle
-stad	Afrikaans, Norwegian, Swedish	Town
-stadt	German	Town
Stara, Stari	Serbo-Croat	Old
Stará, Staré	Czech	Old
Star-aya, oye, -yy, -yye	Russian	Old
Stausee	German	Reservoir
Stenó	Greek	Pass, strait
Step'	Russian	Steppe
Stít	Czech	Peak
Stor-, Stora/Store	Swedish/Danish	Big
Strand	Gaelic, German	Beach
-strand	Danish, Norwegian, Swedish	Beach
Strasse	German	Road
-strede	Norwegian	Passage, strait
Strelka	Russian	Spit
Stretto	Italian	Strait
Sud	French	South
Süd(er)	German	South (southern)
Suhul	Arabic	Plain
Suid	Afrikaans	South
-suido	Japanese	Channel, strait
Sul	Portuguese	South
sul, sull'	Italian	On
Sund	Swedish	Sound, strait
Sungai	Indonesian, Malay	River
-suo	Finnish	Marsh, swamp
Supérieur/Superior	French/Spanish	Upper
Sur	Spanish	South
sur	French	On
Sveti	Serbo-Croat	Saint
Szent-	Hungarian	Saint
-take	Japanese	Peak
Tal	German	Valley
Tall(ât)	Arabic	Hill(s)
Tang	Persian	Pass, strait
Tanjung	Indonesian, Malay	Cape, point
Taraq	Arabic	Hills
Tasek	Malay	Lake
Tau	Russian	Mountain(s)
Tekojärvi	Finnish	Reservoir
Tell	Arabic	Hill
Teluk	Indonesian	Bay
Tengah	Indonesian	Middle
Teniet	Arabic	Pass
Tepe, Tepesi	Turkish	Hill, peak
Tepeler, Tepeleri	Turkish	Hills, peaks
Terre/Tierra	French/Spanish	Land
Thale	Thai	Lake
Tilat	Arabic	Hill
Timur	Indonesian	East, eastern
-tind, -tinderne	Norwegain	Peak, peaks
Tir'at	Arabic	Canal
-tji	Indonesian	Stream
-to	Japanese	Island
-toge	Japanese	Pass
-tong	Korean	Village
Tonle	Cambodian	Lake
-topp	Norwegian	Peak
Torrente	Spanish	Rapids
Travesía	Spanish	Desert
Tulul	Arabic	Hills
Túnel	Spanish	Tunnel
über	German	Above
-udden	Swedish	Cape, point
Új-	Hungarian	New
Ujung	Indonesian	Cape, point
-umi	Japanese	Inlet
Unter-	German	Lower
'Uqlat	Arabic	Well
-ura	Japanese	Inlet
'Urayq	Arabic	Sand ridge
'Uruq	Arabic	Area of dunes

Ust'ye	Russian	Estuary
Utara	Indonesian	North, northern
Uttar	Hindi	Northern
Uul	Mongolian	Mountains
Uval	Russian	Hill
'Uyun	Arabic	Springs
-vaara(t)	Finnish	Hill(s)
-vaart	Flemish	Canal
-våg	Norwegian	Bay
Val, Vall	Italian, Spanish	Valley
Vale	Portuguese, Romanian	Valley
Valle/Vallée	Italian, Spanish/French	Valley
Vallon	French	Small valley
-vann	Norwegian	Lake
-város	Hungarian	Town
-varre	Norwegian	Mountain
Väster, Västra	Swedish	Western
-vatn	Icelandic, Norwegian	Lake
-vatnet	Norwegian	Lake
-vatten, vattnet	Swedish	Lake
Vaux	French	Valleys
Vecchio	Italian	Old
Vechi	Romanian	Old
Velha, Velho	Portuguese	Old
Velik-a, -i	Serbo-Croat	Big
Velik-aya, -iy, -iye	Russian	Big
Vel'k-á, -é, -y	Czech	Big
Verkhn-e, -eye, -iy, -yaya	Russian	Upper
-vesi	Finnish	Lake, water
Vester	Danish	Western
Vest, Vestre	Norwegian	West, western
-vidda	Norwegian	Plateau
Vieja, Viejo/ Vieux	Spanish/French	Old
Vig/-vik	Danish/Norwegian	Bay
Vila	Portuguese	Small town
Ville	French	Town
Víztároló	Hungarian	Reservoir
Vodokhranilishche	Russian	Reservoir
Volcán	Spanish	Volcano
Vorota	Russian	Channel, strait
Vostochn-aya, -oye, -yy	Russian	Eastern
Vozvyshennost'	Russian	Uplands
Vpadina	Russian	Depression
Vrch(y)	Czech	Mountain(s)
Vrchovina	Czech	Mountainous area
Vysocina	Czech	Upland
Vysok-aya, -oye	Russian	Upper
Wad	Flemish	Sand-flat
Wâdi, Wadi	Arabic	Watercourse
Wahat	Arabic	Oasis
Wai	Chinese	Outer
Wald	German	Forest
Wan/-wan	Chinese/Japanese	Bay
Wand	German	Cliff
Wasser	German	Lake, water
Wes-	Afrikaans	West
West, Wester	Flemish, German	West
Wielk-a, -i, -ie, -o	Polish	Big
Wysok-a, -i, -ie	Polish	Upper
Xi	Chinese	Stream, west
Xia	Chinese	Gorge, lower
Xian	Chinese	County
Xiao	Chinese	Small
Xu	Chinese	Islet
-yama	Japanese	Mountain(s)
Yang	Chinese	Ocean
Yarimadasi	Turkish	Peninsula
Yeni	Turkish	New
Yli-	Finnish	Upper
Ytre-	Norwegian	Outer
Ytter-	Norwegian, Swedish	Outer
Yuan	Chinese	Spring
Yugo-	Russian	Southern
Yunhe	Chinese	Canal
Yuzhn-aya, -o, -oye, -yy	Russian	South, southern
-zaki	Japanese	Cape, point
Zalew	Polish	Bay, inlet, lagoon
Zaliv	Russian	Bay
-zan	Japanese	Mountain
Zapadn-aya, -o, -oye, -yy	Russian	West, western
Zatoka	Polish	Gulf
-zee	Flemish	Sea
Zemlya	Russian	Land
-zhen	Chinese	Town
Zhong	Chinese	Middle
Zhou	Chinese	Islet
Zui	Chinese	Point, spit
Zuid	Flemish	South
Zuid-elijk, er	Flemish	Southern

▶ *See also...* Climate maps (16, 57, 115, 127, 155, 186); Urbanization (20); Appendix 4: Glossary of Foreign Geographical Terms (193-195)

The listings above refer to a selection of related themes. For more information, see the Contents (2-7).

6: Glossary of Regional Climate Terms

An alphabetical list of all the terms featured on the regional climate maps.

Benguela Current *Africa maps*
A cold current flowing north along the west coast of South Africa, cooling the coastal region.

Berg Wind *Africa May–October map*
A hot dry wind which blows from the interior to the coastal regions of Namibia and South Africa.

Bora *Europe Winter map*
A cold dry wind which blows from the N and NE, affecting the Adriatic coastlines of Croatia, Italy and Slovenia.

California Current *North America Summer map*
A cold current which flows south along the west coast of California and Mexico, cooling the coastal region, and responsible for the frequent sea fogs particularly during the summer.

Canary Current *Africa maps*
An extension of the North Atlantic Drift (qv), flowing south along the NW Africa coast and moderating temperatures in the coastal region.

Chinook *North America Winter map*
A warm dry wind which blows down the eastern slopes of the Rockies, rapidly melting lying snow.

Crachin *Asia November–April map*
Light rain in the northern mountains and coastal regions of Vietnam.

Cyclone *Asia November–April map*
Tropical cyclones (qv) in the SW Indian Ocean are simply called cyclones. The season lasts from November to May.

El Niño *South America maps*
A change in the ocean-atmosphere system in the Pacific, increasing water temperatures in the central and eastern equatorial Pacific Ocean and bringing rain to the NW coast of South America. A periodic phenomenon, it often affects the western coast of America as far north as California. In some years the weather pattern of the whole American continent can be disrupted, and in exceptional years its effects can be experienced worldwide.

Etesian Wind / Meltemi *Europe Winter map*
A wind blowing from the N and NW in the eastern Mediterranean and the Aegean, often creating rough seas.

Föhn *Europe Winter map*
A wind which blows down Alpine valleys, warming as it descends, and melts snow rapidly.

Garúa *South America November–April map*
A heavy mist on the Pacific slope of the Andes in a normally very dry part of the coast.

Ghibli *Africa May–October map*
Local name for the Sirocco (qv) in Libya.

Guinea Monsoon *Africa May–October map*
Warm humid winds blowing from the SW in West Africa between April and September, associated with the rainy season.

Gulf Stream *North America Summer map*
A warm current which flows NE from the Gulf of Mexico. After passing Newfoundland, it divides and follows three separate routes: 1. northwest towards Europe (the North Atlantic Drift (qv)); 2. southeast; 3. recirculating around an area north of Bermuda.

Harmattan *Africa November–April map*
A dry and dusty NE wind in West Africa blowing from the Sahara, associated with the dry season; cool at night and warm in the day. Opposite of the Guinea Monsoon (qv).

Hurricane *North America Summer map*
The name used for a tropical cyclone (qv) in the N Atlantic and NE Pacific Oceans. The Atlantic hurricane season lasts from June to November, the peak period being August to October. The NE Pacific season is from June to October. For more information on N Atlantic hurricanes, see the N America climate page. (The term is also used in the Beaufort Scale of wind speed: force 12 and above).

Kharif *Asia May–October map*
The rainy season in northern India and Arab countries.

Khamsin / Sharav *Africa May–October map*
A hot dry wind blowing from the S and SE in the eastern Mediterranean, warming the coastal region and helping to create dust storms and a hazy atmosphere.

Labrador Current *North America Summer map*
A cold current flowing south along the east coast of Canada, carrying icebergs and keeping the coastal region relatively cool druing the summer; fogs are caused off the Newfoundland coast where the current meets the warmer Gulf Stream flowing NE from the Gulf of Mexico.

La Niña *South America maps*
The opposite phenomenon to El Niño. Warm surface water flows towards Asia and colder water from the ocean depths moves to the surface in the eastern equatorial Pacific. Evaporation decreases and rainfall in the region is reduced. Often La Niña occurs the year after El Niño, with drought affecting the areas which experienced flooding the year before.

Leveche *Europe Winter map*
A hot, dry and dusty wind in southern Spain which blows from the Sahara.

Mistral *Europe Winter map*
A strong cold dry wind blowing from the north in southern France; known as Cers in Aude département.

Monsoon Winds *Asia maps*
Seasonal winds which change direction during the year; during the dry season in India the NE monsoon blows dry air from the land and during the wet season the SW monsoon blows humid air from the ocean, bringing heavy rain (**Monsoon Rains**). The term is also used in Africa and Australasia.

Mozambique Current / Agulhas Current *Africa May–October map*
A warm current flowing south and west along the coast of Mozambique and eastern South Africa, warming the coastal region.

North Atlantic Drift *Europe Winter map*
An extension of the Gulf Stream (qv) which helps to maintain relatively mild winters in the British Isles and along the Norwegian coast.

Peru Current / Humboldt Current *South America maps*
A cold current flowing north along the west coast of South America and cooling the coastal region as far as the Equator.

Severe Cyclonic Storm *Asia maps*
The name used for a tropical cyclone (qv) in the N Indian Ocean, most likely to occur in May-June & Oct-Nov (Arabian Sea) and Apr-May & Oct-Dec (Bay of Bengal).

Severe Tropical Cyclone *Asia November–April map*
The name used for a tropical cyclone (qv) in the SW Pacific Ocean, peak period December to March and the SE Indian Ocean, where it is also known as a Willy-Willy (qv), peak period January-March.

Shamal *Africa May–October map*
A hot dry wind which blows from the NW in Iraq and The Gulf.

Sirocco *Europe Summer map*
A hot dusty wind blowing towards Europe from north Africa. Known as the Ghibli (qv) in Libya and Leveche (qv) in Spain. Its origins are the same as the Khamsin (qv) or Sharav (qv). On the northern Mediterranean coast, particularly in southern Italy, the wind is moist after crossing the Mediterranean.

Tropical Cyclone *Asia and North America maps*
A storm with low atmospheric pressure at the centre and strong winds blowing around it, accompanied by a great deal of precipitation. It rotates anticlockwise in the northern hemisphere and clockwise in the southern. The central area has light winds and higher temperatures (the 'eye'), feeling oppresive after the strong winds preceding it, but is soon followed by even stronger winds in the opposite direction. Temperate cyclones are much less violent and are usually called depressions or lows. Tropical cyclones which reach winds of at least 17 metres/second (39mph) they are called tropical storms and assigned a name. If winds reach 33 metres/second (74mph) they are called in different parts of the world: hurricane, typhoon, severe tropical cyclone, severe cyclonic storm, willy-willy or simply cyclone.

Typhoon *Asia May-October map*
The term for a tropical cyclone (qv) in the NW Pacific and the China Seas. The typhoon season lasts from May to January but most occur between July and October.

Willy-Willy *Asia November–April map*
The name used for a tropical cyclone (qv) affecting the coasts of northern Australia. Likely to occur between December to April, the peak period is January to March.

7: The World's Major Urban Areas

The list shows the world's largest urban agglomerations, with UN estimates of their population in 2005. The UN defines the term 'urban agglomeration' as a contiguous area inhabited at a density regarded as urban, ignoring administrative boundaries.

The ten largest cities in 1900 and in 1800 are listed at the foot of the page.

Urban area & country	*Pop. ('000)*
Tokyo-Kawasaki-Yokohama, Japan	35,327
Mexico City, Mexico	19,013
New York-Newark, NY, USA	18,498
Mumbai (Bombay), India	18,336
São Paulo, Brazil	18,333
Delhi, India	15,334
Kolkata (Calcutta), India	14,299
Buenos Aires, Argentina	13,349
Jakarta, Indonesia	13,194
Shanghai, China	12,665
Dhaka, Bangladesh	12,560
Los Angeles-Long Beach-Santa Ana, CA, USA	12,146
Karachi, Pakistan	11,819
Rio de Janeiro, Brazil	11,469
Osaka-Kobe, Japan	11,286
Cairo, Egypt	11,146
Lagos, Nigeria	11,135
Beijing, China	10,849
Metro Manila, the Philippines	10,677
Moscow, Russian Fed.	10,672
Paris, France	9,854
Istanbul, Turkey	9,760
Seoul, Rep. of Korea	9,592
Tianjin, China	9,346
Chicago, IL, USA	8,711
Lima, Peru	8,180
London, United Kingdom	7,615
Bogotá, Colombia	7,594
Tehran, Iran	7,352
Hong Kong, China	7,182
Chennai (Madras), India	6,915
Bangkok, Thailand	6,604
Rhine-Ruhr North, Germany *Bochum-Dortmund-Duisburg-Essen*	6,559
Bangalore, India	6,532
Lahore, Pakistan	6,373
Hyderabad, India	6,145
Wuhan, China	6,003
Baghdad, Iraq	5,910
Kinshasa, Dem. Rep. of Congo	5,717
Santiago, Chile	5,623
Riyadh, Saudi Arabia	5,514
Miami, FL, USA	5,380
Philadelphia, PA, USA	5,325
St Petersburg, Russian Fed	5,315
Belo Horizonte, Brazil	5,304
Ahmadabad, India	5,171
Madrid, Spain	5,145
Toronto, OT, Canada	5,060
Ho Chi Minh City, Vietnam	5,030
Chongqing, China	4,975
Shenyang, China	4,916
Dallas-Fort Worth, TX, USA	4,612
Khartoum, Sudan	4,495
Pune (Poona), India	4,485
Barcelona, Spain	4,424
Sydney, NS, Australia	4,388
Singapore	4,372
Boston, MA, USA	4,313
Atlanta, GA, USA	4,284
Houston, TX, USA	4,283
Washington, DC, USA	4,190
Chittagong, Bangladesh	4,171
Hanoi, Vietnam	4,147
Yangon (Rangoon), Myanmar	4,082
Bandung, Indonesia	4,020
Milan, Italy	4,007

Urban area & country	*Pop. ('000)*
Detroit, MI, USA	3,980
Ankara, Turkey	3,953
Guadalajara, Mexico	3,905
Guangzhou, China	3,881
Jeddah, Saudi Arabia	3,807
Pôrto Alegre, Brazil	3,795
Alexandria, Egypt	3,760
Casablanca, Morocco	3,743
Rhine-Main, Germany *Frankfurt-Darmstadt-Wiesbaden*	3,700
Surat, India	3,671
Melbourne, VI, Australia	3,663
Busan, Rep. of Korea	3,527
Recife, Brazil	3,527
Monterrey, Mexico	3,517
Abidjan, Côte d'Ivoire	3,516
Montréal, QU, Canada	3,511
Chengdu, China	3,478
Phoenix-Mesa, AZ, USA	3,393
San Francisco-Oakland, CA, USA	3,342
Brasília, Brazil	3,341
Salvador, Brazil	3,331
Berlin, Germany	3,328
Rhine-Ruhr Middle, Germany *Düsseldorf-Mönchenglad.-Wuppertal*	3,325
Johannesburg, South Africa	3,288
Kabul, Afghanistan	3,288
Pyongyang, DPR of Korea	3,284
Caracas, Venezuela	3,276
Fortaleza, Brazil	3,261
Algiers, Algeria	3,260
Xi'an, China	3,256
Athens, Greece	3,238
Medellín, Colombia	3,236
Nagoya, Japan	3,189
Cape Town, South Africa	3,103
Changchun, China	3,092
Rhine-Ruhr South, Germany *Bonn-Cologne-Leverkusen*	3,084
East Rand (Ekurhuleni), S. Africa	3,043
Kanpur, India	3,040
Tel Aviv-Yafo, Israel	3,025
Seattle, WA, USA	2,959
Katowice, Poland	2,914
Naples, Italy	2,905
Addis Ababa, Ethiopia	2,899
Harbin, China	2,898
Kano, Nigeria	2,884
Curitiba, Brazil	2,871
Luanda, Angola	2,839
San Diego, CA, USA	2,818
Fukuoka-Kitakyushu, Japan	2,815
Nanjing, China	2,806
Jaipur, India	2,796
Zibo, China	2,775
Surabaya, Indonesia	2,735
Dalian, China	2,709
Stuttgart, Germany	2,705
Hamburg, Germany	2,686
Dar es Salaam, Tanzania	2,683
Jinan, China	2,654
Durban, South Africa	2,643
Incheon, Rep. of Korea	2,642
Campinas, Brazil	2,640
Rome, Italy	2,628
Kiev, Ukraine	2,623
Lucknow, India	2,589
Cali, Colombia	2,583
Faisalabad, Pakistan	2,533

1900:

London, United Kingdom	6,500
New York, USA	4,200
Paris, France	3,300
Berlin, Germany	2,700
Chicago, USA	1,700
Vienna, Austro-Hungarian Empire	1,700
Tokyo, Japan	1,500
St Petersburg, Russia	1,400
Manchester, United Kingdom	1,400
Philadelphia, USA	1,400

1800:

Peking, China	1,100
London, Great Britain	900
Canton, China	800
Tokyo (Edo), Japan	700
Constantinople, Ottoman Empire	600
Paris, France	550
Naples, Kingdom of Naples	450
Hangchow, China	400
Osaka, Japan	380
Kyoto, Japan	380

▶ *See also...* Time (18-19); France (86-89); Russia (111); China (136-138); Australia (147-148); USA (161-171); Canada (172-175)

The listings above refer to a selection of related themes. For more information, see the Contents (2-7).

8: US States

ISO‡ abbrev.	*State*	*Nickname*	*Date of admission to the Union*	*State Capital*
AL	**Alabama**	Heart of Dixie	14th Dec 1819	Montgomery
AK	**Alaska**	The Last Frontier	3rd Jan 1959	Juneau
AZ	**Arizona**	Grand Canyon State	14th Feb 1912	Phoenix
AR	**Arkansas**	The Natural State	15th June 1836	Little Rock
CA	**California**	Golden State	9th Sept 1850	Sacramento
CO	**Colorado**	Centennial State	1st Aug 1876	Denver
CT	**Connecticut**	Constitution State	9th Jan 1788 †	Hartford
DE	**Delaware**	First State / Diamond State	7th Dec 1787 †	Dover
DC	**District of Columbia** *(Federal District, coextensive with the city of Washington)*			
FL	**Florida**	Sunshine State	3rd Mar 1845	Tallahassee
GA	**Georgia**	Empire State of the South / Peach State	2nd Jan 1788 †	Atlanta
HI	**Hawaii**	Aloha State	21st Aug 1959	Honolulu
ID	**Idaho**	Gem State	3rd July 1890	Boise
IL	**Illinois**	Land of Lincoln	3rd Dec 1818	Springfield
IN	**Indiana**	Hoosier State	11th Dec 1816	Indianapolis
IA	**Iowa**	Hawkeye State	28th Dec 1846	Des Moines
KS	**Kansas**	Sunflower State	29th Jan 1861	Topeka
KY	**Kentucky**	Bluegrass State	1st June 1792	Frankfort
LA	**Louisiana**	Pelican State	30th Apr 1812	Baton Rouge
ME	**Maine**	Pine Tree State	15th Mar 1820	Augusta
MD	**Maryland**	Old Line State	28th Apr 1788 †	Annapolis
MA	**Massachusetts**	Bay State	6th Feb 1788 †	Boston
MI	**Michigan**	Great Lakes State	26th Jan 1837	Lansing
MN	**Minnesota**	Gopher State / North Star State	11th May 1858	St Paul
MS	**Mississippi**	Magnolia State	10th Dec 1817	Jackson
MO	**Missouri**	Show Me State	10th Aug 1821	Jefferson City
MT	**Montana**	Treasure State	8th Nov 1889	Helena
NE	**Nebraska**	Cornhusker State	1st Mar 1867	Lincoln
NV	**Nevada**	Silver State	31st Oct 1864	Carson City
NH	**New Hampshire**	Granite State	21st June 1788 †	Concord
NJ	**New Jersey**	Garden State	18th Dec 1787 †	Trenton
NM	**New Mexico**	Land of Enchantment	6th Jan 1912	Santa Fe
NY	**New York**	Empire State	26th July 1788 †	Albany
NC	**North Carolina**	Tar Heel State	21st Nov 1789 †	Raleigh
ND	**North Dakota**	Flickertail State / Peace Garden State	2nd Nov 1889	Bismarck
OH	**Ohio**	Buckeye State	1st Mar 1803	Columbus
OK	**Oklahoma**	Sooner State	16th Nov 1907	Oklahoma City
OR	**Oregon**	Beaver State	14th Feb 1859	Salem
PA	**Pennsylvania**	Keystone State	12th Dec 1787 †	Harrisburg
RI	**Rhode Island**	Ocean State	29th May 1790 †	Providence
SC	**South Carolina**	Palmetto State	23rd May 1788 †	Columbia
SD	**South Dakota**	Mount Rushmore State	2nd Nov 1889	Pierre
TN	**Tennessee**	Volunteer State	1st June 1796	Nashville
TX	**Texas**	Lone Star State	29th Dec 1845	Austin
UT	**Utah**	Beehive State	4th Jan 1896	Salt Lake City
VT	**Vermont**	Green Mountain State	4th Mar 1791	Montpelier
VA	**Virginia**	Old Dominion State	25th June 1788 †	Richmond
WA	**Washington**	Evergreen State	11th Nov 1889	Olympia
WV	**West Virginia**	Mountain State	20th June 1863	Charleston
WI	**Wisconsin**	Badger State	29th May 1848	Madison
WY	**Wyoming**	Cowboy State / Equality State	10th July 1890	Cheyenne

† Original 13 states: date of ratification of the Constitution.

9: Canadian Provinces & Territories

ISO‡ abbrev.	*State*	*Language**	*Date of admission to the Dominion*	*State Capital*
AB	**Alberta**	English	1st Sept 1905	Edmonton
BC	**British Columbia**	English	20th July 1871	Victoria
MB	**Manitoba**	English	15th July 1870	Winnipeg
NB	**New Brunswick**	English †	1st July 1867	Fredericton
NL	**Newfoundland and Labrador**	English	31st March 1949	St John's
NT	**Northwest Territories**	English	1870	Yellowknife
NS	**Nova Scotia**	English	1st July 1867	Halifax
NU	**Nunavut** *(Territory)*	Inuktitut **	1st April 1999	Iqaluit
ON	**Ontario**	English	1st July 1867	Toronto
PE	**Prince Edward Island**	English	1st July 1873	Charlottetown
QC	**Québec**	French	1st July 1867	Québec
SK	**Saskatchewan**	English	1st Sept 1905	Regina
YT	**Yukon Territory**	English	13th June 1898	Whitehorse

** Although Canada is officially bilingual (English & French), this column indicates the most commonly-spoken language in each region. † Approx. 35% of the population are French-speaking. ** The language of the Inuit.*

10: Australian States & Territories

ISO‡ abbrev.	*State*	*Nickname*	*Date of granting of responsible gov't*	*State Capital*
AC	**Australian Capital Territory**	Nation's Capital	1911	Canberra *
CL	**Coral Sea Territory** *(External Territory bordering the Queensland coast and Gt. Barrier Reef)*			
NS	**New South Wales**	Premier State	1788 †	Sydney
NT	**Northern Territory**	Outback Australia	1911 **	Darwin
QL	**Queensland**	Sunshine State	1859	Brisbane
SA	**South Australia**	Festival State	1856	Adelaide
TS	**Tasmania**	Holiday Isle	1856	Hobart
VI	**Victoria**	Garden State	1855	Melbourne
WA	**Western Australia**	State of Excitement	1890	Perth

** Canberra became the seat of the Australian government on 9th May 1927. † Date of first settlement: New South Wales originally covered the whole island with the exception of Western Australia. ** Transferred to Commonwealth from South Australia in 1911, self-government within the Commonwealth granted 1978.*

11: Russian Republics (and other administrative areas)

State	*Capital*
Adygeya	Maykop
Altay	Gorno-Altaysk
Bashkortostan	Ufa
Buryatia	Ulan-Ude
Chechnya	Groznyy
Chuvashia	Cheboksary
Dagestan	Makhachkala
Ingushetia	Nazran'
Kabardino-Balkaria	Nal'chik
Kalmykia	Elitsa
Karachay-Cherkessia	Cherkessk
Karelia	Petrozavodsk
Khakassia	Abakan
Komi	Syktyvkar
Mari-El	Yoshkar-Ola
Mordovia	Saransk
North Ossetia (Alania)	Vladikavkaz
Sakha (Yakutia)	Yakutsk
Tatarstan	Kazan'
Tuva	Kyzyl
Udmurtia	Izhevsk
AUTONOMOUS AREAS & REGIONS:	
Agin-Buryat	Aginskoye
Chukot	Anadyr
Evenki	Tura
Khanty-Mansi	Khanty-Mansiysk
Komi-Permyak	Kudymkar
Koryak	Palana
Nenets	Nar'yan-Mar
Taymyr	Dudinka
Ust'-Ordyn-Buryat	Ust'-Ordynskiy
Yamalo-Nenets	Salekhard
Jewish Autonomous Region	Birobidzhan

12: Chinese Provinces (and other administrative areas)

ISO‡ abbrev.	*Type*	*Name*	*Capital*
AH	pr	**Anhui***	Hefei
BJ	mu	**Beijing**	–
CQ	mu	**Chongqing**	–
FJ	pr	**Fujian***	Fuzhou
GS	pr	**Gansu***	Lanzhou
GD	pr	**Guangdong***	Guangzhou
GX	au	**Guangxi Zhuang***	Nanning
GZ	pr	**Guizhou***	Guiyang
HI	pr	**Hainan**	Haikou
HE	pr	**Hebei***	Shijiazhuang
HL	pr	**Heilongjiang**	Harbin
HA	pr	**Henan***	Zhengzhou
HB	pr	**Hubei***	Wuhan
HK	sar	**Hong Kong**	–
HN	pr	**Hunan***	Changsha
JS	pr	**Jiangsu***	Nanjing
JX	pr	**Jiangxi***	Nanchang
JL	pr	**Jilin**	Changchun
LN	pr	**Liaoning**	Shenyang
MO	sar	**Macau**	–
NM	au	**Nei Mongol (Inner Mongolia)**	Hohhot
NX	au	**Ningxia Hui**	Yinchuan
QH	pr	**Qinghai**	Xining
SN	pr	**Shaanxi***	Xilan
SD	pr	**Shandong***	Jinan
SH	mu	**Shanghai**	–
SX	pr	**Shanxi***	Taiyuan
SC	pr	**Sichuan***	Chengdu
TJ	mu	**Tianjin**	–
XJ	au	**Xinjiang Uygur**	Ürümqi
XZ	au	**Xizang (Tibet)**	Lhasa
YN	pr	**Yunnan***	Kunming
ZJ	pr	**Zhejiang***	Hangzhou

** The traditional 18 provinces. pr = province. mu = municipality. au = autonomous region. sar = special autonomous region.*

13: French Départements

Dept. no.	*Département*	*Capital*
01	**Ain**	Bourg-en-Bresse
02	**Aisne**	Laon
03	**Allier**	Moulins
04	**Alpes-de-Hte-Provence**	Digne
05	**Hautes-Alpes**	Gap
06	**Alpes-Maritimes**	Nice
07	**Ardèche**	Privas
08	**Ardennes**	Charleville-Mézières
09	**Ariège**	Foix
10	**Aube**	Troyes
11	**Aude**	Carcassonne
12	**Aveyron**	Rodez
13	**Bouches-du-Rhône**	Marseille
14	**Calvados**	Caen
15	**Cantal**	Aurillac
16	**Charente**	Angoulême
17	**Charente-Maritime**	La Rochelle
18	**Cher**	Bourges
19	**Corrèze**	Tulle
20	**Corse-du-Sud** (2A)	Ajaccio
	Haute-Corse (2B)	Bastia
21	**Côte-d'Or**	Dijon
22	**Côtes-d'Armor**	St-Brieuc
23	**Creuse**	Guéret
24	**Dordogne**	Périgueux
25	**Doubs**	Besançon
26	**Drôme**	Valence
27	**Eure**	Évreux
28	**Eure-et-Loir**	Chartres
29	**Finistère**	Quimper
30	**Gard**	Nîmes
31	**Haute-Garonne**	Toulouse
32	**Gers**	Auch
33	**Gironde**	Bordeaux
34	**Hérault**	Montpellier
35	**Ille-et-Vilaine**	Rennes
36	**Indre**	Châteauroux
37	**Indre-et-Loire**	Tours
38	**Isère**	Grenoble
39	**Jura**	Lons-le-Saunier
40	**Landes**	Mont-de-Marsan
41	**Loir-et-Cher**	Blois
42	**Loire**	St-Étienne
43	**Haute-Loire**	Le Puy
44	**Loire-Atlantique**	Nantes
45	**Loiret**	Orléans
46	**Lot**	Cahors
47	**Lot-et-Garonne**	Agen
48	**Lozère**	Mende
49	**Maine-et-Loire**	Angers
50	**Manche**	St-Lô
51	**Marne**	Châlons-sur-Marne
52	**Haute-Marne**	Chaumont
53	**Mayenne**	Laval
54	**Meurthe-et-Moselle**	Nancy
55	**Meuse**	Bar-le-Duc
56	**Morbihan**	Vannes
57	**Moselle**	Metz
58	**Nièvre**	Nevers
59	**Nord**	Lille
60	**Oise**	Beauvais
61	**Orne**	Alençon
62	**Pas-de-Calais**	Arras
63	**Puy-de-Dôme**	Clermont-Ferrand
64	**Pyrénées-Atlantiques**	Pau
65	**Hautes-Pyrénées**	Tarbes
66	**Pyrénées-Orientales**	Perpignan
67	**Bas-Rhin**	Strasbourg
68	**Haut-Rhin**	Colmar
69	**Rhône**	Lyon
70	**Haute-Saône**	Vesoul
71	**Saône-et-Loire**	Mâcon
72	**Sarthe**	Le Mans
73	**Savoie**	Chambéry
74	**Haute-Savoie**	Annecy
75	**Paris**	Paris
76	**Seine-Maritime**	Rouen
77	**Seine-et-Marne**	Melun
78	**Yvelines** *(canton)*	Versailles
79	**Deux-Sèvres**	Niort
80	**Somme**	Amiens
81	**Tarn**	Albi
82	**Tarn-et-Garonne**	Montauban
83	**Var**	Toulon
84	**Vaucluse**	Avignon
85	**Vendée**	La Roche-sur-Yon
86	**Vienne**	Poitiers
87	**Haute-Vienne**	Limoges
88	**Vosges**	Épinal
89	**Yonne**	Auxerre
90	**Territoire-de-Belfort**	Belfort
91	**Essonne** *(canton)*	Évry
92	**Hauts-de-Seine** *(canton)*	Nanterre
93	**Seine-St-Denis** *(canton)*	Bobigny
94	**Val-de-Marne** *(canton)*	Créteil
95	**Val-d'Oise** *(canton)*	Cergy

‡ International Organisation for Standardisation.

▶ See also... UNESCO Natural Heritage (48-49); UNESCO Cultural Heritage (50-53)

The listings above refer to a selection of related themes. For more information, see the Contents (2-7).

14: The World's Tallest Buildings

Height is measured from the street level of the main entrance to the structural or architectural top of the building, including spires but excluding antennae and flag poles. The list shows the world's tallest traditional buildings (structures intended primarily for human habitation with the great majority of their height divided into occupiable levels). Buildings under construction, TV-tower hybrids and other structures not recognised as traditional buildings are excluded. The world's tallest freestanding structure is Toronto's CN Tower (553m).

Name & location	Height (m)	Date
Taipei 101, Taipei, Taiwan	509	2004
Petronas Tower 1, Kuala Lumpur, Malaysia	452	1998
Petronas Tower 2, Kuala Lumpur, Malaysia	452	1998
Sears Tower, Chicago, IL, USA	442	1974
Jin Mao Tower, Shanghai, China	421	1998
Two International Finance Cent., Hong Kong, China	415	2003
CITIC Plaza, Guangzhou, China	391	1997
Shun Hing Square, Shenzhen, China	384	1996
Empire State Building, New York, NY, USA	381	1931
Central Plaza, Hong Kong, China	374	1992
Bank of China Tower, Hong Kong, China	367	1990
Emirates Office Tower, Dubai, UAE	355	2000
Tuntex Sky Tower, Kaohsiung, Taiwan	348	1997
Aon Center, Chicago, IL, USA	346	1973
The Centre, Hong Kong, China	346	1998
John Hancock Center, Chicago, IL, USA	344	1969
Shimao International Plaza, Shanghai, China	333	2005
Wuhan International Securities Bldg, Wuhan, China	331	2005
Ryugyong Hotel, Pyongyang, DPR of Korea	330	1992
Q1 Tower, Surfers Paradise, QL, Australia	323	2005
Burj al Arab, Dubai, UAE	321	1999
Chrysler Building, New York, NY, USA	319	1930
Nina Tower I, Hong Kong, China	319	2005
Bank of America Plaza, Atlanta, GA, USA	312	1992
US Bank Tower, Los Angeles, CA, USA	310	1989
Menara Telekom, Kuala Lumpur, Malaysia	310	2001
Jumeirah Emirates Towers Hotel, Dubai, UAE	309	2000
AT&T Corporate Center, Chicago, IL, USA	307	1989
JPMorganChase Tower, Houston, TX, USA	305	1982
Baiyoke Tower II, Bangkok, Thailand	304	1997
Two Prudential Plaza, Chicago, IL, USA	303	1990
Kingdom Centre, Riyadh, Saudi Arabia	302	2002
First Canadian Place, Toronto, ON, Canada	298	1976
Yokohama Landmark Tower, Yokohama, Japan	296	1993
Wells Fargo Plaza, Houston, TX, USA	296	1983
311 South Wacker Drive, Chicago, IL, USA	293	1990
SEG Plaza, Shenzhen, China	292	2000
American International, New York, NY, USA	290	1932
Key Tower, Cleveland, OH, USA	289	1991
Plaza 66, Shanghai, China	288	2001
One Liberty Place, Philadelphia, PA, USA	288	1987
Bank of America Tower, Seattle, WA, USA	285	1985
Tomorrow Square, Shanghai, China	285	2003
Chongqing World Trade Centre, Chongqing, China	283	2005
Cheung Kong Centre, Hong Kong, China	283	1999
The Trump Building, New York, NY, USA	283	1930
Bank of America Plaza, Dallas, TX, USA	281	1985
OUB Centre, Singapore	280	1986
Republic Plaza, Singapore	280	1995
UOB (United Overseas Bank) Plaza One, Singapore	280	1992
Citicorp Center, New York, NY, USA	279	1977
Hong Kong New World Tower, Shanghai, China	278	2002
Scotia Plaza, Toronto, ON, Canada	275	1988
Williams Tower, Houston, TX, USA	275	1983
Wuhan World Trade Tower, Wuhan, China	273	1998
Renaissance Tower, Dallas, TX, USA	270	1974
Dapeng International Plaza, Guangzhou, China	269	2004
21st Century Tower, Dubai, UAE	269	2003
Al Faisaliyah Center, Riyadh, Saudi Arabia	267	2000
900 North Michigan Avenue, Chicago, IL, USA	265	1989

15: The World's Longest Bridge Spans

Name & location	Type	Length (m)	Date
Akashi Kaikyo, Kobe–Akashi Island, Japan	Suspension	1,991	1998
Storebælt East, Fyn (Fünen)–Sjælland (Zealand), Denmark	Suspension	1,624	1998
Runyang South, Yangtze River, Zhenjiang, Jiangsu, China	Suspension	1,490	2005
Humber, Kingston upon Hull, England, UK	Suspension	1,410	1981
Jiangyin, Yangtze River, Jiangsu, China	Suspension	1,385	1999
Tsing Ma, Lantau Island–Tsing Yi Island, Hong Kong, China	Suspension	1,377	1997
Verrazano Narrows, Brooklyn–Staten Island, NY, USA	Suspension	1,298	1964
Golden Gate, San Francisco Bay, CA, USA	Suspension	1,280	1937
Höga Kusten (High Coast), Ångermanälven R., Kramfors, Sweden	Suspension	1,210	1997
Mackinac Straits, Mackinaw City–St Ignace, MI, USA	Suspension	1,158	1957
Minami Bisan-Seto, Kojima–Sakaide [Honshu–Shikoku], Japan	Suspension	1,100	1988
Bosporus II (Fatih Sultan Mehmet), Turkey	Suspension	1,090	1988
Bosporus I (Atatürk), Turkey	Suspension	1,074	1973
George Washington, Hudson River, NJ-NY, USA	Suspension	1,067	1931
Kurushima Kaikyo 3;2, Onomichi–Imabari [Honshu–Shikoku], Japan	Suspension	1,030;1,020	1999
Ponte 25 de Abril, Tagus River, Lisbon, Portugal	Suspension	1,013	1966
Forth Road, Edinburgh, Scotland, UK	Suspension	1,006	1964
• LONGEST BRIDGE SPANS OF OTHER TYPES:			
Tatara, Onomichi – Imabari [Honshu – Shikoku], Japan	Cable-stayed	890	1999
Pont de Normandie, Seine River, Le Havre, France	Cable-stayed	856	1995
Pont de Québec, St Lawrence River, QC, Canada	Cantilever Truss	549	1917
Forth Rail, Edinburgh, Scotland, UK	Cantilever Truss	521	1890
Lupu, Huangpu River, Shanghai, China	Steel Arch	550	2003
New River Gorge, Fayetteville, WV, USA	Steel Arch	518	1977

16: The World's Longest Tunnels

Name & location (excludes metro tunnels)	Type	Length (km)	Date
Seikan, Tsugaru Strait [Honshu–Hokkaido], Japan	Rail	53.9	1988
Channel Tunnel, Strait of Dover [England–France]	Rail	50.5	1994
Iwate Ichinohe, Tohoku Shinkansen, Honshu, Japan	Rail	25.8	2002
Lærdal, Lærdal–Aurland, Sogn og Fjordane, Norway	Road	24.5	2000
Shimizu, Joetsu Shinkansen, Honshu, Japan	Rail	22.2	1982
Simplon II; **I**, Brig, Switzerland–Iselle, Italy	Rail	19.8;19.8	1922; '06
Vereina, Selfranga–Sagliains, Switzerland	Rail	19.1	1999
Shin-Kanmon, Sanyo Shinkansen [Honshu–Kyushu], Japan	Rail	18.7	1975
Appennino, 'Direttissima' Bologna–Florence, Italy	Rail	18.5	1934
Qinling I-II, Xi'an–Ankang Line, Shaanxi, China	Rail	18.5	2002
Gotthard (Road), Göschenen–Airolo, Switzerland	Road	16.9	1980
Rokko, Sanyo Shinkansen [Osaka–Kobe], Honshu, Japan	Rail	16.3	1972
Furka Base, Oberwald–Realp, Switzerland	Rail	15.4	1982
Haruna, Joetsu Shinkansen, Honshu, Japan	Rail	15.4	1982
Severomuysk, Baikal-Amur Line, Russian Federation	Rail	15.3	2001
Gorigamine, Hokuriku Shinkansen, Japan	Rail	15.2	1997
Monte Santomarco, Páola–Cosenza, Italy	Rail	15.0	1987
Gotthard (Rail), Andermatt–Airolo, Switzerland	Rail	15.0	1882
Nakayama, Joetsu Shinkansen, Japan	Rail	14.9	1982
Mount Macdonald, Rogers Pass, Glacier Nat. Park, BC, Canada	Rail	14.7	1988
Lötschberg, Kandersteg–Goppenstein, Switzerland	Rail	14.6	1913
Romeriksporten, Oslo–Gardermoen Airport, Norway	Rail	14.6	1999
Dayaoshan, Hengyang–Guangzhou Line, Guangdong, China	Rail	14.3	1987
Arlberg, Langen–St Anton, Austria	Road	14.0	1978

17: World Monuments Fund

The World Monuments Fund (http://wmf.org) is a New York-based non-profit organisation dedicated to the conservation of culturally and historically significant works of art and architecture around the world. The Fund calls attention to imperiled cultural heritage sites by publishing a list every two years of the world's 100 most endangered sites. The 2006 list is shown below.

• UNITED STATES & CANADA
- **Ennis Brown House**, Los Angeles, CA
- **Hanging Flume**, Montrose County, CO
- **Bluegrass cultural landscape**, central KY
- **Cyclorama Center**, Gettysburg, PA
- **Mount Lebanon Shaker Village**, New Lebanon, NY
- **Dutch Reformed Church**, Newburgh, NY
- **2 Columbus Circle**, New York, NY
- **Ellis Island Baggage and Dormitory Building**, New York, NY

• LATIN AMERICA & THE CARIBBEAN
- **Pimería Alta Missions**, Sonora, Mexico
- **San Nicolás Obispo**, Morelia, Mexico
- **Mexico City historic centre**, Mexico
- **Chalcatzingo**, Morelos, Mexico
- **San Juan Bautista Cuauhtinchan**, Puebla, Mexico
- **Naranjo**, El Petén, Guatemala
- **San Miguel Arcangel and Santa Cruz de Roma**, Oanchimalco and Huizucar, El Salvador
- **Panama Canal area**, Panama
- **Finca Vigia (Hemingway's House)**, San Francisco de Paula, Cuba
- **La Guaira historic city**, Venezuela
- **Túcume archaeological site**, Lambayeque, Peru
- **Cajamarquilla**, Lima, Peru
- **Presbitero Maestro Cemetery**, Lima, Peru
- **Quinta Heeren**, Lima, Peru
- **Revash funerary complex**, near Chachapoyas, Peru
- **Convent of San Francisco and Historic Olinda**, Olinda, Brazil
- **Cerros Pintados**, Tarapacá, Chile
- **Tulor Village**, Antofagasta, Chile

• EUROPE (including Turkey)
- **Sandviken Bay**, Bergen, Norway
- **Helsinki-Malmi Airport**, Finland
- **St Vincent's Street Church**, Glasgow, Scotland
- **St Mary's Church**, Stow, Lincolnshire
- **Wonderul Barn**, Kildare, Ireland
- **Segovia Aqueduct**, Spain
- **Teatro Capitolio**, Lisbon, Portugal
- **Santa Maria in Stelle Hypogeum**, Verona, Italy
- **Civita di Bagnoregio**, Bagnoregio, Italy
- **Cimitero Acattolico**, Rome, Italy
- **Temple of Portunus**, Rome, Italy
- **Academy of Hadrian's Villa**, Tivoli, Italy
- **Portici Royal Palace**, Naples, Italy
- **Murgia del Trulli**, Puglia, Italy
- **Jerusalem Hospital of the Teutonic Order**, Malbork, Poland
- **Mausoleum of Karol Scheibler**, Lodz, Poland
- **Lednicke-Rovne Historical Park**, Slovak Republic
- **Novi Dvori Castle**, Zapresic, Croatia
- **St Blaise Church**, Dubrovnik, Croatia
- **Mehmed-Pasha Sokolovic Bridge**, Visegrad, Bosnia-Herzegovina
- **Subotica Synagogue**, Serbia & Montenegro
- **Prizren historic centre**, Serbia & Montenegro
- **Treskavec Monastery and Church**, FYR of Macedonia
- **Oradea Fortress**, Romania
- **Helike archaeological site**, Achaia, Greece
- **Little Hagia Sophia**, Istanbul, Turkey
- **Aphrodisias**, near Denizli, Turkey
- **Riga Cathedral**, Latvia

• RUSSIAN FEDERATION
- **Melnikov's House-Studio**, Moscow
- **Narkomfin Building**, Moscow
- **Semenovskoe-Otrada**, Moscow region

• AFRICA
- **Sabil Ruqayya Dudu**, Cairo, Egypt
- **Tarabay al-Sharify**, Cairo, Egypt
- **Suakin**, Sudan
- **Luxor West Bank**, Egypt
- **Asmara historic city centre and theatre**, Eritrea
- **Massawa historic town**, Eritrea
- **Kidane-Mehret Church**, Senafe, Eritrea
- **Tarrafal Concentration Camp**, Cape Verde
- **Chinguetti Mosque**, Mauritania
- **Old Fourah Bay College**, Freetown, Sierra Leone
- **Benin City earthworks**, Nigeria
- **Bafut Palace**, Bafut, Cameroon
- **Mtwapa heritage site**, Kilifi, Kenya
- **Richtersveld cultural landscape**, northern Cape Province, South Africa

• ASIA
- **Amrit archaeological site**, Syria
- **Shayzar Castle**, Syria
- **Tell Mozan (Ancient Urkesh)**, NE Syria
- **Tripoli International Fairground**, Lebanon
- **Chehabi Citadel**, Hasbaya, Lebanon
- **Tell Balatah (Shechem or Ancient Nablus)**, Nablus, Palestine NRA
- **Jvari Monastery**, Mtshekta, Georgia
- **Cultural heritage sites countrywide**, Iraq
- **Bam**, Iran
- **Haji Piyada Mosque**, Balkh, Afghanistan
- **Thatta monuments**, Pakistan
- **Mian Nasir Mohamed Graveyard**, Dadu district, Pakistan
- **Guru Lhakhang and Sumda Chung Temples**, Ladakh, India
- **Dhangkar Gompa**, Himachal Pradesh, India
- **Watson's Hotel**, Mumbai, India
- **Dalhousie Square**, Kolkata, India
- **Sonargaon-Panam City**, Bangladesh
- **Patan Royal Palace complex**, Nepal
- **Tianshui traditional houses**, Gansu, China
- **Qikou Town**, Shanxi, China
- **Cockcrow Post Town**, Huailai, Hebei, China
- **Lu Mansion**, Dongyang, Zhejiang, China
- **Stone Towers of southwest China**, China
- **Tuanshan Historical Village**, Yunnan, China
- **Chom Phet cultural landscape**, Luang Prabang, Laos
- **Omo Hada**, Nias, Indonesia

• AUSTRALASIA & OCEANIA
- **Dampier Rock Art Complex**, Burrup Peninsula, WA, Australia
- **Pulemelei Mound**, Palauli, Letolo Plantation, Samoa

• ANTARCTICA
- **Sir Ernest Shackleton's Expedition Hut**

The listings above refer to a selection of related themes.
For more information, see the Contents (2-7).

18: City Nicknames

Thousands of cities world-wide have a nickname, and many have more than one. This list has limited itself to a selection of important cities, and to a maximum of four nicknames for each.

Nicknames can have several origins. Some date back centuries, while others are recent and often fanciful inventions by marketing companies or tourist offices. Many refer to a real or imagined pre-eminence in agricultural or industrial production, others to qualiities of architecture, location or nightlife that the city sees itself as possessing. Some may have been given to one city by another in a spirit of rivalry, friendly or otherwise. These are often obsure to anyone not from that area, and occasionally strikingly offensive, and so have generally not been included here. Apologies to any city where a particularly uncomplimentary nickname has slipped in by mistake.

Two of the most popular types of nicknames are, firstly, a comparison with a more famous city such as Athens, Paris or Venice because of similar characteristics; and secondly, the claim to be the 'World capital of...' In some cases this refers more to past glory than present reality. The world capitals which have not been included here include those of fruitcake, hubcaps, rhubarb pie, snacks, polar bears, fire hydrants, curtains, gumboots, horseradish sauce and barbed wire. Whatever the reason for a nickname, and however accurate it may be, each gives a clue as to how a city sees itself, or how it would wish others to do so.

Aberdeen, Scotland	Granite City; Silver City
Abidjan, Côte d'Ivoire	Paris of Africa
Adelaide, SA, Australia	City of Churches
Akron, OH, USA	Rubber City
Albuquerque, NM, USA	Duke City
Alexandria, Egypt	Pearl of the Mediterranean
Allentown, PA, USA	Cement Town; Truck Capital of the World
Alleppey, India	Venice of the East
Amsterdam, The Netherlands	Venice of the North; Gateway to Europe
Anchorage, AK, USA	City of Lights; Anchortown; The End of the World
Ancona, Italy	Princess of the Adriatic; Doric City
Annapolis, MD, USA	Crabtown; Sailing Capital of the World; Naptown
Aosta, Italy	The Rome of the Alps
Århus, Denmark	World's Smallest Metropolis
Asheville, NC, USA	Paris of the South
Atlanta, GA, USA	Athens of the South; Phoenix City of the South; Gate City of the South; Dogwood City
Auckland, New Zealand	City of Sails, Queen City; Big Smoke
Augusta, GA, USA	Home of the Masters; Garden City
Austin, TX, USA	Live Music Capital of the World; City of the Violet Crown
Ávila, Spain	City of Saints and Stones
Bacolod, the Philippines	City of Smiles
Baguio, the Philippines	Summer Capital of the Philippines; City of Pines
Baltimore, MD, USA	Monument City; Charm City; City That Reads; Mob Town
Bangalore, India	India's Silicon Valley; City of Gardens
Bangkok, Thailand	Venice of the East
Bangor, Wales	Athens of Wales
Bari, Italy	Small Paris
Barranquilla, Colombia	The Sandy, Curramba the Beautiful
Basra, Iraq	Venice of the Middle East
Bayamón, Puerto Rico	City of the Cowboys
Beijing, China	The Forbidden City
Beirut, Lebanon	Paris of the Middle East
Belgrade, Serbia & Montenegro	White City
Benares, India	Luminous City
Bérgamo, Italy	City of Garibaldi's Thousand
Berkeley, CA, USA	Athens of the West
Berlin, Germany	Spree-Athens; Grey City
Berne, Switzerland	Zürich West
Billings, MT, USA	Star of the Big Sky Country; Magic City; City Beneath the Rimrocks
Birmingham, AL, USA	Magic City; Pittsburgh of the South
Birmingham, England	Venice of the North; Brum; City of a Thousand Trades
Bogotá, Colombia	Athens of South America
Boise, ID, USA	City of Trees
Bologna, Italy	The Fat One; The Learned One; The Red One
Bolzano, Italy	Door to the Dolomites
Bordeaux, France	Wine Capital of the World
Boston, MA, USA	Puritan City; Cradle of Liberty; Athens of America; Beantown
Braga, Portugal	City of the Bishops
Brandon, MN, Canada	Paris of the Prairies
Bremen, Germany	Key to the World
Bréscia, Italy	Lioness of Italy
Bridgeport, CT, USA	Park City
Brighton, England	Liberal City
Brisbane, QL, Australia	River City; Brisvegas
Bruges, Belgium	Venice of the North
Bucharest, Romania	Little Paris
Budapest, Hungary	Pearl of the Danube
Buenos Aires, Argentina	Paris of Latin America; Queen of the Plata
Buffalo, NY, USA	Bison City; Nickel City; Queen City of the Great Lakes; City of Good Neighbors
Bydgoszcz, Poland	Venice of the North
Caguas, Puerto Rico	Country City
Calgary, AL, Canada	Stampede City; Canada's Oil Capital; Cowtown; Gateway to the Rockies
Cali, Colombia	The Sultaness of the Valley
Cambridge (and area), England	Silicon Fen
Cambridge, MA, USA	Moscow on the Charles
Campbell River, BC, Canada	Salmon Capital of the World
Campinas, Brazil	Brazilian Silicon Valley
Canberra, AC, Australia	Bush Capital
Cape Town, South Africa	Mother City
Carolina, Puerto Rico	Giant City
Caserta, Italy	Versailles of Italy
Casper, WY, USA	Oil Capital of the Rockies; Ghost Town
Cebu, the Philippines	Queen City of the South
Cedar Rapids, IA, USA	City of Five Seasons
Charleston, SC, USA	Palmetto City; America's Most Historic City; Marina City; Holy City
Charleston, WV, USA	Chemicalville
Charlotte, NC, USA	Queen City; Hornet's Nest
Chattanooga, TN, USA	Scenic City; Dynamo of Dixie
Chengdu, China	Brocade City; City of Hibiscus
Cheyenne, WY, USA	Magic City of the Plains
Chicago, IL, USA	Windy City; Second City; City of Big Shoulders; Hog Butcher to the World
Christchurch, New Zealand	Garden City
Cincinnati, OH, USA	Queen City of the West; Porkopolis
Clarksville, TN, USA	Gateway to the New South; Queen City; ClarksVegas
Clearwater, FL, USA	Lightning Capital of the World
Cleveland, OH, USA	Forest City; Mistake on the Lake
Cody, WY, USA	Rodeo Capital of the World
Colorado Springs, CO, USA	Pikes Peak City
Columbus, IN, USA	Athens of the Prairie
Columbus, OH, USA	Crossroads of Ohio; Cowtown
Coober Pedy, SA, Australia	Opal Capital of the World
Corpus Christi, TX, USA	Sparkling City by the Sea
Coventry, England	Concrete Block
Cracow, Poland	Royal Capital City
Cuernevaca, Mexico	City of Eternal Springs
Dakar, Senegal	Paris of Africa
Dalian, China	Hong Kong of the North
Dallas, TX, USA	The Texas Star; Big D; Cowtown
Dallas-Fort Worth, TX, USA	Metroplex
Dayton, OH, USA	Gem City; Birthplace of Aviation
Denver, CO, USA	Mile-High City; Gateway to the Rockies; Queen City of the Plains; Convention City
Detroit, MI, USA	Motor City (Motor-Town/ Motown); Hitsville USA; Amityville; Hockeytown
Dodge City, KS, USA	Cowboy Capital of the World
Dresden, Germany	Florence on the Elbe
Dublin, Ireland	Fair City; The Pale
Dubrovnik, Croatia	Pearl of the Adriatic
Dunedin, New Zealand	Edinburgh of the South
Durham, NC, USA	Bull City; City of Medicine
Edinburgh, Scotland	Athens of the North; Auld Reekie
Edmonton, AL, Canada	Nashville of the North; City of Champions; Gateway to the North; Canada's Festival City
El Paso, TX, USA	Sun City Texas; City with a Legend
Erfurt, Germany	Thuringian Rome
Eskilstuna, Sweden	Smith City
Florence, Italy	City of Lilies; Athens of Italy
Fort Lauderdale, FL, USA	Venice of America; Fort Leatherdale
Fort Wayne, IN, USA	Summit City; City of Churches
Fort Worth, TX, USA	Where The West Begins; Cowtown
Frankfurt, Germany	Mainhattan; Bankfurt
Fredericton, NB, Canada	City of Stately Elms
Fresno, CA, USA	Garden of the Sun; California's New Frontier; Raisin Capital of the World
Gaeta, Italy	Venice of the Tyrrhenian
Galway, Ireland	Venice of the West; City of the Tribes
Genoa, Italy	The Superb
Ghadamis, Libya	Pearl of the Desert
Glasgow, Scotland	Second City of the Empire; Shipbuilding Capital of the World; Dear Green Place
Gothenburg, Sweden	Little London
Grand Rapids, MI, USA	Furniture City; Valley City
Green Bay, WI, USA	Titletown USA
Guadalajara, Mexico	The Tapatian Pearl
Hague, The, The Netherlands	City of Peace and Justice
Hamburg, Germany	Gateway to the World; Venice of the North
Hamilton, New Zealand	Hamiltron
Hamilton, OT, Canada	Steeltown
Harbin, China	Paris of the East
Havana, Cuba	Paris of the Caribbean
Helsinki, Finland	White City of the North
Hershey, PA, USA	Chocolate Town USA; The Sweetest Place on Earth
Ho Chi Minh City, Vietnam	Paris of the Orient
Hollywood (West), CA, USA	Boystown; Creative City
Hollywood, CA, USA	Tinseltown; Showbusiness Capital of the World; Hollyweird
Hong Kong, China	Pearl of the Orient; Asia's World City
Houston, TX, USA	Magnolia City; Space City; Bayou City; Oil Capital of the World
Hyderabad, India	Cyberabad
Indianapolis, IN, USA	Crossroads of America; Naptown; Railroad City; Circle City
Isfahan, Iran	Half of the World
Jackson, MS, USA	Chimneyville
Jacksonville, FL, USA	Bold New City of the South; River City by the Sea; Where Florida Begins
Japiur, India	Pink City
Jeddah, Saudi Arabia	Paris of Arabia
Jerusalem, Israel	City of David; City of Peace; Holy City
Jodhpur, India	Blue City
Johannesburg, South Africa	Egoli (City of Gold)
Jönköping, Sweden	Jerusalem of Småland
Kansas City, MO, USA	City of Fountains; Heart of America; Cowtown
Knoxville, TN, USA	Marble City
Kolkata (Calcutta), India	City of Love; City of Palaces
Kristianstad, Sweden	Little Paris

See also... Urbanization (20)

The listings above refer to a selection of related themes. For more information, see the Contents (2 7).

Kuching, Malaysia	Cat City
Lahti, Finland	Finland's Chicago
Las Vegas (downtown), NV, USA	The Strip; Glitter Gulch
Las Vegas, NV, USA	Entertainment Capital of the World; City of Lights; America's Playground; Sin City
León, Mexico	Shoe Capital of Mexico
Lexington, KY, USA	Horse Capital of the World
Lima, Peru	City of the Kings
Lisbon, Portugal	White City; City with a Future
Little Rock, AR, USA	City of Roses
Livingston (and area), Scotland	Silicon Glen
London (City of), England	The City; The Square Mile
London, England	Big Smoke; Great Wen
London, OT, Canada	Forest City
Londonderry, Northern Ireland	Maiden City
Los Angeles, CA, USA	Big Orange; City of the Angels; Entertainment Capital of the World; City of Flowers & Sunshine
Louisville, KY, USA	Derby City; Falls City; River City; City of Beautiful Churches
Lubbock, TX, USA	Hub of the Plains
Macau, China	Monte Carlo of the East
Madison, WI, USA	Four Lake City; Mad City
Madurai, India	Athens of the East
Manchester, England	Venice of the North
Manchester, NH, USA	Queen City
Manila, the Philippines	Pearl of the Orient; City by the Bay
Mar del Plata, Argentina	Queen of the Coast; La Feliz (The Happy)
Mayagüez, Puerto Rico	Sultan of the West
Mazatlán, Mexico	Pearl of the Pacific
Medellín, Colombia	Orchid City; La Bella Villa
Melbourne, VI, Australia	Paris on the Yarra
Memphis, TN, USA	Home of the Blues; Birthplace of Rock 'n' Roll; Bluff City; River City
Mérida, Mexico	White City
Mexicali, Mexico	City That Captured the Sun
Mexico City, Mexico	City of Palaces
Miami Beach, FL, USA	America's Riviera; Sun and Fun Capital of the World
Miami, FL, USA	Little Cuba; Gateway to the Americas; Capital of Latin America; Magic City
Milan, Italy	Fashion Capital of the World; Factory of the Future; Moral Capital of Italy; Drinkable City
Milwaukee, WI, USA	Cream City; Brew/Beer City; City of Festivals; Flour City
Minneapolis, MN, USA	City of Lakes; Minneapple; Mill City; Flour City
Minneapolis-St Paul, MN, USA	Twin Cities
Mobile, AL, USA	Azalea City; City of Five Flags
Moncton, NB, Canada	Hub City; Monkeytown
Monterrey, Mexico	Sultaness of the North
Montréal, QU, Canada	City of Saints
Mopti, Mali	Venice of Mali
Moscow, Russian Federation	The Third Rome; Big Village
Munich, Germany	Village of a Million Inhabitants; World City with Heart
Nantes, France	Venice of the West
Naples, Italy	Capital of the South
Nashville, TN, USA	Music City USA; Country Music Capital of the World; Athens of the South; Protestant Vatican
New Orleans, LA, USA	Big Easy; Crescent City; Queen of the Mississippi; City That Time Forgot
New York (Lower Manhattan), NY, USA	Silicon Alley
New York, NY, USA	Big Apple; Empire City; City That Never Sleeps; Capital of the World
Newark, NJ, USA	Brick City; Renaissance City
Newcastle upon Tyne, England	The Toon; Georgieland (refers to the Tyneside conurbation)
Niagara Falls, OT, Canada	Honeymoon Capital of the World
Nijmegen, The Netherlands	Oldest City of The Netherlands
Norrköping, Sweden	Peking
Nouméa, New Caledonia	Paris of the Pacific
Oakland, CA, USA	Oaktown
Oklahoma City, OK, USA	Renaissance City
Oporto, Portugal	The Invincible
Orange County, CA, USA	Biotech Beach
Orlando, FL, USA	City Beautiful
Ottawa, OT, Canada	Venice of the North; Silicon Valley of the North; Bytown
Oxford, England	City of Dreaming Spires; Silicon Spires
Paris, France	City of Light; City of Love
Pasadena, CA, USA	City of Roses; Crown City
Penang, Malaysia	Pearl of the Orient
Pensacola, FL, USA	City of Five Flags
Perth, WA, Australia	City of Lights
Petra, Jordan	Rose Red City
Philadelphia, PA, USA	City of Brotherly Love; Philly; Quaker City
Phoenix, AZ, USA	Valley of the Sun; Desert Storm
Pittsburgh, PA, USA	Steel City; Iron City; Birmingham of America; City of Champions
Ponce, Puerto Rico	City of the Lions; Senior City
Port Elizabeth, South Africa	Friendly City; Windy City
Portland, ME, USA	Forest City; Hill City
Portland, OR, USA	City of Roses; Rip City; Bridgetown; Little Beirut; Stumptown
Portsmouth, England	Pompey
Prague, Czech Republic	Golden City; City of 100 Spires; Heart of Europe; Rome of the North
Pretoria, South Africa	Jacaranda City
Providence, RI, USA	Beehive of Industry
Puebla, Mexico	City of Angels; City of Sweet Potatoes; City of Tiles
Qom, Iran	Iran's Vatican
Québec, QU, Canada	Gibraltar of North America; Le Grande Village; La Vieille Capital
Queenstown, New Zealand	Extreme Sports Capital of the World
Raleigh, NC, USA	City of Oaks; Raleighwood
Recife, Brazil	Venice of Brazil
Regina, SA, Canada	Queen City
Reno, NV, USA	Biggest Little City in the World; Neon Babylon
Richmond, VA, USA	Capital of the Confederacy; City of Seven Hills; Easy to Love; Fist City
Riga, Latvia	Paris of the East
Rio de Janeiro, Brazil	Marvellous City
Rochester, NY, USA	Flower City; Kodak City; Snapshot City
Rome, Italy	Eternal City; City of the Seven Hills; City of Love; City of Cats
Rosario, Argentina	Chicago of Argentina
Sacramento, CA, USA	Big Tomato; Camelia Capital of the World; Almond Capital of the World; River City
St John, NB, Canada	Port City
St Louis, MO, USA	Gateway to the West; Mound City; City with a Future
St Paul, MN, USA	Moscow on the Mississippi
St Petersburg, Russian Fed.	Venice of the North; Northern Palmyra
Salem, MA, USA	City of Witches
Salem, OR, USA	Cherry City
San Antonio, TX, USA	Alamo City; Mission City; River City; Venice of the West
San Diego, CA, USA	Plymouth of the West; America's Finest City; The Place Where California Began; The First Great City of the 21st Century
San Francisco (southern bay area), CA, USA	Silicon Valley
San Francisco, CA, USA	Golden Gate City; Shaky Town; City by the Bay; Baghdad by the Bay
San Jose, CA, USA	Garden City; Capital of Silicon Valley
São Paulo, Brazil	Brazil's Locomotive; City That Never Sleeps; Land of Fog
Saskatoon, SA, Canada	City of Bridges; Saskabush
Scarborough, England	Queen of the Yorkshire Coast
Seattle, WA, USA	Emerald City; Jet City; Queen City of the Pacific Northwest
Sète, France	Venice of the South
Shanghai, China	Paris of the Orient
Sheffield, England	Steel City; People's Republic of South Yorkshire
Shibam, Yemen	Manhattan of the Desert
Shiraz, Iran	Athens of Iran; Paris of Iran; City of Roses
Singapore	Lion City
Sioux Falls, SD, USA	Gateway to the Plains
Sitka, AK, USA	The Natural Place to Visit; Paris of the Pacific
Spokane, WA, USA	Lilac City; Spokavegas; The Can; Skybridge City
Springfield, MA, USA	City of Firsts; Birthplace of Basketball
Springfield, MO, USA	Gateway to the Ozarks; Birthplace of Route 66
Stockholm, Sweden	Venice of the North; The Oak
Stockton, CA, USA	California's Sunrise Seaport; Asparagus Capital of the World
Suzhou, China	Venice of the East
Sydney, NS, Australia	Harbour City; Emerald City
Syracuse, NY, USA	Salt City; Central City; City of Bridges; Typewriter City
Tabriz, Iran	City of Uprising
Tacoma, WA, USA	City of Destiny; Tacyoma; America's Number One Wired City
Tai O, Hong Kong, China	Venice of Hong Kong
Tampa, FL, USA	America's Next Greatest City
Tampere, Finland	Manchester of the North
Táranto, Italy	City of the Two Seas
Tarpon Springs, FL, USA	Venice of the South
Taxco, Mexico	Silver Capital of the World
Te Puke, New Zealand	Kiwi Fruit Capital of the World
Tehran, Iran	City of 72 Nations
Tel Aviv, Israel	City That Never Stops
Tijuana, Mexico	Television Capital of the World
Tikal, Guatemala	City That Time Forgot
Toledo, OH, USA	Glass City; Frog Town; Corn City
Toronto, OT, Canada	Queen City; Hogtown; Festival City; Hollywood North
Tromsø, Norway	Paris of the North
Tucson, AZ, USA	The Old Pueblo
Tulsa, OK, USA	Oil Capital of the World
Turin, Italy	Capital of the Alps; First Capital of Italy; Regal City
Udaipur, India	Venice of the East
Umeå, Sweden	City of Birches
Ushuaia, Argentina	The End of the World
Vancouver, BC, Canada	Rainy City; Brollywood; Terminal City; VanCity
Västerås, Sweden	Cucumber City
Venice, Italy	Bride of the Sea; Queen of the Adriatic; La Serenissima
Victoria, BC, Canada	Whale-watching Capital of the World; Little England; Garden City
Vilnius, Lithuania	Athens of the North
Warsaw, Poland	Paris of the North; Phoenix City; Biggest Village in Poland
Washington DC, USA	News Capital of the World; Capital City; Our City, Our Future
Wellington, New Zealand	Harbour Capital; Windy City; Wellywood
Wichita, KS, USA	Emerald City; Air Capital of the World
Wilmington, DE, USA	Chemical Capital of the World
Windsor, OT, Canada	Tijuana North; Sin City Canada
Winnipeg, MN, Canada	Winterpeg
Zákinthos, Greece	Venice of the South
Zamboanga, the Philippines	City of Flowers

The listings above refer to a selection of related themes.
For more information, see the Contents (2 7).

19: Principal International Environmental Treaties

Many issues of environmental importance are the subject of a range of international conventions and treaties. Within some of these, various protocols also exist to provide action plans in specific areas. The list below is a selection of the most important of these agreements. In their various ways, they all seek to encourage environmental awareness and protection, thereby addressing the effects of mankind's impact on the planet. This information was compiled largely by Greenpeace, although any errors or omissions are the responsibility of the publishers. For more information on the work Greenpeace is doing in these areas, visit www.greenpeace.org. For more information on the various treaties, conventions and protocols themselves, see the web site address within each entry.

1/12/59 Date treaty in force 44 Ratifications (at April '06)

Principal Areas of Responsibility:

- Wildlife protection
- Pollution control
- Marine protection
- Bio-diversity
- Ozone depletion/climate change

Antarctic Treaty
1/12/59 44

www.antarctica.ac.uk/about_antarctica/treaty

The treaty is designed to protect the Antarctic continent from the exploitation of its raw materials and to ensure the use of its territory for peaceful purpose only, such as scientific research. In addition to several other objectives, the treaty also prescribes the preservation and conservation of Antarctic living resources.

ASCOBANS
29/3/94 9

Agreement on the Conservation of Small Cetaceans of the Baltic and North Seas

www.ascobans.org

With the establishment of this environmental treaty, Northern European countries such as Denmark, Germany and the UK sought to secure long term protection of small cetaceans in the Baltic and North Seas from hazards such as high bycatch rates and habitat deterioration.

Barcelona Convention
16/1/76 22

The Barcelona Convention for the Protection of the Mediterranean Sea

www.unepmap.gr

Established in 1976 for the protection of the Mediterranean as part of the UNEP Regional Seas Programme. Its objective is to achieve international co operation for a co ordinated and comprehensive approach to the protection and enhancement of the Mediterranean marine environment.

Basel Convention
5/5/92 165

Basel Convention on the Control of Transboundary Movements of Hazardous Wastes and their Disposal

www.basel.int

The Basel Convention provides targets for the reduction of hazardous wastes and the creation of adequate disposal facilities; since 1998, it has also instituted a ban on waste exports from OECD to non-OECD countries.

CBD
29/12/93 188

Convention on Biological Diversity

www.biodiv.org

The Convention's objectives are 'the conservation of biological diversity, the sustainable use of its components and the fair and equitable sharing of the benefits arising out of the utilization of genetic resources.' It is the first comprehensive agreement to address all aspects of biological diversity. Its objectives have led to a broad work plan, involving all primary sectors (forests, oceans, and agriculture) and cross-cutting issues such as genetic engineering, indigenous peoples, technology transfer and intellectual property rights.

CCAMLR
7/4/82 32

Convention on the Conservation of Antarctic Marine Living Resources

www.ccamlr.org

The convention focuses on the conservation of Antarctic marine living resources by attempting to minimise the risk of irreversible changes to the Antarctic marine ecosystem and ensuring an increase in the populations of exploited species.

CITES
1/7/75 169

Convention on International Trade in Endangered Species of Wild Fauna and Flora

www.cites.org

This is the only treaty whose focus is the global protection of plant and animal species from unregulated international trade. A classification of endangered species is constantly monitored and updated to co ordinate protection measures.

HELCOM
17/1/00 10

Convention on the Protection of the Marine Environment of the Baltic Sea Area, 1992

www.helcom.fi

This is the first convention to take into account all aspects of the Baltic marine environment and its protection. It deals with all aspects of pollution, including land based, from ships, from dumping, and from the exploration and exploitation of the sea bed and its subsoil. The convention also regulates co operation in combating marine pollution by oil and other harmful substances.

London Convention
30/8/75 81

London Convention on the Prevention of Marine Pollution by Dumping of Wastes and Other Matter

www.marine.gov.uk/london_convention.htm

This Convention is the principal international instrument to limit marine pollution and ocean contamination by dumping of wastes and other harmful matter.

OSPAR
25/3/98 16

Convention for the Protection of the Marine Environment of the North East Atlantic

www.ospar.org

In 1992, this Commission replaced, and combined the aims of, the Oslo Convention on the Prevention of Marine Pollution by Dumping of Ships & Aircraft (1972) and the Paris Convention for the Prevention of Marine Pollution from Land Based Sources (1974).

Ramsar
2/2/71 151

Ramsar Convention on Wetlands

www.ramsar.org

This convention, signed in Ramsar, Iran, in 1971, is an intergovernmental treaty which provides the framework for international cooperation for the conservation and prudent use of wetlands and their resources. There are presently 1,283 wetland sites, totaling 108.7 million hectares, designated for inclusion in the Ramsar List of Wetlands of International Importance.

Stockholm Convention
22/5/01 49

Stockholm Convention on Persistent Organic Pollutants

www.pops.int

This Convention focuses on the elimination of a priority list of 12 of the most hazardous persistent organic pollutants (POPs), the elimination of other existing POPs and the prevention of the marketing of new chemicals with the characteristics of POPs .

UNCLOS
16/11/94 149

United Nations Convention on the Law of the Sea

www.un.org/depts.los/index.htm

This Convention addresses protection and preservation of the marine environment to reflect customary international law with respect to maritime navigation. In addition, it provides basic obligations to prevent and reduce pollution from land based sources, from sea bed activities subject to national jurisdiction and from ocean dumping.

UNFCCC & Kyoto Protocol
21/3/94 71 **(Kyoto)**

United Nations Framework Convention on Climate Change

www.unfccc.org

The objective of the Convention is to achieve stabilisation of greenhouse gas concentrations in the atmosphere at a level that would prevent dangerous anthropogenic interference with the climate system. Such a level should be achieved within a time frame sufficient to allow ecosystems to adapt naturally to climate change, to ensure that food production is not threatened and to enable economic development to proceed in a sustainable manner. As part of the UNFCCC, the widely discussed Kyoto Protocol commits its signatories to targets in the reduction and limitation of their national greenhouse gas emission.

Vienna Convention & Montréal Protocol
1/1/89 189

Montréal Protocol on Substances that Deplete the Ozone Layer

www.unep.org/unep/secretar/ozone

The Montréal Protocol operates within the framework of the 1985 Vienna Convention, which seeks to protect human health and the environment against adverse effects resulting from depletion of the ozone layer. The Montréal Protocol is specifically concerned with the protection of the ozone layer by taking precautionary measures to control global emissions of substances that deplete it, such as CFCs and halons. It also seeks to promote the exchange of appropriate technological research.

20: A Selection of Anniversaries in 2007

• 1907
- 13 Feb Suffragettes storm the British parliament
- 21 Feb WH Auden born
- 22 Feb Scouting movement founded by Lord Baden Powell
- 15 Mar Finland becomes the first European country to extend the vote to women
- 22 Mar Taxis with meters are first used in London
- 20 Apr Sheffield Wednesday beat Everton 2-1 to win the FA Cup
- 12 May Katherine Hepburn born
- 22 May Laurence Olivier born
- 26 May John Wayne born
- 27 May Bubonic Plague breaks out in San Francisco
- 16 Jul Barbara Stanwyck born
- 18 Jul Premiere of Ziegfeld's *Follies* in New York
- 31 Aug Britain, Russia and France sign the Triple Entente
- 7 Sep Maiden voyage of the *Lusitania* from Liverpool to New York
- 26 Sep New Zealand becomes a Dominion, and effectively independent from the UK
- 16 Nov Oklahoma becomes the 46th state of the USA

• 1807
- 19 Jan Robert E Lee born
- 2 Feb Napoleon's invasion of Russia begins
- 27 Feb Henry Longfellow born
- 4 Mar First performance of Beethoven's 4th Symphony
- 25 Mar First passenger railway service in Britain (in Swansea)
- 25 Mar Abolition of salvery in Great Britain and Ireland
- 22 May First sales of fruit-flavoured fizzy drinks (in Philadelphia)
- 6 Jun Lisbon earthquake

• 1707
- 7 Mar US founding father Stephen Hopkins born
- 22 Apr Novelist Henry Fielding born
- 29 Apr Act of Union creating the Kingdom of Great Britain

• 1607
- 20 Jan Tsunami in the Bristol Channel
- 26 Apr Foundation of Jamestown
- 7 Jul First performance of *God Save the King*

• 1507
- The word 'America' first appears on a map
- 3 Nov Leonardo da Vinci commissioned to paint the *Mona Lisa*

• 1407
- 24 Nov Murder of the Duke of Orleans, leading to civil war in France

• 1307
- 13 Oct Philip IV of France orders the arrest of the Knights Templar

• 1207
- 1 Oct The future Henry III of England born

• 1107
- The Chinese print money in three colours to prevent forgery

• 1007
- Foundation of Songjiang, now Shanghai

▶ See also... page 210 for details of maps directly relating to the figures in this section; Contents (2-7) for details of all maps and charts in this Atlas

These pages provide exact data relevant to many of the thematic maps which appear elsewhere in this atlas. Attention is drawn to the notes at the foot of page 210. Many sources have been used in the compilation of these statistics and these are specified on the maps themselves, as are the year/s to which the information relates.

The matter of deciding what is and what is not a country is by no means clear-cut, but no political or other subjective stance has been adopted. Many countries have dependencies, overseas possessions and the like; for various reasons (mainly connected with the availability, reliability or relevance of statistical data) some have been listed separately, some have had their figures amalgamated with those for their mother country and some have been excluded. As a general, but not infallible, rule, where 'T' appears in the Military Spending column, this indicates that the 'country' has a dependence of some kind on another state (which takes responsibility for its defence). For more information on countries worldwide, consult the latest edition of the Columbus *World Travel Dictionary* or *World Travel Guide*.

The *italic* numbers in the second row for each country (preceded by •) give the world ranking for that category in descending order highest figure ranked number 1). The top 10 countries in each category have their ranking figure in **bold**. Countries whose figures are equal according to whatever rounding has been used have been ranked equally. As data is not always available for all 226 countries, the figures at the bottom of the chart give the lowest ranking figure in that category: as this can be shared by two or more countries, it may therefore not always represent the total number of countries covered.

Throughout, n/a means that, at the time of going to press, data was not available, not reliable or not relevant. In the case of mobile telephone lines and internet usage, it may in a few instances also mean that the country did not have a network or service.

Some countries have more than one capital city or have recently changed their capital or its name. These are referred to in the notes at the foot of the chart on page 210. These notes also specify inclusions and exclusions for offshore islands and the like for some of the more important countries.

Country Map Ref. (pp14-15)	Internet code	Capital	Area '000 sq km	Population '000	Population Density People/sq km	International Arrivals 1997 '000	International Arrivals 2004 '000	Visitor Receipts US$ million	International Departures '000	Visitor Expenditure US$ million	Hotel Bedrooms 2003	Gross Nat'l Income US$ billion	GNI per Person US$	GDP Growth Av. annual % 1997-2006	Energy Production Million tonnes oil equiv.	Energy Consumption Million tonnes oil equiv.	Energy Consumption Tonnes oil equiv./person	Fixed Tel. Lines Lines/100 people	Mobile Tel. Lines Lines/100 people	Internet Usage Subscribers/100 people	Agricultural Land % of national area	Total Health Spending % of GNI	Life Expectancy Years	Military Spending % of GNI
Afghanistan M4	.af	Kabul	652.10 • *41*	29,929 • *38*	45.9 • *150*	n/a • –	n/a • –	n/a • –	n/a • –	n/a • –	n/a • –	5,543 • *122*	185 • *217*	15.3 • ***2***	0.21 • *131*	0.48 • *159*	0.02 • *209*	0.20 • *220*	2.41 • *188*	0.10 • *204*	58.3 • *44*	8.0 • *42*	41.5 • *210*	2.8 • *40*
Albania J3	.al	Tirana	28.70 • *142*	3,563 • *130*	124.2 • *80*	19 • *192*	42 • *144*	673 • *75*	n/a • –	n/a • –	4,161 • *114*	6,641 • *114*	1,864 • *136*	5.4 • *40*	1.39 • *106*	2.44 • *119*	0.68 • *137*	8.30 • *142*	35.80 • *88*	2.35 • *160*	39.7 • *103*	6.1 • *87*	72.0 • *87*	1.2 • *120*
Algeria J4	.dz	Algiers	2,381.70 • *11*	32,532 • *37*	13.7 • *194*	635 • *85*	1,234 • *71*	n/a • –	1,254 • *56*	n/a • –	n/a • –	73,676 • *49*	2,265 • *119*	4.1 • *68*	176.64 • *16*	33.29 • *42*	1.02 • *114*	7.08 • *149*	14.48 • *128*	2.61 • *156*	16.8 • *170*	4.3 • *150*	70.5 • *111*	3.3 • *31*
American Samoa A6	.as	Pago Pago	0.20 • *211*	58 • *205*	289.4 • *40*	26 • *184*	n/a • –	n/a • –	n/a • –	n/a • –	n/a • –	500 • *191*	8,638 • *68*	n/a • –	0.00 • –	0.21 • *176*	3.62 • *48*	25.86 • *85*	4.14 • *174*	n/a • –	24.9 • *149*	n/a • –	76.0 • *55*	T • –
Andorra J3	.ad	Andorra la Vella	0.45 • *196*	71 • *200*	156.8 • *65*	2,347 • *47*	2,791 • *54*	n/a • –	n/a • –	n/a • –	n/a • –	1,900 • *159*	26,932 • *23*	n/a • –	0.00 • –	n/a • –	n/a • –	52.30 • *26*	61.63 • *56*	16.42 • *81*	55.6 • *52*	6.5 • *71*	81.0 • ***4***	T • –
Angola J6	.ao	Luanda	1,246.70 • *23*	11,827 • *69*	9.5 • *204*	45 • *174*	194 • *121*	97 • *103*	n/a • –	n/a • –	9,244 • *83*	14,441 • *83*	1,221 • *148*	9.5 • ***6***	48.99 • *37*	3.37 • *111*	0.28 • *160*	0.67 • *203*	6.68 • *156*	1.22 • *174*	46.0 • *83*	5.0 • *124*	40.0 • *213*	4.7 • *17*
Anguilla F5	.ai	The Valley	0.16 • *215*	13 • *219*	82.8 • *106*	43 • *177*	54 • *141*	69 • *109*	n/a • –	n/a • –	759 • *139*	30 • *220*	2,263 • *121*	n/a • –	0.00 • –	n/a • –	n/a • –	47.69 • *39*	13.85 • *131*	n/a • –	0.0 • –	n/a • –	77.0 • *47*	T • –
Antigua & Barbuda F5	.ag	St John's	0.44 • *197*	69 • *202*	156.2 • *66*	240 • *129*	245 • *115*	n/a • –	n/a • –	n/a • –	n/a • –	800 • *179*	11,641 • *59*	3.7 • *81*	0.00 • –	0.19 • *180*	2.75 • *68*	49.35 • *35*	70.13 • *49*	25.97 • *58*	31.7 • *122*	4.8 • *133*	72.5 • *77*	M • –
Argentina F7	.ar	Buenos Aires	2,780.40 • ***8***	39,538 • *31*	14.2 • *192*	2,764 • *41*	3,353 • *47*	2,563 • *46*	3,088 • *39*	2,964 • *31*	174,629 • *15*	142,338 • *35*	3,600 • *100*	2.2 • *142*	91.17 • *25*	66.76 • *28*	1.69 • *88*	22.76 • *96*	35.35 • *89*	16.10 • *82*	63.7 • *25*	8.9 • *29*	74.5 • *63*	1.2 • *120*
Armenia L3	.am	Yerevan	29.80 • *141*	2,983 • *135*	100.1 • *92*	23 • *188*	n/a • –	n/a • –	169 • *78*	n/a • –	n/a • –	3,424 • *142*	1,148 • *150*	7.7 • *13*	0.95 • *110*	4.31 • *99*	1.44 • *96*	9.09 • *140*	6.66 • *157*	4.91 • *131*	46.9 • *77*	5.8 • *99*	68.5 • *127*	2.7 • *45*
Aruba F5	.aw	Oranjestad	0.18 • *213*	72 • *199*	397.6 • *22*	650 • *81*	728 • *85*	n/a • –	n/a • –	n/a • –	7,731 • *86*	323 • *200*	4,513 • *88*	n/a • –	0.00 • –	0.34 • *169*	4.72 • *27*	35.03 • *60*	73.61 • *46*	33.33 • *43*	10.4 • *188*	n/a • –	79.5 • *17*	n/a • –
Australia P7	.au	Canberra	7,682.30 • ***6***	20,090 • *52*	2.6 • *220*	4,318 • *28*	5,200 • *38*	12,952 • ***10***	3,388 • *37*	9,407 • *17*	204,461 • *12*	541,173 • *14*	26,937 • *22*	3.6 • *85*	256.53 • ***9***	128.46 • *18*	6.39 • *16*	58.55 • *19*	82.76 • *33*	65.28 • ***8***	58.1 • *45*	9.5 • *19*	80.5 • ***7***	1.9 • *77*
Austria J3	.at	Vienna	83.90 • *115*	8,185 • *89*	97.6 • *95*	16,647 • *11*	19,373 • ***10***	15,412 • ***9***	5,060 • *27*	11,416 • *14*	282,614 • ***10***	262,147 • *22*	32,029 • *15*	2.2 • *142*	12.37 • *63*	36.38 • *40*	4.44 • *31*	46.20 • *41*	97.36 • *12*	47.52 • *30*	40.5 • *100*	7.7 • *49*	79.0 • *24*	0.8 • *144*
Azerbaijan L3	.az	Baku	86.60 • *113*	7,912 • *91*	91.4 • *102*	306 • *120*	n/a • –	n/a • –	1,376 • *53*	n/a • –	5,034 • *107*	7,828 • *104*	989 • *161*	11.4 • ***4***	22.77 • *53*	15.86 • *66*	2.00 • *80*	12.28 • *124*	17.44 • *125*	4.89 • *132*	54.2 • *61*	3.7 • *167*	65.0 • *146*	1.9 • *77*
Bahamas F4	.bs	Nassau	13.90 • *159*	302 • *175*	21.7 • *179*	1,618 • *56*	1,561 • *64*	1,884 • *54*	n/a • –	n/a • –	15,393 • *71*	4,684 • *131*	15,521 • *42*	3.2 • *108*	0.00 • –	1.21 • *136*	4.01 • *41*	44.14 • *48*	58.68 • *61*	29.34 • *49*	1.0 • *213*	6.9 • *66*	72.0 • *87*	M • –
Bahrain L4	.bh	Manama	0.71 • *187*	688 • *161*	969.5 • ***10***	1,611 • *57*	n/a • –	740 • *73*	n/a • –	n/a • –	n/a • –	8,834 • *99*	12,834 • *55*	5.2 • *42*	11.19 • *67*	10.22 • *77*	14.85 • ***5***	25.92 • *84*	87.92 • *24*	20.67 • *72*	14.1 • *176*	4.4 • *146*	74.0 • *70*	5.1 • *15*
Bangladesh N4	.bd	Dhaka	148.40 • *93*	144,320 • ***7***	972.5 • ***9***	182 • *136*	271 • *112*	67 • *110*	1,414 • *52*	n/a • –	4,565 • *110*	61,230 • *52*	424 • *188*	5.6 • *36*	10.90 • *68*	15.37 • *67*	0.11 • *179*	0.61 • *205*	2.03 • *193*	0.22 • *198*	61.2 • *35*	3.1 • *179*	63.0 • *154*	1.2 • *120*
Barbados F5	.bb	Bridgetown	0.43 • *198*	279 • *178*	648.5 • *13*	472 • *95*	552 • *95*	810 • *69*	n/a • –	n/a • –	6,210 • *97*	2,507 • *151*	8,990 • *67*	2.4 • *133*	0.08 • *141*	0.55 • *157*	1.97 • *82*	50.09 • *31*	73.85 • *44*	55.35 • *18*	44.2 • *88*	6.9 • *66*	74.5 • *63*	M • –
Belarus K3	.by	Minsk	207.60 • *85*	10,300 • *78*	49.6 • *145*	254 • *126*	68 • *138*	287 • *93*	n/a • –	524 • *54*	n/a • –	20,856 • *73*	2,025 • *131*	6.8 • *23*	2.14 • *99*	30.76 • *45*	2.99 • *63*	32.24 • *65*	22.73 • *114*	24.98 • *59*	43.0 • *91*	6.4 • *75*	69.0 • *126*	1.2 • *120*
Belgium J3	.be	Brussels	30.50 • *139*	10,364 • *77*	339.8 • *28*	6,037 • *23*	6,710 • *28*	9,120 • *18*	7,268 • *18*	13,954 • *11*	63,220 • *34*	322,837 • *18*	31,149 • *18*	2.2 • *142*	12.25 • *64*	67.02 • *27*	6.47 • *15*	46.44 • *40*	88.32 • *23*	40.62 • *37*	49.8 • *69*	9.1 • *26*	78.5 • *30*	1.3 • *113*
Belize E5	.bz	Belmopan	23.00 • *150*	281 • *177*	12.2 • *196*	146 • *142*	231 • *118*	n/a • –	n/a • –	n/a • –	5,050 • *105*	1,115 • *171*	3,967 • *94*	5.7 • *35*	0.02 • *151*	0.32 • *171*	1.14 • *107*	12.92 • *121*	35.12 • *91*	13.41 • *86*	6.6 • *199*	5.2 • *115*	68.0 • *131*	2.0 • *73*
Benin J5	.bj	Porto Novo	112.60 • *100*	7,649 • *93*	67.9 • *121*	148 • *141*	n/a • –	n/a • –	n/a • –	n/a • –	n/a • –	3,667 • *141*	479 • *184*	4.6 • *58*	0.02 • *151*	0.64 • *153*	0.08 • *187*	1.00 • *194*	5.33 • *161*	1.38 • *170*	29.9 • *128*	4.7 • *137*	53.0 • *185*	1.8 • *83*

•: *Ranking* (top 10 in **bold**). **n/a:** Not available, not relevant or not reliable. **T:** See note on page 41. **M:** See note on page 41. For more information, see pages 202 & 210.

Country / Map Ref. (pp14-15)	Internet code	Capital	Area '000 sq km	Population '000	Population Density People/sq km	International Arrivals 1997 '000	International Arrivals 2004 '000	Visitor Receipts US$ million	International Departures '000	Visitor Expenditure US$ million	Hotel Bedrooms 2003
Bermuda F4	.bm	Hamilton	0.05 • 221	65 • 203	1,307.3 • 6	380 • 104	272 • 111	354 • 90	n/a • –	232 • 68	3,100 • 122
Bhutan N4	.bt	Thimphu	46.50 • 131	2,232 • 142	48.0 • 149	5 • 200	9 • 152	12 • 114	n/a • –	n/a • –	1,239 • 136
Bolivia F8	.bo	note 9	1,098.60 • 28	8,858 • 86	8.1 • 208	355 • 112	405 • 105	n/a • –	672 • 61	n/a • –	20,611 • 58
Bosnia-Herzegovina J3	.ba	Sarajevo	51.10 • 127	4,430 • 119	86.7 • 104	76 • 160	190 • 122	490 • 82	n/a • –	126 • 73	n/a • –
Botswana K7	.bw	Gaborone	581.70 • 47	1,640 • 147	2.8 • 218	607 • 88	1,202 • 73	549 • 77	n/a • –	n/a • –	3,589 • 119
Brazil G6	.br	Brasília	8,547.40 • 5	186,113 • 5	21.8 • 177	2,850 • 40	4,725 • 39	3,222 • 42	2,293 • 42	2,871 • 33	n/a • –
British Virgin Is. F5	.vg	Road Town	0.13 • 217	23 • 214	174.2 • 63	244 • 128	332 • 108	n/a • –	n/a • –	n/a • –	2,705 • 126
Brunei O5	.bn	Bandar Seri Begawan	5.80 • 169	372 • 173	64.2 • 130	643 • 83	n/a • –	n/a • –	n/a • –	n/a • –	n/a • –
Bulgaria K3	.bg	Sofia	111.00 • 102	7,450 • 95	67.1 • 122	2,980 • 37	4,630 • 40	2,168 • 49	3,403 • 36	963 • 45	n/a • –
Burkina H5	.bf	Ouagadougou	274.10 • 74	13,492 • 63	49.2 • 146	138 • 145	n/a • –	n/a • –	n/a • –	n/a • –	n/a • –
Burundi K6	.bi	Bujumbura	27.80 • 145	7,795 • 92	280.4 • 42	11 • 198	n/a • –	n/a • –	n/a • –	n/a • –	n/a • –
Cambodia O5	.kh	Phnom Penh	181.00 • 89	13,636 • 62	75.3 • 116	219 • 130	1,055 • 79	n/a • –	n/a • –	n/a • –	n/a • –
Cameroon J5	.cm	Yaoundé	475.40 • 53	16,988 • 58	35.7 • 162	42 • 178	n/a • –	n/a • –	n/a • –	n/a • –	n/a • –
Canada D2	.ca	Ottawa	9,970.60 • 2	32,805 • 35	3.3 • 214	17,669 • 9	19,150 • 11	12,843 • 12	17,739 • 10	16,017 • 9	n/a • –
Cape Verde H5	.cv	Praia	4.00 • 172	418 • 171	104.6 • 90	45 • 175	157 • 124	109 • 102	n/a • –	78 • 75	n/a • –
Cayman Is. E5	.ky	George Town	0.26 • 205	44 • 208	170.3 • 64	381 • 103	260 • 113	n/a • –	n/a • –	n/a • –	5,127 • 104
Central African Rep. K5	.cf	Bangui	622.40 • 43	4,238 • 121	6.8 • 210	17 • 193	n/a • –	n/a • –	n/a • –	n/a • –	n/a • –
Chad J5	.td	Ndjaména	1,284.00 • 21	9,657 • 82	7.5 • 209	27 • 182	n/a • –	n/a • –	n/a • –	n/a • –	n/a • –
Channel Is. I3	.gg, .je	note 10	0.20 • 212	156 • 190	780.2 • 11	n/a • –	n/a • –	n/a • –	n/a • –	n/a • –	n/a • –
Chile F7	.cl	Santiago	736.90 • 39	15,981 • 60	21.7 • 180	1,644 • 55	1,785 • 61	1,091 • 61	2,100 • 47	892 • 47	52,362 • 39
China O4	.cn	Beijing	9,536.70 • 3	1,306,314 • 1	137.0 • 73	23,770 • 6	41,761 • 4	25,739 • 7	20,222 • 9	19,100 • 7	992,804 • 4
China: Hong Kong SAR[1] O4	.hk	-	1.10 • 180	6,899 • 98	6,271.5 • 4	11,273 • 13	21,811 • 7	9,007 • 19	4,428 • 29	13,258 • 12	42,936 • 44
China: Macau SAR[1] O4	.mo	-	0.02 • 222	449 • 167	22,459.9 • 1	3,836 • 33	8,323 • 24	7,452 • 22	156 • 80	n/a • –	9,185 • 84
Colombia F5	.co	Bogotá	1,141.70 • 26	42,954 • 28	37.6 • 159	639 • 84	744 • 84	1,032 • 63	1,177 • 57	1,290 • 41	54,820 • 38
Comoros L6	.km	Moroni	1.90 • 177	671 • 162	353.3 • 26	26 • 184	n/a • –	n/a • –	n/a • –	n/a • –	n/a • –
Congo J6	.cg	Brazzaville	341.80 • 63	3,602 • 128	10.5 • 200	27 • 182	n/a • –	n/a • –	n/a • –	n/a • –	n/a • –

Country / Map Ref. (pp14-15)	Internet code	Capital	Gross Nat'l Income US$ billion	GNI per Person US$	GDP Growth Av. annual % 1997-2006	Energy Production Million tonnes oil equiv.	Energy Consumption Million tonnes oil equiv.	Energy Consumption Tonnes oil equiv./person	Fixed Tel. Lines Lines/100 people	Mobile Tel. Lines Lines/100 people	Internet Usage Subscribers/100 people	Agricultural Land % of national area	Total Health Spending % of GNI	Life Expectancy Years	Military Spending % of GNI
Bermuda F4	.bm	Hamilton	2,710 • 149	41,459 • 4	n/a • –	0.00 • –	0.20 • 178	3.08 • 61	86.15 • 4	79.03 • 37	62.90 • 10	18.9 • 167	n/a • –	n/a • –	T • –
Bhutan N4	.bt	Thimphu	677 • 186	303 • 204	8.2 • 12	0.52 • 119	0.46 • 161	0.21 • 167	3.88 • 169	2.45 • 187	0.04 • 207	12.5 • 183	4.5 • 144	62.5 • 155	1.8 • 83
Bolivia F8	.bo	note 9	8,656 • 101	977 • 163	3.0 • 117	8.72 • 76	4.70 • 93	0.53 • 141	6.97 • 150	20.07 • 116	3.90 • 139	33.6 • 118	7.0 • 62	65.0 • 146	1.7 • 88
Bosnia-Herzegovina J3	.ba	Sarajevo	7,841 • 103	1,770 • 138	9.1 • 7	4.36 • 84	5.51 • 89	1.24 • 102	22.17 • 97	27.40 • 106	5.38 • 127	41.5 • 95	9.2 • 24	72.5 • 77	2.9 • 35
Botswana K7	.bw	Gaborone	7,490 • 107	4,567 • 86	5.5 • 39	0.58 • 116	1.30 • 130	0.79 • 128	7.96 • 145	33.31 • 96	3.50 • 143	44.7 • 87	6.0 • 92	36.5 • 217	4.1 • 26
Brazil G6	.br	Brasília	552,096 • 13	2,966 • 103	2.4 • 133	178.37 • 14	220.81 • 10	1.19 • 106	23.46 • 93	36.32 • 85	12.18 • 90	30.8 • 125	7.9 • 45	69.5 • 123	1.6 • 93
British Virgin Is. F5	.vg	Road Town	265 • 203	11,703 • 57	n/a • –	0.00 • –	0.02 • 204	0.87 • 124	50.87 • 30	34.78 • 93	17.39 • 78	58.8 • 42	n/a • –	76.5 • 53	T • –
Brunei O5	.bn	Bandar Seri Begawan	6,842 • 111	18,375 • 38	2.1 • 149	21.78 • 54	2.36 • 120	6.34 • 17	25.57 • 86	17.74 • 123	15.30 • 83	3.3 • 206	3.5 • 171	77.0 • 47	6.1 • 11
Bulgaria K3	.bg	Sofia	21,326 • 71	2,862 • 104	3.1 • 112	9.73 • 74	22.22 • 57	2.98 • 64	35.13 • 59	60.94 • 57	28.35 • 51	48.0 • 74	7.4 • 56	72.5 • 77	2.6 • 47
Burkina H5	.bf	Ouagadougou	4,436 • 135	329 • 200	5.6 • 36	0.04 • 146	0.45 • 162	0.03 • 202	0.61 • 205	2.97 • 185	0.40 • 192	37.9 • 109	4.3 • 150	45.0 • 201	1.3 • 113
Burundi K6	.bi	Bujumbura	669 • 187	86 • 224	2.4 • 133	0.04 • 146	0.19 • 180	0.02 • 208	0.34 • 212	0.90 • 204	0.35 • 195	78.0 • 9	3.0 • 182	42.5 • 208	5.9 • 12
Cambodia O5	.kh	Phnom Penh	4,430 • 136	325 • 201	7.0 • 19	0.01 • 158	0.21 • 176	0.02 • 210	0.26 • 217	3.52 • 180	0.28 • 196	29.3 • 134	12.0 • 2	53.5 • 184	2.5 • 53
Cameroon J5	.cm	Yaoundé	13,138 • 89	773 • 167	4.2 • 66	4.38 • 83	1.91 • 125	0.11 • 178	0.59 • 207	9.43 • 148	1.02 • 175	19.3 • 166	4.6 • 140	47.5 • 136	1.5 • 102
Canada D2	.ca	Ottawa	905,629 • 8	27,606 • 21	2.5 • 128	460.91 • 5	337.11 • 7	10.28 • 9	64.27 • 15	46.72 • 75	62.36 • 12	6.8 • 198	9.6 • 16	80.0 • 10	1.2 • 120
Cape Verde H5	.cv	Praia	852 • 177	2,037 • 130	7.2 • 17	0.00 • –	0.06 • 195	0.14 • 173	15.56 • 110	13.94 • 130	5.30 • 129	17.4 • 169	5.0 • 124	70.0 • 116	0.7 • 147
Cayman Is. E5	.ky	George Town	1,391 • 166	31,421 • 16	n/a • –	0.00 • –	0.13 • 185	2.95 • 65	86.36 • 3	38.64 • 81	22.50 • 64	11.6 • 186	n/a • –	80.0 • 10	T • –
Central African Rep. K5	.cf	Bangui	1,226 • 169	289 • 206	1.6 • 159	0.02 • 151	0.15 • 184	0.04 • 200	0.26 • 217	1.53 • 198	0.23 • 197	8.3 • 193	3.9 • 161	42.5 • 208	1.3 • 113
Chad J5	.td	Ndjaména	2,277 • 154	236 • 213	8.4 • 10	2.03 • 100	0.07 • 191	0.01 • 211	0.15 • 222	1.39 • 201	0.68 • 184	37.9 • 109	6.5 • 71	45.5 • 198	1.4 • 109
Channel Is. I3	.gg, .je	note 10	6,190 • 119	39,669 • 7	n/a • –	n/a • –	n/a • –	n/a • –	86.00 • 5	83.33 • 32	42.00 • 35	n/a • –	n/a • –	83.0 • 10	T • –
Chile F7	.cl	Santiago	78,407 • 48	4,906 • 82	4.1 • 68	8.39 • 77	27.59 • 49	1.73 • 86	21.53 • 99	62.08 • 54	27.90 • 54	20.2 • 161	86.0 • 99	77.0 • 47	3.5 • 30
China O4	.cn	Beijing	1,676,846 • 6	1,284 • 146	8.4 • 10	1,102.52 • 3	1,137.06 • 2	0.87 • 123	23.98 • 91	25.76 • 110	7.23 • 113	57.9 • 47	5.8 • 99	71.5 • 95	2.3 • 60
China: Hong Kong SAR[1] O4	.hk	-	183,516 • 29	26,602 • 25	3.1 • 112	0.00 • –	21.82 • 61	3.16 • 59	54.42 • 25	118.77 • 2	50.32 • 21	6.4 • 201	n/a • –	79.5 • 17	n/a • –
China: Macau SAR[1] O4	.mo	-	6,717 • 113	14,953 • 44	n/a • –	0.00 • –	0.66 • 151	1.47 • 95	37.38 • 56	92.94 • 17	32.24 • 45	0.0 • –	n/a • –	82.0 • 1	n/a • –
Colombia F5	.co	Bogotá	90,626 • 44	2,110 • 128	2.2 • 142	76.55 • 29	28.83 • 47	0.67 • 138	17.14 • 108	22.95 • 113	8.94 • 103	40.2 • 101	8.1 • 40	72.5 • 77	4.4 • 18
Comoros L6	.km	Moroni	328 • 199	489 • 180	2.4 • 133	0.00 • –	0.04 • 198	0.06 • 192	1.66 • 185	0.25 • 211	1.01 • 176	78.9 • 7	2.9 • 183	64.0 • 151	3.0 • 34
Congo J6	.cg	Brazzaville	2,974 • 147	826 • 165	3.5 • 91	13.11 • 61	0.38 • 165	0.11 • 180	0.36 • 211	10.05 • 147	0.94 • 178	29.9 • 128	2.2 • 187	54.0 • 183	1.4 • 109

•: *Ranking* (top 10 in **bold**). **n/a:** Not available, not relevant or not reliable. **T:** See note on page 41. **M:** See note on page 41. For more information, see pages 202 & 210.

▶ See also... page 210 for details of maps directly relating to the figures in this section; Contents (2-7) for details of all maps and charts in this Atlas

Country (Map Ref. (pp14-15))	Internet code	Capital	Area ('000 sq km)	Population ('000)	Population Density (People/sq km)	International Arrivals 1997 ('000)	International Arrivals 2004 ('000)	Visitor Receipts (US$ million)	International Departures ('000)	Visitor Expenditure (US$ million)	Hotel Bedrooms 2003	Gross Nat'l Income (US$ billion)	GNI per Person (US$)	GDP Growth (Av. annual % 1997-2006)	Energy Production (Million tonnes oil equiv.)	Energy Consumption (Million tonnes oil equiv.)	Energy Consumption (Tonnes oil equiv./person)	Fixed Tel. Lines (Lines/100 people)	Mobile Tel. Lines (Lines/100 people)	Internet Usage (Subscribers/100 people)	Agricultural Land (% of national area)	Total Health Spending (% of GNI)	Life Expectancy (Years)	Military Spending (% of GNI)
Congo, Dem. Rep. *K6*	.zr	Kinshasa	2,344.90 • 12	60,764 • 20	25.9 • 174	30 • 179	30 • 148	1 • 117	n/a • –	n/a • –	5,829 • 100	6,416 • 117	106 • 223	0.9 • 169	2.78 • 94	2.01 • 122	0.03 • 204	0.02 • 223	1.89 • 194	0.09 • 205	9.7 • 189	4.0 • 159	44.5 • 205	1.0 • 134
Cook Is. *A6*	.ck	Avarua	0.23 • 210	21 • 215	93.0 • 99	50 • 171	83 • 136	n/a • –	10 • 90	n/a • –	1,152 • 137	531 • 189	24,827 • 27	n/a • –	0.00 • –	0.02 • 204	0.95 • 119	29.52 • 73	7.14 • 155	17.14 • 79	25.3 • 146	4.6 • 140	71.0 • 99	T • –
Costa Rica *E5*	.cr	San José	51.10 • 128	4,016 • 123	78.6 • 112	811 • 74	1,453 • 67	1,357 • 58	373 • 70	404 • 58	35,003 • 52	18,969 • 78	4,723 • 84	4.5 • 59	2.22 • 97	4.25 • 100	1.06 • 109	31.62 • 69	21.73 • 115	23.54 • 61	56.1 • 50	9.3 • 21	77.5 • 41	M • –
Côte d'Ivoire *I5*	.ci	note[11]	320.80 • 68	17,298 • 57	53.9 • 142	274 • 122	n/a • –	n/a • –	n/a • –	n/a • –	n/a • –	13,263 • 88	767 • 168	1.0 • 168	3.40 • 90	2.53 • 117	0.15 • 171	1.43 • 188	9.07 • 149	1.78 • 165	23.6 • 155	6.2 • 81	45.5 • 198	1.5 • 102
Croatia *J3*	.hr	Zagreb	56.50 • 126	4,496 • 117	79.6 • 111	4,178 • 31	7,912 • 25	6,973 • 23	n/a • –	841 • 48	77,113 • 29	29,700 • 61	6,606 • 75	3.6 • 85	4.32 • 85	9.95 • 78	2.21 • 79	42.74 • 51	58.37 • 63	29.51 • 48	55.6 • 52	7.4 • 56	74.5 • 63	2.1 • 66
Cuba *F4*	.cu	Havana	110.90 • 103	11,347 • 72	102.3 • 91	1,153 • 63	2,017 • 58	n/a • –	113 • 82	n/a • –	43,696 • 43	25,501 • 66	2,247 • 123	3.7 • 81	3.76 • 88	11.78 • 74	1.04 • 111	6.78 • 151	0.67 • 206	1.32 • 171	60.1 • 39	7.5 • 55	77.0 • 47	n/a • –
Cyprus[2] *K4*	.cy	Nicosia	9.30 • 166	780 • 158	83.9 • 105	2,088 • 52	2,349 • 55	2,096 • 50	629 • 63	208 • 70	46,706 • 41	13,633 • 85	17,475 • 40	3.5 • 91	0.00 • –	2.83 • 114	3.63 • 47	51.84 • 27	79.37 • 36	36.93 • 41	1.1 • 212	7.0 • 62	78.5 • 30	1.5 • 102
Czech Rep. *J3*	.cz	Prague	78.90 • 117	10,241 • 79	129.8 • 76	4,976 • 27	6,061 • 33	4,169 • 37	36,074 • **5**	2,271 • 39	97,282 • 23	93,155 • 42	9,096 • 66	2.2 • 142	28.70 • 49	43.46 • 38	4.24 • 37	33.58 • 62	105.64 • **5**	49.97 • 25	54.2 • 61	7.0 • 62	75.5 • 59	2.2 • 63
Denmark *J3*	.dk	Copenhagen	43.10 • 133	5,432 • 108	126.0 • 78	2,158 • 51	3,358 • 46	5,669 • 29	5,564 • 25	n/a • –	41,729 • 45	219,422 • 27	40,392 • **6**	2.0 • 153	29.41 • 47	22.17 • 58	4.08 • 39	64.46 • 14	95.51 • 15	60.41 • 14	61.9 • 31	8.8 • 31	77.5 • 41	1.5 • 102
Djibouti *L5*	.dj	Djibouti	23.20 • 149	477 • 165	20.5 • 181	20 • 191	n/a • –	n/a • –	n/a • –	n/a • –	n/a • –	739 • 183	1,550 • 141	2.2 • 142	0.00 • –	0.66 • 151	1.38 • 100	1.63 • 186	5.07 • 164	1.32 • 171	56.1 • 50	6.3 • 77	54.5 • 182	4.3 • 20
Dominica *F5*	.dm	Roseau	0.75 • 184	69 • 201	92.0 • 100	65 • 167	n/a • –	n/a • –	n/a • –	n/a • –	n/a • –	261 • 204	3,781 • 98	0.9 • 169	0.01 • 158	0.05 • 197	0.72 • 135	29.40 • 74	58.68 • 61	28.75 • 50	29.3 • 134	6.4 • 75	73.5 • 75	M • –
Dominican Republic *F5*	.do	Santo Domingo	48.40 • 130	9,050 • 84	187.0 • 57	2,211 • 50	3,450 • 45	3,180 • 43	321 • 72	n/a • –	56,378 • 35	18,443 • 79	2,038 • 129	4.9 • 48	0.35 • 125	7.27 • 83	0.80 • 127	10.65 • 134	28.82 • 101	9.10 • 102	76.3 • 12	6.1 • 87	68.5 • 127	1.1 • 129
East Timor *P6*	.tp	Dili	14.60 • 158	1,041 • 155	71.3 • 119	n/a • –	n/a • –	n/a • –	n/a • –	n/a • –	n/a • –	506 • 190	486 • 181	4.0 • 73	n/a • –	n/a • –	n/a • –	n/a • –	n/a • –	n/a • –	19.6 • 162	9.7 • 13	58.0 • 176	n/a • –
Ecuador *F6*	.ec	Quito	275.80 • 73	13,364 • 64	48.5 • 148	529 • 92	793 • 83	367 • 89	613 • 64	391 • 59	38,237 • 47	28,783 • 63	2,154 • 127	2.6 • 126	24.69 • 50	9.73 • 80	0.73 • 134	12.22 • 126	26.86 • 108	4.73 • 133	29.7 • 130	4.8 • 133	71.0 • 99	2.4 • 57
Egypt *K4*	.eg	Cairo	997.70 • 30	77,506 • 15	77.7 • 114	3,656 • 34	7,051 • 26	6,125 • 26	3,644 • 34	1,257 • 43	136,510 • 18	90,129 • 45	1,163 • 149	4.9 • 48	67.62 • 32	58.06 • 29	0.75 • 132	13.52 • 117	10.92 • 143	5.57 • 126	3.4 • 205	4.9 • 128	67.0 • 137	2.6 • 47
El Salvador *E5*	.sv	San Salvador	21.00 • 152	6,705 • 99	319.3 • 32	387 • 102	966 • 80	337 • 91	940 • 58	240 • 67	4,578 • 109	15,613 • 81	2,329 • 117	2.5 • 128	0.89 • 111	2.98 • 113	0.44 • 146	13.42 • 119	27.71 • 105	8.88 • 104	81.0 • **5**	8.0 • 42	70.0 • 116	0.7 • 147
Equatorial Guinea *J5*	.gq	Malabo	28.10 • 144	529 • 164	18.8 • 185	n/a • –	n/a • –	n/a • –	n/a • –	n/a • –	n/a • –	323 • 201	611 • 171	34.8 • **1**	11.47 • 66	1.24 • 134	2.34 • 75	1.77 • 181	10.95 • 142	0.99 • 177	11.9 • 185	1.8 • 191	51.0 • 190	2.5 • 53
Eritrea *K5*	.er	Asmara	93.70 • 109	4,670 • 115	49.8 • 144	410 • 100	87 • 134	73 • 106	n/a • –	n/a • –	4,139 • 115	806 • 178	173 • 219	1.4 • 163	0.00 • –	0.24 • 175	0.05 • 196	9.30 • 139	4.74 • 168	11.84 • 91	61.7 • 32	5.1 • 119	59.5 • 169	19.4 • **1**
Estonia *K3*	.ee	Tallinn	45.20 • 132	1,333 • 151	29.5 • 169	730 • 77	1,750 • 63	806 • 70	2,075 • 48	365 • 61	12,445 • 74	9,435 • 98	7,079 • 71	6.5 • 25	3.07 • 92	5.59 • 87	4.19 • 38	33.95 • 61	96.00 • 13	51.22 • 20	15.4 • 173	5.1 • 119	71.0 • 99	1.9 • 77
Ethiopia *L5*	.et	Addis Ababa	1,104.30 • 27	73,053 • 16	66.2 • 126	139 • 144	n/a • –	n/a • –	n/a • –	n/a • –	3,497 • 120	7,747 • 105	106 • 222	4.4 • 61	0.52 • 119	1.94 • 123	0.03 • 207	0.63 • 204	0.25 • 211	0.16 • 201	27.1 • 141	5.7 • 107	50.0 • 192	4.3 • 20
Falkland Is. *G8*	.fk	Stanley	12.20 • 160	3 • 225	0.2 • 225	n/a • –	n/a • –	n/a • –	n/a • –	n/a • –	n/a • –	32 • 217	10,785 • 61	n/a • –	0.00 • –	0.01 • 207	3.33 • 55	80.00 • **6**	n/a • –	50.00 • 23	92.8 • **1**	n/a • –	0.0 • –	T • –
Faroe Is. *I2*	.fo	Tórshavn	1.40 • 179	47 • 207	33.5 • 164	n/a • –	n/a • –	n/a • –	n/a • –	n/a • –	n/a • –	1,008 • 173	21,464 • 32	n/a • –	0.02 • 151	0.26 • 173	5.53 • 22	49.76 • 34	85.78 • 28	66.47 • **5**	2.1 • 211	n/a • –	79.5 • 17	T • –
Fiji Is. *R6*	.fj	Suva	18.30 • 155	893 • 156	48.8 • 147	359 • 110	507 • 99	n/a • –	104 • 83	n/a • –	6,142 • 98	2,281 • 153	2,553 • 108	2.5 • 128	0.16 • 134	0.68 • 148	0.76 • 131	12.35 • 123	13.31 • 134	7.20 • 114	25.1 • 147	4.2 • 158	68.5 • 127	2.2 • 63
Finland *K2*	.fi	Helsinki	338.10 • 64	5,223 • 111	15.4 • 189	1,832 • 54	2,840 • 53	2,060 • 51	5,585 • 24	n/a • –	55,767 • 37	171,024 • 30	32,742 • 14	3.6 • 85	10.49 • 70	30.48 • 46	5.84 • 20	45.40 • 44	95.63 • 14	63.00 • **9**	6.6 • 199	7.3 • 59	78.5 • 30	1.2 • 120
France[3] *J3*	.fr	Paris	549.10 • 49	60,656 • 21	110.5 • 85	66,591 • **1**	75,121 • **1**	40,842 • **3**	17,426 • 11	28,636 • **5**	603,279 • **7**	1,858,731 • **5**	30,644 • 19	1.7 • 156	128.38 • 21	281.05 • **8**	4.63 • 28	56.04 • 22	73.72 • 45	41.37 • 36	54.3 • 59	9.7 • 13	80.0 • **10**	2.6 • 47
French Guiana *G5*	.gf	Cayenne	85.50 • 114	196 • 184	2.3 • 222	68 • 164	n/a • –	n/a • –	n/a • –	n/a • –	n/a • –	2,282 • 152	11,672 • 58	n/a • –	0.00 • –	0.36 • 167	1.84 • 84	30.22 • 72	53.55 • 67	20.77 • 70	0.3 • 215	n/a • –	77.5 • 41	n/a • –

•: *Ranking* (top 10 in **bold**). **n/a:** Not available, not relevant or not reliable. **T:** See note on page 41. **M:** See note on page 41. For more information, see pages 202 & 210.

▶ *See also...* page 210 for details of maps directly relating to the figures in this section; Contents (2-7) for details of all maps and charts in this Atlas

Country Map Ref. (pp14-15)	Internet code	**Capital**	**Area** '000 sq km	**Population** '000	**Population Density** People/sq km	**International Arrivals 1997** '000	**International Arrivals 2004** '000	**Visitor Receipts** US$ million	**International Departures** '000	**Visitor Expenditure** US$ million	**Hotel Bedrooms 2003**	**Gross Nat'l Income** US$ billion	**GNI per Person** US$	**GDP Growth** Av. annual % 1997-2006	**Energy Production** Million tonnes oil equiv.	**Energy Consumption** Million tonnes oil equiv.	**Energy Consumption** Tonnes oil equiv./person	**Fixed Tel. Lines** Lines/100 people	**Mobile Tel. Lines** Lines/100 people	**Internet Usage** Subscribers/100 people	**Agricultural Land** % of national area	**Total Health Spending** % of GNI	**Life Expectancy** Years	**Military Spending** % of GNI
French Polynesia B7	.pf	Papeete	4.20 • 171	270 • 180	64.4 • 129	180 • 137	212 • 119	n/a • –	n/a • –	n/a • –	3,221 • 121	3,794 • 138	14,027 • 50	n/a • –	0.02 • 151	0.27 • 172	1.00 • 115	21.48 • 100	29.24 • 100	18.15 • 75	10.8 • 187	n/a • –	76.0 • 55	T • –
Gabon J6	.ga	Libreville	267.70 • 76	1,394 • 150	5.2 • 212	167 • 139	n/a • –	n/a • –	236 • 75	n/a • –	n/a • –	5,415 • 123	3,884 • 96	4.7 • 53	13.30 • 59	0.98 • 140	0.70 • 136	3.17 • 173	36.20 • 86	2.96 • 153	19.3 • 165	4.3 • 150	57.5 • 177	0.3 • 162
Gambia, The H5	.gm	Banjul	10.70 • 164	1,595 • 148	149.1 • 70	85 • 156	n/a • –	n/a • –	n/a • –	n/a • –	n/a • –	414 • 193	260 • 208	4.7 • 53	0.00 • –	0.10 • 188	0.06 • 189	2.89 • 177	11.97 • 138	3.35 • 146	63.2 • 27	7.3 • 59	57.5 • 177	0.6 • 152
Georgia L3	.ge	Tbilisi	69.70 • 121	4,677 • 114	67.1 • 123	313 • 118	n/a • –	n/a • –	n/a • –	n/a • –	n/a • –	4,683 • 132	1,001 • 159	6.0 • 30	1.96 • 101	3.49 • 109	0.75 • 133	13.47 • 118	16.57 • 126	3.46 • 144	43.1 • 90	3.8 • 163	71.0 • 59	1.1 • 129
Germany J3	.de	Berlin	357.00 • 62	82,431 • 14	230.9 • 50	15,837 • 12	20,137 **• 9**	27,657 **• 5**	74,600 **• 1**	72,271 **• 1**	892,302 **• 5**	2,488,974 **• 3**	30,194 • 20	1.2 • 165	132.43 • 19	356.03 **• 5**	4.32 • 34	66.15 • 12	86.42 • 27	42.67 • 33	47.5 • 75	10.9 **• 7**	79.0 • 24	1.4 • 109
Ghana I5	.gh	Accra	238.50 • 81	21,946 • 50	92.0 • 101	325 • 115	n/a • –	n/a • –	n/a • –	n/a • –	n/a • –	8,090 • 102	369 • 197	4.8 • 50	1.53 • 105	3.14 • 112	0.14 • 174	1.47 • 187	7.93 • 152	1.72 • 166	61.5 • 33	5.6 • 109	58.5 • 175	0.7 • 147
Gibraltar I4	.gi	Gibraltar	0.01 • 225	28 • 213	4,647.3 **• 5**	n/a • –	n/a • –	n/a • –	n/a • –	n/a • –	n/a • –	498 • 192	17,860 • 39	n/a • –	0.00 • –	1.32 • 129	47.14 **• 2**	87.50 **• 2**	35.00 • 92	22.14 • 65	0.0 • –	n/a • –	80.0 **• 10**	T • –
Greece K4	.gr	Athens	132.00 • 96	10,668 • 75	80.8 • 107	10,070 • 16	13,787 • 16	12,872 • 11	n/a • –	2,874 • 32	330,970 **• 9**	183,917 • 28	17,239 • 41	3.4 • 98	10.38 • 71	35.57 • 41	3.33 • 54	57.84 • 20	84.77 • 29	17.81 • 77	64.0 • 23	9.5 • 19	78.5 • 30	4.1 • 26
Greenland G2	.gl	Nuuk	2,166.10 • 14	56 • 206	0.0 • 226	n/a • –	n/a • –	n/a • –	n/a • –	n/a • –	n/a • –	764 • 181	13,552 • 53	n/a • –	0.00 • –	0.20 • 178	3.57 • 49	44.69 • 46	35.15 • 90	66.32 **• 6**	0.1 • 216	n/a • –	n/a • –	T • –
Grenada F5	.gd	St George's	0.34 • 202	90 • 196	263.2 • 46	111 • 148	134 • 126	n/a • –	n/a • –	n/a • –	1,758 • 131	397 • 194	4,436 • 89	3.4 • 98	0.00 • –	0.09 • 189	1.00 • 115	31.75 • 68	42.05 • 78	7.77 • 110	37.6 • 111	5.7 • 107	67.5 • 135	M • –
Guadeloupe F5	.gp	note **12**	1.70 • 178	449 • 168	263.9 • 45	660 • 80	n/a • –	n/a • –	n/a • –	n/a • –	7,603 • 90	6,006 • 120	13,385 • 54	n/a • –	0.00 • –	0.67 • 149	1.49 • 94	48.73 • 36	71.04 • 48	17.83 • 76	28.2 • 139	n/a • –	78.0 • 39	n/a • –
Guam O5	.gu	Agaña	0.54 • 191	169 • 188	312.2 • 33	1,382 • 60	1,160 • 75	n/a • –	n/a • –	n/a • –	7,227 • 93	3,120 • 146	18,509 • 36	n/a • –	0.00 • –	1.00 • 139	5.92 • 19	50.89 • 29	19.29 • 119	47.88 • 29	40.1 • 102	n/a • –	78.5 • 30	T • –
Guatemala E5	.gt	Guatemala City	108.90 • 104	12,014 • 68	110.3 • 86	576 • 89	1,182 • 74	770 • 72	658 • 62	649 • 50	17,519 • 64	26,945 • 64	2,243 • 124	3.3 • 103	1.95 • 102	4.35 • 97	0.36 • 151	8.94 • 141	25.02 • 111	5.97 • 123	41.4 • 97	4.8 • 133	66.5 • 140	0.5 • 156
Guinea I5	.gn	Conakry	245.90 • 78	9,453 • 83	38.4 • 158	17 • 193	45 • 143	30 • 111	n/a • –	n/a • –	n/a • –	3,681 • 140	389 • 195	3.7 • 81	0.11 • 137	0.56 • 156	0.06 • 193	0.34 • 212	1.44 • 199	0.53 • 186	49.8 • 69	5.8 • 99	52.0 • 187	2.9 • 35
Guinea-Bissau I5	.gw	Bissau	36.10 • 137	1,413 • 149	39.2 • 156	n/a • –	n/a • –	n/a • –	n/a • –	n/a • –	n/a • –	250 • 207	177 • 218	-0.3 • 175	0.00 • –	0.13 • 185	0.09 • 183	0.82 • 196	0.10 • 215	1.99 • 164	45.1 • 85	6.3 • 77	46.5 • 197	3.1 • 32
Guyana G5	.gy	Georgetown	215.00 • 84	765 • 160	3.6 • 213	76 • 160	122 • 127	n/a • –	n/a • –	n/a • –	n/a • –	765 • 180	1,000 • 160	1.1 • 167	0.00 • –	0.60 • 155	0.78 • 129	13.39 • 120	13.64 • 132	18.90 • 73	8.1 • 194	5.6 • 109	62.5 • 155	0.9 • 138
Haiti F5	.ht	Port-au-Prince	27.80 • 146	8,122 • 90	292.1 • 39	149 • 140	n/a • –	n/a • –	n/a • –	n/a • –	n/a • –	3,380 • 143	416 • 192	0.9 • 169	0.06 • 144	0.67 • 149	0.08 • 188	1.71 • 182	4.87 • 166	6.09 • 122	57.3 • 48	7.6 • 52	53.0 • 195	0.9 • 138
Honduras E5	.hn	Tegucigalpa	112.10 • 101	7,168 • 96	63.9 • 131	307 • 119	672 • 87	396 • 87	277 • 73	210 • 69	18,590 • 62	7,321 • 108	1,021 • 157	3.4 • 98	0.44 • 121	2.52 • 118	0.35 • 154	5.57 • 157	10.10 • 146	3.18 • 152	26.1 • 143	6.2 • 81	67.0 • 137	0.4 • 159
Hungary J3	.hu	Budapest	93.00 • 110	10,007 • 81	107.6 • 87	2,887 • 39	12,212 • 17	4,061 • 38	14,283 • 14	2,864 • 34	64,091 • 33	83,315 • 46	8,326 • 70	4.0 • 73	9.73 • 74	26.86 • 50	2.68 • 69	35.43 • 58	86.43 • 26	26.74 • 56	63.1 • 28	7.8 • 48	72.5 • 77	1.8 • 83
Iceland I2	.is	Reykjavik	103.00 • 105	297 • 176	2.9 • 217	202 • 132	836 • 82	372 • 88	n/a • –	n/a • –	7,330 • 92	11,199 • 96	37,740 **• 8**	n/a • –	2.50 • 95	3.50 • 108	11.78 **• 8**	65.01 • 13	99.00 **• 10**	77.00 **• 2**	22.1 • 159	9.9 • 11	80.0 **• 10**	M • –
India **19** M4	.in	New Delhi	3,065.00 **• 7**	1,080,264 **• 2**	352.5 • 27	2,374 • 45	3,457 • 44	4,739 • 35	5,351 • 26	5,072 • 24	91,720 • 25	674,580 • 11	624 • 170	6.0 • 30	253.66 • 11	350.75 **• 6**	0.32 • 156	4.07 • 167	4.37 • 170	3.24 • 151	55.1 • 55	6.1 • 87	61.5 • 158	2.1 • 66
Indonesia O6	.id	Jakarta	1,919.40 • 16	241,974 **• 4**	126.1 • 77	5,185 • 25	5,322 • 37	4,798 • 34	n/a • –	3,507 • 28	263,014 • 11	248,007 • 23	1,025 • 156	2.7 • 124	216.96 • 12	117.97 • 20	0.49 • 144	4.49 • 162	13.48 • 133	6.52 • 120	23.3 • 156	3.2 • 177	66.5 • 140	1.5 • 102
Iran L4	.ir	Tehran	1,648.00 • 18	68,018 • 18	41.3 • 153	764 • 76	n/a • –	n/a • –	n/a • –	n/a • –	n/a • –	153,984 • 33	2,264 • 120	4.8 • 50	281.68 **• 6**	150.98 • 16	2.22 • 78	21.97 • 98	6.16 • 158	7.88 • 108	37.1 • 112	6.0 • 92	69.5 • 123	3.8 • 28
Iraq L4	.iq	Baghdad	438.30 • 58	26,075 • 44	59.5 • 137	15 • 197	n/a • –	n/a • –	n/a • –	n/a • –	n/a • –	n/a • –	#VALUE! • –	n/a • –	71.44 • 31	24.40 • 53	0.94 • 120	4.00 • 168	2.22 • 191	0.14 • 202	23.0 • 157	1.5 • 192	55.5 • 180	n/a • –
Ireland I3	.ie	Dublin	70.30 • 120	4,016 • 124	57.1 • 139	5,587 • 24	6,982 • 27	4,279 • 36	4,929 • 28	5,200 • 23	n/a • –	137,761 • 36	34,306 • 12	7.7 • 13	0.88 • 112	15.20 • 68	3.78 • 44	49.94 • 33	93.49 • 16	29.63 • 47	62.7 • 29	7.3 • 59	78.5 • 30	1.0 • 134
Israel **20** K4	.il	Jerusalem	21.90 • 151	6,277 • 101	286.6 • 41	2,010 • 53	1,506 • 65	2,383 • 47	3,299 • 38	2,976 • 30	46,368 • 42	118,124 • 37	18,819 • 34	n/a • –	0.20 • 132	22.28 • 56	3.55 • 50	43.72 • 49	105.25 **• 6**	46.63 • 32	25.6 • 145	9.1 • 26	80.0 **• 10**	9.1 **• 4**

•: *Ranking* (top 10 in **bold**). **n/a:** Not available, not relevant or not reliable. **T:** See note on page 41. **M:** See note on page 41. For more information, see pages 202 & 210.

▶ *See also...* page 210 for details of maps directly relating to the figures in this section; Contents (2-7) for details of all maps and charts in this Atlas

Country (Map Ref. (pp14-15))	Internet code	Capital	Area ('000 sq km)	Population ('000)	Population Density (People/sq km)	International Arrivals 1997 ('000)	International Arrivals 2004 ('000)	Visitor Receipts (US$ million)	International Departures ('000)	Visitor Expenditure (US$ million)	Hotel Bedrooms 2003
Italy *J3*	.it	Rome	301.30 • 71	58,103 • 23	192.8 • 55	34,692 • **4**	37,071 • **5**	35,658 • **4**	26,817 • **7**	20,544 • **6**	999,722 • **3**
Jamaica *F5*	.jm	Kingston	11.40 • 162	2,736 • 138	240.0 • 49	1,192 • 62	1,415 • 68	1,437 • 57	n/a • –	287 • 64	20,827 • 57
Japan *P4*	.jp	Tokyo	377.80 • 61	127,417 • **10**	337.3 • 29	4,218 • 30	6,138 • 32	11,294 • 13	13,296 • 15	38,129 • **4**	1,562,867 • **2**
Jordan *K4*	.jo	Amman	91.90 • 111	5,760 • 105	62.7 • 133	1,127 • 64	2,853 • 52	826 • 67	1,533 • 51	n/a • –	19,698 • 61
Kazakhstan *M3*	.kz	Astana	2,717.30 • **9**	15,186 • 61	5.6 • 211	1,471 • 59	n/a • –	n/a • –	2,374 • 41	n/a • –	11,104 • 77
Kenya *K5*	.ke	Nairobi	582.60 • 46	33,830 • 34	58.1 • 138	907 • 70	1,132 • 77	495 • 81	n/a • –	n/a • –	n/a • –
Kiribati *A6*	.ki	Bairiki	0.72 • 186	103 • 195	143.2 • 71	5 • 200	n/a • –	n/a • –	n/a • –	n/a • –	n/a • –
Korea, DPR (North) *P3*	.kp	Pyongyang	122.80 • 98	22,912 • 47	186.6 • 58	n/a • –	n/a • –	n/a • –	n/a • –	n/a • –	n/a • –
Korea, Rep. (South) *P4*	.kr	Seoul	99.40 • 107	48,641 • 24	489.3 • 19	3,908 • 32	5,818 • 35	5,697 • 28	7,086 • 19	9,499 • 16	56,196 • 36
Kuwait *L4*	.kw	Kuwait City	17.80 • 156	2,336 • 140	131.2 • 75	79 • 159	91 • 132	180 • 98	n/a • –	n/a • –	n/a • –
Kyrgyzstan *M3*	.kg	Bishkek	199.90 • 86	5,146 • 112	25.7 • 175	87 • 155	n/a • –	n/a • –	n/a • –	n/a • –	n/a • –
Laos *O5*	.la	Vientiane	236.80 • 82	6,217 • 102	26.3 • 173	193 • 134	236 • 117	119 • 101	n/a • –	n/a • –	12,289 • 76
Latvia *K3*	.lv	Riga	64.60 • 124	2,290 • 141	35.5 • 163	635 • 85	1,080 • 78	267 • 94	2,286 • 43	377 • 60	7,618 • 89
Lebanon *K4*	.lb	Beirut	10.50 • 165	3,826 • 126	364.4 • 25	558 • 90	1,278 • 70	1,278 • 59	n/a • –	n/a • –	16,202 • 69
Lesotho *K7*	.ls	Maseru	30.40 • 140	2,031 • 144	66.8 • 124	144 • 143	n/a • –	n/a • –	n/a • –	n/a • –	n/a • –
Liberia *I5*	.lr	Monrovia	99.10 • 108	2,900 • 136	29.3 • 170	n/a • –	n/a • –	n/a • –	n/a • –	n/a • –	n/a • –
Libya *J4*	.ly	Tripoli	1,775.50 • 17	5,766 • 104	3.2 • 215	50 • 171	n/a • –	n/a • –	n/a • –	n/a • –	12,405 • 75
Liechtenstein *J3*	.li	Vaduz	0.16 • 216	34 • 210	210.7 • 52	57 • 170	50 • 142	n/a • –	n/a • –	n/a • –	591 • 141
Lithuania *K3*	.lt	Vilnius	65.30 • 123	3,597 • 129	55.1 • 140	1,012 • 67	1,800 • 60	817 • 68	3,502 • 35	639 • 51	7,694 • 87
Luxembourg *J3*	.lu	Luxembourg	2.60 • 174	469 • 166	180.2 • 60	778 • 75	874 • 81	3,666 • 41	n/a • –	3,347 • 29	7,626 • 88
Macedonia, FYR *K3*	.mk	Skopje	25.70 • 148	2,045 • 143	79.6 • 110	121 • 147	165 • 123	72 • 107	n/a • –	55 • 76	6,825 • 94
Madagascar *L8*	.mg	Antananarivo	587.00 • 45	18,040 • 56	30.7 • 167	101 • 151	200 • 120	n/a • –	n/a • –	n/a • –	9,325 • 82
Malawi *K6*	.mw	Lilongwe	118.50 • 99	12,707 • 65	107.2 • 88	207 • 131	414 • 104	n/a • –	n/a • –	n/a • –	20,871 • 56
Malaysia *O5*	.my	Kuala Lumpur	329.80 • 66	23,953 • 46	72.6 • 117	6,211 • 22	15,703 • 13	8,198 • 20	32,201 • **6**	n/a • –	144,380 • 16
Maldives *M6*	.mv	Malé	0.30 • 204	349 • 174	1,163.7 • **8**	366 • 108	617 • 90	479 • 83	44 • 87	n/a • –	8,557 • 85
Mali *I5*	.ml	Bamako	1,248.60 • 22	11,415 • 71	9.1 • 205	75 • 162	113 • 129	n/a • –	n/a • –	n/a • –	3,907 • 116

Country	Gross Nat'l Income (US$ billion)	GNI per Person (US$)	GDP Growth (Av. annual % 1997-2006)	Energy Production (Million tonnes oil equiv.)	Energy Consumption (Million tonnes oil equiv.)	Energy Consumption (Tonnes oil equiv./person)	Fixed Tel. Lines (Lines/100 people)	Mobile Tel. Lines (Lines/100 people)	Internet Usage (Subscribers/100 people)	Agricultural Land (% of national area)	Total Health Spending (% of GNI)	Life Expectancy (Years)	Military Spending (% of GNI)
Italy	1,503,562 • **7**	25,878 • 26	1.2 • 165	31.19 • 45	199.05 • 12	3.43 • 52	44.75 • 45	108.19 • **4**	49.78 • 26	51.2 • 67	8.5 • 35	81.0 • **4**	1.9 • 77
Jamaica	7,738 • 106	2,829 • 106	1.3 • 164	0.05 • 145	3.84 • 106	1.40 • 99	14.60 • 113	82.21 • 34	39.87 • 38	46.7 • 81	6.0 • 92	72.5 • 77	0.4 • 159
Japan	4,749,910 • **2**	37,278 • **9**	0.9 • 169	98.56 • 23	560.53 • **4**	4.40 • 33	46.00 • 43	71.58 • 47	50.20 • 22	13.7 • 177	7.9 • 45	81.5 • **2**	1.0 • 134
Jordan	11,629 • 92	2,019 • 132	4.4 • 61	0.37 • 123	5.96 • 85	1.03 • 112	11.00 • 131	28.41 • 104	10.69 • 98	12.8 • 181	9.3 • 21	71.0 • 99	8.9 • **6**
Kazakhstan	33,780 • 60	2,224 • 125	7.1 • 18	104.38 • 22	52.22 • 33	3.44 • 51	16.23 • 109	17.91 • 122	2.60 • 157	76.1 • 13	3.5 • 171	61.5 • 158	1.1 • 129
Kenya	14,987 • 82	443 • 186	2.8 • 123	1.00 • 108	3.84 • 106	0.11 • 177	0.92 • 195	7.85 • 153	4.63 • 135	45.6 • 84	4.9 • 128	49.5 • 193	1.7 • 88
Kiribati	95 • 215	922 • 164	4.2 • 66	0.00 • –	0.01 • 207	0.10 • 182	5.11 • 158	0.59 • 207	2.35 • 160	48.1 • 73	8.0 • 42	64.5 • 150	T • –
Korea, DPR (North)	11,047 • 97	482 • 183	n/a • –	20.45 • 55	22.04 • 59	0.96 • 118	4.10 • 166	n/a • –	n/a • –	22.4 • 158	4.6 • 140	66.5 • 140	n/a • –
Korea, Rep. (South)	673,036 • 12	13,837 • 52	4.7 • 53	33.93 • 42	215.84 • 11	4.44 • 32	55.31 • 23	76.09 • 41	65.68 • **7**	19.5 • 163	5.0 • 124	76.5 • 53	2.5 • 53
Kuwait	43,052 • 58	18,433 • 37	3.0 • 117	130.29 • 20	23.45 • 54	10.04 • **10**	19.47 • 103	78.34 • 38	23.50 • 62	8.5 • 191	3.8 • 163	77.5 • 41	9.0 • **5**
Kyrgyzstan	2,050 • 157	398 • 193	5.6 • 36	3.46 • 89	4.63 • 94	0.90 • 122	8.18 • 144	5.17 • 162	5.16 • 130	54.3 • 59	4.3 • 150	63.5 • 152	2.9 • 35
Laos	2,239 • 155	360 • 198	6.2 • 28	1.11 • 107	1.24 • 134	0.20 • 168	1.30 • 190	3.53 • 179	0.36 • 194	7.9 • 195	2.9 • 183	59.0 • 172	2.1 • 66
Latvia	12,570 • 90	5,489 • 80	6.8 • 23	0.54 • 118	3.90 • 103	1.70 • 87	28.45 • 77	67.22 • 51	n/a • –	38.3 • 107	5.1 • 119	71.0 • 99	1.7 • 88
Lebanon	22,668 • 69	5,925 • 78	3.0 • 117	0.26 • 129	5.74 • 86	1.50 • 93	17.75 • 105	25.01 • 112	16.90 • 80	31.5 • 124	11.5 • **3**	70.0 • 116	4.3 • 20
Lesotho	1,336 • 167	658 • 169	2.0 • 153	0.09 • 139	0.17 • 183	0.08 • 186	2.07 • 180	8.83 • 150	2.39 • 159	76.9 • 11	6.2 • 81	37.5 • 216	2.6 • 47
Liberia	391 • 196	135 • 221	n/a • –	0.00 • –	0.18 • 182	0.06 • 190	0.21 • 219	1.40 • 200	0.03 • 208	26.6 • 142	2.1 • 188	41.5 • 210	7.5 • **8**
Libya	25,257 • 68	4,381 • 90	3.5 • 91	83.91 • 26	18.15 • 65	3.15 • 60	13.56 • 116	2.30 • 189	3.62 • 141	8.7 • 190	3.3 • 175	63.5 • 152	2.0 • 73
Liechtenstein	1,252 • 168	37,133 • **10**	n/a • –	n/a • –	n/a • –	n/a • –	n/a • –	n/a • –	n/a • –	56.3 • 49	n/a • –	79.5 • 17	T • –
Lithuania	19,727 • 75	5,485 • 81	5.9 • 32	4.63 • 81	10.95 • 75	3.04 • 62	23.80 • 92	99.29 • **9**	28.09 • 52	53.4 • 65	5.9 • 96	72.0 • 87	1.6 • 93
Luxembourg	25,302 • 67	53,998 • **1**	5.2 • 42	0.04 • 146	4.46 • 96	9.51 • 13	79.75 • **7**	119.38 • **1**	59.00 • 15	24.0 • 152	6.2 • 81	79.0 • 24	0.9 • 138
Macedonia, FYR	4,855 • 127	2,374 • 113	2.4 • 133	1.56 • 104	2.77 • 115	1.35 • 101	25.19 • 89	37.23 • 82	7.70 • 111	48.3 • 72	6.8 • 69	72.0 • 87	2.5 • 53
Madagascar	5,181 • 124	287 • 207	3.2 • 108	0.14 • 136	0.92 • 144	0.05 • 197	0.33 • 214	1.87 • 195	0.50 • 187	46.9 • 77	2.1 • 188	57.0 • 179	1.4 • 109
Malawi	1,922 • 158	151 • 220	5.9 • 32	0.32 • 126	0.61 • 154	0.05 • 198	0.75 • 200	1.80 • 196	0.37 • 193	36.2 • 114	9.8 • 12	35.0 • 219	0.8 • 144
Malaysia	117,132 • 38	4,890 • 83	4.4 • 61	93.04 • 24	57.85 • 30	2.42 • 73	17.38 • 106	57.12 • 66	38.62 • 40	23.9 • 153	3.8 • 163	72.5 • 77	2.8 • 40
Maldives	752 • 182	2,154 • 126	6.9 • 20	0.00 • –	0.85 • 145	2.44 • 72	9.60 • 138	34.53 • 94	5.79 • 124	43.6 • 89	5.8 • 99	65.0 • 146	5.5 • 13
Mali	4,335 • 137	380 • 196	5.2 • 42	0.17 • 133	0.38 • 165	0.03 • 203	0.68 • 202	3.60 • 177	0.45 • 190	28.0 • 140	4.5 • 144	45.0 • 201	1.9 • 77

•: *Ranking* (top 10 in **bold**). **n/a:** Not available, not relevant or not reliable. **T:** See note on page 41. **M:** See note on page 41. For more information, see pages 202 & 210.

▶ See also... page 210 for details of maps directly relating to the figures in this section; Contents (2-7) for details of all maps and charts in this Atlas

Country (Map Ref. (pp14-15))	Internet code	Capital	Area ('000 sq km)	Population ('000)	Population Density (People/sq km)	International Arrivals 1997 ('000)	International Arrivals 2004 ('000)	Visitor Receipts (US$ million)	International Departures ('000)	Visitor Expenditure (US$ million)	Hotel Bedrooms 2003	Gross Nat'l Income (US$ billion)	GNI per Person (US$)	GDP Growth (Av. annual % 1997-2006)	Energy Production (Million tonnes oil equiv.)	Energy Consumption (Million tonnes oil equiv.)	Energy Consumption (Tonnes oil equiv./person)	Fixed Tel. Lines (Lines/100 people)	Mobile Tel. Lines (Lines/100 people)	Internet Usage (Subscribers/100 people)	Agricultural Land (% of national area)	Total Health Spending (% of GNI)	Life Expectancy (Years)	Military Spending (% of GNI)
Malta J4	.mt	Valletta	0.32 • 203	399 • 172	1,245.4 • **7**	1,111 • 66	1,156 • 76	779 • 71	174 • 77	256 • 65	n/a • –	4,913 • 126	12,328 • 56	2.5 • 128	0.00 • –	0.98 • 140	2.46 • 71	51.63 • 28	76.52 • 40	75.25 • **4**	31.6 • 123	9.6 • 16	78.5 • 30	0.7 • 147
Marshall Is. R5	.mh	Majuro	0.18 • 214	59 • 204	328.2 • 30	6 • 199	7 • 153	n/a • –	n/a • –	n/a • –	n/a • –	142 • 210	2,404 • 112	n/a • –	0.00 • –	note 1 • –	n/a • –	8.27 • 143	1.11 • 203	3.51 • 142	77.3 • **10**	10.6 • **8**	61.5 • 158	T • –
Martinique F5	.mq	Fort-de-France	1.10 • 181	433 • 170	393.5 • 24	513 • 93	471 • 100	n/a • –	n/a • –	n/a • –	6,766 • 95	6,346 • 118	14,659 • 47	n/a • –	0.00 • –	0.72 • 146	1.66 • 90	44.47 • 47	74.78 • 43	27.09 • 55	30.0 • 127	n/a • –	79.0 • 24	n/a • –
Mauritania I5	.mr	Nouakchott	1,030.70 • 29	3,087 • 133	3.0 • 216	24 • 187	n/a • –	n/a • –	n/a • –	n/a • –	n/a • –	1,210 • 170	392 • 194	7.4 • 15	0.01 • 158	1.25 • 133	0.40 • 147	1.31 • 189	17.53 • 124	0.47 • 189	38.6 • 106	3.9 • 161	50.5 • 191	1.6 • 93
Mauritius L7	.mu	Port Louis	2.00 • 176	1,231 • 152	615.3 • 15	536 • 91	719 • 86	853 • 66	161 • 79	255 • 66	9,647 • 81	5,730 • 121	4,656 • 85	5.0 • 45	0.03 • 150	1.30 • 130	1.06 • 110	28.69 • 75	41.36 • 79	14.60 • 84	55.4 • 54	3.5 • 171	72.5 • 77	0.2 • 163
Mayotte L6	.yt	Dzaoudzi	0.37 • 200	194 • 185	523.3 • 18	n/a • –	n/a • –	n/a • –	n/a • –	n/a • –	n/a • –	881 • 175	4,550 • 87	n/a • –	0.00 • –	n/a • –	n/a • –	6.24 • 154	28.80 • 102	n/a • –	n/a • –	n/a • –	61.5 • 158	T • –
Mexico D4	.mx	Mexico City	1,967.20 • 15	106,203 • 11	54.0 • 141	19,351 • **8**	20,618 • **8**	10,753 • 14	11,044 • 17	6,959 • 22	496,292 • **8**	703,080 • **10**	6,620 • 74	3.5 • 91	254.19 • **10**	169.79 • 13	1.60 • 91	17.22 • 107	36.64 • 84	13.38 • 87	54.9 • 56	6.1 • 87	74.5 • 63	0.5 • 156
Micronesia, Fed. States Q5	.fm	Palikir	0.70 • 188	108 • 194	154.4 • 67	17 • 193	19 • 150	n/a • –	n/a • –	n/a • –	n/a • –	252 • 206	2,331 • 115	n/a • –	0.00 • –	n/a • –	n/a • –	10.81 • 133	11.52 • 140	10.81 • 97	67.1 • 21	6.5 • 71	69.5 • 123	T • –
Moldova K3	.md	Chisinău	33.70 • 138	4,455 • 118	132.2 • 74	21 • 190	24 • 149	95 • 104	67 • 85	135 • 71	2,559 • 127	2,563 • 150	575 • 175	3.3 • 103	0.09 • 140	4.34 • 98	0.97 • 117	20.25 • 101	18.46 • 121	9.52 • 100	75.0 • 14	7.0 • 62	67.0 • 137	0.4 • 159
Monaco J3	.mc	Monaco-Ville	0.002 • 226	32 • 211	16,204.5 • **2**	259 • 124	246 • 114	n/a • –	n/a • –	n/a • –	2,212 • 130	870 • 176	26,844 • 24	n/a • –	0.00 • –	n/a • –	n/a • –	105.31 • **1**	60.31 • 59	50.00 • 23	0.0 • –	11.0 • **6**	81.5 • **2**	T • –
Mongolia O3	.mn	Ulan Bator	1,565.00 • 19	2,791 • 137	1.8 • 223	82 • 157	n/a • –	n/a • –	n/a • –	n/a • –	n/a • –	1,484 • 165	532 • 179	4.4 • 61	1.72 • 103	2.35 • 121	0.84 • 126	5.62 • 156	12.98 • 136	7.60 • 112	83.4 • **3**	6.3 • 77	65.5 • 145	2.1 • 66
Montserrat F5	.ms	Plymouth[13]	0.10 • 219	9 • 222	93.4 • 98	5 • 200	10 • 151	n/a • –	n/a • –	n/a • –	n/a • –	21 • 221	2,248 • 122	n/a • –	0.00 • –	0.02 • 204	2.22 • 77	n/a • –	n/a • –	n/a • –	29.4 • 133	n/a • –	79.0 • 24	T • –
Morocco[21] I4	.ma	Rabat	458.70 • 55	32,726 • 36	71.3 • 118	3,072 • 36	5,501 • 36	3,921 • 40	1,694 • 50	568 • 53	75,284 • 30	46,518 • 56	1,421 • 143	3.3 • 103	0.32 • 127	12.39 • 73	0.38 • 150	4.38 • 164	31.23 • 98	11.71 • 92	42.6 • 92	4.6 • 140	71.0 • 99	4.2 • 24
Mozambique K7	.mz	Maputo	799.40 • 35	19,407 • 54	24.3 • 176	n/a • –	n/a • –	95 • 104	n/a • –	134 • 72	n/a • –	4,710 • 130	243 • 211	8.5 • **9**	3.92 • 86	4.16 • 102	0.21 • 164	0.42 • 209	3.73 • 176	0.73 • 182	60.6 • 36	5.8 • 99	45.0 • 201	1.3 • 113
Myanmar (Burma) N4	.mm	Yangon[14]	676.60 • 40	46,997 • 26	69.5 • 120	189 • 135	242 • 116	136 • 100	n/a • –	n/a • –	17,039 • 65	13,785 • 84	293 • 205	n/a • –	10.14 • 72	4.58 • 95	0.10 • 181	0.79 • 198	0.17 • 214	0.12 • 203	16.1 • 172	2.2 • 188	59.5 • 169	2.3 • 60
Namibia J7	.na	Windhoek	824.30 • 34	2,031 • 145	2.5 • 221	502 • 94	n/a • –	403 • 86	n/a • –	87 • 74	2,749 • 125	4,813 • 128	2,370 • 114	3.5 • 91	0.36 • 124	1.26 • 132	0.62 • 139	6.36 • 153	14.23 • 129	3.73 • 140	47.1 • 76	6.7 • 70	51.5 • 189	2.8 • 40
Nauru R6	.nr	Yaren District	0.02 • 223	13 • 220	652.4 • 12	n/a • –	n/a • –	n/a • –	n/a • –	n/a • –	n/a • –	32 • 218	2,452 • 110	n/a • –	0.00 • –	0.06 • 195	4.62 • 29	14.62 • 112	11.54 • 139	0.02 • 209	0.0 • –	7.6 • 52	61.5 • 158	T • –
Nepal N4	.np	Kathmandu	140.80 • 95	27,677 • 40	196.6 • 54	422 • 97	360 • 107	n/a • –	258 • 74	n/a • –	20,063 • 60	6,538 • 116	236 • 212	3.7 • 81	0.57 • 117	1.55 • 128	0.06 • 194	1.69 • 183	0.47 • 208	0.48 • 188	34.2 • 116	5.2 • 115	60.5 • 166	1.6 • 93
Netherlands J3	.nl	Amsterdam[15]	41.50 • 134	16,407 • 59	395.4 • 23	7,841 • 18	9,646 • 20	10,081 • 16	16,463 • 12	16,539 • **8**	88,146 • 26	515,148 • 15	31,397 • 17	2.3 • 139	63.20 • 34	100.47 • 22	6.12 • 18	48.44 • 38	91.21 • 18	61.63 • 13	46.9 • 77	8.8 • 31	78.5 • 30	1.6 • 93
Netherlands Antilles F5	.an	Willemstad	0.80 • 183	220 • 181	274.9 • 43	705 • 78	n/a • –	919 • 64	n/a • –	477 • 57	n/a • –	2,154 • 156	9,793 • 63	1.7 • 156	0.00 • –	3.87 • 105	17.59 • **4**	37.23 • 57	90.09 • 20	n/a • –	8.3 • 192	n/a • –	76.0 • 55	T • –
New Caledonia R7	.nc	Nouméa	18.60 • 154	216 • 182	11.6 • 199	105 • 149	100 • 130	n/a • –	78 • 84	n/a • –	n/a • –	3,158 • 145	14,587 • 48	n/a • –	0.08 • 142	0.70 • 147	3.24 • 58	22.98 • 95	50.19 • 69	n/a • –	13.4 • 178	n/a • –	74.0 • 70	T • –
New Zealand R7	.nz	Wellington	270.50 • 75	4,035 • 122	14.9 • 191	1,497 • 58	2,348 • 56	4,951 • 33	1,374 • 54	2,360 • 38	20,072 • 59	82,465 • 47	20,435 • 33	3.1 • 112	17.12 • 56	21.87 • 60	5.42 • 23	46.11 • 42	77.52 • 39	81.95 • **1**	63.7 • 25	8.5 • 35	79.5 • 17	1.1 • 129
Nicaragua E5	.ni	Managua	130.70 • 97	5,465 • 107	41.8 • 151	358 • 111	615 • 91	10 • 115	562 • 65	n/a • –	4,418 • 112	4,452 • 134	815 • 166	3.8 • 79	0.22 • 130	1.60 • 127	0.29 • 159	3.77 • 171	13.00 • 135	2.20 • 162	58.0 • 46	7.9 • 45	70.5 • 111	0.9 • 138
Niger J5	.ne	Niamey	1,186.40 • 25	12,163 • 66	10.3 • 201	44 • 176	n/a • –	n/a • –	n/a • –	n/a • –	1,472 • 133	2,836 • 148	233 • 214	3.6 • 85	0.11 • 137	0.40 • 163	0.03 • 205	0.19 • 221	1.19 • 202	0.19 • 199	13.0 • 180	4.0 • 159	41.5 • 210	1.1 • 129
Nigeria J5	.ng	Abuja (9)	923.80 • 32	128,766 • **9**	139.4 • 72	611 • 87	n/a • –	21 • 112	n/a • –	n/a • –	n/a • –	53,983 • 54	419 • 191	4.1 • 68	140.10 • 18	24.62 • 51	0.19 • 169	0.81 • 197	7.20 • 154	1.39 • 169	78.2 • **8**	4.7 • 137	45.5 • 198	1.2 • 120
Niue A6	.nu	Alofi	0.26 • 206	2 • 226	8.3 • 207	2 • 204	3 • 154	n/a • –	n/a • –	n/a • –	n/a • –	4 • 224	1,847 • 137	n/a • –	0.00 • –	0.00 • 211	0.50 • 143	55.00 • 24	20.00 • 117	n/a • –	30.4 • 126	9.7 • 15	71.0 • 99	T • –

•: *Ranking* (top 10 in **bold**). **n/a:** Not available, not relevant or not reliable. **T:** See note on page 41. **M:** See note on page 41. For more information, see pages 202 & 210.

▶ See also... page 210 for details of maps directly relating to the figures in this section; Contents (2-7) for details of all maps and charts in this Atlas

Country	Map Ref. (pp14-15)	Internet code	Capital	Area '000 sq km	Population '000	Population Density People/sq km	International Arrivals 1997 '000	International Arrivals 2004 '000	Visitor Receipts US$ million	International Departures '000	Visitor Expenditure US$ million	Hotel Bedrooms 2003	Gross Nat'l Income US$ billion	GNI per Person US$	GDP Growth Av. annual % 1997-2006	Energy Production Million tonnes oil equiv.	Energy Consumption Million tonnes oil equiv.	Energy Consumption Tonnes oil equiv./person	Fixed Tel. Lines Lines/100 people	Mobile Tel. Lines Lines/100 people	Internet Usage Subscribers/100 people	Agricultural Land % of national area	Total Health Spending % of GNI	Life Expectancy Years	Military Spending % of GNI
Northern Mariana Is.	Q5	.mp	Saipan	0.46 • 194	80 • 198	174.7 • 62	685 • 79	525 • 97	n/a • –	n/a • –	n/a • –	4,231 • 113	117 • 212	1,456 • 142	n/a • –	0.00 • –	n/a • –	n/a • –	26.25 • 82	3.75 • 175	n/a • –	28.4 • 138	n/a • –	76.0 • 55	T • –
Norway	J2	.no	Oslo	323.80 • 67	4,593 • 116	14.2 • 193	2,702 • 42	3,600 • 42	3,087 • 44	2,588 • 40	8,428 • 19	67,114 • 32	238,398 • 25	51,904 • **2**	3.0 • 117	260.06 • **8**	44.51 • 36	9.69 • 12	48.64 • 37	90.89 • 19	39.37 • 39	3.2 • 207	9.6 • 16	79.5 • 17	2.0 • 73
Oman	L5	.om	Muscat	309.50 • 70	3,002 • 134	9.7 • 203	376 • 105	n/a • –	n/a • –	n/a • –	n/a • –	6,473 • 96	20,508 • 74	6,832 • 72	4.0 • 73	59.36 • 36	9.75 • 79	3.25 • 57	10.05 • 136	33.32 • 95	10.14 • 99	3.5 • 204	3.4 • 174	74.0 • 70	12.2 • **2**
Pakistan	M4	.pk	Islamabad	796.10 • 36	162,420 • **6**	204.0 • 53	375 • 106	648 • 89	186 • 97	n/a • –	1,275 • 42	36,451 • 49	90,663 • 43	558 • 176	4.5 • 59	31.62 • 43	47.69 • 35	0.29 • 158	2.95 • 176	3.29 • 182	1.31 • 173	34.1 • 117	3.2 • 177	62.0 • 157	4.4 • 18
Palau	P5	.pw	Koror	0.51 • 192	20 • 217	39.8 • 155	74 • 163	89 • 133	n/a • –	n/a • –	n/a • –	n/a • –	137 • 211	6,748 • 73	n/a • –	n/a • –	n/a • –	n/a • –	33.50 • 63	5.00 • 165	n/a • –	17.7 • 168	9.1 • 26	68.0 • 131	T • –
Palestine NAR[4]	K4	.ps	Jerusalem[16]	6.20 • 168	3,762 • 127	606.8 • 16	201 • 133	n/a • –	n/a • –	n/a • –	n/a • –	5,919 • 99	3,771 • 139	1,002 • 158	n/a • –	n/a • –	n/a • –	n/a • –	9.70 • 137	26.44 • 109	4.34 • 138	61.5 • 33	n/a • –	72.5 • 77	n/a • –
Panama	E5	.pa	Panama City	75.50 • 118	3,140 • 132	41.6 • 152	421 • 98	652 • 88	685 • 74	227 • 76	n/a • –	16,766 • 68	13,468 • 86	4,289 • 91	4.1 • 68	0.72 • 115	4.99 • 90	1.59 • 92	11.85 • 129	26.98 • 107	9.46 • 101	29.5 • 132	8.9 • 29	75.5 • 59	1.2 • 120
Papua New Guinea	Q6	.pg	Port Moresby	462.80 • 54	5,545 • 106	12.0 • 198	66 • 166	59 • 140	18 • 113	n/a • –	n/a • –	2,830 • 124	3,262 • 144	588 • 173	0.6 • 174	2.95 • 93	1.17 • 137	0.21 • 166	1.13 • 193	0.27 • 210	2.91 • 154	2.3 • 209	4.3 • 150	60.5 • 166	0.6 • 152
Paraguay	G7	.py	Asunción	406.80 • 59	6,348 • 100	15.6 • 188	395 • 101	309 • 109	70 • 108	153 • 81	n/a • –	4,899 • 108	6,752 • 112	1,064 • 155	1.7 • 156	13.13 • 60	10.64 • 76	1.68 • 89	4.73 • 160	29.38 • 99	2.49 • 158	61.0 • 36	8.4 • 38	72.0 • 87	0.9 • 138
Peru	F6	.pe	Lima	1,285.20 • 20	27,926 • 39	21.7 • 178	649 • 82	1,203 • 72	1,078 • 62	889 • 59	620 • 52	123,252 • 19	65,043 • 50	2,329 • 116	3.4 • 98	10.04 • 73	14.22 • 69	0.51 • 142	7.39 • 147	14.75 • 127	11.61 • 93	24.4 • 151	4.4 • 146	70.5 • 111	1.3 • 113
Philippines	P5	.ph	Manila	300.00 • 72	87,857 • 12	292.9 • 38	2,223 • 49	2,291 • 57	2,012 • 52	1,803 • 49	1,315 • 40	21,409 • 55	96,930 • 41	1,103 • 154	3.9 • 76	10.63 • 69	31.30 • 44	0.36 • 153	4.16 • 165	39.85 • 80	5.32 • 128	40.7 • 99	2.9 • 183	68.0 • 131	0.9 • 138
Poland	J3	.pl	Warsaw	312.70 • 69	38,558 • 32	123.3 • 81	19,520 • **7**	14,290 • 15	5,828 • 27	38,730 • **4**	3,906 • 27	68,588 • 31	232,398 • 26	6,027 • 77	3.8 • 79	75.82 • 30	91.20 • 23	2.37 • 74	31.85 • 67	59.91 • 60	23.35 • 63	58.7 • 43	6.1 • 87	75.0 • 62	2.0 • 73
Portugal[5]	I3	.pt	Lisbon	91.90 • 112	10,566 • 76	115.0 • 82	10,172 • 15	11,617 • 19	7,788 • 21	n/a • –	2,767 • 35	105,986 • 21	149,790 • 34	14,176 • 49	2.5 • 128	4.58 • 82	27.92 • 48	2.64 • 70	40.25 • 55	98.41 • 11	28.03 • 53	44.9 • 86	9.3 • 21	77.5 • 41	2.1 • 66
Puerto Rico	F5	.pr	San Juan	8.90 • 167	3,911 • 125	439.5 • 21	3,242 • 35	3,541 • 43	3,024 • 45	1,272 • 55	499 • 56	12,788 • 73	4,468 • 133	1,142 • 152	n/a • –	0.07 • 143	13.07 • 71	3.34 • 53	28.53 • 76	68.82 • 50	22.12 • 66	32.8 • 120	n/a • –	n/a • –	T • –
Qatar	L4	.qa	Doha	11.40 • 163	863 • 157	75.7 • 115	435 • 96	n/a • –	498 • 80	n/a • –	n/a • –	3,858 • 117	19,490 • 77	22,583 • 30	9.9 • **5**	77.43 • 27	12.40 • 72	14.37 • **6**	25.45 • 87	65.38 • 52	22.00 • 67	6.2 • 202	3.1 • 179	74.5 • 63	10.0 • **3**
Réunion	L7	.re	Saint-Denis	2.50 • 175	777 • 159	310.8 • 34	374 • 107	430 • 103	448 • 85	333 • 71	n/a • –	2,910 • 123	8,755 • 100	11,268 • 60	n/a • –	0.15 • 135	1.10 • 138	1.42 • 98	41.04 • 53	75.51 • 42	26.08 • 57	19.5 • 163	n/a • –	74.5 • 63	n/a • –
Romania	K3	.ro	Bucharest	236.40 • 83	22,330 • 49	94.5 • 97	2,957 • 38	3,739 • 41	505 • 79	6,497 • 20	512 • 55	97,320 • 22	63,910 • 51	2,862 • 105	2.4 • 133	29.02 • 48	42.12 • 39	1.89 • 83	20.25 • 101	47.13 • 73	20.76 • 71	62.2 • 30	6.3 • 77	71.5 • 95	2.4 • 57
Russian Federation	M2	.ru	Moscow	17,075.40 • **1**	143,420 • **8**	8.4 • 206	17,463 • **10**	9,164 • 21	5,226 • 31	20,468 • **8**	15,730 • **10**	177,200 • 14	487,335 • 16	3,398 • 101	4.7 • 53	1,230.03 • **2**	726.61 • **3**	5.07 • 25	27.47 • 78	51.61 • 68	11.10 • 95	12.7 • 182	6.2 • 81	65.0 • 146	4.3 • 20
Rwanda	K6	.rw	Kigali	26.30 • 147	8,441 • 88	320.9 • 31	104 • 150	n/a • –	n/a • –	n/a • –	n/a • –	n/a • –	1,875 • 160	222 • 215	6.4 • 26	0.02 • 151	0.34 • 169	0.04 • 199	0.27 • 215	1.64 • 197	0.45 • 190	70.2 • 16	5.3 • 114	44.5 • 205	2.8 • 40
St Helena	I7	.sh	Jamestown	0.12 • 218	7 • 223	62.2 • 134	n/a • –	n/a • –	n/a • –	n/a • –	n/a • –	n/a • –	18 • 222	2,413 • 111	n/a • –	0.00 • –	0.01 • 207	1.43 • 97	31.43 • 70	n/a • –	7.14 • 115	29.3 • 134	n/a • –	78.0 • 39	T • –
St Kitts & Nevis	F5	.kn	Basseterre	0.26 • 207	39 • 209	149.8 • 69	88 • 154	n/a • –	n/a • –	n/a • –	n/a • –	n/a • –	357 • 197	9,164 • 65	3.2 • 108	0.00 • –	0.04 • 198	1.03 • 113	50.00 • 32	20.00 • 117	21.41 • 68	38.2 • 108	5.5 • 112	70.5 • 111	M • –
St Lucia	F5	.lc	Castries	0.62 • 190	166 • 189	268.2 • 44	248 • 127	298 • 110	325 • 92	n/a • –	n/a • –	3,749 • 118	706 • 184	4,245 • 92	2.1 • 149	0.00 • –	0.13 • 185	0.78 • 130	31.95 • 66	62.00 • 55	36.67 • 42	32.5 • 121	5.0 • 124	72.0 • 87	M • –
St Pierre et Miquelon	G3	.pm	St Pierre	0.24 • 208	7 • 224	29.2 • 171	n/a • –	n/a • –	n/a • –	n/a • –	n/a • –	n/a • –	108 • 214	15,402 • 43	n/a • –	0.00 • –	0.03 • 202	4.29 • 35	68.57 • 11	n/a • –	n/a • –	12.4 • 184	n/a • –	70.0 • 116	T • –
St Vincent & the Gren.	F5	.vc	Kingstown	0.39 • 199	118 • 191	301.4 • 37	65 • 167	87 • 134	n/a • –	n/a • –	n/a • –	1,680 • 132	396 • 195	3,369 • 102	3.5 • 91	0.01 • 158	0.07 • 191	0.59 • 140	13.72 • 115	47.07 • 74	6.61 • 119	41.1 • 98	5.9 • 96	70.0 • 116	M • –
Samoa	S6	.ws	Apia	2.80 • 173	177 • 187	63.3 • 132	68 • 164	98 • 131	n/a • –	n/a • –	n/a • –	939 • 138	333 • 198	1,878 • 135	3.3 • 103	0.02 • 151	0.07 • 191	0.40 • 148	7.29 • 148	5.76 • 160	3.33 • 147	46.3 • 82	6.2 • 81	68.5 • 127	T • –
San Marino	J3	.sm	San Marino	0.06 • 220	29 • 212	481.3 • 20	28 • 181	42 • 146	n/a • –	n/a • –	n/a • –	683 • 140	653 • 188	22,611 • 29	n/a • –	0.00 • –	n/a • –	n/a • –	71.03 • **9**	57.93 • 65	49.31 • 27	16.4 • 171	7.7 • 49	81.0 • **4**	T • –

•: *Ranking* (top 10 in **bold**). **n/a:** Not available, not relevant or not reliable. **T:** See note on page 41. **M:** See note on page 41. For more information, see pages 202 & 210.

▶ *See also...* page 210 for details of maps directly relating to the figures in this section; Contents (2-7) for details of all maps and charts in this Atlas

Country / Map Ref. (pp14-15)	Internet code	Capital	Area '000 sq km	Population '000	Population Density People/sq km	International Arrivals 1997 '000	International Arrivals 2004 '000	Visitor Receipts US$ million	International Departures '000	Visitor Expenditure US$ million	Hotel Bedrooms 2003	Gross Nat'l Income US$ billion	GNI per Person US$	GDP Growth Av. annual % 1997-2006	Energy Production Million tonnes oil equiv.	Energy Consumption Million tonnes oil equiv.	Energy Consumption Tonnes oil equiv./person	Fixed Tel. Lines Lines/100 people	Mobile Tel. Lines Lines/100 people	Internet Usage Subscribers/100 people	Agricultural Land % of national area	Total Health Spending % of GNI	Life Expectancy Years	Military Spending % of GNI
São Tomé e Príncipe *J6*	.st	São Tomé	1.00 • *182*	187 • *186*	187.4 • *56*	5 • *200*	n/a • –	n/a • –	n/a • –	n/a • –	n/a • –	60 • *216*	320 • *202*	3.3 • *103*	0.00 • –	0.04 • *198*	0.21 • *165*	4.59 • *161*	3.17 • *183*	12.20 • *89*	54.9 • *56*	11.1 • ***5***	59.0 • *172*	0.8 • *144*
Saudi Arabia *L4*	.sa	Riyadh	2,200.00 • *13*	26,418 • *43*	12.0 • *197*	n/a • –	8,580 • *22*	6,542 • *24*	4,104 • *31*	4,406 • *26*	81,197 • *28*	242,180 • *24*	9,167 • *64*	3.4 • *98*	580.17 • ***4***	142.30 • *17*	5.39 • *24*	14.83 • *111*	36.82 • *83*	6.36 • *121*	n/a • –	4.3 • *150*	71.0 • *59*	8.7 • ***7***
Senegal *I5*	.sn	Dakar	196.20 • *87*	11,706 • *70*	59.7 • *136*	314 • *117*	363 • *106*	n/a • –	n/a • –	n/a • –	10,268 • *80*	6,967 • *109*	595 • *172*	5.4 • *40*	0.04 • *146*	1.64 • *126*	0.14 • *175*	2.37 • *179*	10.85 • *144*	4.66 • *134*	41.5 • *95*	5.1 • *119*	55.5 • *180*	1.5 • *102*
Serbia & Montenegro *K3*	.yu	Belgrade	102.20 • *106*	10,829 • *74*	106.0 • *89*	298 • *121*	580 • *92*	220 • *95*	n/a • –	55 • *77*	37,101 • *48*	21,715 • *70*	2,005 • *133*	2.0 • *153*	13.34 • *58*	19.23 • *63*	1.78 • *85*	32.94 • *64*	58.01 • *64*	18.61 • *74*	54.7 • *58*	8.1 • *40*	72.5 • *77*	4.2 • *24*
Seychelles *L6*	.sc	Victoria	0.46 • *195*	81 • *197*	176.5 • *61*	130 • *146*	121 • *128*	172 • *99*	50 • *86*	n/a • –	2,435 • *129*	685 • *185*	8,437 • *69*	0.7 • *173*	0.00 • –	0.40 • *163*	4.94 • *26*	26.16 • *83*	60.78 • *58*	24.69 • *60*	15.4 • *173*	5.2 • *115*	72.0 • *87*	1.8 • *83*
Sierra Leone *I5*	.sl	Freetown	73.30 • *119*	5,867 • *103*	80.0 • *108*	23 • *188*	44 • *144*	n/a • –	13 • *88*	n/a • –	1,457 • *134*	1,113 • *172*	190 • *216*	5.0 • *45*	0.00 • –	0.35 • *168*	0.06 • *191*	0.48 • *208*	2.28 • *190*	0.19 • *199*	39.0 • *105*	2.9 • *183*	38.0 • *215*	1.7 • *88*
Singapore *O5*	.sg	Singapore	0.65 • *189*	4,426 • *120*	6,808.8 • ***3***	6,531 • *21*	8,328 • *23*	5,090 • *32*	4,221 • *30*	7,744 • *21*	35,930 • *50*	104,994 • *39*	23,724 • *28*	n/a • –	0.00 • –	43.92 • *37*	9.92 • *11*	43.20 • *50*	89.47 • *21*	56.12 • *16*	3.0 • *208*	4.3 • *150*	61.5 • *158*	5.2 • *14*
Slovak Rep. *K3*	.sk	Bratislava	49.00 • *129*	5,431 • *109*	110.8 • *84*	814 • *72*	1,401 • *69*	901 • *65*	408 • *68*	745 • *49*	35,853 • *51*	34,907 • *59*	6,427 • *76*	4.1 • *68*	7.07 • *79*	20.04 • *62*	3.69 • *46*	23.22 • *94*	79.39 • *35*	42.27 • *34*	49.6 • *71*	5.9 • *96*	74.0 • *70*	1.9 • *77*
Slovenia *J3*	.si	Ljubljana	20.30 • *153*	2,011 • *146*	99.1 • *94*	974 • *68*	1,499 • *66*	1,630 • *55*	2,114 • *46*	911 • *46*	15,534 • *70*	29,555 • *62*	14,696 • *46*	3.6 • *85*	7.55 • *78*	7.68 • *82*	3.82 • *43*	40.68 • *54*	87.09 • *25*	47.96 • *28*	24.9 • *149*	8.3 • *39*	77.0 • *47*	1.5 • *102*
Solomon Is. *R6*	.sb	Honiara	28.40 • *143*	538 • *163*	18.9 • *184*	16 • *196*	n/a • –	4 • *116*	n/a • –	n/a • –	n/a • –	260 • *205*	483 • *182*	-0.5 • *176*	0.00 • –	0.07 • *191*	0.13 • *176*	1.31 • *190*	0.31 • *209*	0.61 • *185*	4.2 • *203*	4.8 • *133*	71.0 • *99*	M • –
Somalia *L5*	.so	Mogadishu	637.70 • *42*	8,592 • *87*	13.5 • *195*	n/a • –	n/a • –	n/a • –	n/a • –	n/a • –	n/a • –	n/a • –	#VALUE! • –	n/a • –	0.00 • –	0.26 • *173*	0.03 • *206*	1.67 • *184*	4.17 • *173*	1.67 • *167*	69.1 • *19*	n/a • –	44.0 • *207*	n/a • –
South Africa *K7*	.za	note [17]	1,224.70 • *24*	44,344 • *27*	36.2 • *161*	5,170 • *26*	6,678 • *29*	5,648 • *30*	5,692 • *23*	2,668 • *36*	52,329 • *40*	165,326 • *31*	3,728 • *99*	3.1 • *112*	147.89 • *17*	122.54 • *19*	2.76 • *67*	10.40 • *135*	43.13 • *77*	7.89 • *107*	81.7 • ***4***	8.7 • *33*	49.0 • *194*	1.6 • *93*
Spain [6] *I4*	.es	Madrid	504.80 • *51*	40,341 • *29*	79.9 • *109*	39,553 • ***3***	53,599 • ***2***	45,248 • ***2***	4,094 • *32*	12,156 • *13*	740,747 • ***6***	875,817 • ***9***	21,710 • *31*	3.1 • *112*	37.99 • *39*	154.30 • *15*	3.82 • *42*	41.52 • *52*	89.46 • *22*	33.18 • *44*	59.8 • *40*	7.6 • *52*	79.5 • *17*	1.2 • *120*
Sri Lanka *N5*	.lk	note [18]	65.60 • *122*	20,065 • *53*	305.9 • *36*	366 • *108*	566 • *93*	513 • *78*	561 • *66*	296 • *62*	16,973 • *66*	19,618 • *76*	978 • *162*	4.7 • *53*	0.75 • *114*	4.90 • *91*	0.24 • *161*	5.10 • *159*	11.37 • *141*	1.44 • *168*	36.0 • *115*	3.7 • *167*	7[illegible].5 • *35*	2.7 • *45*
Sudan *K5*	.sd	Khartoum	2,505.80 • ***10***	40,187 • *30*	16.0 • *187*	30 • *179*	n/a • –	n/a • –	n/a • –	n/a • –	n/a • –	18,152 • *80*	452 • *185*	8.7 • ***8***	12.85 • *62*	3.46 • *110*	0.09 • *185*	2.98 • *175*	3.04 • *184*	3.30 • *150*	53.4 • *64*	4.9 • *128*	59.5 • *169*	2.4 • *57*
Surinam *G5*	.sr	Paramaribo	163.80 • *91*	438 • *169*	2.7 • *219*	61 • *169*	138 • *125*	n/a • –	n/a • –	n/a • –	n/a • –	997 • *174*	2,276 • *118*	3.2 • *108*	0.96 • *109*	0.98 • *140*	2.24 • *76*	18.52 • *104*	48.48 • *71*	6.83 • *118*	0.5 • *214*	8.6 • *34*	66.0 • *143*	0.7 • *147*
Swaziland *K7*	.sz	Mbabane	17.40 • *157*	1,138 • *153*	65.4 • *127*	269 • *123*	459 • *101*	n/a • –	n/a • –	n/a • –	1,339 • *135*	1,859 • *162*	1,633 • *140*	2.9 • *122*	0.28 • *128*	0.53 • *158*	0.47 • *145*	4.43 • *163*	10.43 • *145*	3.32 • *148*	80.1 • ***6***	6.0 • *92*	34.5 • *220*	1.7 • *88*
Sweden *J2*	.se	Stockholm	450.00 • *56*	9,002 • *85*	20.0 • *182*	2,388 • *44*	3,003 • *49*	6,167 • *25*	12,579 • *16*	10,123 • *15*	96,372 • *24*	321,401 • *19*	35,704 • *11*	2.7 • *124*	30.27 • *46*	52.01 • *34*	5.78 • *21*	71.54 • ***8***	108.47 • ***3***	75.46 • ***3***	7.0 • *197*	9.2 • *24*	80.5 • ***7***	1.8 • *83*
Switzerland *J3*	.ch	Bern	41.10 • *135*	7,489 • *94*	182.2 • *59*	10,600 • *14*	6,578 • *30*	10,309 • *15*	n/a • –	8,797 • *18*	139,969 • *17*	356,052 • *17*	47,541 • ***3***	1.5 • *160*	15.97 • *57*	31.86 • *43*	4.25 • *36*	70.97 • ***10***	84.63 • *31*	47.20 • *31*	36.9 • *113*	11.2 • ***4***	83.5 • ***7***	1.0 • *134*
Syria *K4*	.sy	Damascus	185.20 • *88*	18,449 • *55*	99.6 • *93*	891 • *71*	3,032 • *48*	2,220 • *48*	3,997 • *33*	n/a • –	16,966 • *67*	21,125 • *72*	1,145 • *151*	3.0 • *117*	36.99 • *40*	22.69 • *55*	1.13 • *108*	14.60 • *113*	12.87 • *137*	4.39 • *137*	74.3 • *15*	5.1 • *119*	71.5 • *95*	7.1 • ***9***
Taiwan *P4*	.tw	Taipei	36.20 • *136*	22,894 • *48*	632.4 • *14*	2,372 • *46*	2,950 • *50*	4,040 • *39*	5,923 • *22*	8,170 • *20*	21,896 • *54*	317,070 • *20*	13,849 • *51*	4.3 • *65*	11.89 • *65*	104.43 • *21*	4.56 • *30*	59.63 • *18*	100.31 • ***8***	53.81 • *19*	25.0 • *148*	5.6 • *109*	77.0 • *47*	2.6 • *47*
Tajikistan *M4*	.tj	Dushanbe	143.10 • *94*	7,164 • *97*	50.1 • *143*	2 • *204*	n/a • –	n/a • –	n/a • –	n/a • –	n/a • –	1,779 • *163*	248 • *210*	7.4 • *15*	3.92 • *86*	6.45 • *84*	0.90 • *121*	3.75 • *172*	0.73 • *205*	0.08 • *206*	29.7 • *130*	3.3 • *175*	61.0 • *165*	2.2 • *63*
Tanzania *K6*	.tz	Dodoma	945.00 • *31*	36,766 • *33*	38.9 • *157*	347 • *113*	566 • *93*	595 • *76*	n/a • –	n/a • –	10,525 • *79*	11,560 • *93*	314 • *203*	6.4 • *26*	0.79 • *113*	1.94 • *123*	0.05 • *195*	0.42 • *209*	4.35 • *172*	0.88 • *179*	42.4 • *93*	4.9 • *128*	45.0 • *201*	2.1 • *66*
Thailand *O5*	.th	Bangkok	513.10 • *50*	64,186 • *19*	125.1 • *79*	7,294 • *20*	11,651 • *18*	10,034 • *17*	2,152 • *45*	4,517 • *25*	n/a • –	158,703 • *32*	2,473 • *109*	2.6 • *126*	39.81 • *38*	78.09 • *25*	1.22 • *104*	10.97 • *132*	44.18 • *76*	11.25 • *94*	39.3 • *104*	4.4 • *146*	70.0 • *116*	1.3 • *113*
Togo *J5*	.tg	Lomé	56.80 • *125*	5,400 • *110*	95.1 • *96*	92 • *153*	83 • *136*	n/a • –	n/a • –	n/a • –	4,480 • *111*	1,868 • *161*	346 • *199*	2.3 • *139*	0.00 • –	0.48 • *159*	0.09 • *184*	1.21 • *192*	4.40 • *169*	4.41 • *136*	63.9 • *24*	10.5 • ***9***	52.0 • *187*	1.6 • *93*
Tonga *S6*	.to	Nuku'alofa	0.75 • *185*	112 • *192*	149.9 • *68*	26 • *184*	41 • *147*	n/a • –	n/a • –	n/a • –	n/a • –	186 • *208*	1,654 • *139*	2.1 • *149*	0.00 • –	0.04 • *198*	0.36 • *152*	11.29 • *130*	3.38 • *181*	2.88 • *155*	69.5 • *18*	6.9 • *66*	71.0 • *99*	M • –

•: *Ranking* (top 10 in **bold**). **n/a:** Not available, not relevant or not reliable. **T:** See note on page 41. **M:** See note on page 41. For more information, see pages 202 & 210.

▶ *See also...* Contents (2-7) for details of all maps and charts in this Atlas

Country Map Ref. (pp14-15)	Internet code	Capital	Area '000 sq km	Population '000	Population Density People/sq km	International Arrivals 1997 '000	International Arrivals 2004 '000	Visitor Receipts US$ million	International Departures '000	Visitor Expenditure US$ million	Hotel Bedrooms 2003	Gross Nat'l Income US$ billion	GNI per Person US$	GDP Growth Av. annual % 1997-2006	Energy Production Million tonnes oil equiv.	Energy Consumption Million tonnes oil equiv.	Energy Consumption Tonnes oil equiv./person	Fixed Tel. Lines Lines/100 people	Mobile Tel. Lines Lines/100 people	Internet Usage Subscribers/100 people	Agricultural Land % of national area	Total Health Spending % of GNI	Life Expectancy Years	Military Spending % of GNI
Trinidad & Tobago *F5*	.tt	Port of Spain	5.10 • *170*	1,075 • *154*	210.8 • *51*	324 • *116*	443 • *102*	n/a • –	n/a • –	n/a • –	5,378 • *102*	11,360 • *94*	10,567 • *62*	6.9 • *20*	31.51 • *44*	13.28 • *70*	12.35 • ***7***	24.58 • *90*	49.82 • *70*	12.24 • *88*	25.9 • *144*	3.7 • *167*	70.0 • *116*	0.6 • *152*
Tunisia *J4*	.tn	Tunis	154.50 • *92*	10,075 • *80*	65.2 • *128*	4,263 • *29*	5,998 • *34*	1,910 • *53*	2,274 • *44*	326 • *62*	110,009 • *20*	26,301 • *65*	2,611 • *107*	5.0 • *45*	6.25 • *80*	8.56 • *81*	0.85 • *125*	12.11 • *127*	35.86 • *87*	8.40 • *106*	59.7 • *41*	5.8 • *99*	72.0 • *87*	1.6 • *93*
Turkey *K4*	.tr	Ankara	779.50 • *37*	69,661 • *17*	89.4 • *103*	9,040 • *17*	16,826 • *12*	15,888 • ***8***	5,928 • *21*	2,524 • *37*	201,510 • *13*	268,741 • *21*	3,858 • *97*	3.9 • *76*	22.81 • *52*	83.32 • *24*	1.20 • *105*	26.45 • *81*	47.99 • *72*	14.13 • *85*	53.5 • *63*	6.5 • *71*	70.5 • *111*	4.9 • *16*
Turkmenistan *L4*	.tm	Ashgabat	488.10 • *52*	4,952 • *113*	10.1 • *202*	257 • *125*	n/a • –	n/a • –	n/a • –	n/a • –	n/a • –	6,615 • *115*	1,336 • *145*	11.7 • ***3***	65.16 • *33*	18.46 • *64*	3.73 • *45*	7.73 • *146*	0.19 • *213*	0.73 • *182*	66.8 • *22*	4.3 • *150*	60.5 • *166*	2.9 • *35*
Turks & Caicos Is. *F4*	.tc	Cockburn Town	0.50 • *193*	21 • *216*	41.1 • *154*	93 • *152*	n/a • –	n/a • –	n/a • –	n/a • –	2,473 • *128*	117 • *213*	5,692 • *79*	n/a • –	0.00 • –	0.01 • *207*	0.24 • *163*	27.14 • *80*	8.10 • *151*	n/a • –	2.3 • *209*	n/a • –	74.5 • *63*	T • –
Tuvalu *R6*	.tv	Funafuti	0.02 • *224*	12 • *221*	581.8 • *17*	1 • *206*	1 • *155*	n/a • –	n/a • –	n/a • –	n/a • –	13 • *223*	1,117 • *153*	n/a • –	0.00 • –	n/a • –	n/a • –	5.83 • *155*	n/a • –	10.83 • *96*	0.0 • –	4.4 • *146*	61.5 • *158*	M • –
Uganda *K5*	.ug	Kampala	241.00 • *80*	27,269 • *41*	113.2 • *83*	175 • *138*	512 • *98*	n/a • –	n/a • –	n/a • –	n/a • –	6,911 • *110*	253 • *209*	5.8 • *34*	0.44 • *122*	0.94 • *143*	0.03 • *201*	0.27 • *215*	4.36 • *171*	0.75 • *181*	51.1 • *68*	7.4 • *56*	48.5 • *195*	2.3 • *60*
Ukraine *K3*	.ua	Kyyiv (Kiev)	603.70 • *44*	46,997 • *25*	77.8 • *113*	7,558 • *19*	15,629 • *14*	1,141 • *60*	14,795 • *13*	996 • *44*	32,572 • *53*	60,297 • *53*	1,283 • *147*	4.8 • *50*	76.81 • *28*	156.41 • *14*	3.33 • *56*	25.22 • *88*	28.52 • *103*	7.79 • *109*	68.6 • *20*	4.7 • *137*	67.5 • *135*	2.9 • *35*
United Arab Emirates *L4*	.ae	Abu Dhabi	83.70 • *116*	2,563 • *139*	30.6 • *168*	2,476 • *43*	6,394 • *31*	1,593 • *56*	n/a • –	n/a • –	38,402 • *46*	48,007 • *55*	18,729 • *35*	6.2 • *28*	178.24 • *15*	54.19 • *31*	21.14 • ***3***	27.32 • *79*	84.71 • *30*	31.85 • *46*	7.3 • *196*	3.1 • *179*	73.5 • *75*	3.1 • *32*
United Kingdom[7] *I3*	.uk	London	243.50 • *79*	60,441 • *22*	248.2 • *48*	25,515 • ***5***	27,755 • ***6***	27,299 • ***6***	61,424 • ***2***	55,930 • ***3***	n/a • –	2,016,393 • ***4***	33,361 • *13*	2.3 • *139*	265.24 • ***7***	245.87 • ***9***	4.07 • *40*	56.35 • *21*	102.16 • ***7***	62.88 • *11*	69.8 • *17*	7.7 • *49*	78.5 • *30*	2.8 • *40*
United States of America[8] *D3*	.us	Washington DC	9,372.60 • ***4***	295,734 • ***3***	31.6 • *165*	47,752 • ***2***	46,082 • ***3***	74,481 • ***1***	56,175 • ***3***	65,635 • ***2***	4,415,696 • ***1***	12,150,931 • ***1***	41,087 • ***5***	2.2 • *142*	1,762.39 • ***1***	2,471.07 • ***1***	8.36 • *14*	60.60 • *17*	62.11 • *53*	55.58 • *17*	42.0 • *94*	14.6 • ***1***	77.5 • *41*	3.8 • *28*
United States Virgin Is. *F5*	.vi	Charlotte Amalie	0.35 • *201*	109 • *193*	310.6 • *35*	411 • *99*	544 • *96*	n/a • –	n/a • –	n/a • –	5,044 • *106*	1,602 • *164*	14,737 • *45*	n/a • –	0.00 • –	5.52 • *88*	50.64 • ***1***	63.86 • *16*	n/a • –	n/a • –	28.8 • *137*	n/a • –	79.0 • *24*	T • –
Uruguay *G7*	.uy	Montevideo	176.20 • *90*	3,416 • *131*	19.4 • *183*	2,316 • *48*	1,756 • *62*	455 • *84*	495 • *67*	n/a • –	18,160 • *63*	13,414 • *87*	3,927 • *95*	1.5 • *160*	2.19 • *98*	4.20 • *101*	1.23 • *103*	30.85 • *71*	18.51 • *120*	20.98 • *69*	84.5 • ***2***	10.0 • ***10***	75.5 • *59*	1.6 • *93*
Uzbekistan *M3*	.uz	Tashkent	447.40 • *57*	26,851 • *42*	60.0 • *135*	960 • *69*	n/a • –	n/a • –	400 • *69*	n/a • –	7,332 • *91*	11,860 • *91*	442 • *187*	3.5 • *91*	61.64 • *35*	53.54 • *32*	1.99 • *81*	6.70 • *152*	2.05 • *192*	3.32 • *148*	60.5 • *38*	5.5 • *112*	66.0 • *143*	0.5 • *156*
Vanuatu *R6*	.vu	Port Vila	12.20 • *161*	206 • *183*	16.9 • *186*	50 • *171*	61 • *139*	n/a • –	13 • *88*	n/a • –	10,793 • *78*	287 • *202*	1,395 • *144*	1.5 • *160*	0.00 • –	0.03 • *202*	0.15 • *172*	3.11 • *174*	4.84 • *167*	3.46 • *144*	13.3 • *179*	3.8 • *163*	68.0 • *131*	T • –
Venezuela *F5*	.ve	Caracas	916.50 • *33*	25,375 • *45*	27.7 • *172*	814 • *72*	n/a • –	n/a • –	832 • *60*	n/a • –	82,366 • *27*	104,958 • *40*	4,136 • *93*	2.1 • *149*	188.88 • *13*	72.88 • *26*	2.87 • *66*	12.78 • *122*	32.17 • *97*	8.84 • *105*	23.7 • *154*	4.9 • *128*	74.0 • *70*	1.3 • *113*
Vietnam *O5*	.vn	Hanoi	331.70 • *65*	83,536 • *13*	251.8 • *47*	1,114 • *65*	2,928 • *51*	n/a • –	n/a • –	n/a • –	n/a • –	45,082 • *57*	540 • *178*	6.9 • *20*	36.46 • *41*	24.62 • *51*	0.29 • *157*	12.28 • *124*	6.01 • *159*	7.12 • *116*	n/a • –	5.2 • *115*	71.0 • *99*	2.6 • *47*
Wallis & Futuna *S6*	.wf	Matu Utu	0.24 • *209*	16 • *218*	66.8 • *125*	n/a • –	n/a • –	n/a • –	n/a • –	n/a • –	n/a • –	32 • *219*	1,997 • *134*	n/a • –	0.00 • –	n/a • –	n/a • –	11.88 • *128*	n/a • –	5.63 • *125*	21.9 • *160*	n/a • –	n/a • –	T • –
Western Sahara *I4*	.eh	al-Aioun	252.10 • *77*	273 • *179*	1.1 • *224*	n/a • –	n/a • –	n/a • –	n/a • –	n/a • –	n/a • –	159 • *209*	582 • *174*	n/a • –	0.00 • –	0.09 • *189*	0.33 • *155*	0.73 • *201*	n/a • –	n/a • –	15.1 • *175*	n/a • –	n/a • –	n/a • –
Yemen *L5*	.ye	San'a	555.00 • *48*	20,727 • *51*	37.3 • *160*	80 • *158*	n/a • –	n/a • –	n/a • –	n/a • –	13,280 • *72*	11,218 • *95*	541 • *177*	3.9 • *76*	23.42 • *51*	3.88 • *104*	0.19 • *170*	3.85 • *170*	5.17 • *163*	0.87 • *180*	33.0 • *119*	3.7 • *167*	59.0 • *172*	7.1 • ***9***
Zambia *K6*	.zm	Lusaka	752.60 • *38*	11,262 • *73*	15.0 • *190*	341 • *114*	n/a • –	n/a • –	n/a • –	n/a • –	5,202 • *103*	4,748 • *129*	422 • *190*	3.6 • *85*	2.25 • *96*	2.71 • *116*	0.24 • *162*	0.79 • *198*	2.75 • *186*	2.11 • *163*	46.9 • *77*	5.8 • *99*	39.0 • *214*	0.6 • *152*
Zimbabwe *K6*	.zw	Harare	390.70 • *60*	12,161 • *67*	31.1 • *166*	1,281 • *61*	1,853 • *59*	194 • *96*	n/a • –	n/a • –	5,766 • *101*	5,150 • *125*	423 • *189*	-4.3 • *177*	3.40 • *90*	4.71 • *92*	0.39 • *149*	2.67 • *178*	3.56 • *178*	6.90 • *117*	52.6 • *66*	8.5 • *35*	36.5 • *217*	2.1 • *66*
• Lowest rank			**• 226**	**• 226**	**• 226**	**• 206**	**• 161**	**• 117**	**• 90**	**• 77**	**• 141**	**• 224**	**• 224**	**• 177**	**• 158**	**• 211**	**• 211**	**• 223**	**• 215**	**• 209**	**• 216**	**• 192**	**• 220**	**• 163**

Some country names have been shortened for reasons of space. For more information on sources and dates, see the pages referred to in the next column. Every attempt has been made to obtain the most recent relaible figures. In some cases, however, these are estimates (official or otherwise). See also the notes below and at the top of the chart. Maps relating to many of the topics covered in this chart may be found on the following pages:

Countries & Capitals: *pages 14-15.*
Area, Population & Population Density: *page 20.*
Travel: *pages 24-25; also the regional introductions.*
GNI & GDP Growth: *page 22.*
Energy: *pages 28-29.*
Telecom & Internet: *pages 36-37.*
Health: *page 38.*
Agricultural Land: *page 17.*
Military: *page 41.*

NOTES:

1 Special Administrative Region of China.
2 Figures exclude Northern Cyprus.
3 All figures exclude overseas Départements and other dependencies listed separately here.
4 National Autonomous Region.
5 All figures include Madeira and the Azores.
6 All figures include Balearic and Canary Islands.
7 All figures exclude the Channel Islands and the Isle of Man.
8 All figures exclude overseas possessions and other dependencies listed separately here.
9 La Paz (seat of government); Sucre (judicial).
10 St Peter Port (Guernsey) & St Helier (Jersey).
11 Yamassoukro (official); Abidjan (administrative & commercial).
12 Basse-Terre (administrative) & Pointe-à-Pitre (commercial).
13 Plymouth was largely destroyed in 1997 by volcanic eruption. A temporary administrative centre has been established at Brades.
14 Formerly called Rangoon.
15 Amsterdam (capital); The Hague (seat of government).
16 East Jerusalem has been declared the capital by the Palestinian Authority. Currently, the legislature is in Ramallah and the Palestinian Authority executive is is Gaza City.
17 Pretoria (City of Tshwane) (administrative), Cape Town (legislative), Bloemfontein (judicial). This arrangement is currently under review.
18 Colombo (administrative & commercial); Sri Jayewardenepura Kotte (legislative).
19 Population and area figures exclude the disputed territory of Jammu & Kashmir.
20 Population and area figures include the Golan Heights and East Jerusalem.
21 Population and area figures exclude Western Sahara.

•: *Ranking* (top 10 in **bold**). **n/a:** Not available, not relevant or not reliable. **T:** See note on page 41. **M:** See note on page 41. For more information, see pages 202 & 210.

Index

COMPREHENSIVE INDEX TO THE COMPLETE ATLAS

The index lists all locations and features which appear throughout this atlas, with the exception of the following special-subject maps/map pages:

- World climate
- World time
- World statistical maps
- Film locations
- Business
- Health risks
- Sport
- Airports*
- Flight times
- Cruising
- Europe climate
- Europe 'empires'
- European Union
- Europe airports & high-speed rail
- Europe rail & ferries
- Europe museums & art galleries*
- London airports & connections
- UK attractions
- Belgium attractions
- The Western Front
- The Dutch vs the Sea
- The Netherlands attractions
- Germany attractions
- France attractions
- Spain & Portugal attractions
- Italy attractions
- Africa climate
- Asia climate
- Asia historical
- Asia museums & art galleries*
- North America climate
- North America historical
- USA & Canada airports & railways
- USA & Canada museums & art galleries*
- South America climate
- South America historical
- South America museums & art galleries*

Maps marked * include a list of locations on the page itself

GENERAL ABBREVIATIONS

(for Australian, Canadian, Chinese and US state/province abbreviations, see appendices)

Arch.	Archaeological
Hist.	Historic/Historical
I.	Island, Ile and equivalents
Int.	International
Is.	Islands, Iles and equivalents
Mem.	Memorial
Mon.	Monument
Mt	Mount/Mont
Mtn	Mountain/Montagne
Mtns	Mountains/Monts
Nac.	Nacional
Nat.	National
Naz.	Nazionale
Prov.	Provincial
St	Saint/Sankt/Sint

(all 'St' entries are treated as if spelt 'Saint' and are located in the index accordingly)

Ste	Sainte

(all 'Ste' entries are treated as if spelt 'Sainte' and are located in the index accordingly)

Vdkhr.	Vodokhranilishche

Countries and significant dependencies and possessions are shown in CAPITALS

Hyphens and some accents have been removed in certain cases for consistency and ease of viewing. The correct form appears on the maps themselves.

The following names, which appear in bold, indicate the entry is a featured location on one of the special subject maps:

Beach	Beach map
Dive	Diving site maps
Heritage C	UNESCO cultural heritage maps
Heritage N	UNESCO natural heritage map
Hill Sta	Hill station map (India)
Ind Res	Indian Reservation map (USA)
Park L	Leisure/Theme park maps
Park N	National Park maps
Russ Adm	Russian administrative map

The following abbreviations appear occasionally to distinguish features with the same name:

[Adm]	Administrative region
[Apt]	Airport
[Riv]	River

C

D

E

F

G

H

J

L

M

Q

R

S

T

U

V

W

X

Y